BUSINESS LAW

FOURTH EDITION

BUSINESS LAW

FOURTH EDITION

JORDAN L. PAUST

PH.B., M.A., J.D.

Professor of Law Emeritus, Los Angeles City College

Attorney at Law

Member of the California and Wisconsin Bars

ROBERT D. UPP

B.S.J., M.A., M.S., J.D.

Professor of Law Emeritus, Los Angeles City College

Attorney at Law

Member of the California Bar

JOHN E.H. SHERRY

J.D.

Associate Professor of Law, School of Hotel Administration,

Cornell University

Member of the Ohio, New York, and Supreme Court

of the United States Bars

WEST PUBLISHING COMPANY

St. Paul   New York   Los Angeles   San Francisco

Library of Congress Cataloging in Publication Data

Paust, Jordan L.
  Business law.

  Rev. ed. of: Business law text. 3rd ed. 1979.
  Includes index.
  1. Commercial law—United States. I. Upp, Robert D.
II. Sherry, John E.H. III. Paust, Jordan L. Business
law text. IV. Title.
KF888.P3   1984   346.73'07   83–21778
ISBN 0–314–77944–2

3rd Reprint—1987

CONTENTS IN BRIEF

CONTENTS

Part II   THE LAW OF CONTRACTS

Part III   AGENCY

Part IV   PROPERTY

Part V THE LAW OF SALES

Part VIII   COMMERCIAL PAPER

APPENDIXES

PREFACE

Law in modern society, especially in the business environment, holds an expanding importance and influence upon most activities. Increased governmental regulation, the proliferation of legislation, and the growing accumulation of reported court decisions have resulted in so vast a body of legal principles that scholars, executives, and even lawyers feel overwhelmed. Aware of this, the authors have sifted through the voluminous amounts of available material to extract and focus upon those points deemed most relevant to the beginning college and university student.

The best way to understand the law is to examine it as applied by the courts to actual situations. In this fourth edition, excerpts of such examples have been integrated into the text to illustrate the stated rules. Following the textual material in each chapter there are several published opinions which have been selected and edited carefully to assure that the fact situations are interesting, that the language used by the court is understandable, and that all extraneous matter is deleted. Each of these cases is preceded by a heading which indicates the rule of law being applied. Citations and footnotes have been omitted to avoid possible confusion. At the end of each chapter there are situation type problems that challenge the reader's grasp of the legal principles studied. These are practical examples based on true happenings. Many, which have stood the test of time, are carried over from the previous edition.

In addition to bringing all of the material up to date and adding the excerpt cases, a few minor changes have been made in this fourth edition. The law of agency has been placed in Part III in the first half of the book, while the law of sales has been moved farther back. This was done to conform to the present trend of including agency with contracts in a one semester course. Material has been added on labor law, employment regulation, and the new bankruptcy act because of the obvious impact these areas now have on the business community.

The resulting fourth edition is a book that a beginning college student can understand; one that is interesting and readable; one that states the relevant points of law in a direct, concise manner; and one that is accurate in the presentation of the law.

The Student Workbook, tailored for use with this volume, is a valuable aid to the student and to the instructor for preparation, review, and examination. Use of this combination makes for greater simplicity of teaching methods and stimulates higher motivation for the learner. The workbook contains questions based on each chapter that are true-false, multiple choice, case decision analysis, and short essays.

In determining which critical areas of the law to include in this work, the authors were guided by their many years of teaching experience and law practice; by a nation-wide survey of business law instructors conducted by the West Publishing Company; and by the advice of numerous consultants who assisted with this revision.

Many schools use this book for a two semester course, covering the first half as Law 1, and completing the balance during the following term as Law 2. However, the conciseness of the material is such that it may be compressed into a single semester.

While every effort has been made to assure the accuracy of this edition, the authors realize that errors may occur. They invite and would certainly appreciate reader advice concerning any corrections or suggestions for the improvement of future editions.

In the completion of this revised and updated fourth edition, the authors have received much input and many valuable contributions for which they wish to express their thanks and gratitude.

First: To the thousands of students who have contributed so much to the popularity of the book.

Second: To Denise Simon, editor; Tad Bornhoft, assistant production editor; and the many others at West Publishing Company who helped in bringing this work into final form.

Third: To the very able reviewers of the drafts of this book for their most helpful comments and additions. They were Professor Edward T. Burda, Cabrillo College, California (M.A., Stanford University); Professor Rudolph H. Cartier, Jr., Suffolk Community College, New York, and a practicing attorney; Professor Jack D. Dokey, Department of Business, City College of San Francisco, California; Larry E. Suimstra (J.D., University of California, Davis), a practicing attorney; Professor Jane Kelley, CPA, Richland College, Texas; Professor Martin A. Kron, Saint Francis College, New York; Professor Craig C. Milnor, Clark College, Washington; Professor Mary Ellen Pangonis, Los Angeles Valley College, California, and a practicing attorney; Professor Richard Perry, Santa Rosa Junior College (J.D., University of California, Berkeley); and Professor Nicholas Sarris, Essex Community College, Maryland.

Fourth: To the following persons who were among the many who have made valuable contributions for each edition: Professor Charles O. Stapleton III, Chairman, Law Department, Los Angeles City College; E. V. Brinegar, M.A., Banking, University of Washington; Professor Robert Cheng, LL.M., J.S.D., Yale University School of Law; Professor L. Edmund Kellogg, J.D., practicing attorney; Professor Louis D. Igo, J.D., University of Tulsa, practicing attorney; Professor Jordan J. Paust, Law Center, University of Houston; Richard M. Paust, M.A., J.D., practicing attorney; Professor Vanita M. Relerford, J.D., Texas Southern University; Professor Carl Ross, Head of Business Department, Southwest College, California; and Professor John Weaver, J.D., University of Arizona, practicing attorney.

J.L.P.

R.D.U.

J.E.H.S.

BUSINESS LAW
FOURTH EDITION

Part I

LAW AND THE COURTS

Chapter 1

INTRODUCTION

As a business law student you might first ask what law is, how one finds it, and how one learns its content and utility in the business world. Although you have probably asked a set of questions that nearly every student of law has asked for years, such questions have never been answered completely, nor can they be "answered" with mathematical certainty. The simple question, "What is law?" has provided lawyers, philosophers, and social scientists years of inquiry and intense debate. For our purposes it is important to realize that no definition of law is true or false; some definitions are merely more helpful because they provide a useful focus. All are incomplete, for law is ultimately as complex as social process, ever changing and of varied content, patterns, and effects.

The origins of the law and the law's useful application are equally complex. But isn't there a useful focus for the student? What generally is the nature of business law, and how is it created? Also, how does law function in the business world? For our purposes in the field of business law, we can define law as norms, rules, or principles used to guide or regulate business transactions that can be created by courts, legislatures, and administrative agencies or, ultimately, self-generated by business persons or entities.

One function and objective of business law is to provide stability or consistency so that business entities and persons can utilize law to guide decisions and act within the common interest. Imagine the chaos that might occur in our society of each of us had the complete freedom to act as we pleased. For example, think of the confusion that would result if anyone could drive an automobile on either side of the road at any time or ignore business contracts at will. Imagine the confusion in the business world if each business had a different set of legal rules for deciding whether it was bound to sell or buy materials. No one would know what to expect from others or how to plan business operations. In the area of commercial disputes, imagine the confusion if there were no rules to guide their settlement. Finally, consider the chaos if there were no penal or consumer laws for the protection of society from illegal business practices. On the other hand, imagine the impracticalities of rigid, out-of-date laws. Rules that are inflexible might also be harmful to business and society. Often the rules must change to meet old needs in new fact situations to meet new social needs, or to reflect new business patterns and expectations.

The student should keep in mind that lawmakers are human beings possessing biases, prejudices, and limitations. Consequently, continual change and error should be expected. Law reflects our thoughts, our actions, our expectations, and our practices. Consider the change in the laws relating to the automobile. With the replacement of the horse and buggy, we developed a whole new body of law contained in the Motor Vehicle Code. As the automobile became more powerful and faster, we had to change the laws to keep pace with the new power and speed. This, in turn, resulted in new types of roads and highways and, thus, the Streets and Highways Code. Demands for automobile pollution controls and safety features have led to new laws. Other examples of changes in the law or new laws resulting from changes in society can be found in the fields of human rights, Social Security, food and drugs, welfare, unemployment compensation, monopolies, insurance, consumer protection, environmental control, zoning, business practices, and the extensive use of computers that may result in more efficiency but may also result in the invasion of privacy.

Some students experience frustration because of the confusion and the uncertainty in the law. But when an attempt is made to understand the confusion, it becomes more palatable. Since the law is continually changing, a rule must be researched before use in order to determine whether or not the law has been changed or modified by legislative action, administrative regulation, or court interpretation. There are at least two sides to contested legal issues. The same legal problem may have several answers, any one of which might be correct depending upon the particular circumstances, time, and place.

The facts upon which a specific case is based are often as important as the law to be applied. One situation may invoke several relevant rules. Attorneys for each side of a lawsuit usually make conflicting arguments to the judge requesting him or her to apply opposite rules to the facts at issue. Law does not supply arithmetical answers that are the same for each problem. Most legal disputes have more than one answer, and some may have no answer at all. The student should not be upset by this uncertainty, which provides a challenge to one's imagination and initiative. Those forceful persuaders who convince the court or the legislature that they have the right answer, whether or not one exists, are the individuals who shape the course of future legal action.

Justice is depicted as being blind, which means that law should be totally objective. To judge properly, one must consider carefully the claims of both sides of a controversy as well as the common interest involved. As you read the cases, you may notice that the court seldom explains the loser's legal position. This is logical, since the matter has been decided the other way. However, the loser must have thought he or she had a valid legal position, since hiring an attorney for the trial and then appealing the case is an expensive process. Analyze the loser's reasoning in these cases, since it might become future law. Perhaps the Court erred in its decision. Judges are human and can also make mistakes. If you disagree with any case or rule, express your dissent, provided that it is based on reason rather than on emotion.

QUESTIONS

1. Define the term "law."

2. Why do we need stability in the law?

3. State one example of change in the law and the reason for the change.

4. State an example of a "new" law and the reason it came into existence.

5. If you had the power, what new law would you make and why?

6. What are the factors that can influence a legislator to vote for passage of a law?

7. A judge asks a prospective juror in a criminal case whether he has any particular feelings one way or another in this case. The juror responds, "No, I have not; however, it is difficult for me to ignore the fact that the defendant has been arrested for this crime and the district attorney saw fit to prosecute him." What are your feelings about this answer?

8. Some cases—particularly criminal cases—attract a great deal of attention in the media that results in some people making definite statements as to how a case should end even before it is tried. What are your feelings regarding the statements of the following people:

    (a) your barber

    (b) the plaintiff's attorney to the media

    (c) the defendant's attorney to the media

    (d) the local politician

    (e) your law professor

Chapter 2

LAW IN THE
UNITED STATES

The main sources of law are the federal and state constitutions, federal and state statutes, federal and state court decisions, the rules and regulations of federal and state administrative agencies, and the ordinances of local governments. This text emphasizes (1) judicial decisions, also called "case law," and (2) legislative enactments, also called "statutory law" or "code law." Administrative law is covered in Chapter 5.

A. THE U.S. CONSTITUTION

Superseding and shaping all of our law, whether case law, statutory law, or administrative law, is the U.S. Constitution and the fundamental expectations of the people. As the U.S. Constitution declares, the people of the United States formed the Constitution. They are the ultimate source of all authority and the ultimate source of law, for they will shape the law, follow it or break it, and make it effective or obsolete. Although the entire process of government or of law involves the authority of the people, under our system, the U. S. Constitution is the supreme law of the land. No state, federal, or other law is valid in this country if it violates the U. S. Constitution. The final arbiter as to the constitutionality of any law, the final interpreter of the Constitution, is the U. S. Supreme Court, although realistically the Court is influenced by public expectation and, thus, by the primary source of law—the people themselves.

The Constitution provides that powers not delegated to the United States by the people are reserved for the states or the people themselves (Amendments Nine and Ten). Generally, this means that each state may make its own laws regarding matters that are purely intrastate. However, any state law that violates the U. S. Constitution or substantially thwarts federal rights is invalid. Examples are found when human or civil rights clash with local statutes, ordinances, or business practices.

Each state has a constitution that is the supreme law of the state. Statutes passed by the legislature and case law decided by the judiciary are subordinate to the state constitution.

B. JUDICIAL LAW

Judicial law is created by the courts in the process of deciding disputes that come before them. It is called "case law," "judge-made law," or "common law" and serves as a precedent for the determination of later controversies. It is referred to as the unwritten law, although voluminously recorded and in great part republished in statutory or code form in subsequent years. To give continuity to this system, judges imposed on themselves an unwritten doctrine called *stare decisis,* which means to stand by or apply the rule of decided cases instead of changing the rule. For example, if a case was tried before a judge involving a legal problem that had never been decided upon before, the judge's decision was called a "precedent" or an original rule of law. In later cases involving the same problem, other judges might follow the same rule, whether or not they agreed with it, thus adhering to the judicial doctrine of *stare decisis.* The result was that the precedent became the law. It was called the common law, since it was applied to all persons, and was therefore a law common to all people. The doctrine of *stare decisis* is not, however, completely rigid. In any society, the courts must be flexible to meet new expectations and needs. For example, the reason for the original decision may have changed so that the judge would not be bound to follow the decision. The factual situation before the judge might be different from the one in the original case so that the judge would not have to follow the same rule. Finally, the judge might feel that the original decision was wrong and refuse to follow it. The result of these latter decisions is the making of new and conflicting law that creates a certain amount of confusion until a higher court decides which ruling is controlling and hence becomes "the law." In business law, we see a constant tension between the need for *stare decisis* so that law can guide business decisions and the need for flexibility and change so that the law meets new business expectations and needs as well as those of the entire community. In the long run, all law is dynamic.

C. LEGISLATIVE LAW

Legislative law, also known as statutory law or code law, is law that is enacted by Congress, and the various state legislative bodies. Legislative law is the primary source of new law and ordered social change in the United States today.

Each state has a constitution supplemented by case law and a system of codes. California, for example, has 27 codes: Food and Agricultural Code, Business and Professions Code, Civil Code, Code of Civil Procedure, Commercial Code, Corporations Code, Education Code, Elections Code, Evidence Code, Financial Code, Fish and Game Code, Government Code, Harbors and Navigation Code, Health and Safety Code, Insurance Code, Labor Code, Military and Veteran's Code, Penal Code, Probate Code, Public Resources Code, Public Utilities Code, Revenue and Taxation Code, Streets and Highways Code, Unemployment Insurance Code, Vehicle Code, Water Code, and Welfare and Institutions Code.

D. THE UNIFORM COMMERCIAL CODE

In recent years, a great effort has been made to make the laws of the states uniform in certain areas. The most recent example is the Uniform Commercial Code, which has been adopted with variations in all 50 states (see Appendix A). The purpose of the code is to simplify, clarify, and modernize the law governing commercial transactions; to permit the continued expansion of commercial practices through custom, usage, and agreement of the parties; and to make uniform the law among the states. Thus, the code itself permits change in laws regulating business transactions while attempting to provide uniform guidance for business decisions.

The code is restricted to transactions involving various aspects of the sale, financing, and security in respect to PERSONAL property, which generally consists of moveable things. Except for isolated instances, the code does not apply to real property (i.e., interests in land and those things permanently attached thereto).

Under the code, if the parties express intent to contract, some of the technical requirements for entering into a contract become unnecessary. The code provides rules and principles that will become part of the contract if the parties have not otherwise agreed. Although the parties can tailor their contract to suit their needs, they cannot change the code obligations of good faith, diligence, reasonableness, and due care.

The student should note in the material on contracts and sales that most contracts must still adhere to the accepted principle that a contract must be certain to be enforceable. The liberality in the area of certainty applies only to the sale of goods, and even in that area exceptions can exist (e.g., the sale of automobiles and installment sales of consumer goods other than motor vehicles.

QUESTIONS

1. Name two of the main sources of law in the United States.

2. What supersedes all law?

3. Must a state statute comply with the U.S. Constitution if it complies with the state constitution?

4. What is judicial law?

5. What is common law?

6. What does *stare decisis* mean?

7. What is legislative law also known as?

8. What is the purpose of the Uniform Commercial Code (U.C.C.)?

9. The U.C.C. is generally restricted to what transactions?

10. How many states have adopted the U.C.C.?

Chapter 3

THE COURT SYSTEM

The United States has two major court systems, consisting of the broad federal system and the courts of the fifty individual states.

A. THE FEDERAL SYSTEM

The Constitution created the Supreme Court and authorized such inferior courts as Congress may from time to time establish. Congress, pursuant to this authority, has established the United States Court of Appeal, the United States District Courts of which there is at least one in each state, and other courts, such as the Court of Tax Appeals, the U.S. Court of International Trade, and the U.S. Claims Court. The following chart illustrates the federal court system.

FEDERAL COURT SYSTEM

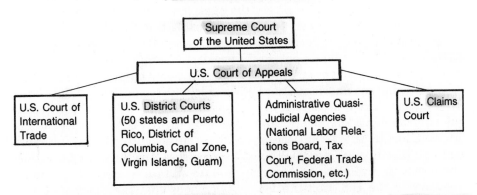

The District Courts are courts of original jurisdiction or "trial courts" (the courts in which proceedings are commenced and tried). The District Courts have jurisdiction of, among other things, cases that arise under the U.S. Constitution or federal laws and treaties that involve personal rights, cases involving federal crimes, and civil cases in which the matter in controversy exceeds the sum or value of $10,000 and is based on diversity of citizenship (e.g., citizens of different states).

The Court of Appeal is a review court and a court to which an appeal may be taken from the District Courts, the Claims Court, the U.S. Court of International Trade, the Patent and Trademark Office, the U.S. International Trade Commission, the Merit System Protection Board, and agency boards of contract appeals. A Court of Appeal will review the case and will either affirm, reverse, or modify the judgment of the trial court.

From the Court of Appeal, the case may then be appealed to the U.S. Supreme Court, which has the final word on the legal problems involved. The Supreme Court consists of a Chief Justice and eight Associate Justices.

An appeal to the U.S. Supreme Court is largely a matter of privilege rather than of right, since this Court may either allow or deny a petition for hearing. The Court will give a full hearing to a case only if four of the nine justices vote to hear it (called the "rule of four"). Two procedures are used for bringing a case before the Court, namely, by *appeal* and by *writ of certiorari.*

Few cases are brought to the Court by *appeal.* An individual has the right to appeal in the following cases: (1) when a U.S. Court of Appeals holds a state statute to be in violation of the Constitution, treaties, or laws of the United States; (2) when the highest court of a state declares a federal statute or treaty invalid or when the highest state court upholds the validity of a state statute that has been challenged as violating the Constitution, treaties, or laws of the United States; (3) when a federal court declares that an act of Congress is unconstitutional and the federal government or one of its employees is a party; and (4) when an appeal is for an injunction in a civil action that Congress requires a district court of three judges to determine.

A *writ of certiorari* is a written order by the Supreme Court issued to a lower court requiring the lower court to produce a certified record of a particular case that was tried in the lower court. The Court uses the writ as a discretionary device to choose the cases it will hear. Most of the cases heard by the Court are by the writ procedure. Writs are granted when there is an important federal question involved or when there is a conflict in the decisions of U.S. Circuit Courts of Appeals. Generally, only petitions for *writs of certiorari* that raise important constitutional questions are granted.

Although the Supreme Court work is primarily appellate, it does have original jurisdiction in cases in which the states may be a party, and in cases affecting ambassadors, public ministers, and consuls. The power of the Supreme Court to review the decisions of the state courts, however, is limited to those that involve a federal question. However, the Supreme Court has the power to invalidate any federal or state statute by declaring it to be contrary to the U.S. Constitution. It is obvious that the Supreme Court wields enormous influence and has great power. The legal principles enunciated by the Court are followed by other federal courts in controversies that come before those courts. If the decision involves a constitutional problem, the Court's decision will be followed by all of the various courts of the United States, both federal and state.

B. THE STATE SYSTEMS

Most states follow the basic federal system and have trial courts of original jurisdiction, intermediate appellate courts, and the highest court of the state as the one of final appeal.

1. COURTS OF ORIGINAL LIMITED JURISDICTION

Trial courts of limited jurisdiction might be city or municipal courts and justices' or commissioners' courts whose jurisdiction is limited to the city and which may hear criminal cases involving only misdemeanors and civil cases for money damages up to a limited amount.

Some states have a *small claims court* system in which the courts have a limited money jurisdiction (e.g., $1,500); and where the litigants handle their own cases, since the parties may not be represented by attorneys. This has been a very useful court to relieve the municipal courts, which are so crowded that it often takes up to one year to have a case tried. Although small claims courts dispense justice on an assembly-line basis, the system is quite successful.

Persons going to small claims court must prove liability on the part of the defendant (e.g., that the defendant was negligent). The plaintiff must also prove the amount of damages (e.g., loss of wages due to injury caused by the defendant). Proof must be made by a preponderance of the evidence (i.e., 51%). Once the plaintiff has proven his or her case, the defendant must put on evidence to disprove the plaintiff's evidence (e.g., that the plaintiff lost wages due to illness and not from an injury). If the defendant has a claim against the plaintiff, he or she must file a cross-complaint after being served the plaintiff's complaint. See Chapter 4 for court procedures.

A party to the case can prove his or her case by witnesses (if a witness cannot go to court, the party should bring a statement of the witness under penalty of perjury with his or her signature notarized). Obviously, a witness in court carries greater weight than does a written statement. Generally, it is better practice to subpoena the witness. A person is permitted to pay a witness fee as set by statute. However, if someone offers to pay the witness a fee based on the outcome of a case, the credibility of the witness may be destroyed. A person may have to pay an expert a fee based on the expert's time in court, not on the outcome of the case. If the expert cannot or will not go to court, the expert's statement can be presented in written form. In property damage cases, if the expert cannot appear, it is customary to bring three estimates of the money damages to court.

A party should have his or her case prepared in an organized manner. An outline of what he or she intends to say can be helpful. The court will be impressed with receipts, diagrams, and photographs. A photo copy of the law, or at least a reference to the law, is very helpful.

A case may hinge on a substantive legal point. For example, is a bus company liable when a bus driver strikes a passenger? Is the parent of a young child liable when the child hits another child with a stick? Is a tenant liable for rent when the rented premises become uninhabitable because of failure of the landlord to make necessary repairs? What can a creditor do when he or she receives a check from a debtor stating "Paid in Full" on the back of the check and the check is for a smaller amount than the creditor believes is due? If you read through the table of contents and the index of this law book, you will probably find material that will help you prepare your case.

2. COURTS OF ORIGINAL UNLIMITED JURISDICTION

Trial courts that have unlimited jurisdiction might hear cases involving unlimited amounts of money, probate, equity, divorce, and felony cases rather than merely misdemeanors. They are called by various names: Circuit Courts (Illinois, Indiana, Michigan), Superior Courts (California, Massachusetts), Supreme Courts (New York), District Courts (Iowa, Minnesota, Oklahoma, Wyoming), Courts of Common Pleas (Ohio, Pennsylvania).

3. APPELLATE COURTS

A. Intermediate Courts of Appeal

These courts have been created in some states to relieve the highest state court of some of the cases that it reviews. They are usually called District Courts of Appeal or Courts of Appeal and are found in Arizona, California, Illinois, Louisiana, Michigan, New York, North Carolina, Ohio, and Pennsylvania. These are the courts to which a litigant would file his or her initial appeal from the trial court. In general, appellate courts do not hear witnesses. They examine the record of a case on appeal to determine whether the trial court committed a prejudicial error, and if so, to reverse the judgment.

B. Highest Court

Every state has a court that it designates as its highest court of appeals. California, Illinois, and most states call it the Supreme Court. Kentucky, Maryland, and New York call it the Court of Appeals. Massachusetts and Maine call it the Supreme Judicial Court. The losing litigant in the intermediate court of appeal can file an appeal in this court. An appeal from this court to the U.S. Supreme Court is possible only if a constitutional law question is involved, which means that a state statute or decision is asserted to be in violation of the U.S. Constitution.

4. ARBITRATION

Arbitration is a procedure by which a dispute is brought before one or more arbitrators who make a decision that the parties may agree to accept as final. The case is presented in an informal manner, and the arbitrator has discretion in admitting evidence that would otherwise be inadmissible in a court proceeding. For example, an arbitrator may admit hearsay evidence (for definition of "hearsay," see the dictionary of terms in Appendix C). Arbitration is encouraged as a means of avoiding expensive and timely litigation and relieving congestion and delay in the courts. Arbitration agreements have been widely used in commercial disputes and labor disputes.

Generally speaking, virtually every state has some kind of arbitration statute. The "modern" arbitration acts provide for the irrevocability of agreements to submit disputes to arbitration and provide for the means of compelling arbitration, staying suits at law, and confirming awards with limited review. Most of the states have adopted the modern act. The U.S. government has adopted the U.S. Arbitration Act, which applies in any state if the transaction involves interstate commerce and diversity of citizenship exists. Information regarding the rules of arbitration and wording of arbitration clauses to be used in a contract can be obtained from the American Arbitration Association, a private, nonprofit organization founded in 1926 to foster the study of arbitration and to perfect the techniques of this method of settling disputes.

QUESTIONS

1. What are the two main court systems in the United States?

2. What is the difference between the District Court and the Court of Appeals?

3. What are the two procedures for bringing a case before the Supreme Court?

4. What is a *writ of certiorari?*

5. Which court has the final word on constitutional problems?

6. What is an arbitration procedure?

7. What is the advantage of arbitration?

8. You want to put an arbitration clause into a contract. How would you get help in this area?

9. While you are driving your automobile down a public street, your vehicle is struck at an intersection by another vehicle that is turning left. Your vehicle is damaged in the amount of $750. You are injured but do not go to a doctor. You lose three days' work as a result of your injury, which costs you $300. You sue in small claims court for the sum of $1,050. What will you do to prepare your case?

10. Will you need additional preparation if the vehicle the defendant is driving is a truck belonging to the driver's employer, a plumbing contractor, and the defendant is driving from the plumber's place of business to a job? If so, what additional preparation would you need?

Chapter 4

TAKING A CASE TO COURT

The judicial procedure that must be followed in taking a case to court varies from state to state and between state and federal courts. It can be complicated. Our purpose in this part of the text is to give a general summary of some of the common characteristics of judicial procedure in the United States. Although this material may give the student some insight into judicial procedure, it is not intended to give a person sufficient knowledge to handle his or her own litigation.

A. THE PARTIES

The person who brings the lawsuit in the trial court is generally called the "plaintiff" or "petitioner," and the person against whom the suit is brought is called the "defendant" or "respondent."

Usually the plaintiff or petitioner is listed first in the title of the case, and the defendant or respondent listed second. In some states, the appellant is listed first, even though he or she was the defendant in the trial court. A notation has been made in those cases where this has been done to avoid possible confusion for the student.

B. THE PLEADINGS

The plaintiff's first pleading is called a "complaint," "petition," or "declaration." (see dictionary of terms in Appendix C for further explanation of terms used in this and other chapters). The type of lawsuit dictates the type and form of the pleading. Many volumes of pleading forms are available for use by attorneys in preparing pleadings. Some states are standardizing some forms (e.g., probate, dissolution of marriage) so that the attorney can merely check off certain items and with a few typewritten additions file an acceptable pleading.

The complaint, or other first pleading, alleges the facts upon which the plaintiff bases his or her cause of action. It must be prepared pursuant to prescribed rules and be filed with the proper governmental authority within a prescribed period of time or the cause of action is generally barred forever. When suing a governmental body, such as a city, statutes generally provide that a claim for damages be presented to that entity within a certain number of days as a prerequisite to filing a lawsuit against the entity. For a discussion of possible causes of action in business cases, see Chapter 17. After the complaint is filed, together with a summons, a copy of the complaint and summons is served upon the defendant.

If the defendant wishes to contest the action, he or she must file an answer or demurrer. Usually the defendant files an answer rather than a demurrer. Generally the answer merely denies the allegations in the plaintiff's complaint.

After the defendant files an answer and it is served on the plaintiff or his or her attorney pursuant to local rules, the case is at issue and is ready for pretrial proceedings.

C. PRETRIAL PROCEEDINGS

The main function of a pretrial procedure is to discover the basic issues and facts before the trial. The theory behind discovery rules is that a lawsuit should be an intensive search for the truth, not a game to be determined in outcome by consideration of tactics and surprise. The five main discovery devices are depositions, written interrogatories, motions for inspection, physical and mental examinations, and demands for admission.

After the issues are joined, it is customary for the attorneys to take depositions of the respective adverse parties and of key witnesses. The most popular type of deposition consists of oral testimony under oath given in answer to oral interrogatories of one or more attorneys that is later reduced to writing and authenticated. It is usually taken in the office of one of the attorneys. Its main function is to discover the facts upon which the opposition is relying so that preparation can be made to dispute or disprove those facts in the trial of the action. It is also useful to impeach testimony given at the trial. That is, a statement testified to in the deposition can be used to contradict conflicting testimony given at the trial. It is extremely important for a person to be prepared as to the facts before his or her deposition is taken.

A deposition can also be taken upon written interrogatories (written questions propounded to the adverse party or to a witness that he or she must answer under oath). Written interrogatories are usually not so effective as oral interrogatories, which provide for on-the-spot cross-examination, since the person has more time to prepare an answer, often with the help of an attorney.

A motion for inspection permits the court to order any party to produce and permit the inspection and copying by the party bringing the motion of certain designated documents, papers, books, accounts, letters, photographs, and other objects or tangible items.

In an action in which the mental or physical condition or the blood relationship of a party or of certain other persons is in controversy, the court may order the party to submit to a physical or mental or blood examination by a physician. This discovery device is commonly used in accident cases by insurance companies to prevent fraud on the part of claimants.

A significant tool in helping to avoid unnecessary expense and labor in trial preparation and in proof at the trial is the demand for admissions. This is a request by one party against the other to admit the genuineness of any relevant documents described in the request or of the truth of any relevant matters of fact set forth in the request.

It should be apparent that modern discovery devices provide tools for all sides to a contest that make surprises unnecessary at the trial. The issues can be narrowed and practically all of the testimony of the parties elicited in advance.

In addition to requests for the above discovery procedures, a pretrial conference can be requested in many cases. At this conference, which is held before a judge or commissioner, the parties attempt to settle the case or, failing that, to narrow the issues so that the trial can be shorter and more orderly.

D. THE TRIAL

The trial is the time when the witnesses, parties, and attorneys congregate outside the courtroom door for amenities and last-minute discussions. It is the time when the nervous wish they had settled.

Most judges want to see the attorneys in chambers before trial in an effort to make a last-minute settlement. If that fails, the judge may want to discuss the case in an effort to narrow the issues and thereby shorten the time of trial.

If the case is to be tried by a jury, the attorneys and the judge examine the prospective jurors in an attempt to select competent and unbiased jurors. After the jury is selected, each attorney makes an opening statement in which the attorney states what he or she expects to prove during the trial.

The plaintiff's attorney then presents his or her case by examining each of the witnesses and introducing documentary evidence. As the plaintiff's attorney finishes direct examination of each witness, the defendant's attorney has the right to cross-examine. After the defendant's attorney finishes cross-examination, the plaintiff's attorney may redirect and the defendant's attorney may then re-cross. The plaintiff's attorney presents all the evidence and rests his case, and the defendant puts on his or her case as outlined above. All of the above proceedings are subject to strict rules of procedure and evidence so that the trial may proceed in an orderly manner.

After all of the evidence has been introduced and various motions have been made, the plaintiff's attorney makes his final argument to the jury in which he reviews the evidence and relates the evidence to the instructions that the judge will give the jury. After the plaintiff's attorney finishes his argument, the defendant's attorney follows the same procedure. A short rebuttal is then available to the plaintiff's attorney.

After the arguments are concluded, the judge instructs the jury on the law applicable to the case. The jury then retires to consider and render a verdict.

After the judgment is rendered, the attorney for the losing party may file a motion for judgment notwithstanding the verdict; i.e., the losing party claims that the winning party did not even produce a *prima facie* case (insufficient evidence to support a judgment).

Either attorney can move for a new trial on one or more of several grounds (e.g., excessive or inadequate damages, irregularity in proceedings, misconduct of jury, newly discovered evidence, insufficient evidence, verdict against the law, error in the law).

E. THE APPEAL

After the judgment is entered and motions, if any, are decided, the party who feels aggrieved may appeal. This party may be the one who lost the case or the party who won the case but did not get as much as he or she had hoped. Some of the grounds for an appeal are that the court erred in admitting or excluding certain evidence, erred in instructing the jury, or erred in refusing the appellant a directed verdict or that the evidence was insufficient to sustain the verdict.

The appellate court hears the case without a jury and without witnesses. The attorneys for the appellant and appellee submit written briefs to the court in which they state their arguments supported by citations of previous court decisions and statutes. In addition, the attorneys are usually permitted to make an oral argument to the court. The court examines the briefs of the attorneys and the record of the proceedings before the lower court, including the pleadings, the testimony of the witnesses, documentary evidence, and the lower judge's instructions to the jury. After a review of the case, the appellate court renders its decision and writes its opinion. These opinions are preserved in permanently bound volumes or reports. It is these opinions that we will be studying in the cases in this book. The court in its decision may affirm the lower court's decision, reverse it, or remand the case back to the lower court with directions to hold a new trial pursuant to certain instructions or with directions to enter a new judgment in accordance with the opinion given by the appellate court.

F. ENFORCEMENT OF THE JUDGMENT

If the losing party does not pay the judgment after it has been entered or after an appeal has been decided, the winning party must take steps to execute or carry out the judgment. Two common procedures for enforcing the judgment are the issuance of a writ of execution for the seizure and sale of property of the loser and a garnishment proceeding.

A writ of execution directs the sheriff to levy upon sufficient property of the judgment debtor to satisfy the judgment plus costs of the execution.

If the sheriff finds sufficient property, he will seize and sell it at public auction in accordance with state statutes. Certain property of the judgment debtor is exempt from levy and execution by statutory exemptions (e.g., furnishings, personal clothing, tools of trade, a certain amount of money). If the judgment is for the recovery of specific property, the judgment will direct the sheriff to deliver the property to the winning party.

A garnishment is a statutory proceeding whereby the judgment debtor's property, usually money, in possession or under control of another is applied to payment of the debtor's obligation. For example, the winning party may run a garnishment against the judgment debtor's employer to obtain a portion of the debtor's wages. Statutes specify the amount that can be taken under the garnishment.

QUESTIONS

1. In a lawsuit:

    (a) who is the plaintiff?

    (b) who is the defendant?

1. What is the first step in commencing a lawsuit:

    (a) against a person or corporation?

    (b) against a city?

3. What is the function of pretrial procedures?

4. What is the theory behind discovery rules?

5. What are the two common procedures for enforcing a judgment?

Chapter 5

ADMINISTRATIVE AGENCIES

A. IN GENERAL

An administrative agency is a governmental authority, other than a legislative or judicial body, that has the power to affect the rights of private parties either through the formation of rules or through adjudication.

Administrative law is that branch of public law that regulates administrative agencies in the exercise of their various powers. Such agencies include the Internal Revenue Service, the Federal Trade Commission, the Interstate Commerce Commission, the National Labor Relations Board, the Federal Communications Commission, the Social Security Administration, the Workers' Compensation Board, and the Securities and Exchange Commission. Literally hundreds of such federal, state and local agencies exist.

Administrative agencies are involved in one way or another in practically every aspect of business. The scope of administrative law is expanding because of the increasing complexity of the economic, industrial, and social life in the United States. Legislatures and courts have neither the technical knowledge nor the time to deal with the many complicated problems that face the nation today. Advances in technology require special training and experience to attempt to solve the problems. It is obvious that every legislator, judge, and executive cannot have all of the knowledge required in handling problems in such complicated fields as taxation, atomic energy, labor relations, consumer rights, transportation, and communications. Also, the merging of many of the legislative, judicial, and executive functions saves money.

Members of administrative agencies are usually appointed. In the case of federal agencies, they are by the President with the consent of two thirds of the members of the Senate.

B. POWERS

Most administrative agencies are created by and receive their powers from the legislature; that is, the legislature delegates its power to the administrative agency. They may have executive power, legislative power, judicial power, or any combination thereof.

1. EXECUTIVE POWER

Most administrators have the power to investigate and administer. For example, they may subpoena witnesses to appear and testify, subpoena documents, and administer its rules. The power is a continuing one; thus, the agency can put a party on probation and require that he make periodic reports to show whether or not he complied with the law.

2. LEGISLATIVE POWER

Most administrators have the power to make appropriate regulations to cope with the problems within the jurisdiction of the agency. Thus, the agency may make rules regarding taxes, unfair methods of competition, fish and game, prices, and contracts, to name a few. This is similar to a legislature's enacting a statute.

3. JUDICIAL POWER

Most administrators have the power to hear cases within the jurisdiction of the subject matter of the agency (e. g., tax liability, unfair competition, and unfair labor practice). This is similar to a court of law's hearing and rendering a decision in a case.

The Internal Revenue Service is an example of an agency having all three powers. The IRS enacts rules regarding taxes (a legislative function). It investigates, collects taxes, and administers its rules (an executive function). It makes determinations on tax liabilities (a judicial function).

C. ADMINISTRATIVE PROCEDURE

1. RIGHT TO A HEARING

The function of a hearing is to bring information to the determining body.

Due process under the fifth and fourteenth Amendments to the Constitution requires that federal and state governments provide notice and a hearing before taking action that would deprive a person of liberty or property. The right to a hearing is basic in administrative law and is a vital protection against governmental arbitrariness. Due process does not require that there be a *trial* but requires only a *hearing* at some point in the procedure. There is no right to a jury trial.

Examples of the types of adjudicatory action that *require* a hearing are discharge of a public employee, revocation of a license to practice for a professional person, the right of a tenured teacher to continued employment, the right of a person to qualify for welfare benefits, the right of a parolee to remain on parole, the right of an unwed father to obtain custody of his children, and the right to seize allegedly obscene books.

On the other hand, a hearing may be *denied* a public employee where the person's position involves access to secret information or policy making, the denial being made on the grounds of national interest. If a hearing would mean the disclosure of informants whose identity must be concealed in the interests of national security, the hearing may be denied.

2. THE HEARING

A. IN GENERAL

The government must generally provide a hearing *before* acting in a manner that will cause serious injury to a party (e.g., suspending a driver's license). However, in some cases, the government can act and provide a hearing later (e. g., cutting off disability benefits, discharging a civil service employee, effecting an emergency bank seizure, or calling a public health emergency, such as destruction of spoiled poultry). If the agency acts before a hearing, it can have practical consequences. The party seeking a hearing later has the burden of proof and the cost of going forward. Often this is a deterrent to any action by the party.

The hearing must be conducted at a time when the parties have had an opportunity to prepare their cases, and the hearing must be conducted in a meaningful manner. The parties must have had timely and adequate notice detailing the reasons for the proposed hearing.

A hearing officer can be disqualified by a showing that he or she is actually biased. Also, an ex parte contact with one of the parties would violate hearing procedure (e.g., having dinner with one of the parties and discussing the case).

The Federal Administrative Procedure Act of 1946, Section 554(b), contains a typical notice provision:

> Persons entitled to notice of an agency hearing shall be timely informed of—
>
> (1) The time, place, and nature of the hearing;
>
> (2) The legal authority and jurisdiction under which the hearing is to be held; and
>
> (3) The matters of fact and law asserted.
>
> When private persons are the moving parties, other parties to the proceedings shall give prompt notice of issues controverted in fact or law; and in other instances, agencies may by rule require responsive pleading. In fixing the time and place for hearings, due regard shall be had for the convenience and necessity of the parties or their representatives.

A person called as a witness has a right to counsel in all agency proceedings if they are adjudicative, but not if they are merely investigatory and not a criminal trial.

Unless there is a special statutory provision or special administrative regulation, there is generally no procedure for pretrial discovery.

B.   EVIDENCE

The trend is to admit all *relevant and useful* evidence at the discretion of the hearing officer. The normal rules of evidence do not apply in administrative hearings. The hearings are usually informal and similar to a legislative inquiry. However, the parties must be given an opportunity to defend and to cross-examine the witnesses.

In general, the hearing officer may consider only the evidence introduced at the hearing and not that from another source. For example, the hearing officer cannot go to the scene of an airplane crash, discuss the accident with the controller, and form an opinion based on that discussion, since it would not be on the record subject to cross-examination. If the hearing officer needs an expert to help in forming an opinion, he or she must have the expert testify on the record subject to cross-examination. An exception is where the evidence is best established by physical inspection (e.g., the hearing officer visits the scene of the accident).

Statistical data is often proper proof (e.g., publications of the Bureau of Labor Statistics). *Hearsay evidence* (statements made by another out of court, not under oath, and not subject to cross-examination) is generally admissible provided it is relevant. This means that evidence that would normally be inadmissible may be included as part of an administrative hearing for its probative value. However, it has been held that a driver's license cannot be suspended by a motor vehicle department when the only evidence presented at the hearing was an unauthenticated report made to the department by the driver of the other vehicle.

An agency may use material in its own files (annual reports of the railroad carriers in determining a reasonable rate for the transportation of ice) as proof. However, it is not permissible to make an unspecified reference to files without providing an opportunity for the parties to contradict.

A hearing officer may take official notice of facts concerning special skills and judgment that are in the field in which the agency usually operates (e. g., technical principals). In a court of law, this is known as judicial notice.

A hearing officer can generally evaluate evidence by using his or her own expertise and reach a conclusion based primarily on that expertise. This is especially common where difficult technical questions exist in an area in which the agency is experienced.

Except as otherwise provided by statute, the proponent of a rule or order has the burden of proof.

C.   FINDINGS

In both federal and state courts, administrative decisions are required to be based on adequate findings; i.e., the grounds upon which the agency acted must be clearly disclosed and adequately sustained.

In adjudicatory proceedings, A.P.A. Section 557(c) provides that "All decisions, including initial, recommended, and tentative decisions, are a part of the record and shall include a statement of—(A) findings and conclusions, and the reasons or basis therefor, on all the material issues of fact, law, or discretion presented on the record; and (B) the appropriate rule, order, sanction, relief, or denial thereof."

Several reasons exist for requiring findings:

1.   The findings as to certain facts may be necessary to establish the agency's powers or jurisdiction.

2.   Requiring the fact finder to state findings and reasons assures that he or she will carefully evaluate the evidence (helps prevent arbitrary action).

3.   Without findings, reviewing courts would have the very time-consuming task of scouring the record to ascertain if the ultimate decision had a reasonable basis.

4.   The findings give the parties a basis as to the reason for the decision, thereby simplifying petitions for rehearing and ultimately for judicial review.

3.   JUDICIAL REVIEW

A.   IN GENERAL

Generally, in order for one to qualify for judicial review, the administrative agency action must be a final one or must be made reviewable by statute.

Generally, a statute that creates a federal agency prescribes the procedure for judicial review of agency decisions (e. g., appeal to the Court of Appeals). In many states, a single state statute will set forth the general procedure for judicial review of state agency decisions.

Where there is no statutory procedure, the parties must use one of the common law writs (e. g., injunction and declaratory judgment, mandamus, habeas corpus).

Generally, the right of judicial review is granted to any person suffering a legal wrong because of agency action. The exceptions are when the statute precludes judicial review or when agency action is by law committed to agency discretion.

When the judicial review involves a question of *law*, the court will reverse the agency it if disagrees. However, if the question is one of *fact*, the court will seldom reverse.

Generally, the reviewing court is required to act in certain cases:

1.   To compel the agency to act when it unlawfully or unreasonably refuses to act.

2.   To set aside any agency actions that are
     (a) In excess of lawful authority.
     (b) Contrary to constitutional rights.
     (c) In violation of procedural requirements.
     (d) Arbitrary.
     (e) Unsupported by the evidence.

Pending review, the administrative agency may postpone the effective date of any action taken by it.

B. Exhaustion of Remedies

The doctrine of *exhaustion of administrative remedies* occurs when a person attempts to block an administrative proceeding about to begin, or interrupt one that has already begun, by going to court for relief rather than by seeking relief at the administrative level. The general rule is that a person cannot seek judicial review for a threatened injury until the prescribed administrative remedy has been exhausted. The reasons for the rule are as follows:

1. It permits full development of the facts prior to judicial review.

2. It enables the agency to employ the discretion or expertise expected of it.

3. It avoids piecemeal appeals from administrative agencies.

4. Administrative proceedings will not be circumvented by appeal to the courts.

5. It helps prevent the court dockets from being clogged.

6. It recognizes the autonomy of the agency and its right to transact business without undue interruption.

Exceptions to the exhaustion rule exist (a person can bypass the agency and appeal directly to the court) in the following instances:

1. The matter is in the general public interest.

2. The administrative procedure is constitutionally defective, beyond its jurisdiction, or illegal.

3. The administrative remedy is useless because the agency is deadlocked.

4. Pursuing administrative remedies will cause irreparable injury.

5. An appeal within the agency is not required by statute or agency rule.

D. CRITICISM OF ADMINISTRATIVE AGENCIES

Some of the complaints against administrative agencies are as follows:

1. The government, through its agencies, has become too big and too hard to control and supervise. As the size of these agencies increases, the ability of the people to control those in political power becomes less and less.

2. The same persons who establish the agency's rules act as prosecutor and as judge to determine whether or not the rules have been violated. One of our basic constitutional provisions is the separation of the powers of the government. Yet administrative agencies have in most cases legislative, judicial, and executive powers that violate this basic premise.

3.   The agencies do not follow the rules of courts. They reject the exclusionary rules of evidence. They use witnesses who are not available for cross-examination. They use extra-record information at arriving at decisions.

QUESTIONS AND PROBLEMS

1.   (a)   What is an administrative agency?

       (b)   How is one usually created?

       (c)   What powers may it have?

2.   Richard applies for a license as a pilot. The license application remains with the FAA for two years, and the FAA refuses to act upon it. Can Richard go to court to force the FAA to act?

3.   The Federal Highway Administrator is given statutory power to determine the routes of new highways. The administrator must consider such factors as cost, traffic movement, traffic safety, and potential disruption of neighborhoods. The administrator approves the decision to construct a certain highway that passes through a poor neighborhood in City. The people of the neighborhood protest that their neighborhood will be disrupted but admit that an alternate route will be much more expensive. Do you believe the court will set aside the decision of the administrator?

4.   The rules of Law and Order College provide that students must not disrupt class activities, and students who do are subject to expulsion. The rules also provide that before expulsion can occur, the students have the right to a conference with the dean of students. Richard, who has been accused of disruption, claims that the dean is biased against him because of statements attributable to the dean in which he said that Richard was a menace and should be kicked out of school.

       (a)   Should the dean hear the case?

       (b)   Does Richard have the right to cross-examine adverse witnesses?

5.   A statute requires the granting of licenses to all qualified real estate brokers. The state denies Alice a license on the grounds that she is not qualified because she is incompetent. Is Alice entitled to a hearing?

6.   The FAA is considering whether or not to revoke Richard's pilot's license because he recently crashed his plane.

       (a)   Would it be proper for the FAA members to examine the runways at the airport and rely on evidence from this personal inspection?

       (b)   Would it be proper for the members to discuss the accident with the air controller at the airport and rely on his opinion as to the cause of the accident?

7. In a procedure to set new rates, can the FCC use the following as evidence:

   (a) the consumer price index published by the Bureau of Labor Statistics?

   (b) its own files, without indicating exactly what materials in its files it examined and used?

8. A proceeding is brought against D, a doctor, in an administrative hearing to revoke his license for dispensing illegal drugs. One of his patients who allegedly used some of the drugs is now dead. However, before she died, she stated to investigators that the doctor prescribed the drugs to her. Assuming there is considerable other evidence against the doctor, would it be an error to admit and rely on her statement?

9. The Environmental Protection Agency is considering the revocation of the license of a pesticide on the grounds that the pesticide causes cancer. During the hearing, a great deal of scientific evidence is introduced that tends to confuse the examiner, who telephones the staff chemist at EPA and asks for an explanation of some of the evidence. Could the examiner's decision be reversed?

10. During the hearing on rate setting, the hearing officer accepts an invitation to dinner by the president of the company seeking a rate hike. During dinner the two discuss the reasons for the rate hike. Is this sufficient to have a decision reversed?

Chapter 6

TORTS AND CRIMES IN BUSINESS

Since people in business may become involved in torts or crimes, it is necessary to have some basic knowledge in these fields of law.

A tort can be defined as a private or civil wrong or injury; it is a violation of some duty to the plaintiff and a wrongful act for which a civil suit can be brought. The purpose of tort law is to compensate the person injured, not to punish the wrongdoer, as is the case in criminal law. It differs from a crime in that a crime is a positive or negative act in violation of a penal law. It is an offense against the state or society as a whole, rather than against the individual. An act can be a tort and a crime (e.g., false imprisonment).

A. TORTS IN BUSINESS

As stated above, a tort is any wrongful act consisting of the violation of a right for which a civil suit can be brought. Following are some of the common types of torts found in the business environment.

1. NEGLIGENCE

Negligence is the failure to use reasonable care that causes harm to a person or property. Reasonable care means the care that an ordinary prudent person would exercise under similar circumstances.

Four basic requirements are necessary for negligence: (1) there must be a duty owed; (2) it must be breached; (3) the breach must be the proximate cause of the harm; and (4) there must be damages.

The *duty* requirement generally arises by operation of law; for example, the legislature passes a statute regulating the speed of a motor vehicle. The *proximate cause* of an injury is that cause which, in natural and continuous sequence, unbroken by any efficient intervening cause, produces the injury and without which the result would not have occurred. It is the efficient cause the one that necessarily sets in operation the factors that accomplish the injury. Proximate cause remains an elusive concept, and both its rules and their application have been the subject of continual debate by courts and legal writers. A simple example of proximate cause is where the driver of an automobile runs a red light and strikes a pedestrian crossing the street in the crosswalk. Running the red light was the proximate cause of the harm to the pedestrian.

Examples of negligence in business are injuries caused by foods, drugs, and other products; malpractice by accountants, lawyers, and doctors; and motor vehicle collisions while the vehicle is used for a business purpose.

In most states, if the plaintiff is also negligent and that negligence contributed to his or her injuries, he or she cannot recover. This is called the doctrine of contributory negligence. Many states have discarded this doctrine in negligence cases and instead compare the negligence of the parties. That is, the plaintiff's negligence reduces the amount recovered in proportion to the degree of his or her own negligence.

Another possible defense is assumption of risk by the plaintiff. This involves a case where the plaintiff voluntarily enters into a risky situation knowing the risk involved. For example, a baseball fan voluntarily sits in a section where a foul ball often lands. The fan knows he might be hit but still sits there. The doctrine of assumption of risk should preclude the plaintiff from recovering a judgment. However, if a person sits in an unprotected area not knowing the danger, recovery should take place.

2. STRICT LIABILITY

Strict liability is discussed in Chapter 30 on products liability. It means that a person who commits such a tort is liable whether there was any negligence or intention to cause harm. Examples are injuries resulting from a defective product and abnormally dangerous activities such as dynamiting, crop dusting, fumigating, keeping wild animals, and emitting noxious gases or fumes into a settled community.

3. INTERFERENCE WITH CONTRACT OR BUSINESS RELATIONSHIP

The tort of wrongful *interference with a contract* arises when a third party intentionally and unjustifiably interferes with the performance of a contract between two other persons which causes one of the persons to the contract not to perform. For example, coach Chuck Fairbanks has a five-year contract with the New England Patriots. The University of Texas wants to hire Fairbanks to coach its team and offers Fairbanks $75,000 more per year than he is getting with the Patriots. The university makes this offer knowing that Fairbanks has four more years to run on his contract. If the offer by the university interferes with the Fairbanks-Patriot contract, the university will be liable for intentional interference with contractual relations.

The tort of wrongful *interference with a business relationship* arises when a person intentionally interferes with a business relationship between two parties. This relationship is not based on contract, because there is no binding contract between the parties. For example, while Fairbanks is negotiating a new contract with the Patriots, the university untruthfully tells Fairbanks that a person who knows nothing about football is buying the

Patriots, that this will ruin the team, and that he, Fairbanks, should get out while he can and sign with the university. Fairbanks, concerned that the new owner will ruin the team, signs a contract with the university. The university is guilty of the tort of interfering with a business relationship.

Not every interference is actionable. For the defendant's conduct to be privileged, however, it must be for justifiable ends and he or she must use justifiable means. For example, the end may be justifiable when the defendant carries on such an effective advertising campaign that one party breaches the contract with another party. The means may be justifiable by use of honest advertising.

4.   FRAUD

The essential elements of fraud are (1) a false representation of a material fact, (2) made with knowledge of its falsity or made with inexcusable ignorance of its truth, (3) with intention that it be acted upon by the party deceived, (4) that the party deceived reasonably relied upon the representation and acted upon it, and (5) that the party was thereby injured.

It is one of the most frequently committed business torts. A person defrauded can recover damages for the harm caused or rescind the contract. Fraud can also be a crime if it is in violation of a penal statute.

A more detailed discussion of fraud appears in Chapter 11.

5.   DEFAMATION

Defamation is a communication by the defendant to a third person that injures the plaintiff in his or her good name or reputation. There are two types of defamation: libel and slander. Libel is written and slander is oral.

The plaintiff must show that the defamatory matter was intentionally communicated by the defendant to some third person who understood it or that the defendant communicated through failure to exercise due care (e. g., left defamatory writing where it was reasonably forseeable that a third person may see it).

A publisher is one who is responsible for the original publication of a defamation and is strictly liable for that defamation unless he or she has a valid defense. One who repeats or republishes a defamation is also a publisher.

A disseminator merely circulates, sells, rents or otherwise distributes the material (e.g., dealer or distributor of books or newspapers). A disseminator is held only to a standard of due care (i. e., is liable only if he or she knew or should have known of the defamatory nature of the material).

Defamation has four defenses: (1) the plaintiff consented to the defamation; (2) the defamatory statement was true; (3) absolute privilege existed (statements made in the course of a judicial proceeding, statements made in a legislative proceeding, statements made by top rank executives as to a relevant communication in the discharge of their official duties, and defamatory statements uttered by either spouse about a third person to the other spouse); and (4) conditional or qualified privilege existed (e. g., most courts hold that credit-rating agencies have a conditional privilege if acting in good faith to provide information upon request to those having a legitimate interest).

A person may in good faith defame where reasonably necessary to protect an interest of his own (reporting a crime believed to have been committed against him, falsely informing his attorney that a customer owes him money).

Is a *computer mistake* a good defense to the charge of defamation? If the computer contains wrongful information communicated as a poor credit rating to third persons that harms a person, the credit bureau is liable. *Ford Motor Credit Company v. Swarens* (Ky., 447 S.W.2d 53) held no defense to an improper repossession of an automobile.

Defamation can also be a crime.

6.   DISPARAGEMENT

Disparagement is a false statement intentionally made to others that causes harm to the plaintiff. The false statement explicitly reflects on the plaintiff and tends to disparage the plaintiff's product or service. For example, a buyer contemplates purchasing seller's stock of merchandise but does not purchase because the buyer has read an advertisement in a newspaper in which a third party falsely asserts that he has a lien on the merchandise. The third party has disparaged the seller's property in the goods.

Disparagement differs from defamation in that defamation is generally available as a defense to reputation of a person, whereas disparagement usually involves business or property (defendant states that plaintiff's watch has only 10 jewels when it really has 21 jewels). It differs from fraud in that the statement in fraud is made directly to the plaintiff, whereas in disparagement, the statement is made to a third party.

7.   INTENTIONAL INFLICTION OF MENTAL DISTRESS

Intentional infliction of mental distress permits a person to recover from one who by an extreme and outrageous act causes the plaintiff to suffer serious mental distress (e. g., a bloody, dead rat wrapped up as a loaf of bread for a sensitive person to open, a collection agency using threatening language designed to harass the debtor, abusive and threatening conduct used by an evicting landlord or an insurance adjuster).

8.   FALSE IMPRISONMENT

False imprisonment is the unlawful confinement of one person by another. It is a misdemeanor at common law.

Confinement can consist of forcibly restraining a person within an enclosure with no reasonable means of escape. It can occur when a person is under no physical restraint but submits to a threat of force or asserted legal authority.

In *National Bond and Investment Co. v. Whithorn* (276 Ky. 204, 123 S.W.2d 263 [1939], the court held that the repossessors of cars were guilty of false imprisonment when they stopped Whithorn (owner of the car) while he was driving on a street and told him not to move the car. Shortly thereafter, a tow truck, which had been called by the repossessors, pulled up, hooked on to the car, and started pulling the car away. Whithorn objected vehemently, put on the emergency brake, and put the car into reverse, thereby stalling the wrecker and bringing the car to a stop after it had been towed about 100 feet. The court said that Whithorn did not have to leave his car and that the repossessors had no right to take the car over Whithorn's protests. While Whithorn was in his car, he was in a place he had the legal right to be.

A victim who consents to the confinement and is not coerced by threats of force or legal authority is not unlawfully confined.

A merchant has the legal right to detain a person the merchant reasonably believes has shoplifted merchandise. Most states have statutes that absolve the merchant of liability provided that the merchant detains the suspect in a reasonable manner, for only a reasonable time, and only if he or she has a reasonable cause. The following case is an example of false imprisonment, because the merchant did not have reasonable cause.

> **FACTS** Plaintiff picked out and paid for candy at defendant's store. The store manager suddenly grabbed her as she was about to leave the store, accusing her of stealing certain articles. He forcibly took her into custody against her will, detained her, and deprived her of her right to freedom. He publicly searched her and her shopping bag, but when he found nothing except what she had paid for, he released her.

> **DECISION** A merchant operating a self-service store does not have the right to apprehend and detain a customer and inspect parcels and packages upon mere suspicion of shoplifting based only upon a failure to heed or comply with some rule or regulation of the self-service store requiring customers to present for checking the merchandise they are carrying, regardless of whether it was purchased elsewhere or paid for when purchased.

> *Great Atlantic & Pacific Tea Co. et al. v. Smith,* (136 S.W.2d 759 [Ky. 1939])

False imprisonment can also be a crime.

9. ASSAULT AND BATTERY

An *assault* is the intentional action or conduct by one person directed at another that places him or her in apprehension of immediate bodily harm or offensive contact. For example, a manager of a store threatening a customer with a punch in the nose would constitute an assault. The person in danger of the assault must have knowledge of the danger and be apprehensive of an imminent threat to his or her safety. For example, if a store manager tells a fellow employee that he is going to punch a customer in the nose, there is no assault, since the customer is not aware of the threat. An assault can also be a crime.

A *battery* is the intentional act by a person to cause harmful or offensive bodily contact and the contact is actually made. For example, a store manager who actually hits a customer has committed a battery. A battery can also be a crime.

10. INVASION OF PRIVACY

Generally the tort of intentional invasion of privacy can occur in four situations: (1) when a person uses another's name or likeness for profit without permission; (2) when an unreasonable publication occurs placing a person in a false light, such as putting a sign on the victim's place of business accusing him or her of criminal activity that is not true; (3) when there is a disclosure of private facts, such as a merchant's putting a sign in his or her store window stating that a customer will not pay his or her bill;or (4) when there is an intrusion on the solitude or seclusion of another, such as eavesdropping on another's private conversations.

11. NUISANCE

A nuisance is the unreasonable interference with the possessory interest of an individual in the use or enjoyment of his or her land. The defendant's conduct or use of the property may have been intentional, negligent, or neither. Nearly anything can be a nuisance (e. g., pollution of air with noxious fumes, gases, vapors, smoke, or soot; loud noise from a race track, especially at night; the storing of explosives in a residential neighborhood). The interference must be annoying, offensive, or inconvenient to a "normal" person in the community. An unduly sensitive person would not have a case. Also, the gravity of the harm must outweigh the utility of the defendant's conduct. Factors considered are the type of neighborhood, relative value of the properties, and the existence of alternatives by which the defendant might achieve his or her goals.

12. CONVERSION

Conversion is the unauthorized and unjustified interference with the dominion and control of another's personal property. It is a civil action for theft. Conversion can be committed by taking property wrongfully or fraudulent; destroying property; using another's property without authority; buying, receiving, or selling stolen property; delivering property to the wrong person; or refusing to surrender property to the rightful owner on demand.

13. TRESPASS

A. REAL PROPERTY

Real property is land and anything attached thereto, such as minerals, trees, and buildings. The law protects the rights of the possessor of land to its exclusive use and quiet enjoyment.

Section 158 of the Restatement of Torts, Second, provides the following: One is subject to liability to another for trespass, irrespective of whether he thereby causes harm to any legally protected interest of the other, if he intentionally does any of the following:

1. Enters land in the possession of the other or causes a thing or a third person to do so.

2. Remains on the land.

3. Fails to remove from the land a thing which he is under a duty to remove.

It is no defense that the intruder acted upon the mistaken belief of law or fact that he was not trespassing. If the intruder intended to be upon the particular property, it is irrelevant that he reasonably believed that he owned the land or had permission to enter upon the land (Restatement of Torts, Second, Section 164). An intruder is not liable if his presence on the land of another is not caused by his own actions. For example, if A is thrown onto B's land by C, A is not liable to B for trespass, but C is. By the same token, if a heavy gust of wind carries A's garbage can onto B's land, A is not liable to B for trespass.

A trespass may be committed on, beneath, or above the surface of the land. Although it has been stated, *cujus est solum, ejus est usque ad coelum* (he who owns the soil owns upward into heaven), the advent of aviation has made this legal proposition obsolete. The law now regards the upper air, above the prescribed minimum altitude of flight, as a public highway. No trespass occurs unless the aircraft enters into the immediate reaches of the air space and substantially interferes with the landowner's use and enjoyment of it (Restatement of Torts, Second, Section 159).

B. PERSONAL PROPERTY

A chattel or personal property is any type of property other than an interest in land. The law protects a number of interests in the possession of chattels, including an interest in their physical condition and usability, an interest in the retention of possession, and an interest in their availability for future use.

Trespass to personal property or chattels consists of the intentional dispossession or unauthorized use of the chattel of another. The interference with the right to exclusive use and possession may be direct or indirect, but liability is limited to instances in which the trespassor (1) dispossesses the other of the chattel, (2) substantially impairs the condition, quality, or value of the chattel, (3) deprives the possessor of the use of the chattel for a substantial time, or (4) causes bodily harm to the possessor or harm to some person or thing in which the possessor has some legal interest (Restatement of Torts, Second, Section 218).

A major distinction between trespass to personal property and conversion is the measure of damages. In trespass, the possessor recovers damages for the actual harm to the chattel or as compensation for the loss of possession. In conversion, the possessor recovers the full value of the chattel and the convertor takes possession of it upon payment of the judgment.

14. UNFAIR COMPETITION

Unfair competition is an intentional tort enabling the victim to sue for damages or for an injunction to stop the unfair practice. The tort does not attempt to prevent all competition, only that which the court deems unfair.

The use of an employer's trade secret by a former employee is an example of unfair competition, since it gives other competitors in the same business a competitive advantage.

Other examples are imitating a competitor's packaging of products, signs, advertisements, trade name, or trademarks.

B. CRIMES IN BUSINESS

A crime is an act or omission plus criminal intent or negligence prohibited by law and enacted for the protection of the public. The wrong is against the public rather than against the individual, as is the case in a civil wrong. Following are some of the common types of crimes found in the business environment.

1. LARCENY

Larceny is taking and carrying away by trespass (wrongfully) the personal property of another with the intent to permanently deprive him or her of it. The defendant may act directly or by an agent (e. g., a child). He or she may obtain possession directly, as in the case of robbery, or by trick (e. g., where he uses false tokens or pretenses).

It is no defense that the person from whom the property was taken was not the owner so long as that person had the right of possession. Statutes in many states provide that an act is larceny even when the defendant intends to return the property (e. g., joyriding statutes).

It is not larceny where the defendant receives or takes the goods by mistake unless he had a wrongful intent at the time he acquired the goods.

2. ROBBERY AND BURGLARY

Robbery and burglary are two different crimes. *Robbery* at common law was the unlawful taking and carrying away of personal property of another from his person or in his presence, by force or fear, with the intent to permanently deprive him of his property.

A purse snatcher is usually guilty of larceny rather than of robbery, because the requisite force is not present. However, if the victim is shoved, the crime can be robbery.

Burglary at common law was the breaking and entering of a dwelling at night with intent to commit a felony. Most states have statutes covering the crime of burglary. For example, the California Penal Code, Section 459, does not require that there be a breaking, does not require that the crime be committed at night, expands the word "dwelling" to practically any type of building, and includes intent not only to commit "any felony" but also to commit "grand or petit larceny." Thus, it is much easier to commit the crime of burglary under our modern statutes than it was at common law. A typical example of a burglary is the entering of a home or store to take and carry away personal property.

3. EMBEZZLEMENT

Embezzlement is the wrongful appropriation of personal property of another by one who has been entrusted with it and who has lawful possession. It is a statutory offense. It is common for the statute to specify the persons to whom they apply: clerk, servant, agent, executor, officer, public official. Intent to return the property or its equivalent, or the fact it is returned, is generally no defense.

4. RECEIVING STOLEN PROPERTY

This crime is committed when the defendant takes property into his or her possession with knowledge that it has been stolen and with intent to permanently deprive the owner.

It is not generally required that the defendant be certain that the goods were stolen; it is sufficient if he or she strongly suspects that the goods were stolen. Although the test is whether the defendant actually had the required knowledge, this knowledge can be proven by circumstantial evidence (e. g., purchase of goods for grossly inadequate price or prior purchases of stolen goods from the thief).

5. OBTAINING PROPERTY BY FALSE PRETENSES

This crime consists of obtaining title to personal property through false representations with intent to defraud. The representation must be untrue and the defendant must know it is untrue. The representation must relate to a past or present fact. The victim must rely on the false representation and must intend to relinquish title to the property as well as possession.

6. FORGERY

Forgery is the false making or material alteration of any writing having apparent legal significance with intent to defraud. Typical examples are checks, deeds, mortgages, contracts, and wills. Signing another's name without authority to an instrument is forgery. Raising the amount of a check is forgery.

7. ARSON

Arson is the burning of the dwelling house of another with malice. The slightest burning will suffice. Modern statutes in most jurisdictions have expanded the crime to include any buildings or structures, whether owned by the defendant or by others, or any personal property in excess of a certain value (e. g., $25.00). Property burned with intent to defraud an insurance company is a separate crime in most jurisdictions.

8.   COMPOUNDING CRIMES

This crime consists of accepting money or anything of value from one who has committed a crime pursuant to an agreement not to report or prosecute the crime. The victim himself may be guilty of compounding (e. g., the victim of embezzlement agrees not to prosecute the embezzler if he returns the money). If the victim institutes the agreement by threats to prosecute, he or she may also be guilty of extortion. The obvious procedure for the victim of a crime is to report it to the proper authorities. The reason behind making the above actions of the victim a crime is that the commission of a crime is not a crime against the victim (he or she may have an action in tort), but rather a crime against the people (i. e., the state). Therefore, only the people through their proper representatives (the police, district attorney, judge, governor) have the right to "forgive" a crime (e. g., upon restitution of the money). Statutes in many states provide that certain crimes, usually misdemeanors, may be compromised with the approval of the court.

9.   INCOME TAX EVASION

It is a crime to knowingly annd willfully cause the filing of a false and fraudulent income tax return. This crime is committed by understating gross income, overstating expenses, or a combination the two.

PROBLEMS

1.   Defendant, a plumber, while driving to a job in the truck he uses in his business, fails to observe a stop sign and enters an intersection without stopping. Plaintiff, a college student who is in a hurry to get to class because he is late, enters the interesection at 25 miles per hour above the posted speed limit and strikes defendant's vehicle in the front fender. Plaintiff sues for damages. Was defendant negligent? Was plaintiff negligent? If there was negligence, was it the proximate cause of the accident? Was there any contributory negligence? If there was contributory negligence, would that operate as a bar to recovery? Would comparative negligence be a bar to recovery?

2.   Al, a business competitor of Discount Stores, Inc., tells Crocker, who has a contract with Discount Stores, Inc., that Discount's products are of inferior quality and that Discount's promises are no good. Al's false statements cause Crocker to break his contract with Discount. Has Discount any legal remedies against Al or Crocker?

3.   S sells his automobile new-parts store to B telling B that all of the boxes under the counter are filled with parts. B, relying on this statement, purchases the store. Later B learns that the boxes are filled with used parts not fit for sale. B seeks rescission of the contract. Decision?

4. P, a young woman who suffered a neck injury when struck by an automobile while crossing the street at an intersection crosswalk, is told by the insurance adjuster, who represents the owner of the automobile, that he believes P is a faker. He threatens her that if she does not accept a settlement in the amount of $100 right now, he will not give her "one red cent" later. Does P have any cause of action against the adjuster?

5. (a) A merchant is informed by a customer that the customer thinks that D put one of the merchant's products in his coat pocket. The merchant orders D to accompany him to his office, where he orders D to empty his pockets. What tort or crime, if any, has the merchant committed?

(b) On two separate occasions, eyewitness employees of a fabric mill reported to their employer that Barbara Farut, a fellow employee, had been seen secreting employer's cloth in her purse. After the second report, security guards delayed Farut for about 20 minutes at the mill gatehouse as she attempted to leave work. The delay was to investigate the reports. The security guards requested that she open her purse; she refused to do so. After some discussion, she left the mill gatehouse without further hindrance. Farut files action for false imprisonment based upon the delay at the gatehouse. Discuss.

6. The chimneys of the XYZ factory emit soot and smoke that cause damage to the paint on nearby houses. The chimneys can be equipped to prevent the soot and smoke from escaping at relatively inexpensive cost. The owners of the houses seek your advice.

7. D gives the cashier at the college cafeteria a $2 bill. The cashier in her haste gives D change for a $20 bill. D takes his tray of food and the change and walks away. Has D commited any crime?

8. Employee needs money for medicine for his sick child and "borrows" $10 from the employer's cash register intending to pay the money back when he receives his pay check. When employee receives his pay check he returns the $10. Has he committed any crime?

9. B, the owner of a junk yard, purchases four Cadillac hub caps in excellent condition from a 12-year-old boy for $2 each. Has B committed any crime?

10. D, over a period of many months, embezzles thousands of dollars from his employer. When the employer learns of D's actions, he tells D that if D will return all of the money, he will not inform the police as to what D has done. D returns the money. Has the employer committed any crime?

Chapter 7

LEGAL ANALYSIS OF CASES

The study of cases or court opinions is one of the best methods of learning the law. Most law schools use the case method for presentation of subject matter. The study of cases is the inductive method of learning; i.e., it starts with the cases that contain specific fact situations and application of legal principles from which the student learns to reason and reach a conclusion.

In reading the title of a case (e.g., *Smith v. Jones*), the "v." means versus or against. Thus, in the trial court, Smith is the plaintiff who brought the suit and Jones is the defendant against whom the suit was brought. When the case is appealed, some courts place the name of the party who appeals (called "appellant") first. Thus, in our example, if Jones lost the case at the trial level and then appealed, the title of the case would read *Jones v. Smith*. Because this can be confusing, a notation has been made in each case where the defendant appealed and his or her name is first in the title.

Mose cases used in law books are many years old. Authors use these older cases for many reasons:

1. The facts in the chosen case best demonstrate the legal point involved.

2. The facts are interesting and practical.

3. The court's discussion of the law is clear and is still used to define the law.

4. The case lends itself to class discussion.

5. The authors can edit down a lengthy case to one or two pages without losing the point of the case.

6. The case was the first to be decided on that particular legal point.

7. A more recent case involving similar facts or law has not been tried.

A. IN GENERAL

Subsequent chapters contain text material, edited appellate cases, and problems. Before you read the cases or the problems, study the text material. This brief material will give you a summary of the law involved in the chapter. If you are familiar with this material, it will be easier to brief the cases and answer the problems.

B. HOW TO BRIEF A CASE

A standard procedure is followed in reciting on a law case. The procedure consists of using a brief of the case in the book. Before class, the student reads the case very carefully. When the student feels that he or she understands the case, the student prepares a brief of the case. The format of the brief follows (made for the first case in the book).

RICHARDSON v. J. C. FLOOD COMPANY

190 A.2d 259 (D.C.App.1963)

ACTION: Suit for labor and material furnished for a new water line.

FACTS: Defendant (the appellant) requested the plaintiff plumbing company to correct a stoppage in the sewer line of her house. During the cleaning of the line, plaintiff discovered that a water pipe running parallel with the sewer line was defective. Defendant was informed of the defective water line and told that it had to be replaced then or at a later date when the yard would have to be redug for that purpose. Plaintiff replaced the defective water line. Defendant, through daily inspections of the repairs, knew of the magnitude of the work required and made no objection to the replacement of the water line until after the entire job was finished, at which time defendant refused to pay any part of the total bill submitted. She defends on the ground that she did not authorize the replacement of the water line.

QUESTION: Did the failure of the defendant to object to plaintiff's conduct create an implied agreement to pay for the replacement of the water line?

DECISION: Yes. Judgment for plaintiff.

RULE: A contract for work to be done is implied when arising from a mutual agreement and promise not set forth in words. A contract may be presumed from the acts and conduct of the parties.

In preparing the brief, be certain that you incorporate all important facts; however, remember that the brief is supposed to be brief. If you understand all important facts, you will find that the rule usually follows quite logically. If you change one important fact, you can change the result of the case.

The question or issue in the case is extremely important. Ask yourself, "What is this fight all about? Why are they in court?" If you do not know, you do not have the case.

Finally, be able to state the court's reason for the decision and be ready to defend or challenge it.

What do the numbers and abbreviations called a "citation" under the title of the case mean? The first number means the volume in the reporter where the case can be found. The last number means the page. The letters indicate the name of the state appellate court. In our example, the citation would mean "District of Columbia Court of Appeals, Volume 190, Atlantic Reporter Second Series, Page 259." Thus, the entire decision in the *Richardson v. Flood Company* case can be found in Volume 190, Page 259, of the Second Series of the Atlantic Reporter. For purposes of classroom study, the complete decision has been edited, as indicated by the asterisks in the case.

Trial court decisions are generally not published as reported decisions, although there are a few exceptions (e.g., federal court decisions, New York decisions). Trial court decisions are filed only in the office of the clerk of the court where the trial took place.

The decisions of the appellate courts are found both in state reports of that particular state and in a series of reporters embracing the whole United States comprising the National Reporter System, published by West Publishing Company. The National Reporter System divides the states into seven regional reporter groups: Atlantic (Atl. or A.), North Eastern (N.E.), North Western (N.W.), Pacific (Pac. or P.), Southern (So.), South Eastern (S.E.), and South Western (S.W.). Consolidating reported cases by area makes it much simpler to research cases.

The federal court decisions are found in the Federal Reporter (Fed. or F.), Federal Supplement (F.Supp.), Federal Rules Decisions (F.R.D.), and United States Supreme Court Reports (U.S.), Supreme Court Reporter (S.Ct.), Lawyers Edition (L.Ed.).

Part II

THE LAW OF CONTRACTS

Chapter 8

NATURE OF CONTRACTS

A contract is an agreement, express or implied, to do or not to do a particular thing. The Restatement, *Contracts,* Section 1, gives the following definition: "A contract is a promise or a set of promises for the breach of which the law gives a remedy, or the performance of which the law in some recognizes as a duty." The U.C.C. definition of a contract is: " 'Contract' means the total legal obligation which results from the parties' agreement as affected by this Act and any other applicable rules of law." Section 1–201(11). Also see Section 1–201(3), Appendix A, for definition of "agreement."

Generally, the following elements are required in a legal contract: (1) two or more competent parties, (2) their consent, (3) consideration, (4) a proper subject matter, and (5) mutuality of obligation. These requirements are considered in subsequent chapters.

For our purposes, we can classify contracts as follows: (1) express or implied, (2) unilateral or bilateral, (3) executed or executory, and (4) void, voidable, or unenforceable.

An express contract is one in which its terms are stated *in words* oral or written. An implied in fact contract is one in which the existence and terms are manifested *by conduct.* The distinction between an express contract and an implied in fact contract relates only to the manner in which the consent was made evident by the parties. To illustrate: A man waves to a taxi, gets in, and gives the driver an address. No other words are spoken. This is an implied contract that the driver will receive compensation for taking the man to the address.

Another type of contract is one that is implied in law, normally referred to as a "quasi-contract." In this case, the law imposes an obligation on a party to prevent an unjust enrichment. That is, the law may imply a promise to pay for benefits or services rendered even though no such promise may have been made or intended. For example, a nurse furnishes beneficial services to a person who has been insane for many years. There is no contract as such. However, if the nurse rendered the services in good faith with no intention of making a gift of such services, the nurse could recover the reasonable value of the services in a quasi-contract or, as is also said, as if there were a contract. The following case is an example of a quasi-contract.

FACTS A contractor furnished labor and materials used in the construction of a bathroom in a home owned by Mr. and Mrs. Dozier. The contractor had acted upon a request by the Doziers' daughter who lived in the home with her parents. The materials and labor were furnished with the full knowledge and consent of the homeowners. The daughter refused to pay, and the contractor sued the Doziers, who defended on the grounds that they did not have a contract with the contractor.

DECISION The court gave judgment for the contractor for the reasonable value of the improvements. A benefit was conferred on the defendants by the plaintiff, and appreciation given by the defendants of such benefit, and acceptance made of such benefit under such circumstances that it would be inequitable for the defendants to retain the benefit without payment of its value.

Actions brought upon theories of unjust enrichment, quasi-contracts, contracts implied in law, and *quantum meruit* ("as much as he deserved") are essentially the same, and courts frequently employ the various terminology interchangeably to describe that class of implied obligations where, on the basis of justice and equity, the law will impose contractual relationship between the parties, regardless of their assent thereto. [Judgment for the plaintiff.]

Paschall v. Dozier (219 Tenn. 45, 407 S.W.2d 150 [1966])

A unilateral contract is one in which a promise is given in exchange for an act or the forebearance of an act, with only one promisor. An example of a unilateral contract is the reward type of case. The law enforcement agency offers a reward for the capture of a criminal. The promise is the offer of the reward, and the act is the capture of the criminal.

A bilateral contract is one in which mutual promises are given. One promise is given in consideration for the other promise. Most contracts are bilateral. An attorney promises to perform certain services for a client. The client promises to pay money for the services. This is a bilateral contract.

An executed contract is one in which the object of the contract is fully performed (e. g., a cash sale). All others are executory (i. e., a contract that is wholly performed on one side but unperformed on the other side) or unperformed on both sides in whole or in part). The distinction is important in certain cases such as illegality, modification of a written contract by executed oral agreement, consideration, and the statute of frauds. In such cases (discussed in detail in later chapters), the defenses normally available to performance of the contract are no longer available if the contract has been executed.

A void contract is a nullity and cannot be enforced by either party; for example, the victim of fraud in the inception did not know she was signing a legal document. A voidable contract is void or valid at the option of the parties. For example, a contract induced by fraudulent misrepresentations would be voidable at the option of the victim. (See Chapter 11, B., for discussion of fraud.)

An unenforceable contract is one that cannot be enforced because of some legal technicality, such as the failure to satisfy the statute of frauds (failure to put the contract in writing which the statute of frauds requires of certain contracts) or because the statute of limitations has run on the contract (failure to file the lawsuit within the time prescribed by local statute). Such contracts are unenforceable rather than void or voidable.

A contract or clause therein, can also be unenforceable because it is unconscionable (i. e., an absence of meaningful choice on the part of one of the parties together with unreasonable contract terms favoring the other party). (See the U.C.C., Sections 2–302, and 2–719(3), Appendix A.) The basic test is whether the clauses involved are so one-sided as to be unconscionable under the circumstances existing at the time the contract was made and in light of the general commercial needs of the particular trade or case. Examples of unconscionable contracts are those involving grossly excessive prices, particularly when the buyer is a person of limited income and education, or contracts with clauses hidden in fine print and unknown to the consumer. Most courts do not limit the test of unconscionability to the sale of goods but will apply it to any agreement. The following case is an example of an unconscionable clause in a commercial setting.

FACTS Plaintiff brought this action against the oil company to recover losses suffered when the service station that he operated under defendant's retail dealer contract was destroyed by fire allegedly caused by defendant's delivery of gasoline containing water. Plaintiff seeks to recover the loss of his inventory and other consequential damages.

Defendant moves to dismiss plaintiff's claim for consequential damages relying on a clause in the retail dealer contract that provides: "In no event shall Seller be liable for prospective profits or special, indirect or consequential damages."

The plaintiff claims the clause is unconscionable.

DECISION The court stated, "We believe the law in Michigan to be that, where goods or services used by a significant segment of the public can be obtained from only one source, or from limited sources on no more favorable terms, an unreasonable term in a contract for such goods or services will not be enforced as a matter of public policy."

The court found the clause to be unconscionable and not binding on the plaintiff, noting that the plaintiff could not read well and therefore could not understand the significance of the clause and that the clause was not brought to the plaintiff's attention nor was its legal significance explained to him.

Johnson v. Mobil Oil Corporation (415 F.Supp. 264 [1976])

ILLUSTRATIVE CASES

1. Contract Implied When Failure to Object

RICHARDSON v. J. C. FLOOD COMPANY

190 A.2d 259 (D.C.App.1963)

MYERS, Judge. This is an appeal by a property owner [defendant Richardson] from a judgment against her for costs of labor and material furnished by appellee [plaintiff] plumbing company.

Appellant contends there was error in the findings of the trial court that all work done by appellee was authorized by her and that there was sufficient competent evidence to substantiate the amount of recovery.

Appellant requested appellee to correct a stoppage in the sewer line of her house. In the course of the work a "snake" used to clear the line leading to the main sewer became caught and to secure its release a portion of the sewer line in the backyard was excavated. It was then discovered that the instrument was embedded in pieces of wood which had become lodged in a sewer trap from surface debris. At this time numerous leaks were found in a rusty, defective water pipe which ran parallel with the sewer line. In order to meet District regulations, the water pipe, of a type no longer approved for such service, had to be replaced then or at a later date when the yard would have to be redug for that purpose. Appellee's agent testified he so informed appellant's agent. Appellant testified she had requested appellee to clear the sewer line but denied she was told about the need for replacement of the water line and contested the total amount of the charges for all the work done by appellee.

In the absence of a written contract, but with appellant admitting she had requested correction of a sewer obstruction but denying she had agreed to replace the water pipe, the existence of an implied agreement between the parties to replace the water pipe at the same time became an issue for the trial court.

It seems clear from the record that there was evidence to support a finding that appellant and her agent through daily inspections of the repairs knew of the magnitude of the work required and made no objection to the performance of the extra work in replacing the water pipe until after the entire job was finished when appellant refused to pay any part of the total bill submitted.

Contracts for work to be done are either express or implied—*express* when their terms are stated by the parties, *implied* when arising from a mutual agreement and promise not set forth in words. Direct evidence is not essential to prove a contract which may be presumed from the acts and conduct of the parties as a reasonable man would view them under all the circumstances. The testimony was conflicting but we cannot say that the trial court was wrong in holding that the burden of proving its right to recover had been carried by appellee.

With respect to the costs of both jobs the record reveals that no testimony was offered by appellant to show that itemized amounts for labor and materials furnished by appellee were wrong or excessive and unreasonable or that the work performed was either unnecessary or unsatisfactory. Appellee produced testimony that the charges were fair and reasonable and that the work on both the sewer and the water lines was fully completed. We find no merit in appellant's claim of error that the evidence on the costs of labor and material was insufficient to support the finding on this point.

[Affirmed.]

2. Quasi-Contract: Retention Must Be Inequitable

PUTTKAMMER v. MINTH

83 Wis.2d 686, 266 N.W.2d 361 (1978)

HANSEN, Justice. The defendant, Minth, is the owner of the Hiawatha Supper Club in Eagle River, Wisconsin, which he leased during 1972 and 1973 to James Piekarski. During the period of the lease, the plaintiff, at the request of Piekarski, resurfaced the access and service areas of the supper club, providing labor and materials with a reasonable value of $2,540, and increasing the value of the property by the same amount.

The defendant was aware that this work was being done and "stood by and acquiesced" in its completion. Piekarski did not pay for the work and was subsequently adjudged bankrupt, with no assets in his estate for the payment of plaintiff. The defendant now has the benefit of the improvements but refuses to pay for them, and the plaintiff has not been paid for any portion of the work.

The complaint further alleges that the plaintiff has exhausted his remedy against Piekarski and that if the defendant is not required to pay for the improvements, he will be unjustly enriched at the plaintiff's expense. The amended complaint therefore prays for damages in the amount of $2,540, plus costs and disbursements.

*   *   *

The plaintiff maintains that the complaint states a cause of action in equity for unjust enrichment. The elements of such a cause of action are: (1) a benefit conferred upon the defendant by the plaintiff; (2) an appreciation or knowledge by the defendant of the benefit; and (3) acceptance or retention by the defendant of the benefit under circumstances making it inequitable for the defendant to retain the benefit without payment of its value.

*   *   *

In an action for unjust enrichment, " '[r]ecovery is based upon the universally recognized moral principle that one who has received a benefit has the duty to make restitution when to retain such benefit would be unjust.' " [Citations.] It is not enough to establish that a benefit was conferred and retained; the retention must be inequitable.

The law in this state thus recognizes the principle set forth in the Restatement, *Restitution,* sec. 1, Comment c., p. 13, that:

Even where a person has received a benefit from another, he is liable to pay therefor only if the circumstances of its receipt or retention are such that, as between the two persons, it is unjust for him to retain it. The mere fact that a person benefits another is not of itself sufficient to require the other to make restitution therefor.

*　　　*　　　*

The general rule of the authorities which have come to our attention is summarized in 98 C.J.S. *Work & Labor* § 42, pp. 779, 780, as follows:

[A] landlord or lessee [sic] cannot be held liable for materials furnished and labor performed by plaintiff on the leased premises where plaintiff entered into the undertaking looking only to the tenant or lessee for payment in the absence of anything to show that the landlord ordered the work, or authorized anyone to have it done, or ratified the work after it was done, and notwithstanding the landlord ultimately benefits from the work that was done by reason of his ownership of the property.

3. Unconscionable Contracts Not Enforceable (U.C.C. 2-302)

JONES v. STAR CREDIT CORP.

59 Misc.2d 189, 298 N.Y.S.2d 264 (1969)

Action brought by buyers, welfare recipients, to reform sales contract which was allegedly unconscionable. The Supreme Court, Special Term. Sol M. Wachtler, J., held that selling for $900 ($1,439.69 including credit charges and $18 sales tax) a freezer unit having an actual retail value of $300 was, under the Uniform Commercial Code, unconscionable as a matter of law.

WACHTLER, Justice.　On August 31, 1965 the plaintiffs, who are welfare recipients, agreed to purchase a home freezer unit for $900 as the result of a visit from a salesman representing Your Shop At Home Service, Inc. With the addition of the time credit charges, credit life insurance, credit property insurance, and sales tax, the purchase price totalled $1,234.80. Thus far the plaintiffs have paid $619.88 toward their purchase. The defendant claims that with various added credit charges paid for an extension of time there is a balance of $819.81 still due from the plaintiffs. The uncontroverted proof at the trial established that the freezer unit, when purchased, had a maximum retail value of approximately $300. The question is whether this transaction and the resulting contract could be considered unconscionable within the meaning of Section 2–302 of the Uniform Commercial Code which provides in part:

(1) If the court as a matter of law finds the contract or any clause of the contract to have been unconscionable at the time it was made the court may refuse to enforce the contract, or it may enforce the remainder of the contract without the unconscionable clause, or it may so limit the application of any unconscionable clause as to avoid any unconscionable result.

(2) When it is claimed or appears to the court that the contract or any clause thereof may be unconscionable the parties shall be afforded a reasonable opportunity to present evidence as to its commercial setting, purpose and effect to aid the court in making the determination.
* * *

There was a time when the shield of "caveat emptor" would protect the most unscrupulous in the marketplace—a time when the law, in granting parties unbridled latitude to make their own contracts, allowed exploitative and callous practices which shocked the conscience of both legislative bodies and the courts.

The effort to eliminate these practices has continued to pose a difficult problem. On the one hand it is necessary to recognize the importance of preserving the integrity of agreements and the fundamental right of parties to deal, trade, bargain, and contract. On the other hand there is the concern for the uneducated and often illiterate individual who is the victim of gross inequality of bargaining power, usually the poorest members of the community.

The law is beginning to fight back against those who once took advantage of the poor and illiterate without risk of either exposure or interference. From the common law doctrine of intrinsic fraud we have, over the years, developed common and statutory law which tells not only the buyer but also the seller to beware. This body of laws recognizes the importance of a free enterprise system but at the same time will provide the legal armor to protect and safeguard the prospective victim from the harshness of an unconscionable contract.

Section 2–302 of the Uniform Commercial Code enacts the moral sense of the community into the law of commercial transactions. It authorizes the court to find, as a matter of law, that a contract or a clause of a contract was "unconscionable at the time it was made", and upon so finding the court may refuse to enforce the contract, excise the objectionable clause or limit the application of the clause to avoid an unconscionable result. "The principle", states the Official Comment to this section, "is one of the prevention of oppression and unfair surprise". It permits a court to accomplish directly what heretofore was often accomplished by construction of language, manipulations of fluid rules of contract law and determinations based upon a presumed public policy.

There is no reason to doubt, moreover, that this section is intended to encompass the price term of an agreement. In addition to the fact that it has already been so applied * * * the statutory language itself makes it clear that not only a clause of the contract, but the contract in toto, may be found unconscionable as a matter of law. Indeed, no other provision of an agreement more intimately touches upon the question of unconscionability than does the term regarding price.

Fraud, in the instant case, is not present; nor is it necessary under the statute. The question which presents itself is whether or not, under the circumstances of this case, the sale of a freezer unit having a retail value of

$300 for $900 ($1.439.69 including credit charges and $18 sales tax) is unconscionable as a matter of law. The court believes it is.

Concededly, deciding the issue is substantially easier than explaining it. No doubt, the mathematical disparity between $300, which presumably includes a reasonable profit margin, and $900, which is exorbitant on its face, carries the greatest weight. Credit charges alone exceed by more than $100 the retail value of the freezer. These alone, may be sufficient to sustain the decision. Yet, a caveat is warranted lest we reduce the import of Section 2–302 solely to a mathematical ratio formula. It may, at times, be that; yet it may also be much more. The very limited financial resources of the purchaser, known to the sellers at the time of the sale, is entitled to weight in the balance. Indeed, the value disparity itself leads inevitably to the felt conclusion that knowing advantage was taken of the plaintiffs. In addition, the meaningfulness of choice essential to the making of a contract, can be negated by a gross inequality of bargaining power. * * *

Having already paid more than $600 toward the purchase of this $300 freezer unit, it is apparent that the defendant has already been amply compensated. In accordance with the statute, the application of the payment provision should be limited to amounts already paid by the plaintiffs and the contract be reformed and amended by changing the payments called for therein to equal the amount of payment actually so paid by the plaintiffs.

QUESTIONS AND PROBLEMS

1. What is the difference between an express contract and an implied in fact contract?

2. State an example of an implied in fact contract.

3. Why does the law impose an obligation in the case of a quasi-contract?

4. What is the difference between a void and voidable contract?

5. What are some of the facts that may lead a court to hold that a clause in a contract, or the contract itself, is unconscionable?

6. With particular reference to the discussion in *Jones v. Star Credit Corp.*:

(a) Should the courts protect people who enter into contracts that are unfair to those persons? Why?

(b) Why let a person out of a contract because the contract provides for a price that is grossly excessive or contains important provisions in fine print? So long as there is no fraud, why not enforce it?

(c)   Does this type of holding encourage people to not read the fine print, knowing they might be able to get out of the contract later if the fine print makes the contract unfair? Does it encourage people not to see an attorney regarding the meaning of the contract?

7.   Sosa Crisan was an 87-year-old widow of Roumanian origin without any relatives. While shopping at her grocer's on March 17, she collapsed and was moved by the Detroit police department to its receiving hospital, where she was admitted and remained for 14 days. On March 31, she was transferred to Central Hospital, where she died, without ever regaining consciousness, on February 9, some 11 months later. The City of Detroit had a contract with the receiving hospital which gives the City the right to charge for services rendered by the receiving hospital. The City presented a claim against Crisan's estate for services rendered. The executor of the estate contends that the estate does not have to pay, because there was no meeting of the minds of the parties as to charges for services rendered because Crisan was unconscious at all times. Decision?

8.   Richard was seriously injured in an automobile accident. A bystander called Dr. Meine to render medical treatment while Richard was unconscious. Dr. Meine sent Richard a bill for the reasonable value of his medical services. Richard refuses to pay. Decision?   Quasi - Unjust enrichment

9.   Debtor paid money to X by mistake, intending to pay the money to Creditor. X has no right to the money but refuses to return it to Debtor. Can Debtor obtain a judgment for return of the money?

10.   Seller, a dealer, sold Buyer a seven-year-old Buick for $939.75 plus a credit service charge of $242.47. During the first week that Buyer operated the automobile, the steering post on the front end of the car was loose, the wheel bearing on the right front made an unusual noise, the shock absorbers were defective, and the ignition would not always start. Buyer spent $570 to repair the automobile. Buyer seeks your advice as to his right to relief under U.C.C. Section 2–302.

Chapter 9

REACHING THE AGREEMENT

A. INTENTION OF THE PARTIES

1. MANIFESTATION OF ASSENT

Every contract must have mutual assent or consent. Mutual assent is determined by the acts and the reasonable meaning of the words of the parties and not from the unexpressed intentions of the parties. This is referred to as the objective test for ascertaining intent. In other words, it is not necessary to have an actual meeting of the minds of the parties to have a valid contract. It is sufficient if there is an apparent meeting of the minds. The following case illustrates the point that an expression can be reasonably understood as manifesting an intent to make an offer and not to be a joke.

> **FACTS** Seller and buyer were each dealers in cattle. During an extremely hot spell, seller was worried over the fact that he had too many cattle on the market. Buyer discovering this fact jokingly offered to buy the cattle. After some dickering as to price, the parties apparently came to an agreement. Buyer later insisted that the whole transaction was a joke. Seller believed that buyer's offer to buy the cattle was made seriously. Seller sues for damages.

> **DECISION** The court held for the seller. Under the objective test for ascertaining intent, all that is needed is an apparent meeting of the minds for a valid contract. Undisclosed intentions of one party are not part of the contract. If the law were otherwise, a party might successfully escape his obligations on a contract by stating that he or she was only joking.

> *Deitrick v. Sinnott* (189 Iowa 1002, 179 N.W. 424 [1920])

2. NEGLIGENCE IN SIGNING OR ACCEPTING A CONTRACT

As a general rule, one who signs or accepts a contract which on its face, is a contract is deemed to assent to all of its terms. The party cannot escape liability on the grounds that he or she has not read the contract. Of course, if fraud was present in procuring the signature, or if a fiduciary relationship

51

existed between the parties giving rise to an affirmative duty of disclosure, the signer would not be liable but would probably end up in expensive litigation. A common complaint in a contract dispute is either "I didn't read the contract" or "I didn't understand the contract." Generally this is no excuse. Therefore, it is very important to remember that you should never sign a legal document of any kind unless you understand it. If you do not understand the document, take it to an attorney, who can advise you as to its legal consequences. The following case illustrates the point that failure to read the contract generally is no defense.

> **FACTS** In June 1940, Vargas entered into an employment contract with Esquire by which he agreed to furnish Esquire with certain art material. Vargas understood that he was signing a contract fixing the terms and compensation. There were only six paragraphs to the contract. It was written in plain and ordinary language.

> **DECISION** In the absence of fraud, a person in possession of all his faculties who signs a contract cannot relieve himself from the obligations of the contract by saying he did not read it when he signed it or did not know or understand what it contained. It is a well-settled rule of law that a party to a contract who is able to read and has the opportunity to do so cannot thereafter claim ignorance of its terms and conditions.

Vargas v. Esquire, Inc. (166 F.2d 651 [7th Cir. 1948])

B. THE OFFER

1. IN GENERAL

A contract results from an offer and the acceptance thereof. No particular formality is required. An offer is a proposal to enter into a contract, and it may be expressed by acts as well as by words. The person who makes the offer or proposal is the offeror; the person to whom it is made is the offeree.

To be legally sufficient, an offer must meet the following criteria:

1. The words must show a present contractual intent.

2. The terms of the offer must be sufficiently clear and complete so that a court can determine the parties' intentions.

3. The offer must be communicated to the offeree, and the offeree must have knowledge of the offer.

For example, John offers a reward for the return of his lost ring. If Bob returns the ring without knowledge of the offer, he cannot claim the reward. Or if John writes a letter offering to sell his ring to Bob but does not mail the letter, Bob has no power to accept the offer even if he learns of it, since the offer was never communicated to him. If John inadvertly mails the offer to Bob, there a valid offer would exist, because communication is determined *objectively,* and not by what the offeror subjectively intended.

2. OFFER IN JEST

A proposal obviously made in jest, an invitation to a purely social function, or a remark made in the course of a family discussion, which a reasonable person would not be justified in treating as an offer to enter into a contract, is not an offer. There is a conflict of authority as to whether a proposal made under great emotional stress is a valid offer. Some courts hold that the offeree cannot take advantage of such an offer when he or she knows or should know that the offeror was unable to formulate a rational intent to contract. Other courts hold that the offeror is bound, since to do otherwise is to open the door and permit the offeror another method of escaping from the offer.

3. PRELIMINARY NEGOTIATIONS

When a party suggests the terms of a possible contract by a letter, circular, display, or advertisement *without making a definite proposal,* the result is a mere invitation to the other party to make an offer. For example, such language as "We can quote you" is generally considered merely a statement of terms and not an offer. However, a quotation may be sufficiently specific and promissory to constitute an offer. Thus, it may add the statement that the quotation is "For immediate wire acceptance" and could be construed as an offer.

An estimate usually does not suggest a binding proposal; however, where the word "estimate" is in the heading and not in the body of the document, and the body contains words such as "We propose to furnish to" and "The signature herein is an authorization to install such equipment as described in the above estimate," the court can call the estimate an offer.

4. CERTAINTY OF OFFER

A. IN GENERAL

An offer must be sufficiently definite so that the performance required by the offeree is reasonably certain. The offer must describe the subject matter and the quantity and should state the price. However, the complete absence of any mention of the price is not necessarily fatal, as the court may interpret the contract to mean the market price or a reasonable price. The offer should state the time and place. However, failure to so state does not necessarily render the contract void if the intent of the parties is otherwise ascertainable. In determining whether a contract is sufficiently enforceable, the court will liberally interpret laypersons' agreements or nontechnical language. The court will attempt to make the contract valid if uncertainty exists by carrying into effect the reasonable intentions of the parties if they can be ascertained.

The following case is an example of an oral promise that was too uncertain to be enforceable.

FACTS   Alice Sherman, niece of George Sherman, entered into an oral agreement with George whereby George would give Alice 100 acres of land if she would keep house for him until her marriage. Alice did her part, but George refused to convey the land to her. George dies and Alice sues to recover the land. George's administrator contends that it had never been made certain just what land that plaintiff was to receive, as George had many parcels of land.

DECISION   A contract must be certain to be enforceable. An action brought upon an express promise lies only when a person assumes to do a certain thing, and this means a certainty to a common intent. The words must show that the understanding was certain. In this case, the action fails because the alleged contract did not state which 100 acres George was to give Alice.

Sherman v. Kitsmiller, Administrator (17 Serg. & Rawle 45 [Penn.])

B.   UNDER THE U.C.C.

Under the Uniform Commercial Code, fundamental changes have been made in contracts involving the sale of personal property. A word of caution: These changes affect only personal property sales and not other contracts, such as contracts for personal services and real estate contracts (see Chapter 2, D.).

The most fundamental changes relaxing the requirements of certainty in a contract for the sale of goods under the U.C.C. can be found in the following sections set out in full in Appendix A:

1.   Section 2–204, *Formation in General* provides that a contract for sale of goods may be made in any manner sufficient to show agreement, including conduct by the parties. In other words, if the parties act as if a contract exists, there may be one.

This section also provides that even though one or more of the terms of the contract are left open, the contract is still enforceable if the parties intended a contract and if the court can given an appropriate remedy.

2.   Section 2–305, *Open Price Term* supplies a price if nothing is paid as to price. This usually means the market price at the time and place of delivery.

3.   Section 2–306, *Output, Requirements and Exclusive Dealings,* supplies a quantity where the parties have not stated a definite quantity, but instead the buyer agrees to buy the seller's entire output or agrees to buy all that the buyer may require. "Requirements" means actual good faith requirements. For example, the buyer cannot demand a disproportionate quantity in relation to his or her normal prior requirements or to his or her stated estimate. See Sections 1–203, 2–103(1)(b).

4.   Section 2–308, *Absence of Specified Place for Delivery,* supplies the place of delivery if omitted in the contract.

5.   Section 2–309, *Absence of Specific Time,* supplies a time if one is omitted in the contract. For example, seller agrees to purchase 500 crates of oranges from buyer for $3,000 cash. Nothing is said regarding time for payment or

delivery. In such a situation, the courts would imply an agreement to perform within a commercially reasonable period of time.

6.　Section 2–310, *Open Time for Payment or Running of Credit: Authority to Ship Under Reservation,* supplies payment terms and delivery terms if omitted in the contract.

7.　Section 2–208, *Course of Performance or Practical Construction,* provides that repeated conduct by the parties shall be relevant to determine the meaning of the agreement.

8.　Section 1–205, *Course of Dealing and Usage of Trade,* provides that a course of dealing between the parties and any usage of trade in the vocation or trade in which they are engaged shall be used to supplement or qualify the terms of the contract.

5.　DURATION OF OFFER

A communicated offer continues until it lapses or expires, becomes illegal or impossible by operation of law, is revoked by the offeror, is revoked by the counteroffer, is rejected by the offeree, or is accepted by the offeree. The following case is an example of an offer revoked by a counteroffer.

> **FACTS**　Defendant manufacturer, in reply to an inquiry from plaintiff, sent a letter dated December 8 stating terms upon which it would sell 2,000 to 5,000 tons of 50-pound iron rails. On December 16, plaintiff sent a telegram to defendant ordering 1,200 tons of rails on those terms. On December 18, defendant sent a telegram to plaintiff rejecting the order. The next day plaintiff sent defendant a telegram stating, "Please enter an order for 2,000 tons rails as per your letter of the eighth." Defendant refused the order, and plaintiff sued for breach of contract.

> **DECISION**　For defendant. Plaintiff's telegram of December 16, refering to the terms stated in defendant's letter of the 8th, varied the number of tons, and was therefore a counteroffer. A counteroffer is in law a rejection of the original offer. On December 18 the defendant declined to fulfill the plaintiff's order, thus the negotiations between the two parties was closed. The plaintiff's attempt to fall back on the defendant's original offer by the telegram of December 19, therefore, created no rights against the defendant.

> *Minneapolis & St. L. Ry. Co. v. Columbus Rolling-Mill Co.* (119 U.S. 149, 7 S.Ct. 168, 30 L.Ed. 376 [1886])

A.　LAPSE

The offer is revoked if the offeree fails to accept the offer within the prescribed period of time stated in the offer. If the offer prescribes no particular time for its acceptance, it is revoked by the lapse of a reasonable time. What is a reasonable time is a question of fact depending upon the nature of the particular offer, the usages of business, and the circumstances of the case. An offer to purchase real estate would not require as prompt an acceptance as an offer to purchase personal property of a perishable nature or of fluctuating value. The Restatement of the Law of Contracts, Section 40, cites the following regarding reasonable time:

1.   Whether three days is too long to accept an offer to sell land is a question of fact under the circumstances.

2.   Where the buyer receives the offer at the close of business hours for the sale of ordinary goods, an acceptance by letter promptly the next morning creates a contract.

3.   A telegraphic offer to sell oil, which at the time is subject to rapid fluctuation in price, received near the close of business hours is not accepted in time by a telegraphic reply sent the next day.

The following case is an example of an offer terminated by lapse of a specified time.

> **FACTS**   Plaintiff sent a letter to defendant in which he offered to sell certain lots to him for $300. The letter stated, "Let me know by return mail [the next mail pick-up]." The letter was received by the defendant on September 6. On September 9 the defendant wrote a letter accepting the offer.

> **DECISION**   The offer was not accepted according to its terms. When an individual makes an offer by post stipulating that the answer must be by return mail, the offer terminates if the answer is not by return mail.

> *Ackerman v. Maddux* (26 N.D. 50, 143 N.W. 147 [1913])

B.   ILLEGAL OR IMPOSSIBLE BY OPERATION OF LAW

If the subject matter of a contract becomes illegal, the offer is revoked (e.g., the legislature passes a law making the subject illegal). Destruction of the subject matter prior to acceptance revokes the offer.

Death or insanity of the offeror prior to acceptance revokes the offer, since at the time of acceptance, there is no offeror capable of contracting. Death of the offeree also revokes the offer, since only the person to whom the offer was made can accept it.

C.   REVOCATION

The general rule is that an offer may be revoked at any time before the communication of acceptance, even though the offer is stated to be good or irrevocable for a specified period. For example, seller tells his friend Richard that he will sell his rifle to him for $150 and will give him 10 days to accept the offer. Three days later, seller informs Richard that he has sold the rifle to another person. Richard cannot accept the offer, as it was revoked by the seller when he sold the rifle and informed Richard of that fact.

Some exceptions to revocation are as follows:

1.   An option where consideration is given for an agreement to keep the offer open for a stated period of time or until a certain date.

2. A unilateral contract after substantial part performance by the offeree. Normally in a unilateral contract, no acceptance is made until the offeree performs the act requested (e.g., catching the criminal in a reward type of case). However, to prevent the injustice that would occur if the offeror revoked the offer after substantial performance on the part of the offeree, most courts will protect the offeree in some way, such as making the offer irrevocable or permitting the offeree to recover in quasi-contract for the reasonable value of his or her performance up to the time of revocation. To alleviate this problem in the sale of goods, the U.C.C. provides the following in Section 2–206(2): "Where the beginning of a requested performance is a reasonable mode of acceptance, an offeror who is not notified of acceptance within a reasonable time may treat the offer as having lapsed before acceptance."

3. Firm offers under the U.C.C. Section 2–205 of the U.C.C. states that a merchant's written and signed offer to buy or sell goods giving assurance by its terms that it will be held open is not revocable for the time stated and, if no time is stated, for a reasonable time (in either case, not over three months), even though there is no consideration. For definition of "merchant," see U.C.C. Section 2–104.

The general rule is that a revocation must be communicated to the offeree before it is effective (i.e., received by the offeree). The minority rule, followed in California (Civil Code, Section 1587(1)), states that revocation is effective upon posting. Thus, if the offeror mails the revocation before the offeree mails the acceptance, there is no contract. In the United States, posting can be effective as early as handing the revocation to the mailcarrier, since in this country the mailcarrier is under a duty to accept the mail. The California rule is not favored, since the offeree does not know of the revocation until he or she receives it; and in the meantime, the offeree might have committed himself or herself to other contracts relying on a contract that never became effective. Thus, such a rule slows the economy, since the offeree cannot make other contracts until he or she is certain that the offeror has not mailed a revocation of his or her offer.

An offer made to the public may generally be revoked in the same manner in which it was made (e. g., an offer made by television may be withdrawn in the same manner).

D. REJECTION AND COUNTEROFFER

A rejection of an offer is an act by the offeree that shows his or her unwillingness to accept the offer. It may consist of express language, or it may be implied from the language or conduct of the offeree. A rejection terminates the offeree's right to accept the offer. A rejection is not effective until it is *received* by the offeror. The right of rejection in a sales contract case must be exercised seasonably. "An act is taken 'seasonably' when it is taken at or within the time agreed or if no time is agreed at or within a reasonable time" (U.C.C. §1–204(3)). A racehorse was purchased at a 3:00 p.m. auction one day and rejected before 1:00 p.m. on the following day. The court held that the rejection came too late. *Miron v. Yonker's Raceway* (400 F.2d. 112 [U.S. Ct. App. 2d Cir], 5 U.C.C. Rep. 673 [1968])

A *counteroffer* is a counterproposal by the offeree upon terms different from those contained in the offer. For example, seller offers to sell his television set for $250 to buyer. Buyer tells seller that he will give him $200 for the set. This is a counteroffer, which terminates the offer. However, if seller responds to buyer's counteroffer by saying "I can't take less than $250," this impliedly renews the offer.

If the offeree's reply does not show an unwillingness to accept the original offer, no rejection or counteroffer exists. For example, in answer to the seller's offer, buyer says, "I will consider your offer. In the meantime will you consider selling the set to me for $200?" This is considered to be a mere inquiry.

For special rules under the U.C.C., see C., 3., infra.

C. THE ACCEPTANCE

1. IN GENERAL

An offer must be accepted before a contract exists. Acceptance is an expressed or communicated overt act by the offeree indicating that he or she assents to the terms of the offer. It may, if the offer permits, take the form of performing the act called for in the offer (unilateral contract), a promise communicated to the offeror (bilateral contract), or the formal act of both parties signing a written document. Mere words, such as "O.K.," can constitute an acceptance. Where the offeror signs and delivers a contract to the offeree and the latter accepts it, the offeree will be bound even though he or she does not sign it (e. g., landlord hands lease to tenant, who accepts it without objection).

The right to accept an offer cannot be assigned and therefore can be accepted only by the person to whom it was made.

The student should remember that once an offer is accepted, a contract exists unless there is a valid defense. In the case of a fluctuating market, the offeree is in the better bargaining position, because he or she can reject or accept the offer. It is usually better procedure, therefore, to send out a quotation of prices (making it clear that it is not an offer) rather than an offer.

2. ACCEPTOR MUST HAVE KNOWLEDGE OF THE OFFER

The rule that the acceptor-offeree must have knowledge of the offer applies to both unilateral and bilateral contracts. In a unilateral contract (reward type), no recovery of the reward can be made unless the offeree knew of the reward.

The following case is one of the classic reward cases in the common law.

FACTS The defendants (dealers in a device for the cure of influenza known as "The Carbolic Smoke Ball"), to induce the sale of their product, offered to pay $500 to any person who contracted influenza after having used the smoke ball in a specified manner. The plaintiff, on the faith of the advertisement containing the offer, bought one of the smoke balls and used it according to instructions but still contracted influenza. The defendants refused to pay her on the grounds that no contract existed, because the offer was not made to anybody in particular and because she did not notify them of her acceptance.

DECISION An offer of a reward is made to anybody who performs the conditions named in the advertisement, and anybody who does perform accepts the offer. No notice to the offeror is expected in the reward type of case. In a unilateral contract, it is ordinarily not necessary for the offeree to notify the offeror of his or her acceptance.

Carlill v. Carbolic Smoke Ball Co. (Law Reports, 1 Q.B.Div. 256)

With a bilateral contract, identical offers to buy and sell goods that cross in the mails can create a contract even though the parties are each ignorant of the other's offer. Suppose the owner of an automobile sends a letter to Alice offering to sell the vehicle for $500. In the meantime, Alice had sent an offer to buy the automobile for $500. Will these crossover offers result in a contract? Under the objective theory and U.C.C. Section 2–204, a contract exists. The U.C.C. does not demand that a person be able to pinpoint the exact moment of the contract's creation. Under the code, the court is more interested in whether the parties intended to make a contract, and whether the court can fashion a remedy.

3.   ACCEPTANCE MUST BE UNQUALIFIED

In contracts where the U.C.C. is not involved, the acceptance must be positive and unequivocal. It may not change any of the terms of the offer or qualify it in any way. A qualified acceptance is a new proposal and constitutes a rejection of the original offer, after which the original offer cannot be accepted by the offeree.

However, under the U.C.C., Section 2–207(1)(2), the offeree may state additional terms from those contained in the offer; and the acceptance may still be valid, assuming it complies with the other requirements of a valid acceptance, as these terms are merely considered as *proposals* for additions to the contract. They do not amount to a counteroffer. In other words, the offeree accepts the offer but wants the offeror to consider some additional terms (e. g., the wire of acceptance adds "Ship by Thursday" or "Rush"). A frequent example is the exchange of printed purchase order and acceptance forms. Often the seller's form contains different terms from the buyer's form; nevertheless, the parties proceed with the transaction.

If the offeror and offeree are both merchants, the additional terms become part of the contract unless:

1.   The offer expressly limits acceptance to its terms.

2.   They materially alter the offer.

3.   The offeror objects to them within a reasonable time.

   An example of a clause that materially alters the contract and is thus not included unless expressly agreed to by the other party is a clause negating such standard warranties as that of merchantability or fitness for a particular purpose under circumstances in which either warranty normally attaches. Arbitration clauses have been held to be material alterations of the offer. An example of a clause not material is a clause fixing a reasonable time for complaints within customary limits. An astute offeror will insert a clause in the offer incorporating number 1, thus obviating the problem of 2 and 3.

   In many cases, goods are shipped, accepted, and paid for before any dispute arises. In such cases, if the writings of the parties do not establish a contract, Section 2–207(3) establishes the contract by conduct and governs the question as to what terms are included.

4.   ACCEPTANCE BY SILENCE

In a bilateral contract, ordinarily silence cannot constitute acceptance of an offer. This is true even though the offer states that silence will be taken as consent, for the offeror cannot force the offeree to make an express rejection.

   The rule has several exceptions:

1.   Previous dealings between the parties place the offeree under a duty to act or be bound (e.g., failure to object to a billing statement from a creditor). Similarly, if Seller has offered lamps to Buyer on three prior occasions under identical terms, with Buyer's remaining silent and paying for the goods, Buyer must affirmatively reject the present offer.

2.   Use of services or goods by the offeree when he or she had freedom to reject them amounts to an acceptance. Note that the Federal Postal Reorganization Act, Section 3009, 1970, provides that a person who receives unsolicited goods in the mail, except from a charity, has the right to retain, use, discard, or dispose of them in any manner he or she sees fit without any obligation to the sender. Some states have passed similar laws (e. g., Arizona, California, Illinois, Louisiana, Oklahoma).

3.   Complete performance or tender thereof by the offeree is equivalent to a promise of acceptance resulting in a contract.

4.   The terms of the offer may expressly *waive* any communication of acceptance. For example, a mail order company sends an *offer* that states, "Your order is only an offer and must be accepted by our home office before there is a binding contract." The order becomes a contract without notice to the customer when the home office accepts the order.

5.   Under the Contracts Restatement Rule, Section 72(1) (b), if the offeror prescribes silence as the means of assent, and the offeree remains silent intending to accept, a contract results; however, little authority exists approving this position.

In a unilateral contract, it is ordinarily not necessary for the offeree to notify the offeror of his or her acceptance, as the offer normally requests an act rather than a promise. Even if the offeree does give one, a notification has no legal effect.

Under the U.C.C., Section 2–206(1)(b), an order or offer to buy goods for prompt shipment may be accepted by a promise to ship the goods or by the prompt shipment of conforming or nonconforming goods. For example, buyer sends a telegram to seller that states, "Send me one dozen business law books. Ship on or before August 5." The order is received on August 2. On the same day seller receives the telegram, he begins packing the order and sends the following telegram to buyer: "Your order received and promise shipment within 48 hours." On August 3, seller receives the following telegram from buyer: "Cancel business law book order." Under the U.C.C., seller's prompt promise to ship the goods constitutes an acceptance, which cuts off the buyer's power to revoke the offer.

A seller who ships nonconforming goods (goods that deviate from the order in quality or quantity) should notify the buyer that the shipment is an *accommodation* shipment. If the seller does not do so, he or she may be in breach of the contract that was accepted by the act of shipping.

5.   EFFECTIVE TIME OF ACCEPTANCE

If the offer involves a bilateral contract, acceptance is effective when it is placed in the course of transmission. If the mails are used, acceptance is effected when the offeree mails the acceptance in an envelope properly addressed and stamped.

As stated, "mailing" takes place when the acceptance is placed in a U.S. mail box or handed to the mailcarrier. However, is placing the acceptance in an office outbox for mailing sufficient mailing? In *Cushing v. Thomson* (118 N.H. 292, 386 A.2d 805 [1978]), the court held that placing the acceptance in the outbox was sufficient. The court said, "Moreover plaintiff's counsel represented to the court that it was customary office practice for outgoing letters to be picked up from the outbox daily and put in the U.S. mail. * * * Thus the representation that it was customary office procedure for the letters to be sent out the same day that they are placed in the office outbox * * * supported the implied finding that the completed contract was mailed before the attempted revocation."

If a telegram is used, acceptance is effected when the telegram is handed to the telegraph operator. In most states, it is immaterial that the letter or telegram is delayed or not received by the offeror. Once the acceptance has been completed by posting or transmitting the telegram, it cannot be countermanded or withdrawn. If the acceptance is made too late or in an unauthorized manner, the offeror cannot waive the defect and treat the acceptance as valid. Instead, it is merely treated as a counteroffer, which would have to be accepted by the original offeror.

The *manner* in which the acceptance is to be communicated can be specified in the offer. If an unauthorized mode of acceptance is used, some courts treat the attempted acceptance as a counteroffer, while others treat it as an acceptance but delay the time of effectiveness until the offeror receives it. The risk that the acceptance will not be received in time rests with the acceptor. If the offer does not prescribe a specified manner, any reasonable manner may be used, Section 2–206(1) of the U.C.C. Hence, it would be proper to answer a letter with a telegram.

An offer must be accepted within a reasonable time unless otherwise specified in the offer. An offer by telegram should be accepted by telegram rather than by letter and ordinarily sent the same day as the offer is received. If an offer by mail calls for a reply "by return mail," a letter of acceptance must be sent either by the next mail or during the day that the offer is received. If an offer states that it is "open for 10 days," the 10-day period begins on the date that appears on the offer. Thus, if the offer is delayed for 10 days, it never becomes effective. However, if the offer states that the offeree has 10 days in which to accept, the 10-day period does not begin until the offer is received. In the latter case, if the offer is delayed and the offeree knew or had reason to know of the delay, the offeree will have 10 days minus the delay to accept the offer. If an offer by mail does not specify "by return mail" or any other time, the offeree has a reasonable period of time to respond as determined by the type of offer, the type and usages of business, and all other surrounding circumstances. The following case is an example of an offer stipulating that acceptance was not valid until received.

> **FACTS**   The plaintiffs filed suit for death benefits under a policy issued by the Franklin Life Insurance Company. Decision for plaintiffs, and the company appeals. The policy contained an offer allowing the owner to cancel the policy and receive its cash value. The policy required that a written request to terminate be received at the home office. The insured plaintiff requested by letter that the insurer send the cash value of the policy. However, the letter was not received by the company until after the insured was killed in an airplane crash. The letter was mailed by the insured two days before his death.
>
> **DECISION**   The court held that the acceptance by the insured never became effective, since it was received after the insured's death. The court said, "An offeror can specify any mode of acceptance he pleases and can require that the acceptance of his offer shall not be operative until received by him."
>
> *Franklin Life Insurance Company, Appellant v. Winney, Appellee* (469 S.W.2d 21 [Tex. 1971]).

The time of acceptance may be proved by the oral testimony of the offeree or his or her secretary that the acceptance was mailed at a particular time and place. A letter correctly addressed and properly mailed is presumed to have been received in the ordinary course of mail. A copy of the acceptance can be introduced in evidence to show the contents of the acceptance.

6. ACCEPTANCE AFTER SENDING REJECTION

A rejection is effective when it is received. An acceptance is effective when it is sent. If the offeree sends a rejection, then later changes his or her mind and sends an acceptance, is the acceptance valid?

The validity of the acceptance depends upon whether the acceptance or the rejection arrived first. The acceptor lost the right to have the acceptance effective when it was sent because he or she previously sent a rejection. Under these circumstances, an overtaking acceptance is effective upon receipt subject to the condition that the acceptance must be made timely. That is, if the offeree waits too long to send the acceptance or the acceptance takes an unreasonable time to arrive, the acceptance would be ineffective.

ILLUSTRATIVE CASES

1. Intent Determined by Words and Acts

LUCY v. ZEHMER

196 Va. 493, 84 S.E.2d 516 (1954)

BUCHANAN, Justice.   This suit was instituted by W. O. Lucy and J. C. Lucy, complainants, against A. H. Zehmer and Ida S. Zehmer, his wife, defendants, to have specific performance of a contract by which it was alleged the Zehmers had sold to W. O. Lucy a tract of land owned by A. H. Zehmer in Dinwiddie county containing 471.6 acres, more or less, known as the Ferguson farm, for $50,000.

The instrument sought to be enforced was written by A. H. Zehmer on December 20, 1952, in these words: "We hereby agree to sell to W. O. Lucy the Ferguson Farm complete for $50,000.00, title satisfactory to buyer," and signed by the defendants, A. H. Zehmer and Ida S. Zehmer.

*   *   *

The answer of A. H. Zehmer admitted that at the time mentioned W. O. Lucy offered him $50,000 cash for the farm, but that he, Zehmer, considered that the offer was made in jest; that so thinking, and both he and Lucy having had several drinks, he wrote out "the memorandum" quoted above and induced his wife to sign it; that he did not deliver the memorandum to Lucy, but that Lucy picked it up, read it, put in his pocket, attempted to offer Zehmer $5 to bind the bargain, which Zehmer refused to accept, and realizing for the first time that Lucy was serious, Zehmer assured him that he had no intention of selling the farm and that the whole matter was a joke. Lucy left the premises insisting that he had purchased the farm. *   *   *

The discussion leading to the signing of the agreement, said Lucy, lasted thirty or forty minutes, during which Zehmer seemed to doubt that Lucy could raise $50,000. Lucy suggested the provision for having the title examined and Zehmer made the suggestion that he would sell it "complete,

everything there," and stated that all he had on the farm was three heifers.
* * *

    Lucy took a partly filled bottle of whiskey into the restaurant with him for the purpose of giving Zehmer a drink if he wanted it. Zehmere did, and he and Lucy had one or two drinks together. Lucy said that while he felt the drinks he took he was not intoxicated, and from the way Zehmer handled the transaction he did not think he was either. * * *

    The defendants insist that the evidence was ample to support their contention that the writing sought to be enforced was prepared as a bluff or dare to force Lucy to admit that he did not have $50,000; that the whole matter was a joke; that the writing was not delivered to Lucy and no binding contract was ever made between the parties. * * *

    In his testimony Zehmer claimed that he "was high as a Georgia pine," and that the transaction "was just a bunch of two doggoned drunks bluffing to see who could talk the biggest and say the most." That claim is inconsistent with his attempt to testify in great detail as to what was said and what was done. * * * The record is convincing that Zehmer was not intoxicated to the extent of being unable to comprehenbd the nature and consequences of the instrument he executed, and hence that instrument is not to be invalidated on that ground. * * *

    Not only did Lucy actually believe, but the evidence shows he was warranted in believing, that the contract represented a serious business transaction and a good faith sale and purchase of the farm. * * *

    In the field of contracts, as generally elsewhere, "We must look to the outward expression of a person as manifesting his intention rather than to his secret and unexpressed intention. 'The law imputes to a person an intention corresponding to the reasonable meaning of his words and acts.'"
* * *

    The mental assent of the parties is not requisite for the formation of a contract. If the words or other acts of one of the parties have but one reasonable meaning, his undisclosed intention is immaterial except when an unreasonable meaning which he attaches to his manifestations is known to the other party.

*   *   *

    Reversed and remanded [for entry of a proper decree requiring defendants to perform the contract].

2. Failure to Read Baggage and Claim Checks Can Be a Defense

KERGALD v. ARMSTRONG TRANSFER EXP. CO.

330 Mass. 254, 113 N.E.2d 53 (1953)

LUMMUS, Justice.   This is an action of contract, in which the plaintiff sues for the loss of her trunk and its contents. The defendant is an intrastate common carrier. There was evidence that the plaintiff arrived with her trunk at the South Station in Boston late in an evening in May, 1949, and went to the defendant's office there. She was not asked the value of her trunk, but was given a small pasteboard check by the defendant which was not read to her and which she did not read, but put in her purse. The trunk was to be delivered at her home in Boston. The defendant failed to deliver her trunk, and admitted that it had been lost. The small check had on one side the order number and the words "Read contract on reverse side," and on the other the words, "The holder of this check agrees that the value of the baggage checked does not exceed $100 unless a greater value has been declared at time of checking and additional payment made therefor."

The defendant excepted [see dictionary in Appendix C] to the denial of its motion for a directed verdict for the plaintiff in the sum of $100.

Where what is given to a plaintiff purports on its face to set forth the terms of a contract, the plaintiff, whether he reads it or not, by accepting it assents to its terms, and is bound by any limitation of liability therein contained, in the absence of fraud.

On the other hand, where as in this case what is received is apparently a means of identification of the property bailed, rather than a complete contract, the bailor is not bound by a limitation upon the liability of the bailee unless it is actually known to the bailor. * * * (limitation on back of railroad ticket); * * * (schedule as to baggage, no knowledge warranting inference of assent); * * * (identification check for automobile given by parking station). * * * In our opinion no error is disclosed by the record.

Exceptions overruled [judgment for plaintiff].

[Many states have statutes that limit the amount of liability on the part of the bailee. See Chapter 23 on bailments.]

3. An Ad Generally Not an Offer

O'KEEFE v. LEE CALAN IMPORTS, INC.

128 Ill.App.2d 410, 262 N.E.2d 758 (1970)

McNAMARA, Justice.

Christopher D. O'Brien brought suit against defendant for an alleged breach of contract. O'Brien died subsequent to the filing of the lawsuit, and the administrator of his estate was substituted in his stead. * * * Plaintiff and defendant filed cross-motions for summary judgment. The court denied plaintiff's motion for summary judgment and granted defendant's motion. * * *

On July 31, 1966, defendant advertised a 1964 Volvo Station Wagon for sale in the Chicago *Sun-Times*. Defendant had instructed the newspaper to advertise the price of the automobile at $1,795. However, through an error of the newspaper and without fault on part of defendant, the newspaper inserted a price of $1,095 for said automobile in the advertisement. O'Brien visited defendant's place of business, examined the automobile and stated that he wished to purchase it for $1,095. One of defendant's salesmen at first agreed, but then refused to sell the car for the erroneous price listed in the advertisement.

Plaintiff appeals, contending that the advertisement constituted an offer on the part of defendant, which O'Brien duly accepted and thus the parties formed a binding contract. * * *

It is elementary that in order to form a contract there must be an offer and an acceptance. A contract requires the mutual assent of the parties.

The precise issue of whether a newspaper advertisement constitutes an offer which can be accepted to form a contract or whether such an advertisement is merely an invitation to make an offer, has not been determined by the Illinois courts. Most jurisdictions which have dealt with the issue have considered such an advertisement as a mere invitation to make an offer, unless the circumstances indicate otherwise. As was stated in Corbin on Contracts § 25 (1963):

> It is quite possible to make a definite and operative offer to buy or to sell goods by advertisement, in a newspaper, by a handbill, or on a placard in a store window. It is not customary to do this, however; and the presumption is the other way. Neither the advertiser nor the reader of his notice understands that the latter is empowered to close the deal without further expression by the former. Such advertisements are understood to be mere requests to consider and examine and negotiate; and no one can reasonably regard them otherwise unless the circumstances are exceptional and the words used are very plain and clear.

* * *

We find that in the absence of special circumstances, a newspaper advertisement which contains an erroneous purchase price through no fault of the defendant advertiser and which contains no other terms, is not an offer which can be accepted so as to form a contract. We hold that such an advertisement amounts only to an invitation to make an offer. It seems apparent to us in the instant case, that there was no meeting of the minds nor the required mutual assent by the two parties to a precise proposition. There was no reference to several material matters relating to the purchase of an automobile, such as equipment to be furnished or warranties to be offered by defendant. Indeed the terms were so incomplete and so indefinite that they could not be regarded as a valid offer.

In *Lefkowitz v. Great Minneapolis Surplus Store,* 251 Minn. 188, 86 N.W.2d 689 (1957) defendant advertised a fur stole worth $139.50 for a sale at a price of $1.00, but refused to sell it to plaintiff. In affirming the judgment for plaintiff, the court found that the advertisement constituted a valid offer and, upon acceptance by plaintiff, a binding contract. However in that case, unlike the instant case, there was no error in the advertisement, but rather, defendant deliberately used misleading advertising. And in *Lefkowitz,* the court held that whether an advertisement was an offer or an invitation to make an offer depended upon the intention of the parties and the surrounding circumstances.

* * *

The judgment of the Circuit Court is affirmed.

* * *

4. The Problem of Conflicting Commercial Forms

APPLICATION OF DOUGHBOY INDUSTRIES, INC.

17 A.D.2d 216, 233 N.Y.S.2d 488 (1962)

Proceeding on a motion to stay arbitration proceedings. [See Chapter 5. B. 4. for discussion of arbitration.]

BREITEL, Justice.　This case involves a conflict between a buyer's order form and a seller's acknowledgment form, each memorializing a purchase and sale of goods. The issue arises on whether the parties agreed to arbitrate future disputes. The seller's form had a general arbitration provision. The buyer's form did not. The buyer's form contained a provision that only a signed consent would bind the buyer to any terms thereafter transmitted in any commercial form of the seller. The seller's form, however, provided that silence or a failure to object in writing would be an acceptance of the terms and conditions of its acknowledgment form. The buyer never objected to the seller's acknowledgment, orally or in writing. In short, the buyer and seller accomplished a legal equivalent to the irresistible force colliding with the immovable object.

*　　　*　　　*

Of interest in the case is that both the seller and buyer are substantial businesses—a "strong" buyer and a "strong" seller. This is not a case of one of the parties being at the bargaining mercy of the other.

The facts are:

During the three months before the sale in question the parties had done business on two occasions. On these prior occasions the buyer used its purchase order form with its insulating conditions, and the seller used its acknowledgment form with its self-actuating conditions. Each ignored the other's printed forms, but proceeded with the commercial business at hand.

The instant transaction began with the buyer, on May 6, 1960, mailing from its office in Wisconsin to the seller in New York City two purchase orders for plastic film. Each purchase order provided that some 20,000 pounds of film were to be delivered in the future on specified dates. * * * Neither party, orally or in writing, objected to the conditions printed on the other's commercial form. * . * *

The dispute, which has arisen and which the parties wish determined, the seller by arbitration, and the buyer by court litigation, is whether the buyer is bound to accept all the goods orderes. * * * The arbitration would take place in New York City. The litigation might have to be brought in Wisconsin, the buyer's home state.

The buyer's purchase order form had on its face the usual legends and blanks for the ordering of goods. On the reverse was printed a pageful of terms and conditions. The grand defensive clause reads as follows:

> ALTERATION OF TERMS—None of the terms and conditions contained in this Purchase Order may be added to, modified, superseded or otherwise altered except by a written instrument signed by an authorized representative of Buyer and delivered by Buyer to Seller, and each ship-

ment received by Buyer from Seller shall be deemed to be only upon the terms and conditions contained in this Purchase Order except as they may be added to, modified, superseded or otherwise altered, notwithstanding any terms and conditions that may be contained in any acknowledgment, invoice or other form of Seller and notwithstanding Buyer's act of accepting or paying for any shipment or similar act of Buyer.

The buyer's language is direct; it makes clear that no variant seller's acknowledgment is to be binding. But the seller's acknowledgment form is drafted equally carefully. On its front in red typograpy one's attention is directed to the terms and conditions on the reverse side; and it advises the buyer that he, the buyer, has full knowledge of the conditions and agrees to them unless within 10 days he objects in writing.

The seller's clause reads:

IMPORTANT

Buyer agrees he has full knowledge of conditions printed on the reverse side hereof; and that the same are parrt of the agreement between buyer and seller and shall be binding if either the goods referred to herein are delivered to and accepted by buyer, or if buyer does not within ten days from date hereof deliver to seller written objection to said conditions or any part thereof.

On the reverse side the obligations of the buyer set forth above are carefully repeated. Among the conditions on the reverse side is the general arbitrration clause.

This case involves only the application of the arbitration clause.
* * *

As pointed out earlier, an agreement to arbitrate must be clear and direct, and must not depend upon implication, inveiglement or subtlety.
* * * It follows then that the existence of an agreement to arbitrate should not depend solely upon the conflicting fine print of commercial forms which cross one another but never meet. * * *

Consequently, as a matter of law there was no agreement to arbitrate in this case, if one applies existing principles.

But the problem of conflicting commercial forms is one with which there has been much concern before this, and a new effort at rational solution has been made. The new solution would yield a similar result. The Uniform Commercial Code * * *:

§ 2–207 Additional Terms in Acceptance or Confirmation

(1) A definite and seasonable expression of acceptance or a written confirmation which is sent within a reasonable time operates as an acceptance even though it states terms additional to or different from those offered or agreed upon, unless acceptance is expressly made conditional on assent to the additional or different terms.

(2) The additional terms are to be construed as proposals for addition to the contract. Between merchandise such terms become part of the contract unless:

(a) the offer expressly limits acceptance to the terms of the offer;

(b) they materially alter it; or

(c) notification of objection to them has already been given or is given within a reasonable time after notice of them is received.

*   *   *

On this exposition, the arbitration clause, whether viewed as a material alteration under subsection (2), or as a term nullified by a conflicting provision in the buyer's form, would fall to survive as a contract term. In the light of the New York cases, at least, there can be little question that an agreement to arbitrate is a material term, one not to be injected by implication, subtlety or inveiglement. And the conclusion is also the same if the limitation contained in the offer (the buyer's purchase order) is given effect, as required by subsection 2(a) of the new section.

[Motion by buyer to stay arbitration proceedings granted.]

PROBLEMS

1. The vice president of a punchboard corporation publicly stated that he would pay $100,000 to anyone who could find a crooked punchboard. (A punchboard is a small board with many holes, each filled with a rolled-up printed slip of paper. A player pays a nominal sum and chooses a slip to be punched out, hoping that that slip entitles him to a prize.) This offer was carried in the newspaper and specifically restated over the telephone in response to an inquiry concerning whether the offer was serious. Although plaintiff presented two rigged punchboards to the vice president, the vice president claims he made the statement in jest and had no serious contractual intent. Plaintiff sues for the $100,000. Decision?

2. The Lyle School District sent a copy of an unsigned contract to the plaintiff, who is a certified teacher in the district, in a timely manner. The contract stated, "If this contract is not signed by said employee and returned to the Secretary of the school district on or before June 14, 1976, the Board reserves the right to withdraw this offer. In addition, the superintendent of schools personally called the plaintiff and reminded him of the time limit. The plaintiff informed the superintendent that he was considering other employment. Plaintiff did not sign and return the copy of the contract until June 16, 1976. The superintendent informed the plaintiff that the school district would not rehire him. Plaintiff sues. Decision?

3. Lessig discovered that an old set of harness worth about $15 had been stolen from his premises. Angered by the theft, in his excitement he shouted to the bystanders, "I will give $100 to anyone who will find out who the thief is," using rough language and epithets concerning the thief. Higgins, one of the bystanders who heard the remark, catches the thief and now sues for the $100. Decision?

4. Defendant-employer promises plaintiff-employee that he will pay plaintiff in addition to his regular salary part of the profits of the business on a "very liberal basis." When defendant-employer fails to pay the promised share of the profits, plaintiff brings action. Decision?

5.   Buyer and seller make a contract for the purchase and sale of 1,000 bushels of wheat at a certain price. The contract is certain in all respects, except that the parties forget to discuss the place and time of delivery. The price of wheat rises sharply, and the seller refuses to deliver the wheat, contending that the contract is unenforceable since it lacks certainty. Decision?

6.   Seller sends a signed written offer to buyer in which seller offers to sell 1000 number 51 J coats to buyer at a certain price. The offer states that it will be kept open for a period of 60 days. Buyer sends an acceptance 10 days prior to the 60-day period. Thinking the buyer was not going to accept, seller has sold the coats to another retailer. Buyer sues seller for damages. Seller contends he could revoke the offer at any time. Decision?

7.   S mailed an offer to sell certain land to B for the price of $15,000. S mailed the letter on June 4, and B received the letter on June 5. On June 5, B mailed a letter to S which contained the following language: "Will you take less?" S replied in the negative. B then mailed a letter on June 7 which stated, "I accept your offer of June 4." Is there a contract?

8.   On January 15, buyer mailed an offer from Los Angeles to seller in New York for the purchase of 500 dresses at a certain price. On January 18, the buyer mailed a revocation of the offer. On January 19, seller received the offer and mailed an acceptance. Seller immediately purchased sufficient yardage to make the special dresses. On January 22 the seller received the revocation. Is there a contract?

9.   On June 3, S, not a merchant, made an offer to sell an antique vase to B for $500. B asked S if he could have some time to think it over. S stated that he could have until June 5 to accept. On June 5, B called S and told him that he accepted the offer, whereupon S said that he had sold the vase the day before. B sues for breach of contract. Decision?

10.   Seller offers his hot rod to the buyer for $500. Buyer states that he likes the hot rod but cannot afford that much. Buyer then states that he will give the seller $400. The seller tells the buyer that he cannot take the $400 and starts to walk away. The buyer then states, "Oh, all right, I accept your offer of $500." Is there a contract?

11.   On June 5, B made an offer to S to purchase a tract of land. The offer stated that the deed was to be delivered to B on or before July 6. On July 10, S crossed out the date of delivery and inserted June 24. S then signed B's offer indicating his acceptance. Is there a contract?

12.   S received an offer from B to purchase certain real estate that S owned. S sent a telegram to B that stated, "Your offer accepted subject to details to be worked out by you and my attorney." The next day, S sold the property to another buyer at a higher price. B sues for breach of contract. Decision?

Chapter 10

CONSIDERATION

A. NECESSITY FOR CONSIDERATION

In addition to the requirement of intent to contract that is evidenced by an offer and acceptance, consideration is ordinarily required in a contract.

Consideration is something of value that is a benefit to one party or a loss to the other party. It is the inducement to the contract. It is the reason, cause, motive, or price that induces a contracting party to enter into a contract. Consideration may be a benefit conferred or agreed to be conferred upon the promisor or some other person, or a detriment suffered or to be suffered by the promisee or some other person. Consideration may be the giving up of a legal right; e.g., the right to go through bankruptcy. A promise not to sue on a claim may be consideration. Consideration must be bargained for; e.g., if you do something for me, I will do something for you. (I will wash your car if you promise to pay me $5.00. Washing the car is the consideration for the promise to pay $5.00. Promising to pay $5.00 is the consideration for washing the car.)

A promise to make a gift is not consideration and is not enforceable; e.g., Jones promises to give Smith $100 next Tuesday. The promise by Jones is not enforceable, because there is no consideration by Smith. However, an executed gift cannot be set aside for lack of consideration; e.g., Jones gives the $100 to Smith and then requests Smith to give back the money. Smith can keep the money.

The general rule is that a contract must be supported by consideration to be valid and legally enforceable. However, the rule has received criticism, and modern law tends to relax the requirement and to expand the exceptions.

B. AN ACT AS CONSIDERATION

In a unilateral contract, the promise by the offeror is the consideration for the act or forbearance by the offeree. For example, a sheriff promises a reward for the capture of a criminal. The consideration moving from the sheriff is the promise to pay the reward, and the consideration moving from the offeree is the act of capturing the criminal. Or an uncle promises his nephew the sum of $5,000 if the nephew does not smoke until he is 30 years of age. The uncle's consideration is promising to pay $5,000, and the nephew's consideration is giving up the legal right to smoke.

C. A PROMISE AS CONSIDERATION

In a bilateral contract, the promise of one party is the consideration for the promise of the other party. Where mutual promises are made, the one furnishes a sufficient consideration to support an action on the other. For example, S promises to sell his car to B, and B promises to pay S $400 for it. The agreement is binding, since both sides have furnished consideration (i.e., their mutual promises).

D. ILLUSORY OFFER

A proposal by a seller to furnish to a buyer at a specified price all the goods of a certain kind that the buyer may want or desire during a certain period is considered an illusory offer (misleading), which does not, upon acceptance, result in an enforceable contract. The reason is that the offeree may not want any goods during the period and hence is not bound to buy any particular amount. Thus, there is no mutuality of obligation, and hence the contract is not enforceable.

Where the proposal is to furnish all the goods of a certain kind that the other party may need in a certain business for a definite period, acceptance results in a binding contract.

E. ADEQUACY OF CONSIDERATION

As a general rule, so long as the consideration is of some value, however slight, it will be sufficient to sustain a contract in the absence of fraud or unconscionable conduct. The inadequacy is for the parties to consider at the time of making the agreement and not for the court when it is sought to be enforced. For example, a promise of a nephew to name his first son after his uncle is consideration for the uncle's promise to pay the nephew $5,000.

Where the price is so inadequate as to shock the conscience of the court, inadequacy alone may furnish sufficient grounds for granting relief. For example, the seller makes a contract with the buyer to sell a parcel of real estate for $5,000. However, unknown to the seller, the land is really worth $20,000 at the time the contract is made. Before the seller delivers a deed to the buyer, he learns of the true value of the land and refuses to deliver the deed. The buyer sues the seller for specific performance (i.e., the buyer asks the court to order the seller to hand over the deed [specific performance is discussed in Chapter 17]). The seller defends on the ground that the consideration offered by the buyer is grossly inadequate. The court will examine the consideration and, finding it grossly inadequate, will not order specific performance.

Moreover, the existence of gross inadequacy of consideration may indicate fraud, misrepresentation, duress, undue influence, mistake, unconscionability, or overreaching by a dominant party in a fiduciary relationship, in which case the court will grant relief.

In some states (e.g., California Civil Code Section 3391), the courts may refuse to order specific performance on the basis of inadequacy of consideration without a showing that the inadequacy was gross. Adequacy is a question for the jury or other trier of the facts. The consideration does not necessarily have to measure up to the value of the property (e.g., eagerness to sell may explain the discrepancy).

F. DOING WHAT ONE IS BOUND TO DO

Doing or promising to do what one is already legally bound to do cannot be consideration. For example, a police officer while on duty cannot recover a reward offered for the capture of a criminal, since it is the officer's duty to capture criminals. Likewise, when an employee refuses to complete a contract unless the employer promises to pay a bonus in addition to the sum specified in the original contract and the employer promises to pay that bonus, most courts hold that the second promise of the employer is unenforceable because it lacks consideration. However, if the parties mutually rescind the first contract and enter into a new contract that includes the bonus, the second contract is enforceable. Also, if the terms of the original contract are modified so as to vary, even slightly, the employee's performance, the promise to make the additional payment would be enforceable.

G. PAST CONSIDERATION

Past consideration is not sufficient to sustain a promise. Acts or forbearances previously performed cannot be consideration for a new promise. For example, Smith has worked for Jones the past year receiving his salary each week. Jones tells Smith he is so pleased with Smith's work that tomorrow he is going to give Smith $100 as compensation for Smith's excellent work. The promise by Jones is not enforceable, because there is no consideration by Smith. His past excellent performance was paid for and is not sufficient to sustain the new promise by Jones. When Jones made the promise to pay the $100, Smith should have made a promise to do something for Jones (e.g., turning off the lights when he leaves at the end of the day).

H. MORAL OBLIGATION

Generally, a moral obligation cannot be consideration. For example, a nurse without expectation of payment cared for D, an indigent who lived in Illinois, for one month before his death. T, a friend from California, learned of the nurse's care at the funeral and the next day called the nurse and told her that he was going to give her $5,000 for her services. This promise is unenforceable, since it is based on a moral obligation. It is merely a promise to make a gift. There are some exceptions, however, where a moral obligation is sufficient to sustain a promise:

1.   Where a promise to pay a debt is based on a preexisting legal duty, it may be regarded as based on a moral obligation and hence enforceable (e.g., debtor owes creditor $1,000 for which there is no remedy, since it is barred by the statute of limitations). Debtor, however, writes a note to the creditor stating that he will pay the debt. This promise is binding, though without new consideration (most states require that the new promise be in writing). A debt can also be revived by a mere acknowledgment in writing in most states. For example, the debtor sends a note to the creditor stating that she knows the debt is barred by the statute of limitations. However, she acknowledges that she still owes it. Also, a debt can be revived or extended by part payment in most states.

2.   A few states have statutes that state that a moral obligation originating in some benefit conferred upon the promisor, or prejudice suffered by the promisee, is good consideration for a promise to pay the obligation (e.g., California Civil Code Section 1606). For example, Harris, while walking along the beach, sees Segal out in deep water and in trouble. Harris, thinking he might make some money for saving Segal, swims out to Segal and brings him to shore, thereby saving him from drowning. Segal is so happy that he promises to pay Harris $5,000 the next day. The promise by Segal is good consideration for the benefit conferred upon him.

I. LIQUIDATED DEBT

A liquidated debt is one that is for a sum certain (e.g., a patient owes a doctor $100). There is no dispute as to the amount due. In the case of a liquidated debt, payment of a lesser sum will not discharge the balance, since there is no consideration for the release of the balance. This is true even though the creditor orally accepts the lesser sum in full payment. For example, the patient tells the doctor that he has only $75 and asks the doctor if he will accept that amount as payment in full. The doctor states that she will. Since there is no consideration for the release of the $25, the doctor's promise is not enforceable; thus, the patient still owes $25.

  Some states have statutes that provide that if the creditor gives the debtor a written release signed by the creditor, consideration is not necessary to discharge the balance due (e.g., California Civil Code Sections 1524 and 1541). In the previous example, if the doctor had given the patient a signed release of the balance due, the balance in the amount of $25 would have been discharged.

J. UNLIQUIDATED DEBT

An unliquidated debt is one in which the amount is in *good faith dispute*. In such a case, acceptance by the creditor of the lesser sum discharges the balance. For example, the patient believes she owes the doctor $75, but the doctor believes that the patient owes him $100. This is an unliquidated debt. The patient hands the doctor $75 in cash and states that this is payment in full. The doctor takes the $75. By taking the lesser sum, the doctor discharges the balance.

K. "PAID IN FULL" AS ACCORD AND SATISFACTION

When a debtor sends a check to his or her creditor marked "Paid in Full" and the creditor cashes the check, does that preclude the creditor from getting a judgment against the debtor for the balance that the creditor believes is still due? Has there been an "accord and satisfaction"? An *accord* is an agreement for a substituted performance in satisfaction of the original obligation. When the accord is carried out, there is an *accord* and *satisfaction* and the original obligation is discharged. The usual purpose is to settle a claim with a different performance, such as payment of a smaller amount of money than is due.

The following two cases demonstrate the conflict in the interpretation of Section 1–207 of the U.C.C.

1. U.C.C. Section 1–207 is the basis for holdings in New York, and South Dakota (*Scholl v. Tallman* 247 N.W.2d 490 [1976]), that the creditor can maintain an action for the balance due. Note, however, in the following case that New York, unlike many states, has a special annotation to the statute upon which the court also relies to hold that accord and satisfaction has not been made and therefore the creditor can maintain an action for what he or she believes is a balance due.

> **FACTS** Plaintiff and defendant had a dispute as to the amount due on a contract. Defendant sent a check to plaintiff on the back of which was typed: "Endorsement of this check by payee shall constitute a full accord and satisfaction of payee's invoice no. 2767 to maker hereof."
> Plaintiff sent a letter to defendant stating he was not accepting the check as payment in full, that he was accepting the check as partial payment, and that he was accepting the check under protest and specifically reserving his right to collect the balance due.

DECISION The transaction between the plaintiff and the defendant is covered by the U.C.C., Section 1–207. Under the New York Annotations it is stated: "This section permits a party involved in a Code-covered transaction to accept whatever he can get by way of payment, performance, etc., without losing his rights to demand the remainder of the goods, to set-off a failure to quality, or to sue for the balance of the payment, so long as he explicity reserves his rights." The plaintiff's reservation is more than adequate to satisfy the intent of Section 1–207 of the U.C.C.

Kroulee Corp. v. A. Klein & Co., Inc. (426 N.Y.S.2d 206 [1980]). Recent cases in New York have affirmed the *Kroulee* case.

2. The following New Jersey case holds that Section 1–207 does not change the common law; therefore, there is an accord and satisfaction, and the creditor cannot maintain an action for what he or she believes is a balance due.

FACTS Plaintiff and defendant had a dispute as to the amount due on a contract. The defendant sent a check to the plaintiff with a notation on the front "Paid in Full."

DECISION Once a check is deposited by the creditor, no matter what alterations are made on the reverse side, an accord and satisfaction is reached. When a check is tendered as payment in full payment, the creditor is deemed to have accepted this condition by depositing the check for collection notwithstanding any obligeration or alteration.

The New York cases are distinguishable in that the New York Annotations to the Code clearly deals with the effect of Section 1–207 on the "full payment check" and concludes that the rule of accord and satisfaction has been changed. New Jersey did not adopt such an annotation. If the New York rule was followed a convenient and informal device for the resolution of disagreements in the business community would be seriously impeded.

Chancellor, Inc. v. Hamilton Appliance Co., Inc., 175 N.J. Super 345, 418 A.2d 1326 (1980).

The following courts have held in accord with New Jersey: California (*Connecticut Printers, Inc., a Corporation, v. Gus Kroesen, Inc.* [APP., 184 Cal. Rptr. 436 (1982)]); Florida (*Eder v. Yvette B. Gervey Interiors, Inc.* [Fla.Dist.Ct.App.] (33 UCC Reporting Service, 407 So.2d 312 [1981]); North Carolina (*Brown v. Coastal Truckways, Inc.* [44 N.C.App. 454, 261 S.E.2d 266 (1980)]) and Wisconsin (*Flambeau Products Corporation v. Honeywell* [116 Wis.2d 95 (1984)].

Relatively few states have made a direct holding one way or the other on Section 1–207. If the payee of a paid-in-full check is in a state where the section is untested, his alternatives are: (1) to reject the check or instrument and demand payment in full for the amount he claims is due or (2) to accept the check or instrument placing a statement on the back that he accepts the check without prejudice and under protest pursuant to U.C.C. Section 1–207, that he reserves the right to demand the balance of the amount due, and that the negotiation of the check does not effect an accord and satisfaction. The payee will then run the risk that the court will hold there has been an accord and satisfaction.

L. PART PAYMENT WITH ADDITIONAL ADVANTAGE

If a a creditor accepts a lesser sum than is due, prior to due date, offered in full satisfaction of the debt, the balance is discharged because the debtor incurs a legal detriment by paying before the debt is due. Similarly, if the debt is not secured and the creditor accepts a lesser amount if the debtor secures the debt with a mortgage, the balance is discharged (i.e., the giving of such security is something the debtor was not legally bound to do and therefore is sufficient consideration for the creditor's promise to accept the lesser sum).

M. PROMISSORY ESTOPPEL

Most courts hold that promissory estoppel arises when there is a clear and unambiguous promise which the promisor should reasonably expect to induce action or forbearance on the part of the promisee and which does induce such action or forbearance, and such promise is binding if injustice can be avoided only by enforcement of the promise. The promisor is bound when he should reasonably expect a substantial *change of position* (act or forbearance) in reliance on his promise if injustice can be avoided only by its enforcement. In such a case, the promisor is estopped from pleading a lack of consideration for his promise. In other words, promissory estoppel is a substitute for consideration (i.e., the promise is binding even though the promisor received nothing in exchange for his promise). Promissory estoppel is best defined by examples.

A subscription to a charity is an example of the use of promissory estoppel. When the charitable institution, such as a church, makes expenditures or incurs obligations in reliance on the promise of a subscriber, the subscriber is estopped or prevented from using lack of consideration as a defense. As soon as the charity changes its position (e.g., hires an architect in reliance on the promise of the subscriber), the subscriber can be held to his or her promise.

Other examples of promissory estoppel are as follows:

1. A promise not to foreclose on a lien for a specified period of time even though the period of redemption had expired. For example, a woman pledged her mink coat for a $270 loan. After the period of redemption had expired, she was notified by the lien holder that she had one week to repay and reclaim the coat. She stated that she was ready and would do so. Within the one-week period, the lien holder sold the coat. The agreement was binding without consideration, since the representation by the lien holder induced her to forbear redemption immediately in reliance on the promise that was calculated to induce such forbearance.

2.   Where a debtor induces his or her creditor to postpone suit by promising not to invoke the statute of limitations. The debtor is estopped from using the statute of limitations.

3.   Where an insurance adjuster promises to settle a personal injury case with the injured party as soon as the party was discharged by his or her doctor. The insurance company could not rely on the statute of limitations, which had run after one year.

4.   Where a mortgagor makes improvements on his or her property in reliance upon the mortgagee's promise not to foreclose.

5.   Where a donee (recipient of a gift) makes improvements upon land in reliance on a promised gift of the land.

In these examples, promissory estoppel is a substitute for consideration.

The Restatement of the Law of Contracts, Second, § 90, seeks to make the doctrine of promissory estoppel more available as a form of relief by dispensing with the following three earlier requirements:

1.   That the promise must have been gratuitous (i.e., it would apply to promises made in connection with a bargain as well as to gift promises). Historically, the courts have left the parties without relief when they found themselves with a bad bargain (e.g., a contractor runs into unexpected costs demanding more money, which the other party agrees to pay). Under the Restatement, Second, the court could enforce the promise to pay more money in spite of the fact there was no consideration for the promise to pay the contractor additional money.

2.   That the foreseeable reliance has been substantial. Where the reliance is less than substantial, partial enforcement of the promise could be granted. For example, manufacturer agrees to make and sell to the buyer all of the ejectors that the buyer may want during the coming year. This contract is unenforceable because it is illusory. Manufacturer incurs some expenses preparing to manufacture the ejectors. The buyer informs the manufacturer that he does not want any ejectors. The court could grant relief "as justice requires" (e.g., the expenses incurred).

3.   That the gratuitous promise cannot be made for the benefit of a third party (e.g., husband gratuitously promises wife that he will pay the expenses of college for wife's brother). In reliance on the promise, the brother incurs expenses. The promise would be enforceable.

The courts are divided regarding the doctrine as stated in the Restatement; however, it is the modern trend.

N.   EXECUTED TRANSACTIONS

The requirement of consideration applies only to executory contracts. After a contract is fully executed (the obligations of the parties are completed so that nothing remains to be done), it is no longer possible to attack its validity on that particular ground.

O. PROMISES UNDER THE U.C.C. THAT DO NOT REQUIRE CONSIDERATION

The U.C.C. provides that consideration is not required in the following five situations:

1. A claim or right arising out of a breach of contract for the sale of goods can be discharged in whole or in part without consideration by a written waiver or renunciation, signed and delivered by the aggrieved party (Section 1–107).

2. A written offer signed by a merchant to buy or sell goods which by its terms gives assurance that it will be held open is not revocable for lack of consideration during the time stated that it is open and if no time is stated, for a reasonable time, but in no event may the period of irrevocability exceed three months (Section 2–205).

3. No consideration is necessary when a check is accepted in full settlement of disputed debt and probably has the same effect if the debt is not disputed. Official Comment number 2 of Section 3–408 states in part ". . . an instrument given for more or less than the amount of a liquidated obligation does not fail by reason of the common law rule that an obligation for a lesser liquidated amount cannot be consideration for the surrender of the greater" (Section 3–408).

4. The holder of a promissory note or draft or check may discharge any party to the instrument without consideration by (1) intentionally cancelling the instrument, (2) striking out the signature of the party on the instrument, (3) renouncing rights on the instrument in writing signed and delivered, or (4) surrendering the instrument to the party to be discharged (Section 3–605).

5. An agreement modifying a contract for the sale of goods does not need consideration to be binding, however, the modification must meet the test of good faith (§ 1–203, 2–103(1)(b)), and a mere technical consideration cannot support a modification made in bad faith (Section 2–209(1)).

6. No consideration is necessary to establish a letter of credit (see Section 5–103) or to enlarge or otherwise modify its terms (Section 5–105).

P. GUARANTEE FOR DEBT OF ANOTHER

This type of guarantee is a promise made for consideration to be legally responsible for the debts of another (e.g., your friend promises to pay your debt if you tutor him in business law).

If the promise is made as part of a transaction in which the debt is originally incurred, no consideration is needed (e.g., father signs with his son to purchase a car for the son on the installment plan). The seller's reliance on the guarantee of the father as part of the debt-making transaction is sufficient consideration to hold the father liable on his promise.

ILLUSTRATIVE CASES

1. Waiver of a Legal Right as Consideration

HAMER v. SIDWAY

124 N.Y. 538, 27 N.E. 256 (1891)

Action to recover the sum of $5,000 promised by an uncle to his nephew. The promisor had agreed with his nephew that if the latter would refrain from drinking liquor and using tobacco until he reached the age of twenty-one, the uncle would then pay his nephew $5,000. * * * [Hamer is the assignee of the nephew's claim, and Sidway is the Executor of the uncle's estate.]

PARKER, J. The trial court found as a fact that "on the 20th day of March, 1869, * * * William E. Story agreed to and with William E. Story, 2d, that if he would refrain from drinking liquor, using tobacco, swearing, and playing cards or billiards for money until he should become 21 years of age, then he, the said William E. Story, would at that time pay him, the said William E. Story, 2d, the sum of $5,000 for such refraining, to which the said william E. Story, 2d, agreed," and that he "in all things fully performed his part of said agreement."

The defendant contends that the contract was without consideration to support it and, therefore, invalid. He asserts that the promisee by refraining from the use of liquor and tobacco was not harmed but benefited; that that which he did was best for him to do independently of his uncle's promise, and insists that it follows that unless the promisor was benefited, the contract was without consideration. A contention which, if well founded, would seem to leave open for controversy in many cases whether that which the promisee did or omitted to do was, in fact, of such benefit to him as to leave no consideration to support the enforcement of the promisor's agreement. Such a rule could not be tolerated, and is without foundation in the law. * * * Courts "will not ask whether the thing which forms the consideration does in fact benefit the promisee or a third party, or is of any substantial value to anyone. It is enough that something is promised, done, forborne, or suffered by the party to whom the promise is made as consideration for the promise made to him." * * *

"In general a waiver of any legal right at the request of another party is a sufficient consideration for a promise."

* * * "Consideration means not so much that one party is profiting as that the other abandons some legal right in the present or limits his legal

freedom of action in the future as an inducement for the promise of the first."

"Now, applying this rule to the facts before us, the promisee used tobacco, occasionally drank liquor, and he had a legal right to do so. That right he abandoned for a period of years upon the strength of the promise of the testator that for such forbearance he would give him $5,000. We need not speculate on the effort which may have been required to give up the use of those stimulants. It is sufficient that he restricted his lawful freedom of action within certain prescribed limits upon the faith of his uncle's agreement, and now having fully performed the conditions imposed, it is of no moment whether such performance actually proved a benefit to the promisor, and the court will not inquire into it * * *."

[Judgment for plaintiff.]

2. Generally Court Does Not Inquire as to Adequacy of Consideration

WOLFORD v. POWERS, ADMINISTRATRIX

85 Ind. 294 (1882)

Action against the administratrix of Charles Lehman's estate to collect the sum of $10,000 upon a promissory note drawn to the plaintiff's order by the intestate some months prior to his death. Defendant contends that there was no adequate consideration for the promise of the deceased to pay plaintiff this sum. The facts are fully set forth in the opinion.

ELLIOTT, J. The * * * complaint is founded upon a promissory note * * *. The answer * * * alleges that the only consideration for the note sued on was the * * * agreement of the (plaintiff) to bestow upon one of his children the name of Charles Lehman Wolford. The (plaintiff) replied to the answer that Charles Lehman * * * was a widower, about eighty-seven years of age; that he had been the father of one boy who had died many years before the execution of the note; that on the 18th day of April, 1878, a male child was born to (plaintiff); that * * * Lehman requested that it should be given the name of Charles Lehman Wolford; that * * * the (plaintiff) did name the child Charles Lehman * * *; (and) that * * * the * * * note for $10,000 * * * "was executed in consideration of the naming of the child Charles Lehman * * *."

* * * It is the general rule that where there is no fraud, and a party gets all the consideration he contracts for, the contract will be upheld. * * *

The consideration in the case before us was * * * one which the parties alone were competent to measure and determine. Where a party contracts for the performance of an act which will afford him pleasure * * * his estimate of value should be left undisturbed, unless, indeed, there is evidence of fraud. * * * If * * * there is any legal consideration for a promise, it must be sufficient for the one made. * * *

The surrender * * * of the right or privilege of naming the * * * child was * * * consideration. The right to give his child a name was one which the father possessed. * * * If the intestate chose to bargain for the exercise of this right, he should be bound; for by his bargain he limited and restrained the father's right to bestow his own or some other name upon the child. We can perceive no solid reason for declaring that the right with which the father parted at the intestate's request was of no value. * * * In yielding to the intestate's request, and in consideration of the promise accompanying it, the (plaintiff) certainly * * * surrendered some right. * * * As the (plaintiff) suffered some detriment * * * there is a legal consideration.

[Judgment for plaintiff.]

3. Consideration Is Necessary for Subscription Offer

BOARD OF HOME MISSIONS, ETC. v. MANLEY

129 Cal.App. 541, 19 P.2d 21 (1933)

JAMISON, Justice pro tem. This action is upon a rejected claim against the estate of Martha D. Sanders, deceased. The claim is for a subscription or pledge by deceased for the benefit of plaintiff. * * * The case was tried by the court, which found * * * in her favor upon the defense of want of consideration. Judgment was thereupon rendered for defendant, and from this judgment plaintiff appeals.

The question to be determined upon this appeal is whether or not the said claim is supported by a sufficient consideration. On October 30, 1929, the said deceased executed and delivered to appellant the following subscription or pledge: "Estate Pledge. To the Board of Home Missions and Church Extension of the Methodist Episcopal Church. In consideration of my interest in Christian Missions and of the securing by the above named Board of other pledges for its work, and for value received, I hereby promise and agree to pay to The Board of Home Missions and Church Extension of the Methodist Episcopal Church, at 1701 Arch Street, Philadelphia, Pa., the sum of Five Thousand Dollars ($5000.00) which shall become due and payable one day after my death out of my estate." * * *

A subscription is considered as a mere offer until the beneficiary has accepted it, or has acted on the faith thereof so that his conduct implies an acceptance, and until such acceptance the promisor generally has the right to revoke the subscription. The death of the subscriber before the acceptance of the subscription constitutes a revocation of the offer, and the estate of the subscriber will not be liable on the subscription. * * * An acceptance can only be shown by some act on the part of the promisee whereby some legal liability is incurred or money expended on the faith of the promise. * * * However, there is an exception to this rule, and that is that, where there is a mutual promise by several individuals to contribute to the payment of an aggregate sum for the benefit of a charitable, religious, or educational institution in which they are all interested, such mutual promise is generally held to support an adequate consideration authorizing its enforcement by the promisee. * * *

There is no evidence in the case at bar indicating that appellant performed any acts or incurred any obligations or expense in reliance upon the payment of the said subscription of deceased prior to her death, or that other individuals concurred with her in contributing to the payment of an aggregate sum for the benefit of appellant. * * *

There is no showing that between the date of deceased's pledge and the date of her death, that is to say, between October 30, 1929, and June 11, 1930, appellant performed any act or incurred any obligation or expense in reliance upon the payment of the said pledge by deceased. Therefore, we are of the opinion that the said estate pledge was without consideration and was revoked by the death of the said deceased. * * *

The judgment is affirmed [for defendant].

4. Promissory Estoppel as Consideration

BREDEMANN v. VAUGHAN MFG. CO.

40 Ill.App. 232, 188 N.E.2d 746 (1963)

McCORMICK, Justice. This appeal is taken from a summary judgment entered in the Circuit Court of Cook County in favor of the defendant. The plaintiff, Marie Bredemann, had filed a complaint * * * against the defendant, Vaughan Mfg. Company. In the first count she seeks damages for the breach of an alleged oral agreement by the defendant corporation to pay her a monthly salary during her lifetime.

* * *Count I of the complaint alleges that the plaintiff was a loyal and trusted employee of defendant corporation for a period of twenty-five years immediately preceding her retirement in December 1954. It is further alleged that as a part of the consideration for the services rendered to the defendant by her, the defendant, by and through its officers, directors and agents, orally promised to pay her full salary of $375 a month as long as she lived. It is further alleged that the defendant complied with the oral agreement and paid plaintiff her full salary of $375 a month from December 23, 1954, to about June 30, 1957, and that on or about June 30, 1957, the payments were reduced, and in June 1961 the defendant stopped all payments to the plaintiff. * * * About the 15th of December, 1954, she had a conversation with a Mr. Burchill, who told her that Mr. Grace, who was then the president of the company, wanted to see her about a retirement or a pension, and she said that she could not afford to retire on a pension. Burchill then said that she did not have to worry and that Mr. Grace had said that she would receive her full pay for the rest of her life. * * *

The defendant's contention in this court is that the promises to pay the plaintiff her full salary upon retirement were without consideration and are unenforceable. * * * As the parties agree, the consideration sufficient to support a contract may be either a benefit to the promisor or a loss or detriment to the promisee. * * *

It is generally true that one who has led another to act in reasonable reliance on his representations of fact cannot afterwards in litigation between the two deny the truth of the representations, and some courts have sought to apply this principle to the formation of contracts, where, relying on a gratuitous promise, the promisee has suffered detriment. It is to be noticed, however, that such a case does not come within the ordinary definition of estoppel. If there is any representation of an existing fact, it is only that the promisor at the time of making the promise intends to fulfill it. As to such intention there is usually no misrepresentation and if there is, it is not that which has injured the promisee. In other words, he relies on a promise and not on a misstatement of fact; and the term "promissory" estoppel or something equivalent should be used to make the distinction. Williston on Contracts, Rev.Ed., Sec. 139, Vol. 1.

[Judgment for plaintiff].

PROBLEMS

1. Debtor, being in failing circumstances and contemplating bankruptcy, offered the creditor 30 percent of his debt as a settlement in full. The creditor dissuaded the debtor from going into bankruptcy, accepted the alternate offer, and received the money. Creditor now sues for the 70 percent balance, claiming there was no consideration to bind him to the agreement. Discuss.

2. A and B have a contract by which A is to work for B for one year at a salary of $500 a month. Six months after A commenced working for B, he received an offer from another employer. B promised that if A would not leave his employment during the year, he would give him a bonus amounting to $600 at the end of the one-year period. A accepts the promise and does not leave the employment. At the end of the year, A requests the $600 bonus. Is he legally entitled to it?

3. Seyler, a resident of Chicago, owned a building lot located in Milwaukee and which seller thought was worth $1,000. Buyer, who lived near the lot, knew that it was worth $5,000. Buyer went to the seller in Chicago and offered him $1,000 for the lot. In the discussion, buyer did not make any misstatements; he merely remainded silent as to the true value of the lot. The parties then prepared a written contract for the sale of the real estate. Later, when buyer tendered the $1,000 purchase price, seller refused the money and refused to deliver a deed. Buyer sues seller for specific performance. Decision?

4. John and Mary are brother and sister. Upon the death of their mother, it was discovered that the mother's will left the bulk of her estate to Mary. John threatened to contest the will. Mary told him that if he would tell the truth in court, she would give him $10,000. John accepted and told the truth in court; the will was upheld. John now demands the $10,000. Decision?

5. Plaintiff rendered services to her aged and ill father for 27 years. The services took the form of managing an apartment house, marketing, cooking, paying the bills, and generally caring for her father. A few months before her father's death, her brother told her that he was so grateful for what she had done that he would see to it that she was taken care of for life. Plaintiff did not change her position in reliance on her brother's statement but continued to render the same services she had done for the past 27 years. Plaintiff brings suit against her brother for the services rendered for the past 27 years. Decision?

6. Defendant owed plaintiff $10,000, which was evidenced by an unsecured note. The parties agreed that a new note in the amount of $8,000 secured by a mortgage on defendant's property would be executed in place of the note for $10,000. Defendant signed the new note and mortgage, but now plaintiff claims the defendant owes the entire $10,000, as there was no consideration for the release of the $2,000. Decision?

7. In February, defendant signed a pledge to his favorite college in the amount of $50,000. In March, the college signed a contract to have an addition built onto the law school for the amount of the pledge. In April, defendant rescinded the pledge. The college sues for the $50,000. Decision?

8. Red Owl promised plaintiffs that it would build a store building in Chilton, Wisconsin, and stock it with merchandise for plaintiffs to operate. Later, plaintiffs would pay Red Owl the sum of $18,000 for a franchise agreement. In reliance on the promise of Red Owl, plaintiffs sold their bakery building and business in Wautoma, Wisconsin, purchased a building site in Chilton, and rented a residence there. When plaintiffs wanted to enter into the franchise agreement, Red Owl refused. Plaintiffs sue for damages. Red Owl defends on the grounds that there was no consideration for the promise to grant a franchise. Decision?

9. Seller and buyer enter into an agreement in which buyer agrees to buy 1,000 bushels of corn from seller. Prior to delivery of the corn, seller learns he will incur substantial losses in the performance of that agreement because of greatly increased transportation costs and asks the buyer if he will pay $1.00 more per bushel. The buyer agrees to this modification of the agreement. After delivery of the corn, the buyer refuses to pay the additional $1.00 on the grounds there was no consideration for the payment of the extra $1.00 per bushel. Decision?

10. Mr. Elwell signed the following instrument: "I promise to pay to my wife on condition the sum of $5,000 providing she stays with me while I live and take care of things as she always has done; this note not due for six months after my death, and to bear no interest until due." Mr. Elwell died, and Mrs. Elwell now seeks payment of the $5,000 from his estate. Mrs. Elwell continued to live with her husband after the execution of the instrument until his death, and she performed the same household duties she had performed before, such as housekeeping, keeping the simple farm accounts, marketing farm products, collecting and paying out money and drawing checks on the bank, cooking for the hired hands, making trips to town to buy parts for farm implements, and helping to look after and supervise the work of clearing and grubbing more than 200 acres of the land. Does Mrs. Elwell have a legal case for payment of the $5,000?

Chapter 11

REALITY OF CONSENT

A. MISTAKE

To create a contract there must be mutual assent through an offer and acceptance. "Real" assent is lacking if a party is induced to contract by mistake, fraud, duress, or undue influence.

1. MUTUAL MISTAKE AS TO EXISTENCE OR IDENTITY OF SUBJECT MATTER

If both parties are mistaken, and neither is at fault or both are equally at fault, the mistake will prevent the formation of a contract. The mistake may involve the nature of the contract, the identity of the person with whom it is made, or the identity or existence of the subject matter; however, the mistake must relate to a material fact.

In the famous case of *Raffles v. Wichelhaus* (2 H. & C. 906), there was a contract to sell cotton to be shipped to the buyer on the ship, *Peerless*. Unknown to the parties, there were two ships of that name departing from the same port but at different times. The buyer had in mind the ship that sailed earlier; the seller had in mind the ship that sailed later. No contract resulted. Hence, if neither party is to blame, or both are to blame, there is no contract.

Similarly, where the subject matter, or something essential to performance, ceases to exist before the agreement is reached, there is no contract. Thus, S makes a contract to sell a horse to B. However, unknown to either party, the horse has been destroyed. There is no contract. The U.C.C. follows the same rule if the loss is total (all the goods are destroyed). However, if the loss is partial, the buyer may accept the partial amount of goods with due allowances from the contract price but without further right against the seller (Section 2–613).

2. MISTAKE AS TO VALUE

Although a mutual mistake as to price can prevent the formation of a contract, a mutual mistake as to value will not permit rescission. This is the ordinary risk in business transactions, and the courts will not grant relief. For example, a woman in Wisconsin found a rough stone that looked like a topaz. Thinking it might be worth something, she took it to a jewelry store to sell it. The jeweler did not know the true value of the stone but nevertheless offered her one dollar for it, which the woman accepted. Later, it was discovered that the stone was an uncut diamond worth $700. The court held that the sale was valid and could not be set aside. The parties did not know what the stone was or its value. Each party assumed the risk that the value might be more or less than one dollar. There was no fraud or misrepresentation.

3. UNILATERAL MISTAKE

Generally, a unilateral or one-sided mistake is no ground for avoiding a contract. However, it may do so when it is caused by the other party or the other party knows or has reason to know that there is a material mistake. A common example in which relief is granted for a unilateral mistake occurs when a contractor submits a bid for construction and the mistake is material. In such a case, the courts rule that it would be unconscionable to hold the contractor to the bid when the other party knows of the unfairness in ample time to award the contract differently.

4. NEGLIGENCE OF MISTAKEN PARTY IN FAILURE TO READ CONTRACT

Generally, a party is held to what he has signed; i.e., ignorance through negligence or inexcusable trustfulness will normally not relieve a party from his contractual obligations. However, there are exceptions:

1. Fraud or other wrongful act on the part of the other party;

2. Where the other party misrepresents the character of the paper (signer thinks he is signing a receipt, but it is a contract); or,

3. Where a reasonable person would not think that the paper contained contractual provisions; e.g., a hat check stub containing provisions in fine print; or an "Acknowledgment of Order" printed form which contained provisions for arbitration and the exclusion of warranties in fine print at the bottom of the form.

5. MISTAKE OF LAW

In most states, a mistake of law will not afford grounds for rescission (e.g., buying property for a use that would violate a zoning restriction).
The rule has been criticized, and there are exceptions:

1. Where there has been fraud or undue influence.

2.   Where the mistake resulted in a failure of the contract to express the agreement (e.g., parties mutually agree on the terms of a contract and choose legal phrases which in legal effect express a meaning different from that agreed upon.

3.   In those states where, by special statute, a mistake of law is treated as a mistake of fact (e.g., California Civil Code Section 1578).

B.   FRAUD AND MISREPRESENTATION

1.   IN GENERAL

Fraud has been defined as "an intentional perversion of truth for the purpose of inducing another in reliance upon it to part with some valuable thing belonging to him or to surrender a legal right; a false representation of a matter of fact, whether by words or by conduct, by false or misleading allegations, or by concealment of that which should have been disclosed, which deceives and is intended to deceive another so that he shall act upon it to his legal injury" (Black's Law Dictionary, Revised Fourth Edition).

The essentials of fraud are as follows:

1.   A false representation of a *material fact.*

2.   Made with knowledge of its falsity or made with inexcusable ignorance of its truth.

3.   With intention that it be acted upon *by the party deceived.*

4.   That the party deceived reasonably *relied* upon the representation and acted upon it.

5.   That he or she was thereby injured.

A.   MATERIAL FACT

An essential element of fraud is the misrepresentation of a material *fact.* Sales talk is not actionable fraud (e.g., "This is the best car in town," "This is a good car," "This property is worth $75,000"). It is often difficult to distinguish between sales talk, or puffing, and a statement of fact. Generally, a prediction as to what will happen in the future is treated as an opinion and is not a statement of fact (e.g., A in good faith informs B that stock in a corporation is going to rise).

Also, the misrepresentation must be of a *material* fact and must be of such a substantial nature that but for it, the person would not have entered into the contract. A false statement that a horse was not a gelding would be material.

The following case is an example of sales talk.

FACTS   The plaintiff purchased a dwelling from the defendant. After living in the dwelling for six months, the plaintiff discovered the house was seriously damaged by termites. Suit was filed to rescind the sale because the seller had stated the house to be a good house.

DECISION　The representation was merely sales talk. Statements that things are "good" or "large" or "strong" necessarily involve to some extent an exercise of individual judgment, and even though such statements are made absolutely, the hearer must know that they can be only expressions of opinion.

Cannaday et ux. v. Cossey et ux. (228 Ark.1119, 312 S.W.2d 442 [1958])

B.　KNOWLEDGE OF FALSITY

The second element necessary to prove fraud consists of the statement made with knowledge of its falsity or made with inexcusable ignorance of its truth. A statement by a used-car salesperson that a car "does not eat oil" and that "the car does not need oil added between oil changes" when he or she does not know this to be a fact is an example of a statement made with inexcusable ignorance.

It is unjust for a person to retain the benefits of a bargain even though his or her misrepresentation is innocent. Therefore, most courts will permit rescission in this type of case. However, damages in addition to rescission would not be appropriate. In most cases, it would seem unnecessary to rely on the theory of innocent misrepresentation, since the facts usually establish mutual mistake (i.e., one party mistakenly representing the facts and the other believing the representation).

C.　INTENTION IT BE ACTED UPON BY PARTY DECEIVED

Another element of fraud is that the person making the misrepresentation intends that only a certain party be deceived. A third party who overhears the misrepresentation and acts upon it cannot recover, as it was not intended that he or she so act.

D.　JUSTIFIABLE RELIANCE

The plaintiff is under a duty to use reasonable diligence for his or her own protection (i.e., he or she must use reasonable care to keep from being defrauded). If a buyer knows or should know that the representation of the seller is untrue, the court will not grant the buyer relief (e.g., the used-car salesperson tells the buyer that a 1982 Lincoln gets 60 miles to a gallon of gasoline).

E.　INJURY

The plaintiff must suffer damages or he cannot recover money damages for fraud. Generally, the measure of damages is equal to what the value of the property would have been had it been delivered as represented, less the actual price paid for the property.

2. FRAUD IN THE INDUCEMENT

In the usual case of fraud, the defrauded party knows what he is signing, but his consent has been induced by fraud; mutual assent is present and a contract is formed, but the contract is voidable because of the fraud. For example, Seller induces Buyer to purchase Seller's Cadillac for $5,000, representing that the car has been driven only 25,000 miles. Before payment and delivery, Buyer learns that the car was actually driven 95,000 miles. Buyer may rescind the transaction because of Seller's fraud in the inducement.

To avoid the contract, the party must rescind by prompt notice and offer to restore the consideration received, if any.

Under the U.C.C., Section 2–721, the defrauded party may rescind the contract and recover damages, if any, resulting from the fraud.

3. FRAUD IN THE INCEPTION OR EXECUTION

In this type of case, the defrauded party does not know what he or she is signing because of deceit as to the nature of the document or does not intend to enter into a contract at all. Since mutual assent is lacking, the contract is void and may be disregarded without the necessity of rescission. For example, when a party who is unable to read English signs a release relying on the representation of the insurance agent that the instrument is only a receipt, the contract is void.

4. SILENCE OR CONCEALMENT AS FRAUD

Generally, silence is not fraud; however, there are several exceptions:

1. Where the parties are in a fiduciary or confidential relationship with each other, such as an attorney and client, there is a duty to speak and to make full disclosure of all facts relevant to the transaction. Failure to do so can be fraud. For example, an attorney knows that certain land owned by the client is going to increase in value because a certain corporation needs the land and plans to buy it. If the attorney wants to buy the land and later sell it to the corporation, the attorney must inform the client of the fact that the corporation is planning to buy the land.

2. Where there is a hidden defect, there is a duty to disclose (e.g., S sells cattle to B knowing the cattle have Texas fever, which is not easily ascertainable on inspection, without informing B of the disease, or seller fails to inform buyer that a certain house is subject to flooding from the neighboring river).

3. Active concealment, or a half-truth, can be actionable fraud (e.g., auto dealer puts foreign substance in motor to conceal engine defect).

4. Important provisions that are concealed in the fine print are generally unenforceable.

5.　STIPULATION IN THE CONTRACT

A party cannot absolve himself or herself from the effects of fraud by a stipulation in the contract that no misrepresentation has occurred in the contract or that any right based on fraud has been waived. Such a clause is against public policy and is unenforceable.

C.　DURESS AND UNDUE INFLUENCE

1.　DURESS

Duress consists of a wrongful act that compels assent through fear. It makes the contract voidable. Duress can be of the person (i.e., unlawful confinement of the party, spouse, child, etc.) or of goods (i.e., unlawful detention of property of the party). For example, it is duress for an attorney or accountant to refuse to give a client important papers unless the client agrees to pay a higher fee than originally agreed upon. *Thompson Crane & Trucking Co. v. Eyman* (123 Cal.App.2d 904, 267 P.2d 1043 [1954])

The modern tendency is to expand duress in the area of property to coercion in the field of business. However, to prove duress by business or economic compulsion, it is generally necessary to prove that the victim would suffer irreparable loss or near financial ruin for which he or she could not adequately recover from the wrongdoer. For example, seller refuses to deliver needed goods to buyer, who cannot get the goods from any other seller, unless buyer pays a higher price than the price set in the contract.

The general rule is that the act of duress must be unlawful (i.e., it must be a tort or a crime). Threat of criminal prosecution is duress, but not threat of a civil suit. For example, Robert, son of Mr. Jones, embezzles money from Robert's employer. The employer tells Mr. Jones that he will not ask the District Attorney to prosecute Robert if he, Mr. Jones, will make restitution. This threat of criminal prosecution is duress. However, if the employer merely states that he is going to sue Robert and Mr. Jones for the money, it is not duress.

2.　UNDUE INFLUENCE

Undue influence is the unlawful control exercised by one person over another so as to substitute his will for the volition of the victim. It is a kind of mental coercion that destroys the free agency of one and constrains him to do that which is against his will and what he would not have done if left to his own judgment and volition so that his act becomes the act of the one exerting the influence rather than his own act. However, mere appeals to affection or understanding are not considered undue influence, nor are mere advice or fair argument and persuasion. Normally a gift occasioned by gratitude for kindness or affection is not undue influence.

In most states, undue influence makes the contract voidable and subject to ratification. However, in some states, the remedy is limited to rescission (i.e., there can be no affirmance *and* recovery of damages).

In most states where a confidential relationship exists between the parties (e.g., attorney and client, guardian and ward, trustee and beneficiary, parent and child), the confidential relationship raises a presumption of undue influence and places upon the dominant party the burden of establishing fairness of the transaction and that it was the free act of the other party.

In some states, although no presumption of undue influence arises from a parent-child relationship, if dominance of the child is found to exist in fact, the burden is on the parent to establish the fairness of the transaction. In the absence of a presumption of undue influence, the person seeking to set aside the transaction must prove that by misrepresentation and deception the alleged victim was led into doing something that he or she would not have done but for the misrepresentation and deception. In the following case, the court held that undue influence was present and set aside the deed.

FACTS The plaintiff was an 82-year-old invalid, severely ill and completely dependent upon his son, the defendant, and his other 12 children. The plaintiff could not read or write English. The defendant was the primary person who advised the plaintiff and handled his business affairs, although the other sons helped to some degree. Plaintiff deeded his farm to the defendant for $23,500, the original purchase price. However, at the time of the transaction, the farm was worth between $145,000 and $160,000.

DECISION The court found that a confidential relationship existed between the plaintiff and the defendant which resulted in superiority and opportunity for influence, that the plaintiff was an invalid at the time of the conveyance, and the plaintiff's mental acuity was impaired and he sometimes suffered from disorientation and lapse of memory. The court held that the presumption of undue influence was raised by the plaintiff's prima facie case and that the defendant failed to rebut it.

Schaneman v. Schaneman (206 Neb. 113, 291 N.W.2d 412 [1980])

ILLUSTRATIVE CASES

1. Generally Unilateral Mistake Affords No Relief

BEAVER v. ESTATE OF URBAN HARRIS

67 Wn.2d 621, 409 P.2d 143 (1965)

BRADFORD, Judge.   Plaintiff brought this action against Urban Harris and Marjorie Harris, his wife, for personal injuries received in an automobile accident. Urban Harris has since died and his estate substituted as defendant. * * *

The defendant answered and alleged * * * a settlement contract with the plaintiff wherein the plaintiff received $1,750 for a full, complete and final release of the defendant for all injuries known and unknown sustained in the accident. Plaintiff presented his case on the theory there had been a mutual mistake of a material fact and the release should be rescinded. The defendant contended the release was valid and a complete defense, and the court should have determined this as a matter of law.

The primary question raised by this appeal is, can a person who has been injured in an accident caused by another's negligence rescind or set aside a general release and bring an action for damages where there is no allegation or proof of fraud, overreaching, questionable conduct, misrepresentation or any indication of incapacity of the party signing the release?

The facts are that on May 22, 1962, plaintiff was driving his automobile in a southerly direction along Aurora Avenue in Seattle. Urban Harris, at the same time, drove his car from the east side of the street to a traffic channel in the center of Aurora, stopped, and then started on across. There is a dispute as to whether the cars actually made contact. The plaintiff swerved to avoid the defendant driver, left the road, glanced off a pole, jumped the curb and ended up against a concrete abutment. The weather was misty and the pavement was wet. The plaintiff's face was bleeding and he seemed badly shaken. The plaintiff called his doctor, Virgel Anderson, on the evening of the accident and the doctor prescribed muscle relaxants, pain killers and equanil. Plaintiff complained of headaches, painful cervical spine, and pain through his low back area. * * *

Plaintiff consulted regularly with his doctor from the date of the accident until he was discharged to return to work on June 20, 1962. Les Winder, an adjuster for defendant's insurance company, first contacted the plaintiff on May 23, 1962. He and the plaintiff had six or seven talks between this date and June 14, when plaintiff signed a settlement and release, receiving a check for $1,750. * * *

When plaintiff signed the release, he believed he had a strained back. Medical testimony, based on examinations made after August 12, indicated plaintiff had a herniated disc when he settled.

It is a well recognized principle of law that, before a plain, unambiguous instrument can be set aside on the ground of mutual mistake, the evidence must be clear and convincing. * * *

Although this specific question has not been directly decided, we have repeatedly emphasized the value of amicable settlements of claims of this character, especially when the settlement has been secured without fraud, misrepresentation or overreaching. * * *

Mutual mistake is one of the recognized grounds whereby any contract may be set aside or vacated. What constitutes a mutual mistake must be clearly established.

There is ample authority holding a mutual mistake must be one involving both parties, a mistake independently made by each party.

In the case now being considered, the only information of plaintiff's condition was from the plaintiff himself. Defendant had no independent knowledge and he accepted plaintiff's own diagnosis and opinion of his injuries. If there was a mistake, it was a unilateral mistake, rather than a mutual mistake. * * *

The judgment is reversed and plaintiff's complaint dismissed on the merits.

2. Active Concealment as Fraud

DE JOSEPH v. ZAMBELLI

392 Pa. 24, 139 A.2d 644 (1958)

DANNEHOWER, President Judge.   This is an action in equity by a purchaser of real estate seeking a rescission and cancellation of a deed, and the recovery of the purchase price, $18,000.00, together with costs and expenses incidental thereto, from the defendant vendors, on the grounds of false and fraudulent representations inducing the sale. * * *

The evidence discloses that the defendants' vendors had knowledge of the existence of termites in their premises as early as May, 1952, and that they persisted in attempts to check and abate them until May, 1955, when the property was sold to the plaintiff. This is established clearly by the testimony of the tenants in the second floor apartment who were disinterested parties to the controversy. * * *

It was further disclosed that the basement had been given a heavy application of paint or whitewash shortly before the plaintiff first inspected the premises in February, 1955. According to the description of one witness, the basement looked like a "white sepulcher". In addition, the joists were partially obscured by shelves laden with jars and articles of clothing, and in some areas, strips of wood had been attached with the apparent purpose of concealing the more obvious termite damage. As a result of this deception and concealment the latent defects in the joists could not be detected and were not susceptible of discovery except by expert investigation.

The inference is inescapable that the defendants knew that the dwelling was infested with termites and were aware of the serious deterioration of the joists when the property was offered for sale to the plaintiff. The reply to the plaintiff's inquiry that the joists were "as good as new" was therefore a false, material and erroneous statement of fact.

* * * Where a party is induced to enter into a transaction with another by means of the latter's fraud or material misrepresentation, such a transaction can be avoided by the innocent party. Fraud arises where the misrepresentation is knowingly false, where there is a concealment calculated to deceive, or where there is a nonprivileged failure to disclose. * * *

Applying the above principles to the case at bar, we are of the opinion that the defendants are guilty of fraud in the purposeful concealment of the termite condition in the premises, and in misrepresenting to the plaintiff that the joists in the basement were "as good as new". This being true we must conclude that the plaintiff is entitled to avoid the transaction and be returned to status quo.

3. Silence Is Fraud When Duty to Disclose

GRIGSBY v. STAPLETON
94 Mo. 423, 7 S.W. 421 (1888)

Action to recover the contract price of 100 cattle sold by plaintiff to defendant. The defendant sets up plaintiff's failure to disclose the fact that the cattle were suffering from Texas fever, (deadly cattle fever disease, caused by tick bites, and difficult to detect) * * * and contends that silence as to this defect is fraudulent. The rest of the facts appear in the opinion.

Black, J. * * * Plaintiff purchased 105 head of cattle at the stock yards in Kansas City on Friday, July 25, 1884, at $3.60 per hundredweight. He shipped them to Barnard on Saturday. Mr. Ray, plaintiff's agent, attended to the shipment and accompanied the cattle. Ray says it was reported in the yards, before he left Kansas City, that the cattle were sick with Texas fever; some persons said they were sick and some said they were not. When the cattle arrived at Barnard, Ray told the plaintiff of the report, and that the cattle were in bad condition; that one died in the yards at Kansas City before loading, and another died in the cars on the way. On Sunday morning the plaintiff started with them to his home. After driving them a mile or so, he says he concluded to and did drive them back to the yards, because they were wild. One of them died on this drive, and two more died in the pen at Barnard before the sale to defendant. * * * He made no disclosure of the fact that the cattle were sick to defendant, nor that they were reported to have the fever. Defendant bargained for the cattle on Sunday afternoon and on Monday morning completed the contract at $3.75 per hundredweight, and at once shipped them to Chicago. Thirty died on the way, and twenty were condemned by the health officer. It is shown beyond all question that they all had the Texas fever. * * * If defects in the property sold are patent and might be discovered by the exercise of ordinary attention, and the buyer has an opportunity to inspect the property, the law does not require the vendor to point out defects. But there are cases where it becomes the duty of the seller to point out and disclose latent defects. * * * The sale of animals which the seller knows, but the purchaser does not, have a contagious disease, should be regarded as a fraud when the fact of the disease is not disclosed. * * *

There is no claim in this case that defendant knew these cattle were diseased. It seems to be conceded on all hands that Texas fever is a disease not easily detected, except by those having had experience with it. The cattle were sold to the defendant at a sound price. If, therefore, plaintiff knew they had the Texas fever, or any other disease materially affecting their value upon the market, and did not disclose the same to the defendant, he was guilty of a fraudulent concealment of a latent defect. * * * They were circumstances materially affecting the value of the cattle for the purposes for which they were bought, or for any other purpose, and of which defendant, on all the evidence, had no equal means of knowledge. To withhold these circumstances was a deceit * * *.

[Judgment for defendant].

4. Deprivement of Contract Volition Is Duress

McINTOSH v. McINTOSH

209 Cal.App.2d 371, 26 Cal.Rptr. 26 (1962)

SHEPARD, Justice.   This is an appeal from a judgment * * * in regard to enforcement of a divorce decree. * * *

During the trial, sharply conflicting testimony was had regarding whether plaintiff had written and signed an alleged waiver of alimony voluntarily or involuntarily. * * *

It appears from the record that plaintiff, about November 24, 1959, gave birth to an illegitimate child by a man named Glessner. On December 2, 1959, plaintiff wrote, signed and mailed to defendant a waiver of further alimony and a promise that when the family home (which had been awarded her by the divorce decree) was sold, she would divide the proceeds with defendant. The principal controversy between the parties involves the question of validity of said waiver. Defendant's testimony, if believed, would support the conclusion that the waiver was voluntary and for a consideration. However, plaintiff testified that on November 13, 1959, defendant beat plaintiff severely, broke part of the furniture, and threatened to kill her; that thereafter defendant made further and repeated threats to kill her, that he would burn her house down, bring her into court on a charge of adultery, and take her son and daughter away from her; that she was afraid then that if she did not send defendant the written waiver defendant would kill or injure her; that immediately prior to her writing of the waiver, defendant telephoned her and dictated its contents; that when she wrote the waiver she was worried sick and didn't know what she was doing. From the foregoing we are satisfied that the trial court was justified in finding that plaintiff was coerced into writing the waiver by fear of personal injury or death at the hands of defendant; that said fear was induced by the beating of November 13, 1959, coupled with the subsequent threats of defendant; that the waiver was not the voluntary act of plaintiff and was invalid. * * *

> Under the modern doctrine there is no standard of courage or firmness with which the victim of duress must comply at the risk of being without remedy; the question is merely whether the pressure applied did in fact so far affect the individual concerned as to deprive him of contractual volition; if it did there is duress, if it did not there is none * * *.

The judgment is affirmed [for plaintiff].

5. Nagging Can Constitute Undue Influence

TRIGG v. TRIGG

37 N.M. 296, 22 P.2d 119 (1933)

The case was tried before the district court of San Miguel county, where the issues were found for the plaintiff from which judgment and decree the issue is here on appeal.

ZINN, Justice.   The plaintiff * * * brought suit against the defendant to cancel deeds of conveyance. * * *

That conveyances and other instruments may be set aside because procured by the exercise of undue influence upon the party executing them is not questioned, and the exercise of such undue influence does not necessarily mean the infliction or threat of any physical injury or mischief. In the general sense of the term, undue influence would seem to be a species of duress, or, if this be not quite accurate, the two would at least seem to run together so that the precise line where one begins and the other stops is not easily definable. * * * Generally, the cases cited are where the husband obtained the property from the wife, where the guardian obtained property from the ward, where children obtained the property from the aged father or mother, the attorney from the client; generally the weaker or subservient having conveyed to the stronger or dominant, and equity has granted relief because of undue influence, duress, or fraud.

Here, however, we have the reverse, the clinging vine inducing the oak to convey to her all his interest in fourteen thousand broad acres on the Pablo Montoya grant, the weaker sex importuning, "nagging," and obtaining from the stronger and dominating member of the life partnership a conveyance of community real estate. She adopted the device, as alleged by the plaintiff of threatening abandonment of his bed and board, and dissolving the marriage by securing a divorce unless he gave her a deed to the ranch.

* * * The affection, confidence, and gratitude which inspires the gift from a husband to a wife, being a natural and lawful influence, does not render the gift voidable, unless the influence has been so used as to confuse the judgment and control the will of the donor.

* * * Plaintiff on cross-examination testified that the defendant abandoned him without cause, refusing to occupy the same bed with him, that it was without reason, "just her temper and mad all the time, and she was displeased about something always, and the atmosphere she made, just made it impossible to have any affection, and she would lock her bedroom doors and if I attempted to caress or pet her, she would scream for the servants to come."

Plaintiff testified that he deemed it necessary to place the title in Mrs. Trigg, the appellant, to preserve his home and happiness, without any intention to vest the same in [her] * * * Domestic tranquillity, the companionship and affection of a companionable mate and a peaceful household are more priceless than jewels, and cannot be measured in dollars and cents, and a social or domestic force exercised in such a manner as might put fear into the mind of a husband that, unless a conveyance is made of property so as to vest the same in the wife, a divorce would follow, with the consequences attendant thereto upon the domestic and social affairs of the threatened husband, might be considered as such undue influence and force as preventing the true and free action of his will and consent, and, where a deed of conveyance has been made after persistent "nagging," followed by threats of divorce and abandonment unless the deed is executed, it is a legitimate inference that such deed was made under the exercise of a domestic or social force which prevented the free action of the will of the donor and that such gift was made as the result of undue influence, and, if such gift be made in consideration of the fraudulent promise of a wife to return home and live with the grantor as his wife, and such promise is not fulfilled, it will amount to fraud. * * *

Constant importunities and "nagging" amount to an undue influence which can overcome the mind of the strongest willed person, and such constant importuning and "nagging" does amount to an undue influence. Such persistent urging amounts to "nagging," and "nagging" is the exercise of a domestic force by which the mind becomes irritated, disturbed, ruffled, wearied, and troubled, so that the judgment may become confused and the free action of the will is out of normal control, and a chancellor can set aside a conveyance of property made under such improper conditions. * * *

Finding no error, the judgment of the district court is affirmed, and it is so ordered.

PROBLEMS

1. Husband had an insurance policy on his life for $10,000 payable to his wife as beneficiary. Husband did not return home one day and subsequently was missing for two years. Wife was having trouble paying the premiums on the policy. After a discussion with the insurance company's agent, wife decided to take a paid-up policy for $2,500 instead of the $10,000 policy. It was discovered later that husband had been dead before the conversion to the $2,500 paid-up policy. Wife now demands the $10,000 payment from the insurance company. The insurance company will pay her only $2,500. Decision?

2. Builder submits a written offer to homeowner to erect a building for $54,000, and homeowner accepts the offer. Builder later discovers that he made a mistake of $20,000 and that the offer should have been for $74,000. Builder now seeks to be allowed to withdraw his offer and to have the contract rescinded because of this mistake. Decision?

3. Mrs. Reed was injured in a train accident. The insurance agent had her examined by a company physician shortly after the accident and while she was en route to her destination. The physician told her that she was not seriously injured. The insurance

agent requested her to sign a release for damages for the consideration of $100, which she did. After completing her journey, she discovered that she sustained serious injuries requiring hospitalization. She now seeks to have the release set aside by reason of the false representations made to her by the insurance agent and the physician. She testified that she could neither read nor write and signed the release with an X mark; that she knew little about the contents of the release; that she signed it a few hours after the accident without a chance to consult with friends, a doctor, or an attorney; and that she signed at the urgent solicitation of the claims agent who was with her on the train at the time of the accident. Decision?

4. To induce buyer to purchase a tract of land, seller stated that the land was low enough to be readily irrigable from a nearby irrigation ditch. Seller knew that his statement was false. Buyer consulted an irrigation expert about the possibility of getting water upon the land from the ditch and, apparently satisfied with the expert's opinion, purchased the land. Later, buyer discovers that the land was too high for irrigation from the nearby irrigation ditch and sues seller for damages for deceit. Decision?

5. To induce buyer to purchase a herd of cattle ranging over an extensive territory, seller told buyer the number of animals he had branded the preceding season. However, he failed to inform buyer that many of the cattle had since been lost or killed. When buyer sought to determine the number in the herd for himself, seller put various obstacles in the way of buyer's inspection, as a result of which buyer was unable to learn of the extensive losses among the cattle. Buyer now sues seller for fraud. Decision?

6. Seller built a dwelling house directly over an old cesspool and, without making any reference to the unsanitary pit beneath the cellar floor, sold the new house to buyer. The house soon became uninhabitable because of the odor from the hidden refuse. Buyer sues seller for the deceit. Seller contends that he was merely silent as to the cesspool, and silence is not fraud. Decision?

7. Debtor owed creditor $1,000. Creditor tried every friendly gesture possible to get the debtor to pay but with no result. Finally, the creditor sent the debtor a letter as follows: "I have tried to be nice about this, but you simply will not cooperate. This is to inform you that unless I receive payment in full on or before Friday at 4:00 p.m., I am going to file a civil suit against you on Monday." Debtor claims creditor is using duress to collect the money. Decision?

8. B purchased four tires from the B. F. Goodrich Tire Company advertised as guaranteed 40,000-mile radials. The local salesman made the same representation to B. In fact, the company did not begin to market guaranteed 40,000-mile radials until some eight months later. The tires sold to B carried a warranty only against defects and road hazards which at the time of sale was applicable to all grades of Goodrich tires. B sues for damages on the basis of fraud. Decision?

9. Plaintiff contracted to buy a large herd of cattle from defendant and made an initial payment of $200,000. On the day of delivery of the cattle when plaintiff was to pay the balance of the purchase price, plaintiff discovered that 460 head of cattle were missing. Plaintiff insisted on deducting the value of the missing cattle from the purchase price. Defendant refused to deliver any of the cattle unless the entire balance called for by the contract was paid. Winter was approaching, and the cattle might be exposed to great loss unless properly cared for during the winter season. To obtain the cattle and to protect his initial payment, plaintiff paid the entire sum. Plaintiff now sues for the value of the missing 460 head of cattle. Defendant claims that since plaintiff paid for all of the cattle, he has no claim. Decision?

10. Sallie Beard, 70 years of age, a widow, feeble, in ill health, and entirely without business experience, made up her mind to withdraw her extensive funds from the X bank and use them elsewhere. The bank officials, close relatives of Sallie's deceased husband, and their attorney, worried that the withdrawal would injure the bank and repeatedly urged Mrs. Beard not to withdraw the money but rather to sign a deed of trust with the bank as trustee. Mrs. Beard wanted to see her attorney but was persuaded not to see him. She was told that if she withdrew the money, the bank would not survive and her father-in-law would probably be influenced to ignore her in his will if she refused to execute the deed of trust. Finally, she executed the deed of trust. Later, she discovered that the deed she signed took away all control over the funds and deprived her forever of any power to revoke the trust. She brings an action to have the deed declared void on the grounds of undue influence. Decision?

Chapter 12

CAPACITY OF PARTIES

One of the requirements of a binding contract is that the parties have legal capacity to contract (i.e., that they are competent). However, many contracts involve persons under a legal disability (e.g., minors, intoxicated persons, persons of unsound mind, aliens, convicts, partnerships, and corporations). The limitations on partnerships and corporations are found in later chapters. This chapter considers the limitations on persons.

A. MINORS

1. MINOR'S RIGHT TO AVOID A CONTRACT

Under common law, a person who had not attained the age of 21 was considered a minor. Today, by statute in most jurisdictions, persons are given adult status at the age of 18 for most purposes (e.g., the right to make binding contracts, to make a will, and to marry without parental consent).

Generally, a minor can avoid a contract he or she has entered into any time during the period of minority or within a reasonable time thereafter. What is a reasonable time depends upon the intelligence of the minor, his or her means of knowledge, the nature of and relation to the transaction, and the purpose to be attained thereby. There is no hard and fast rule. Seven months after reaching majority has been held to be unreasonable, whereas 14 years has been held to be reasonable. Generally, several months can be safely considered reasonable.

Until the minor avoids the contract, the adult party is bound by it. The following case is an example of the right of a minor to rescind a contract.

> **FACTS** The plaintiff Adams, while a minor, purchased an automobile from the defendant Barcomb. The plaintiff operated the car for approximately two weeks and was dissatisfied with it. She disaffirmed the contract and requested her money back. The defendant refused to return her money. The plaintiff sued for the return of the money.

DECISION   The law in Vermont has always been that a minor can disaffirm a contract, if not for necessities, while a minor or within a reasonable time after arriving at adult age. After disaffirmance, the plaintiff is entitled to the return of the consideration paid for the automobile.

Adams v. Barcomb (125 Vt. 380, 216 A.2d 648 [1966])

2.   RESTITUTION ON AVOIDANCE

After the minor disaffirms the contract by notice to the other party, must he or she return the consideration? Under the majority rule, the minor does not have to return the consideration if the contract is for a luxury and he or she no longer has it. For example, a minor buys an automobile from a dealer and then disaffirms the contract. Must the minor return the automobile? Most courts hold that he or she must return the automobile if he or she still has it. If the minor has wrecked it, he or she need only to return the wrecked automobile. If the minor has sold it but no longer has the money received for the car, most courts will not require the car's return.

By statutes, and by court decisions in some states, the minor must account for the property's value if he or she cannot return the consideration.

Suppose a minor trades in his Ford automobile and purchases a new Chevrolet from a dealer, and the dealer sells the Ford to an innocent third party. Upon disaffirmance, can the minor get the Ford back from the third party? Under Section 2–403 of the U.C.C., the minor cannot.

3.   CONTRACTS FOR NECESSITIES

A minor is liable for the reasonable value of necessities actually furnished him or her by another person at the minor's request. The minor is not bound by the terms of the contract but is required to pay the reasonable value of the necessities on the theory of quasi-contract.

What is a necessity depends on the surrouding circumstances of the minor, such as age, actual need, and financial or social status. Necessities include food, clothing, shelter, medical care, tools of a trade, vocational education, and possibly a college education.

There has been a tendency to expand the concept of necessities to include property and services necessary for the minor to make a living (e.g., farm implements, employment agency fee). It is likely the trend will continue to include as necessities items that under modern living standards are associated with necessities of life. Of course, as the courts expand the concept of necessities, the minor becomes liable for more types of contracts.

4.   CONTRACTS MINOR CANNOT AVOID

A minor cannot avoid a contract if he or she ratifies it when no longer a minor. A ratification may be made expressly by the minor or by his or her conduct. For example, a minor purchases an automobile and after becoming an adult sells it; the act of selling is a ratification by conduct.

By statutes or court decisions in many states, minors cannot avoid certain types of contracts (e.g., contracts for legal or medical services; loans by a governmental agency made for the purpose of obtaining a higher education; life insurance contracts; credit union, bank, or building and loan association contracts; contracts that involve the transfer of shares of stock; contracts for the purchase of homes and farms with the Veterans' Welfare Board; contracts for services in the field of sports or dramatics approved by the proper court; and contracts arising from a business the minor operates). The U. S. Supreme Court has held that a minor's enlistment in the armed forces may be binding subject to statutory qualifications as to age.

5. MISREPRESENTATION OF AGE

Under the majority rule, the fact that a minor misrepresents his or her age will not preclude him or her from disaffirming the contract. This rule has been changed by statute in some states. The general rule is that even though the minor can disaffirm the contract, he or she is still liable in damages for the tort (civil wrong or injury not arising out of contract) of deceit on the theory that the tort is independent of the contract and that minors generally should be held liable for their torts.

By the majority view, a minor is not liable for a tort that involves a breach of a duty flowing from the contractual status. For example, a minor rents an automobile under a contract that requires him to use reasonable care in the operation of the automobile. Through negligence, the minor damages the car, thus breaching the contract. His contractual immunity absolves him from liability on the contract. Can the adult recover in a suit for damages based on the minor's tort (negligence in damaging the automobile)? In most states (e.g., Michigan, New Jersey) the adult cannot. However, if the minor goes beyond the contract (by making an unauthorized use, for example) and during this unauthorized use negligently damages the automobile, most courts would hold that the tort was independent of the contract and allow recovery.

6. PARENTAL LIABILITY FOR CONTRACTS

Ordinarily, a parent is not liable for the contracts of a minor child. The parent is liable, however, if the child acted as the parent's agent.

If a parent has not provided the child with necessities, the parent is liable to third persons for the reasonable value of the necessities furnished to the minor.

If a parent joins in a contract with a minor (e.g., to purchase an automobile), the parent is liable even though the minor may be able to disaffirm.

7. PARENTAL LIABILITY FOR TORTS

Generally, a parent is not liable for the tortious acts of the minor child even though the child may be liable. There are exceptions.

1. A parent is liable for the torts of the child when the child is acting as an agent or servant of the parent.

2.   Where the negligence of the parent made the injury possible, the parent is liable on the basis of theordinary rules of negligence, but not on the parent-child relationship.

3.   Where the parent directs, consents to, or sanctions the tort.

4.   In most states, by statute the parents are liable for willful, malicious, intentional, or unlawful acts of the minor child.

5.   In some states, the parent is liable by special statute (e.g., limited amount associated with a driver's license).

B.   INTOXICATED PERSONS

If a person is so intoxicated or under the influence of drugs at the time he enters into a contract that he is unable to comprehend the nature and effect of the transaction, the contract is voidable at the person's option.

C.   PERSONS OF UNSOUND MIND

If a person is so deranged mentally that he does not know that he is making a contract or does not understand the consequences of the transaction, the contract is voidable.

Most states by special statute (e.g., California Civil Code Section 38–40) provide that if a person had been *judicially* declared insane, the contract is void. If the person is incompetent, but not judicially declared insane, the contract is voidable.

By case law in California, it has been held that where a person in a hospital signed an insurance release while in a dazed and semi-conscious condition as a result of injuries sustained in an automobile accident, the release was wholly void.

D.   ALIENS

Generally, aliens who are legally in this country have the same right to contract as citizens. Thus, they can contract for the transfer of land; can be admitted to the practice of law, which involves entering into contracts; can receive state educational and welfare benefits; and can be employed in nonpolicymaking civil service jobs.

Laws generally provide, however, that aliens cannot vote, hold high public office, act as jurors, or be employed in sensitive areas with broad discretionary powers, such as police officers. The United States Supreme Court has given the states wide latitude in excluding aliens legally in the United States from public employment.

E. CONVICTS

Generally, convicts are accorded full contractual capacity. The law varies from state to state. In some states, a convict under a life sentence cannot contract except to sell real property he or she may own. The trend is to liberalize the contract rights of prisoners and convicts.

Parole generally restores limited civil rights including the right to contract, the right to vote, and the right to hold public office.

ILLUSTRATIVE CASES

1. Minor Not Required to Restore Consideration on Rescission
(Majority Rule)

ROBERTSON v. KING

225 Ark. 276, 280 S.W.2d 402 (1955)

ROBINSON, Justice.   The principal issue here is whether [defendant], a minor, may rescind a contract to purchase a pick-up truck. On the 20th day of March, 1954, L. D. Robertson, a minor, entered into a conditional sales agreement whereby he purchased from Turner King and J. W. Julian, doing business as the Julian Pontiac Company, a pick-up truck for the agreed price of $1,743.85. On the day of the purchase, Robertson was 17 years of age, and did not have his 18th birthday until April 8th. Robertson traded in a passenger car for which he was given a credit of $723.85 on the purchase price, leaving a balance of $1,020 payable in 23 monthly installments of $52.66 plus one payment of $52.83. He paid the April installment of $52.66. * * *

It appears that Robertson had considerable trouble with the wiring on the truck. He returned it to the automobile dealers for repairs, but the defective condition was not remedied. On May 2nd, the truck caught fire and was practically destroyed. He notified the automobile concern * * *.

On June 7th, [plaintiffs] filed suit to replevy the damaged truck from Robertson. By his father and next friend, Robertson filed a cross-complaint in which he alleged that he is a minor and asked that the contract of purchase be rescinded and sought to recover that part of the purchase price he had paid, * * * There was a judgment for King and Julian on the complaint and the cross-complaint. On appeal, Robertson contends that he was 17 years of age at the time of the alleged purchase and that he has a right under the law to rescind the contract and to recover the portion of the purchase price he has paid.

[Plaintiffs] also contend that * * * a minor cannot rescind a contract of purchase without reimbursing the seller for any loss that he may have sustained by reason of such rescission. This statute deals with situations where a minor is 18 years of age at the time of making a purchase. The statute is not applicable here because according to the undisputed evidence Robertson was only 17 years of age at the time of entering into the purchase agreement. * * *

The automobile dealers have disposed of the car they received in the trade, and cannot restore it to the minor. In a situation of this kind, the weight of authority is that the actual value of the property given as part of the purchase price by the minor is the correct measure of damages. Neither side is bound by the agreement reached as to the value of the car at the time the trade was made. * * * Hence, the court erred in finding for the automobile dealers, and the cause is therefore reversed and remanded for a new trial.

[A minor does not have to return the consideration when he does not have it and the contract is for a luxury].

2. Minors' Employment Agency Contract May Be a Necessity

GASTONIA PERSONNEL CORP. v. ROGERS

276 N.C. 279, 172 S.E.2d 19 (1970)

On May 29, 1968, [defendant was a minor,] emancipated and married. He needed only "one quarter or 22 hours" for completion of the courses required at Gaston Tech for an A.S. degree in civil engineering. His wife was employed as a computer programmer at First Federal Savings and Loan. He and she were living in a rented apartment. They were expecting a baby in September. Defendant had to quit school and go to work.

For assistance in obtaining suitable employment, defendant went to the office of plaintiff, an employment agency, on May 29, 1968. After talking with Maurine Finley, a personnel counselor, defendant signed a contract containing, *inter alia,* the following: "If I ACCEPT employment offered me by an employer as a result of a lead (verbal or otherwise) from you within twelve (12) months of such lead even through it may not be the position originally discussed with you, I will be obligated to pay you as per the terms of the contract." Under the contract, defendant was free to continue his own quest for employment. He was to become obligated to plaintiff only if he accepted employment from an employer to whom he was referred by plaintiff.

After making several telephone calls to employers who might need defendant's services as a draftsman, Mrs. Finley called Spratt-Seaver, Inc., in Charlotte, North Carolina. It was stipulated that defendant, as a result of his conversation with Mrs. Finley, went to Charlotte, was interviewed by Spratt-Seaver, Inc., and was employed by that company on June 6, 1968, at an annual salary of $4,784.00. The contract provided that defendant would pay plaintiff a service charge of $295.00 if the starting annual salary of accepted employment was as much as $4,680.00.

* * *

Plaintiff sued to recover a service charge of $295.00. In his answer, defendant admitted he had paid nothing to plaintiff; alleged he was not indebted to plaintiff in any amount; and, as a further answer and defense, pleaded his infancy.

* * *

BOBBITT, Chief Justice. * * *

In general, our prior decisions are to the effect that the "necessaries" of an infant, his wife and child, include only such necessities of life as food, clothing, shelter, medical attention, etc. In our view, the concept of "necessaries" should be enlarged to include such articles of property and such services as are reasonably necessary to enable the infant to earn the money required to provide the necessities of life for himself and those who are legally dependent upon him.

* * * To hold, as a matter of law, that such a person cannot obligate himself to pay for services rendered him in obtaining employment suitable to his ability, education and specialized training, enabling him to provide the necessities of life for himself, his wife and his expected child, would place him and others similarly situated under a serious economic handicap.

In the effort to protect "older minors" from improvident or unfair contracts, the law should not deny to them the opportunity and right to obligate themselves for articles of property or services which are reasonably necessary to enable them to provide for the proper support of themselves and their dependents. The minor should be held liable for the reasonable value of articles of property or services received pursuant to such contract.

Applying the foregoing legal principles, which modify *pro tanto* the ancient rule of the common law, we hold that the evidence offered by plaintiff was sufficient for submission to the jury for its determination of issues substantially as indicated below.

To establish liability, plaintiff must satisfy the jury by the greater weight of the evidence that defendant's contract with plaintiff was an appropriate and reasonable means for defendant to obtain suitable employment. If this issue is answered in plaintiff's favor, plaintiff must then establish by the greater weight of the evidence the reasonable value of the services received by defendant pursuant to the contract. Thus, plaintiff's recovery, if any, cannot exceed the reasonable value of its services to defendant.

Accordingly, the judgment of the Court of Appeals is reversed and the cause is remanded to that Court with direction to award a new trial to be conducted in accordance with the legal principles stated herein.

Error and remanded.

3. The Problem of Parental Tort Liability

GISSEN v. GOODWILL

80 So.2d 701 (Fla., 1955)

KANNER, Associate Justice.

* * *

It is averred [these are merely allegations of the plaintiff which he must prove at the trial] in the second amended complaint that at the time of the appellant's injury, he was employed as a clerk at the Gaylord Hotel in the City of Miami Beach, Florida, and the appellees were residing as business invitees at the same hotel; that the minor child, Geraldine Goodwill, 8 years of age, "did wilfully, deliberately, intentionally and maliciously" swing a door "with such great force and violence against the plaintiff so that the middle finger on plaintiff's left hand was caught in the door and a portion of said finger was caused to be instantaneously severed and fell to the floor." It is further averred that

> owing to a lack of parental discipline and neglect in the exercise of needful paternal influence and authority, the defendants, Albert Goodwill and Mrs. Albert Goodwill carelessly and negligently failed to restrain the child, Geraldine Goodwill, whom they knew to have dangerous tendencies and propensities of a mischievous and wanton disposition; that said parents had full knowledge of previous particular acts committed by their daughter about the hotel premises, such as striking, knocking down and damaging objects of furniture and furnishings and disturbing and harassing the guests and employees of the hotel and that the defendant Geraldine Goodwill did commit other wanton, wilfull and intentional acts of a similar nature to the act committed against the plaintiff, such as striking guests and employees of the aforesaid hotel, which acts were designed or resulted in injury, so that the child's persistent course of conduct would as a probable consequence result in injury to another. Said parents, nevertheless, continually failed to exercise any restraint whatsoever over the child's reckless and mischievous conduct, thereby sanctioning, ratifying and consenting to the wrongful act committed by the defendant, Geraldine Goodwill, against the plaintiff herein.

This is a case of first incidence in this Court's jurisdiction, posing as it does the problem of whether the specific set of circumstances here can render the parents of the minor child accountable at law for the tort alleged to have been committed by the child.

It is basic and established law that a parent is not liable for the tort of his minor child because of the mere fact of his paternity. * * * However, there are certain broadly defined exceptions wherein a parent may incur liability: (1) Where he intrusts his child with an instrumentality which, because of the lack of age, judgment, or experience of the child, may become a source of danger to others. (2) Where a child, in the commission of a tortious act, is occupying the relationship of a servant or agent of its parents. (3) Where the parent knows of his child's wrongdoing and consents to it, directs or sanctions it. (4) Where he fails to exercise parental control over his minor child, although he knows or in the exercise of due care should have known that injury to another is a probable consequence. * * *

In the case of *Norton v. Payne* (154 Wash. 241, 281 P. 991, 992 [1929]), action was brought by infant, aged 5, by his guardian for injuries sustained when he was struck in the eyeball with a stick by defendants' child, aged 7, who had the *habit* of striking smaller children in the face with sticks. It was alleged that parents knew about and encouraged her *habit* of striking other children with sticks. The appellate court reversing the lower court's dismissal of the case said, "* * * we think parents should be held responsible and liable for a *dangerous habit* of a child of which they have knowledge and take no steps to correct, or restrain. It is that which constitutes the negligence on the part of the parent." It was pointed out by the court that, although the evidence in the case is that the father did not know that the child was committing this particular tort, the parents did nevertheless know that such child was in the habit of perpetrating this particular kind of tort and that the father encouraged her in so doing, the implication being that since he made no effort to restrain the child, he must therefore be deemed to have consented to its commission by her at any time.

* * *

In the case of *Ellis v. D'Angelo* (116 Cal.App.2d 310, 253 P.2d 675, 679 [1953]), it is alleged that the parents, employing plaintiff for the first time as a baby sitter for their 4 year old son and knowing that their son *habitually* engaged in violently attacking and throwing himself forcibly and violently against other people, violently shoving and knocking them, nevertheless failed to warn the plaintiff of such habitual conduct on the part of their infant; and that shortly after plaintiff entered on her duties in the home, the son attacked and injured her. The appellate court reversed the lower court's dismissal of the complaint, holding that a cause of action had been stated, and said, "While it is the rule in California, as it is generally at the common law, that there is no vicarious liability on a parent for the torts of a child there is 'another rule of law relating to the torts of minors which is somewhat in the nature of an exception, and that is that a parent may become liable for an injury caused by the child, where the parent's negligence made it possible for the child to cause the injury complained of, and probable that it would do so.' *Buelke v. Levenstadt* (190 Cal. 684, 689, 214 P. 42, 44 [1923])."

* * *

One common factor from the foregoing cases appears salient in the assessment of liability to the parents, that the child had the habit of doing the particular type of wrongful act which resulted in the injury complained of. In the instant case, the cause of action sought to be established fails in that the negligence charged with relation to parental restraint is not claimed to flow from the commission of an act or course of conduct which the child habitually engaged in and which led to the appellant's injury. It is nowhere claimed that the child here involved had a propensity to swing or slam doors at the hazard of persons using such doors. The deed of a child, the enactment of which results in harm to another and which is unrelated to any previous act or acts of the child, cannot be laid at the door of the parents simply because the child happened to be born theirs. However, a wrongful act by an infant which climaxes a course of conduct involving similar acts may lead to the parents' accountability. A deed brought on by a totally unexpected reaction to a situation which is isolated of origin and provocation could not have been foretold or averted and hence could not render the parents responsible.

[Judgment for defendants.]

4. Must Prove Insanity to Avoid Contract

HANKS v. McNEIL COAL CORP.

114 Colo. 578, 168 P.2d 256 (1946)

STONE, Justice.   Lee A. Hanks, who was a prosperous farmer and business man in Nebraska, came to Colorado with his family in 1918, at first settling on a farm in Weld county, which included the coal lands involved in this proceeding; then, in 1920 moving to Boulder where he purchased a home, engaged in the retail coal business, and thereafter resided. His son, J. L. Hanks, continued to operate and live on the farm as a tenant. * * * Shortly after 1922 Lee Hanks discovered that he was afflicted with diabetes, and members of his family noticed a progressive change in his physical and mental condition thereafter. He became irritable and easily upset, very critical of his son's work, and increasingly interested in the emotional type of religion. He began to speculate in oil and other doubtful ventures with money needed for payment of debts and taxes. About 1934 he sent his son what he denominated a secret formula for the manufacture of medicine to cure fistula in horses, which was compounded principally of ground china, brick dust, burnt shoe leather and amber-colored glass. If the infection was in the horse's right shoulder, the mixture was to be poured in the animal's left ear, and if on the left shoulder then in the right ear. In 1937 Mr. Hanks started to advertise this medicine through the press under the name of Crown King Remedy. Thereafter he increasingly devoted his efforts and money to the compounding and attempted sale of this concoction, his business judgment became poor and he finally deteriorated mentally to the point that on May 25, 1940, he was adjudicated insane and his son was appointed conservator of his estate.

* * * Hanks learned that the defendant coal company, which had leased other lands lying to the north of his property, was extracting coal from their other leased lands and conveying it by means of the open haulage way through his lands to its shaft located to the south thereof. Hanks made demand for payment of royalty on the coal so transported across his land and there was extended argument and controversy which finally led to discussion of outright purchase of the Hanks property and the ultimate signing of the contract here involved on July 21, 1937, between Hanks and the defendant companies. * * *

The present action was brought by the conservator seeking to have the court set aside this contract. * * * The record is voluminous; the case was carefully considered by the court below and judgment of dismissal entered on findings against plaintiff on the question of insanity.

There is always in civil, as well as in criminal, actions a presumption of sanity. * * * Insanity and incompetence are words of vague and varying import. Often the definition of the psychiatrist is at variance with that of the law. The legal test of Hanks' insanity is whether "he was incapable of understanding and appreciating the extent and effect of business transactions in which he engaged." * * *

The legal rule does not recognize degrees of insanity. It does not presume to make a distinction between much and little intellect. * * * One may have insane delusions regarding some matters and be insane on some subjects, yet capable of transacting business concerning matters wherein such subjects are not concerned, and such insanity does not make one incompetent to contract unless the subject matter of the contract is so connected with an insane delusion as to render the afflicted party incapable of understanding the nature and effect of the agreement or of acting rationally in the transaction.

    * * * Patently Hanks was suffering from insane delusion in 1937 with reference to the efficacy of the horse medicine, but there is no evidence of delusions or hallucinations in connection with this transaction or with his transaction of much of his other business at that time; there is no basis for holding voidable his sale here involved on the ground of his insanity, and the trial court correctly so held. * * *

    Accordingly, the judgment is affirmed.

PROBLEMS

1.   Buyer, a minor, purchased a used automobile for $1,000 from a dealer. The minor used the automobile for three months and then damaged it in an accident. The automobile is now worth $250. Buyer takes the automobile back to the dealer and demands the return of the purchase price. Decision?

2.   Buyer, a minor, badly in need of an overcoat, purchases one on credit for $100. The coat is really only worth $75. The buyer wears the coat for three months during the winter season and then attempts to return the coat and disaffirm the contract. Seller sues buyer for purchase price. Decision?

3.   Buyer, a minor, purchases furniture on credit. After he becomes an adult, he sells the furniture and uses the proceeds of the sale to purchase an automobile. He defaults on the furniture payments, contending that he purchased the furniture when he was a minor and therefore he can rescind the contract. Seller sues for the balance due on the contract. Decision?

4.   Buyer, a minor, wishes to purchase a new "Cool" automobile. He knows, however, that Cool dealers will not sell a Cool to a minor and informs the dealer that he is 22 years of age. The dealer sells the minor the automobile for cash. Six months later, and while the buyer is still a minor, he returns the automobile requesting disaffirmance of the contract. Decision?

5.   A minor owns and operates a filling station. An adult drives his automobile to the station and requests an oil change and a lube job. The minor drains the oil from the crankcase and lubricates the necessary parts of the automobile. Because of having to wait on a gas customer, the minor forgets to fill the crankcase with oil. The adult pays the minor for the work and drives his car from the filling station. After being driven a short distance, the motor becomes seriously damaged. The adult

demands that the minor pay to have the motor repaired, but the minor is only willing to return the amount paid for the oil change and the lube job. The adult sues the minor in tort for the damage. Decision?

6. Defendant, a minor, gave a catered dinner for his university friends. His father was a man of great wealth. Defendant refuses to pay for the dinner, and caterer brings suit. Discuss.

7. Defendant, a married minor with a child, purchased from plaintiff certain farm machinery consisting of a tractor, disc, and cultipacker. Defendant was engaged in farming and used the machinery so that he might earn a living for himself, wife, and child. The machinery was destroyed by a fire through no fault of defendant. Plaintiff sues for the value of the machinery. Discuss.

8. Alice, a minor, borrowed $20,000 from her aunt for the express purpose of attending the state university and obtaining a degree in home economics, as she felt that such a degree would help her become a better homemaker. Alice, while still a minor, finished the required work and was awarded the degree. Although Alice has recently become an adult and has married a wealthy man, she refuses to repay the loan. Can Alice's aunt get a judgment against Alice?

9. Richard, a minor who likes to impress his girlfriends, purchased a used automobile on an installment contract. He has defaulted in payments, and the seller seeks payment from Richard's father. Discuss.

10. Two brothers, ages 10 and 12, while playing football on the sidewalk collided with plaintiff who received injuries. There was no evidence that either boy had previously played with a football on the public streets or conducted himself in a disorderly manner. Plaintiff claims that a parent's failure to exercise proper supervision renders liability for acts of a minor even though there is lack of evidence of unrestrained conduct. Discuss.

Chapter 13

LEGALITY OF SUBJECT MATTER

A. ILLEGALITY IN GENERAL

As a general rule, contracts that involve a violation of the law or are contrary to public policy are unenforceable. Examples of illegal contracts include restraints of trade, bribery of public officials, usury, an agreement to perform services without the required regulatory license, an agreement to injure or defraud someone, and gambling. It is interesting to note that even though the contract is expressly permitted by statute, it may still be unenforceable.

The following case is an example of a decision in which the court held that gambling debts are not enforceable because gambling is against public policy (i.e., tends to be injurious to the interests of the public).

> **FACTS** The plaintiff, Corbin, seeks to recover $20,000 on a winning bet of $100 at 200-to-1 odds that the Boston Red Sox would win the American League pennant. The defendant refuses to pay on the grounds that gambling debts are not collectible through the courts.
>
> **DECISION** This is a court action for recovery of a gambling debt. This court has refused to aid in the collecting of gambling debts for nearly a century and we will not depart from those cases.
>
> *Corbin v. O'Keefe* (484 P.2d 565 [Nev. 1971])

If part of the consideration for a contract is illegal, the entire contract is unenforceable unless the contract is divisible, in which case the legal part will be upheld. For example, an employee is to receive $100 a week for sweeping the floor and for drawing beer, but the latter act is illegal, because the employer does not have a license. The employee will be unable to recover any money, because part of the consideration is illegal and the contract is not divisible. If he were to receive $50 for sweeping the floor and $50 for drawing the beer, he would be able to recover $50 for sweeping the floor, as the contract is divisible.

When parties are not equally at fault, the court will not intercede to help the more innocent party where the agreement was morally wrong or inherently evil (i.e., the contract was *malum in se*). For example, Mrs. X hires Hood to kill her husband. Hood kills Mrs. X's husband but cannot collect the fee, because murder is morally wrong and inherently evil.

If the contract were only *malum prohibitum* (against some statute or regulation but not inherently evil), quasi-contractual recovery may be had. For example, employer hires firefighter to do part-time work, knowing that the firefighter would violate a departmental regulation regarding part-time work. The firefighter can recover for the value of his other services, since the violation did not involve an affront to public morals.

Mere knowledge of wrongful use will not preclude recovery. For example, a seller can recover for the price of sugar sold even though she knew the buyer was going to use it to make illegal whiskey; or a lender can recover money loaned even though he knew the borrower was going to use it for illegal gambling. Of course, the seller or lender must not do anything in furtherance of the unlawful design or participate in the unlawful venture.

A lottery has been defined as "a chance for a prize for a price." Lotteries are usually prohibited by statute, but there are exceptions (e.g., New York). A lottery is illegal regardless of the name attached to it, since the law will look through the form to the substance. If participation in the game does not require the participant to purchase anything or to give anything of value, it is not a lottery (e.g., giveaway plans and games). Insurance contracts are not lotteries, as they share existing risks of loss from a possible future event, such as a fire, and are therefore for the good of the public.

B.   AGREEMENT TO COMMIT A CRIME

An agreement to commit a crime is illegal. If A promises B $5,000 if B will kill T, and B in reliance on the promise kills T, the court will not enforce A's promise to pay the $5,000.

C.   AGREEMENT NOT TO PROSECUTE FOR A CRIME

An agreement not to prosecute for a crime not only is illegal but is a crime itself. An employer learns that E, his employee, has embezzled some of his goods and sold them to B. B and E sign a promissory note for the employer on his promise that he will not prosecute E for the crime. The employer will not be able to enforce the note in an action on it and can be held guilty of the crime of Compounding a Felony. This is based on the principle that the employee committed the crime against the state; the employer therefore does not have the right to make an agreement to refrain from the criminal prosecution (or conceal the crime or withhold evidence) for the promise of reimbursement. The employer can also be guilty of the crime of extortion under these facts.

D. AGREEMENT TO COMMIT A TORT

An agreement to commit a tort (civil wrong or injury not arising out of contract) is illegal. A politician promises a newspaper editor that he will pay the editor $5,000 if the editor will publish a false story indicating that the politician's opponent is a communist. Such a promise is unenforceable; and if the story is published, the editor would be guilty of the tort of libel (which may also be a crime).

E. AGREEMENT INTERFERING WITH A PUBLIC DUTY

An agreement that tends to be against the public interest is unenforceable (e.g., corrupting a public official to influence legislation or to get a government contract).

Generally, lobbying contracts are upheld if the lobbyist is not to use improper methods of influencing legislation, such as secret, personal influence; bribery; threat of loss of votes; or a contingency fee based on success.

F. FAILURE TO OBTAIN LICENSE REQUIRED BY LAW

Every state has laws requiring persons engaged in certain types of occupations to be licensed (e.g., lawyers, doctors, accountants, brokers, contractors, architects). Such laws are either regulatory in nature or merely for revenue purposes.

If a law is regulatory in nature and the person does not have a license, he or she cannot enforce a contract made without the license. If the law is merely to provide revenue, the person can enforce the contract even though he or she does not have the revenue license. The occupations listed in the preceding paragraph all require regulatory licenses.

If a painting contractor does not have the required regulatory license and she paints your house pursuant to a contract, can she enforce the contract? The answer is no, since the license was required so that the state could regulate the particular business. However, suppose that you pay the painter for her work and then you discover that she did not have a license. Can you recover the money paid? The answer is no, since there can be no recovery of money paid on an executed contract involving an unlicensed person. The typical city business license is one for revenue purposes only, since the city does not attempt to regulate the particular business. Thus, if the painter had her state regulatory license, she would be able to enforce the contract even though she did not have the revenue license.

The following case is an example of a void and unenforceable contract for failure to obtain a regulatory license.

FACTS The plaintiff sued the defendant hospital for breach of contract to hire him as a full-time resident physician. The defendant's agents had told him that he would have the position for as long as the hospital needed a resident physician. Plaintiff began work on August 1, 1972, and was discharged on August 15, 1972, because plaintiff did not have a license to practice medicine in Illinois. It was proven that although he was well-qualified for the position, he did not have the necessary license.

DECISION The court held that plaintiff could not recover for breach of contract or for damages in quasi-contract, since his agreement with the hospital was illegal and void as contrary to public policy. The purpose of the statute requiring a physician to be licensed is to protect the public by assuring it of adequately trained practitioners.

Tovar v. Paxton Community Memorial Hospital (330 N.E.2d 247 [Ill. 1975])

G. STIPULATION AGAINST LIABILITY FOR NEGLIGENCE

A provision in a contract that relieves a party of liability for his or her own ordinary negligence is not favored by the law, is strictly construed against the party relying on it, and is often declared illegal by statutes or courts as contrary to public policy. For example, California Civil Code Section 1668 provides that all contracts that have as their object, directly or indirectly, to exempt anyone from responsibility for his or her own fraud, or willful injury to the person or property of another, or violation of law, whether willful or negligent, are against the policy of the law. The California Supreme Court has ruled that an exculpatory clause in a residential lease violates public policy and therefore does not operate to relieve an owner of liability for injuries caused to his or her tenants while on a common stairway in an apartment building. When such a clause is declared illegal, it is usually because the public interest is involved (e.g., a charity patient in a nonprofit medical research center, release of surgeons and hospital invalid where surgeons were only ones in area capable of performing particular operation, public carrier, theatre, parking lots). Thus, if a parking lot attempts to avoid liability due to the negligence of one of the parking lot drivers, it will generally fail for one of the following reasons: (1) a reasonable person would not be aware and would not have understood that the parking ticket was a contract relieving the lot of liability, (2) there has been a violation of a statute such as that found in California, or (3) the exculpatory clause is unconscionable. However, it has been held that the parking lot can *limit* liability to a reasonable amount (it has been held that $1,000 was not a sufficient amount when automobile was stolen from lot).

Where the public interest or some statutory limitation is not involved, the Restatement of the Law of Contracts and many courts take the position that the clause is valid. Exceptions exist: A person cannot contract out of *gross* negligence; an employer cannot contract to relieve himself or herself from liability for injuries to employees; and a person cannot excuse himself or herself for fraud, willful injury, or a violation of the law by an exculpatory clause.

H. SUNDAY LAWS

Many states have enacted laws that make contracts entered into on Sunday unenforceable ("blue laws"). Excluded from the law, however, are acts that must be done on Sunday to protect health, life, or property and contracts entered into on a Sunday but ratified on a weekday.

I. DISCRIMINATION CONTRACTS

The Federal Civil Rights Act of 1964 provides that public accommodations and facilities (e.g., restaurants and hotels) may not discriminate on the basis of race, religion, color, or national origin.

The Fourteenth Amendment to the federal Constitution (by court interpretation) prohibits discrimination in the sale of property.

J. PROMISES NOT TO COMPETE

A promise by a seller of a business not to compete with the buyer is enforceable if it is reasonable in time and in area. Thus, if a contract for the sale of a grocery store in the city of New York contains a clause that prohibits the seller from entering into the grocery business in that city for a period of one year, the clause would be enforceable by an injunction against the seller. However, if the clause provides for a time that is too long or an area that is too great, a problem can arise.

Many courts "blue pencil" the unreasonable part and leave the rest of the clause when the clause is divisible. For example, if the above sale had a covenant that provided that the seller could not enter into the business for a period of one year in the cities of New York, Albany, Syracuse, and Rochester, these courts would blue pencil the cities of Albany, Syracuse, and Rochester and hold the rest of the clause valid.

Many courts (e.g., California, Delaware, Florida, Massachusetts, Mississippi, New Jersey, New York, Texas, Washington, and Wisconsin) redo the clause by inserting *reasonable* restrictions. For example, if the clause prohibited the seller from engaging in the grocery business for 30 years in the entire state of New York, these courts would insert a reasonable time and a reasonable area. This is the modern tendency. Its objection is that it tends to encourage employers and purchasers possessing superior bargaining power over that of their employees and vendors to insist upon unreasonable and excessive restrictions, secure in the knowledge that the promise may be upheld in part, if not in full, and if not, they will at least get reasonable restrictions inserted by the court. The solution to this objection can be found in *McLeod v. Meyer* (237 Ark. 173, 372 S.W.2d 220 [1963]), where the court held that a covenant deliberately unreasonable and oppressive, whether severable or not, is invalid. In some states, the courts use all of the above rules depending upon the facts and circumstances of the case.

A clause incident to a contract of *employment* that restricts an employee from discussing trade secrets or engaging in competition after employment has terminated has been a prolific source of litigation. Some of the criteria generally considered by the courts in determining whether or not such a clause is valid are as follows:

1. Is the restraint reasonable in the sense that it is no greater than necessary to protect the employer in some legitimate interest?

2. Is the restraint reasonable in the sense that it is not unduly harsh and oppressive on the employee?

3. Does the employee's work for the rival party irreparably injure the employer or threaten to injure him or her irreparably?

In *Washington Capitols Basketball Club, Inc. v. Barry* (304 F.Supp. 1193 [N.D.Cal. 1969]), a star basketball player signed one contract too many, and his original employer sought a restraining order to prevent him from playing for his new employer. The court, in granting the temporary injunction, held that the contract was not unconscionable, unenforceable, or otherwise void and stated, "The precedents for granting injunctive relief against 'star' athletes 'jumping' their contracts—and certainly defendants do not deny that Barry is a unique, a 'star' athlete—are numerous."

By statute in a few states, an employer cannot restrict an ordinary employee from engaging in competition after the employment ends. For example, California B. & P. C., Section 16600, provides that a covenant not to compete between an employer and an employee after termination of employment is void.

Other state and federal statutes governing restraint of trade are covered in subsequent chapters.

K. USURY

1. IN GENERAL

Usury means an illegal contract for a loan in which illegal interest is reserved (i.e., a rate of interest greater than allowed by statute). Intent to violate the law is not necessary.

Most states strictly regulate the interest rates on loans by statute. The maximum chargeable interest rate allowable varies from 6 percent to 30 percent in the various jurisdictions. If the lender charges interest over the permitted maximum rate, the contract is illegal. Although most states deny the lender any interest at all if he or she charges an illegal amount, a few states permit the lender to recover the maximum legal amount that has been established by statute. In a few states, the lender forfeits the entire amount of the principal and the interest. If the interest has been paid by the borrower, jurisdictions differ as to whether he or she recovers merely the amount of the interest paid or whether he or she recovers two or three times that amount as a penalty.

Most states have statutes that provide for so many exceptions to the general rule of usury that the purpose of the law (i.e., to protect debtors from excessive interest) has been largely nullified.

2.　WHAT IS NOT USURY

A few of the many exceptions to the usury laws are as follows:

1.　Installment sales (i.e., sales on credit) generally do not come within the usury statutes. The theory is that in such cases the seller does not lend money to the buyer but agrees that he or she is to be paid by the buyer later. Since no loan is made, the usury law does not apply. The seller is free to sell for cash at one price and on credit at a different price that is much higher. However, many states (e.g., California) have adopted statutes that regulate the differential between cash and time prices that may be charged by the seller.

If the sale is going to be financed by a bank and the credit sale contract provides that the buyer is to make payments directly to the bank, it is considered a loan, and the unpaid balance is subject to the usury law.

2.　Reasonable expenses or service fees incidental to the loan may be charged in addition to the maximum rate of interest (e.g., inspecting of property, investigating the credit of the borrower, and drawing necessary documents). However, points (the fee or charge a lender sometimes makes for the privilege of making a loan and which is one or more of the percentages of the principal amount of the loan) are considered interest and are prorated over the term of the loan to determine if the points added to the regular interest is usurious.

Finance or carrying charges on long-term loans are also allowable. There is a conflict in the court decisions as to late charges: Some courts hold that late charges are not interest and therefore not subject to usury laws, while others hold they are interest on the theory that they are payments due because the money was not repaid on time.

3.　Most statutes provide that collecting interest in advance, compound interest, or accelerated maturity for nonpayment of installments is not usury so long as the total interest does not exceed the maximum rate per annum for the full period of the loan.

4.　The purchase of a note at a discount greater than the maximum interest with no intent to evade the law is not usury.

5.　Where the borrower has the option to pay the principal of the debt before due date, together with some months' unearned interest, there is no usury.

6.　Most states have enacted statutes that permit licensed moneylenders, such as banks, to charge more interest than is permissible in ordinary business transactions.

ILLUSTRATIVE CASES

1. Agreement Not to Prosecute Crime is Unenforceable

GRASSO v. DEAN

171 Neb. 648, 107 N.W.2d 421 (1961)

SPENCER, Justice.   This is an action by plaintiff, Grasso, against defendants, Adolph, Gladys, and Joan Dean, and defendant corporations, State Finance Company, Postal Finance Company, and First Loan Company. It seeks to foreclose a mortgage on the home owned by defendants Adolph and Gladys Dean, in which the three defendant corporations are alleged to claim some interest. The mortgage was given to secure an installment promissory note signed by the three defendants Dean.

The defense raised by defendants Adolph and Gladys Dean, is that the promissory note and mortgage * * * were obtained by the use of duress and threats. * * *

The essential facts are: Defendant Joan entered the employ of plaintiff, a dentist, in 1954 as an office clerk, receptionist, and technician. Plaintiff had been in practice but a few months. Joan was 16 years of age but represented herself to be 18. During the years 1956 and 1957, Joan embezzled funds belonging to plaintiff. According to plaintiff's testimony, Joan admitted "about the fourth or sixth month * * * of 1957," that she had been taking money, but could not give the amount. Audits were made by plaintiff's accountant. On October 24, 1957, Joan, in the office of plaintiff's accountant and in his presence, and in the presence of plaintiff, signed an "affidavit of admission," but no amount was stated. During December 1957, Joan made two payments on the obligation. Subsequent to these payments, plaintiff insisted that Joan bring her father to his office. About 2 weeks previous to February 18, 1958, Joan brought Adolph to plaintiff's office. Previous to this time, Joan had not wanted her folks informed. At this visit, plaintiff discussed Joan's difficulty with her father, who, according to plaintiff's testimony, said, "he would help her in any way he could, and he was appreciating what I was doing." On February 18, 1958, Joan and Adloph met plaintiff at the home of plaintiff's accountant, and signed a note for $7,974, and Adolph executed a mortgage on the Dean home.

* * * The evidence in this case is undisputed that Joan did embezzle funds of plaintiff. However, in considering the defense of duress herein, the question of her guilt or innocence is immaterial. The question is whether the facts and circumstances, as disclosed by the record involved, constitute duress. * * * the law is well established that where a parent or other relative is induced to execute an instrument by threats and fear of criminal punishment of a child or relative, the instrument is the result of duress and the contract may be voided. * * *

Plaintiff testified: "* * *

Q. Just tell us what you said, just what you said in regard to paper. A. *That we wanted to try to rehabilitate her, we didn't want to persecute her, we wanted to do everything to help her. In other words, just because she is down we didn't want to trample her, we wanted to help her."* (Italics supplied.)

The word "persecute" as used by the witness would ordinarily have an entirely different meaning, but as used here could logically be calculated to induce fear of prosecution. * * * What was plaintiff doing that Joan's father appreciated? * * *

When we consider the substance of the testimony adduced by plaintiff, we can readily conclude the obvious answer must be the correct one. There was a threat of prosecution under plaintiff's evidence, and while not stated in so many words, it certainly produced the desired condition of mind. * * * We believe the consideration for the giving of the note and mortgage was the suppression of a criminal prosecution, and find the transaction illegal and void and that no recovery can be had thereon. * * *

[Judgment for defendant.]

[Query: what possible crimes were committed? Embezzlement by Joan? Compounding a felony by the plaintiff? Extortion by the plaintiff? Conspiracy to the crime of compounding a felony by all the parties? If the accountant prepared the note and mortgage he could have committed the crime of practicing law without a license.]

2. Agreement to Commit a Tort Is Unenforceable

ATKINS v. JOHNSON

43 Vt. 78 (1870)

The defendant had written a defamatory article about one Gregory, and to induce the plaintiff, a publisher, to print it in his newspaper, the defendant had agreed to protect him against any action for damages brought by Gregory, or any other liability that might arise from the publication. The plaintiff, having been sued successfully by Gregory, brings this action upon the defendant's promise to indemnify him.

PIERPOINT, C.J.   * * * The plaintiff is here seeking to compel the defendant to indemnify him for the damage which he has sustained in consequence of publishing a libel, at the request of the defendant, and from the consequences of which the defendant agreed to save him harmless. The question is whether such an agreement as the plaintiff sets out in his declaration can be legally enforced.

In this case, these parties in the outset conspired to do a wrong to one of their neighbors, by publishing a libel upon his character. The publication of a libel is an illegal act upon its face. This both parties are presumed to have known. The publication not only subjects the party publishing to a prosecution by the person injured for damages, but also to a public prosecution by indictment. * * *

Both these parties knew that they were arranging for and consummating an illegal act, one that subjects them to legal liability, hoping, to be sure, that they might defend it; but the plaintiff, fearing they might not be able to do so, sought to protect himself from the consequences by taking a contract of indemnity from the defendant. To say under such circumstances that these parties were not joint wrongdoers, within the full spirit and meaning of the general rule, would be an entire perversion of the plainest and simplest proposition. This being so, the law will not interfere in aid of either. It will not inquire which of the two are most in the wrong, with a view of adjusting the equities between them, but regarding both as having been understandingly engaged in a violation of the law, it will leave them as it finds them, to adjust their differences between themselves as they best may.
* * *

[Case dismissed.]

3. Failure to Obtain License Required by Law

ELEPHANT LUMBER CO. v. JOHNSON

120 Ohio App. 266, 202 N.E.2d 189 (1964)

COLLIER, Presiding Judge.   The Elephant Lumber Company, a corporation, * * * herein designated the plaintiff, brought this action on June 10, 1963, in the Chillicothe Municipal Court to recover for services rendered * * * Helen Johnson, herein referred to as the defendant, in preparing and drawing plans, specifications and material lists for the erection of a building to be used as a nursing home. * * *

No answer or other pleading was filed by the defendant and, on July 15, 1963, a default judgment was entered in favor of plaintiff for the full amount claimed in the petition. * * * The defendant now seeks a reversal of that judgment. * * *

The defendant's contentions are that the petition does not state a cause of action for the reason it is not alleged in the petition that the plaintiff is an architect or has as its employee an architect authorized to draw and furnish plans and specifications and to charge for such services; that the alleged contract is in violation of statute and therefore void; that a valid default judgment may not be rendered upon such defective petition. Section 4703.18, Revised Code, provides:

> No person shall enter upon the practice of architecture, or hold himself forth as an architect or registered architect, unless he * * * is the holder of a certificate of qualification to practice architecture issued or renewed and registered under such sections.

* * * Ohio is one of the many states that have enacted statutes regulating architects in the practice of their profession. It is generally held that designing a building for another, or furnishing the plans and specifications for such a building for another, constitutes architectural services. It is also well settled that such legislation is a proper exercise of the police power.

* * * The general rule is that a contract entered into by a person engaged in a business without taking out a license as required by law is void and unenforceable and that where a license or certificate is required by statute as a requisite to one practicing a particular profession, an agreement of a professional character without such license or certificate is illegal and void. * * *

It is also a well established rule that a contract which cannot be performed without a violation of a statute is void. * * *

Our conclusions are that the plaintiff's claim is for services rendered as an architect; that to practice the profession of architecture in Ohio and to recover in an action for such services, it is necessary to obtain a license as prescribed by law; that a contract for such services entered into by one who is not so licensed and registered is void; that a default judgment, rendered on a petition to recover for such services in which it is not alleged that the plaintiff is a licensed and registered architect, is void. The judgment will be reversed and final judgment rendered for the defendant.

4. Cannot Waive Negligence When Public Interest Involved

HUNTER v. AMERICAN RENTALS, INC.

189 Kan. 615, 371 P.2d 131 (1962)

WERTZ, Justice. This was an action for damages brought by Everett L. Hunter, plaintiff against American Rentals, Inc., defendant. * * *

The petition alleged that the defendant corporation was engaged in the business of renting trailers to the general public, including trailer hitches and all other attendant equipment necessary to connect trailers to automobiles; that plaintiff went to defendant's place of business for the purpose of renting a trailer, told defendant's agent that he knew little about trailers, had never pulled a trailer behind an automobile, and that he would have to rely on defendant's agent's superior knowledge and skill to determine the size of the trailer and other necessary equipment to transport enumerated items from Wichita to Oklahoma City. * * * [T]hat defendant's agent returned to the office and advised plaintiff the trailer was ready for the trip and that it would not be necessary for plaintiff to do anything further to the trailer or the hitch. Plaintiff then paid the rental charges. * * *

Driving his automobile and the trailer loaded with the furniture and items previously described, plaintiff departed from Wichita, and when he reached a point near Edmond, Oklahoma, the trailer hitch broke, leaving the trailer and automobile attached only by the safety chain. This chain had been attached by the defendant's agent in such a manner that it permitted the trailer to start moving from one side of the highway to the other, causing plaintiff's car to overturn, and by reason thereof plaintiff received personal injury and damage to the automobile for which he seeks recovery.

* * *

By its answer defendant seeks to avoid liability to plaintiff, contending that the plaintiff entered into a written rental agreement for the use of one of defendant's trailers and at the time the rental agreement was entered into plaintiff paid the defendant the rental charge. A portion of the rental agreement reads:

> The renter hereby absolved the AMERICAN RENTALS of any responsibility or obligation in the event of accident, regardless of causes or consequence, and that any costs, claims, court or attorney's fees, or liability resulting from the use of described equipment will be indemnified by the renter regardless against whom the claimant or claimants institute action.

* * *

Contracts for exemption for liability from negligence are not favored by the law. They are strictly construed against the party relying on them. The rule is unqualifiedly laid down by many decisions that one cannot avoid liability for negligence by contract. The rule against such contracts is frequently limited to the principle that parties cannot stipulate for the protection against liability for negligence in the performance of a legal duty or a duty of public service, or where the public interest is involved or a public duty owed, or when the duty owed is a private one where public interest requires the performance thereof. * * * There is no doubt that the rule that forbids a person to protect himself by agreement against damages resulting from his own negligence applies where the agreement protects him against the consequences of a breach of some duty imposed by law.

G.S.1949, Chapter 8, Article 5, contains the uniform act regulating traffic on the highway. Section 8–5, 118 provides:

> (a) When one vehicle is towing another the drawbar or other connection shall be of sufficient strength to pull, stop and hold all weight towed thereby, * * *. (b) In addition to the drawbar connections between any two such vehicles there shall be provided an adequate safety hitch. * * *

* * * It is apparent that the mentioned statute was passed for the protection of the public; that the business in which the defendant is engaged, i.e., that of renting trailers to the public, is one where the interest and safety of the public must be kept in view; and, where one violates a duty owed to the public, he may not come into a court of law and ask to have his illegal contract, exempting him from liability to comply with such duty, carried out. * * *

If an agreement binds the parties, or either of them, to do something opposed to the public policy of the state, it is illegal and absolutely void. * * *

For the reasons stated, this court is of the opinion that the contract pleaded, being in contravention of the statute and the public policy of this state, is void and unenforceable and constitutes no defense to plaintiff's cause of action, * * * and the judgment must be affirmed.

5. Can Waive Negligence in Private Contracts

CIOFALO v. VIC TANNEY GYMS, INC.

10 N.Y.2d 294, 220 N.Y.S.2d 962, 177 N.E.2d 925 (1961)

FROESSEL, Judge.   This action by plaintiff wife for personal injuries, and by plaintiff husband for medical expenses and loss of services, stems from injuries which the wife sustained as the result of a fall at or near the edge of a swimming pool located on defendant's premises. Plaintiff claimed that because of excessive slipperiness and lack of sufficient and competent personnel she was caused to fall and fractured her left wrist. * * *

At the time of the injury, plaintiff wife was a "member" or patron of the gymnasium operated by defendant, and in her membership contract she had agreed to assume full responsibility for any injuries which might occur to her in or about defendant's premises, "including but without limitation, any claims for personal injuries resulting from or arising out of the negligence of" the defendant.

Although exculpatory clauses in a contract, intended to insulate one of the parties from liability resulting from his own negligence, are closely scrutinized, they are enforced, but with a number of qualifications. Whether or not such provisions, when properly expressed, will be given effect depends upon the legal relationship between the contracting parties and the interest of the public therein. * * * [W]here the intention of the parties is expressed in sufficiently clear and unequivocal language * * * and it does not come within any of the * * * categories where the public interest is directly involved, a provision absolving a party from his own negligent acts will be given effect.

* * * Here there is no special legal relationship and no overriding public interest which demand that this contract provision, voluntarily entered into by competent parties, should be rendered ineffectual. Defendant, a private corporation, was under no obligation or legal duty to accept plaintiff as a "member" or patron. Having consented to do so, it had the right to insist upon such terms as it deemed appropriate. Plaintiff, on the other hand, was not required to assent to unacceptable terms, or to give up a valuable legal right, as a condition precedent to obtaining employment or being able to make use of the services rendered by a public carrier or utility. She voluntarily applied for membership in a private organization, and agreed to the terms upon which this membership was bestowed. She may not repudiate them now. * * *

The judgment appealed from should be affirmed, without costs.

PROBLEMS

1.   The Encino Woman's Club wants to raise scholarship money for indigent college students. The club plans on having a party at which it will sell tickets for $100 each on a new automobile. The holder of the winning ticket will receive the automobile. The tickets will have the word "Donation" at the top. What is your advice as to the legality of this transaction?

2.   Las Vegas Hacienda, Inc., made a public offer to pay $5,000 to any person who, having paid 50 cents for the opportunity of attempting to do so, shot a hole in one on its golf course pursuant to certain conditions. Gibson complied with the conditions, including the payment of the money, and shot a hole in one. Hacienda refuses to pay contending the contract was a wagering contract. Gibson claims the shooting of the hole in one was a feat of skill and not a feat of chance. Decision?

3.   Seller sold buyer a quantity of candy and silverware. The candy had been put up by seller in prize packages, some of which contained tickets. Buyer was to resell the packages at a price greater than their real value, each purchaser taking a chance that he or she would get a ticket that would entitle him or her to a piece of silverware. Buyer refuses to pay for the candy and the silverware, contending that the contract was illegal and unenforceable. A statute provided that every lottery, game, or device of chance in the nature of a lottery, by whatsoever name it may be called, other than such as have been authorized by law, shall be deemed unlawful. Decision?

4.   Defendant wished to delay action by the board of supervisors for the purchase of certain real estate in which defendant was interested. He made a contract with plaintiff to pay him $50,000 if plaintiff could get the supervisors to postpone action. The plaintiff gave a majority of the supervisors and their wives a party at Las Vegas, at which time the plaintiff gave each of the wives a cloth coat and convinced the wives to speak to their husbands regarding a postponement of the purchase of the real estate. Subsequently, the supervisors postponed the purchase. Defendant refuses to pay the $50,000. Decision?

5.   Richie and Cody were the opposing nominees for the office of jailer of Knott County, Kentucky. Shortly before the election, Cody secretly agreed to withdraw his candidacy if Richie would agree to appoint him his deputy and divide the fees of the office. Richie agreed. To guarantee his performance of the contract, he deposited the sum of $500 with a third party with the understanding that the money was to be repaid when he had fully performed his agreement. Richie was elected and has fully complied with his obligations to Cody. He now seeks to recover the $500 from the third party. The third party refuses to give Richie the $500. Decision?

6.   The XYZ Insurance Company contracted to insure a surgeon against personal liability for his negligence in connection with his surgical work. During an operation, the surgeon carelessly injured a patient. The surgeon now sues the insurance company to compel it to protect him from loss as a result of such injury. The company's defense is that the surgeon's contract for protection against responsibility for his own negligence is illegal and void. Decision?

7. Lally sold his barbershop to Mattis "together with all good will." The contract contained a clause that provided that Lally would not engage in the barbering business for a period of two years in the city of Rockville, where the barbershop was located. Nine months after the sale, Lally set up a one-chair barbershop in his own home, which was approximately 300 yards from the shop he sold to Mattis. Mattis seeks an injunction. Decision?

8. Blackman, a real estate salesman, signed an employment contract with Abramson, a real estate broker, which provided that "The salesman shall not after the termination of this contract, use to his advantage any information gained verbally or from the files of the broker." Blackman wants to leave Abramson and seeks your advice as to whether he can work for a different broker in the same area.

9. Plaintiff, an employee of the department of mental health for the State of Kansas, was informed that the defendant hospital in Illinois wished to hire a resident physician. Plaintiff was not licensed to practice in Illinois. Plaintiff informed the defendant of her education, training, and licensing as a physician. Defendant told plaintiff that her credentials were satisfactory and represented to her that the position would last for her natural life or for so long as the hospital required the services of a resident physician, and as long as she was able to do the work competently. Plaintiff resigned his position in Kansas and entered defendant's employment. Two weeks later she was discharged. Plaintiff sues damages for breach of contract. Discuss.

10. B is induced into purchasing a used car by misrepresentations of the seller. The contract B signed stated that he had read the contract and that there had been no misrepresentations that induced the sale of the car. Assuming B can prove the misrepresentations and that they induced him into purchasing the car, will the clause in the contract prevent rescission?

Chapter 14

THE STATUTE OF FRAUDS (WRITINGS)

A. NATURE AND EFFECT

Some students believe that all contracts must be in writing. Otherwise, they wonder, how will the contract be proven in court? Actually, only relatively few contracts must be in writing, and even then there are exceptions.

When a contract is not in writing, it is proven in court by the testimony of the parties to the contract and by witnesses, if any. In court, there is often conflicting testimony and confusion about the actual terms of the contract, in which case it is very difficult for the judge to make a correct decision. Also, if the contract is in writing, there is much less chance of litigation on the contract.

Some contracts are so important, or there is such an opportunity for fraud in the making of the contract, that every state has a Statute of Frauds declaring which contracts must be in writing. The statutes differ only in the types of contracts that must be in writing. In the following sections, you will find the most common and important types of these contracts.

Perhaps the Statute of Frauds is a misnomer, since the statute has nothing to do with the *law of frauds* discussed in Chapter 11. However, the original Statute of Frauds was passed in England in 1677 as "An Act for the Prevention of Frauds and Perjuries," and the name still continues. Perhaps a better name for this statute would be the Statute of Writings, since the statute states that certain contracts must be in writing and signed by the party to be charged (the defendant in the lawsuit), or the contract is unenforceable (not unlawful).

The writing required may be a note or memorandum, may be informal, and may consist of one or more writings (e.g., separate escrow instructions and signed by one of the parties, or two letters). The writing may be made at the time the agreement is entered into or at a later date. The writing should meet the test of reasonable certainty and should contain the names of the parties, the subject matter, the terms and conditions of all the promises, and by whom and to whom made. Under this rule, the absence of a description of the property or the names of the parties in the sale of real estate is fatal.

Under the U.C.C., which is applicable to the sale of goods, the test of reasonable certainty has been greatly relaxed. A check in the seller's hands may be held to be a sufficient memorandum of the sale if it refers to the goods in question. The seller's indorsement is evidence of receipt and acceptance.

Under the U.C.C., signature of the party includes any symbol executed or adopted by a party with the intention of authenticating a writing (Section 1–201(39)). Authentication may be printed, stamped, or written. It may be by initials or by thumbprint. In *Automotive Spares Corp. v. Archer Bearings Co.* (382 F.Supp. 513 [(N.D.Ill. 1974]), the court held that it may be on any part of the document and in appropriate cases may be found in a billhead or letterhead.

B. SALE OF GOODS

1. IN GENERAL

Section 2–201(1) of the U.C.C. states that a contract for the sale of goods for the price of $500 or more is not enforceable unless there is some writing sufficient to indicate that a contract for sale has been made between the parties. (See U.C.C. Section 2–105 in Appendix A for definition of "goods.") The writing must be signed by the party against whom enforcement is sought. The writing may be informal, since the only purpose of the section is for the parties to establish that there is in fact a contract for sale and purchase. Although the details regarding price, place of delivery, etc., may be omitted, the quantity must be stated unless it is a "need" or "output" contract (see Chapter 10.,A.,4.).

There are exceptions to the above rule.

1.   Section 2–201(2) states that as between merchants, an oral contract of sale is enforceable if one of the merchants sends a written confirmation of the contract to the other merchant and the merchant receiving the information does not object to the contents of the confirmation within 10 days after receiving it. Both merchants are bound (i.e., the merchant who signed the confirmation and the merchant who received it and failed to object). (For a definition of "merchant," see U.C.C. Section 2–104 in Appendix A. A farmer has been held to be a merchant in *Campbell v. Yokel* [313 N.E.2d 628 (Ill. 1974)].)

2.   Section 2–201(3)(a) states that a writing is not necessary if the goods are to be specially manufactured for the buyer and if, before receiving repudiation by the buyer, the seller has made a substantial beginning of their manufacture or has made commitments for their procurement and the goods are not suitable for sale to others in the ordinary course of the seller's business. The following case illustrates this section.

FACTS Plaintiff sued defendant for damages because defendant refused to accept certain shoes manufactured for him. Defendant ordered one hundred dozen "brog. oxford" shoes from plaintiff. The shoe is specially made, very fancy, and of an unusual size. The shoes were not suitable for sale in the ordinary course of business. The price was over $500.

DECISION Because the transaction comes within Section 2–201(3)(a), the contract did not have to be in writing.

Adams v. Cohen (242 Mass. 17, 136 N.E. 183 [1922])

3. Section 2–201(3)(c) states that the contract does not have to be in writing if payment for the goods has been made and accepted or they have been received and accepted by the buyer. If the goods have been partly paid for or partially delivered, the oral contract is enforceable only to the extent of the partial payment or partial delivery. However, when the goods are not divisible, such as an automobile, part payment will be sufficient to make the contract totally enforceable.

2. MINERALS, STRUCTURES, GROWING TIMBER, CROPS

Section 2–107(1) states that a contract for the sale of minerals (including oil and gas) or the sale of a structure or its materials to be removed from the land is a contract for the sale of goods IF the goods are to be severed by the seller. Thus, Section 2–201 applies. However, if the goods are to be severed by the buyer, the contract is one affecting land and Section 2–201 does not apply.

Section 2–107(2) states that a contract for the sale of growing timber or growing crops is a contract for the sale of goods whether severed by the seller or the buyer.

3. SALE OF SECURITIES

Section 8–319 provides that every contract for the sale of securities, regardless of the amount, must be in writing and signed by the party to be charged (normally the defendant in the lawsuit) or his or her authorized agent or broker. Delivery of the securities or a confirmatory writing will satisfy the Statute.

4. SALES OF OTHER KINDS OF PERSONAL PROPERTY

Section 1–206 provides that other types of personal property sales, such as royalty rights, patent rights, and general intangibles in an amount over $5,000 are within the Statute (i.e., must be in writing and signed by the party to be charged).

C. SALE OF LAND

Contracts for the sale of land, or any interest therein, must be in writing and signed by the party to be charged regardless of the amount involved. This also applies to mortgages, easements, and real estate brokers' commission contracts. However, construction contracts are service contracts and do not come within this section. Most states have statutes that provide that a lease of real property for a longer period than one year must be in writing.

A few courts hold that in the case of a sale of land, the seller must sign the contract or the contract is unenforceable against either party. If the seller does sign, both parties are bound.

On occasion, a buyer and seller enter into an *oral* contract for the sale of land; and the buyer, in reliance on the oral contract, goes into possession of the land and/or makes valuable improvements on the land. In other words, the buyer, relying on the oral contract, changes his or her position in equity. Can the seller use the Statute of Frauds as a basis for refusal to perform the contract? Most courts will hold for the buyer under the doctrine of part performance even though there is nothing in the statute that aids the buyer in this situation. Since it would be inequitable to permit the seller to use the statute after such reliance by the buyer, the seller is estopped from using the Statute as a defense to the oral contract. A few courts, relying on the literal language that provides no provisions regarding part performance, refuse to grant relief to the buyer and will not enforce the oral contract.

Most courts demand that the buyer go into possession *and* make improvements before the oral contract will be enforced. Many courts also require that the buyer make payment as required by the oral contract. Generally, payment alone is insufficient to constitute part performance.

Some courts require only that the buyer go into possession *or* make improvements in reliance on the oral contract to make the oral contract enforceable. It has been held in California that possession alone, without payment, is sufficient.

D. CONTRACT NOT TO BE PERFORMED WITHIN A YEAR

An agreement that by its terms is not possible to perform within a year from the making thereof is within the Statute and must be in writing and signed by the party to be charged (the defendant when a lawsuit is filed).

The period begins when the agreement is made and not when performance begins. Thus, an agreement to perform services for exactly one year beginning on the date the contract is entered into can be oral. However, if the services are to begin two days after the contract is made, the contract is not possible to perform within a year from its making and hence is unenforceable. Most states permit one day's grace. The following case is an example of an unenforceable oral contract not performable within a year from the making thereof.

> **FACTS**   Hanan sued Corning Glass Works on an oral employment contract entered into in March that was to begin on May 1 of that year and end on April 30 of the following year.
>
> **DECISION**   The court held for the defendant on the basis that the contract was not performable within one year from the making (March) and hence unenforceable because of the Statute of Frauds.
>
> *Hanan v. Corning Glass Works* (35 A.D.2d 697, 314 N.Y.S.2d 804 [1970])

If it is possible to perform the contract within one year, the Statute does not apply. For example, a promise by A to loan money to B when A receives her inheritance from her father who is still living could be performed within a year because the father could die within a year. To service and maintain equipment "as long as you need it" could be completed within a year by not needing it within a year. To support another person until he or she dies could be performed within a year by the death of the person to be supported.

Requirement and output contracts are not subject to the Statute, because the party could go out of business within a year and thus have no more requirements and no output.

Employment contracts of indefinite duration (employee is hired but not for any period of time) are enforceable although oral, since either party could terminate the contract within one year from the making thereof. This has been held even where the employer promised "permanent" employment but retained the right to discharge for cause or otherwise.

It is generally held that a contract to make a will must be in writing where it involves the devise of land or of personal property where the Statute requires the sale of personalty over a certain amount to be in writing and the amount has been exceeded. Some statutes require a contract to make a will be in writing in any event.

There are two main exceptions to this section of the Statute of Frauds.

1.   Where one party has fully performed in a bilateral contract, most courts hold that the contract is enforceable, even though the contract was not possible to perform within a year. For example, B purchases an automobile from S on a contract that provides that B will pay the price in 15 monthly payments and B is given immediate possession of the automobile. After B obtains possession of the automobile, his oral promise to pay the installments is binding.

2.   The modern tendency is to enforce the oral contract if the plaintiff, in reliance on the contract, has so changed his or her position that pecuniary or unconscionable injury would be suffered, or the defendant, having accepted the benefits of the contract, would be unjustly enriched by plaintiff's legal inability to enforce the oral contract. It has been said that part performance

is available when a restitutionary remedy is wholly inadequate and the facts are virtual fraud for the defendant not to perform (e.g., plaintiff leased property for two years and went into possession making permament improvements).

The following case is an example of the equitable enforcement of an oral contract.

> **FACTS**   The plaintiff, Lucas, sued to recover the balance due him on an alleged two-year oral employment contract. An oral agreement was reached between the plaintiff and the defendant whereby the plaintiff was to act as general manager for the defendant company at an annual salary of $27,000 for a fixed period of two years. In reliance on the oral contract, plaintiff resigned his employment in Missouri and moved his family to Colorado, where he assumed his new duties. After 13 months, he was discharged without cause. The defendant invokes the Statute of Frauds as a defense.
>
> **DECISION**   The court held that the defendant was estopped to invoke the Statute of Frauds as a defense, because the plaintiff suffered unconscionable injury as a result of his reliance on the oral agreement. The plaintiff had resigned from a secure job with a company for whom he had worked for nine years. The plaintiff had sold a custom-built house in which he and his family had lived for only eight months. He gave up business and social contacts.
>
> *Lucas v. Whittaker Corporation* (470 F.2d 326 [1972])

E.   PROMISE TO PAY DEBT OF ANOTHER

Generally, a promise to the creditor to pay the debt of another must be in writing and signed by the party to be charged. For example, Richard wants to buy a car, so he and his father go to the "Honest John" used-car lot. Richard chooses a car, makes a down payment, and signs an installment contract for the balance. "Honest John" is concerned about Richard's ability to pay and asks the father if he will guarantee payment. The father says, "If Richard doesn't pay, I will." This promise made to the creditor must be in writing, or it is not enforceable.

There are exceptions to this type of agreement:

1.   Where the third party makes the promise to the *debtor,* the oral promise is enforceable. For example, if the father tells his son (for consideration) that he will pay the son's debt to "Honest John", the promise is enforceable, as the Statute of Frauds does not apply.

2.   Where the *leading benefit* of the transaction is for the promisor, the Statute does not apply, even though the promise is made to the creditor. For example, the father wants his son to buy a car so that the father does not have to drive his son and two other children to and from three different

schools, because the time involved conflicts with the father's law practice, especially when he has court appearances. An oral promise to "Honest John" by the father is enforceable, because the father receives a benefit that he did not previously enjoy.

3. Where there has been a *novation* or substitution of debtors, the Statute does not apply. For example, if "Honest John", the father, and the son all agree orally that the father will take over the son's debt and the son will be discharged, the oral agreement is enforceable.

4. Where the promisor is the original debtor, the Statute does not apply. For example, if the father calls a jeweler and tells her to send a $400 watch to his son as a birthday gift, the promise is enforceable, because the father is promising to pay his own debt and not the debt of another.

F.   PROMISE MADE IN CONSIDERATION OF MARRIAGE

If a person makes a promise to pay a sum of money or to give property to another in consideration of that person's promise to marry, the agreement must be in writing. For example, if "Honest John" promises the father's daughter that if she will marry him he will give her the choice of any car on his lot, and she agrees, the oral contract is not enforceable. It is universally held that the marriage itself does not constitute such part performance as to make the oral ante-nuptial contract valid. This provision of the statute does not apply to mutual promises to marry.

G.   MODIFICATION OF WRITTEN CONTRACT

Generally, a contract that is required to be in writing under the Statute of Frauds cannot be modified except in writing.

Under the U.C.C., Section 2–209(3), if the contract as modified is within the Statute of Frauds, Section 2–201 must be satisfied. For example, buyer and seller orally agree to buy and sell certain goods for a price of $400 and later wish to increase the quantity of goods in an amount that will increase the price to $600. The modified agreement must meet the requirements of writing under the Statute of Frauds.

If the contract is in writing, but did not have to be under the Statute of Frauds, would the modification have to be in writing? In most courts it would not. However, the modification would need the essential elements of a contract to be valid. By statute in some jurisdictions, the modification must be in writing, although there are exceptions (e.g., fully executed oral modification; one party induced into changing his or her position creating an equitable estoppel). (The admissibility of oral evidence that may change a written contract is discussed in Chapter 15, B., The Parol Evidence Rule.)

ILLUSTRATIVE CASES

1. Check Stub Is Not a Written Memorandum

PRESTI v. WILSON

348 F.Supp. 543 (D.C.N.Y.1972)

JUDD, District Judge.

A motion by defendant seller in this diversity contract action asks summary judgment against plaintiff buyer on the basis of the Statute of Frauds. The action is one for damages for failure to complete the sale of a race horse.

The complaint asserts that plaintiff made an oral agreement with the defendant by a telephone call in October 1970 to buy a thoroughbred "Goal Line Stand" for the sum of $60,000, that he sent defendant a form of bill of sale and a check for the $60,000, post-dated December 1, 1970, and that defendant retained the check. It is asserted that defendant told plaintiff in a later conversation that he wished not to consummate the transaction until after January 1, 1971 for tax reasons, and that he would send the foal certificate in February 1971. The check was neither deposited nor negotiated, but plaintiff asserts that he kept money in his account to meet it.

Defendant asserts by answer and by affidavit that he never agreed to sell "Goal Line Stand" to plaintiff, that he never received a check from plaintiff for "Goal Line Stand," and that he never received the bill of sale which plaintiff describes.

Plaintiff's claim is supported by a copy of his check stub and by the affidavit of his executive assistant, who says that he monitored both telephone calls and prepared and mailed the bill of sale and the check.

The sale of a horse is governed by the Uniform Commercial Code covering sales of goods. The statute of frauds contained therein, U.C.C. § 2–201, states:

> (1) * * * a contract for the sale of goods for the price of $500 or more is not enforceable by way of action or defense unless there is some writing sufficient to indicate that a contract for sale has been made between the parties and signed by the party against whom enforcement is sought or by his authorized agent or broker * * *.

>   *   *   *

> (3) A contract which does not satisfy the requirements of subsection (1) but which is valid in other respects is enforceable * * *

> > (b) if the party against whom enforcement is sought admits in his pleading, testimony or otherwise in court that a contract for sale was made * * *.

or

(c) with respect to goods for which payment has been made
and accepted or which have been received and accepted.

Plaintiff seeks to avoid the statute of frauds on the basis of the two
exceptions quoted, first that the statute would not apply if defendant admits
that the contract was made, and second that it does not apply where payment was made and accepted.

*   *   *

* * * [T]he exception for a party who admits the making of a contract
is not applicable here, since the defendant has denied under oath that any
agreement for sale was ever made with plaintiff.

Plaintiff's second argument depends on establishing that the receipt
and retention of a post-dated check constitutes payment and acceptance,
even though the seller denies receiving the check and never negotiated it,
and the check was stale before the suit was brought.

The statute of frauds permits a party to welch on an oral bargain, in
order to avoid the risk that an oral contract may be proved by fraudulent
testimony. The exceptions for part performance or payment and acceptance
both involve mutual participation and not unilateral acts.

Defendant's liability should be tested by the rule set forth by the New
York Court of Appeals in *Young v. Ingalsbe* (208 N.Y. 503, 507, 102 N.E. 590,
591 [1913]) that

The design of the statute requires that neither party can create the
evidence which shall prove the unwritten contract as against the other.

The cases indicate that both the copy of plaintiff's check stub and the asser-
tions of plaintiff and his executive assistant are ineffective as evidence
which could be created by the plaintiff.

*   *   *

Two threads run throughout the cases considering part performance or
payment as an escape from the statute of frauds. First, payment without
acceptance of the payment is not sufficient; tender alone does not constitute
payment. Second, there must be some objective manifestation referable to
payment and acceptance.

Assuming here that plaintiff made a tender of payment, the only alleged act by defendant which would manifest an acceptance of the payment
is his statement that the check would be held until 1971 to gain a tax
advantage. This is evidence which the plaintiff could create, and therefore
is not an objective manifestation of assent to the contract.

*   *   *

It is ordered that defendant's motion be granted and that the complaint
be dismissed.

2. Party Payment Satisfies Statute of Frauds

STARR v. FREEPORT DODGE, INC.

54 Misc.2d 271, 282 N.Y.S.2d 58 (1967)

BERNARD TOMSON, Judge. These cross motions for summary judgment raise, apparently for the first time in this state, the important question as to whether, under the Uniform Commercial Code, part payment exempts an indivisible contract from the operation of the statute of frauds. * * *

Plaintiff's action is for breach of contract and arises out of the attempted purchase by him of a new automobile from the corporate defendant, a car dealer, through the individual defendant, the salesman involved in the transaction. The plaintiff alleges that he signed an order form for a new automobile which described the subject matter of the sale, the price, which was in excess of $500, and the identity of both buyer and seller. The form is not signed by the dealer. * * *

It further appears that the plaintiff made a $25 down payment to the dealer, which was accepted by the dealer and for which deposit a credit was noted on the form. * * *

The defendants urge that there was no contract between the parties and that the order form, unsigned as it is by the dealer, falls within the purview of Section 2–201 of the Uniform Commercial Code as unenforceable since it was not signed by the party to be charged.

Section 2–201 of the U.C.C. provides in part as follows:

> (1) Except as otherwise provided in this section a contract for the sale of goods for the price of $500 or more is not enforceable by way of action or defense unless there is some writing sufficient to indicate that a contract for sale has been made between the parties and signed by the party against whom enforcement is sought or by his authorized agent or broker. * * *

> (3) A contract which does not satisfy the requirements of subsection (1) but which is valid in other respects is enforceable

>   *   *   *

> (c) with respect to goods for which payment has been made and accepted or which have been received and accepted (Section 2–606). * * *

Under the code, part payment takes the case out of the statute only to the extent for which payment has been made. * * *

Even if subparagraph (c) validates, as the writers seem unanimously to agree, a divisible contract only for as much of the goods as have been paid for, it does not necessarily follow that such a rule invalidates an indivisible oral contract where some payment has been made and accepted. To paraphrase Hawkland—It is difficult (here) to see how the contract could have contemplated less than one (automobile), assuming as the Court did, that (automobiles) are indivisible. Any other conclusion would work an unconscionable result and would encourage rather than discourage fraud if the facts as pleaded (known as "low balling" in the trade) were proven at a trial.

The statute of frauds would be used to cut down the trusting buyer rather than to protect the one who, having made his bargain, parted with a portion of the purchase price as an earnest of his good faith. Certainly here the $25 deposit was not intended as a purchase of a portion of the automobile. It was intended as payment towards the purchase of the entire article if the facts alleged in the complaint are proven at the trial.

[Part payment will take the case out of the Statute of Frauds for all of the goods when the goods are not divisible. Judgment for plaintiff.]

3. Delivery Satisfies Statute of Frauds

COHEN SALVAGE CORP. v. EASTERN ELECTRIC SALES CO.

205 Pa.Super. 26, 206 A.2d 331 (1965)

DOTY, Judge.   In the latter part of June, 1963, plaintiff, located in Bladensburg, Maryland, and defendant, located in Philadelphia, both acting by a duly authorized agent, had a telephone conversation in which plaintiff advised defendant that it had a quantity of electric cable for sale. Arrangements were made for defendant to send one of its employees to Bladensburg, Maryland to examine the cable. After this employee examined the cable and returned to Philadelphia, another oral conversation transpired as a result of which plaintiff shipped the cable, weighing 36,440 pounds, to defendant in Philadelphia. The cable was run off plaintiff's reels to defendant's reels, and was taken by defendant's employees and placed in defendant's warehouse, where it still remains. * * *

The plaintiff brought this action in assumpsit for the cable allegedly sold and delivered. The defendant's position at trial was * * * even if there was a contract it is unenforceable because of the statute of frauds. * * *

Defendant's reliance on the Statute of Frauds to vitiate this contract is misplaced. Section 2–201(1) of the Uniform Commercial Code provides that a contract for the sale of goods in excess of $500 is not enforceable.

> Unless there is some writing sufficient to indicate that a contract for sale has been made between the parties and signed by the party against whom enforcement is sought, or by his authorized agent or broker. * * *

In this case plaintiff introduced into evidence a written sales order which contained plaintiff's name, the notation, "SOLD TO: Eastern Electric," the date, the name of the shipper, the quantity and description of the goods, and the weight of the goods, as well as the notation, "Your Order Number," and "Our Sales Number." This form was admittedly signed by an authorized agent of the defendant's company. This writing was sufficient to satisfy the requirements of the Statute of Frauds.

> All that is required is that the writing afford a basis that the offered oral evidence rests on a real transaction.

*   *   *

Its object is the elimination of certain formalistic requirements adherence to which often resulted in injustice, rather than the prevention of fraud.

This writing clearly afforded a basis for believing that the oral evidence rests on a real transaction. The fact that price was omitted (and it was the only relevant term omitted) is not fatal since "A writing is not insufficient because it omits * * * a term agreed upon. * * *"

There is another reason why the Statute of Frauds does not preclude a verdict for plaintiff in this case. Section 2–201(3)(c) of the Code provides:

> A contract which does not satisfy the requirements of subsection (1) but which is valid in other respects is enforceable with respect to goods which have been received and accepted.

That the cable was received there can be no doubt. After it was received by defendant it was run from one reel to another by several of the defendant's employees who admitted they inspected it at that time. It was then tagged and placed in the defendant's warehouse, where it remains. * * *

[Judgment for plaintiff.]

4. Leading Benefit to Promisor Not Within Statute of Frauds

YARBRO v. NEIL B. McGINNIS EQUIPMENT CO.

101 Ariz. 378, 420 P.2d 163 (1966)

BERNSTEIN, Vice Chief Justice.   * * * McGinnis Equipment Co., brought suit to recover payments due it pursuant to a conditional sales contract for the sale of one used Allis-Chalmers Model HD–5G tractor. The contract was negotiated in August of 1957 and called for twenty-three monthly installments of $574.00 each. The buyer, Russell, failed to make the first monthly payment, and on his suggestion a McGinnis company representative met with the appellant, Yarbro, to ask if he would help with the payments. As a result of this meeting Yarbro agreed to, and did, pay the September installment.

In the months that followed there was a continued failure on the part of Russell to make any of the monthly installment payments. * * *

In May, 1958 when McGinnis Co. indicated that the tractor soon would have to be repossessed, Yarbro again assured the company that it would be paid as soon as two pending real estate escrows were closed. This promised payment was not made. A similar promise was made by Yarbro in July on the strength of proceeds that were to be forthcoming from an oat crop in New Mexico but again no payment was made. * * * The tractor was finally repossessed in January of 1959. Subsequently, the McGinnis Co. brought an action to recover the payments due under the conditional sales contract, naming Russell and Yarbro as defendants. A default judgment was entered against Russell and the only question before this court now concerns the liability of the defendant, Yarbro. The trial court found Yarbro liable for the entire balance under the conditional sales contract. * * *

Although the promises made by Yarbro clearly were of the type covered in [the Statute of Frauds] the plaintiff contends that the leading object or primary purpose exception is applicable. * * * Simply stated, this rule provides that where the leading object of a person promising to pay the debt of another is actually to protect his own interest, such promise if supported by sufficient consideration, is valid, even though it be oral.

* * * Although a third party is the primary debtor, situations may arise where the promisor has a personal, immediate and pecuniary interest in the transaction, and is therefore himself a party to be benefitted by the performance of the promisee. In such cases the reason which underlies and which prompted the above statutory provision fails, and the courts will give effect to the promise. Recognizing the leading object rule as a well reasoned exception, the question remains whether the facts presently before this court make the exception applicable. There are no easy, mathematical guidelines to such a determination. To ascertain the character of the promise in question and the intention of the parties as to the nature of the liability created, regard must be had to the form of expression, the situation of the parties, and to all the circumstances of each particular case. * * * Further evidence of Yarbro's interest in the tractor comes from the fact that after its purchase he had borrowed it on a series of occasions. When repairs were needed shortly after Yarbro had made the first installment payment, the McGinnis Co. repairman found the machine on Yarbro's land. * * * Yarbro had asked on several occasions that the McGinnis Co. not repossess the tractor because he needed it. These requests were usually in conjunction with a promise to pay what was owing on the tractor. * * * It is when the leading and main object of the promisor is *not* to become surety or guarantor of another, even though that may be the effect, but is to serve some purpose or interest of his own, that the oral promise becomes enforceable. * * *

[Judgment for plaintiff affirmed.]

5. Ante-nuptial Contract Must Be in Writing

TELLEZ v. TELLEZ, ET AL.

51 N.M. 416, 186 P.2d 390 (1947)

COMPTON, Justice.   This is a suit by appellee, Guadalupe Diaz Tellez, seeking relief in the nature of specific performance of an oral ante-nuptial contract. From an adverse judgment, appellants bring this appeal.

Eusebio Tellez, now deceased, in July, 1940, orally proposed marriage to appellee, then Guadalupe Diaz, now his widow, promising that if she would marry and care for him, as his wife, until death, that he would give her all his property, both real and personal. * * * Pursuant to the agreement, the deceased executed a will on or about August 1, 1940, whereby all his property was devised and bequeathed to appellee. In consideration of his promise, the marriage took place August 8, 1940.

Thereafter, while the parties were living together, and without the knowledge or consent of appellee, Eusebio Tellez conveyed the real estate here involved, to his children and grandchildren by a former marriage. This was a voluntary conveyance. Eusebio Tellez suffered a paralytic stroke on August 11, 1943, which required the constant care and attention of a nurse and other assistants. For convenience he was moved from his home to the home of a daughter, where he lived until his death, November 7, 1944. Soon after being taken to the daughter's home, difficulties arose between appellee and his children by the former marriage, causing appellee to leave the home of the daughter. She did not see her husband for about a year prior to his death. * * *

The question is whether the oral ante-nuptial contract stated in the findings may be enforced against the appellants who are the heirs at law of the deceased and grantees in a deed made by him after appellee and deceased married, by which he conveyed to them all of his property. * * *

The deceased's agreement to leave his property to appellee for the consideration stated, implied that his property would be devised and bequeathed to her, in consideration of her marrying him and caring for him until his death. * * *

The contract was within the * * * Statute of Frauds, in that it was an oral contract made upon consideration of marriage. * * *

The judgment of the district court is reversed with directions to the trial court to reinstate the case upon its docket and enter an order dismissing appellee's complaint, and it is so ordered.

PROBLEMS

1.   On June 1, Buyer and Seller entered into an oral contract for the sale of 100 office chairs at $50 each, delivery by freight. On June 3, Seller sent a signed letter to Buyer that reaffirmed the terms of the oral contract. Buyer received the letter on June 4. On June 4, Seller shipped the chairs to Buyer. On June 15, before the chairs arrive, Buyer changes his mind and wants to get out of the oral contract. Discuss.

2.   Defendant made an oral contract with plaintiff for a tombstone to be made according to a pattern and design in a catalog at a price of $600. After the plaintiff selected the proper design and cut the inscription upon it the defendant refused to accept it although it was complete and ready for delivery. Defendant pleads the Statute of Frauds. Discuss.

3.   Buyer and Seller entered into an oral contract for the sale of a boat at a price of $1,000. Buyer made a down payment in the amount of $50. Now Buyer desires to cancel the contract, arguing that the contract should have been in writing. Discuss.

4.   Buyer orally orders from the Reynolds Television Manufacturing Company a color television set for the price of $2,000. The set will be specially manufactured so that it will receive only educational channels and will be able to make a visual and sound tape of any program. Mr. Reynolds has personally built the chassis for the set and is about to install the fine-tuning mechanism when he receives a telephone call from the buyer stating that he has lost his job at the college where he is employed and wants nothing more to do with education, including the television set he had ordered. Mr. Reynolds states that he has spent a lot of money on the set and must insist on payment. The buyer contends that since he has not signed anything, he is not bound due to the Statute of Frauds. Decision?

5. Buyer orally contracts with seller to purchase a garage on the seller's property for the sum of $450. Seller is to dismantle the garage and have it ready for pickup within three months from the date of the contract. Seller dismantles the garage and has it ready for pickup within the period; however, buyer refuses to pick up or pay for the garage. Seller brings suit, and buyer defends on the ground that the contract was for real estate and is unenforceable under the Statute of Frauds. Decision?

6. Seller and Buyer entered into an oral contract for the sale of a parcel of land for the price of $499, to be paid in monthly installments. In reliance on the oral contract, buyer goes into possession and builds a cabin on the land. After buyer has paid $200 in monthly installments, he discovers gold on the land. Seller brings an action to evict the buyer on the grounds that the contract was for real estate, and there was nothing in writing. Decision?

7. In the middle of March, A orally employs B to manage a farm for one year upon specified terms commencing April 1. In December, A discharged B without cause. B brings suit for breach of contract. Decision?

8. Buyer purchased from Seller a dry-goods and grocery business which was located in Excelsior, Wisconsin. Buyer paid $500 to Seller in addition to the purchase price for Seller's oral promise not to engage in a similar business for one year in Excelsior, Wisconsin. A few months after the sale, Seller starts a similar business in Excelsior. Buyer sues to enforce the oral promise. Seller pleads the one-year Statute of Frauds section. Decision?

9. Employer, in California, orally promised employment to Employee in Alabama. The term of employment was two years. Employee sold his furniture at a loss, gave up his permanent employment in Alabama, moved his family to California, and worked at an "inferior" job for nine months while waiting for the position to open that he had been promised. After nine months, Employer discharges Employee as part of a reduction in overhead. Employee sues for breach of contract. Decision?

10. Annie and Horace Roderick are contemplating a divorce and seek your advice as to the ownership of a certain automobile that Horace purchased with his own funds shortly before marriage. Annie states that Horace told her that if she would marry him he would give the automobile to her. He never gave her the automobile, and she now wants either the automobile or its value. Horace admits making the statement. Decision?

Chapter 15

INTERPRETATION OF CONTRACTS

A. IN GENERAL

A contract should contain all of the important terms, which should be clearly stated, since ambiguous terms can result in different interpretation by the parties and can, in turn, result in unnecessary litigation. If the differences of the parties cannot be resolved and the case is litigated, the court applies certain principles of construction and interpretation to the contract.

1. INTENTION OF THE PARTIES

The purpose of the interpretation of a contract is to determine and give effect to the mutual intention of the parties. The modern approach is to look for the *expressed* intent (i.e., the words used). The secret or undisclosed intention of a party has no effect. In other words, we are interested only in what the parties said and not in their undisclosed thoughts.

An interpretation that gives a reasonable, lawful, and effective meaning to manifestations of the intent of the parties is preferred to an interpretation that makes such manifestations unreasonable, unlawful, or of no effect.

2. INTERPRETATION AS A WHOLE

A contract must be read and interpreted as a whole or in its entirety so as to give effect to every part. The intention of the parties is to be gathered from the entire instrument and not from detached or isolated words or parts.

If several writings exist between the parties regarding one transaction, they are all to be construed as one writing.

However, terms in a printed letterhead or billhead or on the reverse side of a printed contract form are not part of the contract unless a reasonable person would regard such terms as part of the contract. Likewise, important provisions placed in fine print are generally unenforceable. Provisions that are called to the attention of the buyer after the contract has been entered into may not be binding on the buyer (e.g., an invoice shown after the contract is entered into for an employer's manual shown to the employee after the employment contract is entered into).

3.   WRITTEN AND PRINTED TERMS

When a contract is partly handwritten or typewritten and partly printed and the written part conflicts with the printed part, the written part prevails.

When there is a conflict between an amount expressed both in words and figures, the amount expressed in words prevails (e. g., One Hundred and Twenty Dollars [$1.20]), the One Hundred and Twenty Dollars would prevail.

Punctuation and rules of grammatical construction may be used to aid in the ascertaining of intent but are not used when they are in conflict with the real intent of the parties.

4.   USAGE AND CUSTOM

Usage and custom may be used to explain the meaning of language in a contract and to imply terms when no contrary intention appears from the terms of the contract (e. g., in agency agreement to sell automobiles, the custom of taking used cars as trade-ins established such authority of agent; in a sale of real estate, custom may properly determine details regarding opening of escrow, furnishing of deeds and title insurance, and prorating of taxes; a lay-away or will-call plan customarily means that the buyer has an option to purchase the goods within a specified time during which the seller will not sell the goods).

To enable custom to be used to interpret a contract, the parties must agree to it, or one party must know or have reason to know that the other party intends custom to govern the contract, or it must be so well known that a reasonable person would be aware of it.

5.   SUBSEQUENT CONDUCT OF PARTIES

Acts of the parties that take place after the execution of the contract but before any controversy arises may be looked to in determining the meaning of the contract. The parties themselves are most likely to be correct as to their real intent.

6.   PARTY CAUSING UNCERTAINTY

The language of a contract should be interpreted most strongly against the party who caused the uncertainty to exist (i.e., the person who prepared the contract). The rule is particularly applicable in the case of a contract prepared by an expert or experienced party, and especially where the party using the ambiguous language seeks to defeat the contract because of such language. The rule is also particularly applicable where the contract is on a printed form prepared by one of the parties. However, this rule of interpretation is to be used only after all other rules of interpretation have been used and no satisfactory result has been obtained.

7. INSURANCE CONTRACTS

Insurance contracts are interpreted against the insurance company because the company prepared the contract and because the policy of the law favors coverage for losses to which the policy of insurance relates. It has been said that courts construe against insurance companies because people do not read their policies and would not understand them if they did. Whether the coverage relates to the peril insured against, the amount of liability, or the person or persons protected, the language will be interpreted in its most inclusive sense for the benefit of the insured.

Exception clauses are construed strictly. In other words, if the insurance company does not want to cover a particular loss related to the policy, the company must clearly exclude this loss or the insured will be covered.

B. THE PAROL EVIDENCE RULE

1. IN GENERAL

Prior to the signing of a written contract, the parties generally negotiate the various terms orally. After the oral discussion, the contract is reduced to writing and signed by the parties. All negotiations and oral understandings are merged into the written contract. It is logical that the signed written contract correctly contain the oral terms agreed upon by the parties, therefore, it does not seem reasonable for one party to claim that the parties agreed to something other than that which is stated in the written contract.

The parol evidence rule states that oral testimony is not admissible to vary the terms of a written contract when the oral testimony relates to oral statements made prior to the signing of the contract or at the same time as the signing of the contract.

The parol evidence rule should stand out as a warning to parties to a contract, especially to buyers. *Never* sign a contract unless you are certain that it contains *all* of the terms agreed upon. You may find that the salesperson's oral promise will be denied when it comes time to enforce it; and even if you can prove the promise in court, the cost of litigation might well be more than the promise involved. Also, remember that an innocent-looking document, such as a purchase order of goods or a deposit receipt, can be a contract.

2. EXCEPTIONS TO THE PAROL EVIDENCE RULE

A. AMBIGUITY

If ambiguity is present in any of the words or provisions of a written contract, oral testimony is admissible to explain the ambiguity. For example, seller agreed to sell buyer a reaper, which seller warranted in writing to be capable of cutting and raking from 12 to 20 acres of grain a day with one good person and a team of horses. Seller orally told buyer prior to the written contract that he meant a team like that the buyer owned. However, the buyer's team could not make the machine do the work satisfactorily. Seller claims if *any* sort of team can pull the machine, the buyer is bound by the contract. The buyer will be permitted to testify as to the seller's statement (i. e., that the *buyer's* team could pull the machine).

B. MISTAKE, FRAUD, DURESS, UNDUE INFLUENCE, ILLEGALITY, OR LACK OF CAPACITY

If a mistake is made in reducing the contract to writing, oral testimony is admissible regarding the mistake (e.g., the typist uses the wrong figures in the written contract, and the parties do not notice the error when they sign it).

Fraud, duress, undue influence, and illegality can always be testified to in the making of a contract (e. g., salesperson states that a contract contains a certain warranty whereas it does not). In *Ganley Bros., Inc. v. Butler Bros. Building Co.* (170 Minn. 373, 212 N.W. 602 [1927]), the plaintiff contractor signed a contract that contained the following clause: "[The contractor] is not relying upon any statement made by the company." The contractor was permitted to testify that the contract was procured by fraud. The testimony is not admitted to vary the terms of the contract but rather to show that the contract should be avoided because it was induced by fraud.

Testimony is admissible to prove lack of capacity (e. g., that the party was a minor or insane).

C. INCOMPLETE CONTRACT

If the written contract is not complete on its face (e.g., important terms are obviously missing), oral testimony is admissible to supply the missing terms.

D. CONDITION PRECEDENT

If the parties orally agree that the written contract is not to be enforceable unless a certain event occurs, this condition precedent to the validity of the contract can be testified to, since the party is not trying to vary or change the written contract but is attempting to prove that there is no contract, since the condition precedent to its validity did not take place. For example, a politician promises a person employment if elected to office. In such a case, the election to office is a condition precedent to the employment. Or a buyer of real estate inserts a clause in the contract that the purchase of the property is contingent upon the buyer's being able to procure a loan in a certain amount at a certain interest and upon certain terms, such as monthly payments and length of loan. A buyer who is unable to obtain such a loan does not have to purchase the property. Another conditional clause frequently found in real estate contracts is that the sale is contingent upon the buyer's approval of a report regarding the plumbing, electrical system, soil, roof, and general construction of the property.

E. LATER ORAL CHANGES OR ADDITIONS

The rule applies only to oral clauses made prior to or contemporaneous with the written contract and not to later oral changes or additions. Although the parol evidence rule would not apply, certain other rules might prevent the later oral change or addition from being effective (e.g., statute of frauds). Although the later oral changes may be testified to in court, the other party may deny that oral changes were made and the court may believe this denial. The point to remember here is that all potential oral changes should be put in writing.

F. CONSIDERATION

Frequently, certain types of instruments, such as deeds, leases, notes, and bonds, will contain a statement that the consideration has been received when in fact it has not; or the instrument will contain a nominal recital of consideration, whereas it is greater. Generally, in these cases, the courts will permit parol evidence to show that the consideration was not paid or that it is different than stated. This is because the document was not intended to be an integration of the agreement supplanting prior negotiations. Under this rule, it would be proper to permit testimony to show that in addition to the consideration stated in the deed, there was an oral promise to convey certain land by a will.

However, if the terms are fully and correctly embodied in the contract, parol evidence is not generally admissible. Under this rule, if the contract sets out the purchase price, payable pursuant to certain terms, oral testimony is inadmissible to vary the contract.

G. THE UNIFORM COMMERCIAL CODE

In addition to the rules stated above, the U.C.C. contains provisions relating to the interpretation of contracts for the sale of goods. The U.C.C. Sections 1–205, 2–202, and 2–208 provide that in a sale of goods, a written contract may be explained or supplemented in four ways: (1) by a prior course of dealing between the buyer and the seller, (2) by usage of trade, (3) by the course of performance between the parties, or (4) by evidence of consistent additional terms used by the parties. Although a single occasion of conduct does not fall within the language of Section 2–208 relating to the course of performance, other sections, such as those on silence after acceptance and failure to specify particular defects, can affect the parties' rights on a single occasion (see 2–605 and 2–607). (For use of the term "as is" in a contract, see U.C.C. Section 2–316(3)(a).)

C. CONFLICT OF LAWS

A conflict of laws exists when there is a difference in the laws between municipalities, between states, or between countries. The law of New York is different from the law of California regarding revocation of an offer. If the buyer (offeror) is in Los Angeles and the seller (offeree-acceptor) is in New York, and no intent is indicated as to which law should apply, which law do we use? The validity of the contract is ordinarily determined by the law of the place where the contract was made, and this would be where the last act is necessary for its validity. This has been called the "more favored rule". In our example, we would use the law of New York, since the last act necessary to make the contract, namely the acceptance, would take place in New York. If the contract is entered into by telephone, the place of making is the place where the acceptor speaks.

Some courts follow the rule that the place where the contract is to be performed governs. Some courts follow the rule that the intent of the parties govern (i. e., the law of the place where the parties intended or presumed to have intended).

A growing tendency by the courts is to follow the "center of gravity" or "grouping of contacts" theory, under which the courts emphasize the law of the place that has the most significant contacts with the matter in dispute. Even under this theory, the courts place heavy emphasis on the parties' intention, the place of making the contract, and the place of performance. Under this theory, the courts examine all of the points of contact that the transaction has with the two or more states involved, with a view to determining that aspect of the contract immediately before the court. When the court has identified the state with which the matter at hand is predominantly or most intimately concerned, it concludes that this is the proper law of the contract that the parties intended at the time of the contracting.

Under the U.C.C., Section 1–105(1), the parties have the right to choose their own law. This right is subject to the firm rules stated in subsection (2) and is limited to jurisdictions to which the transaction bears a "reasonable relation." Ordinarily, the law chosen must be that where a significant enough portion of the making or performance of the contract is to occur.

ILLUSTRATIVE CASES

1. Interpretation by Subsequent Conduct of Parties

CRESTVIEW CEMETERY ASS'N v. DIEDEN

54 Cal.2d 744, 8 Cal.Rptr. 427, 356 P.2d 171 (1960)

PETERS, Justice. [Action to recover portion of legal fee paid. Defendant countered for the balance due under the contract.] The sole question presented on this appeal is whether the trial court correctly interpreted the contract admittedly existing between the parties.

The record shows that, in 1956, Crestview owned some real property in an unincorporated area of Alameda County near the city of Hayward that it desired to develop as a cemetery. This was difficult under the existing county zoning laws, which Crestview and McKeever, [counsel for Crestview] found to be confusing.

In April of 1956 Leonard Dieden was recommended to McKeever * * * as an attorney who might be able to secure the desired result. * * * As a result of several later telephone conversations the figure of $7,500 was agreed upon as the contingent fee. It was agreed that Dieden should have three months to try and secure the desired result. * * *

After the parties agreed upon the contingent fee on May 14, 1956, Dieden started to work. He prepared a letter to the Hayward Planning Commission, which was executed by McKeever, requesting a rezoning of the property. Dieden then prepared and filed an application for rezoning and actively argued in favor of the application at several hearings at which vigorous opposition to his position developed. * * * After the ordinance had passed by a vote of four to three a recess was called. At that time a woman who had opposed the rezoning ordinance told McKeever and Dieden that her group intended to continue to attack the ordinance by referendum. * * * McKeever congratulated Dieden on having completed his job so successfully and Dieden said "There's your permit. Send me a check." This McKeever promised to do. Three days later, on July 27, 1956, and after McKeever knew that the referendum was pending, he sent Dieden a check for $5,000. In determining what the parties agreed upon and intended by their agreement of May 14, 1956, we are not to determine what the words used by the parties may mean to us but if possible to ascertain what those words meant to the parties. Moreover, in interpreting those words we must keep in mind that McKeever and Dieden were not novices or inexperienced. Both are practicing attorneys.

* * * While there is substantial evidence that McKeever wanted to be assured the land would be available for cemetery purposes, the evidence is capable of being interpreted as meaning that Dieden was to secure the passage of a rezoning ordinance. While this may not be the interpretation that we might place upon the terms of the contract, it is the interpretation placed upon it by the parties before any controversy arose between them. This contract is not to be interpreted in a vacuum. These two lawyers knew what they meant and intended. By their actions, and by their performance under the contract, their intent was disclosed with crystal clarity. * * *

In the first place McKeever insisted that Dieden must perform within a period of three months. That period of time may be a reasonable one for securing an amendment to an ordinance but is not reasonable if it was intended that Dieden, after passage of the ordinance, was to protect it against attacks that might be made on it. * * * Dieden, in the presence of McKeever, argued the matter before the council against strong opposition, and finally, again in the presence of McKeever, secured passage of the controversial ordinance. Then, most significantly, McKeever congratulated Dieden on a job well done. Dieden, in the obvious belief that his job was completed, requested his money. McKeever, even though he knew the opponents were contemplating a referendum, and knew the required number of signatures for a referendum, in the obvious belief that Dieden had completed the job contemplated, promised to pay. Three days later, and after McKeever knew the opponents to the ordinance were working on a referendum, McKeever sent the $5,000 check to Dieden "on account of your legal fee * * *"

The only reasonable interpretation of these actions is that both parties then believed, and acted on the belief, that the work contemplated had been completed and that Dieden had earned his fee.

* * * The trial court found that the contract of May 14, 1956, was fully performed. * * *

Certainly the parties so interpreted the contract. As already pointed out both Dieden and McKeever obviously believed the contract had been fully performed even after they knew that a referendum was to be attempted and was in process. * * *

The judgment is affirmed [for defendant.]

2. Exception Clause Strictly Construed

GRAY v. ZURICH INSURANCE CO.

65 Cal.2d 263, 54 Cal.Rptr. 104, 419 P.2d 168 (1966)

TOBRINER, Justice.   Plaintiff, Dr. Vernon D. Gray, is the named insured under an insurance policy issued by defendant. * * *

The policy contains a provision that "[T]his endorsement does not apply * * * to bodily injury or property damages caused intentionally by or at the direction of the insured."

The suit which Dr. Gray contends Zurich should have defended arose out of an altercation between him and a Mr. John R. Jones. * * * Dr. Gray notified defendant of the suit, stating that he had acted in self-defense, and requested that the company defend. Defendant refused on the ground that the complaint alleged an intentional tort which fell outside the coverage of the policy. Dr. Gray thereafter unsuccessfully defended on the theory of self-defense; he suffered a judgment of $6,000 actual damages although the jury refused to award punitive damages.

Dr. Gray then filed the instant action charging defendant with breach of its duty to defend.

The * * * court rendered judgment in favor of defendant. * * * In interpreting an insurance policy we apply the general principle that doubts as to meaning must be resolved against the insurer and that any exception to the performance of the basic underlying obligation must be so stated as clearly to apprise the insured of its effect. * * *

* * *

* * * No one can determine whether the third party suit does or does not fall within the indemnification coverage of the policy until that suit is resolved; in the instant case, the determination of whether the insured engaged in intentional, negligent or even wrongful conduct depended upon the judgment in the Jones suit, and, indeed, even after that judgment, no one could be positive whether it rested upon a finding of plaintiff's negligent or his intentional conduct. The carrier's obligation to indemnify inevitably will

not be defined until the adjudication of the very action which it should have defended. * * * The insured is unhappily surrounded by concentric circles of uncertainty: the first, the unascertainable nature of the insurer's duty to defend; the second, the unknown effect of the provision that the insurer must defend even a groundless, false or fraudulent claim; the third, the uncertain extent of the indemnification coverage. Since we must resolve uncertainties in favor of the insured and interpret the policy provisions according to the layman's reasonable expectations, and since the effect of the exclusionary clause is neither conspicuous, plain nor clear, we hold that in the present case the policy provides for an obligation to defend and that such obligation is independent of the indemnification coverage.

* * * The judgment is reversed and the trial court instructed to take evidence solely on the issue of damages alleged in plaintiff's complaint including the amount of the judgment in the Jones suit, and the costs, expenses and attorney's fees incurred in defending such suit.

3. Parol Evidence Is Admissible to Prove Condition Precedent to Validity of Written Contract

LONG v. JONES

319 S.W.2d 292 (Ky. 1958)

MILLIKEN, Judge. The appellee, Mrs. Jones, recovered a judgment of $800, with interest, covering the down payment made by her on the proposed purchase of a house from the appellant, Dan Long, in Lexington. A written contract covering the terms of the proposed purchase was signed by her and by the vendor through his agent, and the $800 down payment was referred to therein "as evidence of good faith to bind this contract" and it was "to be applied on the purchase price upon passing of deed, or refunded, should title prove not merchantable, or acceptable, or if this offer is not accepted." * * *

As an explanation of her failure to go through with the purchase within the terms of the agreement, Mrs. Jones testified that at the time she signed the printed contract form and made the $800 down payment it was understood between her and the agent of the appellant-seller that she could not complete the proposed purchase within the time allotted unless she sold her home in Flemingsburg, and the trial court accordingly instructed the jury to find for Mrs. Jones if they believed what she said. It was proper for such testimony to be admitted for the consideration of the jury, not for the purpose of varying the terms of a written agreement, but on the issue of whether a contract in fact existed. * * *

> Evidence is generally held admissible to show that the parties made an agreement before or at the time they entered into a written contract of sale that such contract of sale should become binding only on the happening of a certain condition or contingency, the theory being that such evidence merely goes to show that the writing never became operative as

a valid agreement and that there is therefore no variance or contradiction of a valid written instrument. * * *

The motion for an appeal is overruled, and the judgment is affirmed. [Caveat: put the clause in the written contract and avoid litigation.]

PROBLEMS

1. Plaintiff was insured by X Automobile Insurance Company. The policy had a provision whereby the company would pay all "reasonable medical expenses" incurred by the plaintiff as a result of an automobile accident. The plaintiff was injured in an automobile accident, and his doctor prescribed medicines and an orthopedic (very hard) mattress and spring for the plaintiff's low back injury. The plaintiff submitted all medical bills as requested by the company; however, the company will not pay for the special mattress and spring. What decision?

2. L leased an apartment to T for a period of one year. The lease provided that the rent was due and payable on the first day of each and every month. Immediately prior to the signing of the lease by L and T, T informed L that he was paid every two weeks so he would usually pay his rent several days after the first of the month. L told T that this was all right with him. For several months T paid the rent several days after the first with no objection from L. Now L insists that T pay the rent on the first day of the month. If this case goes to court, will T be able to testify as to the oral arrangement with L?

3. Seller and buyer enter into a contract for a used automobile. A few minutes before the contract was signed, the buyer asked the seller if the automobile had a warranty. The seller stated: "It sure does. If any parts in the motor need replacing during the next 10,000 miles, bring the car in and we will furnish free labor and parts." The contract, however, stated that the automobile was being sold as is and there were no warranties of any kind in the sale. After 8,000 miles, the automobile developed motor trouble requiring extensive repairs. Seller refuses to acknowledge the warranty. Decision?

Would your answer be different if the buyer made the inquiry five minutes after he signed the contract?

4. Seller and buyer entered into a written contract for the sale of a truck. The contract provided that the writing contained the whole agreement and that anything not incorporated therein was not to be regarded as part of the agreement between the parties. The seller fraudulently substituted a different motor for the one that he had led the buyer to believe he was buying. The buyer now sues for the fraud, but the seller contends that in view of the provisions in the written contract, oral testimony as to the alleged fraud may not be heard by the court. What should the court decide?

5. A, an architect, made a written contract with B to design a building for which A was to be paid 10 percent of the cost of the building. There was nothing in the written contract as to the maximum cost of the building. After A finished his work, he demanded payment based on the actual cost of the building. B claims, however, they had agreed on a maximum cost for the building and that A's fee could not exceed 10 percent of that maximum cost, which was considerably lower than the actual cost. Will the court permit B to testify as to the oral agreement?

6.   C, a contractor, made a contract with O, the owner, to construct a building. The contract provided that no charges would be made for work in addition to that stated in the contract unless the additional work and the charge for it was put in writing and signed by the parties. From time to time during the construction of the building, O requested certain additional work which was performed by C. However, none of this was in writing. When C finished the construction, he requested payment for the additional work. O refuses on the grounds it was not in writing. Decision?

7.   Seller gave buyer a deed for a tract of land. The deed stated that the consideration for the land was $5,100.00 and that the sum had been paid. Seller now contends that buyer never paid him for the land. Buyer attempts to testify to the fact that the parties had really agreed that payment was to be made in merchantable bar iron. Seller contends that this testimony should not be admitted because of the parol evidence rule. Decision?

8.   A and B entered into a written contract in which A was to manufacture and install a canopy in front of B's restaurant. It was orally agreed at the time the contract was entered into that A was to obtain the permission of the owner of the building prior to manufacture and installation of the canopy. A manufactured and installed the canopy without obtaining the owner's permission. B refuses to pay, since the owner objects to the canopy. At the trial, B wants to testify as to the oral agreement. May he do so?

9.   Employee was employed by Employer and in the course of employment was injured. Employer made a contract with Employee to pay him $100 per week until he was able to return to normal work. The contract provided that such payments would be paid back to Employer from any recovery obtained in a lawsuit against the person who caused his injury, with payments to be made upon the "successful conclusion of the case." Employee recovered $20,000 in the suit against the third party but does not believe that the recovery was a successful conclusion of the case and refuses to pay. Decision?

10.   Tenant signs a printed form lease stating that a garage is not included in the apartment rent. In a blank space at the end of the lease above the signatures of the parties, the landlord writes "garage included in rent." A dispute arises as to whether the printed words in the lease prevail or the written words. Decision?

Chapter 16

TERMINATION OF CONTRACTS

Ordinarily a contract is terminated by performance of the terms by the parties. Termination may also occur by acts of the parties, by impossibility of performance, or by operation of law.

A. BY PERFORMANCE

1. PAYMENT

When payment is required by the contract, performance is completed by the payment of the money. Payment by check is a conditional payment and is not a discharge of the debt until it is paid (i.e., credited to the bank account of the creditor). The creditor can refuse payment by check on the grounds that it is not legal tender. The U. C.C. Sections 2–511 and 3–802(1)(b) take the same position.

A valid tender of payment consists of an unconditional offer by the debtor to the creditor of the exact amount due on the date the debt or claim is due. If the tender is refused, the debt is not discharged. The refusal stops the running of interest, discharges liens, and prevents the awarding of court costs if the debtor is sued, although the debtor must keep the tender open (i.e., keep the money available for the creditor). Statutes in some states provide that when tender is refused, the debtor can deposit the money in a bank in the name of the creditor and thereafter notify the creditor, at which time the obligation is extinguished (California C.C. 1500).

On occasion a debtor will owe one creditor more than one debt, and the debtor will send the creditor a partial payment. The question then arises as to which debt the payment should be applied to. This may be important, because one of the debts may be barred by the statute of limitations, and if the creditor applies the payment to that debt, it will be revived in most states. The debtor can specify how the payment should be applied, and the creditor is bound by the debtor's selection. However, if the debtor does not specify, the creditor may apply the payment to any one or more of the debts in such manner as he or she chooses.

2. TIME

If the date of performance is stated in the contract, performance should be made on that date. A short delay normally does not justify rescission or a suit for damages. The nature of the contract might be such that even a short delay is actionable. For example, in contracts of a mercantile nature (for manufacture and sale of goods) or where there is a sale of property of a speculative or fluctuating value (oil, gas, or mining rights), time is considered to be of the essence, and a short delay is actionable. The contract itself may contain a clause stating that "time is of the essence," in which case delayed performance is treated as a breach of contract unless to delay would be unconscionable.

In contracts for the manufacture of special products or in building contracts, time is not of the essence, and a reasonable delay is permitted because of the great hardship that might otherwise occur. In the usual real estate contract, time is not regarded to be of the essence.

The following case is an example of a delay in performance excused because it involved a contract for skill.

> **FACTS** The plaintiff contracted with the defendant to furnish certain fine stationery and advertising matter "in the course of the year." The work was not finished in time, and delivery was not made until one week after the expiration of the year. The defendant refused to pay for the goods on the grounds that the goods were not furnished within the time specified in the contract. Plaintiff sued for the price [of the goods].

> **DECISION** In contracts for work or skill, and the materials upon which the work or skill is to be bestowed, a statement fixing the time of performance of the contract is not ordinarily of its essence, and a failure to perform within the time stipulated, followed by substantial performance after a short delay, will not justify the aggrieved party in repudiating the entire contract but will simply give the party his or her action for damages for the breach of the stipulation.
> Judgment for plaintiff.

> *Beck & Pauli Lithographing Co. v. Colorado Milling Co.* (3 C.C.A. 248, 52 F. 700 [1893])

3. SUBSTANTIAL PERFORMANCE

When one party fails to perform his or her part of the contract, the other party may terminate the contract and sue for breach of contract. In such a case, there has been a failure of consideration. However, to apply the rule strictly could result in a great hardship. For example, if a building contractor constructed a home for a party and complied with the contract except for some minor detail, it would be unfair to permit the party to rescind the contract. In this type of case, the party could not rescind the contract because of substantial compliance by the builder. The party would, however, be able to obtain a judgment for damages (see Chapter 17 for rule of damages).

4. PERFORMANCE TO SATISFACTION OF PROMISEE OR THIRD PARTY

A. SATISFACTION OF PROMISEE

If a party contracts to "personally satisfy" the promisee and the promisee is not satisfied, the courts look to the type of contract to make a decision. If the contract is one in which the personal taste or fancy of the promisee is involved (e.g., painting a portrait of the promisee), the courts generally hold that the promisee has the final word, and there can be no recovery unless he or she is personally satisfied (but the promisee must act in good faith). If the contract involves operative fitness or mechanical utility (e.g., contractor agrees to build a garage to promisee's satisfaction), the courts usually apply the term "reasonably satisfactory"; and if a reasonable person would be satisfied under the circumstances, the promisor can recover.

In the following case, the court held that the personal satisfaction of the buyer was required.

> **FACTS** Plaintiff purchased a Cadillac from the defendant. It was agreed that if the plaintiff was "not happy with the car" he could return the car. The car was in very bad condition, and the plaintiff demanded that the defendant take it back, which the defendant refused to do.
>
> **DECISION** The court held for the plaintiff, stating the words "not happy with the car" meant "not satisfied with the Cadillac."
>
> *Fulcher v. Nelson* (159 S.E.2d 519 [N.C. 1968])

B. SATISFACTION OF THIRD PARTY

Suppose a doctor makes a contract with a contractor for the construction of her expensive home and the doctor, realizing that she knows very little about construction, has her attorney place a clause in the contract that states that the doctor does not have to pay the contractor until the doctor's architect is satisfied with the construction and issues an architect's certificate of approval. Must the certificate be issued before the contractor has the right of payment? Yes, unless the certificate is withheld through mistake or fraud or in bad faith, in which case the contractor can recover without the certificate.

B. BY ACT OF PARTIES

1. BY CONDITION IN CONTRACT

The contract may provide that it shall terminate upon the happening of a certain event (e.g., provision in insurance policy that provides that the insured shall give the insurance company notice of a loss by fire within a stated period and if it is not done, the right to recover on the policy is lost; a seller may sell property agreeing that the property may be returned if it does not comply with certain specifications, thus giving the buyer title subject to rescission; a builder agrees to perform certain construction if the city council passes a pending ordinance; a provision in the contract that either party can terminate the contract upon giving a 30-day written notice).

2. BY MUTUAL RELEASE

The parties to a contract may agree to rescind the contract and place each other in status quo by returning any property or money that had been delivered or paid. An oral mutual rescission is valid except in the case of a sale of an interest in land, in which case the mutual rescission must be in writing pursuant to the same formalities as required by the statute of frauds.

For a discussion of an oral modification of a written contract refer to Chapter 14, G.

3. SUBSTITUTION OF NEW AGREEMENT

The parties may agree to replace the original contract with a new one. If they do so, the original contract is terminated by substitution.

4. NOVATION

A novation is a substitution of a new contract or obligation for an old one, which is thereby extinguished. It can involve the substitution of a new debt or obligation where the debtor and creditor remain the same (debtor to paint creditor's house instead of paying creditor a certain sum of money), where the debt remains the same but a new creditor is substituted for the previous creditor, or where the debt remains the same but a new debtor is substituted for the previous debtor.

Novation of debtors is the most frequent form of novation. For example, John purchases a new car on an installment contract. While still owing $1,000 on the contract, John loses his job and is unable to keep up the payments on the car. Richard, John, and the finance company agree that Richard will take over the payments and the ownership of the car and John will be released from the installment contract.

Although a novation can be oral, it is better practice to put the substitution agreement in writing.

5. ACCORD AND SATISFACTION

An *accord* is an agreement for a substituted performance in satisfaction of the original obligation. When the accord is carried out, there is an *accord and satisfaction* and the original obligation is discharged. The usual purpose is to settle a claim with a different performance. Thus, debtor owes creditor $1,000. The parties agree that debtor shall paint creditor's house in satisfaction of the debt. The agreement is an accord. When the house is painted, there has been an accord and satisfaction and the debt is discharged.

6. ACCOUNT STATED

An account is a right to payment under a contract. An account *stated* is an agreement between parties who have transacted business with each other as to the amount of the final balance due from one to the other. This is a new and independent executory contract. The items in the original accounts are merged into the account stated. No right or action remains as to the items. For example, A and B have been doing business with each other over a period of time, which has created a relationship of debtor and creditor between them. A and B agree that a certain amount is due, and B promises to pay that amount. This is called an account stated. The agreement discharges the obligations arising under the prior transactions.

The account stated may be implied, as where a creditor renders a statement to the debtor and the debtor fails to object within a reasonable time. The debtor will be liable for the amount stated in the account. A creditor can also be bound. In *Levy v. Prinzmetal* (134 C.A.2d Supp. 919, 286 P.2d 1023 [1955]), the creditor sent the debtor a bill for a certain amount. The debtor sent the creditor a check for a lesser amount with a notation on the check "in full." The creditor *accepted the check as payment without objection*. This resulted in an account stated, and the creditor could not recover the additional sum. Refer to Chapter 10, K., for discussion of "Paid in Full" cases.

7. MATERIAL ALTERATION OF EXISTING CONTRACT

Generally a material, fraudulent alteration of a written contract by one who asserts a right under the contract extinguishes the person's right to recover on the contract. The test of materiality is whether the alteration makes any change in the meaning or legal effect of the contract. The following are exceptions to the general rule: (1) where the alteration is not material, (2) where it is made by a stranger to the instrument, (3) where it is made accidentally or innocently, (4) where it is made to show the actual agreement of the parties, or (5) where the alteration is ratified by the other party.

Where the alteration is intentional but not fraudulent, the effectiveness of the instrument is destroyed. The party who made the innocent alteration can generally recover on the original consideration. For example, A borrowed $10,000 from B and signed a note and mortgage, which created a lien on his farm. B innocently made a material alteration of the mortgage document without A's knowledge. Under the general rule, B will be able to get a judgment on the note, but will not be able to enforce the mortgage lien against the farm.

Where one party signs an incomplete instrument containing blanks and the other party without authority fills them in, a fraudulent alteration has occurred that prevents the formation of any contract.

8. PREVENTION OR WAIVER

Where one party prevents the other party from performing, the latter is excused from performance. Also, where one party waives performance by the other, performance is excused. For example, landlord habitually accepts rental payments many days after payments are due. In such a case, before the landlord can insist that the payments be made on due date, the landlord must give a timely notice to the tenant of the reinstatement of the requirement. The following case is an example of prevention of performance constituting a breach of contract.

> **FACTS** Velma Jacobs, owner of a farm, entered into a contract with Earl Walker in which Walker agreed to paint the barns and improvements on the farm. Walker purchased the paint from Charles Jones, doing business as Chas. Jones Lumber Company. Before the work was completed, Jacobs ordered Walker to stop because she was dissatisfied with the results. Offers were made by Jones and Walker to complete the job, but Jacobs declined to permit Walker to fulfill his contract.
>
> **DECISION** Jacobs, by her order to Walker to cease work and by refusing to permit either Walker or Jones to complete the work, which the trial court found they were willing to do, breached the contract and excused further performance on the part of Walker. Under the circumstances the law implies a promise on the one party not to prevent, hinder, or delay the performance of the other party.
>   Under the facts, as found by the trial court, Jones was entitled to be paid for the value of the paint furnished for use and used upon Jacobs' barns and improvements, and Walker was entitled to recover for the reasonable value of the work completed by him in accordance with the contract.
>
> *Jacobs v. Jones* (161 Colo. 505, 423 P.2d 321 [1967])

9. ANTICIPATORY BREACH

An actual breach does not take place until the time for performance has arrived; there may, however, be a total breach by anticipatory repudiation. A repudiation of a contract prior to the date fixed by the contract for performance is called an "anticipatory breach." For example, in February, Jones and Elwell enter into a contract in which Elwell will act as a lifeguard for Jones during the months of May through September. In March, Jones informs Elwell that he has hired someone else to be the lifeguard. This action by Jones is an anticipatory breach of the contract between Jones and Elwell.

If a party to a contract informs the other party prior to performance date that he is not going to perform, the aggrieved party has an election of remedies: (1) he may wait until the time for performance and exercise his remedies for the actual breach, or (2) he may treat the repudiation as an anticipatory breach and exercise his remedies immediately. Remedies available are discussed in Chapter 17.

The doctrine does not apply to unilateral contracts. For example, debtor owes creditor $100 on a note that is not yet due and informs the creditor that he is not going to pay the note when it becomes due. Creditor cannot bring suit until after the note is due.

The doctrine does not ordinarily apply to a lease between a landlord and tenant. In the absence of a special provision in the lease, the lessor cannot sue at once to recover damages based on the entire balance due when the tenant defaults.

An anticipatory breach can be retracted if the injured party has not changed his position in the meantime. The injured party does not waive his remedies by urging performance.

Section 2–610 of the U.C.C. provides that the aggrieved party may suspend performance on his part and maintain an action for breach of contract although he has urged retraction of the repudiation.

Section 2–611 of the U.C.C. provides that if the aggrieved party has not changed his position or cancelled the contract, the repudiation may be retracted. However, although the repudiation may be retracted, the aggrieved party can demand assurance of due performance and until he receives such assurance may suspend any further performance on his part (Section 2–609, U.C.C.)

C. BY IMPOSSIBILITY

1. IN GENERAL

If performance of a contract was physically impossible at the time the contract was made and this fact was not known to the parties, performance is excused. For example, T leases a dance hall from L. Unknown to the parties, the building had been destroyed by fire. This is usually referred to as "objective" impossibility (i.e., impossible in the nature of things rather than because of the inability of the party to perform).

Impossibility because a party is or becomes financially unable or because he or she personally lacks the capability or competence to perform is usually referred to as "subjective" impossibility and generally does not excuse performance. The following case is an example of subjective impossibility.

> **FACTS**   Plaintiff and defendant entered into a contract for the sale of plaintiff's apartment house to defendant. When the time arrived for performance by the defendant, he was unable to raise the necessary funds due to a decline in his used-car business. He was, however, solvent.
>
> **DECISION**   Proof of this kind does not establish the type of impossibility that constitutes a defense. Financial inability to pay does not discharge the contractual duty.
>
> *Christy v. Pilkinton* (224 Ark. 407, 273 S.W.2d 533 [1955])

2. ACT OF GOD OR NATURE

Many courts hold that an act of God or nature (flood, tornado) does not excuse performance of a contract unless performance is excused in the contract. By statute or case law in many jurisdictions, an act of God or nature that renders a contract impossible of performance is a defense to performance.

3. STRIKES AND OTHER HAZARDS

Unless provided for in the contract, strikes, picketing, riots, fire, business threats, inevitable or unavoidable accidents, breaking of machinery or equipment, or similar hazards generally do not constitute a defense for failure to perform. This type of hazard is generally foreseeable or only of a temporary nature. For a strike to be used as a defense, two things are necessary: (1) the strike must be unexpected and unforeseeable, and (2) the strike must have rendered performance commercially impracticable.

The act of an enemy is generally no defense unless it renders performance impossible or illegal or destroys the basis or subject matter of the contract, in which case most courts excuse performance.

Regarding strikes and other hazards constituting a defense in a contract for the sale of goods under the U.C.C., see Section 5B, infra.

4. DESTRUCTION OF SUBJECT MATTER

When a contract requires the transfer of a *specific* thing, the destruction of the thing makes the performance impossible and excuses performance (e.g., a contract to manufacture goods in a particular factory is discharged by the destruction of the factory; a contract to paint a specific building is discharged by the destruction of the building; a contract to carry goods by a particular ship is discharged by the loss of the ship; a sale of the wheat crop growing on a specific parcel of land is discharged if the crop is destroyed). (See U.C.C. Section 2–613(a).)

If there is a contract to sell only a given quantity of wheat and not a particular crop of wheat, the seller is not discharged by the destruction of the wheat. In such a case, the seller makes an absolute undertaking to deliver the wheat, which is not limited or restricted in any way to any particular wheat. Thus, if the seller is unable to deliver the quantity of wheat, he or she is liable for breach of contract. Moral: Sellers, put in an escape clause (e.g., destruction of the wheat excuses performance); buyers, keep it out.

5. EXTRAORDINARY DIFFICULTY OR EXPENSE

A. IN GENERAL

Mere unforeseen difficulty or expense does not constitute impossibility and ordinarily is not a defense. The modern trend, however, is to allow the defense of impossibility when performance is impracticable because of excessive and unreasonable expense or extraordinary difficulty that was not reasonably foreseeable. The following case illustrates the rule.

> **FACTS** The plaintiff entered into a contract with the defendant in which the plaintiff agreed to repair and upgrade the upstream face of Cooper Lake Dam. The contract provided that the plaintiff would quarry at a designated site across the lake. The parties assumed that the rock could be transported to the dam during the winter across the frozen ice. However, in attempting the crossing, the plaintiff lost three trucks and the lives of two drivers when the trucks broke through the ice.
>
> **DECISION** The court held the contract was impossible to perform and that the plaintiff was discharged. The court said: "[A] party is discharged from his contract obligations, even if it is technically possible to perform them, if the costs of performance would be so disproportionate to that reasonably contemplated by the parties as to make the contract totally impractical in a commercial sense."
>
> *Northern Corp. v. Chugach Electric Ass'n* (518 P.2d 76 [Alaska 1974])

The doctrine of commercial frustration is similar to the doctrine of impossibility or impracticability in that both require extreme hardship in order to excuse performance. Commercial frustration is different in that it assumes the possibility of literal performance but excuses performance because a supervening event that was not contemplated by the parties and not reasonably foreseeable essentially destroyed the purpose for which the contract was made (e.g., lease of neon advertising sign followed by governmental blackout order frustrating primary purpose justified termination). Commercial frustration cannot be used to withdraw from a poor bargain (e.g., tenant leases a gas station that does not produce the profit anticipated because of governmental regulations).

B. SALE OF GOODS UNDER THE U.C.C.

Section 2–614 of the U.C.C. provides that substituted performance is permissible when the agreed manner of shipping becomes commercially impracticable or the agreed manner of payment fails because of a governmental regulation.

Section 2–615 of the U.C.C. provides that delay in delivery or nondelivery is excused when it has been made impracticable under certain conditions. The Official Comment to this section states that the "section excuses a seller from timely delivery of goods contracted for, where his performance has become commercially impracticable because of unforeseen supervening circumstances not within the contemplation of the parties at the time of contracting. * * * Increased cost alone does not excuse performance unless the rise in cost is due to some unforeseen contingency which alters the essential nature of the performance. Neither is a rise or collapse in the market in itself a justification, for that is exactly the type of business risk which business contracts made at fixed prices are intended to cover. But a severe shortage of raw materials or of supplies due to a contingency such as war, embargo, local crop failure, unforeseen shutdown of major sources of supply, or the like, which either causes a marked increase in cost or altogether prevents the seller from securing supplies necessary to his performance, is within the contemplation of this section."

6. DEATH OR DISABILITY

When one party to a contract must perform an act that requires personal skill (author, painter, lawyer), death or disability of the person who was to perform the act discharges the contract.

But if all the work or services are of such a character that they may be performed by others as well, the obligation will not be discharged (e.g., building contract). The following case is an example of disability as an excuse for performance.

> **FACTS** Plaintiff entered into a contract with the Arthur Murray Dance Studio. The contract stated in bold-type words "NON-CANCEL-LABLE NEGOTIABLE CONTRACT" and "I UNDERSTAND THAT NO REFUNDS WILL BE MADE UNDER THE TERMS OF THIS CONTRACT." Plaintiff was severely injured in an automobile collision rendering him incapable of continuing his dancing lessons. At that time, he had contracted for a total of 2734 hours of lessons for which he had paid $24,812.80. Despite written demands defendant refused to return any of the money.
>
> **DECISION** Defendants do not deny that the doctrine of impossibility of performance is generally applicable to this type of case. Rather the defendants contend that the bold-type words were a waiver of the doctrine of impossibility and that the words indicated a contrary intention. The court held that this type of construction was unacceptable. Judgment for plaintiff.
>
> *Parker v. Arthur Murray*, Inc. (10 Ill.App.3d 1000, 295 N.E.2d 487 [1973])

D. BY OPERATION OF LAW

1. IN GENERAL

Generally, a contract is discharged and performance is excused if, after the contract has been entered into, the performance is made unlawful by a governmental order or decree. Under such circumstances, performance would constitute a violation of public policy (e.g., change in zoning law prior to beginning of construction prohibited construction of apartment building in that locality).

2. BANKRUPTCY

A discharge in bankruptcy is the result of a proceeding in a federal court by which the bankrupt is released from the obligation of certain provable debts. He or she is not released from such debts as back taxes accruing within three years prior to bankruptcy, claims based on willful or malicious injury to the person or property of another, alimony and child support, certain claims involving fraud, certain fines and penalties payable to governmental units, and certain student loans.

A debtor may voluntarily pay debts discharged in bankruptcy. However, before creditors can enforce a debt discharged in bankruptcy, the Bankruptcy Reform Act of 1978, Section 524, sets forth the following requirements:

1.   The debtor's promise must be made before the discharge of the debt is granted.

2.   The debtor does not revoke the promise within 30 days after the promise becomes enforceable.

3.   The debtor, if an individual, must be informed by the bankruptcy court of his or her legal rights and the effects of his or her new promise.

4.   The debtor's promise, if the debtor is an individual and the debt is a consumer obligation, must be approved by the bankruptcy court as being in the best interests of the debtor. Section 101 of the Act defines a consumer debt as a "debt incurred by an individual primarily for a personal, family, or household purpose".

3.   STATUTE OF LIMITATIONS

Statutes provide that if you do not file a lawsuit within a specified time after the right accrues, you are forever barred from bringing the suit. Since the time varies, local statutes must be consulted. The U.C.C., Section 2–725, specifies a four-year period for actions on contracts for sales of goods.

In most states, the debtor may waive the Statute of Limitations by a promise to pay the debt (in most states, the new promise must be in writing) or by part payment of the debt which then revives the debt. In addition, there are certain other exceptions where the Statute cannot be used (e.g., against the government or where a party has been misled [insurance agent promises to settle suit and thereby misleads injured party into not filing lawsuit in time]).

A customer may owe a seller on an open account for goods purchased at different times over a period of many years. When the customer sends a partial payment to the seller, the general rule is that the seller can apply the payment to the oldest items in the account, thereby preventing the statute of limitations from running on the oldest items. However, the debtor can change that rule by instructions accompanying the payment (e.g., a notation on the check "By endorsement this check when paid is accepted in full payment of the following account [here state the specific items or invoice numbers and amounts so that the payment is made on current accounts and not on those barred or about to be barred by the statute of limitations]"). A letter containing similar instructions should accompany the check.

Some contracts (e.g., insurance contracts) contain a time limitation within which suit must be brought, such as 90 days. Because suits against the government or its agencies are allowed by consent only, all statutory requirements, including time for filing, must be strictly followed.

4. INSOLVENCY

Section 1–201(23) of the U.C.C. states that a person is insolvent when he or she cannot pay his or her debts as they become due or has ceased to pay his or her debts in the ordinary course of business, or if the person comes within the definition of insolvency in the Federal Bankruptcy Act which means that his or her liabilities exceed his or her assets.

Authorities differ as to whether insolvency constitutes a breach of contract. Some courts hold that there is an implied condition in every contract that the promisor will not permit himself to be disabled from making performance through insolvency, and that insolvency is a breach of the contract.

Other courts hold that insolvency does not result in a breach of contract unless there is an express provision in the contract to the contrary. In the latter courts, if the seller is selling on credit and the buyer becomes insolvent, the seller must deliver the goods if the buyer can make payment (i.e., the seller is not excused from performance by the insolvency).

Under the U.C.C., Section 2–702, the seller may demand cash from an insolvent buyer prior to delivery and may reclaim goods sold to an insolvent buyer. Under the U.C.C., Section 2–502, the buyer can recover identified goods from an insolvent seller when the buyer has paid all or part of the purchase price.

ILLUSTRATIVE CASES

1. Substantial Performance of Building Contract Can Be Sufficient

SURETY DEVELOPMENT CORP. v. GREVAS

42 Ill.App.2d 268, 192 N.E.2d 145 (1963)

Smith, Justice.   When is a house a home? In our context a house is a home when it can be lived in. But when is that: When substantially completed or completely completed? We posit the question, because the answer is decisive.

Plaintiff sells prefabricated houses. Defendants selected one of their models, styled "Royal Countess, elevation 940". A contract was signed. The cost was $16,385.00; completion date September 27, 1961. Around 4:00 P.M. on that date defendants refused to accept the house asserting non-completion. Plaintiff then sued for the balance due and defendants counter-claimed for their downpayment. Both alleged performance by them and non-performance by the other. The legal issue is therefore relatively simple: Who performed and who didn't. The facts are more elusive—plaintiff at times says one thing, defendants another. We narrate them briefly.

On the morning of the twenty-seventh, "Royal Countess, elevation 940" was far from being a house, let alone a home. Racing the clock, plaintiff initiated a crash program. When defendants arrived on the scene at 4:00, at plaintiff's behest for final inspection, the crash program was still crashing—workmen were all over the place, slapping on siding, laying the floors, bulldozing the yard, hooking up the utilities, and so on. Defendants' tour was not a success, to put it mildly. Instead of a home, they found, to their dismay, a hive buzzing with activity. They did not tarry, in spite of the foreman's assurances that all would be right by 5:30. Nor did they come back. They should have. Believe it or not, the foreman was right. The job was substantially completed by 5:30, with only a service walk, some grading and black-topping left undone.

The trial court found that the house had been substantially completed and concluded that there had been, therefore, substantial compliance with the contract and with this we agree. But because the house was not completely completed, it found that there had not been *complete* compliance. With this, too, we agree, but such finding is beside the point. Substantial—not complete—compliance in a construction contract is all that is required. By 5:30, there had been just that, in other words, substantial performance of the contract. Plaintiff's contretemps in having inspection set for 4:00 o'clock was hardly the way to make friends and influence people, but such happenstance is of no moment in determining whether or not there had been substantial compliance, unless such can be said to indicate bad faith. We do not think that it does. What it indicates is bad timing, not bad faith. * * *

No substantial sum was required to complete the items left undone. Nor were they of so essential a character that defendants could not have been esconced in their new home that night if they had so desired. We have thus answered our question: A house is ready to be lived in, to become a home, when it has been substantially completed.

[Judgment for plaintiff.]

2. When Personal Satisfaction Is Not Required

JOHNSON v. SCHOOL DISTRICT NO. 12

210 Or. 585, 312 P.2d 591 (1957)

KESTER, Justice. This is an action to recover damages for breach of contract, in which plaintiff appeals from a judgment of nonsuit.

* * * Plaintiff was a school-bus operator in the Wallowa area, and on September 1, 1951, he entered into a contract with School District No. 4 of Wallowa county for the operation of a school bus during the two school years 1951–52–53. * * * The contract contained the following option:

> The said second party [Johnson] is to have option the next 3 years if a bus is run and his service has been satisfactory.

It is agreed that plaintiff operated a bus during the two-year period of the contract, and for that he was fully paid.

* * * On June 9, 1953, after preliminary negotiations, plaintiff wrote to the board of District No. 12 stating that he elected to exercise his option [District No. 4 and 12 had been consolidated]. Defendant, however, refused

to accept plaintiff's services, and instead defendant has operated its own bus, over the same route, since that time. * * *

In granting the nonsuit, the trial court held that the contractual provision that plaintiff's service be "satisfactory" was akin to those contracts where fancy, taste, or personal judgment are involved, and where lack of satisfaction on the part of the promisor is not reviewable. * * *

Plaintiff's option to renew the contract if his service has been satisfactory presents a question similar to those arising under contracts giving one party a right to terminate or be relieved from obligation if performance is unsatisfactory. Such contracts are generally grouped into two categories: * * *

> 1. Those which involve taste, fancy or personal judgment, the classical example being a commission to paint a portrait. In such cases the promisor is the sole judge of the quality of the work, and his right to reject, if in good faith, is absolute and may not be reviewed by court or jury.

> 2. Those which involve utility, fitness or value, which can be measured against a more or less objective standard. In these cases, although there is some conflict, we think the better view is that performance need only be "reasonably satisfactory," and if the promisor refuses the proffered performance, the correctness of his decision and the adequacy of his grounds are subject to review. * * *

Where, in a given contract, it is doubtful whether the promise is intended to be conditional on the promisor's personal satisfaction or on the sufficiency of the performance to satisfy a reasonable man, the latter interpretation is adopted.

* * * Even in cases where the right to terminate is absolute, the dissatisfaction must be actual and honest, and not merely feigned in order to escape liability. * * *

And where a right to renewal is predicated upon the existence of mutually satisfactory conditions at the expiration of the original period, one party cannot defeat the option by unreasonable refusal to cooperate in making the operation satisfactory. * * *

After study of the contract in question here, we are of the opinion that the standard of performance involved is not the mere personal satisfaction of the school board, unsupported by reason, but it is such performance as would satisfy a reasonable man under the circumstances. * * *

In our opinion, therefore, plaintiff would establish a prima facie case for renewal of the contract by proving that his performance was of a quality that should have satisfied a reasonable man under the circumstances.

[Nonsuit affirmed on procedural grounds; i.e., plaintiff should have exhausted his administrative remedies by filing his complaint with the school board before proceeding with his court action.]

3. Anticipatory Breach of Contract

KLEEB v. BURNS

5 Ariz.App.566, 429 P.2d 453 (1967)

HATHAWAY, Chief Judge. Jeanette M. Kleeb, defendant below, has appealed from a judgment against her, awarding the full real estate broker's commission to Robert Hilgenberg dba [doing business as] Hilgenberg Realty Company, and ordering her to return the $1,000 earnest money to the plaintiff, Robert W. Burns. * * * The trial court found that the commission had been earned in a real estate transaction which was not carried out.

*   *   *

Viewing the evidence * * * we find that the appellee, Hilgenberg, acting under a written listing, signed by the appellant, brought the buyer and seller together.

On June 17, 1964, the appellant, Jeanette Kleeb, entered into a "DEPOSIT RECEIPT AND AGREEMENT" to sell a house in Tucson to Robert W. Burns. The pertinent provisions of the agreement provided:

Closing date—June 23, 1964; possession date—June 24, 1964.

*   *   *

Time is of the essence.

On June 23, a meeting relating to the closing of the transaction was held in Mr. Hilgenberg's office. Mrs. Kleeb was on a trip to Guadalajara, Mexico, but her attorney John W. Ross attended the meeting. Others present were Mr. Burns and his attorney J. Mercer Johnson, Mr. Hilgenberg and his secretary, Yvonne Hutchins.

Mr. Johnson stated that the buyer was ready and willing to complete the closing at that time, if the seller, Mrs. Kleeb, could deliver possession on June 24 according to the contract. A discussion ensued relating to Mrs. Kleeb's failure to take steps to remove any of her personal possessions and furnishings from the seven room and two and a half bath home. At this time Mr. Ross stated that he refused to take any responsibility for removing the personal property of Mrs. Kleeb from the premises. Mr. Ross then called his client in Mexico and advised her about the complication. She gave Mr. Ross authority to remove her personal possessions from the home, but left the decision up to him. An impasse developed between the parties and the closing did not take place.

Mrs. Kleeb returned from Mexico at 5 p.m. on the 24th of June and went immediately to Mr. Hilgenberg's office. Mr. Hilgenberg testified that Mrs. Kleeb told him that she was willing to do anything to complete the transaction that was not taken care of on the 23d. He further testified that he had a mover who would remove all of her property from the premises but that she refused to have this done as it would take "several days" and that "she said it is impossible to do it [to move the furniture on the 24th] at that time."

Mrs. Kleeb's testimony revealed that she had made no arrangements to have the furnishings removed. * * *

*   *   *

The buyer's attorney delivered a letter on June 24 to both Mr. Ross and the Hilgenberg Realty offering to complete the agreement on June 24. Mr. Johnson received a telephone call from Mr. Hilgenberg at his home on the evening of June 24 informing him that Mrs. Kleeb could deliver possession of the premises on June 26. * * *

*   *   *

We believe that the evidence shows that Mrs. Kleeb anticipatorily breached the contract by putting herself in a position making it impossible for her to deliver possession of the premises on June 24. Time being of the essence of the contract, delivery of possession was required of her on the date to fulfill the performance required of her under the contract.

It is clearly the law that a party to a contract need not perform where his performance would be useless in the face of the opposite party's manifesting his inability to perform his part of the agreement.

*   *   *

For the foregoing reasons the judgment is affirmed.

4. Mere Increase in Difficulty and Costs Not Impossibility

KENNEDY v. REECE

225 Cal.App.2d 717, 37 Cal.Rptr. 708 (1964)

CONLEY, Presiding Justice. This is an appeal by the plaintiff from a judgment adverse to him on his complaint and favorable to the defendants on their counterclaim. The plaintiff, Fred Kennedy, made a contract with Reece and Thomas, mining partners, to drill a water well for them * * *

*   *   *

The cause was tried by the court sitting without a jury, and resulted in a judgment for the defendants on their counterclaim in the sum of $1,307.15, besides interest and costs.

*   *   *

The evidence shows that Mr. Kennedy was an experienced water well driller carrying on his trade in the area; that he assured Mr. Reece that he was certain of getting an acceptable well and that there would be no trouble in reaching the 400-foot level contemplated by the written contract. However, the first hole drilled by the plaintiff, after being carried to a depth of 130 feet, was abandoned at the instance of the appellant because he claimed that he had struck hard rock. The plaintiff told Mr. Reece that he would move, without charging him any additional sum, to a new point on the land of a neighbor, if Mr. Reece would dig a sump hole at the proposed location and construct a passable roadway to the place where the well was to be drilled. The defendants accordingly secured permission to drill the well on the neighbor's property, and the second hole was carried down to a depth of 270 feet; Mr. Kennedy claimed that he there struck the same hard formation, which he said was granite but which the evidence on behalf of the defendants showed was a relatively brittle rock that could be drilled through. Mr. Kennedy removed his equipment without any preliminary notice to defendants and left the area; he did not complete the well, and he did not insert any casing or cap either of the holes. No consent was given by Mr. Reece for the abandonment of the operations by Kennedy. In this respect as well as in others, there was a conflict in the testimony, but, of course, the trial court's findings, being sustained by substantial evidence, must prevail.

The defendants did not complete the well, although the evidence indicates that two contractors stated to Mr. Reece that they would be willing to drill to the 400-foot level at a cost estimated at $5.00 per foot, besides the necessary expense of setting up and taking down their equipment. * * *

* * *

It is obvious that the finding that the plaintiff failed to comply with the terms of his contract is supported by substantial evidence; the well driller did not dig the well to a depth of 400 feet; he did not case it; he did not gravel pack, or wash, or bail it. Appellant contends, however, that he was relieved from the duty of completing his contract because of "impossibility" resulting when he hit hard rock at the 270 foot level.

The enlargement of the meaning of "impossibility" as a defense, (which at common law originally meant literal or physical impossibility of performance) to include "impracticability" is now generally recognized. * * * However, this does not mean that any facts, which make performance more difficult or expensive than the parties anticipated, discharge a duty that has been created by the contract * * * Facts which make performance harder or more costly than the parties contemplated when the agreement was made do not constitute a ground for the successful interposition of the defense of "impracticability" unless such facts are of the gravest importance. If it be noted that this is merely a difference of degree rather than a difference in kind, such notation is accurate.

* * *

[I]ncreased difficulties and heightened costs of a reasonable nature, even though originally unforeseen, do not render the performance of a contract "impracticable". * * * For example, if a contractor agrees to build a structure and it is destroyed by fire or other casualty when only partly completed, the contractor is not relieved from his duty to rebuild merely because of the additional expense he must incur or the added difficulties he must overcome. * * *

In the present case, neither the pleadings nor the facts as found by the court warrant the application of the doctrine of impossibility, or impracticability. * * *

* * *

[Judgment for defendant.]

5. Doctrine of Commercial Frustration No Defense to Lease of Real Property

WOOD v. BARTOLINO

48 N.M. 175, 146 P.2d 883 (1944)

BRICE, Justice.   The appellant leased a building to appellees "for use solely as a filling station and not for restaurant or lunch counter purposes," at a rental of $100 per month for a term of five years commencing June 1, 1939. It was operated by sub-lessees until February 1, 1941, and thereafter until July 1, 1942 by appellees, when the latter ceased its operation and offered to restore possession of the premises upon the alleged ground that the lease contract had been terminated because of "commercial frustration" resulting from government rules, regulations, and orders freezing automobiles, tires and tubes and rationing the sale of gasoline, so that it was "impossible and impracticable to use or operate the leased premises as a filling station" at any time after the first of December, 1942; and that such "impossibility and impracticability" still continued and would continue throughout the term of the lease. * * *

As a direct and proximate consequence of the governmental rules, regulations and orders concerning the "freezing" of tires, tubes and automobiles, it became and was impossible and impracticable to use or operate the leased premises as a filling station during the months of July, August, September, October and November, 1942, and by reason thereof, and of the rationing of gasoline, it became and was impossible and impracticable to use or operate the leased premises as a filling station during the months of December, 1942, January, 1943, or any time thereafter, and that such impossibility and impracticability still continues and will continue throughout the term of the lease contract.

*   *   *

The parties, at the time the lease contract was entered into, did not contemplate, and could not reasonably have contemplated, that such laws, rules and regulations would be enacted, promulgated or enforced, or that they would materially and substantially change the conditions of the business operated in the leased premises. * * *

The doctrine of "commercial frustration," or, as more often called by the courts of this country, the doctrine of "implied condition," has been developed by a process of evolution from the rules: * * *

"(1) Impossibility due to domestic law;

"(2) Impossibility due to the death or illness of one who by the terms of the contract was to do an act requiring his personal performance.

"(3) Impossibility due to fortuitous destruction or change in character of something to which the contract related, or which by the terms of the contract was made a necessary means of performance." * * * [T]he essence of the modern defense of impossibility is that the promised performance was at the making of the contract, or thereafter became, impracticable owing to some extreme or unreasonable difficulty, expense, injury, or loss involved, rather than that it is scientifically or actually impossible. * * * The impor-

tant question is whether an unanticipated circumstance has made performance of the promise vitally different from what should reasonably have been
within the contemplation of both parties when they entered into the contract. If so, the risk should not fairly be thrown upon the promisor."

* * *

The courts of this country, Federal and State, have cited with approval,
and generally followed, the decisions of the English courts on the doctrine
of "commercial frustration," involving commercial transactions. It is held by
the English courts that the doctrine has no application to an ordinary lease
of real property. * * *

There are no Federal regulations prohibiting the sale of gasoline, oil,
tires, tubes and other merchandise ordinarily sold at filling stations, though
the enforcement of such regulations has drastically reduced appellees' income, which before was less than operating expenses; nor has any Federal
law, rule or regulation deprived appellees of the use of the premises as a
filling station. * * * It follows that the trial court erred in denying recovery
of rent by appellant. * * *

In such cases relief lies only in the conscience of the landlord, to which
in this case, it appears, fruitless appeals for relief have been made.

[Judgment for plaintiff.]

PROBLEMS

1. Russell promises to paint Smith's portrait on or before July 15, and Smith
promises to pay Russell the sum of $500, "provided I am satisfied with your work."
Russell completes his work on July 14, whereupon Smith examines the painting,
declares that he is "not satisfied," and refuses to pay. Russell's work is excellent.
Smith is in good faith. Discuss.

2. Moore had a fire policy on his home with the Phoenix Insurance Company that
had a clause as follows: "If the above-mentioned premises shall become vacant and
unoccupied for a period of more than ten days, this policy shall be void". Moore and
his family left the premises for a two-week vacation. One month after their return,
the home burned to the ground. The insurance company refuses to pay on the
grounds that the policy was terminated by a violation of the policy. Decision?

3. XYZ Corporation had a contract with B whereby XYZ would deliver certain
types of motors to B on or before June 1. On February 1, XYZ informed B that it
would not be able to deliver the motors, because the company was having financial
problems. B ignored this information. In March, XYZ was able to get a governmental
subsidy to continue operations. In April XYZ informed B that it was going to deliver
pursuant to the contract. B, believing he can purchase the motors at a lower price,
desires to cancel the contract on the grounds of anticipatory breach under U.C.C.
2–610. Decision?

4. The Weather Construction Company contracted to construct a building for O at a certain price. Abnormal rainfall resulted in the flooding of the job site, and the contractor incurred extra expense, which he now demands that O pay. O claims that Weather is bound by the contract. Decision?

5. Seller contracts with buyer to sell buyer all of his corn crop to be grown on seller's land known as "Sweetacre." After the crop is grown and identified, but before it is time to be harvested, an unusual windstorm destroys the crop. Buyer insists that seller get corn from another source or pay damages. Seller claims he is excused from performance. Decision?

6. The Mineral Park Land Company owned a bed of gravel in a ravine. Howard, who was about to build a concrete bridge nearby, made a contract with the company by which he agreed to take from the company's gravel bed all the gravel required for the bridge at a price of five cents per cubic yard. After Howard had removed about half of the total amount required for the bridge, he discovered that the rest of the gravel was below the level of the ground water in the ravine and that to remove it would necessitate the use of a steam dredge at an expense of 10 or 12 times more than the usual cost per yard. Howard, therefore, refuses to take any more gravel, and the company sues him for his failure to go on with the performance of the contract. Decision?

7. "Whirlwind" White had a contract to fight "Madman" Morris at the Forum on June 14. On June 10, while hitting the punching bag, Morris sprained his wrist, causing a postponement of the fight. The prefight ticket purchasers now sue Morris for spraining his wrist, White for refusing to fight a man with a sprained wrist, and the Forum for postponing the fight. Result?

8. T leased a neon advertising sign from L for a period of one year. A few days after T and L entered into the lease, a governmental order forbid the use of neon signs in T's area. T seeks to rescind the lease. Decision?

9. B contracts to purchase 100 copper-covered tables from S. B is aware that S must obtain the copper from a certain manufacturer in a foreign country. Shortly after the contract is made, the supplier of the copper is forced to shut down his factory because of a riot and a strike. B sues S for breach of contract in failing to deliver the tables, contending that S should have provided an escape clause in the contract, since neither a riot nor a strike is a defense. Decision?

10. Debtor filed a Petition in Bankruptcy and was discharged of his debt to his doctor-creditor. Later the doctor called the debtor and asked him to please pay the debt, since it was the doctor's skill that saved his life. The debtor said the doctor was right and that he would pay the entire debt. Now debtor has second thoughts and seeks your advice.

Chapter 17

REMEDIES IN GENERAL

A. DAMAGES

1. COMPENSATORY DAMAGES

A. IN GENERAL

When one party breaches a contract, the other party may be entitled to damages. In this situation, the law attempts to compensate the plaintiff so he or she will be placed in as good a position as if the defendant had performed the contract. The theory is just compensation for losses that are the immediate, direct, and natural result of the act complained of and that are usual and might have been expected. For example, an electrical power company was held liable to food stores for spoiling of perishable food items when the company interrupted service without warning for six hours during a summer heat wave.

The injured party is entitled only to damages that were within the contemplation of the parties at the time the contract was made. Unusual or unexpected damages resulting from facts unknown to the defendant or that he or she could not foresee at the time the contract was made are not recoverable. For example, plaintiff, a flour mill, sent a broken crank shaft to a nearby town by the defendant, a common carrier. Plaintiff did not inform defendant that it would be unable to operate without the shaft. Defendant promised to bring the shaft back as soon as it was repaired; however, defendant neglected to make prompt delivery as promised. As a result of defendant's delay, the plaintiff lost several days of profits. Plaintiff sued for the lost profits. The court held for the defendant on the grounds that the fact that the plaintiff would be unable to operate without the shaft was not communicated to the defendant and that the carrier would not reasonably foresee that the plaintiff would be shut down as a result of the delay in transporting the broken shaft.

The amount of damages recoverable is for the jury to decide and for the court if there is no jury. Court costs (e.g., filing fees, witness fees, jury fees, deposition costs) are usually assessed against the losing party. If the plaintiff did not suffer a loss or cannot prove a loss, the court may award him or her nominal damages (e.g., one dollar, plus court costs).

In construction contracts, where the contractor breaches the contract, damages are generally measured by the reasonable cost of completion in accordance with the contract (the amount extra it costs above the contract price to get the building done), plus reasonable compensation for any delay in performance. Generally this is true whether the contractor refused to finish the work or not and whether the breach was total or partial. However, if there would be an unreasonable economic waste (tearing down the building and starting over), generally the damage rule is based on the difference between the value of full performance as promised and the value of the defective performance actually rendered. Some courts refuse to follow the economic waste rule if the contractor is guilty of wilful or intentional breach. In such courts, the contractor is thus liable for the actual cost of completion.

When a contractor delays in completing performance of the contract, the general rule is that the injured party may recover the cost of renting other premises. It is usually advisable in this type of contract to have a liquidated damage clause (see A. 3. of this chapter).

Generally, *attorney fees* are not recoverable for breach of contract. Reasonable fees can be granted, however, when provided for in the contract, by statute, or when punitive damages are awarded. Some states (California by statute) provide for attorney fees to the prevailing party when there is a clause in the contract providing for attorney fees whether the attorney is named or not. For example, a lease provides that the landlord can recover reasonable attorney fees if he or she brings suit against the tenant, but there is nothing in the lease stating that the tenant can recover attorney fees. Under this statute, the tenant would recover attorney fees if he or she prevailed in the suit even though this was not stated in the lease.

Emotional reactions peculiar to a particular individual that might flow from a breach of a contract are too subjective and variable to be contemplated prior to a breach of contract or ascertainable afterwards and therefore are generally not recoverable.

Is a *computer mistake* a good defense against a claim for damages? In *Ford Motor Credit Company v. Swarens* (447 S.W.2d 53 [1969]), Swarens sued Ford Motor Credit Company, appellant, for damages for the wrongful repossession of his automobile. Ford defended on the grounds that the repossession was the result of a computer mistake. The court said, "Men feed data to a computer and men interpret the answer the computer spews forth. In this computerized age, the law must require that men in the use of computerized data regard those with whom they are dealing as more important than a perforation on a card. Trust in the infallibility of a computer is hardly a defense, when the opportunity to avoid the error is as apparent and repeated as was here presented."

B. LOSS OF PROFITS

The injured party may recover for loss of profits if he or she can establish them with reasonable certainty. Reasonable certainty, not mathematical certainty, is all that is required. Where there is no uncertainty as to the *fact* of damages, it is no objection that the *amount* cannot be exactly determined.

Speculative profits, as any speculative damages, are not recoverable (e.g., loss of future profits from a *new* business). However, loss of future profits from an *established* business would be recoverable if there is a reasonably certain basis for the calculation of plaintiff's probable loss resulting from the breach.

Where plaintiff is unable to prove loss of profits, courts frequently award the amount of expenditures plus the value of his or her own services in preparation and performance in reliance on the contract.

c. INTEREST

Interest at the legal rate (the rate set by statute) is recoverable from the time of breach where the amount of money is liquidated or from the time it becomes liquidated, otherwise from the date of the judgment. Even though the demand is not for a specific sum, interest may be recovered where the damages are capable of being made certain by calculation (e.g., reference to market value). If the damages are neither certain nor capable of being made certain by calculation, interest is not allowed prior to judgment.

2. PUNITIVE DAMAGES

Exemplary or punitive damages are awarded to one party in order to punish the other party and to discourage others from similar wrongful conduct. Generally, punitive damages are limited to certain situations involving willful, wanton, or malicious torts, such as fraud or libel. Cases have awarded punitive damages for willful breach of a fiduciary duty, persistent and repeated wrongful conduct in the operation of a business (where the conduct has been sufficiently intentional, reckless, wanton, willful, or gross as to permit a reasonable inference of malice), and fraud arising from a contract.

Generally, punitive damages are not recoverable for breach of contract. *Brown v. Coates* (253 F.2d 36 [1958]) involved a breach of a fiduciary duty. The defendant, a real estate broker, held himself out to the public as experienced and competent. He induced the plaintiffs, who were homeowners, to enter into a contract with him for exchange of their old house for a new one, with resulting effect that the homeowners received no money for the equity in the old house. When the plaintiffs told him they ought to get a lawyer to advise them, he said he was a lawyer and he would take care of them. The court held that where the breach of the agent's fiduciary duties under contract merges with and assumes the character of a willful tort, calculated, and in disregard of the obligations of trust, punitive damages may be allowed.

In awarding punitive damages, the more reprehensible the acts, the greater the appropriate punishment, and thus the higher award of punitive damages is justified. Another yardstick is the amount of compensatory damages; if the actual harm suffered is small, even a very reprehensible act would not support a very high punitive damage award.

3. LIQUIDATED DAMAGES

The parties may stipulate in the contract that a certain amount shall be paid
to the injured party in case of default (known as a "liquidated damage
clause"). The amount stated must be as a result of a reasonable endeavor by
the parties to state an amount that bears a reasonable relationship to actual
damages. If the amount specified is not so excessive as to be in the form of
a penalty, the clause will be valid. Also, the nature of the contract must be
such that it would be extremely difficult or impractical for the court to
ascertain the actual amount of damages.

A common example of a liquidated damage clause is found in building
contracts where the contractor is required to pay a stated sum for each day
of delay. In *Oregon State Highway Commission v. DeLong Corp.* (9 Or.App.
550, 495 P.2d 1215 [1972]), the court held that $2,000 a day for each day of
delay by the contractor was reasonable in view of the losses by the state.

In *Vincent v. Chef Joe's* (273 Or. 814, 541 P.2d 469 [1975]), the court held
that a clause in an exclusive listing agreement requiring the real estate
broker to be paid a commission if the property was sold within the exclusive
listing period even though sales were made through the efforts of others was
a valid liquidated damage clause.

In *Garrett v. Coast* (9 Cal.3d 731, 108 Cal.Rptr. 845, 511 P.2d 1197
[1973]), the court held that a late payment charge based on the percentage
of unpaid balance of the loan obligation was punitive in character and
unenforceable. However, the court said the plaintiff could recover damages
for a late payment based on the period of time the money was wrongfully
withheld, plus the administrative costs reasonably related to collecting and
accounting for the late payment. Under Section 2–718 of the U.C.C., a liquidated damage clause is valid if it is reasonable under specified circumstances.

4. DUTY TO MINIMIZE DAMAGES

The injured party is under a duty to mitigate his damages, and this duty
requires that the injured party take whatever steps are reasonably necessary to reduce the actual loss as much as possible. The injured party cannot
add to the damages when it is reasonably within his or her power to mitigate
damages. For example, a person who is wrongfully discharged from an
employment contract before the term expires must use reasonable means to
find similar employment (i.e., he cannot sit idly by and expect to draw a
salary). If the person cannot find similar suitable employment, he is entitled
to recover his full salary for the balance of the contract term.

A buyer who receives inferior goods under a contract cannot increase
the damages by continuing to use the goods after learning of their unfitness.
And a buyer who does not receive goods or services according to a contract
cannot recover damages resulting from his or her doing without such goods
or services when it is possible to substitute other goods or services from
someone else. Sections 2–602(2)(b) and 2–603(1) of the U.C.C. cover a buyer's
duties to minimize damages under certain conditions.

B. EQUITABLE RELIEF

1. SPECIFIC PERFORMANCE

There are times when a plaintiff is not interested in money damages because he or she feels that money per se is not the solution to the defendant's breach. For example, plaintiff finds a rare Rembrandt painting that she wishes to add to her art collection. Plaintiff makes a contract with defendant for the purchase of the painting. Later, when plaintiff tenders the money, the defendant refuses to deliver the painting. In such a case, plaintiff is not interested in money damages, which could be only nominal, but wants the painting. Courts have the power to order the defendant to deliver the painting and, if he refuses, to sentence him to prison for contempt of court. This order is called a "decree of specific performance." This decree is not granted lightly. There are five requirements to a decree for specific performance:

1.   The contract must be definite and certain.

2.   Money damages must be inadequate.

3.   The agreement must be legal and without fraud or immorality.

4.   The decree must not work a hardship or injustice on the defendant (e.g., consideration grossly inadequate at the time the contract was entered into or contract unconscionable).

5.   The court must be able to supervise the performance of the ordered act.

Courts will generally order specific performance of real estate contracts (because each parcel of real estate is unique) and contracts for unique personal property.

Contracts for ordinary personal property are not specifically enforceable, because the plaintiff can purchase identical goods on the open market. If he has a loss, money damages will be adequate.

Personal services contracts are ordinarily not specifically enforceable because of the difficulty of supervision by the court and because of the Thirteenth Amendment, which prohibits involuntary servitude.

The court will not order specific performance of a building contract, because enforcement of the decree would require too much supervision of the details of construction.

Section 2–716 of the U.C.C. provides for specific performance in the sale of goods where it is equitable to do so.

2. RESCISSION

Rescission is the unmaking of the contract. A contract may not be unilaterally rescinded unless legal grounds for rescission exist. Some jurisdictions enumerate the grounds for rescission by statute.

The common grounds for rescission are illegality, commercial frustration, fraud, undue influence and duress, mistake, insanity, intoxication, entire or substantial failure of consideration, substantial nonperformance or breach by the other party (failure of a building contractor to duly and properly perform his or her contract), and cases whereby if one party places it out of his or her power to perform, the other party may treat the contract as terminated.

A right to rescind must be exercised promptly or within a reasonable time after discovery of the facts that entitle the person to rescission. Failure to act promptly can be considered a waiver of the right of rescission. In *City of Baltimore v. De Luca-Davis Construction Co.* (210 Md. 518, 124 A.2d 557 [1956]), the defendant submitted a bid for the construction of storm conduits. However, a clerical error caused the bid to be $600,000 too low. When the bids were announced, the defendant realized his bid was in error and immediately informed the city of that fact and requested a return of the bid and the certified check for $50,000 that had accompanied the bid. The court held for the defendant, stating that rescission does not require a mutual mistake. Rescission may be granted a contractor's bid "based on clerical, material, palpable, bona fide mistakes." However, the mistake must be brought to the attention of the contracting authority before the acceptance of the bid.

When a rescission takes place, the successful party is entitled to restitution (i.e., to recover any consideration he or she gave plus any other compensation necessary to make him or her whole). Thus, a buyer who placed improvements on land was entitled to the value of the improvements when he rescinded the contract because of the seller's failure to perform. Under U.C.C. Section 2–721, a party can rescind a contract and also recover damages.

3.   REFORMATION

A party may want reformation of a contract rather than rescission (i.e., have the contract corrected to show the true intent of the parties). Typical cases in which the court will reform a contract are where there has been mutual mistake or fraud in the making of the contract.

4.   INJUNCTION

A contract for personal services ordinarily is not specifically enforceable for several reasons: difficulty of enforcement, the fact that the services would be unsatisfactory under compulsion, and where physical labor is contracted for (the Thirteenth Amendment prohibits involuntary servitude).

A negative covenant in a contract may, under some circumstances, be enforced by injunction. For example, an opera singer agreed to sing at plaintiff's theatre and nowhere else for a certain time, then contracted to sing for another. Court held that she could not be forced to sing at the theatre but could be prevented from singing anywhere else during that period. Generally, an injunction in this type of case will be granted only if the services are "unique" or "extraordinary" (e.g., opera singer, ball player, actor). Also, an injunction should not be granted when it would cause unjust or harmful results (e.g., defendant is left without a reasonable means of livelihood).

A number of states, by statute, limit equity's power to enjoin breach of negative covenants in certain types of contracts. For example, under California Civil Code Section 3423, the breach of a contract for personal services will be restrained only if the services are unique and the salary is $6,000 or more per year. In *Foxx v. Williams* (244 Cal.App.2d 223, 52 Cal.Rptr. 896 [1966]), Redd Foxx was not enjoined, because his royalty contract for making phonograph records did not guarantee a minimum of $6,000 a year.

The modern rule does not require an express negative covenant in a contract for injunctive relief. This is because an affirmative promise *implies* a promise not to do anything that defeats the required performance (Restatement of Contracts, Section 380, Comment a.).

ILLUSTRATIVE CASES

1. Emotional Reaction Generally Not Recoverable in Breach of Contract

PETTAWAY v. COMMERCIAL AUTOMOTIVE SERVICE

49 Wn.2d 650, 306 P.2d 219 (1957)

FINLEY, Justice.   This is an action for damages for the breach of an alleged contract for the purchase and sale of an automobile.

The defendant company displayed a special model, a 1953 Buick "Skylark," automobile in its show window. The plaintiff saw the car and discussed its purchase with a Mr. Shaw, one of defendant corporation's salesmen. Thereafter, the plaintiff signed one of the defendant corporation's order forms on which the price of the new car was stated as $5,667, and $1,500 was designated as a credit allowance for plaintiff's 1948 Chrysler.

* * * Plaintiff's testimony further indicated that, when he returned from the voyage of some two or three months' duration, he tendered a cash payment to Mr. Shaw in an amount in excess of the five hundred dollars; that he was informed the defendant corporation had sold the 1953 Buick "Skylark" model to someone else. Apparently, the manufacturer had allotted only three automobiles of the particular model to the defendant company, and defendant company failed to produce one for the plaintiff. Thereupon, plaintiff commenced this action for damages for breach of contract. * * *

The jury awarded $1,325 to plaintiff. By answer to special interrogatories, it set (a) $825 as the market value of plaintiff's Chrysler; (b) $300 for plaintiff's disappointment, mental anguish, loss of sleep, humiliation, and damages to his reputation, allegedly resulting from the breach of the contract and the deprivation of the allegedly unique chattel; and (c) $200 by reason of deprivation of use of an automobile. The defendant corporation appealed.

* * * Now, as to the question of damages: Appellant contends that the court erred in submitting to the jury the issue of damages for deprivation of the use of respondent's Chrysler. The evidence was inadequate for the jury

to make an award in any amount for that item. There is testimony in the record that respondent hired a taxicab a couple of times for six dollars; but these events were not connected with the breach of the contract in question. The award is the result of pure speculation. * * *

The jury awarded respondent three hundred dollars for the mental anguish occasioned by the failure to deliver the "Skylark" for "conspicuous consumption." The appellant contends that the court erred in submitting that issue to the jury and instructing upon it. We agree. Consequential damages are sustainable if they flow naturally and inevitably from a breach of contract and are so related to it as to have been within the contemplation of the parties when they entered into it. * * * The emotional reactions peculiar to a particular individual which might flow from a breach of a contract of sale of an automobile are too subjective and variable to be contemplated prior to a breach of contract, or ascertainable afterward. Such suffering, if any, is not compensable in an action for damages for breach of contract. * * *

For the reasons stated hereinbefore, it was error to allow the respondent damages in the amounts of $300 for mental anguish and $200 for loss of use of an automobile, and the judgment must be modified and reduced in this respect. [Note: Loss of use is recoverable in many jurisdictions.]

2. Liquidated Damages Recoverable When Not a Penalty

MEDAK v. HEKIMIAN

241 Or. 38, 404 P.2d 203 (1965)

HOLMAN, Justice.   Plaintiffs were real estate agents and leased from defendants in January of 1952 premises for a business office in a building on the southeast corner of Tenth and Broadway in the city of Portland. * * *

In 1954 defendants were approached by the promoters of Lloyd Center, a proposed integrated shopping complex of enormous proportions. They wished to purchase the premises, a portion of which plaintiffs occupied, for inclusion in the planned complex. * * * As a result, plaintiffs and defendants entered into another contract whereby defendants agreed to construct another building on the southwest corner of the same intersection on property also owned by them and to rent a portion of the premises to plaintiffs for a period of five years commencing in January 1957 at the expiration of plaintiffs' lease on the premises which was being sold to the Lloyd Center. * * * The agreement also provided that in the event defendants did not construct the building defendants would pay plaintiffs $5,000 as liquidated damages for their failure to perform.

Defendants failed to erect the building as agreed, and this action was brought to recover the $5,000 provided as liquidated damages for the contract's breach. The defendants appeal from a judgment of $5,000 entered upon a jury verdict. * * *

The defendants claim the provision in the contract providing they would pay to plaintiffs the sum of $5,000 as liquidated damages if defendants did not construct the building was in fact a penalty and therefore not enforceable and that the court erred in not so finding as a matter of law.

* * * Two criteria seem to be paramount in determining whether the sum provided to be paid is for the purpose of securing performance of the contract, and therefore a penalty, or whether it is intended to be paid in lieu of performance, and therefore liquidated damages. At the time of the making of the contract would the sum provided seem to bear any reasonable relationship to the anticipated damages and would the actual damages be difficult or impossible of ascertainment? If both answers are "yes," the sum provided would normally be considered liquidated damages.

* * * The agreed value of the five year extension of the lease in the old building which plaintiffs gave up was $100 per month, or a total of $6,000. Would two and one-half times the space in a new building be worth $5,000 more over the five-year period of the extension? The sum is not so grossly disproportionate to the probable actual damages resulting from failure to perform as to require it to be called a penalty. * * * Two and one-half years hence would there be other space in the same locality of like size and condition which would serve as a guide to prove plaintiffs' damage? Could the parties be sure that at that time the damage could be accurately estimated? If no space were available, it was possible plaintiffs could suffer actual damage because of loss of business which would not be compensable under the usual measure of damage. There would appear to be nothing reprehensible or unreasonable in the parties agreeing to a sum which would compensate plaintiffs for such actual anticipated loss in case of breach. * * *

These imponderables at the time of making a contract would seem to justify the use of a sum as liquidated damages as long as it was not disproportionate to actual anticipated damages.

The trial judge refused to say it was a penalty. We do not disagree. * * *

[Judgment for plaintiff.]

3. Damaged Party Has Duty to Mitigate Damages

AMERICAN BROADCASTING–PARAMOUNT THEATRES, INC. v. AMERICAN MFRS. MUTUAL INS. CO.

48 Misc.2d 397, 265 N.Y.S.2d 76 (1965), affirmed 24 App.Div.2d 851, 265 N.Y.S.2d 577, affirmed 17 N.Y.2d 849, 271 N.Y.S.2d 284, 218 N.E.2d 324, certiorari denied 385 U.S. 931, 87 S.Ct. 291

GELLER, Justice. This is an action for breach of a sponsorship contract brought by plaintiff, herein referred to as "ABC", against defendant insurance companies, collectively known as The Kemper Insurance Companies and herein referred to as "Kemper."

On August 15, 1962, the parties entered into a television network contract whereby Kemper agreed to sponsor one program per week of the ABC Evening Report news program over a 26-week period beginning October 17, 1962. On November 9, 1962, the fourth telecast under Kemper's contract, a "promotional announcement" was made at the end of the sponsored program and just before the scheduled time was up, regarding the Howard K. Smith program on November 11 entitled "The Political Obituary of Richard M. Nixon," evidently occasioned by his recent defeat in the contest for the California governorship. Alger Hiss appeared on that program and attacked Richard M. Nixon. This caused considerable public controversy.

Protesting the appearance of Hiss on the ABC–TV Network and, in particular, the promotional announcement at the close of its sponsored Evening Report program and referring to the numerous complaints received from its agents and policyholders, Kemper cancelled its participating sponsorship of Evening Report by telephone on November 13, 1962 and letter on November 14, 1962. ABC replied that same day that it intended to hold Kemper "fully responsible for any and all sums due and to become due to us under the terms of the agreement between us dated August 15, 1962."
* * *

However, market value is not always the measure of recovery—as for example, where there is no market for the type of goods involved, or where it is a contract for personal services, or where the subject matter of the contract is perishable. * * *

Advertising contracts have been held to fall into the latter category, so that upon wrongful withdrawal by an advertiser the publisher is entitled to recover the contract price, reduced, as though the contract was one for services, by such amount as was or could have been obtained in the exercise of reasonable efforts to minimize damages by the use of that space for other advertisements * * * Moreover, the subject matter—commercial minutes or time—is perishable, since, if not sold in time, it has vanished and is of no value to anyone. Furthermore, there has been no showing that there is a market or market value for commercial television minutes in the same sense as there is a market and market value for goods and commodities.

* * * To keep the subject in perspective, it should be pointed out that the price in Kemper's contract dated August 15, 1962 amounted to about $7,500 net per commercial minute (after deducting 15% agency commission); that ABC's selloffs of 13 1/2 of the 55 minutes were at an average net price of $4,080 per minute; * * *

The court determines that ABC made reasonable efforts, in light of the existent circumstances and consistent with its regular business practice, to selloff the available Kemper 55 minutes. * * *

The period from November to April is off-season for the procurement of television sponsorship. The major contracts are negotiated months before the fall season, which commences about the latter part of September.
* * *

The selloffs by ABC, less the station compensation payments attributable thereto, and by its 5 owned and operated stations realized $36,664.04. Thus, ABC's recoverable damages are in the sum of $265,047.21. * * *

4. Specific Performance Proper When Property Unique

COCHRANE v. SZPAKOWSKI

355 Pa. 357, 49 A.2d 692 (1946)

DREW, Justice. The learned court below having decreed specific performance of a written contract entered into by defendant, Mary Szpakowski, and
plaintiff, John F. Cochrane, for the sale of her restaurant and retail liquor
business, she took this appeal. * * * Following a verbal agreement entered
into by appellant and appellee on May 18, 1945, they executed a written
contract four days later for the sale on or before June 15, 1945, by appellant
to appellee of this business, together with all fixtures and contents, except
stock, for $7,000. The agreement also provided that appellant would transfer
to appellee as part of the consideration, her liquor license, if approved by the
Pennsylvania Liquor Control Board, and further that she would surrender
the leased premises to him. * * *

The general rule undoubtedly is that the specific performance of contracts for the sale of personal property will not be enforced for the reason
that ordinarily compensation for the breach of the contract may be had by
way of damages. A well-recognized exception to the rule is where the thing
contracted for cannot be purchased in the market, and, because of its nature
or the circumstances, the delivery of the thing itself, and not mere pecuniary
compensation, is the redress practically required. * * * In the instant case,
it is obvious that equity does have jurisdiction because a similar restaurant
and liquor business to the one in question could not be purchased in the
market, and therefore could not be reproduced by money damages.
* * * Furthermore, this contract involves the transfer and ownership of a
retail liquor license, the value of which cannot be accurately determined in
an action at law. It seems unrealistic to us to close our eyes to the fact that
* * * retail liquor licenses cannot be issued by the Board in the City of
Pittsburgh because the number allowed * * * is greatly exceeded by the
existing licenses. This gives to the license, here involved a peculiar value
depending upon the business ability and the popularity of the owner, which
cannot be accurately or adequately measured or compensated for in an
action at law. * * *

Decree affirmed, at appellant's costs.

PROBLEMS

1. Plaintiff ordered from defendant two dresses for his prospective bride to be made
after model 46A and to be used on the honeymoon. Plaintiff told defendant at the
time that the wedding was to take place on January 10 and that he was incurring
great expense for the wedding. Defendant promised to have the gowns ready on or
before January 9 but did not do so. Plaintiff alleges that as a result of the defendant's

failure, his prospective bride changed the wedding date, and he suffered a loss in the amount of $1,000 for foods, wines, entertainment, and other expenses. Decision?

2.   Defendant signed a contract with plaintiff for the installation of a fire detection system on their premises for $498. The contract had a cancellation clause that read, "In the event of cancellation of this agreement, the owner agrees to pay 1/3 of the contract price as liquidated damages." About 9:00 the next morning, following the signing of the contract and before the plaintiff had done anything in respect to the contract, defendant cancelled. Plaintiff sues to enforce the liquidated damage clause. Decision?

3.   Plaintiff wrote a telegram in a secret code and tendered it to the telegraph company for transmission to T. Due to the carelessness of the telegraph company employee, the message never reached T. As a result, plaintiff lost a very valuable business deal with a profit of $10,000. Plaintiff now sues the telegraph company for the loss of profit. Decision?

4.   Plaintiff purchased a demonstrator automobile from defendant. The odometer on the car was set back by defendant approximately 7,000 miles showing mileage of only 165 miles. Defendant represented to plaintiff that the mileage on the odometer was the correct mileage. Immediately upon learning of the true mileage, plaintiff sued for rescission, compensatory damages, and punitive damages. Defendant claims punitive damages should not be awarded. Discuss.

5.   Seller and buyer entered into a written contract for the sale of real estate on certain terms. After the contract was entered into, the buyer changed her mind because of financial reverses and asked the seller to be relieved of the contract. Seller was anxious for the sale to be completed because he had tried without success to sell the property for a long time. Furthermore, although the consideration for the contract was adequate, the value of the real estate dropped slightly after the contract was entered into. Seller sues buyer for specific performance. Decision?

6.   "Tricky" Blowhard was a candidate in the primary election for the U. S. Senate. He had a contract with the XYZ television corporation to televise two important political speeches one week before the election. Through a mixup in programming, the speeches were never televised. "Tricky" lost the election and now sues for breach of contract, claiming damages consisting of campaign expenses and the salary he would have received as a senator. Decision?

7.   Primo Carnera, a heavyweight boxer, had a contract with the Madison Square Garden Corporation to fight the winner of the Schmeling-Scribling contest. The contract provided that Carnera could not render services as a boxer in any major boxing contest pending the fight between Schmeling and Scribling. Thereafter, Carnera made a contract to fight Jack Sharkey on a date prior to the S-S fight. Madison Square Garden Corporation seeks an injunction to prevent the Carnera-Sharkey fight. Carnera claims the prohibition violates the Thirteenth Amendment. Decision?

8.   S and B enter into a written contract whereby S agrees to sell certain real property to B. Through a mutual mistake, an incorrect description is inserted in the contract. B prefers the mistaken description, because he will obtain more land for the price agreed upon. S, however, seeks reformation of the contract to show the correct description. Decision?

9. (a) Alice hires a contractor to remodel her kitchen for a total price of $5,000 due on completion. After an insignificant part of the work is finished, the contractor quits. It costs Alice $6,000 to get another contractor to finish the job. Alice claims damages in the amount of $1,000. Decision?

(b) Under the same contract, contractor substantially completes the contract and then he quits. The value of his work is $3,500. It costs Alice $2,500 to get another contractor to finish the job. Contractor sues Alice for $3,500. Decision?

10. C, a professional football coach, is fired by M without due cause after three years on a five year contract. His salary is $200,000 per year. He attempts to find similar employment but is unable to do so. After one year of searching, he is finally offered a job as coach of the Podunk High School football team at $40,000 a year. He refuses the job. At the end of two years he brings suit against M for $400,000. Decision?

Chapter 18

THIRD PARTIES

A. THIRD PARTY BENEFICIARIES

1. IN GENERAL

Often contracts are made between two parties for the express purpose of benefiting a third party. A common example is a contract between an insurance company and a husband under which the husband's life is insured so that on his death the amount of the policy will be paid to his wife. In such a case, his wife is the beneficiary of the contract. Even though she is not a party to the insurance contract, she has a direct, personal cause of action for any breach of the promised performance.

The third party cannot enforce the contract unless it was made expressly for his or her benefit. Also, the beneficiary can recover only if there was an enforceable contract between the original parties to the contract. Thus, any defense between the original parties will also be effective against the third party.

There are three types of third-party beneficiary contracts: (1) donee, (2) creditor, and (3) incidental. Although nearly all jurisdictions permit donee or creditor beneficiaries to bring an action to enforce a contract, courts will not enforce an incidental beneficiary contract.

2. DONEE BENEFICIARY

If the purpose of the contract is to make a gift to the third party, it is called a third-party donee beneficiary contract. Thus, the insurance illustration is an example of a donee beneficiary contract. The wife is the donee beneficiary of the contract.

3. CREDITOR CONTRACT

If the purpose of the contract between the original parties is to satisfy an obligation to a third party, it is a creditor beneficiary contract. A creditor beneficiary is a creditor of the promisee whose obligation will be discharged to the extent that the promisor performs his or her promise. Thus, where a tenant assigns a lease to a subtenant and the subtenant agrees to perform all of the terms of the lease, the agreement between the tenant and the subtenant is for the benefit of the lessor (landlord). The landlord may sue the subtenant as a creditor beneficiary (the landlord also maintains his or her legal rights against the original tenant).

Similarly, when a business is sold and the buyer assumes the liabilities of the seller's business, the creditors of the business are creditor beneficiaries of the agreement between the seller and the buyer. The creditors have a cause of action against the buyer of the business and maintain their right to recover against the seller of the business if the buyer does not pay. As another example, if the owner of an automobile that was financed by a bank and upon which there is still an amount due makes a contract to sell the automobile to a buyer and the buyer agrees to pay off the balance of the loan, the bank is a third-party creditor beneficiary of the contract between the seller and the buyer and can hold the buyer to his or her promise.

4. INCIDENTAL OR REMOTE BENEFICIARIES

A person who is only remotely benefited by a contract cannot enforce it. In such case, it is not the intention of either the promisee or the promisor that the third person benefit from the contract. Thus, where a city makes a contract with a contractor to pave Balboa Avenue, property owners living along Balboa Avenue cannot sue the contractor if he fails to perform, because they are only incidental beneficiaries. The city made the contract to benefit all the members of the public and not primarily for the individual property owners on Balboa Avenue. Similarly, if Mary promises John that she will marry him if he gives her a new Cadillac and John fails to purchase and give her the Cadillac after the marriage, General Motors cannot sue John, since it is only a remote or incidental beneficiary of the contract. Other examples: Smith hires Jones to paint and relandscape his house. Jones' performance may well increase the value of an adjoining house owned by Dickson, but Dickson is only an incidental beneficiary and cannot enforce the contract between Smith and Jones. Or Jordan promises Paula a box of candy from the local store if she will care for his pet dog. Again, the store is only an incidental beneficiary of the Jordan/Paula contract.

5. RESCISSION

Under the modern view, most courts, and the Second Restatement of Contracts, both donee and creditor beneficiaries of a contract are classified as *intended beneficiaries*. The promisor and promisee (the parties to the contract that creates the donee or creditor beneficiary) lose their power to modify or revoke the contract made for an intended beneficiary whenever the beneficiary learns of the contract *and* (1) brings suit against the promisor, *or* (2) materially changes his or her position in reasonable reliance on the contract, *or* (3) manifests his or her assent to the benefits at the request of either the promisor or the promisee.

Some states have special statutes regarding insurance policies (e.g., California Insurance Code Section 10170(e) provides that the contract may be rescinded unless the rights of the beneficiary have been expressly declared *irrevocable;* thus, in California the beneficiary of an insurance policy *can* be changed unless otherwise stated).

B. ASSIGNMENTS

1. IN GENERAL

An assignment is a transfer by one party to a contract of some or all of his or her rights under the contract to a person who is not a party to the contract (e.g., patient owes doctor $100 for services rendered and does not pay, and doctor assigns the right to the money to a collection agency). The party making the assignment is called the "assignor," and the party to whom the assignment is made is called the "assignee."

No special language or form is necessary to make an assignment. Thus, an oral assignment is valid unless required by statute to be in writing (e.g., wage assignments generally must be in writing).

An assignment can be total or partial (e.g., a creditor may assign part of a claim and retain the remainder of the claim).

Consideration is not necessary to make an assignment; thus, an assignment may be made as a gift.

2. CONTRACTS ORDINARILY ASSIGNABLE

Whether a contract is assignable depends upon its terms and the nature of the contract. Ordinarily, a contract is assignable. Thus, a contract for the sale and delivery of all the grapes of a certain quality that the seller was to raise on a certain vineyard for 10 years was assignable to the person who purchased the seller's land.

Under the U.C.C. Section 2–210, contracts are assignable subject to certain restrictions. See Chapter 3. E. infra.

Although an offer is not assignable, an option contract, which is a contract whereby the seller keeps the offer open, is assignable.

3. CONTRACTS NOT ASSIGNABLE

A. PERSONAL SERVICE CONTRACTS

If the contract calls for the skill, credit, or other personal quality of the promisor, it is not assignable since the performance received from the assignee would be different from that required by the contract; e.g., a famous singer cannot assign his contract to sing at a certain night club to another singer.

B. EXPRESS PROVISION

If the contract contains an express provision against assignment ("This contract is not assignable by either party and any attempted assignment will make this contract void"), generally, the provision will be upheld and the contract will not be assignable (e.g., lease containing express provision against assignment without written permission of landlord is generally upheld). However, this clause can be waived (e.g., implied waiver when nonassigning party [landlord] accepted rent from assignee [new tenant]).

A provision against assigning a contract would not prohibit an assignment of the money due or to become due under the contract, nor of money damages for breach of the contract.

c. Rights Under Contract of Employment

Where there is an existing contract of employment, money to become due or other rights thereunder may be assigned. However, where the contract of employment is not yet in existence, the general rule is that the assignment is not enforceable (e.g., cannot assign future wages unless presently employed under an enforceable contract).

d. Claims for Personal Wrongs

A right of action founded on a wrong of purely personal nature is not assignable (e.g., slander, assault and battery, negligent personal injuries). However, the *judgment* based on such action is assignable.

e. Under the U.C.C.

Under Section 2–210(2), a court can prohibit an assignment in any one of the following cases:

1.   Where it would materially affect the duty of the nonassigning party. For example, A contracts to sell to B all of B's requirements of a certain product during a certain period. If B's requirements are materially different from C's, a potential assignee, B cannot assign the contract to C.

2.   Where the assignment would increase the burden or risk on the nonassigning party. For example, A contracts to sell B goods according to B's specifications as to quality. B assigns to C, whose specifications as to quality vary materially from B's. B cannot assign to C, as this would materially increase the burden or risk on A.

3.   Where the assignment would impair materially the nonassigning party's chance of obtaining a return performance. For example, S, a seller, has a continuing obligation in regard to goods already delivered under contract to B, who is to pay part of the price at a future date. S may not assign his right to payment, since assignment may diminish his interest in continuing his obligation in regard to the goods.

Under Section 2–210(2), a right to money damages for breach of contract may be assigned despite agreement otherwise.

Under Section 9–318(4), sums due and to become due under contracts of sale can be assigned despite a provision to the contrary, even if made to an assignee who took with full knowledge that the account debtor had sought to prohibit or restrict assignment of the claims. The Official Comment states "as accounts and other rights under contracts have become the collateral which secures an ever increasing number of financing transactions, it has been necessary to reshape the law so that these intangibles, like negotiable instruments and negotiable documents of title, can be freely assigned."

4. EFFECT OF ASSIGNMENT

A. LIABILITY OF ASSIGNOR

The assignor cannot escape his or her burdens on the contract by an assignment and still remains liable as a surety to the original party. This is true even though the assignee assumes the obligations of the contract. In other words, the assignor can assign the benefits of the contract but is still liable for the burdens. For example, a buyer of goods assigns her right to purchase the goods to a new buyer (assignee). The original buyer remains liable on the original contract if the new buyer defaults.

U.C.C. Section 2–210(1) states, "No delegation of performance relieves the party delegating of any duty to perform or any liability for breach."

B. LIABILITY OF ASSIGNEE

Under the minority and traditional view, the assignee does not become bound to perform the obligations of the assignor by merely accepting the assignment. However, if the assignee expressly assumes the assignor's promise to perform, he or she is liable to the creditor, since the creditor would be a third-party beneficiary to such an assignment if it appeared that it was made for the creditor's benefit. For example, S sells his business to B and as part of the contract, B promises to pay off all of the existing creditors of the business. B has assumed the seller's promise to perform. If B fails to pay off the debts, he is also liable to S for breach of the assumption agreement.

Under the modern view, the Restatement of Contracts, and Section 2–210(4) of the U.C.C., an acceptance by the assignee of an assignment of a contract constitutes a promise by the assignee to perform the duties of the assignor (in the absence of language or circumstances to the contrary). The promise is enforceable by either the assignor or the other party to the original contract. This type of assignment is the normal commercial assignment (substitution of the assignee for the assignor both as to rights and duties). For example, S sells, transfers, and assigns to B all of his rights and obligations in connection with a specified business. Although B promised nothing, it will be implied that he promised to pay off the obligation from the acceptance of the assignment.

Under Section 2–210(5) of the U.C.C., the nonassigning original party has a stake in the reliability of the person with whom he or she has closed the original contract and is therefore entitled to due assurance that any delegated performance will be properly forthcoming. Thus, he or she may treat the assignment as creating reasonable grounds for insecurity and demand assurances from the assignee. For example, a purchaser of goods to be specially manufactured feels insecure when the manufacturer assigns the contract to a second unknown manufacturer. The purchaser thus demands a provision for withholding stated amounts of the purchase price until satisfactory completion of the stated performance.

c. Rights of Assignee

After the assignment, the assignee has all of the legal rights of the assignor. However, to assert these rights, the assignee must give notice to the nonassigning original party. After notice of the assignment, performance by the obligor to the assignor does not extinguish the obligation (i.e., the obligor must perform his obligation to the assignee after actual notice of the assignment). For example, after the seller learns that the buyer has assigned his right to purchase the goods to the new buyer (assignee), the seller must deliver to the new buyer to extinguish his obligation. Or, after the doctor assigns his fee to a collection agency, the debtor must pay the collection agency to extinguish the obligation.

After the assignment, the assignee "stands in the shoes" of the assignor. In other words, the assignee takes all the rights of the assignor subject to any defenses that the obligor has against the assignor prior to the notice of the assignment. For example, a painter may assign his claim for payment resulting from the painting of a home to a collection agency, but the homeowner may assert against the collection agency-assignee any claims for damages sustained by the owner because the painter did not properly perform the contract, necessitating the owner's paying a second painter to correct the defective work.

Clauses are frequently inserted in installment contracts that provide that the buyer will not assert any defenses he may have (such as a defective product) against an assignee of the contract (a financing company). These clauses have led to litigation, and their present validity under case law is in confusion. The majority rule, and the modern trend, is that the clause is ineffective. In some jurisdictions, the clauses have been held void as attempts to create negotiable instruments outside the framework of Article 3, or on grounds of public policy. In many states, such waivers have been invalidated by consumer protection statutes (e.g., California Civil Code Section 1804.2). In some states, courts have found such waivers invalid because of the close connection the assignee of the contract has with the original transaction.

In 1977, the Federal Trade Commission invalidated waiver of defense provisions in consumer credit transactions. Also, under the Uniform Consumer Credit Code Section 2–404, Alternative A, the clause is ineffective.

Under the U.C.C. Section 9–206(1), such waivers are enforceable only if the assignee (finance company or lender) purchased the contract *for value,* in *good faith,* and *without notice* of any defenses that the obligor might have against the assignor.

For defenses an account debtor has against an assignee of an account where the debtor has not made an enforceable agreement not to assert defenses or claims as provided in Section 9–206, see U.C.C. Section 9–318(1).

5.　PRIORITIES AMONG SUCCESSIVE ASSIGNEES

Sometimes the assignor, because of mistake or fraud, assigns the same claim to more than one assignee. For example, creditor assigns a claim for $1,000 to A on January 10 and then assigns the same claim to B on January 12. Which assignee prevails against the debtor?

A.　Assignee First in Time

The so-called American rule, adopted in most states, including New York, gives priority to the assignee first in time on the theory that the legal title passed from the assignor after the first assignment. Thus the assignor has nothing left to assign to the second assignee. Of course, the second assignee will have a cause of action against the assignor.

B.　First Assignee to Give Notice

The minority rule, followed by California and Florida, gives priority to the assignee who first gives notice to the obligor on the theory that an assignment should be governed by equitable rules (i.e., the first assignee should perfect his or her right by giving notice to the debtor, since by failure to do so, he or she leaves the assignor with the power to deceive the second assignee, an innocent party, by another assignment.

C.　The U.C.C.

In the area of accounts receivable, the U.C.C. (Article 9) attempts to alleviate the problem of priorities by requiring the filing of the assignment of accounts receivable in a "financing statement." This gives notice to all prospective purchasers of the accounts receivable that they have previously been assigned. While detailed rules govern priority as to specialized types of contract rights, the basic rule is that assignments are protected in order of time of their filing.

ILLUSTRATIVE CASES

1. Third Party Donee Beneficiary Contracts Are Enforceable

SAYLOR v. SAYLOR
389 S.W.2d 904 (Ky. 1965)

PALMORE, Judge.　This is a declaratory judgment action to determine the ownership of a bank savings account. The facts are stipulated. The contest is between the administrator and the widow of Adrian M. Saylor. The trial court found in favor of the widow, and the administrator appeals.

The account was opened by Mr. Saylor on March 19, 1962, with the deposit of $6,540.65 derived from the sale of government bonds owned exclusively by him. The pass book issued by the bank to Mr. Saylor on March 19, 1962, was made out in the names of "Mr. or Mrs. Adrian M. Saylor," and the bank's ledger card for the account was established and thenceforth maintained in the names of "Adrian M. Saylor or Kathleen B. Saylor." Kathleen is the widow.

On June 15, 1963, Mr. Saylor deposited $2,132.60 of his own money in the account, and the deposit was entered in the pass book. There were no other deposits, and for purposes of this opinion it may be assumed that there were no withdrawals whatever prior to the death of Mr. Saylor on May 15, 1964.

The question is whether the balance of the account at Mr. Saylor's death is payable wholly to the administrator, wholly to the widow, or half to each. The trial court held it was a survivorship account, passing wholly to the widow.

It is recognized in this state that a person may by depositing his own money in the names of himself and another create the equivalent of a tenancy in common or a tenancy by the entirety, depending upon his intent. [Citations.] As in the case of other intangibles such as bonds or stock certificates, the right gratuitously conferred on the other party is recognized and is enforceable on the theory of third party beneficiary contract. It is not necessary that such a contract be supported by a consideration moving from the beneficiary, and it is not necessary that a "gift" be proved. [Citation.]

"The prevailing modern view is that a donee-beneficiary has a right of action to enforce a promise made for his benefit. In this respect, the courts so holding have rejected any requirement of consideration, privity, or obligation as between the promisee and the third person." [Citation.]

"In this jurisdiction a party beneficiary of a contract may look to the promisor directly and sue him in his own name to enforce a promise made for plaintiff's benefit, even though he is a stranger, it being sufficient that there is a consideration between the parties who made the agreement for the benefit of the third party." [Citations.]

"It is not essential, in order to enable a third person to recover on a contract made and intended for his benefit, that he knew of the contract at the time it was made." [Citation.] A fortiori, that Mrs. Saylor did not sign the signature card or otherwise participate in the establishment of the account is immaterial.

By his deposit of money a contract was created between Mr. Saylor and the bank. By causing the account to be established and maintained in the names of himself and his wife, in the absence of evidence to the contrary there is a rebuttable presumption that Mr. Saylor intended to and did make his wife a third party beneficiary of the contract.

That Mr. Saylor did not have Mrs. Saylor sign the signature card may indicate that he did not wish her to make any withdrawals. If so, that circumstance is consistent with a purpose to give her the right of survivorship, because otherwise there would have been no reason at all for him to establish a joint account.

The judgment is affirmed.

2. Assignee May Perform Contract When No Special Skill

LA RUE v. GROEZINGER

84 Cal. 281, 24 P. 42 (1890)

HAYNE, C. This was an action for damages for the breach of a contract to buy grapes. The substance of the material portions of the contract was as follows:

One Hopper agreed to sell all the grapes which he might raise during a period of ten years * * *. In consideration whereof the defendant agreed to accept the grapes and pay for them (after delivery) at the rate of $25 per ton * * *.

The parties performed this contract for five years. At the end of that time, * * * Hopper conveyed the vineyard and assigned the contract to the plaintiff. * * * The crop of the following year was grown, gathered, and tendered by the plaintiff. The defendant refused to accept it, saying that he had no contract with the plaintiff, and * * * that the contract was not assignable. * * * The Civil Code of this state provides that written contracts "for the payment of money or personal property" may be transferred * * *. It is clear, however, that the provision cannot be construed to render assignable all contracts whatever, regardless of their nature or effect, but must be taken with some qualification.

In the first place, it was not intended to render null any agreement that the parties may have made on the subject. Hence, if the contract itself provides in terms that it is not transferable, it certainly cannot be transferred, although it otherwise might be so. * * *

In the next place, although the language may not show an intention that the contract should not be assigned, yet the nature of the case may be such that performance by another would be *an essentially different thing* from that contracted for. Thus a picture by one artist is an essentially different thing from a picture on the same subject by another artist; and so of a book composed by an author, or any other act or thing where the skill, credit, or other personal quality of circumstance of the party is a distinctive characteristic of the thing contracted for, or a material inducement to the contract. * * *

If, therefore, the case before us comes within either of the qualifications above stated, then it must be conceded that the contract was not assignable. * * * There is nothing in the language which excludes the idea of performance by another * * * and * * * there is nothing in the nature or circumstances of the case which shows that the skill or other personal quality of the party was a distinctive characteristic of the thing stipulated for, or a material inducement to the contract. There is no evidence that grapes for wine-making, containing a specified amount of saccharine matter, raised upon a particular vineyard by one man, would necessarily or probably be different from grapes raised from the same vines by another man. * * *

It is not impossible that one man might have some peculiar skill or secret by which he could raise better grapes from the same vines than other men could. But there is no evidence that there was any such peculiarity about the original owner of this vineyard, and we do not think that the court will *assume*that there was. * * * We cannot see any reason that would make this contract nonassignable * * *.

[Judgment for plaintiff.]

3. Ratification of Assignment of Personal Service Contracts

SEALE v. BATES

145 Colo. 430, 359 P.2d 356 (1961)

DOYLE, Justice.   Plaintiffs in error will be referred to by name or as they were designated in the trial court where they were plaintiffs in an action against John Bates, individually, the Bates Dance Studio, Inc. and the Dance Studio of Denver, Inc. The Seales sought to recover $2,040 which had been paid to the Bates Dance Studio to defray the cost of 300 hours of dance instruction. * * * From their complaints it would appear that the contracts which the plaintiffs entered into with the Bates Dance Studio had been assigned to the Dance Studio of Denver, doing business as Dale Dance Studio. * * * The Seales were told that the "students and the instructors, the entire organization was transferred to the Dale Studios; that we would have the same instructors, the same instruction, a continuation of what we had had at Bates." They proceeded to take lessons at Dale, but after some 30 one-half hours of instruction they became dissatisfied with the conditions. * * * This dissatisfaction arose from the fact that the room was much smaller and more crowded and the music from another room interfered with the lessons. Each of the Seales did not have his or her own instructor, Mr. Seale being required to take his lessons from a male instructor; there were difficulties in getting appointments and on some occasions when appointments were made an instructor would not be available. * * * As a result of this dissatisfaction, Mr. and Mrs. Seale stopped taking lessons in May of 1957. The following August they complained to Mr. John Bates of the Bates Studio and demanded that he refund their money or make proper arrangements for completing their contract. Bates informed them that his school was then closed and that there was no money to reimburse them.

   * * * The basis for dispositions as to the Bates and Dale Studios was the assent of the plaintiffs to the assumption by Dale of the obligations under the contracts; that this acceptance of Dale was apparent from the plaintiffs' conduct. * * *

   In seeking reversal, plaintiffs assert that the trial court erred * * * * * * *

   In failing to hold that the duties under these contracts were personal, therefore non-assignable.

   * * * The argument of plaintiffs that this was a personal service contract and therefore non-assignable without their consent is valid. * * * This, however, does not furnish a reason for holding that plaintiffs are now entitled to recover. On the contrary, there is evidence to support the trial court's

finding and conclusion that the plaintiffs accepted the assignment as such; they did not elect to rescind when it was brought to their attention that the contracts had been assigned to Dale Dance Studio. The undisputed evidence shows that they accepted the assignment and proceeded to take lessons from the Dale Dance Studio. This conduct is inconsistent with plaintiffs' present theory that they at all times objected to the assignment. Had they refused to receive instruction from Dale and had they taken the position that their contract was with Bates and no other, there would be substance to their present contention that this violation justified the rescission. * * * Accordingly the trial court's finding and conclusion that the plaintiffs waived any rights which may have arisen from the assignment must be upheld. * * *

[Judgment for defendant.]

PROBLEMS

1. Mr. Smith takes out a policy of insurance on his life with his mother as the beneficiary. Several years later, Mr. Smith marries and desires to change the beneficiary of the policy to his wife. Discuss his right to do so without permission of his mother.

2. S entered into a contract with B to sell a going business to him. The sales price was to be paid in installments. Shortly thereafter, B assigned the contract to T, who assumed all the liabilities and obligations under the contract. Prior to complete payment of the sales price, T assigned the contract to X, who assumed all the liabilities and obligations. Shortly thereafter, X became insolvent. S seeks a judgment against B and T. B defends on the grounds that he is under no obligation to pay, since T assumed all liabilities and obligations. T defends on the grounds that the second assignment operated as a rescission of the agreement between B and T. Decision?

3. A has been injured in an automobile accident and retains B as his attorney to represent him. Later B assigns the retainer contract to T without A's permission. A seeks your advice as to whether he must accept T as his new attorney.

4. Seller and buyer enter into a contract for the sale of a carload of tomatoes. The contract states that the right of either party to money damages in case of breach of contract cannot be assigned. The seller delivers buyer inferior goods, causing him $1,000 in damages. Buyer assigns his action to a collection agency for collection. Seller defends on the grounds the contract prohibited assignment of the claim. Decision?

5. S sold an automobile to B by a contract which contained a clause prohibiting S from assigning the money due under the contract. S needs money and desires to assign the contract to T, who knows of the prohibiting clause. Can S assign the contract without B's permission?

6. Tenant assigns the balance of his five-year store lease to assignee, who assumes all of the burdens of the lease. Shortly after the assignment, the assignee becomes bankrupt. The landlord seeks unpaid and future rentals for the balance of the term from the tenant. Tenant defends on the grounds that he had assigned the lease and the assignee expressly assumed the burdens of the lease. Decision?

7. A contracted with B to do some plumbing work in B's home. A did not have a license, although a statute required a license as a condition to recovering for plumbing work. After A completed the work, he assigned the right to the money for the work to T. B refuses to pay T, so T sues B on the contract between A and B. Decision?

8. Debtor owes creditor $1,000. Creditor assigns the claim to T, who promptly mails notice to the debtor. The debtor, however, fails to read the notice of the assignment from T and pays the creditor in full without knowing of the assignment. T seeks payment from debtor, and debtor contends that his payment to creditor without notice is a defense. Decision?

9. Debtor owes creditor $1,000. Creditor assigns the claims to A on June 1 and then by mistake assigns the same claim to B on June 4. On June 4, B gives notice of the assignment to debtor. On June 5, A gives notice of the assignment to the debtor. Both A and B claim the $1,000 from debtor. Who prevails?

10. Buyer purchased a new car from the seller on the installment plan. The installment contract contained a clause waiving any defenses the buyer had in the sale against any assignee of the contract. The bank purchased the installment contract for value, in good faith, and without notice of the buyer's defense. Buyer does not want to pay on the installment contract because the car has proven defective. Discuss.

Part III

AGENCY

Chapter 19

INTRODUCTION

A. NATURE OF AGENCY

1. IN GENERAL

Agency is the fiduciary relationship between two persons in which one person (the agent) acts for or represents another (the principal) in dealings with third persons (e.g., real estate broker representing homeowner).

2. SERVANT OR EMPLOYEE

Although most of the laws relating to servants and employees are the same as those relative to agents, the relationship is not identical. Normally, a servant or employee is one who gives personal service as a member of a business or domestic household and is subject to control by the employer as to his or her physical duties or activities. A servant or employee usually does work that is more ministerial in nature, has no discretion as to the means to accomplish the end for which he or she is employed, and seldom has authority to represent the master or employer in business dealings. A servant or employee sells or gives his or her time, while a nonservant agent is paid primarily for results rather than for the time it takes to accomplish them. At times, an employee will act in a dual relationship as an agent (e.g., the store manager is an employee regarding internal affairs but is an agent when purchasing inventory). Often the lines are not clearly drawn as to whether a person is acting as an employee or as an agent.

The agency relationship is created when the servant or employee represents the employer in transactions with third persons. The employee or servant then becomes the agent and the employer or master is the principal.

3. INDEPENDENT CONTRACTOR

An independent contractor is a person who contracts to do a piece of work according to his or her own methods and without being subject to the control of his or her employer except as to the result of the work (e.g., building contractor), whereas in an agency, the right of the principal to direct what the agent shall do or not do is basic. Also, an independent contractor does not represent the employer in business dealings.

It is important to distinguish between an agent, servant, or employee on the one hand, and an independent contractor on the other hand. Under the doctrine of *respondeat superior,* the principal, master, or employer is liable for the tort of his or her agent, servant, or employee committed while acting within the scope of his employment, whereas, the employer generally is not liable for the tort of an independent contractor. Also, the benefits of the Workers' Compensation laws do not apply to independent contractors.

The following case illustrates the general rule concerning liability of independent contractors:

> **FACTS** Plaintiff was injured by tripping over a piece of wire left on a sidewalk by a newsboy. The issue was whether the newsboy was an agent of the newspaper under the doctrine of *respondeat superior* or was operating as an independent contractor.
>
> **DECISION** The court observed that ruling on control exercised over newspaper carriers was a difficult problem. It found in this case that the managers sold papers directly to the newspaper carriers, who then resold the papers at a profit. Any losses on unpaid accounts were borne by the newspaper carriers, who had no assigned territories and could sell competitors' papers. Finding practically no control to exist, the judge found the newsboy to be an independent contractor and granted the newspaper's motion for summary judgment.
>
> *Mirto v. News-Journal Co.* (50 Del. (11 Terry) 103, 123 A.2d 863 [1956])

(Compare this with Illustrative Case no. 2, *Peairs v. Florida Publishing Co.* at the end of the chapter.)

However, the courts have applied several exceptions to this rule and have found employers liable for the acts of the independent contractors. Exceptions to this rule have been held in the following instances:

1. The employer was negligent in the selection, instruction, or supervision of the contractor.

2. Situations in which strict liability is imposed by law.

3. The contractor is participating in an inherently dangerous activity, such as blasting.

B. CREATION OF AGENCY

1. IN GENERAL

An agency can be created by agreement, by estoppel, by ratification, or by operation of law.

Since the law treats one who acts through an agent as doing the act himself, the capacity to act by an agent depends on the capacity of the principal to do the act himself if he were present. Thus, a person who has capacity to contract may appoint an agent, but an appointment by a person without capacity (e.g., a minor) would be voidable.

Any person can act as an agent except a person who does not understand the legal importance of making contracts for another. For example, a minor can act as an agent but not if he is an infant of tender years. Thus, agents are not required to possess the same qualifications as are principals. That is, a person can act as an agent for someone else although he is not capable of acting for himself. The principal cannot complain of the lack of mental capacity of one whom he has chosen to represent him. Generally, anyone except a lunatic, imbecile, or infant of tender years is capable of acting as an agent.

2. BY AGREEMENT

The usual method of creating an agency is by agreement (i.e., one person expressly authorizes another to act for him or her). In most instances, the authorization may be oral. If the agent is authorized to enter into a contract for the sale of real property for the principal, most states require that such an authorization be in writing. In some states, the authorization must be in writing in any case in which the agent will enter into any of the types of contracts required by the Statute of Frauds to be in writing (e.g., sale of real property, sales of goods of a value of $500 or more). This is called the *equal dignities* rule (i.e., if the agent is to make contracts required to be in writing, his or her authorization must be created by a method of equal dignity, namely, a written instrument).

3. BY ESTOPPEL

Agency by estoppel (apparent authority) arises when the principal intentionally or by want of ordinary care causes a third person to believe another to be his or her agent who is not really employed by him or her. For example, if the owner of a store places another person in charge of the store, third persons might assume that the person in charge is the agent of the owner of the store. The agent has apparent authority, because he or she appears to be the agent and the principal is estopped from denying the agency, even if none exists.

The situation of agency by estoppel also occurs where there is an actual agency but the principal leads third persons to believe that the agent has greater powers than actually exist.

4. IMPLIED AGENCY

An agency agreement may also be implied from the parties actions, and the courts may find an actual agency relationship to exist notwithstanding a denial by the principal. Such an agency may be indicated by the prior habits or course of dealing between the two persons, subsequent acts, or the acquiescence or ratification of previous similar acts.

Although implied agencies are similar to those created by estoppel, the latter can be invoked by a third person only when he or she knew or relied upon the conduct of the principal. Since an implied agency is an *actual* agency, this limitation does not apply. The following case illustrates an implied agency:

FACTS Plaintiff's Cadillac was parked by Buster Douglas and was stolen while plaintiff dined in defendant's restaurant. The issue of the case was whether defendant restaurant, by permitting an individual to park patrons' cars thereby held him out as its employee for such purposes. Buster Douglas was not an employee in the usual sense, but with the knowledge of defendant, he did station himself in front of the restaurant, wore a doorman's uniform (which he himself had purchased), and had been parking defendant customers' autos.

DECISION The court held that the restaurant owner knew of and did not object to Buster Douglas's parking cars. Therefore, although Buster was not an actual employee, he had been held out to customers as being an authorized agent to park their vehicles. Because no suitable disclaimer was posted, plaintiff was justified in assuming that Buster Douglas represented the restaurant. Motion to dismiss was denied and the case set for trial.

Weingart v. Directoire Restaurant, Inc. (70 Misc. 2d 419, 333 N.Y.S.2d 806 [1972])

5. BY RATIFICATION

An agency may be created by ratification (i.e., acceptance by the principal of the benefits of the acts of the purported agent). Nearly all courts hold that the agent must be purporting to act for the principal at the time of the contract with the third person as prerequisite for ratification.

Ratification may be express or implied. It is implied when the principal, with knowledge of the material facts surrounding the agent's unauthorized act, receives and retains the benefits thereof.

The principal must ratify before the third person withdraws from the transaction. Until the principal ratifies, the third person can withdraw for any reason. This is because until affirmance, the third person and the purported principal are similar to an offeror and an offeree before acceptance. No mutuality of obligation exists until the principal ratifies the transaction; if the principal cannot be bound, neither can the third person. Since the agent acted without authority, the principal may repudiate the act if he or she chooses to do so.

The following case is an example of the failure to meet the prerequisite for ratification:

FACTS Plaintiff brings this action to compel defendant, Armiger Body Shop, to transfer and deliver to him the title certificate evidencing ownership of a certain 1960 Ford Falcon. On September 30, 1960, plaintiff purchased the car from Roy Hitchens, a dealer in used automobiles, for $1,995. The Falcon was delivered to plaintiff on the day of the sale and has been in plaintiff's possession ever since. The vehicle is titled in the name of defendant, and the title certificate is in defendant's possession.

DECISION The court held that there had been no proof of an actual principal-agent relationship between the defendant body shop and Hitchens, granting the latter the authority to sell the Falcon. Plaintiff could recover only if he could establish an agency authority by ratification. However, at the time of sale, Hitchens purported to act as the owner, not as an agent. The general agency rule is that acts done by one in his or her individual capacity cannot be ratified by another. Judgment for defendant.

Taylor v. Armiger Body Shop (40 Del. Ch. 22, 172 A.2d 572 [1961])

6. BY OPERATION OF LAW

Agency implied by law can arise by statute. For example, most states have adopted a nonresident motorist statute that provides that the operation of a motor vehicle upon the highway of a state is an appointment of the Secretary of that state as the agent of the nonresident for service of process in any action arising out of the operation of the motor vehicle in the state.

Agency can also be implied by law when the acts of a self-constituted agent are, by reason of the neglect of the principal or an act of God, necessary for the self-preservation of the principal or the well-being of society. Examples are a principal's being so incapacitated by injuries that he or she cannot act for himself or herself or a merchant's furnishing necessities to a wife and charging them to her husband's account (no agency relationship exists, but the husband is liable for the necessities by virtue of a social policy that is in furtherance of the welfare of the neglected wife and the well-being of society as a whole).

C. TERMINATION OF AGENCY

An agency may be terminated by act of the parties or by operation of law.

1. ACT OF THE PARTIES

A. MUTUAL AGREEMENT

Since the agency was created by an agreement, it can be terminated in the same manner.

B. EXPIRATION OF CONTRACT

The contract of agency may provide that it shall terminate at a definite time (e.g., one year). In such case, the agency terminates in one year by virtue of the terms of the contract. Or the agency may be created for a particular purpose, in which case the agency terminates when the agent accomplishes the particular purpose (e.g., real estate broker sells the house).

C. REVOCATION OF AUTHORITY

The principal may at any time revoke the authority given his or her agent by reasonable notice with or without good cause. When the agency is created for an indefinite time, it can be revoked by either party after reasonable notice without incurring liability. However, when the agency is contracted for a definite period of time, revocation without cause by either party may result in damages for the breach.

D. RENUNCIATION BY THE AGENT

The agent may also at any time, with or without good cause, renounce the power conferred upon him or her by giving reasonable notice to the principal. If the agency is created for a definite period, renunciation by the agent prior to the expiration of the period subjects the agent to liablity for damages for breach of contract.

E. OPTION OF A PARTY

An agency agreement may provide that either party may terminate the agency by giving a specified notice or paying a specified sum of money.

2. OPERATION OF LAW

A. DEATH

Because an agency is a personal service contract with a fiduciary responsibility, the authority given to an agent terminates upon the principal's death. Also, the agent's death ends the agency relationship. To avoid the hardship that might result from personal liability of the agent for an unwitting breach of his or her implied warranty of authority, some states have modified the rule and will not terminate the agency until the agent is notified of the principal's death.

Under the U.C.C., Section 4-405, death of a customer does not revoke the authority of a bank to accept, pay, collect, or account until the bank is notified of the death and has a reasonable opportunity to act on it.

In many states, a third person can rely on the agent's authority until the third person receives notice of the principal's death. An exception may exist where there is an irrevocable agency (see Section D in this chapter).

Ordinary contracts already made do not terminate upon death but become an obligation of the principal's estate.

B. INSANITY

Insanity of the principal or the agent generally terminates an ordinary agency. In some states, a third person who has no knowledge of the principal's insanity and who deals in good faith with the agent will be protected if it would work an injustice on him or her. However, if the principal has been judicially declared insane, the third person is not protected, since all persons are deemed to know the status of a judicially declared incompetent. Under the U.C.C., Section 4-405, incompetency of a customer does not revoke the authority of a bank to accept, pay, collect, or account until the bank is notified of the incompetency.

c. Bankruptcy

Bankruptcy of the principal terminates the agency as to matters affected by the bankruptcy. Bankruptcy of the agent terminates the agency if the agent should realize that the state of his credit would so affect the interests of his or her principal that the principal, if he or she had knowledge of the facts, would no longer consent to the agency.

d. Impossibility

The agency terminates when it becomes impossible to perform the agency (e.g., change in the law that makes the performance of the authorized act illegal or criminal, destruction of the subject matter, death of the third person with whom the agent has been dealing, insanity of the third person).

e. War

If the outbreak of war places the principal and agent in the position of alien enemies, the agency is terminated, or at least the agent's authority is suspended until peace is restored. War can also make it impossible or impractical for the agency to continue, in which case the agency will terminate.

f. Change in Business Conditions

The agency is terminated by the occurrence of an unusual event or a change in value or business conditions of such a nature that the agent should reasonably infer that the principal would not desire him or her to continue to act under the changed circumstances (e.g., broker to sell land at a certain price should regard authority to sell the land at that price as terminated if the land suddenly doubles in value).

D. IRREVOCABLE AGENCY

An agency coupled with an interest in the subject matter or as a power given as a security is generally irrevocable and is not terminated by death or insanity of the principal or the agent (e.g., a mortgage on real property or a pledge of goods given to the agent as security for an advance of funds on behalf of the principal). Suppose that P owns valuable real estate or diamonds and wishes to borrow money from A. As security for the loan, P gives to A a mortgage on the land or a pledge on the diamonds, together with the power to sell in the event the money is not repaid. If A then sells the property or the diamonds, he gives the purchaser a deed to the land or a bill of sale for the diamonds in P's name by A as agent. Such an arrangement is irrevocable. However, unless the principal actually has transferred some sort of ownership interest in the subject matter to the agent, such as the mortgage or pledge, together with a power of sale, most courts will terminate the agency upon the death or insanity of either of the parties.

E. FRANCHISES

The terms "agent" and "agency" are often used in everyday conversation to refer to franchise relationships that usually are not intended to be agencies. Franchising is a major modern business phenomenon. With nearly a million franchises operating varied enterprises around the world, many new legal problems have been created. The attractiveness of a franchise is that it enables a person to operate a small, local business with expert managerial help and mass media advertising from a central source.

A franchise is a contract by which a franchisee is given the right to engage in the business of offering, selling, or distributing goods or services under a marketing plan or system prescribed in substantial part by the franchisor and associated with the franchisor's trademark, service mark, trade name, or other commercial symbol.

Although the degree and quality of control exercised by the franchisor may be decisive in determining success, they also lead to many legal questions of agency.

Because of the varying degrees of control imposed by the contracts, courts tend to classify franchisees as either "independent" or as "agents." If the franchisee is an agent, under agency law, the franchisor could become liable both for contract and tort obligations of the franchisee.

Most franchises are designed to permit extensive control of the system by the franchisor. If the contract is too one-sided or unfair, it may be stricken as unconscionable under the U.C.C.

State disclosure laws and other regulatory measures have been applied to franchise contracts. This is a rapidly evolving area of the law that surely will be subject to much statutory regulation and judicial interpretation.

ILLUSTRATIVE CASES

1. Creation of Agency Relationship

OSTRANDER v. BILLIE HOLM'S VILLAGE TRAVEL INC.

87 Misc.2d 1049, 386 N.Y.S.2d 597 (1976)

NEWMARK, Judge.   In this action the plaintiff arranged for return limousine service from the airport in connection with airline tickets that she purchased from the defendant. In evidence is the receipt or voucher issued by the defendant for the services. The plaintiff's plane arrived approximately three (3) hours late and in accordance with the instructions given to the plaintiff by the defendant she telephoned the limousine service but was unable to make contact for she received no answer. After several further attempts to reach the limousine service plaintiff attempted to make comparable arrangements but found that there was no limousine service functioning at that hour and was compelled to take a taxi at a charge of $45.00.

Defendant disclaims responsibility and explained that it sold the services, issued the voucher and notified the limousine service that the transaction had been made, and would subsequently be billed for the service.

Keeping in mind defendant's acknowledgement that it is not unusual for aircraft to be three hours late, the obvious question is whether the travel agent should be held liable for the failure to furnish limousine service. That ultimate answer must, in turn, be premised on the nature of the relationship between a travel agency and its clients.

* * * "Obviously the travel agent is an agent, but the question comes, whose agent?"

The possible bases for the liability of the travel agent to a traveler have been summarized as follows:

> The legal responsibility of travel agents to the clients whom they service may be based on one or more of three bodies of legal principles: negligence, agency, or contract. The law of negligence will supply the minimum legal duty of the travel agent no matter what his legal status is said to be. The remainder will hinge on a determination of his legal status vis-à-vis the other participants in the scheme of travel distribution.

*   *   *

"An agent is a person authorized by another to act on his account or under his control. An agent is one who acts for or in the place of another by authority from him. He is one who, by the authority of another, undertakes to transact some business or manage some affairs on account of such other." Although the client of the travel agent seldom exercises control over the specifics of the arrangements necessary to accomplish his travel goals he has the right as part of the relationship to be specific as to the most minute elements of the travel arrangements should he choose to do so. Also, "there is not the slightest indication that an express agreement creating agency is ever entered into between travel agent and client. They do not generally address themselves to the matter * * * and whatever relationship exists between them appears to be either assumed by the parties to exist or never enters their minds at all." Nevertheless, this Court is constrained to follow the holding that a travel agency is the agent of the traveler.

* * * The limousine service cannot be considered a sub-agent of defendant since no delegation of the responsibility assumed by the travel agent took place.

An independent contractor is "one who, exercising an independent employment, contracts to do a piece of work according to his own methods, and without being subject to the control of his employer except as to the result of his work * * *."

Such was the relationship between this defendant and the limousine service retained by it to transport the plaintiff from the airport to her residence upon the latter's return. The travel agent was only interested in accomplishing this result and presumably had no control over the manner of its accomplishment by the limousine service.

In general, an employer or principal is not liable for damages caused by an independent contractor. There exist, however, at least six recognized exceptions to this exemption:

> Thus, it can be said, the hirer or principal remains liable (1) where the thing contracted to be done is unlawful, (2) where the acts performed create a public nuisance, (3) where a duty is imposed by statute or ordinance, (4) where the hirer is under a nondelegable duty to perform the services promised, (5) where the work to be performed is inherently dangerous and (6) where the principal or hirer assumes a specific duty by contract.

Exception (6) is applicable to the case at bar. "[W]hen the client asks the travel agent to secure reservations for him he is making an offer for a bilateral contract to the travel agent which is accepted by the latter when he agrees to try to secure the reservations requested." Here the defendant arranged for the transportation of the plaintiff and issued a confirmation form which was represented to entitle plaintiff to the transportation she desired. The court finds the defendant liable for the failure of the performance.

Judgment in favor of plaintiff in the amount of $45.00.

2. Agent or Independent Contractor

PEAIRS v. FLORIDA PUBLISHING COMPANY

132 So.2d 561 (1961)

CARROLL, Chief Judge.

* * *

The plaintiffs alleged in their complaint that prior to November 23, 1957, the defendant, a newspaper publisher, in the course of distributing its papers carelessly and negligently permitted a wire loop used for binding bundles of its papers, to remain and be on the parking lot of a certain restaurant in the City of Jacksonville, and that on that date the plaintiff Louise Peairs, a patron of the said restaurant, while walking from the restaurant to her car in the parking lot, tripped upon the said wire loop and fell, fracturing the bones in both of her wrists. * * *

* * *

The defendant, the publisher of a Jacksonville newspaper, distributed its newspapers to route carriers under a carrier lease contract in which the defendant leased to the carrier a certain route, together with its subscription list, and the carrier undertook to deliver the papers to the subscribers on the route. Under this contract the defendant sold the papers to the carrier at a stipulated price and agreed not to interfere with or attempt to control the carrier with respect to the ways, means, or methods of performance, distribution, solicitation, or collection. * * *

* * * * * *

There was evidence also that, unless a distribution point was cleaned up, wires and trash would be left about a drop area. It was against the defendant's policy to leave wires and other trash around the distribution points, and the defendant's circulation manager had given instructions to the district managers to see that the wires and trash were picked up at the distribution points. Some of the carrier lease contracts had been terminated by the defendant because of the carriers' failure to pick up trash at the distribution points after being told to do so. If the carriers did not pick up the trash, usually the defendant's district managers would do so.

* * * * * *

When, at the close of the plaintiffs' case, the trial court granted the defendant's motion for a directed verdict, the court said, "* * * but this is the basis of the Court's feeling, that the carriers themselves were independent contractors and independent of the defendant's negligence for which they alone are responsible." * * *

* * * * * *

A major apparent exception to the general rule that a person is not liable for the torts of his independent contractor occurs when the employer has the right to direct or control the performance of the work or the manner of its accomplishment, for then the master and servant relationship arises as a basis for imposing liability upon the employer. [Citations.] This exception, basically considered, is more apparent than real, for, when such control exists, the worker may bear the relation of servant or employee to the employer rather than that of independent contractor. * * *

* * * * * *

Another exception to the general rule of nonliability for the torts of an independent contractor arises when the act contracted for is tortious. * * *

* * * * * *

In their brief the appellants have called our attention to another recognized exception, which they claim is applicable to the facts of the present appeal—"Where a company gains knowledge of a dangerous situation created by its independent contractor, it may incur liability through its failure to halt the operation or correct it * * *." * * *

* * * * * *

The courts of this state have recognized several other exceptions, not pertinent here, to the general rule that a person is not liable for the torts of his independent contractor.

* * * * * *

Applying these principles to the case before us, we are of the opinion that the jury could have fairly and reasonably concluded from the evidence produced at the trial that the defendant-appellee was liable to the plaintiffs for the negligent acts of the newsboy carriers, even though those carriers bore the relation of independent contractors to the defendant, under one or more of the exceptions to the general rule of nonliability for acts of independent contractors, as discussed above.

*　　　*　　　*

Our conclusion is that the trial court erred in taking the case away from the jury and directing a verdict for the defendant. * * *

Reversed and remanded.

3. Agency by Estoppel

LINDSTROM v. MINNESOTA LIQUID FERTILIZER CO.

264 Minn. 485, 119 N.W.2d 855 (1963)

MURPHY, Justice.　Action for labor and materials furnished by plaintiff, Anund T. Lindstrom, to defendant Minnesota Liquid Fertilizer Company, a Minnesota corporation. The jury returned a verdict in plaintiff's favor for $2,338.90, and defendant appeals from an order denying its motion for judgment notwithstanding the verdict or for a new trial.

The labor and material furnished by plaintiff were ordered by one Hurley Weaver, who represented to plaintiff that he was acting for defendant in the transactions. Defendant denies that he was its agent or employee and contends that the evidence compelled a finding that his status was merely that of a lessee of defendant's plant and equipment, without authority to bind defendant in any way. * * *

Weaver undertook to use defendant's equipment solely for the sale of defendant's products under defendant's trade name, and to maintain a sales volume in the area, which, in defendant's opinion, would represent a reasonable amount of business. He was directed to promote the sale of defendant's products in cooperation with defendant and to use defendant's equipment in applying the products sold. He agreed to furnish defendant with copies of invoices covering all sales and of contracts with the customers and to deposit the proceeds of such sales in defendant's name in the local bank. Therein defendant agreed to promote the sales of its products in Weaver's area; to act as consultant with respect thereto; and to provide sales and technical instructions therein at all reasonable times. It reserved the right to conduct an advertising program in the area and required that Weaver furnish it with a mailing list of all of his prospective customers. Any provisions in the agreement constituting a limitation on Weaver's authority were certainly unknown to the public or to plaintiff.

* * * Further, at all times its corporate name was painted in large letters on the buildings, tanks, and equipment of this branch, with nothing thereon to indicate that Weaver was lessee of such business or operated it as an independent contractor. It is well settled that, in so far as third parties are concerned, the relationship of principal and agent may be evidenced by acts on the part of the alleged principal or appearances of authority he permits another to have which lead to the belief that an agency has been created. * * * It has been held that, where a party permits his name to be used on property or equipment which is placed under the control or direction

of another and thus makes such other an ostensible agent, an agency by estoppel will result. * * *

The jury's finding that a principal and agent relationship existed between defendant and Weaver would render defendant liable for acts performed by Weaver within the scope of his apparent authority as plant manager. Any secret limitations placed thereon by defendant would not absolve it from liability to third persons such as plaintiff who dealt with Weaver as defendant's manager and who were unaware of any limitations upon his authority as such. * * *

Affirmed.

4. Effect of Termination of Agency

ZUKAITIS v. AETNA CASUALTY & SURETY CO.

195 Neb. 59, 236 N.W.2d 819 (1975)

BLUE, J.   This is an action for a declaratory judgment brought to determine whether defendant-appellee, the Aetna Casualty and Surety Company, was obligated under its professional liability insurance policy to defend plaintiff-appellant, Raymond R. Zukaitis, in a medical malpractice suit.

*   *   *

* * * Raymond R. Zukaitis was a physician practicing medicine in Douglas County, Nebraska. Aetna issued Dr. Zukaitis a policy of professional liability insurance through its agent, the Ed Larsen Insurance Agency, Inc. This policy was for a period from August 31, 1969, to August 31, 1970.

On August 7, 1971, Dr. Zukaitis received a written notification of a claim for malpractice which allegedly occurred on September 27, 1969. On August 10, 1971, Dr. Zukaitis telephoned the Ed Larsen Insurance Agency. At the request of the agency the written claim was forwarded to it by Dr. Zukaitis. This was received on August 11, 1971, and was erroneously referred to the St. Paul Fire and Marine Insurance Company on that date by the agency.

Dr. Zukaitis was insured with St. Paul Fire and Marine Insurance Company from August 31, 1970, to August 31, 1971. But on the date of the alleged malpractice, he was insured with Aetna. Apparently without notice to Dr. Zukaitis, the agency contract between Ed Larsen Insurance Agency and Aetna had been cancelled effective August 1, 1970. At that time the agency placed Dr. Zukaitis' insurance with St. Paul.

*   *   *

Aetna contends that it is relieved from its obligation to Dr. Zukaitis since notice was not given as required by paragraph 4(b) of the policy which provides: "If claim is made or suit is brought against the insured, the insured shall immediately forward to the company every demand, notice, summons or other process received by him or his representative."

Dr. Zukaitis contends that under the circumstances, notice to Aetna was given within a reasonable period in that the agent who wrote the policy was given notice, and further that a delay in giving notice does not defeat policy obligations unless the insurer is prejudiced by the delay.

*   *   *

Dr. Zukaitis made demand upon Aetna on May 28, 1974, for it to undertake the defense of Dr. Zukaitis, but this demand was refused.

Dr. Zukaitis retained his own attorney to represent him in the malpractice case. A motion for summary judgment was filed by Dr. Zukaitis in that case, which motion was sustained. This action for a declaratory judgment against Aetna therefore resolved itself into an effort to recover attorney's fees and costs. The District Court found for Aetna.

*   *   *

Ordinarily notice to a soliciting agent who countersigns and issues policies of insurance is notice to the insurance company.

*   *   *

The question then is whether this is true after the agency contract between the insurance company and the agent has been terminated as it was in this case. To answer this, it is necessary to refer to the general law of agency.

The rule is that a revocation of the agent's authority does not become effective as between the principal and third persons until they receive notice of the termination.

*   *   *

Here, Dr. Zukaitis did what most reasonable persons would do in this situation; he notified the agent who sold him the policy. There is no evidence that notice of the termination was sent to him or that he knew the agency contract had been canceled.

*   *   *

We conclude that under the facts and circumstances of this case, the notice given by the plaintiff to the agent of the defendant constitutes notice to the defendant and would obligate defendant to carry out the terms of its insurance contract with plaintiff. The District Court was in error when it determined to the contrary.

*   *   *

[Reversed and remanded.]

5. Franchisee as Agent

NICHOLS v. ARTHUR MURRAY, INC.

248 Cal.App.2d 610, 56 Cal.Rptr. 728 (1967)

COUGHLIN, Associate Justice.   Defendant appeals from a judgment awarding plaintiff the amount prepaid by the latter under contracts for dancing lessons which were not furnished.

Plaintiff had entered into five such contracts with "Arthur Murray School of Dancing" at San Diego, operated by Burkin, Inc., a corporation, under a franchise agreement with defendant Arthur Murray, Inc., a corporation.

Defendant Arthur Murray, Inc., was engaged in the business of licensing persons to operate dancing studios using its registered trade name "ARTHUR MURRAY" and the Arthur Murray method of dancing.

The franchise agreement between defendant, therein referred to as Licensor, and Burkin, Inc., therein referred to as Licensee, conferred upon the latter a license "to use the 'ARTHUR MURRAY METHOD' and name in connection with a dancing school" to be conducted by it in San Diego.

The judgment herein is premised upon the conclusion defendant was the undisclosed principal in the transaction between plaintiff and the "Arthur Murray School of Dancing" in San Diego. An undisclosed principal is liable for the contractual obligations incurred by his agent in the course of the agency * * * even though the obligee did not know there was a principal at the time the obligations were incurred.

* * *

The issue on appeal is whether the evidence supports the conclusion, as found by the trial court, that Burkin, Inc., was the agent of defendant when the former executed the contracts for dancing lessons with plaintiff, and accepted the latter's prepayments on account of these contracts. Defendant contends Burkin, Inc., was only its licensee, and not its agent.

* * *

Whether the relationship between parties to a written agreement is that of principal and agent, at least insofar as this relationship affects a stranger to the agreement as in the case at bench, is dependent upon the intention of the parties determined from the writing and the accompanying circumstances.

* * *

In determining whether an agency relationship exists between parties to a business enterprise, which is the subject of an agreement between them, the right to control is an important factor. If, in practical effect, one of the parties has the right to exercise complete control over the operation by the other an agency relationship exists; the former is the principal and the latter the agent. [Citations.]

* * *

In the case at bench defendant depreciates the importance of the element of control, contending in a franchise agreement conferring the right to use a trade name controls are essential to the protection of the trade name; the controls provided by the instant agreement were for this purpose; the franchise holder was given some freedom of action; and, for these reasons, the court should have concluded the controls in question did not establish an agency relationship.

* * *

The subject agreement, in substance, conferred upon defendant the right to control the employment of all employees of the franchise holder whether or not their duties related to teaching or supervising dancing instruction; to fix the minimum tuition rates to be charged; to select the financial institution handling, financing or discounting all pupil installment contracts; to designate the location of the studio, its layout and decoration; to make refunds to pupils and charge the amounts paid to the franchise holder; to settle and pay all claims against defendant arising out of the operation of the contemplated enterprise; to reimburse itself for the payment of any such refunds or claims, and the expense of any litigation in connection therewith, from a fund consisting of weekly payments by the franchise holder to defendant in an amount equal to 5% of the gross receipts; to invest the proceeds of this fund and pay the franchise holder only such portion of the income therefrom as defendant "shall determine should be properly allocated"; to control all advertising by the franchise holder, which was required to be submitted to defendant for approval prior to use; and to exercise a broad control over the operation of the enterprise under a provision requiring the franchise holder "to conduct the studio, to be maintained and managed by Licensee, in accordance with the general policies of the Licensor as established from time to time", and directing that failure to maintain such policies shall be sufficient cause for immediate cancellation of the agreement.

* * *

Many of the controls conferred were not related anywise to the protection of defendant's trade name, including its dancing and teaching methods, good will and business image. Other controls, although related to the protection of the trade name, because the exercise thereof was not limited to effecting such purpose, enabled defendant to impose its will upon the franchise holder in areas wholly unrelated to that purpose.

* * *

Defendant directs attention to provisions in the agreement which it claims expressly declare the intention of the parties that no agency relationship is intended; refers to the established principle that agency is a consensual relationship; and contends these circumstances dictate the conclusion no agency was created by the subject agreement. This contention disregards the fact that the agreement, as such, was consensual; both parties consented to the provisions imposing controls; and the agency relationship was created by the legal effect of those provisions.

* * *

Our conclusion is that the controls imposed upon the franchise holder by defendant completely deprived the former of any independence in the business operation subject to the agreement. * * *

The evidence adequately supports the conclusion that in executing the subject contract and receiving the prepayment thereon, Burkin, Inc., was acting as agent for defendant.

The judgment is affirmed.

6. Termination of Agency by Death

MUBI v. BROOMFIELD
108 Ariz. 39, 492 P.2d 700 (1972)

UDALL, Vice Chief Justice.   This case is before us on a Petition to Review a ruling by the Court of Appeals (No. 1 CA–CIV 1755) wherein the Court declined to accept jurisdiction in a special action for the reason that prior to the time of the service of the written acceptance of offer on August 11, 1970, William Mubi, plaintiff's husband, had died. The Court of Appeals ordered the petition dismissed. We also conclude the petitioner's prayer for relief must be denied.

The undisputed facts are that William Mubi, husband of petitioner in this case, commenced a civil suit in Superior Court, Maricopa County, against Walter W. Tribble and Jane Doe Tribble for personal injuries and property damages resulting from a motor vehicle collision. On August 5, 1970, after this action was filed, defendants through their attorney filed an answer and an Offer of Judgment in the amount of $3,150.

Under Rule 68, Rules of Civil Procedure, 16 A.R.S., this offer had to be accepted, if at all, within 10 days or it was deemed withdrawn. William J. Mubi died at approximately 9:00 A.M. on the 11th day of August, 1970, 6 days after the offer was made. Prior to his death he had advised his wife Sharon Mubi to accept the offer of settlement of $3,150, and she in turn advised the secretary of Mubi's attorney, Robert Spillman, that the offer was accepted. Because Spillman was out of town on vacation he did not receive the notice of the offer of judgment until 2:00 P.M. on August 11th, whereupon Spillman authorized an office associate to immediately accept the offer of judgment pursuant to Rule 68, which acceptance of offer was duly mailed to the defendants on August 11, 1970 and was received in due course. Upon Spillman's return to his office he caused an acceptance of offer of judgment to be mailed to the law firm representing defendants on August 17, 1970, which acceptance of offer was duly receipted by the attorneys for the defendants.

It appears, thus, that while the decision to accept the Offer was communicated to decedent's attorney before he died, the written acceptance as required by Rule 68 was not made until after Mubi died.

*   *   *

Since written acceptance as required by Rule 68 was not made prior to death, we must inquire into whether it was validly made after death in view of our holding that death did not terminate the offer. We hold that acceptance was not properly made.

The power to accept after Mubi's death was transferred to his estate and upon its command the acceptance, if made in writing and within the 10-day period would have been valid. Since this did not occur, the only question remaining is whether the decedent's attorney could accept on behalf of Mubi after his death. With very few exceptions, none of which are applicable here, the death of the principal acts as an instantaneous revocation by operation of law of the authority of the agent. * * * When a person has authority as an attorney to do an act, he must do it in the name of the one who gave him that authority. The principal appoints the attorney to act in his place and represent his person. Thus, where there is only a naked authority, not coupled with an interest, the death of the principal without notice ends the agent's authority to act in his principal behalf. In short, the agent's power is a derivative one and simply cannot last longer than the original authority except in a few unrelated instances.

Since the existence of a contingent fee contract does not create an agency coupled with an interest nor otherwise create an interest in the suit sufficient to create an exception to this rule, we hold that the power of the attorney to answer on behalf of Mubi terminated at Mubi's death. * * * Since the acceptance, made first by Mr. Spillman's office associate and then by Mr. Spillman, could not bind Mubi or his estate, the offer was not accepted within the 10-day period and pursuant to Rule 68 was "deemed withdrawn".

It is ordered that petitioner's prayer for relief be denied.

PROBLEMS

1. Defendant, a milk route distributor, struck and injured plaintiff while defendant was on his milk route. The defendant distributed milk for the Mt. Meadow Creameries, but the Mt. Meadow company had no control over the activities of the defendant. Plaintiff joins the company in the lawsuit. Company defends on the grounds that the defendant was an independent contractor, and therefore the doctrine of *respondeat superior* does not apply. Decision?

2. Plaintiff, owner of an antique shop, asked his friend Richard to mind the store while he went to the post office to mail a package. While the plaintiff was gone, a woman came into the store and purchased a rare painting for a very low price. When the plaintiff returned, Richard told him about the sale. Plaintiff brings action against the woman for the return of the painting on the grounds that Richard did not have authority to make the sale. Decision?

3. Jones, the secretary of defendant's corporation, purchases some personal property for the corporation that he knows the corporation needs. Jones does not have authority to make the purchase. Defendant, after learning of the purchase, accepts the benefits of the purchase and is pleased to get the goods. Plaintiff, seller of the goods, brings action against the corporation for the purchase price. Defendant takes the position that Jones acted without authority. Decision?

4. Plaintiff, a real estate broker, asks defendant, a homeowner, if he wants to sell his house. Defendant replies that he does. Plaintiff asks defendant if he can represent him and make a sale of the house for him. Defendant tells him that it is all right with him if the price is at least $25,000 and if the commission is not over 5 percent. Plaintiff agrees. A few days later, plaintiff enters into a contract for the sale of the house with a third party; however, defendant refuses to confirm the sale. Plaintiff brings action to force defendant to specifically perform the oral contract and the sale and to pay the commission. Decision?

5. P, a manufacturer, employs A as a traveling salesman to contract for the sale of goods manufactured by P. P is killed, but A does not know of this and continues to make contracts. A makes a contract with T, who now brings action against P's estate. Decision?

6. As the result of negligence of a concessionaire, plaintiff's small daughter was injured while riding on a kiddie ride owned and operated by the concessionaire as a component of a carnival owned and operated by the defendant. Defendant had nothing to do with the actual operation of the ride but did make rules and regulations for the concessionaires and had the right to require the correction of anything wrong with the equipment used or its mode of operation or to remove it entirely from the carnival. Plaintiff sues for damages. Decision?

7. Atwood employed Bade, aged 17, as an agent. Acting within the scope of his authority and on behalf of Atwood, Bade made a contract with Sibley. Sibley demanded that Atwood perform the contract. Atwood sues to rescind on the ground that Sibley's contract was made with a minor. Decision?

8. The National Life Insurance Company employed Brown as its district agent. Brown died and in his will stated that his son was to carry on his work as district agent. When the son attempted to write an insurance policy for Sullivan, Sullivan claimed that the son could not legally do so. Decision?

9. Bill, the driver of a school bus carrying 50 small children to school, discovered that the brakes did not work. To avoid disaster, Bill drove into a garage and had the brakes repaired, then drove on to the school. The garage sues Mac, the bus owner, for the cost of the repairs. Decision?

10. Joe, a skilled photographer, was hired by the ABC Company to photograph the new models of equipment it was preparing for market. Before Joe could take the pictures, he was arrested for a felony, failed to make bail, and was put in prison. ABC claims its agency contract with Joe is terminated. Decision?

Chapter 20

RELATIONSHIP BETWEEN PRINCIPAL AND AGENT

A. IN GENERAL

The agent is a fiduciary (i.e., the agent owes a duty of scrupulous good faith and candor to his or her principal). The agent-principal relationship is one of trust.

B. DUTIES OF AGENT

Generally, the agent owes certain duties to the principal.

1. DUTY OF CARE

The agent owes a duty to use reasonable care, diligence, and skill in his work. However, the agent is not obliged to render perfect service; and errors in judgment not due to want of care, fraud, or unfair dealing, are alone not actionable against him or her. For example, an insurance agent must not neglect to keep insurance in force for the specified amount to which he or she had agreed; an attorney should file a lawsuit or an appeal within the required time; an insurance broker must obtain insurance covering the designated risk.

2. DUTY OF GOOD CONDUCT

The agent owes a duty to conduct himself or herself in such a manner so as not to bring discredit or disrepute upon the principal or his or her business or to make it impossible to continue friendly relations (e.g., a waitress should not become a call girl).

3. DUTY TO GIVE INFORMATION

It is the duty of an agent to keep the principal informed of all facts relevant to the agency so that the principal can protect his or her interests (e.g., broker must reveal all offers to purchase property). Since notice to the agent is generally held to be the same as notice to the principal, it is obvious that the agent must keep the principal informed. The following case is an example:

> **FACTS** Mr. & Mrs. Miles were buying a house, and Mr. Russell was their agent for procuring a loan. A termite inspection had been made for Russell and the lender savings and loan company for $15. Later that day, the savings and loan company and Russell were advised that the house was termite infested and treatment would cost $450. Mr. and Mrs. Miles were not told about the termites and did not discover them until after the sale was completed and they had taken possession of the property.
>
> **DECISION** The court held that an agent owes the principal a duty to disclose all material information that the agent learns concerning the subject matter of the agency relation and about which the principal is uninformed. Russell and the savings and loan company were agents to secure the termite inspection, and they had a duty to inform the plaintiffs of the result. Since they were duty bound to disclose the facts relating to the termite infestation prior to recording the deed and distributing the funds, they were liable to the plaintiffs for the cost of repairing the termite damage.
>
> *Miles v. Perpetual Savings and Loan Company,* (58 Ohio St. 2d 93, 388 N.E.2d 1364 [1979])

4. DUTY TO KEEP AND RENDER ACCOUNTS

It is the duty of an agent to account to the principal for all property or money belonging to the principal that comes into the agent's possession.

5. DUTY TO ACT ONLY AS AUTHORIZED

The agent owes a duty not to act in the principal's affairs except in accordance with all lawful instructions given to the agent by his or her principal.

6. DUTY NOT TO ATTEMPT THE IMPOSSIBLE OR IMPRACTICABLE

The agent owes a duty not to continue to render service that subjects the principal to risk of expense if it reasonably appears to the agent to be impossible or impracticable to accomplish the objects of the principal and if the agent cannot communicate with the principal.

7. DUTY TO OBEY

The agent is subject to a duty to obey all reasonable and lawful directions in regard to the manner of performing a service that he or she has contracted to perform. If the agent disobeys a reasonable order, the principal can terminate the employment.

8. DUTY OF LOYALTY

An agent must be loyal and faithful to the principal. The agent must not obtain any secret profit or advantage from the agency relationship. An agent must not enter into any transaction within the scope of the agency in which he or she has a personal interest unless he or she obtains the consent of the principal. An agent must not compete with the principal concerning the subject matter of the agency or represent a person whose interests conflict with the principal. Unless otherwise agreed, an agent has a duty to act in the principal's name and not to appear as the owner of the principal's property (e.g., attorney must not put money he or she has collected for a client in his or her own personal bank account. The agent's loyalty must be undivided.

Real estate brokers are agents licensed by the state to represent sellers and buyers of real property. Their authority is usually limited to identifying the property and quoting a price in accordance with the seller's listing agreement. However, in many instances, as when a buyer comes into a realty office to purchase property, the broker may have a loyalty problem when trying to get the best price for the seller and the lowest for the buyer. A solution to this dual agency dilemma is to classify such a broker as either a "seller's" or "buyer's" agent.

9. DUTY AFTER TERMINATION OF AGENCY

An agent is subject to a duty not to act as such after the termination of his or her authority.

C. DUTIES OF PRINCIPAL

1. DUTY TO PERFORM CONTRACT

The principal has the duty to perform the contract made with the agent.

2. DUTY NOT TO INTERFERE WITH AGENT'S WORK

A principal has a duty to refrain from unreasonably interfering with the agent's work (e.g., terminating the agent's authority to act, supplying the agent with inferior goods, competing with the agent when the agent's services are exclusive [appointing an agent to collect a debt and then collecting it himself or herself]).

8. DUTY TO GIVE AGENT INFORMATION

The principal owes a duty to use care to inform the agent of risks of physical harm or pecuniary loss that exist in the performance of authorized acts and that he has reason to know are unknown to the agent. The principal's duty to give other information to the agent depends on their agreement or on the custom of the business (e.g., furnishing list of prospective customers to selling agent).

4. DUTY TO KEEP AND RENDER ACCOUNTS

A master has a duty to keep and render accounts of the money due from the master to the servant. An agent can sue a principal for an accounting as an equitable remedy. However, the extent of the principal's duty in this area depends upon the contract between them, custom of the business, method of compensation, whether the agent operates an independent business, and other similar factors.

5. DUTY OF GOOD CONDUCT

The principal owes a duty to conduct himself in such a manner so as not to harm the agent's reputation or to make it impossible for the agent, consistent with his reasonable self-respect or personal safety, to continue in the employment (i.e., agent does not have to continue to act for one whom he discovers to be an unsavory person or for one who physically or verbally abuses or insults him).

6. DUTY TO INDEMNIFY

It is the duty of the principal to indemnify the agent for any losses or damages suffered without his or her fault (e.g., payments of damages to third persons that the agent is required to make on account of the authorized performance of an act that constitutes a tort or a breach of contract; expenses of defending actions by third persons brought because of the agent's authorized conduct, such actions being unfounded but not brought in bad faith; obligations arising from the possession of things that the agent is authorized to hold on account of the principal; authorized payments made by the agent on behalf of the principal; payments resulting in benefit to the principal made by the agent under such circumstances that it would be inequitable for indemnity not to be made; and losses caused by the failure of the principal to give the agent required information, such as failure to give agent proper instructions for grading a street).

7. DUTY TO COMPENSATE

The principal is under a duty to pay the agent the compensation agreed upon. If no sum was agreed upon, the agent may recover the customary compensation for such services; and if there is no customary compensation, the agent may recover the reasonable value of his or her services. The following case illustrates how the court determines when the compensation is due:

> **FACTS** Floyd sued Morristown European Motors, Inc., for commissions he claimed were due. Between January 8 and February 13, at a time when the new models were not in stock and prices had not been set on them, Floyd took signed orders for three cars, and the buyers paid 10 percent of the expected price. Floyd took a leave of absence in March and was gone when the cars arrived and the buyers took delivery. Morristown refused to pay Floyd the $721.25 commissions, claiming that when the

cars were paid for and turned over to the customers, Floyd was not an employee.

DECISION The court held that so long as a salesperson is the "procuring cause of the sale," he or she is entitled to the commission even though the actual consummation was by the principal or through another agent. Judgment for Floyd.

Floyd v. Morristown European Motors, Inc. (138 N.J.Super. 588, 351 A.2d 791 [1976])

8. DUTY NOT TO TERMINATE

A principal has a duty not to repudiate or terminate the agency relationship in violation of the contract of employment.

ILLUSTRATIVE CASES

1. Duty of Agent to Principal

GENERAL AUTOMOTIVE MANUFACTURING CO. v. SINGER
19 Wis.2d 528, 120 N.W.2d 659 (1963)

BROWN, Chief Justice. Study of the record discloses that Singer was engaged as general manager of Automotive's operations. Among his duties was solicitation and procurement of machine shop work for Automotive. Because of Singer's high reputation in the trade he was highly successful in attracting order. * * * As time went on a large volume of business attracted by Singer was offered to Automotive but which Singer decided could not be done by Automotive at all, for lack of suitable equipment, or which Automotive could not do at a competitive price. When Singer determined that such orders were unsuitable for Automotive he neither informed Automotive of these facts nor sent the orders back to the customer. Instead, he made the customer a price, then dealt with another machine shop to do the work at a lesser price, and retained the difference between the price quoted to the customer and the price for which the work was done. Singer was actually behaving as a broker for his own profit in a field where by contract he had engaged to work only for Automotive. We concur in the decision of the trial court that this was inconsistent with the obligations of a faithful agent or employee.

Singer finally set up a business of his own, calling himself a manufacturer's agent and consultant, in which he brokered orders for products of the sort manufactured by Automotive,—this while he was still Automotive's employee and without informing Automotive of it. Singer had broad powers of management and conducted the business activities of Automotive. In this capacity he was Automotive's agent and owed a fiduciary duty to it.

* * * Under his fiduciary duty to Automotive Singer was bound to the exercise of the utmost good faith and loyalty so that he did not act adversely to the interests of Automotive by serving or acquiring any private interest of his own. * * * He was also bound to act for the furtherance and advancement of the interest of Automotive.

* * * If Singer violated his duty to Automotive by engaging in certain business activities in which he received a secret profit he must account to Automotive for the amounts he illegally received. * * *

The present controversy centers around the question whether the operation of Singer's side line business was a violation of his fiduciary duty to Automotive. * * *

The trial court found that Singer's side line business, the profits of which were $64,088.08, was in direct competition with Automotive. However, Singer argues that in this business he was a manufacturer's agent or consultant, whereas Automotive was a small manufacturer of automotive parts. The title of an activity does not determine the question whether it was competitive but an examination of the nature of the business must be made. In the present case the conflict of interest between Singer's business and his position with Automotive arises from the fact that Singer received orders, principally from a third-party called Husco, for the manufacture of parts. As a manufacturer's consultant he had to see that these orders were filled as inexpensively as possible, but as Automotive's general manager he could not act adversely to the corporation and serve his own interests. * * *

Rather than to resolve the conflict of interest between his side line business and Automotive's business in favor of serving and advancing his own personal interests, Singer had the duty to exercise good faith by disclosing to Automotive all the facts regarding this matter. * * * By failing to disclose all the facts relating to the orders from Husco and by receiving secret profits from these orders, Singer violated his fiduciary duty to act solely for the benefit of Automotive. Therefore he is liable for the amount of the profits he earned in his side line business.

2. Nature of Fiduciary Relationship

MOON v. PHIPPS

67 Wn.2d 948, 411 P.2d 157 (1966)

HALE, Judge. Joanna Moon had never met Dr. Woolery until the day after her stroke. Sixty-one years of age, widowed, and living with her 91-year-old aunt in the latter's home, she awoke the morning of May 19, 1962, to find her entire left side paralyzed; she could move neither her left leg nor arm. * * * Dr. Woolery sent Mrs. Moon to the hospital for four days and then transferred her to a nursing home for continuous observation, treatment and rehabilitation during the next four months. On leaving the nursing home, she continued treatments from Dr. Woolery, reporting at intervals to his office. During the course of and as a part of his therapy, he sought to alleviate her feelings of financial insecurity by advising her to sell her farm, and recommended his father-in-law as the agent to help her. * * *

Dr. Woolery's treatment included drugs and psychotherapy, for he believed her emotional symptoms were interrelated to her physical problems. * * *

He employed a kind of therapy whereby the patient is said to ventilate her feelings by talking about personal problems; and in so doing he noted that her ownership of a run-down farm was the source of several unhappy emotional responses. * * *

Mrs. Moon, acting on this suggestion, telephoned defendant Everett R. Phipps, Dr. Woolery's father-in-law, who came from his home in Portland a few days before Christmas, 1962, to look the farm over.

* * * In 1955, the land alone had been appraised at $18,700 by three realtors. The trial court found it had a value of $25,000 in 1962.

In January, Phipps drove Mrs. Moon to his home in Portland where his wife served her coffee and cookies, and he prepared a one page written legal instrument which Mrs. Moon testified she thought to be a listing agreement. * * * The instrument, which Mrs. Moon says she thought to be simply a listing agreement, turned out to be a 60-day, irrevocable option to Mr. Phipps to buy the farm for $12,500 at $1,000 down and $150 per month. * * * Plaintiff brought this action to rescind * * *. The court did, however, grant full relief on the basis of breach of fiduciary trust * * *.

A simple reposing of trust and confidence in the integrity of another does not alone make of the latter a fiduciary. There must be additional circumstances, or a relationship that induces the trusting party to relax the care and vigilance which he would ordinarily exercise for his own protection. * * * Nor would the circumstances that plaintiff was a widow in poor health, without family, under severe emotional stress, and taking a number of powerful drugs, convert an ordinary agency into a fiduciary relationship, for every sick and emotionally dependent person of advanced years does not, merely in listing his property for sale with a real estate agent, make of the latter a fiduciary with respect to the listed property.

* * * Loyalty is the chief virtue required of an agent. * * *

The evidence in this case discloses a number of circumstances which, when added to the agency, support the court's finding of a fiduciary relationship. First, we have evidence of special trust and confidence generated by the doctor and patient relationship. Then, we have a vicarious transfer of that trust and confidence through the doctor's psychotherapy and advice from the plaintiff to defendant Phipps, and her engaging him to procure a purchaser for her property at the best price and terms obtainable. Finally, instead of employing Phipps as her agent, she unwittingly conferred upon him a temporary legal title to her farm, giving him both the power of alienation over and the profits to be derived therefrom. * * *

When, therefore, by virtue of an agency relationship, an agent, without the knowledge and consent of his principal, acquires dominion over and control of his principal's property in such a way that the agent possesses a legal power to alienate the principal's interests in or possessory rights thereto, the agent has transformed the agency into a fiduciary relationship. A fiduciary, in handling another's property, must exercise the utmost good faith, disclose fully all facts relating to his interest in and his actions affecting the property involved in the fiduciary relationship, and deliver over to the party for whom he is acting all benefits derived from or inuring to the property from the breach.

The judgment is, therefore, affirmed.

3. Duty of Principal to Agent

McKINNON AND MOONEY v. FIREMAN'S FUND INDEMNITY CO.

288 F.2d 189 (6th Cir., 1961)

PER CURIAM. Plaintiff-appellee, as agent for The Fireman's Fund Indemnity Company, defendant-appellant, issued a liability policy for the appellant on an automobile owned by Fitzgerald. On October 17, 1954, it cancelled the policy for nonpayment of premium. On October 23, 1954, Fitzgerald was involved in an automobile accident in which one Davis was injured.

Davis recovered a $10,000.00 judgment in the state court against Fitzgerald, and thereafter filed a supplemental petition against the Indemnity Company asserting that Fitzgerald was covered by the insurance policy of the Indemnity Company in that the alleged cancellation of the policy was fraudulent. At the request of the Indemnity Company, appellee's employees testified in this action with respect to the cancellation of the policy. The Indemnity Company was successful in its defense of the action.

Thereafter, Davis sued appellee in the United States District Court alleging that appellee fraudulently conspired to manufacture evidence depriving him of a recovery under the supplemental petition in the state court. Appellee notified the Indemnity Company of this suit and requested it to defend the action, which the Indemnity Company refused to do. Appellee employed its own attorney and successfully defended this action on the ground of res judicata.

* * * The attorney submitted his bill for attorney's fee for his services in the matter and expenses in the amount of $5,236.09, which the appellee paid. Appellee then brought the present action against the Indemnity Company for reimbursement of this expense.

The District Judge rendered judgment for the appellee in the amounts of $4,000.00 for a reasonable attorney's fee plus $500.00 for expenses. This apeal followed.

We agree with the reasoning of the District Judge that an agent may recover from his principal any expenditures necessarily incurred in the transaction of his principal's affairs and that under this well settled rule of principal and agent, an agent, compelled to defend a baseless suit, grounded upon acts performed in his principal's business, may recover from the principal the reasonable and necessary expenses of his defense. * * * The judgment is affirmed.

PROBLEMS

1. Roumel, the owner of an apartment building, employed Robbins as manager to live in the building and, among other things, to collect rent from the tenants. Robbins kept the rental money in an unlocked desk in her apartment although banking facilities were available nearby. Tenants and workers had frequent access to the desk. Rent money in the amount of $200 was left in the desk and apparently stolen. Roumel brought action against Robbins for the rent money. Decision?

2. Homeowner employed broker to sell his home. Broker sold the home to his own wife for $10,500. Some months later, broker sold the home to a third person for $11,500. Homeowner sues broker for the $1,000 profit. Decision?

3. Principal gave agent an exclusive territory to sell principal's products. During the exclusive contract, the principal invaded the territory and made sales of his own. Agent brings action against principal for the profits he would have made on the sales. Decision?

4. Isaacs bought chances on an automobile, which was to be presented to the winner at a picnic on a certain date. Isaacs offered Leake $25 to take his tickets to the picnic and receive the car for him if he was the winner. Leake agreed. One of Isaacs' tickets was the lucky one, and the car was turned over to Leake, who refused to give the car to Isaacs, maintaining that the lottery was illegal and that by the rules the winner had to be present. Isaacs sues for the car. Decision?

5. As an agent for Alberts, Doyle received $1,000 from the sale of certain merchandise. He deposited this amount in his personal bank account. The bank failed, and Alberts sued Doyle for the $1,000. Decision?

6. Evans, the credit manager for ABC Corporation, attended a regional credit meeting held in San Francisco. He submitted an expense account, including reasonable amounts for air fare, hotel, meals, taxi, and registration fee. The firm's accountant questions these expenses, and Evans claims he is entitled to reimbursement. Decision?

7. Moe, hired by Super TV as a repairman, went on a house call and, while repairing the television set, received a high-voltage shock that resulted in medical care and a long period of curative treatments. Moe claims that Super TV is liable for these expenses. Decision?

8. Custom Video Games hired Benjamin as sales manager at a salary of $5,000 a month. After working with the company for several years and building up a large sales volume, Benjamin quit and immediately went to work for nearby competition. Custom Video Games claims that Benjamin has violated his fiduciary duty as an agent. Decision?

9. Wilbur opens a store and hires Oscar as his general manager. Before leaving on a lengthy cruise, Wilbur tells Oscar not to spend over $2,000 on any noninventory item during his absence. Shortly after Wilbur sailed, Oscar received a call from the city building inspector indicating that certain wiring in the store had to be replaced within 24 hours or their business permit would be cancelled. If the lowest bid on the rewiring is $3,000, is Oscar authorized to have it done?

10. Williams instructed his agent, Shoreham, to ship goods from Los Angeles to San Francisco on the Southern Pacific Railroad. Shoreham checked rail schedules and decided that the goods would get to San Francisco faster if he shipped them on the Santa Fe Railway. The goods were lost en route and never arrived. Williams sues Shoreham for the value of the goods. Decision?

Chapter 21

AGENCY RELATIONSHIP WITH THIRD PARTIES

A. LIABILITY OF PRINCIPAL FOR AGENT'S CONTRACTS

A principal is liable to third persons on contracts made by the agent on behalf of the principal within the scope of the agent's authority. The principal is liable whether the agent's authority was actual or apparent and whether the principal's existence was disclosed or undisclosed. Also, a principal is liable to a third party for the unauthorized transaction made by the agent if the agent was acting within his or her apparent authority, the principal is estopped, or the principal has been unjustly benefited. Representations, declarations, and admissions of an agent, made within the agent's actual or apparent authority while acting on behalf of the principal, are also binding on the principal.

B. AUTHORITY OF THE AGENT

Once the agency relationship has been created, the existence and extent of the authority of the agent to act for the principal in a manner that makes the principal liable for the actions of the agent are based on the words and conduct of the principal. Although courts and writers have not been uniform in the terms used to classify types of authority, the usual categories are referred to as "express," "implied," or "apparent."

1. EXPRESS AUTHORITY

Express authority is the actual authority given to the agent in words or in writing. The principal must express to the agent those acts that the agent is to perform. Express authority may also be inferred from silence if the agent informs the principal of acts he or she intends to do and the principal has no objections.

2. IMPLIED AUTHORITY

Unless the principal expressly limits the authority of the agent by orders or by clear implication, the authority to carry out a task or an instruction includes the authority to do those things that are usually or customarily done by an agent to reasonably accomplish the objective. Implied authority may be inferred from the words or conduct of the principal (e.g., the principal employs an agent to manage an apartment building at a certain salary per month; and the agent has implied authority to employ necessary labor to keep the apartment building clean, to make minor repairs when needed, to purchase fuel for heating, and to arrange for rubbish pickup).

Implied authority is often referred to as incidental authority, meaning the right to do those acts incidental to carrying out an assignment. For example, if an agent is asked to buy goods but given no money to pay for them, authority to buy on credit would be implied as incidental to such purchase.

Implied authority is sometimes referred to as customary authority— that which is customary in a particular community for the type of activity involved. The following case is an example of customary authority.

> **FACTS** A hotel manager offered a reward for information leading to the arrest of the murderer of one of his night clerks. Jackson located the killer and claimed the reward but was turned down on the basis that the manager had no authority to make the offer. Jackson sued and won a jury verdict, which was set aside by the judge as a matter of law. Jackson appealed.
>
> **DECISION** The court stated that the authority to contract for rewards may be inferred from the authority to manage a business. Such authority is limited to those contracts that are incident to the business, are usually made in it, or are reasonably necessary in its conduct. The judge added that a factor to be considered is the custom of similar businesses at the same time and place. Since a jury reflects the community sense of a locale and the jury in this case had decided that the plaintiff had reasonably believed the authority to exist, the court found for the plaintiff and reinstated the verdict.

Jackson v. Goodman (69 Mich.App. 225, 244 N.W.2d 423 [1976])

3. APPARENT AUTHORITY

Apparent authority results when the principal, by words or conduct, manifests that another is the agent and such manifestation is made to a third person rather than to the agent. It is that authority that is apparent to the third persons with whom the agent deals (i.e., the authority that a third party might reasonably attribute to the agent). For example, a landowner writes a letter to a broker hiring the broker as agent to sell a piece of property and sends a copy of the letter to a prospective buyer. The broker now has actual authority to sell the property to anyone, but as to the prospect, the broker has apparent authority.

4. OSTENSIBLE AUTHORITY

Ostensible authority (or authority by estoppel) is similar to apparent authority, and the terms are often confused or used interchangeably. The difference is that ostensible authority is not really authority at all but a rule applied to prevent a principal who has misled another from profiting thereby. It is invoked whenever a principal has intentionally or negligently caused or allowed a third person to believe that an agent has authority to do that which, in fact, he or she is not authorized to do and the third person reasonably relies thereon. Under such circumstances, it would be unjust to allow the principal to deny the agent's authority. For example, a local manager of a business had express authority to receive checks but no authority to endorse and cash them. He did so for some time, however, without complaint from his principal. The court found ostensible authority by estoppel and held the principal to be liable.

5. UNDISCLOSED PRINCIPAL

Where the principal is named in the contract and not excluded by its terms and the fact of agency appears, the principal will be liable for the acts of the agent, actually or apparently authorized as a *disclosed* principal. However, on occasion, an agent may enter into a transaction on behalf of a principal without disclosing to the third party that he or she is acting only as an agent. For example, a movie star wants to purchase a certain house but realizes that if the owner of the house knows who the prospective purchaser is, he may raise the price. The movie star appoints an agent to make the purchase for her without disclosing that he is an agent. This would be a transaction by an agent for an *undisclosed* principal. In the case of an undisclosed principal, the contract can be enforced by the principal against the third party, and the third party can enforce the contract against *either* the agent or the undisclosed principal, but not against both.

Suppose that an agent enters into a contract with a third party disclosing that he or she is an agent but not disclosing the name of the principal (e.g., agent signs contract "John Doe, agent"). The general rule is that oral evidence may be introduced at the trial to show that the parties intended to bind only the principal and not the agent. However, absent such showing, the principal is still undisclosed.

C. LIABILITY OF PRINCIPAL

1. DOCTRINE OF *RESPONDEAT SUPERIOR*

A principal, employer, or master is liable for torts of an agent, employee, or servant committed within the scope of his or her agency or employment. This is a form of liability without fault and is based on the doctrine of *respondeat superior* (i.e., let the superior respond). It is immaterial that the agent acted in excess of his or her authority or contrary to instructions. The main justification for the doctrine is that the employer can spread the risk of loss through insurance and carry the cost as part of his or her overhead.

A. WITHIN SCOPE OF EMPLOYMENT

(1) In General

To impose liability on the principal or employer, it is essential that the agent or employee be acting for the principal within the scope of the employment when the tort is committed. Scope of employment means that the act was done in the course of the agency and by virtue of the authority as agent with a view to the principal's business. The agent in performing the act is endeavoring to promote the principal's business within the scope of the actual or apparent authority conferred on him or her for that purpose. The act may be within the scope of the agent's authority and not be in the interest of the principal or in the prosecution of the principal's business and still be within the scope of employment. It is also said that the conduct of an agent is within the scope of employment if it is not a serious departure from authorized conduct in manner or space and is actuated in part by a motive to serve the principal. For example, a truck driver is delivering gasoline for the principal. The driver throws a lighted cigarette to the ground onto which a pool of gasoline has dripped from the truck during the process of delivery. The principal is liable for the resulting damage, as it occurred within the scope of employment.

(2) Acts for Personal Convenience or Pleasure

Acts necessary for the comfort, convenience, health, and welfare of the employee while at work, though strictly personal, do not take the employee outside the scope of his or her employment. Cessation of work for such acts as eating, drinking, and warming oneself is necessary to employment and contributes to the furtherance of an employee's work.

(3) Deviation and Departure

Only a substantial deviation or departure to take care of one's own business or engage in activities for one's own pleasure will take the employee outside the scope of his or her employment. If the main purpose of the activity is still the employer's business, it is within the scope of the employment even though there are incidental personal acts, slight delays, or a deviation from the most direct route. For example, a truck driver starts out on a direct route from the employer's factory to the railroad depot to deliver some goods. On the way, he stops at his home, which is one block off the direct route. As he is driving away from his home, he has an accident. The employer is liable, as the deviation was slight.

(4) Going and Coming Rule

The going and coming rule describes the rule in which there is a substantial deviation or departure by the agent. For example, an employee going to and from work or to meals is considered outside the scope of his or her employment. However, some exceptions exist to the rule:

1. *Bunkhouse rule.* An employee who lives at his or her place of work (e.g.,

ranch hand living on ranch) is generally regarded as within the scope of employment when going to or returning from the work area (e.g., the fields) to his or her living quarters.

2.   *Traveling salespeople.* Traveling salespeople are generally regarded within the scope of their employment the entire time that they are away, even while not actually at work.

3.   *Special errand or dual purpose.* Where the employee's going or coming has some additional business purpose, the employee may be considered within the scope of employment during the entire trip. For example, an employee who works nights goes gome to get certain tools and then goes to dinner. On the way back, he has an accident. His dual purpose was to obtain the tools and to eat and was therefore within the scope of his employment.

4.   *Employer provides travel.* Where the employer provides transportation to the worker, compensates the worker for travel time, or defrays travel expenses, the courts have held that such employee is exempt from the going and coming rule.

B.   INTENTIONAL TORTS

(1)   In General

The employer is liable for the malicious acts of the employee within the scope of employment or connected with the employment.

(2)   Over Business Dispute

The employer is liable for the assault and battery by an employee committed against a third person arising over a business dispute connected with the employment. However, where the tort results from a personal grudge unrelated to the employment, the principal will not be liable, even though the assault takes place on the employer's premises during business hours.

(3)   To Maintain Order or to Protect Property

The employer is liable for the employee's torts where the employment involves the risk of force and the act is connected with the employment (e.g., bouncer in a nightclub assaults noisy customer; employee in charge of property trying to safeguard equipment throws a stone at a boy trespassing on the property, injuring the boy).

C.   FRAUD

Generally, the principal is liable for fraudulent representations of a type that are normally incidental to sales (i.e., those that the principal might reasonably expect would be the subject of representations by the agent). However, the principal is not liable for representations that are unusual or exceptional unless the principal with knowledge of the fraud retains the benefits of the transactions. For example, the owner of a business employs a broker to sell the business for him. The broker misrepresents to a buyer that the net income is much greater than it really is and that the Exxon Corporation is purchasing the surrounding area to erect a tract of homes that will greatly increase the business. The first misrepresentation is one that a principal might reasonably expect a salesperson to make, and the principal is thus liable for the fraud of the agent. However, the second misrepresentation is so unusual to the sale of a business that there would be no liability on the part of the principal.

In some states, the principal is held liable for the fraud of an agent even when the fraudulent statement is unusual or extreme under the doctrine of *respondeat superior.*

In some states (e.g., California), the courts hold that an innocent principal is not liable for the fraud of the agent if the written contract provides that the agent has no authority to make any representations not contained in the written contract, which the seller must sign. Such a provision gives notice to the third person that the agent's representations are not authorized. In such a case, although the third party cannot hold the principal liable for fraud, he or she can hold the agent for fraud and can rescind the contract.

D.   AUTOMOBILE STATUTES

Many states have statutes that provide that the owner of an automobile who has permitted another to drive the vehicle is liable up to a certain amount of money for the negligent act of the driver as though the driver were the agent, creating the relationship by operation of law.

Many states require that parents sign the application for a minor's driver's license. In such a situation, the parents undertake financial responsibility up to a limited amount for the negligent acts of the minor while driving the vehicle.

D.   LIABILITY OF AGENTS

A number of situations exist in which an agent may become personally liable to third persons.

1.   TORTS

An agent is personally liable for any torts he or she commits regardless of the liability of the principal. For example, a truck driver who negligently injures a person in a crosswalk is liable to the injured person even though the principal may also be liable.

The agent is liable even though he or she acted pursuant to the principal's directions. However, an innocent agent who is required to pay damages for such a tort is entitled to reimbursement from the principal.

2. CONTRACT IN NAME OF AGENT

A. UNDISCLOSED AGENCY AND UNDISCLOSED PRINCIPAL

If the agent's name appears alone on the contract without either the name of the principal or a statement of the fact of agency, the agent is personally liable.

B. DISCLOSED AGENCY AND PARTIALLY DISCLOSED PRINCIPAL

Under the Restatement of Agency and the law of nearly all of the states, an agent who signs as an agent but does not set forth the name of the principal is liable on the contract unless otherwise agreed. However, extrinsic evidence is permitted to show the intent of the parties (i.e., that the agent was not to be bound).

Other courts (e.g., California) go further and hold the agent liable regardless of the disclosure of the agency unless the name of the principal is disclosed so that it appears on the face of the instrument that only the principal is to be bound (e.g., plaintiff proposed a contract to "Hotel Berry Systems," and defendant Berry wrote on the contract as follows: "Signed and accepted, B. S. Berry"). Plaintiff knew that the defendant was acting only as an agent. Defendant was held personally liable, since he had signed his name without disclosure of the principal or of the fact of agency. The fact that the proposed contract was submitted to the hotel company was not enough, since the contract may have intended to hold the agent as well.

After the third person has discovered the identity of the undisclosed or partially disclosed principal, he or she may hold either the principal or the agent on the contract but not both of them. The third party has a choice, and once the choice is made, he or she is bound by it.

The following example illustrates the necessity of disclosing the principal if the agent seeks to avoid personal liability:

> **FACTS** Defendants had placed orders for materials furnished on credit by plaintiff in the amount of $20,711.95, ordered before and after the date defendants incorporated. Defendants now state that they were acting as agents for the corporation and are not liable personally for the bill.

> **DECISION** The court held that at the time the first purchases were made the defendants were individually liable, because the corporation had not yet been formed and thus could not exist as a principal. After incorporation, no notice was given to the plaintiff of the corporate status. Where agents fail to disclose their principal when it is within their power to do so, the agents are personally liable. Judgment for plaintiff.

> *Tarolli Lumber Co., Inc. v. Adreassi* (59 A.D.2d 1011, 399 N.Y.S.2d 739 [1977])

3. LACK OF AUTHORITY

Every agent implicitly warrants or guarantees that he or she is authorized by the principal to do what he or she is doing. An agent who does not have authority to bind the principal is bound by the contract unless the principal ratifies it.

4. INCOMPETENCY OF PRINCIPAL

Under the majority rule, the agent does not warrant the competency of the principal (e.g., that the principal is a minor or is mentally incompetent). However, the agent has a duty to inform third persons of the principal's lack of capacity and is liable for fraud in the form of nondisclosure if he or she does not do so.

5. WRONGFUL RECEIPT OF MONEY

If an agent obtains a payment of money from a third person by the use of illegal methods, the agent is liable to the third person. When a third person makes an overpayment to the agent or a payment when none is due, the agent who knows that the payment was not proper is liable to the third person.

E. LIABILITY OF THIRD PERSON TO PRINCIPAL

The third person can be liable to the principal in contract or in tort.

1. IN CONTRACT

A third person who has contracted with an agent representing a disclosed principal is as liable to the principal as though the contract had been made personally with the principal. Where the contract was unauthorized, it is not binding on the third party until the principal ratifies it.

A third person is liable to an undisclosed principal on a contract made on his or her behalf by the agent unless the terms of the contract expressly bar any principal or unless the third party would not contract with that particular principal and the agent or the principal knows this. In such a case, it is fraudulent for the agent not to reveal the principal's identity. However, in the normal case where the agent enters into a contract in his or her own name, concealing the fact that he or she is an agent and contracting as if he or she were the principal, the contract inures to the benefit of the principal, who may at any time come forward and claim all of the benefits from the third party.

2. IN TORT

A third person is liable in tort to a principal for injuries he or she commits to the principal's property or interests in the hands of an agent, whether or not the principal had been disclosed at the time, in the same manner and to the same extent as though such agency did not exist and as if the third person had dealt with him or her directly.

A person who knowingly induces or assists an agent to violate a fiduciary duty to the principal is liable to the principal (e.g., bribing an agent for obtaining confidential information).

A third person who colludes with the agent to have the agent act for the third person rather than the principal is liable for fraud in the absence of a reasonable belief that the principal acquiesces.

A third person who causes an agent to fail in his or her performance (e.g., to leave his or her employment prematurely) will be liable to the principal for damages.

F. LIABILITY OF THIRD PERSON TO AGENT

An agent who makes a contract with a third person on behalf of a disclosed principal has no right of action against the third person for breach of contract, and likewise, the third person normally has no right of action against the agent. Some exceptions exist, however.

1. UNDISCLOSED AND PARTIALLY DISCLOSED PRINCIPAL

If an agent executes a contract without informing the third person of the existance of the agency and the identity of the principal, the agent may maintain an action against the third person for breach of contract. Of course, if the principal asserts his or her rights under the contract, the rights of the agent are extinguished.

2. AGENT INTENDS TO BE BOUND

If the parties intend that the agent be bound to the contract even though the third person knew the agent was acting as an agent, the agent may bring action against the third person for breach of contract.

3. TORTS

The third person is liable for fraudulent or other wrongful acts causing injury to the agent. If the third person wrongfully injures the agent's property or person, the agent has a cause of action against the third person. If the third person wrongfully causes the agent to be discharged, the agent has a cause of action against the third person.

4. AGENT AS ASSIGNEE

When the principal has assigned or otherwise transferred his or her claim or right to the agent (e.g., for purpose of collecting money for the principal), the agent has a cause of action against the third person for breach of his or her obligation to the principal.

5.   FOR INJURY TO PRINCIPAL'S PROPERTY

An agent, such as a bailee, in possession of the principal's property has a general or special interest in the property and, therefore, may maintain an action against a third person who disturbs his or her possession or unlawfully injures the property. The third person's liability is not merely to the extent of the agent's special interest but is also for the full measure of damages caused by the injury, the agent being liable to account to the principal for the balance beyond his or her own interest.

ILLUSTRATIVE CASES

1. "Actual" Authority of Agent

COBLENTZ v. RISKIN
74 Nev. 53, 322 P.2d 905 (1958)

MERRILL, Justice.   Appellants are owners of the Thunderbird Jewel Shop in Clark County, Nevada. Respondent Riskin is a diamond broker and wholesale jeweler of Los Angeles, California. In August, 1955 appellants employed Hyman Davidson for services in connection with their store. In January, 1956 Davidson entered into a consignment agreement with Riskin pursuant to which he received, for purposes of retail sale, two expensive items of jewelry. In his dealings with Riskin, Davidson represented himself as manager of the jewel shop with full authority to receive merchandise on consignment. Riskin did not check these representations with appellants but did check with others in the jewelry trade and satisfied himself as to Davidson's authority. The jewelry pieces were reconsigned by Davidson without Riskin's approval or consent. The person to whom they were reconsigned has disappeared. Riskin demanded of appellants the return of the jewelry or its agreed value pursuant to the terms of the agreement. Upon failure of appellants to comply with his demand this action was brought. Judgment in favor of Riskin was given in the sum of $16,300. * * *

Riskin testified that it was the custom in the jewelry trade to take expensive pieces of jewelry on consignment rather than by purchase at wholesale. * * * By consignment retail merchants are not financially committed to the purchase of expensive items until they have themselves resold the items. Until resale their only financial commitment is that of safekeeping. Thus there is substantial benefit to be realized at the minimum of financial commitment. It can hardly be questioned that the engaging in consignment transactions would be regarded by those in the jewelry trade as a customary, proper and necessary function of store management. * * *

Davidson testified positively that he had been employed as manager of the store with instructions to run the store as he saw fit; that he had discussed with appellants the matter of taking merchandise on consignment and that appellants had approved; * * * that appellants had indicated approval of Davidson's success in securing such quality pieces and had never said anything about restrictions upon his authority to deal on consignment.

* * * Actual authority includes both implied authority and incidental authority. * * * Implied authority is that which the agent reasonably believes himself to possess as a result of representations by the principal or of acts of the agent permitted by the principal over a course of time in which the principal has acquiesced. * * * Incidental authority is that which is reasonably necessary, proper and usual to carry into effect the main authority granted. * * *

The trial court has found that Davidson was employed to serve as manager and that he did so serve. The evidence we have recited presents a clear case of both implied authority and incidental authority. We conclude that the trial court's determination of actual authority is supported by the record and that appellants are bound by Davidson's actions in their behalf in committing them to the consignment agreement with Riskin.

Affirmed.

2. "Ostensible" Authority of Agent

MIDWAY MOTORS v. PERNWORTH

141 Cal.App.2d 929, 296 P.2d 130 (1956)

Patrosso, Judge.   Action upon a sight draft drawn in favor of plaintiff's assignor, Berl Berry, Inc., by one F. H. Bradbury, purporting to act as agent for and in the name of the defendant, issued in payment for an automobile purchased from said assignor. The sole question is whether the trial court was warranted in concluding that Bradbury was not authorized to purchase and accept delivery of the automobile and to execute and deliver the draft upon behalf of the defendant.

Berl Berry, Inc., is a dealer in automobiles with its place of business in Kansas City, Missouri. Defendant is a physician having his office in Compton, California, and also was Secretary of Bradbury Motor Corporation, of which Bradbury was President. Prior to the events with which we are here concerned, the defendant established an account with funds provided by him and in his own name in the Compton National Bank for the purpose of paying for automobiles to be purchased by Bradbury who alone was authorized to draw thereon. The defendant testified that the account was opened for the purpose of providing funds for the purchase of cars by Bradbury Motor Corporation but due to the fact that it was in financial difficulties the account previously mentioned was maintained in defendant's individual name. * * *

The evidence * * * leaves no doubt but that Bradbury was authorized by defendant to purchase automobiles in the latter's name and to issue in payment thereof drafts in defendant's name drawn upon the defendant through the Compton National Bank; that Bradbury, pursuant to such authorization, proceeded to purchase automobiles, taking title thereto in the name of defendant and issuing in payment thereof drafts drawn upon the defendant which were accepted by the latter. This, if it does not establish actual authority in Bradbury to bind defendant, establishes that he was clothed with ostensible authority so to do. "Ostensible authority to do a particular act may be established by showing that the principal approved similar acts of the agent." * * *

Accepting as true defendant's statement that the purpose of establishing the account in the name of defendant individually was to permit the corporation to purchase automobiles because of the financial difficulties in which it found itself, it would be a gross fraud upon those who in good faith sold automobiles in the belief that the defendant individually was the purchaser thereof to permit defendant to say after the automobiles were purchased in his name that such cars were in fact purchased for the corporation, for it is only reasonable to assume that under the circumstances they would have refused to do so upon the credit or promise of a financially embarrassed corporation. More important, however, is the fact that, whether the automobiles were purchased for the defendant or the corporation, according to defendant's own testimony Bradbury was authorized to draw drafts on defendant in payment of such cars as he might purchase. * * *

The judgment is reversed.

3. Liability of Principal for Torts of Agent

EDGEWATER MOTELS, INC v. GATZKE

277 N.W.2d 11 (Minn., 1979)

Edgewater Motels, Inc. (plaintiff), brought an action against A. J. Gatzke and the Walgreen Company (defendants) for damages sustained in a fire allegedly caused by Gatzke's negligence.

A. J. Gatzke was a district manager for the Walgreen Company. He spent several weeks in Duluth, Minnesota, supervising the opening of a new Walgreen restaurant there. He remained at the restaurant approximately 17 hours a day and was on call 24 hours a day to handle problems arising in other Walgreen restaurants in his district. While in Duluth he lived at the Edgewater Motel at Walgreen's expense.

On August 23, 1977, Gatzke had been at the restaurant with a district manager from another district all day. At about 12:30 A.M. they used a company car to return to the Edgewater. They went across the street to a bar where Gatzke had four brandy Manhattans in about an hour, three of them doubles. While there they discussed drink mixing and prices with the bartender since the new Walgreen restaurant had a bar. Witnesses testified that Gatzke acted normal and sober when he returned to the motel. He went directly to his room and spent some time at a desk filling out the expense account required by Walgreen. Shortly after Gatzke went to bed, his room caught on fire. He escaped, but damage to the motel was over $330,000.

Gatzke smoked a cigarette after completing the expense account. He habitually smoked about two packs a day, and the motel maid testified that his room was usually full of cigarette butts and that often there were butts in the plastic wastebasket next to the desk. A fire reconstruction specialist placed the origin of the fire in or near the wastebasket.

Edgewater sued Walgreen as well as Gatzke, arguing that it was liable for Gatzke's negligence based on *respondeat superior*. Walgreen's motion for judgment notwithstanding, a jury verdict favoring Edgewater was based on its claim that Gatzke was not acting within the scope of his employment at the time the fire was started.

SCOTT, Justice.　To support a finding that an employee's negligent act occurred within his scope of employment, it must be shown that his conduct was, to some degree, in furtherance of the interests of his employer.

Other factors to be considered in the scope of employment determination are whether the conduct is of the kind that the employee is authorized to perform and whether the act occurs substantially within authorized time and space restrictions.

The initial question raised by the instant factual situation is whether an employee's smoking of a cigarette can constitute conduct within his scope of employment.

A number of courts which have dealt with the instant issue have ruled that the act of smoking, even when done simultaneously with work-related activity, is not within the employee's scope of employment because it is a matter personal to the employee which is not done in furtherance of the employer's interests.

Other courts which have considered the question have reasoned that the smoking of a cigarette, if done while engaged in the business of the employer, is within an employee's scope of employment because it is a minor deviation from the employee's work-related activities, and thus merely an act done incidental to general employment.

We agree with this analysis and hereby hold that an employer can be held vicariously liable for his employee's negligent smoking of a cigarette if he was otherwise acting in the scope of his employment at the time of the negligent act.

The expense account was, of course, completed so that Gatzke could be reimbursed by Walgreen's for his work-related expenses. In this sense, Gatzke is performing an act for his own personal benefit. However, the completion of the expense account also furthers the employer's business in that it provides detailed documentation of business expenses so that they are properly deductible for tax purposes. In this light, the filling out of the expense form can be viewed as serving a dual purpose: that of furthering Gatzke's personal interests and promoting his employer's business purposes. Accordingly, it is reasonable for the jury to find that the completion of the expense account is an act done in furtherance of the employer's business purposes.

Additionally, the record indicates that Gatzke was an executive type of employee who had no set working hours. He considered himself a 24-hour-a-day man; his room at the Edgewater Motel was his "office away from home."

It was therefore also reasonable for the jury to determine that the filling out of his expense account was done within authorized time and space limits of his employment.

Reversed for Edgewater and against Walgreen.

4. Torts That Are Agent's Sole Responsibility

CITY OF GREEN COVE SPRINGS v. DONALDSON
348 F.2d 197 (5th Cir., 1965)

JONES, Circuit Judge.   This action was brought against appellant, a Florida municipal corporation, by the appellee, Mrs. Yvonne Donaldson, to recover damages sustained as a result of the actions of an employee of the City of Green Cove Springs. Jurisdiction was based upon diversity of citizenship. A judgment was recovered in the amount of $9,000, and costs. * * * At about 9:00 o'clock in the evening of July 10, 1960, Mrs. Donaldson and a companion, Mrs. Wells, left the Donaldson home in Mayport, Florida, and drove to Green Cove Springs. After arriving there and driving around for several hours, the two women began their journey home, and were then stopped by two police officers employed by the City and driving an official vehicle. The officers were on duty at the time. The record shows that the initial reason for the arrest was that Mrs. Donaldson was slightly exceeding the speed limit, for which the officers intended to give her a mere warning. Upon further investigation it appeared that there was something irregular about the automobile license tag, and Mrs. Donaldson was requested to follow the officers to the city jail so the tag could be checked.

* * * At no time was the plaintiff booked or issued a citation; nor was she ever taken into the jail. When they arrived at the jail, [Officer] Mosely said there was no one there, and drove to a point near a railroad track, a short distance away. Mosely stopped the car, "propositioned" Mrs. Donaldson several times, and then assaulted her. According to the plaintiff's testimony, she resisted for approximately forty-five minutes, until Mosely overcame her and succeeded in raping her. The next thing she remembered was driving home. The jury returned a verdict for Mrs. Donaldson, and the City has appealed from the judgment entered on the verdict. * * * Subsequent to the oral argument before this Court, the Supreme Court of Florida held that Florida municipal corporations are liable for intentional torts of their police officers to the same extent as private corporations. * * *

The imposition upon an employer of vicarious liability for the torts of its agents is limited by the proposition that the tort must have been committed while the agent was acting within the scope of his employment. * * * Although the scope of employment is considerably broader than explicitly authorized acts of the employee, it does not extend to cases in which "the servant has stepped aside from his employment to commit a tort which the master neither directed in fact, nor could be supposed, from the nature of his employment, to have authorized or expected the servant to do." * * * We hold that the acts of Officer Mosely in his assault and rape of the plaintiff were outside the scope of his employment as a police officer for the City of Green Cove Springs. Consequently, the City is not liable, as a matter of law, for her injuries.

* * * It is generally held that liability for an assault by an employee that bears no relation to the real or apparent scope of his employment or to the interest of his employer is not imposed upon the employer under the doctrine of respondeat superior. * * *

The facts, construed most favorably for the appellee, will admit of no inference other than that in his rape of the plaintiff, Officer Mosely stepped aside from his employment to accomplish his own, rather than the City's purpose. Accordingly, the judgment is reversed and the cause remanded to the district court for entry of a judgment in favor of the City of Green Cove Springs.

Reversed and remanded.

5. Issue of the Lunch Hour Rule

GIPSON v. DAVIS REALTY CO.

215 Cal.App.2d 190, 30 Cal.Rptr. 253 (1963)

MOLINARI, Justice.　This is an appeal from a judgment in favor of the defendant, Davis Realty Company, a corporation, in an action for damages for personal injuries. * * *

On April 4, 1957, Mrs. Jane Gipson, who was pregnant with child, was being transported by ambulance to the Stanford Hospital where her child was to be delivered. A collision between the ambulance and an automobile owned and driven by Roland Shugg occurred at the intersection of 26th Avenue and Clement Street in San Francisco. The accident occurred at about 12:20 p. m. The child was born about 40 minutes after the accident. The child showed signs of brain damage immediately after the accident, it being subsequently determined that such damage was permanent and that the child was suffering from a disability diagnosed as cerebral palsy. * * * A personal injury action was thereafter instituted by the child's father, Edward T. Gipson, as guardian ad litem on behalf of the child, * * * and against Shugg and Davis Realty Company, a corporation, as the alleged employer of Shugg. * * *

The important question is whether, at the time of the accident in question, Shugg, as such agent, was acting within the course and scope of his employment. * * *

The facts leading up to the accident appear to be undisputed. Shugg testified: that on the morning of the accident he was at the office of Davis Realty; that he left the office for the purpose of going to 38th Avenue and Clement Street to try to obtain a listing on a house at that corner on behalf of Davis Realty; that his sole intention upon leaving the office was to look at that property; * * * that as he started out on Clement Street he noticed it was around noon, so he decided to stop by at his home for lunch and then continue out to look at the property after lunch; * * * that the respondent did not instruct its salesmen as to when or where they should eat lunch; that it was the usual practice to stop at a convenient location for lunch and then continue on with the business of Davis Realty; that he ate lunch at home if he happened to be in the area; * * *.

* * * Therefore, whether or not the principal or employer is responsible for the act of the agent or employee at the time of the injury depends upon whether the agent or employee was engaged at that time in the transaction of the business of his principal or employer, or whether he was engaged in an act which was done for his own personal convenience or accommodation and related to an end or purpose exclusively and individually his own. * * * Accordingly, it is the general rule that an employee on his way to lunch, even though he is driving an automobile which is the property of the master, is not engaged in furthering any end of the employer, and that therefore under such circumstances, the servant is not acting within the scope of his employment. * * *

The so-called "lunch hour rule," * * * is, however, subject to an exception termed the "dual or combined purpose rule." * * *

> "[W]here the servant is combining his own business with that of his master, or attending to both at substantially the same time, no nice inquiry will be made as to which business the servant was actually engaged in when a third person was injured; but the master will be held responsible, unless it clearly appears that the servant could not have been directly or indirectly serving his master."

* * * In the instant case it cannot be said that at the time of the accident Shugg was engaged in an act which was done for his own personal convenience or accommodation and related to an end or purpose exclusively and individually his own. The testimony shows that, initially, his sole intent was to attend to the business of his principal at 38th Avenue and Clement Street. Enroute, he decided to combine his business with that of Davis Realty. This is the extent of his deviation. * * * The extent and substantiality of Shugg's deviation, if any, was a question of fact for the jury.

The judgment is reversed.

6. Liability of Principal Where Agency Disclosed

GUILLORY v. COURVILLE

158 So.2d 475 (La.App., 1963)

CULPEPPER, Judge. This is a suit on an open account. From an adverse judgment the plaintiff appeals.

The substantial issue is whether defendant has proved his defense that he was acting as a disclosed agent of a corporation.

* * * There is no dispute as to the law. An agent is responsible to those with whom he contracts when he does not disclose that he is acting as an agent. * * *

Furthermore, the special defense of agency, cannot be proved by the

mere testimony of defendant. He must be corroborated by other evidence.
* * *

The facts show that in January of 1958 the defendant, Claude Courville, and several other parties formed a corporation known as "Basile Flying Service, Inc.", domiciled in Evangeline Parish, Louisiana, for the purpose of engaging in the business of providing flying services to farmers. This concern purchased gasoline from the plaintiff at various times, from February, 1958 down through July of 1959, on an open account. Although occasionally delinquent, the account was paid except for the sum of $1,834.48 for purchases made during the period July 4, 1959 through July 30, 1959. Plaintiff's statements of account were addressed to "Basile Flying Service."

Plaintiff testified that he did not know the business was incorporated and that he was relying on the credit of defendant, with whom he had done satisfactory business before. Defendant testified that he personally told plaintiff before the purchases in question were made, that the business was incorporated. At least one other witness corroborated defendant in this respect. Furthermore, several checks received by plaintiff's office, in payment of previous amounts on this open account, were clearly marked "Basile Flying Service, Inc.", although plaintiff denied seeing any of these checks.
* * *

The record amply supports the following finding of facts by the district judge:

> "The court is of the opinion that plaintiff was informed by the defendant and other stockholders of the corporation of the fact that he was doing business with the corporation; that plaintiff cashed checks from the corporation; that an account was opened for the corporation and a credit check was made on the corporation. It is further the opinion of the court that the present action against defendant is a result of plaintiff's inability to effect collection against the corporation to whom the gasoline was originally billed or charged. The court is of the opinion that no action of defendant in this matter created a personal obligation toward plaintiff."

For the reasons assigned the judgment appealed is affirmed.

PROBLEMS

1. P is a bread manufacturer. He employs A to purchase wheat for him, but he instructs A not to purchase any wheat in a quantity greater than 100 bushels without first contacting P for approval of the price. A represents to T, who knows he is P's agent, that he has authority to purchase 500 bushels of wheat for P. However, he does not inform T that he has no such authority without approval of P. Without obtaining P's approval, A purchases 500 bushels of wheat from T. P now refuses to take the wheat, and T sues P for breach of contract. Decision?

2. S, a deliveryman for M's liquor store, delivers a case of whiskey to a customer's home. After leaving the customer's home, S drives five miles farther to a hospital to visit his sick mother. As he is driving out of the hospital parking lot, he negligently runs into a child in the crosswalk. The child, through her guardian ad litem, brings suit against M. Decision?

3. Pacific Tuna Company hired Charlie as a purchasing agent to buy fish for it. After several transactions, Pacific Tuna Company advised Charlie that future purchases should be made only on consignment but did not notify the suppliers of the change. Despite these instructions, Charlie bought some fish outright and then bought ice to keep the fish fresh. Discuss Charlie's authority and Pacific Tuna Company's liability.

4. A bus driver for a local bus company asked a passenger who was slightly intoxicated to please get off of the bus because he was making a general nuisance of himself. The passenger refused. The bus driver and the passenger exchanged words and tempers flared. Finally, the bus driver pushed the passenger off the bus. With that, the passenger referred to the bus driver's ancestors with some unkindly remarks. The bus driver then got off the bus and hit the passenger in the mouth breaking some front teeth. Passenger brings action against the bus company. Bus company defends on the grounds that the bus driver went beyond the scope of employment, since the company does not hire bus drivers to go around hitting people. Decision?

5. Burkovits sued Morton Gregson Co. and Kleeburger for return of overpayments for meat. Kleeburger was a salesman for Morton Gregson Co., delivering meat to Burkovits and collecting weekly. Over a period of time, Kleeburger wrongfully altered statements to Burkovits, and in consequence Burkovits made large overpayments. Burkovits sued Morton Gregson to recover the amounts overpaid, which had been retained by Kleeburger. Decision?

6. Reilly, president of Rock Wool Insulating Company, borrowed money from Huston on behalf of the corporation and executed a promissory note for the amount of the loan. The minute book of the corporation showed that Reilly had general authority to make loans for the company but indicated nothing regarding execution of notes. When Huston sued on the note, Rock Wool Insulating Company claimed that Reilly had no authority to execute the note. Decision?

7. Pete operated a service station for the Southern Oil Company and was one of their most successful retailers. Pete told several customers that the products of his neighboring competitors were from foreign-owned companies, were inferior, and tended to cause irreparable damage to motors when used. Southern Oil had permitted Pete to make these statements, knowing that they were false and slanderous. The competitors sued Southern Oil Company for damages due to Pete's misrepresentations. Decision?

8. A contract was put on the letterhead of a corporation principal and signed, "The Feldheym Co., Inc. *Dave Schwebel.*" T brings action against Dave Schwebel personally. T contends that Schwebel did not indicate by his signature that he was acting only as an agent and that he should have used the word "by" before his signature. Schwebel contends that he was acting only as an agent and that this fact is easily inferred from the letterhead and from the name of the company before the signature. Decision?

9. Luke was fired by the ABC Company because of arguments he had with the sales manager. Shortly thereafter, Luke visited the XYZ Company, one of the accounts he had serviced for the ABC Company, and collected $250 which was due the ABC Company. Luke absconded with the money. No notice had been given to XYZ Company concerning Luke's discharge. ABC Company sues XYZ Company for the $250. Decision?

10. Ace Corporation, wishing to acquire an adjoining site for its factory expansion but without provoking a rise in price, hired Lott Realty to purchase the land without disclosing Ace's name. Lott Realty did so and signed a contract in its own name with Landers to purchase the site. If Ace changes its mind and refuses to complete the sale, what are Landers' legal rights?

Part IV

PROPERTY

Chapter 22

PERSONAL PROPERTY

A. NATURE

In our individualistic society, *property* refers to the rights one has in anything that may be owned. Property may be classified as *real* property, consisting of land and those things intended to be permanently attached thereto by people or by nature, such as buildings and vegetation; or *personal* property, referring to all other things, including tangible movable items and certain intangibles, such as contract rights. A single piece of property might be classified as either real or personal, depending upon its nature and intended use.

B. PERSONAL PROPERTY DEFINED

Personal property includes all things that are not real property and that are generally movable. Such things may be either tangible or intangible.

1. TANGIBLE PERSONAL PROPERTY

Tangible personal property consists of those objects that we recognize through our physical senses. Some examples are furniture, automobiles, books, food, perfume, and stereo equipment. The legal term "chattel" refers to such items.

2. INTANGIBLE PERSONAL PROPERTY

Intangible personal property is that which has no physical dimension but does represent a legal right to receive ownership or possession. Some examples are patent rights, shares of stock, negotiable instruments, currency, insurance policies, and executory contract rights. Such documents are not intrinsically valuable but represent specific rights. Accounts receivable (unpaid obligations owed by one party to another) are also intangible.

C. ACQUISITION OF TITLE

Title and right to possession of personal property may be acquired in many different ways. The U.C.C. has standardized the law on the sale of goods (see Part 5, The Law of Sales). The U.C.C. also sets forth the legal rules for the acquisition and transfer of title to negotiable instruments (see Part 8, Commercial Paper). In addition to acquisition by these standard commercial transactions, personal property rights may be acquired by gift, through creation, because of accession or confusion of movable goods, and by operation of law.

1. GIFTS

A gift is the voluntary transfer of property from the owner (the donor) to another (the donee) without payment of compensation. This lack of consideration is the basic difference between a gift and a contract. To be effective, a gift must be completed by delivery and acceptance. A gratuitous promise to make a gift in the future would not be enforceable. Gifts of personal property may be *inter vivos, causa mortis,* or testamentary. The latter occurs when the property is made as a gift through a validly executed will of a deceased person.

A. GIFT *INTER VIVOS*

An *inter vivos* gift is one made between two living persons. The legal requirements are as follows:

1. Donor's expressing an intent to transfer title.

2. Delivery of property by the donor.

3. Right of the donee to disclaim the gift and divest title within a reasonable time after notice of the gift.

The delivery may be actual or symbolic. A symbolic delivery would be the handing over of the keys to a new automobile, thereby making a gift of the vehicle.

Since there is no consideration, a prospective donee cannot sue to compel the gift, and if the donor dies before making delivery, the gift fails.

A gift may also be conditional, requiring that some condition occur before the transfer of title to the gift is completed. The typical example is the gift of an engagement ring, which usually is made in contemplation of the condition of subsequent marriage. Consequently, if the party who received such a conditional gift of the ring breaks the engagement, the ring would have to be returned.

B. GIFT *CAUSA MORTIS*

A *causa mortis* gift is one made when the donor, believing he or she is nearing death, delivers personal property to a donee intending that the donee shall retain it after the donor dies. This is a conditional gift, and the property must be returned under the following circumstances:

1. Donor does not die.

2. Donor revokes gift before his or her death.

3. Donee predeceases the donor.

c. UNIFORM GIFTS TO MINORS ACT

All states have enacted laws providing for the making of gifts of money or securities to minors. Under the Uniform Gifts to Minors Act, adopted by a majority of jurisdictions, adults can make a gift to the minor by depositing the cash or registering the securities with another adult, broker, or financial institution with trust powers, as custodian for the minor. This is considered an irrevocable gift but may be used by the custodian for the minor's benefit.

2. CREATION

Artists and inventors may obtain exclusive rights to their creations under patent, copyright, and trademark laws.

A. PATENT LAW

A creator who has given physical expression to an idea may be granted a patent by the U.S. Patent Office. A patent is the grant of a monopoly to the inventor for a period of 17 years and is not renewable. The item must be something new and useful, not previously known and used. The Patent Office, after making a thorough examination of the prior art and determining that the invention, process, product, or design does not conflict with a prior pending or issued patent, may grant the monopoly.

A patentee who believes that an infringement of his or her patent rights has occurred may be required to sue in Federal Court to determine the validity of the patent.

B. COPYRIGHT LAW

A copyright is a grant by the government of the exclusive right to print, publish, and sell books, written material, musical compositions, lectures, works of art, photographs, motion pictures, data systems, videotapes, and other creations in a tangible medium of expression. The Copyright Revision Act of 1976 was the first major change in the law since 1909 and changed the former time period of 28 years plus a 28-year renewal to the life of the person plus 50 years. Existing copyrights in their first 28-year period may be extended for an additional 47 years.

The exclusive right now attaches upon creation rather than publication. Fair use is permitted but not infringement upon creator's rights. Reproduction for classroom use is fair if certain tests are met. In making such a determination, the following factors are considered:

1. Purpose and character of the use (commercial or nonprofit).

2. Nature of the work.

3. Proportion of the work used.

4. Effect of use upon the potential market and value of the work.

Where an anthology has been compiled, the copyright belongs to each original author for his or her contribution unless it has been expressly granted to the compiler.

The following case is an example of the application of fair use in connection with historical biographies:

FACTS　Gardner, author of *The Rosenberg Story*, sued Nizer, author of *The Implosion Conspiracy*, for copyright infringement, alleging that Nizer copied material from Gardner's book while writing about the Rosenbergs' case.

DECISION　The court held that historical facts, as such, are not protected by copyright. Biographies are similar of necessity and infringement occurs only where there is a substantial or material taking from a copyrighted work. Also, the fair use doctrine applied in this case. Fair use is the right to use copyrighted matter in a reasonable manner. Since the rule is liberally applied to biographies because of the public benefit from such works, infringement requires similarity that is virtually complete or verbatim. The case was dismissed.

Gardner v. Nizer (391 F. Supp. 940 [D.C.N.Y., 1975])

c. TRADEMARK LAW

The United States Code defines a trademark as any "word, name, symbol, or device or combination thereof adopted and used by a manufacturer or merchant to identify his goods to distinguish them from those manufactured or sold by others."

Under federal law, a trademark may be registered by its owner or user. Such registration will entitle the registrant to its exclusive use for a period of 20 years. To qualify for registration, a name or symbol must be distinctive in style, unless long public use has identified the product with a common name. Anyone using a registered trademark without the consent of the owner is liable for damages for such unauthorized use.

When a trademark becomes so common that it is used in a generic sense and becomes a part of the language, the exclusive rights to its use are lost. Some examples of such former trade names are linoleum, aspirin, trampoline, and brassiere.

3. ACQUISITION BY ACCESSION OR CONFUSION

Acquisition of title by accession or by confusion has special legal significance related to the moveable nature of personal property.

A. ACCESSION

Accession refers to an owner's right to any increase in the value of his or her property caused by man-made or natural means. Examples are the newborn young of animals, repairs made by a finder of a lost watch, or equipment added to a stolen automobile. When courts are asked to rule on whether title to the added value goes to the rightful owner of the property, an equitable result is sought by analyzing such factors as intent and willfulness. The following case illustrates rightful ownership of property with added value:

> **FACTS**   Lane bought a dump truck on credit and had its bed and hoist replaced by Texas Hydraulic. When the finance company repossessed the truck, it claimed the improvements by accession. The court agreed. Texas Hydraulic appealed.
>
> **DECISION**   Although Texas Hydraulic claimed that it could remove the body and the hoist without damaging the truck, the court held that since the work had been completed and delivered to the owner without the requirement of a security document, the sale was complete and the items had become part of the truck by accession.
>
> *Texas Hydraulic and Equipment Co. v. Associates Discount Corp.* (414 S.W. 2d 199 [Tex., 1967])

B. CONFUSION

Confusion of goods occurs when property belonging to different owners is commingled. If the mixing is done willfully and wrongfully by one of the parties so that the total mass is indistinguishable, the innocent party acquires title to all. This rule does not apply if the following circumstances exist:

1.   Commingling was done by consent of all owners.

2.   Commingling was done by accident or mistake.

3.   When the goods are of equal kind and grade of fungibles (oil, grain, etc.).

4.   When the owners can still identify their goods.

4. POSSESSION

Under certain circumstances, the taking of physical possession of property, if done lawfully, creates ownership rights. If lost property is found, the finder has title that is good against everyone except the owner. Title to property that has been abandoned or over which no prior title rights have been established rests with the person who takes and holds possession.

A. LOST PROPERTY

Property is lost or mislaid when its rightful owner cannot locate it but does not intend to give up title or ownership. However, "finders keepers, losers weepers" is not the law, and title remains with the loser. To acquire legal title, the finder, who is considered an involuntary bailee, must comply with the requirements of local statutes, which usually require that the item be turned over to the police or other authority for a period of time. If the owner does not claim the property, it is ordinarily returned to the finder. If the owner reclaims the property, the finder is not entitled to a reward or compensation unless a contract has been made with the owner or statutory provision grants such award.

(1) Property Found on Privately Owned Property

The general rule that the finder's rights to goods are superior to all but the rightful owner may not apply when the goods are discovered on privately owned property. Under certain circumstances, the owner of the place, rather than the finder, is entitled to the goods.

1.   If the goods are found in a private, rather than a public, area of the place (e.g., a private room for examining safe deposit boxes in a bank, rather than the bank's public lobby).

2.   If the goods are determined to be mislaid, placed somewhere, and then forgotten, rather than lost, since the owner, if and when he or she remembers, would probably return to the place where he or she left them.

3.   If they are found by an employee, such as a chambermaid, who has the duty to turn the goods over to the employer.

4.   Where the finders are trespassers.

(2) Buried Property

Where lost property is found buried in the ground, the owner of the land generally has a claim superior to the finder. An exception is the common law treasure trove rule, followed in many jurisdictions, which gives the finder of bullion or coin in the soil the right to possession.

B. ABANDONMENT

Personal property is abandoned when the owner gives up possession with an intent to disclaim title. The items you put in your trash can are usually abandoned. The first person to take possession and control of abandoned property becomes the property's owner.

C. WILD ANIMALS

Wild animals and fish, living freely in nature, are not owned by any person. However, under the state's police power, most wildlife is protected by game regulations and conservation laws. Absent such restrictions, anyone who legally obtains possession and control of such wild creatures becomes their owner. If the animal should be captured or killed while the hunter is trespassing on private property, title would belong to the landowner.

5. OPERATION OF LAW

Title to personal property may be transferred by operation of law. For example, it may be sold by a trustee in bankruptcy for the benefit of creditors.

Personal property not exempted by statute may be seized by proper authority and sold to satisfy court-awarded damages of the judgment creditor. Ordinarily, judgments against personal property have no effect upon the title unless the determination of title was the purpose of the lawsuit. A person claiming ownership of personal property in the possession of another may elect to either sue to recover the property, thereby determining title, or treat the matter as an involuntary transfer and sue for the value of the property together with any money damages in an action for conversion (the wrongful conversion of another's property to one's own use).

If a person dies without having disposed of his or her property by will, the personal property will go to the heirs by operation of law in accordance with the laws of succession in the state where the person resided at the time of his or her death. If there were no heirs, the property will go to the state by *escheat*. Various state escheat laws also provide that the title to unclaimed property, such as stock dividends, bank deposits, and insurance payments, shall revert to the state after a prescribed period of time. It is estimated that over a billion dollars a year of such intangibles are never claimed by those entitled to ownership.

D. FIXTURES

Fixtures are usually defined as personal property that has been affixed to the land or made a part of buildings in such a way that they are considered part of the real property.

The key test for making such a determination is the intent of the parties concerned. The method of attachment, the purpose for which placed, and the ordinary custom and usage may all be considered in ascertaining the intent. This can be an issue involving ordinary household appliances, as illustrated by the following case:

FACTS Plaintiff sued to foreclose on a mortgage on defendant's house and also alleged (1) that Sears had removed a hot water heater, range, and other kitchen equipment that Sears had installed in the house under a conditional sales contract and (2) that Sears had replaced the original equipment. The issue was whether the items were personal property that Sears could remove or fixtures that should remain in the house and be included with the foreclosure.

DECISION The lower court in its final judgment held the items to be personalty, stating that there was no evidence of intent to "make the annexation a permanent accession to the freehold." Since the intention of the party making the annexation had been held to be a primary test in determining whether an article is a fixture, a finding of no evidence of intent requires a ruling that the articles were in fact not fixtures. The judgment for Sears is accordingly affirmed.

First Federal Savings and Loan Association of Okaloosa County v. Stovall (289 So. 2d 32 [Fla.App., 1974])

Trade fixtures are those fixtures placed in a rented building by a tenant for use in business or trade. They may ordinarily be removed by the tenant if done before the expiration of the lease and if they can be removed without doing injury to the property. These factors were considered by the court in the following case:

FACTS　The city of Rockford had condemned an office building, and the appraisal included a payment for immovable fixtures. The tenant, an architectural firm, had installed decorative wall coverings, carpets, and cabinets, which it claimed were trade fixtures entitling them to the sum paid by the city. The corporate landlord also claimed the money, contending that the items were part of the building. No material damage resulted to the building by removal of these items.

DECISION　Deciding that these items were trade fixtures, the court held that when tenants add fixtures to premises, there is a presumption that they so do for their own benefit and not for that of the landlord. This rule is construed liberally, and the tenant is allowed to remove such fixtures if the tenant does so before the lease expires and without causing any material damage to the property. Judgment for tenant.

Empire Building Corp. v. Orput and Associates, Inc. (336 N.E. 2d 82, 32 Ill. App. 3d 839 [1975])

E.　MULTIPLE OWNERSHIP OF PROPERTY

The ownership of property, personal or real, may be held by one individual, in severalty, or it may be held concurrently by two or more persons or entities. Joint owners are referred to as co-tenants, with each entitled to an undivided interest in the entire item and no one having a sole claim to any specific portion.

Concurrent ownerships are generally classified as tenancy in common or as joint tenancy. Married persons may hold property jointly in some states as community property and in other states, to real property only, as tenancy by the entirety.

1.　TENANCY IN COMMON

When title to property is transferred or deeded to two or more persons, in the absence of an express statement to the contrary, the majority rule is that such property is held as tenants in common. The distinctive feature of such tenancy is that it is an estate of inheritance. Upon the death of any joint owner, his or her interest in the property passes to the heirs or devisees. The ownership shares do not have to be co-equal but may be in any proportion, and profits and costs are shared in the same proportion as the ownership interest. The only common right that is shared equally is the right of possession. In the case of real property, a tenant in common may petition the court to divide the land in kind between the tenants. Such an action is called "partition."

2. JOINT TENANCY

Joint tenancy is created when exactly equal interests are transferred at the same time by one instrument that expressly states that the parties are to take possession as joint tenants.

The important characteristic of this tenancy is the right of survivorship. Upon the death of one of the joint tenants, his or her interest passes equally to the surviving joint tenants or tenant.

A transfer by one of the joint tenants of his or her interest to another destroys the joint tenancy and transforms the status to one of tenants in common.

Joint tenancy property does not go through probate, since title is assumed to pass automatically to the survivors upon the death of a joint tenant. The property is, however, subject to the payment of appropriate estate and inheritance taxes.

3. COMMUNITY PROPERTY

In some states, including all of those in the southwestern United States area acquired from Mexico, the system of community property is followed. This refers to all property, real and personal, acquired by the earnings or efforts of the husband or the wife during the marriage, which each then owns co-equally with the other. In addition, each spouse may have separate property. This refers to that property owned by either at the time of marriage, acquired by gift or inheritance, or community property that has been converted by agreement. Commingling separate property with community property to the extent that it can no longer be traced may also change the separate property to community property. Originally, the husband was designated the manager of the community and its property. Recent sex discrimination court decisions have declared equal management rights to both spouses.

Several states permit married persons to take title to real property as tenants by the entirety. Upon the death of either spouse, the entire property goes to the other. Neither spouse can transfer title or force a partition without the written consent of the other. In the event of a divorce, title is then held as tenants in common.

ILLUSTRATIVE CASES

1. Creating Patent Property Rights

DIAMOND v. CHAKRABARTY

447 U.S. 303, 100 S.Ct. 2204, 65 L.Ed.2d 144 (1980)

BURGER, Chief Justice.

*   *   *

In 1972, respondent Chakrabarty, a microbiologist, filed a patent application * * * related to Chakrabarty's invention of "a bacterium from the genus Pseudomonas containing therein at least two stable energy-generating plasmids, each of said plasmids providing a separate hydrocarbon degradative pathway." This human-made, genetically engineered bacterium is capable of breaking down multiple components of crude oil. Because of this property, which is possessed by no naturally occurring bacteria, Chakrabarty's invention is believed to have significant value for the treatment of oil spills.

*   *   *

The Constitution grants Congress broad power to legislate to "promote the Progress of Science and useful Arts, by securing for limited Times to Authors and Inventors the exclusive Right to their respective Writings and Discoveries." The patent laws promote this progress by offering inventors exclusive rights for a limited period as an incentive for their inventiveness and research efforts. * * * The authority of Congress is exercised in the hope that "[t]he productive effort thereby fostered will have a positive effect on society through the introduction of new products and processes of manufacture into the economy, and the emanations by way of increased employment and better lives for our citizens."

*   *   *

The relevant legislative history also supports a broad construction. The Patent Act of 1793, authored by Thomas Jefferson, defined statutory subject matter as "any new and useful art, machine, manufacture, or composition of matter, or any new or useful improvement [thereof]." The Act embodied Jefferson's philosophy that "ingenuity should receive a liberal encouragement."

*   *   *

This is not to suggest that [the patent law] has no limits or that it embraces every discovery. The laws of nature, physical phenomena, and abstract ideas have been held not patentable. * * * Thus, a new mineral discovered in the earth or a new plant found in the wild is not patentable subject matter. Likewise, Einstein could not patent his celebrated law that $E=mc$; nor could Newton have patented the law of gravity. Such discoveries are "manifestations of . . . nature, free to all men and reserved exclusively to none."

*   *   *

Judged in this light, respondent's micro-organism plainly qualifies as patentable subject matter. His claim is not to a hitherto unknown natural phenomenon, but to a nonnaturally occurring manufacture or composition of matter—a product of human ingenuity "having a distinctive name, character [and] * * * use."

* * * A rule that unanticipated inventions are without protection would conflict with the core concept of the patent law that anticipation undermines patentability. Mr. Justice Douglas reminded that the inventions most benefiting mankind are those that "push back the frontiers of chemistry, physics, and the like."

                              *   *   *

To buttress its argument, the petitioner * * * points to grave risks that may be generated by research endeavors such as respondent's. The briefs present a gruesome parade of horribles. Scientists, among them Nobel laureates, are quoted suggesting that genetic research may pose a serious threat to the human race, or, at the very least, that the dangers are far too substantial to permit such research to proceed apace at this time. We are told the genetic research and related technological developments may spread pollution and disease, that it may result in a loss of genetic diversity, and that its practice may tend to depreciate the value of human life. These arguments are forcefully, even passionately presented; they remind us that, at times, human ingenuity seems unable to control fully the forces it creates—that, with Hamlet, it is sometimes better "to bear those ills we have than fly to others that we know not of." * * *

* * * The grant or denial of patents on micro-organisms is not likely to put an end to genetic research or to its attendant risks. The large amount of research that has already occurred when no researcher had sure knowledge that patent protection would be available suggests that legislative or judicial fiat as to patentability will not deter the scientific mind from probing into the unknown any more than Canute could command the tides. Whether respondent's claims are patentable may determine whether research efforts are accelerated by the hope of reward or slowed by want of incentives, but that is all.

Accordingly, the judgment of the Court of Customs and Patent Appeals [allowing the patent] is affirmed.

2. Mislaid Property Rule

DOLITSKY v. DOLLAR SAVINGS BANK

203 Misc. 262, 118 N.Y.S.2d 65 (1952)

This was an action by Betty Dolitsky (plaintiff) against Dollar Savings Bank (defendant) to recover $100 allegedly found by Dolitsky.

Betty Dolitsky rented a safe-deposit box from Dollar Savings Bank. The safe-deposit vault of the bank was in the basement, and the vault area was walled off from all other parts of the bank. Only box renters and officers and employees of the bank were admitted to this area. To gain access to the area, a box renter had to obtain an admission slip, fill in the box number and sign the slip, have the box number and signature checked by an employee against the records of the bank, and then present the slip to a guard who admitted the renter to the vault area.

On November 7, 1951, Dolitsky requested access to her box. While Dolitsky was in the booth she was looking through an advertising folder which the bank had placed there and found a $100 bill, which she turned over to the attendant. Dolitsky waited one year, and during that time the rightful owner of the $100 bill made no claim for it. Dolitsky then demanded that the bank surrender the bill to her, claiming that she was entitled to the bill as finder. The bank claimed that the bill was mislaid property and that it owed a duty to keep the bill for the rightful owner.

TRIMARCO, Justice.   At common law property was lost when possession had been casually and involuntarily parted with, so that the mind had no impress of and could have no knowledge of the parting. Mislaid property was that which the owner had voluntarily and intentionally placed and then forgotten.

Property in someone's possession cannot be found in the sense of common-law lost property. If the article is in the custody of the owner of the place when it is discovered it is not lost in the legal sense; instead it is mislaid. Thus, if a chattel is discovered anywhere in a private place where only a limited class of people have a right to be and they are customers of the owner of the premises, who has the duty of preserving the property of his customers, it is in the possession of the owner of the premises.

In the case of mislaid property discovered on the premises of another, the common-law rule is that the proprietor of the premises is held to have the better right to hold the same for the owner, or the proprietor has custody for the benefit of the owner, or the proprietor is the gratuitous bailee of the owner. The effect of the cases, despite their different description of the relationship, is that the proprietor is the bailee of the owner. Thus, the discoverer of mislaid property has the duty to leave it with the proprietor of the premises, and the latter has the duty to hold it for the owner. New York statutory requirements do not change this rule.

The bank is a gratuitous bailee of mislaid property once it has knowledge of the property. As such the bank has the duty to exercise ordinary care in the custody of the articles with a duty to redeliver to the owner.

The recent case of *Manufacturers Savings Deposit Co. v. Cohen*, which held that property found on the floor of a booth located in an outer room used by a safe-deposit company in conjunction with a bank, access thereto not being limited to box holders or officials of the safe-deposit company, was lost property and as such should have been turned over to the property clerk of the Police Department, can be distinguished from the present case. In the *Cohen* case the court found that the booth on the floor of which the money was found was not located within the safe-deposit vault but rather in an outer room adjoining said vault and in a part of the bank which was accessible to the ordinary customer of the bank for the purchase of bonds and the opening of new accounts; as such the court considers the room in which the booth was located a public place which was not restricted to safe-deposit officials and persons having safe-deposit boxes in the vault. The case is further distinguished from the present case since its facts disclose that the money was found on the floor of the booth, which indicated to the court that the money was not mislaid.

Judgment for Dollar Savings Bank.

3. Ownership of Wild Animals

STATE EX REL. VISSER v. STATE FISH AND GAME COMMISSION

150 Mont. 525, 437 P.2d 373 (1968)

HARRISON, Justice.   This is an appeal from a judgment entered upon findings of fact and conclusions of law finding that the defendant appellant, State Fish and Game Commission, wrongfully confiscated and sold two elk belonging to plaintiffs and also, from a peremptory writ of mandate which issued, ordering the Commission to pay to plaintiffs the reasonable value of such elk and reasonable attorney's fees.

Early in the morning of January 13, 1967, a hunting party set out from a place known as the Rainbow Ranch in Gallatin County, Montana. The members of the party were the plaintiffs Visser and Kroon, Floyd Thomas, and a licensed guide known as Duke Hobart. Unknown to the other three men, Floyd Thomas was a game warden in plain clothes sent to the area to investigate suspected illegal hunting practices of the guide Hobart. Hobart was charged with the illegal killing and pleaded guilty. * * *

This was during a special elk hunting season called by the Montana Fish and Game Commission. Visser and Kroon each had a valid license to kill an elk on that particular day. Hobart did not.

The party hunted, with Hobart on horseback, and the other three men on foot. At about 10:45 a.m., Hobart was over a rise and out of sight of the three other men when they heard some shooting.

They met Hobart and asked him if he had shot anything. He said that he had dropped one elk and thought he had wounded another. The men proceeded on and came upon the animal Hobart had dropped. Its back was broken, but it was still alive. Hobart shot it again from close range and killed it. The three men then field-dressed the animal and Mr. Kroon placed his elk tag on the carcass. * * *

The party then set out in pursuit of the elk Hobart had wounded at the time he killed the first elk. Hobart, being on horseback, got to the animal first and killed it at about 1:00 p.m. * * *

The next day the plaintiffs learned that Floyd Thomas was a game warden and that the Fish and Game Commission had confiscated the two elk which they had tagged. Representatives of the Commission arranged for the bringing of the elk down from the mountain. The carcasses were then sold as confiscated meat as is provided by law. * * *

Does the assumption of possession and the placing of a valid elk tag on the carcass of an elk killed by another divest the State of Montana of its ownership? * * *

The ownership of wild animals is in the state, and these animals are not subject to private ownership except insofar as the State shall choose to make them so. So long as constitutional limitations are not infringed, the Legislature may impose such terms and conditions as it sees fit on the acquiring of ownership of these wild animals. It is the plaintiffs' contention that the requirements of the law were met when they tagged the elk.

When a person has the proper license he is authorized to "pursue, hunt, shoot and kill the game animal or animals authorized by the license held and to possess the dead bodies of game animals of the State which are so authorized by the regulation of the commission." * * * The tagging of a game animal that someone else has killed, or so far brought under control that one can walk up to it and cut its throat, is not the method of acquiring ownership contemplated by the statute authorizing a licensed hunter to pursue, hunt, shoot and kill a game animal and then to possess the carcass.

In Montana, big game hunting is a sport. The licensed sportsman-hunter must kill his own animal; he cannot have it done for him. When he has the proper license, and has himself taken an animal he may then tag and possess the carcass. When one hunter reduces the animal from its wild state another hunter may not legally possess it. If the person who reduces the animal from the wild state does so in compliance with the law he gains ownership of it. If the animal is not taken and tagged lawfully its ownership remains in the state.

The Montana Fish and Game Commission was acting within its authority when it confiscated the two elk in question. This being true, the plaintiffs' prayer must fail. The cause is reversed and remanded to the district court of Gallatin County with orders to vacate the writ of mandate and dismiss the action.

4. Identification of Trade Fixtures

MARSH v. BORING FURS, INC.
275 Or. 579, 551 P.2d 1053 (1976)

O'CONNELL, Justice. This is an action for the conversion of mink pens which plaintiff contends are personal property and which defendant contends are fixtures and therefore a part of the real property which he acquired as purchaser. The trial court entered a judgment in favor of defendant and plaintiff appeals.

The pens or cages in question and the sheds which house them were used in the operation of the Marsh farm before it was sold. The pens were arranged in batteries which were suspended within the sheds by means of nails, wires or staples. In the regular operation of the mink farm it is necessary from time to time to remove the pens for cleaning and repairs. This is accomplished without material injury to the pens or the sheds. The pens were designed to fit the sheds on the farm so that each battery of pens fit between the support members of the shed. This type of construction is typical, each rancher building his pens for his particular sheds and creating his own design of pens and shed. When pens other than those designed by plaintiff were used on the Marsh farm, the sheds had to be modified to hold them. To remove the pens from the sheds one had to cut wires, pull out boards with the use of a hammer or crowbar, unhook plumbing and dismantle pipe. The pens in question had never been removed from the Marsh ranch. For property tax purposes, the pens were appraised as part of the sheds and were taxed as real property. The sheds on the Marsh farm were developed as part of a mink ranch and were suitable for that purpose only. On the basis of these facts the trial court held that there was no conversion. We agree.

In numerous previous cases we have laid down the test for determining when a chattel which is annexed to the land continues to retain its separate identity as personal property in spite of the annexation. In making this determination, three factors have been employed: (1) annexation, (2) adaptation, and (3) intention. A more recent formulation of essentially the same test is found in Brown on Personal Property (3d ed. 1975) § 16.1, p. 517:

> * * * Would the ordinary reasonable person validly assume that the article in question belongs to and is a part of the real estate on which it is located—such assumption to be based on a consideration of the nature of the article itself, permanent or temporary; the degree of its attachment, firm or slight, and whether, according to the custom of the time and place the article was an appropriate and ordinary adjunct to the land or building in which it was located?

The degree of annexation necessary to transform a chattel into realty depends upon the circumstances of the particular case. In some cases the transformation may be effected without any annexation at all. Thus it is explained:

> * * * Where the element of the suitability of the particular article to the use to which the realty is put is particularly strong, the factor of physical annexation is liberally construed or even entirely dispensed with.

The fact that the former chattel rests in a space in a building specially prepared for it creates a strong inference that it was intended to become a part of the realty.

In the present case the fact that the building was designed for one purpose which could be fulfilled only by attaching the mink pens raises the inference that the owner intended to integrate the building and pens into a single economic unit.

Plaintiff adduced evidence to show that he did not intend to treat the pens as a part of the realty. We have made it clear that the factor of intention is not to be treated by the owner's actual subjective intent, but "an objective and presumed intention of that hypothetical ordinary reasonable person, to be ascertained in the light of the nature of the article, the degree of annexation, and the appropriateness of the article to the use to which the realty is put."

The evidence is sufficient to establish that the mink pens were fixtures and that defendant purchased the real property without notice of any interest which plaintiff might have retained by agreement with defendant's predecessors in title.

Judgment affirmed.

5. Fixtures and Appurtenances

PAUL v. FIRST NATIONAL BANK OF CINCINNATI

52 Ohio Misc. 77, 369 N.E. 2d 488 (1976)

BLACK, Judge.

As the purchaser for $575,000 of an elegant residence known as Long Acres, located in Indian Hill, Hamilton County, plaintiff Lawrence M. Paul sues the defendants for removing and converting from the buildings and grounds certain items of property * * *.

* * *

On July 13, 1971, plaintiff entered into a purchase contract with the defendant Executor, which contained the following provisions, among others:

> 1. *Purchase and Sale of Real Estate.* The Bank agrees to sell and Paul agrees to purchase certain residential real estate situated in the Village of Indian Hill, Hamilton County, Ohio, more particularly described on Exhibit 'A' attached hereto and made a part hereof, *improvements, fixtures, and appurtenances* being also described on Exhibit 'A', all of which is herein referred to as 'The Real Estate.' (Emphasis added.)

Exhibit "A" contains the following * * *: *"II.* Together with * * * *all fixtures relating to said real estate * * *."* (Emphasis added.)

* * *

When possession was delivered to plaintiff on January 15, 1972, he noticed that a number of items were missing that had been on the property both before and after the date of the purchase contract. The defendants admit that these items had been removed by the individual defendants before surrendering possession.

Decedent Augustine J. Long, his wife and one of his children died on September 9, 1969, in an airplane accident. * * * The First National Bank of Cincinnati was duly appointed Executor of the Long Estate.

The will left to the decedent's surviving children "*all household furnishings, appliances, decoration and equipment* owned by me and used in or about any principal or seasonal residence." (Emphasis added.)

* * *

The converted items must be considered in two groups, as follows:

(1) 4 Handmade lighting fixtures around swimming pool
    Lighting fixture in living quarters of apartment over stable
    2 Lighting fixtures removed from chapel
    3 Metal cranes

4 Garden statues.

(2) Ornamental housing over well

Mercury statue

Walnut organ bench

In the court's judgment, group (1) are legally classified as "fixtures," and group (2) are "appurtenances," under the intent and meaning of the purchase contract. This conclusion is based on three considerations: the law of fixtures, the intent and meaning of the purchase contract, and the intent and meaning of the testamentary gift to the children.

* * *

In *Masheter v. Boehm*, the Ohio Supreme Court designated, in paragraph two of the syllabus, six "facts" to be considered in determining whether an item is a fixture:

1. The nature of the property;

2. The manner in which the property is annexed to the realty;

3. The purpose for which the annexation is made;

4. The intention of the annexing party to make the property a part of the realty;

5. The degree of difficulty and extent of any loss involved in removing the property from the realty; and

6. The damage to the severed property which such removal would cause.

As the Supreme Court ruled, the expression of "a comprehensive and generally applicable rule of law" about fixtures has bedevilled the courts for years and is complicated by the need for different definitions in those situations where the relationship between the parties is different.

Using the Supreme Court's considerations, the light "fixtures" (there is no other available word) from the swimming pool, the stable apartment and the chapel are clearly fixtures in contemplation of law. * * * But they were designed and produced solely and only for the swimming pool, from the same design as was used for the light fixture in the porte cochere (which was not removed). Further, the poles from which they were taken are barren and incomplete without them.

* * *

These cranes and statues were not items moved about at the whim of the owner or according to the seasons: they were permanent implacements, intended to be part of the continuing visual effect of the estate. While no great difficulty was encountered in removing any of them, their absence is a source of loss. * * *

* * *

Group (2), being the ornamental well housing, the Mercury statue and the organ bench, were not attached in a permanent way. However, interpreting the contract from its four corners, in the light of all the facts and circumstances in evidence, the Court concludes that these items were "appurtenances" to the real estate, both in contemplation of law and in interpretation of this word as used in the purchase contract.

The word "appurtenance" means more than rights of way or other incorporeal rights: it includes an article adapted to the use of the property to which it is connected and which is intended to be a permanent accession to the freehold. [Citations.]

All three items in group (2) form a part of the character of Long Acres and enhance the style of its elegance. They are appurtenant to Long Acres in the sense that they are necessarily connected with the use and enjoyment of this country estate. * * *

To allow the heirs to walk off with an organ bench, leaving the built-in organ behind would be plainly ridiculous. You cannot play an organ while standing up, and no ordinary bench will do.

The Mercury statue is pictured in two photographs included in the appraisal of Long Acres which was considered by plaintiff before purchase. * * *

* * *

As fixtures [group (1)] and appurtenances [group (2)], these articles are classified legally as items which pass to the purchaser on sale of the real estate. * * *

* * *

The plaintiff is entitled to recover the sum of $9,675 (with interest at the legal rate from January 15, 1972) from The First National Bank of Cincinnati, as Executor, for breach of contract * * *.

* * *

PROBLEMS

1. Homer Havens, owner of an apartment hotel, leased an apartment to Hal Turner. One night, Sheila Hart, Hal's mother-in-law, was invited to spend the night and to sleep in the folding bed in the living room. While Sheila was making up the bed, she found a diamond ring caught in the springs under the mattress. When the true owner could not be found following diligent search, Homer, Hal, and Sheila each claimed the ring. Who is entitled to its possession? Would it make any difference if Sheila had been a maid employed by Homer instead of being Hal's mother-in-law?

2. Ruth purchased a female pedigreed miniature poodle dog from Pierre's Kennels. Unknown to either party, the dog was pregnant. When the litter was born, both Ruth and Pierre claimed the right of ownership. Who is correct?

3. Happy Hunter and his hounds were lawfully fox hunting on Rolling Acres farm with the landowner's consent. The dogs rousted a fox and were chasing it with Hunter in hot pursuit. Hiram Gunn was also hunting on the farm at the same time, lawfully and with the owner's consent. Gunn saw the fox come over the hill with Hunter and his hounds following, whereupon Gunn shot the fox and took possession. Who owned the dead fox? Suppose that Hunter had reached the carcass first after Gunn had shot it, would it have made any difference?

4. Ken Watts had an old electric motor that wouldn't work, and he dumped it in a ditch alongside the public highway. Rod Walker found it, took it home, repaired it, and put it to use in his workshop. Watts discovers that the motor is now in working order and demands that Walker return it to him at once. Who owns the motor? Why?

5. Handler, shopping in a department store, takes his purchase to a cashier's check-stand and while waiting for a clerk to assist him, notices a billfold on the counter. He examines it and finds that it contains $100 but no identification. The clerk arrives and demands that the billfold and money be turned over to the store. Does Handler have a better right to it than the store? Would it make any difference if Handler had found it on the floor in an aisle?

6. Arnold and Jack were playing golf and Jack complained that his putter was no good. Arnold then promised Jack that when they played next week Arnold would give him an old putter that Jack had always admired. Before they finished their game, they got into an argument over their scores and Arnold told Jack that he could forget all about the putter. Jack claims that Arnold must either deliver the putter or pay damages. Decision?

7. Hy Perkins was going to the hospital for an operation on what had been diagnosed as a malignancy. Hy called over his friend, Will Givens, endorsed over the title to his car, handed him the keys, and said: "If I don't make it, I want you to have my car." The doctor discovered the cancer was inoperable and sent Hy home. Three months later Hy died from the tumor. Both Will and the executor of Hy's estate claim the car. Does Will have to turn it over to the executor?

8. Bernie asked Gracie to marry him and Gracie accepted. Bernie thereupon gave Gracie a valuable two-carat diamond engagement ring. Later, Gracie got mad at Bernie, broke the engagement, and married another man. Bernie demanded that the ring be returned. Is Gracie required to give it back? Would the result be the same if Bernie had broken the engagement? What result if they mutually agreed to call the engagement off?

9. Sears provided Seven Palms Motor Inn with drapes which were installed on steel traverse rods attached to the walls of the rooms above the windows and with matching bedspreads made out of the same material as the drapes. In asserting a mechanic's lien, Sears claims that these items were fixtures that had become a part of the real property and were therefore subject to the lien. What decision?

10. Roy, Gene, and Hoot owned a horse as tenants in common. Hoot kept the horse on his ranch, fed him, and used him for farm work. Gene visited the ranch one day and saw that the horse was hauling heavy loads of produce. Gene claimed that Hoot was working the horse too hard and ordered him to take it easier. Hoot told Gene that care of the horse was his responsibility and none of Gene's business. Is Hoot correct?

Chapter 23

BAILMENTS

A. NATURE

1. BAILMENTS DEFINED

A bailment is the transfer of possession of personal property for a particular purpose. For example, the owner of a watch gives the watch to a jeweler for repair. No transfer of title is made. The owner and the transferor of the property is the bailor; the person receiving the property is the bailee. Real property cannot be the subject matter of a bailment.

2. ESSENTIALS OF BAILMENT

The essential elements of a bailment are as follows:

1. Retention of title by bailor.

2. Delivery of possession to the bailee.

3. Acceptance of possession by the bailee.

4. Possession and temporary control of property by the bailee for a specific purpose.

5. Ultimate possession of the property to revert to bailor unless bailor orders it transferred to another person.

The necessity of acceptance of possession by the bailee is illustrated by the following case:

FACTS Trushin loaned his car to Acker, who drove it to the Harbor Lounge. When Acker stopped at the front of the lounge, he left the lights on and the motor running. Acker waved to one of the attendants who waved back. Acker then entered the lounge. None of the attendants parked the car, which was not seen thereafter; the car was stolen.

While the thief was allegedly operating the vehicle in a negligent manner, plaintiffs were injured; they sued several defendants, including the Harbor Lounge.

The trial court entered summary judgment in favor of the lounge and plaintiffs appealed.

DECISION   The court held that the keys had been left in the car by Acker and there was no evidence that the car had been accepted by any employee of the lounge, nor was there any proof that any of the employees of the lounge were negligent.

Almeida v. Trushin (368 So. 2d 346 [Fla., 1979])

3. BAILMENT DISTINGUISHED

A bailment should be distinguished from a sale, a pledge or a pawn, and a lease or a license.

A. SALE

A bailment differs from a sale in three ways:

1.   A sale is a transfer of title. A bailment is a transfer only of possession; it is still a bailment, even though the goods are to be returned in a different form (e.g., wheat taken to a mill to be ground into flour and returned). However, if the person to whom the goods are given is to return only similar goods, the transaction may be a sale (e.g., a five-year lease of a farm and a herd of cows, with the provision that the lessee return cows of equal age and quality at the expiration of the lease).

2.   A sale requires consideration. A bailment may be either for consideration or gratuitous.

3.   A sale contemplates a permanent change of possession. A bailment is only a temporary change.

B. PLEDGE OR PAWN

A pledge or a pawn is a security device by which an owner of personal property gives possession of the property to secure a debt or to assure the performance of some obligation (e.g., debtor gives possession of a ring to a pawnshop owner to secure a loan). The debtor is the pledgor, and the pawnshop owner is the pledgee. A pledge arises when stocks, bonds, or negotiable paper is put up as security for a debtor, whereas, a pawn exists when any other type of personal property is used as security for a loan. A pledge is similar to a bailment in that neither the pledgee nor the bailee has title to the property but has merely a special interest. However, there are two differences:

1.   In a pledge, the pledgee can assign the interest in the property to another person even without permission of the pledgor. In a bailment, the bailee cannot assign the property to anyone else.

2.   In a pledge, the pledgee always has the right to sell the property if the debtor does not pay the debt. In a bailment, the bailee cannot sell the property to satisfy money due unless expressly permitted by statute. See Division 9 of the U.C.C., Appendix A, for the pledgee's rights in the event of default by the pledgor.

c. Lease or License

In a lease or license, the "acceptor" of the owner's goods has neither the right to possession nor the exclusive control of the goods. The lessor or licensor is merely making space or goods available for the lessee or licensee.

4. BAILEE'S DUTY OF CARE

The amount of care owed towards the property by the bailee depends on the type of bailment, local statutes, and the contract of bailment. While the type of bailment may be important in determining the liability of the bailee for loss or damage to the bailed property, the modern trend is for courts to consider the overall question of negligence rather than to rely on these distinctions.

a. Type of Bailment

(1) Sole Benefit to Bailor

In this type of bailment, the sole benefit of the bailment is for the bailor (e.g., bailor leaves his dog with a neighbor while bailor goes away on a vacation). In this case, the bailee owes a duty of *slight* care towards the property.

(2) Benefit to Both Parties

In this type of bailment, both the bailor and the bailee benefit from the bailment (e.g., bailor leaves his dog with bailee with the understanding that the bailee can use the dog to go hunting while the bailor is on vacation). In this case, the bailee owes a duty of *ordinary* care. Ordinary care means reasonable care under the circumstances.

(3) Sole Benefit to Bailee

In this type of bailment, the sole benefit of the bailment is for the bailee (e.g., bailee borrows the bailor's dog to go hunting, but bailor is not going on a vacation and is receiving nothing for the use of his dog). In this type of bailment, the bailee owes a duty of *great* care.

b. Local Statutes

Many local statutes contain exemptions from, or limitations on, liability in the case of certain bailees and in certain situations (e.g., California Civil Code Section 1840, which provides that where the bailee is informed of the value by the bailor, or has reason to assume its actual value, the liability cannot exceed such amount).

c. Contract of Bailment

The act of bailment may be accompanied by an agreement that enlarges the liability of the bailee (e.g., "You are responsible for any damages to any of our cylinders while in your possession or care"). A lease of a furnished house provided that lessee would redeliver furniture in good condition and that lessee "assumes all liability"; the court held that lessee was an insurer and liable for a stolen rug.

Except where permitted by statute, contracts that attempt to exclude or limit liability are illegal if the bailee is quasi-public in character (e.g., common carrier, public parking lot, public warehouse, hotel). Even where local statutes permit limitation of liability, the amount must be reasonable or the limitation is ineffective. Private bailees can limit their liability if the clause does not defeat the real purpose of the contract. However, any such limitation must be brought to the attention of the bailor before the property is bailed. A limitation by a private bailee contained in a stub or ticket given to the bailor or posted on a sign or on the walls of the bailee's place of business ordinarily will not bind the bailor unless the bailee calls the bailor's attention to the writing and informs him or her that it contains a limitation of liability. See Part 2, Chapter 13, G., "Stipulation Against Liability for Negligence."

5. BAILEE'S LIEN

By statute in most states, the bailee is given the right to a lien on the goods for payment for work or services rendered in connection with the bailed goods. The lien carries with it the right to sell the goods at public sale if the bailor does not pay for the work or services.

In the absence of a statute to the contrary, the lien is lost if the bailee voluntarily returns the goods to the bailor.

No lien arises on the goods when the work is done on credit.

6. BAILEE'S DUTY TO RETURN PROPERTY

The bailee has a duty to return the bailed property to the bailor upon termination of the bailment, with a few exceptions:

1. Where the goods are taken by legal process while in the bailee's possession (e.g., attached by the sheriff for a debt due by bailor).

2. Where the person to whom the bailee delivers the property is better entitled to its possession than the bailor. In such a situation, if the bailee is in doubt as to which of two claimants is entitled to the goods, he or she is protected in most states by being permitted to interplead the parties (surrendering the goods to a court and requiring the claimants to establish their rights in court) or by requiring the claimant who was not the bailor to indemnify the bailee against any liability to his or her bailor.

3. Where the goods are lost, stolen, or destroyed through no fault of the bailee.

4. A bailee who has a lien on the goods is entitled to keep possession of them until paid the amount of the lien.

B. TERMINATION

A bailment may be terminated by performance, acts of the parties, destruction of the bailed property, or operation of law.

1. BY PERFORMANCE

Complete performance by both parties of the bailment contract terminates the bailment. This may occur by completion of the particular purpose of the bailment or, where the bailment was created for a particular time, by the expiration of the period of time.

2. BY ACTS OF THE PARTIES

The bailment may be terminated by a subsequent agreement of the parties or when it was created for an indefinite time, by the will of either party or, when it was created for the sole benefit of one party, by the will of either party.

　　If either party causes a material breach of the bailment, the other party may terminate (e.g., bailee sells the bailed property to a third person). If the bailor elects not to terminate the bailment, the bailee remains liable for any damages caused by his or her breach.

3. DESTRUCTION OF BAILED PROPERTY

If the bailed property is destroyed by a third person or by an act of God, or if it becomes unfit for use for the purpose of the bailment, the bailment is terminated.

4. OPERATION OF LAW

Death terminates a bailment at will. Insanity and bankruptcy terminate a bailment at will if it becomes impossible for the bailee to perform his or her duties. However, if the bailment is for a definite period, death or incapacity will not terminate the bailment, but rather the rights of the deceased party pass to his or her estate.

C. SPECIAL BAILMENTS

1. HOTEL KEEPERS

Liability of hotel keepers is largely controlled by statute. The typical statute provides that if the proprietor provides a fireproof safe or some similar place for the keeping of valuable property, and if the proprietor notifies the guests of such depositary, he or she is not liable for the loss of any property that the guest may fail to turn over to the proprietor for safekeeping. A guest who delivers valuables to the proprietor must inform the proprietor that the articles are of unusual value, or there will not be any extraordinary liability.

　　When wearing apparel is left in the guest's room and is stolen, some statutes provide that the proprietor is liable only if he or she was negligent. Even when the proprietor is liable, most statutes permit him or her to limit the liability to a certain amount, which is usually rather small (e.g., $100 for each trunk; $50 for each traveling bag and contents; $10 for each box, bundle, or package and contents; and $250 for all other personal property of any kind).

The hotel keeper is liable for an employee's theft of a guest's property if the theft was within the scope of the employee's employment (e.g., clerk in charge of safe steals valuables deposited by guest). However, even where the theft is within the scope of the employment, the hotel keeper's liability is limited to the sums specified in the statute.

The hotel keeper has a lien on the baggage of guests for the agreed charges and, if no express agreement was made, for the reasonable value of the accommodations that were furnished.

2. COMMON CARRIERS

A common carrier is that who holds itself out to the public as carrying goods and passengers from place to place for compensation. Common carriers are regulated by state governmental authority (e.g., Public Utilities Commission) and, if engaged in interstate transportation, by the Interstate Commerce Commission.

A. LIABILITY OF COMMON CARRIERS

A common carrier is absolutely liable for any loss or damage to goods in its possession unless it can prove that the loss or damage was solely due to one of the following five exceptions:

1. *Act of God.* Unforeseen, unusual, violent, and superhuman events or catastrophes, such as an unprecedented wind or storm, earthquake, extreme temperature, severe flood, or stroke of lightning (a fire of human origin has been held not to be an act of God).

2. *Act of Public Enemy.* Nations, persons, or groups engaged in violent activities directed at an attempt to overthrow the government are the public enemy. Thieves, rioters, arsonists, and other criminals are not included in this definition unless they are attempting to overthrow the government.

3. *Acts of State or Public Authority.* Seizure of narcotics by the government and attachment of goods by the sheriff.

4. *Acts of Shippers.* Improper packing; however, if this is apparent upon visual inspection and the carrier still accepts the goods, it has full liability for them.

5. *Inherent Nature of the Goods.* Carrier is not liable for perishable fruits and vegetables when shipper fails to obtain refrigerated or heated cars, nor is carrier liable for normal percentage of evaporation of oil or other liquids in transit.

If the carrier unnecessarily exposed the goods to damage by incorrect routing, it will be liable even though the damage was caused by one of the five exceptions stated.

B. Termination of Strict Liability

Three different rules are followed as to when the strict liability terminates. Some states hold that it ends when the goods are unloaded from the car into the freight house, at which time the duties of the warehouseperson begin. Some states hold that it ends after the consignee (person to whom the shipment has been made) has had a reasonable time to inspect and remove the goods. Some states hold that the consignee has the right to notice of the arrival of the shipment and that the strict liability of the carrier does not end until after notice and after the consignee has a reasonable time in which to remove the goods.

When the goods remain in possession of the carrier after strict liability terminates, the carrier's liability is reduced to that of a warehouseperson (ordinary care) until the goods are claimed.

C. Limitation of Liability

A carrier can limit its liability as follows:

1. *Under Federal Law.* Carriers in interstate commerce are subject to federal law. Under the Carmack Amendment to the Interstate Commerce Act, the carrier may limit its liability to a stated amount by a provision in the bill of lading provided that the shipper is allowed to obtain a higher amount at an increased rate.

2. *Under State Laws.* Most states provide by statute that a common carrier may, in intrastate commerce, limit its liability for injury to or loss of baggage or packages from ordinary negligence but not for such loss or injury caused by gross negligence. U.C.C. Section 7–309(2) provides that damages may be limited "if the carrier's rates are dependent upon value and the consignor by the carrier's tariff is afforded an opportunity to declare a higher value."

D. Common Carriers of Passengers

Common carriers of passengers are not insurers of the safety of the passengers. However, because of the public nature of the business, they are held to the highest degree of care, skill, and diligence. Common carriers of passengers are subject to extensive state and federal regulation.

3. WAREHOUSEMEN

A person engaged in the business of storing goods of others for compensation is a warehouseman. In the absence of special statute, the warehouseman owes a duty of *ordinary* care towards goods in his or her possession. Because of the public nature of their activities, warehousemen are subject to extensive state and federal regulation.

U.C.C. Section 7–203 places a duty on the warehouseman to deliver goods that conform to the description in the warehouse receipt or to answer in damages. The warehouseman may avoid this liability, however, by an honest disclaimer on the receipt to the effect that he or she does not know whether the goods conform to the description. This can be done by writing *conspicuously* such words as "said to contain" or "contents unknown."

4. LESSEE OF PERSONAL PROPERTY

In this type of bailment (e.g., automobile rental), the lessee is the bailee and the lessor is the bailor. The bailor must deliver the personal property in a condition fit for the purpose of letting, must repair all deteriorations not caused by the bailee or the natural result of use, and must secure quiet title in the bailee from any lawful claimant.

If the bailee is injured or his or her property is damaged due to a defective condition of the bailed property, the bailor may be liable as follows:

1. The bailor of dangerous personal property is liable to the bailee for injuries resulting from negligence (bailee may be barred by contributory negligence or assumption of the risk).

2. The bailor of personal property warrants that the property is fit for its particular use, and if it is not, the warranty is breached for failure to exercise reasonable care to ascertain that it was safe. For example, in hiring a horse for riding purposes, there is an implied warranty that the stable keeper used reasonable care to ascertain the habits of the horse. A stable keeper who should have discovered the horse's dangerous propensities and did not is liable (*Kersten v. Young* [52 Cal.App.2d 1, 125 P.2d 501 (1942)]). Modern cases have extended the bailor's liability of fitness for a particular use at the time of the bailment to a fitness during the entire period of the bailment and to third persons.

Where property is leased for a particular use and the bailee uses it for another purpose, the bailor may recover damages or terminate the hiring. Most courts hold the bailee absolutely liable for injury or loss occurring during such unauthorized use even though the bailee was not negligent.

5. PARKING LOTS

The courts have generally held that when the owner locks his or her automobile and takes the keys, there is no bailment, since the parking lot attendant is not given sufficient physical control over the car to constitute him or her a bailee. However, when the owner leaves the key in the automobile at the request of the parking lot attendant, a bailment is created and the bailee owes a duty of ordinary care towards the car.

6. CHECKROOMS

The courts generally hold that when a patron hangs his or her coat on a hook in a restaurant, barber shop, or similar place, no bailment is created. The reasoning is that there was no actual delivery of the coat to the proprietor. However, if the establishment provides an attendant to receive the coat, a bailment is created. A question arises as to whether the proprietor is liable for something in the pocket of the coat that is lost or stolen. Courts generally hold that there is no liability, because the proprietor did not intend to assume possession of the property in the bailor's pocket, unless the proprietor was advised of the contents or reasonably should have known of their existence when he or she accepted custody of the coat. The following case illustrates a typical checkroom bailment situation:

FACTS Plaintiff and a companion went to the defendant's restaurant for dinner. Some time after they were seated, they decided to check their coats, and took the coats to the checkroom. The room was full, and Patty, the checkroom attendant, said that she was out of checks but that she knew plaintiff and would accept the coats. When plaintiff started to leave the restaurant the checkroom was unattended. Patty later appeared, but could not find plaintiff's black Persian lamb coat. The trial court awarded $500 damages to plaintiff, and defendant appealed.

DECISION The court held that checkroom service was incident to the restaurant business and that Patty had the implied authority to accept the coat without giving a claim check. Since Patty had left the coatroom unattended, she failed to exercise the ordinary care required of a bailee under a mutual benefit bailment. Judgment was affirmed.

Johnson v. B. and N., Inc. (190 Pa. Super. 586, 155 A.2d 232 [1959])

7. SAFE DEPOSIT BOX

A person who rents a safe deposit box will have one key for access to the box, while the bank retains the other. Both keys are necessary to gain admittance to the box. The bank has control of the premises. Nearly all courts hold that the customer is the bailor and the bank is the bailee. Since this is a mutual benefit type of bailment, the bank must use ordinary care regarding the contents of the box.

8. CONTENTS OF CONTAINER

Whether the contents of a safe deposit box are bailed, whether the bailment of a coat is a bailment of the contents of its pockets, whether a bailment of an automobile is a bailment of the personal property on the seats, are questions of whether the contained articles are of a nature that are reasonably or normally found within the container. If they are, it is a bailment; if they are not, it is not a bailment. Thus, a bailee of a container is not liable for the contents of a container that are not visible when the container is bailed to him or her, unless from the nature of the container itself or from the surrounding circumstances the bailee ought to have anticipated the presence of such contents as a reasonable person or unless he or she had express notice of the contents. This rule is illustrated in the following case:

FACTS The plaintiff left his car in the defendant's parking lot. The keys, including the trunk key, were left in the car. The car was taken from the lot by persons unknown. The car was later recovered, but the plaintiff's golf clubs, valued at $373.53, which had been locked in the trunk, were missing and were not recovered. The plaintiff was not asked and did not voluntarily advise the defendant about the presence of the golf clubs when he left his car in the defendant's lot.

The plaintiff brings this civil action for the value of the golf clubs.

DECISION   The court held that a parking lot bailee's duty depends upon notice, actual or constructive, of the presence of golf clubs or other items in a vehicle. Since no actual notice was given, constructive notice might be established by the property's being in plain view. But where, as in this case, the property was locked out of sight in the trunk, it would not be reasonable to assume that a driver would be carrying golf clubs in the trunk of the car. Judgment for defendant.

Allen v. Houserman (250 A.2d 389 [Del. Super., 1969])

9.   CONSTRUCTIVE BAILMENTS

The law recognizes certain types of bailments wherein the bailee's obligation is imposed by law rather than by agreement of the parties and the courts usually hold that he is a gratuitous bailee (e.g., finder of lost or misplaced property; police officer taking possession of stolen goods; animal from one farm strays upon land of adjoining farm owner; property placed on property of another by mistake). A seller of goods who has not yet delivered the goods to the buyer is a bailee of the goods if the title has passed to the buyer. Similarly, the buyer who is in possession of goods but does not have title is a bailee of the goods.

In the finder, or voluntary, type of bailment, the finder must take possession of and care for the lost property. However, the finder will be entitled to recover for the value of his or her time and expense in caring for the property.

In the unwilling type of bailment, where property is thrust upon a stranger through some agency beyond the control of either party, such as a tornado or other act of God, most courts hold that the bailee has only a moral duty to care for the property. A person who undertakes to do so becomes a bailee and is liable for negligence in caring for the personal property. Some states, by statute, impose a duty of care on the unwilling bailee regardless of his or her undertaking to care for the property.

These are all constructive bailments made by law.

ILLUSTRATIVE CASES

1. Degrees of Liability Under Bailments

CLOTT v. GREYHOUND LINES, INC.

278 N.C. 378, 180 S.E.2d 102 (1971)

Plaintiff, a merchant seaman, testified, that he bought a ticket in Bushnell, Florida, to go to New York City, by Greyhound bus. * * * [He] changed buses in Jacksonville, Florida, because he had only five minutes between buses, and all baggage had to be checked twenty minutes before departure time. He testified that his bag contained $2,209 in cash, a camera, two watches, perfume, certain seaman's papers, and other personal effects. He described his bag as "a brown bag, valise type, satchel type bag. I had locks on the bag. I had a padlock on it, on the two handles, and also a key lock on the small latch * * *." When he got on the bus in Jacksonville he got in the last seat and put the bag between the seat and the motor wall. He did not think anyone saw him deposit the bag. When the bus arrived in Columbia, South Carolina, at about 6:30 A.M., he heard the announcement about a stopover, but paid no attention to it because he was half asleep. It was later announced over the bus loud speaker that the bus would be delayed about twenty minutes because of a dead battery. He then went into the coffee shop to get coffee and doughnuts, and while he was walking out with the doughnuts he saw the bus pulling out. He heard no announcement of the departure after he left the bus. The dispatcher told him that he knew the bus was one passenger short. He asked the dispatcher to get a police car or a taxi so that he might stop the bus, and then told the dispatcher about his bag containing valuables and money and about its location on the bus. The dispatcher told plaintiff that he would wire Raleigh. Plaintiff further testified that about two hours later he took the next scheduled bus to Raleigh, and upon arrival he talked to Mr. Rackley, the Raleigh dispatcher. "I asked for my bag, and I told him and asked him where my bag was, and he said to me, 'Here's a hat here.' He said, 'But the bag,' he said, 'My God, I gave it away.' He said, 'I must have made a mistake.' "

He received his bag from defendant company about six months later. When it was returned, "the lock was gone off and the small lock there was jimmied, * * *" Everything was gone except some papers, including his empty pay envelope.

* * *

BRANCH, Justice. Plaintiff contends that the trial judge erred when he granted defendant's motion for a directed verdict.

* * * We must, however, consider the possibility of liability upon a showing of negligence where other relationships of bailor and bailee exist.

This Court has classified bailments as those (1) for the sole benefit of bailor, or in which relationship the bailee will be liable only for gross negligence, (2) for the bailee's sole benefit, in which relationship the bailee will be liable for slight negligence, and (3) those for the mutual benefit of both parties, in which relationship the bailee will be liable for ordinary negligence. However, "the terms 'slight negligence,' 'gross negligence,' and 'ordinary negligence' are convenient terms to indicate the degree of care required; but, in the last analysis, the care required by the law is that of the man of ordinary prudence. This is the safest and best rule, and rids us of the technical and useless distinctions in regard to the subject; ordinary care being that kind of care which should be used in the particular circumstances and is the correct standard in all cases. It may be high or low in degree, according to circumstances, but is, at least, that which is adapted to the situation." A bailment solely for the benefit of the bailee—a gratuitous bailment—may be effected with respect to baggage when the property comes into the hands of a carrier as an involuntary trust through accident or mistake. When a passenger stops or lies over at an intermediate point on his journey, without consent of the carrier, and permits his baggage to go on without him, the carrier is liable as a gratuitous bailee.

*   *   *

Ordinarily, a passenger leaving personal baggage in a carrier upon alighting therefrom cannot hold the carrier responsible, but where it is shown that a subsequent loss was the proximate result of conduct of carrier's employees in failing to exercise ordinary care, through failure to take care of the baggage after full knowledge of the facts, the carrier may be held liable.

*   *   *

The bus driver was "given information of baggage that was left on the bus" belonging to plaintiff. Pursuant to this information he delivered a small bag to the dispatcher. *He noticed nothing unusual about the bag, and the dispatcher received the bag without comment.* There is no evidence that any other passenger on the bus ever reported a missing bag. The dispatcher in Raleigh received the bag with information that it contained money and valuable contents. When plaintiff arrived about two hours later, the dispatcher was unable to deliver the bag which the driver had delivered to him.

*   *   *

We think this evidence is sufficient to support a finding that the baggage removed from the bus by defendant's driver was plaintiff's baggage, and was received by defendant's agents before the locks were broken and the bag rifled.

When the above rules of law are applied to plaintiff's evidence, we think defendant is a bailee for the sole benefit of the bailor, i.e., a gratuitous bailee. However, we conclude that classification of bailments is of little import since the degree of care required in all classes of bailments is, in truth, the care of the man of ordinary prudence as adapted to the particular circumstances. The care must be "commensurate care" having regard to the value of the property bailed and the particular circumstances of the case. The standard of care is a part of the law of the case which the court must apply and explain. The degree of care required by the circumstances of the particular case to measure up to the standard is for the jury to decide. * * *

Thus, when a bailor, whether classified as gratuitous or otherwise, offers evidence tending to show (1) that the property was delivered to the bailee, (2) that bailee accepted it and therefore had possession and control of the property, and (3) that bailee failed to return the property, or returned it in a damaged condition, a prima facie case of actionable negligence is made out and the case must be submitted to the jury. * * *

           *   *   *

The decision of the Court of Appeals is reversed. The case is remanded to that Court to be certified to the trial court for a new trial in accord with this opinion.

2. Parking Lot Bailment

PARKING MANAGEMENT, INC. v. GILDER

343 A.2d 51 (D.C.App., 1975)

GALLAGHER, Associate Judge.

           *   *   *

Appellee parked his car at the Parking Management, Inc. parking area which is enclosed within the Washington Hilton Hotel in this city. He was directed to a space by an attendant. He locked his car and kept the keys. He then opened the trunk in plain view of a group of employees and placed his lady friend's cosmetic bag in it and then locked the trunk. The rear of the car was exposed to the aisle. Upon his return, he found the trunk lid damaged from being pried open and reported it to the management.

The principal question for the court, initially at least, is the nature of the legal relationship of the parties. More particularly, it must be determined at the outset whether the parking lot operator owed the car owner any duties and, if so, what they were. In order to resolve this, it is necessary to examine the nature of the parking operation. It is not enough simply to ascertain whether the car owner locked his car and kept the keys ("park and lock"). These are material factors to be considered, but they do not end the inquiry.

When the car owner entered, he was handed a ticket by one of three attendants and directed to a particular parking space. There were about 160 lined spaces on one level and about 150 lined spaces on a second level. These were self-service to the extent that the driver places the car in a space at the direction of an attendant. If additional spaces are needed, *the aisle spaces are utilized* and according to the parking operator (PMI) these are "not self-service," which may only be construed as meaning that the attendants park the cars in the aisles and retain the keys. There is thus a mixed arrangement here, one being self-service and the other nonself-service, depending upon the volume of customers. Under appellant's theory of the case, there would be the anomaly of a bailment for the cars parked in the aisle but not for those in the lined spaces on the same floor in the same garage.

When appellee entered the garage, a number of PMI employees were on duty including a manager, a cashier, and three attendants. According to the Supervisor of Plans and Operations for Parking Management, Inc. (PMI):

> A PMI employee is a uniformed employee. He is a public relations man for our company. He is a service man for our company. * * * He is there to control the parking, guide the parking *and control whatever is necessary in respect to housekeeping and any general operations that might pertain to the parking industry.* (Emphasis added.)

> *　　　*　　　*

He said that thefts are "not necessarily a big problem, but, of course, damages and thefts, *security is a major concern*"(emphasis added). He also agreed that watching the area and acting as a "kind of security" is a part of the employees' job.

The trial court in this nonjury case concluded that the evidence established either (a) a bailment or (b) that the protection which the patron was led to believe existed was not provided. The court thereupon entered judgment for the car owner.

*　　　*　　　*

Appellant is correct in its assertion that this court has stated in those cases that a bailment did not exist where the car owner (a) parked his car and (b) kept the car keys. However, those cases simply involved those two factors and nothing more. Here there was additional evidence on the parking arrangement involved, *e. g.,* the presence of 5 employees to service the customers in an enclosed area of the hotel and the acknowledgment that security of the cars is a major concern of PMI, which, according to the PMI supervisor, includes watching for thefts and tampering with the vehicles, as well as the acknowledged exertion of "control * * * in respect to housekeeping and any general operations that might pertain to the parking industry." Although, strictly speaking, the finding that a bailment existed may be open to debate, we believe the trial court reached the correct result in any event by way of its alternative finding that the protection the car owner was entitled to believe existed was not provided.

The car owner was entitled under the circumstances to expect that reasonable care would be utilized to prevent tampering with his auto; and that this was not an unreasonable expectation on his part was demonstrated by testimony of the management of PMI to the effect that this was in fact among the duties of the employees. * * *

While there has been a tendency to consider a showing of a "park and lock" arrangement as creating a lease agreement, we doubt the sophistication of this doctrine. Unlike the usual tenant of realty, the car owner has utterly no control of the so-called lease space as he is by definition always absent and helpless to protect his property, for all practical purposes. There is in most instances no fixed term, the duration of the parking being usually at the option of the car owner. Lastly, the car owner may not remove the car until the parking fee is paid. * * *

The owner of the car cannot observe and protect the car since he is always absent from it. It is the operator, not the car owner, who is in a position to have the superior knowledge.

*　　　*　　　*

On the facts here presented, we believe an operator may be required to exercise reasonable care to avoid malicious mischief to, or theft of, vehicles parked on a commercial parking lot (a going concern), even though the arrangement was "park and lock." The car owner was necessarily absent when the car damage occurred and should not be disadvantaged as a matter of law because of this reality. We do not feel that a car owner may fairly be regarded as a virtual stranger to the lot operator except for the payment of a parking fee.

*　　　*　　　*

* * * Consequently, the judgment is affirmed.

3. Liability Limitation Requires Notice

SCHROEDER v. AUTO DRIVEAWAY COMPANY

11 Cal.3d 908, 114 Cal.Rptr. 622, 523 P.2d 662 (1974)

TOBRINER, J.　Defendants appeal from a judgment following jury verdict for plaintiff Madeleine Schroeder awarding her $25,000 in compensatory damages and $10,000 in punitive damages. We uphold the judgment as to liability for the reasons stated in the opinion of the Court of Appeal, which, as to the issue of liability, we adopt as our opinion. * * *

In 1971, plaintiffs Mr. and Mrs. Schroeder, an elderly couple, decided to move from Phoenix, Arizona to Susanville, California. Mrs. Schroeder had purchased a large quantity of new and secondhand goods, and intended to open a store in Susanville for the sale of this merchandise. Plaintiffs also bought a van for the purpose of transporting the goods to Susanville, and sought to hire a driver for the van.

Defendant Auto Driveaway Company is a common carrier that furnishes drivers for hire. Mrs. Schroeder contacted defendant Trimble, the Phoenix representative of Auto Driveaway, to arrange for a driver for the van. Trimble called at the plaintiff's home on August 13, 1971, observed the partially loaded van, and filled out a shipping order and freight bill which he gave to plaintiffs. This document provided that for a consideration of $189 ($139 in advance; $50 on delivery) Auto Driveaway would pick up the loaded van and drive it to Susanville.

On the back of the form appeared 15 conditions, all but one, which required a full gas tank at time of pick-up, in exceedingly small print. Condition number four stated a limitation of liability and read as follows:

> 4. Unless a greater value is declared hereon, the owner hereby agrees and declares that the value of the baggage, personal effects and sporting equipment described herein is released to a value not exceeding $50.00 per shipment. * * *

According to Mrs. Schroeder, neither she nor her husband read the reverse side of the contract. Trimble did not call their attention to the provisions on the back of the contract, discuss the weight or contents of the van, or inform them of any limitation upon Auto Driveaway's responsibility for the value of the goods carried.

*   *   *

Trimble hired defendant Roberts to drive the van to Susanville. Under both Interstate Commerce Regulations and the contract between Auto Driveaway and plaintiffs, the driver was required to proceed by the most expeditious and suitable route. Instead she and her companion, defendant Linnuste, decided to detour to the Grand Canyon for sightseeing. About 20 miles north of Flagstaff, on their way to the Grand Canyon, the van skidded off a mountain road. The van itself was totally destroyed, and much of the contents damaged.

*   *   *

The load occupied the interior of a van 8-1/2 feet high and 14 feet long, and weighed about 3,840 pounds. Trimble was in a position to observe the extent and weight of the load.

*   *   *

Several days later an unidentified person notified plaintiffs, who had arrived in Susanville, of the accident. Defendants did not tell plaintiffs the location of the van or its goods nor attempt to complete the transportation of the goods to Susanville. When plaintiffs engaged an attorney to communicate with Auto Driveaway that defendant responded that it was not responsible for the accident. Finally, after suit was filed in January of 1972, Auto Driveaway told plaintiffs where their goods were stored and made arrangements with plaintiffs' attorney for transportation of the goods to Susanville. When the goods arrived in February large quantities were missing, and much of that received was broken, wet, and mildewed.

* * * The Schroeders were not informed of conditions and limitations which had been imposed by the Interstate Commerce Commission upon Auto Driveaway if it was to contract with a shipper to carry goods for which it would be liable for less than full value of loss. Before it could so contract, it was required by law and by the Interstate Commerce Commission not only so to advise the shipper of such limitation but also to [inform] that shipper of his alternative to pay a greater price for carrier liability to reimburse for the full value of all loss. Trimble, according to Mrs. Schroeder, deceived the Schroeders because he knew that the value of the goods in the van was greatly in excess of $250, and its weight greatly in excess of 500 pounds. He also knew that the Schroeders would not have authorized Auto Driveaway to transport the van and its contents had they known of the terms, hidden from them, which were superimposed upon the written instrument by Trimble. * * *

The foregoing items of damages total $21,414.85. In addition to that figure, Mrs. Schroeder is entitled to compensation for pain, suffering, and emotional distress. Consequently the jury award of $25,000 for compensatory damages falls well within that permitted by the evidence.

*   *   *

For the foregoing reasons the judgment as to both liability and damages is affirmed.

4. Effect of Statutes on Liability of Interstate Carriers

BLAIR v. DELTA AIR LINES, INC.

344 F.Supp. 360 (D.C.Fla., 1972)

FULTON, Chief Judge. * * * The plaintiff alleges in the original complaint that the defendant airline was negligent in shipping and transporting the casket and remains of the plaintiff's deceased wife from Miami to Vicksburg, Mississippi. Plaintiff claims that as a result of defendant's negligence in loading and unloading the shipment was damaged by rain. Damages are sought for physical damage to the casket, the attempted restoration of the deceased and great mental anguish to the plaintiff. The defenant's answer set forth as an affirmative defense the tariff filed with the Civil Aeronautics Board [hereinafter C.A.B.] as constituting an absolute bar, or alternatively a limitation upon the damages recoverable by the plaintiff. * * *

Defendant's [motion] for summary judgment [was] filed May 4, 1972, and [was] accompanied by affidavits in support thereof, a copy of the airbill under which the remains of plaintiff's deceased wife were shipped, and a copy of the tariff of Delta Air Lines on file with the C.A.B., which tariff was in effect on the date of the shipment. Airbill No. 006–MIA–1311 2712 was issued May 3, 1970, as to one casket of human remains of Agnes Blair weighing 265 pounds at a charge of $54.48. No specific value was declared.
* * *

The basis for the defendant's motion for summary judgment is that the tariff filed with the C.A.B. pursuant to 49 U.S.C. § 1373 constitutes a limitation upon the damages recoverable by the plaintiff as a matter of law and that under the tariff provisions cited earlier the maximum liability of the defendant is $132.50. The plaintiff makes the following assertions: (1) that state law, not federal, is applicable to this lawsuit; (2) that this claim does not fall into the category covered by the defendant's tariff; and (3) that the tariff cannot bar a claim for gross negligence and that if such a bar exists, it is against public policy.

First, it is clear that a tariff, required by law to be filed, constitutes the law and is not merely a contract, * * * and that with respect to such tariff federal law governs the loss of or damage to baggage or freight as a result of an air carrier's negligence. * * * It is also clear that tariffs, if valid and accepted by the C.A.B., may contain exculpatory clauses for certain classes of freight and limitations of liability for loss or damage to specified property regardless of fault, and that such provisions are not prohibited by the Federal Aviation Act of 1958, 49 U.S.C. §§ 1301 et seq. * * * The established rule is that the tariffs, if valid, constitute the contract of carriage between the parties and "conclusively and exclusively govern the rights and liabilities between the parties." * * * Thus, federal, not state, law is controlling, and the tariff filed by the defendant with the C.A.B. governs the shipment in this cause.

* * *

The plaintiff asserts that he does not fall within the tariff provisions of the defendant in that the tariff is applicable only to claims of ordinary negligence and does not bar a claim of gross negligence on the part of the air carrier. It is apparent that plaintiff's contention must fail. The language of tariff Rule 30(B) does not distinguish between ordinary or gross negligence on the part of the air carrier. The Rule excludes the air carrier from liability except as to its actual negligence, of whatever degree. Further, tariff Rule 30(C) expressly states that the carrier shall not be liable in any event for special or consequential damages, and the limitation of liability provision of Rule 32(A) unambiguously states that the total liability of the carrier shall in no event exceed the value of the shipment as determined under Rule 52. The tariff provisions are clearly applicable to claims for both ordinary and gross negligence on the part of the defendant. * * *

Finally, the plaintiff asserts that the imposition of the tariff as a bar to a claim against the defendant for gross negligence is against public policy and that such a bar would deprive the plaintiff of his constitutional right of due process. * * *

The tariff limiting liability in this lawsuit is not contrary to public policy. Defendant's tariff provisions are valid and cover all aspects of this cause. Plaintiff had the opportunity to declare a higher value upon the shipment if he so desired. Failing to do so, the plaintiff's loss is subject to the limitations in the Air Tariff Rules which provide in Rule 32(A) that the total liability of the carrier shall in no event exceed the value of the shipment as determined in Rule 52. Rule 52, "Charges for Declared Value," provides that a shipment shall have a declared value of $0.50 per pound, but not less than $50.00, where a higher value is not declared. Since plaintiff did not declare a higher value, the shipment weighing 265 pounds results in a declared value of $132.50. Tariff Rule 32(C) provides that the total liability of the carrier shall not exceed either the value of the shipment under Rule 52, or the actual value of the shipment, or the amount of damages actually sustained, whichever is the least. In accord with the above provisions of the Official Air Freight Rules, Tariff No. 1–B, defendant's maximum liability in this cause is limited to $132.50 as a matter of law.

[NOTE: Some courts distinguish between experienced travellers and those who would reasonably be unaware of such tariffs. *Muelder v. Western Greyhound Lines* (8 Cal. App 3d 319, 87 Cal.Rptr. 297 [1970]) held that the limitation did not apply to lost baggage, but the 1980 case of *Steinburg v. PSA,* also in California, held that tariff limitations applied to businessmen who travelled often.]

5. Warehouseman Lien

FLORES v. DIDEAR VAN & STORAGE COMPANY, INC.

489 S.W. 2d 406 (Tex.Civ.App., 1972)

NYE, Chief Justice.

This is a suit for conversion of personalty brought about by a wrongful foreclosure of a warehouseman's lien. Aurora Flores and her husband, Jesse Flores, Jr., sued Didear Van and Storage Company, Inc. for the value of their stored household goods and for exemplary damages. The case was tried to a jury. Based on the jury verdict, the trial court entered a take nothing judgment. * * *

On April 15, 1967 Jesse Flores, Jr. arranged with the defendant storage company to store his family's household goods for the duration of his military service. He executed a storage agreement, a warehouse receipt and an inventory of his household effects on that date. He listed his mother-in-law's address as his mailing address since he was renting his own residence while he was away. He stated that his mother-in-law, Mrs. Alaniz, would always know how to contact him. Flores was inducted into the service on April 21, 1967. Flores paid only the first monthly storage bill in the amount of $50.80. From April 21, 1967 to December 17, 1967, Flores was assigned to several posts in the United States for basic training and schooling. Mrs. Flores joined him for a nine week period in July and August. On December 17, 1967, Jesse Flores was sent to West Germany and in March of 1968 Mrs. Flores joined him there. In March of 1969 he and Mrs. Flores returned to the United States and Mr. Flores continued on to Vietnam for a one year tour of duty lasting until April 1970. He was then discharged from the Army.

In April and May of 1968, the Storage Company instituted statutory proceedings to foreclose its lien on the stored household goods, because of non-payment of storage fees. On May 18, 1968 the goods were sold at public auction.

In July 1969, about three months after returning from West Germany, Mrs. Flores went to the defendant's place of business to make a payment on the storage bill. She was told that their goods had been sold fourteen months previously for non-payment of storage costs. The Flores then brought suit against the storage company. They alleged that they stored their goods with appellee for a valuable consideration, that they made a demand for such goods, that defendant refused to deliver those goods (because they had wrongfully sold their goods) to their damage. * * *

During the course of trial, the plaintiffs proved their ownership, proved defendant's possession of the goods, proved that the defendant exercised dominion over those goods and proved that the defendant refused to surrender them on demand. The Flores thereby made out a prima facie case of conversion. It was then incumbent upon the defendant Storage Company to prove its right to the goods by a valid foreclosure of its warehouseman's lien.

The defendant Storage Company claimed that Sections 7.209 and 7.210, Bus. & C., V.T.C.A. gave them a statutory lien on the property and the authority for the enforcement of that lien by foreclosure because of non-payment of storage charges. [The] Uniform Commercial Code, Documents of Title, states in part:

*   *   *

A warehouseman's lien on goods other than goods stored by a merchant in the course of his business *may be enforced only as follows:*

(1) All persons known to claim an interest in the goods must be notified.

(2) The notification must be delivered in person or sent by registered or certified letter to the last known address of any person to be notified.

(3) *The notification must include* an itemized statement of the claim, a description of the goods subject to the lien, *a demand for payment within a specified time not less than ten days after receipt of the notification,* and a conspicuous statement that unless the claim is paid within that time the goods will be advertised for sale and sold by auction at a specified time and place.

(4) *The sale must conform to the terms of the notification.* (Emphasis supplied.)

The notice of sale dated April 15, 1968 * * * was sent by the defendant by certified mail but was returned to the sender unopened.

*   *   *

A warehouseman has no personal remedy for selling property for collection of charges at common law. His remedy lies by foreclosure as is provided by statutory law. The enforcement of such lien under summary foreclosure procedures, must be accompanied in strict compliance with the terms of the statute upon which such power is granted. [Citations.] The letter notifying Flores of the impending sale failed to comply with the requirement of the code which says that ten days notice *"must"* be given to the owner within which time he could pay for the goods. Since the notice was dated April 15, 1968, it would have been impossible to have given the plaintiffs the time specified by law by requiring them to pay "on or before the 24th day of April." Because the defendant failed to comply with the requirements of the statute, the sale is void. [Citations.]

The judgment of the trial court is reversed. Judgment is rendered awarding appellants damages in the amount of $1220.00. * * *

6. Innkeeper's Liability

NORTH RIVER INS. CO. v. TISCH MANAGEMENT, INC.
64 N.J.Super. 357, 166 A.2d 169 (1960)

CONFORD, S. J. A. D.   Plaintiff paid the insurance claim of Mr. and Mrs. Louis Cohen for loss of Mrs. Cohen's mink coat while guests at the Traymore Hotel in Atlantic City December 24, 1957, and now, as subrogee, brings this action to recover for the loss against the defendant operator of the hotel on its common-law liability. The Law Division of the Superior Court granted a motion for judgment in favor of the defendant at the end of the case, and plaintiff appeals therefrom.

Plaintiff's proofs were that the Cohens had been guests at the hotel since December 21, 1957, and that when they returned to the room on the evening of December 24, 1957 they discovered that the coat was missing from the hanger in the closet where it had been placed by Mr. Cohen.
* * *

It has long been a principle of English law, accepted by most American jurisdictions, that in the absence of statute an innkeeper is practically the insurer of the safety of property entrusted to his care by a guest, exoneration being had only by showing the loss was due to an act of God or the public enemy, or to the fault of the guest himself. * * *

It remains to be considered whether, as argued by defendant, the result below should be confirmed because of the application to the facts of the case of the special statute affecting liability of hotels to guests. * * *

* * * This provision ordains that whenever a hotelkeeper provides a safe or other depository for safekeeping valuables of types specified in the act, including furs, and "shall place, in a conspicuous position in the room or rooms occupied by such guests, a notice stating the fact that such safe or other depository is provided" in which the valuables may be deposited, and a guest neglects so to deposit the articles, the hotelkeeper is not liable for loss of the property. If the goods are thus deposited the liability of the hotelkeeper for loss is limited to $500.

Defendant's principal dependence in this regard is upon a document which, according to its proofs, was left under the glass on a dresser in the hotel room at the time it was occupied by the Cohens. This paper is about 11½ inches square. Commanding its top-center space, in the style of a title, is the prominent designation, "The Traymore Directory." * * *

What defendant relies upon is a box of about 2½ inches in the lower righthand corner of the "Directory," bearing the caption, "Notice to Guests," in type substantially less prominent than that of the five captions for featured facilities set forth in much more prominent positions elsewhere on the paper. This notice contains the statutory information concerning the availability of a "safe" and of the absence of liability of the hotel for valuables not left there.

The question before us is whether this notice satisfied the statute as a matter of law. We hold it did not. The "notice" constituted a minor appendage of what in primary purport was a hotel directory. A guest whose eye should be caught by this document might very well stop reading it as soon as he gathered its general import, if not interested therein, and before reaching the lower corner where the "notice" is set out. The express requirement in the statute that the notice be placed "in a conspicuous position" evidences an intent that the notice itself be conspicuous and a serious question is presented as to whether this notice can be regarded as conspicuous, in the light of the diverting character of the main substance of the data on the paper on which it appears. * * *

Evidence of actual knowledge by the guest of the availability of a hotel depository and of the limited statutory liability, is, by the weight of authority, with which we agree, not an acceptable substitute for strict compliance with the statute as to notice by the hotelkeeper. * * *

Reversed and remanded for a new trial.

7. Constructive Bailment

SHAMROCK HILTON HOTEL v. CARANAS

488 S.W.2d 151 (Tex.Civ.App., 1972)

BARRON, Justice. This is an appeal in an alleged bailment case from a judgment in favor of plaintiffs below.

Plaintiffs, husband and wife, were lodging as paying guests at the Shamrock Hilton Hotel in Houston on the evening of September 4, 1966, when they took their dinner in the hotel restaurant. After completing the meal, Mr. and Mrs. Caranas, plaintiffs, departed the dining area leaving her purse behind. The purse was found by the hotel bus boy who, pursuant to the instructions of the hotel, dutifully delivered the forgotten item to the restaurant cashier, a Mrs. Luster. The testimony indicates that some short time thereafter the cashier gave the purse to a man other than Mr. Caranas who came to claim it. There is no testimony on the question of whether identification was sought by the cashier. The purse allegedly contained $5.00 in cash, some credit cards, and ten pieces of jewelry said to be worth $13,062. The misplacement of the purse was realized the following morning, at which time plaintiffs notified the hotel authorities of the loss.

Plaintiffs filed suit alleging negligent delivery of the purse to an unknown person and seeking a recovery for the value of the purse and its contents.

*   *   *

We find after a full review of the record that there is sufficient evidence * * * to support the jury findings on the special issues to the effect that the misdelivery was negligence and a proximate cause of the loss to appellees. Article 4592, Vernon's Tex.Rev.Civ.Stat.Ann. (1960), does not apply to limit the hotel's liability to $50.00 since its proviso declares that the loss must not occur through the negligence of the hotel, and such limiting statute is not applicable under the circumstances of this case.

Contrary to appellants' contention, we find that there was indeed a constructive bailment of the purse. The delivery and acceptance were evidenced in the acts of Mrs. Caranas' unintentionally leaving her purse behind in the hotel restaurant and the bus boy, a hotel employee, picking it up and taking it to the cashier who accepted the purse as a lost or misplaced item. * * *

As stated above, the evidence conclusively showed facts from which there was established a bailment with the Caranases as bailors and the hotel as bailee. The evidence also showed that the hotel, as bailee, had received Mrs. Caranas' purse and had not returned it on demand. Such evidence raised a presumption that the hotel had failed to exercise ordinary care in protecting the appellees' property. When the hotel failed to come forward with any evidence to the effect that it had exercised ordinary care, that the property had been stolen, or that the property had been lost, damaged or destroyed by fire or by an act of God, the appellees' proof ripened into proof by which the hotel's primary liability was established as a matter of law. * * *

Further, this bailment was one for the mutual benefit of both parties. Appellees were paying guests in the hotel and in its dining room. Appellant hotel's practice of keeping patrons' lost personal items until they could be returned to their rightful owners, as reflected in the testimony, is certainly evidence of its being incidental to its business, as we would think it would be for almost any commercial enterprise which caters to the general public. Though no direct charge is made for this service there is indirect benefit to be had in the continued patronage of the hotel by customers who have lost chattels and who have been able to claim them from the management.

Having found this to have been a bailment for the mutual benefit of the parties, we hold that the appellants owed the appellees the duty of reasonable care in the return of the purse and jewelry, and the hotel is therefore liable for its ordinary negligence. * * *

Appellants urge that if a bailment is found it existed only as to "the purse and the usual petty cash or credit cards found therein" and not to the jewelry of which the hotel had no actual notice. * * *

We believe appellants' contention raises the question of whether or not it was foreseeable that such jewelry might be found in a woman's purse in a restaurant of a hotel such as the Shamrock Hilton under these circumstances.

* * * It is known that people who are guests in hotels such as the Shamrock Hilton, a well-known Houston hotel, not infrequently bring such expensive jewelry with them, and it does not impress us as unreasonable under the circumstances that one person might have her jewelry in her purse either awaiting a present occasion to wear it or following reclaiming it from the hotel safe in anticipation of leaving the hotel.

* * * Appellants were on notice that recovery was sought primarily for the value of the jewelry and that the only ground for recovery was the hotel's negligence with respect to the bailment, purse and contents. * * *

* * * It follows that the findings of negligence and proximate cause of the loss of the purse apply to the jewelry as well, which is deemed to be a part of the bailment. * * *

*　　　　*　　　　*

The bus boy and cashier assumed possession and control of the purse per instructions of the hotel with respect to articles misplaced or lost by customers. The active cause which produced the loss was wholly independent of the negligence of Mrs. Caranas, and the hotel's primary duty of ordinary care to its paying guest was clear.

The judgment of the trial court is affirmed.

PROBLEMS

1. Plaintiff, brewery, sold cartons of beer to consumers with the understanding that there would be a refund of all deposits on returned cartons. The consumer was not required to return the cartons. The state claims that the cartons were sold to the consumers, and thus the seller owed a sales tax. The seller contends that the cartons were not sold but bailed to the consumers, and thus no sales tax was due. Decision?

2. Plaintiff left her diamond ring with the defendant jeweler for cleaning. Prior to closing his store, the defendant placed the ring in the safe and locked the safe. During the night, a burglar opened the safe and stole the contents, including the plaintiff's ring. Plaintiff brings action for the value of the ring. Decision?

3. Plaintiff parked his car in a parking lot operated by defendant. A sign at the entrance to the lot stated that the owner was not liable for theft or any damages to the cars from any cause and that all parking was entirely at the risk of the owner. Plaintiff did not read the sign because of the heavy traffic in getting into the lot. Defendant also handed plaintiff a parking ticket which had the same type of liability exemption on the back in small print. Plaintiff did not read the statement on the back, as he believed the ticket was merely a token of identification. Plaintiff's car was stolen from the parking lot while the attendant was away from the lot aiding victims of an automobile accident that occurred nearby. Plaintiff brings action for the value of his car. Defendant contends that he is not liable because of the sign and ticket, which exempted him from liability. Decision?

4. Ace Rudder, while flying his private plane, had an engine failure and made an emergency landing in Rudy Hayes's oat field. Ace returned to the wrecked plane to disassemble it for salvage, but Rudy refused to allow Ace to remove the plane until he paid for the damages done to his field. Several days later, an insurance agent representing Ace came by and paid for the damages, whereupon Rudy allowed Ace and the agent to remove the plane. During the interval, no one had been watching the site, and many people had visited the oat field to view the spot. About $2000 worth of equipment had been stolen from the plane. Ace sued Rudy for the damage caused by the thefts, claiming a bailment and negligence. Decision?

5. Brown delivered a large quantity of wheat to the mill owned and operated by Smith. It was understood by the parties that the wheat would be ground into flour and that Smith would return a certain amount of flour for each bushel of wheat. The flour would not necessarily be processed from Brown's wheat, since it was the custom to commingle the wheat prior to grinding it into flour. It was further agreed that Brown would call for his flour the following day. During the night, without the fault of anyone concerned, the mill and all the wheat and flour were destroyed by fire. Brown sues Smith for the loss. Decision?

6. Marsh left a package containing costume jewelry worth over $2,000 in a railroad station locker while he had lunch. On his return, the package was gone. He sued the locker company, contending that it was under a duty to keep the package safely and had negligently failed to do so. The locker was of the common type that permits the individual user to deposit a coin and withdraw the key. The company retained a right of access to remove parcels left for more than 24 hours. Marsh sues to recover the value of the jewelry. Decision?

7. Plaintiff was a guest in the defendant's hotel. She left a valuable fur piece in her locked room when she went downstairs to dinner. On her return, she found the fur piece missing. The bedroom had a notice posted on the inside of the entrance door which she had not read stating that the hotel provided a safe, free of charge, for the deposit of all valuable articles and that the hotel would not be liable for any valuable articles stolen from a room. Plaintiff brings action against the hotel for the value of her fur. Decision?

8. Plaintiff ships goods from New York to Chicago by defendant's railroad. During transit, the goods are destroyed by rioters. Plaintiff sues railroad as an insurer for the value of the goods. Defendant contends that it is not liable, since the damage was beyond its control. Decision?

9. Mrs. Chown saw a brood of turkeys along the highway that she believed to be hers and took them to the protection of her chicken yard. She then learned that the turkeys belonged to Ryan, her neighbor, and she put them back on the highway where they were all killed. Ryan sues Chown for the value of the turkeys. Decision?

10. Ike stored a sealed box in Lyons' warehouse, stating that the box contained books. Lyons issued a negotiable warehouse receipt for books. Ike negotiated the receipt to Don, who bought in good faith for value. Don surrendered the warehouse receipt to Lyons, and the warehouseman delivered the sealed box. When opened, the box was found to contain worthless pieces of wood. Don sued Lyons for the value of the books. Decision?

Chapter 24

REAL PROPERTY

A. NATURE

Real property is land; those things intended to be affixed permanently thereto or embedded therein; and various interests in its ownership, use, or possession.

B. ESTATES IN REAL PROPERTY

Estates in real property are generally classified as either freehold or leasehold. Leasehold estates pertain to the law of landlord and tenant, discussed in Chapter 25. Other interests in land may be easements or licenses. A modern trend of ownership is in condominiums.

1. FREEHOLD ESTATES

Freehold estates are usually classified as either fee simple estates or life estates.

A. FEE SIMPLE ESTATES

A fee simple estate is the greatest interest one can possess in land and gives the owner the absolute right of disposal or of transmitting by inheritance. It is possible, however, to grant a fee simple subject to a condition, such as "until a person remarries" or for "so long as used for church purposes" and then provide that upon the occurrence of the condition, the property reverts to the grantor or his or her heirs.

B. LIFE ESTATES

The typical life estate is the grant or devise of real property to a grantee "for life," creating an estate that will terminate upon the death of the grantee, called the life tenant. In such cases, upon the death of the life tenant, the property would revert to the grantor or his or her heirs, called a reversionary interest. However, the grantor may designate some other party to take the estate upon the death of the life tenant, in which event the one so named would be a remainderman, and the estate received, a remainder. Although a life tenant may transfer his or her interest, he or she can grant only what he or she has—an estate for the duration of his or her lifetime.

In some states, the common law rules of dower and curtesy create by operation of law what amounts to a life estate to a spouse of a one-third interest in all the real property owned by the couple during marriage. This rule does not apply in community property states, where each spouse has a half interest in all the property acquired by the work and efforts of either or both during marriage.

2.　EASEMENTS

An easement is a limited right to make use of the land of another in a specific manner and is created either by the acts of the parties or by operation of law.

A.　EASEMENT BY DEED

Easements may be granted in writing by an express grant, reservation, or exception in the deed transferring title to the property, or they may be granted in a separate document.

For example, the grantor may transfer title to a portion of his or her land and also expressly grant an easement for right of way over the rest of the land, or the grantor might reserve a right of way easement for himself or herself over the land granted.

Easements may be for many purposes, such as the laying of utility lines or the use of a common driveway.

Easements that relate to adjoining land are usually called appurtenant. The land benefited is known as the dominant tenement, while the one giving up the right is designated as the servient tenement. Such easements usually are said to run with the land and are transferred with it in subsequent change of ownership.

Easements not tied to adjoining land but granted to an individual, such as rights of way for utility companies, are called easements in gross, and their transferability varies according to the laws of the state in which they occur.

B.　EASEMENT BY PRESCRIPTION

An easement by prescription is similar to the acquisition of title by adverse possession and may be obtained by the actual use of the land for easement purposes openly and notoriously, in a manner adverse to the rightful owner's use, continuously and uninterruptedly for the period of time set forth in the state's statute of limitations. The continuous and uninterrupted use requirement can usually be stopped by the owner's placing an obstruction blocking the user's path.

c. Easement By Implication

An easement by implied grant or reservation may arise when an owner of adjacent properties establishes an apparent and permanent use, such as a common driveway, in the nature of an easement and then transfers one of the properties without mention of any easement.

Another implied easement may be created through reason of necessity. Where an owner grants part of his or her land to another and the portion granted is so situated that there is no access to it except across the grantor's remaining land, the law implies a grant of the right-of-way easement. However, it must be based on necessity rather than mere inconvenience.

The following case illustrates an easement by implication:

FACTS The trial court awarded the Millers and the Howells an easement for ingress and egress over the land of the Burrows, and the latter have appealed.

The opposing parties are coterminous landowners. Their common source of title is J. C. Clark. The Howells' land is located south of the Burrows'.

The Howells' right of ingress and egress was a road separating the lands of the Burrows and of Flurrie Shotts. Testimony was given to the effect that this road was the only one to the Howells' land and that it had been continuously used since 1948.

DECISION The court held that the two requirements for an easement of necessity had been established. First, the property came from a common source, J. C. Clark. Second, reasonable necessity existed, since this was the only practical avenue of ingress and egress. Although necessity does not of itself create a right of way, it is evidence of the grantor's intention to do so. The underlying principle is that anyone who conveys property also conveys whatever is necessary for its beneficial use, realizing that it is for the public good that land be occupied. Affirmed.

Burrow v. Miller (340 So.2d 779 [Ala., 1976])

3. LICENSES

A license is the right to use the land of another based upon the permission granted by the owner. It creates no interest in property and in most cases is exercised only at the will of, and subject to revocation by, the owner at any time. However, when use or occupation of property is under license, no adverse or prescriptive rights will accumulate.

4. CONDOMINIUMS

Condominium ownership is a combination of both sole and joint ownership. Individuals owning an office or living quarters in a condominium complex are co-owners of the land and commonly shared areas, but each person owns his or her specific office or living quarters. Participation in management and the sharing of expenses are determined by agreement or statute. Unit owners all have an equal right to use the common areas. The condominium unit is freely transferable, subject to legal restrictions that might be contained in the original agreement. Ownership generally has some advantages over ordinary rental in that an investment is obtained and the allowable expense deductions provide an income tax benefit.

C. ACQUIRING TITLE TO REAL PROPERTY

Ownership and title to real property may be acquired by original occupancy, voluntary transfer by the owner, involuntary transfer through operation of law, adverse possession, will or lawful succession, or action of nature.

1. ORIGINAL OCCUPANCY

A nation, through its power, is the ultimate owner of all the land within its boundaries; and in many totalitarian countries, the state retains title to most of the real property. Most governments, however, permit private ownership of land with the right to transfer title freely in such manner as the owner chooses. In the United States, the government still owns much land; has the right under eminent domain to retake whatever it deems desirable for public use, provided payment is made to the owner; and has the ability to take what is considered necessary under its police power, without payment. If an owner dies, leaving neither will nor heirs, the property returns to the state by escheat.

All original title to land in the continental United States was acquired either by grant or patent from the federal government under homestead laws or from a nation that had previously held the land.

2. VOLUNTARY TRANSFERS BY OWNER

The most common way by which title to real estate is transferred to another is through sale by the owner. However, since consideration is not required, a gift may be made of land and an individual may also transfer property to a public agency by dedication.

Most sales of real estate are negotiated through licensed brokers. Although their services are not required, brokers usually obtain listing agreements from prospective sellers and, for a commission, seek buyers who are ready, willing, and able to buy at the listed terms.

Actual transfer of real property is accomplished by the execution and delivery of a deed of conveyance. The person who transfers his or her interest is called the grantor, and the recipient is called the grantee.

A quitclaim deed or a warranty deed, sometimes called grant deed, are those commonly used in the voluntary transfers of real property.

A. PROPERTY CONVEYANCE BY DEED

Under early English common law, real property was transferred symbolically by the grantor, standing on the described land, delivering a twig or piece of soil therefrom to the grantee, and announcing the transfer. Later, a written instrument describing the land being sold was delivered in lieu of the symbolism and became the deed or means of title transfer still in use.

Most deeds contain the following elements:

1. Names of the grantor and grantee.

2. The consideration paid, if any.

3. Words of conveyance, such as "grant and convey," or a similar statement of intent.

4. Property description, which should be formal, describing the actual land, not the street address, and expressed either by lot and block number, metes and bounds, or government survey.

a. Most subdividers of real estate file plat maps with the clerk of the county in which the land is located, identifying the parcels by lot and block number.

b. Metes (measures) and bounds (direction) describe land by beginning at a certain point and then, by direction and measured distance, circumscribing the parcel until the point of beginning is reached.

c. Most of the United States has been surveyed by the government into a grid system, wherein the north and south lines are called meridians and the east and west lines are called parallels or base lines. These grids are then broken down into townships of six square miles each, which, in turn, are divided into 36 numbered sections of one square mile each, containing approximately 640 acres. Once the section is identified by number, regular parcels to be described by acreage may be expressed in halves or quarters, referring to the north, east, south, or west halves and the northeast, northwest, southeast, or southwest quarters.

5. Listing of any exceptions or reservations that might be excluded from the grant, such as mineral rights.

6. Quantity of the estate conveyed, usually with the words, "To have and to hold."

7. Covenants or promises of warranty, however, in many states, these are implied from the words of conveyance.

8. Executed and signed by the grantor or grantors. For a deed to be recorded, it must be acknowledged before a competent officer, usually a notary public, who guarantees that the signature is genuine.

B. Quitclaim Deed

Quitclaim is the simplest form of deed. It states that the grantor transfers to the grantee all of his or her rights, if any, in the property described. This instrument could then transfer the entire estate, any part thereof, or nothing, depending upon what the grantor owns.

c. Warranty or Grant Deed

A warranty deed, or grant deed, is one by which the owner warrants or guarantees that he or she has a good and merchantable title to the described property being conveyed. Such a deed implies several additional promises or covenants, such as the right to quiet enjoyment of the property and no existing encumbrances other than those stated in the deed. If any of these covenants are broken, the grantee has the right to recover damages from the grantor.

d. Completion of Conveyance

Actual conveyance is not completed until the deed has been delivered. This may be done directly to the grantee, or it may be done in escrow to a third person for delivery to the grantee upon the completion of the escrow instructions by all of the parties.

Recordation, although not required to effect transfer, serves to give notice to the world of the conveyance, and if the same property has been deeded to more than one grantee, the first one to record has the good title.

Recording is accomplished by depositing the deed with the proper authority for that purpose, usually the recorder or clerk of the county where the land is situated.

In addition to obtaining recordation, a buyer may seek further protection by procuring a policy of title insurance in many states or, in others, by obtaining an abstract of title, usually prepared by a lawyer, which is a summarized report of the recorded transactions concerning the property.

3. INVOLUNTARY TRANSFER BY OPERATION OF LAW

Title to land may be obtained by a buyer at a sale conducted by a sheriff or other proper official. This may be brought about by a judgment sale under a writ of execution obtained by a judgment creditor to secure money for payment of the amount owed. It may also result from a foreclosure action on an unpaid mortgage or trust deed. A worker or materials supplier who has contributed to making improvements on the property may force a sale under statutory mechanic's lien rights to recover payment for their goods or services. Nonpayment of property taxes or of special assessments against the realty may also lead to forced sale of the property.

The government, under the power of eminent domain, may take private property for public use but is required to pay the owner the reasonable value thereof. However, if property is taken by public authority under its police power for the protection of the public health, safety, and welfare, no compensation is required.

The government may also, through zoning and city-planning laws, restrict the use that an owner may make of his or her property, if the interest of the state is more compelling than that of the owner and if the restrictions are reasonable.

4. ADVERSE POSSESSION

Title may also be acquired by adverse possession, which occurs when a person enters into actual possession of the land of another and remains there openly and notoriously for the period of time prescribed by the state's statute of limitations. This time period varies from state to state, ranging from five to thirty years.

Such possession must be hostile to that of the true owner and must be continuous for the time period. Some states also require that the holding be under claim of title, and others require payment of taxes on the property during the occupation. An individual who is on another's land with permission of the owner occupies by license, and the holding is not hostile or adverse. Although it is not essential that the owner be actually aware that the land is being occupied, the possession must be of such a nature that a reasonably diligent owner would know of the adverse claim. Government-owned land is exempt from adverse possession.

5. WILL OR DESCENT

Real property, as well as personal property, may be transferred by an owner through his or her will, a written expression of his or her desires for the distribution of property after death. In addition to disposing of property, the will may cover such items as the conduct of the funeral, a gift of the body or parts thereof for scientific or medical use, the choice of a guardian for any minor children, and the appointment of an executor or executrix for the estate.

When a person dies leaving a will, he or she is said to have died testate. If the deceased were male, he is called a testator; if female, a testatrix. Real property granted by will is called a devise and the recipient is a devisee. A gift of money is a legacy made to a legatee, and any other form of personal property is designated a bequest.

Any person of legal age and sound mind may make a will. It can be either a formal, witnessed will, drafted by a lawyer in accordance with the laws of the state of the testator's residence and witnessed by either two or three witnesses as the pertinent statute requires. In many states, it may be a valid holographic will, one that must be dated, written, and signed entirely in the handwriting of the testator or testatrix.

Under our system of property ownership, when the owner dies, the property must pass to someone else. If the person dies intestate, (without a will), the property passes to the heirs by descent under the laws of succession of the state of residence at the time of death. Priority of distribution is usually to the decedent's spouse and surviving descendants, followed, if necessary, by the most nearly blood-related next of kin.

State probate laws provide for descent and for the administration of the estate. The person charged with this function is the personal representative, who may be the executor or executrix named in a will or, in the absence thereof, the administrator or administratrix, usually the nearest heir, appointed by the court for that purpose. The personal representative is charged with gathering the assets, paying the creditors' claims, filing and paying the tax returns, and assuring that the distribution of the remaining property is made in accordance with the will or by the laws of succession.

6. ACTION BY NATURE

Action by nature through water flow or floods may add to property or take away property from an adjacent owner, either gradually or suddenly. Gradual deposits of land by water along the water's banks is known as accretion. Soil being washed up and deposited on the land is known as alluvium. Under such circumstances, the addition or deletion of property falls upon the owner abutting the water course. However, a severe storm or flood causing a river to change its course suddenly is called avulsion, and there is no change in the title to the land so shifted.

D. JOINT OWNERSHIP OF REAL PROPERTY

Real property may be held by co-owners as joint tenants, tenants in common, tenants by the entirety, and community property in the same manner as personal property. (See the discussion of joint ownership in Chapter 22, E). Co-owners of real property may terminate the joint ownership through the legal action of partition, as set forth in the following case:

> **FACTS**   Plaintiff sued her brother seeking to partition 500 acres of farmland in Nebraska. The trial court held that the parties were owners as joint tenants with right of survivorship rather than as tenants in common and that the property should be partitioned equally between them. Defendant brother appeals.
>
> **DECISION**   Brother argued that a distinction should be made between a "joint tenancy" grant and their deed, which was "joint tenancy with right of survivorship." The court held that the survivorship phrase made no difference. Once a joint title to real property has been established, partition is a legal right. When a joint tenant acts to end any of the required coexisting unities, as by partition or deed, the joint tenancy and the right of survivorship are ended. Affirmed.
>
> *Yunghans v. O'Toole* (199 Neb. 317, 258 N.W.2d 810 [1977])

E. NATURAL RIGHTS IN LAND

Under operation of law, without regard to the intent of the parties, certain rights are attached to the ownership of land. Some of the more common refer to space, riparian, lateral support, disposition, and freedom from nuisance.

1. SPACE RIGHTS

Before the advent of modern air traffic, a landowner was deemed to own his or her land and the rights thereto from the center of the earth to the outermost limits of space. However, aviation law has changed the outer range to a height within which the owner has reasonable control. Air rights are now being sold for the construction of buildings in the space over other structures. Subterranean rights still belong with the land and include such oil and minerals as might lie thereunder. The boring or drilling under the property of another without his consent, regardless of the depth, constitutes an illegal trespass.

2. RIPARIAN RIGHTS

The rights of landowners to a natural watercourse within their property are referred to as "riparian" rights. An owner may not pollute, divert, or diminish the flow of such stream to the detriment of other downstream landowners. If the stream is not navigable, adjoining owners have title to the soil to the middle of the stream. If the waterway is navigable, the landowners have title to the low water mark but the stream belongs to the federal government.

Percolating waters are those under the earth's surface. At common law, the owner of property had an absolute right over such water; however, this use is now regulated by statute. In most states, the reasonable use rule is followed (i.e., the landowner can take as much as is reasonably needed for the ordinary purposes of living on the land but not for commercial use).

3. LATERAL SUPPORT

Enjoyment and use of land depends upon the lateral support it receives from adjacent land. No owner is allowed to excavate so near to the boundary as to cause his or her neighbor's land to cave in or the buildings to be damaged.

The California Supreme Court has imposed a duty on a landowner to use reasonable care to protect a neighboring lot from any condition on his or her own land, whether natural or artificial, that might damage the neighbor (*Sprecher v. Adamson Cos.* [636 P.2d 1121 (1981)].)

4. USE AND DISPOSITION OF LAND

In theory, the owner of land has the right to freely use and dispose of it as he or she wishes. However, this right is subject to government controls and restrictions such as planning, zoning, and building construction standards laws. Furthermore, many private restrictive covenants may be placed in deeds or subdivision plans that further limit this right. They may include setting set-back limits, prohibiting construction within a certain distance from the property lines; controlling the size, cost, and architectural design of any houses to be built; and prohibiting the sale of liquor thereon. Although restrictions are not popular in law, if it appears that they will operate to the general benefit of all concerned landowners, the courts will usually enforce them. However, racial, religious, and ethnic restrictive covenants have been declared unconstitutional.

5. ABATEMENT OF NUISANCES

Nuisances are such things as loud noises, polluted air, obnoxious odors, continual vibrations, and similar results from activities that unreasonably interfere with the enjoyment of property by adjacent landowners. If the condition affects the entire neighborhood or community, it is a public nuisance; if it affects only one or a few property owners, it is a private nuisance. Victims of such impositions have the right to seek a court order abating the nuisance and to recover damages suffered as a result of the condition. An example of the nuisance problem is set forth in the following case:

> **FACTS** Del Webb built Sun City in Arizona on a site near a large stock-feeding operation. People hesitated to buy property near the feedlot because of the odor and the flies. Webb brought suit to abate the nuisance.

> **DECISION** The court held that the difference between a private nuisance and a public nuisance was generally one of degree, the former affecting a few but the latter affecting the rights of many citizens as a part of the public. Since the entire community of the southern portion of Del Webb's Sun City was concerned, a public nuisance was created and the court ordered it to be abated. However, since Spur Industries feeding operation had been located there first, Del Webb was required to pay to Spur a reasonable amount for the cost of moving or shutting down.

> *Spur Industries, Inc. v. Del E. Webb Development Co.* (108 Ariz. 178, 494 P.2d 700 [1972])

F. REAL ESTATE SECURITY TRANSACTIONS

Secured transactions involve a debt or obligation to pay money secured by an interest in specific property belonging to the debtor. Such transactions involving personal property are discussed in Chapter 31. Mortgages, deeds of trust, or land contracts are the most commonly used documents when real property is the security for the debt.

1. MORTGAGES

The purchase of homes and other real estate involves so much money today that few people would be able to pay the total purchase price with their own funds. Therefore, it is necessary for the buyer to borrow part of the money and defer payment over a period of time. The realty itself is the security as evidenced by the promissory note for the loan together with another document, usually a mortgage or a trust deed.

The mortgage instrument is in the form of a conveyance given by the debtor (the mortagor) to the creditor (the mortgagee). A mortgage is executed with the same formalities used in the completion of deeds. It differs from other conveyances in that there is usually a statement that the mortgage is void and of no effect when the mortgagor completes payment of the debt. Such a provision is referred to as a "defeasance." The same result may be accomplished by a separate document called a "reconveyance." If an instrument, on its face, purports to be a deed or outright transfer of the property, but the evidence establishes that it was, in fact, intended as a security transaction, defeasance will be implied.

Most states follow the lien theory of mortgages, in which the mortgagor retains title and possession even when in default of payment. Only by foreclosure sale or by court appointment of a receiver can the right of possession be taken from the mortgagor.

Some states follow the common law title theory that upon the making of the mortgage, title passes to the mortgage subject to a condition subsequent of payment of the debt. When the obligation is paid, title reverts to the mortgagor. During the mortgage period, the mortgagor is usually entitled to possession. Mortgagors in possession are responsible for dealing with the property in a manner so as not to impair the value of the security.

If a mortgagor sells the land without paying off the mortgage, the interests under the mortgage may also be passed to the buyer by assignment, depending upon the agreement of the parties and the state law protecting the creditor. Unless the buyer expressly assumes the mortgage, he or she is not personally liable for the mortgage debt. Otherwise, the property is transferred subject to the mortgage, and the buyer's liability exposure is limited to loss of the property.

When the mortgagor fails to make payments, the remedy for the mortgagee is through foreclosure of the mortgage. At common law, an immediate strict foreclosure with title given to the mortgagee was permitted. Since this often permitted creditors to obtain property for inequitably low sums, the practice is no longer followed. Instead, most states have a procedure of foreclosure by public judicial sale through an officer of the court. In many jurisdictions, the mortgagor has a statutory right (equity of redemption) to recover the property from the sale within a specified time thereafter by paying all of the arrears and costs. Some states permit a power of sale clause in the mortgage that permits the mortgagee to foreclose by a sale without obtaining a court order. This is used most commonly in the trust deed type of mortgage.

If foreclosed property sells for more than the amount due on the secured note, the surplus should be returned to the mortgagor. However, if it sells for less, the difference is a deficiency that normally remains the liability of the original mortgagor or any subsequent purchaser who had expressly assumed the mortgage.

A purchase money mortgage is one given by the buyer to the seller of real property to secure a note for the difference between the down payment and the purchase price. In many states, the purchase money mortgagee will not be permitted a deficiency judgment upon foreclosure, but as the original seller in the transaction, must be satisfied with whatever the property brings at the sale.

2. DEED OF TRUST

In many states, a deed of trust or trust deed is used to secure real property loans. It is created by a conveyance made to a third person (the trustee) with instructions to hold the property in trust as security for the payment of the debt.

The purposes are the same as with a mortgage, the practical difference being in the method of foreclosure. Instead of using a judicial sale (although that option may be followed as an alternative in some jurisdictions) foreclosure is by virtue of sale conducted by the trustee, who has a fiduciary obligation to act impartially and fairly towards both parties. The trustee sells at public auction, applies the proceeds to the payment of the debt to the creditor beneficiary, and accounts to the borrower trustor for any surplus money. Generally, there is no right of equity of redemption.

3. LAND CONTRACT

Another method of financing, common where the seller retains the security interest or where the buyer can make only a small down payment, is the installment land contract. This is a contract between buyer and seller where the seller retains the title to the land and the buyer, although usually given possession, does not acquire the title until the last payment has been made. The seller may include in the contract clauses that time is of the essence; that the buyer must keep the property insured and repaired and pay all taxes; and that upon default by the buyer, the seller can declare a forfeiture, retake possession of the land, and retain all payments made. Because of the possibility of unfairness in this type of arrangement, some states will treat the seller as a mortgagor and permit the buyer an equity of redemption.

ILLUSTRATIVE CASES

1. Title by Adverse Possession

HANKINS v. PONTOON BEACH AMUSEMENT PARK, INC.

28 Ill.App.3d 512, 328 N.E.2d 714 (1975)

CARTER, Justice.

This is an appeal from a judgment of the Circuit Court of Madison County in favor of the plaintiff in an action to quiet title.

The complaint alleged that defendant-appellant, Pontoon Beach Amusement Park, Inc., is the owner of record to a certain tract of land known and described as lot 29 in the subdivision of lots 13 and 16 of Pontoon Place, as it appears on the plat thereof recorded in the Recorder's Office of Madison County; that the plaintiff for more than twenty years has enjoyed actual possession of the above-described real estate, which possession was hostile, actual, visible, exclusive and continuous for the statutory period and under a claim of title inconsistent with that of the possessor of the record title; and that, as a result thereof, plaintiff is the legal owner of the above-described tract of land.

The facts of the case indicate that the defendant purchased lots 13 and 16 of Pontoon Place in 1946 by a contract for deed and obtained legal title in 1948. In 1951 lots 13 and 16 were subdivided into lots numbering 17 to 29. A 20 foot gravel road separates lots 17 to 22, which are on the south side of the road, from lots 23 to 29, which are on the north side of the road. The plaintiff negotiated the purchase of lots 18 and 28 from one Ferro in February, 1951, and Ferro was not related to or connected with the defendant or its officers in any manner. The plaintiff received a deed to lots 18 and 28, but was shown lots 17 and 29 by Ferro, and she believed she was obtaining title to lots 17 and 29 by her purchase. In February, 1951, the plaintiff moved into a house which was located on lot 17. The twenty foot gravel road separates lots 17 and 29. Plaintiff testified that she bought lot 17 for taxes in 1972, and she paid six years' taxes on lot 29, four years being at one time to redeem it.

To support plaintiff's claim of title by adverse possession, the claim must include five elements: it must be (1) hostile or adverse, (2) actual, (3) visible, notorious and exclusive, (4) continuous, and (5) under claim of ownership. If the record does not establish all of those conditions plaintiff cannot prevail. * * *

The evidence indicates that since February, 1951, when plaintiff moved into the house located on lot 17, only the plaintiff and members of her family have maintained lot 29. Her son worked for a person for a year who filled the hole on lot 29 so the children could play on the property. There was a privy on lot 29 maintained by the plaintiff from February, 1951 until 1961. Since February, 1951, plaintiff and her family are the only persons who have mowed the weeds on lot 29, and they also attempted to grow grass and raise a garden. Since 1951, lot 29 has been used for many of the outdoor recreational needs of the family of the plaintiff.

*   *   *

"For possession to be hostile in its inception, no spirit of animosity or hostility is required nor need the adverse claimant be guilty of deliberate or wilful tortious conduct. The essence of such possession is that it be in opposition to the possession of the true owner and not be subordinate thereto." * * * The very nature of plaintiff's entry and possession of lot 29 is an assertion of her own title and a denial of the title of all others. It matters not that the possessor was mistaken, and that, had she been better informed, she would not have entered on the land. We therefore reject defendant's allegation that the claim of ownership asserted by the plaintiff is insufficient to support hostile adverse possession.

Most of the cases discussing title by adverse possession maintain that the extent or degree of dominion or control required is largely determined by the nature of the property. From the evidence and testimony produced in the trial court, it was clearly shown that all five elements necessary for adverse possession to constitute a bar to the assertion of a legal title by the owner were present in plaintiff's case. * * *

Judgment affirmed.

2. Restrictive Covenants Strictly Construed

NORTH CHEROKEE VILLAGE MEMBERSHIP v. MURPHY

71 Mich.App. 592, 248 N.W.2d 629 (1977)

RILEY, Judge.

We are asked to decide whether a restrictive covenant banning "house trailers and tents" can be interpreted to include within its prohibition the placement of a "double-wide" mobile home on appellants' lot.

Appellants' deed, like those of all other property owners in the North Cherokee Village subdivision, contains the following restrictive covenant:

No house trailers or tents allowed on subdivision.

Aware of the restriction, appellants consulted their real estate agent and township officials to ask whether a "double-wide" mobile home would fall within the language of the covenant. In addition, they made somewhat half-hearted but unsuccessful attempts to seek the advice of the president of the homeowners association in their subdivision. The real estate agent advised them that as long as the structure complied with other deed restrictions, they could place the mobile home on their lot. They did so.

The mobile home, manufactured in two halves and carted separately to the premises, bore a certificate of title denominating it as a "trailer coach, double-wide". Pursuant to a Denton Township building permit the two sections were placed on a concrete block foundation and bolted together after removal of the two separate chassis. As conjoined the edifice has dimensions of 44 feet by 24 feet with three bedrooms, two baths, living room, dining room and kitchen, totaling 1,056 square feet of living space. Its purchase price was $12,000. It is equipped with connections to gas, electric, water and sewage lines. The roof is gabled with asphalt shingles. In all other respects, the structure complies with applicable deed restrictions, namely, clauses prohibiting structures with less than 900 square feet of usable floor space or those with flat roofs.

Two months after the mobile home had been placed on the lot, appellee brought suit seeking removal of the structure. The court below, holding that the wording of the restriction could reasonably be construed to embrace appellants' dwelling, issued an injunction commanding appellants to remove or raze the structure.

We begin with recognition of the general rule that covenants are construed strictly against those claiming the right of enforcement and all doubts are resolved in favor of the free use of property. In addition, it is well settled that a court of equity will not enlarge the scope of a covenant beyond the clear meaning of the language employed.

* * *

* * * The instant prohibition against "house trailers and tents" pales in comparison to the more comprehensive language of the restrictive covenants considered by the Illinois and Montana courts. Despite the dubious rationale of the Illinois appellate court, (a mobile home is a mobile home is a mobile home), the court there could at least cite restrictive language specifically banning mobile homes, whereas, this Court is asked to engage in semantic sleight of hand by declaring a two piece mobile home, bereft of its chassis and securely joined together, to be a house trailer. We decline the invitation.

*　　*　　*

Even assuming *arguendo* we were to infer an intent to ban transient structures by reading the phrase "house trailer and tent" in a light most favorable to plaintiff, we do not believe appellants' modular unit can accurately be described as any less permanent than other kinds of sectional, prebuilt dwellings currently on the market. Surely, factory-built housing would not violate the covenant; we discern, therefore, no significant reason why the appellants' summer home is any greater encroachment on the sparse language of the restriction.

*　　*　　*

This cause is reversed and remanded to the trial court for rescission of the injunction.

3. Restriction to Adults Held Reasonable

RILEY v. STOVES

22 Ariz.App. 223, 526 P.2d 747 (1974)

HATHAWAY, Chief Judge.

Defendants James W. and Lois Riley appeal from a judgment against them which enjoined their further violation of a restrictive covenant * * *.

Plaintiffs and defendants are all owners of lots comprising Enchanted Acres Subdivision, Unit One, a mobile home subdivision, consisting of 39 lots. At the time the defendants purchased their lot, it was subject to a recorded Declaration of Restrictions which included the following:

> Restricted to persons 21 years of age and older. One family unit per lot. Developers are not restricted in regard to age until subdivision is completed.

It was admitted at trial that defendants lived on their lot with two children under 21 years of age. On appeal, they assert that the above-quoted restriction is invalid upon several grounds.

*　　*　　*

In the case at hand, the phrase "restricted to persons 21 years of age and older" is to be construed in its popular sense and in relation to the circumstances of its use. The trial court properly received evidence of such circumstances. Plaintiffs introduced a promotional brochure prepared by the common grantor who recorded the restrictions which states that the subdivision is "restricted to adult living." Each plaintiff who testified stated he had understood before purchasing his lot that the restriction in question effectively precluded children from living in the subdivision. Plaintiffs relied upon the age-limit restriction in purchasing their lots.

*   *   *

From the language of the restriction and the circumstances of its use, it appears self-evident that what was being sought was the prohibition against persons under 21 years of age residing in the subdivision. We believe the evidence presented compelled the trial court's interpretation of the restriction as a mutual agreement by each lot owner that persons under the age of 21 years would not be allowed to live in the subdivision.

*   *   *

The restriction flatly prevents children from living in the mobile home subdivision. The obvious purpose is to create a quiet, peaceful neighborhood by eliminating noise associated with children at play or otherwise. The testimony given by the plaintiffs indicates that they prefer to live away from children, that children living in their neighborhood tend to disturb them, and that they bought their respective lots upon the assumption that Enchanted Acres, Unit I, would be an "adult community."

*   *   *

Here, the common developer subdivided a large tract of land. He obviously felt that a portion of the market for mobile home lots desired an adult community. He therefore set aside a portion of the mobile home lots in Unit One for exclusive adult living. * * * It fulfilled a legitimate need of older buyers who sought to retire in an area undisturbed by children.

*   *   *

It is of interest here to note that the United States Congress has recognized the need of elderly Americans for adult communities. It has adopted several programs to provide housing for the elderly. An age minimum of 62 years has been set for occupancy of these housing developments. These sections represent an implicit legislative finding that not only do older adults need inexpensive housing, but also that their housing interests and needs differ from families with children. The age limitation is designed in part to prevent the distractions and disturbances often caused by a large number of children living in the development.

We do not think the restriction is in any way arbitrary. It effectively insures that only working or retired adults will reside on the lots. It does much to eliminate the noise and distractions caused by children. We find it reasonably related to a legitimate purpose and therefore decline to hold that its enforcement violated defendants' rights to equal protection.

*   *   *

Affirmed.

4. Life Estate

MARTIN v. HEARD

239 Ga. 816, 238 S.E.2d 899 (1977)

PER CURIAM. The plaintiffs appeal from a judgment rendered in favor of the defendants refusing to reform a warranty deed and refusing to issue an injunction.

On October 19, 1970, Mr. Coy Martin executed an option to Waymon Heard Farms, Inc., to convey 612 acres of land "reserving a life estate for himself and his wife on 12 acres which is to include the home site" * * *. Heard Farms exercised the option. The warranty deed, however, does not describe the reservations in the same terms as the option. Following a description of the 612 acres, the deed provides: "Grantor reserves unto himself and his wife the right to reside in the residence located on the following described property for and during their natural life." A description of the 12 acres follows and then a forfeiture clause: "In the event that the grantor or his wife should discontinue the use of the house on the above described property for their personal residence, then and in that event all rights herein reserved will be forfeited to the grantee." * * *

In 1975 the Martins learned of the variances between the reservations in the option and the reservations in the deed. They filed suit to reform the deed to conform with the option and to enjoin Mr. Heard and the Heard corporation from interfering with the Martins' exercise of their rights. After a trial without a jury, the court held the deed valid as written, and interpreted the forfeiture clause to mean that if either Mr. or Mrs. Martin discontinued use of the property by death or otherwise, the remaining party would have to vacate the property within a reasonable time. * * * Finally the court ruled that the reservation of fishing privileges to the Martins terminated when their right to use the 12 acres ended. The Martins appeal.

*   *   *

We conclude that the Martins each have a life estate subject to divestiture in the house and acreage * * *.

The appellant owned a large tract of land, conveying out of himself title to all except the interests reserved. He reserved unto himself and his wife "[T]he right to reside in the residence located on the following described property for and during their natural life." Then the deed described a definite 12.5 acres of land carved out of the larger 612 acre tract. The term of the reservation was for life, subject to forfeiture only if the grantor or his wife should discontinue the use of the house on the property for their personal residence. It is not reasonable to conclude that these parties who owned the land in fee, intended to reduce their rights thereon to rights comparable to those that may be granted to a tenant. Although the reservation is not as clear as the words contained in the original option to sell, they are clear enough to indicate that the granting parties were reserving to themselves, full use and enjoyment of the house for their lifetime.

*   *   *

We also conclude that the condition upon which the life estates termi-

nate occurs when the Martins *both* cease living on the property, whether by both vacating it or by the death or removal of the survivor of them. This conclusion follows in part from a reading of the testimony of the attorney who drew the deed, who stated that it was the parties' intent to incorporate into the deed in substance the same provisions as were contained in the option contract. The mere fact that the estate may terminate on some condition earlier than death does not destroy its character as a life estate.
* * *

* * *

* * * The trial court erred * * *.

5. Land Sale Contract

KOSLOFF v. CASTLE

115 Cal. App. 3d 369, 171 Cal.Rptr. 308 (1981)

This appeal arises out of a dispute over real property in Sonoma County. After a nonjury trial, the court granted recovery to respondent on her complaint to quiet title and recover possession and denied recovery to appellant on her cross-complaint for specific performance.

Appellant contends that a willfully defaulting vendee under an installment land contract is legally entitled to an equity of redemption, i.e., that she should have been allowed to reinstate the contract and tender full performance. She also maintains that an installment land contract is in fact a mortgage under Civil Code section 2924, giving a right of redemption to mortgagors.

For the most part the facts are not disputed. In 1966, respondent purchased a home in Sonoma County for $15,000 which she rented to appellant in 1970 for $150 per month. Appellant continued to rent the house at that rate for the next three years. On July 1, 1973, the parties entered into a written agreement for the sale of the property to appellant for $15,000. The purchase price was payable in installments of $150 per month for two years, and the balance of $11,400 in a single balloon payment was due on or before July 1, 1975. There was no provision for interest. The respondent would retain title to the property until the final payment was made, and appellant would forfeit her interest in the property if she breached the contract. In the event of a breach appellant's monthly payments would be deemed rental payments for the use of the property. Time was of the essence.

From July 1, 1973, until April 1976, appellant paid $114 per month directly to the lending institution for the monthly loan installment and impound account and remitted the balance of $36 to respondent. Appellant failed to tender the balloon payment of $11,400 on July 1, 1975, when due. From May 1976 through January 1977, she paid a reduced monthly amount of $98.77 to the lending institution and continued to remit $36 to respondent. From February 1977 through September 1977 appellant paid only the $98.77 and failed to make any payments to respondent; after suit was filed, appellant paid to respondent $288, representing the $36 per month for this latter eight-month period. From December 1976 through February 1978, appellant paid directly to the county treasurer three installments totalling $808 on property taxes.

*   *   *

Respondent took no steps to enforce payment of the $11,400 until December 15, 1976, at which time respondent's attorney informed appellant by letter that her rights under the contract had terminated. Respondent served appellant with a notice to quit in April 1977 and filed an action for unlawful detainer and to quiet title in August 1977.

In September of 1977, appellant tendered the amount of $9,372.72 which sum represented the $11,400 minus the payments made from July 1975 to September 1977, with an allowance for interest on the $11,400. The offer was refused.

Over appellant's objections, the court found that respondent believed, following the breach of contract, that appellant had once again assumed the role of tenant. The court also found that the value of the property at the time of the contract was $20,000 to $22,000 and that the reasonable rental in April 1977 was $200 per month.

*   *   *

Along with the mortgage and deed of trust, the Legislature has categorized the installment land contract as a security instrument in the subordination legislation (Civ. Code § 2953.1), and as a security device within the purchase-money anti-deficiency limitation of Code of Civil Procedure section 580b. It is appellant's contention that an installment land contract used as a security device is a "mortgage" under Civil Code section 2924 and that she should have the relief available to a mortgagee.

The trend has been toward judicial recognition that where the installment land contract is used as a security device, it is for all intents and purposes a mortgage; the total judicial equation of the two, however, has never been completed.

It is obvious from its memorandum of intended decision that the trial court weighed the equities in this case and concluded that they did not favor appellant's reinstatement of the contract. The trial court found that appellant's continuing failure to pay the $11,400 subsequent to July 1975 was a willful and grossly negligent breach of contract. During the more than two years in which appellant was in default, she often did not even make the $150 payments required under the contract. There was no evidence of improvement to the property, which had in fact fallen into a state of disrepair. With regard to respondent's delay in enforcing her rights, the court found that it was reasonable under the circumstances for respondent to have believed that upon appellant's failure to make the balloon payment their relationship reverted to that of landlord-tenant. No restitution was owing in this case where the monthly installments were no more than the equivalent of the rental value of the property. Thus there was no forfeiture of partial payment in this case.

The court properly weighed the equities of which there was substantial evidence to justify the trial court's decision that "It is just and equitable to enforce the terms of the land sale contract as set forth."

*   *   *

Appellant urges us to complete the land sale reform initiated by *Barkis v. Scott, supra,* 34 Cal.2d 116, and ending prematurely with *MacFadden v. Walker, supra,* 5 Cal.3d 809, by today holding that the land sale contract is a mortgage under Civil Code section 2924. That section states in part that, "Every transfer of an interest in property, other than in trust, made only as a security for the performance of another act, is to be deemed a mortgage . . ." If we were to so hold, appellant would then be entitled to a right of redemption under Civil Code 2924c. One of the area's foremost commentators argues persuasively for appellant's position. (Hatland, Secured Real Estate Transactions (1974) § 2.12, pp. 59–61.)

We decline to hold that the agreement in the case before us is a mortgage as defined in Civil Code section 2924. We believe that any reform in this area is more appropriately initiated by the Legislature which is in a better position to effect and coordinate comprehensive answers to the many-faceted questions that such a determination would evoke.

6. Zoning Ordinances must be Reasonable

HERRINGTON v. TOWN OF MEXICO

91 Misc.2d 861, 398 N.Y.S.2d 818 (1977)

EDWARD F. McLAUGHLIN, Justice. Petitioner initiated this proceeding * * * seeking relief from an adverse determination by the respondent, Town of Mexico, concerning an application for a permit to place a mobile home on a certain site in the Town of Mexico.

Petitioner contends that denial of the application by the Town Zoning Board of Appeals is arbitrary and capricious and attacks the constitutional validity of Section 540(4)(D) of the Town Zoning Ordinance. Respondent contends that the Ordinance is a valid exercise of the Town's police power in promoting the health, safety and general welfare of the community, and that it was enacted to prevent the danger of arbitrary determinations by individual zoning officers.

*   *   *

Petitioner resides in the Town of Mexico and is the owner of twenty (20) acres of open farm land situated in that town. On April 8, 1977, petitioner applied to the zoning officer of the Town of Mexico for a permit to place a 1973 model mobile home on his farm property. The mobile home, which was owned by petitioner's brother and sister-in-law, was to be placed on the site for the purpose of renting it to tenants who are neither parties to this proceeding nor related to petitioner.

Section 540(4)(D) of respondent's Land Use Ordinance enacted May 5, 1976, provides as follows:

4. A mobile home must be:

*   *   *

D. Original owner units.

*   *   *

Once emplaced to conform to the above standards, an original unit, which
for the purpose of this ordinance is defined as a mobile home manufactured within a year prior to the date of emplacement, and not previously
occupied, may be resold in place provided that it otherwise complies with
the above standards.

The zoning officer denied petitioner's application on the sole ground
that petitioner's mobile home did not comply with the definition of "original
owner units" under Subdivision 4D in that the mobile home was manufactured more than one year prior to the proposed date of placement.

*   *   *

Zoning ordinances are enacted for the purposes of promoting the
health, safety, morals or general welfare of the community. Town Boards are
empowered by statute to regulate and restrict the height, number of stories
and size of buildings and other structures, the percentage of lot that may be
occupied, the size of yards, courts and other open spaces, the density of
population and the location and use of buildings, structures and land for
trade, industry, residence or other purposes. Furthermore, Section 130(21)
of the Town Law permits a town to pass ordinances regulating house trailer
camps and house trailers. The statute provides for regulation of sewer connection, water supply, toilets, garbage removal, registration of occupants
and inspection of camps.

*   *   *

There is a presumption that a duly enacted zoning ordinance is constitutional and the burden of establishing otherwise rests upon the petitioner.
Petitioner must show the ordinance is not justifiable under the police power
of the State by any reasonable interpretation of the facts. If the judgment
of the legislative body is fairly debatable, it must control. When, however,
the restrictions upon the free use of property become so harsh as to be
unreasonable and arbitrary, unnecessary to the preservation of the scheme
and purpose as a whole, approaching the point where an owner is deprived
of any beneficial or profitable use of his property, then the Court should step
in * * *.

The Court finds that Section 540(4)(D) of the Zoning Ordinance of the
Town of Mexico is an arbitrary and unreasonable restraint upon petitioner's
use of his property. It cannot reasonably be contended that only those mobile
homes built within a year of placement are sufficiently safe and aesthetically pleasing to satisfy even the most rigorous health, safety and welfare
standards of the community. It is unreasonable to conclusively presume that
a high-quality mobile home built two or three years before emplacement is
per se unfit for location within the Town.

The mobile home in question has a value of approximately $7,000.00
and is in excellent condition. As a 1973 model, it can hardly be said to be
antiquated or obsolete or aesthetically unacceptable. The arbitrary nature
of the ordinance restriction is readily apparent. For example, a nine-month

old mobile home with a cost of $4,000.00 would be eligible for placement in the Town, while a well kept two-year old mobile home with a cost of $10,-000.00, or an even newer model which had once changed hands, would not.

*   *   *

Under the circumstances, the Court cannot view the "original owner units" requirement as having a reasonable relation to the health, safety and welfare of the community. Furthermore, it appears that a restriction allowing only those mobile homes emplaced within one year of manufacture is much more arbitrary than would be the decision of a zoning officer based on reasonable, articulated standards of construction, safety, placement and exterior appearance.

* * * Subdivision 4D of Section 540 is declared to be null and void, and the respondent is restrained from acting pursuant to it.

PROBLEMS

1. Houseman deeded his land to Koehler "for the term of Koehler's life." Two years later, Koehler deeded the land to Quentin "for the term of Quentin's life." A year later, Koehler died and Houseman claimed the land from Quentin under Houseman's reversion. Does Houseman have the title? Why?

2. In 1950, Grizzly Ben built a cabin on some remote forest land in California belonging to the U.S. government. Government agents discovered Ben at the site in 1979 and learned that he had been living there openly and continuously during the entire period. When the government attempted to evict him, Grizzly Ben claimed that he had title to the property by adverse possession. Is Grizzly Ben right?

3. Archer gave Gonzales permission to take a shortcut over Archer's land to reach Gonzales' orchard, thereby saving Gonzales a long trip around Archer's farm. Gonzales had been taking this shortcut regularly for 10 years. Archer then sold his farm to Sharp, who fenced the farm in and told Gonzales that he could no longer use the shortcut. Gonzales claims that Sharp is required to permit him to use the shortcut, since Gonzales had been using it for 10 years and the statute of limitations in the state for easement by prescription was only seven years. Is Gonzales legally entitled to continue to use the shortcut? Suppose he had been using it for 10 years without Archer's consent, express or implied. Would it make a difference?

4. Pop Wise wanted to make a gift of his mountain lot to his daughter Vera. Vera had a grant deed to the lot drawn up and gave it to Pop, who later signed it before a notary public and put it in his desk drawer. Pop died before doing anything else. His will didn't mention the lot, but the residuary clause of the will left everything not otherwise disposed of to Pop's son Les. Both Vera and Les claim title to the lot. Who gets it?

5. Rod Reddy wasn't sure whether or not he owned Rancho Dunrovin, but Owen Fields wanted to buy it from him. Rod sold it to Owen and conveyed it by means of a quitclaim deed, which Owen had recorded. Later, Rod discovered that he actually had owned the full title to Rancho Dunrovin in fee simple. He sold the property to Hy Walls and gave Hy a general warranty grant deed to the property. Hy took the warranty grant deed and sued to evict Owen from the property on the theory that his general warranty grant deed gave him better title to Rancho Dunrovin than Owen's quitclaim deed. Is Hy entitled to the land?

6. Wil Wright died, leaving as his only last will and testament a document typed on his typewriter, signed by Wil in his own handwriting, but unwitnessed. The will purported to leave all Wil's real property to his sister Ruth. Wil's brother Art claims that the will is void and that the land must be distributed under the laws of succession of the state. Is Art correct?

7. Heavenly Acres, Inc., subdividers, put restrictive covenants in the grant deeds delivered to all purchasers of lots or houses in their development. Included among the restrictions placed in all of the deeds were the following: (1) No laundry may be hung outside for drying. (2) No animal pets may be kept inside or outside the premises. (3) No more than four people can be in any house at any one time. (4) Houses or lots cannot be sold to anyone except members of the Caucasian race. Are any of these restrictions enforceable? Are any unenforceable? Why?

8. Ray Kane came home from work one day and found that the city had installed parking meters in front of both his home and the other homes in the block. Ray disregarded the meter and did not put in the required money. When he got a traffic ticket, Ray argued to the court that by the deed to his house he owned the land to the middle of the street and that the city had no right to make him pay for parking on his own property. Is Ray correct?

9. The Fountain of Youth Drinking Water Company, serving thousands of customers throughout the county, drilled three artesian wells near Pine Mountain on some land the company owned. When Fountain of Youth started pumping, many property owners at Pine Mountain complained that the water level in their wells had dropped too low to provide for their domestic needs. The other property owners seek an injunction to stop Fountain of Youth from pumping. What result?

10. Jerry Gold bought an office building from Rob Baker for $200,000. Jerry took the building subject to a preexisting $150,000 mortgage held by the Fidelity Trust Company. Jerry's business failed, and the office building was sold through foreclosure by the Fidelity Trust Company. At public auction, the building brought $140,-000. Fidelity Trust Company got a deficiency judgment in the amount of $10,000. Does Jerry have to pay this $10,000 out of his other personal assets? Would it make any difference if he had assumed the mortgage?

Chapter 25

LANDLORD AND TENANT

When the owner of property (the lessor) gives up the right to possession of the property to another (the lessee) the agreement accomplishing this purpose is called a "lease" and the consideration normally paid is called "rent." When the lessee actually takes possession, he or she becomes the tenant and the lessor is the landlord. The lease may be express or implied and is required to be in writing only if a period of time is set that falls within the statute of frauds, usually that exceeding one year. (See Statute of Frauds, Chapter 14.)

A. LEASEHOLD TENANCIES

Leasehold estates are of four types: (estate for years, periodic tenancy, tenancy at will, and tenancy at sufferance).

1. ESTATE FOR YEARS

An estate for years is one fixed for a definite period of time, with a stated date for beginning and ending. Since a lease is a contract, it may be ended at any time during its term by mutual agreement of the parties, by a condition stated in the lease, by operation of law such as bankruptcy, or by a merger if the lessee acquires fee simple title to the leased property.

2. PERIODIC TENANCY

A periodic tenancy is often referred to as a tenancy from year to year or from month to month, depending on the period of time for which rental payment is made. Usually the period is from month to month, from one month to the next. It may be either written or oral and may be terminated at the end of any period by giving notice, usually of equal length of time as the period stated. In the absence of any notice to the contrary, it automatically renews for the next period.

3. TENANCY AT WILL

A tenancy at will is one that may be terminated by either party at any time. Since no period of time is stated, it is "at the will" of either party and may be either express or implied. Most states require that notice be given to terminate the tenancy relationship.

4. TENANCY AT SUFFERANCE

A tenancy at sufferance exists when a tenant continues to occupy the premises after the expiration of the lease. If the tenant continues to remain on the premises, it is at the sufferance of the landlord. However, most states require that notice to quit be given such tenants, and if they are permitted to stay, the leasehold implicitly becomes a periodic tenancy. An example of this type of tenancy is set forth in the following case.

FACTS The plaintiff brought an action for damages against the defendants alleging that she was the widow of W. R. Teston, who died May 30, 1973; that the defendants are her stepsons; that her deceased husband had deeded their homeplace to the defendants reserving therein a life estate; that on the day after W. R. Teston's death the defendants threw her out of the house, took certain property, padlocked the house containing the plaintiff's clothing and other personal property, and told the plaintiff not to come back. The complaint set forth special damages sustained by the plaintiff and prayed for such damages plus $10,000 punitive damages for mistreatment of the plaintiff.

DECISION The court held that the plaintiff did not become an intruder after the death of her husband. Where a husband was a tenant at sufferance, after his death his wife and children succeeded to that same relation. If another has the right of possession, he or she may recover damages even from the owner. A tenant holding over wrongfully may not be "... forcibly dispossessed by the landlord without subjecting the latter to an action of trespass; he having an appropriate remedy for her summary dispossession." Judgment for plaintiff.

Teston v. Teston (135 Ga.App. 321, 217 S.E.2d 498 [1975])

B. LEASE COVENANTS

Covenants are the clauses, or promises, in a lease that set forth the rights and obligations of the parties. Like any contract provision, they may be drafted to cover almost any contingency that is not unlawful or against public policy. Some of the more common covenants found in the usual lease are for rent, security or cleaning deposits, use of the premises, duty to make repairs, assignment and subleasing, fixtures, option to renew or purchase, and quiet enjoyment.

1. RENT

Rent is the compensation paid or furnished the landlord in return for the use and possession of the leased premises. Most agreements now provide that rent be paid in advance, many requiring that the last month or two be advanced as a hedge against the possibility of the tenant's unlawfully detaining the property. If no figure is stated as rent, a reasonable amount is due, payable at the end of the lease period.

The usual lease is a gross lease, which calls for rental at a fixed rate per month. Some businesses operate with a net lease, under which the tenant pays the taxes, assessments, and all operating expenses in connection with the premises, turning the balance net figure over to the landlord. Many modern store leases are percentage leases, a type in which the rental is based on either a flat fee plus a percentage of gross or a percentage of the net income received from the tenant's business conducted on the premises. The latter type may contain a recapture clause permitting the landlord to take back the premises if the tenant's business does not reach a certain gross or net.

2. SECURITY OR CLEANING DEPOSIT

A security deposit or cleaning deposit is a sum required to be paid in advance to cover possible damage, breakage, or cost of cleaning when the tenant moves. When the term expires and the tenant leaves, if no rent is due, nothing has been damaged or broken beyond fair wear and tear, and the premises have been properly cleaned, the landlord must return the deposit. In many states, an improper refusal by the landlord to refund the deposit may result in punitive damages. A few courts have held that the landlord must also pay the state's legal rate of interest on the deposit for the time it was held.

3. USE OF PREMISES

For most practical purposes, the tenant becomes the owner of the premises during the period of the lease and may use the property in any legal manner unless there is a covenant in the lease to the contrary. An exception is that the tenant is not permitted to damage or injure the landlord's interest, and any diminishment of the property's value because of damage caused by the tenant is known as waste, for which the tenant is liable. The owner may include a covenant stating that the use of the premises will be limited to "no other use" or "only for," such as "clothing store and no other use" or "use only for a clothing store," and provide for forfeiture in the event of breach.

The following case considers an interesting problem regarding proper use of leased premises:

> **FACTS**   Landlord claims that tenant has violated a substantial obligation of his tenancy by sharing his apartment with a young lady "without the benefit of clergy" (or even the blessings of a Civil Court judge). However, she was the tenant's fiancee.

DECISION The tenant breached a substantial obligation of the tenancy by permitting undertenant, a person other than a member of his immediate family, to occupy the apartment. The breach is material and sufficient to warrant termination of the tenancy. If, however, undertenant becomes a member of tenant's immediate family (as appears imminent), or removes from the apartment, within 60 days, issuance of the warrant will be stayed.

Fraydun Enterprises v. Ettinger (91 Misc.2d 119, 397 N.Y.S.2d 301 [1977])

4. ASSIGNMENT OR SUBLEASE

In the absence of a provision to the contrary, a tenant may assign the lease or sublet the premises to another. A sublease is something less than all of the tenant's leasehold rights. To prevent the obtaining of undesirable tenants, the landlord usually insists on a covenant by which the tenant agrees not to sublet or assign without the written consent of the landlord. To avoid arbitrary action, the tenant may request an addition that the landlord will not unreasonably withhold such consent. The modern rule followed in many courts is that the landlord's covenant is unenforceable where the withholding of consent is deemed unreasonable.

If the landlord accepts rent from an assignee or sublessee, it is considered a waiver of the restriction against assignment or subletting and amounts to a ratification by the landlord.

5. QUIET ENJOYMENT

Most leases, either expressly or by implication, carry a covenant for quiet enjoyment. This means that the tenant will not lose possession by any act of the landlord through failure of the landlord's title or by the enforcement of any lien superior to the landlord's title. It also implies that the landlord will not personally disturb the possession of the tenant. Any breach of this covenant constitutes an eviction of the tenant and the tenant has a right to recover damages and the option of terminating the lease. The following case is an example of failure to provide quiet enjoyment of the premises:

FACTS Tenant's dog had disturbed neighbors who complained to the apartment house manager. Management asked tenant to move out. When she refused to move, management cut off her electricity. The weather was cold, so she took her children to her parent's home for the night, leaving the dog on the patio at the apartment. The manager let the dog inside the apartment, where the dog caused extensive damage to the tenant's property. Tenant sued landlord for damages; the trial court awarded tenant $1745 actual damages and $1200 punitive damages. Landlord appeals.

DECISION The court found this to be a violation of tenant's quiet enjoyment right. Since a wrong had been committed as well as breach of contract, the award of both actual and punitive damages was affirmed.

Clark v. Sumner (559 S.W.2d 914 [Tex.Civ.App., 1977])

C. TERMINATION OF LEASE

A lease may be terminated in accordance with the terms stated in the body of the lease by destruction or loss of the premises and by the breach of certain covenants.

1. TERMINATION UNDER LEASE TERMS

An estate for years is terminated in accordance with the terms set forth in the lease. Periodic tenancies renew automatically unless notice is given by one party to the other, generally at least one period in advance. However, most states have statutes governing the maximum length of notice required, usually either 30 days or 60 days, regardless of the period involved. In a tenancy at will, no notice was required at common law for termination. Today, however, most states require legal notice, which makes the tenancy practically identical to a period-to-period type. In a tenancy at sufferance, since the tenant has already held over beyond the terms of the lease, notice should not be required. Nevertheless, if the landlord has not commenced formal eviction, the tenancy converts to a periodic one and must be ended with proper notice and legal action.

2. DESTRUCTION OR LOSS OF PREMISES

At common law, destruction of the premises did not terminate the lease, because the land was still available. Today, however, destruction of all or a material part of the premises terminates the lease under the doctrine of commercial frustration. Where changes in zoning laws have required the business to cease or to remove to another location, the same rule applies. Most leases have covenants providing for this contingency.

When land is taken by the government for public use under the right of eminent domain in a condemnation proceeding, the tenant usually has no claim against the landlord. To avoid legal entanglements and the difficulty of apportioning damages, each lease should have a clause either stating that the lessee receives nothing or setting a distribution ratio agreeable to all parties.

If the premises were mortgaged at the time the lease was made, the mortgage has priority and a foreclosure would end the tenancy. However, if the leases were already in effect when the mortgage was executed, the mortgage is subject to the tenancies and a foreclosure would not affect the leases.

3. BREACH OF COVENANT

Most covenants of a lease are generally made conditions, and as such, any breach thereof is justification for termination of the lease. When a condition, such as payment of rent, is breached, the landlord has the right to dispossess the tenant by eviction.

Eviction may be accomplished lawfully by giving legal statutory notice; serving the necessary papers on the tenants; proceeding to a court hearing for unlawful detainer, usually summary in nature; obtaining a judgment; and, if necessary, accomplishing actual ejectment through the appropriate law enforcement agency.

A modern rule followed in many states prohibits retaliatory eviction. For example, when a tenant reports illegal or substandard conditions to the proper authorities and the landlord is required to make the necessary corrections, an eviction of the tenant for revenge is held to be against public policy and will not be enforced.

A. BREACH OF COVENANT BY TENANT

When a tenant defaults in the performance of any major covenant of the lease, particularly the one requiring payment of rent, the landlord has the option of terminating the tenancy. If the landlord elects to evict, a notice of default must be served on the tenant demanding either that the breach be corrected or that the tenant quit. If the tenant fails to do either, the landlord may then proceed with legal action to terminate the tenancy and recover possession. The following case is an example of a tenant's breach:

> **FACTS** Landlord seeks to evict tenant, claiming a violation of a lease covenant prohibiting tenant from defacing the premises or making any alteration, addition, or improvement without the prior written consent of the landlord. Tenant had installed a permanent air-conditioning unit.
>
> **DECISION** The court noted that the landlord and the tenant were unfriendly but observed that lack of a "mutual admiration" society was no reason for terminating a lease. However, the judge found that the lease had been violated by the installation of a permanent type of air conditioner that had defaced the premises. He noted that cases permitting the placement of a window type of air-conditioner were different, since no alterations were required. The tenant was ordered to remove the air conditioner and to restore the property to its original condition within 60 days or the court would order the lease terminated.

Kaminoff v. Spiegel (93 Misc.2d 458, 402 N.Y.S.2d 777 [1978])

B. BREACH OF COVENANT BY LANDLORD

The failure of the landlord to perform covenants in the lease does not alone entitle the tenant to terminate, but the tenant's remedy is generally only for damages for breach of covenant. There are exceptions to this rule when the landlord breaches the covenant for quiet enjoyment or causes a constructive eviction.

The landlord's failure to perform a covenant that materially impairs the tenant's ability to enjoy the premises will be treated by analogy as a breach of quiet enjoyment and as a constructive eviction of the tenant. A constructive eviction may also exist if the premises have been made uninhabitable because of some act or omission of the landlord.

D. RESPONSIBILITY FOR PROPERTY CONDITION

At common law, the landlord was held to have no responsibility concerning the condition of the premises, since the lease transferred his or her interest to the tenant for the period of the leasehold. The tenant's only obligation was to not damage or commit waste upon the property.

Today's building, housing, and zoning laws require that someone be responsible for the condition of the premises, and statutes may place the liability on either the landlord or the tenant. Covenants, unless prohibited by state or local law, may also fix this obligation.

The tenant's liability exists only to that part of the premises leased to him or her and the landlord is responsible for the common areas, as they are deemed to have remained with the landowner. Common areas are those parts where no individual tenant is entitled to exclude any other from use or enjoyment, including entryways, common stairs, halls, parking lots, and other facilities shared by all of the tenants. Exterior walls, heating, air conditioning, and plumbing systems have also been placed in this category.

Most states now have habitability statutes requiring the landlord of residential premises to keep the premises in a habitable condition. Such laws usually permit the tenant, after giving notice, to make the required repairs and deduct up to one month's rent to cover the cost. If the landlord covenants to make repairs and refuses to do so, the tenant would be entitled to make them and recover the entire cost from the landlord as damages for breach of contract.

E. TORT LIABILITY

Tort liability of landowners and occupiers of premises refers to the responsibility for damages or injury suffered by an individual because of substandard conditions on the property resulting from a negligent act or omission by the party having the duty of care for the premises.

The older rules of law set different standards of reasonable care, depending upon whether the injured person was a licensee, invitee, or trespasser. However, the modern view followed in most states establishes the test of due care as the reasonable application of all facts and circumstances, with the status of the injured party as only one of the considerations. Therefore, an injured party is now usually referred to as a "visitor," irrespective of the various status categories.

1. TENANT'S LIABILITY

The tenant, as the possessor and occupier of leased premises, has the primary liability to other persons who are injured because of the unreasonable conditions of the premises.

2. LANDLORD'S LIABILITY

Although there was no common law of responsibility for the landlord over leased premises, the modern rule treats the lessor as a seller to the tenant, and new rules have been applied that are similar to those found in products liability (see Chapter 30). As a result, landlords have been found liable in many situations.

When the lease has a covenant charging the landlord with the duty to repair, the landlord has been held liable for failure to maintain the premises in a proper condition. Under such circumstances, both the landlord and the tenant may be liable to the injured visitor.

Violations of building codes that lead to injury of a visitor have been held to be the landlord's responsibility. Since they involve safety statutes, it is reasoned that visitors are a class intended to be protected and may sue as beneficiaries. At the same time, the tenant may also be liable for negligence in failing to care for the premises.

Latent, or hidden, defects are also the landlord's problem, if they were known to the landlord and not disclosed to the tenant. This rule is based on the fraud theory of the duty to disclose such information. Some recent court decisions have expanded this logic to require warning against dangerous social conditions, such as the high incidence of burglary and rape in a building or its vicinity.

Most states now hold that the landlord must use due care in maintaining the premises, and the fact that he or she is not in actual possession is merely one of the factors to be considered in determining the question of fault in a negligence action.

ILLUSTRATIVE CASES

1. Term and Periodic Tenancies

WALDROP v. SIEBERT

286 Ala. 106, 237 So. 2d 493 (1970)

McCALL, Justice. The appellees brought this action to recover possession of leased premises from the appellant. * * * The trial court rendered judgment for the plaintiff and the defendant has appealed therefrom. The basic question in the case being one of law, is "Does the lease between the parties give the appellant lessee the right to perpetually renew it."

On July 20, 1963, the appellees executed a written lease of the premises to the appellant for an original term of two years to run from July 20, 1963 to July 19, 1965. The rent was $720, payable in equal monthly installments of $30 on July 20, 1963, and on the 20th day of each month thereafter. The lease provides for an optional tenancy in the following language:

Lessor grants to Lessee the option to renew at end of term for an additional term of Three (3) years, and year to year thereafter.

*　　　*　　　*

The original term of this lease created a leasehold estate in the lessee
for two years. The estate granted, being one limited to endure for a definite
and ascertained period, fixed in advance, is what is known as a term for
years. * * * By the provisions of the lease, the appellant is granted an
option, at the end of the first term of two years, to renew or continue his
tenancy "for an additional term of Three (3) years, and year to year thereafter." A tenancy from year to year is a periodic tenancy, measured by the year.
This optional tenancy is part of the original demise.

While the language of the renewal clause may be susceptible of different meanings, we construe it to grant the appellant a single option, to renew
"* * * for an additional term of Three (3) years, and year to year thereafter."
The renewal creates a term of three years, which thence proceeds with a
year to year tenancy, constituting one leasehold estate. The words of controversial import are "and year to year thereafter." We conclude that the
conjunction joins this periodic tenancy from year to year to the tenancy for
three years, not to the option to renew. After the appellant exercised the
option, there was no second option or consecutive options conferred for
subsequent renewals from year to year. The singular, "option," is employed.
These words "and year to year thereafter" indicate to us the parties' intention, at the expiration of the three years, to continue the leasehold estate as
transformed from a term of years to a year to year tenancy. The year to year
tenancy continues in being for successive periods of a year until terminated
by either party at his will at the end of any year by giving the previous legal
notice.

*　　　*　　　*

* * * Therefore the additional term is at least for the three definite
years plus one year, because such specifies for three years, and year to year
thereafter. * * *

Having decided upon this the appellant had four additional years under
the renewal option rather than three. Therefore, appellees' notice to quit the
premises on July 19, 1968, was premature and inefficacious to terminate the
lease, because the notice was given when appellant's leasehold estate was
yet to run for another year, to wit, to July 19, 1969.

For this reason the case must be reversed and remanded.

2. Eviction by Landlord Action

OSTROW v. SMULKIN

249 A.2d 520 (D.C.App., 1969)

Hood, Chief Judge.　This appeal is from a judgment for rent against appellant who, with four other persons and a corporation (hereafter called the
tenants), leased an apartment building for a term of twenty years from

appellees' testator (hereafter called the landlord). The tenants did not lease the building for occupancy by themselves but for the purpose of subleasing the apartments to others as a commercial venture. After managing the property for about three years with apparently limited success, the tenants in 1963 engaged the Davis Company, a real estate company, to handle management and rental of the building. Operation of the building under the Davis management also appears not to have been completely successful because the tenants became delinquent in payment of rent. As a result, the landlord brought an action for possession because of nonpayment of rent allegedly in the amount of $3250. The tenants did not answer and judgment for possession by default was entered on July 13, 1965.

The tenants, apparently satisfied with what they considered the termination of their unprofitable lease, notified the Davis Company that they no longer had any interest in the building and thereafter they received no checks from the Davis Company and had no "dealings with the property."

* * *

Three months after obtaining judgment for possession, the landlord brought this action against Ostrow, one of the tenants, for $5850, alleged to be due as rent for the period of February 1, 1965 to October 30, 1965. After trial, the court awarded the landlord judgment for the full amount claimed.

Ostrow asserts that the judgment was erroneous in that it allowed recovery for rent beyond August 13, the date judgment for possession was entered. His contention is that when the judgment for possession was entered and in compliance therewith the tenants gave up possession, the tenancy was terminated and their liability to pay future rent ended. For reasons hereafter stated, we agree.

There are two basic incidents to a tenancy: the right to possession by the tenant and the corresponding right to rent by the landlord. If the landlord retakes possession by legal process or by accepting a voluntary surrender of possession by the tenant, the obligation of the tenant to pay future rent ceases. Of course, a tenant cannot escape his obligation to pay rent by a mere tender of possession to the landlord or by abandonment of possession. Unless a landlord accepts a tender or reenters after abandonment, the tenant's obligation to pay rent continues. And, depending upon the circumstances and contractual provisions of the lease, the tenant may be liable for damages even after the landlord has retaken possession, but this liability is for damages for breach of contract and not for rent.

Here the landlord filed an action for, and obtained judgment for, possession. It is true the landlord made no attempt to enforce his judgment by eviction process, but when a landlord by judicial proceeding asserts his right to possession, he is in no position to say that the tenant has no right to surrender possession. When the tenants received notice of the landlord's action for possession, did not oppose it, let judgment go by default, and then notified Davis Company, the managing agent, that they no longer had any interest in the property, we think as a matter of law there was a surrender of possession in compliance with the landlord's demand, and this constituted a termination of the lease and the tenants were not liable for rent thereafter.

As the lease was terminated by the surrender and not by the commencement of the action or the entry of the judgment, and the record before us does not show the exact date of the surrender, the judgment must be reversed with instructions to determine the date of surrender and the amount of rent due at that date, and to enter judgment for the landlord for such amount.

Reversed * * *.

3. Reasonable Sublease Requires Landlord's Consent

HOMA-GOFF INTERIORS, INC. v. COWDEN

350 So.2d 1035 (Ala., 1977)

JONES, Justice.　This summary judgment case involves a counterclaim filed by the appellants, Homa-Goff Interiors, Inc., against Geraldine Cowden, the appellee, claiming interference with a contractual relationship and unlawful refusal, by Mrs. Cowden, to grant consent to a sublease agreement between Homa-Goff and certain named prospective subtenants.

In February of 1974, a lease was entered into by Mrs. Cowden and Homa-Goff, John Goff, Pal Shoemaker, Henry Goff, and Thomas Gallion for a ten-year period. * * * The lease contained a clause which restricted the lessees' power to sublet subject to the landlord's written consent.

In October, Homa-Goff opened a furniture store on the leased premises. After several months in business, however, it became apparent to the appellants that, because of financial problems, they could not continue their operation. Therefore, they began seeking a subtenant. After some negotiation with the State of Alabama, the appellants, according to their counterclaim, reached a tentative agreement with the State to sublease the premises at a rental rate in excess of the rate paid by the lessees. Mrs. Cowden, exercising her option provided in the lease, refused to approve the State as a sublessee.

*　　　*　　　*

* * * [T]he trial Judge ruled: "[t]he landlord's withholding of consent can be arbitrary and unreasonable." From the order based on these rulings, Homa-Goff appeals. We reverse.

The threshold question is whether Mrs. Cowden, pursuant to ¶ 15(a) of the lease, may arbitrarily and capriciously reject a subtenant proposed by the lessee. * * *

*　　　*　　　*

The general rule throughout the country has been that, when a lease contains an approval clause, the landlord may arbitrarily and capriciously reject proposed subtenants. This rule, however, has been under steady attack in several states in the past twenty years; and this for the reason that, in recent times, the necessity of reasonable alienation of commercial building space has become paramount in our ever-increasing urban society.

Ohio has expressly rejected the general rule. * * * The Ohio Court, in ruling on whether the landlord could arbitrarily withhold consent, stated:

(W)here provision is made in a lease permitting assignment of rights thereunder, limited only by the requirement of prior consent of the lessor, such consent may not be withheld unless the prospective assignee is unacceptable, using the same standards applied in the acceptance of the original lessee.

The arbitrary and capricious rule has also been rejected in Illinois.

*   *   *

Guided by this rationale, we hold that, even where the lease provides an approval clause, a landlord may not unreasonably and capriciously withhold his consent to a sublease agreement. The landlord's rejection should be judged under a test applying a reasonable commercial standard. This question, of course, becomes a question of fact to be determined by the jury. Therefore, we hold that the trial Judge erred in granting a summary judgment in favor of Mrs. Cowden regarding appellant's claim alleging Mrs. Cowden was arbitrary and capricious in rejecting the prospective subtenants. It is a jury question whether Mrs. Cowden acted reasonably, and there is sufficient conflict of material fact to mandate a reversal.

*   *   *

ALMON, Justice (dissenting): I would adhere to the view adopted by a majority of jurisdictions in this country. Citizens should have the right to contract.

In my judgment, the court has rewritten this contract so as to rid it of its alleged moral harshness. There are many valid reasons why a lessor would insist that a lease-contract contain a provision to prevent subletting without the consent of the lessor. Why should a lessor be obligated to accept a sub-tenant chosen by a defaulting original tenant on the basis of "commercial standards," (whatever they may be) when the lessor's contract plainly gives him a contrary right?

4. Landlord Responsible for Common Areas

SHACKETT v. SCHWARTZ

77 Mich.App. 518, 258 N.W.2d 543 (1977)

O'BRIEN, Judge. Jack H. Kaufman was a tenant in an office building owned by Charles E. Schwartz. Kaufman is a doctor. One of Kaufman's patients slipped, fell and injured herself in the parking lot behind the office in question. She brought action against both, alleging joint and several liability.

The lease here devised only a portion of the premises to Kaufman. The other portion of the building was vacant at the time of the accident. The lease states that the vacant area at the rear of the building is to be used in common with other tenants. This portion would appear to be the parking lot.

The lease requires the lessee to maintain his own premises, and the lessor the roof and outer walls. At trial, Kaufman stated that he did not maintain the parking lot. Schwartz testified he made no arrangements for parking lot maintenance.

*   *   *

The trial court instructed the jury on the question of control of the parking lot. The jury returned a verdict for the plaintiff against both defendants for $25,000.

*   *   *

A general statement of the landlord's duties is stated as follows:

The first question is the nature of the duty owed by defendants to plaintiff. *At common law, a landlord's duty depends upon the facts and circumstances of each case. The element of control is of prime importance.* The common-law duty is predicated upon the concept that a lease is equivalent to a sale. *The lessor, absent agreement to the contrary, surrenders possession and holds only a reversionary interest. Under such circumstances, he is under no obligation to look after or keep in repair premises over which he has no control.*

An exception to the general lack of obligation is that a landlord has a duty to keep in safe condition any portion of a building under his control. The duty extends to a tenant's invitees, such as plaintiff.

*   *   *

However, the landlord has retained his responsibility for the common areas of the building which are not leased to his tenants. The common areas such as the halls, lobby, stairs, elevators, etc., are leased to no individual tenant and remain the responsibility of the landlord. It is his responsibility to insure that these areas are kept in good repair and reasonably safe for the use of his tenants and invitees.

The existence of this relationship between the defendant and its tenants and invitees placed a duty upon the landlord to protect them from unreasonable risk of physical harm.

The lease here demised only a portion of the premises to Kaufman. The other portion of the building was vacant at the time of the accident. The lease states that the vacant area at the rear of the building is to be used in common with other tenants. This portion would appear to be the parking lot.

While it is true that Kaufman was the only tenant, the provisions of the lease stated the amount of control of the premises surrendered under the lease. The fact that Kaufman was the only tenant should not change the result.

It would seem clear that under the general rule the landlord is responsible for common areas. The fact that there were no other tenants using the common area should be of no consequence.

*   *   *

* * * The lease taken as a whole shows that Kaufman had exclusive control of *only* the rooms enumerated in the lease.

Here, the lease is silent as to any allocation of risk. Since the lease did not transfer any right of control over the parking lot to the tenant, Kaufman, risk should remain with Schwartz, the landlord.

Reversed [as to Kaufman].

5. Landlord's Duty to Maintain Habitable Premises

GREEN v. SUPERIOR COURT OF CITY AND COUNTY OF SAN FRANCISCO

10 Cal.3d 616, 111 Cal. Rptr. 704, 517 P.2d 1168 (1974)

TOBRINER, Justice. Under traditional common law doctrine, long followed in California, a landlord was under no duty to maintain leased dwellings in habitable condition during the term of the lease. In the past several years, however, the highest courts of a rapidly growing number of states and the District of Columbia have reexamined the bases of the old common law rule and have uniformly determined that it no longer corresponds to the realities of the modern urban landlord-tenant relationship. Accordingly, each of these jurisdictions has discarded the old common law rule and has adopted an implied warranty of habitability for residential leases. * * *

On September 27, 1972, the landlord Jack Sumski commenced an unlawful detainer action in the San Francisco Small Claims Court seeking possession of the leased premises and $300 in back rent. The tenant admitted non-payment of rent but defended the action on the ground that the landlord had failed to maintain the leased premises in a habitable condition. The small claims court awarded possession of the premises to the landlord and entered a money judgment for $225 against the tenant. * * * [Following unsuccessful appeals] the tenant thereafter sought a hearing in this court; because of the statewide importance of the general issues presented, we exercised our discretion and issued an alternative writ of mandate.

* * * [I]n testimony at trial, petitioner and his roommate detailed a long list of serious defects in the leased premises which had not been repaired by the landlord after notice and which they claimed rendered the premises uninhabitable. Some of the more serious defects described by the tenants included (1) the collapse and non-repair of the bathroom ceiling, (2) the continued presence of rats, mice, and cockroaches on the premises, (3) the lack of any heat in four of the apartment's rooms, (4) plumbing blockages, (5) exposed and faulty wiring, and (6) an illegally installed and dangerous stove. The landlord apparently did not attempt to contest the presence of serious defects in the leased premises, but instead claimed that such defects afforded the tenant no defense in an unlawful detainer action.

*   *   *

At common law, the real estate lease developed in the field of real property law, not contract law. Under property law concepts, a lease was considered a conveyance or sale of the premises for a term of years, subject to the ancient doctrine of caveat emptor. Thus, under traditional common law rules, the landlord owed no duty to place leased premises in a habitable condition and no obligation to repair the premises. * * * Furthermore, because the law of property crystallized before the development of mutually dependent covenants in contract law, a lessee's covenant to pay rent was considered at common law as independent of the lessor's covenants. Thus even when a lessor expressly covenanted to make repairs, the lessor's breach did not justify the lessee's withholding of the rent.

* * * We have suggested that in the Middle Ages, and, indeed, until the urbanization of the industrial revolution, the land itself was by far the most important element of a lease transaction; this predominance explained the law's treatment of such leases as conveyances of interests in land. In today's urban residential leases, however, land as such plays no comparable role. The typical city dweller who frequently leases an apartment several stories above the actual plot of land on which an apartment building rests, cannot realistically be viewed as acquiring an interest in land; rather, he has contracted for a place to live. * * *

First, the increasing complexity of modern apartment buildings not only renders them much more difficult and expensive to repair than the living quarters of earlier days, but also makes adequate inspection of the premises by a prospective tenant a virtual impossibility; complex heating, electrical and plumbing systems are hidden from view, and the landlord, who has had experience with the building, is certainly in a much better position to discover and to cure dilapidations in the premises.

Second, unlike the multi-skilled lessee of old, today's city dweller generally has a single, specialized skill unrelated to maintenance work. Furthermore, whereas an agrarian lessee frequently remained on a single plot of land for his entire life, today's urban tenant is more mobile than ever; a tenant's limited tenure in a specific apartment will frequently not justify efforts at extensive repairs. Finally, the expense of needed repairs will often be outside the reach of many tenants for "[l]ow and middle income tenants, even if they were interested in making repairs, would be unable to obtain any financing for major repairs since they have no long-term interest in the property." * * * For one thing, the severe shortage of low and moderate cost housing has left tenants with little bargaining power through which they might gain express warranties of habitability from landlords, and thus the mechanism of the "free market" no longer serves as a viable means for fairly allocating the duty to repair leased premises between landlord and tenant. For another, the scarcity of adequate housing has limited further the adequacy of the tenant's right to inspect the premises; even when defects are apparent the low income tenant frequently has no realistic alternative but to accept such housing with the expectation that the landlord will make the necessary repairs. Finally, the shortage of available low cost housing has rendered inadequate the few remedies that common law courts previously have developed to ameliorate the harsh consequences of the traditional "no duty to repair" rule.

*   *   *

We have concluded that a warranty of habitability is implied by law in residential leases in this state and that the breach of such a warranty may be raised as a defense in an unlawful detainer action. Under the implied warranty which we recognize, a residential landlord covenants that premises he leases for living quarters will be maintained in a habitable state for the duration of the lease.

*   *   *

In most cases substantial compliance with those applicable building and housing code standards which materially affect health and safety will

suffice to meet the landlord's obligations under the common law implied
warranty of habitability we now recognize.

[Judgment vacated and remanded for trial.]

6. Landlord's Duty to Provide Security

HOLLEY v. MT. ZION TERRACE APARTMENTS, INC.

382 So. 2d 98 (Fla. App., 1980)

SCHWARTZ, Judge.   On May 31, 1976, the plaintiff-appellant's decedent,
Shirley Bryant, was raped and murdered while a tenant in the defendant-
appellee's apartment complex. The crime was committed by an intruder,
thought to have been a co-tenant, who apparently gained access into Ms.
Bryant's second story apartment through a window which fronted onto a
common outside walkway. The basis of the plaintiff's wrongful death action
against the landlord was its allegedly negligent failure to provide reasonable
security measures in the building's common areas. The trial judge entered
summary judgment for the defendant and the plaintiff has taken this appeal. We reverse.

The Mt. Zion Terrace Apartments consists of twelve separate two-story
buildings with over 130 apartments in all. It is located in the heavily popu-
lated Opa-Locka-Carol City area of Dade County. For a long period prior to
the tragedy involved in this case, the complex had been plagued by the high
incidence of serious crime which is unfortunately all too characteristic of our
urban society. In the calendar year immediately before the murder, it had
been the scene of no less than twenty "class one" crimes, those involving
violence, which were reported to the police. Of these, there were six cases
of violent assaults and seven in which apartments in the project were burgla-
rized. The record shows that the landlord had itself recognized the dangerous nature of its premises in at least two ways. First, it would accept no cash
at its office in the complex and took only checks or money orders in rental
payments. Second, and far more importantly, Mt. Zion had in the past taken
significant steps, which had been abandoned by the time that Ms. Bryant
was killed, to safeguard the security of its apartments. Between 1972 and
1974 (Ms. Bryant moved in during 1973), it hired uniformed armed guards
to patrol and protect the complex. During these years, the landlord had
charged each tenant an additional five dollars a month for this service.
Although the Federal Housing Administration put a stop to the practice,
there is an unresolved indication in the record that the charge was thereafter added to and included in the rent. Notwithstanding the guard service was
terminated. In 1974, Mt. Zion spent $4,924 for security; in 1975, $1,113; in
1976, the year of the murder, nothing.

On these facts, we hold that the defendant failed to carry its required
burden to demonstrate conclusively that it was not liable for Ms. Bryant's
death. * * * Without repeating the extensive legal analyses they contain, we
approve and follow those cases in other jurisdictions which have recognized
such potential liability in similar circumstances. [California, District of Co-

lumbia, Georgia, Hawaii, Illinois, Michigan, New Jersey, New York, and Wisconsin.] Furthermore, two particular features of this case make the plaintiff's position even more convincing than in most, if not all, of the prior precedents:

1.   Mt. Zion's prior practice of providing armed guards constitutes an admissible indication of the defendant's own "knowledge of the risk and the precautions necessary to meet it." W. Prosser, Law of Torts, § 33 at 168 (4th ed. 1971); and

2.   The showing that part of Ms. Bryant's rent may have been expressly for security creates a genuine issue concerning the landlord's contractual responsibility to provide that protection.

For these reasons, the judgment under review is reversed and the cause remanded for further consistent proceedings.

PROBLEMS

1.   Larry Lease made an oral agreement with Tommy Tate under which Tommy would take over possession of Larry's beach house for five years at a monthly rental of $300. After Tommy had moved in and lived there for six months, Tony Trapp offered Larry $400 a month rent for the house; Larry gave Tommy a 30-day notice to quit. Tommy says that Larry cannot break their valid lease. Who wins?

2.   Lucy Lesser rented a furnished apartment to Tim Teller for the period of one year under a written lease. There was no covenant in the lease concerning liability for the furniture during the period of the tenancy. Tim liked to give wild parties, and the furniture suffered during his occupancy. When Tim moved out at the end of the lease, Lucy sued him for the loss in value of the furniture during Tim's tenancy. Is Tim liable?

3.   Theus Temple leased one of the 20 apartments in the Hamilton House for two years. After he had lived there for six months, the building caught fire and burned to the ground. Theus stopped making rent payments, and the landlord sued him for the rents due under the balance of the lease. Is Theus liable for these payments?

4.   Ted Tinsley rented a suite of rooms in a luxury apartment building, redecorated them, stocked the place with antiques, and advertised that he was opening an interior decorating business. City inspectors contacted Ted and advised him that the building was in an area zoned for residential purposes only and the business could not be conducted on the premises. Ted advises the landlord that he considers the lease broken, since he had rented the suite for business purposes. Is Ted correct? Would it make any difference if the suite had been zoned for commercial purposes at the time Ted made the lease and had been rezoned as residential only after he had taken possession?

5.   Thelma Thorne leased an apartment for one year beginning on April 1 at a rental of $300 per month. When the lease expired the following April, Thelma did not move but paid the landlord another $300 for the next month, which was accepted. In June, the landlord gave Thelma a 30-day notice to vacate. Thelma refuses to move, saying that she has a binding lease until the next April 1. Does Thelma have to give up the apartment before the following March 31?

6.   Les Lockett leased an apartment to Tessie Todd. There was no provision in the lease giving Les the right to enter and make inspections. Tessie suspected that Les was entering the premises and making inspections during her absence, so Tessie had the locks changed. When Les discovered this fact, he sought to evict Tessie on the grounds that he is entitled to make reasonable inspections but that she has prevented it by locking him out. Does Les have the right he claims?

7.   Leroy Little, a carpenter and handyman, built his own home. Later, he leased the house to Tyrone Tripp, who moved in with his family. One afternoon, Tyrone's small daughter got up on a chair to remove a toy from a marble mantel above the brick fireplace in the living room. The mantel was not attached in any way to the wall or fireplace and fell away to the floor, falling on the child and causing her serious injuries. Tyrone claims that Leroy is liable, but Leroy says that he is not responsible for the condition of the leased premises. Who is correct?

8.   Travis Thatcher had a lease for two years of a house from Liza Lott. When the lease still had four months to run, Liza entered the house with a passkey and noticed that some of Travis' furnishings had been removed. Liza then changed the locks on the house. A week later, Travis returned, broke one of the locks and removed the remainder of his belongings. He then wrote to Liza and said that he no longer would be responsible for the lease. Liza then sued Travis for the unpaid rent for the balance of the term of the lease. What result?

9.   Lilly Lodge covenanted to keep her tenant's premises in good repair. Terry Taylor, the tenant, noticed that the hot water faucet handle in the bathroom shower was loose and asked Lilly to have it fixed, Lilly did nothing about the condition; a few weeks later, while a guest of Terry's was taking a shower, the handle and faucet broke and the guest was scalded. The guest sued both Lilly and Terry for damages for his injuries. Who is liable?

10.   Tillie Tyson leased a house from Louise Lowe on a month-to-month tenancy. Louise orally agreed to make reasonable repairs within a reasonable time. Tillie notified Louise by mail, demanding repair of leaky pipes, kitchen ceiling, and back porch, stating that rent would be withheld if the repairs were not made within 30 days. Two weeks later, Tillie obtained an inspection by the city building and safety officer, who cited Louise for eight violations of the city housing and maintenance code. Louise, at the end of the month, served Tillie with a proper 30-day notice to quit. Tillie withheld the rent for the ensuing month and deposited it with the court. At the end of the 30 days, Louise brought an unlawful detainer action to evict Tillie. What result?

Part V

THE LAW OF SALES

Chapter 26

NATURE OF SALES

A. IN GENERAL

A sale consists of the passing of title from the seller to the buyer for a price (U.C.C., Section 2–106(1)) (e.g., housewife buys a bottle of milk at the store). Although the basic principles of the law of contracts apply to the law of sales, the Uniform Commercial Code contains many variations, a number of which were covered in Part Two, The Law of Contracts. Others are covered in Part Five, which contains the most important laws relating to sales.

B. CONTRACT TO SELL

There is a distinction between a sale and a contract to sell. In a sale, title can pass at the time the contract is made, whereas in a contract to sell, title passes at a future time (e.g., contract to sell crops to be grown in the future). The importance of title is discussed in Chapter 27.

There can be no sale of goods not in existence (e.g., fish to be caught in the ocean or goods to be manufactured). Such an attempted sale only operates as a contract to sell the goods (U.C.C. Section 2–105(2)). Of course, a seller who cannot perform the contract to sell will be liable for breach of contract unless he or she has a valid and legal defense.

C. FUNGIBLE GOODS

"Fungible" with respect to goods or securities means goods or securities of which any unit is, by nature or usage of trade, the equivalent of any other like unit." (U.C.C., Section 1–201(17)). For example, oil, corn, flour, and wheat are considered fungible goods by nature. Goods such as bales of cotton, sacks of sugar, and cases of canned goods, can be considered as fungible by usage of trade.

In the case of fungible goods where the seller purports to sell a portion of the mass to the buyer, the buyer becomes an owner in common with the seller in the proportion the amount sold bears to the amount in the mass at the time of the sale. For example, the seller has 1,000 bushels of wheat in a bin. The buyer and the seller enter into a contract whereby the buyer purchases 500 of the bushels in the bin. When the contract is entered into, the seller and the buyer own the wheat in common even though the wheat has not been divided (U.C.C. Section 2–105(4)). The buyer cannot own title to a specific 500 bushels of wheat until that amount of wheat has been separated from the mass. Precisely how and when title passes to the buyer is discussed in Chapter 27.

D. SALES BETWEEN MERCHANTS OR WHEN MERCHANT IS A PARTY

A merchant is a person who deals in goods that are the subject of the contract or who holds himself or herself out as having special knowledge or skill regarding such goods or employs an agent who holds himself or herself out as having special knowledge or skill (U.C.C., Section 2–104(1)).

The U.C.C. contains 15 sections that apply to sales between merchants or when a merchant is a party (the sections do not apply to nonmerchants). The rules demand a higher standard of conduct on the part of merchants, because merchants set the standards for business practices and they have special knowledge in the field of trade and commerce. Some of these sections were discussed in earlier chapters (e.g., Statute of Frauds, 2–201(2), Firm Offers, 2–205). Others are discussed in later chapters under appropriate headings. The numbers of the sections are as follows: 2–201(2) (Statute of Frauds), 2–205 (Firm Offers), 2–207(2) (Additional Terms), 2–209(2) (Modification), 2–231(3) (Warranty of Title), 2–314(1) (Implied Warranty), 2–326(3) (Sale on Approval), 2–327(1)(c) (Special Incidents of Sale), 2–402(2) (Rights of Sellers' Creditors), 2–403(2) (Entrusting of Possession), 2–509(3) (Risk of Loss), 2–603(1)(2) (Buyer's Duties), 2–605(1)(b) (Waiver), 2–606(1)(2) (Acceptance), 2–609(2) (Assurance).

E. BULK SALES

A bulk sale is a transfer in bulk (not in the ordinary course of the transferor's business) of a substantial part of the materials, supplies, merchandise, or other inventory, including equipment, of the enterprise (U.C.C., Section 6–102).

To protect the creditors of the merchant from the possibility that the merchant may sell all of the inventory and disappear with the money, the U.C.C., Article 6, sets up two requirements. First, a bulk transfer is ineffective against a creditor unless the buyer requires the seller to furnish a list of existing creditors, signed and sworn to by the seller (Section 6–104). Second, the buyer must send a notice containing the pertinent information to all the creditors listed at least 10 days before either taking possession of the goods or paying for them, whichever is done first (Section 6–105).

More than a third of the states have adopted an additional requirement in their bulk sales statutes that states that the buyer must hold off payment to the seller for 30 days after the sale. During this period, omitted creditors are likely to find out about the sale and can put in their claims against the money still held by the buyer. For those states that have not adopted this additional requirement, it is advisable to place this clause in the contract of sale.

A sale that does not comply with Article 6 is still valid between the buyer and the seller, however, since this legislation is only for the protection of the creditors of the seller.

The following case illustrates a typical bulk sale dispute.

FACTS Johnson entered into a two-year employment contract with Mid States Screw and Bolt Company in 1974. In 1975, Johnson was terminated for reasons other than cause and brought suit under the employment contract to recover his compensation. After the suit was filed, Vincent Brass and Aluminum Company contracted to buy the assets of Mid States. As part of the sale, Mid States agreed to remain liable to Johnson. In addition, it did not include Johnson in the list of creditors it furnished to Vincent Brass (U.C.C. Section 6–104). Therefore, Johnson did not receive formal notice of the transfer of Mid States' assets. The trial court awarded Johnson his compensation against Mid States. Johnson subsequently filed a garnishment action against Vincent Brass.

DECISION The court concluded that Johnson can collect from Vincent Brass. The Uniform Commercial Code requires that the transferor, Vincent, provide formal notice to all creditors and "To all other persons who are known to the transferee to hold or assert claims against the transferor" (U.C.C. Section 6–107(3)). Although Johnson was not included in the list of creditors, Vincent Brass had actual knowledge (U.C.C. Section 1–201(25)) that Johnson had asserted a claim against Mid States. Therefore, Vincent Brass was required to provide Johnson formal notice. That was not done.

Johnson v. Vincent Brass & Aluminum Co. (244 Ga. 412, 260 S.E. 2d 325 [1979])

F. AUCTION SALES

Auction sales are covered by Section 2–328 of the U.C.C. In a sale by auction, if goods are put up in separate lots, each lot is the subject of a separate sale. Title passes when the auctioneer so announces by the fall of the hammer or in other customary manner.

An auction with reserve is the normal procedure, and in such a sale the auctioneer may withdraw the goods at any time until announcing completion of the sale. If the sale is without reserve, the auctioneer cannot withdraw the article or lot after calling for bids unless no bid is made within a reasonable time. An auction is with reserve unless the goods are in explicit terms put up without reserve.

G. CONDITIONAL SALE OR SECURITY AGREEMENT

A conditional sale is a transfer of title on a condition, usually the payment of money (e.g., the seller sells a television set to the buyer transferring the possession at the time of the contract but withholding the transfer of the title until the buyer makes complete payment). The contract provides the seller with the right to peaceably retake possession of the property if the buyer defaults. If the property is destroyed before full payment, the seller loses his or her security and the buyer loses the property but must still pay the balance due on the contract. To cover this loss, the typical contract provides that the buyer take out an insurance policy with a loss payable clause to the seller.

Under the Code, a conditional sales contract is known as a "security agreement" rather than as a conditional sale. A security agreement is an agreement that creates or provides for a security interest. (see Chapter 31 "Secured Transactions").

H. CONTRACT FOR LABOR OR SERVICES

The U.C.C. does not govern contracts to provide services or contracts to sell real estate. Rather, the Code speaks of "transactions in goods." Nonetheless, some courts have applied U.C.C. principles to service transactions where the transaction is mixed (i.e., contains elements of both a sale of goods and services). The test applied is whether the major or predominant transaction was a sale or merely a service. If a sale is found to predominate, the courts are more likely to apply the U.C.C. In a recent case, the plaintiffs purchased movie film for family use from the defendants (dealer and manufacturer). The Supreme Court of Washington found the U.C.C. to apply, in particular Section 2–302, to what the court concluded was a nonsales transaction.

> **FACTS** Plaintiffs took 32 reels of previously developed movie film to the camera department of a drugstore to be spliced together into four reels. Upon delivery, plaintiffs said to the manager: "Don't lose these. They are my life." The manager gave plaintiffs a receipt containing the language: "We assume no responsibility beyond retail cost of film unless otherwise agreed to in writing." He sent the film to the manufacturer for service. The film was lost by the manufacturer. Plaintiffs sued for the loss of their films, which could not be replaced or reproduced.

> **DECISION** The court awarded plaintiffs $7,500. It held that the disclaimer was unconscionable under the U.C.C. Section 2–302 and therefore not enforceable. Article 2 of the U.C.C., it concluded, goes considerably beyond the basic sale of goods and includes such transactions as bailments and leases (U.C.C. Section 2–102).

Mieske v. Bartell Drug Co. (92 Wn. 2d 40, 593 P.2d 1308 [1979])

The Code provides that serving food or drink to be consumed either on or off the premises is a sale (§ 2–314(1)).

The Code also states that when goods are to be specially manufactured it is a sale and not a service (§ 2–105(1)).

I. BAILMENTS

A bailment is a transfer of the possession of personal property without a transfer of title (e.g., when a watch is taken to the jeweler for repairs, it is only a bailment). Transfer of title is necessary in a sale, although transfer of possession is not.

J. OPTION TO BUY

In an option to buy, there is no transfer of title. It is a privilege existing in one person for which he or she has paid money and which gives him or her the right to buy certain property from another person, if he or she chooses, at any time within an agreed period and at a fixed price, or to sell such property to such other person at an agreed price and time.

K. GIFT

A gift is a gratuitous transfer of the title to property with no consideration (bargaining). A promise to make a gift is unenforceable for lack of consideration. There must be delivery of the property in a gift, whereas delivery is not necessary in a sale.

To determine the effectiveness of a gift, two tests must be met. The giver (donor) must intend to make a gift of the property and intent may be established in writing, orally, or by conduct. Delivery is the second requirement of a gift. Delivery can be not just the manual transfer of the property from the donor to the donee. Delivery to a third person with instructions to give the property to the donee is sufficient. Where the property cannot be delivered manually because it is bulky or located at a distance, delivery of a symbolic item or document, called a constructive delivery, will satisfy the requirement.

In the following case, the court was confronted with the question of whether an engagement ring, given in contemplation of marriage, could be recovered by the estate of the donor from the donee where the marriage did not occur because of the death of the donor.

> **FACTS** Richard Rothchild gave Carol Cohen an engagement ring. Shortly before the wedding date, Richard was killed in an auto accident. Richard's estate sought to recover the ring.

DECISION   Courts are split on the issue of whether the donor's estate can recover an engagement ring under such circumstances. One view treats the exchange as a gift subject to the condition that if the marriage does not occur the ring shall be returned. This court treated the exchange as a gift. It reasoned that Richard gave the ring as a symbol of his love and that he obviously intended that Carol have the ring.

Cohen v. Bayside Federal Savings and Loan Association (62 Misc. 2d 738, 309 N.Y.S. 2d 980 [1970])

ILLUSTRATIVE CASES

1. Contract to Sell

LOW v. PEW

108 Mass. 347 (1871)

The owner of a fishing schooner purported to make a present sale to Low of all the halibut to be caught during the next trip of the vessel to the Grand Banks. Low paid the full price of the fish at the time the contract was made. The schooner made a successful voyage but the owner became bankrupt before the vessel returned. Low now seeks to obtain possession of the fish, contending that title passed to him when the contract was made. The defendant, who represents the bankrupt, contends that no title could pass to property not owned by the seller at the time the contract was made, and that the transaction at most was a mere contract to sell.

MORTON, J. * * * The question in the case therefore is whether a sale of halibut afterwards to be caught is valid, so as to pass to the purchaser the property in them when caught. It is an elementary principle of the law of sales, that a man cannot grant personal property in which he has no interest or title. To be able to sell property, he must have a vested right in it at the time of the sale. * * *

*   *   *

In the case at bar, the sellers, at the time of the sale, had no interest in the thing sold. There was a possibility that they might catch halibut; but it was a mere possibility and expectancy, coupled with no interest. We are of opinion that they had no actual or potential possession of, or interest in, the fish; and that the sale to the plaintiff was void. * * *

[Judgment for defendant.]

2. Sales by and Between Merchants

CBS, INC. v. AUBURN PLASTICS, INC.

67 A.D.2d 811, 413 N.Y.S.2d 50 (1979)

In September, 1973 defendant submitted price quotations to plaintiff for the manufacture of eight cavity molds to be used in making parts for plaintiff's toys. * * *

The face of each price quotation was headed by the word "PROPOSAL" and specified, * * *, in part, that: "In consideration of the engineering services necessary in the designing of molds and tools, the customer hereby agrees to pay Auburn Plastics, Inc., an additional charge of thirty per cent above the quoted price of sale molds and tools when and if the customer demands delivery thereof."

Thereafter, in December, 1973 and January, 1974 plaintiff sent detailed purchase orders to defendant for the eight molds. The orders recited on their face that * * * plaintiff reserved the right to remove the molds from the defendant at any time without a withdrawal charge. The reverse side of the purchase orders similarly recited that the molds will be subject to removal without additional cost to the buyer, and also that no modification of the conditions of the contract shall be binding upon the buyer unless made in writing and signed by the buyer's representative.

In response to the purchase orders, defendant sent acknowledgements which described the molds, the price and the terms of payment and delivery essentially as contained in the purchase orders. However, the acknowledgements also stated that "[t]his sale subject to the terms and conditions of our quotation pertinent to this sale."

Thereafter plaintiff paid for the molds and ordered toy parts from the defendant which were fabricated from the molds. In May, 1978, however, as a result of defendant's announcement of a price increase, plaintiff requested delivery of the molds. Defendant refused to do so on the ground that it was entitled to a 30% engineering charge. Plaintiff obtained an order directing the sheriff to seize the molds. * * *

*   *   *

In our view, plaintiff's purchase orders constituted offers to buy the molds, and defendant's acknowledgements of those orders represented its acceptance of the offers. * * *

Whether the condition in defendant's acknowledgements calling for an additional 30% charge became a part of the contracts requires the application of subdivision 2 of section 2–207. The parties are clearly merchants * * *, and, therefore, since the purchase orders expressly limited acceptance to their terms * * *, and also because notification of objection to a withdrawal charge was implicitly given by plaintiff * * *, the provision for such a charge did not become a part of the contracts.

Order unanimously affirmed, with costs.

3. There Is No Bulk Sale When No Inventory

BROOKS v. LAMBERT

10 D. & C.2d 237 (Pa., 1957)

DIGGINS, J. This is an action * * * wherein plaintiffs are judgment creditors against Louis Lambert and have two judgments against John S. McCleary Republican Club as well.

The record also discloses that on or about August 10, 1956, Louis Lambert entered into a written agreement with Isadore Gus Weinberg, transferring, for a consideration of $1,500, personal property, equipment, and fixtures, excluding the club liquor license, of the Delaware County Athletic Association, and these are the same goods which are the subject matter of this action. * * *

The bill of complaint seeks to set aside the * * * alleged sale by Lambert to Weinberg on the ground that neither complied with the bulk sales provisions of the Uniform Commercial Code. * * *

> (1) A 'bulk transfer' is any transfer in bulk and not in the ordinary course of the transferor's business of a major part of the materials, supplies, merchandise or other inventory. * * *

> (2) A transfer of a substantial part of the equipment of such an enterprise is a bulk transfer if it is made in connection with a bulk transfer of inventory, but not otherwise.

The question of whether or not the Uniform Commercial Code applies to a business which has a liquor license has been the subject of interpretation by lower courts during the operation of the old Bulk Sales Act * * *, of which, for all practical purposes, the pertinent sections of the Uniform Commercial Code are reenacted. These cases hold that even though the liquor inventory is not the subject of any normal sale, the other inventory is, that is to say, a restaurant business with a liquor license or a combination bar and taproom, or a combination restaurant and taproom, is within the contemplation of the act as to all save presumably the liquor itself which under the liquor control board's regulations, can only be sold to another licensee under its supervision and approval. * * * However, the Uniform Commercial Code * * * provides that a transfer of a substantial part of the equipment of such an enterprise is a bulk transfer if it is made in connection with the bulk transfer of inventory, but not otherwise. Since by its very terms, unchallenged here, this sale included only personal property, equipment and fixtures, without reference to stock in trade, which would seem normal under the circumstances, because the little stock in trade that such a business enterprise as here involved would have consisted of goods unsaleable in bulk. * * *

It therefore follows that the sale covered by the agreement dated August 10, 1956, between Louis Lambert and Isadore Gus Weinberg was not prohibited by the Uniform Commercial Code. * * *

[Judgment for defendant.]

4. Sale by Auction

HAWAII JEWELERS ASSOCIATION v. FINE ARTS GALLERY, INC.

51 Hawaii 502, 463 P.2d 914 (1970)

ABE, Justice.   The defendant, Fine Arts Gallery, Inc., commenced business on July 5, 1968, at 2270 Kalakaua Avenue, in Waikiki, Honolulu, Hawaii, advertising its business as "auction." It also gave notice of "auction" to the public by bulkmail. At the premises there were several signs reading "auction."

The plaintiff, Hawaii Jewelers Association, an unincorporated trade association, brought this action against the defendant corporation and Stanton M. Bier, as principal stockholder and "auctioneer," pursuant to HRS § 445–32 to enjoin the operation by the defendants of a public auction without having first obtained a license as required by HRS § 445–7; without designating a public auction room as required by HRS § 445–29; and without obtaining a bond as required by HRS § 445–31.

The defendants contended in the trial court that the following statement or notice "OUR GOLDEN RULE 30 day money back guarantee on every sale" appearing in newspaper advertisements and on the inside back cover of the catalogue gave a buyer a right to return any article for any or no reason within 30 days and to a refund of the purchase price. Therefore, they argue that though the sale was conducted by competitive bidding, they were not conducting an auction.

The trial court on July 15, 1968, * * * issued a preliminary injunction.

Subsequently, after a hearing on October 25, 1968, the preliminary injunction was made permanent and the final order was entered on November 6, 1968. Defendants appealed.

*   *   *

The defendants' contention is that the "thirty day money back guarantee" postpones the transfer to purchasers of title to articles and therefore the operation was not an auction within the provisions of the Uniform Commercial Code, HRS § 490:2–328. The pertinent portion of the provision reads as follows:

Sale by auction. (1) In a sale by auction if goods are put up in lots each lot is the subject of a separate sale.

(2) A sale by auction is complete when the auctioneer so announces by the fall of the hammer or in other customary manner. * * *

The section defines sale by auction, but we believe that it does not mean that one cannot enter into a sales contract or an agreement of sale by way of an auction; or that where all other incidents of an "auction" are present, the transaction is not an auction if title to the chattel is not transferred upon the fall of the hammer.

There are cases holding that upon the acceptance of a bid by a fall of the hammer at an auction, one has contractual rights which may be enforced, but title to a chattel auctioned is not transferred to a successful bidder. The relationship between a vendor and a vendee, upon the acceptance of the vendee's bid at an auction, is the same as between a promissor and a promissee of an executory contract of sale conventionally entered into. * * *

However, for the determination of this action it is not necessary for this court to decide that point because here we hold that upon the fall of the hammer, title to a chattel auctioned was transferred to a successful bidder. We believe that defendants and successful bidders intended that title would pass upon the fall of the hammer and that purchasers could do as they pleased with the goods purchased—give or sell them to third parties. The "thirty day money back guarantee" was either an option given a successful bidder to return the goods and get a refund of money paid within 30 days or a continuing offer of defendants to repurchase the goods for a period of 30 days from the date of sale. It was similar to a satisfaction or money back guarantee given purchasers under a "sale or return" contract which gives the buyer an option or right to return the goods. * * *

As we have stated the "thirty days money back guarantee" did not prevent or postpone the transfer of the title to chattels upon the fall of the hammer and we hold that defendants were conducting a public auction within the meaning of HRS §§ 445–21 to 38, but without meeting the requirements of HRS §§ 445–7, 445–29, and 445–31. Therefore, the trial court properly issued a permanent injunction under the provisions of HRS § 445–32 to enjoin from conducting an auction. * * *

PROBLEMS

1. P was a patient in the XYZ hospital. During the course of his treatment he was given a blood transfusion. The transfusion was listed as a separate item on his hospital bill. P contracted serum hepatitis from the blood used in the transfusion, resulting in his death. P's heirs bring suit against the hospital on the theory that the transfusion was a sale of blood which carried with it an implied warranty that the blood was fit for use. XYZ does not argue the law of implied warranty but claims that the transfusion was merely a service and not a sale. Decision?

2. Buyer and seller entered into a contract whereby the seller is to sell all of the wheat to be grown on his land to the buyer. After the contract is entered into but before the wheat is harvested, the price of wheat rises dramatically. Both buyer and seller claim the crop. Discuss.

3. C, a customer at a local hamburger stand, discovers a half-eaten fly in his hamburger. C gets sick. He seeks your advice as to whether or not he must prove that the owner of the stand was negligent.

4. S agreed to sell and deliver five carloads of lumber to B at a certain railroad siding designated as track location XYZ. S sued B for the purchase price contending that it delivered all five carloads to B at the siding agreed upon. B admitted receiving four carloads but not the fifth carload. It later transpired that the fifth carload was unloaded by mistake by third persons after S had notified B of delivery on a normal business day. Is S entitled to recover the price agreed upon?

5. B contracted to buy a motorcycle from S's motorcycle shop. The seller was to deliver the motorcycle within ten days. B paid the full purchase price, registered and insured the vehicle before the delivery date. The motorcycle was then stolen by looters from S's shop during a power blowout. B exercised no dominion or control over the motorcycle. Who bears the loss of the vehicle?

6. P a book publisher, sold its entire book inventory to B. At that time P owed D and others sums greatly in excess of the sale price. No notice of the sale was sent to P's other creditors. The entire proceeds of the sale were credited to D. These creditors seek your advice as to their respective rights against B and D.

7. Moreland contracted to install overhead doors in a factory for Hoyt. Moreland agreed to "furnish all labor materials, tools and equipment to satisfactorily complete the installation of all overhead doors." Five years later the work had not been done. Hoyt sued Moreland for breach of contract. Hoyt argued that the contract was for the sale of goods, and that the lawsuit was time-barred by the four-year U.C.C. statute of limitations. Moreland claimed that the contract was for services, and thus within the 6-year limitations period provided in such cases. Decision?

8. Murphy, owner of an automobile accessory and appliance business, sold his business to Evans before paying business debts owed to Johnson. Evans mixed the Murphy inventory with his own so that the two could not be identified. Johnson sued Evans personally for payment of the entire debt, alleging that Evans violated the bulk sales law. Assuming a U.C.C. Article 6 violation by Evans, is Evans personally liable to Johnson?

9. Gross gave $4,000 to his son Martin. Martin thereupon opened two custodial accounts under the Uniform Gifts to Minors Act (UGMA) for his minor children, naming himself as custodian. Later the accounts were closed and the balance paid to Gross. Jean, mother of the children, sued Martin to recover the value of the custodial accounts withdrawn, claiming that both deposits were irrevocable gifts. Martin argued that no gifts were intended, but that the accounts were opened as tax shelters. Decision?

10. Buyer purchases a refrigerator-freezer combination from Seller on an installment plan, whereby Seller is to retain legal-security title until Buyer completes all payments. Shortly after the purchase the appliance is destroyed by fire in Buyer's home. Buyer refuses to pay the balance, arguing that since Seller retained legal title, Seller must bear the loss. Decision?

Chapter 27

TRANSFER OF TITLE
AND RISK OF LOSS

1. When does title transfer to the buyer so that the creditors of the seller can no longer seize the goods?

2. At what point does the buyer have an insurable interest in the goods?

3. When goods are destroyed through no fault of the buyer or seller, who must suffer the loss?

The parties can and should provide the answers to these questions by inserting appropriate clauses in the contract (U.C.C., Sections 1–102(4), 2–303, 2–401(1), 2–509(4)). In the absence of an explicit agreement, the U.C.C. attempts to provide the answers.

Under the U.C.C., title has limited importance in determining the rights, duties, and remedies of the seller and the buyer. Under the U.C.C. title and risk of loss are treated separately. Risk of loss may exist independently of ownership (e.g., buyer may have title to identified goods in a deliverable state in seller's possession, but risk of loss is on seller until buyer takes physical possession of the goods [Section 2–401(3)(b)]).

Title is still important in determining (1) whether the seller can recover the goods or recover the purchase price of the goods, (2) which party is liable for taxes, and (3) which creditors can seize the goods.

The Supreme Court of New Hampshire has noted the difference in treatment of title under common law contract rules and the U.C.C. in the following case.

> **FACTS** Shabny shipped goods to Hargo, but Hargo did not want to purchase the goods at that time. Hargo agreed to store the goods on its premises until it needed the goods. Hargo subsequently went bankrupt. At issue was who owned the goods. The lower court applied U.C.C. Section 2–401(1) and held that title had passed from seller to buyer upon delivery.
>
> **DECISION** The Supreme Court reversed. The common law viewed title as the main factor in solving sales problems. The U.C.C. deliberately deemphasizes that view (U.C.C. Section 2–101). The parties' agreement concerning the delivered goods created no contract for sale. The parties showed no intent to pass title, and therefore title remained with Shabny.

Meinhard-Commercial Corp. v. Hargo Woolen Mills (112 N.H. 500, 300 A.2d 321 [1972])

The U.C.C. states specific rules that apply to various transactions regarding the rights, duties, and remedies of the buyer and the seller.

A. IDENTIFICATION OR DESIGNATION

1. IN GENERAL

Identification means the designation of particular existing goods as the goods to which the contract refers. Goods can be identified in many ways (e.g., by being described in the contract, by sending the goods to the buyer, by being marked, or by being set aside). In other words, identification means that the parties can say that these are the goods involved in the sale (see U.C.C. 2–501).

The Official Comment to Section 2–501 states, "In view of the limited function of identification there is no requirement in this section that the goods be in a deliverable state or that all of the seller's duties with respect to the processing of the goods be completed in order that identification occur. For example, despite identification the risk of loss remains on the seller under the risk of loss provisions until completion of his duties as to the goods and all of his remedies remain dependent upon his not defaulting under the contract."

Identification alone does not necessarily pass title, but title cannot pass to the buyer until the goods have been identified. Identification and passage of title can occur at the same time, but often identification precedes the passage of title and gives the seller and the buyer certain rights that are independent of title.

2. RIGHTS OF BUYER

Identification invests the buyer with a special property and an insurable interest in the goods (Sections 2–401(1), 2–501(1)).

The special property interest includes the right of the buyer to reclaim goods from an insolvent seller (Section 2–502), the right of the buyer to inspect the goods (Section 2–513(1), the right of possession (Section 2–716), and the right to sue third parties for injuries to the goods (Section 2–722). These rights are discussed in Chapter 29.

The insurable interest created in the buyer on identification of the goods is the interest a person must have in property to be able to insure it. Without an insurable interest, the insurance policy would be invalid as a wagering contract. The buyer can insure goods to the extent of his or her interest even though the goods are still in the seller's possession (Section 2–501(1)). For example, the buyer may carry insurance as protection from damage to the business by interruption due to nondelivery of necessary materials. This could be a loss not collectible from the seller because the seller is excused by casualty or unforeseen circumstances under Section

2–613. The practical solution regarding insurance is to have a clause in the contract stating which party is to obtain the policy and who is to pay the premiums. Such a policy should name the buyer and the seller as insureds, with benefits payable according to their respective interests.

3.   RIGHTS OF SELLER

If the buyer repudiates or breaches the contract after identification is made, the seller can shift to the buyer the risk of loss that occurs within a reasonable time and for which the seller is not insured (Section 2–510(3)).

Identification of goods that are subsequently destroyed through no fault of the seller before passage of risk of loss to the buyer relieves the seller of liability for breach of contract (Section 2–613). Identification entitles the seller to fix damages by reselling the goods at a public sale (Sections 2–706(4), 2–704(2)).

4.   WHEN IDENTIFICATION OCCURS

It is important to know when identification of existing goods as the goods to which the contract refers occurs, since title cannot pass to the buyer until the goods are identified to the contract, and because the buyer and the seller do not obtain the rights as stated in Sections 2 and 3 above until the goods are identified to the contract.

In the absence of specific agreement, identification of the goods to the contract occurs in the following ways:

1.   When the contract is made, if it is for the sale of goods already existing and identified (e.g., undivided shares in an identified fungible bulk—grain in an elevator or oil in a storage tank—can be sold, and the mere making of the contract would be sufficient to effect an identification, even though the seller has not yet performed his or her duties to segregate and deliver the amount stated in the contract [buyer and seller become owners in common] [Section 2–105(3)(4)]).

2.   If the contract is for the sale of future goods (existing goods not yet identified or not yet in existence), other than unborn young or future crops, identification occurs when the goods are shipped, marked, or otherwise designated by the seller as the goods to which the contract refers (Section 2–501(1)(b)).

3.   Unborn young or future crops are identified to a contract when the crops are planted or otherwise become growing crops or when the young are conceived (Section 2–501(1)(c)). If the contract is made after the young are conceived or the crops are planted, such goods are identified by the making of the contract (Section 2–501(1)(a)).

B. DELIVERY REQUIRING MOVEMENT OF GOODS

The underlying general policy is that the risk of loss falls upon the person who has control of the goods, since that person is the most likely to insure the goods. In the absence of an agreement to the contrary or a sale on approval, risk of loss depends on whether the contract requires or authorizes the seller to ship goods by carrier in the form of a shipment contract or a destination contract.

The general rule is that title passes to the buyer at the time and place at which the seller completes his or her performance with reference to the physical delivery of the goods (Section 2–401(2)).

Additional provisions apply when the seller is to ship the goods to the buyer. The transaction may then take place either as a shipment contract or as a destination contract.

1. SHIPMENT CONTRACTS

A shipment contract requires or authorizes the seller to send the goods to the buyer but does not require him or her to deliver them to a particular place. The shipment contract is the normal shipping arrangement. The seller's duties in a shipment contract are generally stated in Section 2–504 (discussed in Chapter 28). They can be varied by the use of shipment terms (e.g., F.O.B.); by an agreement by the parties; or by the open term provisions of the U.C.C. (e.g., delivery in single or multiple lots [Section 2–307], seller's choice of shipment arrangements [Section 2–311(2)], and time for delivery [Section 2–309(1)].

Title passes on completion of the seller's duty of physically putting the goods into the carrier's possession (Section 2–401(2)(a)). This duty sometimes includes actually loading the goods. The seller usually loads rail carloads, but any load smaller than a carload is usually loaded by the railroad.

Risk of loss to the buyer passes on delivery to the carrier (Section 2–509(1)(a)).

F.O.B. (free on board) place of shipment requires the seller to bear the expense and the risk of putting the goods into possession of the carrier, and title and risk pass when physical delivery to the carrier is completed (Section 2–319(1)(a)). F.O.B. carrier requires the seller to bear the expense and risk of loading the goods on board the carrier (Section 2–319(1)(c)) (i.e., title and risk pass after loading).

F.A.S. (free alongside) vessel requires the seller to deliver the goods alongside the vessel, and title and risk pass when that is completed (Sections 2–319(2)(a), 2–401(2)(a)).

C.I.F. (cost, insurance, freight) means that the price includes the cost of the goods, the insurance, and the freight to the named destination. Title and risk pass on shipment (i.e., when the seller completes the duty of physical delivery to the carrier [Sections 2–320(1), 2–401(2)(a)]).

The following case illustrates risk-of-loss factors in shipment contracts.

FACTS A California clothing manufacturer sued to recover the purchase price of merchandise sold to a Connecticut retail clothing store owner. All orders filled by the manufacturer were shipped "F.O.B. Los Angeles" and "Via Denver-Chicago," a common carrier. All orders contained the printed phrase, "Goods shipped at purchaser's risk." Ultimately, the final connecting carrier attempted to deliver the merchandise to the retailer's store. The carrier refused to place the merchandise inside the store premises, and the shipment was not delivered. The merchandise thereupon disappeared. Defendant argued that plaintiff's refusal to deliver inside the store excused payment for the merchandise, since risk of loss remained with the seller absent a proper delivery.

DECISION Judgment for plaintiff. The use of the phrase "F.O.B. Los Angeles" was the controlling factor as to risk of loss of the merchandise upon delivery to Denver-Chicago. Title to the goods and the right to possession passed to defendant at Los Angeles. In addition, the terms of the contract placed the risk of loss on the purchaser, the defendant.

Ninth Street East, Ltd. vs. Harrison (5 Conn. Cir. 597, 259 A.2d 772 [1968])

2. DESTINATION CONTRACT

A destination contract is one that requires the seller to deliver the goods at a named destination (e.g., contract provides that seller deliver goods to buyer's warehouse at a certain address). Title and risk of loss pass to the buyer when the goods are tendered at destination (Sections 2–401(2)(b), 2–509(1)(b)). It is the tender of delivery and not the delivery itself that causes title to pass. The seller must perform certain duties before title can pass at destination; such duties are stated in Section 2–503 (e.g., put and hold goods at the buyer's disposition at a reasonable hour and for a reasonable time, give buyer notice so he or she can take delivery, tender appropriate documents).

F.O.B. destination requires the seller to transport the goods to the destination and tender them there in the manner required under destination contracts (Section 2–319(1)(b)). Title and risk of loss under F.O.B. destination contracts pass on tender at destination (Sections 2–401(2)(b), 2–509(1)(b)).

Ex ship (from the carrying vessel) contracts require the buyer to receive the goods alongside the incoming vessel. Risk of loss does not pass to the buyer until the goods are off the ship at destination (Section 2–322(2)(b)). Ex ship contracts are presumably governed by the same rules as destination contracts, and title therefore transfers to the buyer on tender at destination (Sections 2–401(2)(b), 2–322(2)(a)). However, it can be argued that Section 2–401(2)(a) delays passage of title until the seller unloads the goods from the ship. In ex ship contracts, it is advisable for the parties to explicitly state when title passes.

No arrival, no sale, means the seller must ship conforming goods properly and must tender them to the buyer when they arrive. However, the seller is not liable for breach of contract if the goods do not arrive unless the seller has caused the nonarrival. Title and risk of loss do not pass until the seller properly tenders the goods (Sections 2–324, 2–401(2)(b), 2–509(1)(b)).

3. COLLECT ON DELIVERY CONTRACTS

In a C.O.D. contract, the seller retains control over possession of the goods by preventing the buyer from obtaining delivery until he or she pays for them.

The U.C.C. fails to define C.O.D. or state whether it creates a shipment contract or a destination contract. The courts will probably treat C.O.D. contracts as shipment contracts, which means that title and risk will pass on delivery to the carrier (see Section B, 1, Shipment Contracts). In C.O.D. contracts, the parties should use a shipping term (e.g., F.O.B. place of shipment or F.O.B. destination) or insert an explicit term in the contract regarding title and risk of loss to avoid the problem.

C. DELIVERY WITHOUT MOVING GOODS

1. WITH DOCUMENT OF TITLE

When the goods are in possession of a bailee (100,000 bushels of wheat with a warehouseperson) and the seller is to deliver a document of title (an instrument showing title to the wheat, such as a bill of lading or warehouse receipt), title and risk of loss pass to the buyer when taking possession of the document of title (Sections 1–201(14)(15), 2–401(3)(a), and 2–509(2)(a)(c)).

The following case illustrates the rule that risk of loss remains on a buyer accepting delivery of goods shipped with a document of title without surrendering the document to the carrier, the agent of the seller.

> **FACTS** Capitol agreed to sell beef to Consolidated. Capitol shipped the beef by train to Boston, at which point Consolidated's agent took the beef and delivered it by truck to Consolidated. The railroad never delivered the order bill of lading. The beef was stolen. Capitol has not been paid for the beef. It has the bill of lading.
>
> **DECISION** The court held that the sale was complete when the railroad delivered the goods to the buyer's agent. It concluded that the seller, Capitol, is entitled to recover the sale price from either the buyer or the railroad. The buyer is primarily liable.
>
> *Capitol Packing Co. v. Smith* (270 F. Supp. 36 [D.C.Mass., 1967])

(For further discussion of documents of title see Chapter 31.)

2. WITHOUT DOCUMENT OF TITLE

If goods already identified are to be delivered without a document of title and without being moved (e.g., buyer to load and haul away without seller's help) title passes as soon as the contract is made (Section 2–401(3)(b)). If the contract is for the sale of future goods without a document of title and without being moved, title passes when the goods are identified. The goods do not have to be in a deliverable state. Thus, title to a machine to be specially manufactured may pass as soon as it is in an identifiable form, even though it is not finished. Title to crops may pass as soon as they are planted (Section 2–501(1)(c)).

If the seller is to help load the goods, title does not pass until the seller completes the physical duties (Section 2–401(2)).

Risk of loss passes to the buyer on receipt of the goods if the seller is a merchant (usual case). If the seller is a nonmerchant, risk of loss passes on tender of delivery to the buyer (Section 2–509(3)).

If the goods are in possession of a bailee, risk of loss passes when the bailee acknowledges the buyer's right to possession of the goods (Section 2–509(2)(b)).

D. EFFECT OF BREACH OF CONTRACT

The underlying policy of the effect of breach of contract on risk of loss is that the risk falls, within certain qualifications, on the one who has breached the contract for sale.

1. BUYER'S BREACH

When the buyer repudiates or is otherwise in breach of contract, the seller may pass the risk of loss to the buyer (Section 2–510(3)). In the case of an anticipatory breach, title remains with the seller (Section 2–610). In the case of a wrongful refusal to accept the goods, title revests in the seller (Section 2–401(4)). In the case of a breach after acceptance or wrongful attempt to revoke acceptance, title remains with the buyer.

2. SELLER'S BREACH

If the seller breaches the contract before the buyer accepts or rejects the goods (seller ships nonconforming goods), risk of loss remains with the seller (Section 2–510(1)) (title probably passes to the buyer pursuant to Section 2–401, subject to revesting in the seller pursuant to Sections 2–601 and 2–608).

E. SALE ON APPROVAL

In a sale on approval, neither title nor risk of loss passes to the buyer until he or she indicates approval of the goods (Section 2–327(1)(a)). Obviously, this is the best method of making a purchase as far as the buyer is concerned. If the buyer decides not to accept the goods, he or she must seasonably notify the seller of his or her election to return them. The risk and expense of returning the goods is on the seller, but a merchant buyer must follow any reasonable instructions (Section 2–327(1)(b)(c)). "Seasonably" means an action taken at or within the time agreed or, if no time is agreed, at or within a reasonable time (Section 1–204(3)).

F. SALE OR RETURN

In a sale or return contract, the goods are delivered to the buyer with an option to return them. Title and risk pass to the buyer pursuant to rules stated in Sections B and C, Delivery Requiring Movement of Goods and Delivery Without Moving Goods. The return of the goods is at the buyer's risk and expense (Section 2–327). Title probably revests in the seller when the goods are delivered at destination (i.e., place from which they were sent [Section 2–401(2)(b)]).

Sale or return contracts are usually between a manufacturer and a dealer who will use the goods for resale.

G. CONSIGNMENT

In a consignment, goods are delivered to a dealer and the dealer is a sales agent who is empowered to sell the goods and return the proceeds, less commissions, to the principal. Title does not pass to the dealer. When the goods are sold, title passes from the principal to the buyer. (Section 2–401).

H. AUTOMOBILES

The U.C.C. does not specifically refer to automobiles, nor does it attempt to set out a specific line of interpretation where a public regulation is concerned. Thus, it does not expressly affect preexisting motor vehicle registration statutes.

The modern trend followed by most courts is that ownership does not pass until requirements of the motor vehicle statutes have been complied with. Thus, tort liability remains with the seller until the statute is complied with.

Some courts hold that title passes pursuant to the provisions of the U.C.C., particularly Section 2–401(2), upon physical delivery of the vehicle without completion of the statutory registration formalities. Most of these cases are from states that do not have statutes providing a mandatory and exclusive method of transferring title to motor vehicles.

I. SALE BY NONOWNER

1. IN GENERAL

It is a fundamental rule of law that a thief, finder, or bailee of goods cannot transfer title even to a bona fide purchaser for value. This principle is illustrated by the following case.

FACTS   Connelly acquired a refrigeration trailer at a judicial foreclosure sale to satisfy his mechanic's lien for repair and storage costs. He then sold the trailer to a good faith purchaser, Marvin, for value. Unknown to both seller and buyer, the trailer had been stolen from its rightful owner. The original owner claimed title to the trailer, and the buyer sued the seller to recover the purchase price.

DECISION   The seller purchased only title rights belonging to his predecessor, the thief. Thus, he obtained no title. Under U.C.C. Section 2–312, there is an implied warranty that the title conveyed is good unless otherwise stated. The court held that the seller breached that warranty of good title and found for the buyer.

Marvin v. Connelly (272 S.C. 425, 252 S.E.2d 562 [1979])

An exception as to a bailee is found in the U.C.C. Section 2–403(2)(3), which provides that an owner of goods who entrusts the possession of them to a merchant who deals in goods of that kind gives the merchant the power to transfer all rights of the owner to a buyer in the ordinary course of business. For example, B purchases a watch from a jeweler and leaves it with the jeweler to have his initials engraved on it, but the jeweler sells it to a buyer in the ordinary course of business. Some states (California U.C.C. Section 2403(3) have enacted legislation giving greater protection to the owner by providing that the entrustment must be for the purposes of sale, obtaining offers to purchase, locating of buyer, etc., for the owner's rights to be defeated by a sale to a bona fide purchaser for value. Thus, in the example above, the owner could reclaim the watch.

2.   RESALE BY FRAUDULENT BUYER

The general rule is that when the buyer of goods perpetrates a fraud on the seller and thereby gains possession of the goods, a sale of the goods by the fraudulent buyer to a bona fide purchaser for value passes title to the goods to the purchaser. The theory for passing a good title to the bona fide purchaser for value is that as between two innocent persons, namely the seller and the bona fide purchaser, the person who permitted the transaction to take place should suffer the loss (i.e., the innocent seller). The exception to the rule is in the case of fraud in the execution (e.g., the buyer obtains the seller's signature by trick so that the seller either does not know he is signing a legal document or believes he is signing a document different from the one he is actually signing).

The general rule has been expanded by Section 2–403(1) of the U.C.C., which provides that the bona fide purchaser prevails over the seller when the seller has been deceived as to the identity of the buyer, when delivery of the goods was in exchange for a check which is later dishonored, or when it was agreed that the transaction was to be a cash sale and the buyer did not pay cash.

TRANSFER OF TITLE AND RISK OF LOSS

TYPE OF DELIVERY OR SALE	WHEN TITLE PASSES	WHEN RISK PASSES
DELIVERY BY MOVEMENT OF GOODS		
1. *Shipment contract* (Usual type of sale) between merchants)	Delivery to carrier	Delivery to carrier
2. *Destination contract*	Tender at destination	Tender at destination though in possession of carrier
3. Other contracts requiring physical delivery by seller		
a. Merchant seller (Usual type of sale between merchant and nonmerchant)	Completion of seller's duties of delivery	Buyer's taking physical possession of goods
b. Nonmerchant seller	Same as (a)	Tender of delivery
DELIVERY WITHOUT MOVEMENT OF GOODS		
1. Goods in seller's possession		
a. Merchant seller (Usual type of sale) between merchant and nonmerchant)	Identification of goods or making sales contract (whichever occurs later)	Buyer's taking physical possession of goods
b. Nonmerchant seller	Same as above	Tender of delivery
2. Goods in bailee's possession		
a. Delivery by negotiable document of title	When buyer takes possession of document	When buyer takes possession of document
b. Delivery by non-negotiable document of title	Same as above	Honoring of document by bailee or buyer's inaction for reasonable time after receiving it
c. Delivery by procuring bailee's acknowledgment without a document of title	Identification of goods or making of contract (whichever occurs later)	Bailee's acknowledgment
d. Delivery by giving buyer written direction to bailee	Same as above	Honoring of document by bailee or buyer's inaction for reasonable time after receiving it
SALE ON APPROVAL	Signifies approval	Signifies approval
SALE OR RETURN	Title passes pursuant to rules above except sale on approval	Risk of loss passes pursuant to rules above except sale on approval

---

ILLUSTRATIVE CASES

1. Risk of Loss Passes to Buyer Upon Acceptance of the Goods

MEAT REQUIREMENTS COORDINATION, INC. v. GGO, INC.

673 F.2d 229 (8th Cir., 1982)

BRIGHT, Circuit Judge.   GGO, Inc., appeals from an adverse judgment in this action instituted by Meat Requirements Coordination, Inc. (MRC). MRC successfully sought to recover money from its sale of frozen beef trimmings to GGO. As buyer, GGO maintains that the terms of its purchase contract with MRC allocated the risk of loss to MRC, the seller. As a consequence, GGO argues that it was absolved from liability for payment once it revoked its acceptance of the meat. * * * We reject GGO's contentions and, accordingly, affirm.

MRC and GGO, both meat brokers, traded extensively with each other * * *.

* * * On September 13, 1977, GGO and MRC conducted telephone conversations concerning the purchase of 38,000 pounds of boneless beef trimmings. On about the same date, GGO sent MRC its purchase order, which contained its standard terms and conditions on the reverse side. MRC then sent GGO its confirmation and transferred title to the meat in storage to GGO. GGO did not inspect the meat, but the record indicates that the meat was inspected before it left storage, at GGO's direction, for delivery to an Armour & Company packing plant in Wisconsin. On September 23, 1977, Armour inspected 4,300 pounds of the 38,000 pound load to determine whether it met the fat content specifications of its contract to GGO. While Armour's inspection indicated that the meat was in excellent condition, it nevertheless rejected the uninspected portion of the load because the meat did not satisfy the requirements of Armour's contract with GGO.

The portion of the load Armour rejected remained at the Armour facility until September 29, when GGO shipped it to Illinois. From there it was shipped to Kelly Foods in Tennessee on October 3, 1977. Kelly rejected the load as "old," and on October 5, 1977, GGO informed MRC of the condition of the meat. GGO placed the load in storage, and on November 9, 1977, United States Department of Agriculture (USDA) officials examined it. The USDA impounded the meat, and on November 22, 1977, GGO formally revoked its acceptance of the meat * * *. * * *

MRC instituted this action after GGO refused to pay the contract price of the meat. * * *

*   *   *

GGO contends that the terms contained in its purchase order permitted it to shift the risk of loss to MRC by revoking its acceptance after the USDA inspection disclosed that the meat was spoiled. We do not believe that the terms of the purchase order can be interpreted to shift the risk of loss to MRC under these circumstances.

While parties are free to alter the effect of the Uniform Commercial Code by contract, * * * (UCC § 1–102(3)), none of the terms of GGO's purchase order purports to displace the requirements of the Uniform Commercial Code governing timely revocation of acceptance.

> (2) Revocation of acceptance must occur within a reasonable time after the buyer discovers or should have discovered the ground for it and before any substantial change in condition of the goods which is not caused by their own defects. It is not effective until the buyer notifies the seller of it. (UCC § 2–608(2)).

The reference in the purchase order permitting GGO "to obtain certificates * * * of inspection of the product from applicable governmental agencies *at any time* after the product leaves the possession of the Seller," [emphasis added] does not relieve GGO of its duties to conduct its own inspection within a reasonable time to discover defects in the product and to revoke acceptance before a substantial change in the condition of the goods occurs. (UCC § 2–608(2)).

Here, the magistrate found that the beef trimmings were in excellent condition when delivered to GGO. The magistrate further found that the spoilage occurred as a result of mishandling the meat after Armour inspected the meat for fat content and rejected the load. Under these circumstances, neither the terms of GGO's purchase order, nor the Uniform Commercial Code, permits GGO to shift the risk of loss to MRC. Comment to section 2–608 of the Uniform Commercial Code states: "[t]he buyer may not revoke his acceptance if the goods have materially deteriorated except by reason of their own defects."

In addition, the purchase order, which provides that "[u]pon notice by Purchaser [GGO] to Seller [MRC] of rejection of products or any part thereof, Seller shall then bear the risk of loss for the rejected product[,]" would not shift the risk of loss to MRC in this case. This provision governs the rejection of goods, not revocation of acceptance. * * * GGO has never contended that it did not accept the meat. Thus, any rights it may have against MRC must be based on its right to revoke acceptance, which we have already determined adversely to it.

Accordingly, we conclude that even if the terms of GGO's purchase order became part of its contract with MRC, those terms did not shift the risk of loss to MRC for deterioration of the meat that occurred after GGO accepted the goods and after GGO had a reasonable opportunity to inspect the meat.

*   *   *

2. Transfer of Title on Delivery to Carrier

MORAUER v. DEAK & CO., INC.

26 UCC Rep. 1142 (D.C. Super., 1979)

On March 12, 1975, Marauer contracted with Deak, a dealer in foreign currency, to purchase for investment purposes * * * a quantity of gold coins. He paid for his purchase with personal checks totaling $35,000. After his checks had cleared, he came to Deak's place of business to take delivery. Morauer had a discussion with Deak's assistant manager about the District of Columbia tax on the sale of gold. Both parties agreed that in order to avoid the tax, an admittedly legal endeavor, Deak would ship all of Morauer's gold coins to his residence in suburban Maryland. * * *

Deak packaged the coins in two packages and sent the coins per Morauer's authorization to Morauer's house by registered mail, return receipt requested. Deak did not insure the packages with the U.S. Postal Service, but rather, per its custom, relied on its own insurance * * * to cover any risk of loss. Only one package was received by Morauer; however, he did not open it and thus did not realize at the time that he had received only a portion of his gold coins. More than two years later, while making an inventory of his collection, Morauer discovered the problem and notified Deak. By that time the Post Office had destroyed its records of the shipment and Deak's insurance coverage for that particular shipment had expired. Morauer then brought a lawsuit asking the value at the time of purchase of the gold coins he had not received.

SMITH, Judge.   The court must determine whether the risk of loss of the gold coins in question passed from defendant Deak to Morauer upon Deak's delivery of the coins to the Post Office for shipment to Morauer. If so, then Deak is not liable to Morauer for the value of the lost shipment. If the risk of loss did not pass, however, then Deak is liable for the full value of the coins at time of purchase.

The case is governed by § 2–509(1) of the UCC, and the court must determine whether paragraph (a) or paragraph (b) of subsection (1) controls. If the contract was a so-called "shipment" contract, then the risk of loss passed to Morauer, the buyer, on Deak's delivery to the carrier, § 2–509(1)(a), provided, however, that Deak also satisfied the UCC's requirements for a valid "shipment" contract. § 2–504. If, on the other hand the contract called for delivery at a particular destination, then the risk of loss never passed to Morauer, because the goods were never delivered, and Morauer must prevail. § 2–509(1)(b).

The fact that the parties had agreed that Deak would ship the coins to Morauer's residence in Maryland is not dispositive of this controversy. A "ship to" term in a sales contract has no significance in determining whether the agreement is a "shipment" or a "destination" contract. Moreover, there is a preference in the UCC for "shipment" contracts. * * *

* * * The seller is not obligated to deliver at a named destination and bear the concurrent risk of loss until arrival, unless he has specifically

agreed so to deliver or the commercial understanding of the terms used by the parties contemplates such delivery.

Here we have an order and payment by Morauer in person to Deak with receipts * * *, indicating Morauer's home address and, * * *, including the further instruction, "c/o Mrs. Geraldine Morauer." * * * Deak also included the cost of postage as part of Morauer's total bill. Therefore, we hold that Deak was authorized by the contract to ship the gold coins to Morauer by carrier, and that the risk of loss passed from Deak to Morauer on delivery of the packages of coins to the Post Office.

            *   *   *

Judgment in favor of Deak.

3. Risk of Loss Does Not Necessarily Pass to Buyer at the Same Time That Title Passes

MARTIN v. MELLAND'S, INC.
283 N.W. 2d 76 (N.D., 1979)

ERICKSTAD, C. J.   The narrow issue on this appeal is who should bear the loss of a truck and an attached haystack mover that was destroyed by fire while in the possession of the plaintiff, Israel Martin (Martin), but after certificate of title had been delivered to the defendant, Melland's Inc. (Melland's). The destroyed haymoving unit was to be used as a trade-in for a new haymoving unit that Martin ultimately purchased from Melland's. * * *

Martin entered into a written agreement with Melland's, a farm implement dealer, to purchase a truck and attached haystack mover * * * Martin was given a trade-in allowance * * * on his old unit * * * The agreement provided that Martin "mail or bring title" to the old unit to Melland's "this week." Martin mailed the certificate of title to Melland's pursuant to the agreement, but he was allowed to retain the use and possession of the old unit "until they had the new one ready." * * *

Fire destroyed the truck and the haymoving unit in early August, 1974, while Martin was moving hay. The parties did not have any agreement regarding insurance or risk of loss on the unit and Martin's insurance on the trade-in unit had lapsed. Melland's refused Martin's demand for his new unit and Martin brought this suit. * * *

            *   *   *

Martin argues * * * that title * * * and risk of loss passed to Melland's and the property was then merely bailed back to Martin who held it as a bailee. * * *

One of the hallmarks of the pre-Code law of sales was its emphasis on the concept of title. The location of title was used to determine, among other things, risk of loss, insurable interest, place and time for measuring damages, and the applicable law in an interstate transaction. This single title or "lump" title concept proved unsatisfactory because * * * the concept of single title did not reflect modern commercial practices, *i.e.* although the single title concept worked well for "cash-on-the-barrelhead sales", the introduction of deferred payments, security agreements, financing from third parties, or delivery by carrier required a fluid concept of title with bits and pieces held by all parties to the transaction.

Thus the concept of title under the U.C.C. is of decreased importance. * * *

Section 2–401 U.C.C., * * * provides in relevant part:

> Each provision of this chapter with regard to the rights, obligations and remedies of the seller, the buyer, purchasers or other third parties applies irrespective of title to the goods except where the provision refers to such title. * * *

*   *   *

Thus, the question in this case is not answered by a determination of the location of title, but by the risk of loss provisions in Section 2–509 U.C.C. Before addressing the risk of loss question in conjunction with Section 2–509 U.C.C., it is necessary to determine the posture of the parties with regard to the trade-in unit, *i.e.* who is the buyer and the seller and how are the responsibilities allocated. It is clear that a barter or trade-in is considered a sale and is therefore subject to the Uniform Commercial Code. It is also clear that the party who owns the trade-in is considered the seller. * * * [E]ach party is a seller of the goods which he is to transfer.

Martin argues that he had already sold the trade-in unit to Melland's and, although he retained possession, he did so in the capacity of a bailee * * * White and Summers in their hornbook on the Uniform Commercial Code argue that the seller who retains possession should not be considered bailee within Section 2–509.

*   *   *

The courts that have addressed this issue have agreed with White and Summers.

It is undisputed that the contract did not require or authorize shipment by carrier pursuant to Section [2–509(1)] therefore, the residue section, subsection 3, is applicable:

> In any case not within subsection 1 or 2, the risk of loss passes to the buyer on his receipt of the goods if the seller is a merchant; otherwise the risk passes to the buyer on tender of delivery.

Martin admits that he is not a merchant; therefore, it is necessary to determine if Martin tendered delivery of the trade-in unit to Melland's.* * *

It is clear that the trade-in unit was not tendered to Melland's in this case. The parties agreed that Martin would keep the old unit "until they had the new one ready."

*   *   *

We hold that Martin did not tender delivery of the trade-in truck and haystack mover to Melland's pursuant to Section 2–509 U.C.C., consequently, Martin must bear the loss.

We affirm the district court judgment.

4. Sale of Goods on Consignment

BUFKOR, INC. v. STAR JEWELRY CO., INC.

552 S.W. 2d 522 (Tex.Civ. App., 1977)

This was an action brought by Star Jewelry Company, Inc. (plaintiff) against Bufkor, Inc. (defendant), to recover possession of certain jewelry. On January 15, 1975, Bufkor obtained a judgment against James T. Dolleslanger individually and doing business as Tavernier Jewelers. On February 20, 1975, Star Jewelry Company, Inc., delivered certain items of jewelry to "Tavernier Jewelers 1704 S. Post Oak Houston, Texas." The invoice contained these words: "Goods must be purchased or returned within 5 days of receipt or they may be automatically invoiced to your account." On April 2, 1975, Bufkor levied execution upon the jewelry which Star had placed in Tavernier's possession. On March 12, 1976, Star Jewelry, Inc., filed suit against Bufkor, contending that it owned the jewelry because it had been delivered to Tavernier on consignment.

DIES, Chief Judge, Star Jewelry contends title did not pass to Tavernier because of a consignment arrangement. It is true that the term "consignment" was used in the dealings of the parties, but it is also true that Tavernier maintained a place of business for the purpose of selling jewelry merchandise, had authority to sell this merchandise, and Star did not seek return of the merchandise.

Transactions which once might have been regarded as consignments are now regarded as sales by the Uniform Commercial Code. The purpose of this change was to permit people to deal with a debtor upon the assumption that all property in his possession is unencumbered, unless the contrary is indicated by their own knowledge or by public records.

Chapter 9 of the Texas Uniform Commercial Code provides a method by which Star could have given notice of its lien, i.e., by filing a financing statement with the Secretary of State. Tavernier's president, Dolleslanger, gave Star the form and suggested that such a statement be filed. This was not done by Star. Tex. Bus. & Comm. Code Ann. § 2–326 (1968) provides:

> (a) Unless otherwise agreed, if delivered goods may be returned by the buyer even though they conform to the contract, the transaction is

> * * *

> (2) a "sale or return" if the goods are delivered primarily for resale.

> (b) Except as provided in Subsection (c), goods held on approval are not subject to the claims of the buyer's creditors until acceptance; goods held on sale or return are subject to such claims while in the buyer's possession.

> (c) Where goods are delivered to a person for sale and such person maintains a place of business at which he deals in goods of the kind involved, under a name other than the name of the person making delivery, then with respect to claims of creditors of the person conducting the business the goods are deemed to be on sale or return. The provisions of this

subsection are applicable even though an agreement purports to reserve title to the person making delivery until payment or resale or uses such words as "on consignment," or "on memorandum."

The intention of the parties is no longer determinative of the question of whether a transaction is a sale or a consignment. Consequently, we hold that these goods should be held to have been delivered for "sale or return," and thus, that neither the title nor the right to possession of these goods was retained by Star Jewelry Company. Star, having neither title nor right to possession, may not prevail in a trial of right of property.

Judgment for Star Jewelry reversed.

5. Invalid Sale of Goods By Bailee

PORTER v. WERTZ

68 A.D.2d 141, 416 N.Y.S. 2d 254 (1979)

This was an action brought by Samuel Porter (plaintiff) against Peter Wertz and Richard Feigen (defendants) to recover either possession of a painting or its equivalent value.

Porter, a collector of artworks, was the owner of a painting by Maurice Utrillo entitled *Château de Lion-sur-Mer*. In 1972–73 he had a number of transactions with a Harold Von Maker, who was using the name Peter Wertz—a real person who was an acquaintance of Von Maker. Von Maker bought one painting from Porter, paying $50,000 cash and giving him a series of 10 promissory notes for $10,000 each. Von Maker also convinced Porter to let him hang the Utrillo in Von Maker's home, while Von Maker decided whether or not to buy it.

When payment on the first of the $10,000 notes was not made when due, Porter investigated and found that he was not dealing with Peter Wertz, but rather with Von Maker, a man with a history of fraudulent dealings. A letter Porter obtained from Von Maker, which was signed using the name Peter Wertz, acknowledged receipt of the Utrillo. The letter also stated that the painting was on consignment with a client of Von Maker and that within 30 days Von Maker would either return the painting or pay Porter $30,000. However, at the time Von Maker had given this assurance to Porter, he had already disposed of the Utrillo by using the real Peter Wertz to sell it to Feigen's gallery for $20,000. Wertz delivered the painting to a Ms. Drew-Bear at the Feigen gallery after being introduced to Feigen by a man named Sloan, another art associate of Von Maker.

BIRNS, Judge.   The provisions of statutory estoppel are found in section 2–403 of the Uniform Commercial Code. Subsection 2 thereof provides that "any entrusting of possession of goods to a merchant who deals in goods of that kind gives him power to transfer all rights of the entruster to a buyer in the ordinary course of business." Uniform Commercial Code, section 1–201, subdivision 9, defines a "buyer in [the] ordinary course of business" as "a person who in good faith and without knowledge that the sale to him is in violation of the ownership rights or security interest of a third party in the goods buys in ordinary course from a person in the business of selling goods of that kind. . . ."

In order to determine whether the defense of statutory estoppel is available to Feigen, we must begin by ascertaining whether Feigen fits the definition of "[a] buyer in [the] ordinary course of business." (UCC, § 1–2–1 [9].) Feigen does not fit that definition, for two reasons. First, Wertz, from whom Feigen bought the Utrillo, was not an art dealer—he was not "a person in the business of selling goods of that kind." (UCC, § 1–201[9].) Second, Feigen was not "a person. . . in good faith" (UCC, § 1–201[9]) in the transaction with Wertz. Uniform Commercial Code, § 2–103, subdivision (1)(b), defines "good faith" in the case of a merchant as "honesty in fact and the observance of reasonable commercial standards of fair dealing in the trade." Although this definition by its terms embraces the "reasonable commercial standards of fair dealing in the trade," it should not—and cannot—be interpreted to permit, countenance or condone commercial standards of sharp trade practice or indifference as to the "provenance," i.e., history of ownership or the right to possess or sell an object d'art, such as is present in the case before us.

We note that neither Ms. Drew-Bear nor her employer Feigen made any investigation to determine the status of Wertz, i.e., whether he was an art merchant, "a person in the business of selling goods of that kind." (UCC, § 1–201[9].) Had Ms. Drew-Bear done so much as call either of the telephone numbers Wertz had left, she would have learned that Wertz was employed by a delicatessen and was not an art dealer. Nor did Ms. Drew-Bear or Feigen make any effort to verify whether Wertz was the owner or authorized by the owner to sell the painting he was offering. Ms. Drew-Bear had available to her the Petrides volume on Utrillo which included *Château de Lion-sur-Mer* in its catalogue of the master's works. Although this knowledge alone might not have been enough to put Feigen on notice that Wertz was not the true owner at the time of the transaction, it should have raised a doubt as to Wertz's right of possession, calling for further verification before the purchase by Feigen was consummated. Thus, it appears that statutory estoppel provided by Uniform Commercial Code, § 2–403(2), was not available as a defense to Feigen.

Judgment for Porter and case remanded to trial court to assess damages.

PROBLEMS

1. Bay Lines orally agreed to purchase from Lager, a dealer in trucks, a new model. Bay Lines also agreed, as part of the purchase price, to trade in its old truck. Nothing was said about delivery of either the old or new vehicle. When Lager's agents went to Bay Line's terminal to pick up the used truck, Bay had not yet changed some of the tires as they had promised. After the tire change, and while the old truck was being driven by Bay Line's employee to Lager's place of business, the truck was damaged in an accident. Who owned the truck and thus was liable for any loss?

2. B, a commercial grain grower, agreed to buy a silo and other grain storage equipment from S. The contract of sale carried a "one-year warranty of customer satisfaction". The silo and equipment were installed on B's property. Within the one-year warranty period, B rejected the silo and equipment and asked S to remove them from his property, alleging they failed to conform to his written specifications. Did B accept the goods sold, or could he still reject them?

3. Kuehn, a beer brewer, contracted with Griffith to provide food at Kuehn's concession stand at the Knoxville World's Fair based on samples presented to Kuehn. The contract called for delivery of food platters in installments over a one year period. Kuehn rejected the first installment and permitted Griffith to deliver a second installment to correct the variation in quality from the samples. This installment was also rejected as totally unacceptable, at which point Kuehn cancelled the entire contract. Griffith sued to recover out-of-pocket losses and loss of profits. Decision?

4. C, a general contractor, orally asked B to bid on a generator needed to complete work on an airport runway. Although a memorandum as to the terms was later signed by B, no agreement was reached on terms of payment. No payment was made when the order was placed. When C demanded performance, B refused, arguing that the memorandum did not mention a specific term of payment. Is B right?

5. S sold goods on credit to B. After delivery of some of the goods, S learned that B had a bad record for performance. S thereupon demanded payment on delivery as adequate assurance for future performance, even though the sales were to be on credit. Adequate assurance was not given, and S refused to make more deliveries required by its contract. B sued S for failure to perform. Decision?

6. Buyer, a business law student, and seller enter into a contract whereby buyer purchases a typewriter on thirty-days approval. Twenty days after the purchase, the typewriter is stolen from the buyer's locked room due to no fault of the buyer. Buyer immediately notifies seller of the theft and states that he does not approve of the typewriter and disclaims all liability for the purchase price. Seller brings suit. Decision?

7. Mickey Smith steals a watch and sells it for value to a bona fide purchaser who has no knowledge that it has been stolen. The owner of the watch demands the return of the watch from the bona fide purchaser. Decision?

8. Buyer purchases and pays for a large, expensive painting from seller who deals in goods of that kind. Since the buyer does not have the facilities to take the painting with him he leaves it with the seller with the understanding that he will pick it up the next day. Later that day, seller wrongfully sells the painting to a bona fide purchaser for value in the ordinary course of business. Seller absconds with the money from the two sales. Buyer sues the bona fide purchaser to recover the painting. Decision?

9. Buyer, representing himself to be Henry Ford II, offers to purchase a stereo from seller on credit. Seller, quite willing to sell to Ford on credit, sells the stereo to buyer. Buyer then sells the stereo to T, a bona fide purchaser for value, who has no knowledge of the buyer's fraud. When seller discovers the fraud, he attempts to repossess the stereo. Decision?

10. B in New York ordered 1,000 pitons for use in mountain climbing from S in Chicago. B sent a check for partial payment of the purchase price with the order. S put the pitons aside in his factory and put B's name on the box containing them. Eight days later S became insolvent. B tendered the balance of the purchase price and demanded the pitons. C, a creditor of S, wants to seize all of the goods, including the pitons, as they have gone up in value since B's order. Who should get the pitons, and why?

Chapter 28

PERFORMANCE OF THE CONTRACT

In every sale, the obligation of the seller is to transfer and deliver the goods and the obligation of the buyer is to accept and pay in accordance with the contract (Section 2–301). This is true whether the sale involves a bottle of milk at the neighborhood grocery store or a sale involving millions of bushels of wheat. Section 2–301 is adequate to govern performance in almost all sales transactions. Only mercantile sales (e.g., between manufacturer and wholesaler, distributor and retailer) are likely to involve difficult problems regarding delivery, acceptance, or payment.

A. SELLER'S PERFORMANCE

1. DUTY TO SHIP

In a shipment contract, the seller's obligation is performed when the seller starts the goods on their way by delivery to the carrier. The seller does not guarantee arrival of the shipment (Section 2–504). In a destination contract, however, the seller has the duty to get the goods to their destination (Section 2–503). In the absence of a special provision, the contract will be considered a shipment contract rather than a destination contract.

The seller's duties in a shipment contract are as follows:

1. The seller must make a reasonable contract with a reasonable carrier (Section 2–504(a)) (e.g., the seller cannot ship perishable goods from New York to Los Angeles by a slow freighter going around the Horn); the seller must also provide for the care of the goods in transit if needed (e.g., refrigeration of perishables and feeding and watering of livestock).

2. The seller must have the goods classified and described as to their true worth.

3. The seller must arrange for the goods to be properly loaded.

4. The seller must promptly procure and offer to the buyer any document the buyer needs to obtain possession of the goods when they arrive, such as a bill of lading (Section 2–504(b)).

5. The seller must promptly notify the buyer that the shipment has been

made (Section 2–504(c)). A standard manner of notification is sending an invoice or bill of lading to the buyer. Frequently the agreement expressly requires prompt notification (e.g., by wire or cable). Failure of the seller to promptly notify the buyer that shipment has been made or to make a reasonable contract for the transportation of the goods is grounds for rejection of the goods, but only if the failure results in material delay or if loss ensues.

2.   SHIPMENT WITH RESERVATION

Shipment with reserve is a shipment in which the seller reserves a security interest in the goods. For example, instead of sending the bill of lading directly to the buyer, which would enable the buyer to pick up the goods when they arrive without paying the seller for them, the seller makes the bill of lading payable to the order of his or her agent located in the buyer's city or to a financing agency or bank at destination. In such a situation, the buyer cannot obtain the goods until he or she pays for and receives the bill of lading. Thus, the seller retains control of the goods in transit without paying the freight or assuming the risk of loss (Section 2–505). Title and risk pass to the buyer under the normal rules in the absence of an agreement to the contrary.

3.   MERCANTILE SHIPPING TERMS

The U.C.C. defines mercantile shipping terms in Sections 2–319 through 2–324. Sometimes these definitions conflict with those in the American Foreign Trade Definitions (AFTD). In case of conflict, the parties should incorporate one or the other in the contract. The AFTD definitions can be obtained from the National Foreign Trade Commission, Inc., 10 Rockefeller Plaza, New York, NY 10020.

● F.O.B. shipment point. Seller must arrange the shipping; buyer pays the cost of freight, cost of loading unless carrier requires the seller to load, insurance, export and import charges, custom duties, fees, and document expenses needed to bring the goods into the country (Sections 2–311(2), 2–319(1)(a), 2–504).

● F.O.B. vessel, car, or other vehicle. Seller must arrange the shipping and pay for the loading; buyer pays for everything else (Sections 2–311(2), 2–319(1)(a)(c), 2–504).

● F.A.S. vessel. Buyer must arrange shipping and pay for everything (Sections 2–319(3), 2–319(2)(a)).

● C.I.F. Seller must arrange shipping and pay for everything except import duties (Sections 2–311(2), 2–504, 2–320(2)(b), 2–320(c)).

● C. & F. Seller must arrange shipping and pay for loading, freight, and cost of export licenses, fees, and similar exportation charges, while buyer must pay for insurance and cost of import charges, custom duties, fees, and document expenses to bring the goods into the country (Sections 2–311(2), 2–320(2)(b), 2–320(3)).

- F.O.B. destination. Seller must arrange shipping and pay freight and insurance (Sections 2–319(1)(b)).

- No arrival, no sale. Seller must arrange shipping and pay for everything (Section 2–324).

- Ex ship. Seller must arrange shipping and pay for everything (Section 2–322(2)(a)).

4. TENDER OF DELIVERY

A. IN GENERAL

In the absence of an agreement to the contrary, the seller must tender his or her performance under the contract if he or she wants to be paid.

There are two requirements to a valid tender of delivery (as used in this section, "tender" contemplates an offer coupled with a present ability to fulfill all the conditions resting on the tendering party and must be followed by actual performance if the other party shows himself or herself ready to proceed):

1. The seller must put and hold conforming goods at the buyer's disposition.

2. The seller must give the buyer any notification reasonably necessary to enable the buyer to take delivery (Sections 2–503(1), 2–503(3)).

The tender must be at a reasonable hour and must be kept available for a reasonable time so the buyer can take delivery (Section 2–503(1)(a)).

The tender must be at the place stated in the contract and, if no place is stated, at the seller's place of business (Sections 2–308, 2–503(1)).

If there are documents (e. g., bill of lading), the seller must tender all documents in correct form (Section 2–503(5)).

B. EFFECT OF VALID TENDER

The effect of tender of delivery is to entitle the seller to the buyer's acceptance of the goods at the place and time of tender (Section 2–507(1)).

Unless expressly stated in the contract to the contrary, tender of delivery and payment are concurrent conditions (i.e., neither party is required to perform until the other performs or tenders performance [Sections 2–507(1), 2–511(1)]). Neither party can claim the other party is in default until he or she first tenders performance. However, if one party refuses to perform, the other party does not have to tender performance, as this would be a useless act (Section 2–610).

Many contracts provide for credit (i.e., goods are to be delivered to buyer on 60 days credit). In credit cases, the seller must perform his or her part of the contract before he or she can demand performance from the buyer.

C. EFFECT OF IMPERFECT TENDER

If the goods fail to conform to the contract in any respect (e.g., greater quantity than ordered or goods of a different description mixed with the goods ordered), the buyer may (1) reject the whole, (2) accept the whole, or (3) accept any commercial unit or units and reject the rest (Section 2–601). Exact performance by the seller may be tempered, however, by usage of trade, prior course of dealing, or course of performance, any one of which may permit commercial leeway in performance.

Some courts apply a perfect tender rule and reject the doctrine of substantial performance in contracts for the sale of goods. In the following case, the Supreme Judicial Court of Maine stated that perfect tender required that the vendor's tender conform to all the specifications of the contract.

> **FACTS** Plaintiff agreed to sell molds meeting certain specifications to defendant Lyn-Flex. Plaintiff delivered the goods and sued to recover the contract price. At issue was whether the molds were delivered on time and whether they met the buyer's specifications. The trial judge instructed the jury that plaintiff's performance did not need to be one hundred percent complete to entitle plaintiff to enforce the contract. He said that Maine law required "substantial performance." The jury awarded plaintiff the contract price.

> **DECISION** The appellate Court reversed and ordered a new trial. The judge's instruction was incorrect, as Maine law applies a perfect tender rule. U.C.C. Section 2–601 gives the buyer the right to reject "if the goods or the tender of delivery fail in any respect to conform to the contract." The court held that the jury must decide whether plaintiff is liable under the standard.

> *Moulton Cavity & Mold, Inc. v. Lyn-Flex Industries, Inc.* (396 A. 2d 1024 [Me., 1979])

The above rule has two important exceptions:

(1) installment contracts (buyer can reject only if nonconformity substantially impairs the value of that installment and cannot be cured) (Section 2–612) and (2) limitations of remedy (parties can contract to limit the buyer's rights) (Sections 2–718 and 2–719).

If the tendered goods do not conform to the contract and the buyer refuses to accept them, the seller can "cure" his defective performance if time for performance has not yet expired by (1) giving reasonable notice to the buyer of his or her intention to cure and (2) making a conforming delivery within the contract time (Section 2–508). However, the seller does not have the right to cure unless he or she had reasonable grounds to believe that the tender would be accepted. Such reasonable grounds can be in prior course of dealing, course of performance, usage of trade, or in the particular circumstances surrounding the making of the contract. Also, if the buyer does not inform the seller as to the nonconforming defect, he or she may not assert such defect as an excuse for nonperformance if the defect is one that is curable (Section 2–605).

The following case illustrates that the seller must cure defects in his or her performance within a reasonable period of time. After a certain time, the buyer may reject the goods and recover damages.

FACTS   Plaintiff seller agreed to custom-make two molds to be used in manufacturing plastic containers. Plaintiff had difficulty meeting the buyer's specifications. Time and again the seller remade the molds, but they were never suitable. The trial court held that the seller had breached the contract and awarded the buyer damages.

DECISION   Time was of the essence in the performance of the contract. The court held that the time for performance had expired and therefore plaintiff no longer had the unfettered right to "cure" pursuant to U.C.C. Section 2–508(1). Although U.C.C. Section 2–508(2) gives a seller some opportunity to extend the time for performance and cure—within a reasonable time—the seller here in no way complied with that section.

Hayes v. Hettinga (228 N.W. 2d 181 [Iowa, 1975])

A merchant buyer who rightfully rejects delivered goods must follow the reasonable instructions of the seller regarding the disposition of the goods unless the seller has an agent or place of business at the market of rejection. If the goods are perishable or threaten to decline speedily in value, the buyer must make reasonable efforts to sell the goods for the seller even in the absence of instructions. The buyer is entitled to reimbursement for reasonable expenses (Sections 2–603, 2–604).

A nonmerchant buyer who rightfully rejects delivered goods is only under a duty to hold the goods with reasonable care at the seller's disposition for a time sufficient to permit the seller to remove them (Section 2–602(2)(b)(c)).

"Where without fault of either party the agreed berthing, loading or unloading facilities fail or an agreed type of carrier becomes unavailable or the agreed manner of delivery otherwise becomes commercially impracticable but a commercially reasonable substitute is available, such substitute performance must be tendered and accepted" (Section 2–614(1)). Neither party is excused from performance, because the express manner of delivery is impractical when there is a substitute available.

In case either party repudiates the contract before performance is due, the other party may either (1) wait for performance by the repudiating party, (2) resort to any remedy for for breach of contract, or (3) suspend his or her own performance (Section 2–610).

When reasonable grounds for insecurity arise with respect to the performance of either party (e. g., financial problems or strike against manufacturer-seller), the other may in writing demand adequate assurance of performance and until receiving such assurance may suspend his or her own performance (Section 2–609). Adequate assurance of due performance depends on the factual situation. Where the buyer can make use of a defective delivery, a mere promise by a seller of good repute that he or she will give the matter his or her immediate attention and that the defect will not be repeated is sufficient assurance. However, this would probably be insufficient if the statement were made by a known corner cutter, unless accompanied by a surety bond or, if so demanded by the buyer, by a speedy replacement of the defective product. If the defective product cannot be used by the buyer, a mere verbal assurance would not be adequate unless accompanied by replacement or other commercially reasonable cure.

D. DELIVERY IN POSSESSION OF SELLER

The U.C.C. does not specifically provide rules for tender of delivery when the goods are in the possession of the seller and are not to be moved by him or her. For passage of title, see Section 2–401(3).

If the seller tenders delivery by putting and holding conforming goods for the buyer and gives required notice, and if the buyer accepts the goods, probably the seller has completed delivery (Sections 2–503(1), 2–606).

E. DELIVERY WITHOUT MOVEMENT OF GOODS HELD BY BAILEE

When the goods are to be picked up by the buyer from a bailee, a valid tender of delivery can be made either by tendering to the buyer a negotiable document of title (bill of lading or warehouse receipt covering the goods) or by an acknowledgment from the bailee that the buyer is entitled to possession of the goods (Section 2–503(4)(a)).

F. DELIVERY UNDER INSTALLMENT CONTRACTS

"An 'installment contract' is one which requires or authorizes the delivery of goods in separate lots to be separately accepted" (Section 2–612(1)). The buyer may reject any installment that is nonconforming *if* the nonconformity substantially impairs the value of that installment *and* cannot be cured (Section 2–612(2)). If the nonconformity of an installment does not impair the value of the whole contract, the buyer must accept that installment if the seller gives adequate assurance of its cure. Impairment of the value of an installment can turn not only on the quality of the goods but also on such factors as quantity, time, and assortment.

In *Holiday Manufacturing Company v. B.A.S.F. Systems, Inc.,* the seller did not conform strictly to the terms of an installment contract. The court analyzed the buyer's behavior and concluded that the nonconforming deliveries did not substantially impair the value of the whole contract.

> **FACTS** Defendant agreed to purchase six million plastic cassettes in installments. From the start, plaintiff had trouble meeting defendant's specifications, and delays occurred. During the following year, plaintiff delivered only a fraction of the ordered cassettes. Seller corrected many quality problems. Buyer continued to work with the seller and even increased its order. Finally, buyer cancelled all orders, citing "continuous quality problems and delivery delays."

DECISION   Judgment for seller. The Court held that buyer's cancellation was improper under U.C.C. Section 2–612(3). Throughout the year, buyer did not protest or communicate any dissatisfaction. Rather, it encouraged seller to continue production and ever ordered more. Buyer saw in these cassettes a potentially profitable business venture and tolerated the delays. Seller was able to cure all the problems over time. The court concluded that the nonconformities with respect to the installments did not "substantially impair the value of the whole contract" (U.C.C. Section 2–612(3)). Therefore, buyer did not have any right to cancel.

Holiday Manufacturing Co. v. B.A.S.F. Systems, Inc. (380 F. Supp. 1096 [D.C.Neb., 1974])

B.   BUYER'S PERFORMANCE

1.   PAYMENT

The buyer must tender payment before he or she has the right to obtain the goods (Sections 2–507(1), 2–511(1)). Unless the seller has refused to deliver, tender of payment is a prerequisite to putting the seller in default. All sales are for cash unless the seller agrees to extend credit.

Tender of payment is sufficient when made by any means or in any manner current in the ordinary course of business, including check, unless the seller demands payment in legal tender and gives the buyer a reasonable amount of time to procure it (Section 2–511(2)).

Payment by check is conditional (i. e., it is defeated as between the parties by dishonor of the check on due presentment) (Section 2–511(3)). If the check is dishonored, the buyer has no right to retain the goods or dispose of them (Section 2–507(2)). A seller who has been paid by a dishonored check may sue for breach of contract or sue on the instrument itself (Sections 1–106(2), 3–802(1)(b)).

A good faith purchaser from a buyer who has paid for the goods with a bad check will prevail over the seller (Section 2–403(1)). However, the buyer's creditors do not prevail over the seller.

2.   PAYMENT UNDER INSTALLMENT CONTRACTS

If the buyer defaults on an installment payment and if the breach substantially impairs the value of the whole contract to the seller, there is a breach of contract (Sections 2–612(3), 2–703). What is substantial impairment is a difficult question of fact. However, it has been held that nonpayment of an installment can be a substantial impairment of the value of the contract either by creating financial difficulties for the seller, making it virtually impossible for the seller to assign the contract for financing, or giving the seller reasonable apprehension that the buyer would not make future payments.

If the buyer fails to pay for one or more installments, the seller can stop delivery of the goods not paid for. If the seller is uncertain about future performance, he or she can demand adequate assurances of performance from the buyer (e.g., demand that buyer post a surety bond or submit a good credit report from the bank [Section 2–609]).

If the buyer persists over the seller's objections in wrongfully rejecting installments or failing to pay for them, the buyer will then be held to have repudiated the contract permitting the seller to exercise his or her remedies (see Chapter 29). However, if the seller accepts the payments without notification of cancellation of the contract, or if the seller brings an action with respect to past installments or demands performance as to future installments, he or she reinstates the contract (Section 2–612(3)). The seller's acceptance of late payments may also be regarded as a waiver or modification of the contract (Sections 1–205(3), 2–208(3)).

3.　PAYMENT AND INSPECTION

If a sale involves a documentary transaction (bill of lading) and the contract terms call for payment upon presentation of the bill of lading or for C.O.D., the buyer must pay for the goods before inspecting the goods (Section 2–513(3)(b)).

If the sale is F.O.B. vessel, F.A.S. vessel, C.I.F., or C.F. terms, the buyer must pay before inspection of the goods (Section 2–310(c), Section 2–319(4), and Section 2–320(4)). In a sale using C.I.F. or C.F. terms, but the documents are not to be presented for payment until after arrival of the goods, Section 2–321(3) provides for preliminary inspection before payment when this is feasible.

In all other cases, the buyer may inspect the goods before making payment (Section 2–513(1)). The buyer is allowed a reasonable time to inspect the goods and may test or analyze them in the process of inspecting them. Although the buyer must pay for the inspection, if the goods do not conform to the contract, the buyer may recover from the seller necessary expenses of inspection (Section 2–513(2), 2–515(a)).

If the goods are nonconforming and the buyer knows this, the buyer does not have to pay for the goods before inspection (Section 2–512(1)). Section 2–512(1) does not provide any remedy for a seller against an alert buyer who refuses to pay for nonconforming goods. Furthermore, the seller's suit for damages would be ineffective, because the seller could not prove damages. The buyer can be aware that the goods are nonconforming by simple observation (this is not considered inspection), for example, damaged boxes that rattle, wrong quantity, or routine weighing before unloading that reveals an incorrect weight.

In cases where the buyer does not have the right of inspection before payment of the goods and the goods are nonconforming, the buyer must pay first and complain later of the defects.

C. EXCUSING PERFORMANCE

As stated in Chapter 16, hazards such as strikes, financial problems, unforeseen shutdown of sources of supply, governmental regulations, and delay due to fire generally do not excuse performance unless expressly provided for in the contract. However, it may have been within the contemplation of the parties at the time the contract was made that the goods to be manufactured and sold to the buyer were to be manufactured in a designated factory that is subsequently damaged or destroyed through an act such as an earthquake or fire. Under such circumstances, unless the seller has expressly guaranteed performance in spite of the happening of the "presupposed condition," the seller need not perform. (Section 2–615(a)).

ILLUSTRATIVE CASES

1. Seller's Duty to Ship

SIMPSON FEED CO. v. CONTINENTAL GRAIN CO.

199 F.2d 284 (8th Cir., 1952)

SANBORN, Circuit Judge.   The defendant in this action for damages for the alleged breach of a sales contract has appealed from the judgment in favor of the plaintiff. * * *

There is little dispute as to the facts which gave rise to this controversy. On October 30, 1950, the defendant had a carload of beans (about 2,000 bushels) for the plaintiff and called for shipping instructions which the plaintiff was obligated to furnish. These instruction were promptly given and the car was shipped. The defendant sent the plaintiff a draft for 90% of the purchase price, which was paid upon presentation. The balance of the purchase price, amounting to $441.87, has not been paid.

On the night of October 30, 1950, the defendant loaded another car of beans for the plaintiff, and on October 31, by telephone, asked the plaintiff's agent for shipping instructions. There is a dispute in the evidence as to this telephone conversation. The plaintiff's version is that the defendant's agent was informed that the plaintiff was seeking a permit for shipment to New Orleans, but had not yet received it; that the defendant's agent asked when the permit would be obtained and was told that it might be in thirty minutes or in a day or two; that he then said, "Let me know as soon as possible." The defendant's testimony was that the plaintiff's agent stated over the telephone that the plaintiff would furnish shipping instructions within thirty minutes, and that nothing was said about a New Orleans permit.

Shipping instructions were not received by the defendant from the plaintiff until November 2, or about 48 hours after they had been requested. When the plaintiff furnished the instructions, it was advised by the defendant that it considered the contract breached by virtue of the plaintiff's delay and that no more beans would be shipped under the contract. The plaintiff refused to accept this renunciation of the contract and insisted on performance.

It appears that there was a car shortage at the time that shipping instructions for the second carload were requested, and that the defendant was under pressure from the railroad to move the car and billed it out to another of its customers. It thereafter continued to refuse to ship any more soy beans to the plaintiff.

* * *

The District Court concluded that, under the evidence and the applicable law, the attempted renunciation of the contract because of the plaintiff's delay in giving shipping instructions was not justified; that the defendant was indebted to the plaintiff for the difference between the contract price of the beans and their market price on November 30; and that the plaintiff was indebted to the defendant for the balance due upon the carload of beans shipped on October 30, amounting to $441.87. Judgment was entered accordingly, and this appeal followed.

* * * It seems obvious to us, as it did to the District Court, that the plaintiff's delay in furnishing shipping instructions was of no serious or prejudicial consequence to the defendant, but was seized upon by it as an excuse for refusing to furnish the plaintiff with the beans at the contract price which was much lower than the market price which prevailed at the time the delay occurred. * * *

[Judgment affirmed.]

2. Effect of Commercial Impracticability on Seller's Duty to Deliver

MISSOURI PUBLIC SERVICE CO. v. PEABODY COAL CO.

583 S.W. 2d 721 (Mo. App., 1979)

This was an action brought by Missouri Public Service Company (plaintiff) against Peabody Coal Company (defendant) seeking specific performance of a contract to supply Public Service with coal for the generation of electricity.

In 1967 Peabody made an offer to supply the coal needs of one of Public Service's plants for 10 years at a base price of $5.40 per net ton, subject to certain price adjustments from time to time relating to the cost of labor, taxes, compliance with government regulations, and increases in transportation costs as reflected in railroad tariffs. Peabody's offer also included an inflation cost escalator based on the U.S. Department of Labor's Consumer Price Index. Public Service rejected the use of the Consumer Price Index but did agree to the use of an escalator based on the Industrial Commodities Index, also published by the Department of Labor. The parties signed an agreement on December 22, 1967.

Performance of the contract was profitable for Peabody for two year, but then production cost increases outpaced the price adjustment features of the contract. In 1974 Peabody requested a number of modifications in the price adjustment mechanisms. Public Service rejected this request but did offer a $1 a ton increase in the original cost per net ton. Following further discussions between the parties, on May 6, 1975, Peabody notified Public Service by letter that all coal shipments would cease in 60 days unless the modifications it sought were immediately agreed to by Public Service. Public Service treated the letter as an anticipatory repudiation and brought suit against Peabody for specific performance.

At the trial Peabody introduced evidence that its losses under the contract were $3.4 million. It also claimed that the Industrial Commodities Index, which prior to the execution of the contract had been an accurate measure of inflation, had ceased to be an effective measure because of the 1973 oil embargo, runaway inflation, and the enactment of new mine safety regulations.

SWOFFORD, Chief Judge.   Peabody's final allegation of error is that the trial court erred in refusing to relieve or excuse it from its obligations under the contract upon the basis of "commercial impracticability" under Section 2–615(UCC), which section reads, in part:

> Excuse by failure of presupposed conditions
>
> Except so far as a seller may have assumed a greater obligation and subject to the preceding section on substituted performance:
>
> (a) Delay in delivery or nondelivery in whole or in part by a seller who complies with paragraphs (b) and (c) is not a breach of his duty under a contract for sale *if performance as agreed has been made impracticable by the occurrence of a contingency the nonoccurrence of which was a basic assumption on which the contract was made* or by compliance in good faith with any applicable foreign or domestic governmental regulation or order whether or not it later proves to be invalid. [Emphasis supplied.]

The comments accompanying this section treat it as dealing with the doctrine of "commercial impracticability," and central to this concept is that the doctrine may be applicable upon the occurrence of a supervening, unforeseen event not within the reasonable contemplation of the parties at the time the contract was made. Such occurrence must go to the heart of the contract.

  * * * Comment No. 4, accompanying that section, * * * states:

> 4. *Increased cost alone does not excuse performance* unless the rise in cost is due to some unforeseen contingency which alters *the essential nature of the performance.* Neither is a rise or a collapse in the market in itself a justification, *for that is exactly the type of business risk which business contracts made at fixed prices are intended to cover.* But a severe shortage of raw materials or of supplies due to a contingency such as war, embargo, local crop failure, unforeseen shutdown of major sources of supply or the like, which either causes a marked increase in cost or altogether prevents the seller from securing supplies necessary to his performance, is within the contemplation of this section. [Emphasis added.]

*   *   *

The facts as shown by the record lead to the conclusion that at least some of the loss resulted from the fact that for some unexplained reason the Industrial Commodities Index lagged behind the Consumer Price Index, the measuring factor first proposed by Peabody, in reflecting inflationary costs increases. That such indexes were based upon different commercial and economic factors was presumably known by both parties since each was skilled and experienced in those areas and the divergence between the indexes could not be said to be unforeseeable. Be that as it may, Peabody agreed to the use of the Industrial Commodities Index factor.

The other claim made by Peabody, alleged to bring it within the doctrine of "commercial impracticability," is the Arab oil embargo. Such a possibility was common knowledge and had been thoroughly discussed and recognized for many years by our government, media economists and business, and the fact that the embargo was imposed during the term of the contract here involved was foreseeable. Peabody failed to demonstrate that this embargo affected its ability to secure oil or petroleum products necessary to its mining production albeit at inflated cost. In fact, as previously stated, this embargo can reasonable be said to have, at least indirectly, contributed to the marked appreciation to the value of Peabody's coal reserves by forcing the market value of that alternative source of energy upward in this country.

It is apparent that Peabody did make a bad bargain and an unprofitable one under its contract with Public Service, resulting in a loss, the cause and size of which is disputed. But this fact alone does not deal with either the "basic assumption" on which the contract was negotiated or alter the "essential nature of the performance" thereunder so as to constitute "commercial impracticability." The court below properly decreed specific performance.

Judgment for Public Service affirmed.

3. Payment and Delivery Are Concurrent

VIDAL v. TRANSCONTINENTAL & WESTERN AIR, INC.
120 F.2d 67 (3d Cir., 1941)

GOODRICH, Circuit Judge.   * * * This appeal by the plaintiffs is from the action of the trial court in dismissing their complaint. By the terms of the contract, which bears date of April 14, 1937, the defendant agreed to sell and the plaintiff agreed to buy four used airplanes of a specified type belonging to the seller. The price was stipulated and payment was to be made by certified check upon delivery of the airplanes to the buyer at the Municipal Airport, Kansas City, Missouri. The date for delivery was stated to be June 1, 1937. * * *

The trial court found as a fact that on June 1 the defendant was ready, able and willing to deliver one of the planes described in the contract to the plaintiffs at Municipal Airport in Kansas City, Missouri, and that after June 1 and on and prior to July 10 the defendant was ready, able and willing to deliver all of the four airplanes at the place specified. It was also found as a fact that the plaintiffs did not on June 1 or any other date either tender payment on any or all of the machines nor request delivery. * * *

What are the respective rights and duties of the parties in a contract of this kind? * * * [T]here was a simple contract promising delivery by the seller to the buyer of specified goods at a definite time and place and neither party demanded performance from the other or tendered his own. Has either a right against the other? Payment and delivery are concurrent conditions since both parties are bound to render performance at the same time. Restatement, Contracts, § 251. In such a case, as Williston points out, neither party can maintain an action against the other without first making an offer of performance himself. Otherwise, if each stayed at home ready and willing to perform each would have a right of action against the other. "* * * to maintain an action at law the plaintiff must not only be ready and willing but he must have manifested this before bringing his action, by some offer of performance to the defendant, * * * It is one of the consequences of concurrent conditions that a situation may arise where no right of action ever arises against either party * * * so long as both parties remain inactive, neither is liable * * *." This statement by the learned author not only has the force of his authority and that of many decisions from many states, but is also sound common sense. It is not an unfair requirement that a party complaining of another's conduct should be required to show that the other has fallen short in the performance of a legal obligation.

*   *   *

The conclusion is, therefore, that the defendant is not in default. Neither side having demanded performance by the other, neither side is in a position to complain or to assert any claim in an action of law against the other. This view of the case makes it unnecessary to examine the testimony which asserts that the buyers either abandoned or repudiated the contract prior to the time of the performance.

The judgment is affirmed.

4. Seller Has Right to Cure Nonconforming Delivery

WILSON v. SCAMPOLI

228 A.2d 848 (D.C.App., 1967)

MYERS, Associate Judge.   This is an appeal from an order of the trial court granting rescission of a sales contract for a color television set and directing the return of the purchase price plus interest and costs.

[Plaintiff] purchased the set in question on November 4, 1965, paying the total purchase price in cash. The transaction was evidenced by a sales ticket showing the price paid and guaranteeing ninety days' free service and replacement of any defective tube and parts for a period of one year. Two days after purchase the set was delivered and uncrated, the antennae adjusted and the set plugged into an electrical outlet to "cook out." When the set was turned on, however, it did not function properly, the picture having a reddish tinge. Appellant's delivery man advised the buyer's daughter, Mrs. Kolley, that it was not his duty to tune in or adjust the color but that a service representative would shortly call at her house for that purpose.

On November 8, 1965, a service representative arrived, and after spending an hour in an effort to eliminate the red cast from the picture advised Mrs. Kolley that he would have to remove the chassis from the cabinet and take it to the shop as he could not determine the cause of the difficulty from his examination at the house. * * * Mrs. Kolley refused to allow the chassis to be removed, asserting she did not want a "repaired" set but another "brand new" set. Later she demanded the return of the purchase price, although retaining the set. [Defendant] refused to refund the purchase price, but renewed his offer to adjust, repair, or, if the set could not be made to function properly, to replace it. * * * [Uniform Commercial Code, § 2–508]:

> (1) Where any tender or delivery by the seller is rejected because non-conforming and the time for performance has not yet expired, the seller may seasonably notify the buyer of his intention to cure and may then within the contract time make a conforming delivery.

> (2) Where the buyer rejects a non-conforming tender which the seller had reasonable grounds to believe would be acceptable with or without money allowance the seller may if he seasonably notifies the buyer have a further reasonable time to substitute a conforming tender.

A retail dealer would certainly expect and have reasonable grounds to believe that merchandise like color television sets, new and delivered as crated at the factory, would be acceptable as delivered and that, if defective in some way, he would have the right to substitute a conforming tender. The question then resolves itself to whether the dealer may conform his tender by adjustment of minor repair or whether he must conform by substituting brand new merchandise. * * * Here the adamant refusal of Mrs. Kolley, acting on behalf of appellee, to allow inspection essential to the determination of the cause of the excessive red tinge to the picture defeated any effort by the seller to provide timely repair or even replacement of the set if the difficulty could not be corrected. The cause of the defect might have been minor and easily adjusted or it may have been substantial and required replacement by another new set—but the seller was never given an adequate opportunity to make a determination.

We do not hold that appellant has no liability to appellee, but as he was denied access and a reasonable opportunity to repair, appellee has not shown a breach of warranty entitling him either to a brand new set or to rescission.

[Judgment for defendant.]

5. Buyer Has Reasonable Time to Inspect Goods

ZABRISKIE CHEVROLET, INC. v. SMITH

99 N.J.Super. 441, 240 A. 2d 195 (1968)

Smith bought a new 1966 Chevrolet from Zabriskie Chevrolet, making a cash deposit of $124 and thereafter tendering his check in full payment on February 9. The car was delivered to Mrs. Smith on February 10. The transmission seriously malfunctioned a short distance from the dealer's lot. On February 11, Smith called Zabriskie to tell him that he had sold him a lemon and that he was stopping payment on the check and cancelling the sale. Later Zabriskie replaced the transmission. Smith refused to accept the repaired car. Zabriskie sued for the purchase price.

DOAN, J.   Plaintiff urges that defendant accepted the vehicle and therefore under the Code (Section 2–607(1)) is bound to complete payment for it. Defendant asserts that he never accepted the vehicle and therefore under the code properly rejected it; further, that even if there had been acceptance he was justified under the code in revoking the same. Defendant supports this claim by urging that what was delivered to him was not what he bargained for, i.e., a new car with factory new parts, which would operate perfectly as represented and, therefore, the code remedies of rejection and revocation of acceptance were available to him. * * * [T]he primary inquiry is whether the defendant had "accepted" the automobile prior to the return thereof to the plaintiff.

Section 2–606 states in pertinent part:

(1) Acceptance of goods occurs when the buyer

    (a) after a reasonable opportunity to inspect the goods signifies to the seller that the goods are conforming or that he will take or retain them in spite of their non-conformity; or

    (b) fails to make an effective rejection (subsection (1) of 2–602), but such acceptance does not occur until the buyer has had a reasonable opportunity to inspect them, or

    (c) does any act inconsistent with the seller's ownership; but if such act is wrongful as against the seller it is an acceptance only if ratified by him.

It is clear that a buyer does not accept goods until he has had a "reasonable opportunity to inspect." Defendant sought to purchase a new car. He assumed what every new car buyer has a right to assume—and, indeed, has been led to assume by the high-powered advertising techniques of the auto industry—that his new car, with the exception of very minor adjustments, would be mechanically new and factory-furnished, operate perfectly, and be free of substantial defects. The vehicle delivered to defendant did not measure up to these representations. Plaintiff contends that defendant had "reasonable opportunity to inspect" by the privilege to take the car for a typical "spin around the block" before signing the purchase order. If by this contention plaintiff equates a spin around the block with "reasonable opportunity to inspect," the contention is illusory and unrealistic. To the layman, the complicated mechanisms of today's automobiles are a complete mystery. To have the automobile inspected by someone with sufficient expertise to disassemble the vehicle in order to discover latent defects before the contract is signed, is assuredly impossible and highly impractical.

Consequently, the first few miles of driving become even more significant to the excited new car buyer. This is the buyer's first reasonable opportunity to enjoy his new vehicle to see it it conforms to what it was represented to be and whether he is getting what he bargained for. How long the buyer may drive the new car under the guise of inspection of new goods is not an issue in the present case. It is clear that defendant discovered the nonconformity within seven tenths of a mile and minutes after leaving plaintiff's showroom. Certainly this was well within the ambit of "reasonable opportunity to inspect." That the vehicle was grievously defective when it left plaintiff's possession is a compelling conclusion, as is the conclusion that in a legal sense defendant never accepted the vehicle.

Even if defendant had accepted the automobile tendered, he has a right to revoke under U.C.C. Section 2–608

> (1) The buyer may revoke his acceptance of a lot or commercial unit whose non-conformity substantially impairs its value to him if he has accepted it. . . .

Accordingly, and pursuant to U.C.C. Section 2–711 judgment is rendered on the main case in favor of defendant. On the counterclaim judgment is rendered in favor of defendant and against plaintiff in the sum of $124, being the amount of the deposit, there being no further proof of damages.

PROBLEMS

1. Buyer in Michigan and seller in New York enter into a contract for the sale of 1,000 coats #J 23 on credit. Nothing is stated as to whether it is a shipment or destination contract. Seller properly packs the coats and puts them in possession of the carrier, at which time he makes a proper contract for their transportation. Seller obtains a bill of lading representing title to the goods and promptly mails it to the buyer via air mail. While the coats are in transit they are destroyed by fire. Seller demands payment for the coats citing Section 2–509(1)(a). Buyer refuses citing Section 2–504(c). Decision?

2. Carter was an experienced wheat grower. Carter contracted with Bishop, a grain dealer, to deliver 25,000 bushels of wheat, planted by Carter in April, to Zahn in July or August at an agreed price. June was particularly hot and dry. In July Carter notified Bishop that he was going to be short of wheat as a result of the weather conditions. In August, after harvesting his wheat, Carter was only able to deliver 5,000 of the 25,000 bushels promised. Bishop, having previously contracted to sell

Carter's total harvest in reliance on Carter's contract to a grain exporter, covered from other sources and then sued Carter. Carter defended on the ground that the unusually hot weather excused performance of his contract. Decision?

3. B placed an order with S, a valve manufacturer, for certain valves and fittings, all of which were to be made of steel. The order was made up of four different sizes of valves and one size of flange. Upon delivery, B discovered that the flanges were made of iron and rejected them, but paid for the balance of the order, which he retained. S sues to recover the contract price of the flanges. Decision?

4. Seller in New York enters into a contract for the sale of 1,000 bushels of wheat with a buyer in Florida. Seller takes out a negotiable bill of lading in his own name and ships the goods by reasonable contract to the buyer in Florida by independent carrier. Seller immediately notifies buyer of the shipment. The goods are destroyed while in transit. Buyer refuses to pay for the wheat on the grounds that the seller reserved title in his own name by the use of the bill of lading, and, therefore, the seller also retained the risk of loss. Decision?

5. Buyer in Kansas ordered a prefabricated house to be delivered "F.O.B., building site" from a seller in Minnesota. The seller brought the house to the building site and unloaded it. The state of Kansas taxed the buyer on the theory that the sale was made in Kansas. Buyer contends the sale took place in Minnesota. Decision?

6. Buyer and seller entered into a contract for the sale of sheep of specified ages. At the place of delivery in Oregon the buyer requested that he be permitted to inspect the sheep to ascertain the age of each. The seller would not permit a detailed inspection but would permit the buyer to "gate run" them and reject sick or crippled sheep. Buyer refuses to take the sheep without a detailed inspection. Decision?

7. Buyer and seller enter into a contract for the sale of 100 cases of Beefeater Gin. On the contracted delivery date at 4:30 p.m., the seller delivers by truck to the buyer's place of business 80 cases of Beefeater Gin and 20 cases of Gordon's Gin. The buyer tells the truck driver that he will not accept delivery because he ordered 100 cases of Beefeater Gin, and there are only 80 cases on the truck. The truck driver returns the shipment to the seller the next morning, explaining to his employer why the shipment was refused. Five days later, the seller attempts to cure his improper tender by delivering 100 cases of Beefeater Gin; however, the buyer refuses the shipment stating that he has purchased the goods from someone else. Decision?

8. B ordered equipment from S for installation in a new building which B was having built under the supervision of an architect. When the equipment was delivered, B refused to accept it, arguing that his architect had made a mistake and the equipment ordered could not be installed in the new building. S sued for breach of contract. Decision?

9. B ordered 40,000 feet of half-inch, new steel pipe from S. The order specified that "the pipe not to be plugged." The order was shipped C.O.D. upon arrival. B permitted the carrier to unload a small portion of pipe and discovered that the pipe was plugged. B refused to accept the pipe. S sued, contending that the designation of shipment C.O.D. required B to accept and pay for the pipe. Decision?

10. C Corporation, a contractor, was under contract to build a structure for the U. S. Navy. C purchased fuel separating equipment from F Corporation, a manufacturer of such equipment, and installed the equipment in the structure. When F sued for the purchase price of the units, C defended on the ground that the Navy had rejected the units as defective. Decision?

Chapter 29

REMEDIES UNDER THE U.C.C.

If the sales agreement does not specifically provide for remedies on breach of contract, the U.C.C. attempts to meet the problem in Part 7, Sections 2–701 through 2–724. Remedies provided by the U.C.C. are to be liberally administered to the end that the aggrieved party may be put in as good a position as if the other party had fully performed (Section 1–106(1)).

Some of the courses of action open to the buyer and the seller were treated in Chapter 28, e.g., Section 2–602 [(Buyer's rejection of nonconforming goods)], Section 2–609 [Right to adequate assurance by either party], and Section 2–508 [Seller's right to cure an improper tender or delivery].

A. REMEDIES OF THE SELLER

1. WITHHOLD DELIVERY OF THE GOODS

Section 2–703(a) permits the seller to withhold delivery of the goods when:

1. The buyer wrongfully rejects or revokes acceptance of the goods.

2. The buyer fails to make a payment due on or before delivery.

3. The buyer repudiates the contract in whole or in part.

4. The buyer fails to cooperate with the seller so as to enable the seller to perform (Section 2–311(3)(a)).

If the seller discovers the buyer is insolvent, the seller can withhold delivery until he or she is paid cash for the goods. A seller who has already delivered can demand cash (Section 2–702 (1)). Since the Code does not state what constitutes discovery, the seller must have good evidence before using this remedy or the seller will be in breach of contract if the buyer is solvent. Therefore, if the seller is not quite certain that the buyer is insolvent, it would be better for him or her to use the remedy of demanding assurances of performance under Section 2–609(1).

2. STOP DELIVERY WHEN GOODS IN POSSESSION OF CARRIER

The seller can stop delivery of goods when:

1. The buyer is insolvent (Section 2–702(1)).

2. The buyer repudiates or fails to make a payment due before delivery (Section 2–705(1).

3. The seller has any other right to withhold or reclaim the goods (e.g., when the buyer fails to cooperate or when the seller is waiting for justifiably demanded assurances [Section 2–705(1)]).

The right of the seller to stop delivery ends when:

1. The buyer or someone holding under the buyer such as a subpurchaser, actually receives the goods (Section 2–705(2)(a)).

2. A bailee of the goods, except the original carrier, acknowledges to the buyer that it holds the goods for the buyer, thereby obligating the bailee to deliver the goods to the buyer (Section 2–705(2)(b)) (an example of such a bailee would be a warehouseperson).

3. A reshipping carrier or a carrier acting as a warehouseperson acknowledges to the buyer that it holds the goods for the buyer (Section 2–705(2)(c)). A diversion of a shipment is not a reshipment when it is merely an incident to the original contract of transportation and an acknowledgment by the carrier as a warehouseperson requires a contract of a truly different character from the original shipment (i. e., a contract not in extension of transit but as a warehouseperson).

4. A negotiable document of title covering the goods is negotiated to the buyer (Section 2–705(2)(d)).

To stop delivery, the seller must notify the carrier or other bailee so that the bailee by reasonable diligence can prevent delivery (Section 2–705(3)). To stop delivery, the seller usually notifies the freight agent who handled the shipment. The agent will need information from the bill of lading, such as names of the shipper and consignee, the routing, the car number, the shipping point, and the destination point. If a negotiable bill of lading is outstanding, the carrier will probably demand a bond. The seller can probably avoid this, however, by simply diverting the goods to some other destination (Section 7–303). Although the seller is not required to notify the buyer that he or she is stopping delivery, it is usually good practice to give such a notice.

3. RECLAIM THE GOODS

A seller can reclaim goods sold on credit to the buyer if he or she discovers that the buyer was insolvent when receiving the goods. To reclaim the goods, the seller must demand return of the goods within 10 days after the buyer has received them (Section 2–702(2)).

The seller loses the right to reclaim if the buyer has resold the goods to third persons in the ordinary course of business or to other good faith purchasers (Section 2–702(3)).

4. IDENTIFY GOODS TO CONTRACT ON BUYER'S BREACH

The seller may identify goods to the contract (refer to Chapter 27) on the buyer's breach if conforming goods are in the seller's possession or control when learning of the breach.

The effect of identification to the contract is that the seller can resell the goods and hold the buyer for damages (Section 2–704). A seller who cannot resell the goods, can hold the buyer for the contract price (Section 2–709(1)(b)).

5. RESELL THE GOODS

The seller may resell the goods when the buyer wrongfully rejects them or revokes acceptance, fails to make a payment due on or before delivery, or repudiates the contract in whole or in part (Section 2–706).

The seller may recover from the buyer the difference between the resale price and the contract price together with any incidental damages (Section 2–706(1)).

In *Cohn v. Fisher,* the court awarded the seller the difference between the resale price and the contract price plus incidental damages pursuant to U.C.C. Section 2–706.

> **FACTS** Defendant agreed to buy seller's boat for $4,650. The parties agreed that payment would be made on Saturday, May 25. Prior to that date, buyer breached the contract. Seller resold the boat for $3,000.

> **DECISION** The court awarded seller $1,650, representing resale damages (U.C.C. Section 2–706) and incidental damages of $29.50 (U.C.C. Section 2–710). The resale was made in good faith and in a commercially reasonable manner with reasonable notification of the resale to the defaulting buyer.

> *Cohn v. Fisher* (118 N.J. Super. 286, 287 A. 2d 222 [1972])

The resale may be at public or private sale (Section 2–706(2)). If at private sale, the seller must give the buyer reasonable notice of intention to resell (Section 2–706(3)). If at public sale, the seller must give the buyer reasonable notice of the time and place of the resale unless the goods are perishable or threaten to decline speedily in value (Section 2–706(4)(b)).

The seller may purchase the goods at a public sale (Section 2–706(4)(d)). The seller is not accountable to the buyer for any profit made on a resale (Section 2–706(6)).

6. CANCEL THE CONTRACT

When the buyer wrongfully rejects the goods or revokes acceptance, fails to make a payment due, or repudiates the contract, the seller may cancel the contract (Section 2–703(f)). Cancellation permits the seller to end his or her obligations while retaining the right to damages for breach of contract.

7. RECOVER DAMAGES

The seller is entitled to recover damages after the buyer's wrongful rejection of the goods, revocation of acceptance, failure to make a payment due, or repudiation of the contract (Sections 2–703(d)(e), 2–706(1), 2–708).

The normal measure of damages is the difference between the contract price and the market price at the time and place for tender, plus any incidental damages sustained, less any expenses saved as a result of the buyer's breach (Section 2–708(1)).

If the seller resells the goods, the damages will be the difference between the contract and the resale price, plus any incidental damages, less any expense saved as a result of the buyer's breach (Section 2–706(1)).

If the measure of damages (difference between contract price and market price, or between contract price and resale price) is inadequate to put the seller in as good a position as performance would have done, the U.C.C. attempts to remedy the situation by providing the seller with an alternative measure of damages. Section 2–708(2) provides that the seller may recover his or her profit, including reasonable overhead, which he or she would have realized from full performance by the buyer, plus any incidental damages, less expenses saved as a result of the buyer's breach.

In *Detroit Power Screwdriver Company v. Ladney,* the Michigan Court of Appeals authorized recovery of profit where the goods are custom-built or made to nonstandard specifications.

> **FACTS**   Plaintiff seller and defendant buyer agreed to the sale of a very complex piece of equipment. Before seller completed the project, buyer repudiated the agreement. Seller sued for damages. The trial court dismissed, concluding that plaintiff had failed to prove damages with sufficient certainty to permit a recovery.
>
> **DECISION**   The Court of Appeals remanded. Under U.C.C. Section 2–708(1), a seller is entitled to recover the difference between the contract price and the market price. If the measure of damages is inadequate, seller may recover its lost profit under U.C.C. Section 2–708(2). The court held that if the goods are specialty items, there is no market and 2–708(1) damages are inadequate. The court remanded for the trial court to determine whether the machine is a specialty item. If it is not, the case should be dismissed. If it is, seller recovers lost profits.
>
> *Detroit Power Screwdriver Co. v. Ladney* (25 Mich. App. 478, 181 N.W.2d 828 [1970])

8. RECOVER PRICE OF THE GOODS

The seller can recover the price of the goods and incidental damages in three situations:

1. When the buyer has accepted the goods (Section 2–709(1)(a)).

2. When conforming goods are lost or damaged after risk of loss has passed to the buyer (Section 2–709(1)(a)).

3. When the goods have been identified to the contract and the seller is unable to resell them for a reasonable price (Section 2–709(1)(b)).

B. REMEDIES OF THE BUYER

1. COVER

When the seller fails to make delivery or repudiates the contract, or when the buyer rightfully rejects goods or justifiably revokes acceptance (and the seller does not cure his or her defective performance), the buyer has the right to cover (i.e., to purchase goods in substitution for those due under the contract [Sections 2–711(a), 2–712]).

The buyer is not required to cover, and failure to do so does not affect any of the other remedies under the U.C.C. (Section 2–712(3)).

The buyer's damages are the difference between the contract price and the cost of cover, plus incidental or consequential damages, less expenses saved (Section 2–712(2)).

The Supreme Court of South Dakota has ruled that the cover rule is available to a nonmerchant as well as a merchant buyer. Also, the buyer must cover in a reasonable manner, as in the following case.

> **FACTS** Before delivery was due, the seller notified the buyer that he would not deliver the equipment. The parties disagreed as to whether this was a breach or whether seller's refusal to deliver was justified. Buyer covered, paying $1,000 more than the original contract price. Trial court directed a verdict for seller.
>
> **DECISION** The court reversed and remanded, holding that the case presented issues of fact for the jury to decide. A buyer may recover as damages the difference between the cost of cover and the contract price (U.C.C. Section 2–712(2)). The buyer must act in good faith and in a reasonable manner. Also, the cover remedy is available to both merchant and consumer buyer (U.C.C. Section 2–712(1) and comments 2 and 4).
>
> *Thorstenson v. Molbridge Iron Works Co.* (87 S.D. 358, 208 N.W. 2d 715 [1973])

2. REVOKE ACCEPTANCE

A buyer who has accepted goods that later prove to be defective can revoke his or her acceptance (i.e., withdraw his or her previous assent) (Section 2–608). See Section 2–607(2) regarding acceptance of nonconforming goods. The buyer can revoke his or her acceptance only when the nonconformity is such as will cause a substantial impairment of value to the buyer. Generally, this remedy is resorted to only after attempts at adjustment have failed.

The buyer must revoke his or her acceptance within a reasonable time. Five months was held to be an unreasonable time when the buyer knew of the defect immediately after purchase and did nothing. However, this did not preclude him from suing for breach of warranty. A new Lincoln-Continental automobile purchased by plaintiff had spent six to eight weeks during the first year of ownership in defendant dealer's garage receiving substantial repairs caused by inherent defects in the car. Each time, plaintiff was told that the car war in good working order. The car had five times become undriveable on the highway and had to be towed to dealer's. Plaintiff was entitled to revoke his acceptance, because the nonconformity of the car substantially impaired its value to him (*Conte v. Dwan Lincoln-Mercury, Inc.* [172 Conn. 112, 374 A.2d 144 (1976)]).

The effect of a revocation of acceptance is that the buyer is in the same position as if he or she had rejected the goods and, therefore, has the same remedies and duties as a rejecting buyer (Section 2–608(b)—holding goods for seller; Section 2–603(1)—disposing of goods; (3)). (See Section 2–711(3)—security interest; Section 2–602(2) Section 2–604—salvaging goods; Section 2–602(a)—using goods; Section 2–401(4)—revesting title in seller; Sections 1–201(26), 2–327(1)(c), 2–327(2)—sales on approval and sale or return; Section 2–721—remedies for fraud.)

After a proper revocation of acceptance, the buyer is not liable for the price of the goods (Section 2–607(1)).

3. OBTAIN SECURITY INTEREST

A buyer who has rightfully rejected goods or justifiably revoked acceptance of nonconforming goods that remain in his or her possession has a security interest in the goods to cover payments made on the price and the costs of inspection, receipt, transportation, care, and custody. The buyer may resell the goods in the same manner as an aggrieved seller (Section 2–711(3)).

4. OBTAIN IDENTIFIED GOODS FROM INSOLVENT SELLER

Insolvency of the seller gives the buyer specific rights to the goods (Sections 2–502, 2–711(2)(a)). However, for the buyer to have these rights, all of the following four conditions must exist:

1. Buyer has paid all or part of the price, and if he or she has not paid all of the price, he or she has tendered the unpaid portion of the price (Section 2–502(1)).

2. Seller has failed to deliver the goods or has repudiated the contract (Sections 2–502(1), 2–711(2)).

3. The goods have been identified to the contract by the seller (Section 2–502(1)).

4. Seller became insolvent within 10 days after receiving the first install-ment on the price (Section 2–502(1)).

A buyer who is concerned that the seller is having financial trouble should demand assurances of performance (Section 2–609).

5. DEDUCTION OF DAMAGES FROM THE PRICE

A buyer who is damaged by the seller's breach may, after notice to the seller, offset all or part of the damages from the price still due on the contract (Section 2–717).

6. CANCEL THE CONTRACT

The buyer, after notice to the seller, may cancel the contract if the seller fails to deliver the goods or repudiates the contract, or the buyer rightfully revokes acceptance (Section 2–711(1)). The right to cancel is subject to the seller's right to cure a defective performance.

Cancellation excuses further performance by the buyer but does not deprive him or her of any remedy for past breaches (e.g., the buyer may cover, claim damages for breach, obtain conforming goods through replevin —see Section 8 this chapter—or obtain specific performance—see Section 9 this chapter).

In addition to allowing the right to cancel, the Uniform Commercial Code enables the buyer to escape responsibility for the costs of removal of the goods, as in the following case.

> **FACTS** Defendant seller delivered defective flooring to plaintiff. Plain-tiff rejected the goods within a reasonable time and notified the seller. The flooring was not removed. Seller argued that plaintiff's continued use of the goods bars a rescission of the contract.
>
> **DECISION** Judgment for plaintiff. The rejection was justified, and plaintiff was therefore entitled to recover the purchase price of the mer-chandise. The plaintiff's only obligation was to hold the goods with rea-sonable care to permit the seller to remove them. The U.C.C. puts the burden on the merchant to remove the rejected goods (U.C.C. Section 2–602).
>
> *Garfinkel v. Lehman Floor Covering Co.* (60 Misc. 2d 72, 302 N.Y.S.2d 167 [1969])

7. DAMAGES

On the seller's repudiation of the contract, failure to deliver the goods, nonconforming delivery, or breach of warranty, the buyer is entitled to recover damages (Sections 2–711 through 2–715).

The normal measure of damages is the difference between the contract price and the market price of the cost of cover, plus incidental and conse-quential damages, less expenses saved (Sections 2–713, 2–714, 2–715).

In case of breach of warranty, the buyer's measure of damages is the difference between the value of the goods accepted and the value they would have had if the goods had been as warranted (Section 2–714(2)).

The burden of proof rests upon the buyer to establish the damages caused by the alleged breach of warranty. Courts will not allow recovery unless buyer presents sufficient evidence of damages to the jury. See *State v. Travelers Indemnity Company* (250 Or. 356, 442 P.2d 612 [1968]).

Punitive or exemplary (penalty) damages are not covered in the code. Normally, such damages are not recoverable in contract cases.

8. REPLEVIN THE GOODS

Replevin is an action to recover specific goods in which the buyer has an interest and which are unlawfully withheld from the buyer. The buyer's right to such action is stated in Section 2–716(3) of the U.C.C. This remedy is given the buyer in cases in which cover is reasonably unavailable and goods have been identified to the contract. This right is in addition to the buyer's right to recover identified goods on the seller's insolvency. The purpose of this section of the Code is to give a buyer rights to goods that are comparable to a seller's rights to the price.

9. SPECIFIC PERFORMANCE

The buyer can get specific performance of a contract when the goods are unique or in other proper circumstances (Section 2–716(1)). Thus, the U.C.C. broadens the right to obtain specific performance. For example, various situations that could justify specific performance are output and requirement contracts involving a particular or peculiarly available source or market, unavailability of cover, and insolvency of the seller.

The decree for specific performance may include such terms and conditions as to payment, damages, or other relief as the Court may deem just (Section 2–716(2)).

ILLUSTRATIVE CASES

1. Seller Can Reclaim Goods From Insolvent Buyer

AMOCO PIPELINE CO. v. ADMIRAL CRUDE OIL CORP.
490 F. 2d 114 (10th Cir., 1974)

Amoco Pipeline Company agreed to transport and store oil sold by certain crude oil producers to the Admiral Crude Oil Corporation. Admiral did not pay Amoco for gathering, transporting, and storing the oil. Amoco then asserted a lien against a portion of the total crude oil it had stored in its facilities. Later Admiral tendered the crude oil to Admiral, subject to the outstanding lien claim. Admiral refused to accept the oil. Six days after tender, Admiral filed for bankruptcy in Texas. Its parent company filed for bankruptcy in Oklahoma. The Oklahoma bankruptcy trustee sought to claim the oil in Amoco's possession. Amoco brought an action in a New Mexico federal District Court to determine who was entitled to the oil. The District Court found in favor of Amoco and against the trustee. The trustee appealed.

SETH, C.J.   Prior to February 10, 1972, the oil producers discovered that Amoco had received oil from them for Admiral when Admiral was insolvent; the checks which had been tendered to the oil producers by Admiral in payment for oil sold to it in December 1971, were dishonored by the drawee bank and returned marked "insufficient funds." The oil producers therefore notified Amoco and other interested parties to stop delivery of crude oil to or for the benefit or account of Admiral, thus exercising a right of stoppage in transitu and reclamation. Amoco notified the producers that it would enforce its lien against the oil in its possession as Admiral had refused to pay the lien claim and accept delivery of the oil.

Amoco thereafter sold 13,000 barrels of crude oil which it had in its possession on March 15, 1972, to satisfy its common carrier lien against Admiral of $39,564.52, and continued to assert a lien against the balance of the proceeds of sale and 36,953.98 barrels in storage for unpaid demurrage and storage charges against Admiral.

The New Mexico court found that at all material times the crude oil, or the proceeds from its sale, was in the sole and exclusive possession of Amoco, the carrier, or in the registry of the court. This finding is supported by the record.

In the case at bar, the New Mexico district court necessarily had to consider the merits of at least one portion of the case before it. It had to decide who had possession, and who had title to the oil in issue, in order to ascertain if it had jurisdiction of the case and whether it should stay its proceedings. Thus as often happens, a determination of jurisdiction necessarily also decides a substantive issue.

As decided by the district court, the sale of the crude oil by the producers was a sale of goods, and was thus governed by Article 2 of the Uniform Commercial Code. If the Uniform Commercial Code is applied, Admiral, when it refused on February 10, 1972, to accept the tender of the crude oil from Amoco conditioned upon payment by Admiral of Amoco's common carrier lien, caused thereby title to the oil to revest, if indeed it ever passed to Admiral, in the oil producing sellers. Section 2–401(4). Similarly, upon the notice given by the sellers to Amoco, prior to February 10, 1972, to stop delivery of the crude oil to Admiral based upon the previous dishonoring by the drawee bank of Admiral's "insufficient funds" checks to the sellers, the sellers thereby timely exercised their rights of stoppage in transitu under sections 2–702 and 2–705. Thus, regardless of whether title ever passed to Admiral or whether it had a special property interest in the oil, section 2–501, the sellers could reclaim the oil upon demand and notice to Amoco as given herein. Sections 2–702(1), (2) and 2–705(1). This was effective for several reasons. The trial court found, and it is borne out by the record that the tender of the "insufficient funds" checks constituted a written misrepresentation of solvency. From the record it is clear, as the trial court found, that the oil at all material times was in possession of a third party, the carrier. Thus Admiral never had possession, constructive or otherwise, of the oil and under the above-cited provisions of New Mexico's Uniform Commercial Code even if it could be said to have had constructive possession, it did not so have it after February 10, 1972, when Admiral refused tender of the oil and the sellers exercised their rights of stoppage of delivery in transitu and reclaim. The same considerations govern the question of Admiral's "property" or "title" in the oil. The bankruptcy petition was filed, at the earliest, on February 16, 1972, so that upon the date of billing, the title to the oil was not in Admiral. It was not the "property" of the debtor. The Oklahoma district court's stay order thus could not reach the oil, not in the debtor's possession nor its property. 11 U.S.C. § 511. * * *

(Accordingly, the judgment of the district court is in all respects affirmed.)

2. Seller's Damages Under U.C.C. 2–708

PLINE v. ASGROW SEED COMPANY

102 Idaho 827, 642 P.2d 64 (1982)

SWANSTROM, Judge.   In 1975 the parties entered into two contracts whereby Paul E. Pline agreed to grow "Commander" seed corn for Asgrow Seed Company. After Pline grew the corn it was delivered to Asgrow and processed for seed purposes, but Asgrow rejected most of the seed, claiming it failed to meet Asgrow's germination standards and was "unfit for seedmen's use."

The payment Asgrow offered for the seed was unacceptable to Pline, and he brought suit. The trial court found Pline's seed crops met Asgrow's germination standards and Asgrow had breached the contract. The court awarded judgment to Pline for the full amount he claimed due. Asgrow has appealed and has assigned numerous errors by the trial court in admitting evidence and in making its findings and conclusions.

There were two contracts signed by Pline and Asgrow, each covering a separate tract of land farmed by Pline, one of eleven acres and one of seventeen acres. The contracts were otherwise identical. Each contract consisted of a printed "ASGROW SEED COMPANY BAILMENT CONTRACT TO GROW SEED" form supplied by Asgrow and a "ASGROW SEED COMPANY BAILMENT CONTRACT RIDER" which was drafted by one of Agrrow's employees.

Asgrow supplied the seed stock that Pline planted and grew in 1975. The crop was harvested on October 29 and 30, and delivered to Asgrow. After drying and milling Asgrow netted 18,095 pounds of seed from the seventeen acre tract. Asgrow refused to pay Pline the full contract price for these crops contending that they were damaged before harvest by an early freeze.

Asgrow contends that due to the pre-harvest freeze the harvested seed did not meet Asgrow's "normally accepted standard" of germination for seedmen's use [of 85%], and therefore, * * * Asgrow was not obligated to pay the full contract price.

* * *

Asgrow conducted its own germination tests, and submitted evidence at trial that the seed germinated at levels ranging from 68% to 85% with only a small portion of the crops germinating at the 85% level. Pline submitted evidence that the seed germinated at the level of 91% for one crop and 94% for the other. The trial court found that the crops germinated at the level of 91% and 94% and concluded that Asgrow breached its contracts with Pline.

* * *

We conclude that the evidence supports the trial court's finding of fact that the seed met Asgrow's standards. In view of this conclusion, we hold the trial court properly found that Asgrow breached its contracts with Pline.

Asgrow next argues that the evidence does not support the amount of damages awarded to Pline. We disagree. The trial court awarded a total of $20,993.25 to Pline. This figure is found by multiplying the poundage of corn seed, realized by Asgrow after cleaning and processing, by the agreed twenty-five cents per pound contract price, and adding to this the guarantee of $500 per acre contained in the rider attached to each contract. To arrive at the total, the court deducted the amount of seed furnished by Asgrow and the picking expense paid by Asgrow. Twenty-eight acres of corn seed were covered under the two contracts for a total, under the rider of $14,000. The net per pound contract price equalled $6,993.25, making the total of $20,-993.25 due.

At trial the parties disputed the meaning and effect of the contract riders. The trial court found the language of the riders to be ambiguous and susceptible of more than one interpretation. It can be seen that one possible ambiguity is whether the guarantee of $500 per acre was intended to be a bottom limit of what Pline could expect on his contracts, or whether it was intended as a bonus. * * *

* * * The trial court construed the contract rider language to mean that Pline was entitled to receive $500 for each of the twenty-eight acres upon which he produced corn for Asgrow. In addition, the court found that Pline was entitled to twenty-five cents per pound for the net weight of the seed produced. * * * [W]e cannot say the trial court committed error in its interpretation of the contract rider language. * * *

* * *

3. Seller Can Recover Loss of Profits

GENERAL MATTERS, INC. v. PENNY PRODUCTS, INC.

651 F. 2d 1017 (5th Cir., 1981).

GODBOLD, Chief Judge. This suit for breach of contract arises out of an agreement between General Matters, Inc., d/b/a York Associates (York), plaintiff-appellant, and Penny Products, Inc., defendant-appellee. The parties generally agree on the underlying facts, with one or two exceptions. York is a Florida corporation engaged in buying and reselling various types of food items, primarily closeouts and surplus inventory from factories throughout the United States. Normally the products are resold and shipped directly from the factory to York's customers. Leon Kellman is the president of York. Penny Products is a "contract food packer," a company that packs food items for other companies and distributes them to the market. Thomas M. Talbott is the president of Penny Products.

In January 1978, Talbott was given an opportunity by Continental Can Corporation to buy at a reduced price empty cans, some of which had been water-damaged during a warehouse fire. The cans had been produced for the financially troubled Indian River Processors and bore the trademark "Riversweet." Talbott subsequently telephoned Kellman to discuss the possibility of Penny Products' buying the cans and filling them with orange and grapefruit juice for sale to York at reduced prices. York, in turn, could resell the juices to its customers in a brokerage-type operation for less than the prevailing market price. The parties disagree, however, about the number of cases of juice discussed in the telephone conversation. Kellman testified that Talbott offered to sell him 25,000 cases of grapefruit juice and 10,000 cases of orange juice. Although Talbott implied that a figure of 35,000 cases had been discussed, he testified that he had informed Kellman that the precise number of cases to be sold would depend upon how many cans had been damaged beyond use.

January 8, 1978, a day or two after the telephone conversation, York issued a purchase order to Penny Products for 25,000 cases of Indian River unsweetened grapefruit juice, at $3.50 a case, and 10,000 cases of Indian River orange juice, at $4.25 a case. Both parties agreed at trial that Penny Products made no written objection at any time to this purchase order. However, Talbott testified that he called Kellman after receiving the purchase order to warn him that Penny Products could not "guarantee" a "pack-out" of 35,000 cases because of uncertainty about the number of cans damaged beyond use.

During approximately a month after the submission of the purchase order Penny Products shipped 7,000 cases of grapefruit juice and 3,815 cases of orange juice to York's customers. During this same period Penny Products sold 3,456 cases to another customer, MAV Sales.

York paid all invoices submitted by Penny Products except a final invoice in the amount of $16,078.00, which York refused to pay after learning that Penny Products would not make any more shipments under the purchase order. As a result of Penny Products' failure to supply the balance of the 35,000 cases York was unable to fill orders from its customers for more than 20,000 cases.

York sought specific performance of the contract or damages for breach of contract. Penny Products counterclaimed for York's nonpayment of the final invoice.

Relying on Talbott's testimony, the district court found that the parties' agreement was "necessarily limited to the availability of usable cans . . . so that [York] was on notice that it was not within the power of [Penny Products] to keep on producing Indian River cans beyond the availability of the undamaged cans in this salvage lot."

*   *   *

Because the district court found that the agreement was limited to the number of usable cans it held that York was not entitled to recover damages based upon Penny Products' failure to deliver 35,000 cases. On the counterclaim, the court held that Penny Products was entitled to recover the amount of its unpaid invoice, $16,078, subject, however, to a setoff. Since the court also concluded that Penny Products should have made all usable cans available to York it awarded York profit that would have been made on the 3,456 cases sold by Penny Products to MAV Sales. This amount was determined by the district court to be "$1.00 per case, divided by 1/2," an apparent reference to a separate agreement between York and Kandy Man Sales Company (not a party to this suit or to the agreement between York and Penny Products) to divide equally profits from all sales made by either company. The amount of the setoff thus was $1,728. York appeals from the district court's ruling on its damage claim in favor of Penny Products and the court's reduction of the amount of the setoff by one-half.

The only evidence in the record that could support a finding that the purchase order was intended as a final expression of agreement as to quantity is Kellman's testimony that Talbott offered 35,000 cases in the initial phone conversation. However, Kellman's testimony conflicted with Talbott's on this precise point, and the district court credited Talbott's testimony. That credibility resolution, along with the district court's concomitant finding that the parties' agreement was limited to the number of usable cans in the salvage lot, is not clearly erroneous, *see Western Beef, Inc. v. Compton Investment Co.*, 611 F.2d 587, 590 (5th Cir. 1980). Accordingly, we find that the district court properly ruled against York on its claim for breach of contract and in favor of Penny Products on its counterclaim.

Although the district court correctly awarded counterclaim damages to Penny Products subject to a setoff for the cans sold to MAV Sales, it erred in reducing by 50% the amount of the setoff. Presumably this reduction was occasioned by evidence that York had entered into an agreement to split its profits from this and other sales with Kandy Man. An agreement to split its profits from this and other sales with Kandy Man. An agreement between York and one not party to this suit concerning the disposition of York's profits from all its sales contracts has no bearing on the amount of profit York would have realized if Penny Products had fully performed. In Florida the "purpose of an award of damages in a breach of contract action is to place the injured party in the same financial position as he would have occupied if the contract ha[d] been fully performed." Stated another way, the aim of a breach of contract action is to award the nonbreaching party "a sum which is equivalent to the performance of the bargain." Had Penny Products not breached the contract York would have received profits of $3,456.00. The ultimate destination of those profits is of no significance in this suit and should have been disregarded in the computation of the setoff.

We reverse and remand the district court's computation of York's setoff with instructions to allow appellant a setoff equal to the total profits lost because of Penny Products' sale of cans to MAV Sales. The remainder of the judgment if affirmed.

4. Limitations on Right of Seller to Recover Price

WILSON TRADING CORP. v. DAVID FERGUSON LTD.

23 N.Y. 2d 398, 297 N.Y.S. 2d 108, 244 N.E. 2d 685 (1968)

JASEN, J.   The plaintiff, Wilson Trading Corporation, entered into a contract with the defendant, David Ferguson, Ltd., for the sale of a specified quantity of yarn. After the yarn was delivered, cut and knitted into sweaters, the finished product was washed. It was during this washing that it was discovered that the color of the yarn had "shaded"—that is, "there was a variation in color from piece to piece and within the pieces." This defect, the defendant claims, rendered the sweaters "unmarketable".

This action for the contract price of the yarn was commenced after the defendant refused payment. As a defense to the action and as a counterclaim for damages, the defendant alleges that "[p]laintiff has failed to perform all of the conditions of the contract on its part required to be performed, and has delivered * * * defective and unworkmanlike goods".

The sales contract provides in pertinent part:

> "2. No claims relating to excessive moisture content, short weight, count variations, twist, quality or shade shall be allowed *if made after weaving, knitting, or processing*, or more than 10 days after receipt of shipment. * * * The buyer shall within 10 days of the receipt of the merchandise by himself or agent examine the merchandise for any and all defects." [Emphasis supplied.]

*   *   *

Special Term granted plaintiff summary judgment for the contract price of the yarn sold on the ground that "notice of the alleged breach of warranty for defect in shading was not given within the time expressly limited and is not now available by way of defense or counterclaim." The Appellate Division affirmed, without opinion.

The defendant on this appeal urges that the time limitation provision on claims in the contract was unreasonable since the defect in the color of the yarn was latent and could not be discovered until after the yarn was processed and the finished product washed.

Defendant's affidavits allege that its sweaters were rendered unsaleable because of latent defects in the yarn which caused "variation in color from piece to piece and within the pieces." * * * Indeed, the plaintiff does not seriously dispute the fact that its yarn was unmerchantable, but instead, like Special Term, relies upon the failure of defendant to give notice of the breach of warranty within the time limits prescribed by paragraph 2 of the contract.

Subdivision (3) (par. [a]) of section 2–607 of the Uniform Commercial Code expressly provides that a buyer who accepts goods has a reasonable time after he discovers or should have discovered a breach to notify the seller of such breach. * * *

However, the Uniform Commercial Code allows the parties, within limits established by the code, to modify or exclude warranties and to limit remedies for breach of warranty. * * *

We are, therefore, confronted with the effect to be given the time limitation provision in paragraph 2 of the contract. * * *

Parties to a contract are given broad latitude within which to fashion their own remedies for breach of contract (Uniform Commercial Code, § 2–316, subd. [4]; §§ 2–718–2–719). Nevertheless, it is clear from the official comments to section 2–719 of the Uniform Commercial Code that it is the very essence of a sales contract that at least minimum adequate remedies be available for its breach. * * *

* * * [C]ontractual limitations upon remedies are generally to be enforced unless unconscionable. * * *

However, it is unnecessary to decide the issue of whether the time limitation is unconscionable on this appeal for section 2–719 (subd. [2]) of the Uniform Commercial Code provides that the general remedy provisions of the code apply when "circumstances cause an exclusive or limited remedy to fail of its essential purpose". As explained by the official comments to this section: "where an apparently fair and reasonable clause because of circumstances fails in its purpose or operates to deprive either party of the substantial value of the bargain, it must give way to the general remedy provisions of this article." (Uniform Commercial Code, § 2–719, official comment 1.) Here, paragraph 2 of the contract bars all claims for shade and other specified defects made after knitting and processing. Its effect is to eliminate any remedy for shade defects not reasonably discoverable within the time limitation period. It is true that parties may set by agreement any time not manifestly unreasonable whenever the code "requires any action to be taken within a reasonable time" (Uniform Commercial Code, § 1–204, subd. [1]), but here the time provision eliminates all remedy for defects not discoverable before knitting and processing and section 2–719 (subd. [2]) of the Uniform Commercial Code thereform applies.

Defendant's affidavits allege that sweaters manufactured from the yarn were rendered unmarketable because of latent shading defects not reasonably discoverable before knitting and processing of the yarn into sweaters. If these factual allegations are established at trial, the limited remedy established by paragraph 2 has failed its "essential purpose" and the buyer is, in effect, without remedy. The time limitation clause of the contract, therefore, insofar as it applies to defects not reasonably discoverable within the time limits established by the contract, must give way to the general code rule that a buyer has a reasonable time to notify the seller of breach of contract after he discovers or should have discovered the defect. (Uniform Commercial Code, § 2–607, subd. [3], par. [a].) * * *

In sum, there are factual issues for trial concerning whether the shading defects alleged were discoverable before knitting and processing, and, if not, whether notice of the defects was given with a reasonable time after the defects were or should have been discovered. If the shading defects were not reasonably discoverable before knitting and processing and notice was given within a reasonable time after the defects were or should have been discovered, a further factual issue of whether the sweaters were rendered unsaleable because of the defect is presented for trial.

The order of the Appellate Division should be reversed, with costs, and plaintiff's motion for summary judgment should be denied.

5. Right of Buyer to Revoke Acceptance

VENTURA v. FORD MOTOR CORP.

180 N.J. Super 45, 433 A.2d 801 (1981)

BOTTER, P.J.A.D.   Ford Motor Company (Ford) appeals from the final judgment in this action in which plaintiff, the purchaser of a new 1978 Mercury Marquis Brougham, sued Ford's authorized dealer, Marino Auto Sales, Inc. (Marino Auto) and Ford, as manufacturer, for damages due to defects in the vehicle. Marino Auto cross-claimed against Ford for indemnification. The final judgment (a) granted plaintiff rescission of the purchase and damages of $6,745.59 against Marino Auto Sales (representing the purchase price of $7,847.49 less an allowance for plaintiff's use of the car and the sales tax), (b) awarded damages in favor of Marino Auto against Ford on the cross-claim in the sum of $2,910.59 (representing $6,745.59 less the resale value of the car), and (c) awarded counsel fees to plaintiff against Ford in the sum of $5,165. Plaintiff's demands for interest, punitive damages in excess of $2,-000,000 and treble damages were denied.

*   *   *

Plaintiff took delivery of the automobile on April 12, 1978. According to the testimony of plaintiff and his wife, they experienced engine hesitation and stalling problems early in their use of the car which continued without interruption despite repeated attempts by Marino Auto to cure the problem. Stanley Bednarz, Ford's zone service manager and mechanical specialist who assists dealers in satisfying customers, inspected the vehicle on July 13, 1978 and recommended replacing the exhaust regulator valve. Plaintiff testified that he was told by Bednarz that there was nothing wrong with the car and he would "have to live with this one." Plaintiff also testified that later in July 1978 he returned to Marino Auto intending to ask Mr. Marino to take the car back if it could not be fixed but that he was prevented from doing so and was forcibly removed from the premises.

*   *   *

The contract of sale between Marino Auto and plaintiff conspicuously contained the following legend on its face:

> The seller, MARINO AUTO SALES, Inc., hereby expressly disclaims all warranties, either expressed or implied, including any implied warranty of merchantability of fitness for a particular purpose, and MARINO AUTO SALES, Inc., neither assumes nor authorizes another person to assume for it any liability in connection with the sale of the vehicle.

On the back of this sales order-contract are the following terms which were made part of the contract:

> 7. It is expressly agreed that there are no warranties, express or implied, made by either the selling dealer or the manufacturer on the motor vehicle, chassis or parts furnished hereunder except, in the case of a new motor vehicle the warranty expressly given to the purchaser upon the delivery of such motor vehicle or chassis.
>
> The selling dealer also agrees to promptly perform and fulfill all terms and conditions of the owner service policy.

*   *   *

The Magnuson-Moss Warranty Act provides for two types of written warranties on consumer products, those described as "full" warranties and those described as "limited" warranties. 15 *U.S.C.A.* § 2303. The nature of the "full" warranty is prescribed by § 2304. It expressly provides in subsection (a)(4) that a consumer must be given the election to receive a refund or replacement without charge of a product or part which is defective or malfunctions after a reasonable number of attempts by the warrantor to correct such condition. For the breach of any warranty, express or implied, or of a service contract (defined in 15 *U.S.C.A.* § 2301(8)), consumers are given the right to sue for damages and "other legal and equitable relief" afforded under state or federal law, 15 *U.S.C.A.* § 2310(d); 15 *U.S.C.A.* § 2311(b)(1).

*   *   *

The record does not contain a written description of the "owner service policy" which the dealer agreed to perform. Nevertheless, since Ford is the appellant here, we take its contentions at trial and documents in the record to establish the dealer's obligation to Ford and to plaintiff to make the warranty repairs on behalf of Ford (subject to the right of reimbursement or other terms that may be contained in their agreement). For the purpose of this appeal we are satisfied that the dealer's undertaking in paragraph 7 constitutes a written warranty within the meaning of 15 *U.S.C.A.* § 2301(6)(B). Accordingly, having furnished a written warranty to the consumer, the dealer as a supplier may not "disclaim or modify [except to limit in duration] any implied warranty to a consumer. . . ." The result of this analysis is to invalidate the attempted disclaimer by the dealer of the implied warranties of merchantability and fitness. Being bound by those implied warranties arising under state law, Marino Auto was liable to plaintiff for the breach thereof as found by the trial judge, and plaintiff could timely revoke his acceptance of the automobile and claim a refund of his purchase price. In this connection we note that the trial judge found that plaintiff's attempted revocation of acceptance was made in timely fashion, and that finding has adequate support in the evidence.

*   *   *

[Affirmed.]

6. Revocation of Acceptance Within Reasonable Time (Defective Goods)

ED FINE OLDSMOBILE, INC. v. KNISLEY

319 A.2d 33 (Del. Super., 1974)

O'HARA, J. In February, 1970, the buyer, visiting dealer's place of business, expressed an interest in a 1968 Oldsmobile, 4–4–2, convertible, which was on display. He was seeking reliable transportation and, knowing that such models had high performance reputations, sought to ascertain the history of the used vehicle in question. He feared that a vehicle of this sort might have been used for racing or contain racing equipment, and if so, did not intend to buy the automobile. Buyer clearly stated this to the defendant's sale agents. They assured him that it had been well cared for by its previous owner, one of the dealer's mechanics, and that he had neither raced it nor installed any racing equipment in it.

Relying on those assurances, buyer purchased the automobile, taking delivery on February 26, 1970. He immediately began to have difficulties. It burned an excessive amount of oil, hesitated, and ran poorly. On April 3, 1970, dealer took the automobile into its shop for repairs. It was at this time that buyer discovered that several parts of his automobile had, in fact, been altered for racing. Among other things, it had a special racing transmission, a nonstock cam shaft, and racing weights in the carburetor. The dealer replaced these parts without charge and assured the buyer that all defects caused by racing or the use of racing equipment had been remedied.

Thereafter, buyer continued to have difficulties with the automobile. On May 5, 1970, it was placed in dealer's shop for additional repairs, including replacement of the starter. On June 9, 1970, shortly after those earlier repairs had been completed, it was towed to dealer's for the last time. The engine, which had locked after throwing a rod, was completely inoperative.

On condition that he need pay only for the labor costs, buyer agreed to allow the dealer to install a new engine. However, when that work was completed, in late July or early August, dealer told the buyer that he would also be required to pay an additional $364.00, to replace the transmission which had been stolen while the automobile was in dealer's possession. Confronted with what he considered a final act of bad faith, buyer refused to cooperate any further and left the automobile with the dealer. He then filed suit in the Court of Common Pleas for return of the $2,456.75 he had paid for the automobile. Essentially, dealer bases this appeal on two grounds: 1) that there was no breach of warranty, express or implied; and 2) that buyer failed to make an effective revocation of his acceptance of the automobile.

In the case at bar, the trial judge properly concluded that dealer should not be allowed to profit from his own wrongdoings by strictly holding buyer to the written terms of the sales and warranty agreements. The evidence amply supports the legal conclusion that buyer, at the time he discovered the deception, could have rejected the automobile and had his purchase price refunded.

This leads, however, to the other prong of dealer's attack on the trial court's decision. Buyer did not reject the automobile when he learned that it actually contained several pieces of racing equipment and that it did not otherwise fulfill his reasonable expectations or the dealer's representations. Instead, faced with a dealer who would not return the purchase price and who promised to remedy the nonconformities, buyer continued to use the vehicle while frequently bringing it to dealer for replacement of racing parts and other repairs. Given this history of buyer patience, dealer now claims that buyer failed to make a timely revocation of his acceptance as required by § 2–608.

The provision of the Uniform Commerical Code provides, in pertinent part:

> (1) The buyer may revoke his acceptance of a lot or commercial unit whose non-conformity substantially impairs its value to him if he has accepted it

> (a) on the reasonable assumption that its non-conformity would be cured and it has not been seasonably cured: . . .

> (2) Revocation of acceptance must occur within a reasonable time after the buyer discovers or should have discovered the ground for it and before any substantial change in condition of the goods which is not caused by their own defects. It is not effective until the buyer notifies the seller of it.

There is no doubt that buyer was persuaded to withhold his revocation from early April, when the non-conformities were discovered, until that summer by dealer's refusal to rescind the sale and its assurances that those non-conformities could and would be corrected. Nor is there any question that the final failure of the engine was due to the vehicle's own defects. Therefore, the question must turn on the timeliness of the revocation.
* * *

*   *   *

Here,* * * although the the vehicle had been driven some 1,500 miles, the buyer had had little opportunity for inspection or continued use, since it was so frequently being repaired. Every attempt at revocation was forestalled by dealer's assurances and foot-dragging. Finally, dealer's attempt to foist the cost of the stolen transmission upon buyer is hardly support for now permitting dealer to profit thereby. Patience is admittedly a virtue. Dealer would here change it into a vice.

*   *   *

[Judgment for Kinsley affirmed.]

PROBLEMS

1. Seller, pursuant to a credit contract for the sale of 100 television sets, ships the sets from New York to the buyer in Chicago. Upon arrival of the goods, the freight agent for the carrier calls the buyer and acknowledges to him that they are holding the 100 television sets for him and asks him to pick them up. Before the buyer has an opportunity to pick up the sets, the seller learns that the buyer has become insolvent. The seller calls the representative of the carrier and asks him to stop delivery. The agent of the carrier states that he has already acknowledged to the buyer that they are holding the goods for him. Does the seller have the right to stop delivery?

2. Seller in Kentucky sold to a buyer in Florida a large quantity of tobacco, but the buyer refused delivery. After due notice, the seller sold the tobacco elsewhere for a price less than the contract price between the seller and the buyer. Seller brings suit for the difference between the resale price and the contract price, plus expenses in the transportation, care and custody of the goods after the buyer refused delivery, together with the costs of the resale. Buyer contends that seller's election to resell the property to another buyer released him from all liability on the contract. Decision?

3. S, a seller of soft water equipment, sold a unit to B. Approximately two weeks after the sale the equipment proved defective. B complained to S, who attempted to fix the unit. However, the unit continued to be defective. B continued to complain and S continued to try to fix it. This procedure went on for approximately one year when B finally sent a letter to S requesting him to pick up the equipment and refund the purchase price. S refuses to do either, claiming that B waited too long to revoke his acceptance. Decision?

4. B purchased a large quantity of toys from S to use as stock in his store for Christmas trade. Several shipments of toys were sent to B during October and November; however, the number was less than half of the toys ordered. B called S many times during October and November complaining that he was not receiving all of the toys, and each time was assured by S that the rest of the toys would be forthcoming. Finally, on December 1, B called S and angrily demanded the toys. When S gave B the same reply, an exasperated B said that he wanted no more toys. Apparently this call was too late as B received a large shipment of the toys on December 2. This shipment completed the entire purchase order except for one small lot which was never sent. B did not open this shipment. The other toys were priced, put on display, and sold by B. In February B sent all of the toys not sold to S and demanded S pay their value. S returned the shipment to B. Decision?

5. Buyer purchases twenty motors to be used in the construction of swimming pools. After delivery to the buyer, it is discovered that the motors do not conform to the contract. The buyer revokes his acceptance; however, the seller refuses to recognize the revocation and refuses to take back the motors. Buyer, after due notice to the seller, sells the motors and sues seller for the difference between the price realized on the sale and the price he had paid the seller, plus incidental damages. Seller contends that the buyer's exercise of ownership over the goods in reselling them prevents buyer's action. Decision?

6. B purchased from S, the manufacturer, a walk-in freezer unit for storage of ice cream and similar products. The unit was specially made for B. During the two-year period after purchase the unit developed leaks. S was not completely able to eliminate the leaks. During the spring of the second year, after leaks reoccurred, the unit broke down, causing B the loss of its contents. S refused to take the unit back. B sued for breach of warranty, cancellation, recovery of payments made on the contract, and special damages for lost merchandise. After the start of the litigation, B unsuccessfully attempted to sell the unit. S defended on the ground that B had waited too long before seeking to cancel, and that its attempted sale of the unit forfeited its right to cancel. Decision?

7. B bought a bottle of hair dye from R, a retailer of such products. The label contained warnings to the user and stated that the liability of the retailer and the manufacturer was limited to a refund of the purchase price. After using the dye, B was severely burned. A test of the contents of the dye reveals that there were certain impurities in the bottle B had purchased. B sued R to recover for medical expenses and for pain and suffering. R defended, asserting that B was bound by the limitation B accepted as a purchaser of the product. Decision?

8. Saxon Livestock Co. pursuant to a written order, shipped a carload of livestock to Brink, a cattle dealer, F.O.B. at point of delivery to carrier. The purchase price was due and payable two days after Brink received the shipment. The carrier, P-C, issued a straight bill of lading for the shipment. While enroute, Saxon learned that Brink was insolvent and had filed for bankruptcy. At that moment, Saxon ordered P-C to return the carload. The bankruptcy trustee then sued to recover the cattle on behalf of Brink's creditors. Decision?

9. Seller contracts to sell 100 units of merchandise to buyer at $5.00 per unit. Just prior to delivery, buyer notified seller that they would not accept the merchandise and considered the contract at an end. Seller sold the merchandise at $4.00 per unit, its fair market value, and sued buyer to recover the difference of $100. Buyer claims that they are not liable, since they were not notified of the resale by seller. Decision?

10. Klein, a collector of Mercedes-Benz cars, contracted to purchase a specially fitted Mercedes-Benz touring car from SHA Motors. Klein made a $10,000 deposit on the vehicle. SHA later returned the deposit, informing Klein that the car was no longer available. Klein learned that the automobile *was* available and was being sold to another customer. He sued to compel SHA to deliver the car. SHA defended on the grounds that it had offered to provide Klein with a similar car, but not specially-fitted, since SHA could not duplicate the car Klein had ordered. Decision?

Chapter 30

PRODUCT LIABILITY

Generally, four legal theories exist upon which a person can base a claim for damages when injured by a defective product:

1. Negligence.
2. Violation of a statutory duty.
3. Breach of warranty.
4. Strict liability in tort.

A. NEGLIGENCE

Independently of the U.C.C., a manufacturer will be liable to persons injured by a product when the manufacturer is negligent in the preparation or manufacture of the product and when as a reasonable person he or she could foresee that such negligence would injure such person or persons. Such liability extends to all persons that a reasonable person could foresee would be injured regardless of their relationship to the buyer. Recoveries have been allowed against manufacturers of automobiles on behalf of buyers, users, passengers, and bystanders based on negligence resulting in defective steering wheels, axles, brakes, tires, and other operating components.

B. VIOLATION OF STATUTORY DUTY

State and federal statutes impose duties upon manufacturers of food, drugs, cosmetics, flammable materials, and toxic substances, with respect to branding, labeling, description of contents, advertising, and the selling or offering for sale of adulterated, contaminated, or unwholesome products. (See Chapter 32, Consumer Law.)

These statutes provide for enforcement by criminal sanctions, seizure of goods, and injunctions. They do not expressly impose civil liability based upon injuries to the user or consumer of a product that has been sold in violation of the statute. However, in a civil action for damages, a violation of statutory duty may be alleged, and if established by evidence, many courts hold that it constitutes negligence by itself. Examples are recovery for destruction of property resulting from faulty electrical wiring that did not comply with the building code and recovery for crop damage resulting from mislabeling of packages of seed in violation of a state statute.

C. BREACH OF WARRANTY

1. IN GENERAL

A warranty is a promise by the seller concerning some aspect of the sale, such as the quality of the goods, the quantity, or the title.

There are two types of warranties (i.e., express and implied). An express warranty is made part of the contract by the words or conduct of the seller. An implied warranty is made part of the contract by operation of the law.

Under the U.C.C., a warranty can arise by course of dealing between the parties or by usage of trade (e.g., the obligation to provide pedigree papers in the sale of a pedigreed dog or blooded bull).

A warranty carries with it strict liability (i.e., the seller of goods is liable even though he or she did not know or have reason to know the goods were defective).

In most states, the warranties extend to any person who may reasonably be expected to use, consume, or be affected by the goods. This includes, for example, not only the purchaser of the goods but also a subpurchaser (e.g., a customer of the store can bring suit against the distributor from whom the store purchased the goods). In most states, an employee can bring suit against the manufacturer of the product or equipment purchased by the employer for use by the employee.

In most states, not only the seller of the goods but also the manufacturer of the goods or of the component parts that go into the making of the finished product can be sued.

2. EXPRESS WARRANTIES

A. By Affirmation Or Promise

Section 2–313(1)(a) provides that *"any affirmation of fact or promise* made by the seller to the buyer which relates to the goods and becomes part of the basis of the bargain creates an express warranty that the goods shall conform to the affirmation or promise." [Emphasis added.]

No particular words are necessary to create a warranty. The word "guarantee" is treated as the equivalent of "warranty."

Section 2–313(2) provides that a seller's statement as to the value of the goods or a statement that purports to be merely the seller's opinion or commendation of the goods does not create a warranty, since common experience discloses that such statements cannot fairly be viewed as entering into the bargain. These statements are commonly referred to as "puffing" or "sales talk." However, a statement in which the seller gives market figures relating to sales of similar goods would be a statement of fact, not of value, and hence actionable.

Although not every chance remark of the seller is a warranty, a statement that has in the circumstances and in objective judgment become part of the basis of the bargain can be considered a warranty. Also, the more expert and experienced the seller, the more likely his or her words will be construed to be a warranty.

Examples of words construed to be warranties are as follows: glass is "shatterproof"; the machine is "durable" (a warranty that its parts will not wear out or break when put to use); goods are "number one" (an express warranty of good quality); seller will "stand behind the goods 100 percent"; oil well suspension plug is "as good as" the plug of the competition; "this cloth is all wool."

Examples of statements considered as only opinion are as follows: goods are "first class", peach kernel oil "as good as the best grade of olive oil"; caramel coloring matter "just as good as or perhaps better than any"; jukebox a "good machine" in "workable condition" and "would probably not require repair."

A warranty may be made after the transaction is completed, and it need not be supported by consideration (Section 2–209(1)). However, if the sales contract as modified is within the statute of frauds, it must be in writing (Section 2–209(3)).

Section 2–313(1)(a) states that a warranty is made by a seller to a buyer. Can a buyer rely on a warranty made in a manufacturer's advertising so as to hold the manufacturer liable even though the buyer did not deal directly with the manufacturer? Most courts hold the manufacturer liable on the basis of an express warranty, even though the buyer did not contract with the manufacturer (i.e., the buyer recovers although there is no privity of contract between the buyer and the manufacturer).

B. WARRANTY BY DESCRIPTION

"Any description of the goods which is made part of the basis of the bargain creates an express warranty that the goods shall conform to the description", Section 2–313(1)(b). Thus, a descriptive name constitutes a warranty Section (e.g., "black grapes" warrants black-colored grapes; "Blue Goose" tomatoes; "No. 1 Saigon Long Grain Rice"; "export-cured boneless codfish").

The descriptive word or phrase can be an express warranty even though it is only in the invoice or in an advertisement and not in the sales contract. It has been held that a picture in an advertisement can constitute an express warranty.

C. WARRANTY BY SAMPLE OR MODEL

"Any sample or model which is made part of the basis of the bargain creates an express warranty that the whole of the goods shall conform to the sample or model." Section 2–313(c).

If the seller used the sample merely to suggest the character of the subject matter of the contract, it is not a warranty by sample. However, if the seller used the sample to indicate intent that it was to *be* the character of the subject-matter of the contract, it is a warranty. In other words, if the contract is based on the understanding that the seller will supply goods according to a particular description or that the goods will be the same as the sample or a model, the seller is bound by an express warranty that the goods shall conform to the description, sample, or model. A seller who does not want to make this warranty should label the samples and models in such manner as to indicate that they are only suggestive of the material he or she wishes to sell and that they did not come from the goods to be sold. A sample that has been drawn from an existing bulk is considered as describing values of the goods contracted for unless it is accompanied by a denial of warranty.

D. FEDERAL PROTECTION FOR BUYERS OF CONSUMER PRODUCTS

In 1974, Congress enacted the Magnuson-Moss Warranty Act, effective in January of 1975, to provide purchasers of consumer products adequate information concerning written warranties made for such products and to prevent false and deceptive warranties. The Act is administered and enforced by the Federal Trade Commission (FTC).

The Act was a response to various warranty problems:

1. Many warranties were not understandable.

2. Many implied warranties were disclaimed (no responsibility claimed for breach).

3. Many warranties were unfair.

4. Many warranties were not honored.

To remedy these practices, the Act requires the following:

1. Disclosure clearly stated and in understandable language of the warranty.

2. A statement that the warranty is either full or limited.

3. A prohibition against disclaiming any implied warranty where a written warranty is provided.

4. A means of informally settling warranty disputes which is optional with the warrantor.

The Act is applicable only where a consumer product containing a written warranty is put on the market. A consumer product is defined as any item of tangible personal property normally used for family, household, or personal use that is transmitted in interstate commerce.

The Act differentiates between a full and limited warranty, one of which, for any product costing $10 or more, must be designated on the written warranty itself. A full warranty requires the warrantor to repair without charge the product to conform to the warranty; to place no time limit on the duration of any implied warranty; to give the consumer the option of a full refund or replacement if repair is unsuccessful; and to exclude consequential damages (damages caused by the product's failure to function as warranted) only if such an exclusion is clearly noted. A limited warranty cannot disclaim or modify any implied warranty but can limit its duration to that of the written warranty, provided that any such limitation is reasonable, conscionable (not totally one-sided and oppressive), and conspicuously stated. No other new or expanded remedies are provided.

The Magnuson-Moss Act preempts only provisions of the U.C.C. that conflict with it. However, the Act provides that any state law that is more protective of consumers may prevail and be enforced. In practice, the Act would nullify U.C.C. provisions that permit disclaimers of implied warranties of merchantibility and fitness for intended purpose.

A consumer product buyer who does not give the warrantor a reasonable opportunity to repair the product cannot avail himself or herself of the right to a refund of the purchase price under the Act. In *Pratt v. Winnebago Industries, Inc.* (463 F Supp. 709 [W.D. Pa., 1979]), the requirement that the buyer return the product for repair was found reasonable and voluntarily accepted and thus not an impermissible duty under the Act.

3. WARRANTY OF TITLE

Every sale of goods contains a warranty of title (i.e., the title conveyed shall be good and the goods shall be free from any security interest or other lien of which the buyer has no knowledge) (Section 2–312(1)).

4. WARRANTIES IMPLIED BY LAW

A. WARRANTY OF MERCHANTABILITY

A warranty that the goods shall be merchantable is implied in a contract for their sale if the seller is a merchant with respect to goods of that kind (Section 2–314(1)). Essentially, the goods sold by the merchant must be of medium or average quality and be fit for the ordinary purpose for which such goods are used. (See Section 2–314(2) for specific situations.) Most courts hold that a seller is liable under this implied warranty, even though the goods are sold in a sealed container.

In restaurant cases, the seller can be liable if the goods are not fit for human consumption. Whether food is unfit for human consumption is a question of fact. Food for human consumption need not be actually unfit; it is sufficient if the consumer has adequate grounds for believing that it is. The fact that some person on the witness stand would be willing to eat the food would not be a defense. In many states (California, Louisiana, Massachusetts, North Carolina), the warranty of fitness for human consumption does not apply if there is an object in the food that is not foreign to the food (e.g., cherry pit in cherry pie, bone in fish chowder, oyster shell in oyster soup, chicken bone in chicken pie) (*Mix v. Ingersoll Candy Co.* [6 Cal. 2d 674, 59 P. 2d 144 (1936)]). Other states (Maryland, Pennsylvania, Wisconsin) have rejected the so-called foreign-natural test in favor of what is known as the reasonable expectation test. Under this test, the jury must make a determination whether the buyer could reasonably have expected the object in the food. If he or she could not, the buyer will recover. Examples of recovery under this test are chicken bone in a chicken sandwich, oyster shell in canned oysters used in making oyster stew, and chicken bone in chow mein (*Zabner v. Howard Johnson's, Inc.* [201 So. 2d 824 (Fla. App., 1967)]).

In the case of self-service stores, recent cases have found an implied warranty of merchantability when the customer has removed bottles from the display counter after which one of the bottles exploded causing injury (*Sheeskin v. Giant Foods, Inc.* [20 Md.App. 611, 318 A.2d 874 (1974)]; *Gillispie v. Great Atlantic & Pacific Tea Co.* [14 N.C.App. 1, 187 S.E.2d 441 (1972)]). In the Sheeskin case, the court stated that the offer consisted in placing the goods on the shelf with a price stamped upon them. The acceptance consisted in the act of taking physical possession of the goods with the intent to purchase them which manifested an intent to accept the offer and a promise to take them to the checkout counter and pay for them there.

In the case of used or secondhand goods sold by a dealer, no court has excluded the possibility of an implied warranty of merchantability. However, some courts (because of the particular facts in the cases) have not found such an implied warranty. On the other hand, one court found the implied warranty in the sale of a secondhand airplane where damages were incurred in repairing the plane when a defect in the fuel supply system caused a fire three days after the sale (*Georgia Timberlands, Inc. v. Southern Airways Co.* [125 Ga.App. 404, 188 S.E.2d 108 (1972)]). In accord: *Overland Bond & Investment Corp. v. Howard* (9 Ill.App.3d 348, 292 N.E.2d 168 [1972]), used automobile from a dealer; *Hob's Refrigeration and Air Conditioning, Inc. v. Poche* (304 So.2d 326 [La.,1974]), rebuilt compressor not fit for use.

In most courts, leases and bailments of chattels are covered by the implied warranty of fitness for ordinary purpose and, if sufficient facts are presented, by the implied warranty of fitness for a particular purpose.

B. WARRANTY OF FITNESS FOR PARTICULAR PURPOSE

Where the seller has reason to know the particular purpose for which the goods are required and that the buyer is relying on the seller's skill or judgment to select or furnish the goods, there is an implied warranty that the goods shall be fit for such purpose (Section 2–315).

For example, B told S, a retail paint merchant, that the paint on his stucco house was powdery and that he wanted advice as to what paint he should use to cover the walls. S recommended a certain paint, which B purchased and used according to the instructions S gave him. A few months later, the paint began to peel and blister. B has a cause of action for damages, because the seller knew the particular purpose of the buyer and had reason to know that the buyer was relying on the seller's skill and judgment in selecting the appropriate paint.

Robertson Companies, Inc. v. Kenner illustrates that one may sue both to rescind a contract and to recover consequential damages.

> **FACTS**　Plaintiff contracted to build two galvanized steel buildings on defendant's farm. Defendant planned to use the buildings to store his sunflower crop. After first refusing to perform, plaintiff constructed the

buildings. Defendant rejected the buildings as not meeting the proper specifications. Plaintiff sued for the contract price. Defendant counterclaimed for his additional storage expenses, lost sales profits, and other consequential damages.

DECISION   The court rescinded the contract and awarded defendant damages for lost profits. The court held that under the Uniform Commercial Code, rescission and damages are not mutually exclusive remedies.

Robertson Companies, Inc. v. Kenner (311 N.W.2d 194 [N.D., 1981])

On the other hand, construction of a swimming pool has been held not a sale of goods and hence no warranty. Likewise, there is no warranty in the services of a dentist. Nearly all courts hold that a blood transfusion carries no implied warranties. Courts are divided on the question as to whether a beauty treatment is a service or a sale. However, even in those courts that call the treatment a service, a person may still have the remedies of negligence and strict liability in tort available. See *Newmark v. Gimbel's, Inc.* (54 N.J. 585, 258 A.2d 697 [1969]).

5.   EXCLUSION, MODIFICATION, AND DISCLAIMER

Disclaimers or exclusions of both express and implied warranties are construed against the seller. In some states, disclaimers are prohibited by consumer protection laws or by public policy.

U.C.C. Section 2–719(3) provides that a limitation of consequential damages for injury to the person in the case of consumer goods is prima facie unconscionable, but limitation of damages where the loss is commercial is not. An exception is where it is a recognized practice of the trade to exclude them or where they have been consistently excluded in prior dealings.

In *Majors v. Kalo Laboratories, Inc.* (407 F.Supp. 20 [D.C.Ala., 1975]), the court allowed a farmer consequential damages to his crop. It found the exclusionary clause unconscionable, because the damages it allowed (merely a refund of the purchase price) were grossly disproportionate to the damages it knew buyers would suffer if the product (soybean inoculant) did not work. Furthermore, the court noted the product's defects were latent. In *Collins v. Uniroyal, Inc.* (64 N.J. 260, 315 A.2d 16 [1974]), action was brought for death of a tire buyer in an accident occurring when the automobile went out of control due to failure of the manufacturer's tire. In holding for the plaintiff, the court held that the clause that limited buyer's damages to replacement of the tire was unconscionable. To the same effect, see *McCarty v. E. J. Korvette, Inc.* (28 Md.App. 421, 347 A.2d 253 [1975]), citing and following *Collins.*

A.   Warranties Of Description

A clause excluding all warranties, express or implied, will not disclaim the warranty of description unless it is within the contemplation of both parties that such warranty is to be disclaimed. To make the disclaimer effective, the seller should state in conspicuous language that there is no warranty of description and place the disclaimer after the language of description.

B.　Merchantability Warranty

A disclaimer of the implied warranty of merchantability must specifically mention merchantability and, if in writing, must be conspicuous (Section 2–316(2)). "Conspicuous" means clear and distinct language and prominently set forth in large, bold print in such position as to compel notice. An effective disclaimer would state that the seller does not warrant the goods to be merchantable.

C.　Particular Purpose Warranty

A disclaimer of an implied warranty for a particular purpose must be in writing and must be conspicuous. In *Smith v. Sharpenstein,* (13 UUC Reporting Service 609 [C.A.Okl., 1973]), plaintiff entered into a written equipment lease with an option to purchase a used truck-tractor from defendants. The court held that the inconspicuous disclaimer of the implied warranty of fitness for a particular purpose was ineffective, even though the plaintiff had read the disclaimer. (See Section 2–316(2) for an example of an effective disclaimer.)

D.　Trade Usage Warranties

An effective disclaimer in the course of dealing or trade usage should be conspicuous and should state that the buyer acknowledges that (1) no warranties implied by custom or usage have become part of the contract, (2) in their trade, it is customary not to give warranties, and (3) prior dealings do not imply any warranties.

But note the effect of the Magnuson-Moss Warranty Act, discussed earlier in the chapter.

E.　Title Warranty

A warranty of title can be excluded only by specific language or by circumstances that give the buyer reason to know that the person selling does not claim title in himself or herself or that the seller is purporting to sell only such right or title as he or she or a third person may have (Section 2–312(2)). The language should include the word "title" and be conspicuous.

F.　Exclusion by Inspection

(1) Express warranties.

A buyer does not have to inspect or examine the goods but may rely solely on the seller's express warranties. When the seller makes an express warranty and the buyer does not inspect, although an inspection would have revealed that the seller's representations were false, the seller is liable, since the buyer is justified in believing the seller's representations.

(2) Implied warranties.

In the case of implied warranties, the seller can demand that the buyer inspect the goods or a sample or model; if the buyer refuses, all implied warranties are disclaimed. If the buyer does examine the goods, there is no implied warranty as to defects that such examination should have revealed (Section 2–316(3)(b)).

It has been held that where defects cannot be uncovered by inspection but only after use, the buyer can ignore a clause that requires inspection and still recover for the breach of warranty.

In *Twin Lakes Manufacturing Co. v. Coffey,* the Supreme Court of Virginia held that the implied warranty of merchantability on a mobile home requires more than that the home be habitable.

FACTS The Coffeys inspected and bought a mobile home. After the home was assembled, major defects in the home became evident. It was a mess and beyond repair. Not having another home, the Coffeys began living in the home and sued for damages.

DECISION The court awarded the Coffeys the full purchase price of the home. First, the Coffeys' inspection of the unassembled home did not waive the implied warranty, as the defects were latent and could not have been discovered. Second, that the Coffeys lived in the home did not mean that the sellers had not breached their implied warranty of merchantability (U.C.C. Section 2–314). That the home was habitable was insufficient reason to conclude that the goods were fit for their ordinary use.

Twin Lakes Manufacturing Co. v. Coffey (222 Va. 467,281 S.E.2d 864 [1981])

G. OTHER WAYS OF EXCLUDING IMPLIED WARRANTIES

If the contract states that the buyer is taking the goods "as is" or "with all faults" or "as they stand," all implied warranties are excluded (Section 2–316(3)(a)). However, a catch phrase disclaimer, such as "all warranties, express or implied, are excluded," is probably ineffective to exclude express or implied warranties, especially if the words are not conspicuous (Section 2–316, Comment (1)).

Although a disclaimer may be effective to disclaim warranties, the same disclaimer would be ineffective in a suit based on negligence or strict liability in tort where the product was unreasonably dangerous to the user or consumer. This is the trend even where the product is secondhand.

Usage of trade may disclaim implied warranties (e.g., a buyer who purchased from a junk dealer or at a sheriff's sale cannot rely on implied warranties). Also, course of dealing can exclude implied warranties (Section 2–316(3)(c)).

H. AUTOMOBILE WARRANTIES

Automobile disclaimers of warranties are usually so strict as to be misleading. Liability is usually limited to repair or replacement of defective parts. Although the U.C.C. Section 2–316(4) permits contractual limitation of warranties, the courts treat disclaimers that are too strict as ineffective. One of the leading cases in the United States held an automobile disclaimer void on public policy grounds (because buyer has no bargaining power with automobile manufacturers as to disclaimers) and permitted the wife of the buyer of the automobile to recover for personal injury damages from the manufacturer for breach of implied warranty of merchantability (*Henningsen v. Bloomfield Motors, Inc.* [32 N.J. 358, 161 A.2d 69 (1960)]). Other courts have followed the same reasoning. The California Supreme Court held that not only was the disclaimer invalid but the manufacturer and retailer were strictly liable in tort for the buyer's personal injuries (*Vandermark v. Ford Motor Co.* (61 Cal. 2d 256, 37 Cal.Rptr. 896, 391 P.2d 168 (1964)]). (See Section D in this chapter for a discussion of strict liability in tort.)

I. FAMILY USE OF GOODS

Section 2–318 provides that a seller's warranty extends to any natural person who is in the family or household of his or her buyer or who is a guest in his or her home if it is reasonable to expect that such person may use, consume, or be affected by the goods and thus could be injured by breach of the warranty. The purpose of this section is to give a limited class of beneficiaries the benefit of the same express or implied warranty that the buyer received regardless of lack of privity of contract. Virginia adopted a provision in lieu of Section 2–318 that eliminates the requirement of privity in all actions against the manufacturer and seller of goods for negligence and breach of warranty. California and Utah did not adopt Section 2–318, since prior case law went further and did not require privity of contract in the sale of food and drugs or in the case of an express warranty made by a manufacturer. Some states ignore the requirement that a guest must be in the buyer's home at the time of the damage.

Modern decisions permit recovery for property damage as well as for personal injuries.

The last sentence of Section 2–318 forbids the seller from excluding liability to persons to whom the warranties that benefit the buyer would extend under this section. It does not mean that a seller is precluded from excluding or disclaiming a warranty that might otherwise arise in connection with a sale if the exclusion is permitted under Section 2–316; nor does it preclude the seller from limiting the remedies of his own buyer and therefore of any beneficiaries under Section 2–718 or 2–719. Provisions which exclude or modify warranties, or limit remedies for breach of contract, apply equally to the beneficiaries under this section as well as to the buyer.

6. ASSUMPTION OF THE RISK AS A DEFENSE IN BREACH OF WARRANTY

In an action for breach of warranty, it is necessary for the plaintiff to prove the existence of the warranty, that the warranty was broken, and that the breach was the proximate cause of the loss sustained.

In most courts, assumption of the risk is a defense in an action for breach of warranty, because the plaintiff's conduct, rather than the seller's breach, is the proximate cause of the loss. For example, a buyer who was drinking a soft drink from a bottle gagged on a foreign substance. She spit out the substance and proceeded to finish the drink. As she finished the drink, she gagged again and discovered she had suffered injuries from the foreign substance (ground glass) still in the bottle. Her action in finishing the drink (following an examination of the contents that should have indicated the defect complained of) could be shown as a matter bearing on whether the breach itself (the particles of glass) was the cause of the injury. It could be found that her behavior broke the casual chain between the breach of warranty and her injury. In other words, she assumed the risk of injury.

7. CONTRIBUTORY NEGLIGENCE AS A DEFENSE IN BREACH OF WARRANTY

In most courts, the fact that the plaintiff's actions or inactions contributed to the injury is not available as a defense for the seller of the product. For example, plaintiff was reading a book and began eating a candy bar. She noticed that it did not taste just right. After eating about one-third she looked at it and saw that it was covered with worms and webbing. The court held for the plaintiff and said that in an implied warranty case there is no duty to inspect a candy bar before eating it (*Kassouf v. Lee Brothers, Inc.* [209 Cal. App. 2d 568, 26 Cal. Rptr. 276 (1962)]).

Some courts hold that contributory negligence is a defense relying on U.C.C. Section 2–316(3)(b). An overwhelming majority of courts refuse contributory negligence as a defense in the case of an express warranty.

8. NOTICE OF DEFECT

Section 2–607(3)(a) states that the buyer must notify the seller within a reasonable time after he or she discovers or should have discovered any breach or be barred from any remedy. This notice requirement is not necessary where the buyer does not bring suit against the immediate seller.

9. STATUTE OF LIMITATIONS

An action for breach of any contract for sale must be begun within four years after the cause of action has accrued (Section 2–725(1)). A cause of action accrues when the breach occurs, regardless of the aggrieved party's lack of knowledge of the breach. A breach of warranty occurs when tender of delivery is made (Section 2–725(2)).

D. STRICT LIABILITY IN TORT

1. IN GENERAL

The most important remedy in products liability cases today is strict liability in tort. It has several advantages over breach of warranty:

1. It is a simpler remedy requiring only that the product be defective, that the defect existed at the time it left the seller's hands, and that the defect caused the plaintiff's damages.

2. The requirement of privity of contract is completely eliminated.

3. The injured party does not have to give notice, as in the case of a breach of warranty.

4. The producer of a product cannot use his or her superior bargaining power or knowledge to disclaim liability, as disclaimers are ineffective.

5. The plaintiff may be any person foreseeably affected by the goods (e.g., buyer, user, consumer, employee, or bystander).

6. Contributory negligence generally is not a bar to the action.

The following description of the rules of strict liability in tort has been adoted in most courts. The Restatement, Second, Torts, Section 402A, provides:

1. One who sells any product in a defective condition unreasonably dangerous to the user or consumer or to his or her property is subject to liability for physical harm thereby caused to the ultimate user or consumer, or to his or her property, if

a. The seller is engaged in the business of selling such a product.

b. It is expected to and does reach the user or consumer without substantial change in the condition in which it is sold.

2. The rule stated in (1) applies although

a. The seller has exercised all possible care in the preparation and sale of his product.

b. The user or consumer has not bought the product from or entered into any contractual relation with the seller.

Regarding (1) the courts in some states (e.g., California) hold that it is not necessary to prove the product is unreasonably dangerous.

2. DANGEROUS OR DEFECTIVE PRODUCT

A. DANGEROUS PRODUCT

A retail seller of a product manufactured by a third person who knows or has reason to know that the product is dangerous or is likely to be dangerous is liable for bodily harm caused by the product unless the seller warns of the danger (e.g., failure to warn that prescription drug frequently caused cataracts). Failure to give complete instructions on the use of a product can incur liability.

The product does not have to be defective for liability to attach.

The modern trend is that the seller is liable, even though he or she did not know or had reason to know of the dangerous character, such as in the sale of a product in a sealed container.

In *Matthews v. Campbell Soup Co.* (380 F. Supp. 1061 [S.D. Tex., 1974]), the federal District Court applying *McKisson v. Sales Affiliates Inc.* (416 S.W. 2d 787 [Tex., 1967]) construed unwholesome or unfit food products to be unreasonably dangerous under Restatement, Second, Torts, Section 402A.

B. DEFECTIVE PRODUCT

A product may be defective owing to the careless production of a product involving the failure to follow an adequate design (e.g., a defect in the manufacture of an automobile). A product may also be defective because of improper design (e.g., placing the fuel tank in an automobile in such a location as to cause a fire on impact).

The modern trend is that the supplier of a product must make the product safe for uses other than the ones for which it is primarily intended. The supplier must consider any use that may be anticipated. For example, the manufacturer of paint should have anticipated that the paint might get into the eyes of the painter, causing blindness. Some courts refuse to follow this trend in the case of an automobile, on the basis that the intended purpose of an automobile does not include its participation in collisions with other objects. Those courts hold that the manufacturers are under no duty to protect passengers from the second-collision risk by making the car as crashworthy as possible.

Ordinarily no duty exists on the part of the manufacturer to alter the formula of a product that is a safe for normal use in order to avoid risk to a consumer who is allergic to the product. However, if an appreciable number of potentially allergic consumers may use the product, the seller is under a duty to warn the public where the danger is generally unknown.

3. ALL INVOLVED IN MARKETING PROCESS ARE LIABLE

All parties involved in the marketing process, whether manufacturer, distributor, retailer, manufacturer of the component part, assembler, lessor, licensor, or bailor are liable.

A. WHOLESALER

The Restatement, Second, Torts, Section 402A, provides that strict liability is imposed on any person engaged in the business of selling products for use or consumption who sells a defective product; that includes not only a manufacturer or retail seller but also a wholesaler or distributor.

B. SUPPLIERS OF PARTS

Frequently the manufacturer of a finished product purchased some of the components that went into the finished product from manufacturers of those components. Let us assume that an automobile manufacturer uses a component part for the brake system that has been made by another manufacturer and that the component part was defective. Most courts hold that the manufacturer of the defective component part is liable for injuries sustained by the user of the finished product as a result of that defective part if no essential change has been made in it by the manufacturer of the finished product. The liability is based on strict liability in tort. It is no defense that the manufacturer of the finished product failed to discover the defect by inspection or testing.

The manufacturer of the finished product is not excused from liability because of a defective condition resulting exclusively from a defective component part. Liability is based on breach of warranty, strict liability in tort, or negligence. If the manufacturer of the component part had a good reputation and if there had been no prior complaints or defects with respect to that part, such evidence would tend to show absence of negligence on the part of the manufacturer of the finished product. However, this would not preclude recovery on the grounds of breach of warranty or strict liability in tort.

c.　Secondhand Dealers

The trend is to hold secondhand dealers in strict tort liability for defective products.

d.　Lessor or Bailor

A lessor or bailor of personal property is liable for injuries caused by the defective condition of goods that makes them unreasonably dangerous (Restatement, Second, Torts, Section 408). California has extended its strict liability rule to include these parties (*Price v. Shell Oil Co.* [2 Cal. 3d 245, 85 Cal. Rptr. 178, 466 P. 2d 722 (1970)]).

e.　Seller of Real Estate

Recent decisions have extended the strict liability tort theory to the sale of real estate. In *Schipper v. Levitt & Sons, Inc.* (44 N.J. 70, 207 A.2d 314 [1965]), the court held a home developer liable on the theories of negligence, implied warranty, and strict liability where a hot water system had been installed in an apparently defective manner resulting in the scalding of the infant plaintiff (Schipper negligence principles held applicable to all builders in *Totten v. Gruzen* [52 N.J. 202, 245 A.2d 1 (1968)]). In *Kreigler v. Eichler Homes, Inc.* (269 Cal.App.2d 244, 74 Cal.Rptr. 749 [1969]), the home developer was held liable for the failure of a radiant heating system in a concrete slab foundation that failed after eight years of use. In *Avner v. Longridge Estates* (272 Cal.App.2d 607, 77 Cal.Rptr. 633 [1969]), the defendant was held liable for slope failure and pad subsidence due to inadequate soil compaction.

A builder-seller may be insolvent or uninsured, in which case the only remedy may be against the financier of the project. The lender may be liable (1) on the theory of negligence based on the fact that the lender exercised extensive control over the project and therefore assumed a duty of reasonable care to the ultimate purchasers (*Connor v. Great Western Savings and Loan* [69 Cal.2d 850, 73 Cal.Rptr. 369, 447 P.2d 609 (1968)] (2) as a joint venturer with the builder-developer, or (3) is an independent lot manufacturer who wholesales the subdivided lots to the developer. *Cf. Callaizakis v. Astor Development Co.* (4 Ill.App.3d 163, 280 N.E.2d 512 [1972]).

4. SERVICES

The general trend is to impose strict liability in tort in the case of services (e.g., patron's hair and scalp injured through the application of a permanent wave lotion). However, the doctrine is not used in the case of professional services, although a recent case held a hospital strictly liable for defective services rendered to a patient (*Johnson v. Sears, Roebuck and Co.* [355 F.Supp. 1065 (E.D.Wis., 1973)]).

5. ASSUMPTION OF RISK IN STRICT LIABILITY IN TORT

Generally, the user of a product who voluntarily and unreasonably proceeds to use the product in the face of danger that he or she knows or should know exists is barred from recovery on the grounds he or she assumed the risk of danger. Thus, if a conspicuous warning was on the label of a product, the use of the product could amount to an assumption of the risk and preclude recovery.

Generally, misuse or mishandling of the product will bar recovery (e.g., where a bottled beverage is knocked against a radiator to remove the cap). However, where the misuse is foreseeable, the maker has a duty to protect against the misuse by proper manufacture or design or by warning the user.

The Supreme Court of California in *Daly v. General Motors Corp.* (575 P.2d 1162 [1978]) held that assumption of the risk or product misuse will no longer be a complete bar to recovery and, instead, applied the comparative negligence doctrine (i.e., the plaintiff's recovery is reduced to the extent that his or her own lack of reasonable care contributed to the injury).

6. CONTRIBUTORY NEGLIGENCE IN STRICT LIABILITY IN TORT

Generally, when a plaintiff fails to discover a defect or to guard against the possibility it exists, such negligence is not a bar to recovery. This is true even when the consumer or user is careless in the use of the product, since in most courts, contributory negligence on the part of the plaintiff is no defense to the seller.

However, there can be no recovery when the plaintiff's conduct is the sole proximate cause of the injury (e. g., plaintiff was in a semiconscious state from a sleeping pill and her combustible nightgown caught fire while she was smoking a cigarette in bed).

7. STATUTE OF LIMITATIONS

State law varies as to when an action for strict liability in tort must be filed. The typical statutes provide that the action be filed within one, two, or three years from the date or injury.

8. DAMAGES IN STRICT TORT LIABILITY

It has been held that while an injured or damaged plaintiff can recover for both his or her personal injuries and property damage in an appropriate strict liability case, the plaintiff cannot recover for purely economic or commercial losses. However, the plaintiff may be able to recover under the theory of breach of express warranty, if that is applicable to the facts of the case.

Recent cases have awarded punitive damages and attorney fees in strict liability cases where the defendant has been guilty of concealing material facts concerning the safety of the product, where there has been an intentional misrepresentation of the product, or where the manufacturer has deliberately neglected for business reasons to caution customers and the public of a known defect (e. g., failure to redesign television set or warn of fire hazard that resulted in severe burns to plaintiff. *Gillham v. Admiral Corp.* (523 F.2d 102 [6th Cir., 1976], certiorari denied 424 U.S. 913, 96 S.Ct. 1113, 47 L.Ed.2d 318).

In *Grimshaw v. Ford Motor Co.* (119 Cal.App. 3d 757, 174 Cal Rptr. 348 [1981]), the Court of Appeals of California permitted a passenger who was badly burned in an explosion of a defective Pinto to collect both compensatory and punitive damages but disallowed recovery to the heirs of the deceased driver of the vehicle. The personal representative of the driver could have recovered punitive damages. The court reaffirmed the expectation of safety rule in such cases enunciated in *Barker v. Lull Engineering Co.* (20 Cal. 3d 413, 143 Cal. Rptr. 225, 573 P.2d 443 [1978]).

9. INTENTIONAL TORTS—DAMAGES

In *Sprague v. Frank J. Sanders Lincoln Mercury, Inc.* (120 Cal.App. 3d 412, 174 Cal. Rptr. 608 [1981]), plaintiff, injured by reason of the dealer's failure to repair known defects in a new car, introduced evidence of pain and suffering. The California reviewing court held that the suit was not in contract but properly alleged a tort (deceit, Civil Code sec. 1709), thus supported recovery of punitive damages.

ILLUSTRATIVE CASES

1. Warranty by Sample Includes Warranty of Fitness for Purpose

SWAN ISLAND SHEET METAL WORKS, INC. v. TROY'S CUSTOM SMOKING CO., INC.

49 Or.App. 469, 619 P. 2d 1326 (1980)

Troy, a commercial crab cooker, contracted with Swan to build two stainless steel crab cookers. The manufactured cookers were to be based on crab cookers Troy had in use and were to use gas burners. Swan's president, Bader agreed that Swan would seek outside expert help on the design of the burner. After consulting with knowledgeable persons, Bader sent Troy a brochure illustrating the type of burner selected by Bader's experts. The cooker and burner delivered to Troy never worked properly. The cooker ruined 1200 pounds of crab, due to cooking the crab too slowly and to a gas pilot light that was difficult to ignite and keep burning. Ultimately Troy returned the cooker to Swan without paying for it. Swan sued for the price, and Troy counterclaimed for damages based on breach of warranty for a particular purpose. Troy recovered damages after trial. Swan appealed.

WARREN, J. The following three conditions are necessary to create a warranty of fitness for a particular purpose: (1) The seller must have reason to know the buyer's particular purpose. (2) The seller must have reason to know that the buyer is relying on the seller's skill or judgment to furnish appropriate goods. (3) The buyer must, in fact, rely upon the seller's skill or judgment. [Citation.]

Plaintiff's major contention is that defendant did not rely on the plaintiff's expertise to furnish a suitable product.

The existence of a warranty of fitness for a particular purpose depends in part on the comparative knowledge and skills of the parties. There can be no justifiable reliance by a buyer possessing equal or superior knowledge or skill with respect to the product purchased by him. Since both Bader and Troy admitted ignorance of the design of gas burners, plaintiff argues, there could no justifiable reliance by defendant on plaintiff's expertise.

It is uncontested, however, that defendant relied on plaintiff to assemble the expertise necessary to select a suitable burner and design its placement relative to the crab pot. We conclude that where, as here, the parties expressly agree that the seller will seek outside expert advice with respect to the selection and design of a product to be purchased by the buyer, and the buyer relies on the seller to do so, the requirement of reliance * * * is satisfied. Such reliance by the buyer is reasonable. Commercial necessity also justifies such reliance, since a manufacturer must often consult outside specialists on the design and incorporation of component parts into a larger product built and sold by the manufacturer.

Swan Island also argues that Troy's merely relied on it to duplicate an existing crab cooker supplied by Troy's as a model and, therefore, did not rely on Swan Island's skill and judgment. When goods are manufactured in accordance with specifications supplied by the buyer, there is no warranty of fitness for a particular purpose, because the buyer does not rely on the seller's skill or judgment. [Citation.] Here, however, Swan Island did not simply follow Troy's specifications, since a different burner had to be substituted due to the unavailability of a burner to match the one on the old crab cooker.

Swan Island contends that there was no evidence that it was aware of the particular problems unique to cooking crab, and thus that it had no reason to know the particular purpose for which the cooker was required. Bader's testimony indicates, however, that at the time of contracting he was aware that the cooker required certain controls and that a rapid recovery time was essential in order for the cooker to fulfill its intended purpose.

*   *   *

Affirmed.

2. Implied Warranty That Food Fit for Human Consumption

WILLIAMS v. BRAUM ICE CREAM STORES, INC.

15 UCC Rep. 1919 (Okl. App. 1974), cert. denied 534 P. 2d 700 (1975)

REYNOLDS, J. Plaintiff [Williams] brought this action * * * for breaking a implied warranty of merchantability. Defendant's motion for summary judgment was granted. Plaintiff appeals from that ruling.

The uncontroverted facts in the case show that plaintiff purchased a "cherry pecan" ice cream cone from defendant's retail store. * * * Plaintiff ate a portion of the ice cream, and broke a tooth on a cherry pit contained in the ice cream. Plaintiff notified defendant of her injury and subsequently filed this action.

The trial court held that a cherry seed or pit found in ice cream made of natural red cherry halves was a substance natural to such ice cream * * *

There is a division of authority as to the test to be applied where injury is suffered from an object in food or drink * * *. Some courts hold there is no breach of implied warranty * * * if * * * the substance found in the food is natural to the ingredients of the type of food * * *. This rule, labeled the "Foreign-natural test" by many jurists, is predicated on the view that the practical difficulties of separation of ingredients in the course of food preparation (bones from meat or fish, seeds from fruit, and nutshell from the nut meat) is a matter of common knowledge. Under this * * * theory, there may be a recovery only if the object is "foreign" to the food served. * * *

The other line of authorities hold that the test to be applied is what should "reasonably be expected" by a customer in the food sold to him.

*   *   *

The "reasonable expectation" test as applied to an action for breach of implied warranty is keyed to what is "reasonably" fit. If it is found that the pit of a cherry should be anticipated in cherry pecan ice cream and guarded against by the consumer, then the ice cream was reasonably fit under the implied warranty.

In some instances, objects which are "natural" to the type of food but which are generally not found in the style of the food as prepared, are held to be the equivalent of a foreign substance.

We are not aware of any appellate decision in Oklahoma dealing with this precise issue.

We hold that the better legal theory to be applied in such cases is the "reasonable expectation" theory, rather than the "naturalness" theory * * *. What should be reasonably expected by the consumer is a jury question, and the question of whether plaintiff acted in a reasonable manner in eating the ice cream is also a fact question to be decided by the jury. * * *

Reversed and remanded.

3. Scope of Implied Warranty Liability Under U.C.C.

HARRIS v. THE ATLANTIC & PACIFIC TEA CO., INC.

23 Mass.App.Dec. 169 (1962)

GARVEY, J. * * * This is an action of contract or tort whereby the plaintiff seeks to recover for himself and his minor son for injury received by said minor son, Wayne Harris, *while attempting to open a beer bottle.*

I find that the plaintiff, William W. Harris, the father of Wayne Harris, purchased (on December 31, 1960, the reported evidence states) a quart bottle of beer from the defendant. He took the bottle home and that same evening asked his son, Wayne, a nine year old boy, to take the bottle out of the refrigerator and to open it. The boy did as he was requested and in the process of opening the bottle, the neck broke off inflicting a cut on the boy's finger.

The applicable sections of * * * U.C.C. relating to implied warranties and to whom they extend read:

> Sec. 2–314(1) Unless excluded or modified by section 2–316, a warranty that the goods shall be merchantable is implied in a contract for their sale if the seller is a merchant with respect to goods of that kind. Under this section the serving for value of food or drink to be consumed either on the premises or elsewhere is a sale. [The warranty applies to the bottle.]

> Sec. 2–314(2) Goods to be merchantable must at least be such as are fit for the ordinary purposes for which such goods are used.

> Sec. 2–318 A seller's warranty whether express or implied extends to any natural person who is in the family or household of his buyer or who is a guest in his home if it is reasonable to expect that such person may *use, consume or be affected by* the goods and who is injured in person by breach of the warranty. A seller may not exclude or limit the operation of this section. [Emphasis supplied.]

The plaintiff is one of the class of third parties now made beneficiaries of this warranty. * * * The trial judge's ruling that he found for the defendant on the theory that there "was no privity of contract" between the plaintiff and defendant; *was not correct.*

No case law being found or cited we are of the opinion it was also error to rule "that the defendant had no reason to expect that said minor plaintiff would be affected in any manner by the sale of the bottle of beer".

* * * Apparently the judge was of the opinion that because the bottle contained an alcoholic beverage a nine year old child wouldn't be expected to handle or be affected by it. We don't think merchants share his opinion— we don't. Children of this age are to be observed daily in modern stores handling bottled merchandise of all kinds at the invitation of sellers. It is "reasonable" to expect that they are thereby subject to being "affected" and "injured".

It was of no consequence that the bottle contained beer instead of milk, ginger ale, or one of the many kinds of beverages regularly purchased, used and consumed by members of families. There was nothing illegal, as argued by the defendant, in the plaintiff's handling of the bottle in his home. Bottled beer is part of the legal larder of many homes, and is frequently handled, and sometimes consumed with parental approval, by children. It was to be expected by the seller, in usual circumstances, that a father retained the parental prerogative of having his son fetch him a cold bottle of beer.

Prejudicial error being found, a new trial is ordered.

4. Disclaimer Must Be Conspicuous

DORMAN v. INTERNATIONAL HARVESTER CO.

46 Cal.App.3d 11, 120 Cal.Rptr. 516 (1975)

STEPHENS, J.   * * *Dorman entered into a "Retail Instalment Conditional Sales Contract" with I.H. purportedly on October 31, 1968 (he testified that he executed a second contract on November 3) to purchase a new tractor and backhoe for $12,912.26, including finance charges, and had paid a total of $7,233.68 on the contract. Dorman purchased this equipment for use in his earth-grading business and took delivery on November 4, 1968. The evidence adduced at trial shows that Dorman experienced problems with the tractor from the day he took delivery. The tractor broke down on numerous other occasions during the period of November 7, 1968 to August 21, 1969 and it had to be returned to I.H. for repairs. On August 13, 1969, Dorman sent a notice of rescission and breach of warranty to I.H., and filed suit on December 19, 1969.

At the outset of the trial, the court considered the issue of whether the retail instalment conditional sales contract contained a valid disclaimer of warranties. The disclaimer in question is shown in its context in the facsimile below (appearing after paragraph "9. Terms of Payment"):

The court concluded that the disclaimer provision was sufficiently conspicuous to constitute a valid disclaimer of the implied warranties of merchantability and fitness for particular purpose pursuant to California Uniform Commercial Code section 2316. The court thus limited the issues to be determined at trial to whether I.H. had fulfilled its standard printed warranty.

* * * Although Dorman did not assent to the disclaimer provision and did not read the contract at the time he signed it, the court concluded that the provision was conspicuous and that he should be charged with notice of the disclaimer.

California Uniform Commercial Code section 2316, subdivision (2), provides that an exclusion of the implied warranty of merchantability "in case of a writing must be conspicuous," and that an exclusion of the implied warranty of fitness for particular purpose "must be by a writing and conspicuous." The code defines "conspicuous" as "so written that a reasonable person against whom it is to operate ought to have noticed it. A printed heading in capital letters (as: Non-Negotiable Bill of Lading) is conspicuous. Language in the body of a form is 'conspicuous' if it is in larger or other contrasting type or color * * *. Whether a term or clause is 'conspicuous' or not is for decision by the court." (§ 1201, subd. (10).)

* * * In other words, section 2316 seeks to protect the buyer from the situation where the salesman's "pitch," advertising brochures, or large print in the contract, giveth, and the disclaimer clause—in fine print—taketh away.

Here, the disclaimer provision appears in close proximity to where Dorman signed the contract, but emphasized (italicized) the implied-warranties wording *"merchantability and fitness for particular purpose shall apply."* Although the disclaimer provision was printed in a slightly larger type face than was the preceding paragraph of the contract, it was not in bold face type, and we are of the opinion that it was not sufficiently conspicuous to have negated the implied warranties, particularly where no "standard printed warranty" was in fact given to Dorman at the time of execution of the contract. The slightly larger type face and location of the disclaimer paragraph are not conclusive. * * * The instant disclaimer does not reach that level of conspicuousness so as to exclude the right of the buyer to implied warranties which are an integral part of the transaction. * * * It thus violated the underlying rationale of section 2316 as set forth in the official comment of protecting the buyer from an unbargained for limitation in the purchase of a product. In order to have a valid disclaimer provision it must be in clear and distinct language and prominently set forth in large, bold print in such position as to compel notice. (§ 1201, subd. (10).) In the instant contract, the only large size type (in relation to other type on the page) that may satisfy these criteria is that used for the words "Additional Provisions" on the signature page (in a reference to matters on the reverse side of the contract which are extraneous to the warranties disclaimer). Though the size of the type in those words may be large enough, the remainder of the provision is insufficiently "conspicuous." The contract here also failed to have an adequate heading at the beginning of the disclaimer provision, such as "Disclaimer of Warranties," to call the buyer's attention to the disclaimer clause.

The attempted disclaimer of implied warranties in the instant case is ineffective for another reason. Construing the language of the provision strictly, the construction of the wording is ambiguous and could easily be misleading. A purchaser glancing at the provision would reasonably observe the *italicized* language, which reads: *"merchantability and fitness for the particular purpose shall apply,"* and would be lulled into a sense of security. This is directly contrary to the actual intent of the provision. "An implied warranty * * * must be disclaimed by the most precise terms; in other words, so clear, definite and specific as to leave no doubt as to the intent of the contracting parties."

*   *   *

We conclude that the disclaimer was insufficiently conspicuous to inform a reasonable buyer that he was waiving his right to have a quality product. * * *

The judgments on the complaint and cross-complaint are reversed.

5. Strict Liability in Tort (Defective Product)

VANDERMARK v. FORD MOTOR CO.

61 Cal.2d 256, 37 Cal.Rptr. 896, 391 P.2d 168 (1964)

TRAYNOR, Justice. In October 1958 plaintiff Chester Vandermark bought a new Ford automobile from defendant Lorimer Diesel Engine Company, an authorized Ford dealer doing business as Maywood Bell Ford. About six weeks later, while driving on the San Bernardino Freeway, he lost control of the car [due to a defect in the car]. It went off the highway to the right and collided with a lightpost. He and his sister, plaintiff Mary Tresham, suffered serious injuries. They brought this action for damages against Maywood Bell Ford and the Ford Motor Company, which manufactured and assembled the car. They pleaded causes of action and directed a verdict in favor of Maywood Bell on the warranty causes of action * * *.

Plaintiffs appeal.

Ford contends, however, that it may not be held liable for negligence in manufacturing the car or strictly liable in tort for placing it on the market without proof that the car was defective when Ford relinquished control over it. * * *

Retailers like manufacturers are engaged in the business of distributing goods to the public. They are an integral part of the overall producing and marketing enterprise that should bear the cost of injuries resulting from defective products. * * * In some cases the retailer may be the only member of that enterprise reasonably available to the injured plaintiff. In other cases the retailer himself may play a substantial part in ensuring that the product is safe or may be in a position to exert pressure on the manufacturer to that end; the retailer's strict liability thus serves as an added incentive to safety. Strict liability on the manufacturer and retailer alike affords maximum protection to the injured plaintiff and works no injustice to the defendants, for they can adjust the costs of such protection between them in the course of their continuing business relationship. Accordingly, as a retailer engaged in the business of distributing goods to the public, Maywood Bell is strictly liable in tort for personal injuries caused by defects in cars sold by it. * * *

Since Maywood Bell is strictly liable in tort, the fact that it restricted its contractual liability to Vandermark is immaterial. Regardless of the obligations it assumed by contract, it is subject to strict liability in tort because it is in the business of selling automobiles, one of which proved to be defective and caused injury to human beings. * * *

Accordingly, the trial court erred in directing a verdict for Maywood Bell on the so-called warranty causes of action. * * *

[Judgment for plaintiffs.]

6. Strict Liability in Tort (Defective Design)

HECKMAN v. FEDERAL PRESS CO.

587 F.2d 612 (3d Cir., 1978)

WEIS, J.

*   *   *

Plaintiff's left hand was severely injured when it was caught in a power press he was operating in the course of his employment with the Clark Equipment Company. He brought suit against the Federal Press Company, the manufacturer of the machine, alleging defective design because of the lack of an adequate safety device. A jury returned a verdict in favor of the plaintiff in the amount of $750,000 against Federal * * *.

The accident occurred on September 24, 1972, at the Clark factory in Reading, Pennsylvania as Heckman was using a foot pedal to operate the press. The machine functions by dropping a heavy ram onto a die, cutting or shaping the metal which rests on the lower surface. As plaintiff placed a piece of metal in the machine to be cut, the ram came down on his hand, resulting in the amputation of several fingers and other damage.

The press had been purchased by Clark in 1970. It could be operated in two different ways: with hand controls requiring the use of both hands on switches away from the point of operation, or, alternatively, by the use of a foot pedal, an optional item ordered by Clark. When the manual operation was used, the employee's hands necessarily were protected. However, when the foot pedal was utilized without a guard, there was nothing to prevent the hands from being placed in the operating area directly under the descending ram.

Federal did not provide safety appliances other than the dual buttons for manual operation except upon the customer's specific request and at its expense. When ordered, the guards were secured from other sources and attached by Federal. On delivery of the equipment to Clark, Federal sent a letter suggesting, *inter alia*, that the customer "obtain, install, and use 'point of operation' guarding for greater operator safety." In addition, the press itself had a warning plate with similar instructions for use.

Various types of safeguards designed to protect the operator were available on the market, including some designed to accommodate specific uses of the multi-purpose machine. Clark did in fact purchase a point-of-operation guard for $100, but it was not on the press at the time the injury occurred, and, in any event, its efficacy was challenged. Plaintiff produced expert testimony to establish that at least one type of appliance would be effective in about 95% of the customary uses of the press, and that the failure to supply such a device made the press defective within the meaning of Restatement (Second) of Torts § 402A (1965).

Federal contended it was not customary in the trade to furnish guards except upon request, and the multitude of uses to which the machine could be put made it impracticable to designate any one device as standard equipment. Moreover, Clark's failure to heed Federal's warning was said to be a superseding cause absolving defendant from all liability. Finally, Federal relied upon state regulations placing responsibility for the safe operation of presses upon employers and employees.

*   *   *

In answer to interrogatories, the jury found that Federal had sold a press in a defective condition * * *.

* * * In *Webb v. Zern*, (1966), Pennsylvania adopted the strict liability provisions of § 402A of the Restatement (Second) of Torts. Cases interpreting this section have held that lack of proper safety devices can constitute a defective design which may subject the manufacturer of machinery to liability. [Citations.]

*   *   *

Similarly here, plaintiff's expert maintained that the defendant should have provided safeguards to be used in connection with the foot pedal operation, and that effective implements were available at a reasonable cost. [Citation.]

Federal asserts that the bolster plate which Clark had installed blocked the operator's view of the machine's warning plate, and that this screening constituted a superseding cause insulating the manufacturer from liability. Thus, Federal's theory is that when Clark obscured the warning sign it effected a substantial change that became a superseding cause of the accident. But it cannot be said that as a matter of law the decreased visibility of the plaque was such a major departure from the original design of the machine as to cut off the manufacturer's obligations. [Citation.] Particularly is this so when the sign was addressed to a condition that was not latent. We are unwilling to accept the proposition that the warning plate in and of itself absolved Federal as a matter of law. As we observed in *Schell v. AMF, Inc.*:

> [A]s a matter of policy, it is questionable whether a manufacturer which produces a machine without minimal available safeguards is entitled to escape liability by warning of a dangerous condition which could reasonably have been avoided by a better design.

In the circumstances here, the warning issue was for the jury * * *.

* * * If a manufacturer fails to provide reasonable safety devices for a product and thus creates an unreasonable risk of harm to the user, the fact that the manufacturer may expect the user to provide a protective appliance is not sufficient to preclude liability in most circumstances. [Citations.] The issue is one which should be decided by a jury in light of such matters as the feasibility of incorporating safety features during manufacture of the machine, the likelihood that users will not secure adequate devices, whether the machinery is of a standard make or built to the customer's specifications, the relative expertise of manufacturer and customer, the extent of risk to the user, and the seriousness of injury which may be anticipated.

* * *

We conclude that the questions of liability were for the jury's consideration and it was not error to deny Federal's motion for judgment n.o.v.

* * *

7. Manufacturer Liable When Automobile Not Reasonably Safe in Collision

ARBET v. GUSSARSON

66 Wis.2d 551, 225 N.W.2d 431 (1975)

WILKIE, Chief Justice.   This is a "crashworthiness" products liability case arising from an automobile accident in which plaintiffs-appellants, Jane and Raymond Arbet were burned following the rupture of their vehicle's gasoline tank and ignition of the fuel. The Arbets sued defendant Mark Gussarson, the driver of the car that rear-ended their car, and defendant-respondent American Motors Corporation, the manufacturer of the Arbets' car. Gussarson is not a party to this appeal. The Arbets allege American Motors negligently designed and manufactured their car and that such negligence, while not causing the collision itself, did proximately cause the burn injuries. The trial court sustained American Motors' demurrer to plaintiffs' second amended complaint and judgment was entered accordingly. Plaintiffs appeal and we reverse.

The sole issue raised by this appeal is whether an automobile manufacturer may incur liability for injuries to occupants of a car arising from the manfacturer's negligence in designing the car such that it is unreasonably unsafe in an accident.

We conclude that the automobile manufacturer may, and we therefore uphold the complaint as against the demurrer of American Motors Corporation.

The second amended complaint alleges the following facts: On February 15, 1972, in Kenosha county, Raymond Arbet was driving and his wife Jane was a passenger in a 1967 Rambler Station Wagon that the couple had purchased new directly from American Motors. Raymond was waiting to make a left turn when the allegedly intoxicated defendant Gussarson allegedly negligently rammed his car into the rear of the Arbets' car. The sequence of events following the collision was as follows: The front seat failed, causing Jane Arbet to be propelled into the rearmost portion of the station wagon; all four doors jammed "blocking all possibility of normal exit," and preventing Raymond, who apparently escaped through a window, from quickly freeing his wife. The gas tank ruptured, spreading gasoline on the highway that was ignited by an unknown source; the heat from the fire melted a gas line "plastic vent container in the passenter compartment" causing fire inside the car, severely burning Jane Arbet and also burning Raymond as he tried to free his wife. The complaint then alleges that "neither plaintiff would have been injured by the fire if the station wagon had not been negligently designed."

*   *   *

[Under the doctrine of strict products liability] * * * where plaintiff shows that a manufacturer markets a product in a "defective condition" which is "unreasonably dangerous to the user," the manufacturer then has the burden to prove lack of negligence.

In the instant case, plaintiffs primarily allege that the car was defectively designed so that it was unreasonably dangerous in an accident. Plaintiffs do not ask that cars be built like Sherman tanks; rather, merely that they not contain design features rendering them unreasonably unsafe in an accident.

There is not question that the complaint alleges facts showing the car to be "unreasonably dangerous" in an accident—particularly the allegations concerning the plastic apparatus retaining gasoline in the passenger compartment incidate unreasonable danger.

The fact that the defect relates to *design* rather than *negligent manufacture* makes no difference. It must be noted also that the design characteristics complained of in the instant case were hidden dangers, not apparent to the buyer of the car, and not the subject of a manufacturer's warning. This is a different case, therefore, than a case where a plaintiff sues the manufacturer of a Volkswagen and complains that the car was designed too small to be safe. Such a defect could hardly be said to be hidden. To be an "unreasonably dangerous" defect for strict products liability purposes, comment *i* to sec. 402A, Restatement, 2 Torts 2d, says in part:

> The article sold must be dangerous to an extent beyond that which would be contemplated by the ordinary consumer who purchases it, with the ordinary knowledge common to the community as to its characteristics.

Thus, under this definition, since the ordinary consumer would expect a Volkswagen to be less safe in an accident than, say, a Cadillac, the smallness of the car with the attendant danger would not *per se* render it inherently dangerous. Rather it must contain a dangerous defect whose presence an ordinary consumer would not reasonably expect.

Additionally it is not important that the defect did not actually cause the initial accident, as long as it was a substantial factor in causing injury as alleged in plaintiffs' complaint. * * *

Defendant argues that there can be no liability here because plaintiffs *misused* the car, *i. e.* cars were not intended to be "used" to have an accident. Defendant argues that even though accidents are foreseeable, that does not establish a duty on the part of the manufacturer to design a reasonably safe car.

For two reasons, however, defendant is wrong. First, plaintiffs did not misuse the car. They did not intentionally have an accident or use the car to knock down trees in a forest. The accident occurred while plaintiffs were using the car for the purpose for which it was intended, normal driving on the highway. Second, even if the plaintiffs did misuse the car, that would not *ipso facto* defeat their claim if the misuse, or risk of an accident, was reasonably foreseeable. Clearly the risk that a car may be in a rear-end accident is reasonably foreseeable by defendant. Therefore, defendant has a duty to anticipate that risk. * * *

Thus it is clear that plaintiffs' complaint states a cause of action for strict products liability under Wisconsin law. * * *

* * *

Order and judgment reversed; cause remanded for further proceedings not inconsistent with this opinion.

8. Strict Liability Inapplicable to Commercial Transactions Between Parties of Equal Bargaining Power

SCANDINAVIAN AIRLINE SYSTEM v. UNITED AIRCRAFT
601 F.2d 425 (9th Cir., 1979)

Scandinavial Airline System (plaintiff) sued United Aircraft Corporation (defendant) for damages resulting from the failure of two separate jet aircraft engines on two different occasions.

United Aircraft contended that strict liability was not applicable to a commercial sale between two companies of relatively equal economic strength.

HUG, Circuit Judge. The first California case to adopt strict tort liability was *Greenman v. Yuba Power Products, Inc.* There the court stated:

> The purpose of such liability is to insure that the costs of injuries resulting from defective products are borne by the manufacturers that put such products on the market rather than by the injured persons who are powerless to protect themselves.

In *Price v. Shell Oil Co.,* the court concluded that the risk distribution principle was the fundamental policy behind the doctrine, stating:

> Essentially, the paramount policy to be promoted by the rule is the protection of otherwise defenseless victims of manufacturing defects and the spreading throughout society of the cost of compensating them.

The trial judge's decision does not conflict with the risk distribution rationale in California products liability law. SAS and United are financial equals. Further, both are business entities who sell a product or perform a service which is ultimately paid for by SAS's customers. As a result, "[w]hether the loss is thrust initially upon the manufacturer (United) or consumer (SAS), it is ultimately passed on as a cost of doing business included in the price of the products of one or the other and thus spread over a broad commercial stream." Unlike the consumers in *Greenman* and *Price,* SAS can allocate its risk of loss equally as well as United. Therefore, the societal interest in loss shifting present in those cases is absent here.

Although of less significance than the risk-spreading rationale, several other policies have been identified as underlying the doctrine of strict products liability in California. The consumer's difficulty in inspecting for defects has impliedly been stated as a reason for its application. Another policy concerns the difficulty a consumer faces in trying to prove negligence. . . . About it, the court stated:

> We imposed strict liability against the manufacturers and in favor of the user or consumer in order to relieve injured consumers "from problems of proof inherent in pursuing negligence . . . and warranty . . . remedies. . . ."

Finally, "[t]he rule of products liability is further rationalized as an inducement to manufacturers to design and produce a safe product . . ., and as a means to avoid the artificial conditions to recovery in warranty created by the rules of privity."

Here, SAS had the expertise and personnel to inspect the engines for defects. SAS does not have the lack of technical knowledge and expertise which would burden members of the general public in proving negligence in designing or manufacturing the engines. SAS does not face problems of privity as an artificial barrier which the doctrine of strict liability seeks to avoid. Finally, the fact that United will still be liable to airline passengers for any injuries they receive as the result of defective United products will serve as a significant deterrent from manufacturing unsafe products.

The trial judge's decision finds strong support in *Kaiser Steel Corp. v. Westinghouse Elec. Corp.* There the California Court of Appeals stated:

> . . . [T]he doctrine of products liability does not apply as between parties who: (1) deal in a commercial setting; (2) from positions of relatively equal economic strength; (3) bargain the specifications of the product; and (4) negotiate concerning the risk of loss from defects in it.

Interpreting these four requirements as the court did in *Kaiser* leads us to the conclusion that SAS does not have a claim in strict tort liability against United. SAS, United and McDonnell Douglas dealt in a commercial setting from positions of relatively equal economic strength. The specifications of the engines were negotiated by the parties. Finally, McDonnell Douglas, United and SAS all negotiated the risk of loss for defects in the engines.

Judgment for United Aircraft affirmed.

PROBLEMS

1.   Cutter Laboratories manufactured and sold Salk polio vaccine. One shipment mistakenly contained live virus instead of only inactivated virus. The vaccine was injected into children and caused poliomyelitis. In the action against them, Cutter Laboratories defends on the grounds that there was no privity of contract between the manufacturer and the buyer, since the buyer purchased the vaccine from the pharmacy and not from them; and since the plaintiff's children were not the actual buyers, but their doctors. Decision?

2. P, the manager of a hotel, purchased on behalf of his employer four bottles of champagne produced and bottled by D. The champagne was to be consumed by guests of the hotel. While P was preparing the champagne for use, a cap from one of the bottles suddenly ejected and hit P in the eye, causing serious injury. P sues D for breach of warranty. D defends on the grounds that the warranty does not extend to an employee. Decision?

3. P's wife, after reading a manufacturer's brochure, purchased a combination power tool. Due to defective design and construction, the tool could hurl a piece of wood through the air, hitting the user. P was so injured and brings action for his injuries. The retailer and the manufacturer defend on the grounds that there was no breach of warranty, and that only the wife who purchased the tool can recover. Decision?

4. B purchased a two-year old International Harvester tractor truck "as is" from S. About two years after the purchase, B was doing some work on the engine. To get at the motor required raising the cab and securing it with a latch. The cab suddenly collapsed due to a defective latch, fell on B and killed him. His widow sued both S and International Harvester for breach of warranty and strict liability in tort. Discuss.

5. Buyer informed seller that he wanted a weedkiller to use on some weeds between his orange trees. Seller sold buyer a particular brand that would kill the weeds but could also damage his orange trees, even if used in the normal manner. Seller did not warn the buyer that the product would damage the trees if the buyer used it as he planned. Buyer used the product as he planned and damaged his trees. Decision?

6. B purchased a wooden sailing sloop from S. During the course of negotiations prior to sale, S orally stated that the sloop would "make up" and become watertight within a short time after being put into the water. The sloop leaked after allowance for "make up" in the water. B thereafter sued to cancel the contract and recover back the purchase price. S argued that there was no express warranty of seaworthiness at the time of the sea trial of the sloop, but, if any, only at the time of sale, and that there was no proof of what caused the sloop to leak. Decision?

7. The Hafens purchased a mobile home from Tyson, the owner of the home, who had previously purchased the home from Progress Homes, the manufacturer. Tyson was not an employee or selling agent of Progress Homes. Many defects uncovered by the Hafens after the purchase revealed the home to be substantially less in value than the contract price. The Hafens sued Progress Homes for the difference in value. Progress Homes defended on the ground that they did not sell the home to the Hafens, and that Progress Homes was not liable to the Tysons for economic loss in the absence of a direct contractual relationship. Decision?

8. C, a consumer, purchased from S, a butcher, a raw pork roast sliced into pork chops. C did not ask S for how long and at what temperature pork chops should be cooked to render them free of trichinosis parasites. (Such parasites are present in raw pork and cause serious illness of those who eat improperly cooked pork products.) C prepared the chops by frying them for fifteen minutes and then boiling them for one hour over a medium gas flame. The temperature required to make pork safe for consumption, 137° F, was not achieved by this cooking method. After consumption,

C became very ill and had to be hospitalized. C sued S for strict liability in tort. Decision?

9. While cleaning her home, M put a closed can of crystal drain opener on a table next to her infant's crib. The family cat jumped upon the table and tipped the can of drain opener over into the crib. The impact of the fall caused the can to open. The infant, attracted to the can by its pretty packaging, began to play with the crystals, and suffered serious injuries. M, suing on behalf of the infant, sought to recover damages for faulty packaging of the compound. Decision?

10. Ruth, driving a van manufactured by Elway Motors, suffered a rear-end collision caused by another vehicle. Upon collision, Ruth's head was forced backward against the rear window of the van's cab, causing serious injuries. No head-rest was installed in the van, and no such safety equipment was mandated by law at that time. Ruth sued to recover under strict liability in tort. Decision?

Chapter 31

SECURED TRANSACTIONS UNDER THE U.C.C.

A. IN GENERAL

A secured transaction is "any transaction (regardless of its form) which is intended to create a security interest in personal property or fixtures including goods, documents, instruments, general intangibles, chattel paper or accounts; and also any sale of accounts or chattel paper." (Section 9–102(1)). For example, the owner of a business in need of funds seeks a loan from the bank. The loan officer requires security. The owner puts up his inventory as security. If the owner does not pay the loan, the bank can use the inventory as security for payment. This is one form of a secured transaction.

Prior to the U.C.C., many devices were used for giving a creditor a security interest in personal property (i. e., to permit him or her to reclaim the property on default or to give him or her a preferred interest against other creditors). These security interests were known as pledges, assignments, chattel mortgages, trust receipts, trust deeds, inventory liens, equipment trusts, conditional sales, and leases and consignments intended as security. Although these devices have not been abolished by the U.C.C., their labels now have no legal significance. Whatever name the parties use makes no difference, because the U.C.C. looks through the name to the substance of the transaction. Now these devices are called "security agreements"; the interest created, a "security interest"; the borrower or credit buyer, a "debtor"; and the lender, credit seller, or buyer of accounts, contract rights, or chattel paper, a "secured party" (Sections 1–201(37), 9–105).

Article 9 of the U.C.C. covers nearly all security interests in personal property and fixtures. The principal exceptions are state statutes that regulate consumer installment sales and consumer loans; security interests perfected under a federal statute; wage assignments; interests in real estate, except fixtures; mechanic liens; claims arising out of judicial proceedings; equipment trusts covering railway rolling stock; transfers of claims under insurance policies; transfer of deposit, savings, and other accounts maintained with a bank, savings and loan association, credit union, or similar organization.

B. CREATION OF SECURITY INTEREST

For a secured transaction to be effective, three requirements are necessary:

1. The collateral (e. g., a ring) must be in the possession of the secured party (lender or seller) *or* the debtor must have signed a security agreement.

2. There must be an attachment of the secured party's security interest to the collateral.

3. There must be a perfection of the security interest.

The following case illustrates the creation of a security interest.

FACTS Plant Reclamation sold equipment to Amex-Protein in exchange for a promissory note. The note included the following line: "This note is secured by a security interest in subject personal property per invoices." The referee held that the note did not create a valid security interest.

DECISION The federal court reversed the referee, holding that the language of the note created or provided for a security interest (U.C.C. Section 9–105(h)). No magic words or precise form are necessary to create or provide for a security interest so long as the minimum formal requirements of the Code are met. Although the promissory not did not describe the collateral, it made reference to other available documents that provided an adequate description (U.C.C. Section 9–110).

Matter of Amex-Protein Development Corp. (507 F.2d 1056 [9th Cir., 1974])

C. SECURITY AGREEMENT

Security agreement means an agreement between the secured party (creditor) and the debtor that creates or provides for a security interest (Section 9–105(l)).

The security agreement must be in writing, signed by the debtor, and contain a description of the collateral sufficient to reasonably identify it. However, if the security arrangement is a possessory one and the secured party is in possession of the collateral, the arrangement does not have to be in writing (Section 9–203). The security agreement may contain any terms and provisions that the parties desire, but the agreement must be fair to the debtor.

The importance of a sufficient description of collateral in both the financing statement and the security agreement (and the greater need for it in the security agreement) is discussed in the following case.

FACTS The security agreement between American Restaurant Supply Company (plaintiff) and Wilmark (debtor) described the collateral as "Foodservice equipment and supplies delivered to San Marco Inn at St. Marks, Florida." The trial court held that the description was inadequate

(U.C.C Section 9–203(1)) and that the security interest was not legally enforceable.

DECISION   Affirmed. A security agreement should describe collateral with details sufficient for third parties to be able to reasonably identify the particular assets covered. The agreement here does not make possible the identification of the equipment and was therefore not legally sufficient to be enforced.

American Restaurant Supply Co. v. Wilson (371 So.2d 489 [Fla.App., 1979])

D. ATTACHMENT

The U.C.C. uses the term "attach" to indicate when the security interest in favor of a secured party is created in the debtor's property (i.e., the security agreement becomes enforceable between the parties and is said to "attach"). The security interest attaches and the lender takes a security interest in the debtor's property when three requirements have been met:

1.   There must be a security agreement signed (not in blank).

2.   The secured party must have given value (value is given when the secured party advances the money).

3.   The debtor must have rights in the collateral (e. g., debtor owns the collateral).

These requirements may occur in any order. For example, the creditor may advance money immediately to the debtor on agreement that property to be acquired by the debtor in the future will be subject to a security interest in the creditor's favor (when the debtor acquires the rights in the collateral, the security interest will attach).

Although the three events may occur in any order, they must coexist before the interest attaches. For example, debtor and lender agree on May 1 that lender will loan $10,000 against debtor's inventory. On June 1, debtor receives the money from lender. The security interest did not attach until June 1, when debtor received the value.

Similar to the right to security in after-acquired property is the floating lien (Sections 9–204, 9–205). This is a security interest in constantly changing collateral. It has been called a floating lien, a lien on shifting stock, an inventory lien, a free-handed mortgage, and a floating charge. In this type of lien, the debtor (e. g., retail seller) has the right to use, commingle, or dispose of all or part of the collateral; to collect or compromise accounts, contract rights, or chattel paper; or to use, commingle, or dispose of proceeds. It is not necessary for the secured party to require the debtor to account for the proceeds or to replace the collateral.

The floating lien may be used only with respect to inventory or accounts receivable, but of course, it may be used to tie up all of a debtor's assets. It is a highly useful lien in inventory and accounts receivable financing in that it permits a businessperson to pledge property to be obtained in the future and to use the collateral to make money rather than holding it as a stationary asset and gives the secured party an automatically perfected security interest in each item of after-acquired collateral immediately on its acquisition by the debtor.

E. PERFECTION OF SECURITY INTEREST

After the debtor and the secured party make the security agreement and after the secured party's security interest attaches to the collateral, it is necessary to perfect the security interest to make it valid against third parties (e.g., other secured parties, attaching creditors, or a trustee in bankruptcy). Perfecting is not necessary for the secured party to enforce his or her interest against the debtor. That is done by the security agreement and the attaching of the security interest. However, it is necessary to perfect the security interest to make it good against third parties. The purpose of perfection is to give notice to all persons who may be dealing with the debtor that the secured party has or may have a security interest in the collateral.

Three methods of perfecting a security interest are used. The method used depends on the kind of collateral involved.

1. PERFECTION BY ATTACHMENT

Attachment by itself is sufficient to constitute perfection in a limited number of transactions (e. g., installment sales to consumers) (Section 9–302). This is because the burden that filing would place upon retail sellers who typically advance credit in the form of retail-installment contracts would outweigh any interest in protecting other creditors who might look to the collateral of the debtor in payment of their claims.

Perfection by attachment gives a limited protection to the secured party. It does not give the secured party-creditor protection against the rights of a good faith purchaser who purchases the collateral from the consumer-debtor without knowledge of the secured party's interest, pays value, and purchases for his or her (good faith purchaser's) own family household use or for his or her own farming operation (Section 9–307). Thus, a secured party should file a financing statement for more complete protection.

2. PERFECTION BY POSSESSION

Possession of the collateral (e. g., a ring) by the secured party gives notice of the secured party's security interest, making it unnecessary to file a financing statement (Section 9–302).

Possession is the required and exclusive method of perfecting a security interest in an instrument. The word "instrument" includes the following: (1) negotiable instruments (Section 3–104), (2) securities (Section 8–102), and (3) other rights to payment evidenced by writings that are in the ordinary course of business transferred by delivery with any necessary indorsement or assignment (e. g., government warrants) (Sections 9–304, 9–305).

3. PERFECTION BY FILING A FINANCING STATEMENT

The most common method of perfecting a secured party's security interest in the collateral is by filing a financing statement with the proper governmental agency. A financing statement is a document that is signed by both the debtor and the secured party and contains the names and addresses of the parties and a description of the types or items of collateral covered. Any description of personal property or real estate is sufficient whether or not it is specific if it reasonably identifies what is described. Minor errors that are not seriously misleading will not destroy its effectiveness (see Sections 9–110, 9–402).

A financing statement is *not* a substitute for a security agreement. A security agreement may be filed as a financing statement if it contains the required formalities. But because a security agreement often contains details that the parties prefer not to reveal in a public notice, the parties prefer to file the simple financing statement. A person searching the records to ascertain if the debtor's property is subject to a security interest will learn very little from a financing statement except that the property may be subject to a security interest. The person must therefore go to the parties for further information, and there is a procedure to follow in obtaining such information

Sections 9-401 provides for three alternatives regarding the place where the financing statement is to be filed, for example e.g., local filing (county), central filing (Secretary of State), or a combination of both local and central. Because states have used all three alternatives plus variations, local rules must be consulted in this area.

Filing a financing statement is required in the following secured transactions: (1) intangible collateral (i.e., contract rights, accounts, and general intangibles) (examples of general intangibles are any interest or claim in or under any policy of insurance, goodwill, literary rights, patents, and copyrights) and (2) goods (i.e., inventory and equipment in general) (for definitions, see Sections 9–106, 9–109(1), 9–109(2)(4), and 9–109(3)).

Filing is permissive in secured transactions involving chattel paper and negotiable instruments (Section 9–304).

A filing is effective for only five years. Unless a continuation statement is filed prior to the expiration of the five-year period, the perfection of the security interest terminates. A continuation statement is a declaration by the secured party that identifies the original filing statement by its file number and declares that it is still effective. Successive continuation statements will continue the perfection indefinitely.

F. PRIORITIES

Following are common examples of priorities between conflicting security interests.

1. BETWEEN PERFECTED INTERESTS

Priority goes to the secured party who first files or perfects his or her interest. For example, lender advances funds to debtor and files on June 1, knowing that another creditor, T, has a prior security interest in the same collateral, although T's interest has not been perfected. T files on June 5. Lender's interest is entitled to priority, even though he knew of the prior unperfected interest.

2. BETWEEN NONPERFECTED INTERESTS

When neither of the conflicting security interests has been perfected, the rule is that the first interest that attaches is given priority (i. e., the date of attachment). However, this priority lasts only as long as both interests remain unperfected. If a later interest perfects first, it takes priority.

Between a nonperfected interest and other interests, a nonperfected interest generally loses. For example, a secured party who has not perfected his or her interest loses to a lien creditor or trustee in bankruptcy even if the creditor or trustee had notice of the secured interest. Likewise, the secured party loses to a purchaser or assignee of the collateral to the extent that the purchaser gave value and took without notice of the security interest.

3. PURCHASE MONEY SECURITY INTEREST

A purchase money security interest is a security interest taken or retained by the seller of collateral to secure repayment of all or a part of the purchase price. In other words, the seller of property finances the sale with his or her own property, retaining the right to recover the property so as to satisfy any outstanding loan balance in case the buyer fails or refuses to pay.

A purchase money interest generally takes priority over conflicting security interests in the same collateral if the interest is perfected when the debtor takes possession of the collateral or within 10 days thereafter (Section 9–312(3), (4)). For example, a secured party, A, takes a security interest in equipment owned by D and equipment to be after acquired by D. A promptly files. Later, seller sells new equipment to D and takes back a security interest in the new equipment to secure payment of the unpaid purchase price (a purchase money interest). Seller promptly files. Seller's interest prevails.

The above rule applies whether it is a noninventory (e. g., equipment) purchase or an inventory (held for immediate or ultimate sale) purchase. However, if it is an inventory purchase, the secured party's interest must be perfected at the time the debtor receives the collateral (he or she does not have the 10-day grace period) and the secured party must give written notice to any other security interest holder who has previously filed a financing statement covering the inventory of the same type of goods that will be covered in the purchase money security interest (Section 9–312(3)(a)(b)).

The following case illustrates the purchase money security interest.

FACTS   In March, R. L. Moody executed a security agreement in favor of the Sherman County Bank that included a typical after-acquired property clause that created a security interest in all property subsequently acquired by Moody involving his farming operation. On August 15, Moody purchased certain farm equipment and signed a security agreement with the seller. The seller filed the associated financing statements on September 8 and October 9.

DECISION   The seller had a purchase money security interest in the property. Under U.C.C. Section 9–312, the seller's purchase money security interest has priority over the bank's conflicting security interest if the purchase money security interest is perfected at the time the debtor receives possession of the colleteral or within 10 days thereafter. The trial court had looked only toward the date that the purchaser signed the sales contract, August 15, and held for the bank. The appellate court reversed and remanded the case to determine the date of actual physical possession by the purchaser.

Sherman County Bank v. Kallhoff (205 Neb. 392, 288 N.W. 2d 24 [1980])

4. PRIORITY BETWEEN CONFLICTING SECURITY INTERESTS RE FUTURE ADVANCES

The secured party is protected in making future advances to the debtor so long as he or she originally perfected the security interest by filing or taking possession (Section 9–312(7)). The financing statement need not mention anything about future advances. The statement gives constructive notice that some sort of security interest exists, and it is up to the searcher to find out the nature of the interest and what it secures.

5. PRIORITY RE AFTER-ACQUIRED PROPERTY

As a general rule, the secured party under an after-acquired property clause will prevail against other creditors or interest holders including the debtor's trustee in bankruptcy (Section 9–108). For example, lender loaned money to D and took a security interest in D's inventory (both present and after-acquired). Later D, while insolvent, purchased raw material on credit from sellers. Shortly thereafter, sellers discovered D's insolvency and attempted to reclaim the raw material under Section 2–702. Lender claimed the goods under its after-acquired clause. Lender prevails (Sections 2–702(3) and 9–108).

An exception to the general rule is the purchase money security interest (Section 3 in this chapter).

6. PRIORITY OF CERTAIN CLASSES

Certain classes of creditors and interest holders have a priority over perfected security interests: holders of mechanic liens (Section 9–310); good faith purchasers in the ordinary course of business (Section 9–307(1)); the holder in due course of a negotiable instrument (e. g., a check) (Section 9–309); and certain purchasers of chattel paper and nonnegotiable instruments (Section

9–308). The following is an example of Section 9–308. The dealer of automobiles obtains financing of his inventory from a credit corporation (flooring lender). The flooring lender files a financing statement covering the inventory or its proceeds. The dealer sells an automobile to a private party on a conditional sales contract and then sells the paper to a bank. The competing priorities collide where the dealer gets into financial trouble and still has the collateral (automobile) or its proceeds. In such a case, the bank that financed the retail purchase prevails.

The following case illustrates the priority of a perfected security interest.

> **FACTS**　An automobile dealer sold a car on credit for private use and sold the financing paper to the plaintiff bank. Later the original buyer sold the car to another car dealer, who sold to defendant, Jones. Jones purchased the car in good faith and without notice that his purchase was in violation of the bank's security interest. Plaintiff brought suit in the amount outstanding under the original credit agreement. Defendant argued that he was a buyer in the ordinary course of business (U.C.C. Section 1–201(9)) and thus took free of the perfected security interest.
>
> **DECISION**　Defendant is liable to the plaintiff for the outstanding amount of the original sales agreement. U.C.C. Section 9–307(1) provides that the buyer of goods in the ordinary course of business takes free of a security interest created by the seller. Here, the bank's security interest was created not by the defendant's seller but by the first dealer. Thus, U.C.C. Section 9–307(1) does not apply, and defendant does not take free of plaintiff's security interest.
>
> *National Shawmut Bank of Boston v. Jones* (108 N.H. 386, 236 A.2d 484 [1967])

7.　CONFLICTING STATE REQUIREMENTS

Section 9–302(3) expressly exempts from the filing requirements of Article 9 any personal property covered by a certificate of title (e. g., automobiles, mobile homes, trailers, boats). In those states that have a certificate title system, compliance with that law is the only way in which a security interest can be perfected in collateral subject to such laws. In the few states that do not have a certificate of title system, filing under the U.C.C. is the proper method of perfecting a security interest.

G.　DEFAULT OF DEBTOR

The security agreement determines when the debtor defaults. Some of the typical default clauses that define a debtor's default are noninsurance of collateral, removal of collateral, loss or destruction of collateral, bankruptcy or assignment for benefit of creditors, and nonpayment.

1. BASIC REMEDIES ON DEFAULT

The secured party's remedies and conduct in the event of default are limited by implied standards of good faith and constitutional due process.

The three basic remedies of the secured party are (1) sale or other disposition of the collateral (Section 9–504), (2) retention of the collateral (Section 9–505(2)), and (3) an action for the debt (Section 9–501(1)).

2. SECURED PARTY'S RIGHT TO TAKE POSSESSION

Section 9–503 gives the secured party the right to take possession of the collateral upon the debtor's default; however, the secured party must do so peaceably.

The question has arisen several times as to whether or not Section 9–503 is constitutional. That is, is taking a debtor's property without court proceedings a violation of the constitutional guarantee that property shall not be taken without due process of law under the Fourteenth Amendment to the Constitution of the United States? Is some notice to the debtor and an opportunity for hearing necessary?

The majority of courts have held that Section 9–503 is constitutional. For example, in *Adams v. Southern Calif. First Nat. Bank* (492 F.2d 324 [9th Cir., 1973], certiorari denied 419 U.S. 1006, 95 S.Ct. 325, 42 L.Ed.2d 282), the court held that the state of California was not so significantly involved in the self-help repossession procedures undertaken by the creditors as to permit the court to find the "state action" (conduct under color of state law) required to establish a federal cause of action. In other words, due process is a limitation only where "state action" is involved, and repossessions by private persons pursuant to the provisions of the security agreement do not involve "state action." The United States Supreme Court has refused to decide the constitutionality of Section 9–503 up to this time.

If a creditor repossesses the collateral when the debtor is not in default, the creditor commits a conversion. This is also the case when the creditor repossesses the wrong collateral. In addition to compensatory damages for the conversion, the debtor can recover punitive damages when the creditor has acted recklessly and with willful indifference.

ILLUSTRATIVE CASES

1. Enforcement of Security Interest
AETNA FINANCE CO. v. SUMMERS
642 P.2d 926 (Colo., 1982)

ERICKSON, Justice.

*   *   *

* * * On July 7, 1978, * * * Dorothy Summers, executed and delivered a promissory note in the amount of $1,434.60, payable in thirty monthly installments to the Aetna Finance Company (Aetna). To secure the note, which included an acceleration clause, Aetna acquired a security interest in certain household goods and furnishings belonging to Summers. Thereafter, Summers failed to make the payments on the note which were due in January and February 1979. On February 8, 1979, Aetna mailed a "Notice of Default and Consumer's Right to Cure" to Summers by certified mail, return receipt requested. The notice was mailed to Summers at her residence address which was correctly reflected in Aetna's records and which was set forth in the promissory note. The envelope containing the notice was subsequently returned to Aetna by the postal service marked "unclaimed," and the return receipt was returned unsigned. Summers testified at trial that she had never received a notice from the post office of an attempt to deliver a certified letter to her residence.

Upon receipt of the unclaimed notice, Aetna took no further action to provide notice of default and right to cure to Summers. Even though Summers maintained her residence at the same address and Aetna was aware of her place of employment, Aetna did not send her another copy of the notice by regular mail and did not attempt to personally serve her with a copy at her home or place of employment. Consequently, Summers did not receive notice of default and did not have an opportunity to exercise her right to cure.

* * *

Under the Colorado Consumer Credit Code, a creditor may neither accelerate maturity of the unpaid balance of an obligation nor take possession of or otherwise enforce a security interest in the goods that are collateral until twenty days after a notice of the debtor's right to cure is given.
* * *

The purpose of giving notice of the debtor's right to cure is to permit the debtor-creditor relationship to continue if the default is cured. By requiring notice of the default, the statutory preference is to cure rather than to disrupt the debtor-creditor realtionship by judicial or extra-judicial action against the debtor and the collateral. Even though section 111(1) does not require the creditor to prove that the notice was received by the debtor, and permits mailing of the notice as an alternative to actual delivery, the Colorado Consumer Credit Code evidences a legislative intent to provide debtors with notice of default and of their right to cure the default. When the notice, which Aetna sent by certified mail was returned "unclaimed," Aetna was aware that Summers had not received the notice of default and of her right to cure. To hold that Aetna satisfied the statutory notice requirement when it had actual knowledge that the notice was not received would defeat the purpose and intent of section 111(1).

* * * [O]nce Aetna had actual knowledge that Summers had not received the notice, it was incumbent upon Aetna to satisfy the statutory notice requirement by personal service or by sending the notice by regular mail to Summers' home. Sending the notice by regular mail would have satisfied section 111(1) and raised the presumption that the notice was left at Summers' address in accordance with regular mail delivery procedures and was therefore received.

In this case, Aetna took the precaution of sending the notice to Summers by certified mail, return receipt requested, in an attempt to conclusively establish receipt of the notice by a signed return receipt. However, the limitations of such method of delivery actually create a greater potential of nondelivery and do not necessarily provide the same opportunity for receipt of notice that would be available if regular mail service was used:

> If mailed in the ordinarily unregistered letter, the notice would be delivered at the address named or forwarded and thus reach the party. If directed, however, to an indivicual living at such address in a manner requiring a personal receipt, it is obvious it could not be delivered unless that person were available and the receipt personally given.

In the event that no one is at the debtor's residence when the certified mail arrives, it is returned to the post office and, unless the debtor receives notice of the attempted delivery and subsequently obtains the letter from the post office, notice is not provided as contemplated by section 111(1).

The goal of preserving the debtor-creditor relationship is not furthered by construing section 111(1) to permit a creditor to avoid giving notice by using certified mail and then ignoring irrefutable evidence that the debtor has not received notice. Since Aetna did not comply with section 111(1) by providing notice after the certified letter was returned "unclaimed," Summers was denied her statutory right to cure the default prior to the filing of a legal action against her. Under the circumstance, Aetna was required to deliver the notice to Summers or to effect service by the use of regular mail before declaring a default on the consumer loan.

Accordingly, the judgment of the court of appeals is affirmed.

2. Perfection of Security Interest in Consumer Goods

IN RE McFADDEN

18 B.R. 758 (Bkrtcy. Ark., 1982)

The Bankruptcy Court held herein that a Sony Betamax video cassette recorder, owned by the debtor, was used substantially for business and income purposes of the debtor; and that, since appellant did not file on the equipment with the Secretary of State and the County Clerk, as required for business equipment in Arkansas by *Ark.Stat.Ann.* § 85–9–401(c) (Add.1961), appellant was a general creditor and dismissed its Petition for Reclamation.

Appellant seeks a remand, contending that the Bankruptcy Court refused to allow appellant to present rebuttal testimony and to otherwise present evidence to support its position.

*   *   *

The debtor received the subject video cassette recorder in September, 1977.

*   *   *

Based on * * * testimony, the debtor conclusionarily estimates that 60% of his use of the recorder was for business and 40% was personal. But this opinion is not borne out. * * * Even at the outset of his use of the recorder, from September 8, 1977, to the termination of his employment * * *, the debtor, according to his own testimony, used the recorder for business purposes only on an average of once a week * * *. This testimony, rendered by the debtor who should have had the motive and been willing to specify the average time per week spent on business use if it in fact exceeded the average spent on personal use, warrants an inference that the average weekly hour [sic] spent on personal use exceeded the average per week spent on use for business purposes. This finding is sufficient to warrant a conclusion that the "primary" use * * * was personal rather than business. * * *

Even if the subsequent use of the recorder is relevant to the matter of filing, then the evidence * * * shows that, after the debtor terminated his employment * * * he made * * * no business use of the recorder. All his use of it thereafter was personal. Therefore, inasmuch as his use of the recorder was primarily personal, the recorder is properly classifiable as "consumer goods" within the meaning of § 9–109 of the Uniform Commercial Code and single filing is sufficient under § 9–401 of that Code to perfect the security interest.

*   *   *

But, even if it should be found that the claimant's security interest is not perfected * * * perfection of a security interest is not a necessary element in a creditor's *inter partes* suit to recover specific property from the debtor. Perfection is necessary only to defeat the claim or defense of a third party, such as the trustee in bankruptcy, who it appears, makes no claim to this property on behalf of the creditors or estate. Nor is it anywhere represented that the value of the recorder will be used for the creditors' or the estate's benefit. A security interest has efficacy between the parties without any of the incidents of perfection. Therefore, in the case at bar, it must be held that the plaintiff, Walloch TV, may reclaim the cassette recorder without demonstrating perfection.

*   *   *

3. Perfected Security Interest Prevails Over Tax Lien

PARAMOUNT FINANCE CO. v. UNITED STATES
379 F.2d 543 (6th Cir., 1967)

NEESE, District Judge.   S. & C. Tavern, Inc. procured a loan from the plaintiff [taxpayer] * * * and applied the proceeds to the purchase of a tavern business in Cleveland, Ohio. The taxpayer made its promissory note to the lender, securing the repayment of the loan with a security agreement and financing statement. The lender perfected its security interest in the collateral given by the taxpayer by filings in the respective offices of the recorder of Cuyahoga County, Ohio and the Ohio secretary of state on August 15, 1962.

Within two years therefrom the taxpayer was in default on the loan and deficient in paying its federal taxes. The defendant assessed the taxpayer on April 23, 1964 with a tax deficiency of $4,988.03. Four days afterward, the defendant's agents filed with the aforementioned recorder a lien on the taxpayer's property for federal tax liabilities, and its agents seized, * * * the tavern property, including DA–3 permit no. 3494 of the Ohio Department of Liquor Control, respecting a liquor license which had been issued theretofore to the taxpayer.

* * * The defendant was authorized to collect the tax due it from the taxpayer by levy on and seizure of the state liquor license. * * * However, such lien imposed thereon by 26 U.S.C. § 6321 was invalid against the lender's perfected purchase money security interest under the aforementioned security agreement and the financing statement. * * *

The security interest acquired by the lender was a "purchase money security interest" under the Ohio Commercial Code, which applies " * * * so far as concerns any personal property and fixtures within the jurisdiction of [Ohio]

> * * *: (1) to any transaction, regardless of its form, which is intended to create a security interest in personal property or fixtures including goods, documents, instruments, general intangibles, chattel paper, accounts or contracts rights * * *.

> (A). A * * * "General intangible" means any personal property, including things in action, other than goods, accounts, contract rights, chattel paper, documents and instruments. * * *

The taxpayer could not transfer to the lender title to the liquor license issued to it by the Ohio Department of Liquor Control, * * * but the taxpayer could, and did, transfer to the lender a security interest in the liquor license, as constituting "property" with unique value. * * *

The fund produced by the sale by the defendant of the taxpayer's tavern and its liquor license represents the value of its business which was hypothecated to the lender under a security agreement perfected long before the taxpayer's property was seized by the defendant. We agree with District Court that the fund remaining should be applied to the satisfaction of the lender's rights thereunder.

4. Sufficiency of Notice of Foreclosure Sale

CREST INVESTMENT TRUST, INC. v. ALATZAS

264 Md. 571, 287 A.2d 261 (1972)

Suit by lender, which held restaurant buyer's note secured by recorded financing statement, against restaurant business seller, which had repurchased such business at public sale pursuant to foreclosure proceeding against buyer, seeking damages and alleging failure of seller to give it reasonable notification of the foreclosure sale.

McWILLIAMS, Judge.   When Greek meets Greek then comes the tug of war. Triffona George Alatzas met Peter Angelides and sold him a restaurant, whence comes this tug of war. A year or so later (June 1968) Angelides borrowed $18,333 from the appellant (Crest). When Angelides defaulted Alatzas foreclosed his lien. Crest says no notice of the foreclosure was "sent" to it. Thus is presented for our consideration, for the first time it seems, the nature of the "reasonable notification" required by Code (1964 Repl. Vol.), Art. 95B, § 9–504 (3), the Uniform Commercial Code.

As we shall see, the parties are not in complete agreement in respect of what happened. In early 1967 Alatzas occupied as lessee a building in east Baltimore in which he had a restaurant-cum-bar. In March he sold it to Angelides for $33,000, $16,000 of which was evidenced by a note secured by a recorded financing statement. He assigned the lease to Angelides but, of course, his own liability to the lessor was not thereby diminished. The financing statement evidencing Crest's loan was recorded on 21 June 1968.
* * *

Although Alatzas had sold him "a good business, a very good business," Angelides fell behind in his payments to Alatzas and in mid-1969 he closed his doors. The public foreclosure sale was scheduled for 28 October. The auctioneer (Billig) caused the advertisement of sale to appear in the Baltimore Sun on the two Sundays before the sale and on the day of the sale. Alatzas concedes a written notice was not sent to Crest.

Despite credible evidence to the contrary Crest insists its only notice of the sale was received during a telephone conversation between Dennis Psoras, then of counsel for Alatzas, and Irving Bowers, of counsel for Crest, around 4:00 p. m. on the day before the sale. Bowers said he and Sidney Kaplan, also of counsel for Crest, tried, without success, to inform Crest's management of the impending sale and that as a result Crest was not represented at the sale. * * *

Forty or more persons attended the sale. The bidding began at $10,000; Alatzas, at $13,000, was the highest bidder. The amount due him was $11,-274.01; the expenses were $3,805; the deficiency amounted to $2,079.01. Crest does not claim the sale was not "commercially reasonable" as required by § 9–507(2) or that the collateral was not disposed of in the "good faith" required by § 1–203. The balance due it at the time, including attorney's fees of 15%, was $9,376.27.

* * *

At first glance, to be sure, one does get the impression that "send" connotes a notice in writing but, upon closer inspection, it becomes quite clear, we think, that the receipt or acquisition of actual knowledge within the time a properly sent notification could have arrived amounts to compliance with the requirement of § 9–504(3). Written notification could accomplish no more and, in this regard, it will be observed that § 9–504(3) is satisfied merely by sending the notification; there is no requirement that it be received.

* * *

Since we cannot say Judge Cardin's finding that Crest did have actual notice of the sale was clearly erroneous nor that he misapprehended the applicable law, we do not reach the question whether the notice of one day was reasonable in the circumstances. Maryland Rule 886. We shall affirm the judgment in favor of Alatzas against Crest for costs.

Judgment affirmed.

Costs to be paid by the appellant.

5. No Unjust Enrichment of Purchaser Over Defaulting Mortgagor at Land Foreclosure Sale

GUIDARELLI v. LAZARETTI

305 Minn. 551, 233 N.W.2d 890 (1975)

PER CURIAM. This was an action brought by Elio Guidarelli (plaintiff) against Raymond Lazaretti (defendant) to set aside a mortgage foreclosure sale on the ground that the mortgagee, who purchased the property at the sale, was unjustly enriched.

In 1960 Guidarelli purchased a house. In 1962 he borrowed $50,000 from Lazaretti, executing a promissory note to Lazaretti in that amount which was secured by a mortgage on the house. In 1976 Guidarelli defaulted on the mortgage payments and Lazaretti commenced proceedings to foreclose by advertisement. Following proper notice, a public sale was held at which Lazaretti, the mortgagee, placed the highest bid, $37,782.02, and took title subject to Guidarelli's one-year period of redemption.

Guidarelli failed to exercise his option to redeem by December 18, 1968, and in June 1969 Lazaretti obtained a new certificate of title to the property. In March 1972, over four years after the sheriff's sale, Guidarelli brought this action claiming that Lazaretti was unjustly enriched to the extent that the fair market value of the property at the time of the sale, alleged to be at least $100,000, exceeded the bid-in price of $37,782.02.

The sole issue raised by Guidarelli is whether he as a defaulting mortgagor can maintain an action for unjust enrichment against the purchaser at a foreclosure sale when the action is commenced following expiration of the redemption period, in the absence of any fraud or irregularity in the proceedings.

Guidarelli alleges that he should be allowed to show unjust enrichment, conceding that there was no fraud or other irregularity involved in this foreclosure sale. This claim has been in this court several times and has been rejected each time. In *Kantack v. Kreuer*, relied on by the lower court, we most recently restated the general rule:

> With respect to the claim that the foreclosure sale should be invalidated because the bid was grossly inadequate, about all that needs be said is that the general rule is that a foreclosure sale free from fraud or irregularity will not be held invalid for inadequacy of the price.

The reason or basis for this rule was set forth in *Stearns v. Carlson,* a case in which the mortgagee purchased the realty at the foreclosure sale and then brought an action against the mortgagor for the deficiency on the note. This court held that a claim of inadequate price received at the sheriff's sale could not be asserted as a defense, using language that applies with great force here:

> Defendant does not question the regularity * * * of the foreclosure proceedings, . . . but rests his case on the claim that he was entitled to show, as a defense to the action, that the value of the property exceeded the amount of the note. . . .

> In the present case the sale was made by the sheriff at public auction as required by statute. There is no claim that the sale was not fairly conducted, nor that the plaintiff did anything to prevent or discourage bidding by others, nor that any higher bid could have been obtained. None of the elements constituting unfairness or bad faith . . . are disclosed. Defendant or his assigns had the right to redeem at any time within one year by paying the amount for which the property was bid in with interest thereon. If he was unwilling or unable to redeem himself, he had a year in which to find a purchaser who would pay a higher price. Where a sale is made under such conditions, it is well settled that the mortgagor cannot complain that the mortgagee bid in the property for less than its value.

Under the circumstances of the present case, where Guidarelli did not even allege any fraud or irregularity surrounding the foreclosure sale and where none appears from our examination of the record, we hold that the lower court was correct in ruling that Guidarelli could not maintain a cause of action for unjust enrichment. Guidarelli's remedy was to redeem within the year granted by Minn. St. 580.23. Having failed to do so, he cannot complain unless he can show fraud or irregularity to support his claim of unjust enrichment.

*   *   *

PROBLEMS

1. Secured party A has a perfected security interest in debtor's present and future inventory, pursuant to a properly filed financing statement. S sells new inventory to debtor, taking back a security interest in the new inventory. S files the financing statement eight days later. Debtor becomes insolvent. S claims a priority over A as to the new inventory on the basis that S had a purchase money interest which he perfected. Discuss.

2. Stoddard obtained a new automobile loan from National Bank and gave National a security interest in the automobile to protect his loan. National perfected the security interest in compliance with Article 9 of the U.C.C. Stoddard later took the automobile to Levy Auto Mechanics for repairs. Stoddard then stopped paying loan installments to the bank. National sought to repossess the automobile from Levy. Levy refused to surrender the automobile until its repair bill was paid. National sued Levy to recover the vehicle, claiming its perfected security interest was entitled to priority over Levy's common law possessory lien for unpaid repairs. Decision?

3. B and G each bought automobiles for personal use from S, a private owner. Neither B or G knew that each vehicle was subject to an unfiled security interest in favor of the original seller D, a dealer in such vehicles. When S failed to make payment in accordance with the security interests of D, D repossessed the vehicles. B and G sue D, arguing that they had clear title by reason of their purchase from S. Decision?

4. S sold B a new tractor-truck worth $30,000, with a down payment of $3,000 and the balance to be paid in 30 monthly installments. The agreement provided that upon default in any payment S could take "immediate possession of the property—without notice or demand. For this, vendor may enter upon any premises the property may be. . . ." B defaulted, and S notified him that the truck would be repossessed. B had the truck, attached to a loaded trailer, in a locked loading area of a company that had employed B to drive the loaded trailer to the West Coast. S found the truck. When no one was around, S removed the wire screen over a ventilator hole by unscrewing it from the outside with his penknife. S then reached through the ventilator hole with a stick and unlocked the door of the tractor-truck. He then disconnected the trailer and had the truck towed away. B sued S for unlawful repossession of the truck by committing a breach of the peace. Decision?

5. C's security agreement listed the following property: "one-two pc. living room suite, wine; one-five pc. chrome dinette set, yellow; one-three pc. panel bedroom suite, lime oak, matt. & spgs." The security agreement also stated the address where the items were located. The trustee in bankruptcy claims the lien is invalid because the description was insufficient—a three piece bedroom suite could be twin beds and a dresser, and a chest; a two piece living room suite could be a couch converted into a bed and a chair or overstuffed stool, or some item commonly used in a living room; and a five piece dinette, in addition to being a table and four chairs, could be a table, cabinet for dishes, or some other dining or breakfast room piece and three chairs. Decision?

6. C held a security agreement which covered furniture, fixtures and inventory at the bankrupt's old drugstore. The security agreement contained an after-acquired property clause. The drugstore and its contents were destroyed by fire. The bankrupt purchased a new store eight months later in a community 270 miles away. The bankrupt has now filed bankruptcy and C claims the new inventory as against the trustee in bankruptcy. Decision?

7. Bell purchased second-hand equipment from Pruett. Pruett obtained a security interest by filing a financing statement. Bell returned the equipment for repairs and then refused to take it back. Pruett told Bell over the phone that the equipment would be resold without any further notice and that he would be held liable for any difference between the sales price and the original contract price. The equipment was sold privately three months later, and Pruett sued Bell for the deficiency. Bell argued that the sale was invalid because he had not received written notice. Decision?

8. Kottke is a maker of dyed fabrics from textile goods. She purchased and paid for goods from a third party who had bought the goods from Lang, a textile manufacturer. The goods were still in Lang's warehouse at time of sale. Lang refused to deliver the goods to Kottke because the third party had not paid Lang on other accounts. Kottke sued Lang in tort for conversion of the goods. Lang argued that he had a perfected security interest in the goods. Lang did not dispute that he had been paid for Kottke's purchase. Decision?

9. Beniquez had a security agreement with Dixon covering the sale of certain trailers. Beniquez did not file a financing statement or repossess the property when Dixon defaulted in payment. The United States filed a tax lien on the trailers. Beniquez claimed his prior security agreement prevailed over the tax lien. Decision?

10. Gamble borrowed money from Mutual Bank and gave an interest in the equipment and machinery at his place of business as security. Mutual filed a proper financing statement complete in all respects, including Gamble's business address, except that the statement did not contain Gamble's residence address. Gamble went bankrupt. Mutual sued to recover the collateral. The trustee in bankruptcy argued that the financing statement was ineffective because the statement ommitted Gamble's residence address. Decision?

Chapter 32

CONSUMER LAW

Laws for the protection of consumers have increased substantially in recent years. Many consumer-oriented organizations such as Common Cause and Center for Law in the Public Interest and consumer advocates like Ralph Nader have lobbied successfully for new consumer laws. Some groups have argued buyers' rights cases before the appellate courts. All of this activity has created an increased emphasis on the need to protect the average citizen from sharp operators. Further expansion in these directions should be expected to continue in the foreseeable future.

Some consumer protection laws have been discussed in previous chapters: unconscionability in Chapters 8 and 30; fraud in Chapter 11; illegality in Chapter 13; remedies in Chapters 17 and 29; and products liability in Chapter 30.

The following sections cover additional examples of consumer laws.

A. ADVERTISING

1. ADVERTISING OF PRODUCTS

Most advertising regulations are established under an administrative agency of the federal government, with protection of the consumer rather than punishment of the advertiser as the foremost purpose. An example of this is the Federal Trade Commission (FTC), which is authorized to halt false or misleading advertising of products to the consumer.

The FTC is authorized to require that advertisements be limited to such statements as can be proven by the advertiser, to require the name of a product be changed if it misleads or tends to mislead the public, and to seek voluntary agreement from an organization to stop false and misleading advertising and in some cases to correct such deceptive advertising. The authority to order corrective advertising has been upheld in *Warner-Lambert v. Federal Trade Commission* (562 F. 2d 749 [D.C. Cir., 1977]).

The FTC bases its authority concerning regulation of advertising on Section 5 of the Federal Trade Commission Act (15 U.S.C.A. § 41 et seq.), which reads, "Unfair methods of competition in commerce and unfair or deceptive acts in commerce are declared unlawful."

The term "advertising" extends to written messages contained in newspaper and magazine advertisements, window displays, price tags, and audio-visual messages such as those shown on television and heard on radio.

For example, commercials showing tests of products must actually be the test claimed and not merely a deceptive mock-up (*Federal Trade Commission v. Colgate-Palmolive Co.* [380 U.S. 374, 85 S.Ct. 1035, 13 L.Ed.2d 904 (1965)]).

Under the FTC Improvement Act of 1980 (15 U.S.C. § 45 et seq.), Congress curtailed the FTC's investigative authority with respect to unfair or deceptive practices. Currently, rule making in specified areas may be vetoed by action of both houses of Congress within 90 days after promulgation.

2. ADVERTISING OF CREDIT

Under the Consumer Credit Protection Act (15 U.S.C. 1601 et seq.), also known as the Truth in Lending Act, certain rules must be followed when advertising credit terms. "No advertisement to aid, promote, or assist directly or indirectly any extension of consumer credit may state:

> (1) that a specific periodic consumer credit amount of installment can be arranged, unless the creditor usually and customarily arranges credit payments or installments for that period and in that amount.

> (2) that a specified downpayment is required in connection with any extension of consumer credit, unless the creditor usually and customarily arranges downpayments in that amount" (§ 142).

"No advertisement to aid, promote, or assist directly or indirectly the extension of consumer credit under an open end credit plan (e. g., typical department store credit plan) may set forth any of the specific terms of that plan or the appropriate rate determined under section 127(2) 5 unless it also clearly and conspicuously sets forth all of the following items:

> (1) The time period, if any, within which any credit extended may be repaid without incurring a finance charge.

> (2) The method of determining the balance upon which a finance charge will be imposed.

> (3) The method of determining the amount of the finance charge, including any minimum or fixed amount imposed as a finance charge.

> (4) Where periodic rates may be used to compute the finance charge, the period rates expressed as annual percentage rates.

> (5) Such other or additional information for the advertising of open end credit plans as the Board may by regulation require to provide for adequate comparison of credit costs as between different types of open end credit plans" (§ 143).

Section 144 establishes certain provisions for advertising of credit other than open-end plans. Most important of these is the provision that the finance charge must be expressed as an annual percentage rate.

The burden of following all of the provisions of Chapter 3—Credit Advertising—falls on the advertising body, since there is no liability under this chapter on the part of any owner or personnel, as such, of any medium in which an advertisement appears or through which it is disseminated (§ 145).

A special rule provides that any advertisement to "aid, promote, or assist directly or indirectly the extension of consumer credit repayable in more than four installments shall, unless a finance charge is imposed, clearly and conspicuously state, in accordance with the regulations of the Board;

"THE COST OF CREDIT IS INCLUDED IN THE PRICE QUOTED FOR GOODS AND SERVICES" (§ 146).

The civil penalties provided by Section 130 of the Act do not apply to the advertising requirements (*Jordan v. Montgomery Ward and Co.* [442 F. 2d 78 (8th Cir., 1971), cert. denied 404 U.S. 870, 92 S.Ct. 78, 30 L.Ed.2d 114]).

3. BAIT AND SWITCH

The FTC *Guides on Bait Advertising,* 16 CFR 238 (1968), established the following practices as evidence of bait advertising (i. e., an item is advertised at a very low price, and the consumer finds upon going to buy the item that the salesperson tries to induce him or her to buy another, more expensive item or that the store does not have the advertised item available and never did, in fact, have a significant number of the item advertised). Such tactics are referred to as "bait and switch" advertising.

1. Refusal to show the advertised item,

2. Disparagement of the advertised item,

3. Failure to have the advertised item available in reasonable quantities,

4. Refusal to promise delivery of the advertised item within a reasonable time,

5. Discouraging sales personnel from selling advertised products.

In applying sanctions to this practice, the FTC has not looked solely for evidence of salespersons switching customers to the more expensive item, but rather relied on the number of sales of the less expensive item advertised. If that number is minimal in comparison to the expensive item, the violation is established (*Tashof v. FTC* [437 F. 2d 707 (D.C. Cir., 1970)]).

Section 5 of the FTC Act again gives the enforcement prohibiting deceptive acts and practices in advertising. However, once a complaint is issued, the party involved is given a chance to agree to a formal cease and desist order, or the party may be given a chance to agree informally to discontinue the practice. Recently, however, in a number of advertising cases, the FTC has gone further and ordered corrective advertising.

B. SALES PRACTICE

1. DOOR-TO-DOOR

Because of widespread high-pressure methods by door-to-door salespeople resulting in consumers' buying products they do not want and cannot pay for, many state statutes and federal regulations have been passed for the protection of the consumer.

The FTC provides for a three-day cooling-off period on sales of $25 or more. The salesperson is required to tell the customer verbally of the right to cancel, to give him or her a written contract, and to give him or her two copies of a notice of cancellation form. A customer having second thoughts after the salesperson has left must sign a copy of the cancellation form and send or deliver the form to the seller within three business days. Exceptions include orders placed at the seller's address; sales made entirely by mail or telephone; some emergency repair sales or repairs to personal property in the buyer's home; and sales of real estate, insurance, or securities. This regulation supersedes state laws if they do not give the buyer as much time to cancel, if they permit a fee or penalty for cancellation, or if they do not require substantially the same notice to the buyer.

2. REFERRAL SALES AND LEASES

Referral sales and leases schemes are widespread. Typically, a company will induce a buyer to purchase or a tenant to lease at one price with a promised reduction or "bonus" to the purchaser or lessee for every prospective buyer or lessee furnished by the buyer for the same product. The mere giving of a list of names of persons the buyer feels might be interested in the product at the time of the sale is permitted if the price is not contingent on the fact of whether or not the persons named do purchase or on whether or not other events occur in the future.

C. CREDIT DISCLOSURES—TRUTH IN LENDING REGULATIONS

The Consumer Credit Protection Act (15 U.S.C. 1601 et seq.) (the Truth in Lending Act) is implemented by Regulation Z, prescribed by the Board of Governors of the Federal Reserve System. For a free copy of Regulation Z, write to the Federal Trade Commission, Division of Consumer Credit, Washington, DC 20580, or contact your local office of the FTC.

The purpose of Regulation Z is to let borrowers and customers know the cost of credit so that they can compare costs with other credit sources. It does not fix maximum, minimum, or any charges for credit. The finance charge and the annual percentage rate are the two most important disclosures required by the regulation. It applies to any individual or organization which in the ordinary course of business regularly extends or arranges credit for which a finance charge is or may be payable or which by agreement is repayable in more than four installments. It is enforced by both civil and criminal penalties.

The finance charge in connection with any transaction shall be determined as the sum of all charges, payable directly or indirectly by the consumer and imposed directly or indirectly by the creditor as an incident to or as a condition of the extension of credit, whether paid or payable by the customer, the seller, or any other person on behalf of the customer to the creditor or to a third party. It includes any of the following types of charges:

1. Interest, time price differential, and any amount payable under a discount or other system of additional charges.

2. Service, transaction, activity, or carrying charge.

3. Loan fee, points, finder's fee, or similar charge.

4. Fee for an appraisal, investigation, or credit report.

5. Charges of premiums for credit life, accident, health, or loss of income insurance written in connection with any credit transaction (with certain exemptions).

Certain items are excludable as finance charges. In particular, if itemized and disclosed to the customer, any charges of the following types need not be included in the finance charge:

1. Fees and charges prescribed by law that actually are or will be paid to public officials for determining the existence of or for performing or releasing or satisfying any security related to the credit transaction.

2. Certain premiums payable for any insurance in lieu of perfecting any security interest otherwise required by the creditor in connection with the transaction (with certain limitations).

3. Taxes not included in the cash price.

4. License, certificate of title, and registration fees imposed by law.

In addition, late payment, delinquency, default, and reinstatement charges if imposed for actual unanticipated late payment, delinquency, default, or other such occurrence are not finance charges. Nor are overdraft charges imposed by a bank for paying checks that overdraw or increase an overdraft in a checking account, unless the payment of such checks and the imposition of such finance charges were previously agreed upon in writing.

Certain real property transactions charges, such as appraisal fees, credit reports, title examination, abstract of title, title insurance, required property surveys, fees for preparations of deeds, settlement statements, and notary fees, are not included in the finance charge.

There are certain transactions exempted under Section 226.3 of this regulation.

1. Business or governmental credit, other than agricultural purposes.

2. Certain transactions in security or commodities accounts.

3. Credit transactions, other than real property transactions, in which the amount financed is over the sum of $25,000.

4. Certain public utility bills.

5. Agricultural credit transactions, including real property transactions, in which the amount financed exceeds $25,000 or in which the transaction is pursuant to an express written commitment by the creditor to extend credit in excess of $25,000.

Because the many disclosure requirements of the Truth in Lending Act are very detailed and complex, the student is referred to Regulation Z for further particulars.

D. CREDIT CARDS

Section 226.13 of Regulation Z provides that a credit cardholder is liable for the unauthorized use of the credit card up to $50, and then only if:

1. The credit card is an accepted credit card (an accepted credit card is one that the credit cardholder has requested and received, has signed or has used, or has authorized another to use),

2. The card issuer has given adequate notice to the cardholder of his or her potential liability,

3. The card issuer has provided the cardholder with an addressed notification requiring no postage to be paid by him or her that may be mailed by him or her in the event of the loss, theft, or possible unauthorized use of the credit card,

4. The card issuer has provided a method whereby the user of such card can be identified as the person authorized to use it, such as by signature, photograph, or fingerprint on the credit card or by electronic or mechanical confirmation,

5. The unauthorized use occurred before the cardholder notified the issuer that an unauthorized use occurred or may occur as a result of loss or theft.

Notice may be given to the card issuer or his or her designee in person or by telephone or by letter, telegram, radiogram, cablegram, or other written communication that sets forth the pertinent information.

Some states have legislation similar to the above (e. g., New York [Section 512 of the General Business Law]).

In addition to statutory limitation of liability in credit card cases, courts have refused to permit the card issuer to recover any sums when the person dealing with the cardholder was negligent in assuming that the holder of the card was the lawful owner of it and in failing to take steps to identify the holder.

Regardless of whether a credit card is to be used for personal, family, household, agricultural, business, or commercial purposes, no credit card shall be issued to any person except:

1.　In response to a request or application therefor,

2.　As a renewal of, or in substitution for, an accepted credit card, whether such card is issued by the same or a successor card issuer (§ 226.13(a)).

E.　BALLOON PAYMENTS

A balloon payment is an installment greater than the other installments as a provision of an installment sales contract or in an installment loan. Section 226.8(b)(3) of Regulation Z provides "If any payment is more than twice the amount of an otherwise regularly scheduled equal payment, the creditor shall identify the amount of such payment by the term 'balloon payment' and shall state the conditions, if any, under which that payment may be refinanced if not paid when due."

The consumer, in certain cases, set forth under sections 3.308(1) and 3.308(2) of the Uniform Consumer Credit Code, has the right to refinance, without penalty, the amount of that payment at the time it is due and the terms of the refinancing shall be no less favorable to the consumer than the terms of the original transaction. This does not apply to:

1.　A consumer lease,

2.　A transaction pursuant to open-end credit,

3.　A transaction to the extent that the payment schedule is adjusted to the seasonal or irregular income or scheduled payments or obligations of the consumer,

4.　A transaction of a class defined by rule of the Administrator as not requiring for the protection of the consumer his right to refinance.

However, the UCCC has been adopted in only nine states, and is changed and revised by many of them.

Balloon payments can be helpful to consumers with seasonal or otherwise irregular sources of payment. They can also be deceptive to the consumer since the regularly scheduled payments will be so low that the consumer will be enticed into the agreement because the "day of reckoning" is delayed.

F.　FAIR CREDIT REPORTING ACT OF 1970

In 1970, Congress enacted the Fair Credit Reporting Act, Title VI of the Consumer Credit Protection Act. This focuses on requirements for consumer reporting agencies, requirements for users of consumer reports, the rights of consumers, and remedies.

Section 603(f) of this act defines "consumer reporting agency" as any person which regularly engages in whole or in part in the practice of assembling or evaluating consumer credit information or other information on consumers for the purpose of furnishing consumer reports to a third party or parties, and for which monetary fees or dues are paid, or, when acting on a cooperative nonprofit basis, for the purpose of preparing or furnishing consumer reports.

If the information is being assembled or evaluated for the business or person's own use there would be no third party involved and such a person or business would not be considered a "consumer reporting agency".

Section 606 provides that no one may procure or cause to be prepared an investigative consumer report on any consumer unless

> (1) it is clearly and accurately disclosed to the consumer that an investigative consumer report including information as to his character, general reputation, personal characteristics, and mode of living, whichever are applicable, may be made, and such disclosure (A) is made in a writing mailed, or otherwise delivered, to the consumer, not later than three days after the date on which the report was first requested, and (B) includes a statement informing the consumer of his right to request the additional disclosures provided for under subsection (b) of this section; or

> (2) the report is to be used for employment purposes for which the consumer has not specifically applied.

The consumer can then request in writing, within a reasonable time after receiving notice of the requested report, a complete and accurate disclosure of the nature and scope of the investigation. This disclosure must be in writing, mailed, or otherwise delivered to the consumer not later than five days after the date on which the request for such disclosure was received from the consumer or the date such report was first requested, whichever is the later.

In addition, under Section 609, any consumer upon proper identification can request that the consumer reporting agency clearly and accurately disclose the nature and substance of all information (except medical information) in its files on the consumer at the time of the request. The agency must reveal the sources of the information (with certain exceptions).

The Act provides for procedure in case of disputed accuracy, compliance procedures, restrictions on investigative consumer reports, and requirements on users of consumer reports amoung other provisions.

Section 611 gives the consumer an opportunity to make limited corrections to the information on file.

The Federal Trade Commission has principal responsibility for administrative enforcement of the Fair Credit Reporting Act. Other boards and administrators are each given authority to enforce the requirements of the Act when applicable to concerns subject to their respective federal regulatory provisions.

Section 619 of the Act provides for a fine of not more than $5,000 or imprisonment for not more than one year, or both, for anyone who knowingly and willfully obtains information on a consumer from a consumer reporting agency under false pretenses.

Section 920 provides for a fine of not more than $5,000 or imprisonment for not more than one year, or both, for any officer or employee of a consumer reporting agency who knowingly and willfully provides information concerning an individual from the agency's files to a person not authorized to receive that information.

Sections 616 and 617 provide for certain civil liabilities for willful and for negligent noncompliance with the provisions of this Act. However, there are many problems connected with establishing a cause of action under these sections. Any consumer reporting agency using "reasonable" procedures will be discharging its statutory obligations.

G. FAIR CREDIT BILLING ACT

The Fair Credit Billing Act (15 U.S. C.A. 1666 et seq.) became effective in 1975. Because of the heavy volume of consumer complaints over billing errors in accounts, the Fair Credit Billing Act sets forth various remedies to the consumer. Section 127(b) of the Act requires the disclosure of the address to which billing inquiries shall be sent. Section 127(a) provides that the creditor must provide the consumer with a statement in the form prescribed in Regulation Z 226.7(a)(9), explaining the consumer's rights and obligations under the Fair Credit Billing Act at the time of the opening of the account and at semiannual intervals thereafter.

Section 161 (b) describes billing errors as follows:

1.   An extension of credit not made to the complaining customer or not made in the amount reflected on the billing statement.

2.   Credit extensions for which documentation or clarification is requested.

3.   Undelivered or unaccepted goods or services.

4.   Incorrect payments or credits.

5.   Clerical or computation mistakes.

Section 161 provides for requirements to be followed by the consumer regarding clerical and computation errors. Communication must be:

1.   By a written notice.

2.   Received at the creditor's disclosed address.

3.   Listing information enabling the creditor to identify the name and account number (if any) of the consumer.

4.   Indicating that the consumer believes that there is a billing error.

5.   Setting forth of the amount of such billing error.

6.   Setting forth the reasons for the consumer's belief.

Each creditor who receives such a proper claim of error must either make a written acknowledgement of receipt or a written response within 30 days.

Until the creditor responds to the claim of error, it may not take any action to collect the disputed amount. A creditor cannot restrict the use of an open-end account, pending the response to such claim, solely because the amount disputed has not been paid. Once the information has reached the creditor, the creditor may not report or threaten to report the disputed amount delinquent until 10 days after its response has been sent to the consumer.

If a creditor fails to make the necessary requirements set forth in the Act, the creditor forfeits its right to collect the amount in dispute, whether or not such account was in error, and any corresponding finance charges, provided that the amount so forfeited shall not exceed $50 for each item or transaction on a periodic statement indicated by a customer as being in error.

H. EQUAL CREDIT OPPORTUNITY ACT

Regulations have been issued by the Board of Governors of the Federal Reserve System pursuant to the Equal Credit Opportunity Act (15 U.S.C.A. § 1691 et seq.) stating that a creditor shall not discriminate against any applicant on the basis of sex or marital status with respect to any aspect of a credit transaction. The regulations are known as Equal Credit Opportunity Regulations (Regulation B) Title 12—Banks and Banking, Part 202—Equal Credit Opportunity, and are a part of the Consumer Credit Protection Act. These regulations have been in effect since October 28, 1975.

On March 23, 1977, these regulations were amended to provide that discrimination in this matter cannot be used on the basis of race, color, religion, national origin, age, receipt of income from a public assistance program or good faith exercise of rights under the Consumer Protection Act.

Although a form may ask whether applicant is single, married, or separated on a multi-signature loan, it must state that if application is for a single-signature unsecured loan, no information as to applicant's marital status or spouse is required. The applicant may be requested to furnish this information if the spouse will be liable on the account or will also use the account or if the applicant is relying on spouse's income, community property, alimony, or child support to pay the loan.

Specifically, the creditor cannot do any of the following:

1. Assign a value to sex or marital status in evaluating applications.

2. Assign a value to the existence of a telephone listing in evaluating applications.

3. Request, require, or use information about birth control practices or childbearing capability.

4. Terminate, require reapplication, or change terms based solely on change of name or marital status.

5. Discount all or part of the income (including part-time income) of the applicant or the applicant's spouse.

6. Use prohibited information in evaluating applications.

7. Prohibit an applicant from using any particular name.

8. Fail to act or unreasonably delay action upon an application.

9.   Discourage a "reasonable person" from applying for credit.

Section 202.8 rules on separate accounts in relation to state law. Any provision of state law that prohibits the separate extension of consumer credit to each spouse shall not apply in any case where each spouse voluntarily applies for separate credit from the same creditor. In any case, where such a state law is preempted, each spouse shall be solely responsible for the debt so contracted.

Further, when each spouse separately and voluntarily applies for and obtains a separate account with the same creditor, the accounts shall not be aggregated or otherwise combined for purposes of determining permissible finance charges or permissible loan ceilings under the laws of any state or of the United States. Such loan ceilings shall be construed to permit each spouse to be separately and individually liable up to the amount of the loan ceiling less the amount for which both spouses are jointly liable. For example, in a state in which there is a permissible loan ceiling of $1,000, if a married couple were jointly liable for $250, each spouse could subsequently become individually liable for $750 under this section.

Except for the provisions of Section 202.8 set forth above, the Equal Credit Opportunity Act does not preempt state laws prohibiting credit discrimination based on sex or marital status. To date, over half of the states have adopted such laws. For example, California Civil Code 1812.30 to 1812.35 has been amended to prohibit discrimination on the basis of marital status as well as sex and to include an award of attorney's fees for violation thereof.

I. COLLECTION PRACTICES

The Fair Debt Collection Practices Act (Pub.L.No. 95–109, 91 Stat.874) brings debt collection procedures under federal regulation for the first time. The Act is intended to eliminate abusive debt collection practices in the consumer credit industry. Debt collectors who violate any of the Act's provisions will be subject to civil suits in the federal courts by injured parties or classes, or to administrative enforcement by the Federal Trade Commission or certain other agencies.

Not all debt collectors are subject to the provisions of the Act, which is primarily intended to reach third-party collectors of overdue accounts. The most important exception to the Act's reach is the collection of debts by the original creditor itself or by an employee of the original creditor. Other excluded groups include attorneys-at-law who are collecting on behalf of and in the name of a client and purchasers of a debt that is not in default at the time of purchase.

Only debts arising from transactions that are primarily for personal, family, or household purposes are covered by the Act.

Most of the regulations in the Act concern direct contacts between the collector and the debtor. The collector may not communicate with the debtor at an unusual place or time.

Harassment and abuse of the debtor are prohibited, as are false and misleading representations and unfair practices. The following are among the listed practices:

1.   The use or threat of use of violence or other criminal activity to the person, reputation, or property of the debtor.

2.   The use of obscene language.

3.   The publication of "deadbeat lists."

4.   Excessive or anonymous telephone calls.

5.   The threat of legal action that cannot be taken or is not intended to be taken, including arrest.

6.   Use of collect phone calls, telegrams, etc., concealing the true purpose of the communication.

7.   Taking or threatening to take nonjudicial action upon property.

8.   The use of a postcard or any other sign or symbol or company name on an envelope that would indicate that the communication involves debt collection.

Other federal regulations govern the use of the mail and telephone. For example, collection abuses under use of the mails have been prosecuted under 18 U.S.C.A. § 1341 and 18 U.S.C.A. § 1718 (Mail Fraud Statute).

Section 5.108(2) of the Uniform Consumer Credit Code provides, "With respect to a consumer credit transaction, if the court as a matter of law finds that a person has engaged in, is engaging in, or is likely to engage in unconscionable conduct in collecting a debt arising from that transaction, the court may grant an injunction and award the consumer any actual damages he has sustained."

Section 5.108(5) further provides factors applicable to Subsection (2). A creditor is forbidden to do any of the following:

1.   Use or threaten to use force, violence, or criminal prosecution against the consumer or members of his or her family.

2.   Communicate with the consumer or a member of his or her family at frequent intervals or at unusual hours or under other circumstances so that it is a reasonable inference that the primary purpose of the communication was to harass the consumer.

3.   Use fraudulent, deceptive, or misleading representations that simulate legal process or that appear to have been authorized, issued, or approved by a government, governmental agency, or attorney at law when, in fact, it has not or threaten or attempt to enforce a right with knowledge or reason to know that such right does not in fact exist.

4.   Cause or threaten to cause injury to the consumer's reputation or economic status by disclosing information affecting the consumer's status and reputation for creditworthiness with knowledge or reason to know that the information is false.

Certain further restrictions are set forth in Subsection (5) part (d) and part (e).

Even though a debtor is able to establish all of the elements just discussed, he or she still faces the problem of proving damages.

General state laws are utilized in extreme cases involving assault, blackmail, slander, libel, disorderly conduct, or fraud.

J.   OTHER FEDERAL LEGISLATION

1.   The Magnuson-Moss Warranty—Federal Trade Commission Improvement Act (15 U.S.C.A. § 2301 et seq., 1975) was passed to improve the adequacy of information available to consumers, prevent deception, and improve competition in the marketing of consumer products and to establish rules required in the written warranty of products. The Act designates federal minimum standards for warranties, designates warranties, establishes rules for terms and conditions of service contract disclosure, designates representatives, limits disclaimer of implied warranties, and covers full and limited warranting of a consumer product.

2.   The Interstate Land Sales Full Disclosure Act (15 U.S.C.A. § 1701) requires that anyone selling or leasing 50 or more lots of unimproved land as part of a common promotional plan in interstate commerce or by utilization of the mails must first file a statement of record with the Office of the Interstate Land Sales Registration, a division of the Department of Housing and Urban Development. The statement of record contains very detailed information about the land and the developer.

After the statement of record is approved by HUD as being on its face accurate and containing the required information, a developer may proceed to offer land for sale or lease, but he or she will also be required to furnish each purchaser a property report.

3.   The Real Estate Settlements Procedure Act (12 U.S.C.A. § 2601, effective June 20, 1975) applies to all federally related mortgage loans. Virtually all mortgage lenders are covered. The property must be a one- to four-family residential dwelling. The Act requires disclosure of charges, prohibits kickbacks and splitting of fees except for services actually rendered, and limits the amount that a borrower must pay into a special or escrow fund for taxes and insurance.

4.   The Motor Vehicle Information and Cost Savings Act (15 U.S.C.A. § 1901 et seq., 1972) requires disclosure to the buyer of various elements in the cost of an automobile and prohibits selling an automobile without informing the buyer that the odometer has been reset below the true mileage.

5.   The Fur Products Labeling Act (15 U.S.C.A. Section 69–69j), Textile Fiber Products Act (15 U.S.C.A. Section 70–70k), and the Wool Products Labeling Act (15 U.S.C.A. Section 68–68j) provide standards for the labeling of the various products stated in the respective titles. The FTC has regulatory jurisdiction and has issued regulations directing the manner and form of

disclosing required labeling information. The regulations are enforced by cease and desist orders, restitution, affirmative disclosure, rescission of contracts, seizure of mislabeled goods, and willful violations by criminal penalties (these methods of enforcement are generally true in all of the acts).

6. The Flammable Fabrics Act (15 U.S.C.A. Section 1191–1204) covers wearing apparel, fabric for wearing apparel, and household furnishings. Recent FTC activities have been in the area of carpet and rug standards, bedding and mattress standards, and children's no-burn sleepwear standards.

7. The Federal Hazardous Substances Labeling Act (15 U.S.C.A. Section 1261–73) through regulations issued by the Secretary of H. E. W. declares certain products to be hazardous and subject to labeling requirements to warn consumers of dangers. Some of the children's products relate to thermal, mechanical, electrical, toxic, and eye hazard protection.

8. The Mail Fraud Statute (18 U.S.C.A. Section 1341; 26 Stat. 466; 39 U.S.C. Section 259) provides civil and criminal penalties when a party is found to be conducting a scheme or device of obtaining money or property through the mails by means of fraudulent practices.

9. The Fair Packaging and Labeling Act (15 U.S.C.A. Section 1451–61) assists the consumer in determining values. Foods, drugs, cosmetics, and other consumer commodities must be labeled to show net quantity and other product information.

10. The National Traffic and Motor Vehicle Safety Act of 1966 (15 U.S.C.A. Section 1381–1425) covers motor vehicle safety standards, labeling standards relating to tires, and notification of purchasers of automobile parts, including tires, of defects discovered by the manufacturer.

11. The Radiation Control for Health and Safety Act (42 U.S.C.A. Section 263(b)–263(h)) provides that the Secretary of H. E. W. shall set standards for radiation emission for products covered by the statute. Standards for television receivers manufactured after January 15, 1970, have been set in addition to other electronic products.

12. The Federal Postal Reorganization Act (39 U.S.C.A. § 101 at 3009, 1970) provides that a person who receives unsolicited goods in the mail has the right to retain, use, discard, or dispose of them in any manner he or she sees fit without any obligation to the sender. Some states have similar laws.

13. Under the Consumer Product Safety Act (15 U.S.C.A. § 2051 et seq., 1972), consumer products became subject to federal regulations. The government has authority to set safety standards for products and to ban those products that present real hazards to the consumers. A consumer product is any article or part of an article produced or distributed for sale for personal use, consumption, or enjoyment in a household, school, in recreation or otherwise, except foods, drugs, cosmetics, motor vehicles, insecticides, firearms, cigarettes, radiological hazards, and certain flammable fabrics. The exceptions are covered by the Food, Drug and Cosmetic Act (21 U.S.C.A. §

301), the Poison Prevention Packaging Act of 1970 (70 U.S.C.A. § 1471), and other acts mentioned in this chapter.

The Act provides for civil and criminal penalties. In addition to providing for the usual state court action based upon product liability, the Act provides that suit will lie in any U. S. District Court for a person injured through a failure to knowingly observe a consumer product safety rule.

The Act grants broad power to the Consumer Product Safety Commission to preempt state or local consumer product safety standards but allows the agency to grant an exemption if the proposed local rule imposes a higher standard than the federal standard.

14.   The Wholesome Meat Act (21 U.S.C.A. §§ 601–695 (1967)); The Wholesome Poultry Products Act (21 U.S.C.A. §§ 451–570 (1968)); The Public Health Service Act (42 U.S.C.A. §§ 201–300 u-5 (1974)); and numerous related enactments provide consumers protection in those areas exempt from the Consumer Products Safety Act, unless otherwise noted. Standards are provided, as are civil and criminal remedies.

K.   STATE LEGISLATION

Many states have adopted legislation modeled on the federal enactments, some of which provide stronger remedies than are available under federal law. In general, Congress has authorized an exemption from its own legislation where comparable state laws offer greater consumer protection.

In the following two instances, uniform state enactments have been adopted:

1.   The Uniform Consumer Credit Code (U.C.C.C.) sets forth the regulation of retail installment sales, consumer credit loans, and insurance. When adopted, the U.C.C.C. supersedes all other related enactments and controls consumer transactions in each adopting state. Nine states have adopted the Code: Colorado, Idaho, Indiana, Iowa, Kansas, Maine, Oklahoma, Utah, and Wyoming.

2.   The Uniform Commercial Code (U.C.C.) also provides consumer protection. Referral sales types of contracts where the buyer is given a price reduction for referring customers to the seller have been outlawed as unconscionable under U.C.C. Section 2–302.

ILLUSTRATIVE CASES

1. FTC Authority to Require Corrective Advertising

WARNER LAMBERT CO. v. FEDERAL TRADE COMM.

562 F.2d 749 (D.C. Cir., 1977)

J. SKELLY WRIGHT, J. The Warner-Lambert Company petitions for review of an order of the Federal Trade Commission requiring it to cease and desist from advertising that its product, Listerine Antiseptic mouthwash, prevents, cures, or alleviates the common cold. The FTC order further requires Warner-Lambert to disclose in future Listerine advertisements that: "Contrary to prior advertising, Listerine will not help prevent colds or sore throats or lessen their severity." We affirm but modify the order to delete from the required disclosure the phrase "Contrary to prior advertising."

The order under review represents the culmination of a proceeding begun in 1972, when the FTC issued a complaint charging petitioner with violation of Section 5(a)(1) of the Federal Trade Commission Act by misrepresenting the efficacy of Listerine against the common cold.

Listerine has been on the market since 1879. Its formula has never changed. Ever since its introduction it has been represented as being beneficial in certain respects for colds, cold symptoms, and sore throats. Direct advertising to the consumer, including the cold claims as well as others, began in 1921.

*   *   *

Petitioner contends that even if its advertising claims in the past were false, the portion of the Commission's order requiring "corrective advertising" exceeds the Commission's statutory power. The argument is based upon a literal reading of Section 5 of the Federal Trade Commission Act, which authorizes the Commission to issue "cease and desist" orders against violators and does not expressly mention any other remedies. The Commission's position, on the other hand, is that the affirmative disclosure that Listerine will not prevent colds or lessen their severity is absolutely necessary to give effect to the prospective cease and desist order; a hundred years of false cold claims have built up a large reservoir of erroneous consumer belief which would persist, unless corrected, long after petitioner ceased making the claims.

*   *   *

* * * [I]t is clear that the Commission has the power to shape remedies which go beyond the simple cease and desist order. Our next inquiry must be whether a corrective advertising order is for any reason outside the range of permissible remedies.

*   *   *

The Supreme Court [has] expressly noted that the First Amendment presents "no obstacle" to government regulation of false or misleading advertising. The First Amendment, the Court said, as we construe it today, does not prohibit the State from insuring that the stream of commercial information flow[s] cleanly as well as freely.

* * *

* * *[W]e are not convinced that the corrective advertising remedy is really * * * an innovation. The label may be newly coined, but the concept is well established. It is simply that under certain circumstances an advertiser may be required to make affirmative disclosure of unfavorable facts.

* * *

Having established that the Commission does have the power to order corrective advertising in appropriate cases, it remains to consider whether use of the remedy against Listerine is warranted and equitable. We have concluded that part 3 of the order should be modified to delete the phrase "Contrary to prior advertising." With that modification, we approve the order.

Our role in reviewing the remedy is limited. The Supreme Court has set forth the standard:

> The Commission is the expert body to determine what remedy is necessary to eliminate the unfair or deceptive trade practices which have been disclosed. It has wide latitude for judgment and the courts will not interfere except where the remedy selected has no reasonable relation to the unlawful practices found to exist.

The Commission has adopted the following standard for the imposition of corrective advertising:

> [I]f a deceptive advertisement has played a substantial role in creating or reinforcing in the public's mind a false and material belief which lives on after the false advertising ceases, there is clear and continuing injury to competition and to the consuming public as consumers continue to make purchasing decisions based on the false belief. Since this injury cannot be averted by merely requiring respondent to cease disseminating the advertisement, we may appropriately order respondent to take affirmative action designed to terminate the otherwise continuing ill effects of the advertisement.

We think this standard is entirely reasonable.

* * *

Accordingly, the order, as modified, is affirmed.

2. False Advertising by Means of "Bait and Switch" (Criminal Liability)

PEOPLE v. BLOCK & KLEAVER, INC.

103 Misc. 2d 758, 427 N.Y.S.2d 133 (1980)

Block and Kleaver, Inc., the defendant, was in the business of selling bulk beef at retail. It advertised the meat at prices less than the defendant itself had paid for it and less than those charged by two other retail bulk meat businesses. Each customer who responded to the advertisement was shown the sale beef. It was fatty, discolored, and unappetizing. The customer was told that there would be a weight loss averaging about 54 percent to trim the meat for use. The customer was also shown more appetizing and more expensive beef that had been pretrimmed. Employees represented that its weight loss in preparation for use would be only about 10 percent and that a side of beef would last for about 11 months. As a result customers purchased the more expensive beef. However, the average percentage of its waste in 17 purchases was 31 percent and the beef did not last as long as had been represented.

The defendant was charged with violating sections 190.20 and 190.65 of the Penal Law, proscribing misleading advertising and consumer fraud. After a non-jury trial, the defendant was convicted of both offenses. Pertinent parts of the trial court's opinion follows.

MARK, Judge.   * * * Section 190.20 of the Penal Law may be construed in conjunction with Section 396 of the General Business Law. * * * Both statutes proscribe the sale promotional practice known as "bait and switch advertising," "bait advertising," or "fictitious bargain claims." * * * This practice consists of advertising a product at a very low price; a pattern of conduct discouraging the purchase of the advertised article by disparaging the same and exhibiting a poor-appearing specimen of the advertised article; and the resulting switch to the purchase of a product costing more than the one advertised. * * *

This is the exact factual predicate in the instant case, as it was in *People v. Glubo* [158 N.E.2d 699 (N.Y. 1959)].

In that case, the defendant advertised via television a sewing machine which cost $45, for the price of $29.50. A customer who responded was visited by a salesman who would undertake to prove the advertised machine inoperable and point out that it was basically defective and inferior. The salesman would then attempt to persuade the customer to order a better machine at a much higher price. * * * The sole claim of falsity was that the defendant had no intention whatever of selling the advertised machine. * * * The People's case rested on the fact that the defendant advertised for sale a sewing machine it did not intend to sell in order to obtain leads so that it might sell the higher-priced machine. The defendant made no false representation concerning the machines they did sell and the sewing machines sold by the defendants were worth the money paid therefor.

The Court of Appeals held that the conduct of the defendant constituted false advertising and that it was properly convicted. * * *

Accordingly, the defendant corporation [Block & Kleaver, Inc.] is found guilty of the crime of False Advertising in violation of Section 190.20. * * *

Defrauding of different people over [an] extended period, using different means and representations may constitute a scheme and it makes no difference that various deceptions are practiced. * * *

The fact that the employees of the defendant corporation over a period of nine months induced 29 customers to purchase pretrimmed meat by representing the waste percentage of the sale beef at various high percentages, by misrepresenting the estimated loss of the pretrimmed beef at various low percentages, by erroneously informing customers that they could save money by purchasing pretrimmed beef and by overestimating the length of time the pretrimmed beef would last, indicates that the defendant was engaged in a scheme to defraud. [Section 190.65 of the Penal Law.]

* * * Even the defendant's subjective intent is unimportant if his criminal culpability is based upon reckless indifference to the truth. * * * Included in this category are half truths * * * and statements implying knowledge where there is no knowledge, expressions of opinion when the speaker has no opinion in fact, and promises made without a reasonable basis that they can be fulfilled. * * *

The defendant corporation cannot defend upon the ground that the misrepresentations of its employees were mere seller's talk. * * * The federal courts have constructed two tests for distinguishing fraudulent representations from puffing.

Under the first test, a seller engages in a fraudulent misrepresentation when he actually invents non-existent attributes. * * * False declarations of value constitute fraud because values are facts. * * * Under the second test, the purchaser is entitled to receive a product conforming to his expectation, and he is defrauded if his expectation is not met. * * * When a buyer receives a product not meeting the specifications represented * * * or the value of the product is less than represented * * * he has been defrauded. * * *

Accordingly, the defendant corporation is found guilty of the crime of Scheme to Defraud * * * in violation of Section 190.65(1) of the Penal Law.

3. Referral Sale Contract Unconscionable

FROSTIFRESH CORPORATION v. REYNOSO

52 Misc.2d 26, 274 N.Y.S.2d 757 (1966)

DONOVAN, Judge.   Plaintiff brings this action for $1364.10, alleging that the latter amount is owed by the defendants to the plaintiff on account of the purchase of a combination-refrigerator-freezer for which they agreed to pay the sum of $1145.88. The balance of the amount consists of a claim for attorney fees in the amount of $227.35 and a late charge of $22.87. The only payment made on account of the original indebtedness is the sum of $32.00.

The contract for the refrigerator-freezer was negotiated orally in Spanish between the defendants and a Spanish speaking salesman representing the plaintiff. In that conversation the defendant husband told the salesman that he had but one week left on his job and he could not afford to buy the appliance. The salesman distracted and deluded the defendants by advising them that the appliance would cost them nothing because they would be paid bonuses or commissions of $25.00 each on the numerous sales that would be made to their neighbors and friends. Thereafter there was submitted to and signed by the defendants a retail installment contract entirely in English. The retail contract was neither translated nor explained to the defendants. In that contract there was a cash sales price set forth of $900.00.

To this was added a credit charge of $245.88, making a total of $1145.88 to be paid for the appliance.

The plaintiff admitted that cost to the plaintiff corporation for the appliance was $348.00.

No defense of fraud was set forth in the pleadings and accordingly such defense is not available.

However, in the course of the trial, it did appear to the court that the contract might be unconscionable. The court therefore continued the trial at an adjourned date to afford a reasonable opportunity to the parties to present evidence as to the commercial setting, purpose and effect of the contract.

The court finds that the sale of the appliance at the price and terms indicated in this contract is shocking to the conscience. The service charge, which almost equals the price of the appliance is in and of itself indicative of the oppression which was practiced on these defendants. Defendants were handicapped by a lack of knowledge, both as to the commercial situation and the nature and terms of the contract which was submitted in a language foreign to them.

The question presented in this case is simply this: Does the court have the power under section 2–302 of the Uniform Commercial Code to refuse to enforce the price and credit provisions of the contract in order to prevent an unconscionable result.

* * *

It is normally stated that the parties are free to make whatever contracts they please so long as there is no fraud or illegality * * *

However, it is the apparent intent of the Uniform Commercial Code to modify this general rule by giving the courts power "to police explicitly against the contracts or clauses which they find to be unconscionable. * * * The principle is one of the prevention of oppression and unfair surprise." * * *

In the instant case the court finds that it was "too hard a bargain" and the conscience of the court will not permit the enforcement of the contract as written. Therefore the plaintiff will not be permitted to recover on the basis of the price set forth in the retail installment contract, namely $900.00 plus $245.85 as a service charge.

However, since the defendants have not returned the refrigerator-freezer, they will be required to reimburse the plaintiff for the cost to the plaintiff, namely $348.00. No allowance is made on account of any commissions the plaintiff may have paid to salesmen or for legal fees, service charges or any other matters of overhead.

Accordingly the plaintiff may have judgment against both defendants in the amount of $348.00 with interest, less the $32.00 paid on account, leaving a net balance of $316.00 with interest from December 26, 1964.

4. Nondisclosure of Creditor Security Interest to Retail Installment Buyer Violates Truth in Lending Act

CHAPMAN v. MILLER

575 S.W.2d 581 (Tex. Civ. App., 1978)

KEITH, J.   Defendant below appeals from an adverse judgment rendered in a bench trial of a suit brought under * * * the Federal Truth in Lending Act and Regulation Z promulgated thereunder.

Plaintiff entered into a retail installment contract with Don Chapman Motor Sales for the purchase of a used automobile. The contract provided for a down payment of $200, six weekly payments of $25, and eighteen monthly payments of $70.47. Plaintiff made the down payment and the six weekly payments without too much difficulty. The next five monthly installments were accepted even though they were late; but, when the March 1975 payment became overdue, defendant repossessed the car notifying plaintiff that the entire balance was then due and payable. When plaintiff did not pay the balance due, defendant sold the car * * *. [P]laintiff brought this suit alleging several violations of the cited statute and regulaticn. The trial court agreed and awarded damages, plus attorney's fess * * *.

* * * [D]efendant complains that the trial court erred in conclusion of law number 14 by holding that his contract violated 12 C.F.R. § 226.8(a)(1) [Regulation Z] because the description of the security interest is not on the same side of the paper as the buyer's signature.

The cited section requires that all disclosures which must be made thereunder be made together on:

> (1) The note or other instrument evidencing the obligation on the same side of the page and above or adjacent to the place for the customer's signature; of (2) One side of a separate statement which identifies the transaction.

Defendant chose to make his disclosures on the retail credit contract. However, he failed to put all the required disclosures on one side of the contract above plaintiff's signature, *i.e.,* the description of his retained security interest is located on the reverse side of the contract. * * * [W]e are of the opinion that the trial court correctly found a violation of Regulation Z.

Defendant claims that he did not have to make all required disclosures on the front side because of the Interpretive Ruling of the Federal Reserve Board, 12 C.F.R. § 226.801, which allows the required disclosures to be made on both sides of a combination contract and security agreement. This interpretation, however, has a caveat:

> *Provided,* That the amount of the finance charge and the annual percentage rate shall appear on the face of the document, and, if the reverse side is used, the printing on both sides of the document shall be equally clear and conspicuous, both sides shall contain the statement. "NOTICE: See other side for the important information," *and the place for the cus-*

tomer's signature shall be provided following the full content of the document.

The space provided for the plaintiff's signature is on the front page of the contract only and does not follow "the full content of the document." Therefore, defendant has violated Section 226.801.

Defendant rationalizes that his notices at the top and bottom of the front side allow him to incorporate by reference all disclosures and conditions from the reverse side into the front side above the signature. The notice at the top of the page provides:

> BUYER HAS ELECTED TO PURCHASE FROM SELLER SUBJECT TO THE TERMS AND CONDITIONS AS SET FORTH BELOW AND UPON THE REVERSE SIDE HEREOF, THE FOLLOWING DESCRIBED MOTOR VEHICLE, WHICH BUYER HAS THOROUGHLY INSPECTED AND WHICH MEETS WITH BUYER'S APPROVAL IN ALL RESPECTS:

The notice at the bottom of the page provides: "NOTICE: SEE REVERSE SIDE FOR IMPORTANT INFORMATION, ALL TERMS OF WHICH ARE HEREBY INCORPORATED BY REFERENCE." However, this notice was below plaintiff's signature.

The Truth in Lending Act was enacted and Regulation Z was issued "to assure a meaningful disclosure of credit terms so that the consumer will be able to compare more readily the various credit terms available to him and avoid the uninformed use of credit * * *." Their provisions are detailed and explicit.

As noted in *Charles v. Krauss Co., Ltd.,* 572 F.2d 544, 546 (5th Cir. 1978):

> Moreover, liability flows from even minute deviations from the requirements of the statute and of Regulation Z. The statute aims to assure a meaningful disclosure of credit terms so that consumers may shop comparatively for credit * * *. [Citations.] Therefore, the defendant may not escape liability by means of incorporation by reference. The line provided for plaintiff's signature should have been at the end of the contract; her signature so located would show that she knew to read the entire contract —front and back—for all important provisions before signing it. The fact that she did not read any of the contract is immaterial.

> * * *

The judgment of the trial court * * * is affirmed.

5. Voluntary Transfer of Credit Card by Holder to Another Does Not Constitute 'Unauthorized Use' Under Truth In Lending Act

MARTIN v. AMERICAN EXPRESS, INC.

361 So.2d 597 (Ala. Civ. App., 1979)

This was an action brought by American Express, Inc. (plaintiff), against Robert Martin (defendant) to collect approximately $5,300 for purchases that had been made using his American Express Card.

In April 1975 Martin gave his American Express credit card to a business associate, E. L. McBride, to use in their joint business venture. Martin orally authorized McBride to charge up to $500. However, in June 1975 Martin received a statement from American Express which showed that the amount due on his account was approximately $5,300. Martin refused to pay the bill on the ground that he had not signed any of the credit card invoices. American Express then filed suit against him. Martin claimed that his liability for "unauthorized" use of his credit card was limited to $50 by the Truth in Lending Act.

BRADLEY, Judge.   The issue is whether the use of a credit card by a person who has received the card and permission to utilize it from the cardholder constitutes "unauthorized use" under the Truth in Lending Act, 15 U.S.C.A. § 1620(o) and § 1643(a). We hold that in instances where a cardholder, who is under no compulsion by fraud, duress or otherwise, voluntarily permits the use of his (or her) credit card by another person, the cardholder has authorized the use of that card and is thereby responsible for any charges as a result of that use.

Section 1643(a), which is of principal concern in this case limits a cardholder's liability to $50 for the "unauthorized use of a credit card." However, the statutory limitation on liability comes into play only where there is an "unauthorized use" of a credit card. And section 1602(o) defines "unauthorized use" as the "use of a credit card by a person other than the cardholder [a] who does not have actual, implied, or apparent authority for such use, and [b] from which the cardholder receives no benefit."

We believe Congress clearly indicated that "unauthorized use" of a card would occur only where there was no "actual, implied, or apparent authority" given. * * * Thus, Martin says he gave no authority for McBride to charge the large sum which eventually resulted in this suit.

We cannot accept this contention. McBride was actually authorized by Martin to use the latter's card. Martin admitted this fact. And the authority to use it, if not actual, remained apparent even after McBride ignored Martin's directions by charging over $500 to Martin's credit card account. Consequently, Martin was not entitled to rely on the provision contained in section 1643(a) and he must be held responsible for any purchases made through the use of his card.

The express intent of Congress in enacting the Truth in Lending Act was to protect the consumer or cardholder against charges for the unauthorized use of his or her credit card and to limit his or her liability for such unauthorized use to a maximum of $50 providing, however, that the conditions set forth in the statute are complied with. We believe that section 1643(a) clearly indicates that such protection is warranted where the card is obtained from the cardholder as a result of loss, theft or wrongdoing; however, we are not persuaded that section 1643(a) is applicable where a cardholder voluntarily and knowingly allows another to use his card and that person subsequently misuses the card.

Were we to adopt any other view, we would provide the unscrupulous and dishonest cardholder with the means to defraud the card issuer by allowing his or her friends to use the card, run up hundreds of dollars in charges and then limit his or her liability to $50 by notifying the card issuer. We do not believe such a result was either intended or sanctioned by Congress when it enacted section 1643(a).

Judgment for American Express affirmed.

6. Equal Credit Opportunity Act Violated by Failure to Identify Consumer Reporting Agency

CARROLL v. EXXON CO.

434 F. Supp. 557 (E.D.La., 1977)

This action brought by Kathleen Carroll (plaintiff) against Exxon (defendant) claimed that Exxon violated the Fair Credit Reporting Act and the Equal Credit Opportunity Act in denying a credit card to her.

In August 1976 Carroll, a single working woman, applied for an Exxon credit card. Carroll did not have a major credit card, did not list a savings account on her application, had been employed for only one year, and did not have any dependents. On September 14, she was advised by letter that her application for credit was denied, but no reason for the denial was provided. On September 28, she wrote to Exxon and asked to be advised of the specific reasons for the credit denial. In an undated response she was advised that the credit bureau contacted by Exxon had not responded adversely but had been unable to supply sufficient information concerning her established credit. However, this letter, like the earlier letter, did not contain the name of the credit bureau used by Exxon to investigate her credit. Only after filing the lawsuit was Carroll given the name and address of the credit bureau.

MITCHELL, District Judge.   Carroll * * * contends that Exxon violated the terms of the Equal Credit Opportunity Act (ECOA) by failing to provide her with the specific reasons for the credit denial, and by discriminating against her on the basis of marital status in evaluating her credit application.

The ECOA provides, in pertinent part:

(a) It shall be unlawful for any creditor to discriminate against any applicant, with respect to any aspect of a credit transaction—

(1) on the basis of race, color, religion, national origin, sex or marital status, or age (provided that applicant has the capacity to contract).

The ECOA also provides for the promulgation of regulations by the Federal Reserve Board to carry out the purpose of the Act. One such regulation provides that "[a] creditor shall provide each applicant who is denied credit or whose account is terminated the reasons for such action, if the applicant so requests." Ms. Carroll takes the position that Exxon's undated letter, which was sent to her as a result of her request for specific reasons for the credit denial, violated the plain terms in failing to provide the reasons for the negative action.

Counsel for Exxon argues that Exxon's undated letter and its letter of November 2, 1976, satisfy the requirement to provide reasons for the credit denial. The legal issue before this Court, then, is whether Exxon's responses to Carroll satisfy the notification requirement.

The ECOA, provides that "[a] statement of reasons meets the requirements of this section *only if it contains the specific reasons for the adverse action taken"*[emphasis added]. Our independent examination of the record of this case reveals that a number of factors contributed to the denial of Ms. Carroll's credit card application. For example, Carroll did not have a major credit card, she did not list a savings account on her application, she had been employed for only one year, and she had no dependents. However, for some reason, Exxon chose only to list, as its reasons for the denial of credit, that the Credit Bureau which had been contacted could furnish little or no definitive information regarding Carroll's established credit.

The legislative history of the 1976 amendments to the ECOA is particularly instructive in construing the congressional intent behind the passage of the Act:

> The requirement that creditors give reasons for adverse action is, in the Committee's view, a strong and necessary adjunct to the antidiscrimination purpose of the legislation, for only if creditors know they must explain their decisions will they effectively be discouraged from discriminatory practices. Yet this requirement fulfills a broader need: rejected credit applicants will now be able to learn where and how their credit status is deficient, and this information should have a pervasive and valuable educational benefit. Instead of being told only that they do not meet a particular creditor's standards, consumers particularly should benefit from knowing, for example, that the reason for the denial is their short residence in the area, or their recent change of employment, or their already over-extended financial situation. In those cases where the creditor may have acted on misinformation or inadequate information, the statement of reasons gives the applicant a chance to rectify the mistake.

Therefore, even if we view Exxon's undated response to Carroll to have been properly amended and corrected by the letter of November 2, 1976, it is clear that Exxon has failed to meet the requirements. Exxon's responses to Carroll's request for specific reasons for the credit denial fail to achieve the informative purposes legislated in the ECOA. We do not feel that this decision will place any heavier burden on creditors than that intended by Congress to aid the consumer in the search for reliable and informative credit information.

Judgment for Carroll for actual and punitive damages plus reasonable attorney's fees.

PROBLEMS

1. On Monday a salesman called on an elderly widow at her home and identified himself, the company he worked for, and the product he sold. He made a contract to sell her an expensive vacuum cleaner with a lifetime guarantee. The contract provided that she pay 10% down and the balance within one year. Delivery of the vacuum cleaner was subject to the widow's credit being approved by the home office of the seller. On Tuesday the widow calls you for advice as she wants to cancel the contract. Discuss.

2. In September, B purchased a stero on credit from Montgomery Ward through its catalogue. The catalogue contained a statement, "NO MONTHLY PAYMENTS TILL FEBRUARY when you order stereo on Credit at Wards." It was not disclosed that the credit charge was computed by the seller from the date of purchase in September and not from the February date when payment was due. B claims the seller failed to disclose the financing terms in its advertising making it liable for failure to disclose. Discuss.

3. Colgate-Palmolive Company ran a commercial on television which purported to give viewers visual proof that its shaving cream "Rapid Shave" could soften sandpaper. Unknown to viewers, the substance that appeared to be sandpaper in the commercials was in fact a prop made of plexiglass covered with sand. Could the FTC prohibit the use of this type of undisclosed simulation?

4. B applied for life insurance to the N Company and the S Company. These companies requested credit information on B from the R Credit Company, a mercantile reporting agency. R erroneously reported that B was an excessive drinker. This credit report caused both insurance companies to refuse to insure B. In addition, the report caused B's automobile insurance carrier to cancel his policy. B sues R for damages for defamation. Decision?

5. Ramis, a real estate developer, advertised nationally a massive development of one acre unimproved lots in a southwest state. Griswold, an out-of-state resident, learns of it and requests information about the project. Ramis provides Griswold with a small advertising brochure lacking in information about the company or the land. The brochure makes vague descriptions of the joys of home ownership and nothing else. Griswold purchases a lot. Two weeks later, Griswold wishes to cancel the land sales contract. Ramis sues to enforce the contract. Decision?

6. Plunkett obtains gas credit cards for himself and his wife from Mobil. Each card stated: "This card is valid unless expired or revoked. Named holder's approval of all purchases is presumed unless written notice of loss or theft is received." Later, Plunkett returned his card to Mobil, stating that he was cancelling it, but having separated from his wife, he could not return the card in her possession. Mobil thereafter sued Plunkett for charges made by his wife with the card in her possession. Plunkett defended on the ground that he had lawfully cancelled the credit card agreement, and was not responsible for his wife's credit card purchases. Decision?

7. The management of the Andrews Hotel wished to increase their revenues. They added a 2% "sundries charge" to the bill of every hotel guest. Over time the total charges yielded the hotel $100,000. Gardner, a guest, protested the charge, and complained to the state attorney general's Consumer Frauds Bureau when the hotel refused to remove the charge from his bill. The attorney general sued to compel the hotel to stop this practice and to refund charges already collected to all affected guests. The hotel managers argued that a messenger service used by 77% of the guests justified the charge. Decision?

8. Knopf applied for a loan at a bank, which sought a credit check to assure itself of Knopf's financial responsibility. Howe and Associates, a consumer credit reporting agency, confused Knopf's credit file with that of another individual of the same name, and reported Knopf as bankrupt. This mistake delayed the granting of a bank loan. Knopf sued Howe for damages, claiming that their report, which took 49 days to make, was unreasonably delayed. Howe argued that such a complaint does not state a good cause of action. Decision?

9. Buyer purchased an automobile from Seller on credit. Seller listed a $16.00 charge for "tag, title, and fees" and for a "documentary service fee" under the heading "Official Fees" on the sales contract, but failed to itemize the amounts charged. Buyer complains that because components of the "official fees" were not itemized, the amount charged under that heading should not have been included in the computation of the finance charge. Decision?

10. Webb Foods, a retail grocery outlet, purchased debt collection forms from a collection agency. Although they wrote the collection agency's name and address on the mailing envelope, Webb did not include that address on the form letter or telegram when they mailed the forms to Stack, a debtor. Webb was demanding payment from Stack on checks returned for insufficient funds. Webb did not disclose that they had no legal right to collect certain charges, or the fact that they, and not the collection agency, was sending the dunning notices. Is Stack liable to Webb on the checks?

Part VI

PARTNERSHIPS

Chapter 33

INTRODUCTION

A. NATURE OF PARTNERSHIPS

1. IN GENERAL

A person who starts a business is faced with a choice as to what type of business organization he or she should use (e.g., a sole proprietorship, partnership, or corporation). If the person has sufficient money to get started, he or she will probably use the sole proprietorship, a form that gives a person absolute control of the operation of the business and receipt of all of the profits. However, a person who has insufficient funds will probably have to choose between a partnership and a corporation.

A partnership is an agreement between two or more persons to carry on a business for profit (see Uniform Partnership Act, Appendix B). A corporation is an artificial legal being created by the government and endowed with certain powers. It is treated in the law as a separate person or legal entity separate and distinct from the shareholders, who are the owners of the corporation. The chart on page 485 indicates the main differences between a partnership and a corporation.

2. ELEMENTS OF A PARTNERSHIP

A partnership is an association (joining together) of two or more persons having legal capacity (includes individuals, partnerships, corporations, and other associations as defined in the Uniform Partnership Act, Section 2) to carry on a business (includes every trade, occupation, or profession) as co-owners for the purpose of making profits. Profit sharing is the prima facie test of a partnership.

3. CREATION

A partnership may be created by an oral agreement except where it must be in writing because of the statute of frauds. For example, most courts hold that if the partnership is to continue for more than one year or if it will buy or sell real estate, the partnership agreement must be in writing.

PARTNERSHIP	CORPORATION
1. Created by agreement.	Created by statutory authorization.
2. Not a legal, separate entity in most states.	Legal entity separate and distinct from its owners (i. e., a legal person for the ownership of property and appearance as a party to litigation).
3. Each partner subject to unlimited liability for the debts, contracts, and torts of the other partners arising out of the partnership business.	Shareholders not liable for the debts of the corporation.
4. A partner's interest not transferable without the consent of all of the other partners.	Shares of stock freely transferable.
5. Each partner has a direct and equal voice in the management of the business.	Management indirect through elected directors.
6. The partnership terminated by the agreement, or by the death, bankruptcy, or withdrawal of a partner.	May have perpetual existence.
7. Each partner pays an income tax on his or her share of the net profits whether distributed or not.	Corporation pays an income tax on net profits, and the shareholders pay an income tax on the dividends they receive. There can be a tax advantage depending on the amount of net profits distributed and the shareholder's tax bracket.

Even though an oral partnership agreement is usually valid, it is desirable that the agreement be in writing to avoid subsequent disputes as to mutual rights and duties. The following case is an example of the creation of a partnership by oral agreement.

FACTS Athene Cooper and Jacquelyn Hunt (then Saunders) orally agreed to undertake a business venture of the purchase, renovation, and operation of several rooming houses, a restaurant, and a grocery store. When Saunders became Hunt, her husband urged her to terminate the venture with Cooper, which she did. Cooper argued that the evidence did not establish a partnership between the parties, but at most a joint tenancy of the realty, and claimed that no agreements to operate any businesses were ever made. The court decided that there was a partnership and that Hunt was entitled to the amount she had contributed— $12,250. Cooper appealed.

DECISION The court held that a writing was not a partnership requirement. All that is needed is an association of two or more persons to carry on as co-owners of a business for profit. Receipt by a person of a share of the profits of a business is prima facie evidence that he or she is a partner. Affirmed.

Cooper v. Saunders-Hunt (365 A.2d 626 [D.C.App., 1976])

An agreement to form a partnership may be made between parties. Such an agreement does not of itself create a partnership, nor is a partnership created by the advancement by one party of his or her agreed share of the capital. Persons who have entered into a contract to become partners at a future time do not become partners until the agreed time has arrived. Partnerships may be created as trading, for the buying and selling of goods, or as nontrading.

B. FICTITIOUS NAME

Many partnerships, as well as individuals, operate under fictitious business names. Most states have statutes requiring the registration of such names if a business is conducted under a name that does not include the surname of each of the partners or is one that suggests the existence of additional owners.

The purpose of the requirement is to make a public record of the individuals in the partnership for the benefit of those who deal with the partnership.

Such registration is usually necessary because most banking procedures require such filing before they will open an account under a fictitious name and most courts will not permit lawsuits to be filed in the fictitious name until the required notice is executed, filed, and published.

The normal procedure is to file a fictitious business name statement with the county clerk of the county of the main place of business of the entity, usually on a preprinted form provided by the clerk upon which is listed the names and addresses of all of the partners. After the record is filed with the clerk and the filing fee is paid, the statement must be published in a newspaper of general circulation in that county for a specified period of time (in California, once a week for four consecutive weeks).

C. PARTNERSHIP BY ESTOPPEL

A person who holds himself or herself out as a partner or knowingly allows himself or herself to be held out as a partner becomes liable as such to those who deal with the firm in the belief that he or she is a partner. A partnership by estoppel is similar to an agency created by estoppel covered in Part 3.

The following case illustrates the creation of a partnership by estoppel.

FACTS　Plaintiff delivered mud and materials in connection with the drilling of oil well C & W No. 1. Defendant Walker denies responsibility for any part of the $5,795.28 billed for these materials. The court found that defendant Collins and Walker were partners at the time operating under the firm name of Collins and Walker. Walker appealed.

DECISION　The court found that Walker had stated on several occasions that he was a partner with Collins, that signs on the rigs and trailers around the well site read "Collins-Walker, C & W No. 1," and that Collins had introduced Walker as his partner at different times. The judge stated that where there is no written agreement, a partnership may be evidenced by the conduct of the parties. Affirmed.

Calada Materials Co. v. Collins (184 Cal.App.2d 250, 7 Cal.Rptr. 374 [1960])

D.　JOINT VENTURE

A joint venture, or joint adventure, is similar to a partnership in that its members associate together as co-owners of a business enterprise. However, a partnership is usually intended to continue for a definite or indefinite period as a continuing business, while a joint venture is formed for a single transaction or single series of transactions, not requiring the entire attention of the participants, and thus is more limited in scope and duration. An example of a joint venture is an agreement between an owner of lots and a building contractor to build houses for sale and a division of the profits.

The relationship between the members in a joint venture are governed by the rules applicable to partners (e. g., Uniform Partnership Act applied to dissolution; there is a fiduciary duty to account for profits and joint property; there is a power of representation within the scope of the business; profits earned are taxable income to the members whether or not distributed; tort of one member committed in furtherance of joint enterprise causes all other members to be liable).

The following case illustrates how the court considered tax returns in determining that no joint venture was intended.

FACTS　P & M Cattle Company (plaintiff) brought an action against Rusty Holler (defendant) to recover half the losses suffered in a joint venture in cattle feeding. Judgment for Holler; plaintiff appealed.

DECISION　The court held that joint ventures are governed by partnership laws and that although a share of profits is prima facie evidence of the existence of a partnership, there are exceptions. This rule does not apply if the profits were received in payment of a debt, as wages or rent, as an annuity, as interest on a loan, or as consideration for the sale of goodwill or other property of a business. As in any contract, the intent of the parties controls. Evidence showed that no partnership income tax returns had been filed during 1971–1974, the years in question. On the plaintiff's tax returns, profits paid to Holler had been listed as "contract feeding" expense and for "pasture." Holler had included profit items on his tax return as a sale of crops. Judgment affirmed, as there was no proof of intent for a joint venture.

P & M Cattle Company v. Holler (559 P.2d 1019 [Wyo., 1977])

E. LIMITED PARTNERSHIP

A limited partnership is a statutory form of association, basically the same as a general partnership, with the added provision for investors who wish to share in the profits but not in the management and thereby avoid the personal liability of general partners.

The main differences between limited and general partnerships are that the limited partnership:

1. Must have at least one general partner.

2. Must file a Certificate of Limited Partnership.

3. May not include in its name the surnames of any limited partners without making them liable to creditors.

4. May not permit limited partners to take part in the control of the business.

The limited partners share in the profits but do not share losses beyond their capital investment. Limited partnership acts have been enacted in all states, most of them adopting the Uniform Limited Partnership Act (ULPA). In 1976, the ULPA was revised to resolve uncertainties existing in the original law and to permit certain actions by the limited partners that are not considered to be participation in the management or control of the business, such as being a contractor, employee, or agent of the partnership or general partner; consulting with or advising the general partner; and voting on specified extraordinary matters. Most states have either adopted the revised Act or further expanded their own. For example, California's statute, effective in 1983, treats limited partnerships more like corporations, requires that the firm name include the words "limited partnership," lists various activities that limited partners may engage in without exposing themselves to liability, and specifies new detailed procedures to be followed.

A limited partnership is not created by a mere informal agreement as is possible with a general partnership. It is created by a formal proceeding that must follow the statute. For example, the associates must sign, file, and record a certificate, which must set forth the partnership name, charter, location of business, the term to carry on the business, amount and character of contributions by special or limited partners, the share of profits or compensation of each limited partner, and methods for changing personnel and continuing business after retirement of a general partner.

Limited partnerships are used primarily for investment purposes. The limited partners are not really partners but are investors with no personal liability beyond their investment.

There is an ever-increasing use of this method of acquiring investment capital, particularly in real estate development, oil and gas leases, film production, and the building of medical facilities. The attractiveness of this method of business operation is the low risk involved. However, the status of a limited partner who attempts to participate in the actual management of the business project may be converted to that of a general partner with the attendant personal liability.

F. UNINCORPORATED ASSOCIATION

Social clubs, political parties, and fraternal organizations are common examples of unincorporated associations. No particular form of organization is required. The purpose of the organization is nonprofit. A member is not liable for the debts of the association unless he or she authorized or ratified the particular act which created the liability. The following case is an example of how the courts apply this rule.

FACTS Maine National Guard units held an annual New Year's Eve dance in the Augusta State Armory. Libby was a paying guest at the dance and, on leaving, fell on the ice in the parking lot and was injured. Perry was a member of the Armory Committee, which planned and operated the dance, as was Turner. Turner, however, took no part in the activities and was absent from all committee meetings. Judgment was against the entire committee, and it appealed.

DECISION The court held that although the Armory Committee was a voluntary unincorporated association formed to accomplish a common purpose and was duty bound to use the same care to avoid injury to others as natural persons are individually, mere membership in the body does not create liability. It was error to find Turner responsible with the other defendants on the mere evidence that he was a member of the Armory Committee. All the other defendants actively participated, aided, and abetted in the affair and were responsible to the plaintiff for the wrongful acts of omission of their associates or their agents in carrying out the social event duly authorized by the association. Judgment reversed as to Turner but sustained as to the other defendants.

Libby v. Perry (311 A.2d 527 [Me., 1973])

G. COOPERATIVE

A cooperative is a union of individuals formed for the prosecution in common of some productive enterprise, the profits being shared in accordance with the capital or labor contributed by each. Common examples of cooperatives are farmers, laborers, or small capitalists. In many states, statutes regulate cooperatives. In the absence of statute, the cooperative is similar to an unincorporated association in that the rights and liabilities of the members are the same.

H. PARTNERSHIP PROPERTY

1. IN GENERAL

To ascertain the rights of the partners and the creditors to specific property, it is frequently important, especially when creditors of a partner are involved or upon dissolution, to ascertain exactly what property constitutes partnership property and what constitutes property of the individual partner.

What constitutes partnership property is ascertained from the agreement of the partners, from their conduct, and from the purpose for and the way in which the property is used in the partnership business. The Uniform Partnership Act (U.P.A.) states that all property originally brought into the partnership or subsequently acquired by purchase or otherwise on account of the partnership is partnership property. Unless a contrary intention appears, property acquired with partnership funds is partnership property (U.P.A., Section 8(1) (2)).

Anything that is a proper subject of ownership may be partnership property. Examples of partnership property are cash, land, goods, the rendition of personal services, corporate stock, a seat on the stock exchange, an insurance policy on the life of a partner, and a patent.

2. GOODWILL

When a partnership business is sold or continued with new partners after dissolution, one of the property problems is that of determining the value of the existing goodwill.

In the absence of an express or implied agreement to the contrary, goodwill is a partnership asset. Goodwill means the public favor and patronage built up by the owner of a business. It has been defined as "nothing more than the probability that the old customers will resort to the old place." It includes the right to use the established firm name. In service partnerships, it may be so closely tied to the individual partners that none remains in the business. When a court is required to determine the value of the goodwill of a partnership business, the value is usually placed at what a reasonable person would be willing to pay. The following case is an example of this problem.

> **FACTS** Defendant owned and operated a bar, the Havana Club, in a rented building and made an agreement with the plaintiff for the latter to operate it for a split of the net profits. The building was taken over by the Redevelopment Agency and the parties were unable to relocate the club. The agency paid the club $10,000 damages for disruption of the business, and plaintiff sued for half of this amount. Defendant appeals from a judgment for plaintiff.

> **DECISION** The court found that a profit-sharing joint venture is generally a partnership. In this case, it was largely through the capability, experience, and efforts of the plaintiff that there existed a separate asset of the going concern and goodwill of the business which was lost by its

displacement. The failure of the parties to find another suitable location and the cessation of the operation of the Havana Club resulted in a termination of the partnership. The value of what is called "going concern and goodwill" belonged to the two of them as partners in the enterprise. When the business could not be relocated, the $10,000 should be regarded as compensation for the loss and should be shared equally. Judgment affirmed.

Cutler v. Bowen (543 P.2d 1349 [Utah, 1975])

3. CROPS

Crops growing on partnership land are considered partnership property if that is the express or implied agreement of the partners.

4. PARTNERSHIP CAPITAL

The capital of the partnership is a monetary figure that represents the total of the sums contributed by the partners as permanent investments. It represents a fixed amount that the partnership is obligated to return to the partners at the time of dissolution. Undivided profits that one of the partners may permit to be accumulated in the business do not become part of the capital. Nor do loans made by a partner to the partnership become part of the capital.

It is important for partners to make it clear whether contributions to the partnership are to become partnership property or are to remain the individual's property. This is because creditors of the partnership have first claim on the partnership property, and the creditors of the individual partner have first claim on the individual's property. On dissolution it is important to be able to distinguish the property.

5. TITLE TO PARTNERSHIP PROPERTY

A. PERSONAL PROPERTY

A partnership may hold and transfer title to personal property in the name of the partnership, whether the name is fictitious or consists of the names of the partners.

B. REAL PROPERTY

Under the Uniform Partnership Act (which has been adopted by all states except Georgia and Louisiana), real property may be acquired in the partnership name, whether it is fictitious or not. Title acquired in the partnership name must be conveyed in the partnership name.

Whenever real property is acquired by the partnership for partnership purposes, the rule of out-and-out conversion applies which converts the real property to personalty for all purposes, including descent and distribution.

6. RIGHTS OF PARTNERS IN PARTNERSHIP PROPERTY

A partner is a co-owner with the partners of specific partnership property (e. g., the factory, equipment, trucks). In the absence of an agreement to the contrary between the partners, each partner has an equal right with the partners to possess specific partnership property for partnership purposes. Each partner has no right, however, to possess such property for any other purpose without consent of the partners.

7. ASSIGNABILITY

A partner may sell his or her interest in the assets of the partnership to a third person. Such a transfer does not pass the title of the partnership in the assets but only the interest of the individual partner. The assignee does not become a member of the firm because of the highly personal nature of a partnership and thus is not entitled to interfere in the management of the partnership business, to inspect the partnership books, or to require any information regarding partnership transactions. The assignee is entitled only to receive the profits to which the assignor would otherwise be entitled.

8. EXECUTION

A partner's right in specific partnership property is not subject to execution unless it is a claim against the entire partnership. In other words, a personal creditor of a particular partner cannot have that partner's interest in the partnership attached and sold to pay what is owed. The remedy of a personal creditor of a partner is to attempt to reach other assets of the partner; or if the creditor wishes to proceed against partnership property, he or she should get a charging order under which a receiver will be appointed to collect from the partnership the share of profits of the debtor-partner. The U.P.A., Section 28, provides that the creditor can get a charging order whereby a receiver is appointed and the partner's interest in the profits and in the corpus upon dissolution is applied to satisfy the judgment. If the partnership is a partnership at will (no definite time limit), a dissolution can be brought about immediately.

9. DEATH OF A PARTNER

On the death of a partner, his or her right (not ownership) in specific partnership property vests in the surviving partner or partners, except where the deceased was the last surviving partner, in which case the right in such property vests in the deceased's legal representative. This is to prevent the executor of the deceased's estate from coming into the partnership and taking custody of the deceased partner's interest, which would probably cause confusion and difficulty. The surviving partners do not become the owners of the deceased partner's interest. They merely have the right of exclusive possession during the period that the partnership is liquidated and the net assets distributed to the partners, including the representative of the deceased partner. The liquidation of the partnership and distribution of the net assets must be done immediately after death of one of the partners in the absence of an agreement to the contrary.

ILLUSTRATIVE CASES

1. Creation of Partnership

HOWARD GAULT & SON v. FIRST NATIONAL BANK

541 S.W.2d 235 (Tex.Civ.App., 1976)

ROBINSON, Justice.　Defendant Pitman Grain Company is the maker of a check payable to "Thomas & Gault" drawn on its account in the Defendant First National Bank of Hereford, Texas. The defendant bank accepted the check and deposited it to the account of T. B. Thomas, Jr. upon its presentment with the endorsement

Thomas & Gault

T. B. Thomas, Jr.

*　　　*　　　*

Plaintiff, Howard Gault and Son, Inc., sued the bank for conversion of the check and, in the alternative, sued Pitman on the debt for which the check was given.

*　　　*　　　*

The trial court rendered judgment * * * for Pitman and * * * for the bank. Plaintiff appeals. * * *

Plaintiff alleges that it is a payee on the check and that the endorsement of the check by Thomas was ineffective to authorize payment by the bank.

The evidence shows without dispute that the "Gault" of "Thomas & Gault" is Howard Gault and Son, Inc. The check in question was given by Pitman in payment for milo delivered to Pitman elevators from the farming operation of T. B. Thomas, Jr. and Howard Gault and Son, Inc. The question, then, is whether the endorsement by Thomas was sufficient to authorize the bank to deposit the check to his account. * * *

If plaintiff corporation and Thomas were partners in the farming operation, the bank was authorized to pay the check on Thomas' endorsement.

*　　　*　　　*

The written agreements between plaintiff and Thomas provide for farming certain land, part of it belonging to plaintiff and part of it belonging to J. C. Morrison and leased by Morrison to plaintiff and Thomas as lessees. The Morrison lease was for a cash rental. * * *

Plaintiff was to advance financing including a monthly draw for Thomas to be charged against his share of the net proceeds. Thomas was to furnish his equipment, including upkeep, and his own personal labor. All expenses except those for equipment were to be shared equally. *After payment of the landlord's share* all of the "net revenues, rents, and proceeds" were to be divided equally between plaintiff and Thomas. The writing states that the parties are not engaged in the transaction as partners but as landlord and tenant. Nevertheless, both were tenants of the Morrison land and their agreement provides for a sharing by plaintiff and Thomas of both profits and potential losses, after payment of the stipulated rentals. * * *

It is undisputed that Thomas had the right to obligate plaintiff for debts incurred in the line of farming, that a number of accounts with different businesses were carried in the name of "Thomas and Gault," and that Pitman carried the account on its books as "Thomas & Gault" with the consent of or at the direction of Howard Gault and Son, Inc. Pitman had made previous payments by check payable to "Thomas & Gault." Those checks were accepted by Howard Gault and Son, Inc. without complaint and negotiated with its endorsement and without the endorsement of T. B. Thomas, Jr. * * * No Pitman check was ever endorsed by both plaintiff and Thomas.

*   *   *

The statement in one of the agreements that the farming operation was not a partnership is not conclusive on the question of partnership. It is the intent to do the things that constitute a partnership that determines that the relationship exists between the parties, and if they intend to do a thing which in law constitutes a partnership, they are partners whether their expressed purpose was to create or avoid the relationship.

*   *   *

After reviewing the undisputed evidence as it pertains to the agreements between plaintiff and Thomas, we conclude that, as a matter of law, their farming operation was a partnership.

*   *   *

The judgment of the trial court is affirmed.

2. Partnership by Estoppel

COX ENTERPRISES INC. v. FILIP

538 S.W.2d 836 (Tex.Civ.App., 1976)

Appellant's suit was on a sworn account for $622.78, and attorney's fees, for newspaper advertising services furnished to Trans Texas Properties allegedly at the request of Filip and Elliott. After trial to the court, a take-nothing judgment was entered in favor of Elliott, and a judgment for $622.78 and attorneys' fees was entered against Filip in favor of appellant. Appellant has taken an appeal from the take-nothing judgment in favor of appellee Elliott.

* * * In order to obtain credit for Trans Texas Properties, its employee, Tracey Peoples, represented to appellant that appellee Elliott was an owner of the business. Peoples had no authority from appellee to make that representation. Although appellant relied upon Peoples' representation in ex-

tending credit and rendering the advertising services to Trans Texas Properties, appellant made no effort to verify the accuracy of the representation. Moreover, appellee did not hold himself out to appellant as having an ownership interest in Trans Texas Properties. * * *

Appellant's argument is bottomed upon the Texas Uniform Partnership Act. Section 16(1) provides as follows: * * *

§ 16. Partner by Estoppel

Sec. 16. (1) When a person, by words spoken or written or by conduct, represents himself, or consents to another representing him to any one, as a partner in an existing partnership or with one or more persons not actual partners, he is liable to any such person to whom such representation has been made, who has, on the faith of such representation, given credit to the actual or apparent partnership, and if he has made such representation or consented to its being made in a public manner he is liable to such person, whether the representation has or has not been made or communicated to such person so giving credit by or with the knowledge of the apparent partner making the representation or consenting to its being made. . . .

*   *   *

Prior to the enactment of the Texas Uniform Partnership Act, the rule in Texas was that for liability to be based upon partnership by estoppel, it must be established that the person held out as a partner knew of, and consented in fact to the holding out.

*   *   *

Section 16(1) codifies and enlarges upon the common law of partnership by estoppel. That section imposes a duty on a person to deny that he is a partner once he knows that third persons are relying on representations that he is a partner. We do not read section 16(1) as creating an affirmative duty upon one to seek out all those who may represent to others that he is a partner.

Appellant argues that § 16(1) means that one who negligently holds himself out or permits himself to be held out as a member of a partnership relationship is estopped to deny such partnership relationship as against third persons who in good faith relied on the existence of such apparent partnership and extended credit thereon.

*   *   *

In the case at bar, and in the terms of § 16(1), appellant's factual theory was that appellee consented to Peoples' representation to appellant that appellee was a partner in Trans Texas Properties. Appellant, however, failed in its burden to convince the trier of fact that appellee consented for Peoples to represent that appellee was a partner in Trans Texas Properties. * * *

The judgment is affirmed.

3. Nature of Limited Partnership

DELANEY v. FIDELITY LEASE LIMITED

526 S.W.2d 543 (Tex., 1975)

DANIEL, Justice.　　The question here is whether limited partners in a limited partnership become liable as general partners if they "take part in the control of the business" while acting as officers of a corporation which is the sole general partner of the limited partnership. The trial court, by summary judgment, held that under such circumstances the limited partners did not become liable as general partners. The court of civil appeals affirmed with a dissent and a concurring opinion. We reverse and remand the case for trial on the merits.

Fidelity Lease Limited is a limited partnership organized under the Texas Uniform Limited Partnership Act, to lease restaurant locations. It is composed of 22 individual partners, and a corporate general partner, Interlease Corporation. Interlease's officers, directors and shareholders were W. S. Crombie, Jr., Alan Kahn, and William D. Sanders, who were also limited partners of Fidelity. In February of 1969, plaintiffs Delaney, et al. entered into an agreement with the limited partnership, Fidelity, acting by and through its corporate general partner, Interlease, to lease a fast-food restaurant to the partnership. In accordance therewith, plaintiffs built the restaurant, but Fidelity failed to take possession or pay rent.

Plaintiffs brought suit for damages for breach of the lease agreement, naming as defendants the limited partnership of Fidelity Lease Limited, its corporate general partner Interlease Corporation, and all of its limited partners. * * * Plaintiffs appealed only as to limited partners Crombie, Kahn, and Sanders. Plaintiffs sought to hold these three individuals personally liable alleging that they had become general partners by participating in the management and control of the limited partnership.

Pertinent portions of the Texas Uniform Limited Partnership Act, Article 6132a, provide:

> Sec. 8. A limited partner shall not become liable as a general partner unless in addition to the exercise of his rights and powers as a limited partner, he *takes part in the control of the business.*

It was alleged by plaintiffs, and there is summary judgment evidence, that the three limited partners controlled the business of the limited partnership, albeit through the corporate entity. The defendant limited partners argue that they acted only through the corporation and that the corporation actually controlled the business of the limited partnership. In response to this contention, we adopt the following statements in the dissenting opinion of Chief Justice Preslar in the court of civil appeals:

> I find it difficult to separate their acts for they were at all times in the dual capacity of limited partners and officers of the corporation. Apparently the corporation had no function except to operate the limited partnership and Appellees were obligated to their other partners to so operate the corporation as to benefit the partnership. Each act was done

then, not for the corporation, but for the partnership. Indirectly, if not directly, they were exercising control over the partnership. Truly 'the corporation fiction' was in this instance a fiction.

Thus, we hold that the personal liability, which attaches to a limited partner when "he takes part in the control and management of the business," cannot be evaded merely by acting through a corporation.

*　　*　　*

Crombie, Kahn, and Sanders argue that, since their only control of Fidelity's business was as officers of the alleged corporate general partner, they are insulated from personal liability arising from their activities or those of the corporation. This is a general rule of corporate law, but one of several exceptions in which the courts will disregard the corporate fiction is where it is used to circumvent a statute. * * * That is precisely the result here, for it is undisputed that the corporation was organized to manage and control the limited partnership. Strict compliance with the statute is required if a limited partner is to avoid liability as a general partner. * * *

*　　*　　*

Accordingly, the cause of action against the defendants Crombie, Kahn, and Sanders is severed, and as to that portion of the case the judgments of the lower courts are reversed and such cause as to them is remanded for trial in accordance with this opinion. * * *

4. Charging Order and Execution

TUPPER v. KROC

88 Nev. 146, 494 P.2d 1275 (1972)

BATJER, Justice. Lloyd G. Tupper, appellant and Ray A. Kroc, respondent, entered into three limited partnerships for the purpose of holding title to and leasing parcels of real estate. Tupper was the general partner, Kroc was the limited partner and each held a fifty percent interest.

Kroc filed an action alleging that Tupper had mismanaged and misappropriated funds from these partnerships and requested that they be dissolved and that a receiver be appointed. Pending the final outcome of that action the trial court appointed a receiver to manage the three business organizations. Prior to the date on which the complaint for dissolution had been filed, Tupper had on several occasions been unable to pay his share of the partnerships' obligations. Kroc on those occasions personally contributed the total amounts owed by the partnerships, and in return accepted interest bearing notes from Tupper in amounts equal to one-half of the partnerships' debts paid by him. Kroc thereafter filed an action against Tupper to recover on those notes and was awarded a summary judgment in the amount of $54,609.02.

In an effort to collect on that judgment, Kroc filed a motion requesting the district court to charge Tupper's interest in the partnerships with payment of the judgment and for the sale of Tupper's interest to satisfy the judgment. On June 12, 1969, a charging order was entered directing the sheriff to sell all of Tupper's "right, title and interest" in the three partnerships and to apply the proceeds against the unsatisfied amount of the judgment. Tupper was served with notice of the sale, but he took no action to redeem his interest. The sale was held on June 27, 1969, and Kroc purchased Tupper's interest for $2,500.

Kroc filed a motion to terminate the receivership on March 12, 1970, contending that he was the sole owner of the partnerships and that the need for a receiver had ceased. On May 18, 1970, the appellants filed an objection to the respondents' motion to terminate the receivership, and a motion to set aside the sale conducted pursuant to the charging order. The trial court denied the appellants' motion to set aside the sale, and granted the respondents' motion to terminate the receivership and discharge the receiver. It is from these two orders that this appeal is taken.

* * *

The charging order was properly entered by the district court against Tupper's interest in the three partnerships. * * * The district court also was authorized, in aid of the charging order, to make all orders and directions as the case required. Pursuant to the provisions of this statute the district court was authorized to appoint a receiver to act as a repository for Tupper's share of the profits and surplus for the benefit of Kroc, or as the court did here order the sale of Tupper's interest.

* * *

The appellants' contention that the price paid by Kroc for Tupper's interest in the three partnerships is inadequate, is without merit. The mode for determining the value of Tupper's interest in the partnerships was by a public sale. * * * The fair market value of $2,500 was established by Kroc's bid at the sheriff's sale. * * *

* * *

Finally the appellants contend that because Tupper retained an equity in the partnerships' business and assets, the district court erred when it discharged the receiver. Unfortunately for the appellants this is not true. After Kroc bought all of Tupper's interest in the partnerships, i. e. all of his right and title to the profits and surplus, Kroc was entitled to all of the profits and all of the surplus. "Surplus" is the excess of assets over liabilities. * * * After the sale Tupper had no immediate or future rights to any profits or surplus or any equity whatever in the partnership property, and therefore he had no valid reason to insist on a continuation of the receivership.

Although as a matter of law the respondents were entitled to have the receivership terminated and the receiver discharged, the wisdom of that request, short of the dissolution of the partnerships, is questionable for as soon as the receiver was discharged Tupper had the authority under NRS Ch. 87, as well as the partnerships' agreements to assert his right to participate in the management. By purchasing Tupper's interest in the partnerships Kroc did not divest Tupper of his other property rights.

The receiver was appointed at the request of Kroc, now Tupper wants the receiver to be reappointed to protect Tupper as a general partner from liability that might be incurred through excessive partnership debts. At a glance it might seem that Tupper's fears have some merit. However, as a matter of law, at the moment the receiver was discharged Tupper's right to participate in the management of the partnerships was restored, and as the general partner he would, at least theoretically, be able to prevent the partnerships from incurring liabilities in excess of assets.

The orders of the district court from which these appeals have been taken are affirmed.

PROBLEMS

1. A, B, and C agree that they will form a partnership but that C will not become a partner until he is discharged from the Army in one year. In the meantime, C lends the partnership $5,000 and agrees to take 5 percent of the profits as interest on the loan. A tells T, without C's knowledge, that C is a partner of the firm. T, relying on this information, sells the firm goods on credit. Six months later, the firm becomes insolvent. T brings action against C for the debt still due. Decision?

2. Defendant, a friend of the members of a partnership, was present when the partners requested goods on credit from the plaintiff and when, at the same time, they told plaintiff that defendant was a partner. Although defendant heard the statement, he remained silent. Plaintiff brings action for the goods against defendnat. Decision?

3. A and B are partners in the garage business. They invest part of the profits from their business in land, taking title in their names as tenants in common. The land becomes very valuable, but their business becomes insolvent. B dies leaving a wife. Creditors of the partners seek the land. B's wife and A also claim the land. Decision?

4. A, B, and C are partners. Nothing is said in the partnership agreement regarding the assignability of a partner's interest. C & A get into a dispute after which A sells his entire interest to T, a responsible and wealthy businessman, who is an expert in the business of the partnership. B and C refuse to permit T to participate in the management of the partnership business. Decision?

5. A and B are partners at will. C, a judgment creditor of B, wants to attach B's interest in the partnership property to collect his judgment. What advice would you give C?

6. A, B, C, and D, residents of Illinois, were partners doing business under the trade name of Morning Glory Nursery. A owned one-third interest and B, C, and D owned two-ninths each. The partners acquired three tracts of land in Illinois for the partnership. Two of the tracts were acquired in the names of the partners, "trading and doing business as Morning Glory Nursery." The third was acquired in their individual names without the trade name appearing on the deed. B died intestate, leaving his wife and one son as only heirs. The widow and son sue to have B's interest in the real property transferred to them by descent. Decision?

7. Bolden, a minor, and Allen, an adult, formed a partnership to purchase and operate a machine shop. They purchased the shop from plaintiff, and each contributed $5,000 toward the purchase price and gave the plaintiff a note for $5,000 for the balance. The project was unsuccessful, and the partnership became insolvent. Plaintiff brought an action against the partnership and Bolden and Allen individually to recover the $5,000 due on the unpaid note. Bolden claims that as a minor he has no liability. Decision?

8. Mather, a toy manufacturer, employed Stark as a saleswoman, agreeing to pay her a salary of 20 percent of the profits of the business. The business showed a loss of $1,500 at the end of the year. Mather claimed that since Stark was to get 20 percent of the profits, she was also liable for 20 percent of the losses. Is Mather correct?

9. Penner, Cory, and Sheldon decided to ask for contributions of food, clothing, and money from businesses in their town to be used for the poor. They considered themselves to be partners in the work and so identified themselves to others. All contributions made to the group were distributed by them as soon as received. Sheldon presented to Penner and Cory a bill of $25 for transportation and postage expense and insisted that as partners they must pay their proportionate shares. Are Penner and Cory partners with Sheldon in this enterprise?

10. Price and Mulford formed a partnership for the manufacture and sale of low-priced clocks. Price contributed $5,000, and Mulford contributed $10,000. The articles of co-partnership made no provision for the division of profits. At the end of one year, the profits amounted to $8,000. How should the profits be distributed?

Chapter 34

POWERS, RIGHTS, DUTIES, AND LIABILITIES OF PARTNERS

A. POWERS OF PARTNERS

1. MANAGEMENT OF THE BUSINESS

Decisions on business matters of the partnership are made by the partners. "All partners have equal rights in the management and conduct of the partnership business" (U.P.A., Section 18(e)). Usually, decisions are made by majority vote.

2. POWER OF INDIVIDUAL PARTNER

Every partner is an agent (see Agency, Part 3) of the partnership for the purpose of carrying on the partnership business. An individual partner may have express authority to act for the partnership through the partnership agreement or because of a majority vote of the partners. In addition, a partner has implied authority to do those acts that are customarily done in his or her partnership or that are usual for similar partnerships. The agreement of the partnership determines the partnership's nature and scope of the business. The agreement of the partnership can be changed only by the unanimous consent of the partners. If all of the partners agree to enlarge the scope of their business, the agreement is effective and new powers are then conferred on the partners.

A. CUSTOMARY POWERS

The customary powers of a partner to bind the partnership depend on the nature of the business. The following are examples of customary powers held to bind the partnership due to the nature of the particular partnership:

1. Contracts made by a partner necessary to the transaction of business.

2. Sales of goods of the partnership in the regular course of business with warranties usual to such sales.

3. Purchases of property within the scope of the business, including purchases on credit.

4.   Hiring and firing employees.

5.   Obtaining or canceling insurance.

6.   Borrowing money and executing negotiable instruments in a trading partnership (a business of buying or selling for profit), but not in a nontrading partnership (e. g., lawyers, physicians, real estate business).

7.   Compromising, adjusting, or paying claims against the partnership, and compromising, adjusting, and receiving payment for claims by the partnership.

B.   ACTS NOT WITHIN APPARENT AUTHORITY

An act of a partner that is not apparently necessary for the carrying on of the business of the partnership in the usual way does not bind the partnership unless authorized by the other partners. Examples of acts that are not within the authority of a partner in the usual type of partnership are contracts in which the partner assumes the debt of another, payment of a separate debt of the partner with partnership property, pledging partnership property to secure a partner's separate debt, giving away partnership property, and selling part of the partnership capital.

C.   UNAUTHORIZED ACTS UNDER THE U.P.A.

The U.P.A., Section 9(3), provides that a partner has no authority to perform the following acts unless authorized by the other partners or unless the other partners have abandoned the business:

1.   Make an assignment of the partnership property for the benefit of creditors. Such an assignment may be avoided by the other creditors or by the other partners.

2.   Dispose of the goodwill of the business (e. g., a partner has no implied power to bind the partnership by a promise not to compete with a competitor).

3.   Do any other act that would make it impossible to carry on the ordinary business of the partnership (e. g., disposing of the stock of goods in one of the departments in a department store or agreeing not to compete with a competitor).

4.   Confess a judgment (e. g., one partner cannot abandon defenses in a lawsuit; one partner cannot permit a plaintiff to take a judgment without a contest, since all partners should have the right to defend in court).

5.   Submit a partnership claim or liability to arbitration. It has been held that the partnership is not bound to perform an award unless all partners agreed to the submission, nor can it enforce an award against the third person.

B. RIGHTS OF PARTNERS

1. SHARE OF PROFITS

The partners are entitled to share the profits equally, although the partners can provide by agreement that the profits shall be shared in unequal proportions. Losses are shared in the same proportion as profits.

2. CONTRIBUTIONS

Each partner shall be repaid his or her contributions, whether he or she made them by way of capital or later advances to the partnership property. Partners who have made advances beyond the amount of their agreed capital contributions are to be repaid such advances before anything is distributed to partners.

3. REIMBURSEMENT

The partnership must reimburse or indemnify every partner for all expenditures made and personal liabilities reasonably incurred by the partner in the ordinary and proper conduct of the partnership business or for the preservation of its business or property.

4. MANAGEMENT

All partners have equal rights in the management and conduct of the business.

5. PARTNERSHIP BOOKS

Each partner shall at all times have access to and may inspect and copy any of the partnership books.

6. INFORMATION

Partners shall render on demand true and full information of all things affecting the partnership to any partner or to his or her legal representative. Not only do the partners have the right to demand information, but it is the duty of a partner to voluntarily give information when it affects the partnership (e. g., partner must voluntarily disclose interest he or she has in property that is being purchased by the partnership).

7. RIGHT TO AN ACCOUNT

A partner cannot sue his or her partner on an obligation due the partner by the partnership (e. g., reimbursement for expense incurred or a loan to the partnership). Such items cannot be isolated from the partnership accounts and made the subject of a separate action unless the other partners consent to the suit. The proper remedy for an aggrieved partner is a suit in equity for an accounting, although this remedy is seldom permitted except on dissolution of the partnership. The U.P.A., Section 72, provides for this remedy stating that every partner has the right to a formal account as to partnership affairs:

1. If the partner is wrongfully excluded from the partnership business or from the possession of the partnership property by his or her co-partners.

2. If the right exists under any partnership agreement.

3. If a partner has breached a fiduciary duty (U.P.A., Section 21).

4. Whenever other circumstances render it just and reasonable.

8. PARTNERSHIP PROPERTY

The rights of a partner regarding partnership property were stated in Chapter 33, Section H. 6. In addition, since all partnership property is owned jointly by the partners, one partner cannot be convicted of stealing the property from another, as illustrated in the following case.

> **FACTS** Defendants Bogan and Kerr owned an automobile junkyard. They sold the business to the plaintiff, Patterson, who took possession of the junkyard. Defendants claimed that they had sold Patterson only a one-half interest and that they were his partners. Patterson claimed that he had purchased the entire operation and owed them nothing. To compel the return of the property, the defendants secured a warrant for the plaintiff's arrest for the crime of larceny. Patterson was arrested, but the charges were dismissed. Patterson then sued defendants for the tort of malicious prosecution. Bogan and Kerr claimed that they had not acted maliciously but solely to secure the return of the property. Patterson was awarded $5,000 actual damages and $15,000 punitive damages. Defendants Bogan and Kerr appealed.
>
> **DECISION** The court held that as a general rule, a partner cannot be convicted of larceny of partnership property, since each partner is the ultimate owner of an undivided interest in all of the partnership property. Thus, no partnership property, with reference to any partner, can be said to be the property of another. Patterson testified that he had bought the entire business, while defendants said they sold him only one-half interest and were his partners. In either case, as sole owner or partner, plaintiff could not have been guilty of larceny, and swearing out a warrant for his arrest was an act of malicious prosecution. Affirmed.
>
> *Patterson v. Bogan and Kerr* (261 S.C. 87, 198 S.E.2d 586 [1973])

C. DUTIES OF PARTNERS

1. INFORMATION

The duty of a partner regarding information was discussed in Section B. 6. in this chapter.

2. ACCOUNTABILITY

Each partner must account to the partnership for any benefit and hold as trustee for it any profits derived by him or her without the consent of the other partners from any transaction connected with the partnership. The partners have a fiduciary relationship (i. e., a relationship of trust, loyalty, confidence, and good faith) that prohibits a partner from taking advantage of his or her co-partners in any transaction relating to the partnership business or of secretly profiting from the partnership business. The following case is an interesting example of the duty of a partner to carry out a fiduciary responsibility.

FACTS Plaintiffs Lavin and Dillworth and defendant Ehrlich were partners in a storefront tax preparing business. Ehrlich managed the business; Lavin and Dillworth were essentially investors. By letter dated October 9, 1978, Ehrlich announced his immediate withdrawal from and dissolution of the partnership. Later that month, he contracted to buy the storefront property from the landlord, and in January 1974, he took title. The lease on the storefront ran until April 30, 1971, and Ehrlich would not negotiate a new lease with the partnership, which he considered dissolved. His partners claim that Ehrlich breached his fiduciary duties in buying this property, and they ask the Court to rule that he holds it in constructive trust for the partnership.

DECISION The court held that the opportunity to purchase the property and insure continued possession of the goodwill asset of the location should have been offered to the partnership. Ehrlich breached his fiduciary duty in not making that offer and in appropriating this important partnership asset to himself. He went out and grabbed the building, and hoped, with this maneuver and his possession of the list of names of clients and prospects and past tax return files, to capitalize on the location and goodwill to the exclusion of his partners. The Court found that Ehrlich held the property in constructive trust for the partnership and was ordered to surrender his right, title, and interest to the partnership if offered two thirds of the purchase price by the remaining partners, Lavin and Dillworth.

Lavin v. Ehrlich (80 Misc.2d 247, 363 N.Y.S.2d 50 [1974])

3. FULL TIME AND ENERGY

In the absence of an agreement to the contrary, it is the duty of each partner to give his or her entire time, skill, and energy to the partnership business. A partner is not entitled to compensation for his or her services unless there is an express or implied agreement for such payment.

4. REASONABLE CARE

A partner is under a duty to use reasonable care in the transaction of the partnership business and is liable for any loss resulting from the failure to use reasonable care.

5. OBEDIENCE

A partner is under a contractual obligation to do all that is required of him or her by the partnership agreement. If a loss results from the failure to comply with the agreement, the partner must indemnify the partnership.

D. LIABILITIES OF PARTNERS

1. TORT LIABILITY

The partnership is liable for any wrongful act or omission of any partner acting in the ordinary course of the partnership business with the authority of the co-partners (e. g., partner's negligence in the operation of an automobile during the course of the partnership business causing injury to a third person).

The partnership is bound by a partner's breach of trust, and the partnership must make good the loss (e. g., where one partner acting within the scope of his or her apparent authority receives money from a third person and applies it to his or her own use).

Tort liability of partners is joint and several (i. e., the partners may be sued jointly or severally), whether for torts committed by a partner or by an employee of the partnership. Thus, an action may be brought against any partner without joining the others. However, a judgment against one partner is not generally regarded as *res judicata* (a matter settled by judgment) in a later action against the co-partners, especially when the co-partners were unknown to the third party at the time the partner brought his or her first action.

If a partner commits a tort while acting outside the partnership business, although the partnership is not liable in the absence of ratification, the individual partner is liable to the third party.

2. CONTRACTUAL LIABILITY

The contracts of a partner made for the partnership become the obligation of the partnership. This is true even though the partner made the contract in his or her name instead of in the partnership name, as long as he or she was acting within the scope of his or her authority. However, if a partner personally borrows money and the loan is made solely on his or her personal credit, the fact that he or she uses the money for partnership purposes does not make the partnership liable for such personal loan.

Third-party remedies for breach of contract by a partnership in general include damages, restitution, and specific performance.

Generally, in the absence of a statute to the contrary, the liability of the partners on a contractual obligation is joint. Thus, the action may be brought against the partnership or against all of the individual partners, naming them as defendants.

3. CRIMINAL LIABILITY

Partnerships were not considered separate entities at common law and so were incapable of committing criminal acts. Only the individual partners were personally held accountable for the illegal activities in which they participated.

However, the Uniform Partnership Act recognizes the partnership as an entity for some purposes, such as holding title to property and suing in the partnership name. Also, the U.S. Supreme Court and many state courts have held in recent decisions that some partnerships are entities that can be held guilty of criminal acts, as illustrated by the following case.

> **FACTS** Smithtown General Hospital, a partnership (defendant), was indicted for permitting an unauthorized person to participate in a surgical procedure and falsifying records to conceal the crime. The partnership moved to dismiss on the grounds that as a partnership it could not be indicted.

> **DECISION** The court held that although a partnership has been defined as a relationship with no legal being as distinct from the members it comprises, there are exceptions. The partnership can be either an entity or an aggregate of its members, depending upon the nature of its activities and, in the case of criminal law, depending upon the nature of the infraction. The operation of a hospital is so intertwined with the public interest as to legally justify the imposition of extensive controls by all levels of government. The health care is provided by the facility and not necessarily by any of its proprietors. Accreditation, when given, is provided to the institution and not to the component members of the named proprietor. The hospital is in every sense an entity and not just an aggregate of the 42 individual partners. The judge ruled that the defendant may be charged in an indictment as an entity with the commission of these crimes even though there is no showing of wrong on the part of the individual partners. Motion denied.

> *People v. Smithtown General Hospital* (92 Misc.2d 144, 399 N.Y.S.2d 993 [1977])

4. ADMISSION OR REPRESENTATION BY PARTNER

An admission or representation made by a partner concerning partnership business within the scope of his or her authority is evidence against the partnership (e. g., partner involved in automobile accident while on partnership business admitted it was his fault); the admission is evidence to hold the partnership liable. However, for the admission to be admissible against the co-partners, the making of the admission must be itself a partnership transaction (i. e., the partner must at the time be acting within the scope and course of partnership business). Thus, a partner who is on personal business when the automobile accident takes place cannot make an admission that will bind the partnership.

5. EXTENT OF PARTNER'S LIABILITY

Each partner has unlimited liability and is personally liable to the full extent of his or her personal assets for all obligations and liabilities incurred by the partnership.

A silent partner (i. e., one who does not actively engage in the partnership business and is not known to be a partner to those dealing with the partnership) likewise has unlimited liability. Only a limited partner in a limited partnership can limit his or her liability.

An incoming partner who does not personally assume the prior debts is not personally liable for obligations existing at the time of coming into the partnership, but all of the partnership assets continue to be liable, including the share purchased from the outgoing partner. However, an incoming partner who assumed the prior obligations of the partnership will be liable for them.

An outgoing partner continues to be liable for all partnership debts incurred prior to the transfer to the incoming partner, but not for those after the transfer. The only way the outgoing partner can be rid of prior debts is by a novation with the creditors (i. e., the creditors expressly agree to look to the incoming partner and to release the outgoing partner of all liability).

ILLUSTRATIVE CASES

1. Scope of Partnership Liability

McKINNEY v. TRUCK INSURANCE EXCHANGE

324 S.W.2d 773 (Mo.App., 1959)

STONE, Presiding Judge. Cut to the quick by the indignity inflicted upon him, a bull calf being castrated by one Davis, "sort of an expert" at such matters, rebelled and grievously injured his tormentor, by reason of which Davis filed a claim for benefits under the Missouri Workmen's Compensation Law against Paul McKinney, as employer, and Truck Insurance Exchange (hereinafter referred to as the Exchange), his alleged insurer. The Exchange theretofore had issued a "standard workmen's compensation and employers' liability policy" to "Ralph McKinney & Paul McKinney dba Acme Glass Co., 1647 St. Louis, Springfield, Missouri," as "employer," described in the policy declarations as a "co-partnership"; but, claimant Davis having been employed by Paul in connection with operation of a 167-acre farm in another county owned by Paul and his wife, and Davis' castration of the calf having been wholly unrelated to the business conducted by Acme Glass Company (even though the castrated calf had wreaked as much havoc as the proverbial bull in a china closet), the Exchange insisted that its policy issued to Acme afforded no coverage to Paul with respect to his farm operation and refused to defend him in the compensation proceeding instituted by Davis, although Davis' joinder of the Exchange as a party to the proceeding necessitated a defense on its own behalf. After counsel employed by Paul personally and counsel for the Exchange, presenting a united front against their common antagonist, had concluded upon appeal to this court a successful defense of Davis' claim * * * and thus had put out of the way (if not out of mind) the castrated calf and the contentious claimant, Paul turned on the Exchange and brought the instant suit to recoup the expenses (primarily attorneys' fees) incurred by him personally in such defense. Cast in the trial court on the Exchange's motion to dismiss his petition, Paul appeals from the adverse judgment.

* * * Although other jurisdictions reflect a sharp conflict of authority as to whether or not a partnership is a legal or juristic entity separate and distinct from the individuals who compose it, * * * the courts of this state usually have regarded a partnership as a mere ideal entity with no legal existence apart from its members, and have followed the so-called aggregate or common-law theory of partnership rather than the entity theory. * * * However, the persuasive opinion of informed scholars is that the Uniform Partnership Act does not transform a partnership into a separate legal or juristic entity * * * but "adopts the common law approach with 'modifications' relating to partnership property" so that the Act "is consistent with the entity approach for the purposes of facilitating transfers of property, marshalling assets, and protecting the business operation against the immediate impact of personal involvements of the partners." * * *

But, grave danger lurks in unquestioning acceptance and unguarded application of potentially deceptive generalities; and, although our Missouri courts usually follow the aggregate or common-law theory as to partnerships, we think that it should not and cannot be announced, as an arbitrary, absolute, unqualified and unyielding rule, that under no circumstances and for no purposes may a partnership be considered and treated as an entity. We read that the partnership entity sometimes is recognized with reference to its contracts with third persons. * * *

Thus, in jurisdictions where, as in Missouri, the aggregate or common-law theory as to partnerships usually is followed, the courts have given effect to the intention of contracting parties by treating a partnership as an entity in determining and delimiting the coverage afforded by insurance policies issued to the partnership.

* * * The Exchange had no duty to defend Davis' claim under its policy obligation to defend even groundless, false or fraudulent claims against Acme Glass Company, the employer whose liability the Exchange undertook to insure, for Davis made no claim against Acme but, from the outset, presented his claim as an employee of Paul individually and against Paul individually. * * *

The judgment for defendant is affirmed.

2. Partner's Right to Management

SUMMERS v. DOOLEY

94 Idaho 87, 481 P.2d 318 (1971)

DONALDSON, Justice.   This lawsuit, tried in the district court, involves a claim by one partner against the other for $6,000. The complaining partner asserts that he has been required to pay out more than $11,000 in expenses without any reimbursement from either the partnership funds or his partner. The expenditure in question was incurred by the complaining partner (John Summers, plaintiff-appellant) for the purpose of hiring an additional employee. The trial court denied him any relief except for ordering that he be entitled to one half of $966.72, which it found to be a legitimate partnership expense.

The pertinent facts leading to this lawsuit are as follows. Summers entered a partnership agreement with Dooley (defendant-respondent) in 1958 for the purpose of operating a trash collection business. The business was operated by the two men and when either was unable to work, the non-working partner provided a replacement at his own expense. In 1962, Dooley became unable to work and, at his own expense, hired an employee to take his place. In July, 1966, Summers approached his partner Dooley regarding the hiring of an additional employee but Dooley refused. Nevertheless, on his own initiative, Summers hired the man and paid him out of his own pocket. Dooley, upon discovering that Summers had hired an additional man, objected, stating that he did not feel additional labor was necessary and refused to pay for the new employee out of the partnership funds. Summers continued to operate the business using the third man and in October of 1967 instituted suit in the district court for $6,000 against his partner, the gravamen of the complaint being that Summers has been required to pay out more than $11,000 in expenses, incurred in the hiring of the additional man, without any reimbursement from either the partnership funds or his partner. After trial before the court, sitting without a jury, Summers was granted only partial relief and he has appealed. He urges in essence that the trial court erred by failing to conclude that he should be reimbursed for expenses and costs connected in the employment of extra help in the partnership business.

The principal thrust of appellant's contention is that in spite of the fact that one of the two partners refused to consent to the hiring of additional help, nonetheless, the non-consenting partner retained profits earned by the labors of the third man and therefore the non-consenting partner should be estopped from denying the need and value of the employee, and has by his behavior ratified the act of the other partner who hired the additional man.

The issue presented for decision by this appeal is whether an equal partner in a two man partnership has the authority to hire a new employee in disregard of the objection of the other partner and then attempt to charge the dissenting partner with the costs incurred as a result of his unilateral decision.

*   *   *

In the instant case the record indicates that although Summers requested his partner Dooley to agree to the hiring of a third man, such requests were not honored. In fact Dooley made it clear that he was "voting no" with regard to the hiring of an additional employee.

An application of the relevant statutory provisions and pertinent case law to the factual situation presented by the instant case indicates that the trial court was correct in its disposal of the issue since a majority of the partners did not consent to the hiring of the third man. I.C. § 53–318(8) provides:

> Any difference arising as to ordinary matters connected with the partnership business may be decided by a *majority of the partners* * * *. (emphasis supplied)

* * * A careful reading of the statutory provision indicates that subsection 5 bestows *equal rights in the management and conduct of the partnership business* upon all of the partners. The concept of equality between partners with respect to management of business affairs is a central theme and recurs throughout the Uniform Partnership Law, which has been enacted in this jurisdiction. Thus the only reasonable interpretation of I.C. § 53–318(8) is that business differences must be decided by a majority of the partners provided no other agreement between the partners speaks to the issues.

A noted scholar has dealt precisely with the issue to be decided:

> * * * if the partners are equally divided, those who forbid a change must have their way (Walter B. Lindley, A Treatise on the Law of Partnership, Ch. II, § III, ¶ 24–8, p. 403 [1924]).

*　　　*　　　*

In the case at bar one of the partners continually voiced objection to the hiring of the third man. He did not sit idly by and acquiesce in the actions of his partner. Under these circumstances it is manifestly unjust to permit recovery of an expense which was incurred individually and not for the benefit of the partnership but rather for the benefit of one partner.

Judgment affirmed. Costs to respondent.

3. Tort Liability of Partners

FLYNN v. REAVES

135 Ga.App. 651, 218 S.E.2d 661 (1975)

CLARK, Judge.   The circumstances giving rise to this appeal may be summarized as follows: Seeking damages for medical malpractice, plaintiffs, husband and wife, brought suit only against defendant, Dr. Charles R. Moore, alleging him to have been negligent in his diagnosis and treatment of the eyes of plaintiff wife. Defendant answered, denying the allegations of negligence. Thereafter, defendant initiated a third-party action against his former co-partners, Dr. James T. Flynn, Jr., Dr. Robert E. Fokes, Jr. and Dr.

James R. Paulk. (The events had occurred during the existence of the partnership which had been dissolved by mutual agreement prior to commencement of the present litigation.) * * * This pleading alleges that he had been an equal partner with the three third-party defendants, hereafter referred to as "co-partners," in a medical practice partnership operated under the name of "The Eye, Ear, Nose and Throat Clinic" at the time when he had diagnosed and treated plaintiff wife; that his diagnosis and treatment of plaintiff wife was performed within the course of the partnership business; that he and his co-partners shared equally in the profits and losses of the partnership; and that the three co-partners were liable to him for three-fourths of any sum which plaintiffs might recover against him in the principal suit. * * *

The co-partners also challenged the sufficiency of the third-party complaint via motion for a judgment decreeing that it failed to state a claim entitling defendant to the relief sought against the third-party defendants. This motion was denied and the co-partners have appealed that ruling accompanied by the requisite review certificate.

*   *   *

The law of partnership is the law of agency: " 'Each partner being the agent of the firm, the firm is liable for his torts committed within the scope of his agency, on the principle of *respondeat superior,* in the same way that a master is responsible for his servant's torts, and for the same reason [that] the firm is liable for the torts of its agents or servants.' * * * Thus, "where several physicians are in partnership, they may be held liable in damages for the professional negligence of one of the firm."

*   *   *

In the case at bar, therefore, the co-partners and defendant would be jointly and severally liable to plaintiffs if it were established that defendant in fact negligently diagnosed and treated plaintiff wife in the course of the partnership business. Therefore, plaintiffs had the choice of suing the defendant individually, or all of the partners including defendant jointly. But defendant cannot seek contribution from his co-partners simply because they are jointly liable to plaintiffs.

*   *   *

So in this class of cases it is always relevant to inquire, 'Whose wrong really caused the damge?' * * * Generally speaking, a right of action over in such cases exists only where the negligence of him who has been compelled to satisfy the damages is imputed or constructive only, and the negligence of him against whom the remedy over is asserted was actual or more immediately causal."

*   *   *

Here, the co-partners and defendant are not joint tortfeasors as among themselves. For the co-partners are subjected to liability only by the doctrine of respondeat superior. Thus, defendant whose negligence, if any, was actual, cannot seek contribution from his co-partners, who are merely constructively negligent. Of course, had defendant alleged that his co-partners were actual tortfeasors, a third-party action for contribution would lie. But such is not the case. * * *

Therefore, we hold, as other courts have held, that where a partner is sued individually by a plaintiff injured by the partner's sole negligence, the partner cannot seek contribution from his co-partners even though the negligent act occurred in the course of the partnership business.

*   *   *

Since defendant's third-party complaint failed to state a claim upon which relief can be granted, the denial of the co-partners' motion was error.

4. Partner's Duty to Disclose

STARR v. INTERNATIONAL REALTY, LTD.

271 Or. 396, 533 P.2d 165 (1975)

TONGUE, Justice.   The case involves a group of prominent Portland doctors and others in high income tax "brackets" and in need of "tax shelters." They were persuaded by one Stanley G. Harris, a Portland "expert" in real property investments, that by investing $285,000 and joining with him in a partnership for the purchase of an apartment house then under construction, the entire down payment of $265,000 could be treated for federal income tax purposes as "prepaid interest," thereby saving large amounts otherwise payable in income taxes. * * *

It would serve no useful purpose to summarize the entire transaction for the purchase of this property for the sum of $1,010,000 in all of its details, as "put together" by Harris. . . . Harris did not reveal to his partners that the property could have been purchased for $907,500 "net" to the seller * * *, and that a commission of $100,000, together with an escrow fee of $2,500, was to be paid to International Realty Ltd., of which Harris was president.

*   *   *

The question to be decided in this case * * * is whether the $100,000 commission paid to International, of which Harris was the president, was a "secret" commission. * * *

It appears from the testimony that most of the plaintiffs knew or should have known that Harris and International were in the real estate business and that a realtor's commission in some amount would normally be paid to some realtor on the transaction. Apparently, because their interest in the income tax advantage of the transaction was so dominant and overriding, the doctors did not inquire whether such a commission would be paid to Harris or to International, or in what amount, and Harris did not tell them. It is contended by the doctors, however, that in this case they are entitled to the benefit of the equivalent of a rule more familiar to them in the practice of medicine—that of "informed consent."

When, as in this case, a real estate broker undertakes to join as a member of a partnership or joint venture in the purchase of real property on which he holds a listing, he is also subject to the fiduciary duties of undivided loyalty and complete disclosure owed by one partner to another. Indeed, one of the fundamental duties of any partner who deals on his own account in matters within the scope of his fiduciary relationship is the affirmative duty to make a full disclosure to his partners not only of the fact he is dealing on his own account, but all the facts which are material to the transaction. * * *

It follows that the "consent of the other partners" required by ORS 68,340(1) before any partner may retain "any benefit" from "any transaction connected with the formation [or] conduct" of a partnership must necessarily be an "informed consent" with knowledge of the facts necessary to the giving of an intelligent consent.

In this case, Harris did not inform plaintiffs or disclose to them the fact that this property could have been purchased for $907,500 "net" to the seller or that upon its purchase for $1,010,000 Harris or International (of which Harris was the president) would be paid a commission in the amount of $100,000. In the absence of such a disclosure there could be no effective "consent" by plaintiffs to the payment or retention by Harris of any such "benefit" from that transaction. . . .

For these reasons, we must reject defendants' contention that the broker's commission paid to International was "neither secret nor concealed." For the same reasons, the trial court did not err in requiring defendants to account to the partnership for that commission.

PROBLEMS

1. A and B are partners in the grocery business. A signed notes totaling $24,000.00 in the partnership name, giving as the reason for the loans that the partnership was expanding. A then disappeared, and the notes were discovered by B. The holder of the notes brings action against the partnership. Decision?

2. A and B are partners in a dairy. They purchase their feed from the Edwards Feed Mill. B made a purchase of feed on his own personal credit and charged it to his individual personal account, separate from the partnership business, and executed a personal promissory note for its payment in his name alone. Edwards Feed Mill brings action against both partners on the note on the theory that A is also liable since, the partnership received the benefit of the purchase. Decision?

3. A and B are partners. The creditors of the partnership threatened suit if the debts were not paid. B paid the debts in full from his own funds and then sued A in the name of the partnership for reimbursement. Decision?

4. A and B form a partnership to produce a play on a profit-sharing basis, paying the author certain royalties. A concealed from B an agreement with the author whereby A was the assignee of a share of the royalties. B brings a suit in equity to make A account for a pro rata share of the royalties he received. Decision?

5. A and B are partners. By its contract terms, the partnership is to expire on

January 1. The partnership has a lease on some valuable property that will expire the following July 1. After the partnership expires and immediately prior to the end of the lease, A secures a new lease in his own name. B brings a sujit for an accounting. Decision?

6. A and B are partners. A's son borrows an automobile owned by the partnership and while returning home from a dance has an accident. Attendance at the dance was personal and had nothing to do with the partnership business. A's son admits to the plaintiff at the time of the accident that it was all his fault. Plaintiff brings action against the partnership and seeks to use the admission against the partnership. Decision?

7. A and B are partners. B attempts by peaceful means to get a tenant of the partnership to leave the premises, however, the tenant refuses to leave. B then uses unlawful force and bodily evicts the tenant from the premises. The tenant brings action for the unlawful eviction against the partnership. Decision?

8. A and B are partners. They desire to sell their business to T. A misrepresents the profits and the income of the business to T without B's knowledge. T purchases the business and then learns of the misrepresentations. T elects to affirm the contract of sale and sue the partners for fraud. B defends on the basis that he was innocent of the fraud. Decision?

9. A and B were partners. A spent most of his time fishing, hunting, and golfing, while B took care of the business. Finally, B found it necessary to hire extra help to do the work that A was supposed to be doing. At the end of the fiscal year, B deducted the expense of the extra help from A's share of the profits. A sued B for the share of the profits which B deducted. Decision?

10. A, B, and C are partners. C is a silent, or dormant, partner. T sells goods to the partnership on credit, not knowing that C is a partner. Later, the partnership becomes insolvent, and T brings action against the partnership, including C, for the debt. Decision?

Chapter 35

DISSOLUTION AND WINDING UP

A. IN GENERAL

1. DISSOLUTION

Dissolution designates the point in time when the partners cease to carry on the business together. It is the change in the relationship of the partners caused by a partner ceasing to be associated in the carrying on of the business. On dissolution, the partnership is not terminated but continues until the winding up of the partnership business is completed. The following case illustrates this fact.

> **FACTS** On June 11, at a conference between partners, the Bayer Bros. partnership was dissolved. On August 13, the defendant bought 76 shares of stock of the Montville Finishing Company. The trial court found that the purchase of the stock was a breach of defendant's fiduciary duty to his co-partners.

> **DECISION** The court held that upon the dissolution of the partnership, any fiduciary duty that the defendant owed toward the plaintiffs while the co-partnership existed ceased, and that the defendant was free to purchase the stock. It is not unusual that the courts have failed to distinguish between the terms "dissolution," "winding up," and "termination" of a co-partnership. A co-partnership at will is dissolved when either of the partners expresses an intent not to continue any longer or when the partners decide to cease doing business for their mutual benefit. The partnership affairs are not terminated, however, until the winding up is completed. The partners' energies thereafter are devoted to the winding up of the business affairs of the co-partnership and to reaching an agreement as to the distribution of its assets. Reversed.

> *Bayer, et al. v. Bayer* (215 App.Div. 454, 214 N.Y.S. 322 [1926])

2. WINDING UP

Winding up is the process of settling partnership affairs after dissolution. In the ordinary partnership, when a partner ceases to be associated with the carrying on of the partnership business, it usually has the consequence of winding up the partnership or the formation of a new partnership to carry on the business. During the period of winding up a dissolved partnership, the partnership is still in existence. The property is still held by the partners as tenants. The partners can sue and be sued regarding partnership rights and obligations. However, the partners should not undertake new business after the dissolution but should only liquidate and distribute the partnership property. Any new business transacted by a partner is solely for his or her own account.

B. CAUSES OF DISSOLUTION

1. WITHOUT VIOLATION OF AGREEMENT

A. TERMINATION OF TERM OR UNDERTAKING

A partnership can be dissolved by the partnership agreement (e. g., partnership relation shall end on a certain date or on the happening of a certain condition).

B. DISSOLUTION BY WILL IN PARTNERSHIP AT WILL

A partnership at will can be dissolved by the will of any partner.

C. DISSOLUTION BY AGREEMENT

A partnership can be ended by the mutual unanimous agreement of the partners.

2. IN VIOLATION OF AGREEMENT

Any partner may dissolve the partnership at any time, even though it is in violation of the partnership agreement. This is because the partnership relationship is one of agency and, therefore, so personal that it cannot be specifically enforced. The partner who wrongfully causes a dissolution is subject to liability for damages. To prevent undue hardship on the other partners, the U.P.A., Section 38(2) (b), provides that they can buy out his or her interest.

3. SUPERVENING CAUSES FOR DISSOLUTION

A. SUPERVENING ILLEGALITY

A partnership is dissolved, like any other contract, by supervening illegality (e. g., business become illegal).

B. BANKRUPTCY

A partnership is dissolved by the adjudication of bankruptcy or insolvency of the partnership, or an adjudication of bankruptcy or insolvency by one of the partners. Most courts hold that insolvency of the partnership or of one of the partners without an adjudication will not dissolve the partnership.

c. Death

Death of one of the partners dissolves the partnership. In this area, it might be desirable to provide in the partnership agreement for continuation of the business on death of a partner and compensation to his or her estate.

d. War and Armed Conflict

Where partners are the respective citizens of the belligerent countries in a state of war or armed conflict, the partnership is dissolved. However, this does not affect contracts made prior to the hostilities.

4. DECREE OF COURT

A court may decree the dissolution of a partnership. The grounds are as follows:

1. Where the circumstances render it just and equitable (e. g., insolvency of a partner) or where it becomes unprofitable to carry on the business.

2. Misconduct of a partner to the extent that it is injurious to the partnership or to the other partners (e. g., misappropriation of funds) or excluding other partners from possession of partnership property.

3. Incapacity of a partner to discharge his or her duties (e. g., insanity).

4. Dissension among the partners where it is so serious and persistent as to make the successful continuance of the partnership impractical.

C. EFFECT OF DISSOLUTION

1. IN GENERAL

Dissolution terminates the existence of the partnership except for the purpose of winding up (e. g., performance of existing contracts, collection of money due, payment of debts, administering of firm assets, and the distribution of the assets in accordance with the partnership agreement) (U.P.A., Sections 33–43). The following case illustrates this point.

> **FACTS** Miner and Rogers were partners in the purchase and operation of a motel. In November of 1973 the partnership was dissolved and the parties signed a dissolution agreement. This agreement gave Miner the option to either buy or sell his interest in the partnership, and if he elected to buy, he had until January 1, 1974, to arrange financing. Miner was unable to get the financing, and on January 11, 1974, the parties entered into an agreement of sale by which Rogers assumed all the obligations of both Miner and Rogers involved in the purchase of the Country Manor Motel. Shortly after Rogers took possession, he found evidence of shortages in the rental and telephone income and no record of income from candy and soda pop. He further found that Miner had used the motel fund for his personal income taxes, personal expenses, and motel salaries in violation of their agreement. Rogers filed a complaint for breach of the dissolution contract and the contract of sale. Miner

moved to dismiss the complaint on the grounds that no action would lie between partners except an action for accounting.

DECISION   The court held that in Arizona, generally, the only action that will lie between co-partners in regard to partnership business is an action for accounting. However, as here, a former partner may sue another for any breach of the partnership settlement agreement. Therefore, an accounting was not a prerequisite to this suit.

Miner v. Rogers (115 Ariz. 463, 565 P.2d 1324 [1977])

2. EFFECT ON POWERS OF PARTNERS

Normally, dissolution terminates the power of a partner to bind the partnership except for the purpose of winding up. However, the partner may bind the partnership to third persons as follows:

1.   To those who had extended credit to the firm prior to dissolution and had no knowledge or notice of the dissolution.

2.   To those who had not extended credit but knew of the partnership prior to dissolution and had no knowledge or notice of the dissolution, and the notice of the dissolution had not been advertised in a newspaper of general circulation (U.P.A., Section 35).

3. EFFECT ON RIGHTS OF PARTNERS

A. RIGHT TO WIND UP

Unless otherwise agreed, the partners who have not caused the dissolution have the right to wind up the partnership affairs (U.P.A., Section 37). The partner or partners in charge of the winding up are entitled to a reasonable compensation for such services.

B. RIGHT TO APPLICATION OF PARTNERSHIP PROPERTY

Each partner has the right to insist that all the partnership assets be used first to pay partnership debts (U.P.A., Section 38). After partnership debts are paid, remaining assets are used to return capital investments.

4. LIABILITY OF PARTNERS CONTINUING THE BUSINESS

When the membership of the partnership changes by reason of death or retirement of a partner or the coming in of another member, and the business is continued, the creditors of the first or dissolved partnership are also creditors of the partnership continuing the business, and the new member is liable for all the obligations arising before becoming a partner. However, the liability of the new member for prior obligations shall be satisfied out of partnership property only (U.P.A., Section 41).

D. RULES FOR DISTRIBUTION

1. TO CREDITORS

The liabilities of the partnership are paid in the following order:

1. To creditors other than partners.

2. To partners other than for capital and profits.

3. To partners in respect of capital (U.P.A., Section 40(b)).

If there is insufficient partnership property to satisfy the liabilities, the partners must make contribution to the extent necessary to satisfy the liabilities (U.P.A., Section 40(d)). In the absence of agreement, partners share losses in the same way as they share profits (U.P.A., Section 18(a)).

Where the partnership or a partner is insolvent or in bankruptcy, the rule of marshaling of assets is applied (U.P.A., Section 40(h) (i)). This rule is that partnership assets must be applied first to the satisfaction of the claims of the partnership creditors, and individual or personal assets of a partner to the satisfaction of his or her individual or personal creditors. Any balance of the personal estate of a partner is then applied to the satisfaction of partnership creditors. For example, if A is a partner in an insolvent business, the business creditors must first exhaust whatever interest A has in the business before going after his own personal assets, even though he may be a very wealthy man. Conversely, if A should personally become insolvent, his nonpartnership-related creditors must first proceed against all of his personal assets before levying against his partnership interest. For this reason, many partnership creditors will require the individual partners also to assume personal obligations on partnership debts.

The following case is an example of how the court may make a distribution decision.

> **FACTS** Larsen and Claridge were partners in a farming operation from 1962 until the end of 1967. Claridge provided a net capital contribution of $141,940, plus the use of the land and living quarters for Larsen. Larsen agreed to provide services for the farming operation and the partners agreed to share in profits and losses equally. Upon dissolution, the court awarded Claridge the full return of their capital contribution but would make no allowance for Larsen's contribution of labor. Larsen appealed.

> **DECISION** The court held that there was no proof of any agreement between Larsen and Claridge that would equate the labor as provided by Larsen in monetary value with the actual capital contributed by Claridge. Without such an agreement, the court could not hold that labor was meant to provide an equal one-half contribution to the partnership venture. After the return of the $141,940 capital contribution to Claridge, $10,145 was left for distribution and was divided equally between them.

Larsen v. Claridge (23 Ariz.App. 508, 534 P.2d 439 [1975])

2. TO PARTNERS

The balance of the partnership property after payment of all liabilities and return of capital investment is distributed to the partners as profits pursuant to the partnership agreement.

ILLUSTRATIVE CASES

1. Dissolution and Accounting

RALPH SJO v. COOPER

29 Ill. App. 3d 1016, 331 N.E.2d 206 (1975)

Lorenz, Justice. In 1972, plaintiff filed suit for a partnership dissolution and accounting. The trial court found that the partnership had been dissolved in 1969 and dismissed the complaint for want of equity and ordered a distribution of the assets of the partnership with plaintiff being awarded $1,000 and relieved of any further liability on a partnership mortgage. Plaintiff appeals contending that the finding was in error.

*   *   *

In 1960, plaintiff and defendant entered into an oral partnership agreement to construct a building and operate a restaurant. * * * The partners agreed to share all profits and losses equally and the agreement did not have a fixed term.

From 1961 to 1965 the partnership operated the restaurant and in 1966 leased the premises to other parties. * * *

The partners gave contradictory testimony concerning events in 1969. Defendant testified that on three occasions he requested that plaintiff contribute additional funds to help meet mortgage payments and he offered carbon copies of two requests as proof. Plaintiff testified that additional funds had been requested only once and he had declined because the defendant would not give him an accounting * * *. From December, 1969 to July, 1970 the partners did not communicate and defendant continued to meet all partnership obligations.

In June, 1970 defendant signed a 20-year lease with Brown's Chicken, Inc. In July, 1970, the partnership met and defendant stated that plaintiff's failure to contribute over the preceding 18 months had ended their partnership and plaintiff had no interest in the Brown's lease. Plaintiff then filed suit.

*   *   *

Under the Uniform Partnership Act a partnership for no fixed term may be dissolved at the express will of either party. The dissolving party need not give any reason for his desire to end the partnership, but he must give *notice* of his intention to do so. A search of the record finds that at no time prior to July, 1970, did defendant give any such notice. In fact, defendant testified that he was conducting partnership business in early July, 1970.

Defendant contends that plaintiff's failure to contribute additional funds from April, 1969 to July, 1970, constituted a withdrawal from the partnership resulting in dissolution. While there are no Illinois cases on point, we note that the California courts, which are also guided by the Uniform Partnership Act, have found that a *partner's failure to contribute capital does not in itself constitute a dissolution.*

*   *   *

We, therefore, conclude that the partnership was not dissolved in 1969, but rather defendant's statement caused dissolution in July, 1970. The order dismissing plaintiff's complaint is reversed and the cause is remanded for further proceedings consistent with this opinion.

Reversed and remanded with directions.

2. Reasons for Dissolution of Partnership

JONES v. JONES

15 Misc.2d 960, 179 N.Y.S.2d 480 (1958)

BROWN, Jr., Justice.   In this action for a dissolution of a partnership, accounting, etc., defendant moves for an order * * * dismissing the complaint on the ground that it does not set forth facts sufficient to constitute a cause of action. The action is brought by a wife against her husband. * * *

However, it appears from the complaint that the grounds upon which the action rests are that (1) one of the partners, defendant herein, is guilty of adultery and that an action for divorce has been instituted against him by the other party, and (2) defendant has refused to make a distribution of the assets or to account therefor.

Dissolutions of partnerships can only be brought about as provided by Sections 62 and 63 of the Partnership Law. An examination of Sec. 62 reveals that subdivision 1(b) is the only subdivision of this section that possibly could be applied to the situation presented herein provided the proper facts are pleaded. Subdivision 1(b) reads as follows:

> By the express will of any partner when no definite term or particular undertaking is specified.

The courts, however, have held in order to effect a dissolution of a partnership at will:

> there must have been a mutual agreement to dissolve, *or there must have been notice by a party desiring a dissolution to his copartners 'of his election to terminate the partnership, or his election must be manifested by unequivocal acts or circumstances brought to the knowledge of the other party which signify [the exercise of] the will of the former that the partnership be dissolved'.* * * *

Nowhere in the complaint has the plaintiff set forth such facts even though it may well be that such notice of election was given. The court, however, cannot assume from the facts as pleaded that such notice was given. In addition, while allegations of adultery and the institution of a divorce action could be the basis for terminating an alleged partnership at will, it cannot be said that these are unequivocal acts or circumstances signifying an election to dissolve for it is common knowledge that wives have divorced husbands without terminating businesses in which both parties were interested. * * * In an action for a dissolution of a partnership the accounting, impressing of a trust, appointment of a receiver, etc. are merely incidental relief sought in the dissolution of the partnership. * * *

Accordingly, the motion to dismiss is granted with leave to the plaintiff to serve an amended complaint if so advised within 20 days after service of a copy of the order to be entered herein, with notice of entry.

3. Fiduciary Duty During Dissolution

HILGENDORF v. DENSON

341 So.2d 549 (Fla.App., 1977)

Once again, Hilgendorf appeals from a Final Judgment entered upon Denson's claim for an accounting of the profits earned by Hilgendorf after Hilgendrof dissolved a partnership previously known as "Gateway Realty."

*   *   *

In January, 1972, Hilgendorf and Denson formed a partnership known as "Gateway Realty". The nature of that business was to sell real estate. The partnership was compensated by earning real estate commissions. The partnership was a verbal one, with the understanding that the parties would share expenses and profits. It was not for a fixed period of time and, therefore, was subject to being dissolved at any time by the expressed decision of either party. In January, 1973, Hilgendorf told Denson that the partnership was over and Denson left February 2, 1973.

Hilgendorf and her husband owned the premises where the partnership had previously existed. Hilgendorf remained there and continued to operate a real estate business. * * * Denson set up her own business at a different location. Hilgendorf accounted for and paid to Denson one-half of all the sales which resulted from listings that were in the office at the time of the dissolution of the partnership. The Judgment entered against Hilgendorf was in addition to those figures.

Assuming arguendo that Hilgendorf continued the partnership business for a while, or used its assets, as the trial judge found, * * * Denson had the right to have the value of her interest on the date of dissolution ascertained and to receive the value of that interest or, at her option, to receive the profits attributable to the use of her right in the property of the dissolved partnership. * * *

* * * By accepting the proceeds of the sales from listings which were in the office at the time of the dissolution of the partnership, Denson elected

to receive a part of the profits. Any additional profits which have not been distributed to her would of necessity be limited to that part which her share of the assets of the partnership produced.

It must be borne in mind that the profits of the partnership were the result primarily of the performance of personal services. In the absence of particular circumstances affecting the situation, a partner whose only contribution to the firm is personal services or skill is not entitled to share the profits earned after dissolution of the partnership when his services ended upon the dissolution. * * *

We agree with the proposition that if a surviving or remaining partner continues the partnership business with the partnership assets, the remaining partner is required to account to the withdrawing partner.

The assets remaining at the time of the dissolution were so minimal that except for the listing already accounted for there was no basis upon which one could claim that subsequent earnings by Hilgendorf were derived therefrom.

The judgment of the trial court is, therefore, vacated and set aside.

4. Rights of Partner on Dissolution

FORTUGNO v. HUDSON MANURE CO.

51 N.J.Super. 482, 144 A.2d 207 (1958)

GOLDMANN, S. J. A. D. This proceeding began as an action for the dissolution of a family partnership when Anthony Fortugno, one of the partners, filed his complaint * * * on January 4, 1956 against the partnership and his co-partners. * * *

Defendants are the partnership, Hudson Manure Company, and Anthony's seven co-partners: Sylvia Fortugno (mother of the seven other partners), Daniel, Arthur, Alfred and Adeline Fortugno, Connie (Fortugno) Ruble, and Ann (Fortugno) Campanella. * * * The basic dispute concerned the distribution of partnership assets. The question was whether certain corporations, five in number, were assets of the partnership or owned by the individual partners. * * * Arthur claimed the corporations were assets of the partnership and that he was entitled upon dissolution of the partnership to his proportionate share in cash, rather than to be forced to exchange his position as an equal partner for that of a minority shareholder in the family-controlled corporations whose shares would have no value on an open market. * * *

The other partners contended that distribution should be of the shares of stock. * * * The trial court held that the first four of the above-named corporations were not assets of the partnership, and ordered the equal distribution of their stock to the partners. The fifth corporation, Hudson Farms, Inc., was held to have been fraudulently formed with partnership funds; it belonged to the partnership, and was ordered sold. Arthur appeals this order (as well as all other interlocutory orders), particularly with respect to the finding that the first four corporations were not assets of the partnership. * * *

Arthur's present position, essentially, is that he is entitled to have the partnership pay him for his one-eighth interest. * * *

The partnership's original business was * * * the collection and sale of manure. * * * The partnership sold the manure to mushroom growers in southeastern Pennsylvania; it also derived an income from race tracks and other sources of supply for removing the manure. In the course of its operations the partnership found it convenient to put certain of its activities in corporate form. * * *

The reasons for Arthur's stand are readily understandable. As a member of a partnership that owns several corporations he has an effective voice in partnership policy and operation, but as a minority stockholder he could be overruled by a majority vote. * * *

Our statutes provide that all property originally brought into a partnership or subsequently acquired in any way on its behalf is partnership property and, unless a contrary intention appears, property acquired with partnership funds is partnership property. Uniform Partnership Act, 42:1–8(1) and (2) * * *

Less than all the partners in a partnership may not bind the partnership by an act or acts not performed for the purpose of carrying on the usual business of the partnership, unless authorized by the other partners. Uniform Partnership Act, R.S. 42:1–9 * * * This applies particularly to a situation where one or several partners, but not all, seek to incorporate a partnership and transfer the assets of the partnership to the new corporation. * * *

Co-partners must deal with each other with trust, confidence and good faith; there can be no secret advantages or benefits. A partner has a fiduciary duty to share with the partnership those business opportunities clearly related to the subject of its operations. * * *

Applying the principles, stated earlier, of determining what is partnership property, we conclude that the four named corporations were and presently are assets of the partnership, Hudson Manure Company. * * *

We therefore conclude that the assets of the partnership, including those of all the corporations, should be liquidated, and the proceeds distributed in cash. * * *

We cannot order the remaining partners to buy out Arthur's interest.

* * * If the opposing partners will agree to the entry of an order for the appraisal of the partnership under the direction of the court and directing them to pay Arthur one-eighth of the valuation determined upon, such an order will be entered. Otherwise, there will be a liquidation by sale of all the partnership assets, including those owned by the several corporations.

5. Distribution of Partnership Assets in Kind

LOGOLUSO v. LOGOLUSO
233 Cal.App.2d 523, 43 Cal.Rptr. 678 (1965)

STONE, Justice.   This appeal is from a judgment ordering a sale of assets in a proceeding for dissolution of a copartnership engaged in farming. All of the partnership property, both real and personal, was ordered sold as a unit. Appellants attack that part of the judgment ordering the real property sold as a unit, contending that the court erred in not approving a division in kind made by the partners.

The five Logoluso brothers, under the terms of a written copartnership agreement, owned and farmed 12 parcels of real property valued by the court at $2,000,000, subject to encumbrances of about $166,700. The partnership owns equipment valued at $100,000 and has accounts receivable and interests in revolving funds of cooperatives amounting to approximately $278,000.

Leonard Logoluso, one of the appellants herein, on September 26, 1960, gave notice in accordance with the articles of copartnership, that he was resigning from the partnership and demanded termination thereof within 90 days. * * * [T]he five partners divided the 12 parcels of real property by each making a first-choice selection, followed by a second-choice selection, and an auction of the two remaining parcels. * * *

Division in kind of partnership assets upon dissolution is conditioned, however, upon the satisfaction of all partnership obligations to third parties. Here, the partnership owed approximately $166,700, but the obligations present no obstacle to distribution in kind since there are liquid assets, aside from the real property, sufficient to satisfy all partnership obligations. * * * Thus, an executed agreement for the division of real property in kind must be honored by a court presiding over the dissolution of a partnership, unless the agreement is assailed on the ground of mistake, error or fraud.

* * * Therefore we hold that in a partnership dissolution action a court has authority to make distribution of partnership real property in kind. This power, of course, is conditioned upon a finding that it is not necessary to hold a sale in order to satisfy partnership obligations. Absent a compelling necessity to satisfy partnership obligations, a public sale of assets can be justified only if it is found that distribution in kind would result in great prejudice to the parties. This simply conforms to the tenet of equity that recognizes real property and certain kinds of personal property as unique, which, in turn, impels a court of equity to maintain the ownership of property when feasible. * * *

The judgment is reversed.

PROBLEMS

1. A and B formed a partnership for five years. In the fourth year, A fraudulently converted property of the partnership to his own use. B, on discovering this fact, ousted A from the partnership. A brings an action for dissolution of the partnership, an accounting, and damages for the expulsion and loss of profits. Decision?

2. A and B were partners. They were performing a highway construction contract when A died. B continued performance of the contract. It was necessary for B to borrow a substantial sum of money from the bank to continue the project. When the partnership became insolvent, the bank sued the partnership. A's widow raised the defense that B could not enter into a new transaction, such as borrowing money, and, therefore, the partnership should not be liable for the new loan. Decision?

3. A, B, and C are partners. C retired from the firm. A and B assumed the debts of the firm and paid C the value of his interest. D then became a partner of the firm with A and B, and the partnership of A, B, and D continued the business. T, a creditor of the firm of A, B, and C, brings action against A, B, C, and D for the debt. Decision?

4. A, B, and C formed a partnership. The capital was $5,000 to which A contributed $3,000; B, $2,000; and C, nothing. It was agreed that profits would be shared equally. Later, the partnership became insolvent and was short $4,000 to pay the creditors. How shall the loss be adjusted?

5. A, B, and C were partners. The firm borrowed money from a bank and gave the bank the firm's note for the loan. In addition, each partner guaranteed the note personally. The partnership became insolvent. The bank claims that it has a right to file its claim as a partnership debt and has a right to a lien on the assets of the individual partners before the other general creditors of the partnership can look to the assets of the individual partners. Decision?

6. Phillips, Atkins, and Webb formed a partnership for the term of 10 years. In the sixth year, Phillips withdrew without cause and Webb became bankrupt. A dispute then arose among the partners over the right to liquidate and wind up the firm's business. The exclusive right to do so was claimed by each of the partners and by Webb's trustee in bankruptcy. Who is entitled to wind up the business?

7. Golden was admitted into the partnership firm of Jackson and Smith. At the time of Golden's admission as a partner, the firm was indebted to several creditors, including Armen. The firm thereafter became insolvent, and the assets of the partnership and of the partners were insufficient to pay the partnership debts. Armen seeks to hold Golden personally liable for the deficit in his claim. Decision?

8. Riddle and Mohn form a 10-year partnership to practice surgery. During the second year, Mohn is involved in a serious motor accident, which necessitates the amputation of both arms. Riddle seeks to obtain a decree of dissolution of the partnership in a court of equity. Decision?

9. ABC partnership and its three partners, Ace, Best, and Conn, individually, were adjudged bankrupts. No assets remained in the estates of Ace and Best after the necessary expenses of administration had been paid. As to the estate of Conn and the partnership ABC, however, there remained the sums of $1,000 and $2,000, respectively. Can the ABC partnership creditors share in the assets remaining in the estate of Conn along with Conn's personal creditors?

10. Andy, who owned and operated a variety store, formed a partnership with Bill, who agreed to manage and operate the store as a partnership for half the profits. Bill made no capital investment in the enterprise. Later the partnership was dissolved. What proportion of the business assets should have been distributed to Bill?

Part VII

CORPORATIONS

Chapter 36

INTRODUCTION, FORMATION, AND TERMINATION

A. INTRODUCTION

Corporations are subject to greater governmental formalities and control than any other form of business enterprise. Corporations involve the federal Constitution, federal laws, and state laws. Part VII is intended not to be a comprehensive coverage of the law of corporations but merely a light treatment of the subject, emphasizing material important to the business student.

1. NATURE

A corporation is a legal "person" or entity. It has an existence separate from that of its shareholders. A corporation is a "person" within the meaning of the Fifth (due process) and Fourteenth (equal protection) Amendments to the Constitution of the United States. It is not a "citizen" within that part of the Fourteenth Amendment to the Constitution of the United States that has to do with the protection of privileges and immunities. It is, however, "citizen" for the purpose of determining diversity of citizenship as a basis for jurisdiction of the federal courts in an action to which the corporation is a party.

Obviously, a corporation cannot be a person under a statute contemplating a natural person, such as one requiring mandatory imprisonment or one giving preferences to a person over 65 years of age.

For a comparison with partnerships, refer to Part VI, Chapter 33, Section A.

2. ENTITY

A corporation is a legal entity with separate rights and liabilities. It may sue or be sued. It exists in the eyes of the law as though it were a person separate and distinct from the shareholders. Because the debts of the corporation are not the debts of the shareholders, the directors, or the officers, the corporate entity absolves the shareholders and the managers from the liability of the corporation. This is one of the main advantages of a corporation.

However, this corporate entity or veil can be broken or disregarded in an appropriate case to hold personally liable those individuals who are attempting to use the entity to protect themselves from liability for their wrongs.

The general rule is that the corporate entity will be recognized and not disregarded. The exception is that the entity will be disregarded when it is used to defeat public convenience, protect fraud, justify a wrong, evade the law, or defend crime. The courts will not recognize the entity protection to the managers or the shareholders if to do so would produce unjust or undesirable consequences inconsistent with the purpose of the entity concept. The question of disregarding the corporate entity (or as is often said, "piercing the corporate veil") usually arises with a one-person or family type of corporation. The one-person or close corporation is found where one or two persons own all of the corporation stock. This type of corporation may usually afford grounds for disregarding the entity unless the following two conditions are complied with:

1. The business must be conducted on a corporate rather than a personal basis.

2. The business must be established on an adequate financial basis.

3. KINDS OF CORPORATIONS

A. DE JURE

A *de jure* corporation is formed when there is essential compliance with all of the mandatory provisions of the incorporation statute. The *de jure* corporation is legal for all purposes, even though the corporation is not in compliance with some minor provisions of the statute. Only the Secretary of State might challenge such a corporation's corporate existence and authority.

B. DE FACTO

A *de facto* corporation exists where there has not been substantial compliance with the mandatory provisions of the incorporation statute. In practice, it is a corporation in its dealings with all parties—except the Secretary of State of the state of incorporation, who may attack its corporate status and dissolve the corporation in a *quo warranto* court proceeding for that purpose.

To be a *de facto* organization, there must be the following:

1. A valid statute under which the corporation can be formed.

2. A good faith attempt to organize under such statute.

3. A user of the corporate powers (i.e., business has been transacted as a corporation).

A *de facto* corporation is entitled to act as a corporation until dissolved by direct state action.

c. Corporation by Estoppel

When an association represents itself to be a corporation, it cannot escape liability by denying its own corporate existence. Furthermore, if the association is not a *de jure* or *de facto* corporation, the members have unlimited liability as in a partnership. When a person contracts with an association as if it were a corporation, the general rule is that he or she cannot avoid liability on a contract by denying the corporate existence, since that person thereby admits the legal existence of the corporation for the purpose of any action that may be brought to enforce the contract.

In *Robertson v. Levy* (197 A 2d 443 [D.C. App., 1964]), the Court of Appeals for the District of Columbia noted that the adoption of the Model Business Corporation Act made the issuance of the certificate of incorporation the date on which corporate existence began, and that acts by corporate officers made before that date were their own acts and not those of the corporation.

> **FACTS** Robertson and Levy entered into an agreement whereby Levy agreed to form a corporation, Penn Ave. Record Shack, Inc., which was to purchase Robertson's business. Levy submitted articles of incorporation to the Superintendent of Corporations. Before the certificate of incorporation was issued, Levy, acting as president of the corporation, assumed Robertson's lease and signed a note payable to Robertson. Shortly thereafter, the corporation went bankrupt. Robertson sued Levy personally to recover the balance due on the note. Judgment for Levy was appealed.

> **DECISION** Reversed. The court stated that Section 56 of the Model Act provides that corporate existence begins only upon the issuance of the certificate of incorporation. Hence, before the certificate is issued, there is no corporation *de jure, de facto,* or by estoppel. That Robertson may have intended to deal with a corporation is immaterial. Levy is thus subject to personal liability for the obligations incurred prior to January 17, the date the certificate was issued, since he assumed to act as a corporation without any authority to do so (Model Act Section 146).

Robertson v. Levy (197 A.2d 443 [D.C. App., 1964])

d. Private and Public Corporations

Private corporations are those organized for private purposes. Public corporations are created by the people or government for public purposes, political, or otherwise (e.g., United States, states, cities, towns, counties, school districts).

e. Nonprofit

A nonprofit corporation may be formed for religious, charitable, social, educational, or cemetery purposes. The business can be carried on at a profit as an incident to the main purpose of the corporation, although the corporation cannot distribute any gains, profits, or dividends to any of its members except upon dissolution or winding up. A nonprofit corporation is a nonstock corporation (i.e., it may have memberships but no shares).

F.   DOMESTIC OR FOREIGN

A domestic corporation is one that is created by the laws of a particular state or country in which it does business, whereas a foreign corporation is one created by the laws of one state or country but also doing business in another (the "foreign" state or country). "Doing business" means that the corporation is doing a substantial amount of business with substantial regularity in the state. When it is doing business in the state, it must qualify as a foreign corporation. To qualify, it must, among other things, permit itself to be sued in the state. This is done by filing with the Secretary of State in which it is going to do business a copy of its articles of incorporation, together with a statement setting forth its home office and office within the state and the name and address of a person or corporation within the state upon whom legal process may be served in any legal action against it. Failure to qualify as a foreign corporation can result in fines and the denial of the use of the courts of the state to enforce contracts.

G.   CLOSE CORPORATION

Corporations are not all conglomerate giants. Today, because of the advantages of tax benefits and limited liability, many small firms that normally would be operated as sole proprietorships or partnerships are now incorporated. They may have only a few outstanding shares of stock, or all of the stock may be held by one person, a family, or a few friends. Since the stock is closely held by a few and not sold publicly, the entity is called a "close corporation." Many states now have separate statutes covering this type of corporation that permit simpler operation with less technical tax and accounting problems.

The following case illustrates the duty of a close corporation to its shareholders.

FACTS   Plaintiff, Donahue, was a minority shareholder in Rodd Electrotype. Harry Rodd and his children owned the remaining shares and served as officers and directors. Without informing plaintiff, the board voted to reacquire Harry Rodd's shares. Upon learning of the transaction, plaintiff objected and brought suit claiming that the purchase was an unlawful distribution of corporate assets and that the Rodds breached the fiduciary duties owed by them, as controlling shareholders, to the minority shareholder. The trial court dismissed the suit.

DECISION   On appeal, the court held that the Rodds had breached their fiduciary duty owed to plaintiff. Closed corporations are typified by (1) a small number of shareholders; (2) no ready market for corporate stock; and (3) substantial majority stockholder participation in the management, direction, and operations of the corporation. They resemble partnerships, requiring of the controlling owners utmost good faith, trust, fidelity, and absolute loyalty. Because Rodd was a member of the controlling group of shareholders, the corporation should have offered each stockholder an equal opportunity to sell a ratable number of shares to the corporation at an identical price.

Donahue v. Rodd Electrotype Co. (367 Mass. 578, 328 N.E. 2d 505 [1975])

H. PROFESSIONAL CORPORATION

All states now permit a corporation to be organized for the purpose of conducting a profession, although most will not allow skilled individuals, such as doctors and lawyers, to avoid personal liability by incorporation.

4. PROMOTERS

Large corporations are usually planned and formed by promoters. Their activities include researching the economic feasibility of the new business and assembling the necessary resources, property, and personnel. Promoters often continue in control of the corporation after the corporation's formation.

A. DUTY OF DISCLOSURE

Promoters are fiduciaries who owe a duty of good faith, fair dealing, and full disclosure to the corporation. They are liable to the corporation for any secret profits.

B. CONTRACTS OF PROMOTERS

The acts of the promoters do not bind the corporation prior to the corporation's legal existence, since until the corporation legally exists, there cannot be a principal-agency relationship. The corporation is not liable on promoter contracts until it adopts or ratifies such contracts after incorporation.

The promoters themselves are liable on the contracts if they entered into them as individuals but not if they made the contracts in the name of the *contemplated* corporation and solely on its credit. If the other party to the contract is unaware that the corporation has not come into existence at the time he or she contracts with the promoter, and if the promoter expressly or implicitly holds the corporation out to him or her as existing and that he or she has the right to bind the corporation by contract, the promoter will be personally liable on the contract on the theory that he or she has been guilty of a breach of warranty of his or her agency.

5. PREINCORPORATION STOCK SUBSCRIPTIONS

Before forming the corporation, the promoters may attempt to get people to pledge themselves to purchase stock after the corporation is formed. To take this action, the promoters must first secure a permit from the state to take preincorporation subscriptions. After they obtain the permit, they can solicit prospective investors for their promises to purchase stock.

These pledges (or offers) by the investors to purchase stock are usually revocable by the investor, in the absence of statute, until accepted by the corporation after it comes into legal existence. Modern statutes usually make preincorporation subscriptions irrevocable for a stated period of time (e.g., Model Business Corporation Act, Section 16—six months).

Preincorporation agreements are not in common use. Today, it is more usual to first form the corporation and then attempt to sell the stock.

B. FORMATION

1. ARTICLES OF INCORPORATION

In most states, corporate existence begins with the filing of the articles of incorporation prepared by an attorney at law. In some states, corporate existence does not begin until a formal certificate of incorporation is issued by the state.

The contents of the articles of incorporation are prescribed in the general incorporation statutes of the various states. Typical requirements are found in the Model Business Corporation Act, Section 48:

1.   The name of the corporation.

2.   The period of duration, which may be perpetual.

3.   The purpose for which it is organized.

4.   The number of shares that it shall have authority to issue and the par (equal) value of each share or a statement that the shares are without par value.

5.   If the shares are to be divided into classes, the designation of each class and a statement of preferences, limitations, and relative rights of each class.

6.   A statement that the corporation will not commence business until at least $1,000 has been received for issued shares.

7.   Any provision limiting or denying to shareholders the right to acquire additional or treasury shares of the corporation on a preemptive basis.

8.   Any provision the incorporators may choose to set forth for the regulation of the internal affairs of the corporation.

9.   The address of its initial office and agent.

10.   The number of directors constituting the original board of directors and the names and addresses of the persons who are to serve as the first board of directors until the first annual meeting of shareholders or until successors are elected.

11.   The name and address of each incorporator (usually three or more and of legal capacity).

After the articles are prepared and signed by the incorporators, the attorney files them and the necessary fee with the proper state officer, usually the Secretary of State. If the articles are in order, the Secretary of State issues a certificate of incorporation. The certificate and a copy of the articles are filed with the local county recorder. After they are returned by the recorder, they are placed in the corporation minute book. As soon as the corporation comes into legal existence, the directors can hold their first meeting, at which time they will elect officers, adopt bylaws, choose the type of seal and minute book they desire, and conduct other business, such as requesting permission to issue stock.

2. BYLAWS

Bylaws are the rules enacted by a corporation to regulate and govern its own affairs and its directors, officers, and shareholders. They are not necessary in the formation of a corporation.

Bylaws must conform to the articles of incorporation and local laws. States vary as to the required and the permissible content of bylaws and as to how they are to be adopted or amended. Bylaws vary in content from a brief statement of rules for one corporation to a comprehensive booklet for another.

In most states, the bylaws are not filed in any public office.

C. TERMINATION

Termination of a corporation is usually accomplished by either voluntary or involuntary dissolution, discussed later in this chapter.

1. MERGER AND CONSOLIDATION

A. IN GENERAL

Changes of a fundamental nature that alter the structure of a corporation are beyond the scope of ordinary business transactions entrusted to the board of directors and must be approved by the shareholders. This is so because the value of each shareholder's stock, in terms of dividend income and appreciation of market value, could be adversely affected or could benefit by such extraordinary changes, which may include charter amendments, sale or lease of all or the majority of corporate assets, mergers, and consolidations.

Shareholder approval of such changes requires not unanimous consent but, in most cases, a favorable vote of a majority of shares. In practice, minority shareholders who object are overridden by the majority. To protect their interests, such shareholders may be permitted to dissent and recover the fair value of their shares so long as the statutes authorizing such action (called an "appraisal remedy") are strictly followed.

B. TYPES OF EXTRAORDINARY TRANSACTIONS

(1) Charter Amendments

Most business incorporation statutes permit free amendment of corporate articles. Section 58 of the Model Business Corporations Act governs amendments and authorizes comprehensive changes, such as a change of name, duration, and corporate purposes. The most important additional changes, and the most likely subject of amendment, relate to the capital structure of the corporation:

1. Increase or decrease number of par value of shares.

2. Reclassify shares and change preferential rights of shares.

3. Create new classes of shares.

4. Grant, limit, or deny preemptive rights.

Such a change is accomplished by resolution of the board of directors which must then be approved by a majority shareholder vote. Minority shareholders are not afforded an appraisal remedy in most states. Once approved, the articles of amendment are filed with the Secretary of State for further review and approval, which becomes effective upon the issuance of the certificate of amendment by the Secretary. The existing rights of non-shareholders, such as creditors, are not affected by the adoption and approval of corporate charter amendments.

(2) Purchase or Lease of Another Corporation's Assets

The purchase or lease of one corporation's assets by another corporation does not cause any change in the legal existence of either the purchasing, leasing, or selling corporation. All that has occurred is that the purchasing or leasee corporation has obtained ownership or control of additional physical assets, such as plant, inventory, and equipment. The selling or lessor corporation has received cash, property, or agreed-upon rent in return. Otherwise each corporation operates independently of the other. Only the size or nature of each one's assets is altered.

If the sale or lease of assets is in the usual course of business of the selling or lessor corporation, approval of its board of directors is all that is required. Shareholder approval becomes necessary only when such a sale or lease is not in the corporation's usual course of business.

Dissenting shareholders who strictly comply with any statutory right to obtain appraisal and payment for shares owned are protected. The procedure is discussed in 1. C., Rights of Dissenting Shareholders, *infra*.

FACTS Pampered Beef Midwest, Inc. (PBM) owed substantial sums to Nelson and other creditors. Already deep in debt, PBM transferred its assets to Bryant Beef, Inc. The corporate stock of Bryant Beef was owned entirely by James Bryant, who also owed 47 percent of the stock of PBM. Nelson sued to collect their debts from Bryant Beef and James Bryant.

DECISION The transferor (PBM) did not pay its unsecured debts or make provision for their payment. As unsecured creditors, Nelson therefore had an equitable lien which followed PBM's personal and real property into the hands of Bryant.

The four situations in which a transferee becomes personally liable for transferor-corporation debts are an agreement to assume the debts, a consolidation of two corporations, a mere continuation of the transferor corporation, and fraud in fact. None of these are found in the present case. Neither Bryant nor Bryant Beef, Inc. agreed to assume the unsecured debts; PBM and Bryant Beef, Inc. did not consolidate; no intention existed that the transferees would simply be continuations of PBM, and a marked difference existed between the transferor and transferees; and no actual fraud existed.

Neither Bryant nor Bryant Beef, Inc. became generally personally liable to Nelson.

Nelson, et al. v. Pampered Beef-Midwest, Inc. (298 N.W.2d 281 [Iowa, 1980])

(3) Purchase of Shares of Another Corporation

The purchase of all or substantially all the shares of another corporation does not alter the legal existence of either corporation. A parent-subsidiary corporate relationship is created between purchaser and seller. The parent purchasing corporation purchases the shares through its board of directors. The subsidiary (selling) corporation does not, since the sale is made by its shareholders. The capital structure of the subsidiary remains the same, as does that of the parent, unless altered by the financing needed to acquire the shares. Here the rights of dissenting shareholders are not protected, since they may sell their shares or not, as they wish, and thus adequately protect themselves.

(4) Merger of Corporations

A merger of two or more corporations combines all of their total assets, with title held in one of them, called the surviving corporation. The other corporation or corporations, known as merged corporation(s), cease to exist as separate corporate entities. The debts and obligations of the merged corporation are carried over and assumed by the surviving corporation as a matter of law, irrespective of any agreement to do so. The shareholders of the merged corporation receive stock issued by the surviving corporation, as outlined in the merger plan. The board of directors as well as a majority of the shareholders of each corporation must approve any merger.

As in the case of a purchase of all or substantially all assets, dissenting shareholders of either or both corporations (surviving and merged) are entitled to appraisal rights where authorized by statute.

The difference between a merger requiring shareholder approval and a reorganization agreement (not requiring such approval and thus not entitling shareholders to any appraisal rights) was noted in *Farris v. Glen Alden Corp.* The Supreme Court of Pennsylvania, in finding the transaction to be a merger, looked to the consequences of the transaction in making the determination.

FACTS The complaint stated that the notice of the annual shareholders' meeting did not conform to the requirements of the Business Corporation Law, 15 P.S. § 2852-1 et seq., in three respects: (1) It did not give notice to the shareholders that the true intent and purpose of the meetings was to effect a merger or consolidation of Glen Alden and List; (2)

It failed to give notice to the shareholders of their right to dissent to the plan of merger or consolidation and claim fair value for their shares; and (3) It did not contain copies of the text of certain sections of the Business Corporation Law as required.

By reason of these omissions, plaintiff contended that the approval of the reorganization agreement by the shareholders at the annual meeting was invalid, and unless the carrying out of the plan were enjoined, he would suffer irreparable loss by being deprived of substantial property rights.

DECISION   When use of the corporate form of business organization first became widespread, it was relatively easy for courts to define a "merger" or a "sale of assets" and to label a particular transaction as one or the other. But prompted by the desire to avoid the impact of adverse, and to obtain the benefits of favorable, government regulations, particularly federal tax laws, new accounting and legal techniques were developed by lawyers and accountants which interwove the elements characteristic of each, thereby creating hybrid forms of corporate amalgamation. Thus, it is no longer helpful to consider an individual transaction in the abstract and solely by reference to the various elements therein to determine whether it is a "merger" or a "sale." Instead, to determine properly the nature of a corporate transaction, we must refer not only to all the provisions of the agreement, but also to the consequences of the transaction and to the purposes of the provisions of the corporation law said to be applicable.

We hold that the combination contemplated by the reorganization agreement, although consummated by contract rather than in accordance with the statutory procedure, is a merger within the protective purview of the corporation law. The shareholders of Glen Alden should have been notified accordingly and advised of their statutory rights of dissent and appraisal. The failure of the corporate officers to take these steps renders the stockholder approval of the agreement at the shareholders' meeting invalid. The officers and directors of Glen Alden are enjoined from carrying out this agreement.

Farris v. Glen Alden Corporation (393 Pa. 427, 143 A.2d 25 [1958])

(5)   Consolidation of Corporations

A consolidation combines two or more corporations, including all assets, into a newly created consolidated corporation. The original corporations cease to exist, and the debts and liabilities of each of them are assumed by the new corporation. The shareholders of each of the constituent corporations receive stock or other securities issued by the consolidated corporation. Like a merger, consolidation requires the approval of the board of directors and a majority of the shareholders of each constituent corporation.

C.   RIGHTS OF DISSENTING SHAREHOLDERS

To protect the interest of minority shareholders, many states, including those adopting the Model Business Corporations Act, give a shareholder not wishing to approve a proposed sale or lease of corporate assets—merger or consolidation—the right to dissent. By dissenting and complying exactly with the statutory provisions, the shareholder is entitled to receive the fair value of his or her shares. Three requirements must be met:

1. Filing of a written objection to the proposed transaction prior to the vote of the shareholders.

2. Refraining from voting for the proposed transaction either in person or by proxy.

3. Making a written demand for appraisal upon the corporation within the time period specified by the corporation on the form provided, such time period to be not less than 30 days after the corporation mails the form.

The Model Act defines fair value of shares to mean their value immediately before the completion of the proposed transaction, not to include any appreciation or depreciation that anticipated such action, unless disregarding such price fluctuations would be inequitable.

2. DISSOLUTION AND WINDING UP

Dissolution may be voluntary or involuntary.

A. VOLUNTARY

Shareholders may vote to dissolve a corporation. The proportion of shareholders necessary to cause a dissolution varies with local statutes from one half to two thirds.

Usually, a certificate of election to dissolve the corporation must be filed with the Secretary of State as the first step in winding up. The corporation must cease doing any business except that necessary to wind up its affairs. The directors must liquidate as much of the assets as they believe necessary to effect the winding up. After all the debts have been paid, the directors must distribute the balance of the assets to the shareholders. After distribution, the directors must file a certificate with the Secretary of State showing that the corporation has been wound up, debts paid, and the balance of the assets distributed to the shareholders. Upon the filing of this certificate, the corporation terminates.

B. INVOLUNTARY

Forced dissolution can be caused by creditors of a corporation or by petition of a percentage of the stockholders, which varies from 10 to 50 percent. Some of the reasons are fraud on the part of the directors, deadlocked factions of directors and stockholders, wasting of corporate property, misapplication of corporate property, mismanagement, abuse of authority, and unfairness to minority stockholders.

Involuntary dissolution can also be caused by the act of the state legislature in terminating the corporate existence where the right has been reserved and can be caused by a decree of court initiated by the attorney general of the state of incorporation when it appears that the corporation has violated a corporation law (e.g., failure to pay franchise tax, abuse of powers).

In an involuntary dissolution, the court decrees dissolution and orders the winding up by the directors under the supervision of the court. The procedure for winding up is similar to the voluntary dissolution.

ILLUSTRATIVE CASES

1. Fiduciary Duty of Promoters of Corporation

GOLDEN v. OAHE ENTERPRISES INC.

295 N.W.2d 160 (S.D., 1980)

WOLLMAN, C. J. * * * Emmick is the major figure in the story of Oahe. In years past, Emmick has been involved in the sale of industrial chemicals, the promotion of nursing homes, and the management of various farming activities. Emmick approached one J. B. Morris (now deceased) with a plan whereby Morris' Sully County, South Dakota, ranch would be incorporated and through Emmick's managerial skills made to show a profit. At approximately the same time, Emmick approached Golden, who was then operating the Silver Spur Bar in Ft. Pierre, and proposed that Golden contribute some farm machinery and livestock to Oahe. Golden was not, however, present on October 26, 1966, when Oahe was incorporated at a meeting in the office of George Qualley, Emmick's lawyer, in Sioux City, Iowa.

At this meeting, it was concluded that Oahe shares would be given a $50 par value. Officers of the corporation were elected. Chairman and Secretary-Treasurer, J. B. Morris; President, Emmick; and Vice-President, Milton Morris (J. B. Morris' son). An agreement was signed whereby J. B. and Mary Morris transferred their ranch to Oahe Enterprises. It was concluded that the Morris ranch was worth $168,000.00 Of this amount, Morris' equity was determined to be $120,000.00. As his contribution, Emmick transferred 6,315 shares of Colonial Manors, Inc., stock (CM stock) to Oahe.

Colonial Manors, Inc., is an Iowa corporation that is involved in the promotion and management of nursing homes throughout the Midwest. There is serious disagreement concerning the value this stock had at the time Emmick exchanged it for Oahe stock. Emmick represented to the Morrises that the stock was worth $19 per share. At the March 1966 meeting of the CM Corporation, the board of directors set the value of CM stock for internal stock-option purposes at $19 per share. This figure represented $1 for each nursing home the CM Corporation was involved with. At the September 1966 meeting, the value of the CM stock was reduced by the board of directors to $9.50 per share. Emmick knew of the reduction in value of the CM stock prior to the October 26, 1966, meeting at which Oahe was incorporated. There is, however, no evidence that would suggest that this knowledge was disclosed to the Morrises.

*   *   *

Courts faced with the situation in which a promoter benefits from a violation of his fiduciary duty at the expense of the corporation or its members often characterize the promoter's gain as "secret profit." Such profit is not secret if all interested parties know of and assent to it. But where a promoter through, for example, overvaluation of property exchanged for stock and failure to disclose all material facts regarding such exchange, takes more from the corporation than he transfers in, he is held liable for what courts term secret profit. [Citations.]

As a promoter of Oahe, Emmick stood in a fiduciary relationship to both the corporation and its stockholders and was bound to deal with them in the utmost good faith. "The obtaining of a secret profit by a promoter through the sale of property to a corporation is uniformly held to be a fraud on the corporation and stockholders, and the promoter may be required to account for such profit." [Citation.]

The valuation of the CM stock was based on Emmick's self-serving estimate of matters well known to him as a CM insider and was warped by Emmick's self-interest. Emmick was not trading stock that had an easily ascertainable value; he was not dealing with people experienced in transactions of this type. He failed to make known facts of which he, as an insider of CM, was aware. It is true that Emmick was not the only member of the Oahe board of directors. He was, however, the controlling member and the one in possession of information pertinent to the value of his CM stock not generally available to the public or to the other Oahe board members. In addition to being an insider of CM, he was both a director of and the dominant and controlling force in Oahe. We hold, therefore, that he failed in his duty to the corporation to disclose information regarding stock he intended to transfer into Oahe for Oahe shares and is therefore liable for the shortfall to the corporation therefrom.

*   *   *

Because the total value of the CM stock Emmick transferred to Oahe was less than the value Emmick received in Oahe stock, the difference can be equalized by canceling the number of Oahe shares held by Emmick that is proportional to the overevaluation. [Citations.] We note that this Court has upheld the cancellation of stock under circumstances where original issue stock was transferred for the worthless stock of another corporation or for services to be performed in the future.

*   *   *

The judgment is reversed, and the case is remanded to the circuit court with directions to redetermine the fair market value of the CM stock exchanged by Emmick for Oahe stock * * *.

2. Corporation as a "Person"

UNION SAVINGS ASS'N v. HOME OWNERS AID, INC.

23 Ohio St.2d 60, 262 N.E.2d 558 (1970)

DUNCAN, Justice. The record, briefs and arguments of counsel raise the question: May a corporate litigant maintain a legal action *in propria persona* through an officer of the corporation who is not a licensed attorney? If a corporation cannot appear *in propria persona* through its officer, the order of the Court of Common Pleas, striking the corporate defendant's petition to vacate judgment, was proper.

Appellant, Home Owners, contends that corporate statutes in R.C. Chapter 1701, in essence, either provide or imply that a corporation is the same as a natural person in all respects and has all the capacities of a natural person, including the right to represent itself *in propria persona* through an appointed agent who need not be an attorney at law. Home Owners asserts constitutional protection for the right to litigate in this manner pursuant to its entitlement to due process and equal protection of the law, as guaranteed by the Ohio and United States Constitutions. In addition, Home Owners urges that a denial of the maintenance of this litigation through its officer unconstitutionally impairs the obligation of contract.

We cannot agree with appellant's contentions, which appear to be based upon the premise that a corporation and a natural living person are in all respects equal. A corporation is an artificial person, created by the General Assembly and deriving its power, authority and capacity from the statutes.

It is true that certain statutes make it appear that a corporation is to be treated as a natural person. Many other statutes, however, clearly reveal that the General Assembly did not intend a corporation to have all the attributes and powers of a natural person.

* * *

In other jurisdictions, courts have held that a corporation cannot appear *in propria persona*. * * *

The fallacy of defendant corporation's constitutional arguments is that they rest upon the faulty premise that a corporation is in all respects equal to a natural person.

* * *

Beyond what has been concluded hereinabove in importance as a basis for our decision is the statutory prohibition regarding the practice of law. R.C. 4705.01 prohibits anyone from practicing law or commencing or defending an action "in which he is not a party concerned, * * * unless he has been admitted to the bar by order of the Supreme Court * * *."

It is the responsibility of this court to provide effective standards for admission to the practice of law and for the discipline of those admitted to practice. Litigation must be projected through the courts according to established practice by lawyers who are of high character, skilled in the profession, dedicated to the interest of their clients, and in the spirit of public service. In the orderly process of the administration of justice, any retreat from those principles would be a disservice to the public. To allow a corporation to maintain litigation and appear in court represented by corporate officers or agents only would lay open the gates to the practice of law for entry to those corporate officers or agents who have not been qualified to practice law and who are not amenable to the general discipline of the court.

Judgment affirmed.

3. Corporation by Estoppel

BUKACEK v. PELL CITY FARMS, INC.

286 Ala. 141, 237 So.2d 851 (1970)

James Bukacek was having serious financial problems. Bukacek and others agreed to form "Pell City Farms, Inc." Once formed, the corporation was to pay Bukacek's debts. In exchange, Bukacek was to deed his 300-acre farm to the corporation. Bukacek deeded the land to Pell City Farms, Inc., but its articles of incorporation had not as yet been filed with the designated officer of the state. After the corporation was formed, Bukacek participated in corporate business involving the farm and took an active role as an officer, director, and stockholder. However, he later asserted that at the time he signed the deed, the corporation did not legally exist. He therefore argued that the corporation had been incapable of taking title to real property and that he still owned the farm. Bukacek (plaintiff) sued in equity to quiet title to the land. Judgment for Pell City Farms, Inc. Bukacek appealed.

MADDOX, Justice.   Assuming, without deciding that we would subscribe to the broad view that no corporation was here formed prior to the filing of the Articles of Incorporation, we think the fact situation here presented shows that while Pell City Farms, Inc. may not have been a corporation de jure—or perhaps even de facto—insofar as the transaction here is concerned, it should be regarded practically as a corporation, being recognized as such by the parties themselves. In other words, the incidents of corporate existence may exist as between the parties by virtue of an estoppel. * * *

Bukacek was one of the incorporators; he dealt with the corporation as a corporation both before and after the Articles of Incorporation were filed. Under such facts, Bukacek is estopped to deny the existence of the corporation at the time he voluntarily executed a deed transferring property to the corporation even though the Articles of Incorporation had not been filed at that time.

Our ruling here is limited. It is based on equitable grounds which preclude the [plaintiff] here from denying corporate existence. As against the state, of course, a corporation cannot be created by agreement of the parties * * * but they may, by their agreements or their conduct estop themselves from denying the fact of the existence of the corporation. We hold, therefore, that Bukacek is estopped to deny the existence of Pell City Farms, Inc., even though it may have been neither de facto nor de jure at the time he executed the deed making the corporation, *by its corporate name,* the grantee. * * *

Decree [for Pell City Farms, Inc.] is affirmed.

4. "Piercing the Corporate Veil"

KWICK SET COMPONENTS INC. v. DAVIDSON INDUSTRIES, INC.

411 So.2d 134 (Ala., 1982)

BEATTY, Justice. Plaintiff, Davidson Industries, Inc., filed this action in Russell Circuit Court against Ira Dennis Salter, individually, and Capital Components, Inc., d/b/a Kwick Set Components, Inc., for failure to pay a debt on open account. The trial court heard testimony *ore tenus,* dismissed Ira Dennis Salter as a party defendant, and entered judgment against Capital Components and Kwick Set Components for $20,567.92 together with interest and court costs. Kwick Set appeals. We affirm.

Kwick Set contends that it was never named as a party defendant in this action, but only as a trade alias of the defendant Capital Components. According to Kwick Set, the two entities are separate corporations.

* * *

* * * We disagree. The order holding Kwick Set liable was based upon the following findings made by the trial court:

> That Kwick Set Components, Inc., was a dominant corporation as to Capital Components, Inc. at all times pertinent to this cause of action and that Capital Components, Inc. had become a mere instrumentality of Kwick Set Components, Inc.; that the president of both corporations was one and the same, i.e., Ira Dennis Salter, and that the actions of the dominant corporation caused the plaintiff harm in the damages complained of through misuse of the control of the subservient corporation.

The second element, *i.e.,* harm to plaintiff, has clearly been established in this case. The crucial question to be answered is whether Kwick Set, the alleged dominant corporation, controlled Capital Components. The control required under the "instrumentality" rule amounts to "total domination of the subservient corporation, to the extent that the subservient corporation manifests no separate corporate interests of its own and functions solely to achieve the purposes of the dominant corporation."

In the case before us, plaintiff presented evidence that (1) both corporations have the same president and board of directors and (2) Kwick Set purchased goods through the name of the defunct corporation, Capital Components, and used these goods to perform contracts. The mere fact that some or all of the stockholders or officials of two corporations are identical or because one corporation dominates the other does not, of itself, destroy the corporate identity or merge one into the other. That factor, however, combined with the apparent scheme here of the dominant corporation to avoid payment of the subservient corporation's debts while benefiting from use of the goods causing that debt, indicates a lack of separate corporate purpose or existence on the part of the subservient corporation. The courts will not "allow the corporate entity to successfully masquerade through its officers, stockholders, representatives or associates so as to defeat the payment of its just obligations."

Our review of the record convinces us that the trial court had before it sufficient evidence from which it could have found that Capital Components had become the mere instrumentality of Kwick Set and that justice required the court to look directly at Kwick Set for payment of the injuries and damages caused plaintiff. Those findings and the decree based thereon are entitled to a presumption of correctness which may be overturned only if plainly or palpably erroneous.

* * *

PROBLEMS

1. A, B, and C decide to organize a corporation for the purpose of conducting a television repair service. The articles of incorporation are prepared and signed by A and B and acknowledged by a notary public. The articles are then given to C who signs them but forgets to have his signature acknowledged by a notary as required by statute. C files the articles and the required fee with the Secretary of State. Thereafter, A, B, and C meet as the first directors of the ABC Corporation, elect officers, adopt by-laws, purchase a truck to be used in the business, employ D to drive the truck, and conduct other necessary corporate business. While D is driving the truck during the course of his employment, he negligently runs over a pedestrian. The pedestrian brings action against A, B, C, and D individually. A, B, and C defend on the ground that the corporate liability of the ABC Corporation does not extend to them individually. Decision?

2. A state law provides that any person or persons doing business under an assumed or fictitious name should file their true names in the office of the county recorder. Ace, Best and Conn owned all the stock of the ABC Company, a duly organized corporation within the state. The State prosecutes Ace, Best and Conn for failing to register their names under this statute. Decision?

3. A formed a corporation for the purpose of conducting a newspaper business so that he could publish untrue stories about B, a liberal politician who held a high office. A obtained a stock permit which gave the corporation permission to issue 100 shares of stock at $5.00 a share. The corporation issued 90 sharse to A, 5 shares to A's wife, and 5 shares to A's son. Thereafter, A printed a libelous story about B claiming that B was a communist sympathizer, which A knew was untrue. B brings action against A individually. A defends on the ground that only the corporation is liable. Decision?

4. Mr. and Mrs. Jones and Mr. and Mrs. Smith, all ski enthusiasts, purchased a ski lodge. To avoid liability problems, they formed a corporation. Everything went fine the first year. There was plenty of snow, they all pitched in on the work around the lodge, and the corporation showed a good profit. The second year, however, Mr. Smith spent more time at the ski lift than he did at the lodge. By the close of the second year, relations between the four owners of the corporation became strained. During the third year it was apparent that Mr. Smith was becoming a great skier, Mrs. Smith was becoming an alcoholic, and Mr. and Mrs. Jones were getting "housemaid's knees". At the end of the third year the corporation was still solvent; however, there was such dissension among the shareholders that there was a management deadlock and irreparable injury to the corporation was threatened. Mr. and Mrs. Jones file suit for dissolution. Decision?

5. The State of Oregon indicted the Pacific Powder Company, a corporation, for manslaughter, when a truck load of explosives belonging to the company was negligently parked and blew up during a fire, causing the death of a bystander. Oregon Criminal Statutes say: " 'Person' includes corporations as well as natural persons." The statute on manslaughter states, "Every person convicted of manslaughter shall be punished by imprisonment in the penitentiary for not more than 15 years and by a fine not exceeding $5,000." Can the Pacific Powder Company be convicted of manslaughter?

6. XYZ Lines, a carrier, sued M Truck, Inc., claiming that M was operating without the necessary certificate of the state regulatory body. It was shown that M had obtained its certificate when all of its stock was owned by A, B, and C, all individuals. The stock was then sold the D and E, also individuals. No approval of the regulatory body was obtained for the sale of stock to D and E. XYZ Lines argued that M was not entitled to continue operating under its original certificate. Decision?

7. A and two other persons were promotors for a new corporation: AT company. A retained K to perform legal services in connection with the incorporation of the new business and promised to pay K $1,500. K incorporated AT, and A and the other two promotors became AT's only directors. K was told at a director's board meeting that he should obtain a permit for AT to sell stock because the directors wished to pay him for his prior professional services. When A and the other two failed to pay K, K sued AT. AT defended on the ground that it never obligated itself to pay K, either before or after incorporation. Decision?

8. T and others formed a voluntary association called the OTR Club and were chosen to act as an executive committee. The committee made a contract with U, a utility company, on behalf of the club. U later sued the committee members to collect unpaid club utility bills. T and the other committee members defended on the ground that the club was a corporation, immunizing them from liability. Decision?

9. Walley Corporation is solely owned by A, Mr. and Mrs. W, and J, Mr. W's brother, who comprise the corporate officers and directors. Walley procured a fire insurance policy on a building owned by the corporation. Later, A set fire to the building, which was rendered a total loss. When the insurance company refused to pay, Walley sued to recover on the policy. Decision?

10. L, acting as a promotor, made a preincorporation employment contract with M whereby M was hired as corporate comptroller for a one-year term. The corporation, T Company, was thereafter duly incorporated. M began his duties at that time. No formal action verifying M's contract was made by the board of directors, but all directors, officers and shareholders had knowledge of M's contract. Two months later M was terminated without cause. M sues T Company to recover for breach of contract. Decision?

11. A Inc. was duly merged into B Company. S, a shareholder of A, paid only one-half of his original stock subscription. B Company sued S to recover the balance of the subscription price. S defended on the ground that he took no part in the merger proceedings and that the merger extinguished any obligations he owed to A, since A no longer had any corporate existence. Decision?

12. R sought legal advice from MHV, a professional association duly incorporated under the laws of Maryland. R was a resident of Pennsylvania, and the legal advice was actually rendered in that state. The matter concerned the compromise of a medical disciplinary proceeding instituted against R by R's hospital. R ordered MHV to abandon the representation and then refused to pay a final bill rendered. When MHV sued to recover for its services, R defended on the ground that MHV's failure to register as a foreign corporation prevented MVR from suing R in Pennsylvania. Decision?

13. J, a minority shareholder in R Corporation and others similarly situated objected to a plan whereby the majority of R Corporation's shares were voted to amend R Corporation's articles of incorporation to issue new stock to another corporation. R Corporation shares would be reduced in value and the new stock issued to the other corporation would markedly increase in value over the shares exchanged for the new issue. Under the controlling statutes, a merger required the affirmative vote of two-thirds of the shares outstanding, whereas only a majority was required to amend the articles of incorporation. When J sued to set aside the plan of reorganization, R Corporation defended on the ground that the plan was not a merger and that a bare majority of affirmative shareholder votes had been obtained approving the plan. Decision?

14. D Corporation and E Corporation duly consolidated to form DE Enterprises, Inc. Unpaid creditors of both D and E sued to recover payment against DE Enterprises. DE defended on the ground that the consolidation terminated any liability of D and E to creditors, absent express contractual assumption of such obligations by DE Inc. as part of the plan of consolidation. No such contractual assumption of pre-existing obligations had been made. Decision?

15. V Grocery Corporation acquired its direct competitor, SBF Stores, by taking over all SBF stock and all of its assets in the area. Both are large, retail grocery companies in Los Angeles. The U. S. Attorney General moved to halt the merger on the ground that it tended to concentrate the Los Angeles grocery business into too few hands and would accentuate the decline of small independent operators in that market. V defended on the ground that V or SBF would either fail unless the merger was forthcoming or both would be bought up by a larger national competitor. Decision?

Chapter 37

CORPORATE MANAGEMENT

A. IN GENERAL

Three groups participate in the management of a corporation: the shareholders, the directors, and the officers. The powers, qualifications, functions, and procedures relating to these three groups are prescribed in part by constitutions, statutes, administrative rules and regulations, articles of incorporation, bylaws, various shareholder and director resolutions and agreements, and proxies.

B. POWERS

A corporation's powers are the things it is authorized to do and are derived from the articles of incorporation and the laws of the state under which the corporation was organized. A corporation has only such powers as are expressly or implicitly conferred by its charter. The difference between the powers of a natural person and those of a corporation is that a natural person can do anything not forbidden by law, whereas a corporation can do only what is expressly or implicitly authorized by the state.

Because corporate enterprise now engages in most types of activities, the modern trend is to grant almost unlimited powers. In California, for example, purpose statements are specified by statute. The one most commonly used is, "The purpose of this corporation is to engage in any lawful act or activity for which a corporation may be organized under the General Corporation Law of California other than the banking business, the trust company business or the practice of a profession permitted to be incorporated by the California Corporations Code."

1. EXPRESS POWERS

Express powers may be found in the corporation statutes, which are usually quite explicit and lengthy, or in the articles of incorporation. Common express powers granted by statutes are as follows:

1. To have a corporate name.

2. To have perpetual existence.

3. To have a common seal.

4. To purchase and hold land and personal property for authorized corporate purposes.

5. To make bylaws for the governing of the corporation.

6. To borrow money when necessary to carry out the corporate purpose.

7. To sell, convey, mortgage, pledge, or lease part or all of its property.

8. To make contracts and incur liabilities.

9. To conduct its business within or outside of the state of incorporation.

10. To acquire its own shares.

11. To declare and pay dividends.

12. To amend its articles of incorporation.

13. To effect a merger or consolidation.

14. To have and exercise all powers necessary or convenient to effect any or all of the purposes for which it was formed.

15. To cease its corporate activities and surrender its corporate franchise.

2. IMPLIED POWERS

In addition to the express powers granted by the state, corporations, in the absence of limitation by statute or by the articles, have the implied powers to do all acts that may be necessary to enable them to exercise the express powers. To be implied, the act must tend directly and immediately to accomplish the purpose of the corporation's creation. Examples of implied powers are the following:

1. To take and hold property.

2. To borrow money and issue notes, bonds, or other obligations.

3. To loan corporate funds.

4. To reacquire its own shares of stock.

5. To acquire and hold shares and other securities of other corporations.

6. To contribute to charity.

Implied powers are often made express by statute or by the articles of incorporation.

3. *ULTRA VIRES*

An *ultra vires* act is one that is beyond the scope of the powers of the corporation (e.g. a business corporation engaging in a charitable enterprise, such as operating a church or school, or a corporation in the grocery business lending money to produce a stage or screen theatrical production).

Modern business corporation statutes do not recognize lack of corporate capacity to contract (the original justification for the doctrine employed to defend suits for breach of contract) as a means of avoiding such liability. Today the corporation may, in fact, contract beyond its power but must suffer the consequences of such liability to the other contracting party.

In those states that still recognize the *ultra vires* defense, it is generally limited to executory or wholly unperformed contracts. Contracts fully performed by one side will prevent the other side from raising the defense on the grounds that the party benefited is estopped to do so. Contracts fully performed by both sides are immune to the defense; neither the corporations nor the other side may raise and rely on the *ultra vires* defense in such cases.

C. SHAREHOLDERS

A shareholder or stockholder is one who derives certain rights arising out of the ownership of one or more shares of corporate stock. Voting shareholders have an interest in the control, net earnings, and net assets of the corporation. They elect and remove directors, vote on extraordinary corporate transactions (merger and sale of assets), and vote to amend the articles of incorporation. They are entitled to receive dividends, subject to their being declared by the board of directors. Nonvoting shareholders are also entitled to vote on extraordinary corporate transactions and to receive dividends when declared, but may not elect or remove directors.

In the absence of statute, shareholders cannot act for the corporation either individually or collectively. The management of the corporation is vested in the board of directors, although the shareholders have the indirect managerial powers noted above.

1.   SHAREHOLDER MEETINGS

Shareholders must act at a regular or special meeting or their actions have no legal effect. It has been held, however, that where all of the shareholders act together on behalf of the corporation without a regular meeting or formal vote, the action is valid.

A.   PLACE OF MEETING

The articles, bylaws, or directors may prescribe the place of meeting. Most states permit a shareholders' meeting to be held outside the state of incorporation, and this is the position of the Model Business Corporation Act, Section 26. Shareholders who participate in a meeting improperly held as to place or time waive their right to object to it.

B.   TIME OF MEETING

Regular meetings must be held at the time prescribed in the statute, articles, or bylaws. Statutes normally do not require notice of regular meetings, although it is the usual practice to give notice to all shareholders.

c. Special Meetings

Special meetings are usually called by the board of directors pursuant to the bylaws, articles, or statutes for a special purpose. Notice of the day, hour, and place of the meeting must be given to all shareholders. The notice must state the nature of the business to be transacted at the meeting, and no other business may be conducted unless all of the shareholders waive this limitation. Shareholders who participate in a special meeting improperly called waive their right to object.

d. Quorum

A quorum is necessary to have a valid shareholders' meeting. Articles, bylaws, or statutes may provide that to constitute a quorum, a specified number of shareholders (usually a simple majority) must attend.

e. Voting Rights

In the absence of restrictions, each person who is registered as a shareholder on the corporation books has the right to vote. The general rule is that each shareholder has the right to one vote for each share of stock. The common law rule that each shareholder had one vote, regardless of the number of shares held, has been changed by statute or court decision in practically all jurisdictions.

The most common types of voting rights are (1) straight, (2) cumulative, and (3) class.

Straight voting means that each share has one vote for each business matter, including one vote for each director to be elected. Straight voting is the common method of voting on corporation business, except where cumulative voting is used in the election of directors.

Cumulative voting, which is required in some states, is a system of voting that applies only to the election of the board of directors. Each share has as many votes as there are vacancies to be filled, and the votes can be distributed among the candidates in any way the shareholder wishes, (i.e., the shareholder can cumulate votes). For example, if 10 directors are to be elected, a shareholder who owns one share has 10 votes and may give all ten votes to one candidate or five votes to two candidates, etc. The purpose of cumulative voting is to permit minority shareholders to combine and secure some representation on the board of directors. For this reason, it is necessary that the directors be elected as a board (i.e., all at the same time). Cumulative voting is also permitted in the removal of directors.

Class or series voting is where there are two or more classes or series of stock outstanding and where each class or series of stock votes as a separate unit for one or more purposes (e. g., a classified board of directors with one class of stock voting for its class of directors and the other class voting for its class of directors).

Generally, those shareholders of voting stock in whose names the stock appears on the books of the corporation are entitled to vote. The directors may fix a controlling date to determine such eligibility.

A shareholder who has pledged his or her stock as security for indebtedness. usually may continue to vote the stock unless a transfer has been made to the pledge upon the books of the corporation.

F. Proxy Voting

A proxy is an authority to vote stock. In the absence of an express requirement, a person does not have to be a shareholder to act as a proxy. The person acting as proxy to vote the stock is an agent for voting purposes. Most states permit voting by proxy but require that the proxy be in writing and signed by the shareholder. In the absence of an express requirement, no particular formality is required.

G. Voting Agreements

In most states, an agreement among shareholders to vote in a certain manner so as to concentrate their voting strength for the purpose of controlling the management is valid unless there is fraud or other illegal object. In most states, such agreements are valid, even though they bind the directors in the exercise of their discretion, so long as they do not substantially limit the discretion of the directors.

6. Voting Trusts

A voting trust exists when, pursuant to an agreement, some or all of the shareholders transfer their shares to a voting trustee or trustees to hold and vote for them until the purpose of the trust is fulfilled or for a specified period. It is a device to concentrate shareholder control in one or more persons for the purpose of controlling management. Voting trusts are valid in most states, many of which have enacted statutes that provide for the procedures in setting up the trust, powers and duties of trustees, and the trust's duration.

2. SHAREHOLDER ELECTION AND REMOVAL OF DIRECTORS

At the annual or regular shareholder meeting, shareholders participate in the management of the corporation by electing the directors. In the absence of statute or bylaws to the contrary, shareholders elect directors to fill vacant and newly created directorates.

Shareholders have the power to remove a director for cause. A director can be removed without cause only if such right was reserved at the time the director was elected. The following case is an illustration.

> **FACTS** A shareholder and member of the board of directors of the Willoughby Walk Cooperative Corporation sought to set aside the election of directors held six months previously. The petitioners here claimed that one newly elected director was not a member of the cooperative and was therefore not eligible to be on the board.

DECISION   The court denied the petitions. First, the court held that petitioners, by participating at numerous subsequent meetings, effectively acknowledged the director's membership on the board and waived their rights to contest the election. The petitioners should have voiced their disapproval at an earlier time. Second, if the court were to have overturned the election, it would nullify six months of board work. Such a result would have been highly prejudicial to the members of the cooperative. Finally, the question of petitioner's eligibility was not a clear one, and there was no indication of bad faith.

Petition of Directors of Willoughby Walk Cooperative Apartments, Inc. (104 Misc. 2d 477, 428 N.Y.S. 2d 574 [1980])

3. BYLAWS AND RESOLUTIONS

Shareholders participate in management in some states by the power to adopt the initial bylaws and in most states by the inherent power to amend or repeal the bylaws.

Shareholders may pass resolutions that will affect the management of the corporations (e.g., indorsing the administration of a former president and demanding reinstatement). Shareholder resolutions may cover a wide variety of subject matter.

Shareholders resolutions, unless approved by management, are seldom successful.

4. UNUSUAL MATTERS

Shareholders exercise managerial powers in various unusual corporate business matters (e.g., approval of shareholders required for amendment of articles of incorporation, sale or lease of assets outside the regular course of corporation business, merger, consolidation, or dissolution, where such action is required by the articles, bylaws, or statute).

5. INSPECTION OF BOOKS

A shareholder personally or through an attorney or accountant, has the right to inspect the books of the corporation at reasonable times for any legitimate purposes (e.g., to ascertain the financial condition of the corporation, to compile a list of shareholders to contact for the purchase of their stock so as to increase ownership and voting power, to obtain information in aid of bona fide litigation with the corporation). Improper or hostile purposes will justify a denial of inspection (e.g., to seek information to aid a competitor in business, to secure advertising lists, to secure list of shareholders to use for contact as business prospects).

6. SHAREHOLDERS' ACTIONS

A shareholder can sue the corporation in a direct action to enforce his or her shareholder contract. A shareholder can also sue in a derivative action on behalf of the corporation against persons who have damaged the corporation when the corporation refuses to bring an action (e.g., suit against third persons for breach of contract with corporation). Shareholders may also join in an action on behalf of the corporation when the corporation refuses to defend itself. The following case illustrates this point.

FACTS Convertible debenture holders brought both a derivative action on behalf of the corporation and a class action on behalf of all debenture holders against the corporate directors of Metro-Goldwyn-Mayer, Inc. (MGM) to recover the amount of a dividend declared and paid. Plaintiffs alleged that because the dividend was declared for the financial benefit of certain directors and controlling shareholders, it therefore damaged MGM and holders of corporate debt.

DECISION First, the court dismissed the derivative suit. The plaintiff bondholders were not shareholders and did not have standing to maintain a stockholder's derivative suit. Second, the court held that the bondholders were entitled to a trial on the issue of whether the directors acted fraudulently.

Harff v. Kerkorian (324 A.2d 215 [Del.Ch., 1974], *affirmed in part and reversed in part* 347 A.2d 133 [Del. 1975])

7.   OTHER SHAREHOLDER RIGHTS

Other rights include the rights to have the shares recorded in the stock book of the corporation, to have issued to the shareholder a properly executed certificate as evidence of ownership of shares, to transfer shares as he or she chooses subject to any valid restrictions, to receive a proportion of dividends as they are declared subject to various preferences, and to receive any balance of the net corporate assets upon dissolution.

8.   SHAREHOLDER LIABILITY

Ordinarily, shareholder liability is limited. (Refer to Corporations, Chapter 36, Section A, 2) Thus, in the ordinary case, the shareholder is not personally liable for the debts of the corporation. The risk of the shareholder is limited to his or her capital investment. In some cases, the shareholder may have unlimited or further liability (e.g., when the corporate entity is broken, when a statute provides that a shareholder is liable for wages of corporation employees; when a shareholder has not fully paid his or her stock subscription). When dividends are improperly paid out of capital, the shareholders are generally liable to creditors to the extent of the depletion of the capital.

D.   DIRECTORS

The management of a corporation is usuallly entrusted to a board of directors. Nearly all states require at least three directors. The required number is usually stated in the articles of incorporation.

1. QUALIFICATIONS

Most statutes today make no requirement regarding qualifications. Some statutes require that the directors be of legal age to contract, be citizens of the United States, be residents of the state of incorporation, or be shareholders. Qualifications may be prescribed in the articles of incorporation or the bylaws.

2. ELECTION, TERM, AND REMOVAL

The first directors are usually named in the articles of incorporation or are elected by the incorporators.

The term of office is usually until the next annual meeting and until the successor is elected.

Directors may be removed for cause by the shareholders (e.g., insanity, conviction of a felony, fraud, or gross abuse of authority). Many states have enacted statutes that spell out the removal of directors and often preserve cumulative and class voting rights for the shareholders.

3. COMPENSATION

Directors are not entitled to compensation for ordinary services. If extraordinary services are performed as an officer or agent of the corporation, quasi-contractual recovery may be had. Directors have no inherent authority to vote a salary to any director, although it is becoming more common for director compensation to be provided for by statutes, articles of incorporation, bylaws, or shareholder resolutions. Directors are usually entitled to reimbursement of expenses incurred in furtherance of corporate business.

4. FUNCTIONS AND POWERS

The function of the board of directors is to set major policies and to direct the business of the corporation. The details of the operating management is usually left in varying degrees to the officers. Some of the usual functions and powers of the board of directors are as follows:

1.   To select, supervise, remove, and fix the compensation for officers, including retirement plans.

2.   To determine dividend payments, financing, and capital changes.

3.   To make policy decisions regarding products, prices, services, wages, and labor relations.

The following actions by the board of directors generally require a two-thirds approval of the shareholders:

1.   Amendment of the articles of incorporation.

2.   Increase or decrease of stock.

3.   Consolidation, merger, sale of entire assets, or dissolution.

A director has an absolute right to inspection of the corporation books, and his or her right cannot be denied even though his or her motive is ulterior and his or her purpose is improper.

5. MEETINGS AND BOARD ACTION

A. NOTICE

Notice of a directors meeting is usually necessary, although it may be waived if a quorum is present and if each of the directors present signs a written approval of the meeting. It may also be waived by a director who is not notified of a special meeting but nevertheless attends without complaint as to the illegality of the meeting. A resolution passed at an improperly called board of directors meeting can be enforced by a third party who was unaware that the meeting was improperly called as the corporation is estopped from setting up such a defense. Innocent third persons have the right to assume that the meeting was duly held. Bylaws may dispense with notice of regular meetings but not of special meetings.

B. PLACE

Regular meetings must be held at the place designated in the bylaws except when changed by approval of all the members of the board or by board resolution. Special meetings may be held at a place designated or at the principal office of the corporation.

Meetings usually may be held within or without the state of incorporation unless restricted by statute, the articles, or bylaws.

C. QUORUM

Unless otherwise stated by statute, the articles, or bylaws, a quorum is a majority of the whole number of directors. Board of directors action usually requires a majority vote of the directors present at a meeting at which a quorum of the directors is present.

D. MUST ACT AS A BOARD

Ordinarily, directors can exercise their management functions only when duly convened as a board. This requirement may be waived by the shareholders, as it is mainly for their benefit.

E. PROXY

Directors vote personally as individuals and are not allowed to vote by proxy except where permitted by statute in a few states. This is because directors must attend personally to the business of the corporation and because of the value of their consultation and collective judgment.

6. FIDUCIARIES

Directors are fiduciaries and must exercise their powers in good faith and in the interest of the corporation. A director cannot enter into any competing business with the corporation, cannot take advantage of a business opportunity that could have been utilized by the corporation, cannot have an interest that conflicts with the interest of the corporation, cannot make secret profits, cannot oppress minority shareholders, and in a growing minority of states cannot sell stock to shareholders without revealing important inside information that he or she may have as to the value of the stock or as to the business of the corporation (three federal statutes deal with insider trading: the Securities Exchange Act of 1934, as amended in 1964; the Public Utility Holding Company Act of 1935; and the Investment Company Act of 1940). A director cannot vote at a directors meeting on any financial matter in which he or she has a direct personal interest.

In *Smith v. Citation Manufacturing Company, Inc.,* the Supreme Court of Arkansas ruled on the fiduciary duty of a corporate director and stockholder and conduct constituting a breach of that duty.

> **FACTS** Smith was a director and officer of Citation, an industrial cleaning equipment manufacturer. At the same time, Smith owned a company that distributed equipment. Citation made a series of sales to Smith's firm. Smith's company went bankrupt, and Citation could not collect on all its sales. Citation argued that Smith breached his fiduciary duty as director and officer by not disclosing his company's financial troubles and by accepting deliveries he was unable to pay for. Smith defended that Citation knew or should have known of his financial difficulties.
>
> **DECISION** Citation knew of some of Smith's problems, but Smith did not disclose a great deal of information. Smith knew his company was unable to pay for certain shipments. Furthermore, Smith withdrew funds and equipment from his company to meet his personal debts. Citation knew of none of this. The court concluded that Smith had breached his fiduciary duty and was liable for Citation's losses incurred on these sales.

Smith v. Citation Manufacturing Co., Inc. (266 Ark. 591, 587 S.W.2d 39 [1979])

7. LIABILITY OF DIRECTORS

Directors owe a duty of ordinary and reasonable care to the corporation. When the required duty of care is violated, the directors are liable to the corporation for such corporate damage as was caused by their negligence. Directors are liable for losses caused by their bad faith, willfull and intentional departures from their duty, and fraudulent breaches of trust. Directors are also under a duty to act within their authority and are liable for any loss to the corporation from engaging in activities that are *ultra vires*. Examples of actions that have caused directors to be jointly and severally liable to the corporation are as follows:

1. Negligence in selecting or supervising an officer, agent, or employee.

2. Participation in the wrongful act of another director or officer.

3. Making false reports or entries in the corporate books.

4. Improperly expending corporate funds for management compensation.

5. Wrongful distribution of corporate assets among themselves or the shareholders.

6. Making unauthorized loans to directors, officers, or shareholders of corporate funds or other property.

7. Unauthorized purchase of corporation's own stock.

8. Unauthorized issuance of a dividend.

9. Closing down factory with loss of over one million dollars in furtherance of antilabor policy.

E. OFFICERS

Statutes usually provide that a corporation must have specified officers. Typical are the requirement of a president, vice-president, secretary, and treasurer.

1. QUALIFICATIONS

Some statutes provide that officers must have certain qualifications. In the absence of statute, there are no particular qualifications, except that an officer should have legal capacity, since he or she is an agent of the corporation.

2. ELECTION, TERM, AND REMOVAL

The officers are usually appointed by the directors. In many states, however, by statute, officers are elected by the shareholders. Officers usually serve at the pleasure of the board of directors. In most states, officers are removable with or without cause by the board of directors. When an officer has a valid contract of employment with the corporation, the board of directors has the power to remove the officer without cause but must pay damages for breach of contract.

3. COMPENSATION

Officers who are not directors have the right to reasonable compensation for their services. Their compensation is normally fixed prior to the rendering of services.

Officers who are also directors are presumed to serve without compensation on usual matters but are entitled to reasonable compensation for unusual services. It is becoming common for a director-officer to receive a fixed compensation on a prearranged basis. Sometimes the compensation is ratified by the shareholders.

In addition to fixed salaries and liberal expense accounts, there are other forms of compensation (e.g., profit sharing plans, stock bonuses, stock purchase plans, pensions, annuities, tax reimbursement plans, and deferred compensation plans).

4. FUNCTIONS AND POWERS

Officers have such management functions and powers as are given them by the board of directors. The board is limited in such delegation by statutes, articles of incorporation, and bylaws.

A. PRESIDENT

The president may also be chairman of the board of directors and, if so, is the chief executive officer of the corporation. If not, the president is second in command to the chairman of the board. The president's real power depends on the internal structure of the corporation; the president may be a figurehead or may be the controlling power.

The president usually presides at board of directors and shareholder meetings. Modern cases hold that the president has authority to act as agent on behalf of the corporation within the scope of the business of the corporation. The older cases hold that he or she has no authority to bind the corporation. The president who is also the general manager of the corporation has implied power to do such acts as are necessary to carry out the business of the corporation. In large corporations, the president is usually the presiding officer, and the detailed management of the corporate business is delegated to a general manager.

B. VICE-PRESIDENT

A vice-president assists the president and acts as his or her substitute when the president is unable to act. A vice-president has no authority to bind the corporation. In large corporations, there are usually several vice-presidents whose functions are to act as department heads.

C. SECRETARY

The secretary usually attends meetings of the corporation and keeps minutes and records of corporate transactions. The secretary also gives notices, certifies corporate records, and keeps the corporate seal. The secretary may not bind the corporation.

D. TREASURER

The treasurer has charge of the financial records and disbursement of corporate funds. In most states, he or she may not bind the corporation. In large corporations, there is usually a controller in addition to the treasurer. In such case, the controller keeps the records, while the treasurer handles the money.

5. FIDUCIARIES

Officers, like directors, have a fiduciary relationship with the corporation. The law on the fiduciary relationship between the directors and the corporation is applicable here (i.e., cannot make secret profits, etc.).

6. LIABILITY OF OFFICERS

Officers owe a duty of ordinary and reasonable care to the corporation and are liable for willful or negligent acts that result in corporate loss.

An officer may incur personal liability when contracting on behalf of the corporation without authority. Even when an officer has authority, he or she can be liable on a contract if he or she does not indicate that he or she is contracting as an agent for the corporation.

An officer who commits a tort is personally liable to the victim of the tort; and if the tort is committed within his scope of employment, the corporation will also be liable under the doctrine of respondeat superior.

Statutes in many states provide that officers are liable for corporate taxes, debts, wages, and crimes under specific circumstances (e.g., for failure to withhold taxes; for debts contracted before filing of certificate of paid-in capital; for antitrust violation).

ILLUSTRATIVE CASES

1. Right to Inspect Corporate Books

STONE v. MARTIN

56 N.C.App. 473, 289 S.E.2d 898 (1982)

WHICHARD, Judge. Plaintiffs, shareholders in defendant corporation, filed a complaint against the corporation and the individual defendants, who were officers, directors, and shareholders thereof, alleging numerous improper and unlawful acts and omissions in the operation of the corporation. They sought compensatory damages, punitive damages, and, as to the individual defendants, arrest and bail and execution against the person.

Plaintiffs served on defendant fifty-eight interrogatories and fifteen requests for admission. Defendant claimed with respect to each that because the complaint sought punitive damages, which are in the nature of a penalty, to answer would violate his privilege against compulsory self-incrimination under United States Constitution amendments V and XIV and North Carolina Constitution article 1, section 23. Plaintiffs moved under G.S. 1A–1, Rule 37(a), to compel defendant to comply with discovery. Judge Preston found that three of the interrogatories and three of the requests for admission called for potentially incriminatory answers and denied plaintiffs' motion with respect thereto. He ordered defendant to answer the remaining interrogatories and requests within thirty days.

Upon defendant's failure to comply, plaintiffs moved for imposition of Rule 37(b) sanctions. Judge Lee struck defendant's answer and ordered that he not oppose any claim or allegation set forth in plaintiffs' complaint. He further ordered judgment by default against defendant, the issue of damages being for jury determination.

Defendant contends the orders compelling him to respond, and imposing sanctions for his failure to do so, infringe upon his constitutional privilege against compulsory self-incrimination. He does not contend that answering may subject him to criminal punishment; rather, he contends that because plaintiffs seek punitive damages and body execution, he cannot be compelled to submit to discovery. On this record we find no infringement of defendant's constitutional privilege.

*   *   *

Further, the requested discovery related almost entirely to the operation of defendant corporation, of which plaintiffs had been shareholders for more than six months preceding filing of their complaint. Plaintiffs thus had a statutory right, enforceable by an action in the nature of mandamus, to inspect the records of the corporation. They had the further right, similarly enforceable, to inspect the annual financial statement of the corporation and the record of shareholders. Plaintiffs alleged that defendants had denied their oral and written demands for opportunity to inspect the corporate records. The requested discovery to which the court ordered response sought information which the corporate records should have contained and which plaintiffs thus would have received had defendants complied with the statutory requirements for maintenance of corporate records and observed plaintiffs' right to inspect. "[T]he privilege against self-incrimination is a purely personal one," and "the official records and documents of [a corporation] that are held by [an individual] in a representative rather than in a personal capacity cannot be the subject of the personal privilege against self-incrimination, even though production of the papers might tend to incriminate [the individual] personally." It is thus evident that Judge Preston's order simply granted through discovery procedure access to information which plaintiffs could obtain in any event by mandamus.

It should be evident that tensions adhere within the law applicable to the area in which the problem presented falls, and that the standards prescribed for resolving those tensions are not necessarily easily applied in individual cases. We remain persuaded, however, from a careful examination of the standards and of the record in this case, that the standards were properly applied here.

For the foregoing reasons we affirm the order requiring defendant to comply with discovery. Because defendant failed to comply with that order, we find no abuse of discretion in the order imposing sanctions and judgment by default.

*   *   *

2. Corporate Management by Directors

ABROMOWITZ v. POSNER

672 F.2d 1025 (2d Cir., 1982)

MESKILL, Circuit Judge. In *Burks v. Lasker,* 441 U.S. 471, 480, 99 S.Ct. 1831, 1838, 60 L.Ed.2d 404 (1979), the Supreme Court held that the authority of disinterested directors to terminate shareholder derivative litigation is governed by applicable state law, provided that such law is consistent with the policies of the federal acts upon which the action is based. Our present task is to determine whether the district court properly dismissed appellant Ida Abramowitz's derivative suit after the corporation, by unanimous vote of its disinterested directors, declined to sue on its own behalf. We hold that the district court decision comports with Delaware law as recently set forth in *Zapata Corp. v. Maldonado,* 430 A.2d 779 (Del.1981), that Delaware law does not offend relevant federal policy, and that the district court's findings are supported in the record. Accordingly, we affirm.

*   *   *

While the various courts addressing the issue now confronting us have been forced to predict the views of the Delaware Supreme Court, we have the luxury of having that court's recent opinion in *Zapata,* which squarely sets forth the relevant Delaware law. Our simplified task, then, is to determine whether the district court's decision comports with Delaware law as enunciated in *Zapata,* and, if so, whether such a result is consistent with the policies underlying section 10(b) of the Act and Rule 10b–5.

*   *   *

In sum, whether and how Delaware law permits disinterested independent directors of a corporation to seek termination of derivative litigation brought to redress alleged impropriety by other directors depends upon the type of case. Where demand upon the corporation has been made and refused, a court will defer to the company's business judgment to forgo litigation unless the shareholder can show that the directors acted wrongfully. Where demand has not been made due to futility, however, the company bears the initial burden of establishing its good faith and independence in seeking termination, and even then, its judgment is subject to the court's objective scrutiny.

Having set forth applicable state law, we turn now to the second prong of *Burks v. Lasker.* Abramowitz, citing no supporting case law, contends that to defer to the business judgment of NVF's [the corporate defendant's] disinterested directors in this case without closely and objectively scrutinizing their decision to forgo litigation would offend the policies underlying section 10(b) of the Act. * * *

We agree with the Ninth Circuit, *see Lewis v. Anderson,* 615 F.2d 778 (9th Cir. 1979), *cert. denied,* 449 U.S. 869, 101 S.Ct. 206, 66 L.Ed.2d 89 (1980), that the policies underlying section 10(b) are not offended by interpreting the business judgment rule to bar shareholder derivative litigation when a corporation's disinterested directors, independently and in good faith, determine that the action is not in the company's best interests. Private claims for relief under section 10(b) and Rule 10b–5 serve to supplement enforcement of the securities laws by the SEC. But certainly, the decision whether to pursue such a claim is within the discretion of the private plaintiff. The claim in a shareholder derivative action belongs to the corporation on whose behalf it is brought, not to those shareholders who commence the litigation. Therefore, the decision whether to litigate such a claim is for management to make. Absent bad faith, we find no federal policy underlying section 10(b) which requires a court to second-guess the informed judgment of independent corporate directors. As the New York Court of Appeals stated in *Auerbach v. Bennett:*

> It appears to us that the business judgment doctrine, at least in part, is grounded in the prudent recognition that courts are ill equipped and infrequently called on to evaluate what are and must be essentially business judgments.

In short, "[w]e see no threat to the purity of the securities market" in applying the business judgment rule to allow disinterested, independent directors to terminate derivative litigation.

Our final consideration involves a review of the district court's decision. Abramowitz's demand on NVF was refused by unanimous decision of the board, with the defendant directors not voting. Under *Zapata* the district court's inquiry should therefore have been limited to whether the board's refusal passed muster under the business judgment rule—that is, whether the directors acted independently and in good faith in rejecting Abramowitz's demand.

* * *

We find no error in Judge Haight's conclusion that the rejection by NVF's disinterested directors of Abramowitz's Rule 23.1 demand merits protection under the business judgment rule. As we stated in *Galef v. Alexander,* the rule "bars judicial inquiry into actions of directors taken in good faith and in honest pursuit of the legitimate purposes of the corporation." And it has long been settled that "[w]hether or not a corporation shall seek to enforce in the courts a cause of action for damages is, like other business questions, ordinarily a matter of internal management * * *" Provided that the decision of the NVF directors to reject Abramowitz's demand was reached independently and in good faith, that decision will not be disturbed by this Court. Moreover, we are bound to affirm Judge Haight's finding of good faith and independence absent a showing that his conclusions are "clearly erroneous."

* * *

The decision of the district court is affirmed.

3. Officer Not Liable on Corporation Contract

HERKERT v. STAUBER

106 Wis.2d 545, 317 N.W.2d 834 (1982)

COFFEY, Justice.   This is a review of a decision of the court of appeals, 102 Wis.2d 720, 308 N.W.2d 419, affirming a judgment of the circuit court for Dane county, William F. Eich presiding. The judgment awarded Herman J. Herkert, the plaintiff-respondent, $50,400 in a breach of a contract action concerning a certain contract between himself and Mazer-Stauber Associates, P.C., defendants-appellants-petitioners, for the construction of housing units for the elderly. After trial, the jury returned a verdict finding that Mazer-Stauber Associates, P.C., and Guardian Corporation breached the contract with respect to their obligation to secure approval from the Farmer's Home Administration (FmHA) for financing and awarding damages of $7,500. In a memorandum decision on motions after verdict, the trial court increased the $7,500 damage figure to $50,400 holding that these damages were proven as a matter of law and entered judgment against the defendants, both corporate and individual. The defendants appealed * * * the entry of judgment against the individual defendants.

* * *

Our analysis of this issue is hampered, however, because of the failure of the trial court in its memorandum decision on motions after verdict to recite any rationale, testimony, or legal authority to support the imposition of personal liability on the individual defendants. The plaintiff, agreeing with the trial court's decision, argues that the defendants Robert Stauber and Richard Mazer are personally liable because they are licensed architects and the construction contract was one for professional services and, therefore, the breach thereof was a breach of their professional duties. The plaintiff further contends that the fact that the contract was entered into by M–S Associates, a professional service corporation, does not preclude a finding of personal liability for both the Michigan and Wisconsin Statutes provide for the formation of professional service corporations and expressly preserve the personal liability of professionals practicing in the corporate form. The personal liability of William Mazer, although not an architect, is predicated upon the fact that as an employee he was a principal party to the performance of the alleged professional services assumed under the Herkert project and had responsibility for the Herkert contract.

* * *

Our review of both sec. 443.08(4)(b), Wis. Stats., and sec. 450.226, Michigan Compiled Laws, demonstrates that both statutes only preserve personal liability for "professional services" and, thus, in this case, only support the imposition of liability based upon those services which can be defined as "architectural services" rendered by the architects practicing as professional service corporations. Since neither the Michigan nor the Wisconsin definitions of professional services can be interpreted to include assistance in securing financing or body politic approval within the definition thereof, we reach the question of whether the breach of the contract in the case at bar related to "professional services."

*   *   *

* * * [W]e point out that where an architect also involves himself in the business of securing governmental financing as well as approval of a body politic, a breach of the contract to provide those nonarchitectural services is not a basis for personal liability where the breach does not relate to "professional architectural services" rendered.

* * * The mere fact that a professional, such as a doctor, dentist, lawyer or architect, enters into a contract that involves performing some professional service and some other service not within his professional expertise (financing, etc.) does not necessarily make or change that contract into a contract for "professional services" nor does it automatically transform the breach of the contract into a breach of professional obligations in his field of expertise. In order for the breach of a contract entered into with a professional service corporation to result in personal liability, it must be proved both that the breach relates to "professional services" and that the breach was a negligent or wrongful act committed in the rendition of those professional services. This rule preserves the personal responsibility of a professional for services within his expertise and which the client has every right to expect will be performed in a professional manner.

*   *   *

In light of the fact that plaintiff failed to prove that the services of assisting in securing financing and body politic approval are part of the accepted architect-client relationship or within the legal definitions of professional architectural expertise and the fact that the record is devoid of any evidence establishing that the general practice among architects is to assist a party to secure financing, we hold that the plaintiff has not proved by a preponderance of the evidence that the breach of the contract related to "professional services." Thus, we hold that the trial court erred in imposing personal liability upon the individual defendants for contractual obligations beyond their field of expertise as professional architects.

Our determination that the breach did not relate to "professional services" relieves William Mazer of any liability arising from his status as an employee of a professional service corporation. * * *

*   *   *

The decision of the court of appeals is affirmed in part and reversed in part and the judgment of the circuit court is modified accordingly.

4. Corporate Liability for Improper Use of Insider Information

SEC v. TEXAS GULF SULPHUR CO.

446 F.2d 1301 (2d Cir., 1971) On remand 333 F.Supp. 671

The Texas Gulf Sulphur (TGS) case was an action by the SEC against TGS and thirteen directors, officers, and employees for alleged violations of Section 10(b) of the 1934 Act and Rule 10b–5. In 1963 TGS drilled an exploratory hole near Timmins, Ontario, which produced a remarkably high copper content. TGS sealed the hole and, after acquiring the surrounding land, resumed drilling on March 31, 1964. On April 11, New York papers reported rumors of a rich TGS strike. On April 13, TGS management issued a press release designed to quell the rumors. The release stated that the rumors were without factual basis, that most of the areas drilled in eastern Canada were barren, and that:

> The work done to date has not been sufficient to reach definite conclusions and any statement as to size and grade of ore would be premature and possibly misleading. When we have progressed to the point where reasonable and logical conclusions can be made, TGS will issue a definite statement to its stockholders and the public.

At the time of the core drill of November 12, 1963, TGS directors, officers, employees, and their "tippees," owned only 1,135 shares of TGS stock and no calls (the right to purchase additional shares at a fixed price). By March 31, 1964, when drilling resumed, insiders and tippees had acquired 12,300 calls and an additional 7,100 shares. On February 20, 1964, TGS issued stock options to three members of top management and to two other employees as part of their compensation. Between November 12, 1963, and May 15, 1964, the market price of TGS stock rose from $18 to $58 per share.

The SEC's complaint asked the court to (1) enjoin TGS and individual defendants from publishing deceptive and misleading information such as the April 12 press release and (2) compel rescission of the defendants' purchases and stock options. At the first trial, the court found that the April 12 press release [did not constitute a violation of Section 10(b)(5) or Rule 10(b)].

On appeal, the circuit court interpreted the legislative purpose of Section 10(b) as follows [401 F.2d 833 (2d Cir. 1968), cert. denied 344 U.S. 976]:

> . . . The intent of the Securities Exchange Act of 1934 is the protection of investors against fraud. Therefore, it would seem elementary that the Commission has a duty to police management so as to prevent corporate practices which are reasonably likely fraudulently to injure investors. . . . When materially misleading corporate statements or deceptive insider activities have been uncovered, the courts have broadly construed the statutory phrase 'in connection with the purchase or sale of any security.'

The circuit court interpreted the essence of essence of Rule 10b-5 as follows:

> Anyone who, trading for his own account in the securities of a corporation has access, directly or indirectly, to information intended to be available only for a corporate purpose and not for personal benefit of anyone,' may not take 'advantage of such information knowing it is unavailable to those with whom he is dealing,' i.e., the investing public. Insiders, as directors or management officers, are, of course, by this Rule, precluded from so unfairly dealing, but the rule is also applicable to one possessing the information who may not be strictly termed an 'insider' within the meaning of Section 16(b) of the Act. . . . It is here no justification for

insider activity that disclosure was forbidden by the legitimate objective of acquiring . . . land surrounding the exploration site: if the information was * * * material, its possessors should have kept out of the market until disclosure was accomplished.

The court held that all transactions in TGS stock or calls by individuals who knew of the drilling results were made in violation of 10b–5. * * * The appeals court also concluded that the April 12 press release was issued "in a manner reasonably calculated to affect the market price of TGS stock and to influence the investing public." * * * The case was remanded to the trial court to decide (1) whether the release was misleading to the reasonable investor and, if found to be misleading, whether the court should enjoin further deceptive statements and (2) what remedies should be invoked against individual defendants who profited from inside information in violation of Rule 10b–5.

Following the hearing on remand, the trial court (1) enjoined defendants Clayton and Crawford from future violations of 10b–5; (2) denied injunctions against TGS and other defendants, although each was found to have violated 10b–5; (3) required the stock option of Kline, the one member of top management who had not voluntarily returned his option to the corporation, to be cancelled; and (4) required defendants to disgorge profits on their stock to TGS and also required [one employee] Darke to pay to TGS the profits realized by his tippees. Defendants appealed.

WATERMAN, Circuit J. * * * The district court required Holyk, Huntington, Clayton, and Darke to pay to TGS the profits they had derived (and, in Drake's case, also the profits which his tippees had derived) from their TGS stock between their respective purchase dates and April 17, 1964, when the ore strike was fully known to the public. The payments are to be held in escrow * * *. [The total escrow settlement fund amounted to $2,700,000. Former stockholders who sold shares between the time of the discovery and the public announcement, and who contended they would not have sold had they known of the discovery, were permitted to recover from this fund.] At the end of five years any money remaining undisposed of would become the property of TGS. * * *

[The judgment was affirmed as to each appellant except as to the order cancelling Kline's stock option, which was reversed and remanded for a hearing on the appropriateness of that remedy.]

5. Corporate Liability for Short-Swing Transactions

TYCO LABORATORIES, INC. v. CUTLER-HAMMER, INC.
490 F.Supp. 1 (S.D.N.Y., 1980)

Action by Tyco Laboratories, Inc. seeking a declaratory judgment that it was not liable for short-swing profits realized on the sale of Cutler-Hammer Inc. (C-H) stock. Defendant C-H counterclaimed asserting that Tyco was liable for such profits under section 16(b) of the 1934 Act. Tyco had been purchasing C-H common stock commencing in November, 1977. On April 7, 1978 Tyco purchased additional shares, bringing its total holdings to 12 percent of the total number of outstanding C-H shares, thus qualifying it as a beneficial owner of more than 10 percent of a registered security under section 16(a) of the 1934 Act. A few days later, a rival purchaser, Koppers Company, Inc. acquired approximately 21 percent of the voting stock of C-H. Between April 10 and June 9, 1978, Tyco quickly purchased an additional 1,374,100 shares of C-H stock at a cost of $92,560,997. On June 12, 1978, Tyco sold its entire holdings of C-H common stock to Eaton Corporation for $55 per share.

Thereafter, C-H demanded that Tyco pay over its short-swing profits on the sale of the 1,374,100 shares of C-H stock purchased after April 7, 1978 in the sum of $7,900,410. Tyco admitted that this sum was correct, but claimed (1) that because its buying and selling transactions arose out of a contest for control of C-H, they fell within the "unorthodox transaction" exception to 16(b), and (2) that Congress did not intend to impose automatic liability upon 10 percent shareholders who make short-swing cash-for-stock profits unless they had "access to inside information," and that Tyco did not have or use any inside information in its transactions.

WARD, District Judge.

*   *   *

Section 16(b) of the Act was originally intended to apply to insider trading within the statutory six-month period in an automatic, almost mechanistic fashion, which came to be known as the "objective approach." As the Supreme Court stated:

> In order to achieve its goals, Congress chose a relatively arbitrary rule capable of easy administration. The objective standard of Section 16(b) imposes strict liability upon substantially all transactions occurring within the statutory time period, regardless of the intent of the insider or the existence of actual speculation. This approach maximized the ability of the rule to eradicate speculative abuses by reducing difficulties in proof. Such arbitrary and sweeping coverage was deemed necessary to insure the optimum prophylactic effect. *Reliance Electric Co. v. Emerson Electric Co.*, 404 U.S. 418, 422 (1972).

However, in response to a series of cases requiring the application of the statute to transactions which were not classic purchases and sales for cash, such as stock conversions, mergers, and stock options, the Supreme Court approved a narrow exception to the generally broad and arbitrary reach of section 16(b). The court held that when a transaction is "unorthodox" and not clearly within the reach of the statute, the opportunity for speculative abuse should be assessed before section 16(b) liability is imposed.

> In deciding whether borderline transactions are within the reach of the statute, the courts have come to inquire whether the transaction may serve as a vehicle for the evil which Congress sought to prevent—the realization of short-swing profits based upon access to inside information —thereby endeavoring to implement congressional objectives without

extending the reach of the statute beyond its intended limits. *Kern County Land Co. v. Occidental Petroleum Corp.,* 411 U.S. 582 (1973).

This "subjective" or "pragmatic approach" was designed to mitigate the harshness of the application of section 16(b)'s strict liability standard to situations which, although arguably involving some equivalent of a section 16(b) purchase and sale, could not possibly allow for insider speculation and profiteering on non-public information.

Tyco contends that inasmuch as its purchases of C-H stock and the sale of that stock to Eaton occurred in the context of a "control contest type of situation," the sale was an "unorthodox" transaction within the *Kern County* exception to section 16(b) liability.

The Court finds Tyco's arguments without merit. * * * Congress specifically envisioned a statutory scheme which imposes automatic liability on any and all ten percent shareholders who buy and sell an issuer's securities within a six-month period, irrespective of whether they had access to or misused inside information.

* * * Tyco's claim that the existence of a "control contest type of situation" renders the transaction at issue here "unorthodox" within the meaning of *Kern County* and warrants an inquiry into whether Tyco had access to inside information when it traded in C-H stock is without merit.

* * * [T]wo factors must exist in order to remove even an "unorthodox" transaction from the ambit of section 16(b) liability * * *: (1) the unlikelihood of actual access to inside information in an atmosphere of hostility by a party adverse in interest; and (2) the utter inability of the unsuccessful party to control the course of events.

Tyco's complaint asserting that it lacked access to inside information * * * satisfies part of the test. There are no facts alleged in Tyco's complaint, however, which would indicate that its sale of C-H stock was "involuntary" or that it was "utterly unable to control the course of events." * * *

In conclusion, the Court finds that Tyco's extensive cash purchases of C-H stock after becoming a 10 percent stockholder and subsequent sale of their entire block of C-H stock within approximately two months subjects them to liability under section 16(b).

Accordingly, C-H's motion for judgment on the pleadings upon its counterclaim is granted.

PROBLEMS

1. Plaintiff was the secretary and a director of the defendant corporation. The president and secretary of the corporation were directed by the board of directors to sign certain mortgage papers, but the plaintiff refused to sign them. Thereafter, the full board of directors at a duly called meeting removed plaintiff by majority vote from the office of secretary, but not as a director. Plaintiff brings an action to enjoin the corporation from removing her as secretary. Decision?

2. Potent Products Company had a board of fifteen directors. The board, at a meeting attended by 13 of the directors, voted to declare an illegal dividend. The roll call vote was 9 to 2. The dividend was paid and the company soon became insolvent. The creditors sued the 15 directors personally for the amount paid out in the dividend. Which of the following directors, if any, are liable?

   (a)   Director Hart Manning was present and voted in favor of the dividend even though he knew it was illegal.

   (b)   Director Bill Podesta was present but knew nothing about the interpretation of financial statements. He voted in favor of the dividend because Les Cash, the company treasurer and a C.P.A., assured him that the dividend was legal.

   (c)   Director Les Cash, Treasurer and C.P.A., was present and voted in favor, stating that he thought the dividend was legal.

   (d)   Director Harry Grant was present, but didn't vote.

   (e)   Director Valerie Lewis was present and voted "no".

   (f)   Director Frank N. Ernst didn't attend the meeting because his daughter was getting married. It was the only meeting of the board that he had ever missed.

3.   A, B, and C, each own ten shares of stock in the X Corporation.

   (a)   A demands an inspection of the corporate books so that he can compile a list of shareholders for the purpose of contacting them to sell them some speculative oil stock. Does he have the right?

   (b)   B demands to see the corporate books so that he can obtain information to help his brother, a competitor of the X Corporation. Does he have the right?

   (c)   C demands to see the corporate books so that he can compile a list of shareholders for the purpose of trying to buy shares of stock from them. Does he have the right?

4. The chairman of the board of directors of the defendant corporation called a special meeting of the board to authorize the payment of a compromise agreement regarding a tort committed by an agent of the corporation against an innocent third person. All the directors were present except the plaintiff, who was not notified of the meeting. At the meeting, the board of directors unanimously voted to approve of the compromise. Plaintiff brings action to prevent payment. Decision?

5. Plaintiff, a shareholder in defendant corporation, brings a shareholder derivative action against the directors of his corporation for losses alleged to be caused by mismanagement. The directors had formulated an anti-labor policy which resulted in the closing, dismantling, and removal of plants and equipment of the corporation, curtailing production. This was not done for any legitimate business purpose, but only to punish and intimidate employees. The acts were illegal and intended to evade the obligations of the directors under the National Labor Relations Act; the acts constituted unfair labor practices and caused corporate losses of more than one million dollars. The corporation resists the action. Decision?

6. Petersen was hired as Executive Secretary of Max Industries, Inc. for two years. Six months later he was terminated. Petersen then sued Max Industries, its directors, and some other employees for breach of contract. Petersen argued that the directors and other employees had acted maliciously and therefore were liable to him for malicious interference with his employment contract. The individual directors and employees defended on the ground that the officers, directors, agents, and employees of a corporation may not be held individually liable for malicious inducement of breach of an employment contract, and that the individual defendants were acting only in the best interests of the company, not for their personal gain. Decision?

7. A owned all the stock of GX Corporation, which operated a nursing home. GX's poor financial condition caused A to contract to transfer his stock to the RZ Company, which promised to make GX a wholly-owned subsidiary. Later A learned that RZ was on the verge of bankruptcy and sued to rescind the contract on the grounds that RZ had never expressly authorized or ratified the contract, rendering it unenforceable. RZ defended on the ground that it had vested its corporate agent with *de facto* authority to execute the contract since all of RZ's corporate directors and stockholders were present at the stockholders meeting called for that purpose and did not object to the acquisition of GX stock. Decision?

8. C and his wife were two of the three directors of AF Corporation. C ran the business, while his wife and the other director took no active part in its management. C unlawfully used corporate funds to pay his own obligations, including sums used to pay his wife's debts. AF Corporation sued to recover from C and his wife all the corporate moneys improperly spent for their personal use. C's wife defended on the ground that her liability was limited to the sums actually received by her, a small portion of the total amount diverted by C. Decision?

9. Y was the president of ACE Corporation. As part of his corporate duties, Y arranged financing for ACE. FSF Finance Company drew twelve checks payable to the order of ACE. These checks were then indorsed by Y in his corporate capacity as a president and were cashed at two different banks. The BNB Bank, on which the checks were drawn, charged FSF, its depositor, with the amount of the checks. FSF then sued BNB to restore the amount of the checks to its account, arguing that BNB had improperly made payment to Y because Y had no corporate authority to indorse and cash the checks. Decision?

10. Smith was treasurer of Dram Inc. Smith wanted to buy an expensive automobile for his own use and tendered Jones, the automobile dealer, a corporate check in payment when the car was delivered. Jones asked Smith if he had corporate authority to pay by corporate check. Smith assured him that he controlled Dram's purse strings and could therefore spend Dram's corporate funds as he saw fit. Later Dram Inc. sued Jones to recover back the price of Smith's car, claiming no express or implied authority was granted Smith to use a corporate check in payment of personal obligations. Decision?

Chapter 38

CORPORATE FINANCE

A corporation initially obtains its operating capital principally from investors who receive in return securities issued by the corporation evidencing the security holders' rights in the corporation. After the corporation is launched and in operation, corporate funds may be derived from many sources: retained earnings, reserves, accounts receivable, the government, short-term borrowing, accounts receivable financing, inventory financing, trust receipts financing, field warehousing, sales and leasebacks, sale of unneeded assets, reduction of working capital, leasing and installment purchasing, depreciation and depletion deductions, and acquisition of tax-loss corporations.

Today, less than 20 percent of all corporate funds are derived from the issue of securities, such as bonds, debentures, long-term notes, and preferred and common shares of stock. Securities are defined in U.C.C. Section 8–102 as instruments that are issued in bearer or registered form; are a type commonly dealt with on security exchanges or markets; are either one of a class or series or by their terms are divisible into a class or series of instruments; and evidence a share, participation, or other interest in property or in an enterprise, or evidence an obligation of the issuer.

A. BONDS

Bonds are long-term promissory notes issued by a corporation to people who lend money to the corporation. The bonds are the evidence of the corporation's obligation to repay the bondholders at a future date. The bondholders are the creditors of the corporation. Bonds are described as debt securities, because a creditor-debtor relationship is created.

Sometimes a debt security may be convertible, which involves a privilege, usually of the holder, of converting it into some other security. Debt securities convertible into shares of stock have been issued frequently, because they combine safety (creditor status) with opportunity for possible speculative gain (increase in price of shares beyond conversion price).

The use of bonds in corporate financing is almost limited to governmental agencies, quasi-public corporations, and large industrial corporations, because the sale of bonds requires the debtor-corporation to have very substantial assets to make the offer attractive.

B. STOCKS

A corporation sells its ownership to people by issuing shares of stock. Stock evidences the shareholder's proportionate ownership in the corporation. Whereas bondholders are creditors of the corporation, the shareholders are the owners. Shares of stock are described as equity securities, because they indicate the shareholders' equitable ownership in the corporation.

The shareholders do not own the corporate property as such; the corporation owns its property. The shareholders do have an interest in the corporation in that they have a right to receive dividends, the right to participate in distribution of capital on dissolution, and the right to indirect control (refer to Chapter 37).

1. CERTIFICATE

A certificate of stock is the evidence of the ownership of the shares represented by it. The Model Business Corporation Act, Section 21, requires that the certificate include the following: (1) the state of incorporation; (2) the name of the person to whom issued; (3) the number and class of shares represented by the certificate and the designation of the series, if any; and (4) the par value of each share represented by such certificate, or a statement that the shares are without par value.

2. AUTHORIZED, ISSUED, OUTSTANDING, AND TREASURY SHARES

Authorized shares of stock are the shares that the corporation is authorized to issue by the state of incorporation and the articles of corporation.

Issued shares of stock are authorized shares that have been issued to shareholders.

Outstanding shares of stock are issued shares that are held by the shareholders.

Shares that have been reacquired by the corporation are treasury shares but are not considered outstanding. Treasury shares cannot be voted and do not participate in dividends or distribution of net assets on dissolution.

3. KINDS OF STOCK

The rights and privileges of different classes of stock are controlled by the articles of incorporation in the absence of contrary statute. The most common division of classes of stock is into common stock and preferred stock.

A. COMMON STOCK

Common stock is the ordinary stock of the corporation. It entitles the owner to pro rata dividends, but without priority over other stock. On dissolution, common stockholders are entitled to participate in the distribution of net assets.

The common stock is usually the voting stock. Thus, the common stockholders, rather than the preferred stockholders, elect the board of directors. This is because the preferred stockholders, although owners of the corporation with other stockholders, are primarily interested in a fixed return in the form of a dividend and are not so concerned about management so long as their dividend is paid.

On the other hand, the common stockholder has a greater stake as owner of the corporation, since the common stockholder is taking a greater gamble on the success of the corporation and, therefore, should have the choice of management. The common stockholder has a greater gamble, because if the corporation is a success, he or she may receive the largest dividends, while if the venture fails, he or she must absorb the initial and the heaviest losses.

B. PREFERRED STOCK

Preferred stock is stock that has a preference over other classes of stock. The preference is usually as to dividends, although it can take the form of various rights, powers, and privileges, including a priority on distribution of capital on dissolution of the corporation.

Preferred stock may be made either cumulative (usual) or noncumulative (unusual). Cumulative stock means that if there is no distribution of profits in the form of dividends in a particular year because there are no profits or because the profits are to be used for expansion, etc., the dividends accrue, and both back and current dividends must be paid in full before any dividend may be paid on common stock.

In the case of noncumulative stock, the dividends if unpaid during the current year are lost forever. Even if there is a large surplus legally available, a strong showing of fraud or abuse of discretion by the board of directors will be necessary before a court will compel a declaration of a dividend on common or preferred stock. Thus, unless the preferred stock is cumulative, or unless the noncumulative stockholders have a contract with the corporation that makes a dividend mandatory, the noncumulative stock will lose its dividend unless declared each year.

Preferred stock also may be made participating or nonparticipating. The usual provision for participating stock entitles the preferred shares to participate with the common shares in the annual distribution of surplus earnings after the common shares have received a dividend equal to that payable to the preferred.

Preferred stockholders have residuary policy rights, usually involving extraordinary transactions, such as a sale of corporate assets, dissolution, or other action not taken in the normal course of the corporation's express or implied powers.

In *In re Olympic National Agencies, Inc.*, the Supreme Court of Washington ruled that upon liquidation, the preferred shareholders should receive their stated liquidation preference only and are not entitled to share in the distribution of assets beyond that preference.

FACTS Olympic National Agencies had authorized both common and preferred stock. The corporate articles provided only that the preferred shares were entitled to a liquidation preference up to par value. Upon dissolution, the trial court awarded the preferred shares the par value plus a pro rata share of the remaining assets.

DECISION Reversed. Where one class of stock is afforded a stated preference as to assets on liquidation and the articles of incorporation are silent as to any further participation, the clear implication is that the rights of the preferred stock are exhausted once the preference has been satisfied.

In re Olympic National Agencies, Inc. (74 Wn. 2d 1, 442 P.2d 246 [1968])

4. CAPITAL, CAPITAL STOCK, AND STATED CAPITAL

Capital represents the total value of the assets of a corporation. Stated capital or capital stock (often used interchangeably) refers to the declared value of the outstanding shares of stock of the corporation. Stock and shares also have the same meaning. "Stock" was the original term used, but more modern laws refer to "shares." The term "shares of stock" is also in common usage.

Sometimes, par value stock may be sold at a premium, or a higher price than par, in which case the excess is allocated to a capital surplus account.

Shares of capital stock are represented by certificates that describe a proportionate interest in the corporate enterprise but in no way vest their owner with any title to the corporation's property.

5. CONSIDERATION FOR ISSUANCE OF STOCK

The general rule is that shares of stock cannot be issued without payment in money or money's worth or a valid obligation to pay. In the absence of statute or articles of incorporation to the contrary, the stock can be issued without actual payment at the time of issuance. Statutes or articles of incorporation commonly provide that no stock can be issued except for money, labor done, or property actually received.

Although there is a conflict of authority, the majority rule is that if there is no constitutional, statutory, or charter prohibition, a corporation has the power to issue shares of its stock as fully paid on payment of less than its par value and the agreement under which they are so issued will be binding as between the parties. In some states, corporations cannot legally issue stock for less than par value.

6. PAR VALUE AND WITHOUT PAR VALUE

Par value shares and shares without par value are permitted in most states. The trend has been for corporations to establish low par values (e.g., $10 a share valuation).

Par value means that the shares have a definite value stated on the face of the certificate (e.g., $10).

Without par value means that there is no definite amount stated on the certificate. The amount the stock will sell for is determined by the board of directors.

There are three considerations in determining whether par stock or no par stock should be issued:

1. The corporation may wish that the consideration be fixed at a certain amount per share based on a minimum capital requirement, or it may wish that the board of directors be able to fix the value from time to time depending on capital requirements, book value of the stock (total assets of the corporation divided by the number of outstanding shares of stock), and market value of the stock (the price the stock might be expected to bring if offered for sale in a fair market).

2. In some states, there is a capital tax on the corporation's authorized shares, a tax on the issuance of shares, and a tax on the transfer of shares. The rate of these taxes on stock without par value is often arbitrarily set at a figure of up to $100 a share. If the stock is worth considerably less than that amount, the corporation and the stockholders are paying an unnecessarily high tax.

3. Only a capital surplus (the excess of the net assets of a corporation over its stated capital), and not stated capital or capital, may be distributed as dividends or used by the corporation to purchase its own stock in many states. In such states, it is thus desirable to establish a capital surplus so that the corporation has greater flexibility. Capital surplus can be established by issuing par value shares for more than par value, in which case the par value received is allocated to capital and the excess to capital surplus, or by allocating a part of the money received for shares without par value to capital surplus and the excess to capital. States differ as to the amount received from shares without par value that may be allocated to capital surplus. In New York, for example, the total consideration received for shares without par value without a stated value must be allocated to capital. The Model Business Corporation Act, Section 19, provides that in the case of the issuance of shares having par value, the consideration received shall constitute stated capital to the extent of the par value of such shares, and the excess shall constitute surplus. In case of issuance of shares without par value, the entire consideration shall constitute stated capital unless the corporation shall determine that only a part thereof shall be stated capital and the rest capital surplus.

7. LIABILITY FOR SHARES

Shares issues for proper consideration are usually nonassessable. Shares issued for improper consideration or for no consideration are often declared void by state law. Where permitted by statute, shares may be issued that are only partly paid, subject to assessments until the full amount has been paid. Most states and the Model Business Corporation Act, Section 21, take the position that a stock certificate cannot be issued for stock that is only partly paid.

When a corporation issues shares of stock as fully paid and nonassessable for less than proper consideration, the stock is often described as "watered stock." (This term evolved from an alleged practice of livestock sellers who watered thirsty cattle just before weighing in at the market so that the buyer paid extra for the water.) The record owner of such stock is usually held liable for the unpaid consideration. A good faith transferee of watered stock is not liable for any unpaid balance, and the original purchaser cannot escape liability by such a transfer. Usually a person who holds shares in a fiduciary capacity is not liable for the unpaid balance, nor is a pledgee.

8. ISSUANCE AND TRANSFER OF SHARES

A. ISSUANCE

A person may become a shareholder in three ways: (1) by a preincorporation stock subscription (see Corporations, Chapter 36, Section A, 5), (2) by subscribing to a share in an organized corporation, and (3) by transfer of a share from a shareholder. In the case of a preincorporation subscription and a transfer from a shareholder, there is no shareholder status until the stock certificate has been delivered and paid for. In the case of a subscriber, there is immediate shareholder status at the time of making of the subscription, and the subscription may not have to be in writing pursuant to the statute of frauds. In the case of an executory contract for the purchase of a share of stock, the purchaser usually does not become a shareholder until the closing of the transaction.

B. BLUE SKY LAWS

Prior to the solicitation or issuance of stock, a corporation must get a permit that is required in every state except Delaware and Nevada. These state laws are to protect the public from stock frauds and are known as "blue sky" laws (i.e., to prevent speculative schemes that have no more basis than so many feet of blue sky). The governmental agency, usually a Division of Corporations, will grant the permit only if it finds that the proposed corporate venture and the securities are fair, just, and equitable. Many state laws also have broker-dealer-registration provisions that regulate the persons engaged in the securities business and registration-of-securities provisions that provide for the registration of the securities. Generally, a sale of shares made by a corporation in violation of the blue sky law or other noncompliance is voidable and may be rescinded by the purchaser.

c. Securities Regulation

Congress has passed several laws for the protection of potential investors and stockholders from misrepresentation and manipulation and to establish fair trading practices in the securities market. The following are some of the most important of these Acts:

1. The Securities Act of 1933, which requires a corporation to furnish investors with information about its securities and which prohibits fraudulent acts. The purpose of the Act is to bring about full disclosures of relevant facts to a prospective investor by requiring the corporation to register and publish the information in a prospectus. *Securities and Exchange Commission v. Glenn Turner Enterprises* illustrates how broadly courts define "securities" under the federal securities laws.

> **FACTS** Defendant company offered and sold certain courses. Under different plans, purchasers were privileged to attent seminars and receive course materials. They also had the opportunity to sell the courses to others for a commission. The court found that the courses and seminars had no value. The whole scheme was, in fact, an elaborate confidence game. The trial court held that the plans were securities under the federal securities laws and found certain securities laws violations.

> **DECISION** Affirmed. The Acts' definitions of "securities" include a wide variety of instruments and contracts. The Securities Acts cover uncommon and irregular devices if they are widely offered or dealt with under terms or courses of dealing that establish their character in commerce as investment contracts. Here, the purchasers were really buying the possibility of deriving money from sales commissions. The court concluded that these deals were "investment contracts" and hence "securities" within the 1933 and 1934 Acts.

> *Securities and Exchange Commission v. Glenn Turner Enterprises, Inc.* (474 F. 2d 476 [9th Cir., 1973], *cert. denied,* 414 U.S. 821, 94 S.Ct. 117, 38 L.Ed.2d 53)

The 1933 Act prohibits dissemination of false and misleading material registration statements. Section 11 permits directors, officers, underwriters, and certified public accountants to prove due diligence as a defense, based upon reasonable investigation, being defined under Section 11 (C) of the Act as to officers, directors, and underwriters to mean: "that required of a prudent man in the management of his own property." The only party to whom this defense is not available is the issuer of the securities.

In *Escott v. Bachris Construction Company,* the federal District Court discussed these due diligence defenses with regard to directors, underwriters, and accountants.

> **FACTS** Securities purchasers alleged that defendant's registration statements contained materially false statements and material omissions in violation of the Securities Act of 1933.

DECISION The District Court denied defendant's motion to dismiss, finding that the defendant's directors, underwriters, and accountants did not prove adequately that they exercised due diligence. The purpose of Section 11 is to protect investors. A director must exercise reasonable care to investigate the facts that a prudent person would employ in the management of his or her own property. Here, for example, the reliance of the directors, underwriters, and accountants on management's representations was unjustified. The circumstances required that they seek more information and spend more time investigating the facts surrounding the securities issuance.

Escott v. Bachris Construction Co. (283 F. Supp. 643 [S.D.N.Y., 1968])

In *Rubin v. United States,* the Supreme Court of the United States dealt with the issue of what consitutes an offer or sale of stock so as to come within the antifraud provisions (Section 17(a)) of the 1933 Act.

FACTS Rubin, on behalf of Tri-State Energy, borrowed $475,000 from a bank. He and other officers submitted false and misleading financial statements. He also pledged stock that he represented as being marketable and valued at $1.7 million. The shares were worthless. The District Court and Court of Appeals convicted Rubin on conspiring to violate the Securities Act of 1933. Rubin argued on appeal that pledging securities did not constitute an offer or sale under Section 17(a). The pledge, he argued, was not a transfer or sale.

DECISION The Supreme Court affirmed the conviction. Section 2(3) defines "sale" as a "sale or disposition of [an] interest in a security, for value." Pledging a security, does transfer an interest in that security and therefore falls within Section 17(a).

Rubin v. United States (449 U.S. 424, 101 S.Ct. 698, 66 L.Ed.2d 633 [1981])

2. The Federal Securities Exchange Act of 1934, which was passed to correct many abuses found on the securities exchanges as a result of a Congressional investigation. This law created the Securities and Exchange Commission (S.E.C.) to regulate the securities industry. The Act requires registration with the S.E.C. of all national securities exchanges and stockbrokers. It requires registration, reporting, and honest disclosures on all proxy solicitations. Directors, officers, and persons owning 10 percent or more of a corporation's securities registered under the S.E.C. must file a monthly report concerning all changes in their stockholdings. Any profits made on short-swing trades (those happening within a six-month period) must be turned over to the corporation. The purpose of this rule is to prevent excessive profits being made because of inside information. The rule does not apply if there was a legitimate reason for the sale and no insider information was used.

The Act also provides for the control of margin trading (permitting the setting of limits on the amount of credit banks can give for purchasing securities). Tender offers made to stockholders by those seeking over 5 percent of the stock for merger purposes must be filed containing all information concerning the proposal. The main purpose of the Act is to force disclosure to buyers and sellers of securities and to regulate the market. Brokers can be expelled from an exchange and have their licenses revoked if they indulge in fraudulent or unethical practices.

3. The Public Utility Holding Company Act of 1935, which regulates holding companies and their subsidiaries engaged in the interstate electric utility business or interstate distribution of gas business.

4. The Trust Indenture Act of 1939, which requires that bonds or other debt securities offered for sale through the mails or interstate commerce be secured by an indenture qualified under that Act.

5. The Investment Company Act of 1940, which regulates companies that invest and reinvest in the securities of other companies.

6. The Investments Advisors Act of 1940, which regulates persons engaged for compensation in the business of rendering advice regarding securities.

7. Under Chapter X of the Bankruptcy Act (corporate reorganization), which is administered only by the federal courts, the Securities and Exchange Commission has advisory functions.

8. Several miscellaneous federal statutes regulate the issuance of securities (e.g., Interstate Commerce Commission regulates interstate rail and motor carriers; Comptroller of the Currency regulates national banks; Federal Home Loan Bank Board regulates federal savings and loan associations; and the Federal Power Commission regulates electric utilities engaged in interstate commerce).

D. Transfer of Shares

Unless restricted by statute, the articles, or bylaws, a shareholder may freely transfer his or her shares. Bylaws may contain reasonable restrictions on the right to transfer or hypothecate the shares. The usual restriction is for the purpose of keeping unacceptable outsiders from membership in a close corporation by requiring that the shares first be offered to existing shareholders. A restriction is ineffective unless it is stated on the face of the certificate (U.C.C. Section 8–204).

The share is transferred by a delivery of the certificate indorsed by its owner on the back or on a separate assignment form. Usually the transfer must be recorded on the corporate stock books before the corporation is required to recognize the transferee as a shareholder. Today, owing to the size of corporations and their large number of shareholders, corporations have generally retained a transfer agent, usually a bank or other large financial institution, to keep their stockholder records up-to-date. A transfer of the certificate without an indorsement is valid between the parties, but the transferee is an assignee and not a bona fide purchaser for value as against third parties.

Article 8, Uniform Commercial Code, is a negotiable instrument law dealing with securities (see Appendix A). Securities have the negotiability of commercial paper. For example, a thief or finder can pass good title to a bona fide purchaser (see U.C.C. Section 8–302 for definition of bona fide purchaser); and fraud, mistake, duress, etc., in the original transfer will not prevent good title from passing to a bona fide purchaser in the next transfer as he or she takes the security "free of any adverse claim" (U.C.C. Section 8–301(1)). In one type of case, securities have even greater negotiability. For example, a security with a forged indorsement is passed to a bona fide purchaser who gets a new security issued by the corporation. The bona fide purchaser gets good title to the new security (U.C.C. Section 8–311(a)), while the corporation, transfer agent, or brokerage firm must make good the loss to the rightful owner under most circumstances.

E. PREEMPTIVE RIGHTS

The common-law preemptive right of a shareholder is the right to purchase a prorata share of newly authorized issues of shares before they are offered to others. This rule has the effect of permitting a stockholder to maintain the same prorata interest in the corporation. There are so many exceptions to the rule today that it has lost much of its significance. Most state corporation laws allow charter provisions to permit, limit, or deny the preemptive right.

C. DIVIDENDS

1. IN GENERAL

A dividend is a distribution of cash, property, or shares of stock to the shareholders in proportion to their interests. Usually, dividends are paid in cash. Property dividends (e.g., stock in subsidiary or other corporation, other securities, or products of own corporation), are rather unusual.

2. SOURCES

Dividends are payable from various limited funds as prescribed by statutes (e.g., earned surplus, net profits, and surplus).

A. EARNED SURPLUS

All states permit dividends to be issued from earned surplus (i.e., the undistributed net profits earned by the corporation, including the gains from the sale of fixed assets, traced back to the date of incorporation). A few states restrict the issuance of dividends to the earned surplus fund.

B. NET PROFITS

Some statutes permit dividends to be issued from current net profits without regard to the existence of a deficit from prior years (e.g., California Corporation Code, Section 1500(b)).

c. Surplus

Some statutes permit dividends out of any kind of surplus, earned or unearned. In addition to the limitation placed on the *source* of the dividend, there are other limitations placed on the issuance of a dividend. For example, several statutes prohibit dividends where the corporation is or might thereby become insolvent; some statutes prohibit dividends if it would impair the capital of the corporation; federal statutes place limitations on some types of dividends (e.g., Public Utility Holding Company Act of 1935 and the Investment Company Act of 1940); limitations are frequently imposed by other jurisdictions in which the corporation is doing business; and limitations are frequently imposed by stock exchange requirements, articles of incorporation, bylaws, resolutions, and shareholder agreements.

3. DECLARATION BY BOARD

The declaration of dividends is discretionary with the board of directors. Even where there is a large surplus, the shareholders cannot compel distribution of a dividend unless there has been an obvious abuse of discretion or there has been bad faith.

4. PERSON ENTITLED TO DIVIDEND

The right to a cash dividend vests in the shareholder as of the time it is declared by the corporation. The dividend therefore belongs to the person who is the record owner on that date, even though it is payable at a later time. In the case of a transfer of stock, dividends declared before the transfer belong to the transferor, whereas those declared after the transfer belong to the transferee.

The rule that the right to a cash dividend is the date of declaration of the dividend is subject to modification by the corporation in most states. For example, the corporation may make the dividend payable to those who will be holders of record on a later specified date. In such case, the purchaser of stock from another person would have the right to the dividend if he or she purchased before the record date rather than the declaration date. This record date set by the corporation is known as "X-dividend" day.

If the corporation declares a stock dividend rather than a cash dividend, the ownership is determined by the date of distribution. This is because the declaration of a stock dividend has the effect of diluting the corporate assets among a larger number of shares so that the value of the holding represented by each share is accordingly diminished, and unless the person who owns the stock on the date of distribution receives his or her share of the stock dividend, the net effect will be to lessen his or her holdings.

The right of preferred shareholders was discussed earlier in this chapter (B. 3).

5. STOCK SPLIT

The effect of a stock split is merely to change the form of the stockholder's interest in the company but not the substance of the property. It simply involves a division of the outstanding shares into more units, each with less value. Each shareholder's proportionate share of ownership, his or her rights on dissolution, and the total value of his or her investment in the corporation are maintained. The only significant changes are the issuance of a new certificate and a reduction in the market value of each share unit, which usually increases marketability of the shares. For example, 100 shares of $100 par value common stock, following a 2-for-1 split, would become 200 shares of $50 par value common stock.

The declaration and payment of a stock dividend differs from a stock split. The assets of the corporation are frozen in the stated capital account when a stock dividend is paid, whereas a stock split effects no change in stated capital. Where there is more than one class of shares outstanding, either a stock split or stock dividend in one class may alter the relative voting strength of the different classes.

ILLUSTRATIVE CASES

1. Payment for Stock Shares

EASTERN OKLAHOMA TELEVISION CO v. AMECO, INC.

437 F.2d 138 (10th Cir., 1971)

This was an action for damages brought by Eastern Oklahoma Television Company (plaintiff) against Ameco, Inc. (defendant), in which certain promoters and original subscribers of Eastern Oklahoma Television Company (KTEN) became third-party defendants. The basic issue was whether corporate stock allotted to the promoters in consideration of services rendered and property furnished had been validly issued.

C. C. Morris, Brown Morris, and Bill Hoover were owners and operators of two radio stations in Ada, Oklahoma. In 1953 they organized KTEN to operate a TV station in Ada. They obtained a channel from the Federal Communications Commission, pledging all the assets of the radio stations to "undergird" the venture, personally guaranteed payment to Radio Corporation of America in the amount of $240,000 for equipment, designed the facilities, planned the operations, and hired and trained personnel. The articles of incorporation authorized 650 shares of Class A voting stock and 650 shares of Class B nonvoting stock, both classes having a par value of $500 per share.

The Class B stock was sold to the public at par by the promoters, who were also the directors. Each subscriber was told of the necessary organizational services which had been or were to be performed by the directors and that the Class A stock would be allotted to them. The subscriptions and payments on the Class B stock were to be held in escrow in a local bank until the construction permit from the FCC was received. The Class A stock was issued by a resolution of the directors which recited that the consideration was their experience in broadcasting, their standing with the FCC, and their personal guarantee of the debt to RCA for equipment.

The early years of operation of KTEN were plagued with financial difficulties. The promoters not only returned 250 shares of Class A stock to the treasury to be sold for working capital but also made personal loans to the corporation. In addition, $170,000 worth of preferred stock was issued. One of the original shareholders contested the validity of the stock issued to Bill Hoover, one of the two major Class A shareholders.

PICKETT, Circuit Judge. It is urged that the issuance of the stock to the directors was in violation of the Oklahoma Constitution and statutes as having been made without adequate consideration. The record clearly discloses that the stock transfer was for property, goodwill, extensive valuable services rendered, and the personal guaranty given by the directors for the RCA note. That the corporation received valuable services and property from the organizers cannot be doubted. Apparently from the beginning they contributed their time and abilities, together with the risk of all their personal assets for the corporate success. The goodwill, which included Hoover's experience, expertise, and favorable broadcasting record with the FCC, was extremely valuable in the acquisition of FCC permits by KTEN and in the actual construction of the station, including the design and construction of a signal relay system from Oklahoma City. Where goodwill constitutes property and if actually existent and of value at the time, it may be included in determining a valid consideration for the issuance of stock. * * *

In objecting to the personal guaranty upon the RCA note as part of the consideration for the issuance of shares, appellants rely on the rule in Oklahoma that a promissory note or other obligations of the subscriber [are] not valid consideration for such purposes. but here, the guaranty was for an obligation of the corporation. Absent the guaranty, the essential equipment for the operation of a television station could not have been obtained. The organizers personally furnished the security for the purchase of this property. Without it the cost to the corporation would have been substantial if it had been possible to obtain the security by other means. The record clearly indicates that the result of this security was the completion of the station, which eventually led to a successful corporate operation. The guaranty was valuable property or services within the meaning of the Oklahoma Constitution.

The ruling that the stock was valid was affirmed.

2. Value of Shares of Stock

GINTER v. PALMER & CO.

39 Colo.App. 221, 566 P.2d 1358 (1977)

SILVERSTEIN, Chief Judge.   Plaintiff appeals from a summary judgment for defendant. We affirm.

The Articles of Incorporation of defendant, Palmer and Company, provide:

> In the event of the death of a stockholder, the corporation shall have the option to purchase his stock * * * on the basis of the book value as of the date of death.

Dolorosa Ginter, a stockholder in the company died leaving a will under which she bequeathed to plaintiff her stock, or the proceeds thereof, should the company exercise the above option. The company duly exercised its option, asserting the book value of the stock to be $1.91 per share.

Plaintiff brought this action, contending that the "net asset value" of the stock exceeded $20 per share, and that the book value offered by the company was arbitrary and capricious and the result of a conspiracy by the majority stockholders to enrich themselves unjustly by the repurchase of the stock. He further claimed that if the provision of the Articles of Incorporation were to be interpreted to allow defendant to purchase the stock at the offered price, then the provision would be void as unconscionable, contrary to public policy and contrary to law. He prayed for a declaratory judgment adjudicating the respective rights of the parties.

*   *   *

Plaintiff further contends that the incorporators intended "book value" to mean "net asset value," and that their intent is a factual issue to be decided by a jury. This contention has several flaws. First, plaintiff cites Black's Law Dictionary 227 (4th ed.), defining book value as "the value shown by deducting liabilities and other matters required to be deducted from assets * * *." Although this definition is generally accepted, there is no perceivable distinction between this value and net asset value.

Even assuming there is a diffeence between the two values, where, as here, a document is unambiguous, and the intent of its drafters therefore clear, its interpretation is a matter of law, not fact. Further when a term which has a generally accepted meaning is used, the parties may not claim their intent was otherwise.

Plaintiff next asserts that the provision of the Articles of Incorporation is unconscionable and invalid as a restraint of alienation. We do not agree.

The defendant is a close corporation. Ownership of the stock is limited by the Articles of Incorporation to employees or sales agents of the company and producers of products processed or sold by the company. The Articles also provide that if the company fails to exercise the option, then the stock may be sold to anyone qualified to be a stockholder.

Although absolute restriction against the sale of stock is invalid, reasonable restrictions have been held to be invalid in Colorado.

> [T]he validity of the restriction on transfer does not rest on any abstract motion of intrinsic fairness of price. To be invalid, more than mere disparity between option price and current value of the stock must be shown. * * * Since the parties have in effect agreed on a price formula which suited them, and provision is made freeing the stock for outside sale should the corporation not make, or provide for, the purchase, the restriction is reasonable and valid.

This is an apt statement of the rule followed by a majority of the jurisdictions in which the issue has arisen, and controls here.

Judgment affirmed.

3. Right to Transfer Stock

McMENOMY v. RYDEN

266 Minn. 358, 176 N.W.2d 876 (1970)

Plaintiffs are minority shareholders of Midwest Technical Development Corporation ("Midwest"), a closed-end investment company owning assets consisting principally of securities in companies in technological fields. In June, 1962, plaintiffs filed a shareholders derivative suit against 18 individuals and Midwest, as nominal defendant, to recover on behalf of Midwest the profits realized by the individuals through dealing in stock held in the portfolio of Midwest in breach of their fiduciary duty as officers and directors of Midwest.

In October, 1965, a new corporation, Midtext, Inc. was organized to acquire the assets of Midwest. The transfer of assets to Midtext, Inc., was completed in December, 1965, and the shareholders of Midwest received shares of Midtex, Inc. The transfer included all assets owned by Midwest of every kind and nature "whether or not disclosed, on Midwest's books and records, including any contingent assets or claims arising out of Midwest's operations prior to the Closing Date * * * subject, however, to all of the liabilities or obligations of Midwest."

Plaintiffs' motion to join Midtex, Inc. as a party defendant in the suit was denied by the trial court. On appeal, order of the trial court reversed, and the case remanded.

KNUTSON, C.J.   * * * A stockholder's derivative action of the type that we have here is an invention of equity to permit stockholders to seek relief for breach of fiduciary duty by officers or directors when the corporation itself refuses to bring such action. In *Koster v. Lumbermens Mutual Cas. Co.,* 330 U.S. 518, 522, 67 S.Ct. 828, 830, 91 L.Ed. 1067, 1072, the court said:

> The stockholder's derivative action * * * is an invention of equity to supply the want of an adequate remedy at law to redress breaches of fiduciary duty by corporate managers. Usually the wrongdoing officers

also possess the control which enables them to suppress any effort by the corporate entity to remedy such wrongs. Equity therefore traditionally entertains the derivative or secondary action by which a single stockholder may sue in the corporation's right when he shows that the corporation on proper demand has refused to pursue a remedy, or shows facts that demonstrate the futility of such a request. * * *

The cause of action which such a plaintiff brings before the court is not his own but the corporation's. It is the real party in interest and he is allowed to act in protection of its interest, somewhat as a 'next friend' might do for an individual, because it is disabled from protecting itself.

*　　*　　*

That being so, it should not be possible to frustrate this remedy created by equity by the simple expedient of creating a new corporation and assigning the assets of one for whose benefit suit is brought to the newly created entity. Someone should have the continuing right to seek relief from those guilty of breach of fiduciary duty, if there has been such. The stockholders of Midwest, if there was a breach of fiduciary duty by the managing officers, did not lose the right to recover simply because the assets were transferred to a new corporation.

*　　*　　*

It has been argued that inasmuch as Midtext, after procuring legal advice from independent attorneys, decided not to continue the suit or to join it, plaintiffs are thereby barred from continuing the suit. * * *

*　　*　　*

Here the members of the board of directors of Midtex, only one of whom was a member of the board of Midwest at the time plaintiffs commenced this action, has exercised their judgment in deciding not to join the lawsuit or to continue with it. This they had a right to do. By refusing to become a party to the lawsuit, they undoubtedly have chosen a course that will eliminate liability on the part of Midtext for the payment of expenses of the litigation. However, this should not preclude the joining of Midtex as an involuntary defendant if it is in fact the real party in interest as the assignee of the cause of action brought for the benefit of Midwest.

It may be possible to determine prior to trial whether it was the intention of the parties to assign this cause of action to Midtex. If so, the action should proceed for the benefit of the corporation that will receive the benefit of the recovery, if there is one. Unless that issue is determined before trial, Midtext should be joined as an involuntary defendant and the case proceed with both Midwest and Midtex named as defendants. If there is a recovery, the question as to who shall receive the benefit of it can then be determined after the trial.

The case is therefore remanded to the trial court for disposition in conformity with this opinion.

4. Right of Stockholders to Compel Dividend Payment

TWENTY SEVEN TRUST v. REALTY GROWTH INVESTORS

533 F. Supp. 1028 (D.C. Md., 1982)

MILLER, JR., District Judge.   The plaintiff, the Twenty Seven Trust (Twenty Seven), brought this action against Realty Growth Investors (Realty) and RGI Holding Company, Inc. (RGI) on October 22, 1981. Twenty Seven's four-count complaint alleged violations of the federal securities laws and Maryland common law in connection with RGI's attempt to acquire all of the shares of beneficial interest in Realty. On October 23, 1981, the Chambers Judge denied Twenty Seven's request for a temporary restraining order which, if granted, would have enjoined a special meeting of Realty's shareholders called to approve a "squeeze-out merger" between Realty and a wholly-owned subsidiary of RGI.

Twenty Seven filed an amended complaint on November 12, 1981, adding a fifth count based on an alleged discriminatory distribution of cash and securities by Realty to its shareholders. Twenty Seven also filed a petition for appraisal under *Md. Corps. & Ass'ns Code Ann.* §§ 3–201 to 3 213 (1975 & 1981 Cum.Supp.), for a determination of the "fair value" of its Realty shares.

The defendants have moved, pursuant to Rule 12(b)(6), Fed.R.Civ.P., to dismiss Twenty Seven's amended complaint, leaving Twenty Seven solely to its remedy under the appraisal statute.

*   *   *

Twenty Seven's amended complaint contains five claims for relief: (1) Count I alleges a violation of section 10(b) of the Securities Exchange Act of 1934, 15 U.S.C. § 78j(b), and Securities and Exchange Commission (SEC Rule 10b–5, 17 C.F.R. § 240.-10–5 (1981); (2) Count II alleges that the defendants, as majority shareholders, breached their common law fiduciary duty as to Twenty Seven, the minority shareholder, in connection with the merger; (3) Count III alleges common law fraud in connection with the proxy materials; (4) Count IV alleges a violation of the Maryland Securities Act, *Md. Corps. & Ass'ns Code Ann.* §§ 11–301, 11–703 (1975 & 1981 Cum. Supp.); and (5) Count V alleges unlawful shareholder discrimination in connection with Realty's May, 1981 distribution.

In its memorandum, Twenty Seven states that its primary objectives in this litigation are two-fold:

> 1. To have the merger held illegal and to have the Court, pursuant to its equitable powers, order Realty to issue Twenty Seven shares of beneficial interest equal to 6.9% of the currently issued and outstanding shares; and

> 2. To have the distribution held illegal and to have the Court order Realty to pay Twenty Seven $17.19 per share in cash in exchange for the note and Distribution Certificate Twenty Seven was wrongfully compelled to accept.

*   *   *

In Count V, Twenty Seven contends that the defendant engaged in unlawful shareholder discrimination. Twenty Seven alleges that in connection with RGI's $14.31 per share tender offer, Realty and RGI agreed that Realty would make a distribution to all pre-tender shareholders. According to Twenty Seven, although all of Realty's shareholders were of the same class, shareholders owning 1000 shares or less received $17.19 per share in cash while shareholders owning more than 1000 shares, such as itself, received $15.29 per share in distribution certificates and secured notes.

Like corporations, a real estate investment trust, in accordance with its trust declaration, may issue different classes of ownership shares and afford them differing rights. Consequently, if Realty's declaration of trust had provided for classes of shares with differing distribution rights, and the distribution complained of was made pursuant to that instrument, such would be permissible under Maryland law. Twenty Seven has alleged, however, that the shareholders receiving the differing distributions were all of the same class.

If the distribution at issue were a corporate dividend, it is plain that a claim for relief would be stated. It is hornbook law that unless the corporate charter properly provides otherwise, all shareholders of the same class must participate in dividends on a pro rata basis without discrimination or preference. This rule of nondiscrimination among shareholders of the same class refers not only to the amount of the dividend but also to its form.

Although the distributions made by Realty are not strictly dividends, the court concludes that they are sufficiently analogous to dividends to warrant the application of the nondiscrimination rule.

*   *   *

5. Stock Transfer by Forgery

WELLER v. AMERICAN TELEPHONE AND TELEGRAPH

290 A.2d 845 (Del.Ch., 1972)

MARVEL, Vice Chancellor.   Plaintiff seeks the entry of a judgment against two corporations, namely American Telephone and Telegraph Company and General Electric Company, based on her claim for injuries sustained by her as a result of the alleged unauthorized registration of stock owned by her in each such company. * * *

At the time of the acts complained of plaintiff was the registered holder of 500 shares of common stock of American Telephone and Telegraph Company and 100 shares of common stock of General Electric. Later, the shares of the latter company were split two for one.

In 1968, Gertrude L. Weller, a 94 year old widow, was invited to live in the home of Mr. and Mrs. Kenneth Jumper. This change of residence came about because the plaintiff had known Mrs. Jumper for many years and was also acquainted with Mr. Jumper, who had performed various helpful services for her in the past. Because of her lonely circumstances and advanced age she was more than delighted to accept the Jumpers' proposal. As a token of her appreciation for their apparently unselfish gesture Mrs. Weller, after moving in with them, made a gift of 100 shares of American Telephone and Telegraph stock to Mr. Jumper.

Thereafter, because of her age and poor health, plaintiff gradually surrendered more and more responsibility concerning the details of her business affairs to Mr. Jumper. Thus, she acquiesced when he took upon himself to open her mail, being reassured by him on numerous occasions that he was sending her stock dividend checks and other income receipts to her bank. During this period Mrs. Weller evinced complete trust in the Jumpers notwithstanding momentary worries over the fact that her mail was being opened by Mr. Jumper and that she was not actually being shown the income checks which she had received in the mail. However, she was easily convinced that there was nothing to worry about.

In February, 1970, after having moved to her nephew's to live, following disclosure to some extent of Mr. Jumper's actual nature, Mrs. Weller ascertained that for over a period of almost two years she had been systematically defrauded by Mr. Jumper. In other words she became aware for the first time of the fact that Kenneth Jumper had used a form containing her signature for the purpose of opening a joint trading account with a stockbroker, namely the third party defendant Merrill Lynch, Pierce, Fenner & Smith, Inc., and that Mr. Jumper thereafter had apparently forged her name to the stock certificates here involved for the purpose of selling them on the market.

The trial evidence is to the effect that Mr. Jumper had not only forged plaintiff's name to plaintiff's stock certificates but had also closed out her savings account and terminated her checking account by means of a forged signature. Needless to say the income checks which Mr. Jumper had removed from Mrs. Weller's mail had also been diverted to his own use.

Plaintiff thereupon notified the defendants American Telephone and Telegraph Company and General Electric Company on March 4, 1970 that the stock certificates representing her investments in such companies had been sold by means of forged signatures and requested the issuance to her of replacement certificates. The defendants having declined to issue such certificates as requested, this action ensued, the complaint naming as defendants the issuers of the certificates in question. Merrill Lynch was later joined as a third party defendant in its capacity as the broker which had guaranteed Mrs. Weller's signature.

*　　　*　　　*

Section 8–404(2) of the Uniform Commercial Code provides that where an issuer has registered a transfer of a security in the name of a person not entitled to it, such issuer on demand must deliver a like security to the true owner, provided, inter alia, the owner has acted pursuant to subsection (1) of the section which follows. Section 8–404(2)(b). Subsection (1) of the following section provides that the owner of such a security must notify the issuer of the wrongful taking complained of within a reasonable time after he has notice of a lost or wrongfully taken certificate, Section 8–405(1).

Defendants aregue that in the case at bar plaintiff failed to notify the issuers within a "reasonable time," as such phrase is defined in the statute.

It contends that plaintiff should have known some twenty-two months before she notified the issuing corporations that Mr. Jumper had converted her stock certificates. Defendants go on to point out that had plaintiff made a casual examination of her bank book or bank statement, it would have been brought to her attention that dividend checks accruing on the shares here in issue were not being deposited to her credit.

In order to determine whether or not Mrs. Weller notified the issuer within a "reasoanble time" after she had "noticed" that her shares had been transferred as a result of forgery it is necessary to determine the meaning of these two phrases as employed in the statute.

The definition section of Article 8 provides inter alia: "In addition Article 1 contains general definitions and principles of construction and interpretation applicable throught this Article." Section 8–102(6). Article 1 provides that a person has "notice" of a fact when he has actual knowledge of it, has received notification, or "* * * from all the facts and circumstances known to him at the time in question he has reason to know that it exists." Section 1–201(25). Article 1 also provides: "What is a reasonable time for taking any action depends on the nature, purpose and circumstances of such action." Section 1–204(2).

In the case at bar we are concerned with the affairs of a 94 year old woman, who while a guest in another's home was persuaded to allow one of her hosts, whom she trusted, to handle her affairs. I am accordingly satisfied that Mrs. Weller, a lonely and trusting person of advanced years and of infirm mind and body, had every reasonable right to trust a family which took her in and which she had known intimately before she moved into its home. Furthermore, in light of her reliance on the perpetrator of the acts which deprived her of title to her securities and her own age and decrepitude, she having among other things broken a hip while at the Jumpers, I do not think Mrs. Weller can be charged with unreasonable action in not checking her accounts from time to time. I therefore conclude in view of all of the surrounding circumstances that Mrs. Weller did not have the required statutory notice of Mr. Jumper's dishonesty until February 19 or 20, 1970, and that she thereafter notified the issuers of her stolen securities within a reasonable time.

*   *   *

There being no contention that the issuance of substitute certificates to plaintiff would result in an overissue of stock in this case, plaintiff's relief must be limited to the recovery by her of new certificates. * * *

Accordingly, plaintiff is entitled to the entry of an order providing for the issuance to her of 500 shares of American Telephone and Telegraph Company common stock together with accrued and unpaid dividends as well as 200 shares of General Electric Company common stock together with accrued and unpaid dividends, summary judgment having been earlier granted to the defendants American Telephone and Telegraph Company and General Electric Company on their claim against the third party defendant Merrill Lynch, Pierce, Fenner and Smith, Incorporated on the basis of the latter's guarantee of Mrs. Weller's signature.

PROBLEMS

1. Smith signed a stock subscription agreement to buy 10 shares of stock having a par value of $100 per share of the proposed XYZ Corporation. Two weeks later the company was incorporated. A certificate for 10 shares was duly tendered to Smith but he refused to accept it. He was notified of all the shareholders meetings but never attended. A dividend check was mailed to him but he returned it. XYZ Corporation now sues Smith to recover the $1,000. Smith argues that his subscription agreement was an unaccepted offer, that he had not ratified it, and was therefore not liable. Decision?

2. David subscribed for 200 shares of 8 percent cumulative, participating, redeemable, convertible, preferred shares of the Atlas Hotel Company with a par value of $100 per share. The subscription agreement provided that he was to receive a bonus of one share of common stock of $100 per value for each share of preferred stock. David fully paid his subscription agreement of $20,000 and received the aforementioned 200 shares of preferred and the bonus stock of 200 shares of the par value common. Subsequently the company became insolvent. Rogers, the receiver of the corporation, brings suit for $20,000, the par value of the common stock, against David. Decision?

3. Ray, a shareholder in Swanson Company, a corporation, delivered his stock certificate indorsed in blank to Turpin, a purchaser for value. Ray died the following day. His executor, believing that the certificate was lost, applied to the corporation for a new certificate, which was issued and the share transferred to the executor's name on the books. The executor sold the new certificate to Upson, an innocent purchaser, delivering the certificate to him, indorsed to his name, three weeks after Ray's death. Two days later, Turpin presented the original certificate to the corporation, asking that appropriate action be taken to reflect his ownership of the shares. Turpin brings an action against Swanson Company, demanding that he be adjudged the owner of the stock, that Swanson Company be required to issue a new certificate in his name, and that he be paid a dividend which had accrued since the certificate was transferred to him. Decision?

4. Defendant corporation sold 100 shares of stock for $25,000 to plaintiff without having obtained a permit from the Division of Corporations as required by the Corporate Securities Act. Plaintiff knew the defendant had not obtained a permit to sell the stock. Plaintiff attended and participated in shareholder meetings for two years and accepted dividends. The defendant corporation is now insolvent and plaintiff sues to rescind the sale. Decision?

5. Defendant corporation had a surplus of $112,000,000. Henry Ford, who controlled the board of directors, convinced the board to use the money for business expansion although this would apparently not increase profits but enable the corporation to sell its products cheaper. Some of the stockholders brought an action to compel the directors to declare a cash dividend of $40,000,000. Decision?

6. For services rendered as a corporate promotor, A was issued fully paid-up shares of corporate stock far in excess of the value of A's services. A transferred these shares to B, who bought in good faith with no knowledge of the overvaluation. The corporation and its creditors now sue B to recover the difference between the value of the services and the value of the stock. Decision?

7. S learned that A, B, and C were about to form a corporation to produce and market a line of automobile accessories. S had patented a tamper-proof steering column lock but lacked funds to market it successfully. A, B, and C agreed to purchase his patent rights for cash and 200 shares of preferred stock in the corporation. XYZ Inc., when formed, issued the stock to S, but refused to make the promised cash payment. XYZ was very profitable due to S's patented lock, and had a large earned surplus with a large cash balance on hand. XYZ was about to sell the remainder of the authorized preferred shares, ignoring S's demand to purchase a proportiate share of the stock sold. S sued to recover both the cash payment and to enforce his preemptive rights. Decision?

8. Chase, a certified public accountant, audited the books of Brine's Inc. She negligently certified incorrect information in financial statements on the form required and filed with the SEC. Brine's subsequently went bankrupt. After investigation, stockholders of Brine's discover that Donaldson, president of Brine's, had embezzled large sums from the company and has absconded to parts unknown. These stockholders sue Chase under Rule 10 (b)–5. Chase admits negligence in failing to discover Donaldson's misconduct, but defends on the grounds that she had no actual knowledge of the embezzlement. Decision?

9. Z Inc., in seeking to sell a new issue of common stock, registered the issue but made false statements in both the prospectus and registration statement. O was the underwriter of the stock, and RAF acted as the securities broker-dealer. T purchased shares based on the prospectus. The value of the shares fell drastically when the falsity of the information was made public. T sues Z Inc., O, and RAF under the Securities Act of 1933. Z-Inc., O, and RAF assert the defense of due diligence and lack of knowledge of untrue statements. Decision?

10. Mr. and Mrs. S are shareholders in AB Breweries, Inc. They brought a derivative action against AB Inc. and its president, AB Jr., to require AB Jr. to return to the company the value of salary and perquisites provided him in excess of the reasonable value of the services he rendered as president. AB Jr. and AB Inc. defended and requested dismissal of the action on the grounds that the S's had failed to try to persuade the directors to take the desired action. The S's responded that AB Jr. controlled the directors and that AB Jr. and the board controlled communication with shareholders. Decision?

COMMERCIAL PAPER

Chapter 39

INTRODUCTION

A. IN GENERAL

Modern commercial paper includes (1) instruments payable in money or goods, (2) receipts for and promises to deliver goods, (3) instruments creating rights in personal or real property, and (4) documents of title in goods.

Viable business requires the ready transferability of these documents from person to person without loss of attendant rights. Such transfers may be by (1) assignment, (2) negotiation, (3) sale and delivery of goods, and (4) deeding of real property.

One who takes an assignment of such paper acquires all the rights of the assignor but is also subjected to existing defenses excepting certain equities in sales to innocent third parties. However, when such paper is negotiated, nearly all defenses are cut off.

Today's national and international commerce has dictated the need for uniformity in such paper which has resulted in a major part of the Uniform Commercial Code. The U.C.C. Article 3 (Commercial Paper), Article 7 (Warehouse Receipts, Bills of Lading, and other Documents of Title), and Article 8 (Investment Securities) (Appendix A) set forth the statutory law of negotiable instruments.

It has been estimated that 90 percent of all business transactions involve the use of a check. It is thus apparent that negotiable instruments play a very important role in the business world. Most of the assets of banks, insurance companies, and mortgage companies are in the form of negotiable securities. Corporations participate in the gains and losses of business by means of ownership of negotiable stocks and bonds of other companies. The amount of monetary metal in the United States is very small when compared with the total wealth represented by negotiable securities.

B. TYPES OF COMMERCIAL PAPER

1. PROMISSORY NOTES

A negotiable promissory note is a written unconditional promise by one person (the maker) to pay a sum certain in money to another person (the payee). It may be made payable on demand or at a stated future time. It may be made payable to order (and the payee may order that it be paid to another person) or to bearer (one who has possession) (U.C.C. Section 3–104(1)). It is a two-party instrument.

2. DRAFTS

A draft, or bill of exchange, is an unconditional written order by one party (the drawer) on another party (the drawee) to pay a certain sum in money on demand or at a stated future time to a third party (the payee). (U.C.C. Section 3–104(2)(a)).

3. CHECKS

A check is a draft drawn on a bank and payable on demand (U.C.C. Section 3–104(2)(b)). A cashier's check is drawn by a bank on itself ordering itself to pay a sum certain to the depositor or to the person designated by him or her. A certified check is a personal check of the bank's depositor that the bank has certified that the depositor has such amount on deposit. A bank draft is a check drawn by one bank upon another bank in which the first bank has money on deposit.

4. CERTIFICATES OF DEPOSIT

A certificate of deposit is a written acknowledgment by a bank of receipt of a certain amount of money by a depositor and a promise to pay the holder of the certificate that amount when the certificate, properly indorsed, is surrendered (U.C.C. Section 3–104(2)(c)).

C. PARTIES TO COMMERCIAL PAPER

1. PROMISSORY NOTE

A promissory note has two original parties: the maker and the payee. The maker is the party who promises to pay the money. The payee is the party entitled to receive the money.

2. DRAFT AND CHECK

The draft and check have three original parties: the drawer, the drawee, and the payee. The drawer is the person who executes the instrument. In the case of a check, the drawer is sometimes called a signer. The obligation of the drawer is conditional in the sense that if the instrument is not paid by the drawee, he or she is promising to pay. The drawee is the person or institution to whom the order to pay is directed. In the case of a check, the drawee would be a bank. The obligation of the drawee depends entirely upon the relationship between the drawer and the drawee. The usual checking account obligates the bank to honor all orders for payment of money so long as the account has a sufficient balance. In the case of a draft or check, the obligation of the bank extends directly to the holder once the bank has accepted it or, in effect, agreed to honor it. Where the bank has so accepted, it may be referred to as an acceptor. The payee is the party entitled to payment.

3. INDORSER

In addition to original parties, other parties may be involved in a negotiable instrument. An indorser is the party who transfers a negotiable instrument by signing and delivering it to another person. In the case of a check, the first indorser would be the payee. The usual method of indorsing a negotiable instrument is to sign one's name on the back of it.

4. INDORSEE

The indorsee is the person to whom an indorsement is made. An indorsee may also indorse and negotiate the instrument, in which case the indorsee is also an indorser.

5. BEARER

The bearer is the person who has possession of the instrument payable to bearer or indorsed in blank.

6. HOLDER

The holder is the person who has possession of the instrument issued or indorsed to him or her or to his or her order, or to bearer, or indorsed in blank. A holder for value is a holder who gives consideration for the instrument. A holder in due course is a person who becomes a holder for value in good faith and without notice of any defense to the instrument (U.C.C. Section 3–302(1)).

7. ACCOMMODATION PARTY

An accommodation party is a person who signs the instrument for the purpose of lending his or her name to another party to it (U.C.C. Section 3–415(1)). An accommodation party may be a comaker or an indorser.

8. GUARANTOR

A guarantor is a person who signs the instrument, adding a statement that he or she will pay the instrument under certain conditions (U.C.C. Section 3–416).

D. LIABILITY OF THE PARTIES

1. PROMISSORY NOTE

The liability of the maker is primary, which means that the maker will pay the instrument according to its terms at the time of his or her promise to pay (U.C.C. Section 3–413(1)).

2. DRAFT OR CHECK

The liability of the drawer is secondary in that the drawer promises to pay the amount of the draft or check to the holder thereof or to any indorser if the drawee (bank) does not pay *and* if drawer is given proper notice (U.C.C. Section 3–413(2)). The drawee or acceptor has primary liability if the check or draft is accepted by either of them (U.C.C. Section 3–411(1)).

3. INDORSER

The indorser promises to pay the instrument according to its terms at the time of his or her indorsement to the holder or to any subsequent indorser if the instrument is dishonored and proper notice has been given such indorser (U.C.C. Section 3–414).

A person who transfers the instrument without indorsing it or who indorses it by using such words as "without recourse" above his or her signature is not liable for its payment (U.C.C. Sections 3–401(1), 3–414(1)). However, such a person may be bound by warranties that are involved in the transfer of negotiable instruments (U.C.C. Section 3–417).

Unless otherwise agreed, indorsers are liable to one another in the order in which they indorse, which is presumed to be the order in which their signatures appear on the instrument (U.C.C. Section 3–414(2)).

In *Coulter v. Stewart,* The Supreme Court of Arizona had to decide whether certain language constituted a general or qualified indorsement.

FACTS Sardou executed a promissory note to Harvey, who transferred the note to Stewart by writing on the back of the note, "We hereby assign all our right, title and interest in the within installment note to W.O. Stewart." Payments on the note became delinquent, and Sardou was nowhere to be found. Stewart sued Harvey. The trial court awarded judgment for Stewart, who contended that Harvey, as a general indorser, was liable for the balance on the note. Harvey argued that he had made a qualified indorsement under the statute and that he was not liable to Stewart.

DECISION Judgment for Stewart affirmed. The statute provided that an indorser may make a qualified indorsement by adding to the indorser's signature the words "without recourse" or any words of similar impart. By doing so, an indorser does not promise to pay should the instrument be dishonored upon presentment. The Court held that the language used to transfer this note was not language of limitation under the statute and the signers were merely general indorsers.

Coulter v. Stewart (93 Ariz. 242, 379 P. 2d 910 [1963])

E. WARRANTIES OF THE PARTIES

The transferor of negotiable instruments warrants or guarantees that certain facts exist. The warranties vary according to the manner in which the negotiation is made. Where there is an indorsement, the warranty runs to subsequent holders. If the transfer is made by delivery alone, the warranty runs only to the immediate transferee.

1. WARRANTIES OF INDORSER

The following warranties apply where the indorser has transferred the instrument and has received consideration and where his or her indorsement is not without recourse (e. g., the indorser merely signs his or her name as the indorsement or makes the following indorsement: "Pay to the order of John Smith (signed) Robert Jones"):

1. That the indorser has good title or is authorized to act for one who has such title.

2. That the signatures on the instrument are genuine or executed by authorized agents.

The Supreme Judicial Court of Massachusetts dealt with the effectiveness of a signed indorsement of a note in *Watertown Federal Savings and Loan Assn. v. Spanks.*

FACTS Defendants executed a note to pay for certain materials. The note was indorsed twice, until it finally became payable to the plaintiff bank. Bank sued defendants to recover on the note. Defendants denied the genuineness of their signatures and of all indorsements.

DECISION: Judgment for bank. At trial, evidence showed that defendants' signatures on the note were genuine. Although there were some minor questions regarding one indorsement (the company name was abbreviated), the court ruled that (1) the evidence showed that the indorsement was genuine and (2) only the indorsee, and not the defendant, is in a position to question the genuineness of the indorsements under the Uniform Commercial Code (U.C.C. Section 3–203).

Watertown Federal Savings and Loan Assn. v. Spanks (346 Mass. 398, 193 N.E. 2d 333 [1963])

3. That the instrument has not been materially altered.

4. That the indorser has no knowledge of any insolvency proceeding instituted against the maker or acceptor or the drawer of an unaccepted instrument.

5. That no defense of any party is good against him or her (U.C.C. Section 3–417(2).

2. WARRANTIES OF NONRECOURSE INDORSER

A person who indorses an instrument "without recourse" is still liable for all the warranties of an indorser, except that warranty number 5 is limited by the following: "that he has no knowledge of such a defense" (U.C.C. Section 3–417(3)). The nonrecourse indorser may exclude *all* warranties by inserting "without warranties" above his or her signature.

3. WARRANTIES OF TRANSFEROR BY DELIVERY

When one transfers a negotiable instrument by delivery, the warranties are the same as those made by a nonrecourse indorser, except that they extend to the transferee only if he or she has given consideration.

F. DOCUMENTS OF TITLE

1. IN GENERAL

The document of title to goods developed so that paper representing title to the goods could be transferred between parties rather than transferring possession of the goods, which was too cumbersome. The documents serve an important function in reserving or transferring a security interest in goods represented by the document because of the ease with which they can be handled and transferred.

The U.C.C. does not cover interstate shipments or foreign commerce and is expressly subject to applicable federal statutes, including the Federal Bills of Lading Act, the Interstate Commerce Act, the Harter Act of 1893 regulating offshore ocean commerce, the Carriage of Goods by Sea Act, and the United States Warehouse Act.

Document of title includes bill of lading, dock warrant, dock receipt, warehouse receipt, and any other document that in the regular course of business or financing is treated as adequately evidencing that the person entitled under the document has the right to receive, hold, and dispose of the document and the goods it covers. The document must represent that it was issued by a bailee, (e.g., warehouse or carrier) and must purport to cover goods in the bailee's possession that are identified (Sections 1–201(15), 7–102(a)).

A bill of lading is a document evidencing the receipt of goods for shipment issued by a person engaged in the business of transporting or forwarding goods and includes an airbill (Section 1–201(6)) (i.e., it represents a right to goods from a carrier).

A warehouse receipt is a receipt issued by a person engaged in the business of storing goods for hire (Section 1–201(45)) (i.e., it represents a right to goods from a warehouse).

A warehouseperson is a person engaged in the business of storing goods for hire (Section 7–102(1)(h)).

A negotiable document of title is an effective tool for a seller who does not want to sell on credit. For example, a seller in New York who wants to sell goods to a buyer in California can have a bill of lading issued to the order of himself or herself, in which case he or she is the consignor and the consignee (7–102(b)(3)). The buyer's name will appear on the bill of lading as the person to be notified. Next, the seller draws a draft on the buyer and attaches it to the bill of lading. The seller then takes the draft and the bill of lading to the bank in New York and indorses them. The bank pays the seller his or her money and forwards the documents to its correspondent bank in California. The bank in California presents the draft to the buyer, who pays for the draft and is given the bill of lading. The buyer then surrenders the bill of lading to the carrier and is given the goods.

If the seller is willing to sell to the buyer on credit, he or she can use a nonnegotiable bill of lading, usually referred to as a "straight" bill of lading, in which the buyer is named the consignee. In this case, the carrier will deliver the goods to the buyer without requiring the surrender of the bill of lading.

In *Bishop v. Allied Van Lines, Inc.*, The Appellate Court of Illinois examined the liability of a warehouseman for misdelivery of goods stored under a nonnegotiable bill of lading. The court discussed the warehouseman's duty to act in good faith and observe reasonable commercial standards.

> **FACTS** Husband and wife delivered certain household goods to defendant warehouseman. Defendant issued a nonnegotiable bill of lading, signed by husband. Shortly thereafter, husband and wife filed for divorce. Wife notified defendant not to deliver the goods without further instructions. Defendant, nevertheless, delivered the goods to husband. Wife sued defendant. The trial court dismissed the action.
>
> **DECISION** The Appellate Court reversed. U.C.C. Section 7–404 imposes upon a warehouseman a duty to act in good faith and observe reasonable commercial standards. The warehouseman knew of the adverse claims between husband and wife and should not have delivered until he ascertained the validity of the claims. By delivering to husband, defendant did not meet the duties that the statute imposes and is liable.
>
> *Bishop v. Allied Van Lines, Inc.* (80 Ill. App. 3d 306, 35 Ill. Dec. 632, 399 N.E. 2d 698 [1980])

2. NEGOTIABILITY OF DOCUMENTS OF TITLE

Documents of title are either negotiable or nonnegotiable.

A bill of lading, warehouse receipt, or other document of title is negotiable if by its terms the goods are to be delivered to the bearer or to the order of a named person. If the document does not contain these words of negotiability, it is not negotiable (Section 7–104). Thus, a bill of lading stating that the goods are "consigned to John Smith" would not be negotiable. Although a nonnegotiable document can be assigned, the assignee acquires only the rights of the assignor and takes the assignment subject to defenses that are available against the assignor. In a negotiation of the document of title, the purchaser of the document takes the document free from defects of his or her transferor's title and the claims of third persons (e. g., fraud and theft

[Sections 7–501 and 7–502]). The effect of due negotiation is that it creates new rights in the holder of the document.

There are two ways to negotiate a document of title depending on whether it is an "order" document or a "bearer" document. If it is an order document, it is negotiated by indorsement and delivery of the document. If it is a "bearer" document, it is negotiated by delivery alone. An indorsement is the placing of the transferor's signature on the document, usually on the back of the document. If the indorser only signs his name and writes nothing else on the document, it is called a "blank" indorsement. In such a case, the document can be negotiated by delivery alone. If the indorsement also states that the goods are to be delivered to a certain person, it is called a special indorsement and cannot be negotiated without that person's signature (e.g., indorsement states "Deliver to John Smith" and is signed by the indorser). In such a case, if John Smith wants to negotiate the document further, he must sign the document and deliver it to his transferee. If the document states on its face that it is deliverable to "bearer," or if the indorsement is in blank or states "deliver to bearer," a thief would be able to negotiate the document.

A transferee of a document who wishes to hold the document free from defects must have purchased it in good faith, without notice of a defense against it or claim to it on the part of any person. The transferee must also have paid value for the document in the regular course of business or financing. Such a holder acquires title to the document, title to the goods, and the direct obligation of the issuer (warehouseperson or carrier) to hold or deliver the goods according to the terms of the document free from any defense or claim of the issuer other than those afforded him or her by Article 7 (Section 7–502(1)). The holder's rights cannot be defeated by a stoppage of the goods or surrender of them by the bailee (Section 7–502(2)).

3. WARRANTIES OF TRANSFEROR, INTERMEDIARY, AND INDORSER

The person negotiating or transferring a document of title for value (other than an intermediary or a secured party) warrants to his or her immediate purchaser only that:

1. The document is genuine (e.g., one who purchases a forged document of title may recover from the person who sold it to him or her).

2. The person has no knowledge of any fact that would impair the document's validity or worth.

3. The person's negotiation or transfer is rightful and fully effective with respect to the document and the goods it represents (Section 7–507).

The intermediary (e.g., collecting bank) entrusted with documents warrants only good faith and authority to act (Section 7–508).

The indorser is not liable for any default of the bailee or previous indorsers (Section 7–505). This rule is intended to avoid any reluctance on the part of the transferor about indorsing the document.

4. RIGHTS AND OBLIGATIONS OF BAILEE

A. RIGHTS

The warehouseperson and carrier are entitled to liens to guarantee the collection of unpaid charges (Sections 7–209, 7–307). The right of lien is in addition to any other rights allowed by law to a creditor against his or her debtor.

The bailee's lien is lost if he or she voluntarily delivers the goods or unjustifiably refuses to deliver (Sections 7–209(4), 7–307(3)).

B. OBLIGATIONS

The duty of care of warehousepersons and carriers requires that they act as reasonably careful people would under similar circumstances (Sections 7–204(1), 7–309(1)).

The bailee (warehouseperson or carrier) must deliver the goods to the person entitled under the document who satisfies the bailee's lien and surrenders the negotiable document covering the goods (Section 7–403(1)–(3)). A bailee who delivers to a person who holds a forged document will be liable for misdelivery.

Since a thief or finder of goods cannot pass title, he or she cannot obtain a document of title to goods and thereby defeat the true owner. For example, if a thief deposits stolen goods in a warehouse and receives a negotiable warehouse receipt, the warehouseperson is not liable on the receipt if he or she has surrendered the goods to the true owner, even though the receipt is held by a good faith purchaser, since the receipt does not represent title to the goods.

ILLUSTRATIVE CASES

1. Certified Check or Cashier's Check Not Cash

PERRY v. WEST

110 N.H. 351, 266 A.2d 849 (1970)

KENISON, Chief Justice. The issue in this case is whether a municipality can be compelled to accept a bid for property sold for taxes accompanied by a bank draft or a cashier's check when the municipal ordinance and the announced terms of the auction sale require the bid to be accompanied by "cash or certified check." The facts are not in dispute and the issues have been competently argued and briefed by the parties.

Plaintiffs submitted the highest bid at an auction sale of certain property within the City of Concord conducted by George M. West, Tax Collector, as real estate agent for the City. The City had previously acquired the property by tax sale. * * * The advertisements appearing in the *Concord*

Daily Monitor * * * required that all bids be accompanied "by cash or certified check in an amount to at least 10% of the bid price." Plaintiffs' high bid was accompanied by a bank draft of the New Hampshire Savings drawn on the Mechanicks National Bank and payable to George West, Tax Collector. The second highest bid, submitted by Henry J. Love, was accompanied by a cahsier's check of Concord National Bank payable to the City of Concord. The third highest bid was submitted by Pasquale Alosa and accompanied by United States currency. Lockwood Realty Company submitted the fourth highest bid accompanied by its check certified by the Mechanicks National Bank. * * *

On the day of the auction, November 17, 1969, defendant West, on the advice of the City Solicitor, sent a letter to Alosa and the Perrys advising them that Alosa was the successful bidder. On November 19, 1969, the City executed a quitclaim deed to the property in favor of Alosa, which was never recorded. After a hearing on November 20, 1969, in Merrimack County Superior Court on the petition of the Perrys, the City was ordered to execute and deliver a deed to the Perrys. None of the other bidders was made a party at this hearing. On November 21 the City executed a quitclaim deed in favor of the Perrys which was delivered and recorded.

Alosa filed a petition to enter the action as party defendant which was granted. After a hearing on November 25, 1969, the Court enjoined the Perrys from encumbering, transferring or dealing with any rights of ownership in the property. The other bidders were subsequently added as parties. Defendants' exceptions to the granting of the petition of the Perrys have been reserved and transferred by *Loughlin, J.*

Plaintiffs contend that the bank draft submitted with their bid was "cash" within the modern usage of the term and therefore their bid complied with the terms of the auction. * * *

* * * *

Although the meaning of "cash" may vary with the context of its use, the common meaning is United States currency. * * * Nothing in the present case indicates that the City Council intended to expand this meaning. Indeed the term "certified check" would be unnecessary if "cash" were to include various forms of commercial paper in addition to currency.

The various commercial instruments involved in this case have definite and distinct meanings. A bank draft is merely the instrument of one bank drawing upon its deposits with another bank. A cashier's check is the instrument of a bank drawing upon its own funds. * * * Certification of a check is acceptance by the drawee.

For this case the important distinction among these instruments is the number of parties liable on the instrument. Bank drafts and cashier's checks are "one-name paper." Only the drawer bank is liable on a bank draft until accepted by the drawee. Although a cashier's check is accepted upon issuance, there is only one bank involved and therefore only one party bound on the instrument. * * * However both the drawer and drawee are bound on a certified check. * * * There are therefore accepted and reasonable distinctions among "cash," "certified check," "bank draft" and "cashier's check" upon which the City Council could base its preference for cash or certified check. Within the context of the auction of property sold for taxation the phrase "cash or certified check" had a definite, unambiguous and accepted commercial meaning. * * *

The general rule that a municipality must accept the highest bid, * * * only requires acceptance of the highest bid which conforms to the terms of the auction sale consistent with the governing municipal ordinance. * * * The City did not waive the bidding requirements. It rejected the two highest bids which did not comply with the terms of the auction and accepted the bid accompanied by currency. Subsequent compliance with a court order was not a waiver of the terms by the City. Acceptance of the Perrys' bid by defendant West could have subjected him to personal liability. * * *

Both the City and the public were entitled to rely upon the terms of the auction sale and the controlling ordinance and this Court will not compel the City to waive the conditions in the advertisements and Ordinances. * * * All bidders must have equal opportunity and the city officials must not be required to make subjective evaluations of the apparent financial integrity of the bidders. * * * Certainty in bidding procedures by which all bidders are on an equal basis should not be discouraged in the disposition and sale of municipal property.

Pasquale Alosa, the highest bidder who conformed to the terms of the auction, is therefore entitled to the property upon full payment of his bid price. * * *

Remanded.

2. Note Requires "Words of Negotiability"

FIRST STATE BANK AT GALLUP v. CLARK

91 N.M. 117, 570 P. 2d 1144 (1977)

EASLEY, J.   First State Bank of Gallup (First State), Plaintiff-Appellee sued M. S. Horne (Horne), Defendant-Appellant on a promissory note. The trial court granted summary judgment against defendant and we affirm.

Horne had executed a $100,000 note in favor of R. C. Clark which contained a restriction that the note could not be transferred, pledged or assigned without the written consent of Horne. As part of the transaction between Horne and Clark, Horne gave Clark a separate letter authorizing Clark to pledge the note as collateral for a loan of $50,000 which Clark anticipated making with First State. Clark did make the loan and pledged the note, which was accompanied by Horne's letter authorizing the note to be used as collateral. First State also called Horne to verify that he was in agreement that his note could be accepted as collateral. First State attempted to collect from Horne on Horne's note to Clark which had been pledged as collateral. Horne refused to pay and this suit resulted.

The issues raised on appeal include (1) whether the note was a negotiable instrument for purposes of Article 3 of the Uniform Commercial Code (U.C.C.) * * *. Article 3 of the U.C.C. defines a certain type of readily transferable instrument and lays down certain rules for the treatment of that instrument and rules concerning the rights, remedies and defenses of persons dealing with it.

In order to be a "negotiable instrument" for Article 3 purposes the paper must precisely meet the definition set out in § 3–104, since § 3–104 itself states that, to be a negotiable instrument, a writing "must" meet the definition therein set out. Moreover, it is clear that in order to determine whether an instrument meets that definition *only the instrument itself* may be looked to, *not* other documents, even when other documents are referred to in the instrument. [Citations.] As Hart & Willier, 2 Bender's U.C.C. Service, *Commercial Paper,* § 2.03[1] points out in its text and in footnote 3:

> The applicability of Article 3 must be determined from the instrument itself, without reference to other documents or oral agreements. The "four-corners test" is still applicable: the determination of negotiability under Article 3 must be made by inspecting only the instrument itself.
> * * *
>
> This is clear from the mandatory language of U.C.C. § 3–104, and from the following language from the Official Comment to U.C.C. § 3–105 found under the heading "Purposes of Changes": "The section is intended to make it clear that, so far as negotiability is affected, the conditional or unconditional character of the promise or order is to be determined by what is expressed in the instrument itself. * * *

We recognize the Official Comments to the U.C.C. as persuasive, though they are not controlling authority. [Citation.]

Section 3–104 thus requires that, in order to be a negotiable instrument for Article 3 purposes, one must be able to ascertain without reference to other documents that the instrument:

> (a) [is] signed by the maker or drawer; and (b) contain[s] an unconditional promise or order to pay a sum certain in money and no other promise, order, obligation or power given by the maker or drawer except as authorized by [Article 3]; and (c) [is] payable on demand or at a definite time; and (d) [is] payable to order or to bearer.

The note in question here failed to meet the requirements of § 3–104, since the promise to pay contained in the note was not unconditional. Moreover, the note was expressly drafted to be non-negotiable since it stated:

> This note may not be transferred, pledged, or otherwise assigned without the written consent of M. S. Horne.

These words, even though they appeared on the back of the note, effectively cancelled any implication of negotiability provided by the words "Pay to the order of" on the face of the note. Notations and terms on the back of a note, made contemporaneously with the execution of the note and intended to be part of the note's contract of payment, constitute as much a part of the note as if they were incorporated on its face. [Citation.]

*   *   *

The whole purpose of the concept of a negotiable instrument under Article 3 is to declare that transferees in the ordinary course of business are only to be held liable for information appearing in the instrument itself and will not be expected to know of any limitations on negotiability or changes in terms, etc., contained in any separate documents. The whole idea of the facilitation of easy transfer of notes and instruments requires that a transferee be able to trust what the instrument says, and be able to determine the validity of the note and its negotiability from the language in the note itself. [Citation.] * * *

Since the note in question is not negotiable for Article 3 purposes, First State cannot be a holder in due course under Article 3, and we need not discuss that issue.

*   *   *

The summary judgment of the district court is hereby affirmed for the stated reasons, although we reject the trial court's conclusion that the note in question was a negotiable instrument as contemplated by Article 3.

3. Right To Verify Endorsements

KLOTZ v. FIRST NATIONAL BANK OF TOLEDO
10 Ohio App.2d 62, 226 N.E.2d 804 (1967)

SKEEL, Judge.   This appeal is from a judgment of dismissal of plaintiff-appellant's action seeking damages for an alleged libel. The plaintiff deposited with the defendant-appellee for collection and deposit an instrument in the nature of a bank check or sight draft in the sum of $300, drawn on the Western Federal Savings & Loan Association of Los Angeles, California. The plaintiff's petition alleges that the instrument was doubly endorsed with plaintiff's signature appearing as the second endorsement. It is alleged that the defendant was well informed of plaintiff's standing in the community, his good reputation and impeccable character, and that he was thus recognized and was known as an inventor, physicist and mathematician who has worked for the past several years as an engineering writer.

It is alleged that the defendant wrongfully and with deliberate malice caused to be typed on its (the bank's) collection request form and made known to the bank employees the words, "pay only if payee's endorsement appears genuine." In that form the collection request was sent to Los Angeles.

It is claimed that the defendant therefor and thereby imputed to plaintiff his "possible and probable" forgery of the first endorsement and the possible and probable illegal, unlawful, wrongful, dishonest, fraudulent and criminal possession of the instrument.

It is alleged that by causing such words to be placed on its collection form, the defendant acted with intent to impugn plaintiff's honesty, to ascribe to plaintiff a felonious and criminal personality, to bring plaintiff into disrepute in Toledo and its environs, and with like result in Los Angeles, California. * * * The plaintiff having failed to plead further, the court, upon motion, dismissed plaintiff's action and entered judgment against plaintiff for the costs.

* * * As indicated, this action is based on the conduct of the defendant when plaintiff deposited for collection and deposit a banker's check or sight draft upon which, as he alleged, the plaintiff was the second endorser. There is no claim that he was the payee, nor is the identity of the first endorser or payee disclosed. Without identifying the payee as an endorser, the plaintiff could not claim any clear or absolute right based upon possession of the bank check or draft. The defendant, as it was its right to do, placed on the collection request as indicated, "pay only if payee's endorsement appears genuine." * * *

These paragraphs, as indicated above, allege that the use of the words, "pay only if payee's endorsement appears to be genuine," were intended to attribute to the plaintiff the unlawful forging of the "signatures" appearing as endorsements on the instrument; that such words imputed to plaintiff his "possible and probable" illegal, unlawful, wrongful, dishonest, fraudulent and criminal possession of such instrument; that such words placed on defendant's collection request were intended to impugn plaintiff's honesty and to ascribe to plaintiff a felonious and criminal personality and to bring plaintiff into disrepute in Toledo and Los Angeles. No such interpretation could be reasonably ascribed to the use of such words as used on defendant's collection request. * * *

The possession by an agent for collection of an order for the payment of money gives him the legal right, when in doubt, to seek verification of the genuineness of all endorsers and vests the collection agent with the right to request that his agent verify the genuineness of all endorsements.

*   *   *

Judgment affirmed.

4. Effect of Delivery on Forged Bill of Lading

DAVID CRYSTAL, INC. v. CUNARD STEAM-SHIP CO.

223 F.Supp. 273 (D.C.N.Y., 1963), *affirmed* 339 F.2d 295 (2d Cir.), *certiorari denied* 380 U.S. 976, 85 S.Ct. 1339, 14 L.Ed.2d 271 *and* 380 U.S. 976, 85 S.Ct. 1340, 14 L.Ed.2d 271

Levet, District Judge. This action in admiralty, brought by the libellant, David Crystal, Inc. (Crystal), seeks to recover the value of twenty-eight of its shipment of twenty-nine cases of shirts transported by the respondent, Cunard Steam-Ship Co. (Cunard), pursuant to an ocean bill of lading consigning the goods to Crystal's customs broker in New York, Penson & Company (Penson). * * *

A single sentence suffices to express the essential facts in this case: The cargo in question was discharged from Cunard's vessel to the pier by Clark, the stevedore, and from there misdelivered by Clark upon the presentation of a forged delivery order of the customs broker, Penson, obtained by the thieves through the complicity of one of Penson's employees. While pilferage on the New York docks is not new, the cool assurance with which the conspirators completed the necessary formalities and waited at the pier almost nine hours until the cargo was finally loaded aboard their truck, gives some indication that this was a masterly executed plot to obtain the cargo by persons more than casually familiar with the procedures of the piers and the customs brokers. * * *

At the outset is the question of Cunard's liability. It was undisputed at the trial that the misdelivery occurred after the cargo had been discharged from the vessel in the same good order and condition, segregated on the pier by the stevedore, and notice given to the consignee of the time and place of the delivery.

The bill of lading provides:

> Packages merchandise to be delivered subject to the exceptions, restrictions and conditions of the undermentioned clauses, from the ship's deck where the Shipowner's responsibility shall cease * * *.

* * *

Were a literal reading of the bill of lading permitted, the case would clearly come to a swift end in favor of the carrier. But so easy a solution is not possible. * * *

Cunard's liability as a carrier had ceased and both it and its agent Clark stood as warehouseman in relation to the cargo. The question becomes, what is the liability of a carrier, as warehouseman, for a delivery of the goods to the wrong persons. * * *

The libellant argues that a warehouseman is absolutely liable for a misdelivery without any question as to his negligence. * * * As Professor Braucher of Harvard states, "Delivery to the wrong person, under the Code as under prior law, would seem to subject the bailee to an absolute liablity to the person entitled under the document, even though, for example, the bailee relied on a skillfully forged delivery order."

* * * Libellant Crystal is entitled to an interlocutory decree sustaining its claim for liability against the respondent-petitioner Cunard.

5. Effect of Warehouseman's Exculpatory Clause

KIMBERLY-CLARK CORP. v. LAKE ERIE WAREHOUSE

49 A.D. 2d 492, 375 N.Y.S. 2d 918 (1975)

This was an action brought by a bailor of paper, Kimberly-Clark Corporation (plaintiff), against the warehouseman Lake Erie Warehouse (defendant) to recover for water damage alleged to have been caused by Lake Erie's negligence.

Lake Erie defended on the ground that its Rate Schedule Agreement provided to Kimberly-Clark contained an exculpatory clause. The exoneration paragraphs read as follows:

> Sec. 7(c) Warehouseman shall not be liable for damage to customer's goods which are damaged or destroyed by perils insured against by customer; as evidence of which customer waives any and all right of recovery from warehouseman for losses caused by any other perils against which customer has insured.

Sec. 20 Warehouseman's responsibility for storage and handling is limited to "reasonable care as a reasonably careful owner of similar goods would exercise." Warehouseman shall not be liable for any loss or damage to the goods which could not have been avoided by the exercise of such care nor for loss or damage to insured goods as provided in section 7(c).

DEL VECCHIO, Judge.　The exculpatory provisions were ineffective under § 7–202(3) of the Uniform Commercial Code.

Individually and together the exculpatory provisions were an attempt to exempt the warehouseman from liability for damages to stored goods from perils against which the bailor had secured insurance, even when caused by Lake Erie's negligence. However, a warehouseman's liability is fixed by § 7–204(1) of the Uniform Commercial Code, which states:

> A warehouseman is liable for damages for loss of or injury to the goods caused by his failure to exercise such care in regard to them as a reasonably careful man would exercise under like circumstances but unless otherwise agreed he is not liable for damages which could not have been avoided by the exercise of such care.

Subdivision (2) of the same statutory section provides the extent to and manner in which the liability imposed by the preceding subdivision may be modified:

> Damages may be limited by a term in the warehouse receipt or storage agreement *limiting the amount of liability* in case of loss or damage, *and setting forth a specific liability* per article or item, or value per unit of weight, beyond which the warehouseman shall not be liable; provided, however, that such liability may on written request of the bailor at the time of signing such storage agreement or within a reasonable time after receipt of the warehouse receipt be increased on part or all of the goods thereunder, in which event increased rates may be charged based on such increased valuation, but that no such increase shall be permitted contrary to a lawful limitation of liability contained in the warehouseman's tariff, if any. No such limitation is effective with respect to the warehouseman's liability for conversion to his own use. [Emphasis supplied.]

Section 7–202 of the Code, relating to terms in a warehouse receipt, provides in part:

> (3) A warehouseman may insert in his receipt any other terms which are not contary to the provisions of this Act and *do not impair* his obligation of delivery (Section 7–403) or *his duty of care* (Section 7–204). *Any contrary provisions shall be ineffective.* [Emphasis supplied.]

Thus, the statute imposes on the warehouseman a responsibility for breach of a duty of reasonable care, permits a modification of the amount of liability upon prescribed conditions, compliance with which is prerequisite to such modification, and makes ineffective any other attempt to alter the warehouseman's obligation.

Judgment for Lake Erie Warehouse reversed.

PROBLEMS

1. Ace Holder gave Bill Betton his promissory note for money won by Bill in a game of cards. State law made notes given for gambling debts unenforceable. Bill endorsed the note in due course and for value to California Bank. After due presentment and notice of dishonor, the California Bank sues Bill for the amount of the note. Bill interposes the defense that the note was given for an amount won in an illegal gambling transaction. Decision?

2. Jenson contracted to take a correspondence course and signed an agreement: "In consideration of receiving the lessons in this course, I promise to pay to the order of the Literary Writers Correspondence School $250 in equal installments of $25 each month for ten months, starting one month from the date of this contract."

A few weeks after giving the note to the school, Jenson received a letter from the North American Bank, stating that the bank had purchased his note and instructing him to send all payments to the bank. Jenson refused, claiming that the agreement he had made was a contract with the school, not a negotiable instrument. Decision?

3. The Ace Loan Company's safe contained notes that were signed as follows: (a) Al Baker, Secretary; (b) Harry Rose, cashier of the Midway Department store; (c) Maple Furniture Company, by Moe Woods, treasurer. In reviewing the Ace assets, which, if any, of these notes obligate the signer personally? Why?

4. Liza stored all of her goods in the Watchman Warehouse, obtaining for them a negotiable warehouse receipt making the goods deliverable to Liza's order. Liza then duly negotiated the warehouse receipt to Bill for value. Liza returned to Watchman Warehouse and demanded her goods, which were turned over to her by an employee of the warehouse. Liza then disappeared with the goods and the money Bill had paid her for the receipt. Bill went to pick up the goods and presented the receipt, but, of course, the goods were not available. Bill sued Watchman Warehouse for the wrongful release of the goods. Will Bill be able to collect?

5. Sam Sherman, a debtor from out of town, stopped by the Ace Loan Company to make a payment. He had forgotten his checkbook, and the company had no blanks or counter checks. Sam wrote out what purported to be a check on a plain piece of typing paper, including the requisites of negotiability and his encoded number. Sam claims that this is a valid check when he signs and delivers it to Ace Loan Co. Decision?

6. Boak was a maker of a promissory note payable in installments. The note provided that upon default in the payment of any installment, the holder had the option to declare the entire balance "due and payable on demand." The note was negotiated to Cheryl, who sued Boak for the full debt when he failed to pay a required installment. Boak defended on the ground that no notice of acceleration had been given to him prior to suit. Decision?

7. A and B executed a promissory note as makers. B was in fact an accommodation party. Later S, as a holder, agreed with A to extend the time for payment and to reduce the required monthly payments. A failed to pay. S sued B. B defended on the ground that he was released because A's obligation had been changed by the extension of time granted to A, to which B had not consented. Decision?

8. Lou wanted to pay a bill he owed to Greg but lacked sufficient funds in his bank to do so. Lou drew a post-dated check on his bank account and gave the check to Amos. Amos then gave Lou a check drawn on Amos' bank account for the amount of Lou's check. When Amos was sued on his check by Greg, Amos defended on the ground that he (Amos) was an accomodation party. Decision?

9. National Bank was holder of a note that provided: "This note with interest is secured by a mortgage on real estate, of even date herewith made by the maker hereof in favor of the said payee—The terms of said mortgage are made part hereof by this reference." National eventually sued on the note. Doyle, the defendant, argued that the payee was guilty of fraud in paying the mortgage. National replied that it was a holder in due course. Decision?

10. Davis purchased a lawn mower from Ryan on credit and gave him a promissory note for the balance owing. To induce Ryan to accept the note, Haas wrote on the back "guaranteed" and signed his name. Davis promised Haas that he would never be required to pay the note. Davis defaulted on the note, and Ryan sued Haas. Haas defended on the grounds that Davis' promise immunized him from liability and that, in any case, Ryan could not sue him until Ryan had attempted to collect the balance owing from Davis. Decision?

Chapter 40

NEGOTIABILITY

Negotiable instruments are contracts for the payment of money that must meet certain formal requirements to be classified as negotiable instruments. These contracts can be freely transferred without the normal personal defenses that we find in the assignment of ordinary contracts, and it is in this respect that negotiable instruments differ from ordinary contracts. For example, a thief cannot pass title to stolen goods. However, a thief of a negotiable instrument can pass a good title to the instrument to a purchaser for value without notice of the theft. This chapter covers the requirements of negotiability, the transfer of negotiable instruments, and the holder in due course.

A. REQUIREMENTS OF NEGOTIABILITY

If a written contract is to be negotiable so that its purchaser takes free and clear of personal defenses of the true owner of the instrument, it must conform to the requirements set out in U.C.C. Section 3–104(1):

> Any writing to be a negotiable instrument within this Article must:
>
> (a) be signed by the maker or drawer; and
>
> (b) contain an unconditional promise or order to pay a sum certain in money and no other promise, order, obligation or power given by the maker or drawer except as authorized by this Article; and
>
> (c) be payable on demand or at a definite time; and
>
> (d) be payable to order or to bearer.

1. WRITING AND SIGNATURE

If the instrument is to be negotiable, it must be in writing, which includes typing, printing, and engraving. Ink or pencil may be used; pencil is not advisable, however, because it is not so durable as ink and can be easily altered.

The signature may be in one's own handwriting or printed, engraved, or stamped. The signature may consist of initials, figures, or a mark (U.C.C. Section 1–201(39)). It need not be at the end, but must appear somewhere on the instrument, except in the case of an acceptance of a bill in a separate writing or an indorsement on a paper attached to the instrument.

2. PROMISE OR ORDER

If the instrument is a promissory note, it must contain a promise to pay money; if it is a draft or check, it must contain an order to pay money. An acknowledgment of a debt is not a promise (e. g., "I.O.U., John Smith, the sum of $10,000 (signed) Robert Williams"). An authorization to pay money is not an order (e. g., "We hereby authorize you to pay on our account, to the order of William Smith, the sum of $10,000."). Such instruments are not negotiable, since there is no promise to pay and no order to pay.

3. PROMISE AND ORDER MUST BE UNCONDITIONAL

The promise and the order must not be conditional. For example, an instrument that recites that it is "subject to" the terms of another agreement such as a contract or mortgage is conditional (U.C.C. Section 3–105(2) (a)); an order to pay out of a particular fund is conditional (U.C.C. Section 3–105(2) (b)). However, an instrument that merely indicates a particular account to be debited or any other fund from which reimbursement is expected is not conditional (e. g., "charge my expense account" [U.C.C. Section 3–105(1) (f)]). An instrument that is limited to payment out of a particular fund is not conditional if issued by the government (U.C.C. Section 3–105(1) (g)).

4. SUM CERTAIN

If the instrument is to be negotiable, it must call for the payment of a sum certain (i. e., definite on its face as to how much is to be paid). The sum payable is a sum certain, even though it is to be paid with stated different rates of interest before and after default or a specified date (U.C.C. Section 3–106(1) (b)) or with costs of collection or an attorney's fee, or both, upon default (U.C.C. Section 3–106(1) (e)).

5. IN MONEY

The instrument must call for payment in money. It is payable in money if the medium of exchange in which it is payable is money at the time the instrument is made, if the instrument is payable in currency or current funds, and if it is payable in foreign currency (U.C.C. Section 3–107).

6. TIME OF PAYMENT

The instrument to be negotiable must be payable on demand or at a definite time. An instrument is payable at a definite time if by its terms it is payable at a fixed period after a stated date, at a definite time subject to any acceleration, or at a definite time subject to extension at the option of the holder (U.C.C. Section 3–109). It is not payable at a time certain if it is payable upon the happening of an event that may never happen (e. g., "when John is 21 years old").

An instrument is payable on demand if it states that it is payable on demand, at sight, on presentation, or when no time of payment is expressed (U.C.C. Section 3–108).

7. ORDER AND BEARER

The instrument to be negotiable must be made payable to order or to bearer. When it is stated in the instrument that it is payable to the order of a specified person, it is an order paper (e. g., "Pay to the order of John Smith" or "Pay to John Smith or order"). John Smith would have to deliver and indorse the instrument to negotiate it (U.C.C. Section 3–110, Section 3–202(1)).

An instrument is payable to bearer when it is payable to bearer or the order of bearer, a specified person or bearer, or cash or the order of cash (e. g., "Pay to bearer" or "Pay to John Smith or bearer") (U.C.C. Section 3–111). Bearer paper can be negotiated by delivery alone (U.C.C. Section 3–202(1)).

8. DESIGNATION OF PARTIES

The parties to the instrument must be designated with certainty (i. e., each party must be identified, and the position he or she occupies on the instrument must be indicated). The use of assumed or trade names is sufficient identification.

9. ADDITIONAL RECITALS

Many promissory notes and bonds of corporations contain additional recitals that may or may not affect negotiability. Negotiability is not affected by the following (U.C.C. Section 3–112):

1. Such recitals as an authorization of a confession of judgment (debtor permits judgment to be entered against him or her for a stipulated sum without institution of legal proceedings; such proceedings are not permitted in many states).

2. Statement that collateral has been given for the instrument.

3. Statement that debtor waives the benefit of any law intended for his or her benefit (not permitted in many states).

4. Statement that the indorsement by payee is an acknowledgment of full satisfaction of the debt.

5. Notations on the check as to purpose for which the check was given or the items discharged by the check.

A provision authorizing the holder of the instrument to require an act other than the payment of money (e. g., delivery of goods) makes the instrument nonnegotiable (U.C.C. Section 3–104(1) (b)).

It should be remembered that because an instrument is nonnegotiable does not necessarily mean that it is void. It may still be the basis of a valid contract action. Nonnegotiability means that the instrument is transferred with all defenses, if any, to the transferee; it is the same as an assignment of a contract.

B. TRANSFER OF COMMERCIAL PAPER

Commercial Paper may be transferred from one person to another by negotiation or by an assignment. If transfer is by negotiation, the transferee may get a better legal title than the transferor; if by an assignment, the assignee gets only the title of the assignor. A negotiable instrument is assigned when it is an order instrument and it has been transferred without an indorsement.

Commercial paper is negotiated by delivery or by delivery and indorsement. If the instrument is payable to bearer on its face, it may be negotiated by delivery alone. If the instrument is payable to order, it is negotiated by delivery with the indorsement of the holder. If it is payable to order on its face and the last indorsement is in blank (indorser only signs his or her name), it may be negotiated by delivery alone.

1. INDORSEMENTS

The holder of an instrument may indorse the instrument by merely signing his or her name, or he may add other words to it. The indorsement must be on the back of the instrument, unless it is all filled up, in which case it may be written on a paper attached to the instrument. If a holder adds such words as "I hereby assign the within instrument to John Smith" to his or her signature, such a transfer will constitute a valid negotiation by indorsement and delivery. Such language of assignment does not constitute a restrictive indorsement. When the holder signs a guarantee of payment on the back of the instrument, the character of the indorsement is not affected. The addition of a waiver of presentment and notice does not affect the character of the indorsement (U.C.C. Section 3–202(4)).

When an instrument is made payable to a person under a misspelled name or one other than his or her own name, the person may indorse in that name or his or her own name or both. Signature in both names may be required by a person paying or giving value for the instrument (U.C.C. Section 3–203).

U.C.C. Sections 3–204, 3–205, 3–206, 3–414(1) provide for four kinds of indorsements: special, blank, restrictive, and without recourse.

A. SPECIAL

A special indorsement specifies the person to whom or to whose order the instrument is to be payable (e. g., "Pay to John Smith (signed) Robert Jones" or "Pay to the order of John Smith (signed) Robert Jones"). The special indorsee's indorsement (Robert Jones) is necessary for further negotiation of the instrument. He may also indorse specially or in any other proper form.

A special indorsement transfers title to the instrument, imposes a liability on the indorser to pay the amount of the instrument under certain conditions, and creates certain warranties (U.C.C. Sections 3–414, 3–417).

B. BLANK

A blank indorsement specifies no indorsee and consists of a mere signature. An instrument so indorsed is payable to bearer and may be negotiated by delivery alone. Bearer paper may also be converted to order paper by writing a special indorsement over the blank indorsement (e. g., if John Smith endorses in blank and delivers to Richard Jones, Richard can write above John Smith's signature the words "Pay to Richard Jones"). This will protect Richard Jones in case the instrument is stolen, since his signature is now necessary to transfer the instrument. Although blank indorsements are common, they are dangerous to use, since a finder or thief can negotiate by delivery alone.

The negotiation of a blank indorsement passes ownership of the instrument, imposes on the indorser a liability to pay the amount of the instrument under certain conditions, and creates certain warranties (U.C.C. Sections 3–414, 3–417).

In *Palmer and Ray Dental Supply of Abilene, Inc. v. First Nat'l. Bank,* the Court of Civil Appeals of Texas reviewed the question whether a blank endorsement on a check was an authorized indorsement making the depository bank free of liability for payment to a dishonest employee of the maker.

> **FACTS**   Palmer and Ray's bookkeeper, Wilson, was instructed to deposit certain checks in the company's account. Wilson brought the checks to the bank and dishonestly cashed them and did not account to the company for the money she received. Wilson indorsed the checks with a rubber stamp that printed only Palmer and Ray's company name and address. Palmer and Ray sued the bank for wrongful conversions of the checks.

> **DECISION**   The court dismissed the suit. It held that the indorsements, consisting of only plaintiff's name and address, were authorized blank endorsements (U.C.C. Sections 1–201(43), 3–204). When the bank delivered cash to Wilson, the bearer, it was not guilty of conversion.

> *Palmer & Ray Dental Supply of Abilene v. First National Bank* (477 S.W. 2d 954 [Tex. Civ. App., 1972])

C. RESTRICTIVE

A restrictive indorsement specifies the use to be made of the paper. U.C.C. Section 3–205 makes the following indorsements restrictive:

1. A conditional indorsement states that it is to be effective only upon the satisfaction of a specific condition (e. g., "Pay to John Smith upon completion of building").

2. A purported prohibition of further transfer indorsement *appears* to pro-

hibit further transfer but does not, as it is restrictive in form only (e. g., "Pay to John Smith only") (U.C.C. Section 3–206(1)).

3.   A for collection or deposit indorsement uses such words as "for collection," "for deposit," or "pay any bank" to show an intention as to the use of the instrument. *Fultz v. First National Bank in Graham* illustrates the effect of a bank's failure to comply with such an indorsement.

> **FACTS**   Plaintiff, Fultz, indorsed certain checks "For Deposit Only." Defendant bank paid part of the amount of the checks to an employee, McCoy, who was not authorized to sign checks on the account or to withhold cash amounts from the deposits made for Fultz and who misappropriated the funds.

> **DECISION**   The court held that the bank was liable to Fultz, because it failed to follow his instructions carried on the restricted indorsement "For Deposit Only." The court also ruled that Fultz should have been able to rely on the bank to follow the deposit instructions and was under no further duty to ascertain if the bank had followed his instructions.

> *Fultz v. First Nat'l Bank in Graham* (338 S.W. 2d 405 [Tex., 1965])

4.   A trust indorsement that makes the indorsee the agent or trustee of the indorser is restrictive in that it states that the indorsement is for the benefit or use of the indorser or another person (e. g., "Pay John Smith as agent for Robert Jones (signed) Richard Paul," "Pay John Smith for account of Robert Jones (signed) Richard Paul," "Pay John Smith in trust for Robert Jones (signed) Richard Paul").

A restrictive endorsement can be ignored by a bank except when it has been made by the person presenting the instrument to the bank for payment or transferring it to the bank. However, a restrictive indorsement must be recognized by a depositary bank (i. e., one in which the customer deposits the instrument).

D.   WITHOUT RECOURSE

A nonrecourse indorsement is made by using the following words with the signature: "without recourse" (e. g., "Without recourse (signed) Richard Paul"). Such an indorsement limits the liability of the indorser (e. g., to escape liability to his or her transferee if the maker becomes insolvent and is not able to pay or in the case of an attorney who is merely indorsing to his or her client a check made payable to the client and the attorney by a third person [in such a case, the transferee of the check would not expect the attorney to guarantee the check when he or she is not a party to the transaction]).

A nonrecourse indorsement does not affect the passage of title or the negotiable character of the instrument.

C.   HOLDER IN DUE COURSE

A holder in due course (H.D.C.) is a bona fide purchaser of the instrument for value without notice of any defect in the instrument or wrongdoing in connection with it. A holder in due course takes the instrument free of all personal defense (such as lack of consideration, fraud in the inducement, or that it was stolen) but not of real defenses (such as forgery). U.C.C. Section 3–302 establishes certain requirements for becoming a holder in due course.

1.   WHO MAY BECOME A HOLDER IN DUE COURSE

A.   In General

Almost anyone can become a holder in due course, even a payee. However, the person must take the instrument for value, in good faith, and without notice of any defects. U.C.C. Section 3–302(2) provides that a payee may be a holder in due course (e. g., where he or she deals through a third person). A payee who deals directly with the drawer, as in the typical case, would have knowledge of any defense that the drawer might have and thus could not be an H.D.C.

B.   Holder Through an H.D.C.

A holder who derives his or her title through an H.D.C. and who is not himself or herself a party to any fraud or illegality has all the rights of an H.D.C., even though he or she cannot satisfy the requirements of an H.D.C. For example, a payee by fraud induces a drawer to issue a check to him. The payee negotiates the check to an H.D.C. The H.D.C. negotiates the check to John Smith, who knows of the fraud. Since John Smith takes the rights of the H.D.C., he can enforce the check against the drawer (U.C.C. Section 3–201(1)).

C.   Reacquirer

A reacquirer is a holder of an instrument who negotiates the instrument and then reacquires it. A reacquirer who was an H.D.C. the first time he or she acquired the instrument will hold it as an H.D.C., even though the reacquiror was not an H.D.C. when he or she reacquired it (i. e., the reacquirer is remitted to his or her former position).

D.   Those Who Cannot

A buyer who purchases goods at a sale that is not of an ordinary commercial nature cannot be an H.D.C. (e. g., purchaser at a judicial sale; sale of assets of an estate; or bulk sale not in the regular course of business) (U.C.C. Section 3–302(3)).

2. REQUIREMENTS OF DUE COURSE

To be a holder in due course, the person must have taken the instrument for value, in good faith, and without notice it was overdue or dishonored or had any defense against it or claim to it (U.C.C. Section 3–301(1)).

A. VALUE

A holder takes the instrument for value:

1. To the extent that the agreed consideration has been performed (U.C.C. Section 3–303(a)). For example, on June 1, payee indorses a $2,000 note to H for H's promise that he will pay payee the sum of $1,000 on July 1 and $1,000 on August 1. On July 1, H pays payee $1,000, at which time, H becomes an H.D.C. to the extent of $1,000. If after July 1 and before August 1, H should learn of a defense to the note, he will not be able to improve his position as an H.D.C.

2. When the holder takes the instrument in payment of or as security for an antecedent claim, whether or not it is due (U.C.C. Section 3–303(b)). For example, D owes C $1,000, which is due on June 1. On May 15, D receives a negotiable note for $1,000 from M which he transfers to C as payment for the debt. C is an H.D.C.

Pazol v. Citizens National Bank of Sandy Springs illustrates the rule that a holder who takes a check in payment of a prior debt takes "for value" and becomes an H.D.C.

> **FACTS** Pazol issued a check payable to Eidson Construction Company. Eidson wrote "For Deposit" on the check and deposited it in its checking account with the Citizens National Bank. Eidson promptly withdrew the funds from its account. When Citizens presented the check for payment, the check was dishonored. Citizens sued Pazol to recover a judgment for the amount of the check. Pazol defended on the ground that Citizens was not a holder in due course of the check.
>
> **DECISION** When Eidson withdrew the funds from its account, Citizens became a holder for value (U.C.C. Sections 3–302(1)(a), 4–208, 4–209). The court determined that Citizens met the other requirements of U.C.C. Section 3–302(1) and held it to be a holder in due course. The court concluded that it could therefore enforce payment against the drawer.
>
> *Pazol v. Citizens National Bank of Sandy Springs* (110 Ga. App. 319, 138 S.E.2d 442 [1964])

3. When the holder gives a negotiable instrument for the instrument or makes an irrevocable commitment to a third person (U.C.C. Section 3–303(c)). For example, payee gives holder a $1,000 negotiable note in exchange for holder's guarantee of a $1,000 loan by bank to P. Holder has made an irrevocable commitment to a third person (bank) and so is an H.D.C.

4. When a purchase at a discount is for value (U.C.C. Section 1–201(32)). The courts do not measure the value given unless it is so slight as to be

evidence of fraud. In this respect, value in a negotiable instrument is the same as in an ordinary contract.

B. GOOD FAITH

" 'Good faith' means honesty in fact in the conduct or transaction concerned" (U.C.C. Section 1–201(19)). Giving a small value for the instrument can cause the question of good faith to arise. Bad faith is established by proving that the transferee knew certain facts that rendered it improper for him or her to acquire the instrument (e. g. knew that fraud was involved). What is meant by good faith sufficient to establish H.D.C. status is illustrated in the following case.

> **FACTS** Plaintiff agreed to pay defendant, World Wide Distributors, over $1000 in return for an inexpensive piece of furniture and an opportunity to earn money by advertising World Wide's products. Plaintiff signed a note for the purchase price. World Wide sold the note to People's National Fund. The sales scheme was a fraud, and World Wide disappeared. People's contends that even though World Wide may have been guilty of fraud, it can collect on the note because it was a holder in due course.

> **DECISION** To be a holder in due course, People's must have acted in good faith (U.C.C. Sections 1–201(19), 3–302(1)(b)) and without notice that it has any defense against it (U.C.C. § 3–302(1)(c)). People's had dealt with World Wide in the past, and it had good reason to be suspicious of World Wide's sales practices. Since People's did not inquire further under these suspicious circumstances, the court deemed it to have knowledge of World Wide's fraud and held that it was not a holder in due course.

Norman v. World Wide Distributors, Inc. (202 Pa. Super. 53, 195 A. 2d 115 [1963])

C. NOTICE OF OVERDUE OR DISHONORED INSTRUMENT

To qualify as an H.D.C., the purchaser of an instrument must not know that it was overdue or had been dishonored (refusal to pay instrument when due). When an instrument is not paid when due, it may be for the reason that the debtor has a good defense. Although the H.D.C. may not know this, the law assumes that he or she knows there is a defense when the paper is overdue; hence, the purchaser cannot be an H.D.C. A purchaser of an instrument with a fixed date must take the instrument before that date arrives. A demand instrument must be purchased within a reasonable time after its issue. A reasonable time for a check drawn and payable in the United States is presumed to be 30 days (U.C.C. Section 3–304(3) (c)). A holder cannot be an H.D.C. if he or she has reason to know that an installment of principal is delinquent, or that an acceleration of the instrument has been made (U.C.C. Section 3–304(3) (a) (b)). Knowledge of a delinquint interest installment does not disqualify such a holder. (U.C.C. Section 3–304(4)(f)).

D. IGNORANCE OF DEFENSES AND ADVERSE CLAIMS

A purchaser cannot be an H.D.C. if he or she knows of defenses or adverse claims by prior parties to the instrument (e. g., knows that defective goods were given for the instrument [failure of consideration]).

The purchaser has notice of a claim or defense in the following instances:

1. If the instrument is so incomplete, bears such visible evidence of forgery or alteration, or is otherwise so irregular as to call into question its validity, terms, or ownership or to create an ambiguity (U.C.C. Section 3–304(1)(a)).

2. If the purchaser has notice that the obligation of any party to the instrument is voidable in whole or in part or that all the parties have been discharged (U.C.C. Section 3–304(1)(b)).

3. If the purchaser has notice of misappropriation by an agent or fiduciary, in which case he or she has notice of the claim of the principal (U.C.C. Section 3–304(2)). What constitutes sufficient notice of a claim so as to defeat H.D.C. status is the subject of *Salter v. Vanotti*.

> **FACTS** Defendant Vanotti bought a parcel of land and executed a promissory note secured by a mortgage on the lot. Shortly thereafter, plaintiffs purchased the note at a 40 percent discount. The sellers breached the sales contract, entitling Vanotti to rescind the contract. Vanotti stopped payment on the note. Plaintiffs claimed that they were holders in due course and therefore could collect on the note regardless of the buyer's defenses against the sellers.
>
> **DECISION** The court held that the plaintiffs were not holders in due course. The issue was whether plaintiffs, at the time they bought the note, had notice of any defense against the note on the part of any person (U.C.C. Section 3–302(1)). The Code provides that a holder meet this notice requirement if he or she has actual knowledge or has facts from which he or she has reason to know of the defenses when coming into possession of the note. Here plaintiffs knew, from the contents of many documents delivered with the note, that the buyer had possible defenses against the note.
>
> *Salter v. Vanotti* (42 Colo.App. 448, 599 P.2d 962 [1979])

U.C.C. Section 3–304(4) states that certain facts do not of themselves prevent a purchaser from becoming an H.D.C.:

1. The instrument is antedated or postdated.

2. Consideration for the instrument remains executory (e.g., instrument given for goods not yet delivered).

3. A party has signed as an accommodation party.

4. An incomplete instrument has been properly completed.

5. A person negotiating the instrument is or was a fiduciary.

6. There has been a default in payment of interest on the instrument.

The filing or recording of a document does not of itself give such notice that would prevent a purchaser from becoming an H.D.C. (U.C.C. Section 3–304(5)) (e. g., recording notice of action to cancel a note and mortgage does not give notice to a purchaser).

ILLUSTRATIVE CASES

1. Signature Requirements

TESORO PETROLEUM CORP. v. SCHMIDT

210 Neb. 537, 316 N.W.2d 290 (1982)

PER CURIAM. This was an action to recover judgment on a promissory note brought by the plaintiff, Tesoro Petroleum Corporation, against the defendants, Alvin W. Schmidt and Dean's Service Co., a corporation. Trial to the court alone resulted in judgment in favor of the plaintiff and against Dean's Service Co. in the amount of $19,035.55, but in favor of Schmidt as to whom the action was dismissed. It is from this last action of the District Court that Tesoro has appealed, assigning as error the admission of parol evidence surrounding Schmidt's execution of the note and the sufficiency of the evidence to support a judgment of dismissal in favor of Schmidt.

Dean's Service Company was incorporated by Schmidt's wife, Maxine, who was the president and sole stockholder. Schmidt was the vice president and secretary, as well as manager of the gasoline service station operated by the corporation in Scottsbluff.

The service station was owned by Tesoro and was the subject of a lease between Tesoro and Dean's which was executed for the latter by Schmidt in his representative capacity as vice president. He was the one principally involved with Tesoro in the regular business dealings, and the invoices for goods received from Tesoro were marked with the names "Dean's Service Co." and "A. W. Schmidt." Schmidt paid all the bills from the corporate checking account.

For reasons not apparent on the record, Dean's Service Co., Inc., executed a promissory note on July 1, 1976, payable to Tesoro Petroleum Corporation in the amount of $13,779.09. That note is reproduced in [part on page 625]. Other than the state of the signatures, we would only call attention to the words "jointly and severally" which were apparently added with a typewriter to a printed form near the top of the note.

Tesoro's petition alleged that no payments have been made on the note, that demand had been made upon both parties for payment of the same on December 21, 1976, and prayed for judgment for the face amount of the note plus interest, according to its terms. Schmidt's answer contained a general denial, and he also raised the defense that his signatures on the note were

PROMISSORY NOTE

$ 13,779.09   San Antonio   Texas, *July 1st 1976*

jointly and severally

For value received, I, We, or either of us, as principals/promise to pay to the order of   Tesoro Petroleum Corporation, Post Office Box 17536, 8700 Tesoro Drive

.... in the City of   San Antonio ,   Bexar   County, Texas, the sum of

Thirteen thousand seven hundred seventy nine and 09/100 *************** Dollars ($ 13,779.09),

in legal and lawful money of the United States of America, with interest thereon from date hereof until maturity at the rate of .... eight .... per cent (8 %) per annum; the interest payable .... ; matured unpaid principal and interest shall bear interest at the rate of ten per cent (10%) per annum from date of maturity until paid.

This note is due and payable as follows, to-wit:

    The first payment of $3,779.09 due on ~~September~~ 1, 1976 with the remaining $10,000.00 being retired by thirty-six (36) equal monthly payments of principal and interest in the amount of $ 313.36 each beginning ~~October 1~~, 1976, and each successive payment becoming due and payable on the first day of each succeeding month.

Address   Scottsbluff, Nebraska 69361

Date: *8/1/76*   By: *Dean's Service Co. Inc. Mgr   Alvin W Schmidt*

          Dean's Service Co., Inc.   Alvin W. Schmidt

---

made in a representative capacity and did not give rise to a personal obligation on his part.

At trial Schmidt admitted the authenticity of the signatures and the validity of the debt at the time of execution of the note. He made no claim that any payments had been made. He was permitted, over the objection of Tesoro, to testify that at the time he signed the note he had not intended to become personally obligated on the same. No other testimony was offered to the court. The note, however, was received in evidence.

The note in question comes within the form of a negotiable instrument as it is described in Neb. U.C.C. § 3–104. Therefore, the resolution of the issue regarding Schmidt's personal obligation on the note is governed by Neb. U.C.C. §§ 3–401 et seq. in general, and § 3–403 in particular. * * *

Section 3–403 governs the liability of one who signs an instrument as an authorized representative of another. The record sufficiently establishes that Schmidt was an authorized representative of Dean's Service Co. at the time he signed the note in question. The fact that the note identifies the "person represented," namely Dean's Service Co., Inc., removes subsection (2)(a) from consideration, allowing the focus to be shifted to subsections (2)(b) and (3) only. These sections provide: "(2) An authorized representative who signs his own name to an instrument (a) is personally obligated if the instrument neither names the person represented nor shows that the representative signed in a representative capacity; (b) except as otherwise established between the immediate parties, is personally obligated if the instrument names the person represented but does not show that the representative signed in a representative capacity, or if the instrument does not name the person represented but does show that the representative signed in a representative capacity. (3) Except as otherwise established the name of an organization preceded or followed by the name and office of an authorized individual is a signature made in a representative capacity."

In this case, Schmidt's signature appears on the note twice. The signature, which appears in the following form,

/s/ Alvin W. Schmidt, Mgr.

By /s/ Dean's Service Co., Inc.
Dean's Service Co., Inc.

fits well within the provisions of § 3–403(3). The name of an organization, Dean's Service Co., Inc., is preceded by the name and office of an authorized individual, Alvin W. Schmidt, Mgr. Therefore, this signature was clearly "made in a representative capacity" as a matter of law and need be considered no further.

* * *

Schmidt argues that a reasonable construction of the signature appearing above the typed name of Alvin W. Schmidt, when read in conjunction with the remaining signatures, meets the requirements of § 3–403(2)(b), a section which, he alleges, allows the admission of parol evidence to show that the signature was in fact made in a representative capacity.

The other side of the argument, of course, is that the second signature was entirely superfluous to the obvious representative execution of the note and that the note was drafted with the intent that both Dean's Service Co., Inc., and Alvin W. Schmidt be bound to the note, as is apparent from the typewritten addition to the notes of the words "jointly and severally." As such, the signatures and the note are not ambiguous and do not permit the admission of parol evidence.

[The court ruled that Schmidt's testimony that he did not intend to be personally liable was insufficient] to overcome his burden to prove that the note was not signed in his personal capacity.

* * *

* * * [W]e find that mere subjective intent of the maker of a promissory note not to be personally bound is insufficient to rebut the presumption of personal obligation under § 3–403 when that intent is not shown to have been communicated in some manner to the other party to the note. The trial court was clearly wrong in determining that the evidence, even if admissible, was sufficient to support a dismissal of the action against Schmidt.

* * *

[The court concluded that Tesoro was entitled to judgment in the full amount of the note. By bringing suit, Tesoro signified his election to accelerate the payment of the debt in default.]

The judgment of the District Court in favor of Schmidt is reversed and the cause is remanded with directions to enter judgment for Tesoro in accordance with this opinion.

2. Requirement of Definite Time

McLEAN v. PADDOCK

78 N.M. 234, 430 P.2d 392 (1967)

NOBLE, Justice. The circumstances giving rise to this appeal began in 1958 when Carl R. Paddock and Essie Paddock, his wife (hereafter referred to as Paddocks), executed a real estate listing authorizing Harper Realty Company, a real estate broker (hereafter referred to as Harper), to sell their motel. Harper produced a purchaser acceptable to Paddocks, and a binder agreement was executed, reciting a deposit of $1,000 and providing for a further cash down payment of $8,000 on a total price of $249,000. * * * Paddocks and the purchaser thereafter executed a real estate contract which, among other things, directed the Albuquerque National Bank, escrow agent, to pay Harper $75 per month from the purchaser's monthly installment payments. Concurrently with the execution of the real estate contract, Paddocks executed a promissory note in the principal amount of $12,388.20, payable to Harper in monthly installments of $75, representing the balance of the commission. The note was unconditional in its terms and contained no reference to the real estate contract, nor did the contract refer to the note. Harper negotiated this promissory note to Alexander and William McLean (hereafter referred to as McLeans) in May, 1959. Payments on the note becoming in default in January, 1960, McLeans elected to declare the whole balance due, as provided in the note, and sued Paddocks. * * *

The trial court found that Harper had orally agreed the note would be paid solely from the monthly installments on the purchase price of the motel, and that Paddocks were induced to sign the note by Harper's false representation that a note was required in order to authorize the escrow agent to make these monthly payments to Harper. The court concluded that McLeans were holders in due course, finding they had no knowledge of Harper's misrepresentations. Judgment was, accordingly, entered in favor of McLeans and against Paddocks.

* * * The Paddocks challenge the court's determination that the McLeans were holders in due course of a negotiable instrument on several grounds. * * * The note here involved is dated August 9, 1958, and reads:

> For value received, I, we, or either of us promise to pay to Harper Realty, or order, the sum of Twelve Thousand Three Hundred Eight-eight and 20/100 Dollars, said amount to be paid in equal installments of Seventy-Five and no/100 Dollars, each, payable monthly after date beginning _____ 1, 1958 and on the first day of each month thereafter until the whole amount first herein named and any interest or costs shall have been paid in full. * * *

Two contentions arise from the failure of the note to specify, in the blank space indicated, the month in which payments were to begin. Pointing to the requirement that the instrument "[m]ust be payable on demand, or at a fixed or determinable future time," the Paddocks argue that this note lacks negotiability. Alternatively, they argue the blank space prevents the

McLeans from taking an instrument "[t]hat is complete and regular upon its face" * * *

The Paddocks note is "payable monthly after date." The note is dated August 9, 1958. If the instrument had stopped at this point, it could not be doubted but that payments would have commenced September 9, 1958. The following language making payments due on the first day of each month does not create a fatal ambiguity under either theory of the Paddocks. Construing the instrument as a whole, it seems clear that the first payment was intended to be September 1, 1958. * * *

The judgment in favor of McLeans against Paddocks should be affirmed.

3. Endorsements Must Be on or Attached to Instrument

LAMSON v. COMMERCIAL CREDIT CORPORATION

187 Colo. 382, 531 P.2d 966 (1975)

DAY, J.   A chronology of the transactions and the subsequent court trial and appeal draws the issues into focus. Originally, the drawer Commercial Credit Corporation ("the Corporation") issued the two checks payable to Rauch Motor Company ("Rauch"). Rauch indorsed the checks in blank, deposited them to its account in University National Bank ("the Bank"), and received a corresponding amount of money. The Bank stamped the checks "pay any bank," and initiated collection. However, the checks were dishonored and returned to the Bank with the notation "payment stopped." Rauch was obliged to return the money advanced. Its account with the Bank was then overdrawn, but through subsequent deposits Rauch regained a credit balance, which the Bank used to repay itself.

Some months later, to compromise a lawsuit, the Bank executed a special two-page indorsement of the two checks to the plaintiff Lamson. Lamson sued the defendant drawer Corporation on the checks. The Corporation pled a twofold defense. It affirmatively alleged fraud in the inducement and prior payment by Rauch.

The trial court found that the Corporation failed to prove fraud or any other defense. It concluded the defense of payment was unavailable under the Uniform Commercial Code, Section 1–3–306 . . . 1973. Judgment was entered for Lamson for the face amount of the checks plus the legal interest.

In reversing the trial court the Court of Appeals held as a matter of law the plaintiff Lamson was not a holder of the checks. It arrived at the decision by ruling that the Bank's indorsement to Lamson was not in conformance with the Uniform Commercial Code because it was stapled to the checks.

When Ranch deposited the checks, it indorsed them in blank, transforming them into bearer paper. Section 4–1–201(5) and 4–3–204(2). The Bank in turn indorsed the checks "pay any bank." That is a restrictive indorsement. Section 4–3–205(c). After a check has been restrictively indorsed, "only a bank may acquire the rights of a holder . . . (u)ntil the item has been specially indorsed by a bank to a person who is not a bank." Section 4–4–201(2)(b).

There is no question that the checks were indorsed to Lamson by name, thus qualifying as a special indorsement. Section 4–3–204(1). The problem is whether the special indorsement was correctly and properly affixed to the checks under Section 4–3–202(2). It provides inter alia that "(a)n indorsement must be written * * * on behalf of the holder and on the instrument or on a paper so firmly affixed thereto as to become a part thereof."

The subject indorsement was typed on two legal size sheets of paper. It would have been physically impossible to place all of the language on the two small checks. Therefore, the indorsement had to be "affixed" to them in some way. Such a paper is called an allonge. In this case the allonge was affixed by stapling it to the checks.

We agree with the Court of Appeals' statement that a separate paper pinned or paperclipped to an instrument is not sufficient for negotiation. However, we hold, contra to its decision, that the section does permit stapling as an adequate method of firmly affixing the indorsement. Stapling is the modern equivalent of gluing or pasting. Certainly as a physical matter is it just as easy to cut by scissors a document pasted or glued to another as it is to detach the two by unstaplng. Therefore we hold that under the circumstances described, stapling an indorsement to a negotiable instrument is a permanent attachment to the checks so that it becomes "a part thereof."

Section 4–201(20) defines a holder as "a person who is in possession of * * * an instrument * * * indorsed to him * * *." The Bank's special indorsement stapled to the two checks, effectively made Lamson a holder, although not a holder in due course.

[The judgment is reversed, and the case remanded with directions to reinstate the judgment of the trial court.]

4. "Good Faith" Required of Holder in Due Course

ARCANUM NATIONAL BANK v. HESSLER
69 Ohio St. 2d 549, 433 N.E. 2d 204 (1982)

[Appellant Hessler executed some promissory notes payable to John Smith Grain Company. Without the knowledge or consent of appellant, John Smith Grain Company sold the notes to appellee, Arcanum National Bank. The bank sued Hessler to recover the amount of the notes.]

KRUPANSKY, Justice.   The sole issue in this case is whether appellee is a holder in due course who takes the note free from appellant's defense of want of consideration.

In a suit by the holder of a note against the maker, the holder obtains a great advantage if granted the status of holder in due course. R.C. Chapter 1303 (Article 3, U.C.C.) provides that a holder in due course takes the instrument free from most defenses and claims. One such defense which is of no avail when raised against a holder in due course is want of consideration, the defense raised by appellant.

Whether one is a holder in due course is an issue which does not arise unless it is shown a defense exists. Once it is established a defense exists, the holder has the full burden of proving holder in due course status in all respects.

* * *

Appellant contends appellee has not established holder in due course status because appellee took the instrument with notice of a defense against it. We agree.

* * *

Appellant also contends, in essence, appellee bank failed in its burden of proving holder in due course status because appellee failed to establish it took the note in good faith as required under UCC 3–302(A)(2).

"Good faith" is defined as "honesty in fact in the conduct or transaction concerned" UCC 1–201(19). Under the "close connectedness" doctrine, * * * a transferee does not take an instrument in good faith when the transferee is so closely connected with the transferor that the transferee may be charged with knowledge of an infirmity in the underlying transaction. * * *

* * *

According to White and Summers, noted authorities on the Uniform Commercial Code, the following five factors are indicative of a close connection between the transferee and transferor:

(1) Drafting by the transferee of forms for the transferor; (2) approval or establishment or both of the transferor's procedures by the transferee (e.g., setting the interest rate, approval of a referral sales plan); (3) an independent check by the transferee on the credit of the debtor or some other direct contact between the transferee and the debtor; (4) heavy reliance by the transferor upon the transferee (*e.g.,* transfer by the transferor of all or substantial part of his paper to the transferee) and; (5) common or connected ownership or management of the transferor and transferee.

An analysis of the above factors in relation to the facts of this case, as set forth in the trial court's findings, reveals an unusually close relationship between appellee bank (the transferee), the John Smith Grain Company (the transferor-payee) and J & J Farms, Inc.

Appellee provided John Smith Grain Company with the forms used in the transaction and supplied the interest rate to be charged. At the time of the purchase of the first note, appellee bank ran an independent credit check on appellant. There is evidence of a heavy reliance by John Smith Grain Company upon appellee bank insofar as it was customary for the grain company to transfer substantially all of its commercial paper to appellee bank. There was not only a common director of appellee and John Smith Grain Company, but also common directors or management between John Smith Grain Company and J & J Farms, Inc. H. K. Smith was a director of appellee bank and the president and director of John Smith Grain Company. C. North, Jr., was an officer and director of both John Smith Grain Company and J & J Farms, Inc. John Milton Smith was officer and director of John

Smith Grain Company and officer of J & J Farms, Inc. In addition, the trial court found that B. Henninger, the executive vice-president of appellee who had previously been employed by John Smith Grain Company, frequented John Smith Grain Company several times a week between November 1976 and January 1977 to advise the officers of John Smith Grain Company on business practices. During that time, John Smith Grain Company was experiencing serious financial difficulties.

The facts of this case clearly indicate such close connectedness between appellee bank and John Smith Grain Company as to impute knowledge by appellee bank of infirmities in the underlying transaction. * * *

                              *   *   *

* * * Not only do the facts indicate appellee bank was aware of the impending bankruptcy of John Smith Grain Company, but they also show appellee had reason to know of a fatal infirmity in the underlying transaction, viz, there was no consideration given by John Smith Grain Company for the note. C. North, Jr., an officer and director of both John Smith Grain Company and J & J Farms, Inc., obtained appellant's signature and advised appellant to sign his wife's name on the note. As an officer and director of J & J Farms, Inc., C. North, Jr., undoubtedly was aware that at the time he obtained appellant's signature, the hogs had already been mortgaged by J & J Farms, Inc. It is well-established in Ohio a corporation can act only through its officers and agents, and the knowledge of the officers of a corporation is at once the knowledge of the corporation. If North, as officer and director of both John Smith Grain Company and J & J Farms, Inc., knew there was no consideration for the note, then such knowledge is imputed to both corporations. Thus, H. K. Smith, as president and director of John Smith Grain Company, had ample reason to know of the failure of consideration; and since H. K. Smith was also a director of appellee bank, his knowledge is imputed to appellee bank.

The executive vice-president of appellee bank, B. Henninger, who had previously been employed by John Smith Grain Company, was also in close contact with John Smith Grain Company at the time appellant signed the note. According to the trial court's conclusions, at the time appellant's signature was obtained on the note, B. Henninger was meeting several times a week with the officers of John Smith Grain Company to advise them on business practices. At that time, the officers of John Smith Grain Company included H. K. Smith, who was also a director of appellee bank, and C. North, Jr., who was also an officer and director of J & J Farms, Inc.

Given these facts, one cannot conclude with absolute certainty that appellee bank had actual knowledge of the failure of consideration. As appellant correctly states in his brief, however, the doctrine of close connectedness was developed in part because of the difficulty of proving the transferee's actual knowledge of problems in the underlying transaction. The doctrine allows the court to imply knowledge by the transferee when the relationship between the transferee and transferor is sufficiently close to warrant such an implication.

Under the circumstances of this case, we find the relationship between appellee bank and John Smith Grain Company was so entwined that it was error for the trial court not to apply the doctrine of close connectedness to find appellee bank failed to carry its burden of proving good faith.

If we accept the trial court's findings of fact and apply the close connectedness doctrine, we can reach only one conclusion, viz., appellee bank did not take the note in good faith.

Upon either one or both of the above reasoned theories, *i.e.,* (1) notice of a defense and (2) close connectedness doctrine, we find the Court of Appeals erred in affirming the trial court's finding that appellee bank was a holder in due course. The judgment of the Court of Appeals is, therefore reversed.

5. Warranty on Transfer of Instruments

OAK PARK CURRENCY EXCHANGE, INC. v. MAROPOULOS

48 Ill.App.3d 437, 6 Ill. Dec. 525, 363 N.E.2d 54 (1977)

John Bugay possessed a check drawn to the order of Henry Sherman, Inc., and fraudulently indorsed "Henry Sherman" on the reverse side. Bugay sought the assistance of defendant, James Maropoulos, in cashing it. Defendant took Bugay to the plaintiff, Oak Park Currency Exchange, Inc., where defendant was known. At the currency exchange defendant identified himself, and the exchange agreed to cash the check if defendant would indorse it. He indorsed the check, received the money, and gave it immediately to Bugay.

Plaintiff indorsed and deposited the check in Belmont National Bank. The indorsement "Henry Sherman" was subsequently found to be a forgery. The bank sought and received payment back from plaintiff. Plaintiff, in turn, sought payment from defendant on his indorsement and for breach of warranty and filed this suit. The trial court directed a verdict in favor of defendant, and plaintiff appealed.

GOLDBERG, P.J.   * * * In this court, plaintiff urges that defendant breached his warranty of good title when he obtained payment of a check on which the payee's indorsement was forged and that there was sufficient evidence to support a directed verdict in favor of plaintiff. Plaintiff's contentions are based exclusively on Section 3–417(1) of the Code. Defendant contends that an accommodation indorser does not make warranties under Section 3–417(1) and that the trial court properly directed a verdict for the defendant.

A party who signs an instrument "for the purpose of lending his name to another party to . . ." that instrument is an accomodation party. Section 3–415(1). Such a party "is liable in the capacity in which he has signed * * *" Section 3–415(2). Therefore defendant is an accommodation indorser and would be liable to plaintiff under his indorser's contract, provided that he had received timely notice that the check had been presented to the drawee bank and dishonored. Section 3–414. Because these conditions precedent to the contractual liability of an indorser have not been met, defendant is not liable on his contract as an accommodation indorser.

Furthermore, the drawee bank, American National, did not dishonor the check but paid it. This operated to discharge the liability of defendant as an accommodation indorser.

The portion of the Code upon which plaintiff seeks to hold defendant liable is Section 3–417 entitled "Warranties on Presentment and Transfer." * * * Section 3–417(1) sets out warranties which run only to a party who "pays or accepts" an instrument upon presentment. We note that presentment is defined as "a demand for acceptance or payment made upon the maker, acceptor, drawee, or other payor * * *" Section 3–504(1). As applied to the instant case, the warranties contained in Section 3–417(1) * * * run only to the payor bank and not to any other transferee who acquired the check. In the case before us, plaintiff is not a payor or acceptor of the draft. * * * The case before us involves a transferee, not a party who paid or accepted the instrument. Thus it appears that reliance by plaintiff upon subsection 3–417(1) was misplaced. * * *

An additional theory requires affirmance of the judgment appealed from. Subsection 3–417(2) of the Code provides that one "who transfers an instrument and receives consideration warrants to his transferee * * *" that he has good title. * * * The evidence presented in the case at bar establishes that defendant received no consideration for his indorsement. Though Mrs. Panveno [plaintiff's employee] testified that she saw Bugay hand defendant some money as the two left the currency exchange, she also testified that defendant stated that he was doing a favor for his friend; that she was not paying close attention to the two men and that she did not watch them as they walked away from her. Thus her testimony was considerably weakened by her own qualifying statements and it was strongly and directly contradicted by the positive and unshaken testimony of defendant that he received nothing in return for his assistance. The simple fact standing alone that this witness saw Bugay hand some money to defendant, even if proved, would have no legal significance without additional proof of some type showing that the payment was consideration for defendant's indorsement.

Judgment affirmed.

PROBLEMS

1. The payee of a check endorsed it to Hal for value. At the time of the endorsement, the payee looked like a tramp—he was dressed in old clothes and had a beard of several days growth having just returned from a fishing trip. Hal took the check for a 10% discount. Hal was actually innocent when he purchased the check even though the attendant circumstances looked suspicious. It is contended that Hal cannot be a holder in due course. Decision?

2. Robert Jones had signed the following instrument: "Los Angeles, California, 7/1/83. I promise to pay to the order of Paul Payee Ten Thousand Dollars ($10,000) one year from date with interest at the rate of 7% per annum from date. If this note is not paid at maturity, it shall bear interest at the rate of 9% per annum from maturity until paid and costs of collection and reasonable attorney fees. (Signed) Robert Jones." A dispute arises as to whether or not this is a negotiable instrument. Decision?

3. Randall was a salesman on a business trip to Tokyo. He called upon a client who purchased several thousand dollars worth of supplies from him and offered to Randall in payment a draft properly drawn on a San Francisco correspondent bank and made payable in yen. Randall refuses to accept, arguing that it is nonnegotiable since it is made payable in Japanese yen. Decision?

4. Bill Smith was the payee of a check made out to his order. Before it was endorsed, he lost the check. John Finder found it on the floor of the bank and transferred it without endorsement to Joe Brown, a holder who paid value and took it without notice that it had been lost. Joe claims that it has been transferred to him by negotiation and he is a holder in due course. Decision?

5. Morton Marker writes out in longhand, "I, Morton Marker, promise to pay to Paul Porter or order, $100. Does this instrument meet the requirement that a negotiable instrument must be signed?

6. Wendy sued Harlan for divorce. As a result Wendy received a property settlement. Under its terms, a demand note signed by Harlan, payable to the order of Wendy's father, was to be transferred to Wendy later. Wendy's father delivered the note to her but did not indorse the paper or write anything on the note. When Wendy's father died, Wendy sued Harlan on the note. Harlan refused to pay the note, arguing that Wendy could not sue because she was not the owner of the note. Decision?

7. Martin acquired a check by indorsement. At the time Martin acquired the check, he knew all the circumstances surrounding the original issue of the check. Had he known the legal implications of those circumstances, Martin would have realized that the drawer of the check had a valid defense. Not knowing the law, Martin took the check in good faith, believing that all was well. When Martin sued on the check, Stein, the defendant, argued that Martin was not a holder in due course because Martin knew the facts constituting the defense and that his ignorance of the law is no defense. Decision?

8. Francis issued and delivered a check to Lee in payment of an automobile. On the face of the check was written "car to be free and clear of liens." The check was indorsed and delivered by Lee to the Lance Company. When Lance sued Francis, Francis defended on the grounds that Lance was not a holder in due course because the words "car to be free and clear of liens" gave notice of defenses of fraud in the inducement and failure of consideration. Decision?

9. In settlement of his bill at the Ritzy Hotel, Ralph gave Bill his signed blank check with instructions to cash it for $800 and give the cash to the hotel. The hotel charges totaled $3,000. Bill made the check out for $3,000 and delivered it to the Ritzy Hotel. Ralph later stopped payment on the check. The Ritzy then sued Ralph for the hotel bill. Ralph defended on the grounds that the Ritzy did not take the check in good faith since they should have noticed that the check was signed by Ralph and completed in a different handwriting. The Ritzy replied that they were a holder in due course. Decision?

10. A drew a check on National Bank payable to B for cattle feed. The printed portion of the check incorrectly stated the amount as $3,430. The handwritten amounts were for $13,430. B instructed his wife to go to Federal Bank. The B's did not have an account at Federal, but they were known to the bank. B's wife cashed the check for the larger amount after Federal verified sufficient funds with National Bank. Then A stopped payment on the check after learning of conflicting claims to the proceeds, which B's wife had mentioned to the Federal Bank. National Bank, as drawee, dishonored the check. Federal then sued A as drawer. A defended on the grounds that Federal was not a holder in due course because there was an irregularity on the face of the check; that the check was already indorsed; that it was obviously a business-expense check; and that the bank knew about the conflicting claims to the proceeds. Decision?

Chapter 41

DEFENSES

The maker or drawer of a negotiable instrument may or may not be liable to the payee. For example, the payee may have sold and delivered the drawer defective goods, which would be a defense to the instrument (failure of consideration). Similarly, the maker or drawer may or may not be liable to a holder in due course. A maker or drawer who has only a personal defense to the instrument must pay the H.D.C., although the maker or drawer who has a real defense is not liable to the H.D.C.

A. PERSONAL DEFENSES

There are five personal defenses: failure of consideration, fraud in the inducement, lack of delivery, payment or cancellation, and unauthorized completion. There are two defenses that can be personal or real: illegality and duress.

1. FAILURE OF CONSIDERATION

The most common defense, failure of consideration arises whenever a party to a contract receives less than he or she bargained for (e. g., defective goods (U.C.C. Section 3–408)).

2. FRAUD IN THE INDUCEMENT

A person who knows that he or she is signing a negotiable instrument and knows its contents but is induced into signing it by false representations can raise the defense of fraud only against the party with whom he or she bargained and not against an H.D.C. For example, M signs a promissory note to P for the purchase of a used automobile relying on false representations by P as to the condition of the automobile. P negotiates the note to an H.D.C. M has no defense against the H.D.C. M's remedy will be a suit for fraud against P.

3. LACK OF DELIVERY

Failure to deliver a negotiable instrument is only a personal defense and not good against an H.D.C. (e. g., drawer makes out a check to cash and leaves it on his desk and a thief sells the check to an H.D.C). Lack of delivery of the check is not a good defense (i. e., a thief or finder can pass good title to an H.D.C.) (U.S.C. Sections 3–305, 3–306(c)).

Watkins v. Sheriff of Clark County illustrates that a seller of goods can become a holder in due course of an instrument transferred by someone other than the rightful owner. Furthermore, the transferor is not guilty of the crime of obtaining money under false pretenses.

> **FACTS** Mrs. Bluiett endorsed her payroll check for $185.59 in blank and left it on her dresser at home. The next day, the check and other items were missing. That same day, Watkins used the $185.59 check to purchase goods worth $73.21. Watkins was charged with the crime of obtaining money (the $112.38 change) under false pretenses from the seller.

> **DECISION** Watkins was not guilty of obtaining money under false pretenses. One element of that crime is that the person from whom the money is obtained, the seller, must sustain injury. Here, the seller was a holder in due course, having met the requirements of U.C.C. Section 3–302 (value, good faith, no notice of claim to the instrument). Therefore, seller can cash the check and receive its full value and will not have been injured. (This case does not preclude the state from charging Watkins with other crimes).

> *Watkins v. Sheriff of Clark County* (85 Nev. 246, 453 P.2d 611 [1969])

4. PAYMENT OR CANCELLATION

A person who pays a debt represented by a negotiable instrument should always take possession of the instrument or be certain that it is destroyed. If he or she does not, a dishonest holder can negotiate it; and if the new holder is an H.D.C., he or she takes free of the defense of payment. When a person liable on an instrument and the holder agree to cancel the instrument, the person liable should be certain that he or she takes possession of it or that it is destroyed. Otherwise, the holder can negotiate it to an H.D.C., in which case the defense of cancellation is not valid.

5. UNAUTHORIZED COMPLETION

When a person signs a check or note and leaves blank the name of the payee, the amount, or any other term, and the instrument falls into the hands of a thief or a dishonest person who fills in the check or note and then negotiates it to an H.D.C., the drawer or maker has no defense (U.C.C. Section 3–407(3)).

6. ILLEGALITY

If a statute declares that an instrument is void when issued in a particular type of illegal transaction, illegality is a real defense. In the absence of such a statute, it is only a personal defense (U.C.C. Section 3–305(2) (b)). For example, New York has a statute that provides that an instrument given in payment of a gambling debt is void, but California, which prohibits certain types of gambling, has nothing in its statutes declaring that instruments given in payment of a gambling debt are void. Thus, in New York, the instrument would be void, and the drawer would have a good defense, but not so in California (H.D.C. would prevail). Ordinarily, illegality is only a personal defense. This distinction, in a gambling context, was noted and reaffirmed by the Supreme Court of Nevada in *Sea Air Support, Inc., v. Herrmann.*

> **FACTS**   Herrmann wrote a check to a casino to repay money unknow-ingly advanced for gambling. Sea Air Support, an assignee, sued Herr-mann to recover the amount of the check.

> **DECISION**   Judgment for Herrmann. First, despite the fact that gam-bling, where licensed, is legal in Nevada, debts incurred and checks drawn for gambling purposes are void and unenforceable. Second, Sea Air Support was not a holder in due course, as it had not given value and was on notice of defenses against the check.

> *Sea Air Support, Inc. v. Hermann* (96 Nev. 574, 613 P.2d 413 [1980])

7. DURESS

Duress in the form of threatened great bodily injury or death is a real defense (contract is a nullity), but anything less is only a personal defense (contract voidable) or not a defense at all (U.C.C. Section 3–305(2) (b)). For example, payee tells drawer that if he does not sign the check he will not speak to him again (no defense at all); payee tells drawer that if he does not sign the check he will tell newspapers that his wife is a bigamist (contract voidable and only a personal defense). However, if payee tells drawer that if he does not sign the check he will shoot him in the head and he holds a revolver to his head, the instrument is void and the drawer has a good defense against an H.D.C. Duress in the law of negotiable instruments is the same as in the law of contracts. It is very difficult to draw the line between duress as a personal defense and duress as a real defense.

B. REAL DEFENSES

There are four real defenses: forgery, fraud in the inception or execution, incapacity, and material alteration. As previously stated, illegality and du-ress can also be real defenses.

1. FORGERY

Forgery is treated in negotiable instruments the same way we treat counterfeit money; both are valueless. If a signature is forged or signed without authority, the purported drawer or maker has a real defense against the holder in due course. Forgery may be ratified, in which case the drawer or maker would be liable. The defense of forgery may be lost under the doctrine of estoppel if one permits a forgery by negligence. (U.C.C. Section 4–404).

2. FRAUD IN THE INCEPTION

When a person is induced to sign a negotiable instrument by fraud and does not know the nature of the instrument or does not know the essential terms, it is fraud in the inception and the person has a good defense against an H.D.C. (e. g., an illiterate person signs a negotiable note on the representation it is a receipt) (U.C.C., Section 3–305(2) (c)). However, if a person has reasonable opportunity to obtain knowledge of the character of the instrument or its essential terms and does not do so, his or her defense of fraud will be personal and not available against an H.D.C.

In *Reading Trust Co. v. Hutchison,* the court looked at a number of circumstance to determine whether the seller had fraudulently induced the buyers to sign the sales contract.

> **FACTS**   A salesman for Gracious Living, Inc. used high-pressure sales tactics and got the Hutchisons to sign a sales contract and note. Plaintiff bank sued to collect on the note. The Hutchisons claimed that the salesman had tricked them into signing the note, leading them to believe it was another document.

> **DECISION**   Judgment for bank. The bank was a holder in due course. U.S.C. Section 3–305(2)(c) would permit a buyer to avoid payment on a note where the buyer was fraudulently induced to sign. Here the facts did not support that defense. The Hutchisons were educated and literate, there was no particular reason for them to rely on the salesman's word, and there was no pressing reason for them to sign the note that night. The salesman's words alone were not sufficient to support a defense of fraud.

> *Reading Trust Co. v. Hutchison,* (35 D. & C. 2d 790 [Pa., 1964])

3. INCAPACITY

A minor can avoid an obligation to an H.D.C. on a negotiable instrument as he or she can on a contract (U.C.C. Section 3–305(2) (a)). A mentally incompetent person can avoid his or her obligation to an H.D.C. if state law provides that the contracts are void but not if only voidable. For example, a California statute provides that a *judicially* declared incompetent's contracts are void, but if not declared so judicially, then only voidable. Thus, in California, a judicially declared incompetent would have a real defense against an H.D.C. If incompetent and not judicially declared so, the person would have only a personal defense (U.C.C. Section 3–305(2) (b)).

4. MATERIAL ALTERATION

Where there has been a material fraudulent alteration of an instrument, (e. g., raise in amount), there is a partial defense against an H.D.C. (i. e., the H.D.C. can enforce the instrument according to its original terms). The defense of material alteration can be lost by ratification or by negligence (e. g., leaving blank spaces in which words or figures may be inserted) (U.C.C. Sections 3–407; 3–406).

C. ADVERSE CLAIMS

An adverse claim is a claim by a third person that he or she and not the holder is the real owner of the instrument. For example, a check is made payable to payee. Subsequently, it is indorsed to A, B, and C. A then claims that B induced him into transferring the check to him by fraud, that he rescinds said transfer, and that he is therefore the true owner of the check. A will not prevail against C, the H.D.C.

An H.D.C. takes free of all adverse claims except a forged indorsement. For example, a thief steals a note from payee, endorses payee's name to it, and sells it to H.D.C. Payee will be able to recover the note from H.D.C. (U.C.C. Sections 3–207, 3–305(1), 3–306, 3–404 (1)).

ILLUSTRATIVE CASES

1. Defense Available to Holder in Due Course Against Prior Claims

BRICKS UNLIMITED, INC. v. AGEE

672 F. 2d 1255 (5th Cir., 1982)

TATE, Circuit Judge. * * * In 1976, Ralph Agee and his wife, Shelby Agee, were domiciled in Louisiana. On April 4, 1976, Ralph Agee executed a demand note in favor of Bricks Unlimited, Inc., a Louisiana corporation. Mr. Agee signed the note individually and as president of Agee Construction Co., Inc.

Some time later, the Agees moved to Mississippi and became domiciliaries of that state. They purchased a home in Jackson, Mississippi. The demand note in favor of Bricks Unlimited, however, was left unpaid.

After amicable demands for payment of the note produced no results, Bricks Unlimited brought a diversity action on the note against Ralph Agree in Mississippi federal district court on October 26, 1978. Bricks Unlimited prevailed in its suit and obtained a final judgment, dated September 26,

1979, in the amount of $17,031.80, plus interest. Agee did not appeal.

* * *

After recording its judgment in accordance with Mississippi law, Bricks Unlimited caused a writ of garnishment to be served on Dena Sutton on February 6, 1980. Sutton answered the writ on February 25, 1980. She admitted that she was indebted to Ralph Agee "and [his] wife, Shelby Agee, jointly, in the sum of $15,000 [plus interest], evidenced by a promissory note and deed of trust in said sum payable to said parties."

* * * However, * * * prior to the time Sutton answered the writ, the Agees pledged the note and the deed to the Commercial Bank and Trust Company of Metairie, Louisiana ("the Bank"), as security for a $10,000 loan. * * * The Bank was not aware of the garnishment at the time it accepted the Sutton note as collateral for this $10,000 loan.

* * *

The Bank claims that the Sutton note is a negotiable instrument and that, as a holder in due course of this instrument, it is entitled to priority of payment over Bricks Unlimited, the garnishing creditor. We agree.

* * *

The Bank undisputedly was a "holder" of the Sutton note, because the instrument was delivered to the Bank with the necessary endorsements of both Ralph and Shelby Agee. *See* UCC § 3–202(1). Under the UCC, a holder in due course is a holder who takes a negotiable instrument: 1) for value, 2) in good faith, and 3) without notice that it is overdue or has been dishonored or of any defense against or claim to it on the part of any person. UCC § 3–302. The Bank took the note "for value," because a holder who takes a negotiable instrument as collateral for a loan takes "for value" within the meaning of the UCC. And the bank took in good faith and without notice of any claims, because it is undisputed that the Bank was not aware of the Bricks Unlimited claim at the time the Agees negotiated the note to the Bank. Therefore, the Bank was a holder in due course of the Sutton note, so it took the instrument "free from all claims to it on the part of any person." UCC § 3–305(1).

* * *

Because the Bank was a holder in due course of the Sutton note, it is entitled to first priority with respect to the * * * funds. As noted previously, a holder in due course takes the instrument "free from all claims to it on the part of any person." UCC § 3–305(1). This provision means that the holder in due course "takes the instrument free * * * from all liens, equities or claims of any other kind." UCC § 3–305, Official Comment 2. In effect, therefore, the UCC reaffirms the traditional rule that, in order to protect the marketability of commercial paper, the claim of a holder in due course is superior to that of a garnishing creditor, even if the instrument was negotiated after service of a writ of garnishment.

* * *

2. Defense Available Against Holder in Due Course (Alteration and Lack of Authority)

BROGAN CADILLAC–OLDSMOBILE CORP. v. CENTRAL JERSEY BANK & TRUST CO.

183 N.J. Super. 333, 443 A. 2d 1108 (1981)

SCHWARTZ, J. S. C.   This issue in this case is whether a holder in due course of a check may recover the amount of the check from a defendant whose blank check has been stolen and then completed by forgery.

* * * The court is required to determine whether a motion to dismiss the action must be granted under the circumstances of this case despite plaintiff's contention that a jury question is presented by virtue of *N.J.S.A.* 12A:3–406 which provides:

> Any person who by his negligence substantially contributes to a material alteration of the instrument or to the making of an unauthorized signature is precluded from asserting the alteration or lack of authority against a holder in due course or against a drawee or other payor who pays the instrument in good faith and in accordance with the reasonable commercial standards of the drawee's or payor's business.

Defendant bank had kept a series of unbound prenumbered checks in a vault which was locked each evening and opened each morning by officers who possessed the safe combination. The vault was not located in an area open to the public and a limited number of persons were authorized to enter the vault.

The checks were printed at the instance of defendant bank and used by it for the payment of certain obligations. They were drawn on the Chase Manhattan Bank and were mainly used to reimburse that bank after defendant bank issued to its customers and received payment for money orders drawn against the Chase Manhattan Bank.

On November 16, 1979 defendant learned that two checks of this stock of checks had been cashed in another area of the State, and after investigation found that these checks and 20 others in this group, prenumbered 4092 to 4123, were missing from the vault.

Lower-numbered checks and high-numbered checks were found intact. At no previous time had any bank officer or employee actually examined all of the checks *seriatim* to ascertain if the printer or the Chase Manhattan Bank had delivered all of the checks that were supposed to comprise the large stock of checks.

Defendant bank had no previous larcenous or embezzled loss experience. Neither the bank nor the police authorities were able to ascertain when or how the 22 checks came to be missing. The bank notified all banks in the area to be on the look-out for persons attempting to pass forged checks of this series.

On January 5, 1980 plaintiff sold an automobile to a buyer for $22,000 and accepted in payment one of the checks of this group, numbered 4113, made payable to the buyer and endorsed to plaintiff. The names of the signers on the check were actually the names of the officers of defendant bank. When plaintiff deposited the check and found it was a forged instrument, it sought recovery from defendant bank.

The persons whose names appeared as signatories testified they had no recollection of ever seeing a blank check numbered 4113; that they did not prepare a check made payable to the car buyer, did not sign such check and did not know the buyer.

The legislation refers to negligence, the violation of a duty on the basis of which damage was foreseeable. No testimony was introduced to support a claim of failure on the part of the bank to abide by any standard of due care recognized in bank practices.

Was it reasonably foreseeable that a theft of checks kept in a bank vault would occur? Even if crime is prevalent, does a duty arise to take steps to protect others against it?

Was the bank precluded from asserting the unauthorized signatures as a defense to the claim of the holder in due course in light of the statute providing relief for such holders against any "person who by his negligence substantially contributes * * * to the making of an unauthorized signature"?

By way of analogy, if a woman secures a checkbook from her bank, places it into her handbag, enters the public street and is the victim of a purse-snatcher who subsequently forges her check, should a jury be permitted to determine if she was guilty of negligence? Compare this to a situation where the woman placed the checkbook in her pocket and inadvertently let it fall to the street, where it was picked up and fraudulently used.

It would be unjust to require one to anticipate that a crime will be committed unless there has been a warning or unless a previous criminal act occurred in the same premises. * * *

* * *

* * * [I]n our case no evidence was offered of previous criminal conduct within the bank which would call for special steps to be taken by the bank.

In *Fred Meyer, Inc. v. Temco Metal Products Co.,* (1973), the Supreme Court of Oregon concluded that a company whose checks had been stolen and forged was not negligent in failing to guard against theft or forgery. Although a previous burglary had taken place, the company kept the checks in an unlocked filing cabinet from which they were stolen and signatures forged. A protectograph, by which amounts were imprinted on the stolen checks by the burglar, was kept in an unlocked desk drawer also.

The court said the issue should be withdrawn from the jury when the conduct of defendant falls outside the "community's conception of fault." It further said:

> This is not a case in which conduct may be negligent for failure to foresee that such conduct may involve an unreasonable risk of harm to another person through the *negligent* conduct of a third person. Instead, this is a case in which it is contended that defendant was negligent for failure to foresee that his conduct may involve harm to another through the *criminal* conduct of a third person. See Restatement of Torts (2d) sec. 302A and sec. 302B. Under normal circumstances a person may reasona-

bly assume that no one will violate the criminal law. Restatement, *supra,* sec. 302B, Comment d.

*   *   *

There is a clear absence of evidence in this case to support a factual conclusion of negligence on the part of defendant. The conduct of defendant bank was outside the scope of the law's conception of fault. The statute does not apply.

Further, there is no evidence that check No. 4113 was evern in the hands of the bank officials. It is just as likely that someone employed by the printing firm or the Chase Manhattan Bank withdrew the 22 checks before delivery of the stock of checks to defendant bank.

Defendant's motion for entry of judgment in its favor shall be granted.

3. Fraud and Usury as a Real Defense

RICKS v. BANK OF DIXIE

352 So.2d 798 (Miss., 1977)

[The Bank of Dixie sued J. V. Ricks, Jr., and others for the collection of a promissory note. The note was signed by J. V. Ricks, Jr., and payable to the order of Dixie Machine Works. Dixie Machine Works then indorsed to the Bank of Dixie.

Ricks contended that his signature was obtained by fraud because Dixie Machine Works represented that the document was an order, sold on open account, for additional materials and equipment.]

Sugg, J.   A decision of the issue requires determination of this threshold question, did J. V. Ricks, Jr. sign the note on behalf of the defendants because of misrepresentation which induced him to sign the note with neither knowledge nor reasonable opportunity to obtain knowledge of its character or its essential terms?

*   *   *

The defense authorized by section 75–3–305(2)(c) is a limited defense and may be asserted against a holder in due course only if a party was induced to sign an instrument because of misrepresentation coupled with the fact that the party signing the instrument had neither, (1) knowledge of its character or its essential terms, nor (2) reasonable opportunity to obtain knowledge of its character or essential terms. * * *

*   *   *

* * * In order to determine if the defense in this case meets the * * * test, we must consider the evidence which was before the trial court.

The evidence shows without conflict that J. V. Ricks, Jr. signed a promissory note on October 7, 1974 payable to the order of Dixie Machine Works and plaintiff on behalf of all the defendants. The original note was introduced in evidence and is a negotiable instrument under the requirements of section 75–3–104 Mississippi Code Annotated (1972). Plaintiff purchased the note from Dixie Machine Works for a valuable consideration on October 21,

1974 and the note was negotiated on that date in accord with section 75–3–202 Mississippi Code Annotated (1972). Plaintiff met the requirements of section 75–3–302 and became a holder in due course.

The only witness offered by defendants was J. V. Ricks, Jr., who testified that, on the date the note was executed, he signed numerous purchase orders and he thought the note was a verification of terms. He signed all documents presented to him on that day without reading any of them. The witness has a college education and is a businessman with many years of experience. J. V. Ricks, Jr. did not use ordinary care when he signed the note without reading it and putting it into circulation: he was not prevented from reading the note; therefore, defendants' claim of misrepresentation has no legal substance. His testimony fails to establish that he was induced to sign the note. "[W]ith neither knowledge nor reasonable opportunity to obtain knowledge of its character or its essential terms."

In this case the trial court had before it testimony which was not in conflict on the issues to be resolved. It properly considered the evidence, not in conflict, of both plaintiff and defendants in arriving at its decision to grant the peremptory instruction, and correctly decided the issues of law from nonconflicting facts.

In sum, the defendants executed a promissory note through their partner, the partner was an educated businessman who signed the note without reading it, the note was negotiated to plaintiff for a valuable consideration, plaintiff became a holder in due course, and defendants did not establish their affirmative defenses. The trial court correctly granted the peremptory instruction for the plaintiff.

*   *   *

[Affirmed.]

4. Illegality as a Real Defense

GLASSMAN v. FEDERAL DEPOSIT INSURANCE CORP.
210 Va. 650, 173 S.E.2d 843 (1970)

SNEAD, C.J. The trial court held, first, that if the notes were given for gambling losses, they would be invalid under Code, § 11–14, even in the hands of a holder in due course. Code, § 11–14 declares, in part, that "All * * * contracts and securities whereof the whole or any part of the consideration be money or other valuable thing, won * * * at any game * * * shall be utterly void."

In *Lynchburg Nat'l Bank* v. *Scott,* 91 Va. 652, 22 S.E. 487 (1895), we held that a usurious note, which the applicable Virginia statute declared "illegal," could be enforced against the maker by a holder in due course. We recognized, however, that the holder could not have enforced the note if the statute had declared it "void," rather than illegal.

We therefore agree with the trial court's holding that even though Crown Savings was a holder in due course * * * the note should be held invalid under Code, § 11–14, if Glassman proved that the notes were given for gambling losses.

Glassman testified that the gambling losses resulted from a gin rummy game that took place during August and September of 1963 at the Golden Triangle Motor Hotel in Norfolk, Virginia. He stated that his losses totaled about $100,000. The participants in the game, besides Glassman, were George Vantraub, and the two Halprin brothers, Jack and Burt.

After losing a substantial sum, and after the notes were given, Glassman discovered that the cards with which the game had been played were marked.

Richard B. Keeley testified for Glassman. Keeley at the time of the game was manager of the Golden Triangle Motor Hotel. He stated that of his own knowledge he knew of the gin game and had been present at some of the sessions. He corroborated Glassman's testimony as to the participants in the game, the general period during which it was played, and that the cards were marked. He stated that he saw scores kept and knew that Glassman was losing. He also testified that he did not actually see the notes or any money passed.

Glassman stated that after he had lost all his cash, "I had no money coming in, and I gave these notes, and it was a gambling debt." On advice of counsel Glassman notified the banks with which he did business not to honor the notes. Crown Savings was not among those banks.

Although the trial court sat as a jury and heard the witnesses (with the exception of Ridley) we cannot agree with the determination that Glassman failed to prove by a preponderance of the evidence the facts on which his defense rests. To establish his case by a preponderance it is not necessary that he eliminate every doubt or question in the mind of the trier of fact. In our view his testimony established the existence of the gin game, its participants, its location, the general period during which it was played and the fact that it was rigged against him. All this was corroborated by Keeley.

* * *

[Reversed.]

PROBLEMS

1. Payee representes that certain land is readily irrigable and that the soil is good for raising oranges. M, in reliance on the representations, gives Payee his negotiable note for the purchase price. Payee negotiates the note to an H.D.C. M learns that the property is in the desert, not irrigable, and that the soil is poor for oranges. M refuses to pay the note. Decision?

2. M executes a note payable to bearer and forgets it on a counter at the bank. X finds the note and negotiates it to an H.D.C. May the H.D.C recover from M?

3. D gave an order check to P for $5.00. The check was so drawn that figures could be inserted between the dollar ($) sign and the number 5. On the line where the word "five" appeared, there was room to the left to insert several words. P inserted the numbers "90" next to the number 5, and the words "nine hundred and" next to the word five. P then negotiated the check for the sum of $905 to H. D refused to pay H. Decision?

4. M gave an order check to P for value. P negotiated the check to a minor. The minor negotiated the check to A, who negotiated it to an H.D.C. The minor rescinds the transfer to A and claims the check. Decision?

5. P represented to M that an instrument he was asking M to sign was a contract by which P was hiring M as an employee. M was unable to read, and there was no one nearby to read the instrument to him. M signed the note. P negotiated it to an H.D.C. Can the H.D.C. recover from M?

6. B wished to make major improvements to his home. B contracted with C, a contractor, to do the work. C made numerous false representations that they had already purchased material to be used in doing the job. Relying on these false statements, B executed a check to C's order. On the same day C received the check, they cashed it at National Bank. B soon discovered that no material had been purchased and stopped payment on the check. National sued B on the check. B defended on the grounds that the illegal transaction rendered the check a nullity in the hands of a holder in due course. Decision?

7. The Metropolitan Company purchased three cars at auction from Frascone, for which Metropolitan gave Frascone two checks naming Frascone's Auto Sales as payee. Frascone had an account at S&L Bank where he presented the checks and was given cash for them. Metropolitan stopped payment on the checks. When S&L sued Metropolitan as a holder in due course, Metropolitan argued that S&L forfeited such status because S&L did not take the check in good faith and had not exercised ordinary care in the transaction. Metropolitan charged that S&L had not adhered to its own internal policies in that their teller had failed to obtain branch manager approval of these corporate checks drawn on another bank, as required. Decision?

8. A, by fraudulent representations, induced B to buy 100 shares of Acme Company stock. The shares were worthless. On May 5, B delivered to A a promissory note for $5000 in full payment for the shares, due six months after date. On May 25, A indorsed and sold the note to C for $4800. In October, B, made aware that C held the note, told C of the fraud and stated that he refused to pay the note. On December 1, C negotiated the note to D, who, while not involved in the fraud, knew of the fraud perpetrated upon B. D sues B on the note, claiming holder in due course status. Decision?

9. Based on false representations made to him by S, M, a minor, purchased a used motor boat for his aquatic business from S. M signed an installment contract and gave S a promissory note for $500 as a down payment on the motor boat contract, which read "I promise to pay to the order of S, six months after date, the sum of $500 without interest. This is given as a down payment on installment contract for motor boat. (signed) M." S later sold his boat dealership, including M's note, to H. On the back of M's note S had written, "Collection guaranteed. (signed) S", and handed it to H. H left the note in his office safe, but E, a dishonest employee, stole the note and sold it to F for $300, indorsing the note "(signed) S." M's note, otherwise complete, was left undated. In F's presence, E inserted the current date. F sued M on the note. Decision?

10. Penn installed equipment in Morgan's store. Morgan signed and delivered to Penn a promissory note payable to the order of Penn for $1100, the purchase price, due in 30 days. Ten days later Penn, short of funds, returned to Morgan's store and, told Morgan he would accept $1000 in cash now as full payment for the note. Morgan paid the $1000 but forgot to obtain the note from Penn. Two days after this cash payment, Penn indorsed the note in blank and negotiated it for value to Quinn. The next day, Quinn learned that Morgan had already paid Penn for the note, whereupon Quinn gave the note to his mother as a birthday present, without further indorsment. Quinn's mother was not aware of Morgan's prior payment. Quinn's mother sued Morgan on the note. Decision?

Chapter 42

PRESENTMENT, DISCHARGE, AND BANKING PROCEDURES

A. PRESENTMENT

1. IN GENERAL

Chapter 39 stated that the liability of the drawer of a check and an indorser was secondary (that of the drawee bank is primary). This means that the drawer and the indorser are not liable for payment on the check unless certain conditions precedent are met. If these conditions are met, the drawer or indorser must pay. Since the maker of a note is primarily liable, the conditions precedent to liability for the drawer and the indorser do not apply to him or her. That is, in the case of a maker, payment may be demanded of him or her, and the maker may be sued by the holder as soon as the debt is due, since he or she is under a duty to pay the note at the time and at the place named. The conditions precedent to the liability of the drawer of a check and an indorser are presentment and notice of dishonor.

2. DEFINITION

Presentment is a demand for payment or acceptance made upon the maker, acceptor, drawee, or other payor by the holder (U.C.C. Section 3–504(1)). Presentment is necessary to charge secondary parties unless excused (U.C.C Section 3–501(1)). Sections 3–503 (Time of Presentment), 3–504 (How Presentment Made), 3–505 (Rights of Party to Whom Presentment Is Made), and 3–506 (Time Allowed for Acceptance or Payment) of the U.C.C. detail the procedures and rights of presentment. Some of the more important rules are as follows:

1. An instrument having a fixed maturity date must be presented on or before that date.

2. A demand instrument must be presented within a reasonable time after the party the holder seeks to hold has become liable on the instrument.

3. A reasonable time to hold the drawer of a check is within 30 days after the check has been issued, and a reasonable time to hold an indorser is seven days after indorsement.

4. Presentment must be made at the place specified in the instrument and, if there is none, at the residence or place of business of the party liable.

5. The holder presenting the instrument for payment must be prepared to issue a receipt and to surrender the instrument.

3. NOTICE OF DISHONOR

An instrument is dishonored when presentment has been properly made and payment or acceptance is refused (U.C.C. Section 3–507(1)). Upon dishonor, the holder has an immediate right of recourse against drawers and indorsers upon giving them prompt notice of dishonor (U.C.C. Section 3–508). The notice of dishonor must be given by a bank before its midnight deadline (midnight on the next banking day following the banking day on which it receives notice of dishonor) (U.C.C. Section 4–104(1) (h)) and by any other person before midnight of the third business day after dishonor or receipt of notice of dishonor. The holder should give notice of dishonor to all prior parties so that he or she preserves his or her rights against all of them. The notice may be oral but should be written and a copy retained with a notation as to when and to whom notice was given and the address where the notice was given. If notice is sent by mail, it should be sent registered, and a copy should be retained noting the date it was sent and where it was posted. The notice does not have to be in any particular form, but it must identify the instrument and state that it was dishonored. Failure to give notice of dishonor releases parties secondarily liable.

The Supreme Court of Maryland, in *Hane v. Exten,* reiterated the importance of presentment and notice of dishonor as conditions precedent to holding indorsers liable on negotiable instruments.

FACTS   Hane was an assignee of a note signed by Theta Electronic Labs and indorsed by Exten. Theta defaulted, and Hane sued Exten to recover the balance of the note. Hane waited over a year before presenting the note, and he waited almost two months before giving notice of dishonor. The trial court dismissed the suit.

DECISION   Affirmed. Hane must show that Exten was given notice of presentment and dishonor before he can hold them on their indorsement. Unless presentment or notice of dishonor is waived or excused, unreasonable delay will discharge an endorser (U.C.C. sections 3–502(1)(a) and 3–508(2)). The court affirmed the lower court's finding that Hane had delayed presentment and notice of dishonor and dismissed the suit.

Hane v. Exten (255 Md. 668, 259 A.2d 290 [1969])

4. PROTEST

A protest is a formal presentment and certificate of dishonor (U.C.C. Section 3–509). It declares that the instrument was on a certain day presented for payment or acceptance and that such payment or acceptance was refused, stating the reasons given, if any, for the refusal, whereupon the holder protests against all parties to such instrument and declares that they will be held responsible for all loss or damage arising from its dishonor. It is required only on a draft that is drawn or payable outside the United States, although a holder may protest a dishonor on any instrument. The advantage of a protest is that it is evidentiary in character and may save expenses in obtaining or proving evidence through such devices as depositions. In addition to protests, other documents and records are admissible in court to prove a dishonor (e. g., bank stamps and memorandums—"not sufficient funds"—and bank records kept in the usual course of business).

5. WHEN PRESENTMENT AND NOTICE OF DISHONOR NOT NECESSARY

Presentment and notice of dishonor may be waived by the express or implied agreement of the secondary party (U.C.C. Section 3–511(2) (a)). Waiver may be made before or after the instrument (or notice) is due. It may be oral or written or by conduct of the party liable (e. g., party liable promises to substitute a new note). A waiver is binding on all parties if it appears on the face of the instrument. If the waiver is only part of an indorsement, it binds only the indorser (U.C.C. Section 3–511(6)).

Presentment and notice of dishonor may be excused when the holder is unable through reasonable diligence to locate the person who is to make payment (U.C.C. Sections 3–504(2), 3–511(1), 3–511(2) (c)).

Presentment and notice of dishonor may be excused when the person liable has already refused to pay (U.C.C. Sections 3–511(3) (b), 3–511(2) (b)).

Presentment and notice of dishonor may be excused when the party to be charged has died or gone into insolvency proceedings (U.C.C. Section 3–511(3) (a)).

B. DISCHARGE OF PARTIES

A party to a negotiable instrument may be discharged individually or by some act that discharges all of the parties to the instrument at one time. U.C.C. Section 3–601 lists the 12 grounds for the discharge of parties. These grounds either have been discussed previously or are self-explanatory. It is suggested that the students read Sections 3–601 through 3–606, plus the cited sections in Section 3–601.

C. BANKING PROCEDURES

1. COLLECTION OF CHECKS

Rarely does the holder of a check go to the drawee (payor) bank to cash it. Normally, the holder goes to his or her own bank (depository or collecting bank) and either cashes the check or deposits it in his or her account. This creates a collection situation for the depositary or collecting bank from the drawee or payor bank (a payor bank is a bank by which an item is payable as drawn or accepted—U.C.C. Section 4–105(b)). A depositary bank is the first bank to which an item is transferred for collection, even though it is also the payor bank (U.C.C. Section 4–105(a)). A collecting bank is any bank handling the item for collection except the payor bank (U.C.C. Section 4–105(d)).

The usual practice is for the depositary bank to credit the account of the depositor (holder of check) at the time of the deposit. This credit is a provisional settlement in that if the check is not good and it is dishonored, the depositary bank cancels its credit to the holder, whereas if the check is honored by the payor bank, the settlement is final. The depositary bank may collect either directly from the drawee bank through a clearing house or through one or more intermediary banks. A clearinghouse is any association of banks or other payors regularly clearing items. When the check reaches the payor bank, it debits the account of the drawer of the check. The payor bank then credits the account of the presenting bank and remits the money to it.

Unless a contrary intention appears, a collecting bank is an agent for the depositor of the check (U.C.C. Section 4–201(1)). Thus, the depositor of the check has the risk of loss in the event of nonpayment of the check or insolvency of one of the intermediary collecting banks before final settlement.

A depositary or collecting bank must use ordinary care in presenting the check for payment (U.C.C. Section 4–202(1) (a)).

When a holder has given a depositary bank a check for collection without his or her indorsement, the bank can supply the indorsement to speed up the collecting process (U.C.C. Section 4–205(1)). There are some exceptions to this rule. Government Social Security checks and tax refund checks require personal indorsements or a power of attorney given to the bank authorizing it to make the indorsement. Many bank escrow departments and escrow companies require an indorsement on an escrow check, since they use such indorsements as receipts for the money delivered. Some individual checks may also request or specify that a personal indorsement is required.

The customer and the collecting bank make certain warranties to the payor bank when payment is received (e. g., good title, no knowledge signature not authorized, no material alternation) (U.C.C. Section 4–207).

Birmingham Trust National Bank v. Central Bank & Trust Company involved a breach of warranty suit brought by a drawee bank (Birmingham) against a collecting bank (Central). It is the duty of the collecting bank to warrant that prior indorsements are genuine.

FACTS   Central (the collecting bank) presented to Birmingham (the drawee bank) a check with a forged indorsement. Unable to collect, Birmingham sued Central on the grounds that it had breached its warranty of genuineness of prior indorsements. Central countered that Birmingham was contributorily negligent in issuing and later accepting the check. The trial court entered judgment for Central.

DECISION   Reversed. U.C.C. Section 4–207 provides that the collecting bank warrants to the payor bank that it has good title to the check. A drawee bank has no duty to verify the indorsement of a check that comes to it from a collecting bank under warranty. Thus, Central's plea of contributory negligence is no defense to the breach of warranty action, and Birmingham should prevail.

Birmingham Trust National Bank v. Central Bank & Trust Co. (49 Ala. App. 630, 275 So.2d 148 [1973])

The collecting bank has a security interest in the check or proceeds to protect the bank with respect to advances and payments made in connection with the check (U.C.C. Section 4–208).

Following the receipt of the check by the payor bank, the check must be processed (e. g., photographed, examined as to form and signature) (U.C.C. Section 4–109). During this processing period, the bank may receive notice that the drawer has stopped payment on the check, that his or her account has been attached, or that he or she has gone through bankruptcy. U.C.C. Section 4–303 provides rules to govern the situation as to when checks are subject to notice, stop order, legal process, or setoff, and the order in which items may be charged or certified. Any notice or stop order received by a payor bank, any legal process served on it, or any setoff exercised by the bank comes too late to prevent payment of the check if the bank has done any one of the following:

1. Accepted or certified the check.

2. Paid the check in cash.

3. Settled for the check without having or reserving a right to revoke the settlement.

4. Completed the posting of the check or otherwise evidenced its decision to pay the check.

5. Become liable for the check because of failure to settle for or return the check in time.

2. RELATIONSHIP BETWEEN PAYOR BANK AND ITS CUSTOMER

A. IN GENERAL

The payor bank may charge against a customer's account (i. e., drawer's account) any check that is properly payable, even though it creates an overdraft U.C.C. Section 4–404(1)). If there is an overdraft, the bank has an implied promise from the customer for reimbursement. If a drawer signs his or her name to a check in blank and loses the check, the bank may pay an unauthorized person the full amount of the check (if it pays in good faith and does not know that the completion was improper) and charge the customer the full amount of the check.

B. DUTIES OF BANK

A bank is under a duty to honor checks drawn by a customer when there are sufficient funds in his account to cover the checks, the check is not over six months old, and the check is in proper form. If a bank wrongfully dishonors a check, it is liable in damages to the customer (U.C.C. Sections 4–402, 4–404).

The drawer has the right to stop payment on checks drawn on his or her account U.C.C. Section 4–403). The order to stop payment must be received at such time and in such manner as to afford the bank a reasonable opportunity to act on it prior to any action by the bank with respect to the check (e. g., payment or promise to pay). In most states, an oral stop payment is binding upon the bank, but only for 14 days unless confirmed in writing within that period. A written order is effective for only six months unless renewed in writing. A drawer cannot stop payment on a check that has been certified by the bank. A stop payment agreement between the bank and the drawer that provides that the bank shall not be liable for negligence in failing to stop payment is invalid (U.C.C. Section 4–103(1)). A check payable to cash cannot have a stop payment executed on it, since it becomes a bearer item. In those instances where the drawer has used a check guarantee card for identification or to negotiate cashing of the check, payment cannot be stopped, since the bank has agreed to pay any check up to the guaranteed amount, usually $100, provided that the necessary information has been put on the front or back of the check indicating that a check guarantee card was used.

FJS Electronics, Inc. v. Fidelity Bank illustrates the high standard of care that banks must meet in carrying out its customers' requests for stop payment.

> **FACTS**   FJS wrote a check for $1,844.98. Ten days later, FJS called its bank and stopped payment on the check. FJS provided all the necessary information to the bank but misstated the amount of the check by 50 cents. Because of Fidelity's particular computer system, the 50-cent error was fatal and the stop payment was never recorded. Fidelity honored the check, and FJS sued to recover the amount of the check.

> **DECISION**   Judgment for FJS. U.C.C. Section 4–403(1) requires that a customer ordering a stop payment do so in a reasonable manner. The amount of the check was only one piece of information that FJS provided. FJS had no way of knowing that the perfect accuracy of the amount of the check was crucial. The court concluded that FJS described the check with sufficient particularity and should recover.

FJS Electronics, Inc. v. Fidelity Bank (288 Pa. Super. 138, 431 A.2d 326 [1981])

The death or incompetence of the drawer does not revoke the bank's authority to pay checks drawn by him or her until the bank knows of the death or the adjudication of incompetency and has a reasonable time to act (U.C.C. Section 4–405(1)). Even though the bank knows of the death of a drawer, it may pay or certify checks for a period of 10 days after the death unless ordered to stop payment by a person claiming an interest in the account (U.C.C. Section 4–405(2)). The reason for the rule is to permit holders of checks drawn by the deceased to cash the checks without the necessity of filing a claim against the deceased's estate.

c. Duties of Customer

A customer (drawer) of a payor bank owns a duty to examine his or her bank statement and cancelled checks for forgeries or alterations within a reasonable time after they are returned or made available to him or her (U.C.C. Section 4–406(1)). The U.C.C. does not specify the period of time within which the customer must report forgeries or alterations, but many banks attempt to limit liability by provisions in signature cards that state that errors must be reported within 10 days after receipt of monthly statements and cancelled checks. Most courts hold that these provisions are invalid on one of several grounds (e. g., that 10 days is not sufficient time for examination of the statement and checks, that the provisions are too indefinite, or that the provisions were not called to the attention of the customer and that therefore the customer did not intend to be bound by them).

If the customer does not notify the bank promptly of any forgeries or alterations after receiving the cancelled checks and if the bank establishes that it suffered a loss by reason of such failure, the customer is precluded from asserting against the bank his or her unauthorized signature or the alteration (U.C.C. Section 4–406(2)). However, if the customer notifies the bank promptly, the bank is liable to the drawer, since the bank has the opportunity to examine the check when it is presented for payment. If the bank fails to detect the alteration or forgery, it is responsible for the loss.

If the bank did not use ordinary care in paying on a forged or altered check, the bank cannot assert the defense that the customer did not notify it promptly of the forgery or alteration, unless the customer does not notify the bank within one year of the forgery or alteration, in which case the customer must take the loss (U.C.C. Section 4–406)). If the bank waives its defense of late notification (perhaps for good public relations), it cannot thereafter hold the collecting bank or any prior party for the forgery or alteration (U.C.C. Section 4–406(5)).

A customer who is negligent in permitting a forgery or an alteration (e. g., negligent in caring for an automatic check signing device), is estopped from asserting liability against the bank (U.C.C. Section 3–406).

Winkie, Inc. v. Heritage Bank of Whitefish Bay illustrates that a bank customer's extraordinarily long delay in notifying the bank of forged indorsements will bar recovery against the bank.

FACTS From 1965 to 1973, Winkie's employee forged hundreds of checks. Over that period, Winkie never examined any checks, nor did he reconcile any bank statements. Winkie sued the bank to recover for the amounts of the checks. Winkie argued that the bank was negligent in failing to ascertain whether the checks were properly indorsed.

DECISION   Judgment for bank. Winkie was negligent by his failure to both examine the checks and set up a system of internal control. The forgeries of Winkie's signature caused the loss. Thus, the bank's lack of care with respect to the forged indorsements was of no consequence.

Winkie, Inc. v. Heritage Bank of Whitefish Bay (92 Wis.2d 784, 285 N.W.2d 899 [1979])

Where there are successive forgeries or alterations, the failure of the customer to examine and notify the bank within a period of 14 days after the first statement and checks were delivered or available to the customer would preclude him or her from asserting forgeries or alterations of later checks by the same person paid by the bank, and the customer would suffer the loss (U.C.C. Section 4–406(2) (b)). This rule is intended to help prevent the forger from having an opportunity to repeat the wrongdoing. However, the bank is liable during the 14-day period.

3.   SUBROGATION RIGHTS OF PAYOR BANK

If a payor bank has paid an item (e. g., check) over the stop payment order of the drawer or maker or otherwise under circumstances giving a basis for objection by the drawer or maker, to prevent unjust enrichment and only to the extent necessary to prevent loss to the bank by reason of its payment on the item, the payor bank shall be subrogated (substituted) to the rights of the following parties against the drawer or maker:

1.   Any holder in due course that the bank paid on the item. Thus, when the payor bank is sued for wrongful payment, it can assert the defense that its customer (drawer) did not suffer a loss, because he or she would have been liable to the holder in due course whether the bank had obeyed the stop payment order or not (i. e., even if payment had been stopped by the bank, the drawer would still have had to pay the holder in due course). Thus, the U.C.C. places the payor bank in the position of a holder in due course against the drawer.

2.   The payee or any other holder. Thus, when the payor bank is sued for wrongful payment, it can assert any defense that the payee had (e. g., if the payee received the check as payment for defective goods and the drawer retained the goods, the payee would have a defense to the extent of the value of the goods retained by the drawer.

3.   The drawer or maker against the payee or any other holder of the item with respect to the transaction out of which the item arose. Thus, the bank that has made an improper payment on an item is subrogated to the rights of its own customer (drawer) against the payee (e. g., payee has defrauded the drawer, the drawer stops payment on the check, the bank pays on the check wrongfully, the bank pays the drawer for the mistake, the bank sues payee and takes over the rights of the drawer in the suit against the payee) (U.C.C. Section 4–407(a)(b)(c)).

4. OTHER RECOVERY RIGHTS OF PAYOR BANK

A. FORGED CHECK

If a bank pays on a forged check to a holder who is innocent of the forgery, can the bank recover the money from the holder? U.C.C. Section 4–418 provides that the bank cannot.

B. FORGED INDORSEMENT

If a bank pays on a forged indorsement, can the bank recover the money from the party paid? U.C.C. Section 3–417 provides that it can.

C. ALTERATION

If the bank pays on an altered instrument, can the bank recover the money from the party paid? U.C.C., Section 3–417(c) provides that it can, unless the party paid purchased it after certification and was innocent of the alteration, in which case the bank cannot.

D. FICTITIOUS PAYEE

If the bank pays on a check made out to a fictitious payee (e. g., employee in charge of payroll checks sets up a fictitious employee and draws checks to him which he has his employer sign along with other paychecks and then indorses and cashes the checks), can the bank debit the account of the employer? U.C.C. Section 3–405(1) (c) provides that the bank can.

   If the indorsement is not made "in the name of the payee," the bank will be liable for the amount of the check and the employer will not have to pay. See *Travco Corp. v. Citizens Federal Savings & Loan Ass'n. of Port Huron* (42 Mich. App. 291, 201 N.W. 2d 675 [1972]) (collecting bank liable where indorsement not made in name of payee).

E. IMPOSTER PAYEE

If a bank pays on a check made out to an imposter (e. g., imposter induces customer of bank to give him a check payable to the person impersonated), can the bank debit the account of the customer? U.C.C. Section 3—405(1)(a) provides that it can.

   In *Philadelphia Title Insurance Company v. Fidelity-Philadelphia Trust Company,* the Supreme Court of Pennsylvania applied U.C.C. Section 3–405(1)(a), ruling that the customer must bear the loss when it issues a check to an imposter.

   FACTS Paula Jezemski and a man imitating her husband, Edmund Jezemski, induced the plaintiff to issue a check for a mortgage on certain land owned by Edmund. Paula forged Edmund's signature and cashed the check. Plaintiff sued its bank for honoring the check.

DECISION   Bank wins. Generally, the bank bears the loss resulting from a forged endorsement (U.C.C. Section 3–404(1)). The indorsement, however, is effective if an imposter induced the maker to issue the instrument to him (U.C.C. Section 3–405(1)(a)). Here, the man imitating Edmund was such an imposter and Section 3–405(1)(a) applies. Thus, the maker of the check must bear the loss.

Philadelphia Title Insurance Co. v. Fidelity-Philadelphia Trust Co. (419 Pa. 78, 212 A.2d 222 [1965])

ILLUSTRATIVE CASES

1. Effect of Dishonor by Mail

NEVADA STATE BANK v. FISCHER

93 Nev. 317, 565 P.2d 332 (1977)

THOMPSON, J.   The Nevada State Bank charged Lucile Fischer's account $2,000 when it received notice that a check in that amount, endorsed by her, had been dishonored. Therefore, she commenced this action against the Bank for wrongfully so debiting her account.

The district court ruled that her liability as endorser was discharged since notice of dishonor was not timely given her. Judgment was entered in her favor together with interest, costs, and attorney fees. The Bank appeals from that judgment. We affirm.

The facts are not disputed. On May 1, 1970, Mrs. Fischer endorsed a $2,000 check payable to the drawer and drawn on the Clayton Bank of Clayton, Missouri. She did this as an accommodation to the payee-drawer. The Nevada State Bank cashed the check for the payee-drawer and initiated collection through Valley Bank of Nevada that same day.

On July 28, 1970, the Valley Bank of Nevada notified Nevada State Bank that the check had been dishonored stating "original lost in transit— account closed." On July 29, 1970, the Nevada State Bank debited Mrs. Fischer's account for $2,000 and notified her in writing of the payor bank's dishonor of the check.

The record does not disclose which of the several banks involved in the collection process either lost the check or delayed action with regard to it. It is clear, however, that Nevada State Bank acted promptly upon receiving notice of dishonor. Whether it was permissible in these circumstances for that bank to charge its innocent depositor rather than to look to one of the other banks involved is the issue of our decision.

Lucile Fischer endorsed the check as an accommodation party and is liable in the capacity in which she signed. NRS 104.3415. By endorsing the check she engaged that upon dishonor and any necessary notice of dishonor and protest, she would pay the instrument according to the tenor at the time of her endorsement. NRS 104.3414(1).

An endorser is a secondary party, NRS 104.3102(1)(d), whose liability is subject to the preconditions of presentment, NRS 104.3501(1)(b), and proper notice of dishonor NRS 104.3501(2)(a). Where, without excuse, any necessary presentment or notice of dishonor is delayed beyond the time it is due, an endorser is discharged. Such is the command of NRS 104.3502(1).

It is the contention of Nevada State Bank that since it initiated collection within one day of the endorsement and notified the endorser of dishonor within one day of receipt of such notice by it, "delay" does not exist and Mrs. Fischer, as endorser, is not discharged from liability.

An uncertified check must be presented for payment, or collection initiated thereon, within a reasonable time, which in this case is presumed to be seven days. NRS 104.8503(2)(b). Although the record does not advise us when presentment was made to the proper party, NRS 104.3504, we do know that Nevada State Bank initiated collection within one day after cashing the check. Consequently, bank collection was timely initiated.

In our view, however, the second precondition to liability of the endorser, that is, timely notice of dishonor, was not met. Although the Nevada State Bank notified Mrs. Fischer within its midnight deadline, NRS 104.4104, after receipt of notice of dishonor from Valley Bank of Nevada, this fact, alone, does not resolve the timeliness issue.

The record does not disclose at what point in time the check first was dishonored. We know only that almost ninety days elapsed between Mrs. Fischer's endorsement of the check and her receipt of notice of its dishonor. It is apparent that one of the several banks involved in the collection process violated its midnight deadline in giving notice of dishonor. Had such bank given timely notice, Mrs. Fischer would have learned within a reasonable time that the check had been dishonored.

Prompt action by all parties to the transaction is contemplated before an endorser may be held liable. As stated in the official comment to sec. 3–503 of Uniform Commercial Code (our NRS 104.3503):

> The endorser who has normally merely received the check and passed it on and does not expect to have to pay it, is entitled to know more promptly whether it is to be dishonored, in order that he may have recourse against the person with whom he has dealt.

As already expressed, at sometime in the chain of collection a midnight deadline was violated. Notwithstanding such violation, we are asked to conclude that notice of dishonor given ninety days after initiation of bank collection was timely. We decline to so conclude. Mrs. Fischer's liability as an endorser was discharged when the violation of the midnight deadline by a bank, identity unknown, resulted in unreasonable delay in notice of dishonor. The Nevada State Bank may look to the violator for its recovery. Its customer-endorser should not be held responsible for a violation of law committed by another bank involved in the chain of collection.

*   *   *

2. Rights of Depositary Bank as Holder

DOUGLAS v. THE CITIZENS BANK OF JONESBORO

244 Ark. 168, 424 S.W.2d 532 (1968)

HARRIS, J. This litigation involves two separate causes of action, which however, by agreement, were set forth in one set of pleadings, and disposed of at one hearing. Appellants, Weldon Douglas, and Janie Chandler, each maintained a checking account in the Citizens Bank of Jonesboro. Rees Plumbing Company, Inc. (which is not presently a party to this proceeding), was a customer of the bank, and maintained checking accounts. On August 19, 1966, the plumbing company delivered its check in the amount of $1,000.00 to Douglas. On that same day Douglas presented the check to the bank for deposit to his own checking account; an employee at the teller's window prepared a deposit slip, dated as of that day, reflecting that the check was being deposited to Douglas' account. He was given a duplicate of the deposit slip, and an employee of the bank thereafter affixed to the back of the check a stamp in red ink, denoting the August 19th date, and stating, "Pay to any bank—P.E.G., Citizens Bank of Jonesboro, Jonesboro, Arkansas." Under date of August 20, 1966, the bank dishonored the check because of insufficient funds, and charged the amount back to the account of Douglas. This same statement of facts applies to Mrs. Chandler, except that the check she presented was originally made payable to a Richard R. Washburn (in the amount of $1,600.00) by the same Rees Company, and this check had been properly endorsed by Washburn before coming into the hands of Mrs. Chandler.

* * * After first demurring, and moving to make the complaint more definite and certain, the bank filed an answer setting out that the accounts of Rees were insufficient on August 19 to honor the checks, and further, that both were charged back to the accounts of the respective appellants on August 20, and the appellants so notified. The bank further denied that the endorsement stamp, heretofore mentioned, constituted an acceptance stamp. The bank asserted that the stamp was no more than a method of identification. * * *

The principal question of issue is, "Did the bank, by stamping the endorsement upon the checks deposited by appellants, and by delivering to appellants the deposit slips, accept both of said checks for payment?" The answer is, "No." * * * This case is controlled by the following sections of the Code: Ark.Stat.Ann. §85–4–212(3), 85–4–213and §85–4–301(1) (Add.1961).

Subsection (3) of Section 85–4–212 reads as follows:

A depositary bank which is also the payor may charge back the amount of an item to its customer's account or obtain refund in accordance with the section governing return of an item received by a payor bank for credit on its books (Section 4–301 (§85–301)).

Subsection (1) of Section 85–4—301 provides:

Where an authorized settlement for a demand item (other than a documentary draft) received by a payor bank otherwise than for immediate payment over the counter has been made before midnight of the banking day of receipt the payor bank may revoke the settlement and recover any payment if before it has made final payment (subsection (1) of Section 4–213 (§85–213)) and before its midnight deadline it

(a) returns the item; or

(b) sends written notice of dishonor or nonpayment if the item is held for protest or is otherwise unavailable for return.

Section 85–4–213 simply sets out the time that a payment becomes final, not applicable in this instance.

When we consider the statute above referred to, it is clear that appellants cannot prevail. Clark, Bailey and Young, in their American Law Institute pamphlet on bank deposits and collections under the Uniform Commercial Code (January, 1959), p. 2, comment as follows:

> If the buyer-drawer and the seller-payee have their accounts in the same bank, and if the seller-payee deposits the check to the credit of his account, his account will be credited provisionally with the amount of the check. In the absence of special arrangement with the bank, he may not draw against this credit until it becomes final, that is to say, until after the check has reached the bank's bookkeeper and, as a result of bookkeeping operations, has been charged to the account of the buyer-drawer. (The seller-payee could, of course, present the check at a teller's window and request immediate payment in cash, but that course is not usually followed.) If the buyer-drawer's account does not have a sufficient balance, or he has stopped payment on the check, or if for any other reason the bank does not pay the check, the provisional credit given in the account of the seller-payee is reversed. If the seller-payee had been permitted to draw against that provisional credit, the bank would recoup the amount of the drawing by debit to his account or by other means.

The comment of the commissioners is also enlightening. Comment 4, under Section 85–4–213, states:

> A primary example of a statutory right on the part of the payor bank to revoke a settlement is the right to revoke conferred by Section 4–301. The underlying theory and reason for deferred posting statutes (Section 4–301) is to require a settlement on the date of receipt of an item but to keep that settlement provisional with the right to revoke prior to the midnight deadline. In any case where Section 4–301 is applicable, any settlement by the payor bank is provisional solely by virtue of the statute subsection (1) (b) of Section 4–213 does not operate and such provisional settlement does not constitute final payment of the item.

*   *   *

3. Bank's Liability to Customers

ADVANCED ALLOYS, INC. v. SERGEANT STEEL CORP., et al.

72 Misc.2d 614, 340 N.Y.S.2d 266 (1973)

COHEN, J. The question presented is whether a bank has a duty of inquiry before paying a check which is stale in that it was presented for payment 14 months after issuance. Prior to the enactment of the Uniform Commercial Code, such a duty existed. However, UCC 4–404 states that:

> A bank is under no obligation to a customer having a checking account to pay a check, other than a certified check, which is presented more than six months after its date, but it may charge its customer's account for a payment made thereafter in good faith. This statute appears to change the common law rule.

Under this statute, it must be determined whether this payment was made "in good faith." Since no evidence was presented on this point and since both plaintiff and defendant The Chase Manhattan Bank, N.A. agree that there are no issues of fact—the case having been presented to the Court on affidavits prepared for a summary judgment motion—the Court must simply decide whether a payment of a check by a drawee bank 14 months after issuance is a payment "in good faith" when made without inquiry of the depositor. U.C.C. 1–201(19) defines "good faith" as "honesty in fact in the conduct or transaction concerned." Under this definition, to which the Official Comment to UCC 4–404 makes reference, it appears that the payment of the stale check, without making such inquiry, constitutes a payment "in good faith."

Presumably, if it were intended to place a duty of inquiry upon a bank before it could safely pay a stale check, a broader definition of "good faith" would have been made applicable to this situation. It may very well be that in enacting the Code consideration was given, as defendant argues, to the vast number of checks being issued and the requirement that a bank accept or refuse to honor a check within a short, prescribed time limit (UCC 4–301, 302), leading to the conclusion that a bank should not be liable for paying stale checks as long as the bank was honest in fact.

The court realizes that a determination that there is no duty of inquiry puts a substantial burden upon one who issues a check, and then, even for a good reason—as in this case—does not want it to be paid. Since a stop payment order is good for only six months (UCC 4–403(2), it means that the issuer must, in order to protect himself, either continue to renew the stop payment order every six months or close the account. Apparently, in balancing the problems of the issuer and the bank in this situation, the Code resolved the matter in favor of the bank.

The court notes the statement in the Official Comment (* * * Uniform Commercial Code, § 4–404) that normally a bank will not pay a stale check without consulting the depositor and, further the bank "* * * is given the option to pay because it may be in a position to know, as in the case of dividend checks, that the drawer wants payment made." Plaintiff argues that this option to pay is given only when the drawee bank is in a position to know that the drawer wants the check to be paid; and in this case the bank could only know this if it made inquiry—something it did not do. However, the language of the Code itself, as indicated above, does not support this argument and does not impose a duty of inquiry upon the bank in the situation presented herein.

*   *   *

[On appeal, the Supreme Court, Appellate Term, unanimously reversed the granting of summary judgment and remanded the case for trial in the following *per curiam* opinion (360 N.Y.S.2d 142, 79 Misc.2d 149):]

> While UCC 4–404 protects a bank which pays a stale check so long as it acts in good faith, it does not eliminate the requirement of ordinary care which a bank must observe in all its dealings (*Granite Equipment Leasing Corp. v. Hempstead Bank,* 68 Misc.2d 350, 326 N.Y.S.2d 881, see also, *Novak v. Greater N.Y. Sav. Bank,* 30 N.Y.2d 136, 331 N.Y.S.2d 377, 282 N.E.2d 285). In our opinion, there is an issue of fact as to whether under all the circumstances, defendant Chase Manhattan Bank, N.A. acted with due care in this transaction. * * *

4. Duty of Customer to Notify Bank of Error

ARROW BUILDERS SUPPLY CORP. v. ROYAL NATIONAL BANK OF NEW YORK

21 N.Y.2d 428, 288 N.Y.S.2d 609, 235 N.E.2d 756 (1968)

BURKE, J. Faye Zappacosta was employed as a bookkeeper by plaintiff Arrow Builders Supply Corp. Each month, she drew checks for plaintiff's president LaSala on its account in defendant Royal National Bank, payable to the order of that bank, representing income and social security taxes withheld from the wages of Arrow's employees. Between August, 1962 and June 1964 Zappacosta drew and LaSala purportedly signed 54 such checks, of which only 23 were properly applied. The 31 remaining checks, totaling $132,000, were presented individually by Zappacosta to the bank whereupon the bank would issue its own check for the same amount payable to a person designated by Zappacosta. In most cases the payee she selected was either a friend or a relative who would either indorse over the check to her or cash it and deliver the proceeds.

In furtherance of her scheme, she concealed these unlawful withdrawals, as best she could. As bookkeeper, she was the one who first checked the cancelled vouchers and examined these bank statements. Before submitting a statement and the accompanying checks to plaintiff's accountant, she would withdraw the checks involved, write void on their corresponding checkbook stubs and then prepare a tape which, while excluding the amounts of any checks appropriated by her, nevertheless reflected the proper total for all the checks drawn for that month. Thus the total shown always exceeded the sum of the enumerated checks. The statement, with this tape, was then presented to the accountant who neither compared the checks he received against the debits on the statement, nor totalled these checks himself. Consequently, Zappacosta was able to perpetrate this scheme for 23 months whereas a proper review of the first statement would have exposed the first defalcation. Plaintiff brought this suit to recover the entire sum taken by its bookkeeper Zappacosta, alleging that the defendant bank paid these funds without making any appropriate inquiry as to her authority to direct the application of these checks. Defendant, conceding its carelessness, asserts as an affirmative defense plaintiff's negligence in failing to discover the embezzlement. * * * It is our opinion that, upon this record, a triable issue is presented at least as to plaintiff's negligence in failing to discover these defalcations.

* * *

* * * After the bank began to supply these checks under the advisement of Zappacosta, it continued to supply the plaintiff with monthly statements reflecting all the transactions for this account. Thus, during the 23-month period involved, at least two checks were returned each month, each purportedly issued by the plaintiff to cover its monthly payment for income and social security taxes withheld from the wages of its employees. Indeed, in some months, plaintiff received as many as four cancelled checks, each allegedly drawn to cover this single monthly payment. The issuance of such a statement is not without purpose. Rather, it is intended to inform the plaintiff of the status of his account and to provide him with an opportunity to notify the bank of any discrepancies existing between the statement as presented and the balance as maintained by the drawer. In this regard, the duties of the depositor have been often enumerated in unequivocal terms. Justice Shientag's opinion in *Screenland Mag. v. National City Bank of New York,* is illustrative. There, it was noted that:

> A depositor is under a duty to his bank to examine canceled checks and statements received from the bank and to notify the bank promptly of any irregularities in the account. * * *

> * * * [A] "depositor must be held chargeable with knowledge of all the facts that a reasonable and prudent examination of the returned bank statements, vouchers and certificates would have disclosed had it been made by a person on the depositor's behalf who had not participated in the forgeries."

These rules, which have evolved basically with reference to forged signatures, are also applicable where the plaintiff's negligence may have made the embezzlement possible. Applying these standards to the instant case, it is apparent that there are questions of fact as to whether the depositor used due care in the examination of these statements and vouchers. Thus the depositor will be precluded from recovering from the bank, if the jury should find that the bank was damaged by the drawer's negligence in failing to properly examine the monthly statements.

* * *

5. Liability of Bank Customer for Negligence

DINERMAN v. NATIONAL BANK OF NORTH AMERICA

89 Misc. 2d 164, 390 N.Y.S. 2d 1002 (1977)

HYMAN, J.　Man's inventive genuis and explorations in the Twentieth Century have brought forth many innovations; and now, one of the most sensational of all such—one which if allowable must join the ranks of the great—is how to gamble at Las Vegas, or some other such place which permits gambling, losing money in and to their palatial casinos, without it costing the loser anything. The theory presented is an interesting and novel one, made more so in that it has not been conceived by any mathematical genius, but rather by a member of the Bar.

Plaintiff (Irving P. Dinerman) alleges that on or about April 2, 1973 and prior thereto, he maintained several checking accounts with defendant bank and that on or about the above date (actually March 30, 1973, three days earlier) he entered into an "agreement" or "condition of the account," a "contract" (affirmation of plaintiff dated Oct. 8, 1976) with defendant, wherein defendant agreed not to make payments drawn on plaintiff's checking accounts unless the instrument being presented for payment was on "printed checks of the bank," but that in September 1975 (two and one-half years later) the defendant violated such alleged "agreement-contract," without plaintiff's permission and paid out of his checking account the sum of $1,000 "on instruments which were not on the printed check forms of defendant bank"; thus causing the plaintiff $1,000 in damages.

The documentary proof indicates that on March 30, 1973 the plaintiff did put his instructions into "written" form and forwarded same to defendant; and such instructions were acknowledged to have been "received" by defendant in April 1973. The instructions read as follows [emphasis supplied]:

> In accordance with your request for written authorization, I wish to advise you not to pay any instruments drawn on the above accounts unless they are printed checks from your bank.

* * *

Yours very truly,
/s/ Irving P. Dinerman

Received by National Bank of North America this ＿＿＿ day of April, 1973
By: [signature unreadable] 4/2/73

Having left the tables of the Puerto Rican casinos, plaintiff apparently decided to try his luck at the casino tables of the hotels in Las Vegas, Nevada. This he did in August 1975, some two years and four months *after* his so-called prior written instructions. But, to his consternation, he was no better at the tables in his new found gambling haven than he had been at the former palaces of delight, nor, he contends, was his luck any better with the Las Vegas hotel as with the Puerto Rican hotel, insofar as their so-called agreements were concerned, because he did not obtain an "offset" for airfare and other adjustments (also unnamed) from the Las Vegas hotel at whose tables he gambled but lost $1,000, for which he executed two (2) so-called "markers" (actually printed checks) which read substantially as follows [emphasis supplied]:

To Natl. Bk. of N. America

<u>Customers Check 31502</u>
(For Cash Only)

911324983
Your Account Number

N.Y.C., N.Y.   Date 8–15–1975
City and State

PAY TO THE ORDER OF Sahara Hotel Five Hundred $500.00

I represent that I have received cash for the above amount and that said amount is on deposit in said bank or trust company in my name, is free from claims and is subject to this check.

Signed: Irving P. Dinerman

Except for the fact that the second "check" (marker) bore number 29871, they both were dated the same date, drawn upon the same bank with the same numbered account, and were for the same amount.

The defendant opposes the plaintiff's cross motion and in support of its primary mention to dismiss the complaint, admits that a customer does have a limited right to make a "stop payment order" by statutory authority under section 4–403 of the Uniform Commercial Code, which reads as follows:

(1) A customer may by order to his bank stop payment of any item payable for his account but the order must be received at such time and in such manner as to afford the bank a reasonable opportunity to act on it prior to any action by the bank with respect to the item described in Section 4–303.

(2) An oral order is binding upon the bank *only for fourteen calendar days* unless confirmed in writing within that period. *A written order* is effective for only *six months unless renewed in writing.*

(3) *The burden of establishing the fact and amount of loss* resulting from the payment of an item contrary to a pending stop payment order is on the customer. [Emphasis supplied.]

As stated in the Official Comment (Official Comment 7, McKinney's Cons.Laws of N.Y. Anno., Book 62 1/2, Uniform Commercial Code, § 4–403, p. 612):

The existing statutes all specify a time limit after which any direction to stop payment becomes ineffective *unless it is renewed in writing;* and the majority of them have specified six months. The purpose of the provision is, of course, to facilitate stopping payments by clearing the records of the drawee of accumulated unrevoked stop orders, as where the drawer has * * * settled his controversy with the payee, but has failed to notify the drawee. [Emphasis supplied.]

In the instant matter the bank merely acknowledged "receipt" of the written request (stop payment order) on April 2, 1973; as such it cannot be legally interpreted as a general, unlimited lifetime "agreement", but at best is a receipt of the notice to stop payment within the purview of subdivision (26)(b) of section 1–201 of the Uniform Commercial Code, which provides that, "A person 'receives' a notice or notification when * * * it is duly delivered at the place of business * * * [at] the place for receipt of such communications." At best it is an acknowledgement of the taking into possession of something, a mere admission of a fact in writing of the receipt of something, without containing any affirmative obligation of creating any contractual obligation, except that in the instant case it would create the statutory obligation under section 4–403 of the Uniform Commercial Code; a far cry from any contractual obligation.

In the instant matter, the plaintiff, an attorney learned in the law to an extent far greater than a mere layman, cannot now be permitted to claim a lack of knowledge of the statutory limitation placed upon "stop payment orders," particularly one "in writing," beyond a six-month period without written renewal thereof (Uniform Commercial Code, § 4–403, subd. [2]). To permit the plaintiff to now claim, as he does, that the stop payment order was to extend beyond the statutory limitation by virtue of an alleged "oral agreement" simultaneously made with the written stop payment order would do violence to the statute, the enacting legislative intent, and to the "depositor's contract" entered into when opening the account, which provides as follows:

Written request for stop-payment shall be effective for six (6) months, but renewals may be made from time to time. No stop payment request, renewal or revocation shall be valid unless made in writing and served upon the bank. * * * [Decision for Bank].

6. Authority of Bank to Cash Overdraft

KENDALL YACHT CLUB v. UNITED CALIFORNIA BANK

50 Cal.App. 3d 949, 123 Cal.Rptr. 848 (1975)

[Lawrence and Linda Kendall were officers and the principal shareholders of a corporation formed to build yachts upon special order from customers. The corporation had never issued stock and was undercapitalized.

The corporation had a payroll checking account and a general business checking account with United California Bank. When the corporation ran into some financial problems, Mr. Kendall spoke with Ron Lamperts, a loan officer at the bank, in an effort to obtain financing for the corporation.

The bank agreed to honor overdrafts on the corporate account until such time as the corporation was out of the woods. The Kendalls continued to write checks for supplies, payroll, and other operating expenses of the corporation from about mid-October through December. The corporate bank account was badly overdrawn, and a number of the checks had been dishonored by the bank.

The Kendalls brought this lawsuit against United California Bank, charging that its wrongful dishonor of checks that it had initially agreed to accept as overdrafts caused damage to the Kendalls' personal and credit reputation.]

McDaniel, Associate Justice.

*   *   *

During October, November, and December, the Bank honored overdrafts of the Corporation totaling in excess of $15,000. There were also a number of overdrafts written during these months which were not honored by the Bank. Some of these were to suppliers and others were payroll checks to employees. In addition, the Bank failed to honor a check written to Insurance Company of North America to cover a premium for workmen's compensation insurance. The Kendalls were not aware that this check had been "bounced" until after one of their employees had been injured and they had been notified by Insurance Company of North America that their insurance had been terminated for nonpayment of premium.

After the collapse of the business, the Kendalls understandably had a number of enemies in the community. They were accused of having breached the trust of their former suppliers and employees and of having milked the Corporation of its funds and placed them in a Swiss bank account. They were repeatedly threatened with legal action and physical harm; they suffered acts of vandalism such as eggs and oil being thrown at their cars. Mr. Kendall's subsequent employer was contacted and threatened by creditors of the Corporation. Criminal charges were brought against Mrs. Kendall for writing checks against insufficient funds; the charges were dismissed shortly before she was brought to trial on them. The Kendalls were required to appear and answer charges in administrative proceedings involving dishonored payroll checks and the Corporation's failure to carry workmen's compensation insurance. Each testified to experiencing severe emotional distress and humiliation as a result of these matters. They also testified to marital problems which were allegedly caused by the stress brought on by the failure of the business.

*   *   *

The Bank contends first that under Commercial Code section 4402 the wrongful dishonor of a check of a *corporation* does not give a cause of action for damages to individual officers and shareholders of the corporation. Commercial Code section 4402, which represents section 4–402 of the Uniform Commercial Code, reads as follows: "A payor bank is liable to its customer for damages proximately caused by the wrongful dishonor of an item. When the dishonor occurs through mistake liability is limited to actual damages proved." [Footnote omitted.]

[It] was entirely foreseeable that the dishonoring of the Corporation's checks would reflect directly on the personal credit and reputation of the Kendalls and that they would suffer the adverse personal consequences which resulted when the Bank reneged on its commitments.

*   *   *

[It] has been held in this state that a cause of action for wrongful dishonor of a check sounds in tort as well as in contract, and "if the conduct is tortious, damages for emotional distress may be recovered despite the fact that the conduct also involves a breach of contract."

*   *   *

PROBLEMS

1. D drew a check on June 1 payable to P. P negotiated to an H.D.C. The H.D.C. presented the check to the drawee bank on June 10. The drawee dishonored the check. The H.D.C. did not give D or P notice of dishonor. D and P claim that failure to give due notice of dishonor is an absolute discharge of their liability. Decision?

2. The H.D.C. of a check that had been dishonored sent notice of the dishonor to the drawer by a properly stamped and addressed envelope deposited in a United States Post Office box. The drawer states that he never received the notice. Was the notice valid?

3. The drawer of a check delivered it to the payee who negotiated it to H. H altered the check by increasing the amount from $50 to $500 and cashed it at the payor bank. The payor bank made a debit of the drawer's account in the amount of $500. The drawer promptly notified the bank of the alteration after he received his bank statement and checks. Does the bank have the right to debit the drawer's account for $500?

4. The drawer of a check in the amount of $5,000 delivered it to P who indorsed it to H. H took the check to the payor bank for collection. The drawer had only $4,000 in his account, but the bank paid H the sum of $5,000. The drawer refuses to pay the bank $1,000 since the bank had no authority to pay the additional sum. Decision?

5. A check was forged, negotiated, and paid by the drawee. The drawee debited the account of the purported drawer. A few days after the purported drawer received his bank statement and checks, he noticed the forgery and complained to the bank demanding that the bank remove the debt. Decision?

6. Jones borrowed $3000 from Brown, giving Brown in return a promissory note for $3000 payable to the order of Brown. The note, dated September 15, was due in 30 days. On October 12, Brown indorsed the note to the Acme Company. Three days later, Acme learned that Jones was seriously ill. Acme wrote Jones that they were discharging him from liability on the instrument. On the due date, Acme demanded payment from Brown as an indorser, and sued when Brown refused payment. Brown defended on the grounds that his liability was terminated by Acme's discharge of Jones from liability. Decision?

7. A obtained cashier's checks from Federal Bank and sent them to a Mexican bank. Federal notifed the Mexican bank that the cashier's checks would not be paid, and that Federal requested the return of the checks for cancellation. The checks were thereafter presented for payment, but Federal refused to honor them. A's assets were then seized by legal process to satisfy his debt to the Mexican bank. A's reputation was damaged and A was threatened with criminal prosecution. A sued Federal for wrongful dishonor of the checks. Decision?

8. F, posing as a utility repairman, gained entrance to the home of R, an eighty-year-old widow. F told R that he needed a check for $1.50 to cover the "service charge." As an accomodation to R, F volunteered to fill out the check for her. Using one of R's blank check forms, F wrote the figures and words in such a way as to make the check read "Eighteen Hundred Fifty One and 50/100." R signed the altered check. F subsequently cashed the check at R's bank. R sued the bank to recover the raised amount. The bank defended on the grounds that R's negligence substantially contributed to the alteration. Decision?

9. D sent a $600 check drawn on City Bank to P. D then realized that he had already paid P. D went to City Bank at 9:00 a.m. on the following morning when the bank opened, and notified them to stop payment on the $600 check he had written the day before. At 10:40 a.m. P arrived at the bank with the check. The bank certified the check and charged it to D's account. D sued City Bank to recover the amount so charged. The bank defended on the grounds that D was required to prove that they were negligent. Decision?

10. Booker drew a check on National Bank payable to FMX Corporation. FMX requested National to certify Booker's check, on which basis the bank did so. National later refused to make payment on Booker's check. FMX sued National Bank, which defended on the grounds that a dispute existed between Booker and FMX Corporation as to the amount due the latter. Decision?

Part IX

GOVERNMENT REGULATION OF BUSINESS

43
Federal Laws Applied to Business

44
Bankruptcy

Chapter 43

FEDERAL LAWS
APPLIED TO BUSINESS

Practically all of today's business activities are subject to governmental regulation. New laws are continually being introduced by legislative and executive action to control and direct commercial practices. Much of this direction has been delegated to administrative agencies (refer to Chapter 5). These agencies possess rulemaking, executive, and quasi-judicial powers. The final determination of the legality of such operations is for the courts.

The Commerce Clause (U.S. Constitution, Article I, Section 8) gives the federal government the power to regulate foreign commerce and commerce between the states. Court decisions construing this power have broadened the power considerably and extended Congressional control even to businesses generally considered to be local. The states and their subdivisions obtain their authority to regulate from the Tenth Amendment, granting plenary powers to the states, and from their "police power," which is the inherent power of a governing body to control persons and property within its jurisdiction for the purposes of promoting the health, safety, and welfare of its people.

At times there may be conflict between national and local regulations which creates a priority problem. Court decisions seem to classify these issues in the following categories: those exclusively federal in nature, those where local and federal rules are deemed compatible, and those remaining solely within the state's authority. In the concurrent area, further subdivisions are made of those where Congress has preempted the field by express law, those where federal regulations exist but lack completeness to cover all areas of state interest, and those where no federal law exists and the state has legislated.

A. TAXATION

Government requires revenue to meet its expenses. Backed by the power and authority the government possesses, tax laws, not based on consent, are passed and the levies collected. Although this power can be used only for public purposes, the only real limitations are those imposed by the federal and state constitutions or the possibility of the electorate's replacing its elected representatives. Since taxes are not really debts, the constitutional prohibition against imprisonment for nonpayment is not applicable.

Taxes may be directly imposed, such as the income tax, or indirectly imposed, such as manufacturer's taxes passed on to the consumer. They may be specific on individual items, such as packs of cigarettes, or ad valorem (according to value), such as property taxes on private homes. They may be general, to benefit everybody, or special (such as street lighting assessments), benefiting only those who pay. Taxes not only are placed on the value of property but also may be placed on a privilege, commonly called excise taxes, such as paying a fee to engage in the practice of law.

The power to tax is being used to implement political, social, and economic policy as well as to obtain funds. Tax benefits that encourage investment, import duties that protect business from foreign competition, and estate taxes that break up large fortunes are a few examples. Money raised by taxes may also be spent by the federal government to encourage these ends by making grants for housing, education, roads, and other social improvements, provided certain established standards are met.

Although the validity of taxes is seldom questioned before the courts today, the interpretation and application of the rules and regulations are subject to frequent litigation. However, Congress has delegated this authority to the Internal Revenue Service, and the courts recognize that fact, generally upholding the rulings of the Commissioner.

B.   ANTITRUST LAWS

Contracts in restraint of trade are generally against public policy. However, some are valid if they are reasonable for the parties to the contract and in the best interests of the public. For example, a promise not to compete, made in connection with the sale of a business, is enforceable so long as there is a need and the terms are reasonable both as to time and as to geographical area. During this century, many federal laws, rules, and regulations have been passed in the attempt to protect the public from monopolies. The most important of these have been the Sherman Antitrust Act, the Clayton Act, the Federal Trade Commission Act, and the Robinson-Patman Act.

1.   SHERMAN ANTITRUST ACT

In response to public concern over corporate monopoly, Congress passed the Sherman Antitrust Act in 1890. Its purpose was to break up existing monopolies by making illegal any restraint of trade and by imposing criminal penalties on anyone who attempts to monopolize commerce.

However, the U.S. Supreme Court in an early decision restricted the law by applying the "rule of reason," concluding that Congress intended only to prohibit "unreasonable" monopolies. Application of the rule of reason is set out in the following case.

FACTS   The National Football League (NFL) and Commissioner Pete Rozelle appealed from a district court judgment holding the "Rozelle Rule" in violation of the Sherman Act and enjoining its enforcement. The NFL operated under a reserve system whereby every player who signed a contract with an NFL club was bound to play for that club, and no other, for the term of the contract plus one additional year at the option of the club before he could become a free agent. In 1963, the Rozelle Rule was adopted which provided that if a free agent player signed a contract with a different club in the league, unless mutually satisfactory arrangements were made between the two clubs, the Commissioner at his sole discretion could name and award to the former club one or more players (including future draft choices), and his decision would be final and conclusive.

DECISION   The Court held that the Rozelle Rule, as implemented, violated the rule of reason and was an unreasonable restraint of trade in violation of the Sherman Act, because under the Rozelle Rule, a club would sign a free agent only where there was an agreement with the player's former team as to compensation or risk the awarding of unknown compensation by the Commissioner.

Mackey v. National Football League (543 F.2d 606 [8th Cir., 1976])

The Supreme Court has also held that certain activities constitute automatic, or *per se,* violations of the law because they are presumed to be harmful. These include price fixing, territorial restrictions, boycotts, tying arrangements, and production quotas.

Price fixing is an agreement among competitors to establish the price for which they will sell their product.

Agreements among producers to divide up and keep exclusive certain sales areas are illegal territorial restrictions.

Unlawful boycott occurs when competitors agree among themselves to exclude other businesses from dealing in their products. However, some agreements, such as those creating franchise operations that give the holder the sole right to sell a certain product or service within a given territory, have been held permissible.

Production quotas are agreements that arbitrarily restrict the supply of designated items, thereby increasing prices.

Violations of the act now carry criminal penalties of fines up to $100, 000, up to three years imprisonment, or both. Corporations may be fined up to one million dollars. The Department of Justice's Antitrust Division is responsible for initiating criminal proceedings and may also get court injunctions to stop violations of the act.

Any private person, or group, directly injured by violations of the antitrust law may sue for treble damages and court costs.

When the Sherman Antitrust Act was weakened by the rule of reason, business monopolies continued to grow. Congress then tried to correct the situation by enacting the Clayton Act and the Federal Trade Commission Act.

2. THE CLAYTON ACT

The Clayton Act prohibits agreements that make as a condition of selling products a promise not to buy those of a competitor. It also forbids mergers that create potential monopolies, such as horizontal mergers among competing firms, vertical mergers among companies in a chain of distribution, and certain types of conglomerate mergers. The tests applied by the courts to determine whether a merger is to be approved include consideration of the product involved, the geographical market, and the probable future effects of the proposed combination. The Act also prohibits a person from serving on more than one board of directors of competing large industrial corporations, other than banks, trust companies, and common carriers. The following case interprets the interlocking directorate prohibition rule of the Clayton Act.

> **FACTS**   The United States brought an action against three banks, their holding companies, four mutual life insurance companies, and five individuals who were directors of both a bank and an insurance company. It asserted that interlocking directorates between banks and competing insurance companies violated the Clayton Act. Section 8 of the Act bars a person from being a director of two or more large competing corporations other than banks, trust companies, and common carriers. The Court of Appeals held that this barred all interlocking directorates between banks and nonbanking corporations. This decision was appealed to the U.S. Supreme Court.

> **DECISION**   In a 5 to 3 decision, the Supreme Court held that the interlocking directorate rule applied only to large industrial corporations and was not intended to prohibit such activity involving banks. An individual could therefore be a director of both a bank and an insurance company, even though they competed in the interstate market for mortgage and real estate loans.

> *BankAmerica Corp, et al. v. United States,* (___ U.S. ___, 103 S.Ct. 2266, 76 L.Ed.2d 456 [1983])

3. THE FEDERAL TRADE COMMISSION ACT

The Federal Trade Commission Act declares unlawful unfair methods of competition in commerce and unfair or deceptive practices in business. These methods and practices are not defined but are left up to court determination.

The Act also created the Federal Trade Commission (FTC) to investigate and enforce the laws, providing it with several different remedies.

The FTC may obtain a voluntary consent decree wherein the violating firm agrees to stop the challenged action and the FTC agrees not to impose penalties. Press releases may be distributed to the news media through the FTC Office of Public Information. Advisory opinions may be issued to business firms concerning the legality of a proposed activity or questionable practice.

The FTC may issue a cease and desist order, similar to an injunction, directing some person or entity to stop its alleged violation of the antitrust laws.

Finally, the FTC, through the courts, may order such drastic actions as divestiture of improper holdings, dissolution of a business, or other specific corrective action (e.g., to require publication in the media of notice of errors and misrepresentations in commercial advertising).

4. THE ROBINSON-PATMAN ACT

The Robinson-Patman Act, an amendment to the Clayton Act, attempts to limit the power of large purchasers by prohibiting price discrimination in interstate commerce of commodities of like grade and quality. However, price differentials are permitted if the seller can prove a cost savings or a good faith price reduction to meet lawful competition.

C. ENVIRONMENTAL PROTECTION

Until recently, society assumed that humankind's waste materials could all be absorbed by land, air, and water. It is now obvious that modern products accompanied by rapid population growth and concentration are producing emissions beyond the capacity of nature's processes.

In passing the Environmental Quality Improvement Act of 1970, Congress expressly found that "population increase and urban concentration contribute directly to the pollution and degradation of our environment."

In an effort to check this destructive assault on the planet, Congress has enacted several laws for that purpose.

In December 1970, the President created the Environmental Protection Agency (EPA) to consolidate and implement the proposed legislation.

1. NATIONAL ENVIRONMENTAL POLICY ACT

The National Environmental Policy Act of 1969 requires, among other things, that an environmental impact statement be prepared on every recommendation for legislative or federal action that might significantly affect the quality of the environment.

2. CLEAN AIR ACT

The 1970 Clean Air Act separates air pollution control responsibilities into two categories, those dealing with mobile or transportation sources and others covering generally stationary sources. The law establishes time schedules for a 90 percent reduction of automobile emissions of hydrocarbons and nitrogen oxides. It places primary responsibility for the improvement and enforcement of air quality upon the individual states.

3. FEDERAL WATER POLLUTION CONTROL ACT

The Federal Water Pollution Control Act of 1972 was actually an amendment of the initial Federal Water Pollution Control Act passed in 1948. It proclaims the goals of having all water clean enough for swimming and recreational purposes by July 1, 1983, and by the year 1985 to have no pollutants discharged into the nation's waters. Although enforcement responsibility is primarily with the states, federal guidelines are established with provision for criminal penalties to be imposed for violations. In a criminal prosecution of the Allied Chemical Company for pollution of the James River, the court imposed a fine of $13,400,000. Any person or group whose interests are adversely affected may bring an action against anyone violating the standards set by EPA or a state.

4. FEDERAL ENVIRONMENTAL PESTICIDE CONTROL ACT

The Federal Environmental Pesticide Control Act of 1972 amends the Federal Insecticide, Fungicide, and Rodenticide Act of 1947 and gives to the EPA the responsibility of controlling the use of dangerous pesticides that might affect the environment.

5. NOISE CONTROL ACTS

The Noise Control Acts of 1970 and 1972 mandate the EPA and the Federal Aviation Administration to set standards and regulations for the control of aircraft noise and sonic booms. It delegates to the EPA and the Department of Transportation the same mission for interstate railroad and motor carriers. The Acts declare a policy to have an environment free from excessive noise that jeopardizes health and welfare.

6. MARINE PROTECTION, RESEARCH, AND SANCTUARIES ACT

The Marine Protection, Research, and Sanctuaries Act of 1972 prohibits ocean dumping of any waste or matter containing active chemical, biological, or radioactive agent.

D. EMPLOYMENT REGULATION

The modern employment relationship is regulated by numerous federal, state, and local laws, including labor law, worker safety, and discrimination.

1. LABOR LAW

Historically, workers found it difficult to better their wages and working conditions with the means available to them. After much strife and publicity, Congress yielded to public pressure and enacted laws to protect labor movements.

A. Norris-LaGuardia Act

In 1932, during the great depression, the Norris-LaGuardia Act was passed to limit the power of federal courts to issue injunctions in nonviolent labor disputes, and it declared a national policy encouraging the formation of labor unions without employer interference.

B. Wagner Act

The Wagner Act, passed in 1934, was an affirmative effort by the federal government to support unionization and collective bargaining. The Act prohibits certain unfair labor practices by employers, such as interfering with the right to unionize or bargain collectively, dominating a union, discriminating against union members, and refusing to bargain in good faith with authorized employee representatives.

C. Fair Labor Standards Act

The Fair Labor Standards Act of 1938 requires most employers to pay their employees at least a minimum hourly wage as set by the government and time and a half for hours worked in excess of 40 per week. Executives, administrators, professionals, and outside salespersons are exempt from the Act. Time worked includes that which is "suffered or permitted" as well as that which is actually directed by the employer. The following case illustrates an application of the Act.

> **FACTS**　Gilbert and Wade were employed by the Old Ben Coal Corporation as "mine surveyors," but they were not professionals. They placed wooden plugs into the roof of a mine as directional guides for mining machines. They determined the hours they worked as long as they had sufficient plugs in place for the next shift. Neither they nor the employer kept any records of the time they worked, and the employer considered them to be employees exempt from the FLSA. They claimed that they had worked about 50 hours a week and sued for overtime pay.
>
> **DECISION**　The Court held that the employee was required to prove the actual number of hours worked overtime, and since they had no records to establish that fact, they could not recover.
>
> *Gilbert v. Old Ben Coal Corp.* (85 Ill.App.3d 488, 40 Ill. Dec. 939, 407 N.E.2d 170 [1980])

D. Taft-Hartley Act

The Taft-Hartley, or Labor-Management Relations Act, was passed in 1947 following a large increase in union membership and much labor unrest. The law prohibits certain unfair labor practices by unions, such as secondary boycotts, jurisdictional strikes, refusal to bargain in good faith, requiring pay for work not done (featherbedding), and strikes to force discharge of nonunion employees. The Act also reinstates the power of the court to issue injunctions in labor disputes against an unfair labor practice if such is requested by the National Labor Relations Board.

E.   LANDRUM-GRIFFIN ACT

The Landrum-Griffin Act was passed in 1959 and was aimed at eliminating corruption in labor unions. It establishes an elaborate reporting system and sets forth a union member's bill of rights in an effort to make unions more democratic.

2.   EMPLOYEE PROTECTION

Numerous laws have been passed seeking to protect employees by providing a safe work environment and compensating them in the event of work injury.

A.   WORKERS' COMPENSATION

Prior to government regulation, an injured employee could recover from the employer only by showing that the injury was caused by the negligence of the employer. The employer also had several defenses available in such suits, including the fellow servant rule (no liability if the injury was caused by another worker), contributory negligence by the employee, and the doctrine of assumption of risk by a worker who knowingly takes a dangerous job.

All of the states have now adopted Workers' Compensation Acts to provide a more certain and faster remedy for injured employees. These laws create commissions or boards to determine if the employee is entitled to compensation and, if so, how much. They cover practically all job-related injuries and provide for medical expenses as well as wages for time lost from work because of the incident. In most jurisdictions, claims before the commission are the sole remedy available to the worker who is prohibited from filing a negligence lawsuit against the employer but may do so against third persons. These statutes usually permit employers to self-insure, buy insurance, or participate in a state fund. The following case illustrates the application of these laws.

> **FACTS**   Strother filed a Workers' Compensation claim against Morrison Cafeteria, her employer. She was a cashier and worked each night until 9:00 p.m. On three straight days, she observed two men in the cafeteria who were neither customers nor employees. On the third night she drove directly home from work and when she got out of her car, she was assaulted by one of these men who also stole her purse. She claimed that the assailant thought she was carrying the day's receipts of the cafeteria. The commission denied her claim on the basis that the injuries were not sustained in the course of her employment. She appealed.
>
> **DECISION**   The Court held that the test for coverage was "arising out of and in the course of employment" and that the cause of her injury

arose from her employment and was in the course of employment in the sense of continuity of time, space, and circumstances.

Strother v. Morrison Cafeteria (383 So.2d 623 [Fla., 1980])

B. SAFETY

Congress passed the Occupational Safety and Health Act in 1970 in an attempt to insure that every worker would have a safe and healthful place of employment. An administration was created to develop standards, conduct inspections, monitor complaints, and institute enforcement actions.

3. EMPLOYMENT DISCRIMINATION

Several federal laws have been enacted that prohibit discrimination in employment on the basis of race, sex, religion, ethnic origin, age, or handicap. They include Title VII of the 1964 Civil Rights Act, the Equal Pay Act, the Age Discrimination Act of 1967, and the Rehabilitation Act of 1973. Also, affirmative action programs by employers have been promoted to discourage discrimination in the workplace.

A. TITLE VII—CIVIL RIGHTS ACT OF 1964

Title VII of the Civil Rights Act of 1964 prohibits discrimination on the basis of race, color, sex, religion, or national origin in the hiring, firing, pay, promotion, training, or dismissal of employees. It applies to all employers who affect commerce and who have 15 or more employees. The Act creates the Equal Employment Opportunity Commission (EEOC), which has the power and the responsibility to file actions, attempt to compromise violations, investigate all charges of discrimination, and issue guidelines and regulations. Employers' defenses include the establishment of a bona fide seniority or merit system, a professionally developed ability test, or a bona fide occupational qualification. Remedies available to a person who suffers from such discrimination include the enjoining of an employer from such unlawful behavior, application of affirmative action, and reinstatement of an employee with an award of backpay for a period of up to two years. The following case demonstrates some of the problems in this type of action.

FACTS Alice LaBorde was an assistant professor at the University of California at Irvine. She was considered for promotion to full professor several times but rejected. She brought an action under Title VII of the Civil Rights Act of 1964 alleging that the decision not to promote her was based on an unlawful discrimination against her sex. She presented statistical data showing a shortage of female faculty members at the University which raised an inference of a pattern of discrimination in favor of men. The University stated that she was not promoted because of inadequate scholarship.

DECISION LaBorde established a prima facie case with the statistical evidence which then shifted the burden of proof to the University to show that she was rejected for a legitimate nondiscriminatory reason. The

University then showed that she had failed to meet their standards for scholarship and research. That shifted the proof back to her to show that the articulated reason was "a pretext or discriminatory in its application." Since she was unable to do this to the court's satisfaction, decision was for the University.

LaBorde v. Regents of the University of California (686 F.2d 715 [9th Cir., 1982])

B. Equal Pay Act

The Equal Pay Act requires that sex cannot be used as a basis for paying unequal pay for the same work. Seniority systems, merit systems, shift differentials, and piece rate systems are permitted so long as there is no sex discrimination. The same wages must be paid for equal work on jobs the performance of which requires equal skill, effort, and responsibility, and which are performed under similar working conditions.

C. Age Discrimination in Employment Act

The Age Discrimination in Employment Act prohibits discrimination in hiring, firing, salaries, promotion or other incidents of employment because of age. The principles of Title VII are applied to benefit persons between the ages of 40 and 70 and prohibit mandatory retirement of most employees before they reach age 70.

D. Rehabilitation Act

The Rehabilitation Act of 1973 attempts to assist the handicapped to obtain employment, rehabilitation training, and access to public facilities.

E. Affirmative Action Programs

The EEOC strongly promotes affirmative action programs by employers. All federal contractors are required to institute such programs, and programs are required wherever discrimination is found by EEOC or a court. The programs require the setting of goals to increase the proportions of minority group workers in the labor force by establishing goals and then seeking out members of the protected groups to fill them.

ILLUSTRATIVE CASES

1. Governmental Power to Tax Business

CITY OF PITTSBURGH v. ALCO PARKING CORP.

417 U.S. 369, 94 S.Ct. 2291, 41 L.Ed.2d 132 (1974)

WHITE, Justice.

The issue in this case is the validity under the Federal Constitution of Ordinance No. 704, which was enacted by the Pittsburgh, Pennsylvania, City Council in December 1969, and which placed a 20% tax on the gross receipts obtained from all transactions involving the parking or storing of a motor vehicle at a nonresidential parking place in return for a consideration. * * * Soon after its enactment, 12 operators of offstreet parking facilities located in the city sued to enjoin enforcement of the ordinance, alleging that it was invalid under the Equal Protection and Due Process Clauses of the Fourteenth Amendment, as well as Art. VIII, § 1, of the Pennsylvania Constitution, which requires that taxes shall be uniform upon the same class of subjects. It appears from the findings and the opinions in the state courts that, at the time of suit, there were approximately 24,300 parking spaces in the downtown area of the city, approximately 17,000 of which the respondents operated. Another 1,000 were in the hands of private operators not party to the suit. The balance of approximately 6,100 was owned by the Parking Authority of the city of Pittsburgh * * *. The trial court also found that there was then a deficiency of 4,100 spaces in the downtown area.

*   *   *

In the opinion of the Supreme Court of Pennsylvania, two aspects of the Pittsburgh ordinance combined to deprive the respondents of due process of law. First, the court thought the tax was "unreasonably high" and was responsible for the inability of nine of 14 different private parking lot operators to conduct their business at a profit and of the remainder to show more than marginal earnings. Second, private operators of parking lots faced competition from the Parking Authority, a public agency enjoying tax exemption (although not necessarily from this tax) and other advantages which enabled it to offer offstreet parking at lower rates than those charged by private operators. * * *

We cannot agree that these two considerations, either alone or together, are sufficient to invalidate the parking tax ordinance involved in this case. The claim that a particular tax is so unreasonably high and unduly burdensome as to deny due process is both familiar and recurring, but the Court has consistently refused either to undertake the task of passing on the "reasonableness" of a tax that otherwise is within the power of Congress or of state legislative authorities, or to hold that a tax is unconstitutional because it renders a business unprofitable.

*   *   *

It would have been difficult from any standpoint to have held that the ordinance was in no sense a revenue measure. The 20% tax concededly raised substantial sums of money; and even if the revenue collected had been insubstantial, or the revenue purpose only secondary, we would not necessarily treat this exaction as anything but a tax entitled to the presumption of the validity accorded other taxes imposed by a State.

*　　*　　*

The parking tax ordinance recited that "[n]on-residential parking places for motor vehicles, by reason of the frequency rate of their use, the changing intensity of their use at various hours of the day, their location, their relationship to traffic congestion and other characteristics, present problems requiring municipal services and affect the public interest, differently from parking places accessory to the use and occupancy of residences." By enacting the tax, the city insisted that those providing and utilizing nonresidential parking facilities should pay more taxes to compensate the city for the problems incident to offstreet parking. The city was constitutionally entitled to put the automobile parker to the choice of using other transportation or paying the increased tax.

The judgment of the Pennsylvania Supreme Court is reversed.

2. Franchising and the Antitrust Laws

PRINCIPE v. McDONALD'S CORP.

631 F.2d 303 (4th Cir., 1980)

This suit was brought by Principe Company (plaintiff) against McDonald's Corporation (defendant) for damages under Section 1 of the Sherman Act.

Principe acquired its first McDonald's franchise in 1970. At that time Principe executed a 20-year franchise license agreement and a store lease of equal duration. In 1974 Principe acquired a second franchise in Colonial Heights, Virginia, on similar terms. In 1976 Principe sought to purchase a third franchise in Petersburg, Virginia. Beavers, McDonald's regional manager, concluded that Principe lacked sufficient management depth and capability to take on a third store without impairing the quality of its existing operations. During the next 20 months Principe obtained corporate review and reconsideration of the decision to deny it the franchise. Principe was notified in May 1978 that the Petersburg franchise was being offered to a new franchisee.

PHILLIPS, Circuit Judge.　McDonald's is not primarily a fast food retailer. While it does operate over a thousand stores itself, the vast majority of the stores in its system are operated by franchisees. Nor does McDonald's sell equipment or supplies to its licensees. Instead its primary business is developing and collecting royalties from limited menu fast food restaurants operated by independent business people.

*　　*　　*

Having acquired the land, begun construction of the store and selected an operator, McDonald's enters into two contracts with the franchisee.

Under the first, the franchise agreement, McDonald's grants the franchisee the rights to use McDonald's food preparation system and to sell food products under the McDonald's name. The franchisee pays a $12,500 franchise fee and agrees to remit 3 percent of his gross sales as a royalty in return. Under the second contract, the lease, McDonald's grants the franchisee the right to use the particular store premises to which his franchise pertains. In return, the franchisee pays a $15,000 refundable security deposit (as evidence of which he receives a 20-year non-negotiable non-interest bearing note) and agrees to pay 8 1/2 percent of his gross sales as rent. These payments under the franchise and lease agreements are McDonald's only sources of income from its franchised restaurants. The franchisee also assumes responsibility under the lease for building maintenance, improvements, property taxes and other costs associated with the premises. Both the franchise agreement and the lease generally have 20-year durations, both provide that termination of one terminates the other, and neither is available separately.

Principe argues McDonald's is selling not one but three distinct products, the franchise, the lease and the security deposit note. The alleged antitrust violation stems from the fact that a prospective franchisee must buy all three in order to obtain the franchise.

As evidence that this is an illegal tying arrangement, Principe points to the unfavorable terms on which franchisees are required to lease their stores. * * * It urges that McDonald's can protect the integrity of its trademarks by specifying how its franchisees shall operate, where they may locate their restaurants and what types of buildings they may erect. Customers do not and have no reason to connect the building's owner with the McDonald's operation conducted therein. Since company ownership of store premises is not an essential element of the trademark's goodwill, Principe argues, the franchise, lease and note are separable products tied together in violation of the antitrust laws.

* * * Far from merely licensing franchisees to sell products under its trade name, a modern franchisor such as McDonald's offers its franchisees a complete method of doing business. It takes people from all walks of life, sends them to its management school, and teaches them a variety of skills ranging from hamburger grilling to financial planning. It installs them in stores whose market has been researched and whose location has been selected by experts to maximize sales potential. It inspects every facet of every store several times a year and consults with each franchisee about his operation's strengths and weaknesses. Its regime pervades all facets of the business, from the design of the menu board to the amount of catsup on the hamburgers, nothing is left to chance. This pervasive franchisor supervision and control benefits the franchisee in turn. His business is identified with a network of stores whose very uniformity and predictability attracts customers. In short, the modern franchisee pays not only for the right to use a trademark but for the right to become a part of a system whose business methods virtually guarantee his success. It is often unrealistic to view a franchise agreement as little more than a trademark license.

Given the realities of modern franchising, we think the proper inquiry is not whether the allegedly tied products are associated in the public mind with the franchisor's trademark, but whether they are integral components of the business method being franchised. Where the challenged aggregation is an essential ingredient of the franchised system's formula for success, there is but a single product and no tie-in exists as a matter of law.

*   *   *

* * * The formula that produced systemwide success, the formula that promises to make each new McDonald's store successful, that formula is what McDonald's sells its franchisees. To characterize the franchise as an unnecessary aggregation of separate products tied to the McDonald's name is to miss the point entirely. Among would-be franchisees, the McDonald's name has come to stand for the formula, including all that it entails. We decline to find that it is an illegal tie-in.

Judgment for McDonald's Corporation.

3. Occupational Safety

AMERICAN TEXTILE MFGRS. INST., INC. v. DONOVAN
452 U.S. 490, 101 S.Ct. 2478, 69 L.Ed 2d 185 (1981)

The American Textile Manufacturers Institute, Inc., a trade association representing 175 textile firms, and others (plaintiffs) challenged the validity of the cotton dust standard issued by Raymond Donovan (defendant), secretary of labor, under the Occupational Safety and Health Act.

Cotton dust—consisting of waste fibers, soil, noncotton plant matter, and other contaminants of cotton that are present in the air during the processing of cotton into cloth—causes a respiratory disease called byssinosis (brown lung disease) in a substantial proportion of the workers who are involved in that processing. It is estimated that of the currently employed and retired workers who are or have been involved in preparing the cotton and manufacturing cotton yarn, 1 in 12 suffers from the most disabling form of the disease and 25 percent are victims of the disease to some extent.

In 1976 OSHA published a proposed standard for maximum levels of the cotton dust in textile plants. After hearings had been conducted, comments from interested parties had been reviewed, and two studies estimating the costs of implementation to the industry had been reviewed, the secretary of labor in 1978 issued the final standard. This permitted exposure of textile workers to somewhat more dust than had been proposed originally and it allowed textile plants four years to reach full compliance.

BRENNAN, Justice. * * * The manufacturers urge not only that OSHA must show that a standard addresses a significant risk of material health impairment, but also that OSHA must demonstrate that the reduction in risk of material health impairment is significant in light of the costs of attaining that reduction. The Secretary on the other hand contends that the Act requires OSHA to promulgate standards that eliminate or reduce such risks "to the extent such protection is technologically and economically feasible."

* * *

Although their interpretations differ, all parties agree that the phrase "to the extent feasible" contains the critical language in § 6 (b) (5) for purposes of this case.

The plain meaning of the word "feasible" supports the Secretary's interpretation of the statute. According to Webster's Third New International Dictionary of the English Language, "feasible" means "capable of being done, executed, or effected." Thus, § 6 (b) (5) directs the Secretary to issue the standard that "most adequately assures * * * that no employee will suffer material impairment of health," limited only by the extent to which this is "capable of being done." In effect then, as the Court of Appeals held, Congress itself defined the basic relationship between costs and benefits, by placing the "benefit" of worker health above all other considerations save those making attainment of this "benefit" unachievable. Any standard based on a balancing of costs and benefits by the Secretary that strikes a different balance than that struck by Congress would be inconsistent with the command set forth in § 6 (b) (5). Thus, cost-benefit analysis by OSHA is not required by the statute because feasibility analysis is.

The legislative history of the Act, while concededly not crystal clear, provides general support for the Secretary's interpretation of the Act. The congressional reports and debates certainly confirm that Congress meant "feasible" and nothing else in using the term. Congress was concerned that the Act might be thought to require achievement of absolute safety, an impossible standard, and therefore insisted that health and safety goals be capable of economic and technological accomplishment. Perhaps most telling is the absence of any indication whatsoever that Congress intended OSHA to conduct its own cost-benefit analysis before promulgating a toxic material or harmful physical agent standard. The legislative history demonstrates conclusively that Congress was fully aware that the Act would impose real and substantial costs of compliance on industry, and believed that such costs were part of the cost of doing business.

Affirmed for the secretary of labor.

4. Sexual Discrimination in Employment

FLETCHER v. GREINER

106 Misc.2d 564, 435 N.Y.S.2d 1005 (1980)

LEVITT, J.   This is an action alleging charges of sexual discrimination in employment. * * * Plaintiff alleges that from July 18, 1963 to September, 1977 defendant used his "hegemonic position to importune plaintiff" into engaging in acts of sexual intercourse and deviate sexual behavior. Plaintiff asserts that compliance with defendant's requests were a condition of continuing employment and she feared that refusal of these advances would have an adverse effect.

Plaintiff, however, admits that hegemony notwithstanding, she eventually fell in love with defendant and he expressed love for her. She further alleges that they thereafter discussed a future life together and were contemplating matrimony. Indeed, she claims that at the insistence of defendant she divorced her husband in 1973 and waived alimony.

Plaintiff asserts that, four years later, in August, 1977, she refused to have any further sexual relations with defendant, whereupon defendant told her that he would not marry her and subsequently terminated her employment in September and salary payments in December.

The stated purpose of the "Human Rights Law" is to afford an equal opportunity to enjoy a full and productive life and to obtain employment without discrimination because of age, race, creed, color, national origin, sex, or marital status. It was not enacted to afford redress for breach of promise of marriage and its after-effects which, as plaintiff has cogently revealed, lies at the root of this action.

*   *   *

* * * The statute was not intended as a palliative for blighted love even when the lovers are employer and employee.

The primary purpose of the Civil Rights Act is to require employers to make employment-related determinations about their workers on the basis of each person's characteristics, so as to render irrelevant the employee's social, sexual, ethnic or religious background.

It was the intention of Congress to formally regulate the disparate treatment of men and women resulting from sex stereotypes * * *. * * *

Clearly, plaintiff has, through the facts presented on the present motions, failed to come within the purview of this statute. Her action, which she has characterized as "labor lost through force", should more appropriately be designated, as did Shakespeare, "love's labour's lost."

In the instant matter, plaintiff has failed to meet the requisite criteria of a cause of action based upon sexual harassment. Plaintiff, by her own admissions, supports this finding by stating that she and defendant were lovers and that their relationship included plans for a future marriage. Clearly, during most of plaintiff's association with defendant these advances were welcome in the furtherance of their meretricious relationship. However, statutory protection is afforded only to those who repulse the sexual suggestions and advances.

Plaintiff admits that defendant "stole her life" and that relations with him are bitter. To deny defendant's motion for summary judgment of this cause of action would open the floodgates to litigation by countless employees who have emotional affairs with their superiors that subsequently turn sour.

Dismissed for defendant.

5. Affirmative Action Programs

UNITED STEELWORKERS OF AMERICA v. WEBER

443 U.S. 193, 99 S.Ct. 2721, 61 L.Ed2d 480 (1979)

Brian Weber (plaintiff) brought this class action against United Steelworkers of America (defendant) alleging discrimination on the basis of race in violation of Title VII of the Civil Rights Act of 1964.

The Steelworkers and Kaiser Aluminum & Chemical Corporation entered into a master collective bargaining contract in 1974 that contained an affirmative action plan. The contract covered 15 plants. The aim of the affirmative action plan was to eliminate racial imbalances among craft workers, who were then almost all white. The goal for each plant was to have the percentage of blacks in craft positions equal their percentage in the respective local labor forces. The plan established in each plant an on-the-job training program for craft work and reserved 50 percent of the openings in these programs for blacks.

In the first year that the affirmative action plan was in operation at the Gramercy, Louisiana, plant, 13 trainees were selected from the plant work force. Seven were black, and six were white. The most junior black in the program had less plant seniority than several white workers, including Weber, who had been rejected. Weber brought suit against both the union and the employer, claiming that giving the craft training to blacks in preference to more senior white employees was discrimination on the basis of race in violation of Title VII.

BRENNAN, Justice.   The only question before us is the narrow statutory issue of whether Title VII *forbids* private employers and unions from voluntarily agreeing upon bona fide affirmative action plans that accord racial preferences in the manner and for the purpose provided in the Kaiser-USWA plan.

Weber argues that Congress intended in Title VII to prohibit all race-conscious affirmative action plans. His argument rests upon a literal interpretation of §§ 703(a) and (d) of the Act. Those sections make it unlawful to "discriminate * * * because of * * * race" in hiring and in the selection of apprentices for training programs.

Weber's argument is not without force. But it overlooks the significance of the fact that the Kaiser-USWA plan is an affirmative action plan voluntarily adopted by private parties to eliminate traditional patterns of racial segregation.

*   *   *

The prohibition against racial discrimination in §§ 703(a) and (d) of Title VII must therefore be read against the background of the legislative history of Title VII and the historical context from which the Act arose. Examination of those sources makes clear that an interpretation of the sections that forbade all race-conscious affirmative action would "bring about an end completely at variance with the purpose of the statute" and must be rejected.

* * * [I]t was clear to Congress that "the crux of the problem [was] to open employment opportunities for Negroes in occupations which have been traditionally closed to them" (remarks of Sen. Humphrey), and it was to this problem that Title VII's prohibition against racial discrimination in employment was primarily addressed.

Given this legislative history, we cannot agree with Weber that Congress intended to prohibit the private sector from taking effective steps to accomplish the goal that Congress designed Title VII to achieve. * * * It would be ironic indeed if a law triggered by a Nation's concern over centuries of racial injustice and intended to improve the lot of those who had "been excluded from the American dream for so long" (remarks of Sen. Humphrey), constituted the first legislative prohibition of all voluntary, private, race-conscious efforts to abolish traditional patterns of racial segregation and hierarchy.

We therefore hold that Title VII's prohibition in §§ 703(a) and (d) against racial discrimination does not condemn all private, voluntary, race-conscious affirmative action plans.

We need not today define in detail the line of demarcation between permissible and impermissible affirmative action plans. It suffices to hold that the challenged Kaiser-USWA affirmative action plan falls on the permissible side of the line. The purposes of the plan mirror those of the statute. Both were designed to break down old patterns of racial segregation and hierarchy.

At the same time the plan does not necessarily trammel the interests of the white employees. The plan does not require the discharge of white workers and their replacement with new black hires. Nor does the plan create an absolute bar to the advancement of white employees; half of those trained in the program will be white. Moreover, the plan is a temporary measure; it is not intended to maintain racial balance, but simply to eliminate a manifest racial imbalance. Preferential selection of craft trainees at the Gramercy plant will end as soon as the percentage of black skilled craft workers in the Gramercy plant approximates the percentage of blacks in the local labor force.

Reversed in favor of the Steelworkers.

PROBLEMS

1. Perez was a loan shark who loaned money to people in his neighborhood, charging them extortionate rates of interest and using threats of violence as a means of collection. Congress passed a law making loan sharking a federal crime, stating that the power to make such a law was within the Commerce Clause of the U.S. Constitution. When Perez loaned money to Miranda at an excessive rate of interest and threatened to have him put in the hospital when Miranda couldn't meet the ever increasing payment demands, Perez was arrested, tried, and convicted under this

law. Perez contends that he operates only in his local community and is not engaged in interstate commerce, therefore the law is unconstitutional. Is Perez correct?

2. Five competitors who made and sold most of the stainless steel pipe in the country met together on several occasions to discuss their problems. One of them stated, "I won't fix prices with any of you, but I'm going to put the price of my gidget at 'X' dollars. However, you all do what you want." He then leaves and competitor number two says and does the same. Following that process, all leave and all "fix" their prices for gidgets at "X" dollars. When charged with a criminal conspiracy to fix prices in violation of the Sherman Antitrust Act, they deny that any conspiracy occurred. What result?

3. Pueblo operated bowling alleys in three markets in competition with other bowling centers, some of which had purchased equipment from the Brunswick Corporation, the largest operator of bowling centers in the U. S. When Pueblo's competitor's defaulted on their accounts, Brunswick acquired these centers and continued their operation. Pueblo sued Brunswick for treble damages and injunctive relief on the grounds that Brunswick had lessened competition and that if the centers had been allowed to close, Pueblo would have made more profits. A jury gave a verdict for Pueblo for over two million dollars and Brunswick appealed. What result on appeal?

4. The National Commission on Egg Nutrition published advertising representing that there is no scientific evidence that eating eggs increases the risk of heart disease or heart attack. The Federal Trade Commission sought to enjoin such representations as false and violative of the Federal Trade Commission Act. What result?

5. Which, if any, of the following activities are violations of the antitrust laws?

(a) Two or more manufacturers of stereo equipment agree to sell their products at the same price.

(b) Two manufacturers of greeting cards agree to allocate territories whereby neither will sell its product in the area allocated to the other.

(c) A manufacturer and a distributor agree not to sell to a dealer a particular product or parts necessary for the repair of the product.

(d) Two or more dealers agree not to buy products from a particular manufacturer.

6. The State of Washington was preparing to construct a federally funded highway near Daly's property. Daly and other directly interested parties filed an action against the Secretary of Transportation and the Washington State Department of Highways to enjoin construction of the road on the grounds that the National Environmental Policy Act had been violated in that, among other things, no account had been taken of the impact the highway would have on Kimball Creek Marsh, an adjacent wildlife preserve. Will Daly succeed?

7. Tom Katz was a crane operator. While on the job he negligently climbed out on the arm of the crane to make an adjustment, fell, and was seriously injured. Murphy, his employer, had a safety manual for operators which strictly forbid such conduct, and Katz knew of this provision. Katz had also signed a waiver of liability when he took the job. Murphy denies liability on the basis of Katz's negligence, disobedience, and the waiver. What are Katz's rights?

8. The Duke Power Company had several operating departments but in the past had employed blacks only in the labor department, where the highest wages were lower than the lowest in the other departments. After the passage of the Civil Rights Act of 1964, the company required a high school education and a satisfactory score on two professionally prepared aptitude tests as a prerequisite for entering or transferring into the more desirable departments. Black employees sued on the basis of unlawful race discrimination. What should the U.S. Supreme court decide?

9. Los Angeles County required that age 35 was the maximum entry level age for employment of deputy sheriffs and fire department helicopter pilots. All applicants over 35 were rejected solely on the basis of age. The EEOC brought an action alleging that age under 35 was not a bona fide occupational qualification and the requirement was therefore a violation of the Age Discrimination in Employment Act. What should the court hold?

10. Department stores in New Orleans charge for alterations made to women's clothing but not for those sold in men's departments. A female customer claimed that this policy amounted to unlawful sex discrimination and sued under the Federal Civil Rights Act. Decision?

Chapter 44

BANKRUPTCY

Businesses and individuals frequently experience financial difficulty because of economic conditions, poor management, insufficient credit, or a variety of other factors. The U.S. Constitution provides that "Congress shall have power * * * to establish * * * uniform laws on * * * Bankruptcy throughout the United States." Under this authority, bankruptcy laws have been enacted to either allow a fresh start for an overburdened debtor or to obtain a period of judicial protection from the demands of creditors while the debtor tries to plan a workable reorganization of his or her business or personal financial activities.

In 1978 major changes were made to the existing bankruptcy law when Congress passed the Bankruptcy Reform Act, effective October 1, 1979, with a transition period until April 1, 1984. The Act provided that the new bankruptcy court would be phased in by April 1, 1984, but in 1982 the U.S. Supreme Court held that Congress could not confer such vast powers upon a court whose judges did not have the lifetime tenure and salary protection given to Article III federal judges under the U. S. Constitution. The court was therefore declared to be unconstitutional until corrected by Congressional legislation. Until Congress resolves this issue, the courts are operating under an emergency rule that refers contested legal issues to federal district judges for decision (*Northern Pipeline Construction Company v. Marathon Pipe Line Co.* [102 S. Ct. 2858 1982]).

The Bankruptcy Code consists of eight odd-numbered chapters. Chapters 1, 3, and 5 are administrative in nature and apply to all procedures. Chapter 7 provides for liquidation and was "straight bankruptcy" under the old act. Chapter 9 provides for adjustment of debts of a municipality or similar governing body. Chapter 11 provides for reorganization of businesses. Chapter 13 is for the adjustment of debts of an individual. Chapter 15 provides for a five-year pilot program in selected districts utilizing U.S. trustees.

A. PROCEDURE

The filing of a petition in bankruptcy with the court and payment of the filing fee commences the court's jurisdiction and the operation of the bankruptcy laws.

The Code provides alternatives for most debtors, with a liquidation process under Chapter 7, reorganization under Chapter 11, or debt adjustments of an individual under Chapter 13.

Petitions may be either voluntary or involuntary. Most petitions are voluntarily filed by the debtor, who need not be insolvent.

An involuntary petition may be filed only under Chapter 7 or 11. It may be filed by three or more creditors who have unsecured claims totaling $5,000 or more. If there are fewer than 12 creditors, one or more whose total claims equal at least $5,000 may file. Farmers, banks, insurance companies, and nonprofit corporations are exempt from involuntary petitions. If the debtor contests the petition, the court will order relief only if the debtor is not paying his or her debts as they become due or if within 120 days before filing, a custodian or receiver took possession of the property to enforce a lien. If the debtor does not oppose the petition, the court will enter an order for relief against the debtor.

The debtor is required to file a list of all creditors, a schedule of all assets and liabilities, and a statement of financial affairs.

The judge calls the first meeting of the creditors within a reasonable time after filing the petition or, if an involuntary petition is contested, from the time of the court order for relief. The judge cannot preside at or attend any creditors' meetings. The debtor must appear and submit to examination by the creditors and the trustee concerning debtor's assets and other matters that might affect discharge.

1. AUTOMATIC STAY

The filing of a bankruptcy petition triggers an automatic stay of creditor actions against the debtor's property, such as the beginning or continuing of judicial proceedings against the debtor, actions to obtain possession of debtor's property, liens against debtor's property, and setoffs of prior indebtedness owed to the debtor.

Upon proper complaint, the court may relieve the creditor from an automatic stay if good cause can be shown, such as lack of adequate protection for a secured interest, bad faith filing by the debtor, or lack of the debtor's equity in a security.

2. TRUSTEE'S DUTIES

The trustee, either one appointed by the court or the U.S. trustee, if one is appointed in the district, takes over the property of the debtor, inventories it, has it appraised, sets aside that portion exempt from execution under state law where so required by the state, or, under the Bankruptcy Code, recovers any preferences, voids fraudulent transfers, and reduces the estate to cash.

3. THE ESTATE

The debtor's estate consists of all legal and equitable interest of the debtor in nonexempt property; any property acquired within 180 days by inheritance, from property settlement agreement, divorce decree, or from life insurance proceeds; and property that may be recovered by the trustee by avoiding preferences and setting aside fraudulent transfers.

4. EXEMPTIONS

Although the Bankruptcy Code gives the debtor the option of electing either state or federal exemptions, it also gives the states the right to require that the state exemptions be used; most states have so opted. The following case illustrates how there might be a difference in exemptions.

> **FACTS** Lois Perry filed a voluntary petition under Chapter 7. Among the items of personal clothing that she listed as exempt under Virginia State law was a mink coat with a value of approximately $2,500. The statute included as exempt "all necessary wearing apparel of the debtor and his family." Under the Bankruptcy Code exemption, items of clothing up to $200 each are exempt, but Virginia places no monetary limits. The trustee claims the coat as an asset.
>
> **DECISION** The court decided that since there was no monetary limit, the question of good faith should be considered in determining what is necessary. Since a coat is a reasonably necessary item of clothing, the value should not govern. The exemption was allowed.
>
> *In re Perry* (6 B.R. 263 [Bkrtcy. Va., 1980])

The federal exemptions under the Bankruptcy Code include the following:

1. Equity in a residence up to $7,500.

2. Equity in a motor vehicle up to $1,200.

3. Household furnishings and clothing up to $200 per item.

4. Personal jewelry up to $500.

5. Tools of a trade up to $750.

6. Life insurance contracts.

7. Prescription health aids.

8. Any other property up to $400.

9. Social Security, disability, alimony, and like awards.

5. VOIDABLE PREFERENCES

The trustee has the right to recover any preferential payment made by an insolvent debtor to a favored creditor within 90 days of filing the bankruptcy petition, or if the favored party is an insider, such as a family member, if the payment or transfer was made within one year prior to filing.

6. FRAUDULENT TRANSFERS

The trustee may also avoid transfers of property made by the debtor to hinder, delay, or defraud creditors, including those made for less than reasonable value.

7. CLAIMS

The trustee examines all claims, approves those he or she finds proper, collects amounts due the debtor, and defends those filed against him or her. When paying claims, certain ones are given priority under the Code:

1. Fees and expenses of administering the estate.

2. Unsecured claims for employee wages up to $2,000 earned within 90 days before petition filed.

3. Contribution to employee benefit plan within 180 days of petition.

4. Up to $900 by individuals for deposits on personal goods or services for personal use that were not delivered or provided.

5. Taxes.

8. DISCHARGE IN BANKRUPTCY

Only an individual can be granted a discharge from debts in bankruptcy. If any objections are filed by a creditor or a trustee, a hearing is held. Certain types of obligations are not dischargeable in bankruptcy:

1. Taxes due any political unit.

2. Debts obtained by fraud.

3. Claims not scheduled in time for proof.

4. Embezzlement, larceny, or defalcation while acting in a fiduciary capacity.

5. Alimony and child support.

6. Willful and malicious torts.

7. Fines, penalties, and forfeitures payable to a governmental unit.

8. Student loans, unless due and owing over five years.

9. Claims waived or denied in a prior case.

9. DENIAL OF DISCHARGE

Serious infractions of business ethics may cause the denial of a discharge in bankruptcy, including such things as concealing assets to defraud creditors, falsifying records, committing a bankruptcy crime, and having had a prior voluntary discharge within six years.

10. EFFECT OF DISCHARGE

When a discharge has been obtained, the debtor is relieved from payment of the debts and, if sued for any of them, is entitled to set up the discharge in bankruptcy as an affirmative defense. However, a creditor may get a debtor to agree to pay a debt discharged in bankruptcy if it is reaffirmed before the discharge is granted and is approved by the court, and the debtor is given 30 days within which to rescind the agreement.

B. CHAPTER 11 REORGANIZATIONS

Chapter 11 reorganizations permit debtors to adjust their liabilities, satisfy or modify liens on property, and avoid liquidation. Chapter 11 is primarily intended for businesses but may be used by individuals. Initiation of a Chapter 11 may be either voluntary or involuntary, the same as in a Chapter 7. The court appoints one or more creditors' committees and, if the debtor is a corporation, a committee of the equity stockholders. The trustee consults with the committees; looks into the financial affairs; lists the creditors, liabilities, and assets; and files a plan for reorganization or reports as to why no plan is being filed. The trustee may also recommend conversion to a Chapter 7 plan. The plan of reorganization must be feasible, must protect the interest of the creditors, must be accepted, and must be confirmed by the court. The following case illustrates the need for a realistic plan.

> **FACTS**   Landmark at Plaza Park, Ltd., filed a plan of reorganization under Chapter 11. The debtor was a limited partnership whose only substantial asset was a 200-unit garden apartment complex. City Federal holds a $2,250,000 first mortgage at an interest rate of 9.5 percent. The plan would have Landmark issue a new nonrecourse note at 12.5 percent, secured by the same mortgage, and pay it off in 36 months by a combination of refinancing and accumulation of cash from the project. City Federal is undersecured, rejects the plan, and seeks to complete its foreclosure action.
>
> **DECISION**   The court ruled for City Federal, because the plan cannot be accepted over objection unless the total stream of payments has a value equal to the value of the property. The court felt that the interest rate on a new note should reflect the market rate of 15 percent and then determine whether there would be a reasonable prospect of success. It considered factors of the adequacy of the capital structure, the earning potential of the business, economic conditions, and the ability of management. The court then held that the requirement of confirmation of a plan is intended to prevent unrealistic schemes from being forced on creditors and concluded that if the plan were confirmed it would likely be followed by liquidation or further reorganization proceedings. Confirmation denied.

Matter of Landmark at Plaza Park, Ltd. (7 B.R. 653 [Bkrtcy. N.J., 1980])

C. CHAPTER 13 DEBT ADJUSTMENTS

Chapter 13 allows individuals (including small business owners) with regular income to apply for relief to adjust their debts and make repayment out of future income. The debtor must be an individual and is permitted to adjust both secured and unsecured debts with unsecured less than $100,000 and secured less than $350,000. A trustee is appointed to administer the program. The debtor files a plan that must provide for submission of future income to the trustee sufficient to administer the plan.

The Chapter 13 plan must divide the creditors into classes, set forth how each creditor is to be satisfied, state which claims are impaired or adversely affected by the plan, and provide for the same treatment to each creditor in a class unless they consent otherwise. The plan must provide for payment over a period of three years or less. (Under exceptional circumstances, it may be approved by the court for up to five years.)

The proposed plan is submitted to creditors for approval by the holder of two-thirds in amount and one-half in number of the classes impaired. If the court finds the plan to be fair and reasonable and in the best interest of creditors, and it appears the debtor will be able to make the payments, the plan may be confirmed and will be binding on the debtor and all creditors, whether they approve it or not.

Some plans, called zero plans, have been submitted that provide for no payment to the creditor in excess of what he or she would have received in liquidation (often zero) and the courts are not in agreement whether such plans should be approved. The Ninth Circuit court has held that a zero plan may be discharged even though it provided for no payment on a large debt for embezzlement. However, a bankruptcy court in Texas held that it was improper to use a Chapter 13 for the primary purpose of avoiding nondischargeable debts. After the debts have been paid, or at any time after confirmation, if the debtor is unable to make payments because of circumstances beyond his or her control, the court may grant a discharge.

ILLUSTRATIVE CASES

1. Bankruptcy Notice

UNITED STATES v. DIEZ

428 F.Supp. 1028 (D.C.La., 1977)

RUBIN, District Judge.   This case raises the issue of the dischargeability in bankruptcy of a debt due the United States on a postal service obligation when the address of the creditor was not properly given on the bankruptcy schedules.

In 1973 defendant Diez took two orders of stamps totalling $5,330 value on consignment from the United States Postal Service in Metairie, La. The order forms were signed only by the defendant without any indication that he was acting on behalf of anyone else.

The defendant later tendered two post-dated checks to the United States Postal Service in payment for the stamps, but these were dishonored when they were presented for payment. The Postal Service has recovered stamps worth $304.40 from defendant and now seeks to collect the balance due. The defendant contends he incurred the debt for a corporation, Alto Office Furniture & Supplies, Inc., and not personally.

Two years later the defendant filed a petition in bankruptcy. In his schedule of creditors he listed, among others, "U.S. Post Office $5,000." No address for this creditor was given. The Clerk of the Bankruptcy Court wrote in the address of the main Post Office in New Orleans, Louisiana. Pursuant to 11 U.S.C.A. § 94(e) the clerk's office then mailed a notice to the main post office in New Orleans and to the District Director of Internal Revenue. Notice also was sent to the U.S. Attorney's Office in New Orleans pursuant to Bankruptcy Rule 203(g). The defendant was later discharged.

* * *

A discharge in bankruptcy releases a bankrupt from all his provable debts, except "such as * * * have not been fully scheduled in time for proof and allowance, with the name of the creditor, if known to the bankrupt, unless such creditor had notice or actual knowledge of the proceedings." 11 U.S.C.A. § 35(a) (3).

Whenever the schedules of the bankrupt disclose a debt to the United States "acting through any department, agency, or instrumentality thereof * * *" it is the duty of the court to send a notice "to the head of such department, agency, or instrumentality," 11 U.S.C.A. § 94(e), as well as to the U.S. Attorney for the district in which the case is pending and to the District Director of Internal Revenue.

Diez listed the United States Post Office on his schedule of creditors but did not list an address. The Clerk of Court wrote in the address of the main New Orleans branch and mailed a notice to that office as well as to the District Director of Internal Revenue and to the U.S. Attorney for the Eastern District of Louisiana.

* * *

The question, thus, is whether notice to one branch of the U.S. Postal Service suffices as notice to the head of the agency. The U.S. Attorney, who appears for the Postal Service in this action, does not suggest that the notice should have been mailed to the Postmaster General of the United States in his capacity as Chief Executive Officer of the Postal Service, Washington, D.C. It suggests that the head of the agency involved was the postmistress in Metairie. This is untenable. The debt was not due the postmistress of the Metairie Branch; it was due the Postal Service of the United States. That service is but a single agency.

Moreover, the address was supplied by the Clerk of the Bankruptcy Court, not the debtor. * * *

* * *

For these reasons, the debt has been discharged. Judgment will be entered for the defendant.

2. Nondischargeable Debt

IN RE CONRAD

6 B.R. 151 (Bkrtcy. Ky., 1980)

Paul George Conrad filed a voluntary petition in bankruptcy in October 1979, listing $37,354 in liabilities and $25 in assets.

Conrad's obligations consisted of a loan executed in connection with a business venture, Double Dip Ice Cream Company; signature loans; revolving credit card accounts and a student loan of $4,125.79 owed to the U.S. Department of Health, Education, and Welfare.

Conrad had used the GI Bill of Rights to study at five different colleges and had also obtained three federally guaranteed long-term, low-interest student loans. After receiving his bachelor's degree, he had been employed as a teacher. He was terminated as a full-time teacher in April 1979, and since that time he had been on call as a substitute teacher, for which he was paid $33 a day when he was called. He had not sought other full-time employment. He lived at home with his 75-year-old mother. He did not have a car of his own and used his mother's van.

*   *   *

Accurately describing himself as "overweight", Conrad testified that his physical appearance "turns off a lot of people", including potential employers. * * *

*   *   *

* * * One of the issues in the bankruptcy proceeding was whether the student loan was dischargeable in bankruptcy.

DIETZ, Bankruptcy Judge.   Section 523(a) of the Bankruptcy Code provides that a bankruptcy discharge will not extend:

(8) to a governmental unit, or a nonprofit institution of higher education, for an educational loan, unless . . .

(B) excepting such debt from discharge under this paragraph will impose an undue hardship on the debtor.

Before examining the facts of the case before us, we will briefly review current decisions on the point. Even a cursory reading of them reveals the obvious—that each undue hardship case ultimately rests upon its own facts.

Undue hardship was held to entitle the petitioner to a discharge of student debt in *In re Johnson*. The bankrupt was a young woman who was pregnant, being divorced, had recently been seriously injured in an automobile accident, and had been asked by her parents to move out of their home. She planned to rent a room, give birth to the child, and live on welfare.

The claim of undue hardship in this case rests upon two asserted facts:

(1) Conrad must support and provide for his elderly mother, and (2) he is unable to obtain employment because of his physical appearance.

Upon the first point, we have some question as to who is supporting whom. The mother, who gave birth to this healthy young man while in her 44th year, and who fancies a mode of transportation generally associated with drivers two generations her junior, may be a vital woman indeed. Although the record does not indicate the extent of her income or financial substance, it is at least clear that Union Trust Bank would not extend credit to the son without the mother's hand being put to the note.

Upon the second point, we must observe, with neither cynicism nor cruelty, that corpulence is a condition which may swiftly diminish with continued impecuniosity.

This unemployed former president of the Double Dip Ice Cream Company, having double-dipped the available federal subsidies to obtain a superior education, should consider some alternatives. Enlightened self-interest would seem to suggest the virtue of a vigorous and energetic search for a proper workshop in which to use those intellectual tools which have been well honed at federal expense.

*   *   *

Ordered that the indebtedness of Paul George Conrad to the Department of Health, Education and Welfare, United States of America, is not dischargeable in bankruptcy.

Judgment against Conrad.

3. Effect of Discharge

GIRARDIER v. WEBSTER COLLEGE

563 F.2d 1267 (8th Cir., 1977)

URBOM, Chief District Judge. The issue here is whether a college may refuse to release transcripts of credits to former students for the sole reason that those students have not repaid to the college their National Defense Education Act loans and have obtained discharges in bankruptcy of those loans.

The plaintiff, Robert Girardier, took out a National Defense Student Loan with the defendant, Webster College, under Subchapter II of the National Defense Education Act, 20 U.S.C. sections 421–429. He received his bachelor's degree in May 1972. Thereafter, that plaintiff defaulted on the loan and filed bankruptcy papers, listing the college as an unsecured creditor in the sum of $1,500. He was subsequently discharged in bankruptcy from the payment of the loan. At a later time he applied to the defendant for a transcript of his undergraduate credits, tendering the $2 fee therefor. The defendant refused, for the sole reason that the plaintiff owed the defendant $1,500 from the plaintiff's discharged student loan, citing a provision in the college handbook: "No transcript is released until all accounts are paid." Counsel for the defendant admits that, if the plaintiff were to pay the obligation in full, the college would furnish the requested transcript. The plaintiff alleges that a transcript is necessary for him to receive his master's degree, to which he is otherwise entitled, from the University of Missouri-St. Louis.

Along with the provisions giving the bankruptcy court greater powers to determine the effect of discharge, Congress in 1970 passed 11 U.S.C. section 32(f)(2), which states:

> An order of discharge shall * * *
>
> (2) enjoin all creditors whose debts are discharged from thereafter instituting or continuing any action or employing any process to collect such debts as personal liabilities of the bankrupt.

The plaintiffs urge that the language "employing any process" extends to cover the action of the defendant. They argue that the absence of the adjective "legal" before the word "process" implies a Congressional intent to include informal means of debt collection within the proscription of the statute.

In providing a uniform system of bankruptcy, Congress has made fundamental policy of the Act the providing of a means for (1) the effective rehabilitation of the bankrupt and (2) the equitable distribution of the bankrupt's assets among his creditors. * * *

It is true that the first purpose has been variously stated as giving the debtor a new opportunity in life and a clear field for future effort, unhampered by the pressure and discouragement of preexisting debt. * * *

The plaintiffs urge that they are entitled to be treated in a nondiscriminatory manner by reason of their bankruptcy, unless the disparity in treatment is rationally supported. This may be a proper legislative end for the Congress to consider, but it is not the present law. * * *

The Bankruptcy Act, as now written, does not prohibit a private college's refusing to furnish transcripts to persons who have received a discharge in bankruptcy of their college loans. * * *

The judgment of the district court is vacated and the action is remanded to that court with directions to dismiss the complaints for failure to state a claim on which relief may be granted.

4. Discharge Set Aside for Fraud

APPEAL OF MOYNAGH

560 F.2d 1028 (1st Cir., 1977)

MARKEY, Judge.   This appeal is from an order of the district court entered October 29, 1976, affirming a revocation of appellant's discharge in bankruptcy granted August 12, 1975. We affirm.

On March 19, 1975, Moynagh filed a voluntary petition in bankruptcy. The Referee in Bankruptcy set June 10, 1975 as the date for the first meeting of creditors and July 10, 1975 as the last day for filing of objections to Moynagh's discharge.

At the first meeting of creditors, Moynagh was briefly examined by counsel representing the Guaranty Bank and Trust Co. of Worcester, Massachusetts (Bank), listed in the schedules accompanying the petition as a creditor holding a security interest in Moynagh's accounts receivable. During that examination Moynagh admitted that he had endorsed to his mother checks made payable to himself or his company. In response to questions concerning the total amount of the checks so endorsed, Moynagh stated that the amount, though not known exactly, was insignificant.

* * *

On August 20, 1975, the Bank filed a complaint seeking revocation of the discharge pursuant to § 15(1) of the Bankruptcy Act, 11 U.S.C.A. § 33(1), alleging that Moynagh had fraudulently transferred checks of account debtors totalling in excess of $70,000 to an account in his mother's and sister's names in the Worcester County National Bank (hereinafter the WCNB account).

* * *

* * * After a November 20, 1975 hearing on the merits, the Referee found, inter alia, that Moynagh had made: (1) fraudulent transfers of his property, (2) a false oath in his statement of affairs in matters pertinent to the discovery of assets, and (3) a materially false statement at the first meeting of creditors. For these reasons, the Referee concluded that the discharge should be revoked because it was obtained as a result of fraud upon the bankruptcy court. The district court affirmed, and this appeal followed.

* * *

The dispositive issue is whether Moynagh's discharge in bankruptcy can be revoked for fraud upon the bankruptcy court, and without a finding that the Bank lacked pre-discharge knowledge of Moynagh's transfers.

* * *

Section 15(1) of the Bankruptcy Act requires that an applicant seeking revocation of a discharge in bankruptcy on the ground of fraud establish "that the knowledge of the fraud has come to the applicant since the discharge was granted." This appeal, however, does not involve fraud on an applicant for revocation. The Referee's order, which the district court affirmed, specifically found that Moynagh's conduct throughout the proceedings leading to his discharge constituted a *fraud on the bankruptcy court.* Accordingly, whether or not the Bank had pre- or post-discharge knowledge of Moynagh's fraudulent transfers is irrelevant.

* * *

Bankruptcy legislation is intended to relieve an honest debtor from oppressive indebtedness and to permit him to start afresh. Having realized that Moynagh's discharge had been improvidently granted and that permitting it to stand would contravene the intent of the Bankruptcy Act, the Referee acted within his equity power in revoking it.

Affirmed.

5. Zero Plan—Chapter 13

LAWRENCE TRACTOR COMPANY v. GREGORY

705 F.2d 1118 (9th Cir., 1983)

Gregory filed his Chapter 13 bankruptcy petition on November 8, 1979. At that time he owed appellant Lawrence $16,540.58 as the result of the state court judgment against him for embezzlement.

* * *

The order stated that Gregory's "plan of arrangement" divided creditors into seven groups. Group six was "general unsecured creditors" beneath the list of groups the order stated: "The debtor's plan does not propose payment of unsecured creditors." The order also stated, "The plan proposes payment to the Trustee of $147.71 monthly." Lawrence did not receive a copy of Gregory's plan with the order.

The creditors' meeting and the confirmation hearing were held as scheduled on December 17. Lawrence was not represented at either. On January 2, 1980 the bankruptcy court issued its order confirming the plan. Lawrence did not appeal.

* * *

In March 1980, two months after the plan was confirmed, Lawrence filed its "Complaint to Determine Dischargeability of Debt," alleging that its claim was nondischargeable because: (1) it was derived from embezzlement; (2) only debts "provided for" in a plan are dischargeable under section 1328(a), and a debt for which zero payment is proposed is not so provided for * * *.

* * *

Lawrence's initial argument is that a plan proposing zero payment on unsecured claims is not confirmable under the Bankruptcy Code.

Section 1325, which sets out six conditions that a plan must satisfy before it will be confirmed, does not establish a minimum permissible payment. Section 1325(a)(3), however, requires that the plan be "proposed in good faith."

* * *

If the bankrupt can show good faith, it seems almost pointless to distinguish between nominal-payment and zero-payment plans. In fact, the view from the trenches appears to be that zero-payment plans are administratively preferable. * * *

By stating that "this plan provides for -0- payment to unsecured creditors requesting that said debts be discharged," the plan made a provision regarding or "provided for" those debts, and once the order confirming the plan became final and the required payments were made, they became dischargeable under section 1328(a).

* * *

The total discharge of a claim for almost $17,000 against a convicted embezzler upon completion of a Chapter 13 plan which required only six monthly payments of less than $150 seems grossly unfair. However, the claim is legally dischargeable. Lawrence might have objected to the confirmation of the plan on the ground that it was not proposed in good faith. Having permitted the confirmation order to become final, however, it is precluded from raising that objection in subsequent proceedings. By stating that zero payment was to be made on unsecured debts, the plan "provided for" those debts within the meaning of 11 U.S.C. Sec. 1328(a) and when all payments were completed, they became dischargeable.

PROBLEMS

1. Will Terry has a wife, nine children, no job, and debts of $10,000. He has filed voluntary Chapter 7 bankruptcy. Because he has no assets, a creditor of Terry's claims the action improper, alleging that only business people may file voluntary bankruptcy. Is the creditor correct?

2. Mark Boles filed voluntary bankruptcy and submitted the necessary schedules of assets and liabilities with his petition. He was ordered to appear at the first meeting of his creditors. Here he was asked, under oath, many questions concerning his financial affairs. Boles felt that he shouldn't be required to answer some of these questions, because they invaded his privacy. Can he refuse to answer for this reason?

3. Vera Sharp was injured in an auto accident. She alleged that the accident was Ken Brewer's fault. Sharp filed suit against Brewer for $10,000 in damages, following which Brewer filed voluntary bankruptcy. Sharp then sought to file a $10,000 claim in bankruptcy. May she do so?

4. Willie Hyde, having engaged in embarrassing financial transactions, destroyed all of his records. Later, before he had paid off debts incurred during these transactions, Hyde filed voluntary bankruptcy. The story of the destruction of the records emerged during the conduct of the bankruptcy proceedings. Some of Hyde's creditors claimed he should not be granted a discharge from his debts due to this destruction of records. Were the creditors correct?

5. The debtor had made education loans of $6,635, which she now wants to discharge in bankruptcy. She has a take-home pay of $650 a month and reasonable monthly expenses of $926 for her and her three children. Last winter a church had to pay her gas bill so that she could heat her home. She has many unpaid medical bills. She has been sued, and her wages have been garnished. She filed a voluntary bankruptcy petition. Are the unpaid student loans dischargeable?

6. Northwest Products, Inc. filed a petition for a Chapter 11 reorganization. Sierra Supply Co., one of Northwest's creditors, filed a motion to convert the case to a Chapter 7 liquidation. The court found that the debtor corporation had no place of business, no inventory, no equipment, no employees, and no business phone. Should Northwest be permitted to reorganize under Chapter 11?

7. Danny Wood used his charge account to purchase $700 worth of merchandise

from Sears. Less than two months later, Wood filed a bankruptcy petition and subsequently was discharged from his debt. Sears then sued Wood for the amount of the debt, claiming that the merchandise had been obtained by false pretenses or false representations and that the debt was therefore not discharged. What decision?

8. Okamoto owed money to Hornblower & Weeks-Hemphill, Noyes. Hornblower filed a petition to have Okamoto declared an involuntary bankrupt. Okamoto moved to dismiss the petition on the grounds that he had more than 12 creditors and the petition could therefore not be filed by only one. Hornblower replied that because the claims of the other creditors were too small to count and Okamoto did not have more than 12 creditors, the petition could accordingly be filed by one. Decision?

9. Duffy leased a car from Avis on a long-term basis. Duffy made no payments for a period of time. After a conversation with an Avis representative, Duffy then forwarded to Avis a check for $400 postdated to August 3. The check cleared and was honored by the drawee bank on August 6, which was 88 days before the debtor Duffy filed his Chapter 7 petition for relief in bankruptcy. The check was delivered to Avis more than 90 days before the filing but was cashed within the 90-day period. The trustee seeks to set aside the $400 payment as a voidable preference. Decision?

10. Bingham received a discharge in bankruptcy. Several months later, a creditor of a debt that was discharged in the bankruptcy met Bingham in a bar. After a few drinks, the creditor got Bingham to agree to pay the old debt. However, the next day Bingham refused when the creditor reminded him of the agreement. The creditor sues on the debt. Decision?

APPENDIXES

A

Uniform Commercial Code

B

Uniform Partnership Act

C

Uniform Limited Partnership Act

D

Revised Uniform Limited Partnership Act

E

Model Business Corporation Act

Appendix A

THE UNIFORM COMMERCIAL CODE

(Adopted in 52 jurisdictions; all 50 States, although Louisiana has adopted only Articles 1, 3, 4, and 5; the District of Columbia, and the Virgin Islands.)

The Code consists of 10 Articles as follows:

Art.

1. GENERAL PROVISIONS

2. Sales

3. Commercial Paper

4. Bank Deposits and Collections

5. Letters of Credit

6. Bulk Transfers

7. Warehouse Receipts, Bills of Lading and Other Documents of Title

8. Investment Securities

9. Secured Transactions: Sales of Accounts, Contract Rights and Chattel Paper

10. Effective Date and Repealer

Article 1
GENERAL PROVISIONS

Part 1 Short Title, Construction, Application and Subject Matter of the Act

§ 1—101. **Short Title.**

This Act shall be known and may be cited as Uniform Commercial Code.

§ 1—102. **Purposes; Rules of Construction; Variation by Agreement.**

(1) This Act shall be liberally construed and applied to promote its underlying purposes and policies.

(2) Underlying purposes and policies of this Act are

(a) to simplify, clarify and modernize the law governing commercial transactions;

(b) to permit the continued expansion of commercial practices through custom, usage and agreement of the parties;

(c) to make uniform the law among the various jurisdictions.

(3) The effect of provisions of this Act may be varied by agreement, except as otherwise provided in this Act and except that the obligations of good faith, diligence, reasonableness and care prescribed by this Act may not be disclaimed by agreement but the parties may by agreement determine the standards by which the performance of such obligations is to be measured if such standards are not manifestly unreasonable.

(4) The presence in certain provisions of this Act of the words "unless otherwise agreed" or words of similar import does not imply that the effect of other provisions may not be varied by agreement under subsection (3).

(5) In this Act unless the context otherwise requires

(a) words in the singular number include the plural, and in the plural include the singular;

(b) words of the masculine gender include the feminine and the neuter, and when the sense so indicates words of the neuter gender may refer to any gender.

§ 1—103. **Supplementary General Principles of Law Applicable.**

Unless displaced by the particular provisions of this

Act, the principles of law and equity, including the law merchant and the law relative to capacity to contract, principal and agent, estoppel, fraud, misrepresentation, duress, coercion, mistake, bankruptcy, or other validating or invalidating cause shall supplement its provisions.

§ 1—104. **Construction Against Implicit Repeal.**

This Act being a general act intended as a unified coverage of its subject matter, no part of it shall be deemed to be impliedly repealed by subsequent legislation if such construction can reasonably be avoided.

§ 1—105. **Territorial Application of the Act; Parties' Power to Choose Applicable Law.**

(1) Except as provided hereafter in this section, when a transaction bears a reasonable relation to this state and also to another state or nation the parties may agree that the law either of this state or of such other state or nation shall govern their rights and duties. Failing such agreement this Act applies to transactions bearing an appropriate relation to this state.

(2) Where one of the following provisions of this Act specifies the applicable law, that provision governs and a contrary agreement is effective only to the extent permitted by the law (including the conflict of laws rules) so specified:

> Rights of creditors against sold goods. Section 2—402.
>
> Applicability of the Article on Bank Deposits and Collections. Section 4—102.
>
> Bulk transfers subject to the Article on Bulk Transfers. Section 6—102.
>
> Applicability of the Article on Investment Securities. Section 8—106.
>
> Perfection provisions of the Article on Secured Transactions. Section 9—103.

§ 1—106. **Remedies to Be Liberally Administered.**

(1) The remedies provided by this Act shall be liberally administered to the end that the aggrieved party may be put in as good a position as if the other party had fully performed but neither consequential or special nor penal damages may be had except as specifically provided in this Act or by other rule of law.

(2) Any right or obligation declared by this Act is enforceable by action unless the provision declaring it specifies a different and limited effect.

§ 1—107. **Waiver or Renunciation of Claim or Right After Breach.**

Any claim or right arising out of an alleged breach can be discharged in whole or in part without consideration by a written waiver or renunciation signed and delivered by the aggrieved party.

§ 1—108. **Severability.**

If any provision or clause of this Act or application thereof to any person or circumstances is held invalid, such invalidity shall not affect other provisions or applications of the Act which can be given effect without the invalid provision or application, and to this end the provisions of this Act are declared to be severable.

§ 1—109. **Section Captions.**

Section captions are parts of this Act.

Part 2 **General Definitions and Principles of Interpretation**

§ 1—201. **General Definitions.**

Subject to additional definitions contained in the subsequent Articles of this Act which are applicable to specific Articles or Parts thereof, and unless the context otherwise requires, in this Act:

(1) "Action" in the sense of a judicial proceeding includes recoupment, counterclaim, set-off, suit in equity and any other proceedings in which rights are determined.

(2) "Aggrieved party" means a party entitled to resort to a remedy.

(3) "Agreement" means the bargain of the parties in fact as found in their language or by implication from other circumstances including course of dealing or usage of trade or course of performance as provided in this Act (Sections 1—205 and 2—208). Whether an agreement has legal consequences is determined by the provisions of this Act, if applicable; otherwise by the law of contracts (Section 1—103). (Compare "Contract".)

(4) "Bank" means any person engaged in the business of banking.

(5) "Bearer" means the person in possession of an instrument, document of title, or certified security payable to bearer or indorsed in blank.

(6) "Bill of lading" means a document evidencing the receipt of goods for shipment issued by a person engaged in the business of transporting or forwarding goods, and includes an airbill. "Airbill" means a doc-

ument serving for air transportation as a bill of lading does for marine or rail transportation, and includes an air consignment note or air waybill.

(7) "Branch" includes a separately incorporated foreign branch of a bank.

(8) "Burden of establishing" a fact means the burden of persuading the triers of fact that the existence of the fact is more probable than its non-existence.

(9) "Buyer in ordinary course of business" means a person who in good faith and without knowledge that the sale to him is in violation of the ownership rights or security interest of a third party in the goods buys in ordinary course from a person in the business of selling goods of that kind but does not include a pawnbroker. All persons who sell minerals or the like (including oil and gas) at wellhead or minehead shall be deemed to be persons in the business of selling goods of that kind. "Buying" may be for cash or by exchange of other property or on secured or unsecured credit and includes receiving goods or documents of title under a pre-existing contract for sale but does not include a transfer in bulk or as security for or in total or partial satisfaction of a money debt.

(10) "Conspicuous": A term or clause is conspicuous when it is so written that a reasonable person against whom it is to operate ought to have noticed it. A printed heading in capitals (as: NON-NEGOTIABLE BILL OF LADING) is conspicuous. Language in the body of a form is "conspicuous" if it is in larger or other contrasting type or color. But in a telegram any stated term is "conspicuous". Whether a term or clause is "conspicuous" or not is for decision by the court.

(11) "Contract" means the total legal obligation which results from the parties' agreement as affected by this Act and any other applicable rules of law. (Compare "Agreement".)

(12) "Creditor" includes a general creditor, a secured creditor, a lien creditor and any representative of creditors, including an assignee for the benefit of creditors, a trustee in bankruptcy, a receiver in equity and an executor or administrator of an insolvent debtor's or assignor's estate.

(13) "Defendant" includes a person in the position of defendant in a cross-action or counterclaim.

(14) "Delivery" with respect to instruments, documents of title, chattel paper, or certificated securities means voluntary transfer of possession.

(15) "Document of title" includes bill of lading, dock warrant, dock receipt, warehouse receipt or order for

the delivery of goods, and also any other document which in the regular course of business or financing is treated as adequately evidencing that the person in possession of it is entitled to receive, hold and dispose of the document and the goods it covers. To be a document of title a document must purport to be issued by or addressed to a bailee and purport to cover goods in the bailee's possession which are either identified or are fungible portions of an identified mass.

(16) "Fault" means wrongful act, omission or breach.

(17) "Fungible" with respect to goods or securities means goods or securities of which any unit is, by nature or usage of trade, the equivalent of any other like unit. Goods which are not fungible shall be deemed fungible for the purposes of this Act to the extent that under a particular agreement or document unlike units are treated as equivalents.

(18) "Genuine" means free of forgery or counterfeiting.

(19) "Good faith" means honesty in fact in the conduct or transaction concerned.

(20) "Holder" means a person who is in possession of a document of title or an instrument or a certificated investment security drawn, issued, or indorsed to him or his order or to bearer or in blank.

(21) To "honor" is to pay or to accept and pay, or where a credit so engages to purchase or discount a draft complying with the terms of the credit.

(22) "Insolvency proceedings" includes any assignment for the benefit of creditors or other proceedings intended to liquidate or rehabilitate the estate of the person involved.

(23) A person is "insolvent" who either has ceased to pay his debts in the ordinary course of business or cannot pay his debts as they become due or is insolvent within the meaning of the federal bankruptcy law.

(24) "Money" means a medium of exchange authorized or adopted by a domestic or foreign government as a part of its currency.

(25) A person has "notice" of a fact when

    (a) he has actual knowledge of it; or

    (b) he has received a notice or notification of it; or

    (c) from all the facts and circumstances known to him at the time in question he has reason to know that it exists.

A person "knows" or has "knowledge" of a fact when he has actual knowledge of it. "Discover" or "learn" or a word or phrase of similar import refers to knowledge rather than to reason to know. The time and circumstances under which a notice or notification may cease to be effective are not determined by this Act.

(26) A person "notifies" or "gives" a notice or notification to another by taking such steps as may be reasonably required to inform the other in ordinary course whether or not such other actually comes to know of it. A person "receives" a notice or notification when

(a) it comes to his attention; or

(b) it is duly delivered at the place of business through which the contract was made or at any other place held out by him as the place for receipt of such communications.

(27) Notice, knowledge or a notice or notification received by an organization is effective for a particular transaction from the time when it is brought to the attention of the individual conducting that transaction, and in any event from the time when it would have been brought to his attention if the organization had exercised due diligence. An organization exercises due diligence if it maintains reasonable routines for communicating significant information to the person conducting the transaction and there is reasonable compliance with the routines. Due diligence does not require an individual acting for the organization to communicate information unless such communication is part of his regular duties or unless he has reason to know of the transaction and that the transaction would be materially affected by the information.

(28) "Organization" includes a corporation, government or governmental subdivision or agency, business trust, estate, trust, partnership or association, two or more persons having a joint or common interest, or any other legal or commercial entity.

(29) "Party", as distinct from "third party", means a person who has engaged in a transaction or made an agreement within this Act.

(30) "Person" includes an individual or an organization (See Section 1—102).

(31) "Presumption" or "presumed" means that the trier of fact must find the existence of the fact presumed unless and until evidence is introduced which would support a finding of its non-existence.

(32) "Purchase" includes taking by sale, discount, negotiation, mortgage, pledge, lien, issue or re-issue, gift or any other voluntary transaction creating an interest in property.

(33) "Purchaser" means a person who takes by purchase.

(34) "Remedy" means any remedial right to which an aggrieved party is entitled with or without resort to a tribunal.

(35) "Representative" includes an agent, an officer of a corporation or association, and a trustee, executor or administrator of an estate, or any other person empowered to act for another.

(36) "Rights" includes remedies.

(37) "Security interest" means an interest in personal property or fixtures which secures payment or performance of an obligation. The retention or reservation of title by a seller of goods notwithstanding shipment or delivery to the buyer (Section 2—401) is limited in effect to a reservation of a "security interest". The term also includes any interest of a buyer of accounts or chattel paper which is subject to Article 9. The special property interest of a buyer of goods on identification of such goods to a contract for sale under Section 2—401 is not a "security interest", but a buyer may also acquire a "security interest" by complying with Article 9. Unless a lease or consignment is intended as security, reservation of title thereunder is not a "security interest" but a consignment is in any event subject to the provisions on consignment sales (Section 2—326). Whether a lease is intended as security is to be determined by the facts of each case; however, (a) the inclusion of an option to purchase does not of itself make the lease one intended for security, and (b) an agreement that upon compliance with the terms of the lease the lessee shall become or has the option to become the owner of the property for no additional consideration or for a nominal consideration does make the lease one intended for security.

(38) "Send" in connection with any writing or notice means to deposit in the mail or deliver for transmission by any other usual means of communication with postage or cost of transmission provided for and properly addressed and in the case of an instrument to an address specified thereon or otherwise agreed, or if there be none to any address reasonable under the circumstances. The receipt of any writing or notice within the time at which it would have arrived if properly sent has the effect of a proper sending.

(39) "Signed" includes any symbol executed or adopted by a party with present intention to authenticate a writing.

(40) "Surety" includes guarantor.

(41) "Telegram" includes a message transmitted by radio, teletype, cable, any mechanical method of transmission, or the like.

(42) "Term" means that portion of an agreement which relates to a particular matter.

(43) "Unauthorized" signature or indorsement means one made without actual, implied or apparent authority and includes a forgery.

(44) "Value". Except as otherwise provided with respect to negotiable instruments and bank collections (Sections 3—303, 4—208 and 4—209) a person gives "value" for rights if he acquires them

   (a) in return for a binding commitment to extend credit or for the extension of immediately available credit whether or not drawn upon and whether or not a chargeback is provided for in the event of difficulties in collection; or

   (b) as security for or in total or partial satisfaction of a pre-existing claim; or

   (c) by accepting delivery pursuant to a preexisting contract for purchase; or

   (d) generally, in return for any consideration sufficient to support a simple contract.

(45) "Warehouse receipt" means a receipt issued by a person engaged in the business of storing goods for hire.

(46) "Written" or "writing" includes printing, typewriting or any other intentional reduction to tangible form.

Amended in 1962, 1972 and 1977.

§ 1—202. Prima Facie Evidence by Third Party Documents.

A document in due form purporting to be a bill of lading, policy or certificate of insurance, official weigher's or inspector's certificate, consular invoice, or any other document authorized or required by the contract to be issued by a third party shall be prima facie evidence of its own authenticity and genuineness and of the facts stated in the document by the third party.

§ 1—203. Obligation of Good Faith.

Every contract or duty within this Act imposes an obligation of good faith in its performance or enforcement.

§ 1—204. Time; Reasonable Time; "Seasonably".

(1) Whenever this Act requires any action to be taken within a reasonable time, any time which is not manifestly unreasonable may be fixed by agreement.

(2) What is a reasonable time for taking any action depends on the nature, purpose and circumstances of such action.

(3) An action is taken "seasonably" when it is taken at or within the time agreed or if no time is agreed at or within a reasonable time.

§ 1—205. Course of Dealing and Usage of Trade.

(1) A course of dealing is a sequence of previous conduct between the parties to a particular transaction which is fairly to be regarded as establishing a common basis of understanding for interpreting their expressions and other conduct.

(2) A usage of trade is any practice or method of dealing having such regularity of observance in a place, vocation or trade as to justify an expectation that it will be observed with respect to the transaction in question. The existence and scope of such a usage are to be proved as facts. If it is established that such a usage is embodied in a written trade code or similar writing the interpretation of the writing is for the court.

(3) A course of dealing between parties and any usage of trade in the vocation or trade in which they are engaged or of which they are or should be aware give particular meaning to and supplement or qualify terms of an agreement.

(4) The express terms of an agreement and an applicable course of dealing or usage of trade shall be construed wherever reasonable as consistent with each other; but when such construction is unreasonable express terms control both course of dealing and usage of trade and course of dealing controls usage trade.

(5) An applicable usage of trade in the place where any part of performance is to occur shall be used in interpreting the agreement as to that part of the performance.

(6) Evidence of a relevant usage of trade offered by one party is not admissible unless and until he has given the other party such notice as the court finds sufficient to prevent unfair surprise to the latter.

§ 1—206. Statute of Frauds for Kinds of Personal Property Not Otherwise Covered.

(1) Except in the cases described in subsection (2) of

this section a contract for the sale of personal property is not enforceable by way of action or defense beyond five thousand dollars in amount or value of remedy unless there is some writing which indicates that a contract for sale has been made between the parties at a defined or stated price, reasonably identifies the subject matter, and is signed by the party against whom enforcement is sought or by his authorized agent.

(2) Subsection (1) of this section does not apply to contracts for the sale of goods (Section 2—201) nor of securities (Section 8—319) nor to security agreements (Section 9—203).

§ 1—207. Performance or Acceptance Under Reservation of Rights.

A party who with explicit reservation of rights performs or promises performance or assents to performance in the manner demanded or offered by the other party does not thereby prejudice the rights reserved. Such words as "without prejudice", "under protest" or the like are sufficient.

§ 1—208. Option to Accelerate at Will.

A term providing that one party or his successor in interest may accelerate payment or performance or require collateral or additional collateral "at will" or "when he deems himself insecure" or in words of similar import shall be construed to mean that he shall have power to do so only if he in good faith believes that the prospect of payment or performance is impaired. The burden of establishing lack of good faith is on the party against whom the power has been exercised.

§ 1—209. Subordinated Obligations

An obligation may be issued as subordinated to payment of another obligation of the person obligated, or a creditor may subordinate his right to payment of an obligation by agreement with either the person obligated or another creditor of the person obligated. Such a subordination does not create a security interest as against either the common debtor or a subordinated creditor. This section shall be construed as declaring the law as it existed prior to the enactment of this section and not as modifying it. Added 1966.

Note: *This new section is proposed as an optional provision to make it clear that a subordination agreement does not create a security interest unless so intended.*

Article 2
SALES

Part 1
Short Title, General Construction and Subject Matter

§ 2—101. Short Title.

This Article shall be known and may be cited as Uniform Commercial Code—Sales.

§ 2—102. Scope; Certain Security and Other Transactions Excluded From This Article.

Unless the context otherwise requires, this Article applies to transactions in goods; it does not apply to any transaction which although in the form of an unconditional contract to sell or present sale is intended to operate only as a security transaction nor does this Article impair or repeal any statute regulating sales to consumers, farmers or other specified classes of buyers.

§ 2—103. Definitions and Index of Definitions.

(1) In this Article unless the context otherwise requires

    (a) "Buyer" means a person who buys or contracts to buy goods.

    (b) "Good faith" in the case of a merchant means honesty in fact and the observance of reasonable commercial standards of fair dealing in the trade.

    (c) "Receipt" of goods means taking physical possession of them.

    (d) "Seller" means a person who sells or contracts to sell goods.

(2) Other definitions applying to this Article or to specified Parts thereof, and the sections in which they appear are:

"Acceptance". Section 2—606.
"Banker's credit". Section 2—325.
"Between merchants". Section 2—104.
"Cancellation". Section 2—106(4).
"Commercial unit". Section 2—105.
"Confirmed credit". Section 2—325.
"Conforming to contract". Section 2—106.
"Contract for sale". Section 2—106.
"Cover". Section 2—712.
"Entrusting". Section 2—403.
"Financing agency". Section 2—104.

(3) The following definitions in other Articles apply to this Article:

(4) In addition Article 1 contains general definitions and principles of construction and interpretation applicable throughout this Article.

§ 2—104. Definitions: "Merchant"; "Between Merchants"; "Financing Agency".

(1) "Merchant" means a person who deals in goods of the kind or otherwise by his occupation holds himself out as having knowledge or skill peculiar to the practices or goods involved in the transaction or to whom such knowledge or skill may be attributed by his employment of an agent or broker or other intermediary who by his occupation holds himself out as having such knowledge or skill.

(2) "Financing agency" means a bank, finance company or other person who in the ordinary course of business makes advances against goods or documents of title or who by arrangement with either the seller or the buyer intervenes in ordinary course to make or collect payment due or claimed under the contract for sale, as by purchasing or paying the seller's draft or making advances against it or by merely taking it for collection whether or not documents of title accompany the draft. "Financing agency" includes also a bank or other person who similarly intervenes between persons who are in the position of seller and buyer in respect to the goods (Section 2—707).

(3) "Between merchants" means in any transaction with respect to which both parties are chargeable with the knowledge or skill of merchants.

§ 2—105. Definitions: Transferability; "Goods"; "Future" Goods; "Lot"; "Commercial Unit".

(1) "Goods" means all things (including specially manufactured goods) which are movable at the time of identification to the contract for sale other than the money in which the price is to be paid, investment securities (Article 8) and things in action. "Goods" also includes the unborn young of animals and growing crops and other identified things attached to realty as described in the section on goods to be severed from realty (Section 2—107).

(2) Goods must be both exiting and identified before any interest in them can pass. Goods which are not both existing and identified are "future" goods. A purported present sale of future goods or of any interest therein operates as a contract to sell.

(3) There may be a sale of a part interest in existing identified goods.

(4) An undivided share in an identified bulk of fungible goods is sufficiently identified to be sold although the quantity of the bulk is not determined. Any agreed proportion of such a bulk or any quantity thereof agreed upon by number, weight or other measure may to the extent of the seller's interest in the bulk be sold to the buyer who then becomes an owner in common.

(5) "Lot" means a parcel or a single article which is the subject matter of a separate sale or delivery, whether or not it is sufficient to perform the contract.

(6) "Commercial unit" means such a unit of goods as by commercial usage is a single whole for purposes of sale and division of which materially impairs its character or value on the market or in use. A commercial unit may be a single article (as a machine) or a set of articles (as a suite of furniture or an assortment of sizes) or a quantity (as a bale, gross, or carload) or any other unit treated in use or in the relevant market as a single whole.

§ 2—106. Definitions: "Contract"; "Agreement"; "Contract for Sale"; "Sale"; "Present Sale"; "Conforming" to Contract; "Termination"; "Cancellation".

(1) In this Article unless the context otherwise requires "contract" and "agreement" are limited to those relating to the present or future sale of goods. "Contract for sale" includes both a present sale of goods and a contract to sell goods at a future time. A "sale"

consists in the passing of title from the seller to the buyer for a price (Section 2—401). A "present sale" means a sale which is accomplished by the making of the contract.

(2) Goods or conduct including any part of a performance are "conforming" or conform to the contract when they are in accordance with the obligations under the contract.

(3) "Termination" occurs when either party pursuant to a power created by agreement or law puts an end to the contract otherwise than for its breach. On "termination" all obligations which are still executory on both sides are discharged but any right based on prior breach or performance survives.

(4) "Cancellation" occurs when either party puts an end to the contract for breach by the other and its effect is the same as that of "termination" except that the cancelling party also retains any remedy for breach of the whole contract or any unperformed balance.

§ 2—107. Goods to Be Severed From Realty: Recording.

(1) A contract for the sale of minerals or the like (including oil and gas) or a structure or its materials to be removed from realty is a contract for the sale of goods within this Article if they are to be severed by the seller but until severance a purported present sale thereof which is not effective as a transfer of an interest in land is effective only as a contract to sell.

(2) A contract for the sale apart from the land of growing crops or other things attached to realty and capable of severance without material harm thereto but not described in subsection (1) or of timber to be cut is a contract for the sale of goods within this Article whether the subject matter is to be severed by the buyer or by the seller even though it forms part of the realty at the time of contracting, and the parties can by identification effect a present sale before severance.

(3) The provisions of this section are subject to any third party rights provided by the law relating to realty records, and the contract for sale may be executed and recorded as a document transferring an interest in land and shall then constitute notice to third parties of the buyer's rights under the contract for sale.

Part 2 Form, Formation and Readjustment of Contract

§ 2—201. Formal Requirements; Statute of Frauds.

(1) Except as otherwise provided in this section a contract for the sale of goods for the price of $500 or more is not enforceable by way of action or defense unless there is some writing sufficient to indicate that a contract for sale has been made between the parties and signed by the party against whom enforcement is sought or by his authorized agent or broker. A writing is not sufficient because it omits or incorrectly states a term agreed upon but the contract is not enforceable under this paragraph beyond the quantity of goods shown in such writing.

(2) Between merchants if within a reasonable time a writing in confirmation of the contract and sufficient against the sender is received and the party receiving it has reason to know its contents, its satisfies the requirements of subsection (1) against such party unless written notice of objection to its contents is given within ten days after it is received.

(3) A contract which does not satisfy the requirements of subsection (1) but which is valid in other respects is enforceable

(a) if the goods are to be specially manufactured for the buyer and are not suitable for sale to others in the ordinary course of the seller's business and the seller, before notice of repudiation is received and under circumstances which reasonably indicate that the goods are for the buyer, has made either a substantial beginning of their manufacture or commitments for their procurement; or

(b) if the party against whom enforcement is sought admits in his pleading, testimony or otherwise in court that a contract for sale was made, but the contract is not enforceable under this provision beyond the quantity of goods admitted; or

(c) with respect to goods for which payment has been made and accepted or which have been received and accepted (Sec. 2—606).

§ 2—202. Final Written Expression: Parol or Extrinsic Evidence.

Terms with respect to which the confirmatory memoranda of the parties agree or which are otherwise set forth in a writing intended by the parties as a final expression of their agreement with respect to such terms as are included therein may not be contradicted by evidence of any prior agreement or of a contemporaneous oral agreement but may be explained or supplemented

(a) by course of dealing or usage of trade (Section 1—205) or by course of performance (Section 2—208); and

(b) by evidence of consistent additional terms unless the court finds the writing to have been intended also as a complete and exclusive statement of the terms of the agreement.

§ 2—203. Seals Inoperative.

The affixing of a seal to a writing evidencing a contract for sale or an offer to buy or sell goods does not constitute the writing a sealed instrument and the law with respect to sealed instruments does not apply to such a contract or offer.

§ 2—204. Formation in General.

(1) A contract for sale of goods may be made in any manner sufficent to show agreement, including conduct by both parties which recognizes the existence of such a contract.

(2) An agreement sufficient to constitute a contract for sale may be found even though the moment of its making is undetermined.

(3) Even though one or more terms are left open a contract for sale does not fail for indefiniteness if the parties have intended to make a contract and there is a reasonably certain basis for giving an appropriate remedy.

§ 2—205. Firm Offers.

An offer by a merchant to buy or sell goods in a signed writing which by its terms gives assurance that it will be held open is not revocable, for lack of consideration, during the time stated or if no time is stated for a reasonable time, but in no event may such period of irrevocability exceed three months; but any such term of assurance on a form supplied by the offeree must be separately signed by the offeror.

§ 2—206. Offer and Acceptance in Formation of Contract.

(1) Unless other unambiguously indicated by the language or circumstances

(a) an offer to make a contract shall be construed as inviting acceptance in any manner and by any medium reasonable in the circumstances;

(b) an order or other offer to buy goods for prompt or current shipment shall be construed as inviting acceptance either by a prompt promise to ship or by the prompt or current shipment of conforming or nonconforming goods, but such a shipment of non-conforming goods does not constitute an acceptance if the seller seasonably notifies the buyer

that the shipment is offered only as an accommodation to the buyer.

(2) Where the beginning of a requested performance is a reasonable mode of acceptance an offeror who is not notified of acceptance within a reasonable time may treat the offer as having lapsed before acceptance.

§ 2—207. Additional Terms in Acceptance or Confirmation.

(1) A definite and seasonable expression of acceptance or a written confirmation which is sent within a reasonable time operates as an acceptance even though it states terms additional to or different from those offered or agreed upon, unless acceptance is expressly made conditional on assent to the additional or different terms.

(2) The additional terms are to be construed as proposals for addition to the contract. Between merchants such terms become part of the contract unless:

(a) the offer expressly limits acceptance to the terms of the offer;

(b) they materially alter it; or

(c) notification of objection to them has already been given or is given within a reasonable time after notice of them is received.

(3) Conduct by both parties which recognizes the existence of a contract is sufficient to establish a contract for sale although the writings of the parties do not otherwise establish a contract. In such case the terms of the particular contract consist of those terms on which the writings of the parties agree, together with any supplementary terms incorporated under any other provisions of this Act.

§ 2—208. Course of Performance or Practical Construction.

(1) Where the contract for sale involves repeated occasions for performance by either party with knowledge of the nature of the performance and opportunity for objection to it by the other, any course of performance accepted or acquiesced in without objection shall be relevant to determine the meaning of the agreement.

(2) The express terms of the agreement and any such course of performance, as well as any course of dealing and usage of trade, shall be construed whenever reasonable as consistent with each other; but when such construction is unreasonable, express terms shall control course of performance and course of performance

shall control both course of dealing and usage of trade (Section 1—205).

(3) Subject to the provisions of the next section on modification and waiver, such course of performance shall be relevant to show a waiver or modification of any term inconsistent with such course of performance.

§ 2—209. **Modification, Rescission and Waiver.**

(1) An agreement modifying a contract within this Article needs no consideration to be binding.

(2) A signed agreement which excludes modification or rescission except by a signed writing cannot be otherwise modified or rescinded, but except as between merchants such a requirement on a form supplied by the merchant must be separately signed by the other party.

(3) The requirements of the statute of frauds section of this Article (Section 2—201) must be satisfied if the contract as modified is within its provisions.

(4) Although an attempt at modification or rescission does not satisfy the requirements of subsection (2) or (3) it can operate as a waiver.

(5) A party who has made a waiver affecting an executory portion of the contract may retract the waiver by reasonable notification received by the other party that strict performance will be required of any term waived, unless the retraction would be unjust in view of a material change of position in reliance on the waiver.

§ 2—210. **Delegation of Performance; Assignment of Rights.**

(1) A party may perform his duty through a delegate unless otherwise agreed or unless the other party has a substantial interest in having his original promisor perform or control the acts required by the contract. No delegation of performance relieves the party delegating of any duty to perform or any liability for breach.

(2) Unless otherwise agreed all rights of either seller or buyer can be assigned except where the assignment would materially change the duty of the other party, or increase materially the burden or risk imposed on him by his contract, or impair materially his chance of obtaining return performance. A right to damages for breach of the whole contract or a right arising out of the assignor's due performance of his entire obligation can be assigned despite agreement otherwise.

(3) Unless the circumstances indicate the contrary a prohibition of assignment of "the contract" is to be construed as barring only the delegation to the assignee of the assignor's performance.

(4) An assignment of "the contract" or of "all my rights under the contract" or an assignment in similar general terms is an assignment of rights and unless the language or the circumstances (as in an assignment for security) indicate the contrary, it is a delegation of performance of the duties of the assignor and its acceptance by the assignee constitutes a promise by him to perform those duties. This promise is enforceable by either the assignor or the other party to the original contract.

(5) The other party may treat any assignment which delegates performance as creating reasonable grounds for insecurity and may without prejudice to his rights against the assignor demand assurances from the assignee (Section 2—609).

Part 3 **General Obligation and Construction of Contract**

§ 2—301. **General Obligations of Parties.**

The obligation of the seller is to transfer and deliver and that of the buyer is to accept and pay in accordance with the contract.

§ 2—302. **Unconscionable Contract or Clause.**

(1) If the court as a matter of law finds the contract or any clause of the contract to have been unconscionable at the time it was made the court may refuse to enforce the contract, or it may enforce the remainder of the contract without the unconscionable clause, or it may so limit the application of any unconscionable clause as to avoid any unconscionable result.

(2) When it is claimed or appears to the court that the contract or any clause thereof may be unconscionable the parties shall be afforded a reasonable opportunity to present evidence as to its commercial setting, purpose and effect to aid the court in making the determination.

§ 2—303. **Allocations or Division of Risks.**

Where this Article allocates a risk or a burden as between the parties "unless otherwise agreed", the agreement may not only shift the allocation but may also divide the risk or burden.

§ 2—304. **Price Payable in Money, Goods, Realty, or Otherwise.**

(1) The price can be made payable in money or other-

wise. If it is payable in whole or in part in goods each party is a seller of the goods which he is to transfer.

(2) Even though all or part of the price is payable in an interest in realty the transfer of the goods and the seller's obligations with reference to them are subject to this Article, but not the transfer of the interest in realty or the transferor's obligations in connection therewith.

§ 2—305. Open Price Term.

(1) The parties if they so intend can conclude a contract for sale even though the price is not settled. In such a case the price is a reasonable price at the time for delivery if

(a) nothing is said as to price; or

(b) the price is left to be agreed by the parties and they fail to agree; or

(c) the price is to be fixed in terms of some agreed market or other standard as set or recorded by a third person or agency and it is not so set or recorded.

(2) A price to be fixed by the seller or by the buyer means a price for him to fix in good faith.

(3) When a price left to be fixed otherwise than by agreement of the parties fails to be fixed through fault of one party the other may at his option treat the contract as cancelled or himself fix a reasonable price.

(4) Where, however, the parties intend not to be bound unless the price be fixed or agreed and it is not fixed or agreed there is no contract. In such a case the buyer must return any goods already received or if unable so to do must pay their reasonable value at the time of delivery and the seller must return any portion of the price paid on account.

§ 2—306. Output, Requirements and Exclusive Dealings.

(1) A term which measures the quantity by the output of the seller or the requirements of the buyer means such actual output or requirements as may occur in good faith, except that no quantity unreasonably disproportionate to any stated estimate or in the absence of a stated estimate to any normal or otherwise comparable prior output or requirements may be tendered or demanded.

(2) A lawful agreement by either the seller or the buyer for exclusive dealing in the kind of goods concerned imposes unless otherwise agreed an obligation by the seller to use best efforts to supply the goods

and by the buyer to use best efforts to promote their sale.

§ 2—307. Delivery in Single Lot or Several Lots.

Unless otherwise agreed all goods called for by a contract for sale must be tendered in a single delivery and payment is due only on such tender but where the circumstances give either party the right to make or demand delivery in lots the price if it can be apportioned may be demanded for each lot.

§ 2—308. Absence of Specified Place for Delivery.

Unless otherwise agreed

(a) the place for delivery of goods is the seller's place of business or if he has none his residence; but

(b) in a contract for sale of identified goods which to the knowledge of the parties at the time of contracting are in some other place, that place is the place for their delivery; and

(c) documents of title may be delivered through customary banking channels.

§ 2—309. Absence of Specific Time Provisions; Notice of Termination.

(1) The time for shipment or delivery or any other action under a contract if not provided in this Article or agreed upon shall be a reasonable time.

(2) Where the contract provides for successive performances but is indefinite in duration it is valid for a reasonable time but unless otherwise agreed may be terminated at any time by either party.

(3) Termination of a contract by one party except on the happening of an agreed event requires that reasonable notification be received by the other party and an agreement dispensing with notification is invalid if its operation would be unconscionable.

§ 2—310. Open Time for Payment or Running of Credit; Authority to Ship Under Reservation.

Unless otherwise agreed

(a) payment is due at the time and place at which the buyer is to receive the goods even though the place of shipment is the place of delivery; and

(b) if the seller is authorized to send the goods he may ship them under reservation, and may tender the documents of title, but the buyer may inspect the goods after their arrival before payment is due unless such inspection is inconsistent with the terms of the contract (Section 2—513); and

(c) if delivery is authorized and made by way of documents of title otherwise than by subsection (b) then payment is due at the time and place at which the buyer is to receive the documents regardless of where the goods are to be received; and

(d) where the seller is required or authorized to ship the goods on credit the credit period runs from the time of shipment but post-dating the invoice or delaying its dispatch will correspondingly delay the starting of the credit period.

§ 2—311. **Options and Cooperation Respecting Performance.**

(1) An agreement for sale which is otherwise sufficiently definite (subsection (3) of Section 2—204) to be a contract is not made invalid by the fact that it leaves particulars of performance to be specified by one of the parties. Any such specification must be made in good faith and within limits set by commercial reasonableness.

(2) Unless otherwise agreed specifications relating to assortment of the goods are at the buyer's option and except as otherwise provided in subsections (1)(c) and (3) of Section 2—319 specifications or arrangements relating to shipment are at the seller's option.

(3) Where such specification would materially affect the other party's performance but is not seasonably made or where one party's cooperation is necessary to the agreed performance of the other but is not seasonably forthcoming, the other party in addition to all other remedies

(a) is excused for any resulting delay in his own performance; and

(b) may also either proceed to perform in any reasonable manner or after the time for a material part of his own performance treat the failure to specify or to cooperate as a breach by failure to deliver or accept the goods.

§ 2—312. **Warranty of Title and Against Infringement; Buyer's Obligation Against Infringement.**

(1) Subject to subsection (2) there is in a contract for sale a warranty by the seller that

(a) the title conveyed shall be good, and its transfer rightful; and

(b) the goods shall be delivered free from any security interest or other lien or encumbrance of which the buyer at the time of contracting has no knowledge.

(2) A warranty under subsection (1) will be excluded or modified only by specific language or by circumstances which give the buyer reason to know that the person selling does not claim title in himself or that he is purporting to sell only such right or title as he or a third person may have.

(3) Unless otherwise agreed a seller who is a merchant regularly dealing in goods of the kind warrants that the goods shall be delivered free of the rightful claim of any third person by way of infringement or the like but a buyer who furnishes specifications to the seller must hold the seller harmless against any such claim which arises out of compliance with the specifications.

§ 2—313. **Express Warranties by Affirmation, Promise, Description, Sample.**

(1) Express warranties by the seller are created as follows:

(a) Any affirmation of fact or promise made by the seller to the buyer which relates to the goods and becomes part of the basis of the bargain creates an express warranty that the goods shall conform to the affirmation or promise.

(b) Any description of the goods which is made part of the basis of the bargain creates an express warranty that the goods shall conform to the description.

(c) Any sample or model which is made part of the basis of the bargain creates an express warranty that the whole of the goods shall conform to the sample or model.

(2) It is not necessary to the creation of an express warranty that the seller use formal words such as "warrant" or "guarantee" or that he have a specific intention to make a warranty, but an affirmation merely of the value of the goods or a statement purporting to be merely the seller's opinion or commendation of the goods does not create a warranty.

§ 2—314. **Implied Warranty: Merchantability; Usage of Trade.**

(1) Unless excluded or modified (Section 2—316), a warranty that the goods shall be merchantable is implied in a contract for their sale if the seller is a merchant with respect to goods of that kind. Under this section the serving for value of food or drink to be consumed either on the premises or elsewhere is a sale.

(2) Goods to be merchantable must be at least such as

(a) pass without objection in the trade under the contract description; and

(b) in the case of fungible goods, are of fair average quality within the description; and

(c) are fit for the ordinary purposes for which such goods are used; and

(d) run, within the variations permitted by the agreement, of even kind, quality and quantity within each unit and among all units involved; and

(e) are adequately contained, packaged, and labeled as the agreement may require; and

(f) conform to the promises or affirmations of fact made on the container or label if any.

(3) Unless excluded or modified (Section 2—316) other implied warranties may arise from course of dealing or usage of trade.

§ 2—315. Implied Warranty: Fitness for Particular Purpose.

Where the seller at the time of contracting has reason to know any particular purpose for which the goods are required and that the buyer is relying on the seller's skill or judgment to select or furnish suitable goods, there is unless excluded or modified under the next section an implied warranty that the goods shall be fit for such purpose.

§ 2—316. Exclusion or Modification of Warranties.

(1) Words or conduct relevant to the creation of an express warranty and words or conduct tending to negate or limit warranty shall be construed wherever reasonable as consistent with each other; but subject to the provisions of this Article on parol or extrinsic evidence (Section 2—202) negation or limitation is inoperative to the extent that such construction is unreasonable.

(2) Subject to subsection (3), to exclude or modify the implied warranty of merchantability or any part of it the language must mention merchantability and in case of a writing must be conspicuous, and to exclude or modify any implied warranty of fitness the exclusion must be by a writing and conspicuous. Language to exclude all implied warranties of fitness is sufficient if it states, for example, that "There are no warranties which extend beyond the description on the face hereof."

(3) Notwithstanding subsection (2)

(a) unless the circumstances indicate otherwise,

all implied warranties are excluded by expressions like "as is", "with all faults" or other language which in common understanding calls the buyer's attention to the exclusion of warranties and makes plain that there is no implied warranty; and

(b) when the buyer before entering into the contract has examined the goods or the sample or model as fully as he desired or has refused to examine the goods there is no implied warranty with regard to defects which an examination ought in the circumstances to have revealed to him; and

(c) an implied warranty can also be excluded or modified by course of dealing or course of performance or usage of trade.

(4) Remedies for breach of warranty can be limited in accordance with the provisions of this Article on liquidation or limitation of damages and on contractual modification of remedy (Sections 2—718 and 2—719).

§ 2—317. Cumulation and Conflict of Warranties Express or Implied.

Warranties whether express or implied shall be construed as consistent with each other and as cumulative, but if such construction is unreasonable the intention of the parties shall determine which warranty is dominant. In ascertaining that intention the following rules apply:

(a) Exact or technical specifications displace an inconsistent sample or model or general language of description.

(b) A sample from an existing bulk displaces inconsistent general language of description.

(c) Express warranties displace inconsistent implied warranties other than an implied warranty of fitness for a particular purpose.

§ 2—318. Third Party Beneficiaries of Warranties Express or Implied.

Note: If this Act is introduced in the Congress of the United States this section should be omitted. (States to select one alternative.)

Alternative A

A seller's warranty whether express or implied extends to any natural person who is in the family or household of his buyer or who is a guest in his home if it is reasonable to expect that such person may use, consume or be affected by the goods and who is injured in person by breach of the warranty. A seller may not exclude or limit the operation of this section.

Alternative B

A seller's warranty whether express or implied extends to any natural person who may reasonably be expected to use, consume or be affected by the goods and who is injured in person by breach of the warranty. A seller may not exclude or limit the operation of this section.

Alternative C

A seller's warranty whether express or implied extends to any person who may reasonably be expected to use, consume or be affected by the goods and who is injured by breach of the warranty. A seller may not exclude or limit the operation of this section with respect to injury to the person of an individual to whom the warranty extends. As amended 1966.

§ 2—319. F.O.B. and F.A.S. Terms.

(1) Unless otherwise agreed the term F.O.B. (which means "free on board") at a named place, even though used only in connection with the stated price, is a delivery term under which

(a) when the term is F.O.B. the place of shipment, the seller must at that place ship the goods in the manner provided in this Article (Section 2—504) and bear the expense and risk of putting them into the possession of the carrier; or

(b) when the term is F.O.B. the place of destination, the seller must at his own expense and risk transport the goods to that place and there tender delivery of them in the manner provided in this Article (Section 2—503);

(c) when under either (a) or (b) the term is also F.O.B. vessel, car or other vehicle, the seller must in addition at his own expense and risk load the goods on board. If the term is F.O.B. vessel the buyer must name the vessel and in an appropriate case the seller must comply with the provisions of this Article on the form of bill of lading (Section 2—323).

(2) Unless otherwise agreed the term F.A.S. vessel (which means "free alongside") at a named port, even though used only in connection with the stated price, is a delivery term under which the seller must

(a) at his own expense and risk deliver the goods alongside the vessel in the manner usual in that port or on a dock designated and provided by the buyer; and

(b) obtain and tender a receipt for the goods in

exchange for which the carrier is under a duty to issue a bill of lading.

(3) Unless otherwise agreed in any case falling within subsection (1)(a) or (c) or subsection (2) the buyer must seasonably give any needed instructions for making delivery, including when the term is F.A.S. or F.O.B. the loading berth of the vessel and in an appropriate case its name and sailing date. The seller may treat the failure of needed instructions as a failure of cooperation under this Article (Section 2—311). He may also at his option move the goods in any reasonable manner preparatory to delivery or shipment.

(4) Under the term F.O.B. vessel or F.A.S. unless otherwise agreed the buyer must make payment against tender of the required documents and the seller may not tender nor the buyer demand delivery of the goods in substitution for the documents.

§ 2—320. C.I.F. and C. & F. Terms.

(1) The term C.I.F. means that the price includes in a lump sum the cost of the goods and the insurance and freight to the named destination. The term C. & F. or C.F. means that the price so includes cost and freight to the named destination.

(2) Unless otherwise agreed and even though used only in connection with the stated price and destination, the term C.I.F. destination or its equivalent requires the seller at his own expense and risk to

(a) put the goods into the possession of a carrier at the port for shipment and obtain a negotiable bill or bills of lading covering the entire transportation to the named destination; and

(b) load the goods and obtain a receipt from the carrier (which may be contained in the bill of lading) showing that the freight has been paid or provided for; and

(c) obtain a policy or certificate of insurance, including any war risk insurance, of a kind and on terms then current at the port of shipment in the usual amount, in the currency of the contract, shown to cover the same goods covered by the bill of lading and providing for payment of loss to the order of the buyer or for the account of whom it may concern; but the seller may add to the price the amount of the premium for any such war risk insurance; and

(d) prepare an invoice of the goods and procure any other documents required to effect shipment or to comply with the contract; and

(e) forward and tender with commercial promptness all the documents in due form and with any indorsement necessary to perfect the buyer's rights.

(3) Unless otherwise agreed the term C. & F. or its equivalent has the same effect and imposes upon the seller the same obligations and risks as a C.I.F. term except the obligation as to insurance.

(4) Under the term C.I.F. or C. & F. unless otherwise agreed the buyer must make payment against tender of the required documents and the seller may not tender nor the buyer demand delivery of the goods in substitution for the documents.

§ 2—321. C.I.F. or C. & F.: "Net Landed Weights"; "Payment on Arrival"; Warranty of Condition on Arrival.

Under a contract containing a term C.I.F. or C. & F.

(1) Where the price is based on or is to be adjusted according to "net landed weights", "delivered weights", "out turn" quantity or quality or the like, unless otherwise agreed the seller must reasonably estimate the price. The payment due on tender of the documents called for by the contract is the amount so estimated, but after final adjustment of the price a settlement must be made with commercial promptness.

(2) An agreement described in subsection (1) or any warranty of quality or condition of the goods on arrival places upon the seller the risk of ordinary deterioration, shrinkage and the like in transportation but has no effect on the place or time of identification to the contract for sale or delivery or on the passing of the risk of loss.

(3) Unless otherwise agreed where the contract provides for payment on or after arrival of the goods the seller must before payment allow such preliminary inspection as is feasible; but if the goods are lost delivery of the documents and payment are due when the goods should have arrived.

§ 2—322. Delivery "Ex-Ship".

(1) Unless otherwise agreed a term for delivery of goods "ex-ship" (which means from the carrying vessel) or in equivalent language is not restricted to a particular ship and requires delivery from a ship which has reached a place at the named port of destination where goods of the kind are usually discharged.

(2) Under such a term unless otherwise agreed

(a) the seller must discharge all liens arising out

of the carriage and furnish the buyer with a direction which puts the carrier under a duty to deliver the goods; and

(b) the risk of loss does not pass to the buyer until the goods leave the ship's tackle or are otherwise properly unloaded.

§ 2—323. Form of Bill of Lading Required in Overseas Shipment; "Overseas".

(1) Where the contract contemplates overseas shipment and contains a term C.I.F. or C. & F. or F.O.B. vessel, the seller unless otherwise agreed must obtain a negotiable bill of lading stating that the goods have been loaded on board or, in the case of a term C.I.F. or C. & F., received for shipment.

(2) Where in a case within subsection (1) a bill of lading has been issued in a set of parts, unless otherwise agreed if the documents are not to be sent from abroad the buyer may demand tender of the full set; otherwise only one part of the bill of lading need be tendered. Even if the agreement expressly requires a full set

(a) due tender of a single part is acceptable within the provisions of this Article on cure of improper delivery (subsection (1) of Section 2—508); and

(b) even though the full set is demanded, if the documents are sent from abroad the person tendering an incomplete set may nevertheless require payment upon furnishing an indemnity which the buyer in good faith deems adequate.

(3) A shipment by water or by air or a contract contemplating such shipment is "overseas" insofar as by usage of trade or agreement it is subject to the commercial, financing or shipping practices characteristic of international deep water commerce.

§ 2—324. "No Arrival, No Sale" Term.

Under a term "no arrival, no sale" or terms of like meaning, unless otherwise agreed,

(a) the seller must properly ship conforming goods and if they arrive by any means he must tender them on arrival but he assumes no obligation that the goods will arrive unless he has caused the non-arrival; and

(b) where without fault of the seller the goods are in part lost or have so deteriorated as no longer to conform to the contract or arrive after the contract time, the buyer may proceed as if there had been casualty to identified goods (Section 2—613).

§ 2—325. "Letter of Credit" Term; "Confirmed Credit".

(1) Failure of the buyer seasonably to furnish an agreed letter of credit is a breach of the contract for sale.

(2) The delivery to seller of a proper letter of credit suspends the buyer's obligation to pay. If the letter of credit is dishonored, the seller may on seasonable notification to the buyer require payment directly from him.

(3) Unless otherwise agreed the term "letter of credit" or "banker's credit" in a contract for sale means an irrevocable credit issued by a financing agency of good repute and, where the shipment is overseas, of good international repute. The term "confirmed credit" means that the credit must also carry the direct obligation of such an agency which does business in the seller's financial market.

§ 2—326. Sale on Approval and Sale or Return; Consignment Sales and Rights of Creditors.

(1) Unless otherwise agreed, if delivered goods may be returned by the buyer even though they conform to the contract, the transaction is

(a) a "sale on approval" if the goods are delivered primarily for use, and

(b) a "sale or return" if the goods are delivered primarily for resale.

(2) Except as provided in subsection (3), goods held on approval are not subject to the claims of the buyer's creditors until acceptance; goods held on sale or return are subject to such claims while in the buyer's possession.

(3) Where goods are delivered to a person for sale and such person maintains a place of business at which he deals in goods of the kind involved, under a name other than the name of the person making delivery, then with respect to claims of creditors of the person conducting the business the goods are deemed to be on sale or return. The provisions of this subsection are applicable even though an agreement purports to reserve title to the person making delivery until payment or resale or uses such words as "on consignment" or "on memorandum". However, this subsection is not applicable if the person making delivery

(a) complies with an applicable law providing for a consignor's interest or the like to be evidenced by a sign, or

(b) establishes that the person conducting the business is generally known by his creditors to be substantially engaged in selling the goods of others, or

(c) complies with the filing provisions of the Article on Secured Transactions (Article 9).

(4) Any "or return" term of a contract for sale is to be treated as a separate contract for sale within the statute of frauds section of this Article (Section 2—201) and as contradicting the sale aspect of the contract within the provisions of this Article on parol or extrinsic evidence (Section 2—202).

§ 2—327. Special Incidents of Sale on Approval and Sale or Return.

(1) Under a sale on approval unless otherwise agreed

(a) although the goods are identified to the contract the risk of loss and the title do not pass to the buyer until acceptance; and

(b) use of the goods consistent with the purpose of trial is not acceptance but failure seasonably to notify the seller of election to return the goods is acceptance, and if the goods conform to the contract acceptance of any part is acceptance of the whole; and

(c) after due notification of election to return, the return is at the seller's risk and expense but a merchant buyer must follow any reasonable instructions.

(2) Under a sale or return unless otherwise agreed

(a) the option to return extends to the whole or any commercial unit of the goods while in substantially their original condition, but must be exercised seasonably; and

(b) the return is at the buyer's risk and expense.

§ 2—328. Sale by Auction.

(1) In a sale by auction if goods are put up in lots each lot is the subject of a separate sale.

(2) A sale by auction is complete when the auctioneer so announces by the fall of the hammer or in other customary manner. Where a bid is made while the hammer is falling in acceptance of a prior bid the auctioneer may in his discretion reopen the bidding or declare the goods sold under the bid on which the hammer was falling.

(3) Such a sale is with reserve unless the goods are in explicit terms put up without reserve. In an auction with reserve the auctioneer may withdraw the goods at any time until he announces completion of the sale. In an auction without reserve, after the auctioneer

calls for bids on an article or lot, that article or lot cannot be withdrawn unless no bid is made within a reasonable time. In either case a bidder may retract his bid until the auctioneer's announcement of completion of the sale, but a bidder's retraction does not revive any previous bid.

(4) If the auctioneer knowingly receives a bid on the seller's behalf or the seller makes or procures such as bid, and notice has not been given that liberty for such bidding is reserved, the buyer may at his option avoid the sale or take the goods at the price of the last good faith bid prior to the completion of the sale. This subsection shall not apply to any bid at a forced sale.

Part 4 Title, Creditors and Good Faith Purchasers

§ 2—401. Passing of Title; Reservation for Security; Limited Application of This Section.

Each provision of this Article with regard to the rights, obligations and remedies of the seller, the buyer, purchasers or other third parties applies irrespective of title to the goods except where the provision refers to such title. Insofar as situations are not covered by the other provisions of this Article and matters concerning title became material the following rules apply:

(1) Title to goods cannot pass under a contract for sale prior to their identification to the contract (Section 2—501), and unless otherwise explicitly agreed the buyer acquires by their identification a special property as limited by this Act. Any retention or reservation by the seller of the title (property) in goods shipped or delivered to the buyer is limited in effect to a reservation of a security interest. Subject to these provisions and to the provisions of the Article on Secured Transactions (Article 9), title to goods passes from the seller to the buyer in any manner and on any conditions explicitly agreed on by the parties.

(2) Unless otherwise explicitly agreed title passes to the buyer at the time and place at which the seller completes his performance with reference to the physical delivery of the goods, despite any reservation of a security interest and even though a document of title is to be delivered at a different time or place; and in particular and despite any reservation of a security interest by the bill of lading.

(a) if the contract requires or authorizes the seller to send the goods to the buyer but does not require him to deliver them at destination, title passes to the buyer at the time and place of shipment; but

(b) if the contract requires delivery at destination, title passes on tender there.

(3) Unless otherwise explicitly agreed where delivery is to be made without moving the goods,

(a) if the seller is to deliver a document of title, title passes at the time when and the place where he delivers such documents; or

(b) if the goods are at the time of contracting already identified and no documents are to be delivered, title passes at the time and place of contracting.

(4) A rejection or other refusal by the buyer to receive or retain the goods, whether or not justified, or a justified revocation of acceptance revests title to the goods in the seller. Such revesting occurs by operation of law and is not a "sale".

§ 2—402. Rights of Seller's Creditors Against Sold Goods.

(1) Except as provided in subsections (2) and (3), rights of unsecured creditors of the seller with respect to goods which have been identified to a contract for sale are subject to the buyer's rights to recover the goods under this Article (Sections 2—502 and 2—716).

(2) A creditor of the seller may treat a sale or an identification of goods to a contract for sale as void if as against him a retention of possession by the seller is fraudulent under any rule of law of the state where the goods are situated, except that retention of possession in good faith and current course of trade by a merchant-seller for a commercially reasonable time after a sale or identification is not fraudulent.

(3) Nothing in this Article shall be deemed to impair the rights of creditors of the seller.

(a) under the provisions of the Article on Secured Transactions (Article 9); or

(b) where identification to the contract or delivery is made not in current course of trade but in satisfaction of or as security for a pre-existing claim for money, security or the like and is made under circumstances which under any rule of law of the state where the goods are situated would apart from this Article constitute the transaction a fraudulent transfer or voidable preference.

§ 2—403. Power to Transfer; Good Faith Purchase of Goods; "Entrusting".

(1) A purchaser of goods acquires all title which his transferor had or had power to transfer except that a

purchaser of a limited interest acquires rights only to the extent of the interest purchased. A person with voidable title has power to transfer a good title to a good faith purchaser for value. When goods have been delivered under a transaction of purchase the purchaser has such power even though

(a) the transferor was deceived as to the identity of the purchaser, or

(b) the delivery was in exchange for a check which is later dishonored, or

(c) it was agreed that the transaction was to be a "cash sale", or

(d) the delivery was procured through fraud punishable as larcenous under the criminal law.

(2) Any entrusting of possession of goods to a merchant who deals in goods of that kind gives him power to transfer all rights of the entruster to a buyer in ordinary course of business.

(3) "Entrusting" includes any delivery and any acquiescence in retention of possession regardless of any condition expressed between the parties to the delivery or acquiescence and regardless of whether the procurement of the entrusting or the possessor's disposition of the goods have been such as to be larcenous under the criminal law.

(4) The rights of other purchasers of goods and of lien creditors are governed by the Articles on Secured Transactions (Article 9), Bulk Transfers (Article 6) and Documents of Title (Article 7).

Part 5 Performance

§ 2—501. Insurable Interest in Goods; Manner of Identification of Goods.

(1) The buyer obtains a special property and an insurable interest in goods by identification of existing goods as goods to which the contract refers even though the goods so identified are nonconforming and he has an option to return or reject them. Such identification can be made at any time and in any manner explicitly agreed to by the parties. In the absence of explicit agreement identification occurs

(a) when the contract is made if it is for the sale of goods already existing and identified;

(b) if the contract is for the sale of future goods other than those described in paragraph (c), when goods are shipped, marked or otherwise designated by the seller as goods to which the contract refers;

(c) when the crops are planted or otherwise become growing crops or the young are conceived if the contract is for the sale of unborn young to be born within twelve months after contracting or for the sale of crops to be harvested within twelve months or the next normal harvest season after contracting whichever is longer.

(2) The seller retains an insurable interest in goods so long as title to or any security interest in the goods remains in him and where the identification is by the seller alone he may until default or insolvency or notification to the buyer that the identification is final substitute other goods for those identified.

(3) Nothing in this section impairs any insurable interest recognized under any other statute or rule of law.

§ 2—502. Buyer's Right to Goods on Seller's Insolvency.

(1) Subject to subsection (2) and even though the goods have not been shipped a buyer who has paid a part or all of the price of goods in which he has a special property under the provisions of the immediately preceding section may on making and keeping good a tender of any unpaid portion of their price recover them from the seller if the seller becomes insolvent within ten days after receipt of the first installment on their price.

(2) If the identification creating his special property has been made by the buyer he acquires the right to recover the goods only if they conform to the contract for sale.

§ 2—503. Manner of Seller's Tender of Delivery.

(1) Tender of delivery requires that the seller put and hold conforming goods at the buyer's disposition and give the buyer any notification reasonably necessary to enable him to take delivery. The manner, time and place for tender are determined by the agreement and this Article, and in particular

(a) tender must be at a reasonable hour, and if it is of goods they must be kept available for the period reasonably necessary to enable the buyer to take possession; but

(b) unless otherwise agreed the buyer must furnish facilities reasonably suited to the receipt of the goods.

(2) Where the case is within the next section respecting shipment tender requires that the seller comply with its provisions.

(3) Where the seller is required to deliver at a particular destination tender requires that he comply with subsection (1) and also in any appropriate case tender documents as described in subsections (4) and (5) of this section.

(4) Where goods are in the possession of a bailee and are to be delivered without being moved

(a) tender requires that the seller either tender a negotiable document of title covering such goods or procure acknowledgment by the bailee of the buyer's right to possession of the goods; but

(b) tender to the buyer of a non-negotiable document of title or of a written direction to the bailee to deliver is sufficient tender unless the buyer seasonably objects, and receipt by the bailee of notification of the buyer's rights fixes those rights as against the bailee and all third persons; but risk of loss of the goods and of any failure by the bailee to honor the non-negotiable document of title or to obey the direction remains on the seller until the buyer has had a reasonable time to present the document or direction, and a refusal by the bailee to honor the document or to obey the direction defeats the tender.

(5) Where the contract requires the seller to deliver documents

(a) he must tender all such documents in correct form, except as provided in this Article with respect to bills of lading in a set (subsection (2) of Section 2—323); and

(b) tender through customary banking channels is sufficient and dishonor of a draft accompanying the documents constitutes non-acceptance or rejection.

§ 2—504. **Shipment by Seller.**

Where the seller is required or authorized to send the goods to the buyer and the contract does not require him to deliver them at a particular destination, then unless otherwise agreed he must

(a) put the goods in the possession of such a carrier and make such a contract for their transportation as may be reasonable having regard to the nature of the goods and other circumstances of the case; and

(b) obtain and promptly deliver or tender in due form any document necessary to enable the buyer to obtain possession of the goods or otherwise required by the agreement or by usage of trade; and

(c) promptly notify the buyer of the shipment.

Failure to notify the buyer under paragraph (c) or to make a proper contract under paragraph (a) is a ground for rejection only if material delay or loss ensues.

§ 2—505. **Seller's Shipment Under Reservation.**

(1) Where the seller has identified goods to the contract by or before shipment:

(a) his procurement of a negotiable bill of lading to his own order or otherwise reserves in him a security interest in the goods. His procurement of the bill to the order of a financing agency or of the buyer indicates in addition only the seller's expectation of transferring that interest to the person named.

(b) a non-negotiable bill of lading to himself or his nominee reserves possession of the goods as security but except in a case of conditional delivery (subsection (2) of Section 2—507) a non-negotiable bill of lading naming the buyer as consignee reserves no security interest even though the seller retains possession of the bill of lading.

(2) When shipment by the seller with reservation of a security interest is in violation of the contract for sale it constitutes an improper contract for transportation within the preceding section but impairs neither the rights given to the buyer by shipment and identification of the goods to the contract nor the seller's powers as a holder of a negotiable document.

§ 2—506. **Rights of Financing Agency.**

(1) A financing agency by paying or purchasing for value a draft which relates to a shipment of goods acquires to the extent of the payment or purchase and in addition to its own rights under the draft and any document of title securing it any rights of the shipper in the goods including the right to stop delivery and the shipper's right to have the draft honored by the buyer.

(2) The right to reimbursement of a financing agency which has in good faith honored or purchased the draft under commitment to or authority from the buyer is not impaired by subsequent discovery of defects with reference to any relevant document which was apparently regular on its face.

§ 2—507. **Effect of Seller's Tender; Delivery on Condition.**

(1) Tender of delivery is a condition to the buyer's duty to accept the goods and, unless otherwise agreed, to his duty to pay for them. Tender entitles the seller to acceptance of the goods and to payment according to the contract.

(2) Where payment is due and demanded on the delivery to the buyer of goods or documents of title, his right as against the seller to retain or dispose of them is conditional upon his making the payment due.

§ 2—508. Cure by Seller of Improper Tender or Delivery; Replacement.

(1) Where any tender or delivery by the seller is rejected because non-conforming and the time for performance has not yet expired, the seller may seasonably notify the buyer of his intention to cure and may then within the contract time make a conforming delivery.

(2) Where the buyer rejects a non-conforming tender which the seller had reasonable grounds to believe would be acceptable with or without money allowance the seller may if he seasonably notifies the buyer have a further reasonable time to substitute a conforming tender.

§ 2—509. Risk of Loss in the Absence of Breach.

(1) Where the contract requires or authorizes the seller to ship the goods by carrier

    (a) if it does not require him to deliver them at a particular destination, the risk of loss passes to the buyer when the goods are duly delivered to the carrier even though the shipment is under reservation (Section 2—505); but

    (b) if it does require him to deliver them at a particular destination and the goods are there duly tendered while in the possession of the carrier, the risk of loss passes to the buyer when the goods are there duly so tendered as to enable the buyer to take delivery.

(2) Where the goods are held by a bailee to be delivered without being moved, the risk of loss passes to the buyer

    (a) on his receipt of a negotiable document of title covering the goods; or

    (b) on acknowledgment by the bailee of the buyer's right to possession of the goods; or

    (c) after his receipt of a non-negotiable document of title or other written direction to deliver, as provided in subsection (4)(b) of Section 2—503.

(3) In any case not within subsection (1) or (2), the risk of loss passes to the buyer on his receipt of the goods if the seller is a merchant; otherwise, the risk passes to the buyer on tender of delivery.

(4) The provisions of this section are subject to contrary agreement of the parties and to the provisions of this Article on sale on approval (Section 2—327) and on effect of breach on risk of loss (Section 2—510).

§ 2—510. Effect of Breach on Risk of Loss.

(1) Where a tender or delivery of goods so fails to conform to the contract as to give a right of rejection the risk of their loss remains on the seller until cure or acceptance.

(2) Where the buyer rightfully revokes acceptance he may to the extent of any deficiency in his effective insurance coverage treat the risk of loss as having rested on the seller from the beginning.

(3) Where the buyer as to conforming goods already identified to the contract for sale repudiates or is otherwise in breach before risk of their loss has passed to him, the seller may to the extent of any deficiency in his effective insurance coverage treat the risk of loss as resting on the buyer for a commercially reasonable time.

§ 2—511. Tender of Payment by Buyer; Payment by Check.

(1) Unless otherwise agreed tender of payment is a condition to the seller's duty to tender and complete any delivery.

(2) Tender of payment is sufficient when made by any means or in any manner current in the ordinary course of business unless the seller demands payment in legal tender and gives any extension of time reasonably necessary to procure it.

(3) Subject to the provisions of this Act on the effect of an instrument on an obligation (Section 3—802), payment by check is conditional and is defeated as between the parties by dishonor of the check on due presentment.

§ 2—512. Payment by Buyer Before Inspection.

(1) Where the contract requires payment before inspection non-conformity of the goods does not excuse the buyer from so making payment unless

    (a) the non-conformity appears without inspection; or

    (b) despite tender of the required documents the circumstances would justify injunction against honor under the provisions of this Act (Section 5—114).

(2) Payment pursuant to subsection (1) does not constitute an acceptance of goods or impair the buyer's right to inspect or any of his remedies.

§ 2—513. **Buyer's Right to Inspection of Goods.**

(1) Unless otherwise agreed and subject to subsection (3), where goods are tendered or delivered or identified to the contract for sale, the buyer has a right before payment or acceptance to inspect them at any reasonable place and time and in any reasonable manner. When the seller is required or authorized to send the goods to the buyer, the inspection may be after their arrival.

(2) Expenses of inspection must be borne by the buyer but may be recovered from the seller if the goods do not conform and are rejected.

(3) Unless otherwise agreed and subject to the provisions of this Article on C.I.F. contracts (subsection (3) of Section 2—321), the buyer is not entitled to inspect the goods before payment of the price when the contract provides

   (a) for delivery "C.O.D." or on other like terms; or

   (b) for payment against documents of title, except where such payment is due only after the goods are to become available for inspection.

(4) A place or method of inspection fixed by the parties is presumed to be exclusive but unless otherwise expressly agreed it does not postpone identification or shift the place for delivery or for passing the risk of loss. If compliance becomes impossible, inspection shall be as provided in this section unless the place or method fixed was clearly intended as an indispensable condition failure of which avoids the contract.

§ 2—514. **When Documents Deliverable on Acceptance; When on Payment.**

Unless otherwise agreed documents against which a draft is drawn are to be delivered to the drawee on acceptance of the draft if it is payable more than three days after presentment; otherwise, only on payment.

§ 2—515. **Preserving Evidence of Goods in Dispute.**

In furtherance of the adjustment of any claim or dispute

   (a) either party on reasonable notification to the other and for the purpose of ascertaining the facts and preserving evidence has the right to inspect, test and sample the goods including such of them as may be in the possession or control of the other; and

   (b) the parties may agree to a third party inspection or survey to determine the conformity or condition of the goods and may agree that the findings shall be binding upon them in any subsequent litigation or adjustment.

Part 6 **Breach, Repudiation and Excuse**

§ 2—601. **Buyer's Rights on Improper Delivery.**

Subject to the provisions of this Article on breach in installment contracts (Section 2—612) and unless otherwise agreed under the sections on contractual limitations of remedy (Sections 2—718 and 2—719), if the goods or the tender of delivery fail in any respect to conform to the contract, the buyer may

(a) reject the whole; or

(b) accept the whole; or

(c) accept any commercial unit or units and reject the rest.

§ 2—602. **Manner and Effect of Rightful Rejection.**

(1) Rejection of goods must be within a reasonable time after their delivery or tender. It is ineffective unless the buyer seasonably notifies the seller.

(2) Subject to the provisions of the two following sections on rejected goods (Sections 2—603 and 2—604),

   (a) after rejection any exercise of ownership by the buyer with respect to any commercial unit is wrongful as against the seller; and

   (b) if the buyer has before rejection taken physical possession of goods in which he does not have a security interest under the provisions of this Article (subsection (3) of Section 2—711), he is under a duty after rejection to hold them with reasonable care at the seller's disposition for a time sufficient to permit the seller to remove them; but

   (c) the buyer has no further obligations with regard to goods rightfully rejected.

(3) The seller's rights with respect to goods wrongfully rejected are governed by the provisions of this Article on seller's remedies in general (Section 2—703).

§ 2—603. **Merchant Buyer's Duties as to Rightfully Rejected Goods.**

(1) Subject to any security interest in the buyer (subsection (3) of Section 2—711), when the seller has no agent or place of business at the market of rejection a merchant buyer is under a duty after rejection of

goods in his possession or control to follow any reasonable instructions received from the seller with respect to the goods and in the absence of such instructions to make reasonable efforts to sell them for the seller's account if they are perishable or threaten to decline in value speedily. Instructions are not reasonable if on demand indemnity for expenses is not forthcoming.

(2) When the buyer sells goods under subsection (1), he is entitled to reimbursement from the seller or out of the proceeds for reasonable expenses of caring for and selling them, and if the expenses include no selling commission then to such commission as is usual in the trade or if there is none to a reasonable sum not exceeding ten per cent on the gross proceeds.

(3) In complying with this section the buyer is held only to good faith and good faith conduct hereunder is neither acceptance nor conversion nor the basis of an action for damages.

§ 2—604. Buyer's Options as to Salvage of Rightfully Rejected Goods.

Subject to the provisions of the immediately preceding section on perishables if the seller gives no instructions within a reasonable time after notification of rejection the buyer may store the rejected goods for the seller's account or reship them to him or resell them for the seller's account with reimbursement as provided in the preceding section. Such action is not acceptance or conversion.

§ 2—605. Waiver of Buyer's Objections by Failure to Particularize.

(1) The buyer's failure to state in connection with rejection a particular defect which is ascertainable by reasonable inspection precludes him from relying on the unstated defect to justify rejection or to establish breach

(a) where the seller could have cured it if stated seasonably; or

(b) between merchants when the seller has after rejection made a request in writing for a full and final written statement of all defects on which the buyer proposes to rely.

(2) Payment against documents made without reservation of rights precludes recovery of the payment for defects apparent on the face of the documents.

§ 2—606. What Constitutes Acceptance of Goods.

(1) Acceptance of goods occurs when the buyer

(a) after a reasonable opportunity to inspect the goods signifies to the seller that the goods are conforming or that he will take or retain them in spite of their nonconformity; or

(b) fails to make an effective rejection (subsection (1) of Section 2—602), but such acceptance does not occur until the buyer has had a reasonable opportunity to inspect them; or

(c) does any act inconsistent with the seller's ownership; but if such act is wrongful as against the seller it is an acceptance only if ratified by him.

(2) Acceptance of a part of any commercial unit is acceptance of that entire unit.

§ 2—607. Effect of Acceptance; Notice of Breach; Burden of Establishing Breach After Acceptance; Notice of Claim or Litigation to Person Answerable Over.

(1) The buyer must pay at the contract rate for any goods accepted.

(2) Acceptance of goods by the buyer precludes rejection of the goods accepted and if made with knowledge of a non-conformity cannot be revoked because of it unless the acceptance was on the reasonable assumption that the non-conformity would be seasonably cured but acceptance does not of itself impair any other remedy provided by this Article for non-conformity.

(3) Where a tender has been accepted

(a) the buyer must within a reasonable time after he discovers or should have discovered any breach notify the seller of breach or be barred from any remedy; and

(b) if the claim is one for infringement or the like (subsection (3) of Section 2—312) and the buyer is sued as a result of such a breach he must so notify the seller within a reasonable time after he receives notice of the litigation or be barred from any remedy over for liability established by the litigation.

(4) The burden is on the buyer to establish any breach with respect to the goods accepted.

(5) Where the buyer is sued for breach of a warranty or other obligation for which his seller is answerable over

(a) he may give his seller written notice of the litigation. If the notice states that the seller may come in and defend and that if the seller does not do so he will be bound in any action against him by his buyer by any determination of fact common to the two litigations, then unless the seller after seasonable receipt of the notice does come in and defend he is so bound.

(b) if the claim is one for infringement or the like (subsection (3) of Section 2—312) the original seller may demand in writing that his buyer turn over to him control of the litigation including settlement or else be barred from any remedy over and if he also agrees to bear all expense and to satisfy any adverse judgment, then unless the buyer after seasonable receipt of the demand does turn over control the buyer is so barred.

(6) The provisions of subsections (3), (4) and (5) apply to any obligation of a buyer to hold the seller harmless against infringement or the like (subsection (3) of Section 2—312).

§ 2—608. **Revocation of Acceptance in Whole or in Part.**

(1) The buyer may revoke his acceptance of a lot or commercial unit whose non-conformity substantially impairs its value to him if he has accepted it

(a) on the reasonable assumption that its non-conformity would be cured and it has not been seasonably cured; or

(b) without discovery of such non-conformity if his acceptance was reasonably induced either by the difficulty of discovery before acceptance or by the seller's assurances.

(2) Revocation of acceptance must occur within a reasonable time after the buyer discovers or should have discovered the ground for it and before any substantial change in condition of the goods which is not caused by their own defects. It is not effective until the buyer notifies the seller of it.

(3) A buyer who so revokes has the same rights and duties with regard to the goods involved as if he had rejected them.

§ 2—609. **Right to Adequate Assurance of Performance.**

(1) A contract for sale imposes an obligation on each party that the other's expectation of receiving due performance will not be impaired. When reasonable grounds for insecurity arise with respect to the performance of either party the other may in writing demand adequate assurance of due performance and until he receives such assurance may if commercially reasonable suspend any performance for which he has not already received the agreed return.

(2) Between merchants the reasonableness of grounds for insecurity and the adequacy of any assurance offered shall be determined according to commercial standards.

(3) Acceptance of any improper delivery or payment does not prejudice the aggrieved party's right to demand adequate assurance of future performance.

(4) After receipt of a justified demand failure to provide within a reasonable time not exceeding thirty days such assurance of due performance as is adequate under the circumstances of the particular case is a repudiation of the contract.

§ 2—610. **Anticipatory Repudiation.**

When either party repudiates the contract with respect to a performance not yet due the loss of which will substantially impair the value of the contract to the other, the aggrieved party may

(a) for a commercially reasonable time await performance by the repudiating party; or

(b) resort to any remedy for breach (Section 2—703 or Section 2—711), even though he has notified the repudiating party that he would await the latter's performance and has urged retraction; and

(c) in either case suspend his own performance or proceed in accordance with the provisions of this Article on the seller's right to identify goods to the contract notwithstanding breach or to salvage unfinished goods (Section 2—704).

§ 2—611. **Retraction of Anticipatory Repudiation.**

(1) Until the repudiating party's next performance is due he can retract his repudiation unless the aggrieved party has since the repudiation cancelled or materially changed his position or otherwise indicated that he considers the repudiation final.

(2) Retraction may be by any method which clearly indicates to the aggrieved party that the repudiating party intends to perform, but must include any assurance justifiably demanded under the provisions of this Article (Section 2—609).

(3) Retraction reinstates the repudiating party's rights under the contract with due excuse and allowance to

the aggrieved party for any delay occasioned by the repudiation.

§ 2—612. "Installment Contract"; Breach.

(1) An "installment contract" is one which requires or authorizes the delivery of goods in separate lots to be separately accepted, even though the contract contains a clause "each delivery is a separate contract" or its equivalent.

(2) The buyer may reject any installment which is non-conforming if the non-conformity substantially impairs the value of that installment and cannot be cured or if the non-conformity is a defect in the required documents; but if the non-conformity does not fall within subsection (3) and the seller gives adequate assurance of its cure the buyer must accept that installment.

(3) Whenever non-conformity or default with respect to one or more installments substantially impairs the value of the whole contract there is a breach of the whole. But the aggrieved party reinstates the contract if he accepts a non-conforming installment without seasonably notifying of cancellation or if he brings an action with respect only to past installments or demands performance as to future installments.

§ 2—613. Casualty to Identified Goods.

Where the contract requires for its performance goods identified when the contract is made, and the goods suffer casualty without fault of either party before the risk of loss passes to the buyer, or in a proper case under a "no arrival, no sale" term (Section 2—324) then

(a) if the loss is total the contract is avoided; and

(b) if the loss is partial or the goods have so deteriorated as no longer to conform to the contract the buyer may nevertheless demand inspection and at his option either treat the contract as voided or accept the goods with due allowance from the contract price for the deterioration or the deficiency in quantity but without further right against the seller.

§ 2—614. Substituted Performance.

(1) Where without fault of either party the agreed berthing, loading, or unloading facilities fail or an agreed type of carrier becomes unavailable or the agreed manner of delivery otherwise becomes commercially impracticable but a commercially reasonable substitute is available, such substitute performance must be tendered and accepted.

(2) If the agreed means or manner of payment fails because of domestic or foreign governmental regulation, the seller may withhold or stop delivery unless the buyer provides a means or manner of payment which is commercially a substantial equivalent. If delivery has already been taken, payment by the means or in the manner provided by the regulation discharges the buyer's obligation unless the regulation is discriminatory, oppressive or predatory.

§ 2—615. Excuse by Failure of Presupposed Conditions.

Except so far as a seller may have assumed a greater obligation and subject to the preceding section on substituted performance:

(a) Delay in delivery or non-delivery in whole or in part by a seller who complies with paragraphs (b) and (c) is not a breach of his duty under a contract for sale if performance as agreed has been made impracticable by the occurrence of a contingency the non-occurrence of which was a basic assumption on which the contract was made or by compliance in good faith with any applicable foreign or domestic governmental regulation or order whether or not it later proves to be invalid.

(b) Where the causes mentioned in paragraph (a) affect only a part of the seller's capacity to perform, he must allocate production and deliveries among his customers but may at his option include regular customers not then under contract as well as his own requirements for further manufacture. He may so allocate in any manner which is fair and reasonable.

(c) The seller must notify the buyer seasonably that there will be delay or non-delivery and, when allocation is required under paragraph (b), of the estimated quota thus made available for the buyer.

§ 2—616. Procedure on Notice Claiming Excuse.

(1) Where the buyer receives notification of a material or indefinite delay or an allocation justified under the preceding section he may by written notification to the seller as to any delivery concerned, and where the prospective deficiency substantially impairs the value of the whole contract under the provisions of this Article relating to breach of installment contracts (Section 2—612), then also as to the whole,

(a) terminate and thereby discharge any unexecuted portion of the contract; or

(b) modify the contract by agreeing to take his available quota in substitution.

(2) If after receipt of such notification from the seller the buyer fails so to modify the contract within a reasonable time not exceeding thirty days the contract lapses with respect to any deliveries affected.

(3) The provisions of this section may not be negated by agreement except in so far as the seller has assumed a greater obligation under the preceding section.

Part 7 **Remedies**

§ 2—701. **Remedies for Breach of Collateral Contracts Not Impaired.**

Remedies for breach of any obligation or promise collateral or ancillary to a contract for sale are not impaired by the provisions of this Article.

§ 2—702. **Seller's Remedies on Discovery of Buyer's Insolvency.**

(1) Where the seller discovers the buyer to be insolvent he may refuse delivery except for cash including payment for all goods theretofore delivered under the contract, and stop delivery under this Article (Section 2—705).

(2) Where the seller discovers that the buyer has received goods on credit while insolvent he may reclaim the goods upon demand made within ten days after the receipt, but if misrepresentation of solvency has been made to the particular seller in writing within three months before delivery the ten day limitation does not apply. Except as provided in this subsection the seller may not base a right to reclaim goods on the buyer's fraudulent or innocent misrepresentation of solvency or of intent to pay.

(3) The seller's right to reclaim under subsection (2) is subject to the rights of a buyer in ordinary course or other good faith purchaser under this Article (Section 2—403). Successful reclamation of goods excludes all other remedies with respect to them.

§ 2—703. **Seller's Remedies in General.**

Where the buyer wrongfully rejects or revokes acceptance of goods or fails to make a payment due on or before delivery or repudiates with respect to a part or the whole, then with respect to any goods directly affected and, if the breach is of the whole contract (Section 2—612), then also with respect to the whole un-

delivered balance, the aggrieved seller may

(a) withhold delivery of such goods;

(b) stop delivery by any bailee as hereafter provided (Section 2—705);

(c) proceed under the next section respecting goods still unidentified to the contract;

(d) resell and recover damages as hereafter provided (Section 2—706);

(e) recover damages for non-acceptance (Section 2—708) or in a proper case the price (Section 2—709);

(f) cancel.

§ 2—704. **Seller's Right to Identify Goods to the Contract Notwithstanding Breach or to Salvage Unfinished Goods.**

(1) An aggrieved seller under the preceding section may

(a) identify to the contract conforming goods not already identified if at the time he learned of the breach they are in his possession or control;

(b) treat as the subject of resale goods which have demonstrably been intended for the particular contract even though those goods are unfinished.

(2) Where the goods are unfinished an aggrieved seller may in the exercise of reasonable commercial judgment for the purposes of avoiding loss and of effective realization either complete the manufacture and wholly identify the goods to the contract or cease manufacture and resell for scrap or salvage value or proceed in any other reasonable manner.

§ 2—705. **Seller's Stoppage of Delivery in Transit or Otherwise.**

(1) The seller may stop delivery of goods in the possession of a carrier or other bailee when he discovers the buyer to be insolvent (Section 2—702) and may stop delivery of carload, truckload, planeload or larger shipments of express or freight when the buyer repudiates or fails to make a payment due before delivery or if for any other reason the seller has a right to withhold or reclaim the goods.

(2) As against such buyer the seller may stop delivery until

(a) receipt of the goods by the buyer; or

(b) acknowledgment to the buyer by any bailee of the goods except a carrier that the bailee holds the goods for the buyer; or

(c) such acknowledgment to the buyer by a carrier by reshipment or as warehouseman; or

(d) negotiation to the buyer of any negotiable document of title covering the goods.

(3) (a) To stop delivery the seller must so notify as to enable the bailee by reasonable diligence to prevent delivery of the goods.

(b) After such notification the bailee must hold and deliver the goods according to the directions of the seller but the seller is liable to the bailee for any ensuing charges or damages.

(c) If a negotiable document of title has been issued for goods the bailee is not obliged to obey a notification to stop until surrender of the document.

(d) A carrier who has issued a non-negotiable bill of lading is not obliged to obey a notification to stop received from a person other than the consignor.

§ 2—706. Seller's Resale Including Contract for Resale.

(1) Under the conditions stated in Section 2—703 on seller's remedies, the seller may resell the goods concerned or the undelivered balance thereof. Where the resale is made in good faith and in a commercially reasonable manner the seller may recover the difference between the resale price and the contract price together with any incidental damages allowed under the provisions of this Article (Section 2—710), but less expenses saved in consequence of the buyer's breach.

(2) Except as otherwise provided in subsection (3) or unless otherwise agreed resale may be at public or private sale including sale by way of one or more contracts to sell or of identification to an existing contract of the seller. Sale may be as a unit or in parcels and at any time and place and on any terms but every aspect of the sale including the method, manner, time, place and terms must be commercially reasonable. The resale must be reasonably identified as referring to the broken contract, but it is not necessary that the goods be in existence or that any or all of them have been identified to the contract before the breach.

(3) Where the resale is at private sale the seller must give the buyer reasonable notification of his intention to resell.

(4) Where the resale is at public sale

(a) only identified goods can be sold except where there is a recognized market for a public sale of futures in goods of the kind; and

(b) it must be made at a usual place or market for public sale if one is reasonably available and except in the case of goods which are perishable or threaten to decline in value speedily the seller must give the buyer reasonable notice of the time and place of the resale; and

(c) if the goods are not to be within the view of those attending the sale the notification of sale must state the place where the goods are located and provide for their reasonable inspection by prospective bidders; and

(d) the seller may buy.

(5) A purchaser who buys in good faith at a resale takes the goods free of any rights of the original buyer even though the seller fails to comply with one or more of the requirements of this section.

(6) The seller is not accountable to the buyer for any profit made on any resale. A person in the position of a seller (Section 2—707) or a buyer who has rightfully rejected or justifiably revoked acceptance must account for any excess over the amount of his security interest, as hereinafter defined (subsection (3) of Section 2—711).

§ 2—707. "Person in the Position of a Seller".

(1) A "person in the position of a seller" includes as against a principal an agent who has paid or become responsible for the price of goods on behalf of his principal or anyone who otherwise holds a security interest or other right in goods similar to that of a seller.

(2) A person in the position of a seller may as provided in this Article withhold or stop delivery (Section 2—705) and resell (Section 2—706) and recover incidental damages (Section 2—710).

§ 2—708. Seller's Damages for Non-Acceptance or Repudiation.

(1) Subject to subsection (2) and to the provisions of this Article with respect to proof of market price (Section 2—723), the measure of damages for non-acceptance or repudiation by the buyer is the difference between the market price at the time and place for tender and the unpaid contract price together with any incidental damages provided in this Article (Section 2—710), but less expenses saved in consequence of the buyer's breach.

(2) If the measure of damages provided in subsection (1) is inadequate to put the seller in as good a position as performance would have done then the measure of damages is the profit (including reasonable overhead)

which the seller would have made from full performance by the buyer, together with any incidental damages provided in this Article (Section 2—710), due allowance for costs reasonably incurred and due credit for payments or proceeds of resale.

§ 2—709. Action for the Price.

(1) When the buyer fails to pay the price as it becomes due the seller may recover, together with any incidental damages under the next section, the price

  (a) of goods accepted or of conforming goods lost or damaged within a commercially reasonable time after risk of their loss has passed to the buyer; and

  (b) of goods identified to the contract if the seller is unable after reasonable effort to resell them at a reasonable price or the circumstances reasonably indicate that such effort will be unavailing.

(2) Where the seller sues for the price he must hold for the buyer any goods which have been identified to the contract and are still in his control except that if resale become possible he may resell them at any time prior to the collection of the judgment. The net proceeds of any such resale must be credited to the buyer and payment of the judgment entitles him to any goods not resold.

(3) After the buyer has wrongfully rejected or revoked acceptance of the goods or has failed to make a payment due or has repudiated (Section 2—610), a seller who is held not entitled to the price under this section shall nevertheless be awarded damages for non-acceptance under the preceding section.

§ 2—710. Seller's Incidental Damages.

Incidental damages to an aggrieved seller include any commercially reasonable charges, expenses or commissions incurred in stopping delivery, in the transportation, care and custody of goods after the buyer's breach, in connection with return or resale of the goods or otherwise resulting from the breach.

§ 2—711. Buyer's Remedies in General; Buyer's Security Interest in Rejected Goods.

(1) Where the seller fails to make delivery or repudiates or the buyer rightfully rejects or justifiably revokes acceptance then with respect to any goods involved, and with respect to the whole if the breach goes to the whole contract (Section 2—612), the buyer may cancel and whether or not he has done so may in addition to recovering so much of the price as has been paid

  (a) "cover" and have damages under the next section as to all the goods affected whether or not they have been identified to the contract; or

  (b) recover damages for non-delivery as provided in this Article (Section 2—713).

(2) Where the seller fails to deliver or repudiates the buyer may also

  (a) if the goods have been identified recover them as provided in this Article (Section 2—502); or

  (b) in a proper case obtain specific performance or replevy the goods as provided in this Article (Section 2—716).

(3) On rightful rejection or justifiable revocation of acceptance a buyer has a security interest in goods in his possession or control for any payments made on their price and any expenses reasonably incurred in their inspection, receipt, transportation, care and custody and may hold such goods and resell them in like manner as an aggrieved seller (Section 2—706).

§ 2—712. "Cover"; Buyer's Procurement of Substitute Goods.

(1) After a breach within the preceding section the buyer may "cover" by making in good faith and without unreasonable delay any reasonable purchase of or contract to purchase goods in substitution for those due from the seller.

(2) The buyer may recover from the seller as damages the difference between the cost of cover and the contract price together with any incidental or consequential damages as hereinafter defined (Section 2—715), but less expenses saved in consequence of the seller's breach.

(3) Failure of the buyer to effect cover within this section does not bar him from any other remedy.

§ 2—713. Buyer's Damages for Non-Delivery or Repudiation.

(1) Subject to the provisions of this Article with respect to proof of market price (Section 2—723), the measure of damages for non-delivery or repudiation by the seller is the difference between the market price at the time when the buyer learned of the breach and the contract price together with any incidental and consequential damages provided in this Article (Section 2—715), but less expenses saved in consequence of the seller's breach.

(2) Market price is to be determined as of the place for tender or, in cases of rejection after arrival or revocation of acceptance, as of the place of arrival.

§ 2—714. Buyer's Damages for Breach in Regard to Accepted Goods.

(1) Where the buyer has accepted goods and given notification (subsection (3) of Section 2—607) he may recover as damages for any non-conformity of tender the loss resulting in the ordinary course of events from the seller's breach as determined in any manner which is reasonable.

(2) The measure of damages for breach of warranty is the difference at the time and place of acceptance between the value of the goods accepted and the value they would have had if they had been as warranted, unless special circumstances show proximate damages of a different amount.

(3) In a proper case any incidental and consequential damages under the next section may also be recovered.

§ 2—715. Buyer's Incidental and Consequential Damages.

(1) Incidental damages resulting from the seller's breach include expenses reasonably incurred in inspection, receipt, transportation and care and custody of goods rightfully rejected, any commercially reasonable charges, expenses or commissions in connection with effecting cover and any other reasonable expense incident to the delay or other breach.

(2) Consequential damages resulting from the seller's breach include

(a) any loss resulting from general or particular requirements and needs of which the seller at the time of contracting had reason to know and which could not reasonably be prevented by cover or otherwise; and

(b) injury to person or property proximately resulting from any breach of warranty.

§ 2—716. Buyer's Right to Specific Performance or Replevin.

(1) Specific performance may be decreed where the goods are unique or in other proper circumstances.

(2) The decree for specific performance may include such terms and conditions as to payment of the price, damages, or other relief as the court may deem just.

(3) The buyer has a right of replevin for goods identified to the contract if after reasonable effort he is unable to effect cover for such goods or the circumstances reasonably indicate that such effort will be unavailing or if the goods have been shipped under reservation and satisfaction of the security interest in them has been made or tendered.

§ 2—717. Deduction of Damages From the Price.

The buyer on notifying the seller of his intention to do so may deduct all or any part of the damages resulting from any breach of the contract from any part of the price still due under the same contract.

§ 2—718. Liquidation or Limitation of Damages; Deposits.

(1) Damages for breach by either party may be liquidated in the agreement but only at an amount which is reasonable in the light of the anticipated or actual harm caused by the breach, the difficulties of proof of loss, and the inconvenience or nonfeasibility of otherwise obtaining an adequate remedy. A term fixing unreasonably large liquidated damages is void as a penalty.

(2) Where the seller justifiably withholds delivery of goods because of the buyer's breach, the buyer is entitled to restitution of any amount by which the sum of his payments exceeds

(a) the amount to which the seller is entitled by virtue of terms liquidating the seller's damages in accordance with subsection (1), or

(b) in the absence of such terms, twenty per cent of the value of the total performance for which the buyer is obligated under the contract or $500, whichever is smaller.

(3) The buyer's right to restitution under subsection (2) is subject to offset to the extent that the seller establishes

(a) a right to recover damages under the provisions of this Article other than subsection (1), and

(b) the amount or value of any benefits received by the buyer directly or indirectly by reason of the contract.

(4) Where a seller has received payment in goods their reasonable value or the proceeds of their resale shall be treated as payments for the purposes of subsection (2); but if the seller has notice of the buyer's breach before reselling goods received in part performance, his resale is subject to the conditions laid down in this Article on resale by an aggrieved seller (Section 2—706).

§ 2—719. Contractual Modification or Limitation of Remedy.

(1) Subject to the provisions of subsections (2) and (3) of this section and of the preceding section on liquidation and limitation of damages,

(a) the agreement may provide for remedies in addition to or in substitution for those provided in this Article and may limit or alter the measure of damages recoverable under this Article, as by limiting the buyer's remedies to return of the goods and repayment of the price or to repair and replacement of non-conforming goods or parts; and

(b) resort to a remedy as provided is optional unless the remedy is expressly agreed to be exclusive, in which case it is the sole remedy.

(2) Where circumstances cause an exclusive or limited remedy to fail of its essential purpose, remedy may be had as provided in this Act.

(3) Consequential damages may be limited or excluded unless the limitation or exclusion is unconscionable. Limitation of consequential damages for injury to the person in the case of consumer goods is prima facie unconscionable but limitation of damages where the loss is commercial is not.

§ 2—720. Effect of "Cancellation" or "Rescission" on Claims for Antecedent Breach.

Unless the contrary intention clearly appears, expressions of "cancellation" or "rescission" of the contract or the like shall not be construed as a renunciation or discharge of any claim in damages for an antecedent breach.

§ 2—721. Remedies for Fraud.

Remedies for material misrepresentation or fraud include all remedies available under this Article for non-fraudulent breach. Neither rescission or a claim for rescission of the contract for sale nor rejection or return of the goods shall bar or be deemed inconsistent with a claim for damages or other remedy.

§ 2—722. Who Can Sue Third Parties for Injury to Goods.

Where a third party so deals with goods which have been identified to a contract for sale as to cause actionable injury to a party to that contract

(a) a right of action against the third party is in either party to the contract for sale who has title to or a security interest or a special property or an insurable interest in the goods; and if the goods have been destroyed or converted a right of action is also in the party who either bore the risk of loss under the contract for sale or has since the injury assumed that risk as against the other;

(b) if at the time of the injury the party plaintiff did not bear the risk of loss as against the other party to the contract for sale and there is no arrangement between them for disposition of the recovery, his suit or settlement is, subject to his own interest, as a fiduciary for the other party to the contract;

(c) either party may with the consent of the other sue for the benefit of whom it may concern.

§ 2—723. Proof of Market Price: Time and Place.

(1) If an action based on anticipatory repudiation comes to trial before the time for performance with respect to some or all of the goods, any damages based on market price (Section 2—708 or Section 2—713) shall be determined according to the price of such goods prevailing at the time when the aggrieved party learned of the repudiation.

(2) If evidence of a price prevailing at the times or places described in this Article is not readily available the price prevailing within any reasonable time before or after the time described or at any other place which in commercial judgment or under usage of trade would serve as a reasonable substitute for the one described may be used, making any proper allowance for the cost of transporting the goods to or from such other place.

(3) Evidence of a relevant price prevailing at a time or place other than the one described in this Article offered by one party is not admissible unless and until he has given the other party such notice as the court finds sufficient to prevent unfair surprise.

§ 2—724. Admissibility of Market Quotations.

Whenever the prevailing price or value of any goods regularly bought and sold in any established commodity market is in issue, reports in official publications or trade journals or in newspapers or periodicals of general circulation published as the reports of such market shall be admissible in evidence. The circumstances of the preparation of such a report may be shown to affect its weight but not its admissibility.

§ 2—725. **Statute of Limitations in Contracts for Sale.**

(1) An action for breach of any contract for sale must be commenced within four years after the cause of action has accrued. By the original agreement the parties may reduce the period of limitation to not less than one year but may not extend it.

(2) A cause of action accrues when the breach occurs, regardless of the aggrieved party's lack of knowledge of the breach. A breach of warranty occurs when tender of delivery is made, except that where a warranty explicitly extends to future performance of the goods and discovery of the breach must await the time of such performance the cause of action accrues when the breach is or should have been discovered.

(3) Where an action commenced within the time limited by subsection (1) is so terminated as to leave available a remedy by another action for the same breach such other action may be commenced after the expiration of the time limited and within six months after the termination of the first action unless the termination resulted from voluntary discontinuance or from dismissal for failure or neglect to prosecute.

(4) This section does not alter the law on tolling of the statute of limitations nor does it apply to causes of action which have accrued before this Act becomes effective.

Article 3
COMMERCIAL PAPER

Part 1 Short Title, Form and Interpretation

§ 3—101. Short Title.

This Article shall be known and may be cited as Uniform Commercial Code—Commercial Paper.

§ 3—102. Definitions and Index of Definitions.

(1) In this Article unless the context otherwise requires

(a) "Issue" means the first delivery of an instrument to a holder or a remitter.

(b) An "order" is a direction to pay and must be more than an authorization or request. It must identify the person to pay with reasonable certainty. It may be addressed to one or more such persons jointly or in the alternative but not in succession.

(c) A "promise" is an undertaking to pay and must be more than an acknowledgment of an obligation.

(d) "Secondary party" means a drawer or endorser.

(e) "Instrument" means a negotiable instrument.

(2) Other definitions applying to this Article and the sections in which they appear are:
"Acceptance". Section 3—410.
"Accommodation party". Section 3—415.
"Alteration". Section 3—407.
"Certificate of deposit". Section 3—104.
"Certification". Section 3—411.
"Check". Section 3—104.
"Definite time". Section 3—109.
"Dishonor". Section 3—507.
"Draft". Section 3—104.
"Holder in due course". Section 3—302.
"Negotiation". Section 3—202.
"Note". Section 3—104.
"Notice of dishonor". Section 3—508.
"On demand". Section 3—108.
"Presentment". Section 3—504.
"Protest". Section 3—509.
"Restrictive Indorsement". Section 3—205.
"Signature". Section 3—401.

(3) The following definitions in other Articles apply to this Article:
"Account". Section 4—104.
"Banking Day". Section 4—104.
"Clearing House". Section 4—104.
"Collecting Bank". Section 4—105.
"Customer". Section 4—104.
"Depositary Bank". Section 4—105.
"Documentary Draft". Section 4—104.
"Intermediary Bank". Section 4—105.
"Item". Section 4—104.
"Midnight deadline". Section 4—104.
"Payor Bank". Section 4—105.

(4) In addition Article 1 contains general definitions and principles of construction and interpretation applicable throughout this Article.

§ 3—103. Limitations on Scope of Article.

(1) This Article does not apply to money, documents of title or investment securities.

(2) The provisions of this Article are subject to the provisions of the Article on Bank Deposits and Col-

lections (Article 4) and Secured Transactions (Article 9).

§ 3—104. Form of Negotiable Instruments; "Draft"; "Check"; "Certificate of Deposit"; "Note".

(1) Any writing to be a negotiable instrument within this Article must

(a) be signed by the maker or drawer; and

(b) contain an unconditional promise or order to pay a sum certain in money and no other promise, order, obligation or power given by the maker or drawer except as authorized by this Article; and

(c) be payable on demand or at a definite time; and

(d) be payable to order or to bearer.

(2) A writing which complies with the requirements of this section is

(a) a "draft" ("bill of exchange") if it is an order;

(b) a "check" if it is a draft drawn on a bank and payable on demand;

(c) a "certificate of deposit" if it is an acknowledgment by a bank receipt of money with an engagement to repay it;

(d) a "note" if it is a promise other than a certificate of deposit.

(3) As used in other Articles of this Act, and as the context may require, the terms "draft", "check", "certificate of deposit" and "note" may refer to instruments which are not negotiable within this Article as well as to instruments which are so negotiable.

§ 3—105. When Promise or Order Unconditional.

(1) A promise or order otherwise unconditional is not made conditional by the fact that the instrument

(a) is subject to implied or constructive conditions; or

(b) states its consideration, whether performed or promised, or the transaction which gave rise to the instrument, or that the promise or order is made or the instrument matures in accordance with or "as per" such transaction; or

(c) refers to or states that it arises out of a separate agreement or refers to a separate agreement for rights as to prepayment or acceleration; or

(d) states that it is drawn under a letter of credit; or

(e) states that it is secured, whether by mortgage, reservation of title or otherwise; or

(f) indicates a particular account to be debited or any other fund or source from which reimbursement is expected; or

(g) is limited to payment out of a particular fund or the proceeds of a particular source, if the instrument is issued by a government or governmental agency or unit; or

(h) is limited to payment out of the entire assets of a partnership, unincorporated association, trust or estate by or on behalf of which the instrument is issued.

(2) A promise or order is not unconditional if the instrument

(a) states that it is subject to or governed by any other agreement; or

(b) states that it is to be paid only out of a particular fund or source except as provided in this section.

§ 3—106. Sum Certain.

(1) The sum payable is a sum certain even though it is to be paid

(a) with stated interest or by stated installments; or

(b) with stated different rates of interest before and after default or a specified date; or

(c) with a stated discount or addition if paid before or after the date fixed for payment; or

(d) with exchange or less exchange, whether at a fixed rate or at the current rate; or

(e) with costs of collection or an attorney's fee or both upon default.

(2) Nothing in this section shall validate any term which is otherwise illegal.

§ 3—107. Money.

(1) An instrument is payable in money if the medium of exchange in which it is payable is money at the time the instrument is made. An instrument payable in "currency" or "current funds" is payable in money.

(2) A promise to order to pay a sum stated in a foreign currency is for a sum certain in money and, unless a

different medium of payment is specified in the instrument, may be satisfied by payment of that number of dollars which the stated foreign currency will purchase at the buying sight rate for that currency on the day on which the instrument is payable or, if payable on demand, on the day of demand. If such an instrument specifies a foreign currency as the medium of payment the instrument is payable in that currency.

§ 3—108. **Payable on Demand.**

Instruments payable on demand include those payable at sight or on presentation and those in which no time for payment is stated.

§ 3—109. **Definite Time.**

(1) An instrument is payable at a definite time if by its terms it is payable

(a) on or before a stated date or at a fixed period after a stated date; or

(b) at a fixed period after sight; or

(c) at a definite time subject to any acceleration; or

(d) at a definite time subject to extension at the option of the holder, or to extension to a further definite time at the option of the maker or acceptor or automatically upon or after a specified act or event.

(2) An instrument which by its terms is otherwise payable only upon an act or event uncertain as to time of occurrence is not payable at a definite time even though the act or event has occurred.

§ 3—110. **Payable to Order.**

(1) An instrument is payable to order when by its terms it is payable to the order or assigns of any person therein specified with reasonable certainty, or to him or his order, or when it is conspicuously designated on its face as "exchange" or the like and names a payee. It may be payable to the order of

(a) the maker or drawer; or

(b) the drawee; or

(c) a payee who is not maker, drawer or drawee; or

(d) two or more payees together or in the alternative; or

(e) an estate, trust or fund, in which case it is payable to the order of the representative of such estate, trust or fund or his successors; or

(f) an office, or an officer by his title as such in which case it is payable to the principal but the incumbent of the office or his successors may act as if he or they were the holder; or

(g) a partnership or unincorporated association, in which case it is payable to the partnership or association and may be indorsed or transferred by any person thereto authorized.

(2) An instrument not payable to order is not made so payable by such words as "payable upon return of this instrument properly indorsed."

(3) An instrument made payable both to order and to bearer is payable to order unless the bearer words are handwritten or typewritten.

§ 3—111. **Payable to Bearer.**

An instrument is payable to bearer when by its terms it is payable to

(a) bearer or the order of bearer; or

(b) a specified person or bearer; or

(c) "cash" or the order of "cash", or any other indication which does not purport to designate a specific payee.

§ 3—112. **Terms and Omissions Not Affecting Negotiability.**

(1) The negotiability of an instrument is not affected by

(a) the omission of a statement of any consideration or of the place where the instrument is drawn or payable; or

(b) a statement that collateral has been given to secure obligations either on the instrument or otherwise of an obligor on the instrument or that in case of default on those obligations the holder may realize on or dispose of the collateral; or

(c) a promise or power to maintain or protect collateral or to give additional collateral; or

(d) a term authorizing a confession of judgment on the instrument if it is not paid when due; or

(e) a term purporting to waive the benefit of any law intended for the advantage or protection of any obligor; or

(f) a term in a draft providing that the payee by indorsing or cashing it acknowledges full satisfaction of an obligation of the drawer; or

(g) a statement in a draft drawn in a set of parts

(Section 3—801) to the effect that the order is effective only if no other part has been honored.

(2) Nothing in this section shall validate any term which is otherwise illegal.

§ 3—113. Seal.

An instrument otherwise negotiable is within this Article even though it is under a seal.

§ 3—114. Date, Antedating, Postdating.

(1) The negotiability of an instrument is not affected by the fact that it is undated, antedated or postdated.

(2) Where an instrument is antedated or postdated the time when it is payable is determined by the stated date if the instrument is payable on demand or at a fixed period after date.

(3) Where the instrument or any signature thereon is dated, the date is presumed to be correct.

§ 3—115. Incomplete Instruments.

(1) When a paper whose contents at the time of signing show that it is intended to become an instrument is signed while still incomplete in any necessary respect it cannot be enforced until completed, but when it is completed in accordance with authority given it is effective as completed.

(2) If the completion is unauthorized the rules as to material alteration apply (Section 3—407), even though the paper was not delivered by the maker or drawer; but the burden of establishing that any completion is unauthorized is on the party so asserting.

§ 3—116. Instruments Payable to Two or More Persons.

An instrument payable to the order of two or more persons

(a) if in the alternative is payable to any one of them and may be negotiated, discharged or enforced by any of them who has possession of it;

(b) if not in the alternative is payable to all of them and may be negotiated, discharged or enforced only by all of them.

§ 3—117. Instruments Payable With Words of Description.

An instrument made payable to a named person with the addition of words describing him

(a) as agent or officer of a specified person is payable to his principal but the agent or officer may act as if he were the holder;

(b) as any other fiduciary for a specified person or purpose is payable to the payee and may be negotiated, discharged or enforced by him;

(c) in any other manner is payable to the payee unconditionally and the additional words are without effect on subsequent parties.

§ 3—118. Ambiguous Terms and Rules of Construction.

The following rules apply to every instrument:

(a) Where there is doubt whether the instrument is a draft or a note the holder may treat it as either. A draft drawn on the drawer is effective as a note.

(b) Handwritten terms control typewritten and printed terms, and typewritten control printed.

(c) Words control figures except that if the words are ambiguous figures control.

(d) Unless otherwise specified a provision for interest means interest at the judgment rate at the place of payment from the date of the instrument, or if it is undated from the date of issue.

(e) Unless the instrument otherwise specifies two or more persons who sign as maker, acceptor or drawer or indorser and as a part of the same transaction are jointly and severally liable even though the instrument contains such words as "I promise to pay."

(f) Unless otherwise specified consent to extension authorizes a single extension for not longer than the original period. A consent to extension, expressed in the instrument, is binding on secondary parties and accommodation makers. A holder may not exercise his option to extend an instrument over the objection of a maker or acceptor or other party who in accordance with Section 3—604 tenders full payment when the instrument is due.

§ 3—119. Other Writings Affecting Instrument.

(1) As between the obligor and his immediate obligee or any transferee the terms of an instrument may be modified or affected by any other written agreement executed as a part of the same transaction, except that a holder in due course is not affected by any limitation of his rights arising out of the separate written agreement if he had no notice of the limitation when he took the instrument.

(2) A separate agreement does not affect the negotiability of an instrument.

§ 3—120. Instruments "Payable Through" Bank.

An instrument which states that it is "payable through" a bank or the like designates that bank as a collecting bank to make presentment but does not of itself authorize the bank to pay the instrument.

§ 3—121. Instruments Payable at Bank.

Note: If this Act is introduced in the Congress of the United States this section should be omitted.

(States to select either alternative)

Alternative A—

A note or acceptance which states that it is payable at a bank is the equivalent of a draft drawn on the bank payable when it falls due out of any funds of the maker or acceptor in current account or otherwise available for such payment.

Alternative B—

A note or acceptance which states that it is payable at a bank is not of itself an order or authorization to the bank to pay it.

§ 3—122. Accrual of Cause of Action.

(1) A cause of action against a maker or an acceptor accrues

    (a) in the case of a time instrument on the day after maturity;

    (b) in the case of a demand instrument upon its date or, if no date is stated, on the date of issue.

(2) A cause of action against the obligor of a demand or time certificate of deposit accrues upon demand, but demand on a time certificate may not be made until on or after the date of maturity.

(3) A cause of action against a drawer of a draft or an indorser of any instrument accrues upon demand following dishonor of the instrument. Notice of dishonor is a demand.

(4) Unless an instrument provides otherwise, interest runs at the rate provided by law for a judgment

    (a) in the case of a maker, acceptor or other primary obligor of a demand instrument, from the date of demand;

    (b) in all other cases from the date of accrual of the cause of action.

Part 2 Transfer and Negotiation

§ 3—201. Transfer: Right to Indorsement.

(1) Transfer of an instrument vests in the transferee such rights as the transferor has therein, except that a transferee who has himself been a party to any fraud or illegality affecting the instrument or who as a prior holder had notice of a defense or claim against it cannot improve his position by taking from a later holder in due course.

(2) A transfer of a security interest in an instrument vests the foregoing rights in the transferee to the extent of the interest transferred.

(3) Unless otherwise agreed any transfer for value of an instrument not then payable to bearer gives the transferee the specifically enforceable right to have the unqualified indorsement of the transferor. Negotiation takes effect only when the indorsement is made and until that time there is no presumption that the transferee is the owner.

§ 3—202. Negotiation.

(1) Negotiation is the transfer of an instrument in such form that the transferee becomes a holder. If the instrument is payable to order it is negotiated by delivery with any necessary indorsement; if payable to bearer it is negotiated by delivery.

(2) An indorsement must be written by or on behalf of the holder and on the instrument or on a paper so firmly affixed thereto as to become a part thereof.

(3) An indorsement is effective for negotiation only when it conveys the entire instrument or any unpaid residue. If it purports to be of less it operates only as a partial assignment.

(4) Words of assignment, condition, waiver, guaranty, limitation or disclaimer of liability and the like accompanying an indorsement do not affect its character as an indorsement.

§ 3—203. Wrong or Misspelled Name.

Where an instrument is made payable to a person under a misspelled name or one other than his own he may indorse in that name or his own or both; but signature in both names may be required by a person paying or giving value for the instrument.

§ 3—204. Special Indorsement; Blank Indorsement.

(1) A special indorsement specifies the person to whom or to whose order it makes the instrument payable. Any instrument specially indorsed becomes payable to the order of the special indorsee and may be further negotiated only by his indorsement.

(2) An indorsement in blank specifies no particular indorsee and may consist of a mere signature. An instrument payable to order and indorsed in blank becomes payable to bearer and may be negotiated by delivery alone until specially indorsed.

(3) The holder may convert a blank indorsement into a special indorsement by writing over the signature of the indorser in blank any contract consistent with the character of the indorsement.

§ 3—205. **Restrictive Indorsements.**

An indorsement is restrictive which either

(a) is conditional; or

(b) purports to prohibit further transfer of the instrument; or

(c) includes the words "for collection", "for deposit", "pay any bank", or like terms signifying a purpose of deposit or collection; or

(d) otherwise states that it is for the benefit or use of the indorser or of another person.

§ 3—206. **Effect of Restrictive Indorsement.**

(1) No restrictive indorsement prevents further transfer or negotiation of the instrument.

(2) An intermediary bank, or a payor bank which is not the depositary bank, is neither given notice nor otherwise affected by a restrictive indorsement of any person except the bank's immediate transferor or the person presenting for payment.

(3) Except for an intermediary bank, any transferee under an indorsement which is conditional or includes the words "for collection", "for deposit", "pay any bank", or like terms (subparagraphs (a) and (c) of Section 3—205) must pay or apply any value given by him for or on the security of the instrument consistently with the indorsement and to the extent that he does so he becomes a holder for value. In addition such transferee is a holder in due course if he otherwise complies with the requirements of Section 3—302 on what constitutes a holder in due course.

(4) The first taker under an indorsement for the benefit of the indorser or another person (subparagraph (d) of Section 3—205) must pay or apply any value given by him for or on the security of the instrument consistently with the indorsement and to the extent that he does so he becomes a holder for value. In addition such taker is a holder in due course if he otherwise complies with the requirements of Section 3—302 on what constitutes a holder in due course. A later

holder for value is neither given notice nor otherwise affected by such restrictive indorsement unless he has knowledge that a fiduciary or other person has negotiated the instrument in any transaction for his own benefit or otherwise in breach of duty (subsection (2) of Section 3—304).

§ 3—207. **Negotiation Effective Although It May Be Rescinded.**

(1) Negotiation is effective to transfer the instrument although the negotiation is

(a) made by an infant, a corporation exceeding its powers, or any other person without capacity; or

(b) obtained by fraud, duress or mistake of any kind; or

(c) part of an illegal transaction; or

(d) made in breach of duty.

(2) Except as against a subsequent holder in due course such negotiation is in an appropriate case subject to rescission, the declaration of a constructive trust or any other remedy permitted by law.

§ 3—208. **Reacquisition.**

Where an instrument is returned to or reacquired by a prior party he may cancel any indorsement which is not necessary to his title and reissue or further negotiate the instrument, but any intervening party is discharged as against the reacquiring party and subsequent holders not in due course and if his indorsement has been cancelled is discharged as against subsequent holders in due course as well.

Part 3 **Rights of a Holder**

§ 3—301. **Rights of a Holder.**

The holder of an instrument whether or not he is the owner may transfer or negotiate it and, except as otherwise provided in Section 3—603 on payment or satisfaction, discharge it or enforce payment in his own name.

§ 3—302. **Holder in Due Course**

(1) A holder in due course is a holder who takes the instrument

(a) for value; and

(b) in good faith; and

(c) without notice that it is overdue or has been dishonored or of any defense against or claim to it on the part of any person.

(2) A payee may be a holder in due course.

(3) A holder does not become a holder in due course of an instrument:

    (a) by purchase of it at judicial sale or by taking it under legal process; or

    (b) by acquiring it in taking over an estate; or

    (c) by purchasing it as part of a bulk transaction not in regular course of business of the transferor.

(4) A purchaser of a limited interest can be a holder in due course only to the extent of the interest purchased.

§ 3—303. Taking for Value.

A holder takes the instrument for value

(a) to the extent that the agreed consideration has been performed or that he acquires a security interest in or a lien on the instrument otherwise than by legal process; or

(b) when he takes the instrument in payment of or as security for an antecedent claim against any person whether or not the claim is due; or

(c) when he gives a negotiable instrument for it or makes an irrevocable commitment to a third person.

§ 3—304. Notice to Purchaser.

(1) The purchaser has notice of a claim or defense if

    (a) the instrument is so incomplete, bears such visible evidence of forgery or alteration, or is otherwise so irregular as to call into question its validity, terms or ownership or to create an ambiguity as to the party to pay; or

    (b) the purchaser has notice that the obligation of any party is voidable in whole or in part, or that all parties have been discharged.

(2) The purchaser has notice of a claim against the instrument when he has knowledge that a fiduciary has negotiated the instrument in payment of or as security for his own debt or in any transaction for his own benefit or otherwise in breach of duty.

(3) The purchaser has notice that an instrument is overdue if he has reason to know

    (a) that any part of the principal amount is overdue or that there is an uncured default in payment of another instrument of the same series; or

    (b) that acceleration of the instrument has been made; or

    (c) that he is taking a demand instrument after demand has been made or more than a reasonable length of time after its issue. A reasonable time for a check drawn and payable within the states and territories of the United States and the District of Columbia is presumed to be thirty days.

(4) Knowledge of the following facts does not of itself give the purchaser notice of a defense or claim

    (a) that the instrument is antedated or postdated;

    (b) that it was issued or negotiated in return for an executory promise or accompanied by a separate agreement, unless the purchaser has notice that a defense or claim has arisen from the terms thereof;

    (c) that any party has signed for accommodation;

    (d) that an incomplete instrument has been completed, unless the purchaser has notice of any improper completion;

    (e) that any person negotiating the instrument is or was a fiduciary;

    (f) that there has been default in payment of interest on the instrument or in payment of any other instrument, except one of the same series.

(5) The filing or recording of a document does not of itself constitute notice within the provisions of this Article to a person who would otherwise be a holder in due course.

(6) To be effective notice must be received at such time and in such manner as to give a reasonable opportunity to act on it.

§ 3—305. Rights of a Holder in Due Course.

To the extent that a holder is a holder in due course he takes the instrument free from

(1) all claims to it on the part of any person; and

(2) all defenses of any party to the instrument with whom the holder has not dealt except

    (a) infancy, to the extent that it is a defense to a simple contract; and

    (b) such other incapacity, or duress, or illegality of the transaction, as renders the obligation of the party a nullity; and

    (c) such misrepresentation as has induced the party to sign the instrument with neither knowledge nor reasonable opportunity to obtain knowledge of its character or its essential terms; and

    (d) discharge in insolvency proceedings; and

    (e) any other discharge of which the holder has notice when he takes the instrument.

§ 3—306. Rights of One Not Holder in Due Course.

Unless he has the rights of a holder in due course any person takes the instrument subject to

(a) all valid claims to it on the part of any person; and

(b) all defenses of any party which would be available in an action on a simple contract; and

(c) the defenses of want or failure of consideration, nonperformance of any condition precedent, nondelivery, or delivery for a special purpose (Section 3—408); and

(d) the defense that he or a person through whom he holds the instrument acquired it by theft, or that payment or satisfaction to such holder would be inconsistent with the terms of a restrictive indorsement. The claim of any third person to the instrument is not otherwise available as a defense to any party liable thereon unless the third person himself defends the action for such party.

§ 3—307. Burden of Establishing Signatures, Defenses and Due Course.

(1) Unless specifically denied in the pleadings each signature on an instrument is admitted. When the effectiveness of a signature is put in issue

(a) the burden of establishing it is on the party claiming under the signature; but

(b) the signature is presumed to be genuine or authorized except where the action is to enforce the obligation of a purported signer who has died or become incompetent before proof is required.

(2) When signatures are admitted or established, production of the instrument entitles a holder to recover on it unless the defendant establishes a defense.

(3) After it is shown that a defense exists a person claiming the rights of a holder in due course has the burden of establishing that he or some person under whom he claims is in all respects a holder in due course.

Part 4 Liability of Parties

§ 3—401. Signature.

(1) No person is liable on an instrument unless his signature appears thereon.

(2) A signature is made by use of any name, including any trade or assumed name, upon an instrument, or by any word or mark used in lieu of a written signature.

§ 3—402. Signature in Ambiguous Capacity.

Unless the instrument clearly indicates that a signature is made in some other capacity it is an indorsement.

§ 3—403. Signature by Authorized Representative.

(1) A signature may be made by an agent or other representative, and his authority to make it may be established as in other cases of representation. No particular form of appointment is necessary to establish such authority.

(2) An authorized representative who signs his own name to an instrument

(a) is personally obligated if the instrument neither names the person represented nor shows that the representative signed in a representative capacity;

(b) except as otherwise established between the immediate parties, is personally obligated if the instrument names the person represented but does not show that the representative signed in a representative capacity, or if the instrument does not name the person represented but does show that the representative signed in a representative capacity.

(3) Except as otherwise established the name of an organization preceded or followed by the name and office of an authorized individual is a signature made in a representative capacity.

§ 3—404. Unauthorized Signatures.

(1) Any unauthorized signature is wholly inoperative as that of the person whose name is signed unless he ratifies it or is precluded from denying it; but it operates as the signature of the unauthorized signer in favor of any person who in good faith pays the instrument or takes it for value.

(2) Any unauthorized signature may be ratified for all purposes of this Article. Such ratification does not of itself affect any rights of the person ratifying against the actual signer.

§ 3—405. Impostors; Signature in Name of Payee.

(1) An indorsement by any person in the name of a named payee is effective if

(a) an impostor by use of the mails or otherwise has induced the maker or drawer to issue the instrument to him or his confederate in the name of the payee; or

(b) a person signing as or on behalf of a maker or drawer intends the payee to have no interest in the instrument; or

(c) an agent or employee of the maker or drawer has supplied him with the name of the payee intending the latter to have no such interest.

(2) Nothing in this section shall affect the criminal or civil liability of the person so indorsing.

§ 3—406. Negligence Contributing to Alteration or Unauthorized Signature.

Any person who by his negligence substantially contributes to a material alteration of the instrument or to the making of an unauthorized signature is precluded from asserting the alteration or lack of authority against a holder in due course or against a drawee or other payor who pays the instrument in good faith and in accordance with the reasonable commercial standards of the drawee's or payor's business.

§ 3—407. Alteration.

(1) Any alteration of an instrument is material which changes the contract of any party thereto in any respect, including any such change in

(a) the number or relations of the parties; or

(b) an incomplete instrument, by completing it otherwise than as authorized; or

(c) the writing as signed, by adding to it or by removing any part of it.

(2) As against any person other than a subsequent holder in due course

(a) alteration by the holder which is both fraudulent and material discharges any party whose contract is thereby changed unless that party assents or is precluded from asserting the defense;

(b) no other alteration discharges any party and the instrument may be enforced according to its original tenor, or as to incomplete instruments according to the authority given.

(3) A subsequent holder in due course may in all cases enforce the instrument according to its original tenor, and when an incomplete instrument has been completed, he may enforce it as completed.

§ 3—408. Consideration.

Want or failure of consideration is a defense as against any person not having the rights of a holder in due course (Section 3—305), except that no consideration is necessary for an instrument or obligation thereon given in payment of or as security for an antecedent obligation of any kind. Nothing in this section shall be taken to displace any statute outside this Act under which a promise is enforceable notwithstanding lack or failure of consideration. Partial failure of consideration is a defense pro tanto whether or not the failure is in an ascertained or liquidated amount.

§ 3—409. Draft Not an Assignment.

(1) A check or other draft does not of itself operate as an assignment of any funds in the hands of the drawee available for its payment, and the drawee is not liable on the instrument until he accepts it.

(2) Nothing in this section shall affect any liability in contract, tort or otherwise arising from any letter of credit or other obligation or representation which is not an acceptance.

§ 3—410. Definition and Operation of Acceptance.

(1) Acceptance is the drawee's signed engagement to honor the draft as presented. It must be written on the draft, and may consist of his signature alone. It becomes operative when completed by delivery or notification.

(2) A draft may be accepted although it has not been signed by the drawer or is otherwise incomplete or is overdue or has been dishonored.

(3) Where the draft is payable at a fixed period after sight and the acceptor fails to date his acceptance the holder may complete it by supplying a date in good faith.

§ 3—411. Certification of a Check.

(1) Certification of a check is acceptance. Where a holder procures certification the drawer and all prior indorsers are discharged.

(2) Unless otherwise agreed a bank has no obligation to certify a check.

(3) A bank may certify a check before returning it for lack of proper indorsement. If it does so the drawer is discharged.

§ 3—412. Acceptance Varying Draft.

(1) Where the drawee's proffered acceptance in any manner varies the draft as presented the holder may refuse the acceptance and treat the draft as dishonored

in which case the drawee is entitled to have his acceptance cancelled.

(2) The terms of the draft are not varied by an acceptance to pay at any particular bank or place in the United States, unless the acceptance states that the draft is to be paid only at such bank or place.

(3) Where the holder assents to an acceptance varying the terms of the draft each drawer and indorser who does not affirmatively assent is discharged.

§ 3—413. Contract of Maker, Drawer and Acceptor.

(1) The maker or acceptor engages that he will pay the instrument according to its tenor at the time of his engagement or as completed pursuant to Section 3—115 on incomplete instruments.

(2) The drawer engages that upon dishonor of the draft and any necessary notice of dishonor or protest he will pay the amount of the draft to the holder or to any indorser who takes it up. The drawer may disclaim this liability by drawing without recourse.

(3) By making, drawing or accepting the party admits as against all subsequent parties including the drawee the existence of the payee and his then capacity to indorse.

§ 3—414. Contract of Indorser; Order of Liability.

(1) Unless the indorsement otherwise specifies (as by such words as "without recourse") every indorser engages that upon dishonor and any necessary notice of dishonor and protest he will pay the instrument according to its tenor at the time of his indorsement to the holder or to any subsequent indorser who takes it up, even though the indorser who takes it up was not obligated to do so.

(2) Unless they otherwise agree indorsers are liable to one another in the order in which they indorse, which is presumed to be the order in which their signatures appear on the instrument.

§ 3—415. Contract of Accommodation Party.

(1) An accommodation party is one who signs the instrument in any capacity for the purpose of lending his name to another party to it.

(2) When the instrument has been taken for value before it is due the accommodation party is liable in the capacity in which he has signed even though the taker knows of the accommodation.

(3) As against a holder in due course and without notice of the accommodation oral proof of the accommodation is not admissible to give the accommodation party the benefit of discharges dependent on his character as such. In other cases the accommodation character may be shown by oral proof.

(4) An indorsement which shows that it is not in the chain of title is notice of its accommodation character.

(5) An accommodation party is not liable to the party accommodated, and if he pays the instrument has a right of recourse on the instrument against such party.

§ 3—416. Contract of Guarantor.

(1) "Payment guaranteed" or equivalent words added to a signature mean that the signer engages that if the instrument is not paid when due he will pay it according to its tenor without resort by the holder to any other party.

(2) "Collection guaranteed" or equivalent words added to a signature mean that the signer engages that if the instrument is not paid when due he will pay it according to its tenor, but only after the holder has reduced his claim against the maker or acceptor to judgment and execution has been returned unsatisfied, or after the maker or acceptor has become insolvent or it is otherwise apparent that it is useless to proceed against him.

(3) Words of guaranty which do not otherwise specify guarantee payment.

(4) No words of guaranty added to the signature of a sole maker or acceptor affect his liability on the instrument. Such words added to the signature of one of two or more makers or acceptors create a presumption that the signature is for the accommodation of the others.

(5) When words of guaranty are used presentment, notice of dishonor and protest are not necessary to charge the user.

(6) Any guaranty written on the instrument is enforcible notwithstanding any statute of frauds.

§ 3—417. Warranties on Presentment and Transfer.

(1) Any person who obtains payment or acceptance and any prior transferor warrants to a person who in good faith pays or accepts that

    (a) he has a good title to the instrument or is authorized to obtain payment or acceptance on behalf of one who has a good title; and

(b) he has no knowledge that the signature of the maker or drawer is unauthorized, except that this warranty is not given by a holder in due course acting in good faith

(i) to a maker with respect to the maker's own signature; or

(ii) to a drawer with respect to the drawer's own signature, whether or not the drawer is also the drawee; or

(iii) to an acceptor of a draft if the holder in due course took the draft after the acceptance or obtained the acceptance without knowledge that the drawer's signature was unauthorized; and

(c) the instrument has not been materially altered, except that this warranty is not given by a holder in due course acting in good faith

(i) to the maker of a note; or

(ii) to the drawer of a draft whether or not the drawer is also the drawee; or

(iii) to the acceptor of a draft with respect to an alteration made prior to the acceptance if the holder in due course took the draft after the acceptance, even though the acceptance provided "payable as originally drawn" or equivalent terms; or

(iv) to the acceptor of a draft with respect to an alteration made after the acceptance.

(2) Any person who transfers an instrument and receives consideration warrants to his transferee and if the transfer is by indorsement to any subsequent holder who takes the instrument in good faith that

(a) he has a good title to the instrument or is authorized to obtain payment or acceptance on behalf of one who has a good title and the transfer is otherwise rightful; and

(b) all signatures are genuine or authorized; and

(c) the instrument has not been materially altered; and

(d) no defense of any party is good against him; and

(e) he has no knowledge of any insolvency proceeding instituted with respect to the maker or

acceptor or the drawer of an unaccepted instrument.

(3) By transferring "without recourse" the transferor limits the obligation stated in subsection (2) (d) to a warranty that he has no knowledge of such a defense.

(4) A selling agent or broker who does not disclose the fact that he is acting only as such gives the warranties provided in this section, but if he makes such disclosure warrants only his good faith and authority.

§ 3—418. **Finality of Payment or Acceptance.**

Except for recovery of bank payments as provided in the Article on Bank Deposits and Collections (Article 4) and except for liability for breach of warranty on presentment under the preceding section, payment or acceptance of any instrument is final in favor of a holder in due course, or a person who has in good faith changed his position in reliance on the payment.

§ 3—419. **Conversion of Instrument; Innocent Representative.**

(1) An instrument is converted when

(a) a drawee to whom it is delivered for acceptance refuses to return it on demand; or

(b) any person to whom it is delivered for payment refuses on demand either to pay or to return it; or

(c) it is paid on a forged indorsement.

(2) In an action against a drawee under subsection (1) the measure of the drawee's liability is the face amount of the instrument. In any other action under subsection (1) the measure of liability is presumed to be the face amount of the instrument.

(3) Subject to the provisions of this Act concerning restrictive indorsements a representative, including a depositary or collecting bank, who has in good faith and in accordance with the reasonable commercial standards applicable to the business of such representative dealt with an instrument or its proceeds on behalf of one who was not the true owner is not liable in conversion or otherwise to the true owner beyond the amount of any proceeds remaining in his hands.

(4) An intermediary bank or payor bank which is not a depositary bank is not liable in conversion solely by reason of the fact that proceeds of an item indorsed restrictively (Sections 3—205 and 3—206) are not paid or applied consistently with the restrictive indorsement of an indorser other than its immediate transferor.

Part 5 Presentment, Notice of Dishonor and Protest

§ 3—501. When Presentment, Notice of Dishonor, and Protest Necessary or Permissible.

(1) Unless excused (Section 3—511) presentment is necessary to charge secondary parties as follows:

(a) presentment for acceptance is necessary to charge the drawer and indorsers of a draft where the draft so provides, or is payable elsewhere than at the residence or place of business of the drawee, or its date of payment depends upon such presentment. The holder may at his option present for acceptance any other draft payable at a stated date;

(b) presentment for payment is necessary to charge any indorser;

(c) in the case of any drawer, the acceptor of a draft payable at a bank or the maker of a note payable at a bank, presentment for payment is necessary, but failure to make presentment discharges such drawer, acceptor or maker only as stated in Section 3—502(1)(b).

(2) Unless excused (Section 3—511)

(a) notice of any dishonor is necessary to charge any indorser;

(b) in the case of any drawer, the acceptor of a draft payable at a bank or the maker of a note payable at a bank, notice of any dishonor is necessary, but failure to give such notice discharges such drawer, acceptor or maker only as stated in Section 3—502(1)(b).

(3) Unless excused (Section 3—511) protest of any dishonor is necessary to charge the drawer and indorsers of any draft which on its face appears to be drawn or payable outside of the states, territories, dependencies, and possessions of the United States, the District of Columbia and the Commonwealth of Puerto Rico. The holder may at his option make protest of any dishonor of any other instrument and in the case of a foreign draft may on insolvency of the acceptor before maturity make protest for better security.

(4) Notwithstanding any provision of this section, neither presentment nor notice of dishonor nor protest is necessary to charge an indorser who has indorsed an instrument after maturity.

§ 3—502. Unexcused Delay; Discharge.

(1) Where without excuse any necessary presentment or notice of dishonor is delayed beyond the time when it is due

(a) any indorser is discharged; and

(b) any drawer or the acceptor of a draft payable at a bank or the maker of a note payable at a bank who because the drawee or payor bank becomes insolvent during the delay is deprived of funds maintained with the drawee or payor bank to cover the instrument may discharge his liability by written assignment to the holder of his rights against the drawee or payor bank in respect of such funds, but such drawer, acceptor or maker is not otherwise discharged.

(2) Where without excuse a necessary protest is delayed beyond the time when it is due any drawer or indorser is discharged.

§ 3—503. Time of Presentment.

(1) Unless a different time is expressed in the instrument the time for any presentment is determined as follows:

(a) where an instrument is payable at or a fixed period after a stated date any presentment for acceptance must be made on or before the date it is payable;

(b) where an instrument is payable after sight it must either be presented for acceptance or negotiated within a reasonable time after date or issue whichever is later;

(c) where an instrument shows the date on which it is payable presentment for payment is due on that date;

(d) where an instrument is accelerated presentment for payment is due within a reasonable time after the acceleration;

(e) with respect to the liability of any secondary party presentment for acceptance or payment of any other instrument is due within a reasonable time after such party becomes liable thereon.

(2) A reasonable time for presentment is determined by the nature of the instrument, any usage of banking or trade and the facts of the particular case. In the case of an uncertified check which is drawn and payable within the United States and which is not a draft drawn by a bank the following are presumed to be reasonable periods within which to present for payment or to initiate bank collection:

(a) with respect to the liability of the drawer, thirty days after date or issue whichever is later; and

(b) with respect to the liability of an indorser, seven days after his indorsement.

(3) Where any presentment is due on a day which is not a full business day for either the person making presentment or the party to pay or accept, presentment is due on the next following day which is a full business day for both parties.

(4) Presentment to be sufficient must be made at a reasonable hour, and if at a bank during its banking day.

§ 3—504. How Presentment Made.

(1) Presentment is a demand for acceptance or payment made upon the maker, acceptor, drawee or other payor by or on behalf of the holder.

(2) Presentment may be made

(a) by mail, in which event the time of presentment is determined by the time of receipt of the mail; or

(b) through a clearing house; or

(c) at the place of acceptance or payment specified in the instrument or if there be none at the place of business or residence of the party to accept or pay. If neither the party to accept or pay nor anyone authorized to act for him is present or accessible at such place presentment is excused.

(3) It may be made

(a) to any one of two or more makers, acceptors, drawees or other payors; or

(b) to any person who has authority to make or refuse the acceptance or payment.

(4) A draft accepted or a note made payable at a bank in the United States must be presented at such bank.

(5) In the cases described in Section 4—210 presentment may be made in the manner and with the result stated in that section.

§ 3—505. Rights of Party to Whom Presentment Is Made.

(1) The party to whom presentment is made may without dishonor require

(a) exhibition of the instrument; and

(b) reasonable identification of the person making presentment and evidence of his authority to make it if made for another; and

(c) that the instrument be produced for acceptance or payment at a place specified in it, or if there be none at any place reasonable in the circumstances; and

(d) a signed receipt on the instrument for any partial or full payment and its surrender upon full payment.

(2) Failure to comply with any such requirement invalidates the presentment but the person presenting has a reasonable time in which to comply and the time for acceptance or payment runs from the time of compliance.

§ 3—506. Time Allowed for Acceptance or Payment.

(1) Acceptance may be deferred without dishonor until the close of the next business day following presentment. The holder may also in a good faith effort to obtain acceptance and without either dishonor of the instrument or discharge of secondary parties allow postponement of acceptance for an additional business day.

(2) Except as a longer time is allowed in the case of documentary drafts drawn under a letter of credit, and unless an earlier time is agreed to by the party to pay, payment of an instrument may be deferred without dishonor pending reasonable examination to determine whether it is properly payable, but payment must be made in any event before the close of business on the day of presentment.

§ 3—507. Dishonor; Holder's Right of Recourse; Term Allowing Re-Presentment.

(1) An instrument is dishonored when

(a) a necessary or optional presentment is duly made and due acceptance or payment is refused or cannot be obtained within the prescribed time or in case of bank collections the instrument is seasonably returned by the midnight deadline (Section 4—301); or

(b) presentment is excused and the instrument is not duly accepted or paid.

(2) Subject to any necessary notice of dishonor and protest, the holder has upon dishonor an immediate right of recourse against the drawers and indorsers.

(3) Return of an instrument for lack of proper indorsement is not dishonor.

(4) A term in a draft or an indorsement thereof allowing a stated time for re-presentment in the event

of any dishonor of the draft by nonacceptance if a time draft or by nonpayment if a sight draft gives the holder as against any secondary party bound by the term an option to waive the dishonor without affecting the liability of the secondary party and he may present again up to the end of the stated time.

§ 3—508. Notice of Dishonor.

(1) Notice of dishonor may be given to any person who may be liable on the instrument by or on behalf of the holder or any party who has himself received notice, or any other party who can be compelled to pay the instrument. In addition an agent or bank in whose hands the instrument is dishonored may give notice to his principal or customer or to another agent or bank from which the instrument was received.

(2) Any necessary notice must be given by a bank before its midnight deadline and by any other person before midnight of the third business day after dishonor or receipt of notice of dishonor.

(3) Notice may be given in any reasonable manner. It may be oral or written and in any terms which identify the instrument and state that it has been dishonored. A misdescription which does not mislead the party notified does not vitiate the notice. Sending the instrument bearing a stamp, ticket or writing stating that acceptance or payment has been refused or sending a notice of debit with respect to the instrument is sufficient.

(4) Written notice is given when sent although it is not received.

(5) Notice to one partner is notice to each although the firm has been dissolved.

(6) When any party is in insolvency proceedings instituted after the issue of the instrument notice may be given either to the party or to the representative of his estate.

(7) When any party is dead or incompetent notice may be sent to his last known address or given to his personal representative.

(8) Notice operates for the benefit of all parties who have rights on the instrument against the party notified.

§ 3—509. Protest; Noting for Protest.

(1) A protest is a certificate of dishonor made under the hand and seal of a United States consul or vice consul or a notary public or other person authorized to certify dishonor by the law of the place where dishonor occurs. It may be made upon information satisfactory to such person.

(2) The protest must identify the instrument and certify either that due presentment has been made or the reason why it is excused and that the instrument has been dishonored by nonacceptance or nonpayment.

(3) The protest may also certify that notice of dishonor has been given to all parties or to specified parties.

(4) Subject to subsection (5) any necessary protest is due by the time that notice of dishonor is due.

(5) If, before protest is due, an instrument has been noted for protest by the officer to make protest, the protest may be made at any time thereafter as of the date of the noting.

§ 3—510. Evidence of Dishonor and Notice of Dishonor.

The following are admissible as evidence and create a presumption of dishonor and of any notice of dishonor therein shown:

(a) a document regular in form as provided in the preceding section which purports to be a protest;

(b) the purported stamp or writing of the drawee, payor bank or presenting bank on the instrument or accompanying it stating that acceptance or payment has been refused for reasons consistent with dishonor;

(c) any book or record of the drawee, payor bank, or any collecting bank kept in the usual course of business which shows dishonor, even though there is no evidence of who made the entry.

§ 3—511. Waived or Excused Presentment, Protest or Notice of Dishonor or Delay Therein.

(1) Delay in presentment, protest or notice of dishonor is excused when the party is without notice that it is due or when the delay is caused by circumstances beyond his control and he exercises reasonable diligence after the cause of the delay ceases to operate.

(2) Presentment or notice or protest as the case may be is entirely excused when

    (a) the party to be charged has waived it expressly or by implication either before or after it is due; or

    (b) such party has himself dishonored the instrument or has countermanded payment or otherwise has no reason to expect or right to require that the instrument be accepted or paid; or

(c) by reasonable diligence the presentment or protest cannot be made or the notice given.

(3) Presentment is also entirely excused when

(a) the maker, acceptor or drawee of any instrument except a documentary draft is dead or in insolvency proceedings instituted after the issue of the instrument; or

(b) acceptance or payment is refused but not for want of proper presentment.

(4) Where a draft has been dishonored by nonacceptance a later presentment for payment and any notice of dishonor and protest for nonpayment are excused unless in the meantime the instrument has been accepted.

(5) A waiver of protest is also a waiver of presentment and of notice of dishonor even though protest is not required.

(6) Where a waiver of presentment or notice or protest is embodied in the instrument itself it is binding upon all parties; but where it is written above the signature of an indorser it binds him only.

Part 6 Discharge

§ 3—601. Discharge of Parties.

(1) The extent of the discharge of any party from liability on an instrument is governed by the sections on

(a) payment or satisfaction (Section 3—603); or

(b) tender of payment (Section 3—604); or

(c) cancellation or renunciation (Section 3—605); or

(d) impairment of right of recourse or of collateral (Section 3—606); or

(e) reacquisition of the instrument by a prior party (Section 3—208); or

(f) fraudulent and material alteration (Section 3—407); or

(g) certification of a check (Section 3—411); or

(h) acceptance varying a draft (Section 3—412); or

(i) unexcused delay in presentment or notice of dishonor or protest (Section 3—502).

(2) Any party is also discharged from his liability on an instrument to another party by any other act or agreement with such party which would discharge his simple contract for the payment of money.

(3) The liability of all parties is discharged when any party who has himself no right of action or recourse on the instrument

(a) reacquires the instrument in his own right; or

(b) is discharged under any provision of this Article, except as otherwise provided with respect to discharge for impairment of recourse or of collateral (Section 3—606).

§ 3—602. Effect of Discharge Against Holder in Due Course.

No discharge of any party provided by this Article is effective against a subsequent holder in due course unless he has notice thereof when he takes the instrument.

§ 3—603. Payment or Satisfaction.

(1) The liability of any party is discharged to the extent of his payment or satisfaction to the holder even though it is made with knowledge of a claim of another person to the instrument unless prior to such payment or satisfaction the person making the claim either supplies indemnity deemed adequate by the party seeking the discharge or enjoins payment or satisfaction by order of a court of competent jurisdiction in an action in which the adverse claimant and the holder are parties. This subsection does not, however, result in the discharge of the liability

(a) of a party who in bad faith pays or satisfies a holder who acquired the instrument by theft or who (unless having the rights of a holder in due course) holds through one who so acquired it; or

(b) of a party (other than an intermediary bank or a payor bank which is not a depositary bank) who pays or satisfies the holder of an instrument which has been restrictively indorsed in a manner not consistent with the terms of such restrictive indorsement.

(2) Payment or satisfaction may be made with the consent of the holder by any person including a stranger to the instrument. Surrender of the instrument to such a person gives him the rights of a transferee (Section 3—201).

§ 3—604. Tender of Payment.

(1) Any party making tender of full payment to a holder when or after it is due is discharged to the extent of all subsequent liability for interest, costs and attorney's fees.

(2) The holder's refusal of such tender wholly dis-

charges any party who has a right of recourse against the party making the tender.

(3) Where the maker or acceptor of an instrument payable otherwise than on demand is able and ready to pay at every place of payment specified in the instrument when it is due, it is equivalent to tender.

§ 3—605. **Cancellation and Renunciation.**

(1) The holder of an instrument may even without consideration discharge any party

     (a) in any manner apparent on the face of the instrument or the indorsement, as by intentionally cancelling the instrument or the party's signature by destruction or mutilation, or by striking out the party's signature; or

     (b) by renouncing his rights by a writing signed and delivered or by surrender of the instrument to the party to be discharged.

(2) Neither cancellation nor renunciation without surrender of the instrument affects the title thereto.

§ 3—606. **Impairment of Recourse or of Collateral.**

(1) The holder discharges any party to the instrument to the extent that without such party's consent the holder

     (a) without express reservation of rights releases or agrees not to sue any person against whom the party has to the knowledge of the holder a right of recourse or agrees to suspend the right to enforce against such person the instrument or collateral or otherwise discharges such person, except that failure or delay in effecting any required presentment, protest or notice of dishonor with respect to any such person does not discharge any party as to whom presentment, protest or notice of dishonor is effective or unnecessary; or

     (b) unjustifiably impairs any collateral for the instrument given by or on behalf of the party or any person against whom he has a right of recourse.

(2) By express reservation of rights against a party with a right of recourse the holder preserves

     (a) all his rights against such party as of the time when the instrument was originally due; and

     (b) the right of the party to pay the instrument as of that time; and

     (c) all rights of such party to recourse against others.

Part 7 **Advice of International Sight Draft**

§ 3—701. **Letter of Advice of International Sight Draft.**

(1) A "letter of advice" is a drawer's communication to the drawee that a described draft has been drawn.

(2) Unless otherwise agreed when a bank receives from another bank a letter of advice of an international sight draft the drawee bank may immediately debit the drawer's account and stop the running of interest pro tanto. Such a debit and any resulting credit to any account covering outstanding drafts leaves in the drawer full power to stop payment or otherwise dispose of the amount and creates no trust or interest in favor of the holder.

(3) Unless otherwise agreed and except where a draft is drawn under a credit issued by the drawee, the drawee of an international sight draft owes the drawer no duty to pay an unadvised draft but if it does so and the draft is genuine, may appropriately debit the drawer's account.

Part 8 **Miscellaneous**

§ 3—801. **Drafts in a Set.**

(1) Where a draft is drawn in a set of parts, each of which is numbered and expressed to be an order only if no other part has been honored, the whole of the parts constitutes one draft but a taker of any part may become a holder in due course of the draft.

(2) Any person who negotiates, indorses or accepts a single part of a draft drawn in a set thereby becomes liable to any holder in due course of that part as if it were the whole set, but as between different holders in due course to whom different parts have been negotiated the holder whose title first accrues has all rights to the draft and its proceeds.

(3) As against the drawee the first presented part of a draft drawn in a set is the part entitled to payment, or if a time draft to acceptance and payment. Acceptance of any subsequently presented part renders the drawee liable thereon under subsection (2). With respect both to a holder and to the drawer payment of a subsequently presented part of a draft payable at sight has the same effect as payment of a check notwithstanding an effective stop order (Section 4—407).

(4) Except as otherwise provided in this section, where any part of a draft in a set is discharged by payment or otherwise the whole draft is discharged.

§ 3—802. **Effect of Instrument on Obligation for Which It Is Given.**

(1) Unless otherwise agreed where an instrument is taken for an underlying obligation

    (a) the obligation is pro tanto discharged if a bank is drawer, maker or acceptor of the instrument and there is no recourse on the instrument against the underlying obligor; and

    (b) in any other case the obligation is suspended pro tanto until the instrument is due or if it is payable on demand until its presentment. If the instrument is dishonored action may be maintained on either the instrument or the obligation; discharge of the underlying obligor on the instrument also discharges him on the obligation.

(2) The taking in good faith of a check which is not postdated does not of itself so extend the time on the original obligation as to discharge a surety.

§ 3—803. **Notice to Third Party.**

Where a defendant is sued for breach of an obligation for which a third person is answerable over under this Article he may give the third person written notice of the litigation, and the person notified may then give similar notice to any other person who is answerable over to him under this Article. If the notice states that the person notified may come in and defend and that if the person notified does not do so he will in any action against him by the person giving the notice be bound by any determination of fact common to the two litigations, then unless after seasonable receipt of the notice the person notified does come in and defend he is so bound.

§ 3—804. **Lost, Destroyed or Stolen Instruments.**

The owner of an instrument which is lost, whether by destruction, theft or otherwise, may maintain an action in his own name and recover from any party liable thereon upon due proof of his ownership, the facts which prevent his production of the instrument and its terms. The court may require security indemnifying the defendant against loss by reason of further claims on the instrument.

§ 3—805. **Instruments Not Payable to Order or to Bearer.**

This Article applies to any instrument whose terms do not preclude transfer and which is otherwise negotiable within this Article but which is not payable to order or to bearer, except that there can be no holder in due course of such an instrument.

Article 4
BANK DEPOSITS AND COLLECTIONS

Part 1 **General Provisions and Definitions**

§ 4—101. **Short Title.**

This Article shall be known and may be cited as Uniform Commercial Code—Bank Deposits and Collections.

§ 4—102. **Applicability.**

(1) To the extent that items within this Article are also within the scope of Articles 3 and 8, they are subject to the provisions of those Articles. In the event of conflict the provisions of this Article govern those of Article 3 but the provisions of Article 8 govern those of this Article.

(2) The liability of a bank for action or non-action with respect to any item handled by it for purposes of presentment, payment or collection is governed by the law of the place where the bank is located. In the case of action or non-action by or at a branch or separate office of a bank, its liability is governed by the law of the place where the branch or separate office is located.

§ 4—103. **Variation by Agreement; Measure of Damages; Certain Action Constituting Ordinary Care.**

(1) The effect of the provisions of this Article may be varied by agreement except that no agreement can disclaim a bank's responsibility for its own lack of good faith or failure to exercise ordinary care or can limit the measure of damages for such lack or failure; but the parties may by agreement determine the standards by which such responsibility is to be measured if such standards are not manifestly unreasonable.

(2) Federal Reserve regulations and operating letters, clearing house rules, and the like, have the effect of agreements under subsection (1), whether or not specifically assented to by all parties interested in items handled.

(3) Action or non-action approved by this Article or pursuant to Federal Reserve regulations or operating letters constitutes the exercise of ordinary care and, in

the absence of special instructions, action or nonaction consistent with clearing house rules and the like or with a general banking usage not disapproved by this Article, prima facie constitutes the exercise of ordinary care.

(4) The specification or approval of certain procedures by this Article does not constitute disapproval of other procedures which may be reasonable under the circumstances.

(5) The measure of damages for failure to exercise ordinary care in handling an item is the amount of the item reduced by an amount which could not have been realized by the use of ordinary care, and where there is bad faith it includes other damages, if any, suffered by the party as a proximate consequence.

§ 4—104. **Definitions and Index of Definitions.**

(1) In this Article unless the context otherwise requires

(a) "Account" means any account with a bank and includes a checking, time, interest or savings account;

(b) "Afternoon" means the period of a day between noon and midnight;

(c) "Banking day" means that part of any day on which a bank is open to the public for carrying on substantially all of its banking functions;

(d) "Clearing house" means any association of banks or other payors regularly clearing items;

(e) "Customer" means any person having an account with a bank or for whom a bank has agreed to collect items and includes a bank carrying an account with another bank;

(f) "Documentary draft" means any negotiable or nonnegotiable draft with accompanying documents, securities or other papers to be delivered against honor of the draft;

(g) "Item" means any instrument for the payment of money even though it is not negotiable but does not include money;

(h) "Midnight deadline" with respect to a bank is midnight on its next banking day following the banking day on which it receives the relevant item or notice or from which the time for taking action commences to run, whichever is later;

(i) "Properly payable" includes the availability of funds for payment at the time of decision to pay or dishonor;

(j) "Settle" means to pay in cash, by clearing house settlement, in a charge or credit or by remittance, or otherwise as instructed. A settlement may be either provisional or final;

(k) "Suspends payments" with respect to a bank means that it has been closed by order of the supervisory authorities, that a public officer has been appointed to take it over or that it ceases or refuses to make payments in the ordinary course of business.

(2) Other definitions applying to this Article and the sections in which they appear are:

"Collecting bank" Section 4—105.
"Depositary bank" Section 4—105.
"Intermediary bank" Section 4—105.
"Payor bank" Section 4—105.
"Presenting bank" Section 4—105.
"Remitting bank" Section 4—105.

(3) The following definitions in other Articles apply to this Article:

"Acceptance" Section 3—410.
"Certificate of deposit" Section 3—104.
"Certification" Section 3—411.
"Check" Section 3—104.
"Draft" Section 3—104.
"Holder in due course" Section 3—302.
"Notice of dishonor" Section 3—508.
"Presentment" Section 3—504.
"Protest" Section 3—509.
"Secondary party" Section 3—102.

(4) In addition Article 1 contains general definitions and principles of construction and interpretation applicable throughout this Article.

§ 4—105. **"Depositary Bank"; "Intermediary Bank"; "Collecting Bank"; "Payor Bank"; "Presenting Bank"; "Remitting Bank".**

In this Article unless the context otherwise requires:

(a) "Depositary bank" means the first bank to which an item is transferred for collection even though it is also the payor bank;

(b) "Payor bank" means a bank by which an item is payable as drawn or accepted;

(c) "Intermediary bank" means any bank to which an item is transferred in course of collection except the depositary or payor bank;

(d) "Collecting bank" means any bank handling the item for collection except the payor bank;

(e) "Presenting bank" means any bank presenting an item except a payor bank;

(f) "Remitting bank" means any payor or intermediary bank remitting for an item.

§ 4—106. **Separate Office of a Bank.**

A branch or separate office of a bank [maintaining its own deposit ledgers] is a separate bank for the purpose of computing the time within which and determining the place at or to which action may be taken or notices or orders shall be given under this Article and under Article 3.

Note: The brackets are to make it optional with the several states whether to require a branch to maintain its own deposit ledgers in order to be considered to be a separate bank for certain purposes under Article 4. In some states "maintaining its own deposit ledgers" is a satisfactory test. In others branch banking practices are such that this test would not be suitable.

§ 4—107. **Time of Receipt of Items.**

(1) For the purpose of allowing time to process items, prove balances and make the necessary entries on its books to determine its position for the day, a bank may fix an afternoon hour of two P.M. or later as a cut-off hour for the handling of money and items and the making of entries on its books.

(2) Any item or deposit of money received on any day after a cut-off hour so fixed or after the close of the banking day may be treated as being received at the opening of the next banking day.

§ 4—108. **Delays.**

(1) Unless otherwise instructed, a collecting bank in a good faith effort to secure payment may, in the case of specific items and with or without the approval of any person involved, waive, modify or extend time limits imposed or permitted by this Act for a period not in excess of an additional banking day without discharge of secondary parties and without liability to its transferor or any prior party.

(2) Delay by a collecting bank or payor bank beyond time limits prescribed or permitted by this Act or by instructions is excused if caused by interruption of communication facilities, suspension of payments by another bank, war, emergency conditions or other circumstances beyond the control of the bank provided it exercises such diligence as the circumstances require.

§ 4—109. **Process of Posting.**

The "process of posting" means the usual procedure followed by a payor bank in determining to pay an item and in recording the payment including one or more of the following or other steps as determined by the bank:

(a) verification of any signature;

(b) ascertaining that sufficient funds are available;

(c) affixing a "paid" or other stamp;

(d) entering a charge or entry to a customer's account;

(e) correcting or reversing an entry or erroneous action with respect to the item.

Part 2   Collection of Items: Depositary and Collecting Banks

§ 4—201. **Presumption and Duration of Agency Status of Collecting Banks and Provisional Status of Credits; Applicability of Article; Item Indorsed "Pay Any Bank".**

(1) Unless a contrary intent clearly appears and prior to the time that a settlement given by a collecting bank for an item is or becomes final (subsection (3) of Section 4—211 and Sections 4—212 and 4—213) the bank is an agent or sub-agent of the owner of the item and any settlement given for the item is provisional. This provision applies regardless of the form of indorsement or lack of indorsement and even though credit given for the item is subject to immediate withdrawal as of right or is in fact withdrawn; but the continuance of ownership of an item by its owner and any rights of the owner to proceeds of the item are subject to rights of a collecting bank such as those resulting from outstanding advances on the item and valid rights of setoff. When an item is handled by banks for purposes of presentment, payment and collection, the relevant provisions of this Article apply even though action of parties clearly establishes that a particular bank has purchased the item and is the owner of it.

(2) After an item has been indorsed with the words "pay any bank" or the like, only a bank may acquire the rights of a holder

    (a) until the item has been returned to the customer initiating collection; or

    (b) until the item has been specially indorsed by a bank to a person who is not a bank.

§ 4—202. Responsibility for Collection; When Action Seasonable.

(1) A collecting bank must use ordinary care in

(a) presenting an item or sending it for presentment; and

(b) sending notice of dishonor or non-payment or returning an item other than a documentary draft to the bank's transferor [or directly to the depositary bank under subsection (2) of Section 4—212] *(see note to Section 4—212)* after learning that the item has not been paid or accepted as the case may be; and

(c) settling for an item when the bank receives final settlement; and

(d) making or providing for any necessary protest; and

(e) notifying its transferor of any loss or delay in transit within a reasonable time after discovery thereof.

(2) A collecting bank taking proper action before its midnight deadline following receipt of an item, notice or payment acts seasonably; taking proper action within a reasonably longer time may be seasonable but the bank has the burden of so establishing.

(3) Subject to subsection (1)(a), a bank is not liable for the insolvency, neglect, misconduct, mistake or default of another bank or person or for loss or destruction of an item in transit or in the possession of others.

§ 4—203. Effect of Instructions.

Subject to the provisions of Article 3 concerning conversion of instruments (Section 3—419) and the provisions of both Article 3 and this Article concerning restrictive indorsements only a collecting bank's transferor can give instructions which affect the bank or constitute notice to it and a collecting bank is not liable to prior parties for any action taken pursuant to such instructions or in accordance with any agreement with its transferor.

§ 4—204. Methods of Sending and Presenting; Sending Direct to Payor Bank.

(1) A collecting bank must send items by reasonably prompt method taking into consideration any relevant instructions, the nature of the item, the number of such items on hand, and the cost of collection involved and the method generally used by it or others to present such items.

(2) A collecting bank may send

(a) any item direct to the payor bank;

(b) any item to any non-bank payor if authorized by its transferor; and

(c) any item other than documentary drafts to any non-bank payor, if authorized by Federal Reserve regulation or operating letter, clearing house rule or the like.

(3) Presentment may be made by a presenting bank at a place where the payor bank has requested that presentment be made.

§ 4—205. Supplying Missing Indorsement; No Notice from Prior Indorsement.

(1) A depositary bank which has taken an item for collection may supply any indorsement of the customer which is necessary to title unless the item contains the words "payee's indorsement required" or the like. In the absence of such a requirement a statement placed on the item by the depositary bank to the effect that the item was deposited by a customer or credited to his account is effective as the customer's indorsement.

(2) An intermediary bank, or payor bank which is not a depositary bank, is neither given notice nor otherwise affected by a restrictive indorsement of any person except the bank's immediate transferor.

§ 4—206. Transfer Between Banks.

Any agreed method which identifies the transferor bank is sufficient for the item's further transfer to another bank.

§ 4—207. Warranties of Customer and Collecting Bank on Transfer or Presentment of Items; Time for Claims.

(1) Each customer or collecting bank who obtains payment or acceptance of an item and each prior customer and collecting bank warrants to the payor bank or other payor who in good faith pays or accepts the item that

(a) he has a good title to the item or is authorized to obtain payment or acceptance on behalf of one who has a good title; and

(b) he has no knowledge that the signature of the maker or drawer is unauthorized, except that this warranty is not given by any customer or collecting bank that is a holder in due course and acts in good faith

(i) to a maker with respect to the maker's own signature; or

(ii) to a drawer with respect to the drawer's own signature, whether or not the drawer is also the drawee; or

(iii) to an acceptor of an item if the holder in due course took the item after the acceptance or obtained the acceptance without knowledge that the drawer's signature was unauthorized; and

(c) the item has not been materially altered, except that this warranty is not given by any customer or collecting bank that is a holder in due course and acts in good faith

(i) to the maker of a note; or

(ii) to the drawer of a draft whether or not the drawer is also the drawee; or

(iii) to the acceptor of an item with respect to an alteration made prior to the acceptance if the holder in due course took the item after the acceptance, even though the acceptance provided "payable as originally drawn" or equivalent terms; or

(iv) to the acceptor of an item with respect to an alteration made after the acceptance.

(2) Each customer and collecting bank who transfers an item and receives a settlement or other consideration for it warrants to his transferee and to any subsequent collecting bank who takes the item in good faith that

(a) he has a good title to the item or is authorized to obtain payment or acceptance on behalf of one who has a good title and the transfer is otherwise rightful; and

(b) all signatures are genuine or authorized; and

(c) the item has not been materially altered; and

(d) no defense of any party is good against him; and

(e) he has no knowledge of any insolvency proceeding instituted with respect to the maker or acceptor or the drawer of an unaccepted item.

In addition each customer and collecting bank so transferring an item and receiving a settlement or other consideration engages that upon dishonor and any necessary notice of dishonor and protest he will take up the item.

(3) The warranties and the engagement to honor set forth in the two preceding subsections arise notwithstanding the absence of indorsement or words of guar-

anty or warranty in the transfer or presentment and a collecting bank remains liable for their breach despite remittance to its transferor. Damages for breach of such warranties or engagement to honor shall not exceed the consideration received by the customer or collecting bank responsible plus finance charges and expenses related to the item, if any.

(4) Unless a claim for breach of warranty under this section is made within a reasonable time after the person claiming learns of the breach, the person liable is discharged to the extent of any loss caused by the delay in making claim.

§ 4—208. **Security Interest of Collecting Bank in Items, Accompanying Documents and Proceeds.**

(1) A bank has a security interest in an item and any accompanying documents or the proceeds of either

(a) in case of an item deposited in an account to the extent to which credit given for the item has been withdrawn or applied;

(b) in case of an item for which it has given credit available for withdrawal as of right, to the extent of the credit given whether or not the credit is drawn upon and whether or not there is a right of charge-back; or

(c) if it makes an advance on or against the item.

(2) When credit which has been given for several items received at one time or pursuant to a single agreement is withdrawn or applied in part the security interest remains upon all the items, any accompanying documents or the proceeds of either. For the purpose of this section, credits first given are first withdrawn.

(3) Receipt by a collecting bank of a final settlement for an item is a realization on its security interest in the item, accompanying documents and proceeds. To the extent and so long as the bank does not receive final settlement for the item or give up possession of the item or accompanying documents for purposes other than collection, the security interest continues and is subject to the provisions of Article 9 except that

(a) no security agreement is necessary to make the security interest enforceable (subsection (1)(b) of Section 9—203); and

(b) no filing is required to perfect the security interest; and

(c) the security interest has priority over conflicting perfected security interests in the item, accompanying documents or proceeds.

§ 4—209. When Bank Gives Value for Purposes of Holder in Due Course.

For purposes of determining its status as a holder in due course, the bank has given value to the extent that it has a security interest in an item provided that the bank otherwise complies with the requirements of Section 3—302 on what constitutes a holder in due course.

§ 4—210. Presentment by Notice of Item Not Payable by, Through or at a Bank; Liability of Secondary Parties.

(1) Unless otherwise instructed, a collecting bank may present an item not payable by, through or at a bank by sending to the party to accept or pay a written notice that the bank holds the item for acceptance or payment. The notice must be sent in time to be received on or before the day when presentment is due and the bank must meet any requirement of the party to accept or pay under Section 3—505 by the close of the bank's next banking day after it knows of the requirement.

(2) Where presentment is made by notice and neither honor nor request for compliance with a requirement under Section 3—505 is received by the close of business on the day after maturity or in the case of demand items by the close of business on the third banking day after notice was sent, the presenting bank may treat the item as dishonored and charge any secondary party by sending him notice of the facts.

§ 4—211. Media of Remittance; Provisional and Final Settlement in Remittance Cases.

(1) A collecting bank may take in settlement of an item

(a) a check of the remitting bank or of another bank on any bank except the remitting bank; or

(b) a cashier's check or similar primary obligation of a remitting bank which is a member of or clears through a member of the same clearing house or group as the collecting bank; or

(c) appropriate authority to charge an account of the remitting bank or of another bank with the collecting bank; or

(d) if the item is drawn upon or payable by a person other than a bank, a cashier's check, certified check or other bank check or obligation.

(2) If before its midnight deadline the collecting bank properly dishonors a remittance check or authorization to charge on itself or presents or forwards for collection a remittance instrument of or on another

bank which is of a kind approved by subsection (1) or has not been authorized by it, the collecting bank is not liable to prior parties in the event of the dishonor of such check, instrument or authorization.

(3) A settlement for an item by means of a remittance instrument or authorization to charge is or becomes a final settlement as to both the person making and the person receiving the settlement

(a) if the remittance instrument or authorization to charge is of a kind approved by subsection (1) or has not been authorized by the person receiving the settlement and in either case the person receiving the settlement acts seasonably before its midnight deadline in presenting, forwarding for collection or paying the instrument or authorization,—at the time the remittance instrument or authorization is finally paid by the payor by which it is payable;

(b) if the person receiving the settlement has authorized remittance by a non-bank check or obligation or by a cashier's check or similar primary obligation of or a check upon the payor or other remitting bank which is not of a kind approved by subsection (1)(b),—at the time of the receipt of such remittance check or obligation; or

(c) if in a case not covered by sub-paragraphs (a) or (b) the person receiving the settlement fails to seasonably present, forward for collection, pay or return a remittance instrument or authorization to it to charge before its midnight deadline,—at such midnight deadline.

§ 4—212. Right of Charge-Back or Refund.

(1) If a collecting bank has made provisional settlement with its customer for an item and itself fails by reason of dishonor, suspension of payments by a bank or otherwise to receive a settlement for the item which is or becomes final, the bank may revoke the settlement given by it, charge back the amount of any credit given for the item to its customer's account or obtain refund from its customer whether or not it is able to return the items if by its midnight deadline or within a longer reasonable time after it learns the facts it returns the item or sends notification of the facts. These rights to revoke, charge-back and obtain refund terminate if and when a settlement for the item received by the bank is or becomes final (subsection (3) of Section 4—211 and subsections (2) and (3) of Section 4—213).

[(2) Within the time and manner prescribed by this section and Section 4—301, an intermediary or payor bank, as the case may be, may return an unpaid item directly to the depositary bank and may send for collection a draft on the depositary bank and obtain reimbursement. In such case, if the depositary bank has received provisional settlement for the item, it must reimburse the bank drawing the draft and any provisional credits for the item between banks shall become and remain final.]

Note: Direct returns is recognized as an innovation that is not yet established bank practice, and therefore, Paragraph 2 has been bracketed. Some lawyers have doubts whether it should be included in legislation or left to development by agreement.

(3) A depositary bank which is also the payor may charge-back the amount of an item to its customer's account or obtain refund in accordance with the section governing return of an item received by a payor bank for credit on its books (Section 4—301).

(4) The right to charge-back is not affected by

(a) prior use of the credit given for the item; or

(b) failure by any bank to exercise ordinary care with respect to the item but any bank so failing remains liable.

(5) A failure to charge-back or claim refund does not affect other rights of the bank against the customer or any other party.

(6) If credit is given in dollars as the equivalent of the value of an item payable in a foreign currency the dollar amount of any charge-back or refund shall be calculated on the basis of the buying sight rate for the foreign currency prevailing on the day when the person entitled to the charge-back or refund learns that it will not receive payment in ordinary course.

§ 4—213. Final Payment of Item by Payor Bank; When Provisional Debits and Credits Become Final; When Certain Credits Become Available for Withdrawal.

(1) An item is finally paid by a payor bank when the bank has done any of the following, whichever happens first:

(a) paid the item in cash; or

(b) settled for the item without reserving a right to revoke the settlement and without having such right under statute, clearing house rule or agreement; or

(c) completed the process of posting the item to the indicated account of the drawer, maker or other person to be charged therewith; or

(d) made a provisional settlement for the item and failed to revoke the settlement in the time and manner permitted by statute, clearing house rule or agreement.

Upon a final payment under subparagraphs (b), (c) or (d) the payor bank shall be accountable for the amount of the item.

(2) If provisional settlement for an item between the presenting and payor banks is made through a clearing house or by debits or credits in an account between them, then to the extent that provisional debits or credits for the item are entered in accounts between the presenting and payor banks or between the presenting and successive prior collecting banks seriatim, they become final upon final payment of the item by the payor bank.

(3) If a collecting bank receives a settlement for an item which is or becomes final (subsection (3) of Section 4—211, subsection (2) of Section 4—213) the bank is accountable to its customer for the amount of the item and any provisional credit given for the item in an account with its customer becomes final.

(4) Subject to any right of the bank to apply the credit to an obligation of the customer, credit given by a bank for an item in an account with its customer becomes available for withdrawal as of right

(a) in any case where the bank has received a provisional settlement for the item,—when such settlement becomes final and the bank has had a reasonable time to learn that the settlement is final;

(b) in any case where the bank is both a depositary bank and a payor bank and the item is finally paid,— at the opening of the bank's second banking day following receipt of the item.

(5) A deposit of money in a bank is final when made but, subject to any right of the bank to apply the deposit to an obligation of the customer, the deposit becomes available for withdrawal as of right at the opening of the bank's next banking day following receipt of the deposit.

§ 4—214. Insolvency and Preference.

(1) Any item in or coming into the possession of a payor or collecting bank which suspends payment and which item is not finally paid shall be returned by the receiver, trustee or agent in charge of the closed bank to the presenting bank or the closed bank's customer.

(2) If a payor bank finally pays an item and suspends payments without making a settlement for the item

with its customer or the presenting bank which settlement is or becomes final, the owner of the item has a preferred claim against the payor bank.

(3) If a payor bank gives or a collecting bank gives or receives a provisional settlement for an item and thereafter suspends payments, the suspension does not prevent or interfere with the settlement becoming final if such finality occurs automatically upon the lapse of certain time or the happening of certain events (subsection (3) of Section 4—211, subsections (1)(d), (2) and (3) of Section 4—213).

(4) If a collecting bank receives from subsequent parties settlement for an item which settlement is or becomes final and suspends payments without making a settlement for the item with its customer which is or becomes final, the owner of the item has a preferred claim against such collecting bank.

Part 3 Collection of Items: Payor Banks

§ 4—301. Deferred Posting; Recovery of Payment by Return of Items; Time of Dishonor.

(1) Where an authorized settlement for a demand item (other than a documentary draft) received by a payor bank otherwise than for immediate payment over the counter has been made before midnight of the banking day of receipt the payor bank may revoke the settlement and recover any payment if before it has made final payment (subsection (1) of Section 4—213) and before its midnight deadline it

(a) returns the item; or

(b) sends written notice of dishonor or nonpayment if the item is held for protest or is otherwise unavailable for return.

(2) If a demand item is received by a payor bank for credit on its books it may return such item or send notice of dishonor and may revoke any credit given or recover the amount thereof withdrawn by its customer, if it acts within the time limit and in the manner specified in the preceding subsection.

(3) Unless previous notice of dishonor has been sent an item is dishonored at the time when for purposes of dishonor it is returned or notice sent in accordance with this section.

(4) An item is returned:

(a) as to an item received through a clearing house, when it is delivered to the presenting or last collecting bank or to the clearing house or is sent or delivered in accordance with its rules; or

(b) in all other cases, when it is sent or delivered to the bank's customer or transferor or pursuant to his instructions.

§ 4—302. Payor Bank's Responsibility for Late Return of Item.

In the absence of a valid defense such as breach of a presentment warranty (subsection (1) of Section 4—207), settlement effected or the like, if an item is presented on and received by a payor bank the bank is accountable for the amount of

(a) a demand item other than a documentary draft whether properly payable or not if the bank, in any case where it is not also the depositary bank, retains the item beyond midnight of the banking day of receipt without settling for it or, regardless of whether it is also the depositary bank, does not pay or return the item or send notice of dishonor until after its midnight deadline; or

(b) any other properly payable item unless within the time allowed for acceptance or payment of that item the bank either accepts or pays the item or returns it and accompanying documents.

§ 4—303. When Items Subject to Notice, Stop-Order, Legal Process or Setoff; Order in Which Items May Be Charged or Certified.

(1) Any knowledge, notice or stop-order received by, legal process served upon or setoff exercised by a payor bank, whether or not effective under other rules of law to terminate, suspend or modify the bank's right or duty to pay an item or to charge its customer's account for the item, comes too late to so terminate, suspend or modify such right or duty if the knowledge, notice, stop-order or legal process is received or served and a reasonable time for the bank to act thereon expires or the setoff is exercised after the bank has done any of the following:

(a) accepted or certified the item;

(b) paid the item in cash;

(c) settled for the item without reserving a right to revoke the settlement and without having such right under statute, clearing house rule or agreement;

(d) completed the process of posting the item to the indicated account of the drawer, maker or other person to be charged therewith or otherwise has evidenced by examination of such indicated account and by action its decision to pay the item; or

(e) become accountable for the amount of the item under subsection (1)(d) of Section 4—213 and Section 4—302 dealing with the payor bank's responsibility for late return of items.

(2) Subject to the provisions of subsection (1) items may be accepted, paid, certified or charged to the indicated account of its customer in any order convenient to the bank.

Part 4 Relationship Between Payor Bank and Its Customer

§ 4—401. When Bank May Charge Customer's Account.

(1) As against its customer, a bank may charge against his account any item which is otherwise properly payable from that account even though the charge creates an overdraft.

(2) A bank which in good faith makes payment to a holder may charge the indicated account of its customer according to

(a) the original tenor of his altered item; or

(b) the tenor of his completed item, even though the bank knows the item has been completed unless the bank has notice that the completion was improper.

§ 4—402. Bank's Liability to Customer for Wrongful Dishonor.

A payor bank is liable to its customer for damages proximately caused by the wrongful dishonor of an item. When the dishonor occurs through mistake liability is limited to actual damages proved. If so proximately caused and proved damages may include damages for an arrest or prosecution of the customer or other consequential damages. Whether any consequential damages are proximately caused by the wrongful dishonor is a question of fact to be determined in each case.

§ 4—403. Customer's Right to Stop Payment; Burden of Proof of Loss.

(1) A customer may by order to his bank stop payment of any item payable for his account but the order must be received at such time and in such manner as to afford the bank a reasonable opportunity to act on it prior to any action by the bank with respect to the item described in Section 4—303.

(2) An oral order is binding upon the bank only for fourteen calendar days unless confirmed in writing within that period. A written order is effective for only six months unless renewed in writing.

(3) The burden of establishing the fact and amount of loss resulting from the payment of an item contrary to a binding stop payment order is on the customer.

§ 4—404. Bank Not Obligated to Pay Check More Than Six Months Old.

A bank is under no obligation to a customer having a checking account to pay a check, other than a certified check, which is presented more than six months after its date, but it may charge its customer's account for a payment made thereafter in good faith.

§ 4—405. Death or Incompetence of Customer.

(1) A payor or collecting bank's authority to accept, pay or collect an item or to account for proceeds of its collection if otherwise effective is not rendered ineffective by incompetence of a customer of either bank existing at the time the item is issued or its collection is undertaken if the bank does not know of an adjudication of incompetence. Neither death nor incompetence of a customer revokes such authority to accept, pay, collect or account until the bank knows of the fact of death or of an adjudication of incompetence and has reasonable opportunity to act on it.

(2) Even with knowledge a bank may for ten days after the date of death pay or certify checks drawn on or prior to that date unless ordered to stop payment by a person claiming an interest in the account.

§ 4—406. Customer's Duty to Discover and Report Unauthorized Signature or Alteration.

(1) When a bank sends to its customer a statement of account accompanied by items paid in good faith in support of the debit entries or holds the statement and items pursuant to a request or instructions of its customer or otherwise in a reasonable manner makes the statement and items available to the customer, the customer must exercise reasonable care and promptness to examine the statement and items to discover his unauthorized signature or any alteration on an item and must notify the bank promptly after discovery thereof.

(2) If the bank establishes that the customer failed with respect to an item to comply with the duties imposed on the customer by subsection (1) the customer is precluded from asserting against the bank

(a) his unauthorized signature or any alteration on the item if the bank also establishes that it suffered a loss by reason of such failure; and

(b) an unauthorized signature or alteration by the same wrongdoer on any other item paid in good faith by the bank after the first item and statement was available to the customer for a reasonable period not exceeding fourteen calendar days and before the bank receives notification from the customer of any such unauthorized signature or alteration.

(3) The preclusion under subsection (2) does not apply if the customer establishes lack of ordinary care on the part of the bank in paying the item(s).

(4) Without regard to care or lack of care of either the customer or the bank a customer who does not within one year from the time the statement and items are made available to the customer (subsection (1)) discover and report his unauthorized signature or any alteration on the face or back of the item or does not within three years from that time discover and report any unauthorized indorsement is precluded from asserting against the bank such unauthorized signature or indorsement or such alteration.

(5) If under this section a payor bank has a valid defense against a claim of a customer upon or resulting from payment of an item and waives or fails upon request to assert the defense the bank may not assert against any collecting bank or other prior party presenting or transferring the item a claim based upon the unauthorized signature or alteration giving rise to the customer's claim.

§ 4—407. Payor Bank's Right to Subrogation on Improper Payment.

If a payor bank has paid an item over the stop payment order of the drawer or maker or otherwise under circumstances giving a basis for objection by the drawer or maker, to prevent unjust enrichment and only to the extent necessary to prevent loss to the bank by reason of its payment of the item, the payor bank shall be subrogated to the rights

(a) of any holder in due course on the item against the drawer or maker; and

(b) of the payee or any other holder of the item against the drawer or maker either on the item or under the transaction out of which the item arose; and

(c) of the drawer or maker against the payee or any other holder of the item with respect to the transaction out of which the item arose.

Part 5   Collection of Documentary Drafts

§ 4—501. Handling of Documentary Drafts; Duty to Send for Presentment and to Notify Customer of Dishonor.

A bank which takes a documentary draft for collection must present or send the draft and accompanying documents for presentment and upon learning that the draft has not been paid or accepted in due course must seasonably notify its customer of such fact even though it may have discounted or bought the draft or extended credit available for withdrawal as of right.

§ 4—502. Presentment of "On Arrival" Drafts.

When a draft or the relevant instructions require presentment "on arrival", "when goods arrive" or the like, the collecting bank need not present until in its judgment a reasonable time for arrival of the goods has expired. Refusal to pay or accept because the goods have not arrived is not dishonor; the bank must notify its transferor of such refusal but need not present the draft again until it is instructed to do so or learns of the arrival of the goods.

§ 4—503. Responsibility of Presenting Bank for Documents and Goods; Report of Reasons for Dishonor; Referee in Case of Need.

Unless otherwise instructed and except as provided in Article 5 a bank presenting a documentary draft

(a) must deliver the documents to the drawee on acceptance of the draft if it is payable more than three days after presentment; otherwise, only on payment; and

(b) upon dishonor, either in the case of presentment for acceptance or presentment for payment, may seek and follow instructions from any referee in case of need designated in the draft or if the presenting bank does not choose to utilize his services it must use diligence and good faith to ascertain the reason for dishonor, must notify its transferor of the dishonor and of the results of its effort to ascertain the reasons therefor and must request instructions.

But the presenting bank is under no obligation with respect to goods represented by the documents except to follow any reasonable instructions seasonably received; it has a right to reimbursement for any expense incurred in following instructions and to prepayment of or indemnity for such expenses.

§ 4—504. Privilege of Presenting Bank to Deal With Goods; Security Interest for Expenses.

(1) A presenting bank which, following the dishonor of a documentary draft, has seasonably requested in-

structions but does not receive them within a reasonable time may store, sell, or otherwise deal with the goods in any reasonable manner.

(2) For its reasonable expenses incurred by action under subsection (1) the presenting bank has a lien upon the goods or their proceeds, which may be foreclosed in the same manner as an unpaid seller's lien.

Article 5
LETTERS OF CREDIT

§ 5—101. Short Title.

This Article shall be known and may be cited as Uniform Commercial Code—Letters of Credit.

§ 5—102. Scope.

(1) This Article applies

    (a) to a credit issued by a bank if the credit requires a documentary draft or a documentary demand for payment; and

    (b) to a credit issued by a person other than a bank if the credit requires that the draft or demand for payment be accompanied by a document of title; and

    (c) to a credit issued by a bank or other person if the credit is not within subparagraphs (a) or (b) but conspicuously states that it is a letter of credit or is conspicuously so entitled.

(2) Unless the engagement meets the requirements of subsection (1), this Article does not apply to engagements to make advances or to honor drafts or demands for payment, to authorities to pay or purchase, to guarantees or to general agreements.

(3) This Article deals with some but not all of the rules and concepts of letters of credit as such rules or concepts have developed prior to this act or may hereafter develop. The fact that this Article states a rule does not by itself require, imply or negate application of the same or a converse rule to a situation not provided for or to a person not specified by this Article.

§ 5—103. Definitions.

(1) In this Article unless the context otherwise requires

    (a) "Credit" or "letter of credit" means an engagement by a bank or other person made at the request of a customer and of a kind within the scope of this Article (Section 5—102) that the issuer will honor drafts or other demands for payment upon compliance with the conditions specified in the credit. A credit may be either revocable or irrevocable. The engagement may be either an agreement to honor or a statement that the bank or other person is authorized to honor.

    (b) A "documentary draft" or a "documentary demand for payment" is one honor of which is conditioned upon the presentation of a document or documents. "Document" means any paper including document of title, security, invoice, certificate, notice of default and the like.

    (c) An "issuer" is a bank or other person issuing a credit.

    (d) A "beneficiary" of a credit is a person who is entitled under its terms to draw or demand payment.

    (e) An "advising bank" is a bank which gives notification of the issuance of a credit by another bank.

    (f) A "confirming bank" is a bank which engages either that it will itself honor a credit already issued by another bank or that such a credit will be honored by the issuer or a third bank.

    (g) A "customer" is a buyer or other person who causes an issuer to issue a credit. The term also includes a bank which procures issuance or confirmation on behalf of that bank's customer.

(2) Other definitions applying to this Article and the sections in which they appear are:
    "Notation of Credit". Section 5—108.
    "Presenter". Section 5—112(3).

(3) Definitions in other Articles applying to this Article and the sections in which they appear are:
    "Accept" or "Acceptance". Section 3—410.
    "Contract for sale". Section 2—106.
    "Draft". Section 3—104.
    "Holder in due course". Section 3—302.
    "Midnight deadline". Section 4—104.
    "Security". Section 8—102.

(4) In addition, Article 1 contains general definitions and principles of construction and interpretation applicable throughout this Article.

§ 5—104. Formal Requirements; Signing.

(1) Except as otherwise required in subsection (1)(c) of Section 5—102 on scope, no particular form of phrasing is required for a credit. A credit must be in writing and signed by the issuer and a confirmation

must be in writing and signed by the confirming bank. A modification of the terms of a credit or confirmation must be signed by the issuer or confirming bank.

(2) A telegram may be a sufficient signed writing if it identifies its sender by an authorized authentication. The authentication may be in code and the authorized naming of the issuer in an advice of credit is a sufficient signing.

§ 5—105. Consideration.

No consideration is necessary to establish a credit or to enlarge or otherwise modify its terms.

§ 5—106. Time and Effect of Establishment of Credit.

(1) Unless otherwise agreed a credit is established

(a) as regards the customer as soon as a letter of credit is sent to him or the letter of credit or an authorized written advice of its issuance is sent to the beneficiary; and

(b) as regards the beneficiary when he receives a letter of credit or an authorized written advice of its issuance.

(2) Unless otherwise agreed once an irrevocable credit is established as regards the customer it can be modified or revoked only with the consent of the customer and once it is established as regards the beneficiary it can be modified or revoked only with his consent.

(3) Unless otherwise agreed after a revocable credit is established it may be modified or revoked by the issuer without notice to or consent from the customer or beneficiary.

(4) Notwithstanding any modification or revocation of a revocable credit any person authorized to honor or negotiate under the terms of the original credit is entitled to reimbursement for or honor of any draft or demand for payment duly honored or negotiated before receipt of notice of the modification or revocation and the issuer in turn is entitled to reimbursement from its customer.

§ 5—107. Advice of Credit; Confirmation; Error in Statement of Terms.

(1) Unless otherwise specified an advising bank by advising a credit issued by another bank does not assume any obligation to honor drafts drawn or demands for payment made under the credit but it does assume obligation for the accuracy of its own statement.

(2) A confirming bank by confirming a credit becomes directly obligated on the credit to the extent of its confirmation as though it were its issuer and acquires the rights of an issuer.

(3) Even though an advising bank incorrectly advises the terms of a credit it has been authorized to advise the credit is established as against the issuer to the extent of its original terms.

(4) Unless otherwise specified the customer bears as against the issuer all risks of transmission and reasonable translation or interpretation of any message relating to a credit.

§ 5—108. "Notation Credit"; Exhaustion of Credit.

(1) A credit which specifies that any person purchasing or paying drafts drawn or demands for payment made under it must note the amount of the draft or demand on the letter or advice of credit is a "notation credit".

(2) Under a notation credit

(a) a person paying the beneficiary or purchasing a draft or demand for payment from him acquires a right to honor only if the appropriate notation is made and by transferring or forwarding for honor the documents under the credit such a person warrants to the issuer that the notation has been made; and

(b) unless the credit or a signed statement that an appropriate notation has been made accompanies the draft or demand for payment the issuer may delay honor until evidence of notation has been procured which is satisfactory to it but its obligation and that of its customer continue for a reasonable time not exceeding thirty days to obtain such evidence.

(3) If the credit is not a notation credit

(a) the issuer may honor complying drafts or demands for payment presented to it in the order in which they are presented and is discharged pro tanto by honor of any such draft or demand;

(b) as between competing good faith purchasers of complying drafts or demands the person first purchasing his priority over a subsequent purchaser even though the later purchased draft or demand has been first honored.

§ 5—109. Issuer's Obligation to Its Customer.

(1) An issuer's obligation to its customer includes good faith and observance of any general banking usage but unless otherwise agreed does not include liability or responsibility

(a) for performance of the underlying contract for sale or other transaction between the customer and the beneficiary; or

(b) for any act or omission of any person other than itself or its own branch or for loss or destruction of a draft, demand or document in transit or in the possession of others; or

(c) based on knowledge or lack of knowledge of any usage of any particular trade.

(2) An issuer must examine documents with care so as to ascertain that on their face they appear to comply with the terms of the credit but unless otherwise agreed assumes no liability or responsibility for the genuineness, falsification or effect of any document which appears on such examination to be regular on its face.

(3) A non-bank issuer is not bound by any banking usage of which it has no knowledge.

§ 5—110. Availability of Credit in Portions; Presenter's Reservation of Lien or Claim.

(1) Unless otherwise specified a credit may be used in portions in the discretion of the beneficiary.

(2) Unless otherwise specified a person by presenting a documentary draft or demand for payment under a credit relinquishes upon its honor all claims to the documents and a person by transferring such draft or demand or causing such presentment authorizes such relinquishment. An explicit reservation of claim makes the draft or demand non-complying.

§ 5—111. Warranties on Transfer and Presentment.

(1) Unless otherwise agreed the beneficiary by transferring or presenting a documentary draft or demand for payment warrants to all interested parties that the necessary conditions of the credit have been complied with. This is in addition to any warranties arising under Articles 3, 4, 7 and 8.

(2) Unless otherwise agreed a negotiating, advising, confirming, collecting or issuing bank presenting or transferring a draft or demand for payment under a credit warrants only the matters warranted by a collecting bank under Article 4 and any such bank transferring a document warrants only the matters warranted by an intermediary under Articles 7 and 8.

§ 5—112. Time Allowed for Honor or Rejection; Withholding Honor or Rejection by Consent; "Presenter".

(1) A bank to which a documentary draft or demand

for payment is presented under a credit may without dishonor of the draft, demand or credit

(a) defer honor until the close of the third banking day following receipt of the documents; and

(b) further defer honor if the presenter has expressly or impliedly consented thereto.

Failure to honor within the time here specified constitutes dishonor of the draft or demand and of the credit [except as otherwise provided in subsection (4) of Section 5—114 on conditional payment].

Note: *The bracketed language in the last sentence of subsection (1) should be included only if the optional provisions of Section 5—114(4) and (5) are included.*

(2) Upon dishonor the bank may unless otherwise instructed fulfill its duty to return the draft or demand and the documents by holding them at the disposal of the presenter and sending him an advice to that effect.

(3) "Presenter" means any person presenting a draft or demand for payment for honor under a credit even though that person is a confirming bank or other correspondent which is acting under an issuer's authorization.

§ 5—113. Indemnities.

(1) A bank seeking to obtain (whether for itself or another) honor, negotiation or reimbursement under a credit may give an indemnity to induce such honor, negotiation or reimbursement.

(2) An indemnity agreement inducing honor, negotiation or reimbursement

(a) unless otherwise explicitly agreed applies to defects in the documents but not in the goods; and

(b) unless a longer time is explicitly agreed expires at the end of ten business days following receipt of the documents by, the ultimate customer unless notice of objection is sent before such expiration date. The ultimate customer may send notice of objection to the person from whom he received the documents and any bank receiving such notice is under a duty to send notice to its transferor before its midnight deadline.

§ 5—114. Issuer's Duty and Privilege to Honor; Right to Reimbursement.

(1) An issuer must honor a draft or demand for payment which complies with the terms of the relevant credit regardless of whether the goods or documents conform to the underlying contract for sale or other contract between the customer and the beneficiary.

The issuer is not excused from honor of such a draft or demand by reason of an additional general term that all documents must be satisfactory to the issuer, but an issuer may require that specified documents must be satisfactory to it.

(2) Unless otherwise agreed when documents appear on their face to comply with the terms of a credit but a required document does not in fact conform to the warranties made on negotiation or transfer of a document of title (Section 7—507) or of a certificated security (Section 8—306) or is forged or fraudulent or there is fraud in the transaction:

(a) the issuer must honor the draft or demand for payment if honor is demanded by a negotiating bank or other holder of the draft or demand which has taken the draft or demand under the credit and under circumstances which would make it a holder in due course (Section 3—302) and in an appropriate case would make it a person to whom a document of title has been duly negotiated (Section 7—502) or a bona fide purchaser of a certificated security (Section 8—302); and

(b) in all other cases as against its customer, an issuer acting in good faith may honor the draft or demand for payment despite notification from the customer of fraud, forgery or other defect not apparent on the face of the documents but a court of appropriate jurisdiction may enjoin such honor.

(3) Unless otherwise agreed an issuer which has duly honored a draft or demand for payment is entitled to immediate reimbursement of any payment made under the credit and to be put in effectively available funds not later than the day before maturity of any acceptance made under the credit.

[(4) When a credit provides for payment by the issuer on receipt of notice that the required documents are in the possession of a correspondent or other agent of the issuer

(a) any payment made on receipt of such notice is conditional; and

(b) the issuer may reject documents which do not comply with the credit if it does so within three banking days following its receipt of the documents; and

(c) in the event of such rejection, the issuer is entitled by charge back or otherwise to return of the payment made.]

[(5) In the case covered by subsection (4) failure to reject documents within the time specified in subparagraph (b) constitutes acceptance of the documents and makes the payment final in favor of the beneficiary.]

Amended in 1977.

Note: *Subsections (4) and (5) are bracketed as optional. If they are included the bracketed language in the last sentence of Section 5—112(1) should also be included.*

§ 5—115. Remedy for Improper Dishonor or Anticipatory Repudiation.

(1) When an issuer wrongfully dishonors a draft or demand for payment presented under a credit the person entitled to honor has with respect to any documents the rights of a person in the position of a seller (Section 2—707) and may recover from the issuer the face amount of the draft or demand together with incidental damages under Section 2—710 on seller's incidental damages and interest but less any amount realized by resale or other use or disposition of the subject matter of the transaction. In the event no resale or other utilization is made the documents, goods or other subject matter involved in the transaction must be turned over to the issuer on payment of judgment.

(2) When an issuer wrongfully cancels or otherwise repudiates a credit before presentment of a draft or demand for payment drawn under it the beneficiary has the rights of a seller after anticipatory repudiation by the buyer under Section 2—610 if he learns of the repudiation in time reasonably to avoid procurement of the required documents. Otherwise the beneficiary has an immediate right of action for wrongful dishonor.

§ 5—116. Transfer and Assignment.

(1) The right to draw under a credit can be transferred or assigned only when the credit is expressly designated as transferable or assignable.

(2) Even through the credit specifically states that it is nontransferable or nonassignable the beneficiary may before performance of the conditions of the credit assign his right to proceeds. Such an assignment is an assignment of an account under Article 9 on Secured Transactions and is governed by that Article except that

(a) the assignment is ineffective until the letter of credit or advice of credit is delivered to the assignee which delivery constitutes perfection of the security interest under Article 9; and

(b) the issuer may honor drafts or demands for payment drawn under the credit until it receives a notification of the assignment signed by the beneficiary which reasonably identifies the credit involved in the assignment and contains a request to pay the assignee; and

(c) after what reasonably appears to be such a notification has been received the issuer may without dishonor refuse to accept or pay even to a person otherwise entitled to honor until the letter of credit or advice of credit is exhibited to the issuer.

(3) Except where the beneficiary has effectively assigned his right to draw or his right to proceeds, nothing in this section limits his right to transfer or negotiate drafts or demands drawn under the credit.

§ 5—117. Insolvency of Bank Holding Funds for Documentary Credit.

(1) Where an issuer or an advising or confirming bank or a bank which has for a customer procured issuance of a credit by another bank becomes insolvent before final payment under the credit and the credit is one to which this Article is made applicable by paragraphs (a) or (b) of Section 5—102(1) on scope, the receipt or allocation of funds or collateral to secure or meet obligations under the credit shall have the following results:

(a) to the extent of any funds or collateral turned over after or before the insolvency as indemnity against or specifically for the purpose of payment of drafts or demands for payment drawn under the designated credit, the drafts or demands are entitled to payment in preference over depositors or other general creditors of the issuer or bank; and

(b) on expiration of the credit or surrender of the beneficiary's rights under it unused any person who has given such funds or collateral is similarly entitled to return thereof; and

(c) a charge to a general or current account with a bank if specifically consented to for the purpose of indemnity against or payment of drafts or demands for payment drawn under the designated credit falls under the same rules as if the funds had been drawn out in cash and then turned over with specific instructions.

(2) After honor or reimbursement under this section the customer or other person for whose account the insolvent bank has acted is entitled to receive the documents involved.

Article 6
BULK TRANSFERS

§ 6—101. Short Title.

This Article shall be known and may be cited as Uniform Commercial Code—Bulk Transfers.

§ 6—102. "Bulk Transfer"; Transfers of Equipment; Enterprises Subject to This Article; Bulk Transfers Subject to This Article.

(1) A "bulk transfer" is any transfer in bulk and not in the ordinary course of the transferor's business of a major part of the materials, supplies, merchandise or other inventory (Section 9—109) of an enterprise subject to this Article.

(2) A transfer of a substantial part of the equipment (Section 9—109) of such an enterprise is a bulk transfer it if is made in connection with a bulk transfer of inventory, but not otherwise.

(3) The enterprises subject to this Article are all those whose principal business is the sale of merchandise from stock, including those who manufacture what they sell.

(4) Except as limited by the following section all bulk transfers of goods located within this state are subject to this Article.

§ 6—103. Transfers Excepted From This Article.

The following transfers are not subject to this Article:

(1) Those made to give security for the performance of an obligation;

(2) General assignments for the benefit of all the creditors of the transferor, and subsequent transfers by the assignee thereunder;

(3) Transfers in settlement or realization of a lien or other security interest;

(4) Sales by executors, administrators, receivers, trustees in bankruptcy, or any public officer under judicial process;

(5) Sales made in the course of judicial or administrative proceedings for the dissolution or reorganization of a corporation and of which notice is sent to the creditors of the corporation pursuant to order of the court or administrative agency;

(6) Transfers to a person maintaining a known place of business in this State who becomes bound to pay

the debts of the transferor in full and gives public notice of that fact, and who is solvent after becoming so bound;

(7) A transfer to a new business enterprise organized to take over and continue the business, if public notice of the transaction is given and the new enterprise assumes the debts of the transferor and he receives nothing from the transaction except an interest in the new enterprise junior to the claims of creditors;

(8) Transfers of property which is exempt from execution.

Public notice under subsection (6) or subsection (7) may be given by publishing once a week for two consecutive weeks in a newspaper of general circulation where the transferor had its principal place of business in this state an advertisement including the names and addresses of the transferor and transferee and the effective date of the transfer.

§ 6—104. **Schedule of Property, List of Creditors.**

(1) Except as provided with respect to auction sales (Section 6—108), a bulk transfer subject to this Article is ineffective against any creditor of the transferor unless:

    (a) The transferee requires the transferor to furnish a list of his existing creditors prepared as stated in this section; and

    (b) The parties prepare a schedule of the property transferred sufficient to identify it; and

    (c) The transferee preserves the list and schedule for six months next following the transfer and permits inspection of either or both and copying therefrom at all reasonable hours by any creditor of the transferor, or files the list and schedule in *(a public office to be here identified)*.

(2) The list of creditors must be signed and sworn to or affirmed by the transferor or his agent. It must contain the names and business addresses of all creditors of the transferor, with the amounts when known, and also the names of all persons who are known to the transferor to assert claims against him even though such claims are disputed. If the transferor is the obligor of an outstanding issue of bonds, debentures or the like as to which there is an indenture trustee, the list of creditors need include only the name and address of the indenture trustee and the aggregate outstanding principal amount of the issue.

(3) Responsibility for the completeness and accuracy of the list of creditors rests on the transferor, and the transfer is not rendered ineffective by errors or omissions therein unless the transferee is shown to have had knowledge.

§ 6—105. **Notice to Creditors.**

In addition to the requirements of the preceding section, any bulk transfer subject to this Article except one made by auction sale (Section 6—108) is ineffective against any creditor of the transferor unless at least ten days before he takes possession of the goods or pays for them, whichever happens first, the transferee gives notice of the transfer in the manner and to the persons hereafter provided (Section 6—107).

[§ 6—106. **Application of the Proceeds.**

In addition to the requirements of the two preceding sections:

(1) Upon every bulk transfer subject to this Article for which new consideration becomes payable except those made by sale at auction it is the duty of the transferee to assure that such consideration is applied so far as necessary to pay those debts of the transferor which are either shown on the list furnished by the transferor (Section 6—104) or filed in writing in the place stated in the notice (Section 6—107) within thirty days after the mailing of such notice. This duty of the transferee runs to all the holders of such debts, and may be enforced by any of them for the benefit of all.

(2) If any of said debts are in dispute the necessary sum may be withheld from distribution until the dispute is settled or adjudicated.

(3) If the consideration payable is not enough to pay all of the said debts in full distribution shall be made pro rata.]

Note: *This section is bracketed to indicate division of opinion as to whether or not it is a wise provision, and to suggest that this is a point on which State enactments may differ without serious damage to the principle of uniformity. In any State where this section is omitted, the following parts of sections, also bracketed in the text, should also be omitted, namely: Section 6—107(2)(c).*

    6—108(3)(c).

    6—109(2).

  In any State where this section is enacted, these other provisions should be also.

Optional Subsection (4)

[(4) The transferee may within ten days after he takes

possession of the goods pay the consideration into the (specify court) in the county where the transferor had its principal place of business in this state and thereafter may discharge his duty under this section by giving notice by registered or certified mail to all the persons to whom the duty runs that the consideration has been paid into that court and that they should file their claims there. On motion of any interested party, the court may order the distribution of the consideration to the persons entitled to it.]

Note: *Optional subsection (4) is recommended for those states which do not have a general statute providing for payment of money into court.*

§ 6—107. **The Notice.**

(1) The notice to creditors (Section 6—105) shall state:

(a) that a bulk transfer is about to be made; and

(b) the names and business addresses of the transferor and transferee, and all other business names and addresses used by the transferor within three years last past so far as known to the transferee; and

(c) whether or not all the debts of the transferor are to be paid in full as they fall due as a result of the transaction, and if so, the address to which creditors should send their bills.

(2) If the debts of the transferor are not to be paid in full as they fall due or if the transferee is in doubt on that point then the notice shall state further:

(a) the location and general description of the property to be transferred and the estimated total of the transferor's debts;

(b) the address where the schedule of property and list of creditors (Section 6—104) may be inspected;

(c) whether the transfer is to pay existing debts and if so the amount of such debts and to whom owing;

(d) whether the transfer is for new consideration and if so the amount of such consideration and the time and place of payment; [and]

[(e) if for new consideration the time and place where creditors of the transferor are to file their claims.]

(3) The notice in any case shall be delivered personally or sent by registered or certified mail to all the persons shown on the list of creditors furnished by the transferor (Section 6—104) and to all other persons who are known to the transferee to hold or assert claims against the transferor.

§ 6—108. **Auction Sales; "Auctioneer".**

(1) A bulk transfer is subject to this Article even though it is by sale at auction, but only in the manner and with the results stated in this section.

(2) The transferor shall furnish a list of his creditors and assist in the preparation of a schedule of the property to be sold, both prepared as before stated (Section 6—104).

(3) The person or persons other than the transferor who direct, control or are responsible for the auction are collectively called the "auctioneer". The auctioneer shall:

(a) receive and retain the list of creditors and prepare and retain the schedule of property for the period stated in this Article (Section 6—104);

(b) give notice of the auction personally or by registered or certified mail at least ten days before it occurs to all persons shown on the list of creditors and to all other persons who are known to him to hold or assert claims against the transferor; [and]

[(c) assure that the net proceeds of the auction are applied as provided in this Article (Section 6—106).]

(4) Failure of the auctioneer to perform any of these duties does not affect the validity of the sale or the title of the purchasers, but if the auctioneer knows that the auction constitutes a bulk transfer such failure renders the auctioneer liable to the creditors of the transferor as a class for the sums owing to them from the transferor up to but not exceeding the net proceeds of the auction. If the auctioneer consists of several persons their liability is joint and several.

§ 6—109. **What Creditors Protected; [Credit for Payment to Particular Creditors].**

(1) The creditors of the transferor mentioned in this Article are those holding claims based on transactions or events occurring before the bulk transfer, but creditors who become such after notice to creditors is given (Sections 6—105 and 6—107) are not entitled to notice.

[(2) Against the aggregate obligation imposed by the provisions of this Article concerning the application of the proceeds (Section 6—106 and subsection (3)(c) of 6—108) the transferee or auctioneer is entitled to credit for sums paid to particular creditors of the transferor, not exceeding the sums believed in good faith at the time of the payment to be properly payable to such creditors.]

§ 6—110. Subsequent Transfers.

When the title of a transferee to property is subject to a defect by reason of his non-compliance with the requirements of this Article, then:

(1) a purchaser of any of such property from such transferee who pays no value or who takes with notice of such non-compliance takes subject to such defect, but

(2) a purchaser for value in good faith and without such notice takes free of such defect.

§ 6—111. Limitation of Actions and Levies.

No action under this Article shall be brought nor levy made more than six months after the date on which the transferee took possession of the goods unless the transfer has been concealed. If the transfer has been concealed, actions may be brought or levies made within six months after its discovery.

Note to Article 6: *Section 6—106 is bracketed to indicate division of opinion as to whether or not it is a wise provision, and to suggest that this is a point on which State enactments may differ without serious damage to the principle of uniformity.*

In any State where Section 6—106 is not enacted, the following parts of sections, also bracketed in the text, should also be omitted, namely:
Sec. 6—107(2)(e).
   6—108(3)(c).
   6—109(2).
In any State where Section 6—106 is enacted, these other provisions should be also.

Article 7
Warehouse Receipts, Bills of Lading and Other Documents of Title

Part 1 General

§ 7—101. Short Title.

This Article shall be known and may be cited as Uniform Commercial Code—Documents of Title.

§ 7—102. Definitions and Index of Definitions.

(1) In this Article, unless the context otherwise requires:

(a) "Bailee" means the person who by a warehouse receipt, bill of lading or other document of title acknowledges possession of goods and contracts to deliver them.

(b) "Consignee" means the person named in a bill to whom or to whose order the bill promises delivery.

(c) "Consignor" means the person named in a bill as the person from whom the goods have been received for shipment.

(d) "Delivery order" means a written order to deliver goods directed to a warehouseman, carrier or other person who in the ordinary course of business issues warehouse receipts or bills of lading.

(e) "Document" means document of title as defined in the general definitions in Article 1 (Section 1—201).

(f) "Goods" means all things which are treated as movable for the purposes of a contract of storage or transportation.

(g) "Issuer" means a bailee who issues a document except that in relation to an unaccepted delivery order it means the person who orders the possessor of goods to deliver. Issuer includes any person for whom an agent or employee purports to act in issuing a document if the agent or employee has real or apparent authority to issue documents, notwithstanding that the issuer received no goods or that the goods were misdescribed or that in any other respect the agent or employee violated his instructions.

(h) "Warehouseman" is a person engaged in the business of storing goods for hire.

(2) Other definitions applying to this Article or to specified Parts thereof, and the sections in which they appear are:
"Duly negotiate". Section 7—501.
"Person entitled under the document". Section 7—403(4).

(3) Definitions in other Articles applying to this Article and the sections in which they appear are:
"Contract for sale". Section 2—106.
"Overseas". Section 2—323.
"Receipt" of goods. Section 2—103.

(4) In addition Article 1 contains general definitions and principles of construction and interpretation applicable throughout this Article.

§ 7—103. Relation of Article to Treaty, Statute, Tariff, Classification or Regulation.

To the extent that any treaty or statute of the United States, regulatory statute of this State or tariff, classification or regulation filed or issued pursuant thereto is applicable, the provisions of this Article are subject thereto.

§ 7—104. Negotiable and Non-Negotiable Warehouse Receipt, Bill of Lading or Other Document of Title.

(1) A warehouse receipt, bill of lading or other document of title is negotiable

(a) if by its terms the goods are to be delivered to bearer or to the order of a named person; or

(b) where recognized in overseas trade, if it runs to a named person or assigns.

(2) Any other document is non-negotiable. A bill of lading in which it is stated that the goods are consigned to a named person is not made negotiable by a provision that the goods are to be delivered only against a written order signed by the same or another named person.

§ 7—105. Construction Against Negative Implication.

The omission from either Part 2 or Part 3 of this Article of a provision corresponding to a provision made in the other Part does not imply that a corresponding rule of law is not applicable.

Part 2 Warehouse Receipts: Special Provisions

§ 7—201. Who May Issue a Warehouse Receipt; Storage Under Government Bond.

(1) A warehouse receipt may be issued by any warehouseman.

(2) Where goods including distilled spirits and agricultural commodities are stored under a statute requiring a bond against withdrawal or a license for the issuance of receipts in the nature of warehouse receipts, a receipt issued for the goods has like effect as a warehouse receipt even though issued by a person who is the owner of the goods and is not a warehouseman.

§ 7—202. Form of Warehouse Receipt; Essential Terms; Optional Terms.

(1) A warehouse receipt need not be in any particular form.

(2) Unless a warehouse receipt embodies within its written or printed terms each of the following, the warehouseman is liable for damages caused by the omission to a person injured thereby:

(a) the location of the warehouse where the goods are stored;

(b) the date of issue of the receipt;

(c) the consecutive number of the receipt;

(d) a statement whether the goods received will be delivered to the bearer, to a specified person, or to a specified person or his order;

(e) the rate of storage and handling charges, except that where goods are stored under a field warehousing arrangement a statement of that fact is sufficient on a non-negotiable receipt;

(f) a description of the goods or of the packages containing them;

(g) the signature of the warehouseman, which may be made by his authorized agent;

(h) if the receipt is issued for goods of which the warehouseman is owner, either solely or jointly or in common with others, the fact of such ownership; and

(i) a statement of the amount of advances made and of liabilities incurred for which the warehouseman claims a lien or security interest (Section 7—209). If the precise amount of such advances made or of such liabilities incurred is, at the time of the issue of the receipt, unknown to the warehouseman or to his agent who issues it, a statement of the fact that advances have been made or liabilities incurred and the purpose thereof is sufficient.

(3) A warehouseman may insert in his receipt any other terms which are not contrary to the provisions of this Act and do not impair his obligation of delivery (Section 7—403) or his duty of care (Section 7—204). Any contrary provisions shall be ineffective.

§ 7—203. Liability for Non-Receipt or Misdescription.

A party to or purchaser for value in good faith of a document of title other than a bill of lading relying in either case upon the description therein of the goods may recover from the issuer damages caused by the non-receipt or misdescription of the goods, except to the extent that the document conspicuously indicates that the issuer does not know whether any part or all of the goods in fact were received or conform to the description, as where the description is in terms of marks or labels or kind, quantity or condition, or the receipt or description is qualified by "contents, condition and quality unknown", "said to contain" or the like, if such indication be true, or the party or purchaser otherwise has notice.

§ 7—204. Duty of Care; Contractual Limitation of Warehouseman's Liability.

(1) A warehouseman is liable for damages for loss of or injury to the goods caused by his failure to exercise such care in regard to them as a reasonably careful man would exercise under like circumstances but unless otherwise agreed he is not liable for damages which could not have been avoided by the exercise of such care.

(2) Damages may be limited by a term in the warehouse receipt or storage agreement limiting the amount of liability in case of loss or damage, and setting forth a specific liability per article or item, or value per unit of weight, beyond which the warehouseman shall not be liable; provided, however, that such liability may on written request of the bailor at the time of signing such storage agreement or within a reasonable time after receipt of the warehouse receipt be increased on part or all of the goods thereunder, in which event increased rates may be charged based on such increased valuation, but that no such increase shall be permitted contrary to a lawful limitation of liability contained in the warehouseman's tariff, if any. No such limitation is effective with respect to the warehouseman's liability for conversion to his own use.

(3) Reasonable provisions as to the time and manner of presenting claims and instituting actions based on the bailment may be included in the warehouse receipt or tariff.

(4) This section does not impair or repeal . . .

Note: *Insert in subsection (4) a reference to any statute which imposes a higher responsibility upon the warehouseman or invalidates contractual limitations which would be permissible under this Article.*

§ 7—205. Title Under Warehouse Receipt Defeated in Certain Cases.

A buyer in the ordinary course of business of fungible goods sold and delivered by a warehouseman who is also in the business of buying and selling such goods takes free of any claim under a warehouse receipt even though it has been duly negotiated.

§ 7—206. Termination of Storage at Warehouseman's Option.

(1) A warehouseman may on notifying the person on whose account the goods are held and any other person known to claim an interest in the goods require payment of any charges and removal of the goods from the warehouse at the termination of the period of storage fixed by the document, or, if no period is fixed, within a stated period not less than thirty days after the notification. If the goods are not removed before the date specified in the notification, the warehouseman may sell them in accordance with the provisions of the section on enforcement of a warehouseman's lien (Section 7—210).

(2) If a warehouseman in good faith believes that the goods are about to deteriorate or decline in value to less than the amount of his lien within the time prescribed in subsection (1) for notification, advertisement and sale, the warehouseman may specify in the notification any reasonable shorter time for removal of the goods and in case the goods are not removed, may sell them at public sale held not less than one week after a single advertisement or posting.

(3) If as a result of a quality or condition of the goods of which the warehouseman had no notice at the time of deposit the goods are a hazard to other property or to the warehouse or to persons, the warehouseman may sell the goods at public or private sale without advertisement on reasonable notification to all persons known to claim an interest in the goods. If the warehouseman after a reasonable effort is unable to sell the goods he may dispose of them in any lawful manner and shall incur no liability by reason of such disposition.

(4) The warehouseman must deliver the goods to any person entitled to them under this Article upon due demand made at any time prior to sale or other disposition under this section.

(5) The warehouseman may satisfy his lien from the proceeds of any sale or disposition under this section but must hold the balance for delivery on the demand of any person to whom he would have been bound to deliver the goods.

§ 7—207. Goods Must Be Kept Separate; Fungible Goods.

(1) Unless the warehouse receipt otherwise provides, a warehouseman must keep separate the goods covered by each receipt so as to permit at all times identification and delivery of those goods except that different lots of fungible goods may be commingled.

(2) Fungible goods so commingled are owned in common by the persons entitled thereto and the ware-

houseman is severally liable to each owner for that owner's share. Where because of overissue a mass of fungible goods is insufficient to meet all the receipts which the warehouseman has issued against it, the persons entitled include all holders to whom overissued receipts have been duly negotiated.

§ 7—208. Altered Warehouse Receipts.

Where a blank in a negotiable warehouse receipt has been filled in without authority, a purchaser for value and without notice of the want of authority may treat the insertion as authorized. Any other unauthorized alteration leaves any receipt enforceable against the issuer according to its original tenor.

§ 7—209. Lien of Warehouseman.

(1) A warehouseman has a lien against the bailor on the goods covered by a warehouse receipt or on the proceeds thereof in his possession for charges for storage or transportation (including demurrage and terminal charges), insurance, labor, or charges present or future in relation to the goods, and for expenses necessary for preservation of the goods or reasonably incurred in their sale pursuant to law. If the person on whose account the goods are held is liable for like charges or expenses in relation to other goods whenever deposited and it is stated in the receipt that a lien is claimed for charges and expenses in relation to other goods, the warehouseman also has a lien against him for such charges and expenses whether or not the other goods have been delivered by the warehouseman. But against a person to whom a negotiable warehouse receipt is duly negotiated a warehouseman's lien is limited to charges in an amount or at a rate specified on the receipt or if no charges are so specified then to a reasonable charge for storage of the goods covered by the receipt subsequent to the date of the receipt.

(2) The warehouseman may also reserve a security interest against the bailor for a maximum amount specified on the receipt for charges other than those specified in subsection (1), such as for money advanced and interest. Such a security interest is governed by the Article on Secured Transactions (Article 9).

(3) (a) A warehouseman's lien for charges and expenses under subsection (1) or a security interest under subsection (2) is also effective against any person who so entrusted the bailor with possession of the goods that a pledge of them by him to a good faith purchaser for value would have been valid but is not effective against a person as to whom the document confers no right in the goods covered by it under Section 7—503.

(b) A warehouseman's lien on household goods for charges and expenses in relation to the goods under subsection (1) is also effective against all persons if the depositor was the legal possessor of the goods at the time of deposit. "Household goods" means furniture, furnishings and personal effects used by the depositor in a dwelling.

(4) A warehouseman loses his lien on any goods which he voluntarily delivers or which he unjustifiably refuses to deliver.

§ 7—210. Enforcement of Warehouseman's Lien.

(1) Except as provided in subsection (2), a warehouseman's lien may be enforced by public or private sale of the goods in bloc or in parcels, at any time or place and on any terms which are commercially reasonable, after notifying all persons known to claim an interest in the goods. Such notification must include a statement of the amount due, the nature of the proposed sale and the time and place of any public sale. The fact that a better price could have been obtained by a sale at a different time or in a different method from that selected by the warehouseman is not of itself sufficient to establish that the sale was not made in a commercially reasonable manner. If the warehouseman either sells the goods in the usual manner in any recognized market therefor, or if he sells at the price current in such market at the time of his sale, or if he has otherwise sold in conformity with commercially reasonable practices among dealers in the type of goods sold, he has sold in a commercially reasonable manner. A sale of more goods than apparently necessary to be offered to insure satisfaction of the obligation is not commercially reasonable except in cases covered by the preceding sentence.

(2) A warehouseman's lien on goods other than goods stored by a merchant in the course of his business may be enforced only as follows:

(a) All persons known to claim an interest in the goods must be notified.

(b) The notification must be delivered in person or sent by registered or certified letter to the last known address of any person to be notified.

(c) The notification must include an itemized statement of the claim, a description of the goods subject to the lien, a demand for payment within a specified time not less than ten days after receipt of the notification, and a conspicuous statement that unless the claim is paid within the time the goods will be advertised for sale and sold by auction at a specified time and place.

(d) The sale must conform to the terms of the notification.

(e) The sale must be held at the nearest suitable place to that where the goods are held or stored.

(f) After the expiration of the time given in the notification, an advertisement of the sale must be published once a week for two weeks consecutively in a newspaper of general circulation where the sale is to be held. The advertisement must include a description of the goods, the name of the person on whose account they are being held, and the time and place of the sale. The sale must take place at least fifteen days after the first publication. If there is no newspaper of general circulation where the sale is to be held, the advertisement must be posted at least ten days before the sale in not less than six conspicuous places in the neighborhood of the proposed sale.

(3) Before any sale pursuant to this section any person claiming a right in the goods may pay the amount necessary to satisfy the lien and the reasonable expenses incurred under this section. In that event the goods must not be sold, but must be retained by the warehouseman subject to the terms of the receipt and this Article.

(4) The warehouseman may buy at any public sale pursuant to this section.

(5) A purchaser in good faith of goods sold to enforce a warehouseman's lien takes the goods free of any rights of persons against whom the lien was valid, despite noncompliance by the warehouseman with the requirements of this section.

(6) The warehouseman may satisfy his lien from the proceeds of any sale pursuant to this section but must hold the balance, if any, for delivery on demand to any person to whom he would have been bound to deliver the goods.

(7) The rights provided by this section shall be in addition to all other rights allowed by law to a creditor against his debtor.

(8) Where a lien is on goods stored by a merchant in the course of his business the lien may be enforced in accordance with either subsection (1) or (2).

(9) The warehouseman is liable for damages caused by failure to comply with the requirements for sale under this section and in case of willful violation is liable for conversion.

Part 3 Bills of Lading: Special Provisions

§ 7—301. Liability for Non-Receipt or Misdescription; "Said to Contain"; "Shipper's Load and Count"; Improper Handling.

(1) A consignee of a non-negotiable bill who has given value in good faith or a holder to whom a negotiable bill has been duly negotiated relying in either case upon the description therein of the goods, or upon the date therein shown, may recover from the issuer damages caused by the misdating of the bill or the non-receipt or misdescription of the goods, except to the extent that the document indicates that the issuer does not know whether any part of all of the goods in fact were received or conform to the description, as where the description is in terms of marks or labels or kind, quantity, or condition or the receipt or description is qualified by "contents or condition of contents of packages unknown", "said to contain", "shipper's weight, load and count" or the like, if such indication be true.

(2) When goods are loaded by an issuer who is a common carrier, the issuer must count the packages of goods if package freight and ascertain the kind and quantity if bulk freight. In such cases "shipper's weight, load and count" or other words indicating that the description was made by the shipper are ineffective except as to freight concealed by packages.

(3) When bulk freight is loaded by a shipper who makes available to the issuer adequate facilities for weighing such freight, an issuer who is a common carrier must ascertain the kind and quantity within a reasonable time after receiving the written request of the shipper to do so. In such cases "shipper's weight" or other words of like purport are ineffective.

(4) The issuer may by inserting in the bill the words "shipper's weight, load and count" or other words of like purport indicate that the goods were loaded by the shipper; and if such statement be true the issuer shall not be liable for damages caused by the improper loading. But their omission does not imply liability for such damages.

(5) The shipper shall be deemed to have guaranteed to the issuer the accuracy at the time of shipment of the description, marks, labels, number, kind, quantity, condition and weight, as furnished by him; and the shipper shall indemnify the issuer against damage caused by inaccuracies in such particulars. The right of the issuer to such indemnity shall in no way limit his responsibility and liability under the contract of carriage to any person other than the shipper.

§ 7—302. **Through Bills of Lading and Similar Documents.**

(1) The issuer of a through bill of lading or other document embodying an undertaking to be performed in part by persons acting as its agents or by connecting carriers is liable to anyone entitled to recover on the document for any breach by such other persons or by a connecting carrier of its obligation under the document but to the extent that the bill covers an undertaking to be performed overseas or in territory not contiguous to the continental United States or an undertaking including matters other than transportation this liability may be varied by agreement of the parties.

(2) Where goods covered by a through bill of lading or other document embodying an undertaking to be performed in part by persons other than the issuer are received by any such person, he is subject with respect to his own performance while the goods are in his possession to the obligation of the issuer. His obligation is discharged by delivery of the goods to another such person pursuant to the document, and does not include liability for breach by any other such persons or by the issuer.

(3) The issuer of such through bill of lading or other document shall be entitled to recover from the connecting carrier or such other person in possession of the goods when the breach of the obligation under the document occurred, the amount it may be required to pay to anyone entitled to recover on the document therefor, as may be evidenced by any receipt, judgment, or transcript thereof, and the amount of any expense reasonably incurred by it in defending any action brought by anyone entitled to recover on the document therefor.

§ 7—303. **Diversion; Reconsignment; Change of Instructions.**

(1) Unless the bill of lading otherwise provides, the carrier may deliver the goods to a person or destination other than that stated in the bill or may otherwise dispose of the goods on instructions from

   (a) the holder of a negotiable bill; or

   (b) the consignor on a non-negotiable bill notwithstanding contrary instructions from the consignee; or

   (c) the consignee on a non-negotiable bill in the absence of contrary instructions from the consignor, if the goods have arrived at the billed desti-

nation or if the consignee is in possession of the bill; or

   (d) the consignee on a non-negotiable bill if he is entitled as against the consignor to dispose of them.

(2) Unless such instructions are noted on a negotiable bill of lading, a person to whom the bill is duly negotiated can hold the bailee according to the original terms.

§ 7—304. **Bills of Lading in a Set.**

(1) Except where customary in overseas transportation, a bill of lading must not be issued in a set of parts. The issuer is liable for damages caused by violation of this subsection.

(2) Where a bill of lading is lawfully drawn in a set of parts, each of which is numbered and expressed to be valid only if the goods have not been delivered against any other part, the whole of the parts constitute one bill.

(3) Where a bill of lading is lawfully issued in a set of parts and different parts are negotiated to different persons, the title of the holder to whom the first due negotiation is made prevails as to both the document and the goods even though any later holder may have received the goods from the carrier in good faith and discharged the carrier's obligation by surrender of his part.

(4) Any person who negotiates or transfers a single part of a bill of lading drawn in a set is liable to holders of that part as if it were the whole set.

(5) The bailee is obliged to deliver in accordance with Part 4 of this Article against the first presented part of a bill of lading lawfully drawn in a set. Such delivery discharges the bailee's obligation on the whole bill.

§ 7—305. **Destination Bills.**

(1) Instead of issuing a bill of lading to the consignor at the place of shipment a carrier may at the request of the consignor procure the bill to be issued at destination or at any other place designated in the request.

(2) Upon request of anyone entitled as against the carrier to control the goods while in transit and on surrender of any outstanding bill of lading or other receipt covering such goods, the issuer may procure a substitute bill to be issued at any place designated in the request.

§ 7—306. **Altered Bills of Lading.**

An unauthorized alteration or filling in of a blank in

a bill of lading leaves the bill enforceable according to its original tenor.

§ 7—307. Lien of Carrier.

(1) A carrier has a lien on the goods covered by a bill of lading for charges subsequent to the date of its receipt of the goods for storage or transportation (including demurrage and terminal charges) and for expenses necessary for preservation of the goods incident to their transportation or reasonably incurred in their sale pursuant to law. But against a purchaser for value of a negotiable bill of lading a carrier's lien is limited to charges stated in the bill or the applicable tariffs, or if no charges are stated then to a reasonable charge.

(2) A lien for charges and expenses under subsection (1) on goods which the carrier was required by law to receive for transportation is effective against the consignor or any person entitled to the goods unless the carrier had notice that the consignor lacked authority to subject the goods to such charges and expenses. Any other lien under subsection (1) is effective against the consignor and any person who permitted the bailor to have control or possession of the goods unless the carrier had notice that the bailor lacked such authority.

(3) A carrier loses his lien on any goods which he voluntarily delivers or which he unjustifiably refuses to deliver.

§ 7—308. Enforcement of Carrier's Lien.

(1) A carrier's lien may be enforced by public or private sale of the goods, in bloc or in parcels, at any time or place and on any terms which are commercially reasonable, after notifying all persons known to claim an interest in the goods. Such notification must include a statement of the amount due, the nature of the proposed sale and the time and place of any public sale. The fact that a better price could have been obtained by a sale at a different time or in a different method from that selected by the carrier is not of itself sufficient to establish that the sale was not made in a commercially reasonable manner. If the carrier either sells the goods in the usual manner in any recognized market therefor or if he sells at the price current in such market at the time of his sale or if he has otherwise sold in conformity with commercially reasonable practices among dealers in the type of goods sold he has sold in a commercially reasonable manner. A sale of more goods than apparently necessary to be offered to ensure satisfaction of the obligation is not commercially reasonable except in cases covered by the preceding sentence.

(2) Before any sale pursuant to this section any person claiming a right in the goods may pay the amount necessary to satisfy the lien and the reasonable expenses incurred under this section. In that event the goods must not be sold, but must be retained by the carrier subject to the terms of the bill and this Article.

(3) The carrier may buy at any public sale pursuant to this section.

(4) A purchaser in good faith of goods sold to enforce a carrier's lien takes the goods free of any rights of persons against whom the lien was valid, despite noncompliance by the carrier with the requirements of this section.

(5) The carrier may satisfy his lien from the proceeds of any sale pursuant to this section but must hold the balance, if any, for delivery on demand to any person to whom he would have been bound to deliver the goods.

(6) The rights provided by this section shall be in addition to all other rights allowed by law to a creditor against his debtor.

(7) A carrier's lien may be enforced in accordance with either subsection (1) or the procedure set forth in subsection (2) of Section 7—210.

(8) The carrier is liable for damages caused by failure to comply with the requirements for sale under this section and in case of willful violation is liable for conversion.

§ 7—309. Duty of Care; Contractual Limitation of Carrier's Liability.

(1) A carrier who issues a bill of lading whether negotiable or non-negotiable must exercise the degree of care in relation to the goods which a reasonably careful man would exercise under like circumstances. This subsection does not repeal or change any law or rule of law which imposes liability upon a common carrier for damages not caused by its negligence.

(2) Damages may be limited by a provision that the carrier's liability shall not exceed a value stated in the document if the carrier's rates are dependent upon value and the consignor by the carrier's tariff is afforded an opportunity to declare a higher value or a value as lawfully provided in the tariff, or where no tariff is filed he is otherwise advised of such opportunity; but no such limitation is effective with respect to the carrier's liability for conversion to its own use.

(3) Reasonable provisions as to the time and manner of presenting claims and instituting actions based on

the shipment may be included in a bill of lading or tariff.

Part 4 Warehouse Receipts and Bills of Lading: General Obligations

§ 7—401. Irregularities in Issue of Receipt or Bill or Conduct of Issuer.

The obligations imposed by this Article on an issuer apply to a document of title regardless of the fact that

(a) the document may not comply with the requirements of this Article or of any other law or regulation regarding its issue, form or content; or

(b) the issuer may have violated laws regulating the conduct of his business; or

(c) the goods covered by the document were owned by the bailee at the time the document was issued; or

(d) the person issuing the document does not come within the definition of warehouseman if it purports to be a warehouse receipt.

§ 7—402. Duplicate Receipt or Bill; Overissue.

Neither a duplicate nor any other document of title purporting to cover goods already represented by an outstanding document of the same issuer confers any right in the goods, except as provided in the case of bills in a set, overissue of documents for fungible goods and substitutes for lost, stolen or destroyed documents. But the issuer is liable for damages caused by his overissue or failure to identify a duplicate document as such by conspicuous notation on its face.

§ 7—403. Obligation of Warehouseman or Carrier to Deliver; Excuse.

(1) The bailee must deliver the goods to a person entitled under the document who complies with subsections (2) and (3), unless and to the extent that the bailee establishes any of the following:

(a) delivery of the goods to a person whose receipt was rightful as against the claimant;

(b) damage to or delay, loss or destruction of the goods for which the bailee is not liable [, but the burden of establishing negligence in such cases is on the person entitled under the document];

Note: *The brackets in (1)(b) indicate that State enactments may differ on this point without serious damage to the principle of uniformity.*

(c) previous sale or other disposition of the goods in lawful enforcement of a lien or on warehouseman's lawful termination of storage;

(d) the exercise by a seller of his right to stop delivery pursuant to the provisions of the Article on Sales (Section 2—705);

(e) a diversion, reconsignment or other disposition pursuant to the provisions of this Article (Section 7—303) or tariff regulating such right;

(f) release, satisfaction or any other fact affording a personal defense against the claimant;

(g) any other lawful excuse.

(2) A person claiming goods covered by a document of title must satisfy the bailee's lien where the bailee so requests or where the bailee is prohibited by law from delivering the goods until the charges are paid.

(3) Unless the person claiming is one against whom the document confers no right under Sec. 7—503(1), he must surrender for cancellation or notation of partial deliveries any outstanding negotiable document covering the goods, and the bailee must cancel the document or conspicuously note the partial delivery thereon or be liable to any person to whom the document is duly negotiated.

(4) "Person entitled under the document" means holder in the case of a negotiable document, or the person to whom delivery is to be made by the terms of or pursuant to written instructions under a non-negotiable document.

§ 7—404. No Liability for Good Faith Delivery Pursuant to Receipt or Bill.

A bailee who in good faith including observance of reasonable commercial standards has received goods and delivered or otherwise disposed of them according to the terms of the document of title or pursuant to this Article is not liable therefor. This rule applies even though the person from whom he received the goods had no authority to procure the document or to dispose of the goods and even though the person to whom he delivered the goods had no authority to receive them.

Part 5 Warehouse Receipts and Bills of Lading: Negotiation and Transfer

§ 7—501. Form of Negotiation and Requirements of "Due Negotiation".

(1) A negotiable document of title running to the order of a named person is negotiated by his indorsement and delivery. After his indorsement in blank or to bearer any person can negotiate it by delivery alone.

(2) (a) A negotiable document of title is also negoti-

ated by delivery alone when by its original terms it runs to bearer.

(b) When a document running to the order of a named person is delivered to him the effect is the same as if the document had been negotiated.

(3) Negotiation of a negotiable document of title after it has been indorsed to a specified person requires indorsement by the special indorsee as well as delivery.

(4) A negotiable document of title is "duly negotiated" when it is negotiated in the manner stated in this section to a holder who purchases it in good faith without notice of any defense against or claim to it on the part of any person and for value, unless it is established that the negotiation is not in the regular course of business or financing or involves receiving the document in settlement or payment of a money obligation.

(5) Indorsement of a non-negotiable document neither makes it negotiable nor adds to the transferee's rights.

(6) The naming in a negotiable bill of a person to be notified of the arrival of the goods does not limit the negotiability of the bill nor constitute notice to a purchaser thereof of any interest of such person in the goods.

§ 7—502. **Rights Acquired by Due Negotiation.**

(1) Subject to the following section and to the provisions of Section 7—205 on fungible goods, a holder to whom a negotiable document of title has been duly negotiated acquires thereby:

(a) title to the document;

(b) title to the goods;

(c) all rights accruing under the law of agency or estoppel, including rights to goods delivered to the bailee after the document was issued; and

(d) the direct obligation of the issuer to hold or deliver the goods according to the terms of the document free of any defense or claim by him except those arising under the terms of the document or under this Article. In the case of a delivery order the bailee's obligation accrues only upon acceptance and the obligation acquired by the holder is that the issuer and any indorser will procure the acceptance of the bailee.

(2) Subject to the following section, title and rights so acquired are not defeated by any stoppage of the goods represented by the document or by surrender of such goods by the bailee, and are not impaired even though the negotiation or any prior negotiation constituted a breach of duty or even though any person has been deprived of possession of the document by misrepresentation, fraud, accident, mistake, duress, loss, theft or conversion, or even though a previous sale or other transfer of the goods or document has been made to a third person.

§ 7—503. **Document of Title to Goods Defeated in Certain Cases.**

(1) A document of title confers no right in goods against a person who before issuance of the document had a legal interest or a perfected security interest in them and who neither

(a) delivered or entrusted them or any document of title covering them to the bailor or his nominee with actual or apparent authority to ship, store or sell or with power to obtain delivery under this Article (Section 7—403) or with power of disposition under this Act (Sections 2—403 and 9—307) or other statute or rule of law; nor

(b) acquiesced in the procurement by the bailor or his nominee of any document of title.

(2) Title to goods based upon an unaccepted delivery order is subject to the rights of anyone to whom a negotiable warehouse receipt or bill of lading covering the goods has been duly negotiated. Such a title may be defeated under the next section to the same extent as the rights of the issuer or a transferee from the issuer.

(3) Title to goods based upon a bill of lading issued to a freight forwarder is subject to the rights of anyone to whom a bill issued by the freight forwarder is duly negotiated; but delivery by the carrier in accordance with Part 4 of this Article pursuant to its own bill of lading discharges the carrier's obligation to deliver.

§ 7—504. **Rights Acquired in the Absence of Due Negotiation; Effect of Diversion; Seller's Stoppage of Delivery.**

(1) A transferee of a document, whether negotiable or non-negotiable, to whom the document has been delivered but not duly negotiated, acquires the title and rights which his transferor had or had actual authority to convey.

(2) In the case of a non-negotiable document, until but not after the bailee receives notification of the transfer, the rights of the transferee may be defeated

(a) by those creditors of the transferor who could treat the sale as void under Section 2—402; or

(b) by a buyer from the transferor in ordinary course

of business if the bailee has delivered the goods to the buyer or received notification of his rights; or

(c) as against the bailee by good faith dealings of the bailee with the transferor.

(3) A diversion or other change of shipping instructions by the consignor in a non-negotiable bill of lading which causes the bailee not to deliver to the consignee defeats the consignee's title to the goods if they have been delivered to a buyer in ordinary course of business and in any event defeats the consignee's rights against the bailee.

(4) Delivery pursuant to a non-negotiable document may be stopped by a seller under Section 2—705, and subject to the requirement of due notification there provided. A bailee honoring the seller's instructions is entitled to be indemnified by the seller against any resulting loss or expense.

§ 7—505. Indorser Not a Guarantor for Other Parties.

The indorsement of a document of title issued by a bailee does not make the indorser liable for any default by the bailee or by previous indorsers.

§ 7—506. Delivery Without Indorsement: Right to Compel Indorsement.

The transferee of a negotiable document of title has a specifically enforceable right to have his transferor supply any necessary indorsement but the transfer becomes a negotiation only as of the time the indorsement is supplied.

§ 7—507. Warranties on Negotiation or Transfer of Receipt or Bill.

Where a person negotiates or transfers a document of title for value otherwise than as a mere intermediary under the next following section, then unless otherwise agreed he warrants to his immediate purchaser only in addition to any warranty made in selling the goods

(a) that the document is genuine; and

(b) that he has no knowledge of any fact which would impair its validity or worth; and

(c) that his negotiation or transfer is rightful and fully effective with respect to the title to the document and the goods it represents.

§ 7—508. Warranties of Collecting Bank as to Documents.

A collecting bank or other intermediary known to be entrusted with documents on behalf of another or with collection of a draft or other claim against delivery of documents warrants by such delivery of the documents only its own good faith and authority. This rule applies even though the intermediary has purchased or made advances against the claim or draft to be collected.

§ 7—509. Receipt or Bill: When Adequate Compliance With Commercial Contract.

The question whether a document is adequate to fulfill the obligations of a contract for sale or the conditions of a credit is governed by the Articles on Sales (Article 2) and on Letters of Credit (Article 5).

Part 6 Warehouse Receipts and Bills of Lading: Miscellaneous Provisions

§ 7—601. Lost and Missing Documents.

(1) If a document has been lost, stolen or destroyed, a court may order delivery of the goods or issuance of a substitute document and the bailee may without liability to any person comply with such order. If the document was negotiable the claimant must post security approved by the court to indemnify any person who may suffer loss as a result of non-surrender of the document. If the document was not negotiable, such security may be required at the discretion of the court. The court may also in its discretion order payment of the bailee's reasonable costs and counsel fees.

(2) A bailee who without court order delivers goods to a person claiming under a missing negotiable document is liable to any person injured thereby, and if the delivery is not in good faith becomes liable for conversion. Delivery in good faith is not conversion if made in accordance with a filed classification or tariff or, where no classification or tariff is filed, if the claimant posts security with the bailee in an amount at least double the value of the goods at the time of posting to indemnify any person injured by the delivery who files a notice of claim within one year after the delivery.

§ 7—602. Attachment of Goods Covered by a Negotiable Document.

Except where the document was originally issued upon delivery of the goods by a person who had no power to dispose of them, no lien attaches by virtue of any judicial process to goods in the possession of a bailee for which a negotiable document of title is outstanding unless the document be first surrendered to the bailee or its negotiation enjoined, and the bailee shall not be compelled to deliver the goods pursuant to process until the document is surrendered to him or impounded by the court. One who purchases the document for value without notice of the process or injunction takes free of the lien imposed by judicial process.

§ 7—603. Conflicting Claims; Interpleader.

If more than one person claims title or possession of the goods, the bailee is excused from delivery until he has had a reasonable time to ascertain the validity of the adverse claims or to bring an action to compel all claimants to interplead and may compel such interpleader, either in defending an action for non-delivery of the goods, or by original action, whichever is appropriate.

Article 8
INVESTMENT SECURITIES

Part 1 Short Title and General Matters

§ 8—101. Short Title.

This Article shall be known and may be cited as Uniform Commercial Code—Investment Securities.

§ 8—102. Definitions and Index of Definitions.

(1) In this Article, unless the context otherwise requires:

(a) A "certificated security" is a share, participation, or other interest in property of or an enterprise of the issuer or an obligation of the issuer which is

   (i) represented by an instrument issued in bearer or registered form;

   (ii) of a type commonly dealt in on securities exchanges or markets or commonly recognized in any area in which it is issued or dealt in as a medium for investment; and

   (iii) either one of a class or series or by its terms divisible into a class or series of shares, participations, interests, or obligations.

(b) An "uncertificated security" is a share, participation, or other interest in property or an enterprise of the issuer or an obligation of the issuer which is

   (i) not represented by an instrument and the transfer of which is registered upon books maintained for that purpose by or on behalf of the issuer;

   (ii) of a type commonly dealt in on securities exchanges or markets; and

   (iii) either one of a class or series or by its terms divisible into a class or series of shares, participations, interests, or obligations.

(c) A "security" is either a certificated or an uncertificated security. If a security is certificated, the terms "security" and "certificated security" may mean either the intangible interest, the instrument representing that interest, or both, as the context requires. A writing that is a certificated security is governed by this Article and not by Article 3, even though it also meets the requirements of that Article. This Article does not apply to money. If a certificated security has been retained by or surrendered to the issuer or its transfer agent for reasons other than registration of transfer, other temporary purpose, payment, exchange, or acquisition by the issuer, that security shall be treated as an uncertificated security for purposes of this Article.

(d) A certificated security is in "registered form" if

   (i) it specifies a person entitled to the security or the rights it represents; and

   (ii) its transfer may be registered upon books maintained for that purpose by or on behalf of the issuer, or the security so states.

(e) A certificated security is in "bearer form" if it runs to bearer according to its terms and not by reason of any indorsement.

(2) A "subsequent purchaser" is a person who takes other than by original issue.

(3) A "clearing corporation" is a corporation registered as a "clearing agency" under the federal securities laws or a corporation:

(a) at least 90 percent of whose capital stock is held by or for one or more organizations, none of which, other than a national securities exchange or association, holds in excess of 20 percent of the capital stock of the corporation, and each of which is

   (i) subject to supervision or regulation pursuant to the provisions of federal or state banking laws or state insurance laws,

   (ii) a broker or dealer or investment company registered under the federal securities laws, or

   (iii) a national securities exchange or association registered under the federal securities laws; and

(b) any remaining capital stock of which is held by individuals who have purchased it at or prior to the time of their taking office as directors of the corporation and who have purchased only so much of the capital stock as is necessary to permit them to qualify as directors.

(4) A "custodian bank" is a bank or trust company that is supervised and examined by state or federal authority having supervision over banks and is acting as custodian for a clearing corporation.

(5) Other definitions applying to this Article or to specified Parts thereof and the sections in which they appear are:

"Adverse claim". Section 8—302.
"Bona fide purchaser". Section 8—302.
"Broker". Section 8—303.
"Debtor". Section 9—105.
"Financial intermediary". Section 8—313.
"Guarantee of the signature". Section 8—402.
"Initial transaction statement". Section 8—408.
"Instruction". Section 8—308.
"Intermediary bank". Section 4—105.
"Issuer". Section 8—201.
"Overissue". Section 8—104.
"Secured Party". Section 9—105.
"Security Agreement". Section 9—105.

(6) In addition, Article 1 contains general definitions and principles of construction and interpretation applicable throughout this Article.

Amended in 1962, 1973 and 1977.

§ 8—103. Issuer's Lien.

A lien upon a security in favor of an issuer thereof is valid against a purchaser only if:

(a) the security is certificated and the right of the issuer to the lien is noted conspicuously thereon; or

(b) the security is uncertificated and a notation of the right of the issuer to the lien is contained in the initial transaction statement sent to the purchaser or, if his interest is transferred to him other than by registration of transfer, pledge, or release, the initial transaction statement sent to the registered owner or the registered pledgee.

Amended in 1977.

§ 8—104. Effect of Overissue; "Overissue".

(1) The provisions of this Article which validate a se-

curity or compel its issue or reissue do not apply to the extent that validation, issue, or reissue would result in overissue; but if:

(a) an identical security which does not constitute an overissue is reasonably available for purchase, the person entitled to issue or validation may compel the issuer to purchase the security for him and either to deliver a certificated security or to register the transfer of an uncertificated security to him, against surrender of any certificated security he holds; or

(b) a security is not so available for purchase, the person entitled to issue or validation may recover from the issuer the price he or the last purchaser for value paid for it with interest from the date of his demand.

(2) "Overissue" means the issue of securities in excess of the amount the issuer has corporate power to issue.

Amended in 1977.

§ 8—105. Certificated Securities Negotiable; Statements and Instructions Not Negotiable; Presumptions.

(1) Certificated securities governed by this Article are negotiable instruments.

(2) Statements (Section 8—408), notices, or the like, sent by the issuer of uncertificated securities and instructions (Section 8—308) are neither negotiable instruments nor certificated securities.

(3) In any action on a security:

(a) unless specifically denied in the pleadings, each signature on a certificated security, in a necessary indorsement, on an initial transaction statement, or on an instruction, is admitted;

(b) if the effectiveness of a signature is put in issue, the burden of establishing it is on the party claiming under the signature, but the signature is presumed to be genuine or authorized;

(c) if signatures on a certificated security are admitted or established, production of the security entitles a holder to recover on it unless the defendant establishes a defense or a defect going to the validity of the security;

(d) if signatures on an initial transaction statement are admitted or established, the facts stated in the statement are presumed to be true as of the time of its issuance; and

(e) after it is shown that a defense or defect exists,

the plaintiff has the burden of establishing that he or some person under whom he claims is a person against whom the defense or defect is ineffective (Section 8—202).

Amended in 1977.

§ 8—106. **Applicability.**

The law (including the conflict of laws rules) of the jurisdiction of organization of the issuer governs the validity of a security, the effectiveness of registration by the issuer, and the rights and duties of the issuer with respect to:

(a) registration of transfer of a certificated security;

(b) registration of transfer, pledge, or release of an uncertificated security; and

(c) sending of statements of uncertificated securities.

Amended in 1977.

§ 8—107. **Securities Transferable; Action for Price.**

(1) Unless otherwise agreed and subject to any applicable law or regulation respecting short sales, a person obligated to transfer securities may transfer any certificated security of the specified issue in bearer form or registered in the name of the transferee, or indorsed to him or in blank, or he may transfer an equivalent uncertificated security to the transferee or a person designated by the transferee.

(2) If the buyer fails to pay the price as it comes due under a contract of sale, the seller may recover the price of:

(a) certificated securities accepted by the buyer;

(b) uncertificated securities that have been transferred to the buyer or a person designated by the buyer; and

(c) other securities if efforts at their resale would be unduly burdensome or if there is no readily available market for their resale.

Amended in 1977.

§ 8—108. **Registration of Pledge and Release of Uncertificated Securities.**

A security interest in an uncertificated security may be evidenced by the registration of pledge to the secured party or a person designated by him. There can be no more than one registered pledge of an uncertificated security at any time. The registered owner of an uncertificated security is the person in whose name the security is registered, even if the security is subject

to a registered pledge. The rights of a registered pledgee of an uncertificated security under this Article are terminated by the registration of release.

Added in 1977.

Part 2 **Issue—Issuer**

§ 8—201. **"Issuer"**

(1) With respect to obligations on or defenses to a security, "issuer" includes a person who:

(a) places or authorizes the placing of his name on a certificated security (otherwise than as authenticating trustee, registrar, transfer agent, or the like) to evidence that it represents a share, participation, or other interest in his property or in an enterprise, or to evidence his duty to perform an obligation represented by the certificated security;

(b) creates shares, participations, or other interests in his property or in an enterprise or undertakes obligations, which shares, participations, interests, or obligations are uncertificated securities;

(c) directly or indirectly creates fractional interests in his rights or property, which fractional interests are represented by certificated securities; or

(d) becomes responsible for or in place of any other person described as an issuer in this section.

(2) With respect to obligations on or defenses to a security, a guarantor is an issuer to the extent of his guaranty, whether or not his obligation is noted on a certificated security or on statements of uncertificated securities sent pursuant to Section 8—408.

(3) With respect to registration of transfer, pledge, or release (Part 4 of this Article), "issuer" means a person on whose behalf transfer books are maintained.

Amended in 1977.

§ 8—202. **Issuer's Responsibility and Defenses; Notice of Defect or Defense.**

(1) Even against a purchaser for value and without notice, the terms of a security include:

(a) if the security is certificated, those stated on the security;

(b) if the security is uncertificated, those contained in the initial transaction statement sent to such purchaser or, if his interest is transferred to him other than by registration of transfer, pledge, or release, the initial transaction statement sent to the registered owner or registered pledgee; and

(c) those made part of the security by reference, on the certificated security or in the initial transaction statement, to another instrument, indenture, or document or to a constitution, statute, ordinance, rule, regulation, order or the like, to the extent that the terms referred to do not conflict with the terms stated on the certificated security or contained in the statement. A reference under this paragraph does not of itself charge a purchaser for value with notice of a defect going to the validity of the security, even though the certificated security or statement expressly states that a person accepting it admits notice.

(2) A certificated security in the hands of a purchaser for value or an uncertificated security as to which an initial transaction statement has been sent to a purchaser for value, other than a security issued by a government or governmental agency or unit, even though issued with a defect going to its validity, is valid with respect to the purchaser if he is without notice of the particular defect unless the defect involves a violation of constitutional provisions, in which case the security is valid with respect to a subsequent purchaser for value and without notice of the defect. This subsection applies to an issuer that is a government or governmental agency or unit only if either there has been substantial compliance with the legal requirements governing the issue or the issuer has received a substantial consideration for the issue as a whole or for the particular security and a stated purpose of the issue is one for which the issuer has power to borrow money or issue the security.

(3) Except as provided in the case of certain unauthorized signatures (Section 8—205), lack of genuineness of a certificated security or an initial transaction statement is a complete defense, even against a purchaser for value and without notice.

(4) All other defenses of the issuer of a certificated or uncertificated security, including nondelivery and conditional delivery of a certificated security, are ineffective against a purchaser for value who has taken without notice of the particular defense.

(5) Nothing in this section shall be construed to affect the right of a party to a "when, as and if issued" or a "when distributed" contract to cancel the contract in the event of a material change in the character of the security that is the subject of the contract or in the plan or arrangement pursuant to which the security is to be issued or distributed.

Amended in 1977.

§ 8—203. **Staleness as Notice of Defects or Defenses.**

(1) After an act or event creating a right to immediate performance of the principal obligation represented by a certificated security or that sets a date on or after which the security is to be presented or surrendered for redemption or exchange, a purchaser is charged with notice of any defect in its issue or defense of the issuer if:

(a) the act or event is one requiring the payment of money, the delivery of certificated securities, the registration of transfer of uncertificated securities, or any of these on presentation or surrender of the certificated security, the funds or securities are available on the date set for payment or exchange, and he takes the security more than one year after that date; and

(b) the act or event is not covered by paragraph (a) and he takes the security more than 2 years after the date set for surrender or presentation or the date on which performance became due.

(2) A call that has been revoked is not within subsection (1).

Amended in 1977.

§ 8—204. **Effect of Issuer's Restrictions on Transfer.**

A restriction on transfer of a security imposed by the issuer, even if otherwise lawful, is ineffective against any person without actual knowledge of it unless:

(a) the security is certificated and the restriction is noted conspicuously thereon; or

(b) the security is uncertificated and a notation of the restriction is contained in the initial transaction statement sent to the person or, if his interest is transferred to him other than by registration of transfer, pledge, or release, the initial transaction statement sent to the registered owner or the registered pledgee.

Amended in 1977.

§ 8—205. **Effect of Unauthorized Signature on Certificated Security or Initial Transaction Statement.**

An unauthorized signature placed on a certificated security prior to or in the course of issue or placed on an initial transaction statement is ineffective, but the signature is effective in favor of a purchaser for value of the certificated security or a purchaser for value of an uncertificated security to whom the initial transaction statement has been sent, if the purchaser is without notice of the lack of authority and the signing has been done by:

(a) an authenticating trustee, registrar, transfer agent, or other person entrusted by the issuer with the signing of the security, of similar securities, or of initial transaction statements or the immediate preparation for signing of any of them; or

(b) an employee of the issuer, or of any of the foregoing, entrusted with responsible handling of the security or initial transaction statement.

Amended in 1977.

§ 8—206. Completion or Alteration of Certificated Security or Initial Transaction Statement.

(1) If a certificated security contains the signatures necessary to its issue or transfer but is incomplete in any other respect:

    (a) any person may complete it by filling in the blanks as authorized; and

    (b) even though the blanks are incorrectly filled in, the security as completed is enforceable by a purchaser who took it for value and without notice of the incorrectness.

(2) A complete certificated security that has been improperly altered, even though fraudulently, remains enforceable, but only according to its original terms.

(3) If an initial transaction statement contains the signatures necessary to its validity, but is incomplete in any other respect:

    (a) any person may complete it by filling in the blanks as authorized; and

    (b) even though the blanks are incorrectly filled in, the statement as completed is effective in favor of the person to whom it is sent if he purchased the security referred to therein for value and without notice of the incorrectness.

(4) A complete initial transaction statement that has been improperly altered, even though fraudulently, is effective in favor of a purchaser to whom it has been sent, but only according to its original terms.

Amended in 1977.

§ 8—207. Rights and Duties of Issuer With Respect to Registered Owners and Registered Pledgees.

(1) Prior to due presentment for registration of trans-

fer of a certificated security in registered form, the issuer or indenture trustee may treat the registered owner as the person exclusively entitled to vote, to receive notifications, and otherwise to exercise all the rights and powers of an owner.

(2) Subject to the provisions of subsections (3), (4), and (6), the issuer or indenture trustee may treat the registered owner of an uncertificated security as the person exclusively entitled to vote, to receive notifications, and otherwise to exercise all the rights and powers of an owner.

(3) The registered owner of an uncertificated security that is subject to a registered pledge is not entitled to registration of transfer prior to the due presentment to the issuer of a release instruction. The exercise of conversion rights with respect to a convertible uncertificated security is a transfer within the meaning of this section.

(4) Upon due presentment of a transfer instruction from the registered pledgee of an uncertificated security, the issuer shall:

    (a) register the transfer of the security to the new owner free of pledge, if the instruction specifies a new owner (who may be the registered pledgee) and does not specify a pledgee;

    (b) register the transfer of the security to the new owner subject to the interest of the existing pledgee, if the instruction specifies a new owner and the existing pledgee; or

    (c) register the release of the security from the existing pledge and register the pledge of the security to the other pledgee, if the instruction specifies the existing owner and another pledgee.

(5) Continuity of perfection of a security interest is not broken by registration of transfer under subsection (4)(b) or by registration of release and pledge under subsection (4)(c), if the security interest is assigned.

(6) If an uncertificated security is subject to a registered pledge:

    (a) any uncertificated securities issued in exchange for or distributed with respect to the pledged security shall be registered subject to the pledge;

    (b) any certificated securities issued in exchange for or distributed with respect to the pledged security shall be delivered to the registered pledgee; and

    (c) any money paid in exchange for or in redemption of part or all of the security shall be paid to the registered pledgee.

(7) Nothing in this Article shall be construed to affect the liability of the registered owner of a security for calls, assessments, or the like.

Amended in 1977.

§ 8—208. Effect of Signature of Authenticating Trustee, Registrar, or Transfer Agent.

(1) A person placing his signature upon a certificated security or an initial transaction statement as authenticating trustee, registrar, transfer agent, or the like, warrants to a purchaser for value of the certificated security or a purchaser for value of an uncertificated security to whom the initial transaction statement has been sent, if the purchaser is without notice of the particular defect, that:

(a) the certificated security or initial transaction statement is genuine;

(b) his own participation in the issue or registration of the transfer, pledge, or release of the security is within his capacity and within the scope of the authority received by him from the issuer; and

(c) he has reasonable grounds to believe the security is in the form and within the amount the issuer is authorized to issue.

(2) Unless otherwise agreed, a person by so placing his signature does not assume responsibility for the validity of the security in other respects.

Amended in 1962 and 1977.

Part 3 Transfer

§ 8—301. Rights Acquired by Purchaser.

(1) Upon transfer of a security to a purchaser (Section 8—313), the purchaser acquires the rights in the security which his transferor had or had actual authority to convey unless the purchaser's rights are limited by Section 8—302(4).

(2) A transferee of a limited interest acquires rights only to the extent of the interest transferred. The creation or release of a security interest in a security is the transfer of a limited interest in that security.

Amended in 1977.

§ 8—302. "Bona Fide Purchaser"; "Adverse Claim"; Title Acquired by Bona Fide Purchaser.

(1) A "bona fide purchaser" is a purchaser for value in good faith and without notice of any adverse claim:

(a) who takes delivery of a certificated security in bearer form or in registered form, issued or indorsed to him or in blank;

(b) to whom the transfer, pledge, or release of an uncertificated security is registered on the books of the issuer; or

(c) to whom a security is transferred under the provisions of paragraph (c), (d)(i), or (g) of Section 8—313(1).

(2) "Adverse claim" includes a claim that a transfer was or would be wrongful or that a particular adverse person is the owner of or has an interest in the security.

(3) A bona fide purchaser in addition to acquiring the rights of a purchaser (Section 8—301) also acquires his interest in the security free of any adverse claim.

(4) Notwithstanding Section 8—301(1), the transferee of a particular certificated security who has been a party to any fraud or illegality affecting the security, or who as a prior holder of that certificated security had notice of an adverse claim, cannot improve his position by taking from a bona fide purchaser.

Amended in 1977.

§ 8—303. "Broker".

"Broker" means a person engaged for all or part of his time in the business of buying and selling securities, who in the transaction concerned acts for, buys a security from, or sells a security to, a customer. Nothing in this Article determines the capacity in which a person acts for purposes of any other statute or rule to which the person is subject.

§ 8—304. Notice to Purchaser of Adverse Claims.

(1) A purchaser (including a broker for the seller or buyer, but excluding an intermediary bank) of a certificated security is charged with notice of adverse claims if:

(a) the security, whether in bearer or registered form, has been indorsed "for collection" or "for surrender" or for some other purpose not involving transfer; or

(b) the security is in bearer form and has on it an unambiguous statement that it is the property of a person other than the transferor. The mere writing of a name on a security is not such a statement.

(2) A purchaser (including a broker for the seller or buyer, but excluding an intermediary bank) to whom the transfer, pledge, or release of an uncertificated security is registered is charged with notice of adverse claims as to which the issuer has a duty under Section 8—403(4) at the time of registration and which are noted in the initial transaction statement sent to the purchaser or, if his interest is transferred to him other than by registration of transfer, pledge, or release, the initial transaction statement sent to the registered owner or the registered pledgee.

(3) The fact that the purchaser (including a broker for the seller or buyer) of a certificated or uncertificated security has notice that the security is held for a third person or is registered in the name of or indorsed by a fiduciary does not create a duty of inquiry into the rightfulness of the transfer or constitute constructive notice of adverse claims. However, if the purchaser (excluding an intermediary bank) has knowledge that the proceeds are being used or the transaction is for the individual benefit of the fiduciary or otherwise in breach of duty, the purchaser is charged with notice of adverse claims.

Amended in 1977.

§ 8—305. Staleness as Notice of Adverse Claims.

An act or event that creates a right to immediate performance of the principal obligation represented by a certificated security or sets a date on or after which a certificated security is to be presented or surrendered for redemption or exchange does not itself constitute any notice of adverse claims except in the case of a transfer:

(a) after one year from any date set for presentment or surrender for redemption or exchange; or

(b) after 6 months from any date set for payment of money against presentation or surrender of the security if funds are available for payment on that date.

Amended in 1977.

§ 8—306. Warranties on Presentment and Transfer of Certificated Securities; Warranties of Originators of Instructions.

(1) A person who presents a certificated security for registration of transfer or for payment or exchange warrants to the issuer that he is entitled to the registration, payment, or exchange. But, a purchaser for value and without notice of adverse claims who receives a new, reissued, or re-registered certificated security on registration of transfer or receives an initial transaction statement confirming the registration of transfer of an equivalent uncertificated security to him warrants only that he has no knowledge of any unauthorized signature (Section 8—311) in a necessary indorsement.

(2) A person by transferring a certificated security to a purchaser for value warrants only that:

(a) his transfer is effective and rightful;

(b) the security is genuine and has not been materially altered; and

(c) he knows of no fact which might impair the validity of the security.

(3) If a certificated security is delivered by an intermediary known to be entrusted with delivery of the security on behalf of another or with collection of a draft or other claim against delivery, the intermediary by delivery warrants only his own good faith and authority, even though he has purchased or made advances against the claim to be collected against the delivery.

(4) A pledgee or other holder for security who redelivers a certificated security received, or after payment and on order of the debtor delivers that security to a third person, makes only the warranties of an intermediary under subsection (3).

(5) A person who originates an instruction warrants to the issuer that:

(a) he is an appropriate person to originate the instruction; and

(b) at the time the instruction is presented to the issuer he will be entitled to the registration of transfer, pledge, or release.

(6) A person who originates an instruction warrants to any person specially guaranteeing his signature (subsection 8—312(3)) that:

(a) he is an appropriate person to originate the instruction; and

(b) at the time the instruction is presented to the issuer

(i) he will be entitled to the registration of transfer, pledge, or release; and

(ii) the transfer, pledge, or release requested in the instruction will be registered by the issuer free from all liens, security interests, restrictions, and claims other than those specified in the instruction.

(7) A person who originates an instruction warrants to a purchaser for value and to any person guaranteeing the instruction (Section 8—312(6)) that:

(a) he is an appropriate person to originate the instruction;

(b) the uncertificated security referred to therein is valid; and

(c) at the time the instruction is presented to the issuer

(i) the transferor will be entitled to the registration of transfer, pledge, or release;

(ii) the transfer, pledge, or release requested in the instruction will be registered by the issuer free from all liens, security interests, restrictions, and claims other than those specified in the instruction; and

(iii) the requested transfer, pledge, or release will be rightful.

(8) If a secured party is the registered pledgee or the registered owner of an uncertificated security, a person who originates an instruction of release or transfer to the debtor or, after payment and on order of the debtor, a transfer instruction to a third person, warrants to the debtor or the third person only that he is an appropriate person to originate the instruction and, at the time the instruction is presented to the issuer, the transferor will be entitled to the registration of release or transfer. If a transfer instruction to a third person who is a purchaser for value is originated on order of the debtor, the debtor makes to the purchaser the warranties of paragraphs (b), (c)(ii) and (c)(iii) of subsection (7).

(9) A person who transfers an uncertificated security to a purchaser for value and does not originate an instruction in connection with the transfer warrants only that:

(a) his transfer is effective and rightful; and

(b) the uncertificated security is valid.

(10) A broker gives to his customer and to the issuer and a purchaser the applicable warranties provided in this section and has the rights and privileges of a purchaser under this section. The warranties of and in favor of the broker, acting as an agent are in addition to applicable warranties given by and in favor of his customer.

Amended in 1962 and 1977.

§ 8—307. **Effect of Delivery Without Indorsement; Right to Compel Indorsement.**

If a certificated security in registered form has been delivered to a purchaser without a necessary indorsement he may become a bona fide purchaser only as of the time the indorsement is supplied; but against the transferor, the transfer is complete upon delivery and the purchaser has a specifically enforceable right to have any necessary indorsement supplied.

Amended in 1977.

§ 8—308. **Indorsements; Instructions.**

(1) An indorsement of a certificated security in registered form is made when an appropriate person signs on it or on a separate document an assignment or transfer of the security or a power to assign or transfer it or his signature is written without more upon the back of the security.

(2) An indorsement may be in blank or special. An indorsement in blank includes an indorsement to bearer. A special indorsement specifies to whom the security is to be transferred, or who has power to transfer it. A holder may convert a blank indorsement into a special indorsement.

(3) An indorsement purporting to be only of part of a certificated security representing units intended by the issuer to be separately transferable is effective to the extent of the indorsement.

(4) An "instruction" is an order to the issuer of an uncertificated security requesting that the transfer, pledge, or release from pledge of the uncertificated security specified therein be registered.

(5) An instruction originated by an appropriate person is:

(a) a writing signed by an appropriate person; or

(b) a communication to the issuer in any form agreed upon in a writing signed by the issuer and an appropriate person.

If an instruction has been originated by an appropriate person but is incomplete in any other respect, any person may complete it as authorized and the issuer may rely on it as completed even though it has been completed incorrectly.

(6) "An appropriate person" in subsection (1) means the person specified by the certificated security or by special indorsement to be entitled to the security.

(7) "An appropriate person" in subsection (5) means:

(a) for an instruction to transfer or pledge an uncertificated security which is then not subject to a registered pledge, the registered owner; or

(b) for an instruction to transfer or release an uncertificated security which is then subject to a registered pledge, the registered pledgee.

(8) In addition to the persons designated in subsections (6) and (7), "an appropriate person" in subsections (1) and (5) includes:

(a) if the person designated is described as a fiduciary but is no longer serving in the described capacity, either that person or his successor;

(b) if the persons designated are described as more than one person as fiduciaries and one or more are no longer serving in the described capacity, the remaining fiduciary or fiduciaries, whether or not a successor has been appointed or qualified;

(c) if the person designated is an individual and is without capacity to act by virtue of death, incompetence, infancy, or otherwise, his executor, administrator, guardian, or like fiduciary;

(d) if the persons designated are described as more than one person as tenants by the entirety or with right of survivorship and by reason of death all cannot sign, the survivor or survivors;

(e) a person having power to sign under applicable law or controlling instrument; and

(f) to the extent that the person designated or any of the foregoing persons may act through an agent, his authorized agent.

(9) Unless otherwise agreed, the indorser of a certificated security by his indorsement or the originator of an instruction by his origination assumes no obligation that the security will be honored by the issuer but only the obligations provided in Section 8—306.

(10) Whether the person signing is appropriate is determined as of the date of signing and an indorsement made by or an instruction originated by him does not become unauthorized for the purposes of this Article by virtue of any subsequent change of circumstances.

(11) Failure of a fiduciary to comply with a controlling instrument or with the law of the state having jurisdiction of the fiduciary relationship, including any law requiring the fiduciary to obtain court approval of the transfer, pledge, or release, does not render his indorsement or an instruction originated by him unauthorized for the purposes of this Article.

Amended in 1962 and 1977.

§ 8—309. **Effect of Indorsement Without Delivery.**

An indorsement of a certificated security, whether special or in blank, does not constitute a transfer until delivery of the certificated security on which it appears or, if the indorsement is on a separate document, until delivery of both the document and the certificated security.

Amended in 1977.

§ 8—310. **Indorsement of Certificated Security in Bearer Form.**

An indorsement of a certificated security in bearer form may give notice of adverse claims (Section 8—304) but does not otherwise affect any right to registration the holder possesses.

Amended in 1977.

§ 8—311. **Effect of Unauthorized Indorsement or Instruction.**

Unless the owner or pledgee has ratified an unauthorized indorsement or instruction or is otherwise precluded from asserting its ineffectiveness:

(a) he may assert its ineffectiveness against the issuer or any purchaser, other than a purchaser for value and without notice of adverse claims, who has in good faith received a new, reissued, or re-registered certificated security on registration of transfer or received an initial transaction statement confirming the registration of transfer, pledge, or release of an equivalent uncertificated security to him; and

(b) an issuer who registers the transfer of a certificated security upon the unauthorized indorsement or who registers the transfer, pledge, or release of an uncertificated security upon the unauthorized instruction is subject to liability for improper registration (Section 8—404).

Amended in 1977.

§ 8—312. **Effect of Guaranteeing Signature, Indorsement or Instruction.**

(1) Any person guaranteeing a signature of an indorser of a certificated security warrants that at the time of signing:

(a) the signature was genuine;

(b) the signer was an appropriate person to indorse (Section 8—308); and

(c) the signer had legal capacity to sign.

(2) Any person guaranteeing a signature of the originator of an instruction warrants that at the time of signing:

(a) the signature was genuine;

(b) the signer was an appropriate person to originate the instruction (Section 8—308) if the person specified in the instruction as the registered owner or registered pledgee of the uncertificated security was, in fact, the registered owner or registered pledgee of the security, as to which fact the signature guarantor makes no warranty;

(c) the signer had legal capacity to sign; and

(d) the taxpayer identification number, if any, appearing on the instruction as that of the registered owner or registered pledgee was the taxpayer identification number of the signer or of the owner or pledgee for whom the signer was acting.

(3) Any person specially guaranteeing the signature of the originator of an instruction makes not only the warranties of a signature guarantor (subsection (2)) but also warrants that at the time the instruction is presented to the issuer:

(a) the person specified in the instruction as the registered owner or registered pledgee of the uncertificated security will be the registered owner or registered pledgee; and

(b) the transfer, pledge, or release of the uncertificated security requested in the instruction will be registered by the issuer free from all liens, security interests, restrictions, and claims other than those specified in the instruction.

(4) The guarantor under subsections (1) and (2) or the special guarantor under subsection (3) does not otherwise warrant the rightfulness of the particular transfer, pledge, or release.

(5) Any person guaranteeing an indorsement of a certificated security makes not only the warranties of a signature guarantor under subsection (1) but also warrants the rightfulness of the particular transfer in all respects.

(6) Any person guaranteeing an instruction requesting the transfer, pledge, or release of an uncertificated security makes not only the warranties of a special signature guarantor under subsection (3) but also warrants the rightfulness of the particular transfer, pledge, or release in all respects.

(7) No issuer may require a special guarantee of signature (subsection (3)), a guarantee of indorsement

(subsection (5)), or a guarantee of instruction (subsection (6)) as a condition to registration of transfer, pledge, or release.

(8) The foregoing warranties are made to any person taking or dealing with the security in reliance on the guarantee, and the guarantor is liable to the person for any loss resulting from breach of the warranties.

Amended in 1977.

§ 8—313. **When Transfer to Purchaser Occurs; Financial Intermediary as Bona Fide Purchaser; "Financial Intermediary".**

(1) Transfer of a security or a limited interest (including a security interest) therein to a purchaser occurs only:

(a) at the time he or a person designated by him acquires possession of a certificated security;

(b) at the time the transfer, pledge, or release of an uncertificated security is registered to him or a person designated by him;

(c) at the time his financial intermediary acquires possession of a certificated security specially indorsed to or issued in the name of the purchaser;

(d) at the time a financial intermediary, not a clearing corporation, sends him confirmation of the purchase and also by book entry or otherwise identifies as belonging to the purchaser

(i) a specific certificated security in the financial intermediary's possession;

(ii) a quantity of securities that constitute or are part of a fungible bulk of certificated securities in the financial intermediary's possession or of uncertificated securities registered in the name of the financial intermediary; or

(iii) a quantity of securities that constitute or are part of a fungible bulk of securities shown on the account of the financial intermediary on the books of another financial intermediary;

(e) with respect to an identified certificated security to be delivered while still in the possession of a third person, not a financial intermediary, at the time that person acknowledges that he holds for the purchaser;

(f) with respect to a specific uncertificated security the pledge or transfer of which has been registered to a third person, not a financial intermediary, at the time that person acknowledges that he holds for the purchaser;

(g) at the time appropriate entries to the account of the purchaser or a person designated by him on the books of a clearing corporation are made under Section 8—320;

(h) with respect to the transfer of a security interest where the debtor has signed a security agreement containing a description of the security, at the time a written notification, which, in the case of the creation of the security interest, is signed by the debtor (which may be a copy of the security agreement) or which, in the case of the release or assignment of the security interest created pursuant to this paragraph, is signed by the secured party, is received by

   (i) a financial intermediary on whose books the interest of the transferor in the security appears;

   (ii) a third person, not a financial intermediary, in possession of the security, if it is certificated;

   (iii) a third person, not a financial intermediary, who is the registered owner of the security, if it is uncertificated and not subject to a registered pledge; or

   (iv) a third person, not a financial intermediary, who is the registered pledgee of the security, if it is uncertificated and subject to a registered pledge;

(i) with respect to the transfer of a security interest where the transferor has signed a security agreement containing a description of the security, at the time new value is given by the secured party; or

(j) with respect to the transfer of a security interest where the secured party is a financial intermediary and the security has already been transferred to the financial intermediary under paragraphs (a), (b), (c), (d), or (g), at the time the transferor has signed a security agreement containing a description of the security and value is given by the secured party.

(2) The purchaser is the owner of a security held for him by a financial intermediary, but cannot be a bona fide purchaser of a security so held except in the circumstances specified in paragraphs (c), (d)(i), and (g) of subsection (1). If a security so held is part of a fungible bulk, as in the circumstances specified in paragraphs (d)(ii) and (d)(iii) of subsection (1), the purchaser is the owner of a proportionate property interest in the fungible bulk.

(3) Notice of an adverse claim received by the financial intermediary or by the purchaser after the financial intermediary takes delivery of a certificated security as a holder for value or after the transfer, pledge, or release of an uncertificated security has been registered free of the claim to a financial intermediary who has given value is not effective either as to the financial intermediary or as to the purchaser. However, as between the financial intermediary and the purchaser the purchaser may demand transfer of an equivalent security as to which no notice of adverse claim has been received.

(4) A "financial intermediary" is a bank, broker, clearing corporation, or other person (or the nominee of any of them) which in the ordinary course of its business maintains security accounts for its customers and is acting in that capacity. A financial intermediary may have a security interest in securities held in account for its customer.

Amended in 1962 and 1977.

§ 8—314. Duty to Transfer, When Completed

(1) Unless otherwise agreed, if a sale of a security is made on an exchange or otherwise through brokers:

   (a) the selling customer fulfills his duty to transfer at the time he:

      (i) places a certificated security in the possession of the selling broker or a person designated by the broker;

      (ii) causes an uncertificated security to be registered in the name of the selling broker or a person designated by the broker;

      (iii) if requested, causes an acknowledgment to be made to the selling broker that a certificated or uncertificated security is held for the broker; or

      (iv) places in the possession of the selling broker or of a person designated by the broker a transfer instruction for an uncertificated security, providing the issuer does not refuse to register the requested transfer if the instruction is presented to the issuer for registration within 30 days thereafter; and

   (b) the selling broker, including a correspondent broker acting for a selling customer, fulfills his duty to transfer at the time he:

      (i) places a certificated security in the possession of the buying broker or a person designated by the buying broker;

(ii) causes an uncertificated security to be registered in the name of the buying broker or a person designated by the buying broker;

(iii) places in the possession of the buying broker or of a person designated by the buying broker a transfer instruction for an uncertificated security, providing the issuer does not refuse to register the requested transfer if the instruction is presented to the issuer for registration within 30 days thereafter; or

(iv) effects clearance of the sale in accordance with the rules of the exchange on which the transaction took place.

(2) Except as provided in this section or unless otherwise agreed, a transferor's duty to transfer a security under a contract of purchase is not fulfilled until he:

(a) places a certificated security in form to be negotiated by the purchaser in the possession of the purchaser or of a person designated by the purchaser;

(b) causes an uncertificated security to be registered in the name of the purchaser or a person designated by the purchaser; or

(c) if the purchaser requests, causes an acknowledgment to be made to the purchaser that a certificated or uncertificated security is held for the purchaser.

(3) Unless made on an exchange, a sale to a broker purchasing for his own account is within subsection (2) and not within subsection (1).

Amended in 1977.

§ 8—315. **Action Against Transferee Based Upon Wrongful Transfer**

(1) Any person against whom the transfer of a security is wrongful for any reason, including his incapacity, as against anyone except a bona fide purchaser, may:

(a) reclaim possession of the certificated security wrongfully transferred;

(b) obtain possession of any new certificated security representing all or part of the same rights;

(c) compel the origination of an instruction to transfer to him or a person designated by him an uncertificated security constituting all or part of the same rights; or

(d) have damages.

(2) If the transfer is wrongful because of an unauthorized indorsement of a certificated security, the owner may also reclaim or obtain possession of the security or a new certificated security, even from a bona fide purchaser, if the ineffectiveness of the purported indorsement can be asserted against him under the provisions of this Article on unauthorized indorsements (Section 8—311).

(3) The right to obtain or reclaim possession of a certificated security or to compel the origination of a transfer instruction may be specifically enforced and the transfer of a certificated or uncertificated security enjoined and a certificated security impounded pending the litigation.

Amended in 1977.

§ 8—316. **Purchaser's Right to Requisites for Registration of Transfer, Pledge, or Release on Books**

Unless otherwise agreed, the transferor of a certificated security or the transferor, pledgor, or pledgee of an uncertificated security on due demand must supply his purchaser with any proof of his authority to transfer, pledge, or release or with any other requisite necessary to obtain registration of the transfer, pledge, or release of the security; but if the transfer, pledge, or release is not for value, a transferor, pledgor, or pledgee need not do so unless the purchaser furnishes the necessary expenses. Failure within a reasonable time to comply with a demand made gives the purchaser the right to reject or rescind the transfer, pledge, or release.

Amended in 1977.

§ 8—317. **Creditors' Rights**

(1) Subject to the exceptions in subsections (3) and (4), no attachment or levy upon a certificated security or any share or other interest represented thereby which is outstanding is valid until the security is actually seized by the officer making the attachment or levy, but a certificated security which has been surrendered to the issuer may be reached by a creditor by legal process at the issuer's chief executive office in the United States.

(2) An uncertificated security registered in the name of the debtor may not be reached by a creditor except by legal process at the issuer's chief executive office in the United States.

(3) The interest of a debtor in a certificated security

that is in the possession of a secured party not a financial intermediary or in an uncertificated security registered in the name of a secured party not a financial intermediary (or in the name of a nominee of the secured party) may be reached by a creditor by legal process upon the secured party.

(4) The interest of a debtor in a certificated security that is in the possession of or registered in the name of a financial intermediary or in an uncertificated security registered in the name of a financial intermediary may be reached by a creditor by legal process upon the financial intermediary on whose books the interest of the debtor appears.

(5) Unless otherwise provided by law, a creditor's lien upon the interest of a debtor in a security obtained pursuant to subsection (3) or (4) is not a restraint on the transfer of the security, free of the lien, to a third party for new value; but in the event of a transfer, the lien applies to the proceeds of the transfer in the hands of the secured party or financial intermediary, subject to any claims having priority.

(6) A creditor whose debtor is the owner of a security is entitled to aid from courts of appropriate jurisdiction, by injunction or otherwise, in reaching the security or in satisfying the claim by means allowed at law or in equity in regard to property that cannot readily be reached by ordinary legal process.

Amended in 1977.

§ 8—318. No Conversion by Good Faith Conduct

An agent or bailee who in good faith (including observance of reasonable commercial standards if he is in the business of buying, selling, or otherwise dealing with securities) has received certificated securities and sold, pledged, or delivered them or has sold or caused the transfer or pledge of uncertificated securities over which he had control according to the instructions of his principal, is not liable for conversion or for participation in breach of fiduciary duty although the principal had no right so to deal with the securities.

Amended in 1977.

§ 8—319. Statute of Frauds

A contract for the sale of securities is not enforceable by way of action or defense unless:

(a) there is some writing signed by the party against whom enforcement is sought or by his authorized agent or broker, sufficient to indicate that a contract has been made for sale of a stated quantity of described securities at a defined or stated price;

(b) delivery of a certificated security or transfer instruction has been accepted, or transfer of an uncertificated security has been registered and the transferee has failed to send written objection to the issuer within 10 days after receipt of the initial transaction statement confirming the registration, or payment has been made, but the contract is enforceable under this provision only to the extent of the delivery, registration, or payment;

(c) within a reasonable time a writing in confirmation of the sale or purchase and sufficient against the sender under paragraph (a) has been received by the party against whom enforcement is sought and he has failed to send written objection to its contents within 10 days after its receipt; or

(d) the party against whom enforcement is sought admits in his pleading, testimony, or otherwise in court that a contract was made for the sale of a stated quantity of described securities at a defined or stated price.

Amended in 1977.

§ 8—320. Transfer or Pledge Within Central Depository System

(1) In addition to other methods, a transfer, pledge, or release of a security or any interest therein may be effected by the making of appropriate entries on the books of a clearing corporation reducing the account of the transferor, pledgor, or pledgee and increasing the account of the transferee, pledgee, or pledgor by the amount of the obligation or the number of shares or rights transferred, pledged, or released, if the security is shown on the account of a transferor, pledgor, or pledgee on the books of the clearing corporation; is subject to the control of the clearing corporation; and

  (a) if certificated,

    (i) is in the custody of the clearing corporation, another clearing corporation, a custodian bank, or a nominee of any of them; and

    (ii) is in bearer form or indorsed in blank by an appropriate person or registered in the name of the clearing corporation, a custodian bank, or a nominee of any of them; or

  (b) if uncertificated, is registered in the name of the clearing corporation, another clearing corporation, a custodian bank, or a nominee of any of them.

(2) Under this section entries may be made with respect to like securities or interests therein as a part

of a fungible bulk and may refer merely to a quantity of a particular security without reference to the name of the registered owner, certificate or bond number, or the like, and, in appropriate cases, may be on a net basis taking into account other transfers, pledges, or releases of the same security.

(3) A transfer under this section is effective (Section 8—313) and the purchaser acquires the rights of the transferor (Section 8—301). A pledge or release under this section is the transfer of a limited interest. If a pledge or the creation of a security interest is intended, the security interest is perfected at the time when both value is given by the pledgee and the appropriate entries are made (Section 8—321). A transferee or pledgee under this section may be a bona fide purchaser (Section 8—302).

(4) A transfer or pledge under this section is not a registration of transfer under Part 4.

(5) That entries made on the books of the clearing corporation as provided in subsection (1) are not appropriate does not affect the validity or effect of the entries or the liabilities or obligations of the clearing corporation to any person adversely affected thereby.

Added in 1962; amended in 1977.

§ 8—321. Enforceability, Attachment, Perfection and Termination of Security Interests

(1) A security interest in a security is enforceable and can attach only if it is transferred to the secured party or a person designated by him pursuant to a provision of Section 8—313(1).

(2) A security interest so transferred pursuant to agreement by a transferor who has rights in the security to a transferee who has given value is a perfected security interest, but a security interest that has been transferred solely under paragraph (i) of Section 8—313(1) becomes unperfected after 21 days unless, within that time, the requirements for transfer under any other provision of Section 8—313(1) are satisfied.

(3) A security interest in a security is subject to the provisions of Article 9, but:

(a) no filing is required to perfect the security interest; and

(b) no written security agreement signed by the debtor is necessary to make the security interest enforceable, except as provided in paragraph (h), (i), or (j) of Section 8—313(1). The secured party

has the rights and duties provided under Section 9—207, to the extent they are applicable, whether or not the security is certificated, and, if certificated, whether or not it is in his possession.

(4) Unless otherwise agreed, a security interest in a security is terminated by transfer to the debtor or a person designated by him pursuant to a provision of Section 8—313(1). If a security is thus transferred, the security interest, if not terminated, becomes unperfected unless the security is certificated and is delivered to the debtor for the purpose of ultimate sale or exchange or presentation, collection, renewal, or registration of transfer. In that case, the security interest becomes unperfected after 21 days unless, within that time, the security (or securities for which it has been exchanged) is transferred to the secured party or a person designated by him pursuant to a provision of Section 8—313(1).

Added in 1977.

Part 4 Registration

§ 8—401. Duty of Issuer to Register Transfer, Pledge, or Release

(1) If a certificated security in registered form is presented to the issuer with a request to register transfer or an instruction is presented to the issuer with a request to register transfer, pledge, or release, the issuer shall register the transfer, pledge, or release as requested if:

(a) the security is indorsed or the instruction was originated by the appropriate person or persons (Section 8—308);

(b) reasonable assurance is given that those indorsements or instructions are genuine and effective (Section 8—402);

(c) the issuer has no duty as to adverse claims or has discharged the duty (Section 8—403);

(d) any applicable law relating to the collection of taxes has been complied with; and

(e) the transfer, pledge, or release is in fact rightful or is to a bona fide purchaser.

(2) If an issuer is under a duty to register a transfer, pledge, or release of a security, the issuer is also liable to the person presenting a certificated security or an instruction for registration or his principal for loss resulting from any unreasonable delay in registration or from failure or refusal to register the transfer, pledge, or release.

Amended in 1977.

§ 8—402. Assurance that Indorsements and Instructions Are Effective

(1) The issuer may require the following assurance that each necessary indorsement of a certificated security or each instruction (Section 8—308) is genuine and effective:

(a) in all cases, a guarantee of the signature (Section 8—312(1) or (2)) of the person indorsing a certificated security or originating an instruction including, in the case of an instruction, a warranty of the taxpayer identification number or, in the absence thereof, other reasonable assurance of identity;

(b) if the indorsement is made or the instruction is originated by an agent, appropriate assurance of authority to sign;

(c) if the indorsement is made or the instruction is originated by a fiduciary, appropriate evidence of appointment or incumbency;

(d) if there is more than one fiduciary, reasonable assurance that all who are required to sign have done so; and

(e) if the indorsement is made or the instruction is originated by a person not covered by any of the foregoing, assurance appropriate to the case corresponding as nearly as may be to the foregoing.

(2) A "guarantee of the signature" in subsection (1) means a guarantee signed by or on behalf of a person reasonably believed by the issuer to be responsible. The issuer may adopt standards with respect to responsibility if they are not manifestly unreasonable.

(3) "Appropriate evidence of appointment or incumbency" in subsection (1) means:

(a) in the case of a fiduciary appointed or qualified by a court, a certificate issued by or under the direction or supervision of that court or an officer thereof and dated within 60 days before the date of presentation for transfer, pledge, or release; or

(b) in any other case, a copy of a document showing the appointment or a certificate issued by or on behalf of a person reasonably believed by the issuer to be responsible or, in the absence of that document or certificate, other evidence reasonably deemed by the issuer to be appropriate. The issuer may adopt standards with respect to the evidence if they are not manifestly unreasonable. The issuer is not charged with notice of the contents of any document obtained pursuant to this paragraph (b) except to the extent that the contents relate directly to the appointment or incumbency.

(4) The issuer may elect to require reasonable assurance beyond that specified in this section, but if it does so and, for a purpose other than that specified in subsection (3)(b), both requires and obtains a copy of a will, trust, indenture, articles of co-partnership, by-laws, or other controlling instrument, it is charged with notice of all matters contained therein affecting the transfer, pledge, or release.

Amended in 1977.

§ 8—403. Issuer's Duty as to Adverse Claims

(1) An issuer to whom a certificated security is presented for registration shall inquire into adverse claims if:

(a) a written notification of an adverse claim is received at a time and in a manner affording the issuer a reasonable opportunity to act on it prior to the issuance of a new, reissued, or re-registered certificated security, and the notification identifies the claimant, the registered owner, and the issue of which the security is a part, and provides an address for communications directed to the claimant; or

(b) the issuer is charged with notice of an adverse claim from a controlling instrument it has elected to require under Section 8—402(4).

(2) The issuer may discharge any duty of inquiry by any reasonable means, including notifying an adverse claimant by registered or certified mail at the address furnished by him or, if there be no such address, at his residence or regular place of business that the certificated security has been presented for registration of transfer by a named person, and that the transfer will be registered unless within 30 days from the date of mailing the notification, either:

(a) an appropriate restraining order, injunction, or other process issues from a court of competent jurisdiction; or

(b) there is filed with the issuer an indemnity bond, sufficient in the issuer's judgment to protect the issuer and any transfer agent, registrar, or other agent of the issuer involved from any loss it or they may suffer by complying with the adverse claim.

(3) Unless an issuer is charged with notice of an adverse claim from a controlling instrument which it has elected to require under Section 8—402(4) or re-

ceives notification of an adverse claim under subsection (1), if a certificated security presented for registration is indorsed by the appropriate person or persons the issuer is under no duty to inquire into adverse claims. In particular:

(a) an issuer registering a certificated security in the name of a person who is a fiduciary or who is described as a fiduciary is not bound to inquire into the existence, extent, or correct description of the fiduciary relationship; and thereafter the issuer may assume without inquiry that the newly registered owner continues to be the fiduciary until the issuer receives written notice that the fiduciary is no longer acting as such with respect to the particular security;

(b) an issuer registering transfer on an indorsement by a fiduciary is not bound to inquire whether the transfer is made in compliance with a controlling instrument or with the law of the state having jurisdiction of the fiduciary relationship, including any law requiring the fiduciary to obtain court approval of the transfer; and

(c) the issuer is not charged with notice of the contents of any court record or file or other recorded or unrecorded document even though the document is in its possession and even though the transfer is made on the indorsement of a fiduciary to the fiduciary himself or to his nominee.

(4) An issuer is under no duty as to adverse claims with respect to an uncertificated security except:

(a) claims embodied in a restraining order, injunction, or other legal process served upon the issuer if the process was served at a time and in a manner affording the issuer a reasonable opportunity to act on it in accordance with the requirements of subsection (5);

(b) claims of which the issuer has received a written notification from the registered owner or the registered pledgee if the notification was received at a time and in a manner affording the issuer a reasonable opportunity to act on it in accordance with the requirements of subsection (5);

(c) claims (including restrictions on transfer not imposed by the issuer) to which the registration of transfer to the present registered owner was subject and were so noted in the initial transaction statement sent to him; and

(d) claims as to which an issuer is charged with notice from a controlling instrument it has elected to require under Section 8—402(4).

(5) If the issuer of an uncertificated security is under a duty as to an adverse claim, he discharges that duty by:

(a) including a notation of the claim in any statements sent with respect to the security under Sections 8—408(3), (6), and (7); and

(b) refusing to register the transfer or pledge of the security unless the nature of the claim does not preclude transfer or pledge subject thereto.

(6) If the transfer or pledge of the security is registered subject to an adverse claim, a notation of the claim must be included in the initial transaction statement and all subsequent statements sent to the transferee and pledgee under Section 8—408.

(7) Notwithstanding subsections (4) and (5), if an uncertificated security was subject to a registered pledge at the time the issuer first came under a duty as to a particular adverse claim, the issuer has no duty as to that claim if transfer of the security is requested by the registered pledgee or an appropriate person acting for the registered pledgee unless:

(a) the claim was embodied in legal process which expressly provides otherwise;

(b) the claim was asserted in a written notification from the registered pledgee;

(c) the claim was one as to which the issuer was charged with notice from a controlling instrument it required under Section 8—402(4) in connection with the pledgee's request for transfer; or

(d) the transfer requested is to the registered owner.

Amended in 1977.

§ 8—404. Liability and Non-Liability for Registration

(1) Except as provided in any law relating to the collection of taxes, the issuer is not liable to the owner, pledgee, or any other person suffering loss as a result of the registration of a transfer, pledge, or release of a security if

(a) there were on or with a certificated security the necessary indorsements or the issuer had received an instruction originated by an appropriate person (Section 8—308); and

(b) the issuer had no duty as to adverse claims or has discharged the duty (Section 8—403).

(2) If an issuer has registered a transfer of a certificated security to a person not entitled to it, the issuer

on demand shall deliver a like security to the true owner unless:

(a) the registration was pursuant to subsection (1);

(b) the owner is precluded from asserting any claim for registering the transfer under Section 8—405(1); or

(c) the delivery would result in overissue, in which case the issuer's liability is governed by Section 8—104.

(3) If an issuer has improperly registered a transfer, pledge, or release of an uncertificated security, the issuer on demand from the injured party shall restore the records as to the injured party to the condition that would have obtained if the improper registration had not been made unless:

(a) the registration was pursuant to subsection (1); or

(b) the registration would result in overissue, in which case the issuer's liability is governed by Section 8—104.

Amended in 1977.

§ 8—405. **Lost, Destroyed, and Stolen Certificated Securities**

(1) If a certificated security has been lost, apparently destroyed, or wrongfully taken, and the owner fails to notify the issuer of that fact within a reasonable time after he has notice of it and the issuer registers a transfer of the security before receiving notification, the owner is precluded from asserting against the issuer any claim for registering the transfer under Section 8—404 or any claim to a new security under this section.

(2) If the owner of a certificated security claims that the security has been lost, destroyed, or wrongfully taken, the issuer shall issue a new certificated security or, at the option of the issuer, an equivalent uncertificated security in place of the original security if the owner:

(a) so requests before the issuer has notice that the security has been acquired by a bona fide purchaser;

(b) files with the issuer a sufficient indemnity bond; and

(c) satisfies any other reasonable requirements imposed by the issuer.

(3) If, after the issue of a new certificated or uncertificated security, a bona fide purchaser of the original

certificated security presents it for registration of transfer, the issuer shall register the transfer unless registration would result in overissue, in which event the issuer's liability is governed by Section 8—104. In addition to any rights on the indemnity bond, the issuer may recover the new certificated security from the person to whom it was issued or any person taking under him except a bona fide purchaser or may cancel the uncertificated security unless a bona fide purchaser or any person taking under a bona fide purchaser is then the registered owner or registered pledgee thereof.

Amended in 1977.

§ 8—406. **Duty of Authenticating Trustee, Transfer Agent, or Registrar**

(1) If a person acts as authenticating trustee, transfer agent, registrar, or other agent for an issuer in the registration of transfers of its certificated securities or in the registration of transfers, pledges, and releases of its uncertificated securities, in the issue of new securities, or in the cancellation of surrendered securities:

(a) he is under a duty to the issuer to exercise good faith and due diligence in performing his functions; and

(b) with regard to the particular functions he performs, he has the same obligation to the holder or owner of a certificated security or to the owner or pledgee of an uncertificated security and has the same rights and privileges as the issuer has in regard to those functions.

(2) Notice to an authenticating trustee, transfer agent, registrar or other agent is notice to the issuer with respect to the functions performed by the agent.

Amended in 1977.

§ 8—407. **Exchangeability of Securities**

(1) No issuer is subject to the requirements of this section unless it regularly maintains a system for issuing the class of securities involved under which both certificated and uncertificated securities are regularly issued to the category of owners, which includes the person in whose name the new security is to be registered.

(2) Upon surrender of a certificated security with all necessary indorsements and presentation of a written request by the person surrendering the security, the issuer, if he has no duty as to adverse claims or has discharged the duty (Section 8—403), shall issue to

the person or a person designated by him an equivalent uncertificated security subject to all liens, restrictions, and claims that were noted on the certificated security.

(3) Upon receipt of a transfer instruction originated by an appropriate person who so requests, the issuer of an uncertificated security shall cancel the uncertificated security and issue an equivalent certificated security on which must be noted conspicuously any liens and restrictions of the issuer and any adverse claims (as to which the issuer has a duty under Section 8—403(4)) to which the uncertificated security was subject. The certificated security shall be registered in the name of and delivered to:

(a) the registered owner, if the uncertificated security was not subject to a registered pledge; or

(b) the registered pledgee, if the uncertificated security was subject to a registered pledge.

Added in 1977.

§ 8—408. Statements of Uncertificated Securities

(1) Within 2 business days after the transfer of an uncertificated security has been registered, the issuer shall send to the new registered owner and, if the security has been transferred subject to a registered pledge, to the registered pledgee a written statement containing:

(a) a description of the issue of which the uncertificated security is a part;

(b) the number of shares or units transferred;

(c) the name and address and any taxpayer identification number of the new registered owner and, if the security has been transferred subject to a registered pledge, the name and address and any taxpayer identification number of the registered pledgee;

(d) a notation of any liens and restrictions of the issuer and any adverse claims (as to which the issuer has a duty under Section 8—403(4)) to which the uncertificated security is or may be subject at the time of registration or a statement that there are none of those liens, restrictions, or adverse claims; and

(e) the date the transfer was registered.

(2) Within 2 business days after the pledge of an uncertificated security has been registered, the issuer shall send to the registered owner and the registered pledgee a written statement containing:

(a) a description of the issue of which the uncertificated security is a part;

(b) the number of shares or units pledged;

(c) the name and address and any taxpayer identification number of the registered owner and the registered pledgee;

(d) a notation of any liens and restrictions of the issuer and any adverse claims (as to which the issuer has a duty under Section 8—403(4)) to which the uncertificated security is or may be subject at the time of registration or a statement that there are none of those liens, restrictions, or adverse claims; and

(e) the date the pledge was registered.

(3) Within 2 business days after the release from pledge of an uncertificated security has been registered, the issuer shall send to the registered owner and the pledgee whose interest was released a written statement containing:

(a) a description of the issue of which the uncertificated security is a part;

(b) the number of shares or units released from pledge;

(c) the name and address and any taxpayer identification number of the registered owner and the pledgee whose interest was released;

(d) a notation of any liens and restrictions of the issuer and any adverse claims (as to which the issuer has a duty under Section 8—403(4)) to which the uncertificated security is or may be subject at the time of registration or a statement that there are none of those liens, restrictions, or adverse claims; and

(e) the date the release was registered.

(4) An "initial transaction statement" is the statement sent to:

(a) the new registered owner and, if applicable, to the registered pledgee pursuant to subsection (1);

(b) the registered pledgee pursuant to subsection (2); or

(c) the registered owner pursuant to subsection (3).

Each initial transaction statement shall be signed by or on behalf of the issuer and must be identified as "Initial Transaction Statement".

(5) Within 2 business days after the transfer of an uncertificated security has been registered, the issuer

shall send to the former registered owner and the former registered pledgee, if any, a written statement containing:

    (a) a description of the issue of which the uncertificated security is a part;

    (b) the number of shares or units transferred;

    (c) the name and address and any taxpayer identification number of the former registered owner and of any former registered pledgee; and

    (d) the date the transfer was registered.

(6) At periodic intervals no less frequent than annually and at any time upon the reasonable written request of the registered owner, the issuer shall send to the registered owner of each uncertificated security a dated written statement containing:

    (a) a description of the issue of which the uncertificated security is a part;

    (b) the name and address and any taxpayer identification number of the registered owner;

    (c) the number of shares or units of the uncertificated security registered in the name of the registered owner on the date of the statement;

    (d) the name and address and any taxpayer identification number of any registered pledgee and the number of shares or units subject to the pledge; and

    (e) a notation of any liens and restrictions of the issuer and any adverse claims (as to which the issuer has a duty under Section 8—403(4)) to which the uncertificated security is or may be subject or a statement that there are none of those liens, restrictions, or adverse claims.

(7) At periodic intervals no less frequent than annually and at any time upon the reasonable written request of the registered pledgee, the issuer shall send to the registered pledgee of each uncertificated security a dated written statement containing:

    (a) a description of the issue of which the uncertificated security is a part;

    (b) the name and address and any taxpayer identification number of the registered owner;

    (c) the name and address and any taxpayer identification number of the registered pledgee;

    (d) the number of shares or units subject to the pledge; and

    (e) a notation of any liens and restrictions of the issuer and any adverse claims (as to which the issuer has a duty under Section 8—403(4)) to which the uncertificated security is or may be subject or a statement that there are none of those liens, restrictions, or adverse claims.

(8) If the issuer sends the statements described in subsections (6) and (7) at periodic intervals no less frequent than quarterly, the issuer is not obliged to send additional statements upon request unless the owner or pledgee requesting them pays to the issuer the reasonable cost of furnishing them.

(9) Each statement sent pursuant to this section must bear a conspicuous legend reading substantially as follows: "This statement is merely a record of the rights of the addressee as of the time of its issuance. Delivery of this statement, of itself, confers no rights on the recipient. This statement is neither a negotiable instrument nor a security."

Added in 1977.

Article 9
Secured Transactions; Sales of Accounts and Chattel Paper

Note: *The adoption of this Article should be accompanied by the repeal of existing statutes dealing with conditional sales, trust receipts, factor's liens where the factor is given a nonpossessory lien, chattel mortgages, crop mortgages, mortgages on railroad equipment, assignment of accounts and generally statutes regulating security interests in personal property.*

    Where the state has a retail installment selling act or small loan act, that legislation should be carefully examined to determine what changes in those acts are needed to conform them to this Article. This Article primarily sets out rules defining rights of a secured party against persons dealing with the debtor; it does not prescribe regulations and controls which may be necessary to curb abuses arising in the small loan business or in the financing of consumer purchases on credit. Accordingly there is no intention to repeal existing regulatory acts in those fields by enactment or re-enactment of Article 9. See Section 9—203(4) and the Note thereto.

Part 1 Short Title, Applicability and Definitions

§ 9—101. Short Title.

This Article shall be known and may be cited as Uniform Commercial Code—Secured Transactions.

§ 9—102. Policy and Subject Matter of Article.

(1) Except as otherwise provided in Section 9—104 on excluded transactions, this Article applies

(a) to any transaction (regardless of its form) which is intended to create a security interest in personal property or fixtures including goods, documents, instruments, general intangibles, chattel paper or accounts; and also

(b) to any sale of accounts or chattel paper.

(2) This Article applies to security interests created by contract including pledge, assignment, chattel mortgage, chattel trust, trust deed, factor's lien, equipment trust, conditional sale, trust receipt, other lien or title retention contract and lease or consignment intended as security. This Article does not apply to statutory liens except as provided in Section 9—310.

(3) The application of this Article to a security interest in a secured obligation is not affected by the fact that the obligation is itself secured by a transaction or interest to which this Article does not apply. Amended in 1972.

§ 9—103. Perfection of Security Interest in Multiple State Transactions

(1) Documents, instruments and ordinary goods.

(a) This subsection applies to documents and instruments and to goods other than those covered by a certificate of title described in subsection (2), mobile goods described in subsection (3), and minerals described in subsection (5).

(b) Except as otherwise provided in this subsection, perfection and the effect of perfection or non-perfection of a security interest in collateral are governed by the law of the jurisdiction where the collateral is when the last event occurs on which is based the assertion that the security interest is perfected or unperfected.

(c) If the parties to a transaction creating a purchase money security interest in goods in one jurisdiction understand at the time that the security interest attaches that the goods will be kept in another jurisdiction, then the law of the other jurisdiction governs the perfection and the effect of perfection or non-perfection of the security interest from the time it attaches until thirty days after the debtor receives possession of the goods and thereafter if the goods are taken to the other jurisdiction before the end of the thirty-day period.

(d) When collateral is brought into and kept in this state while subject to a security interest perfected under the law of the jurisdiction from which the collateral was removed, the security interest remains perfected, but if action is required by Part 3 of this Article to perfect the security interest,

(i) if the action is not taken before the expiration of the period of perfection in the other jurisdiction or the end of four months after the collateral is brought into this state, whichever period first expires, the security interest becomes unperfected at the end of that period and is thereafter deemed to have been unperfected as against a person who became a purchaser after removal;

(ii) if the action is taken before the expiration of the period specified in subparagraph (i), the security interest continues perfected thereafter;

(iii) for the purpose of priority over a buyer of consumer goods (subsection (2) of Section 9—307), the period of the effectiveness of a filing in the jurisdiction from which the collateral is removed is governed by the rules with respect to perfection in subparagraphs (i) and (ii).

(2) Certificate of title.

(a) This subsection applies to goods covered by a certificate of title issued under a statute of this state or of another jurisdiction under the law of which indication of a security interest on the certificate is required as a condition of perfection.

(b) Except as otherwise provided in this subsection, perfection and the effect of perfection or non-perfection of the security interest are governed by the law (including the conflict of laws rules) of the jurisdiction issuing the certificate until four months after the goods are removed from that jurisdiction and thereafter until the goods are registered in another jurisdiction, but in any event not beyond surrender of the certificate. After the expiration of that period, the goods are not covered by the certificate of title within the meaning of this section.

(c) Except with respect to the rights of a buyer described in the next paragraph, a security interest, perfected in another jurisdiction otherwise than by notation on a certificate of title, in goods brought into this state and thereafter covered by a certificate of title issued by this state is subject to the rules stated in paragraph (d) of subsection (1).

(d) If goods are brought into this state while a security interest therein is perfected in any manner under the law of the jurisdiction from which the goods are removed and a certificate of title is issued by this state and the certificate does not show that the goods are subject to the security interest or that they may be subject to security interests not shown on the certificate, the security interest is subordinate to the rights of a buyer of the goods who is not in the business of selling goods of that kind to the extent that he gives value and receives delivery of the goods after issuance of the certificate and without knowledge of the security interest.

(3) Accounts, general intangibles and mobile goods.

(a) This subsection applies to accounts (other than an account described in subsection (5) on minerals) and general intangibles (other than uncertificated securities) and to goods which are mobile and which are of a type normally used in more than one jurisdiction, such as motor vehicles, trailers, rolling stock, airplanes, shipping containers, road building and construction machinery and commercial harvesting machinery and the like, if the goods are equipment or are inventory leased or held for lease by the debtor to others, and are not covered by a certificate of title described in subsection (2).

(b) The law (including the conflict of laws rules) of the jurisdiction in which the debtor is located governs the perfection and the effect of perfection or non-perfection of the security interest.

(c) If, however, the debtor is located in a jurisdiction which is not a part of the United States, and which does not provide for perfection of the security interest by filing or recording in that jurisdiction, the law of the jurisdiction in the United States in which the debtor has its major executive office in the United States governs the perfection and the effect of perfection or non-perfection of the security interest through filing. In the alternative, if the debtor is located in a jurisdiction which is not a part of the United States or Canada and the collateral is accounts or general intangibles for money due or to become due, the security interest may be perfected by notification to the account debtor. As used in this paragraph, "United States" includes its territories and possessions and the Commonwealth of Puerto Rico.

(d) A debtor shall be deemed located at his place of business if he has one, at his chief executive office if he has more than one place of business, otherwise at his residence. If, however, the debtor is a foreign air carrier under the Federal Aviation Act of 1958, as amended, it shall be deemed located at the designated office of the agent upon whom service of process may be made on behalf of the foreign air carrier.

(e) A security interest perfected under the law of the jurisdiction of the location of the debtor is perfected until the expiration of four months after a change of the debtor's location to another jurisdiction, or until perfection would have ceased by the law of the first jurisdiction, whichever period first expires. Unless perfected in the new jurisdiction before the end of that period, it becomes unperfected thereafter and is deemed to have been unperfected as against a person who became a purchaser after the change.

(4) Chattel paper.

The rules stated for goods in subsection (1) apply to a possessory security interest in chattel paper. The rules stated for accounts in subsection (3) apply to a non-possessory security interest in chattel paper, but the security interest may not be perfected by notification to the account debtor.

(5) Minerals.

Perfection and the effect of perfection or non-perfection of a security interest which is created by a debtor who has an interest in minerals or the like (including oil and gas) before extraction and which attaches thereto as extracted, or which attaches to an account resulting from the sale thereof at the wellhead or minehead are governed by the law (including the conflict of laws rules) of the jurisdiction wherein the wellhead or minehead is located.

(6) Uncertificated securities.

The law (including the conflict of laws rules) of the jurisdiction of organization of the issuer governs the perfection and the effect of perfection or non-perfection of a security interest in uncertificated securities.

Amended in 1972 and 1977.

§ 9—104. **Transactions Excluded From Article.**

This Article does not apply

(a) to a security interest subject to any statute of the United States, to the extent that such statute governs the rights of parties to and third parties affected by transactions in particular types of property; or

(b) to a landlord's lien; or

(c) to a lien given by statute or other rule of law for services or materials except as provided in Section 9—310 on priority of such liens; or

(d) to a transfer of a claim for wages, salary or other compensation of an employee; or

(e) to a transfer by a government or governmental subdivision or agency; or

(f) to a sale of accounts or chattel paper as part of a sale of the business out of which they arose, or an assignment of accounts or chattel paper which is for the purpose of collection only, or a transfer of a right to payment under a contract to an assignee who is also to do the performance under the contract or a transfer of a single account to an assignee in whole or partial satisfaction of a preexisting indebtedness; or

(g) to a transfer of an interest in or claim in or under any policy of insurance, except as provided with respect to proceeds (Section 9—306) and priorities in proceeds (Section 9—312); or

(h) to a right represented by a judgment (other than a judgment taken on a right to payment which was collateral); or

(i) to any right of set-off; or

(j) except to the extent that provision is made for fixtures in Section 9—313, to the creation or transfer of an interest in or lien on real estate, including a lease or rents thereunder; or

(k) to a transfer in whole or in part of any claim arising out of tort; or

(l) to a transfer of an interest in any deposit account (subsection (1) of Section 9—105), except as provided with respect to proceeds (Section 9—306) and priorities in proceeds (Section 9—312).

Amended in 1972.

§ 9—105. Definitions and Index of Definitions

(1) In this Article unless the context otherwise requires:

(a) "Account debtor" means the person who is obligated on an account, chattel paper or general intangible;

(b) "Chattel paper" means a writing or writings which evidence both a monetary obligation and a security interest in or a lease of specific goods, but a charter or other contract involving the use or hire of a vessel is not chattel paper. When a transaction is evidenced both by such a security agreement or a lease and by an instrument or a series of instruments, the group of writings taken together constitutes chattel paper;

(c) "Collateral" means the property subject to a security interest, and includes accounts and chattel paper which have been sold;

(d) "Debtor" means the person who owes payment or other performance of the obligation secured, whether or not he owns or has rights in the collateral, and includes the seller of accounts or chattel paper. Where the debtor and the owner of the collateral are not the same person, the term "debtor" means the owner of the collateral in any provision of the Article dealing with the collateral, the obligor in any provision dealing with the obligation, and may include both where the context so requires;

(e) "Deposit account" means a demand, time, savings, passbook or like account maintained with a bank, savings and loan association, credit union or like organization, other than an account evidenced by a certificate of deposit;

(f) "Document" means document of title as defined in the general definitions of Article 1 (Section 1—201), and a receipt of the kind described in subsection (2) of Section 7—201;

(g) "Encumbrance" includes real estate mortgages and other liens on real estate and all other rights in real estate that are not ownership interests;

(h) "Goods" includes all things which are movable at the time the security interest attaches or which are fixtures (Section 9—313), but does not include money, documents, instruments, accounts, chattel paper, general intangibles, or minerals or the like (including oil and gas) before extraction. "Goods" also includes standing timber which is to be cut and removed under a conveyance or contract for sale, the unborn young of animals, and growing crops;

(i) "Instrument" means a negotiable instrument (defined in Section 3—104), or a certificated security (defined in Section 8—102) or any other writing which evidences a right to the payment of money and is not itself a security agreement or lease and is of a type which is in ordinary course of business transferred by delivery with any necessary indorsement or assignment;

(j) "Mortgage" means a consensual interest created by a real estate mortgage, a trust deed on real estate, or the like;

(k) An advance is made "pursuant to commitment" if the secured party has bound himself to make it, whether or not a subsequent event of default or other event not within his control has relieved or may relieve him from his obligation;

(l) "Security agreement" means an agreement which creates or provides for a security interest;

(m) "Secured party" means a lender, seller or other person in whose favor there is a security interest, including a person to whom accounts or chattel paper have been sold. When the holders of obligations issued under an indenture of trust, equipment trust agreement or the like are represented by a trustee or other person, the representative is the secured party;

(n) "Transmitting utility" means any person primarily engaged in the railroad, street railway or trolley bus business, the electric or electronics communications transmission business, the transmission of goods by pipeline, or the transmission or the production and transmission of electricity, steam, gas or water, or the provision of sewer service.

(2) Other definitions applying to this Article and the sections in which they appear are:

"Account". Section 9—106.
"Attach". Section 9—203.
"Construction mortgage". Section 9—313(1).
"Consumer goods". Section 9—109(1).
"Equipment". Section 9—109(2).
"Farm products". Section 9—109(3).
"Fixture". Section 9—313(1).
"Fixture filing". Section 9—313(1).
"General intangibles". Section 9—106.
"Inventory". Section 9—109(4).
"Lien creditor". Section 9—301(3).
"Proceeds". Section 9—306(1).
"Purchase money security interest". Section 9—107.
"United States". Section 9—103.

(3) The following definitions in other Articles apply to this Article:

"Check". Section 3—104.
"Contract for sale". Section 2—106.
"Holder in due course". Section 3—302.
"Note". Section 3—104.
"Sale". Section 2—106.

(4) In addition Article 1 contains general definitions and principles of construction and interpretation applicable throughout this Article.

Amended in 1966, 1972 and 1977.

§ 9—106. Definitions: "Account"; "General Intangibles".

"Account" means any right to payment for goods sold

or leased or for services rendered which is not evidenced by an instrument or chattel paper, whether or not it has been earned by performance. "General intangibles" means any personal property (including things in action) other than goods, accounts, chattel paper, documents, instruments, and money. All rights to payment earned or unearned under a charter or other contract involving the use or hire of a vessel and all rights incident to the charter or contract are accounts. Amended in 1966, 1972.

§ 9—107. Definitions: "Purchase Money Security Interest".

A security interest is a "purchase money security interest" to the extent that it is

(a) taken or retained by the seller of the collateral to secure all or part of its price; or

(b) taken by a person who by making advances or incurring an obligation gives value to enable the debtor to acquire rights in or the use of collateral if such value is in fact so used.

§ 9—108. When After-Acquired Collateral Not Security for Antecedent Debt.

Where a secured party makes an advance, incurs an obligation, releases a perfected security interest, or otherwise gives new value which is to be secured in whole or in part by after-acquired property his security interest in the after-acquired collateral shall be deemed to be taken for new value and not as security for an antecedent debt if the debtor acquires his rights in such collateral either in the ordinary course of his business or under a contract of purchase made pursuant to the security agreement within a reasonable time after new value is given.

§ 9—109. Classification of Goods; "Consumer Goods"; "Equipment"; "Farm Products"; "Inventory".

Goods are

(1) "consumer goods" if they are used or bought for use primarily for personal, family or household purposes;

(2) "equipment" if they are used or bought for use primarily in business (including farming or a profession) or by a debtor who is a non-profit organization or a governmental subdivision or agency or if the goods are not included in the definitions of inventory, farm products or consumer goods;

(3) "farm products" if they are crops or livestock or

supplies used or produced in farming operations or if they are products of crops or livestock in their un-manufactured states (such as ginned cotton, woolclip, maple syrup, milk and eggs), and if they are in the possession of a debtor engaged in raising, fattening, grazing or other farming operations. If goods are farm products they are neither equipment nor inventory;

(4) "inventory" if they are held by a person who holds them for sale or lease or to be furnished under con-tracts of service or if he has so furnished them, or if they are raw materials, work in process or materials used or consumed in a business. Inventory of a person is not to be classified as his equipment.

§ 9—110. Sufficiency of Description.

For purposes of this Article any description of personal property or real estate is sufficient whether or not it is specific if it reasonably identifies what is de-scribed.

§ 9—111. Applicability of Bulk Transfer Laws.

The creation of a security interest is not a bulk trans-fer under Article 6 (see Section 6—103).

§ 9—112. Where Collateral Is Not Owned by Debtor.

Unless otherwise agreed, when a secured party knows that collateral is owned by a person who is not the debtor, the owner of the collateral is entitled to receive from the secured party any surplus under Section 9—502(2) or under Section 9—504(1), and is not liable for the debt or for any deficiency after resale, and he has the same right as the debtor

(a) to receive statements under Section 9—208;

(b) to receive notice of and to object to a secured par-ty's proposal to retain the collateral in satisfaction of the indebtedness under Section 9—505;

(c) to redeem the collateral under Section 9—506;

(d) to obtain injunctive or other relief under Section 9—507(1); and

(e) to recover losses caused to him under Section 9—208(2).

§ 9—113. Security Interests Arising Under Article on Sales.

A security interest arising solely under the Article on Sales (Article 2) is subject to the provisions of this Article except that to the extent that and so long as the debtor does not have or does not lawfully obtain possession of the goods

(a) no security agreement is necessary to make the security interest enforceable; and

(b) no filing is required to perfect the security interest; and

(c) the rights of the secured party on default by the debtor are governed by the Article on Sales (Article 2).

§ 9—114. Consignment.

(1) A person who delivers goods under a consignment which is not a security interest and who would be required to file under this Article by paragraph (3)(c) of Section 2—326 has priority over a secured party who is or becomes a creditor of the consignee and who would have a perfected security interest in the goods if they were the property of the consignee, and also has priority with respect to identifiable cash proceeds received on or before delivery of the goods to a buyer, if

(a) the consignor complies with the filing provision of the Article on Sales with respect to consign-ments (paragraph (3)(c) of Section 2—326) before the consignee receives possession of the goods; and

(b) the consignor gives notification in writing to the holder of the security interest if the holder has filed a financing statement covering the same types of goods before the date of the filing made by the consignor; and

(c) the holder of the security interest receives the notification within five years before the consignee receives possession of the goods; and

(d) the notification states that the consignor ex-pects to deliver goods on consignment to the con-signee, describing the goods by item or type.

(2) In the case of a consignment which is not a security interest and in which the requirements of the preced-ing subsection have not been met, a person who de-livers goods to another is subordinate to a person who would have a perfected security interest in the goods if they were the property of the debtor.

Added in 1972.

Part 2 Validity of Security Agreement and Rights of Parties Thereto

§ 9—201. General Validity of Security Agreement.

Except as otherwise provided by this Act a security agreement is effective according to its terms between the parties, against purchasers of the collateral and against creditors. Nothing in this Article validates any charge or practice illegal under any statute or regulation thereunder governing usury, small loans, retail installment sales, or the like, or extends the application of any such statute or regulation to any transaction not otherwise subject thereto.

§ 9—202. Title to Collateral Immaterial.

Each provision of this Article with regard to rights, obligations and remedies applies whether title to collateral is in the secured party or in the debtor.

§ 9—203. Attachment and Enforceability of Security Interest; Proceeds; Formal Requisites

(1) Subject to the provisions of Section 4—208 on the security interest·of a collecting bank, Section 8—321 on security interests in securities and Section 9—113 on a security interest arising under the Article on Sales, a security interest is not enforceable against the debtor or third parties with respect to the collateral and does not attach unless:

    (a) the collateral is in the possession of the secured party pursuant to agreement, or the debtor has signed a security agreement which contains a description of the collateral and in addition, when the security interest covers crops growing or to be grown or timber to be cut, a description of the land concerned;

    (b) value has been given; and

    (c) the debtor has rights in the collateral.

(2) A security interest attaches when it becomes enforceable against the debtor with respect to the collateral. Attachment occurs as soon as all of the events specified in subsection (1) have taken place unless explicit agreement postpones the time of attaching.

(3) Unless otherwise agreed a security agreement gives the secured party the rights to proceeds provided by Section 9—306.

(4) A transaction, although subject to this Article, is also subject to ....*, and in the case of conflict between the provisions of this Article and any such statute, the provisions of such statute control. Failure to comply with any applicable statute has only the effect which is specified therein.

Amended in 1972 and 1977.

Note: *At* * *in subsection (4) insert reference to any local statute regulating small loans, retail installment sales and the like.*

    The foregoing subsection (4) is designed to make it clear that certain transactions, although subject to this Article, must also comply with other applicable legislation.

    This Article is designed to regulate all the "security" aspects of transactions within its scope. There is, however, much regulatory legislation, particularly in the consumer field, which supplements this Article and should not be repealed by its enactment. Examples are small loan acts, retail installment selling acts and the like. Such acts may provide for licensing and rate regulation and may prescribe particular forms of contract. Such provisions should remain in force despite the enactment of this Article. On the other hand if a retail installment selling act contains provisions on filing, rights on default, etc., such provisions should be repealed as inconsistent with this Article except that inconsistent provisions as to deficiencies, penalties, etc., in the Uniform Consumer Credit Code and other recent related legislation should remain because those statutes were drafted after the substantial enactment of the Article and with the intention of modifying certain provisions of this Article as to consumer credit.

§ 9—204. After-Acquired Property; Future Advances.

(1) Except as provided in subsection (2), a security agreement may provide that any or all obligations covered by the security agreement are to be secured by after-acquired collateral.

(2) No security interest attaches under an after-acquired property clause to consumer goods other than accessions (Section 9—314) when given as additional security unless the debtor acquires rights in them within ten days after the secured party gives value.

(3) Obligations covered by a security agreement may include future advances or other value whether or not the advances or value are given pursuant to commitment (subsection (1) of Section 9—105).

Amended in 1972.

§ 9—205. Use or Disposition of Collateral Without Accounting Permissible.

A security interest is not invalid or fraudulent against creditors by reason of liberty in the debtor to use, commingle or dispose of all or part of the collateral (including returned or repossessed goods) or to collect or compromise accounts or chattel paper, or to accept the return of goods or make repossessions, or to use, commingle or dispose of proceeds, or by reason of the failure of the secured party to require the debtor to account for proceeds or replace collateral. This section does not relax the requirements of possession where perfection of a security interest depends upon possession of the collateral by the secured party or by a bailee.

Amended in 1972.

§ 9—206. Agreement Not to Assert Defenses Against Assignee; Modification of Sales Warranties Where Security Agreement Exists.

(1) Subject to any statute or decision which establishes a different rule for buyers or lessees of consumer goods, an agreement by a buyer or lessee that he will not assert against an assignee any claim or defense which he may have against the seller or lessor is enforceable by an assignee who takes his assignment for value, in good faith and without notice of a claim or defense, except as to defenses of a type which may be asserted against a holder in due course of a negotiable instrument under the Article on Commercial Paper (Article 3). A buyer who as part of one transaction signs both a negotiable instrument and a security agreement makes such an agreement.

(2) When a seller retains a purchase money security interest in goods the Article on Sales (Article 2) governs the sale and any disclaimer, limitation or modification of the seller's warranties.

Amended in 1962.

§ 9—207. Rights and Duties When Collateral is in Secured Party's Possession.

(1) A secured party must use reasonable care in the custody and preservation of collateral in his possession. In the case of an instrument or chattel paper reasonable care includes taking necessary steps to preserve rights against prior parties unless otherwise agreed.

(2) Unless otherwise agreed, when collateral is in the secured party's possession

(a) reasonable expenses (including the cost of any insurance and payment of taxes or other charges) incurred in the custody, preservation, use or operation of the collateral are chargeable to the debtor and are secured by the collateral;

(b) the risk of accidental loss or damage is on the debtor to the extent of any deficiency in any effective insurance coverage;

(c) the secured party may hold as additional security any increase or profits (except money) received from the collateral, but money so received, unless remitted to the debtor, shall be applied in reduction of the secured obligation;

(d) the secured party must keep the collateral identifiable but fungible collateral may be commingled;

(e) the secured party may repledge the collateral upon terms which do not impair the debtor's right to redeem it.

(3) A secured party is liable for any loss caused by his failure to meet any obligation imposed by the preceding subsections but does not lose his security interest.

(4) A secured party may use or operate the collateral for the purpose of preserving the collateral or its value or pursuant to the order of a court of appropriate jurisdiction or, except in the case of consumer goods, in the manner and to the extent provided in the security agreement.

§ 9—208. Request for Statement of Account or List of Collateral.

(1) A debtor may sign a statement indicating what he believes to be the aggregate amount of unpaid indebtedness as of a specified date and may send it to the secured party with a request that the statement be approved or corrected and returned to the debtor. When the security agreement or any other record kept by the secured party identifies the collateral a debtor may similarly request the secured party to approve or correct a list of the collateral.

(2) The secured party must comply with such a request within two weeks after receipt by sending a written correction or approval. If the secured party claims a security interest in all of a particular type of collateral owned by the debtor he may indicate that fact in his reply and need not approve or correct an itemized list of such collateral. If the secured party without reasonable excuse fails to comply he is liable for any loss caused to the debtor thereby; and if the debtor has properly included in his request a good faith statement of the obligation or a list of the collateral or both the secured party may claim a security interest only as shown in the statement against persons misled by his failure to comply. If he no longer has an interest in the obligation or collateral at the time the request is received he must disclose the name and address of any successor in interest known to him and he is liable for any loss caused to the debtor as a result of failure to disclose. A successor in interest is not subject to this section until a request is received by him.

(3) A debtor is entitled to such a statement once every six months without charge. The secured party may require payment of a charge not exceeding $10 for each additional statement furnished.

Part 3 Rights of Third Parties; Perfected and Unperfected Security Interests; Rules of Priority

§ 9—301. Persons Who Take Priority Over Unperfected Security Interests; Rights of "Lien Creditor".

(1) Except as otherwise provided in subsection (2), an unperfected security interest is subordinate to the rights of

(a) persons entitled to priority under Section 9—312;

(b) a person who becomes a lien creditor before the security interest is perfected;

(c) in the case of goods, instruments, documents, and chattel paper, a person who is not a secured party and who is a transferee in bulk or other buyer not in ordinary course of business or is a buyer of farm products in ordinary course of business, to the extent that he gives value and receives delivery of the collateral without knowledge of the security interest and before it is perfected;

(d) in the case of accounts and general intangibles, a person who is not a secured party and who is a transferee to the extent that he gives value without knowledge of the security interest and before it is perfected.

(2) If the secured party files with respect to a purchase money security interest before or within ten days after the debtor receives possession of the collateral, he takes priority over the rights of a transferee in bulk or of a lien creditor which arise between the time the security interest attaches and the time of filing.

(3) A "lien creditor" means a creditor who has acquired a lien on the property involved by attachment, levy or the like and includes an assignee for benefit of creditors from the time of assignment, and a trustee in bankruptcy from the date of the filing of the petition or a receiver in equity from the time of appointment.

(4) A person who becomes a lien creditor while a security interest is perfected takes subject to the security interest only to the extent that it secures advances made before he becomes a lien creditor or within 45 days thereafter or made without knowledge of the lien or pursuant to a commitment entered into without knowledge of the lien.

Amended in 1972.

§ 9—302. When Filing Is Required to Perfect Security Interest; Security Interests to Which Filing Provisions of This Article Do Not Apply

(1) A financing statement must be filed to perfect all security interests except the following:

(a) a security interest in collateral in possession of the secured party under Section 9—305;

(b) a security interest temporarily perfected in instruments or documents without delivery under Section 9—304 or in proceeds for a 10 day period under Section 9—306;

(c) a security interest created by an assignment of a beneficial interest in a trust or a decedent's estate;

(d) a purchase money security interest in consumer goods; but filing is required for a motor vehicle required to be registered; and fixture filing is required for priority over conflicting interests in fixtures to the extent provided in Section 9—313;

(e) an assignment of accounts which does not alone or in conjunction with other assignments to the same assignee transfer a significant part of the outstanding accounts of the assignor;

(f) a security interest of a collecting bank (Section 4—208) or in securities (Section 8—321) or arising under the Article on Sales (see Section 9—113) or covered in subsection (3) of this section;

(g) an assignment for the benefit of all the creditors of the transferor, and subsequent transfers by the assignee thereunder.

(2) If a secured party assigns a perfected security interest, no filing under this Article is required in order to continue the perfected status of the security interest against creditors of and transferees from the original debtor.

(3) The filing of a financing statement otherwise required by this Article is not necessary or effective to perfect a security interest in property subject to

(a) a statute or treaty of the United States which provides for a national or international registration or a national or international certificate of title or which specifies a place of filing different from that specified in this Article for filing of the security interest; or

(b) the following statutes of this state; [list any certificate of title statute covering automobiles, trailers, mobile homes, boats, farm tractors, or the like, and any central filing statute.]; but during any period in which collateral is inventory held for sale by a person who is in the business of selling goods of that kind, the filing provisions of this Article (Part 4) apply to a security interest in that collateral created by him as debtor; or

(c) a certificate of title statute of another jurisdiction under the law of which indication of a security interest on the certificate is required as a condition of perfection (subsection (2) of Section 9—103).

(4) Compliance with a statute or treaty described in subsection (3) is equivalent to the filing of a financing statement under this Article, and a security interest in property subject to the statute or treaty can be perfected only by compliance therewith except as provided in Section 9—103 on multiple state transactions. Duration and renewal of perfection of a security interest perfected by compliance with the statute or treaty are governed by the provisions of the statute or treaty; in other respects the security interest is subject to this Article.

Amended in 1972 and 1977.

§ 9—303. When Security Interest Is Perfected; Continuity of Perfection.

(1) A security interest is perfected when it has attached and when all of the applicable steps required for perfection have been taken. Such steps are specified in Sections 9—302, 9—304, 9—305 and 9—306. If such steps are taken before the security interest attaches, it is perfected at the time when it attaches.

(2) If a security interest is originally perfected in any way permitted under this Article and is subsequently perfected in some other way under this Article, without an intermediate period when it was unperfected, the security interest shall be deemed to be perfected continuously for the purposes of this Article.

§ 9—304. Perfection of Security Interest in Instruments, Documents, and Goods Covered by Documents; Perfection by Permissive Filing; Temporary Perfection Without Filing or Transfer of Possession

(1) A security interest in chattel paper or negotiable documents may be perfected by filing. A security interest in money or instruments (other than certificated securities or instruments which constitute part of chattel paper) can be perfected only by the secured party's taking possession, except as provided in subsections (4) and (5) of this section and subsections (2)

and (3) of Section 9—306 on proceeds.

(2) During the period that goods are in the possession of the issuer of a negotiable document therefor, a security interest in the goods is perfected by perfecting a security interest in the document, and any security interest in the goods otherwise perfected during such period is subject thereto.

(3) A security interest in goods in the possession of a bailee other than one who has issued a negotiable document therefor is perfected by issuance of a document in the name of the secured party or by the bailee's receipt of notification of the secured party's interest or by filing as to the goods.

(4) A security interest in instruments (other than certificated securities) or negotiable documents is perfected without filing or the taking of possession for a period of 21 days from the time it attaches to the extent that it arises for new value given under a written security agreement.

(5) A security interest remains perfected for a period of 21 days without filing where a secured party having a perfected security interest in an instrument (other than a certificated security), a negotiable document or goods in possession of a bailee other than one who has issued a negotiable document therefor

(a) makes available to the debtor the goods or documents representing the goods for the purpose of ultimate sale or exchange or for the purpose of loading, unloading, storing, shipping, transshipping, manufacturing, processing or otherwise dealing with them in a manner preliminary to their sale or exchange, but priority between conflicting security interests in the goods is subject to subsection (3) of Section 9—312; or

(b) delivers the instrument to the debtor for the purpose of ultimate sale or exchange or of presentation, collection, renewal or registration of transfer.

(6) After the 21 day period in subsections (4) and (5) perfection depends upon compliance with applicable provisions of this Article.

Amended in 1972 and 1977.

§ 9—305. When Possession by Secured Party Perfects Security Interest Without Filing

A security interest in letters of credit and advices of credit (subsection (2)(a) of Section 5—116), goods, instruments (other than certificated securities), money, negotiable documents, or chattel paper may be perfected by the secured party's taking possession of the collateral. If such collateral other than goods covered by a negotiable document is held by a bailee, the secured party is deemed to have possession from the time the bailee receives notification of the secured party's interest. A security interest is perfected by possession from the time possession is taken without a relation back and continues only so long as possession is retained, unless otherwise specified in this Article. The security interest may be otherwise perfected as provided in this Article before or after the period of possession by the secured party.

Amended in 1972 and 1977.

§ 9—306. "Proceeds"; Secured Party's Rights on Disposition of Collateral.

(1) "Proceeds" includes whatever is received upon the sale, exchange, collection or other disposition of collateral or proceeds. Insurance payable by reason of loss or damage to the collateral is proceeds, except to the extent that it is payable to a person other than a party to the security agreement. Money, checks, deposit accounts, and the like are "cash proceeds". All other proceeds are "non-cash proceeds".

(2) Except where this Article otherwise provides, a security interest continues in collateral notwithstanding sale, exchange or other disposition thereof unless the disposition was authorized by the secured party in the security agreement or otherwise, and also continues in any identifiable proceeds including collections received by the debtor.

(3) The security interest in proceeds is a continuously perfected security interest if the interest in the original collateral was perfected but it ceases to be a perfected security interest and becomes unperfected ten days after receipt of the proceeds by the debtor unless

(a) a filed financing statement covers the original collateral and the proceeds are collateral in which a security interest may be perfected by filing in the office or offices where the financing statement has been filed and, if the proceeds are acquired with cash proceeds, the description of collateral in the financing statement indicates the types of property constituting the proceeds; or

(b) a filed financing statement covers the original collateral and the proceeds are identifiable cash proceeds; or

(c) the security interest in the proceeds is perfected before the expiration of the ten day period.

Except as provided in this section, a security interest

in proceeds can be perfected only by the methods or under the circumstances permitted in this Article for original collateral of the same type.

(4) In the event of insolvency proceedings instituted by or against a debtor, a secured party with a perfected security interest in proceeds has a perfected security interest only in the following proceeds:

(a) in identifiable non-cash proceeds and in separate deposit accounts containing only proceeds;

(b) in identifiable cash proceeds in the form of money which is neither commingled with other money nor deposited in a deposit account prior to the insolvency proceedings;

(c) in identifiable cash proceeds in the form of checks and the like which are not deposited in a deposit account prior to the insolvency proceedings; and

(d) in all cash and deposit accounts of the debtor in which proceeds have been commingled with other funds, but the perfected security interest under this paragraph (d) is

(i) subject to any right to set-off; and

(ii) limited to an amount not greater than the amount of any cash proceeds received by the debtor within ten days before the institution of the insolvency proceedings less the sum of (I) the payments to the secured party on account of cash proceeds received by the debtor during such period and (II) the cash proceeds received by the debtor during such period to which the secured party is entitled under paragraphs (a) through (c) of this subsection (4).

(5) If a sale of goods results in an account or chattel paper which is transferred by the seller to a secured party, and if the goods are returned to or are repossessed by the seller or the secured party, the following rules determine priorities:

(a) If the goods were collateral at the time of sale, for an indebtedness of the seller which is still unpaid, the original security interest attaches again to the goods and continues as a perfected security interest if it was perfected at the time when the goods were sold. If the security interest was originally perfected by a filing which is still effective, nothing further is required to continue the perfected status; in any other case, the secured party must take possession of the returned or repossessed goods or must file.

(b) An unpaid transferee of the chattel paper has

a security interest in the goods against the transferor. Such security interest is prior to a security interest asserted under paragraph (a) to the extent that the transferee of the chattel paper was entitled to priority under Section 9—308.

(c) An unpaid transferee of the account has a security interest in the goods against the transferor. Such security interest is subordinate to a security interest asserted under paragraph (a).

(d) A security interest of an unpaid transferee asserted under paragraph (b) or (c) must be perfected for protection against creditors of the transferor and purchasers of the returned or repossessed goods.

Amended in 1972.

§ 9—307. Protection of Buyers of Goods.

(1) A buyer in ordinary course of business (subsection (9) of Section 1—201) other than a person buying farm products from a person engaged in farming operations takes free of a security interest created by his seller even though the security interest is perfected and even though the buyer knows of its existence.

(2) In the case of consumer goods, a buyer takes free of a security interest even though perfected if he buys without knowledge of the security interest, for value and for his own personal, family or household purposes unless prior to the purchase the secured party has filed a financing statement covering such goods.

(3) A buyer other than a buyer in ordinary course of business (subsection (1) of this section) takes free of a security interest to the extent that it secures future advances made after the secured party acquires knowledge of the purchase, or more than 45 days after the purchase, whichever first occurs, unless made pursuant to a commitment entered into without knowledge of the purchase and before the expiration of the 45 day period. Amended in 1972.

§ 9—308. Purchase of Chattel Paper and Instruments.

A purchaser of chattel paper or an instrument who gives new value and takes possession of it in the ordinary course of his business has priority over a security interest in the chattel paper or instrument

(a) which is perfected under Section 9—304 (permissive filing and temporary perfection) or under Section 9—306 (perfection as to proceeds) if he acts without knowledge that the specific paper or instrument is subject to a security interest; or

(b) which is claimed merely as proceeds of inventory

subject to a security interest (Section 9—306) even though he knows that the specific paper or instrument is subject to the security interest.

Amended in 1972.

§ 9—309. Protection of Purchasers of Instruments, Documents and Securities

Nothing in this Article limits the rights of a holder in due course of a negotiable instrument (Section 3—302) or a holder to whom a negotiable document of title has been duly negotiated (Section 7—501) or a bona fide purchaser of a security (Section 8—302) and the holders or purchasers take priority over an earlier security interest even though perfected. Filing under this Article does not constitute notice of the security interest to such holders or purchasers.

Amended in 1977.

§ 9—310. Priority of Certain Liens Arising by Operation of Law.

When a person in the ordinary course of his business furnishes services or materials with respect to goods subject to a security interest, a lien upon goods in the possession of such person given by statute or rule of law for such materials or services takes priority over a perfected security interest unless the lien is statutory and the statute expressly provides otherwise.

§ 9—311. Alienability of Debtor's Rights: Judicial Process.

The debtor's rights in collateral may be voluntarily or involuntarily transferred (by way of sale, creation of a security interest, attachment, levy, garnishment or other judicial process) notwithstanding a provision in the security agreement prohibiting any transfer or making the transfer constitute a default.

§ 9—312. Priorities Among Conflicting Security Interests in the Same Collateral

(1) The rules of priority stated in other sections of this Part and in the following sections shall govern when applicable: Section 4—208 with respect to the security interests of collecting banks in items being collected, accompanying documents and proceeds; Section 9—103 on security interests related to other jurisdictions; Section 9—114 on consignments.

(2) A perfected security interest in crops for new value given to enable the debtor to produce the crops during the production season and given not more than three months before the crops become growing crops by planting or otherwise takes priority over an earlier

perfected security interest to the extent that such earlier interest secures obligations due more than six months before the crops become growing crops by planting or otherwise, even though the person giving new value had knowledge of the earlier security interest.

(3) A perfected purchase money security interest in inventory has priority over a conflicting security interest in the same inventory and also has priority in identifiable cash proceeds received on or before the delivery of the inventory to a buyer if

(a) the purchase money security interest is perfected at the time the debtor receives possession of the inventory; and

(b) the purchase money secured party gives notification in writing to the holder of the conflicting security interest if the holder had filed a financing statement covering the same types of inventory (i) before the date of the filing made by the purchase money secured party, or (ii) before the beginning of the 21 day period where the purchase money security interest is temporarily perfected without filing or possession (subsection (5) of Section 9—304); and

(c) the holder of the conflicting security interest receives the notification within five years before the debtor receives possession of the inventory; and

(d) the notification states that the person giving the notice has or expects to acquire a purchase money security interest in inventory of the debtor, describing such inventory by item or type.

(4) A purchase money security interest in collateral other than inventory has priority over a conflicting security interest in the same collateral or its proceeds if the purchase money security interest is perfected at the time the debtor receives possession of the collateral or within ten days thereafter.

(5) In all cases not governed by other rules stated in this section (including cases of purchase money security interests which do not qualify for the special priorities set forth in subsections (3) and (4) of this section), priority between conflicting security interests in the same collateral shall be determined according to the following rules:

(a) Conflicting security interests rank according to priority in time of filing or perfection. Priority dates from the time a filing is first made covering the collateral or the time the security interest is first perfected, whichever is earlier, provided that

there is no period thereafter when there is neither filing nor perfection.

(b) So long as conflicting security interests are unperfected, the first to attach has priority.

(6) For the purposes of subsection (5) a date of filing or perfection as to collateral is also a date of filing or perfection as to proceeds.

(7) If future advances are made while a security interest is perfected by filing, the taking of possession, or under Section 8—321 on securities, the security interest has the same priority for the purposes of subsection (5) with respect to the future advances as it does with respect to the first advance. If a commitment is made before or while the security interest is so perfected, the security interest has the same priority with respect to advances made pursuant thereto. In other cases a perfected security interest has priority from the date the advance is made.

Amended in 1972 and 1977.

§ 9—313. **Priority of Security Interests in Fixtures.**

(1) In this section and in the provisions of Part 4 of this Article referring to fixture filing, unless the context otherwise requires

(a) goods are "fixtures" when they become so related to particular real estate that an interest in them arises under real estate law

(b) a "fixture filing" is the filing in the office where a mortgage on the real estate would be filed or recorded of a financing statement covering goods which are or are to become fixtures and conforming to the requirements of subsection (5) of Section 9—402

(c) a mortgage is a "construction mortgage" to the extent that it secures an obligation incurred for the construction of an improvement on land including the acquisition cost of the land, if the recorded writing so indicates.

(2) A security interest under this Article may be created in goods which are fixtures or may continue in goods which become fixtures, but no security interest exists under this Article in ordinary building materials incorporated into an improvement on land.

(3) This Article does not prevent creation of an encumbrance upon fixtures pursuant to real estate law.

(4) A perfected security interest in fixtures has priority over the conflicting interest of an encumbrancer or owner of the real estate where

(a) the security interest is a purchase money security interest, the interest of the encumbrancer or owner arises before the goods become fixtures, the security interest is perfected by a fixture filing before the goods become fixtures or within ten days thereafter, and the debtor has an interest of record in the real estate or is in possession of the real estate; or

(b) the security interest is perfected by a fixture filing before the interest of the encumbrancer or owner is of record, the security interest has priority over any conflicting interest of a predecessor in title of the encumbrancer or owner, and the debtor has an interest of record in the real estate or is in possession of the real estate; or

(c) the fixtures are readily removable factory or office machines or readily removable replacements of domestic appliances which are consumer goods, and before the goods become fixtures the security interest is perfected by any method permitted by this Article; or

(d) the conflicting interest is a lien on the real estate obtained by legal or equitable proceedings after the security interest was perfected by any method permitted by this Article.

(5) A security interest in fixtures, whether or not perfected, has priority over the conflicting interest of an encumbrancer or owner of the real estate where

(a) the encumbrancer or owner has consented in writing to the security interest or has disclaimed an interest in the goods as fixtures; or

(b) the debtor has a right to remove the goods as against the encumbrancer or owner. If the debtor's right terminates, the priority of the security interest continues for a reasonable time.

(6) Notwithstanding paragraph (a) of subsection (4) but otherwise subject to subsections (4) and (5), a security interest in fixtures is subordinate to a construction mortgage recorded before the goods become fixtures if the goods become fixtures before the completion of the construction. To the extent that it is given to refinance a construction mortgage, a mortgage has this priority to the same extent as the construction mortgage.

(7) In cases not within the preceding subsections, a security interest in fixtures is subordinate to the conflicting interest of an encumbrancer or owner of the related real estate who is not the debtor.

(8) When the secured party has priority over all owners and encumbrancers of the real estate, he may, on default, subject to the provisions of Part 5, remove his collateral from the real estate but he must reimburse any encumbrancer or owner of the real estate who is not the debtor and who has not otherwise agreed for the cost of repair of any physical injury, but not for any diminution in value of the real estate caused by the absence of the goods removed or by any necessity of replacing them. A person entitled to reimbursement may refuse permission to remove until the secured party gives adequate security for the performance of this obligation. Amended in 1972.

§ 9—314. **Accessions.**

(1) A security interest in goods which attaches before they are installed in or affixed to other goods takes priority as to the goods installed or affixed (called in this section "accessions") over the claims of all persons to the whole except as stated in subsection (3) and subject to Section 9—315(1).

(2) A security interest which attaches to goods after they become part of a whole is valid against all persons subsequently acquiring interests in the whole except as stated in subsection (3) but is invalid against any person with an interest in the whole at the time the security interest attaches to the goods who has not in writing consented to the security interest or disclaimed an interest in the goods as part of the whole.

(3) The security interests described in subsections (1) and (2) do not take priority over

(a) a subsequent purchaser for value of any interest in the whole; or

(b) a creditor with a lien on the whole subsequently obtained by judicial proceedings; or

(c) a creditor with a prior perfected security interest in the whole to the extent that he makes subsequent advances

if the subsequent purchase is made, the lien by judicial proceedings obtained or the subsequent advance under the prior perfected security interest is made or contracted for without knowledge of the security interest and before it is perfected. A purchaser of the whole at a foreclosure sale other than the holder of a perfected security interest purchasing at his own foreclosure sale is a subsequent purchaser within this section.

(4) When under subsections (1) or (2) and (3) a secured party has an interest in accessions which has priority over the claims of all persons who have interests in the whole, he may on default subject to the provisions of Part 5 remove his collateral from the whole but he

must reimburse any encumbrancer or owner of the whole who is not the debtor and who has not otherwise agreed for the cost of repair of any physical injury but not for any diminution in value of the whole caused by the absence of the goods removed or by any necessity for replacing them. A person entitled to reimbursement may refuse permission to remove until the secured party gives adequate security for the performance of this obligation.

§ 9—315. Priority When Goods Are Commingled or Processed.

(1) If a security interest in goods was perfected and subsequently the goods or a part thereof have become part of a product or mass, the security interest continues in the product or mass if

(a) the goods are so manufactured, processed, assembled or commingled that their identity is lost in the product or mass; or

(b) a financing statement covering the original goods also covers the product into which the goods have been manufactured, processed or assembled.

In a case to which paragraph (b) applies, no separate security interest in that part of the original goods which has been manufactured, processed or assembled into the product may be claimed under Section 9—314.

(2) When under subsection (1) more than one security interest attaches to the product or mass, they rank equally according to the ratio that the cost of the goods to which each interest originally attached bears to the cost of the total product or mass.

§ 9—316. Priority Subject to Subordination.

Nothing in this Article prevents subordination by agreement by any person entitled to priority.

§ 9—317. Secured Party Not Obligated on Contract of Debtor.

The mere existence of a security interest or authority given to the debtor to dispose of or use collateral does not impose contract or tort liability upon the secured party for the debtor's acts or omissions.

§ 9—318. Defenses Against Assignee; Modification of Contract After Notification of Assignment; Term Prohibiting Assignment Ineffective; Identification and Proof of Assignment.

(1) Unless an account debtor has made an enforceable agreement not to assert defenses or claims arising out of a sale as provided in Section 9—206 the rights of an assignee are subject to

(a) all the terms of the contract between the account debtor and assignor and any defense or claim arising therefrom; and

(b) any other defense or claim of the account debtor against the assignor which accrues before the account debtor receives notification of the assignment.

(2) So far as the right to payment or a part thereof under an assigned contract has not been fully earned by performance, and notwithstanding notification of the assignment, any modification of or substitution for the contract made in good faith and in accordance with reasonable commercial standards is effective against an assignee unless the account debtor has otherwise agreed but the assignee acquires corresponding rights under the modified or substituted contract. The assignment may provide that such modification or substitution is a breach by the assignor.

(3) The account debtor is authorized to pay the assignor until the account debtor receives notification that the amount due or to become due has been assigned and that payment is to be made to the assignee. A notification which does not reasonably identify the rights assigned is ineffective. If requested by the account debtor, the assignee must seasonably furnish reasonable proof that the assignment has been made and unless he does so the account debtor may pay the assignor.

(4) A term in any contract between an account debtor and an assignor is ineffective if it prohibits assignment of an account or prohibits creation of a security interest in a general intangible for money due or to become due or requires the account debtor's consent to such assignment or security interest.

Amended in 1972.

Part 4 Filing

§ 9—401. Place of Filing; Erroneous Filing; Removal of Collateral.

First Alternative Subsection (1)

(1) The proper place to file in order to perfect a security interest is as follows:

(a) when the collateral is timber to be cut or is minerals or the like (including oil and gas) or accounts subject to subsection (5) of Section 9—103, or when the financing statement is filed as a fixture filing (Section 9—313) and the collateral is goods which are or are to become fixtures, then in the office where a mortgage on the real estate would be filed or recorded;

(b) in all other cases, in the office of the [Secretary of State].

Second Alternative Subsection (1)

(1) The proper place to file in order to perfect a security interest is as follows:

(a) when the collateral is equipment used in farming operations, or farm products, or accounts or general intangibles arising from or relating to the sale of farm products by a farmer, or consumer goods, then in the office of the . . . . in the county of the debtor's residence or if the debtor is not a resident of this state then in the office of the . . . . in the county where the goods are kept, and in addition when the collateral is crops growing or to be grown in the office of the . . . . in the county where the land is located;

(b) when the collateral is timber to be cut or is minerals or the like (including oil and gas) or accounts subject to subsection (5) of Section 9—103, or when the financing statement is filed as a fixture filing (Section 9—313) and the collateral is goods which are or are to become fixtures, then in the office where a mortgage on the real estate would be filed or recorded;

(c) in all other cases, in the office of the [Secretary of State].

Third Alternative Subsection (1)

(1) The proper place to file in order to perfect a security interest is as follows:

(a) when the collateral is equipment used in farming operations, or farm products, or accounts or general intangibles arising from or relating to the sale of farm products by a farmer, or consumer goods, then in the office of the . . . . in the county of the debtor's residence or if the debtor is not a resident of this state then in the office of the . . . . in the county where the goods are kept, and in addition when the collateral is crops growing or to be grown in the office of the . . . . in the county where the land is located;

(b) when the collateral is timber to be cut or is minerals or the like (including oil and gas) or accounts subject to subsection (5) of Section 9—103, or when the financing statement is filed as a fixture

filing (Section 9—313) and the collateral is goods which are or are to become fixtures, then in the office where a mortgage on the real estate would be filed or recorded;

(c) in all other cases, in the office of the [Secretary of State] and in addition, if the debtor has a place of business in only one county of this state, also in the office of . . . . of such county, or, if the debtor has no place of business in this state, but resides in the state, also in the office of . . . . of the county in which he resides.

Note: *One of the three alternatives should be selected as subsection (1).*

(2) A filing which is made in good faith in an improper place or not in all of the places required by this section is nevertheless effective with regard to any collateral as to which the filing complied with the requirements of this Article and is also effective with regard to collateral covered by the financing statement against any person who has knowledge of the contents of such financing statement.

(3) A filing which is made in the proper place in this state continues effective even though the debtor's residence or place of business or the location of the collateral or its use, whichever controlled the original filing, is thereafter changed.

Alternative Subsection (3)

[(3) A filing which is made in the proper county continues effective for four months after a change to another county of the debtor's residence or place of business or the location of the collateral, whichever controlled the original filing. It becomes ineffective thereafter unless a copy of the financing statement signed by the secured party is filed in the new county within said period. The security interest may also be perfected in the new county after the expiration of the four-month period; in such case perfection dates from the time of perfection in the new county. A change in the use of the collateral does not impair the effectiveness of the original filing.]

(4) The rules stated in Section 9—103 determine whether filing is necessary in this state.

(5) Notwithstanding the preceding subsections, and subject to subsection (3) of Section 9—302, the proper place to file in order to perfect a security interest in collateral, including fixtures, of a transmitting utility is the office of the [Secretary of State]. This filing constitutes a fixture filing (Section 9—313) as to the col-

lateral described therein which is or is to become fixtures.

(6) For the purposes of this section, the residence of an organization is its place of business if it has one or its chief executive office if it has more than one place of business.

Amended in 1962 and 1972.

Note: *Subsection (6) should be used only if the state chooses the Second or Third Alternative Subsection (1).*

§ 9—402. Formal Requisites of Financing Statement; Amendments; Mortgage as Financing Statement.

(1) A financing statement is sufficient if it gives the names of the debtor and the secured party, is signed by the debtor, gives an address of the secured party from which information concerning the security interest may be obtained, gives a mailing address of the debtor and contains a statement indicating the types, or describing the items, of collateral. A financing statement may be filed before a security agreement is made or a security interest otherwise attaches. When the financing statement covers crops growing or to be grown, the statement must also contain a description of the real estate concerned. When the financing statement covers timber to be cut or covers minerals or the like (including oil and gas) or accounts subject to subsection (5) of Section 9—103, or when the financing statement is filed as a fixture filing (Section 9—313) and the collateral is goods which are or are to become fixtures, the statement must also comply with subsection (5). A copy of the security agreement is sufficient as a financing statement if it contains the above information and is signed by the debtor. A carbon, photographic or other reproduction of a security agreement or a financing statement is sufficient as a financing statement if the security agreement so provides or if the original has been filed in this state.

(2) A financing statement which otherwise complies with subsection (1) is sufficient when it is signed by the secured party instead of the debtor if it is filed to perfect a security interest in

    (a) collateral already subject to a security interest in another jurisdiction when it is brought into this state, or when the debtor's location is changed to this state. Such a financing statement must state that the collateral was brought into this state or that the debtor's location was changed to this state under such circumstances; or

    (b) proceeds under Section 9—306 if the security

interest in the original collateral was perfected. Such a financing statement must describe the original collateral; or

    (c) collateral as to which the filing has lapsed; or

    (d) collateral acquired after a change of name, identity or corporate structure of the debtor (subsection (7)).

(3) A form substantially as follows is sufficient to comply with subsection (1):

Name of debtor (or assignor) ....

Address ....

Name of secured party (or assignee) ....

Address ....

1. This financing statement covers the following types (or items) of property:

    (Describe) ....

2. (If collateral is crops) The above described crops are growing or are to be grown on:

    (Describe Real Estate) ....

3. (If applicable) The above goods are to become fixtures on *

*Where appropriate substitute either "The above timber is standing on . . . ." or "The above minerals or the like (including oil and gas) or accounts will be financed at the wellhead or minehead of the well or mine located on . . . ."

    (Describe Real Estate) ....

and this financing statement is to be filed [for record] in the real estate records. (If the debtor does not have an interest of record) The name of a record owner is ....

4. (If products of collateral are claimed) Products of the collateral are also covered.

(use   ....
whichever   Signature of Debtor (or Assignor)

is   ....
applicable)   Signature of Secured Party
                (or Assignee)

(4) A financing statement may be amended by filing a writing signed by both the debtor and the secured party. An amendment does not extend the period of effectiveness of a financing statement. If any amendment adds collateral, it is effective as to the added collateral only from the filing date of the amendment. In this Article, unless the context otherwise requires, the term "financing statement" means the original financing statement and any amendments.

(5) A financing statement covering timber to be cut or covering minerals or the like (including oil and gas) or accounts subject to subsection (5) of Section 9—103, or a financing statement filed as a future filing (Section 9—313) where the debtor is not a transmitting utility, must show that it covers this type of collateral, must recite that it is to be filed [for record] in the real estate records, and the financing statement must contain a description of the real estate [sufficient if it were contained in a mortgage of the real estate to give constructive notice of the mortgage under the law of this state]. If the debtor does not have an interest of record in the real estate, the financing statement must show the name of a record owner.

(6) A mortgage is effective as a financing statement filed as a fixture filing from the date of its recording if

(a) the goods are described in the mortgage by item or type; and

(b) the goods are or are to become fixtures related to the real estate described in the mortgage; and

(c) the mortgage complies with the requirements for a financing statement in this section other than a recital that it is to be filed in the real estate records; and

(d) the mortgage is duly recorded.

No fee with reference to the financing statement is required other than the regular recording and satisfaction fees with respect to the mortgage.

(7) A financing statement sufficiently shows the name of the debtor if it gives the individual, partnership or corporate name of the debtor, whether or not it adds other trade names or names of partners. Where the debtor so changes his name or in the case of an organization its name, identity or corporate structure that a filed financing statement becomes seriously misleading, the filing is not effective to perfect a security interest in collateral acquired by the debtor more than four months after the change, unless a new appropriate financing statement is filed before the expiration of that time. A filed financing statement remains effective with respect to collateral transferred by the debtor even though the secured party knows of or consents to the transfer.

(8) A financing statement substantially complying with the requirements of this section is effective even though it contains minor errors which are not seriously misleading. Amended in 1972.

Note: *Language in brackets is optional.*

Note: *Where the state has any special recording system for real estate other than the usual grantor-grantee index (as, for instance, a tract system or a title registration or Torrens system) local adaptations of subsection (5) and Section 9—403(7) may be necessary. See Mass.Gen.Laws Chapter 106, Section 9—409.*

§ 9—403. **What Constitutes Filing; Duration of Filing; Effect of Lapsed Filing; Duties of Filing Officer.**

(1) Presentation for filing of a financing statement and tender of the filing fee or acceptance of the statement by the filing officer constitutes filing under this Article.

(2) Except as provided in subsection (6) a filed financing statement is effective for a period of five years from the date of filing. The effectiveness of a filed financing statement lapses on the expiration of the five year period unless a continuation statement is filed prior to the lapse. If a security interest perfected by filing exists at the time insolvency proceedings are commenced by or against the debtor, the security interest remains perfected until termination of the insolvency proceedings and thereafter for a period of sixty days or until expiration of the five year period, whichever occurs later. Upon lapse the security interest becomes unperfected, unless it is perfected without filing. If the security interest becomes unperfected upon lapse, it is deemed to have been unperfected as against a person who became a purchaser or lien creditor before lapse.

(3) A continuation statement may be filed by the secured party within six months prior to the expiration of the five year period specified in subsection (2). Any such continuation statement must be signed by the secured party, identify the original statement by file number and state that the original statement is still effective. A continuation statement signed by a person other than the secured party of record must be accompanied by a separate written statement of assignment signed by the secured party of record and complying with subsection (2) of Section 9—405, including payment of the required fee. Upon timely filing of the continuation statement, the effectiveness of the original statement is continued for five years after the last date to which the filing was effective whereupon it lapses in the same manner as provided in subsection (2) unless another continuation statement is filed prior to such lapse. Succeeding continuation statements may be filed in the same manner to continue the effectiveness of the original statement. Unless a statute on disposition of public records provides otherwise, the

filing officer may remove a lapsed statement from the files and destroy it immediately if he has retained a microfilm or other photographic record, or in other cases after one year after the lapse. The filing officer shall so arrange matters by physical annexation of financing statements to continuation statements or other related filings, or by other means, that if he physically destroys the financing statements of a period more than five years past, those which have been continued by a continuation statement or which are still effective under subsection (6) shall be retained.

(4) Except as provided in subsection (7) a filing officer shall mark each statement with a file number and with the date and hour of filing and shall hold the statement or a microfilm or other photographic copy thereof for public inspection. In addition the filing officer shall index the statement according to the name of the debtor and shall note in the index the file number and the address of the debtor given in the statement.

(5) The uniform fee for filing and indexing and for stamping a copy furnished by the secured party to show the date and place of filing for an original financing statement or for a continuation statement shall be $. . . . . . . if the statement is in the standard form prescribed by the [Secretary of State] and otherwise shall be $. . . . . . ., plus in each case, if the financing statement is subject to subsection (5) of Section 9—402, $. . . . . . . The uniform fee for each name more than one required to be indexed shall be $. . . . . . . The secured party may at his option show a trade name for any person and an extra uniform indexing fee of $. . . . . . . shall be paid with respect thereto.

(6) If the debtor is a transmitting utility (subsection (5) of Section 9—401) and a filed financing statement so states, it is effective until a termination statement is filed. A real estate mortgage which is effective as a fixture filing under subsection (6) of Section 9—402 remains effective as a fixture filing until the mortgage is released or satisfied of record or its effectiveness otherwise terminates as to the real estate.

(7) When a financing statement covers timber to be cut or covers minerals or the like (including oil and gas) or accounts subject to subsection (5) of Section 9—103, or is filed as a fixture filing, [it shall be filed for record and] the filing officer shall index it under the names of the debtor and any owner of record shown on the financing statement in the same fashion as if they were the mortgagors in a mortgage of the real estate described, and, to the extent that the law of this state provides for indexing of mortgages under the name of the mortgagee, under the name of the secured party as if he were the mortgagee thereunder, or where indexing is by description in the same fashion as if the financing statement were a mortgage of the real estate described. Amended in 1972.

Note: *In states in which writings will not appear in the real estate records and indices unless actually recorded the bracketed language in subsection (7) should be used.*

§ 9—404. **Termination Statement.**

(1) If a financing statement covering consumer goods is filed on or after . . . ., then within one month or within ten days following written demand by the debtor after there is no outstanding secured obligation and no commitment to make advances, incur obligations or otherwise give value, the secured party must file with each filing officer with whom the financing statement was filed, a termination statement to the effect that he no longer claims a security interest under the financing statement, which shall be identified by file number. In other cases whenever there is no outstanding secured obligation and no commitment to make advances, incur obligations or otherwise give value, the secured party must on written demand by the debtor send the debtor, for each filing officer with whom the financing statement was filed, a termination statement to the effect that he no longer claims a security interest under the financing statement, which shall be identified by file number. A termination statement signed by a person other than the secured party of record must be accompanied by a separate written statement of assignment signed by the secured party of record complying with subsection (2) of Section 9—405, including payment of the required fee. If the affected secured party fails to file such a termination statement as required by this subsection, or to send such a termination statement within ten days after proper demand therefor, he shall be liable to the debtor for one hundred dollars, and in addition for any loss caused to the debtor by such failure.

(2) On presentation to the filing officer of such a termination statement he must note it in the index. If he has received the termination statement in duplicate, he shall return one copy of the termination statement to the secured party stamped to show the time of receipt thereof. If the filing officer has a microfilm or other photographic record of the financing statement, and of any related continuation statement, statement of assignment and statement of release, he may remove the originals from the files at any time after receipt of the termination statement, or if he has no such record, he may remove them from the files at

any time after one year after receipt of the termination statement.

(3) If the termination statement is in the standard form prescribed by the [Secretary of State], the uniform fee for filing and indexing the termination statement shall be $......., and otherwise shall be $......., plus in each case an additional fee of $....... for each name more than one against which the termination statement is required to be indexed. Amended in 1972.

Note: *The date to be inserted should be the effective date of the revised Article 9.*

§ 9—405. Assignment of Security Interest; Duties of Filing Officer; Fees.

(1) A financing statement may disclose an assignment of a security interest in the collateral described in the financing statement by indication in the financing statement of the name and address of the assignee or by an assignment itself or a copy thereof on the face or back of the statement. On presentation to the filing officer of such a financing statement the filing officer shall mark the same as provided in Section 9—403(4). The uniform fee for filing, indexing and furnishing filing data for a financing statement so indicating an assignment shall be $....... if the statement is in the standard form prescribed by the [Secretary of State] and otherwise shall be $......., plus in each case an additional fee of $....... for each name more than one against which the financing statement is required to be indexed.

(2) A secured party may assign of record all or part of his rights under a financing statement by the filing in the place where the original financing statement was filed of a separate written statement of assignment signed by the secured party of record and setting forth the name of the secured party of record and the debtor, the file number and the date of filing of the financing statement and the name and address of the assignee and containing a description of the collateral assigned. A copy of the assignment is sufficient as a separate statement if it complies with the preceding sentence. On presentation to the filing officer of such a separate statement, the filing officer shall mark such separate statement with the date and hour of the filing. He shall note the assignment on the index of the financing statement, or in the case of a fixture filing, or a filing covering timber to be cut, or covering minerals or the like (including oil and gas) or accounts subject to subsection (5) of Section 9—103, he shall index the assignment under the name of the assignor

as grantor and, to the extent that the law of this state provides for indexing the assignment of a mortgage under the name of the assignee, he shall index the assignment of the financing statement under the name of the assignee. The uniform fee for filing, indexing and furnishing filing data about such a separate statement of assignment shall be $...... if the statement is in the standard form prescribed by the [Secretary of State] and otherwise shall be $......, plus in each case an additional fee of $...... for each name more than one against which the statement of assignment is required to be indexed. Notwithstanding the provisions of this subsection, an assignment of record of a security interest in a fixture contained in a mortgage effective as a fixture filing (subsection (6) of Section 9—402) may be made only by an assignment of the mortgage in the manner provided by the law of this state other than this Act.

(3) After the disclosure or filing of an assignment under this section, the assignee is the secured party of record. Amended in 1972.

§ 9—406. Release of Collateral; Duties of Filing Officer; Fees.

A secured party of record may by his signed statement release all or a part of any collateral described in a filed financing statement. The statement of release is sufficient if it contains a description of the collateral being released, the name and address of the debtor, the name and address of the secured party, and the file number of the financing statement. A statement of release signed by a person other than the secured party of record must be accompanied by a separate written statement of assignment signed by the secured party of record and complying with subsection (2) of Section 9—405, including payment of the required fee. Upon presentation of such a statement of release to the filing officer he shall mark the statement with the hour and date of filing and shall note the same upon the margin of the index of the filing of the financing statement. The uniform fee for filing and noting such a statement of release shall be $...... if the statement is in the standard form prescribed by the [Secretary of State] and otherwise shall be $......, plus in each case an additional fee of $...... for each name more than one against which the statement of release is required to be indexed. Amended in 1972.

[§ 9—407. Information From Filing Officer].

[(1) If the person filing any financing statement, termination statement, statement of assignment, or statement of release, furnishes the filing officer a copy thereof, the filing officer shall upon request note upon the copy the file number and date and hour of the filing of the original and deliver or send the copy to such person.]

[(2) Upon request of any person, the filing officer shall issue his certificate showing whether there is on file on the date and hour stated therein, any presently effective financing statement naming a particular debtor and any statement of assignment thereof and if there is, giving the date and hour of filing of each such statement and the names and addresses of each secured party therein. The uniform fee for such a certificate shall be $...... if the request for the certificate is in the standard form prescribed by the [Secretary of State] and otherwise shall be $....... Upon request the filing officer shall furnish a copy of any filed financing statement or statement of assignment for a uniform fee of $...... per page.] Amended in 1972.

Note: *This section is proposed as an optional provision to require filing officers to furnish certificates. Local law and practices should be consulted with regard to the advisability of adoption.*

§ 9—408. Financing Statements Covering Consigned or Leased Goods.

A consignor or lessor of goods may file a financing statement using the terms "consignor," "consignee," "lessor," "lessee" or the like instead of the terms specified in Section 9—402. The provisions of this Part shall apply as appropriate to such a financing statement but its filing shall not of itself be a factor in determining whether or not the consignment or lease is intended as security (Section 1—201(37)). However, if it is determined for other reasons that the consignment or lease is so intended, a security interest of the consignor or lessor which attaches to the consigned or leased goods is perfected by such filing. Added in 1972.

Part 5 Default

§ 9—501. Default; Procedure When Security Agreement Covers Both Real and Personal Property.

(1) When a debtor is in default under a security agreement, a secured party has the rights and remedies provided in this Part and except as limited by subsection (3) those provided in the security agreement. He may reduce his claim to judgment, foreclose or otherwise enforce the security interest by any available judicial procedure. If the collateral is documents the secured party may proceed either as to the documents or as to the goods covered thereby. A secured

party in possession has the rights, remedies and duties provided in Section 9—207. The rights and remedies referred to in this subsection are cumulative.

(2) After default, the debtor has the rights and remedies provided in this Part, those provided in the security agreement and those provided in Section 9—207.

(3) To the extent that they give rights to the debtor and impose duties on the secured party, the rules stated in the subsections referred to below may not be waived or varied except as provided with respect to compulsory disposition of collateral (subsection (3) of Section 9—504 and Section 9—505) and with respect to redemption of collateral (Section 9—506) but the parties may by agreement determine the standards by which the fulfillment of these rights and duties is to be measured if such standards are not manifestly unreasonable:

(a) subsection (2) of Section 9—502 and subsection (2) of Section 9—504 insofar as they require accounting for surplus proceeds of collateral;

(b) subsection (3) of Section 9—504 and subsection (1) of Section 9—505 which deal with disposition of collateral;

(c) subsection (2) of Section 9—505 which deals with acceptance of collateral as discharge of obligation;

(d) Section 9—506 which deals with redemption of collateral; and

(e) subsection (1) of Section 9—507 which deals with the secured party's liability for failure to comply with this Part.

(4) If the security agreement covers both real and personal property, the secured party may proceed under this Part as to the personal property or he may proceed as to both the real and the personal property in accordance with his rights and remedies in respect of the real property in which case the provisions of this Part do not apply.

(5) When a secured party has reduced his claim to judgment the lien of any levy which may be made upon his collateral by virtue of any execution based upon the judgment shall relate back to the date of the perfection of the security interest in such collateral. A judicial sale, pursuant to such execution, is a foreclosure of the security interest by judicial procedure within the meaning of this section, and the secured party may purchase at the sale and thereafter hold the collateral

free of any other requirements of this Article. Amended in 1972.

§ 9—502. Collection Rights of Secured Party.

(1) When so agreed and in any event on default the secured party is entitled to notify an account debtor or the obligor on an instrument to make payment to him whether or not the assignor was theretofore making collections on the collateral, and also to take control of any proceeds to which he is entitled under Section 9—306.

(2) A secured party who by agreement is entitled to charge back uncollected collateral or otherwise to full or limited recourse against the debtor and who undertakes to collect from the account debtors or obligors must proceed in a commercially reasonable manner and may deduct his reasonable expenses of realization from the collections. If the security agreement secures an indebtedness, the secured party must account to the debtor for any surplus, and unless otherwise agreed, the debtor is liable for any deficiency. But, if the underlying transaction was a sale of accounts or chattel paper, the debtor is entitled to any surplus or is liable for any deficiency only if the security agreement so provides. Amended in 1972.

§ 9—503. Secured Party's Right to Take Possession After Default.

Unless otherwise agreed a secured party has on default the right to take possession of the collateral. In taking possession a secured party may proceed without judicial process if this can be done without breach of the peace or may proceed by action. If the security agreement so provides the secured party may require the debtor to assemble the collateral and make it available to the secured party at a place to be designated by the secured party which is reasonably convenient to both parties. Without removal a secured party may render equipment unusable, and may dispose of collateral on the debtor's premises under Section 9—504.

§ 9—504. Secured Party's Right to Dispose of Collateral After Default; Effect of Disposition.

(1) A secured party after default may sell, lease or otherwise dispose of any or all of the collateral in its then condition or following any commercially reasonable preparation or processing. Any sale of goods is subject to the Article on Sales (Article 2). The proceeds of disposition shall be applied in the order following to

(a) the reasonable expenses of retaking, holding, preparing for sale or lease, selling, leasing and the like and, to the extent provided for in the agreement and not prohibited by law, the reasonable attorneys' fees and legal expenses incurred by the secured party;

(b) the satisfaction of indebtedness secured by the security interest under which the disposition is made;

(c) the satisfaction of indebtedness secured by any subordinate security interest in the collateral if written notification of demand therefor is received before distribution of the proceeds is completed. If requested by the secured party, the holder of a subordinate security interest must seasonably furnish reasonable proof of his interest, and unless he does so, the secured party need not comply with his demand.

(2) If the security interest secures an indebtedness, the secured party must account to the debtor for any surplus, and, unless otherwise agreed, the debtor is liable for any deficiency. But if the underlying transaction was a sale of accounts or chattel paper, the debtor is entitled to any surplus or is liable for any deficiency only if the security agreement so provides.

(3) Disposition of the collateral may be by public or private proceedings and may be made by way of one or more contracts. Sale or other disposition may be as a unit or in parcels and at any time and place and on any terms but every aspect of the disposition including the method, manner, time, place and terms must be commercially reasonable. Unless collateral is perishable or threatens to decline speedily in value or is of a type customarily sold on a recognized market, reasonable notification of the time and place of any public sale or reasonable notification of the time after which any private sale or other intended disposition is to be made shall be sent by the secured party to the debtor, if he has not signed after default a statement renouncing or modifying his right to notification of sale. In the case of consumer goods no other notification need be sent. In other cases notification shall be sent to any other secured party from whom the secured party has received (before sending his notification to the debtor or before the debtor's renunciation of his rights) written notice of a claim of an interest in the collateral. The secured party may buy at any public sale and if the collateral is of a type customarily sold in a recognized market or is of a type which is the subject of widely distributed standard price quotations he may buy at private sale.

(4) When collateral is disposed of by a secured party after default, the disposition transfers to a purchaser for value all of the debtor's rights therein, discharges the security interest under which it is made and any security interest or lien subordinate thereto. The purchaser takes free of all such rights and interests even though the secured party fails to comply with the requirements of this Part or of any judicial proceedings

(a) in the case of a public sale, if the purchaser has no knowledge of any defects in the sale and if he does not buy in collusion with the secured party, other bidders or the person conducting the sale; or

(b) in any other case, if the purchaser acts in good faith.

(5) A person who is liable to a secured party under a guaranty, indorsement, repurchase agreement or the like and who receives a transfer of collateral from the secured party or is subrogated to his rights has thereafter the rights and duties of the secured party. Such a transfer of collateral is not a sale or disposition of the collateral under this Article. Amended in 1972.

§ 9—505. Compulsory Disposition of Collateral; Acceptance of the Collateral as Discharge of Obligation.

(1) If the debtor has paid sixty per cent of the cash price in the case of a purchase money security interest in consumer goods or sixty per cent of the loan in the case of another security interest in consumer goods, and has not signed after default a statement renouncing or modifying his rights under this Part a secured party who has taken possession of collateral must dispose of it under Section 9—504 and if he fails to do so within ninety days after he takes possession the debtor at his option may recover in conversion or under Section 9—507(1) on secured party's liability.

(2) In any other case involving consumer goods or any other collateral a secured party in possession may, after default, propose to retain the collateral in satisfaction of the obligation. Written notice of such proposal shall be sent to the debtor if he has not signed after default a statement renouncing or modifying his rights under this subsection. In the case of consumer goods no other notice need be given. In other cases notice shall be sent to any other secured party from whom the secured party has received (before sending his notice to the debtor or before the debtor's renunciation of his rights) written notice of a claim of an interest in the collateral. If the secured party receives objection in writing from a person entitled to receive notification within twenty-one days after the notice was sent, the secured party must dispose of the collateral under Section 9—504. In the absence of such written objection the secured party may retain the collateral in satisfaction of the debtor's obligation. Amended in 1972.

§ 9—506. Debtor's Right to Redeem Collateral.

At any time before the secured party has disposed of collateral or entered into a contract for its disposition under Section 9—504 or before the obligation has been discharged under Section 9—505(2) the debtor or any other secured party may unless otherwise agreed in writing after default redeem the collateral by tendering fulfillment of all obligations secured by the collateral as well as the expenses reasonably incurred by the secured party in retaking, holding and preparing the collateral for disposition, in arranging for the sale, and to the extent provided in the agreement and not prohibited by law, his reasonable attorneys' fees and legal expenses.

§ 9—507. Secured Party's Liability for Failure to Comply With This Part.

(1) If it is established that the secured party is not proceeding in accordance with the provisions of this Part disposition may be ordered or restrained on appropriate terms and conditions. If the disposition has occurred the debtor or any person entitled to notification or whose security interest has been made known to the secured party prior to the disposition has a right to recover from the secured party any loss caused by a failure to comply with the provisions of this Part. If the collateral is consumer goods, the debtor has a right to recover in any event an amount not less than the credit service charge plus ten per cent of the principal amount of the debt or the time price differential plus 10 per cent of the cash price.

(2) The fact that a better price could have been obtained by a sale at a different time or in a different method from that selected by the secured party is not of itself sufficient to establish that the sale was not made in a commercially reasonable manner. If the secured party either sells the collateral in the usual manner in any recognized market therefor or if he sells at the price current in such market at the time of his sale or if he has otherwise sold in conformity with reasonable commercial practices among dealers in the type of property sold he has sold in a commercially reasonable manner. The principles stated in the two preceding sentences with respect to sales also apply as may be appropriate to other types of disposition. A disposition which has been approved in any judicial

proceeding or by any bona fide creditors' committee or representative of creditors shall conclusively be deemed to be commercially reasonable, but this sentence does not indicate that any such approval must be obtained in any case nor does it indicate that any disposition not so approved is not commercially reasonable.

Article 10
EFFECTIVE DATE AND REPEALER

10—101. Effective Date.

This Act shall become effective at midnight on December 31st following its enactment. It applies to transactions entered into and events occurring after that date.

§ 10—102. Specific Repealer; Provision for Transition.

(1) The following acts and all other acts and parts of acts inconsistent herewith are hereby repealed:
(Here should follow the acts to be specifically repealed including the following:

    Uniform Negotiable Instruments Act
    Uniform Warehouse Receipts Act
    Uniform Sales Act
    Uniform Bills of Lading Act
    Uniform Stock Transfer Act
    Uniform Conditional Sales Act
    Uniform Trust Receipts Act
       Also any acts regulating:
    Bank collections
    Bulk sales
    Chattel mortgages
    Conditional sales
    Factor's lien acts
    Farm storage of grain and similar acts
    Assignment of accounts receivable)

(2) Transactions validly entered into before the effective date specified in Section 10—101 and the rights, duties and interests flowing from them remain valid thereafter and may be terminated, completed, consummated or enforced as required or permitted by any statute or other law amended or repealed by this Act as though such repeal or amendment had not occurred.

Note: *Subsection (1) should be separately prepared for each state. The foregoing is a list of statutes to be checked.*

§ 10—103. General Repealer.

Except as provided in the following section, all acts and parts of acts inconsistent with this Act are hereby repealed.

§ 10—104. Laws Not Repealed.

(1) The Article on Documents of Title (Article 7) does not repeal or modify any laws prescribing the form or contents of documents of title or the services or facilities to be afforded by bailees, or otherwise regulating bailees' businesses in respects not specifically dealt with herein; but the fact that such laws are violated does not affect the status of a document of title which otherwise complies with the definition of a document of title (Section 1—201).

[(2) This Act does not repeal . . . .*, cited as the Uniform Act for the Simplification of Fiduciary Security Transfers, and if in any respect there is any inconsistency between that Act and the Article of this Act on investment securities (Article 8) the provisions of the former Act shall control.]

Note: *At * in subsection (2) insert the statutory reference to the Uniform Act for the Simplification of Fiduciary Security Transfers if such Act has previously been enacted. If it has not been enacted, omit subsection (2).*

Article 11
(REPORTERS' DRAFT) EFFECTIVE DATE AND TRANSITION PROVISIONS

This material has been numbered Article 11 to distinguish it from Article 10, the transition provision of the 1962 Code, which may still remain in effect in some states to cover transition problems from pre-Code law to the original Uniform Commercial Code. Adaptation may be necessary in particular states. The terms "[old Code]" and "[new Code]" and "[old U.C.C.]" and "[new U.C.C.]" are used herein, and should be suitably changed in each state.

Note: *This draft was prepared by the Reporters and has not been passed upon by the Review Committee, the Permanent Editorial Board, the American Law Institute, or the National Conference of Commissioners on Uniform State Laws. It is submitted as a working draft which may be adapted as appropriate in each state.*

§ 11—101. Effective Date.

This Act shall become effective at 12:01 A.M. on _____, 19___.

§ 11—102. **Preservation of Old Transition Provision.**

The provisions of [here insert reference to the original transition provision in the particular state] shall continue to apply to [the new U.C.C.] and for this purpose the [old U.C.C. and new U.C.C.] shall be considered one continuous statute.

§ 11—103. **Transition to [New Code]—General Rule.**

Transactions validly entered into after [effective date of old U.C.C.] and before [effective date of new U.C.C.], and which were subject to the provisions of [old U.C.C.] and which would be subject to this Act as amended if they had been entered into after the effective date of [new U.C.C.] and the rights, duties and interests flowing from such transactions remain valid after the latter date and may be terminated, completed, consummated or enforced as required or permitted by the [new U.C.C.]. Security interests arising out of such transactions which are perfected when [new U.C.C.] becomes effective shall remain perfected until they lapse as provided in [new U.C.C.], and may be continued as permitted by [new U.C.C.], except as stated in Section 11—105.

§ 11—104. **Transition Provision on Change of Requirement of Filing.**

A security interest for the perfection of which filing or the taking of possession was required under [old U.C.C.] and which attached prior to the effective date of [new U.C.C.] but was not perfected shall be deemed perfected on the effective date of [new U.C.C.] if [new U.C.C.] permits perfection without filing or authorizes filing in the office or offices where a prior ineffective filing was made.

§ 11—105. **Transition Provision on Change of Place of Filing.**

(1) A financing statement or continuation statement filed prior to [effective date of new U.C.C.] which shall not have lapsed prior to [the effective date of new U.C.C.] shall remain effective for the period provided in the [old Code], but not less than five years after the filing.

(2) With respect to any collateral acquired by the debtor subsequent to the effective date of [new U.C.C.], any effective financing statement or continuation statement described in this section shall apply only if the filing or filings are in the office or offices that would be appropriate to perfect the security interests in the new collateral under [new U.C.C.].

(3) The effectiveness of any financing statement or continuation statement filed prior to [effective date of new U.C.C.] may be continued by a continuation statement as permitted by [new U.C.C.], except that if [new U.C.C.] requires a filing in an office where there was no previous financing statement, a new financing statement conforming to Section 11—106 shall be filed in that office.

(4) If the record of a mortgage of real estate would have been effective as a fixture filing of goods described therein if [new U.C.C.] had been in effect on the date of recording the mortgage, the mortgage shall be deemed effective as a fixture filing as to such goods under subsection (6) of Section 9—402 of the [new U.C.C.] on the effective date of [new U.C.C.].

§ 11—106. **Required Refilings.**

(1) If a security interest is perfected or has priority when this Act takes effect as to all persons or as to certain persons without any filing or recording, and if the filing of a financing statement would be required for the perfection or priority of the security interest against those persons under [new U.C.C.], the perfection and priority rights of the security interest continue until 3 years after the effective date of [new U.C.C.]. The perfection will then lapse unless a financing statement is filed as provided in subsection (4) or unless the security interest is perfected otherwise than by filing.

(2) If a security interest is perfected when [new U.C.C.] takes effect under a law other than [U.C.C.] which requires no further filing, refiling or recording to continue its perfection, perfection continues until and will lapse 3 years after [new U.C.C.] takes effect, unless a financing statement is filed as provided in subsection (4) or unless the security interest is perfected otherwise than by filing, or unless under subsection (3) of Section 9—302 the other law continues to govern filing.

(3) If a security interest is perfected by a filing, refiling or recording under a law repealed by this Act which required further filing, refiling or recording to continue its perfection, perfection continues and will lapse on the date provided by the law so repealed for such further filing, refiling or recording unless a financing statement is filed as provided in subsection (4) or unless the security interest is perfected otherwise than by filing.

(4) A financing statement may be filed within six months before the perfection of a security interest would otherwise lapse. Any such financing statement may

be signed by either the debtor or the secured party. It must identify the security agreement, statement or notice (however denominated in any statute or other law repealed or modified by this Act), state the office where and the date when the last filing, refiling or recording, if any, was made with respect thereto, and the filing number, if any, or book and page, if any, of recording and further state that the security agreement, statement or notice, however denominated, in another filing office under the [U.C.C.] or under any statute or other law repealed or modified by this Act is still effective. Section 9—401 and Section 9—103 determine the proper place to file such a financing statement. Except as specified in this subsection, the provisions of Section 9—403(3) for continuation statements apply to such a financing statement.

§ 11—107. Transition Provisions as to Priorities.

Except as otherwise provided in [Article 11], [old U.C.C.] shall apply to any questions of priority if the positions of the parties were fixed prior to the effective date of [new U.C.C.]. In other cases questions of priority shall be determined by [new U.C.C.].

§ 11—108. Presumption that Rule of Law Continues Unchanged.

Unless a change in law has clearly been made, the provisions of [new U.C.C.] shall be deemed declaratory of the meaning of the [old U.C.C.].

Appendix B

THE UNIFORM PARTNERSHIP ACT

(Adopted in 48 States, all except Georgia and Louisiana; the District of Columbia, the Virgin Islands, and Guam. The adoptions by Alabama and Nebraska do not follow the official text in every respect, but are substantially similar, with local variations.)

The Act consists of 7 Parts as follows:

I. Preliminary Provisions

II. Nature of Partnership

III. Relations of Partners to Persons Dealing with the Partnership

IV. Relations of Partners to One Another

V. Property Rights of a Partner

VI. Dissolution and Winding Up

VII. Miscellaneous Provisions

An Act to make uniform the Law of Partnerships

Be it enacted, etc.:

Part I **Preliminary Provisions**

Sec. 1. **Name of Act**

This act may be cited as Uniform Partnership Act.

Sec. 2. **Definition of Terms**

In this act, "Court" includes every court and judge having jurisdiction in the case.

"Business" includes every trade, occupation, or profession.

"Person" includes individuals, partnerships, corporations, and other associations.

"Bankrupt" includes bankrupt under the Federal Bankruptcy Act or insolvent under any state insolvent act.

"Conveyance" includes every assignment, lease, mortgage, or encumbrance.

"Real property" includes land and any interest or estate in land.

Sec. 3. **Interpretation of Knowledge and Notice**

(1) A person has "knowledge" of a fact within the meaning of this act not only when he has actual knowledge thereof, but also when he has knowledge of such other facts as in the circumstances shows bad faith.

(2) A person has "notice" of a fact within the meaning of this act when the person who claims the benefit of the notice:

(a) States the fact to such person, or

(b) Delivers through the mail, or by other means of communication, a written statement of the fact to such person or to a proper person at his place of business or residence.

Sec. 4. **Rules of Construction**

(1) The rule that statutes in derogation of the common law are to be strictly construed shall have no application to this act.

(2) The law of estoppel shall apply under this act.

(3) The law of agency shall apply under this act.

(4) This act shall be so interpreted and construed as to effect its general purpose to make uniform the law of those states which enact it.

(5) This act shall not be construed so as to impair the obligations of any contract existing when the act goes into effect, nor to affect any action or proceedings begun or right accrued before this act takes effect.

Sec. 5. **Rules for Cases Not Provided for in this Act.**

In any case not provided for in this act the rules of law and equity, including the law merchant, shall govern.

Part II **Nature of Partnership**

Sec. 6. **Partnership Defined**

(1) A partnership is an association of two or more persons to carry on as co-owners a business for profit.

(2) But any association formed under any other statute of this state, or any statute adopted by authority, other than the authority of this state, is not a partnership under this act, unless such association would have been a partnership in this state prior to the adoption of this act; but this act shall apply to limited partnerships except in so far as the statutes relating to such partnerships are inconsistent herewith.

Sec. 7. **Rules for Determining the Existence of a Partnership**

In determining whether a partnership exists, these rules shall apply:

(1) Except as provided by Section 16 persons who are not partners as to each other are not partners as to third persons.

(2) Joint tenancy, tenancy in common, tenancy by the entireties, joint property, common property, or part ownership does not of itself establish a partnership, whether such co-owners do or do not share any profits made by the use of the property.

(3) The sharing of gross returns does not of itself establish a partnership, whether or not the persons sharing them have a joint or common right or interest in any property from which the returns are derived.

(4) The receipt by a person of a share of the profits of a business is prima facie evidence that he is a partner in the business, but no such inference shall be drawn if such profits were received in payment:

    (a) As a debt by installments or otherwise,

    (b) As wages of an employee or rent to a landlord,

    (c) As an annuity to a widow or representative of a deceased partner,

    (d) As interest on a loan, though the amount of payment vary with the profits of the business.

    (e) As the consideration for the sale of a good-will of a business or other property by installments or otherwise.

Sec. 8. **Partnership Property**

(1) All property originally brought into the partnership stock or subsequently acquired by purchase or otherwise, on account of the partnership, is partnership property.

(2) Unless the contrary intention appears, property acquired with partnership funds is partnership property.

(3) Any estate in real property may be acquired in the partnership name. Title so acquired can be conveyed only in the partnership name.

(4) A conveyance to a partnership in the partnership name, though without words of inheritance, passes the entire estate of the grantor unless a contrary intent appears.

Part III **Relations of Partners to Persons Dealing with the Partnership**

Sec. 9. **Partner Agent of Partnership as to Partnership Business**

(1) Every partner is an agent of the partnership for the purpose of its business, and the act of every partner, including the execution in the partnership name of any instrument, for apparently carrying on in the usual way the business of the partnership of which he is a member binds the partnership, unless the partner so acting has in fact no authority to act for the partnership in the particular matter, and the person with whom he is dealing has knowledge of the fact that he has no such authority.

(2) An act of a partner which is not apparently for the carrying on of the business of the partnership in the usual way does not bind the partnership unless authorized by the other partners.

(3) Unless authorized by the other partners or unless they have abandoned the business, one or more but less than all the partners have no authority to:

    (a) Assign the partnership property in trust for creditors or on the assignee's promise to pay the debts of the partnership,

    (b) Dispose of the good-will of the business,

    (c) Do any other act which would make it impossible to carry on the ordinary business of a partnership,

    (d) Confess a judgment,

(e) Submit a partnership claim or liability to arbitration or reference.

(4) No act of a partner in contravention of a restriction on authority shall bind the partnership to persons having knowledge of the restriction.

Sec. 10. **Conveyance of Real Property of the Partnership**

(1) Where title to real property is in the partnership name, any partner may convey title to such property by a conveyance executed in the partnership name; but the partnership may recover such property unless the partner's act binds the partnership under the provisions of paragraph (1) of section 9 or unless such property has been conveyed by the grantee or a person claiming through such grantee to a holder for value without knowledge that the partner, in making the conveyance, has exceeded his authority.

(2) Where title to real property is in the name of the partnership, a conveyance executed by a partner, in his own name, passes the equitable interest of the partnership, provided the act is one within the authority of the partner under the provisions of paragraph (1) of section 9.

(3) Where title to real property is in the name of one or more but not all the partners, and the record does not disclose the right of the partnership, the partners in whose name the title stands may convey title to such property, but the partnership may recover such property if the partners' act does not bind the partnership under the provisions of paragraph (1) of section 9, unless the purchaser or his assignee, is a holder for value, without knowledge.

(4) Where the title to real property is in the name of one or more or all the partners, or in a third person in trust for the partnership, a conveyance executed by a partner in the partnership name, or in his own name, passes the equitable interest of the partnership, provided the act is one within the authority of the partner under the provisions of paragraph (1) of section 9.

(5) Where the title to real property is in the names of all the partners a conveyance executed by all the partners passes all their rights in such property.

Sec. 11. **Partnership Bound by Admission of Partner**

An admission or representation made by any partner concerning partnership affairs within the scope of his authority as conferred by this act is evidence against the partnership.

Sec. 12. **Partnership Charged with Knowledge of or Notice to Partner**

Notice to any partner of any matter relating to partnership affairs, and the knowledge of the partner acting in the particular matter, acquired while a partner or then present to his mind, and the knowledge of any other partner who reasonably could and should have communicated it to the acting partner, operate as notice to or knowledge of the partnership, except in the case of a fraud on the partnership committed by or with the consent of that partner.

Sec. 13. **Partnership Bound by Partner's Wrongful Act**

Where, by any wrongful act or omission of any partner acting in the ordinary course of the business of the partnership or with the authority of his co-partners, loss or injury is caused to any person, not being a partner in the partnership, or any penalty is incurred, the partnership is liable therefor to the same extent as the partner so acting or omitting to act.

Sec. 14. **Partnership Bound by Partner's Breach of Trust**

The partnership is bound to make good the loss:

(a) Where one partner acting within the scope of his apparent authority receives money or property of a third person and misapplies it; and

(b) Where the partnership in the course of its business receives money or property of a third person and the money or property so received is misapplied by any partner while it is in the custody of the partnership.

Sec. 15. **Nature of Partner's Liability**

All partners are liable

(a) Jointly and severally for everything chargeable to the partnership under sections 13 and 14.

(b) Jointly for all other debts and obligations of the partnership; but any partner may enter into a separate obligation to perform a partnership contract.

Sec. 16. **Partner by Estoppel**

(1) When a person, by words spoken or written or by conduct, represents himself, or consents to another representing him to any one, as a partner in an existing partnership or with one or more persons not actual partners, he is liable to any such person to whom such representation has been made, who has, on the faith of such representation, given credit to the actual or apparent partnership, and if he has made

such representation or consented to its being made in a public manner he is liable to such person, whether the representation has or has not been made or communicated to such person so giving credit by or with the knowledge of the apparent partner making the representation or consenting to its being made.

(a) When a partnership liability results, he is liable as though he were an actual member of the partnership.

(b) When no partnership liability results, he is liable jointly with the other persons, if any, so consenting to the contract or representation as to incur liability, otherwise separately.

(2) When a person has been thus represented to be a partner in an existing partnership, or with one or more persons not actual partners, he is an agent of the persons consenting to such representation to bind them to the same extent and in the same manner as though he were a partner in fact, with respect to persons who rely upon the representation. Where all the members of the existing partnership consent to the representation, a partnership act or obligation results; but in all other cases it is the joint act or obligation of the person acting and the persons consenting to the representation.

Sec. 17. Liability of Incoming Partner

A person admitted as a partner into an existing partnership is liable for all the obligations of the partnership arising before his admission as though he had been a partner when such obligations were incurred, except that this liability shall be satisfied only out of partnership property.

Part IV Relations of Partners to One Another

Sec. 18. Rules Determining Rights and Duties of Partners

The rights and duties of the partners in relation to the partnership shall be determined, subject to any agreement between them, by the following rules:

(a) Each partner shall be repaid his contributions, whether by way of capital or advances to the partnership property and share equally in the profits and surplus remaining after all liabilities, including those to partners, are satisfied; and must contribute towards the losses, whether of capital or otherwise, sustained by the partnership according to his share in the profits.

(b) The partnership must indemnify every partner in respect of payments made and personal liabilities reasonably incurred by him in the ordinary and proper conduct of its business, or for the preservation of its business or property.

(c) A partner, who in aid of the partnership makes any payment or advance beyond the amount of capital which he agreed to contribute, shall be paid interest from the date of the payment or advance.

(d) A partner shall receive interest on the capital contributed by him only from the date when repayment should be made.

(e) All partners have equal rights in the management and conduct of the partnership business.

(f) No partner is entitled to remuneration for acting in the partnership business, except that a surviving partner is entitled to reasonable compensation for his services in winding up the partnership affairs.

(g) No person can become a member of a partnership without the consent of all the partners.

(h) Any difference arising as to ordinary matters connected with the partnership business may be decided by a majority of the partners; but no act in contravention of any agreement between the partners may be done rightfully without the consent of all the partners.

Sec. 19. Partnership Books

The partnership books shall be kept, subject to any agreement between the partners, at the principal place of business of the partnership, and every partner shall at all times have access to and may inspect and copy any of them.

Sec. 20. Duty of Partners to Render Information

Partners shall render on demand true and full information of all things affecting the partnership to any partner or the legal representative of any deceased partner or partner under legal disability.

Sec. 21. Partner Accountable as a Fiduciary

(1) Every partner must account to the partnership for any benefit, and hold as trustee for it any profits derived by him without the consent of the other partners from any transaction connected with the formation, conduct, or liquidation of the partnership or from any use by him of its property.

(2) This section applies also to the representatives of a deceased partner engaged in the liquidation of the affairs of the partnership as the personal representatives of the last surviving partner.

Sec. 22. Right to an Account

Any partner shall have the right to a formal account as to partnership affairs:

(a) If he is wrongfully excluded from the partnership business or possession of its property by his co-partners,

(b) If the right exists under the terms of any agreement,

(c) As provided by section 21,

(d) Whenever other circumstances render it just and reasonable.

Sec. 23. Continuation of Partnership Beyond Fixed Term

(1) When a partnership for a fixed term or particular undertaking is continued after the termination of such term or particular undertaking without any express agreement, the rights and duties of the partners remain the same as they were at such termination, so far as is consistent with a partnership at will.

(2) A continuation of the business by the partners or such of them as habitually acted therein during the term, without any settlement or liquidation of the partnership affairs, is prima facie evidence of a continuation of the partnership.

Part V Property Rights of a Partner

Sec. 24. Extent of Property Rights of a Partner

The property rights of a partner are (1) his rights in specific partnership property, (2) his interest in the partnership, and (3) his right to participate in the management.

Sec. 25. Nature of a Partner's Right in Specific Partnership Property

(1) A partner is co-owner with his partners of specific partnership property holding as a tenant in partnership.

(2) The incidents of this tenancy are such that:

(a) A partner, subject to the provisions of this act and to any agreement between the partners, has an equal right with his partners to possess specific partnership property for partnership purposes; but he has no right to possess such property for any other purpose without the consent of his partners.

(b) A partner's right in specific partnership property is not assignable except in connection with the assignment of rights of all the partners in the same property.

(c) A partner's right in specific partnership property is not subject to attachment or execution, except on a claim against the partnership. When partnership property is attached for a partnership debt the partners, or any of them, or the representatives of a deceased partner, cannot claim any right under the homestead or exemption laws.

(d) On the death of a partner his right in specific partnership property vests in the surviving partner or partners, except where the deceased was the last surviving partner, when his right in such property vests in his legal representative. Such surviving partner or partners, or the legal representative of the last surviving partner, has no right to possess the partnership property for any but a partnership purpose.

(e) A partner's right in specific partnership property is not subject to dower, curtesy, or allowances to widows, heirs, or next of kin.

Sec. 26. Nature of Partner's Interest in the Partnership

A partner's interest in the partnership is his share of the profits and surplus, and the same is personal property.

Sec. 27. Assignment of Partner's Interest

(1) A conveyance by a partner of his interest in the partnership does not of itself dissolve the partnership, nor, as against the other partners in the absence of agreement, entitle the assignee, during the continuance of the partnership, to interfere in the management or administration of the partnership business or affairs, or to require any information or account of partnership transactions, or to inspect the partnership books; but it merely entitles the assignee to receive in accordance with his contract the profits to which the assigning partner would otherwise be entitled.

(2) In case of a dissolution of the partnership, the assignee is entitled to receive his assignor's interest and may require an account from the date only of the last account agreed to by all the partners.

Sec. 28. Partner's Interest Subject to Charging Order

(1) On due application to a competent court by any judgment creditor of a partner, the court which entered the judgment, order, or decree, or any other court, may charge the interest of the debtor partner with

payment of the unsatisfied amount of such judgment debt with interest thereon; and may then or later appoint a receiver of his share of the profits, and of any other money due or to fall due to him in respect of the partnership, and make all other orders, directions, accounts and inquiries which the debtor partner might have made, or which the circumstances of the case may require.

(2) The interest charged may be redeemed at any time before foreclosure, or in case of a sale being directed by the court may be purchased without thereby causing a dissolution:

(a) With separate property, by any one or more of the partners, or

(b) With partnership property, by any one or more of the partners with the consent of all the partners whose interests are not so charged or sold.

(3) Nothing in this act shall be held to deprive a partner of his right, if any, under the exemption laws, as regards his interest in the partnership.

Part VI Dissolution and Winding up

Sec. 29. Dissolution Defined

The dissolution of a partnership is the change in the relation of the partners caused by any partner ceasing to be associated in the carrying on as distinguished from the winding up of the business.

Sec. 30. Partnership not Terminated by Dissolution

On dissolution the partnership is not terminated, but continues until the winding up of partnership affairs is completed.

Sec. 31. Causes of Dissolution

Dissolution is caused:

(1) Without violation of the agreement between the partners,

(a) By the termination of the definite term or particular undertaking specified in the agreement,

(b) By the express will of any partner when no definite term or particular undertaking is specified,

(c) By the express will of all the partners who have not assigned their interests or suffered them to be charged for their separate debts, either before or after the termination of any specified term or particular undertaking.

(d) By the expulsion of any partner from the business bona fide in accordance with such a power conferred by the agreement between the partners;

(2) In contravention of the agreement between the partners, where the circumstances do not permit a dissolution under any other provision of this section, by the express will of any partner at any time;

(3) By any event which makes it unlawful for the business of the partnership to be carried on or for the members to carry it on in partnership;

(4) By the death of any partner;

(5) By the bankruptcy of any partner or the partnership;

(6) By decree of court under section 32.

Sec. 32. Dissolution by Decree of Court

(1) On application by or for a partner the court shall decree a dissolution whenever:

(a) A partner has been declared a lunatic in any judicial proceeding or is shown to be of unsound mind,

(b) A partner becomes in any other way incapable of performing his part of the partnership contract,

(c) A partner has been guilty of such conduct as tends to affect prejudicially the carrying on of the business,

(d) A partner wilfully or persistently commits a breach of the partnership agreement, or otherwise so conducts himself in matters relating to the partnership business that it is not reasonably practicable to carry on the business in partnership with him,

(e) The business of the partnership can only be carried on at a loss,

(f) Other circumstances render a dissolution equitable.

(2) On the application of the purchaser of a partner's interest under sections 28 or 29 [should read 27 or 28]:

(a) After the termination of the specified term or particular undertaking,

(b) At any time if the partnership was a partnership at will when the interest was assigned or when the charging order was issued.

Sec. 33. General Effect of Dissolution on Authority of Partner

Except so far as may be necessary to wind up partnership affairs or to complete transactions begun but not then finished, dissolution terminates all authority of any partner to act for the partnership,

(1) With respect to the partners,

(a) When the dissolution is not by the act, bankruptcy or death of a partner; or

(b) When the dissolution is by such act, bankruptcy or death of a partner, in cases where section 34 so requires.

(2) With respect to persons not partners, as declared in section 35.

Sec. 34. Rights of Partner to Contribution from Co-partners After Dissolution

Where the dissolution is caused by the act, death or bankruptcy of a partner, each partner is liable to his copartners for his share of any liability created by any partner acting for the partnership as if the partnership had not been dissolved unless

(a) The dissolution being by act of any partner, the partner acting for the partnership had knowledge of the dissolution, or

(b) The dissolution being by the death or bankruptcy of a partner, the partner acting for the partnership had knowledge or notice of the death or bankruptcy.

Sec. 35. Power of Partner to Bind Partnership to Third Persons After Dissolution

(1) After dissolution a partner can bind the partnership except as provided in Paragraph (3).

(a) By any act appropriate for winding up partnership affairs or completing transactions unfinished at dissolution;

(b) By any transaction which would bind the partnership if dissolution had not taken place, provided the other party to the transaction

(I) Had extended credit to the partnership prior to dissolution and had no knowledge or notice of the dissolution; or

(II) Though he had not so extended credit, had nevertheless known of the partnership prior to dissolution, and, having no knowledge or notice of dissolution, the fact of dissolution had not been advertised in a newspaper of general circulation in the place (or in each place if more than one) at which the partnership business was regularly carried on.

(2) The liability of a partner under paragraph (1b)

shall be satisfied out of partnership assets alone when such partner had been prior to dissolution

(a) Unknown as a partner to the person with whom the contract is made; and

(b) So far unknown and inactive in partnership affairs that the business reputation of the partnership could not be said to have been in any degree due to his connection with it.

(3) The partnership is in no case bound by any act of a partner after dissolution

(a) Where the partnership is dissolved because it is unlawful to carry on the business, unless the act is appropriate for winding up partnership affairs; or

(b) Where the partner has become bankrupt; or

(c) Where the partner has no authority to wind up partnership affairs; except by a transaction with one who

(I) Had extended credit to the partnership prior to dissolution and had no knowledge or notice of his want of authority; or

(II) Had not extended credit to the partnership prior to dissolution, and, having no knowledge or notice of his want of authority, the fact of his want of authority has not been advertised in the manner provided for advertising the fact of dissolution in paragraph (1bII).

(4) Nothing in this section shall affect the liability under Section 16 of any person who after dissolution represents himself or consents to another representing him as a partner in a partnership engaged in carrying on business.

Sec. 36. Effect of Dissolution on Partner's Existing Liability

(1) The dissolution of the partnership does not of itself discharge the existing liability of any partner.

(2) A partner is discharged from any existing liability upon dissolution of the partnership by an agreement to that effect between himself, the partnership creditor and the person or partnership continuing the business; and such agreement may be inferred from the course of dealing between the creditor having knowledge of the dissolution and the person or partnership continuing the business.

(3) Where a person agrees to assume the existing obligations of a dissolved partnership, the partners whose obligations have been assumed shall be discharged

from any liability to any creditor of the partnership who, knowing of the agreement, consents to a material alteration in the nature or time of payment of such obligations.

(4) The individual property of a deceased partner shall be liable for all obligations of the partnership incurred while he was a partner but subject to the prior payment of his separate debts.

Sec. 37. **Right to Wind Up**

Unless otherwise agreed the partners who have not wrongfully dissolved the partnership or the legal representative of the last surviving partner, not bankrupt, has the right to wind up the partnership affairs; provided, however, that any partner, his legal representative or his assignee, upon cause shown, may obtain winding up by the court.

Sec. 38. **Rights of Partners to Application of Partnership Property**

(1) When dissolution is caused in any way, except in contravention of the partnership agreement, each partner, as against his co-partners and all persons claiming through them in respect of their interests in the partnership, unless otherwise agreed, may have the partnership property applied to discharge its liabilities, and the surplus applied to pay in cash the net amount owing to the respective partners. But if dissolution is caused by expulsion of a partner, bona fide under the partnership agreement and if the expelled partner is discharged from all partnership liabilities, either by payment or agreement under section 36(2), he shall receive in cash only the net amount due him from the partnership.

(2) When dissolution is caused in contravention of the partnership agreement the rights of the partners shall be as follows:

(a) Each partner who has not caused dissolution wrongfully shall have,

(I) All the rights specified in paragraph (1) of this section, and

(II) The right, as against each partner who has caused the dissolution wrongfully, to damages for breach of the agreement.

(b) The partners who have not caused the dissolution wrongfully, if they all desire to continue the business in the same name, either by themselves or jointly with others, may do so, during the agreed term for the partnership and for that purpose may possess the partnership property, provided they se-

cure the payment by bond approved by the court, or pay to any partner who has caused the dissolution wrongfully, the value of his interest in the partnership at the dissolution, less any damages recoverable under clause (2a II) of the section, and in like manner indemnify him against all present or future partnership liabilities.

(c) A partner who has caused the dissolution wrongfully shall have:

(I) If the business is not continued under the provisions of paragraph (2b) all the rights of a partner under paragraph (1), subject to clause (2a II), of this section,

(II) If the business is continued under paragraph (2b) of this section the right as against his co-partners and all claiming through them in respect of their interests in the partnership, to have the value of his interest in the partnership, less any damages caused to his co-partners by the dissolution, ascertained and paid to him in cash, or the payment secured by bond approved by the court, and to be released from all existing liabilities of the partnership; but in ascertaining the value of the partner's interest the value of the good-will of the business shall not be considered.

Sec. 39. **Rights Where Partnership is Dissolved for Fraud or Misrepresentation**

Where a partnership contract is rescinded on the ground of the fraud or misrepresentation of one of the parties thereto, the party entitled to rescind is, without prejudice to any other right, entitled,

(a) To a lien on, or right of retention of, the surplus of the partnership property after satisfying the partnership liabilities to third persons for any sum of money paid by him for the purchase of an interest in the partnership and for any capital or advances contributed by him; and

(b) To stand, after all liabilities to third persons have been satisfied, in the place of the creditors of the partnership for any payments made by him in respect of the partnership liabilities; and

(c) To be indemnified by the person guilty of the fraud or making the representation against all debts and liabilities of the partnership.

Sec. 40. **Rules for Distribution**

In settling accounts between the partners after dissolution, the following rules shall be observed, subject to any agreement to the contrary:

(a) The assets of the partnership are:

    (I) The partnership property,

    (II) The contributions of the partners necessary for the payment of all the liabilities specified in clause (b) of this paragraph.

(b) The liabilities of the partnership shall rank in order of payment, as follows:

    (I) Those owing to creditors other than partners,

    (II) Those owing to partners other than for capital and profits,

    (III) Those owing to partners in respect of capital,

    (IV) Those owing to partners in respect of profits.

(c) The assets shall be applied in the order of their declaration in clause (a) of this paragraph to the satisfaction of the liabilities.

(d) The partners shall contribute, as provided by section 18(a) the amount necessary to satisfy the liabilities; but if any, but not all, of the partners are insolvent, or, not being subject to process, refuse to contribute, the other parties shall contribute their share of the liabilities, and, in the relative proportions in which they share the profits, the additional amount necessary to pay the liabilities.

(e) An assignee for the benefit of creditors or any person appointed by the court shall have the right to enforce the contributions specified in clause (d) of this paragraph.

(f) Any partner or his legal representative shall have the right to enforce the contributions specified in clause (d) of this paragraph, to the extent of the amount which he has paid in excess of his share of the liability.

(g) The individual property of a deceased partner shall be liable for the contributions specified in clause (d) of this paragraph.

(h) When partnership property and the individual properties of the partners are in possession of a court for distribution, partnership creditors shall have priority on partnership property and separate creditors on individual property, saving the rights of lien or secured creditors as heretofore.

(i) Where a partner has become bankrupt or his estate is insolvent the claims against his separate property shall rank in the following order:

    (I) Those owing to separate creditors,

    (II) Those owing to partnership creditors,

    (III) Those owing to partners by way of contribution.

Sec. 41. Liability of Persons Continuing the Business in Certain Cases

(1) When any new partner is admitted into an existing partnership, or when any partner retires and assigns (or the representative of the deceased partner assigns) his rights in partnership property to two or more of the partners, or to one or more of the partners and one or more third persons, if the business is continued without liquidation of the partnership affairs, creditors of the first or dissolved partnership are also creditors of the partnership so continuing the business.

(2) When all but one partner retire and assign (or the representative of a deceased partner assigns) their rights in partnership property to the remaining partner, who continues the business without liquidation of partnership affairs, either alone or with others, creditors of the dissolved partnership are also creditors of the person or partnership so continuing the business.

(3) When any partner retires or dies and the business of the dissolved partnership is continued as set forth in paragraphs (1) and (2) of this section, with the consent of the retired partners or the representative of the deceased partner, but without any assignment of his right in partnership property, rights of creditors of the dissolved partnership and of the creditors of the person or partnership continuing the business shall be as if such assignment had been made.

(4) When all the partners or their representatives assign their rights in partnership property to one or more third persons who promise to pay the debts and who continue the business of the dissolved partnership, creditors of the dissolved partnership are also creditors of the person or partnership continuing the business.

(5) When any partner wrongfully causes a dissolution and the remaining partners continue the business under the provisions of section 38(2b), either alone or with others, and without liquidation of the partnership affairs, creditors of the dissolved partnership are also creditors of the person or partnership continuing the business.

(6) When a partner is expelled and the remaining partners continue the business either alone or with others, without liquidation of the partnership affairs,

creditors of the dissolved partnership are also creditors of the person or partnership continuing the business.

(7) The liability of a third person becoming a partner in the partnership continuing the business, under this section, to the creditors of the dissolved partnership shall be satisfied out of partnership property only.

(8) When the business of a partnership after dissolution is continued under any conditions set forth in this section the creditors of the dissolved partnership, as against the separate creditors of the retiring or deceased partner or the representative of the deceased partner, have a prior right to any claim of the retired partner or the representative of the deceased partner against the person or partnership continuing the business, on account of the retired or deceased partner's interest in the dissolved partnership or on account of any consideration promised for such interest or for his right in partnership property.

(9) Nothing in this section shall be held to modify any right of creditors to set aside any assignment on the ground of fraud.

(10) The use by the person or partnership continuing the business of the partnership name, or the name of a deceased partner as part thereof, shall not of itself make the individual property of the deceased partner liable for any debts contracted by such person or partnership.

Sec. 42. **Rights of Retiring or Estate of Deceased Partner When the Business is Continued**

When any partner retires or dies, and the business is continued under any of the conditions set forth in sec-

tion 41 (1, 2, 3, 5, 6), or section 38(2b) without any settlement of accounts as between him or his estate and the person or partnership continuing the business, unless otherwise agreed, he or his legal representative as against such persons or partnership may have the value of his interest at the date of dissolution ascertained, and shall receive as an ordinary creditor an amount equal to the value of his interest in the dissolved partnership with interest, or, at his option or at the option of his legal representative, in lieu of interest, the profits attributable to the use of his right in the property of the dissolved partnership; provided that the creditors of the dissolved partnership as against the separate creditors, or the representative of the retired or deceased partner, shall have priority on any claim arising under this section, as provided by section 41(8) of this act.

Sec. 43. **Accrual of Actions**

The right to an account of his interest shall accrue to any partner, or his legal representative, as against the winding up partners or the surviving partners or the person or partnership continuing the business, at the date of dissolution, in the absence of any agreement to the contrary.

Part VII **Miscellaneous Provisions**

Sec. 44. **When Act Takes Effect**

This act shall take effect on the __ day of __ one thousand nine hundred and __.

Sec. 45. **Legislation Repealed**

All acts or parts of acts inconsistent with this act are hereby repealed.

Appendix C

THE UNIFORM LIMITED PARTNERSHIP ACT

(Adopted in 39 States, all except Arkansas, Colorado, Connecticut, Louisiana, Maryland, Minnesota, Montana, Nebraska, Washington, West Virginia, and Wyoming. Also adopted in the District of Columbia, and the Virgin Islands.)

Sec. 1. Limited Partnership Defined

A limited partnership is a partnership formed by two or more persons under the provisions of Section 2, having as members one or more general partners and one or more limited partners. The limited partners as such shall not be bound by the obligations of the partnership.

Sec. 2. Formation

(1) Two or more persons desiring to form a limited partnership shall

(a) Sign and swear to a certificate, which shall state

I. The name of the partnership,

II. The character of the business,

III. The location of the principal place of business,

IV. The name and place of residence of each member; general and limited partners being respectively designated,

V. The term for which the partnership is to exist,

VI. The amount of cash and a description of and the agreed value of the other property contributed by each limited partner,

VII. The additional contributions, if any, agreed to be made by each limited partner and the times at which or events on the happening of which they shall be made,

VIII. The time, if agreed upon, when the contribution of each limited partner is to be returned,

IX. The share of the profits or the other compensation by way of income which each limited partner shall receive by reason of his contribution,

X. The right, if given, of a limited partner to substitute an assignee as contributor in his place, and the terms and conditions of the substitution,

XI. The right, if given, of the partners to admit additional limited partners,

XII. The right, if given, of one or more of the limited partners to priority over other limited partners, as to contributions or as to compensation by way of income, and the nature of such priority,

XIII. The right, if given, of the remaining general partner or partners to continue the business on the death, retirement or insanity of a general partner, and

XIV. The right, if given, of a limited partner to demand and receive property other than cash in return for his contribution.

(b) File for record the certificate in the office of [here designate the proper office].

(2) A limited partnership is formed if there has been substantial compliance in good faith with the requirements of paragraph (1).

Sec. 3. Business Which May Be Carried On

A limited partnership may carry on any business which a partnership without limited partners may carry on, except [here designate the business to be prohibited].

Sec. 4. Character of Limited Partner's Contribution

The contributions of a limited partner may be cash or other property, but not services.

Sec. 5. A Name Not to Contain Surname of Limited Partner; Exceptions

(1) The surname of a limited partner shall not appear in the partnership name, unless

(a) It is also the surname of a general partner, or

(b) Prior to the time when the limited partner became such the business had been carried on under a name in which his surname appeared.

(2) A limited partner whose name appears in a partnership name contrary to the provisions of paragraph (1) is liable as a general partner to partnership creditors who extend credit to the partnership without actual knowledge that he is not a general partner.

Sec. 6. Liability for False Statements in Certificate

If the certificate contains a false statement, one who suffers loss by reliance on such statement may hold liable any party to the certificate who knew the statement to be false.

(a) At the time he signed the certificate, or

(b) Subsequently, but within a sufficient time before the statement was relied upon to enable him to cancel or amend the certificate, or to file a petition for its cancellation or amendment as provided in Section 25(3).

Sec. 7. Limited Partner Not Liable to Creditors

A limited partner shall not become liable as a general partner unless, in addition to the exercise of his rights and powers as a limited partner, he takes part in the control of the business.

Sec. 8. Admission of Additional Limited Partners

After the formation of a limited partnership, additional limited partners may be admitted upon filing an amendment to the original certificate in accordance with the requirements of Section 25.

Sec. 9. Rights, Powers and Liabilities of a General Partner

(1) A general partner shall have all the rights and powers and be subject to all the restrictions and liabilities of a partner in a partnership without limited partners, except that without the written consent or ratification of the specific act by all the limited partners, a general partner or all of the general partners have no authority to

(a) Do any act in contravention of the certificate,

(b) Do any act which would make it impossible to carry on the ordinary business of the partnership,

(c) Confess a judgment against the partnership,

(d) Possess partnership property, or assign their rights in specific partnership property, for other than a partnership purpose,

(e) Admit a person as a general partner,

(f) Admit a person as a limited partner, unless the right so to do is given in the certificate,

(g) Continue the business with partnership property on the death, retirement or insanity of a general partner, unless the right so to do is given in the certificate.

Sec. 10. Rights of a Limited Partner

(1) A limited partner shall have the same rights as a general partner to

(a) Have the partnership books kept at the principal place of business of the partnership, and at all times to inspect and copy any of them

(b) Have on demand true and full information of all things affecting the partnership, and a formal account of partnership affairs whenever circumstances render it just and reasonable, and

(c) Have dissolution and winding up by decree of court.

(2) A limited partner shall have the right to receive a share of the profits or other compensation by way of income, and to the return of his contribution as provided in Sections 15 and 16.

Sec. 11. Status of Person Erroneously Believing Himself a Limited Partner

A person who has contributed to the capital of a business conducted by a person or partnership erroneously believing that he has become a limited partner in a limited partnership, is not, by reason of his exercise of the rights of a limited partner, a general partner with the person or in the partnership carrying on the business, or bound by the obligations of such person or partnership; provided that on ascertaining the mistake he promptly renounces his interest in the profits of the business, or other compensation by way of income.

Sec. 12. One Person Both General and Limited Partner

(1) A person may be a general partner and a limited partner in the same partnership at the same time.

(2) A person who is a general, and also at the same time a limited partner, shall have all the rights and powers and be subject to all the restrictions of a general partner; except that, in respect to his contribution, he shall have the rights against the other members which he would have had if he were not also a general partner.

Sec. 13. Loans and Other Business Transactions with Limited Partner

(1) A limited partner also may loan money to and transact other business with the partnership, and, unless he is also a general partner, receive on account of resulting claims against the partnership, with general creditors, a pro rata share of the assets. No limited partner shall in respect to any such claim

    (a) Receive or hold as collateral security any partnership property, or

    (b) Receive from a general partner or the partnership any payment, conveyance, or release from liability, if at the time the assets of the partnership are not sufficient to discharge partnership liabilities to persons not claiming as general or limited partners,

(2) The receiving of collateral security, or a payment, conveyance, or release in violation of the provisions of paragraph (1) is a fraud on the creditors of the partnership.

Sec. 14. Relation of Limited Partners Inter Se

Where there are several limited partners the members may agree that one or more of the limited partners shall have a priority over other limited partners as to the return of their contributions, as to their compensation by way of income, or as to any other matter. If such an agreement is made it shall be stated in the certificate, and in the absence of such a statement all the limited partners shall stand upon equal footing.

Sec. 15. Compensation of Limited Partner

A limited partner may receive from the partnership the share of the profits or the compensation by way of

income stipulated for in the certificate; provided, that after such payment is made, whether from the property of the partnership or that of a general partner, the partnership assets are in excess of all liabilities of the partnership except liabilities to limited partners on account of their contributions and to general partners.

Sec. 16. Withdrawal or Reduction of Limited Partner's Contribution

(1) A limited partner shall not receive from a general partner or out of partnership property any part of his contribution until

    (a) All liabilities of the partnership, except liabilities to general partners and to limited partners on account of their contributions, have been paid or there remains property of the partnership sufficient to pay them,

    (b) The consent of all members is had, unless the return of the contribution may be rightfully demanded under the provisions of paragraph (2), and

    (c) The certificate is cancelled or so amended as to set forth the withdrawal or reduction.

(2) Subject to the provisions of paragraph (1) a limited partner may rightfully demand the return of his contribution

    (a) On the dissolution of a partnership, or

    (b) When the date specified in the certificate for its return has arrived, or

    (c) After he has given six months' notice in writing to all other members, if no time is specified in the certificate either for the return of the contribution or for the dissolution of the partnership,

(3) In the absence of any statement in the certificate to the contrary or the consent of all members, a limited partner, irrespective of the nature of his contribution, has only the right to demand and receive cash in return for his contribution.

(4) A limited partner may have the partnership dissolved and its affairs wound up when

    (a) He rightfully but unsuccessfully demands the return of his contribution, or

    (b) The other liabilities of the partnership have not been paid, or the partnership property is insufficient for their payment as required by paragraph (1a) and the limited partner would otherwise be entitled to the return of his contribution.

Sec. 17. **Liability of Limited Partner to Partnership**

(1) A limited partner is liable to the partnership

(a) For the difference between his contribution as actually made and that stated in the certificate as having been made, and

(b) For any unpaid contribution which he agreed in the certificate to make in the future at the time and on the conditions stated in the certificate.

(2) A limited partner holds as trustee for the partnership

(a) Specific property stated in the certificate as contributed by him, but which was not contributed or which has been wrongfully returned, and

(b) Money or other property wrongfully paid or conveyed to him on account of his contribution.

(3) The liabilities of a limited partner as set forth in this section can be waived or compromised only by the consent of all members; but a waiver or compromise shall not affect the right of a creditor of a partnership who extended credit or whose claim arose after the filing and before a cancellation or amendment of the certificate, to enforce such liabilities.

(4) When a contributor has rightfully received the return in whole or in part of the capital of his contribution, he is nevertheless liable to the partnership for any sum, not in excess of such return with interest, necessary to discharge its liabilities to all creditors who extended credit or whose claims arose before such return.

Sec. 18. **Nature of Limited Partner's Interest in Partnership**

A limited partner's interest in the partnership is personal property.

Sec. 19. **Assignment of Limited Partner's Interest**

(1) A limited partner's interest is assignable.

(2) A substituted limited partner is a person admitted to all the rights of a limited partner who has died or has assigned his interest in a partnership.

(3) An assignee, who does not become a substituted limited partner, has no right to require any information or account of the partnership transactions or to inspect the partnership books; he is only entitled to receive the share of the profits or other compensation by way of income, or the return of his contribution, to which his assignor would otherwise be entitled.

(4) An assignee shall have the right to become a substituted limited partner if all the members (except the assignor) consent thereto or if the assignor, being thereunto empowered by the certificate, gives the assignee that right.

(5) An assignee becomes a substituted limited partner when the certificate is appropriately amended in accordance with Section 25.

(6) The substituted limited partner has all the rights and powers, and is subject to all the restrictions and liabilities of his assignor, except those liabilities of which he was ignorant at the time he became a limited partner and which could not be ascertained from the certificate.

(7) The substitution of the assignee as a limited partner does not release the assignor from liability to the partnership under Sections 6 and 17.

Sec. 20. **Effect of Retirement, Death or Insanity of a General Partner**

The retirement, death or insanity of a general partner dissolves the partnership, unless the business is continued by the remaining general partners

(a) Under a right so to do stated in the certificate, or

(b) With the consent of all members.

Sec. 21. **Death of Limited Partner**

(1) On the death of a limited partner his executor or administrator shall have all the rights of a limited partner for the purpose of settling his estate, and such power as the deceased had to constitute his assignee a substituted limited partner.

(2) The estate of a deceased limited partner shall be liable for all his liabilities as a limited partner.

Sec. 22. **Rights of Creditors of Limited Partner**

(1) On due application to a court of competent jurisdiction by any judgment creditor of a limited partner, the court may charge the interest of the indebted limited partner with payment of the unsatisfied amount of the judgment debt; and may appoint a receiver, and make all other orders, directions, and inquiries which the circumstances of the case may require.

In those states where a creditor on beginning an action can attach debts due the defendant before he has obtained a judgment against the defendant it is recommended that paragraph (1) of this section read as follows:

On due application to a court of competent jurisdiction by any creditor of a limited partner, the court may charge the interest of the indebted limited partner with payment of the unsatisfied amount of such claim; and may appoint a receiver, and make all other orders, directions, and inquiries which the circumstances of the case may require.

(2) The interest may be redeemed with the separate property of any general partner, but may not be redeemed with partnership property.

(3) The remedies conferred by paragraph (1) shall not be deemed exclusive of others which may exist.

(4) Nothing in this act shall be held to deprive a limited partner of his statutory exemption.

Sec. 23. **Distribution of Assets**

(1) In settling accounts after dissolution the liabilities of the partnership shall be entitled to payment in the following order:

(a) Those to creditors, in the order of priority as provided by law, except those to limited partners on account of their contributions, and to general partners,

(b) Those to limited partners in respect to their share of the profits and other compensation by way of income on their contributions,

(c) Those to limited partners in respect to the capital of their contributions,

(d) Those to general partners other than for capital and profits,

(e) Those to general partners in respect to profits,

(f) Those to general partners in respect to capital.

(2) Subject to any statement in the certificate or to subsequent agreement, limited partners share in the partnership assets in respect to their claims for capital, and in respect to their claims for profits or for compensation by way of income on their contributions respectively, in proportion to the respective amounts of such claims.

Sec. 24. **When Certificate Shall Be Cancelled or Amended**

(1) The certificate shall be cancelled when the partnership is dissolved or all limited partners cease to be such.

(2) A certificate shall be amended when

(a) There is a change in the name of the partnership

or in the amount or character of the contribution of any limited partner,

(b) A person is substituted as a limited partner,

(c) An additional limited partner is admitted,

(d) A person is admitted as a general partner,

(e) A general partner retires, dies or becomes insane, and the business is continued under Section 20,

(f) There is a change in the character of the business of the partnership,

(g) There is a false or erroneous statement in the certificate,

(h) There is a change in the time as stated in the certificate for the dissolution of the partnership or for the return of a contribution,

(i) A time is fixed for the dissolution of the partnership, or the return of a contribution, no time having been specified in the certificate, or

(j) The members desire to make a change in any other statement in the certificate in order that it shall accurately represent the agreement between them.

Sec. 25. **Requirements for Amendment and for Cancellation of Certificate**

(1) The writing to amend a certificate shall

(a) Conform to the requirements of Section 2(1a) as far as necessary to set forth clearly the change in the certificate which it is desired to make, and

(b) Be signed and sworn to by all members, and an amendment substituting a limited partner or adding a limited or general partner shall be signed also by the member to be substituted or added, and when a limited partner is to be substituted, the amendment shall also be signed by the assigning limited partner.

(2) The writing to cancel a certificate shall be signed by all members.

(3) A person desiring the cancellation or amendment of a certificate, if any person designated in paragraphs (1) and (2) as a person who must execute the writing refuses to do so, may petition the [here designate the proper court] to direct a cancellation or amendment thereof.

(4) If the court finds that the petitioner has a right to have the writing executed by a person who refuses to do so, it shall order the [here designate the responsible official in the office designated in Section 2] in the office where the certificate is recorded to record the

cancellation or amendment of the certificate; and where the certificate is to be amended, the court shall also cause to be filed for record in said office a certified copy of its decree setting forth the amendment.

(5) A certificate is amended or cancelled when there is filed for record in the office [here designate the office designated in Section 2] where the certificate is recorded

(a) A writing in accordance with the provisions of paragraph (1), or (2) or

(b) A certified copy of the order of court in accordance with the provisions of paragraph (4).

(6) After the certificate is duly amended in accordance with this section, the amended certificate shall thereafter be for all purposes the certificate provided for by this act.

Sec. 26. Parties to Actions

A contributor, unless he is a general partner, is not a proper party to proceedings by or against a partnership, except where the object is to enforce a limited partner's right against or liability to the partnership.

Sec. 27. Name of Act

This act may be cited as The Uniform Limited Partnership Act.

Sec. 28. Rules of Construction

(1) The rule that statutes in derogation of the common law are to be strictly construed shall have no application to this act.

(2) This act shall be so interpreted and construed as to effect its general purpose to make uniform the law of those states which enact it.

(3) This act shall not be so construed as to impair the obligations of any contract existing when the act goes into effect, nor to affect any action or proceedings begun or right accrued before this act takes effect.

Sec. 29. Rules for Cases Not Provided for in This Act

In any case not provided for in this act the rules of law and equity, including the law merchant, shall govern.

Sec. 30. Provisions for Existing Limited Partnerships

(1) A limited partnership formed under any statute of this state prior to the adoption of this act, may become a limited partnership under this act by complying with the provisions of Section 2; provided the certificate sets forth

(a) The amount of the original contribution of each limited partner, and the time when the contribution was made, and

(b) That the property of the partnership exceeds the amount sufficient to discharge its liabilities to persons not claiming as general or limited partners by an amount greater than the sum of the contributions of its limited partners.

(2) A limited partnership formed under any statute of this state prior to the adoption of this act, until or unless it becomes a limited partnership under this act, shall continue to be governed by the provisions of [here insert proper reference to the existing limited partnership act or acts], except that such partnership shall not be renewed unless so provided in the original agreement.

Sec. 31. Act [Acts] Repealed

Except as affecting existing limited partnerships to the extent set forth in Section 30, the act (acts) of [here designate the existing limited partnership act or acts] is (are) hereby repealed.

Appendix D

THE REVISED UNIFORM LIMITED PARTNERSHIP ACT

(Adopted August 5, 1976, by the National Conference of Commissioners on Uniform State Laws, subject to style changes; it is intended that it will replace the existing Uniform Limited Partnership Act (Appendix E); as of publication, it has been adopted in Arkansas, Colorado, Connecticut, Maryland, Minnesota, Montana, Nebraska, Washington, West Virginia, and Wyoming.

The Act consists of 11 Articles as follows:

1. General Provisions
2. Formation; Certificate of Limited Partnership
3. Limited Partners
4. General Partners
5. Finance
6. Distribution and Withdrawal
7. Assignment of Partnership Interests
8. Dissolution
9. Foreign Limited Partnerships
10. Derivative Actions
11. Miscellaneous

Article 1
GENERAL PROVISIONS

Sec. 101. **Definitions**

As used in this Act, unless the context otherwise requires:

(1) "Certificate of limited partnership" means the certificate referred to in Section 201, as that certificate is amended from time to time.

(2) "Contribution" means any cash, property, or services rendered, or a promissory note or other binding obligation to contribute cash or property or to perform services, which a partner contributes to a limited partnership in his capacity as a partner.

(3) "Event of withdrawal of a general partner" means an event that causes a person to cease to be a general partner as provided in Section 402.

(4) "Foreign limited partnership" means a partnership formed under the laws of any State other than this State and having as partners one or more general partners and one or more limited partners.

(5) "General partner" means a person who has been admitted to a limited partnership as a general partner in accordance with the partnership agreement and named in the certificate of limited partnership as a general partner.

(6) "Limited partner" means a person who has been admitted to a limited partnership as a limited partner in accordance with the partnership agreement and named in the certificate of limited partnership as a limited partner.

(7) "Limited partnership" and "domestic limited partnership" mean a partnership formed by 2 or more persons under the laws of this State and having one or more general partners and one or more limited partners.

(8) "Partner" means any limited partner or general partner.

(9) "Partnership agreement" means any valid agreement, written or oral, of the partners as to the affairs of a limited partnership and the conduct of its business.

(10) "Partnership interest" means a partner's share

of the profits and losses of a limited partnership and the right to receive distributions of partnership assets.

(11) "Person" means a natural person, partnership, limited partnership (domestic or foreign), trust, estate, association, or corporation.

(12) "State" means a state, territory, or possession of the United States, the District of Columbia, or the Commonwealth of Puerto Rico.

Sec. 102. Name

The name of each limited partnership as set forth in its certificate of limited partnership:

(1) shall contain without abbreviation the words "limited partnership";

(2) may not contain the name of a limited partner unless (i) it is also the name of a general partner or the corporate name of a corporate general partner, or (ii) the business of the limited partnership had been carried on under that name before the admission of that limited partner;

(3) may not contain any word or phrase indicating or implying that it is organized other than for a purpose stated in its certificate of limited partnership;

(4) may not be the same as, or deceptively similar to, the name of any corporation or limited partnership organized under the laws of this State or licensed or registered as a foreign corporation or limited partnership in this State; and

(5) may not contain the following words [here insert prohibited words].

Sec. 103. Reservation of Name

(a) The exclusive right to the use of a name may be reserved by:

(1) any person intending to organize a limited partnership under this Act and to adopt that name;

(2) any domestic limited partnership or any foreign limited partnership registered in this State which, in either case, intends to adopt that name;

(3) any foreign limited partnership intending to register in this State and to adopt that name; and

(4) any person intending to organize a foreign limited partnership and intending to have it registered in this State and to adopt that name.

(b) The reservation shall be made by filing with the Secretary of State an application, executed by the applicant, to reserve a specified name. If the Secretary of State finds that the name is available for use by a domestic or foreign limited partnership, he shall reserve the name for the exclusive use of the applicant for a period of 120 days. Once having reserved a name, the same applicant may not again reserve the same name until more than 60 days after the expiration of the last 120-day period for which that applicant reserved that name. The right to the exclusive use of a reserved name may be transferred to any other person by filing in the office of the Secretary of State a notice of the transfer, executed by the applicant for whom the name was reserved and specifying the name and address of the transferee.

Sec. 104. Specified Office and Agent

Each limited partnership shall continuously maintain in this State:

(1) an office, which may but need not be a place of its business in this State, at which shall be kept the records required by Section 105 to be maintained; and

(2) an agent for service of process on the limited partnership, which agent must be an individual resident of this State, a domestic corporation, or a foreign corporation authorized to do business in this State.

Sec. 105. Records to be Kept

Each limited partnership shall keep at the office referred to in Section 104(1) the following: (1) a current list of the full name and last known business address of each partner set forth in alphabetical order, (2) a copy of the certificate of limited partnership and all certificates of amendment thereto, together with executed copies of any powers of attorney pursuant to which any certificate has been executed, (3) copies of the limited partnership's federal, state, and local income tax returns and reports, if any, for the 3 most recent years, and (4) copies of any then effective written partnership agreements and of any financial statements of the limited partnership for the 3 most recent years. These records are subject to inspection and copying at the reasonable request, and at the expense, of any partner during ordinary business hours.

Sec. 106. Nature of Business

A limited partnership may carry on any business that a partnership without limited partners may carry on except [here designate prohibited activities].

Sec. 107. Business Transactions of Partner With the Partnership

Except as provided in the partnership agreement, a partner may lend money to and transact other business with the limited partnership and, subject to other applicable law, has the same rights and obligations with respect thereto as a person who is not a partner.

Article 2
FORMATION; CERTIFICATE OF LIMITED PARTNERSHIP

Sec. 201. Certificate of Limited Partnership

(a) In order to form a limited partnership two or more persons must execute a certificate of limited partnership. The certificate shall be filed in the office of the Secretary of State and set forth:

(1) the name of the limited partnership;

(2) the general character of its business;

(3) the address of the office and the name and address of the agent for service of process required to be maintained by Section 104;

(4) the name and the business address of each partner (specifying separately the general partners and limited partners);

(5) the amount of cash and a description and statement of the agreed value of the other property or services contributed by each partner and which each partner has agreed to contribute in the future;

(6) the times at which or events on the happening of which any additional contributions agreed to be made by each partner are to be made;

(7) any power of a limited partner to grant the right to become a limited partner to an assignee of any part of his partnership interest and the terms and conditions of the power;

(8) if agreed upon, the time at which or the events on the happening of which a partner may terminate his membership in the limited partnership and the amount of, or the method of determining, the distribution to which he may be entitled respecting his partnership interest, and the terms and conditions of the termination and distribution;

(9) any right of a partner to receive distributions of property, including cash from the limited partnership;

(10) any right of a partner to receive, or of a general partner to make, distributions to a partner which include a return of all or any part of the partner's contribution;

(11) any time at which or events upon the happening of which the limited partnership is to be dissolved and its affairs wound up;

(12) any right of the remaining general partners to continue the business on the happening of an event of withdrawal of a general partner; and

(13) any other matters the partners determine to include therein.

(b) A limited partnership is formed at the time of the filing of the certificate of limited partnership in the office of the Secretary of State or at any later time specified in the certificate of limited partnership if, in each case, there has been substantial compliance with the requirements of this section.

Sec. 202. Amendment to Certificate

(a) A certificate of limited partnership is amended by filing a certificate of amendment thereto in the office of the Secretary of State. The certificate shall set forth:

(1) the name of the limited partnership;

(2) the date of filing of the certificate; and

(3) the amendments to the certificate.

(b) Within 30 days after the happening of any of the following events an amendment to a certificate of limited partnership reflecting the occurrence of the event or events shall be filed:

(1) a change in the amount or character of the contribution of any partner, or in any partner's obligation to make a contribution;

(2) the admission of a new partner;

(3) the withdrawal of a partner; or

(4) the continuation of the business under Section 801 after an event of withdrawal of a general partner.

(c) A general partner who becomes aware that any statement in a certificate of limited partnership was false when made or that any arrangements or other facts described have changed, making the certificate inaccurate in any respect, shall promptly amend the certificate, but an amendment to show a change of address of a limited partner need be filed only once every 12 months.

(d) A certificate of limited partnership may be amended at any time for any other proper purpose the general partners may determine.

(e) No person has any liability because an amendment to a certificate of limited partnership has not been filed to reflect the occurrence of any event referred to in subsection (b) of this Section if the amendment is filed within the 30-day period specified in subsection (b).

Sec. 203. **Cancellation of Certificate**

A certificate of limited partnership shall be cancelled upon the dissolution and the commencement of winding up of the partnership and at any other time there are no remaining limited partners. A certificate of cancellation shall be filed in the office of the Secretary of State and shall set forth:

(1) the name of the limited partnership;

(2) the date of filing of its certificate of limited partnership;

(3) the reason for filing the certificate of cancellation;

(4) the effective date (which shall be a date certain) of cancellation if it is not to be effective upon the filing of the certificate; and

(5) any other information the general partners filing the certificate may determine.

Sec. 204. **Execution of Certificates**

(a) Each certificate required by this Article to be filed in the office of the Secretary of State shall be executed in the following manner:

(1) each original certificate of limited partnership must be signed by each partner named therein;

(2) each certificate of amendment must be signed by at least one general partner and by each other partner designated in the certificate as a new partner or whose contribution is described as having been increased; and

(3) each certificate of cancellation must be signed by all general partners.

(b) Any person may sign a certificate by an attorney-in-fact, but a power of attorney to sign a certificate relating to the admission, or increased contribution, of a partner must specifically describe the admission or increase.

(c) The execution of a certificate by a general partner constitutes an affirmation under the penalties of perjury that the facts stated therein are true.

Sec. 205. **Amendment or Cancellation by Judicial Act**

If a person required by Section 204 to execute a certificate of amendment or cancellation fail or refuse to do so, any other partner, and any assignee of a partnership interest, who is adversely affected by the failure or refusal, may petition the [here designate the proper court] to direct the amendment or cancellation. If the court finds that the amendment or cancellation is proper and that the person so designated has failed or refused to execute the certificate, it shall order the Secretary of State to record an appropriate certificate of amendment or cancellation.

Sec. 206. **Filing in the Office of the Secretary of State**

(a) Two signed copies of the certificate of limited partnership and of any certificates of amendment or cancellation (or of any judicial decree of amendment or cancellation) shall be delivered to the Secretary of State. A person who executes a certificate as an agent or fiduciary need not exhibit evidence of his authority as a prerequisite to filing. Unless the Secretary of State finds that any certificate does not conform to law, upon receipt of all filing fees required by law he shall:

(1) endorse on each duplicate original the word "Filed" and the day, month, and year of the filing thereof;

(2) file one duplicate original in his office; and

(3) return the other duplicate original to the person who filed it or his representative.

(b) Upon the filing of a certificate of amendment (or judicial decree of amendment) in the office of the Secretary of State, the certificate of limited partnership shall be amended as set forth therein, and upon the effective date of a certificate of cancellation (or a judicial decree thereof), the certificate of limited partnership is cancelled.

Sec. 207. **Liability for False Statement in Certificate**

If any certificate of limited partnership or certificate of amendment or cancellation contains a false statement, one who suffers loss by reliance on the statement may recover damages for the loss from:

(1) any person who executes the certificate, or causes another to execute it on his behalf, and knew, and any general partner who knew or should have known, the statement to be false at the time the certificate was executed; and

(2) any general partner who thereafter knows or should have known that any arrangement or other fact described in the certificate have changed, making the statement inaccurate in any respect within a sufficient time before the statement was relied upon reasonably to have enabled that general partner to cancel or amend

the certificate, or to file a petition for its cancellation or amendment under Section 205.

Sec. 208. Notice

The fact that a certificate of limited partnership is on file in the office of the Secretary of State is notice that the partnership is a limited partnership and the persons designated therein as limited partners are limited partners, but is not notice of any other fact.

Sec. 209. Delivery of Certificates to Limited Partners

Upon the return by the Secretary of State pursuant to Section 206 of a certificate marked "Filed," the general partners shall promptly deliver or mail a copy of the certificate of limited partnership and each certificate to each limited partner unless the partnership agreement provides otherwise.

Article 3
LIMITED PARTNERS

Sec. 301. Admission of Additional Limited Partners

(a) After the filing of a limited partnership's original certificate of limited partnership, a person may be admitted as a new limited partner:

(1) in the case of a person acquiring a partnership interest directly from the limited partnership, upon the compliance with the partnership agreement or, if the partnership agreement does not so provide, upon the written consent of all partners; and

(2) in the case of an assignee of a partnership interest of a partner who has the power, as provided in Section 704, to grant the assignee the right to become a limited partner, upon the exercise of that power and compliance with any conditions limiting the grant or exercise of the power.

(b) In each case under subsection (a), the person acquiring the partnership interest becomes a limited partner only upon amendment of the certificate of limited partnership reflecting that fact.

Sec. 302. Voting

Subject to Section 303, the partnership agreement may grant to all or a specified group of the limited partners the right to vote (on a per capita or any other basis) upon any matter.

Sec. 303. Liability to Third Parties

(a) Except as provided in subsection (d), a limited partner is not liable for the obligations of a limited partnership unless he is also a general partner or, in addition to the exercise of his rights and powers as a limited partner, he takes part in the control of the business. However, if the limited partner's participation in the control of the business is not substantially the same as the exercise of the powers of a general partner, he is liable only to persons who transact business with the limited partnership with actual knowledge of his participation in control.

(b) A limited partner does not participate in the control of the business within the meaning of subsection (a) solely by doing one or more of the following:

(1) being a contractor for or an agent or employee of the limited partnership or of a general partner;

(2) consulting with and advising a general partner with respect to the business of the limited partnership;

(3) acting as surety for the limited partnership;

(4) approving or disapproving an amendment to the partnership agreement; or

(5) voting on one or more of the following matters:

(i) the dissolution and winding up of the limited partnership;

(ii) the sale, exchange, lease, mortgage, pledge, or other transfer of all or substantially all of the assets of the limited partnership other than in the ordinary course of its business;

(iii) the incurrence of indebtedness by the limited partnership other than in the ordinary course of its business;

(iv) a change in the nature of the business; or

(v) the removal of a general partner.

(c) The enumeration in subsection (b) does not mean that the possession or exercise of any other powers by a limited partner constitutes participation by him in the business of the limited partnership.

(d) A limited partner who knowingly permits his name to be used in the name of the limited partnership, except under circumstances permitted by Section 102(2)(i), is liable to creditors who extend credit to the limited partnership without actual knowledge that the limited partner is not a general partner.

Sec. 304. Person Erroneously Believing Himself a Limited Partner

(a) Except as provided in subsection (b), a person who

makes a contribution to a business enterprise and erroneously but in good faith believes that he has become a limited partner in the enterprise is not a general partner in the enterprise and is not bound by its obligations by reason of making the contribution, receiving distributions from the enterprise, or exercising any rights of a limited partner, if, on ascertaining the mistake, he:

(1) causes an appropriate certificate of limited partnership or a certificate of amendment to be executed and filed; or

(2) withdraws from future equity participation in the enterprise.

(b) Any person who makes a contribution of the kind described in subsection (a) is liable as a general partner to any third party who transacts business with the enterprise (i) before the person withdraws and an appropriate certificate is filed to show withdrawal, or (ii) before an appropriate certificate is filed to show his status as a limited partner and, in the case of an amendment, after expiration of the 30-day period for filing an amendment relating to the person as a limited partner under Section 202, but in either case only if the third party actually believed in good faith that the person was a general partner at the time of the transaction.

Sec. 305. **Information**

Each limited partner has the right to:

(1) inspect and copy any of the partnership records required to be maintained by Section 105; and

(2) obtain from the general partners from time to time upon reasonable demand (i) true and full information regarding the state of the business and financial condition of the limited partnership, (ii) promptly after becoming available, a copy of the limited partnership's federal, state, and local income tax returns for each year, and (iii) other information regarding the affairs of the limited partnership as is just and reasonable.

Article 4
GENERAL PARTNERS

Sec. 401. **Admission of Additional General Partners**

After the filing of a limited partnership's original certificate of limited partnership, additional general partners may be admitted only with the specific written consent of each partner.

Sec. 402. **Events of Withdrawal**

Except as approved by the specific written consent of all partners at the time, a person ceases to be a general partner of a limited partnership upon the happening of any of the following events:

(1) the general partner withdraws from the limited partnership as provided in Section 602;

(2) the general partner ceases to be a member of the limited partnership as provided in Section 702;

(3) the general partner is removed as a general partner in accordance with the partnership agreement;

(4) unless otherwise provided in the certificate of limited partnership, the general partner: (i) makes an assignment for the benefit of creditors; (ii) files a voluntary petition in bankruptcy; (iii) is adjudicated a bankrupt or insolvent; (iv) files a petition or answer seeking for himself any reorganization, arrangement, composition, readjustment, liquidation, dissolution, or similar relief under any statute, law, or regulation; (v) files an answer or other pleading admitting or failing to contest the material allegations of a petition filed against him in any proceeding of this nature; or (vi) seeks, consents to, or acquiesces in the appointment of a trustee, receiver, or liquidator of the general partner or of all or any substantial part of his properties;

(5) unless otherwise provided in the certificate of limited partnership, [120] days after the commencement of any proceeding against the general partner seeking any reorganization, arrangement, composition, readjustment, liquidation, dissolution, or similar relief under any statute, law, or regulation, the proceeding has not been dismissed, or if within [90] days after the appointment without his consent or acquiescence of any trustee, receiver, or liquidator of the general partner or of all or any substantial part of his properties, the appointment is not vacated or stayed, or within [90] days after the expiration of any such stay, the appointment is not vacated;

(6) in the case of a general partner who is a natural person

(i) his death; or

(ii) the entry by a court of competent jurisdiction adjudicating him incompetent to manage his person or his property;

(7) in the case of a general partner who is acting as a general partner by virtue of being a trustee of a trust, the termination of the trust (but not merely the substitution of a new trustee);

(8) in the case of a general partner that is a separate partnership, the dissolution and commencement of winding up of the partnership;

(9) in the case of a general partner that is a corporation, the filing of a certificate of dissolution, or its equivalent, for the corporation or the revocation of its charter; and

(10) in the case of an estate, the distribution by the fiduciary of all the estate's entire interest in the partnership.

Sec. 403. General Powers and Liabilities

Except as otherwise provided in this Act and in the partnership agreement, a general partner of a limited partnership has the rights and powers and is subject to the restrictions and liabilities of a partner in a partnership without limited partners.

Sec. 404. Contributions by a General Partner

A general partner of a limited partnership may make contribution to the partnership and share in the profits and losses of, and in distributions from, the limited partnership as a general partner. A general partner also may make contributions to and share in profits, losses, and distributions as a limited partner. A person who is both a general partner and a limited partner has the rights and powers, and is subject to the restrictions and liabilities, of a general partner and, except as provided in the partnership agreement, also has the powers, and is subject to the restrictions, of a limited partner to the extent of his participation in the partnership as a limited partner.

Sec. 405. Voting

The partnership agreement may grant to all or certain identified general partners the right to vote (on a per capita or any other basis), separately or with all or any class of the limited partners, on any matter.

Article 5
FINANCE

Sec. 501. Form of Contributions

The contribution of a partner may be in cash, property, or services rendered, or a promissory note or other obligation to contribute cash or property or to perform services.

Sec. 502. Liability for Contributions

(a) Except as otherwise provided in the certificate of limited partnership, a partner is obligated to the limited partnership to perform any promise to contribute cash or property or to perform services even if he is unable to perform because of death, disability or any other reason. If a partner does not make the required contribution of property or services, he is obligated at the option of the limited partnership to contribute cash equal to that portion of the value (as stated in the certificate of limited partnership) of the stated contribution that has not been made.

(b) Unless otherwise provided in the partnership agreement, the obligation of a partner to make a contribution or return money or other property paid or distributed in violation of this Act may be compromised only by consent of all of the partners. Notwithstanding the compromise, a creditor of a limited partnership who extends credit, or whose claim arises, after the filing of the certificate of limited partnership or an amendment thereto which, in either case, reflects the obligation and before the amendment or cancellation thereof to reflect the compromise, may enforce the obligation.

Sec. 503. Sharing of Profits and Losses

The profits and losses of a limited partnership shall be allocated among the partners, and among classes of partners, in the manner provided in the partnership agreement. If the partnership agreement does not so provide, profits and losses shall be allocated on the basis of the value (as stated in the certificate of limited partnership) of the contributions made by each partner to the extent they have been received by the partnership and have not been returned.

Sec. 504. Sharing of Distributions

Distributions of cash or other assets of a limited partnership shall be allocated among the partners, and among classes of partners, in the manner provided in the partnership agreement. If the partnership agreement does not so provide, distributions shall be made on the basis of the value (as stated in the certificate of limited partnership) of the contributions made by each partner to the extent they have not been received by the partnership and have not been returned.

Article 6
DISTRIBUTIONS AND WITHDRAWAL

Sec. 601. Interim Distributions

Except as provided in this Article, a partner is entitled

to receive distributions from a limited partnership before his withdrawal from the limited partnership and before the dissolution and winding up thereof:

(1) to the extent and at the times or upon the happening of the events specified in the partnership agreement; and

(2) if any distribution constitutes a return of any part of his contribution under Section 608(c), to the extent and at the times or upon the happening of the events specified in the certificate of limited partnership.

Sec. 602. **Withdrawal of General Partner**

A general partner may withdraw from a limited partnership at any time by giving written notice to the other partners, but if the withdrawal violates the partnership agreement, the limited partnership may recover from the withdrawing general partner damages for breach of the partnership agreement and offset the damages against the amount otherwise distributable to him.

Sec. 603. **Withdrawal of Limited Partner**

A limited partner may withdraw from a limited partnership at the time or upon the happening of the events specified in the certificate of limited partnership and in accordance with the partnership agreement. If the certificate does not specify the time or the events upon the happening of which a limited partner may withdraw or a definite time for the dissolution and winding up of the limited partnership, a limited partner may withdraw upon not less than 6 months' prior written notice to each general partner at his address on the books of the limited partnership at its office in this State.

Sec. 604. **Distribution Upon Withdrawal**

Except as provided in this Article, upon withdrawal any withdrawing partner is entitled to receive any distribution to which he is entitled under the partnership agreement and, if not otherwise provided in the agreement, he is entitled to receive, within a reasonable time after withdrawal, the fair value of his interest in the limited partnership as of the date of withdrawal based upon his right to share in distributions from the limited partnership.

Sec. 605. **Distribution in Kind**

Except as provided in the certificate of limited partnership, a partner, regardless of the nature of his contribution, has no right to demand and receive any distribution from a limited partnership in any form other than cash. Except as provided in the partnership agreement, a partner may not be compelled to accept a distribution of any asset in kind from a limited partnership to the extent that the percentage of the asset distributed to him exceeds a percentage of that asset which is equal to the percentage in which he shares in distributions from the limited partnership.

Sec. 606. **Right to Distribution**

At the time a partner becomes entitled to receive a distribution, he has the status of, and is entitled to all remedies available to, a creditor of the limited partnership with respect to the distribution.

Sec. 607. **Limitations on Distribution**

A partner may not receive a distribution from a limited partnership to the extent that, after giving effect to the distribution, all liabilities of the limited partnership, other than liabilities to partners on account of their partnership interests, exceed the fair value of the partnership assets.

Sec. 608. **Liability Upon Return of Contributions**

(a) If a partner has received the return of any part of his contribution without violation of the partnership agreement or this Act, he is liable to the limited partnership for a period of one year thereafter for the amount of the returned contribution, but only to the extent necessary to discharge the limited partnership's liabilities to creditors who extended credit to the limited partnership during the period the contribution was held by the partnership.

(b) If a partner has received the return of any part of his contribution in violation of the partnership agreement or this Act, he is liable to the limited partnership for a period of 6 years thereafter for the amount of the contribution wrongfully returned.

(c) A partner receives a return of his contribution to the extent that a distribution to him reduces his share of the fair value of the net assets of the limited partnership below the value (as set forth in the certificate of limited partnership) of his contributions which has not been distributed to him.

Article 7
ASSIGNMENT OF PARTNERSHIP INTERESTS

Sec. 701. **Nature of Partnership Interest**

A partnership interest is personal property.

Sec. 702. **Assignment of Partnership Interest**

Except as provided in the partnership agreement, a partnership interest is assignable in whole or in part. An assignment of a partnership interest does not dissolve a limited partnership or entitle the assignee to become or to exercise any rights of a partner. An assignment entitles the assignee to receive, to the extent assigned, only the distribution to which the assignor would be entitled. Except as provided in the partnership agreement, a partner ceases to be a partner upon assignment of all his partnership interest.

Sec. 703. **Rights of Creditor**

On application to a court of competent jurisdiction by any judgment creditor of a partner, the court may charge the partnership interest of the partner with payment of the unsatisfied amount of the judgment with interest. To the extent so charged, the judgment creditor has only the rights of an assignee of the partnership interest. This Act does not deprive any partner of the benefit of any exemption laws applicable to his partnership interest.

Sec. 704. **Right of Assignee to Become Limited Partner**

(a) An assignee of a partnership interest, including an assignee of a general partner, may become a limited partner if and to the extent that (1) the assignor gives the assignee that right in accordance with authority described in the certificate of limited partnership, or (2) all other partners consent.

(b) An assignee who has become a limited partner has, to the extent assigned, the rights and powers, and is subject to the restrictions and liabilities, of a limited partner under the partnership agreement and this Act. An assignee who becomes a limited partner also is liable for the obligations of his assignor to make and return contributions as provided in Article 6. However, the assignee is not obligated for liabilities unknown to the assignee at the time he became a limited partner and which could not be ascertained from the certificate of limited partnership.

(c) If an assignee of a partnership interest becomes a limited partner, the assignor is not released from his liability to the limited partnership under Sections 207 and 502.

Sec. 705. **Power of Estate of Deceased or Incompetent Partner**

If a partner who is an individual dies or a court of competent jurisdiction adjudges him to be incompetent to manage his person or his property, the partner's executor, administrator, guardian, conservator, or other legal representative may exercise all of the partner's rights for the purpose of settling his estate or administering his property, including any power the partner had to give an assignee the right to become a limited partner. If a partner is a corporation, trust, or other entity and is dissolved or terminated, the powers of that partner may be exercised by its legal representative or successor.

Article 8
DISSOLUTION

Sec. 801. **Nonjudicial Dissolution**

A limited partnership is dissolved and its affairs shall be wound up upon the happening of the first to occur of the following:

(1) at the time or upon the happening of events specified in the certificate of limited partnership;

(2) written consent of all partners;

(3) an event of withdrawal of a general partner unless at the time there is at least one other general partner and the certificate of limited partnership permits the business of the limited partnership to be carried on by the remaining general partner and that partner does so, but the limited partnership is not dissolved and is not required to be wound up by reason of any event of withdrawal if, within 90 days after the withdrawal, all partners agree in writing to continue the business of the limited partnership and to the appointment of one or more additional general partners if necessary or desired; or

(4) entry of a decree of judicial dissolution under Section 802.

Sec. 802. **Judicial Dissolution**

On application by or for a partner the [here designate the proper court] court may decree a dissolution of a limited partnership whenever it is not reasonably practicable to carry on the business in conformity with the partnership agreement.

Sec. 803. **Winding Up**

Except as provided in the partnership agreement, the general partners who have not wrongfully dissolved a limited partnership or, if none, the limited partners, may wind up the limited partnership's affairs; but the [here designate the proper court] court may wind up the limited partnership's affairs upon application of any partner, his legal representative, or assignee.

Sec. 804. **Distribution of Assets**

Upon the winding up of a limited partnership, the assets shall be distributed as follows:

(1) to creditors, including partners who are creditors, to the extent otherwise permitted by law, in satisfaction of liabilities of the limited partnership other than liabilities for distributions to partners under Section 601 or 604;

(2) except as provided in the partnership agreement, to partners and former partners in satisfaction of liabilities for distributions under Section 601 or 604; and

(3) except as provided in the partnership agreement, to partners *first* for the return of their contributions and *secondly* respecting their partnership interests, in the proportions in which the partners share in distributions.

Article 9
FOREIGN LIMITED PARTNERSHIPS

Sec. 901. **Law Governing**

Subject to the Constitution of this State, (1) the laws of the state under which a foreign limited partnership is organized govern its organization and internal affairs and the liability of its limited partners, and (2) a foreign limited partnership may not be denied registration by reason of any difference between those laws and the laws of this State.

Sec. 902. **Registration**

Before transacting business in this State, a foreign limited partnership shall register with the Secretary of State. In order to register, a foreign limited partnership shall submit to the Secretary of State, in duplicate, an application for registration as a foreign limited partnership, signed and sworn to by a general partner and setting forth:

(1) the name of the foreign limited partnership and, if different, the name under which it proposes to register and transact business in this State;

(2) the state and date of its formation;

(3) the general character of the business it proposes to transact in this State;

(4) the name and address of any agent for service of process on the foreign limited partnership whom the foreign limited partnership elects to appoint, the agent must be an individual resident of this State, a domestic corporation, or a foreign corporation having a place of business in, and authorized to do business in this State;

(5) a statement that the Secretary of State is appointed the agent of the foreign limited partnership for service of process if no agent has been appointed under paragraph (4) or, if appointed, the agent's authority has been revoked or if the agent cannot be found or served with the exercise of reasonable diligence;

(6) the address of the office required to be maintained in the State of its organization by the laws of that State or, if not so required, of the principal office of the foreign limited partnership; and

(7) If the certificate of limited partnership filed in the foreign limited partnership's state of organization is not required to include the names and business addresses of the partners, a list of the names and addresses.

Sec. 903. **Issuance of Registration**

(a) If the Secretary of State finds that an application for registration conforms to law and all requisite fees have been paid, he shall:

(1) endorse on the application the word "Filed", and the month, day, and year of the filing thereof;

(2) file in his office a duplicate original of the application; and

(3) issue a certificate of registration to transact business in this State.

(b) The certificate of registration, together with a duplicate original of the application, shall be returned to the person who filed the application or his representative.

Sec. 904. **Name**

A foreign limited partnership may register with the Secretary of State under any name (whether or not it is the name under which it is registered in its state of organization) that includes without abbreviation the words "limited partnership" and that could be registered by a domestic limited partnership.

Sec. 905. **Changes and Amendments**

If any statement in a foreign limited partnership's application for registration a foreign limited partnership was false when made or any arrangements or other facts described have changed, making the application inaccurate in any respect, the foreign limited partnership shall promptly file in the office of the Secretary of State a certificate, signed and sworn to by a general partner, correcting the statement.

Sec. 906. **Cancellation of Registration**

A foreign limited partnership may cancel its registration by filing with the Secretary of State a certificate of cancellation signed and sworn to by a general partner. A cancellation does not terminate the authority of the Secretary of State to accept service of process on the foreign limited partnership with respect to [claims for relief] [causes of action] arising out of the transaction of business in this State.

Sec. 907. **Transaction of Business Without Registration**

(a) A foreign limited partnership transacting business in this State may not maintain any action, suit, or proceeding in any court of this State until it has registered in this State.

(b) The failure of a foreign limited partnership to register in this State does not impair the validity of any contract or act of the foreign limited partnership or prevent the foreign limited partnership from defending any action, suit, or proceeding in any court of this State.

(c) A limited partner of a foreign limited partnership is not liable as a general partner of the foreign limited partnership solely by reason of having transacted business in this State without registration.

(d) A foreign limited partnership, by transacting business in this State without registration, appoints the Secretary of State as its agent for service of process with respect to [claims for relief] [causes of action] arising out of the transaction of business in this State.

Sec. 908. **Action by [Appropriate Official]**

The [appropriate official may bring an action to restrain a foreign limited partnership from transacting business in this State in violation of this Article.

Article 10
DERIVATIVE ACTIONS

Sec. 1001. **Right of Action**

A limited partner may bring an action in the right of a limited partnership to recover a judgment in its favor

if general partners with authority to do so have refused to bring the action or if an effort to cause those general partners to bring the action is not likely to succeed.

Sec. 1002. **Proper Plaintiff**

In a derivative action, the plaintiff must be a partner at the time of bringing the action and (1) at the time of the transaction of which he complains or (2) his status as a partner had devolved upon him by operation of law or pursuant to the terms of the partnership agreement from a person who was a partner at the time of the transaction.

Sec. 1003. **Pleading**

In any derivative action, the complaint shall set forth with particularity the effort of the plaintiff to secure initiation of the action by a general partner or the reasons for not making the effort.

Sec. 1004. **Expenses**

If a derivative action is successful, in whole or in part, or if anything is received by the plaintiff as a result of a judgment, compromise, or settlement of an action or claim, the court may award the plaintiff reasonable expenses, including reasonable attorney's fees, and shall direct him to remit to the limited partnership the remainder of those proceeds received by him.

Article 11
MISCELLANEOUS

Sec. 1101. **Construction and Application**

This Act shall be so applied and construed to effectuate its general purpose to make uniform the law with respect to the subject of this Act among states enacting it.

Sec. 1102. **Short Title**

This Act may be cited as the Uniform Limited Partnership Act.

Sec. 1103. **Severability**

If any provision of this Act or its application to any person or circumstance is held invalid, the invalidity does not affect other provisions or applications of the Act which can be given effect without the invalid provision or application, and to this end the provisions of this Act are severable.

Sec. 1104. **Effective Date, Extended Effective Date and Repeal**

Except as set forth below, the effective date of this Act is _____ and the following Acts [list prior limited partnership acts] are hereby repealed:

(1) The existing provisions for execution and filing of certificates of limited partnerships and amendments thereunder and cancellations thereof continue in effect until [specify time required to create central filing system], the extended effective date, and Sections 102, 103, 104, 105, 201, 202, 203, 204 and 206 are not effective until the extended effective date.

(2) Section 402, specifying the conditions under which a general partner ceases to be a member of a limited partnership, is not effective until the extended effective date, and the applicable provisions of existing law continue to govern until the extended effective date.

(3) Sections 501, 502 and 608 apply only to contributions and distributions made after the effective date of this Act.

(4) Section 704 applies only to assignments made after the effective date of this Act.

(5) Article 9, dealing with registration of foreign limited partnerships, is not effective until the extended effective date.

Sec. 1105. **Rules for Cases Not Provided for in This Act**

In any case not provided for in this Act the provisions of the Uniform Partnership Act govern.

Appendix E

THE MODEL BUSINESS CORPORATION ACT

§ 1. Short Title*

This Act shall be known and may be cited as the ". . . . . .† Business Corporation Act."

§ 2. Definitions

As used in this Act, unless the context otherwise requires, the term:

(a) "Corporation" or "domestic corporation" means a corporation for profit subject to the provisions of this Act, except a foreign corporation.

(b) "Foreign corporation" means a corporation for profit organized under laws other than the laws of this State for a purpose or purposes for which a corporation may be organized under this Act.

(c) "Articles of incorporation" means the original or restated articles of incorporation or articles of consolidation and all amendments thereto including articles of merger.

(d) "Shares" means the units into which the proprietary interests in a corporation are divided.

(e) "Subscriber" means one who subscribes for shares in a corporation, whether before or after incorporation.

(f) "Shareholder" means one who is a holder of record of shares in a corporation. If the articles of incorporation or the by-laws so provide, the board of directors may adopt by resolution a procedure whereby a shareholder of the corporation may certify in writing to the corporation that all or a portion of the shares registered in the name of such shareholder are held for the account of a specified person or persons. The resolution shall set forth (1) the classification of shareholder who may certify, (2) the purpose or purposes for which the certification may be made, (3) the form of certification and information to be contained therein, (4) if the certification is with respect to a record date or closing of

the stock transfer books within which the certification must be received by the corporation and (5) such other provisions with respect to the procedure as are deemed necessary or desirable. Upon receipt by the corporation of a certification complying with the procedure, the persons specified in the certification shall be deemed, for the purpose or purposes set forth in the certification, to be the holders of record of the number of shares specified in place of the shareholder making the certification.

(g) "Authorized shares" means the shares of all classes which the corporation is authorized to issue.

*[By the Editor] The Model Business Corporation Act prepared by the Committee on Corporate Laws (Section of Corporation, Banking and Business Law) of the American Bar Association was originally patterned after the Illinois Business Corporation Act of 1933. It was first published as a complete act in 1950. In subsequent years several revisions, addenda and optional or alternative provisions were added. The Act was substantially revised and renumbered in 1969.

This Act should be distinguished from the Model Business Corporation Act promulgated in 1928 by the Commissioners on Uniform State Laws under the name "Uniform Business Corporation Act" and renamed Model Business Corporation Act in 1943. This Uniform Act was withdrawn in 1957.

The Model Business Corporation Act has been influential in the codification of corporation statutes in more than 35 states. However, there is no state that has totally adopted it in its current form. Moreover, since the Model Act itself has been substantially modified from time to time, there is considerable variation among the statutes of the states that used this Act as a model.

†Insert name of State.

(h) "Employee" includes officers but not directors. A director may accept duties which make him also an employee.

(i) "Distribution" means a direct or indirect transfer

of money or other property (except its own shares) or incurrence of indebtedness, by a corporation to or for the benefit of any of its shareholders in respect of any of its shares, whether by dividend or by purchase, redemption or other acquisition of its shares, or otherwise.

§ 3. **Purposes**

Corporations may be organized under this Act for any lawful purpose or purposes, except for the purpose of banking or insurance.

§ 4. **General Powers**

Each corporation shall have power:

(a) To have perpetual succession by its corporate name unless a limited period of duration is stated in its articles of incorporation.

(b) To sue and be sued, complain and defend, in its corporate name.

(c) To have a corporate seal which may be altered at pleasure, and to use the same by causing it, or a facsimile thereof, to be impressed or affixed or in any other manner reproduced.

(d) To purchase, take, receive, lease, or otherwise acquire, own, hold, improve, use and otherwise deal in and with, real or personal property, or any interest therein, wherever situated.

(e) To sell, convey, mortgage, pledge, lease, exchange, transfer and otherwise dispose of all or any part of its property and assets.

(f) To lend money and use its credit to assist its employees.

(g) To purchase, take, receive, subscribe for, or otherwise acquire, own, hold, vote, use, employ, sell, mortgage, lend, pledge, or otherwise dispose of, and otherwise use and deal in and with, shares or other interests in, or obligations of, other domestic or foreign corporations, associations, partnerships or individuals, or direct or indirect obligations of the United States or of any other government, state, territory, governmental district or municipality or of any instrumentality thereof.

(h) To make contracts and guarantees and incur liabilities, borrow money at such rates of interest as the corporation may determine, issue its notes, bonds, and other obligations, and secure any of its obligations by mortgage or pledge of all or any of its property, franchises and income.

(i) To lend money for its corporate purposes, invest and reinvest its funds, and take and hold real and personal property as security for the payment of funds so loaned or invested.

(j) To conduct its business, carry on its operations and have offices and exercise the powers granted by this Act, within or without this State.

(k) To elect or appoint officers and agents of the corporation, and define their duties and fix their compensation.

(l) To make and alter by-laws, not inconsistent with its articles of incorporation or with the laws of this State, for the administration and regulation of the affairs of the corporation.

(m) To make donations for the public welfare or for charitable, scientific or educational purposes.

(n) To transact any lawful business which the board of directors shall find will be in aid of governmental policy.

(o) To pay pensions and establish pension plans, pension trusts, profit sharing plans, stock bonus plans, stock option plans and other incentive plans for any or all of its directors, officers and employees.

(p) To be a promoter, partner, member, associate, or manager of any partnership, joint venture, trust or other enterprise.

(q) To have and exercise all powers necessary or convenient to effect its purposes.

§ 5. **Indemnification of Directors and Officers**

(a) As used in this section:

(1) *Director* means any person who is or was a director of the corporation and any person who, while a director of the corporation, is or was serving at the request of the corporation as a director, officer, partner, trustee, employee or agent of another foreign or domestic corporation, partnership, joint venture, trust, other enterprise or employee benefit plan.

(2) *Corporation* includes any domestic or foreign predecessor entity of the corporation in a merger, consolidation or other transaction in which the predecessor's existence ceased upon consummation of such transaction.

(3) *Expenses* include attorneys' fees.

(4) *Official capacity* means

(A) when used with respect to a director, the office of director in the corporation, and

(B) when used with respect to a person other than

a director, as contemplated in subsection (i), the elective or appointive office in the corporation held by the officer or the employment or agency relationship undertaken by the employee or agent in behalf of the corporation,

but in each case does not include service for any other foreign or domestic corporation or any partnership, joint venture, trust, other enterprise, or employee benefit plan.

(5) *Party* includes a person who was, is, or is threatened to be made, a named defendant or respondent in a proceeding.

(6) *Proceeding* means any threatened, pending or completed action, suit or proceeding, whether civil, criminal, administrative or investigative.

(b) A corporation shall have power to indemnify any person made a party to any proceeding by reason of the fact that he is or was a director if

(1) he conducted himself in good faith; and

(2) he reasonably believed

(A) in the case of conduct in his official capacity with the corporation, that his conduct was in its best interests, and

(B) in all other cases, that his conduct was at least not opposed to its best interests; and

(3) in the case of any criminal proceeding, he had no reasonable cause to believe his conduct was unlawful.

Indemnification may be made against judgments, penalties, fines, settlements and reasonable expenses, actually incurred by the person in connection with the proceeding; except that if the proceeding was by or in the right of the corporation, indemnification may be made only against such reasonable expenses and shall not be made in respect of any proceeding in which the person shall have been adjudged to be liable to the corporation. The termination of any proceeding by judgment, order, settlement, conviction, or upon a plea of nolo contendere or its equivalent, shall not, of itself, be determinative that the person did not meet the requisite standard of conduct set forth in this subsection (b).

(c) A director shall not be indemnified under subsection (b) in respect of any proceeding charging improper personal benefit to him, whether or not involving action in his official capacity, in which he shall have been adjudged to be liable on the basis that personal benefit was improperly received by him.

(d) Unless limited by the articles of incorporation,

(1) a director who has been wholly successful, on the merits or otherwise, in the defense of any proceeding referred to in subsection (b) shall be indemnified against reasonable expenses incurred by him in connection with the proceeding; and

(2) a court of appropriate jurisdiction, upon application of a director and such notice as the court shall require, shall have authority to order indemnification in the following circumstances:

(A) if it determines a director is entitled to reimbursement under clause (1), the court shall order indemnification, in which case the director shall also be entitled to recover the expenses of securing such reimbursement; or

(B) if it determines that the director is fairly and reasonably entitled to indemnification in view of all the relevant circumstances, whether or not he has met the standard of conduct set forth in subsection (b) or has been adjudged liable in the circumstances described in subsection (c), the court may order such indemnification as the court shall deem proper, except that indemnification with respect to any proceeding by or in the right of the corporation or in which liability shall have been adjudged in the circumstances described in subsection (c) shall be limited to expenses.

A court of appropriate jurisdiction may be the same court in which the proceeding involving the director's liability took place.

(e) No indemnification under subsection (b) shall be made by the corporation unless authorized in the specific case after a determination has been made that indemnification of the director is permissible in the circumstances because he has met the standard of conduct set forth in subsection (b). Such determination shall be made:

(1) by the board of directors by a majority vote of a quorum consisting of directors not at the time parties to the proceeding; or

(2) if such a quorum cannot be obtained, then by a majority vote of a committee of the board, duly designated to act in the matter by a majority vote of the full board (in which designation directors who are parties may participate), consisting solely of two or more directors not at the time parties to the proceeding; or

(3) by special legal counsel, selected by the board of directors or a committee thereof by vote as set forth in clauses (1) or (2) of this subsection (e), or, if the requisite quorum of the full board cannot be obtained

therefor and such committee cannot be established, by a majority vote of the full board (in which selection directors who are parties may participate); or

(4) by the shareholders.

Authorization of indemnification and determination as to reasonableness of expenses shall be made in the same manner as the determination that indemnification is permissible, except that if the determination that indemnification is permissible is made by special legal counsel, authorization of indemnification and determination as to reasonableness of expenses shall be made in a manner specified in clause (3) in the preceding sentence for the selection of such counsel. Shares held by directors who are parties to the proceeding shall not be voted on the subject matter under this subsection (e).

(f) Reasonable expenses incurred by a director who is a party to a proceeding may be paid or reimbursed by the corporation in advance of the final disposition of such proceeding upon receipt by the corporation of

(1) a written affirmation by the director of his good faith belief that he has met the standard of conduct necessary for indemnification by the corporation as authorized in this section, and

(2) a written undertaking by or on behalf of the director to repay such amount if it shall ultimately be determined that he has not met such standard of conduct, and after a determination that the facts then known to those making the determination would not preclude indemnification under this section. The undertaking required by clause (2) shall be an unlimited general obligation of the director but need not be secured and may be accepted without reference to financial ability to make repayment. Determinations and authorizations of payments under this subsection (f) shall be made in the manner specified in subsection (e).

(g) No provision for the corporation to indemnify or to advance expenses to a director who is made a party to a proceeding, whether contained in the articles of incorporation, the by-laws, a resolution of shareholders or directors, an agreement or otherwise (except as contemplated by subsection (j)), shall be valid unless consistent with this section or, to the extent that indemnity hereunder is limited by the articles of incorporation, consistent therewith. Nothing contained in this section shall limit the corporation's power to pay or reimburse expenses incurred by a director in connection with his appearance as a witness in a proceeding at a time when he has not been made a named defendant or respondent in the proceeding.

(h) For purposes of this section, the corporation shall be deemed to have requested a director to serve an employee benefit plan whenever the performance by him of his duties to the corporation also imposes duties on, or otherwise involves services by, him to the plan or participants or beneficiaries of the plan; excise taxes assessed on a director with respect to an employee benefit plan pursuant to applicable law shall be deemed "fines"; and action taken or omitted by him with respect to an employee benefit plan in the performance of his duties for a purpose reasonably believed by him to be in the interest of the participants and beneficiaries of the plan shall be deemed to be for a purpose which is not opposed to the best interests of the corporation.

(i) Unless limited by the articles of incorporation,

(1) an officer of the corporation shall be indemnified as and to the same extent provided in subsection (d) for a director and shall be entitled to the same extent as a director to seek indemnification pursuant to the provisions of subsection (d);

(2) a corporation shall have the power to indemnify and to advance expenses to an officer, employee or agent of the corporation to the same extent that it may indemnify and advance expenses to directors pursuant to this section; and

(3) a corporation, in addition, shall have the power to indemnify and to advance expenses to an officer, employee or agent who is not a director to such further extent, consistent with law, as may be provided by its articles of incorporation, by-laws, general or specific action of its board of directors, or contract.

(j) A corporation shall have power to purchase and maintain insurance on behalf of any person who is or was a director, officer, employee or agent of the corporation, or who, while a director, officer, employee or agent of the corporation, is or was serving at the request of the corporation as a director, officer, partner, trustee, employee or agent of another foreign or domestic corporation, partnership, joint venture, trust, other enterprise or employee benefit plan, against any liability asserted against him and incurred by him in any such capacity or arising out of his status as such, whether or not the corporation would have the power to indemnify him against such liability under the provisions of this section.

(k) Any indemnification of, or advance of expenses to, a director in accordance with this section, if arising out of a proceeding by or in the right of the corporation, shall be reported in writing to the shareholders with or before the notice of the next shareholders' meeting.

§ 6. Power of Corporation to Acquire Its Own Shares

A corporation shall have the power to acquire its own shares. All of its own shares acquired by a corporation shall, upon acquisition, constitute authorized but unissued shares, unless the articles of incorporation provide that they shall not be reissued, in which case the authorized shares shall be reduced by the number of shares acquired.

If the number of authorized shares is reduced by an acquisition, the corporation shall, not later than the time it files its next annual report under this Act with the Secretary of State, file a statement of cancellation showing the reduction in the authorized shares. The statement of cancellation shall be executed in duplicate by the corporation by its president or a vice president and by its secretary or an assistant secretary, and verified by one of the officers signing such statement, and shall set forth:

(a) The name of the corporation.

(b) The number of acquired shares cancelled, itemized by classes and series.

(c) The aggregate number of authorized shares, itemized by classes and series, after giving effect to such cancellation.

Duplicate originals of such statement shall be delivered to the Secretary of State. If the Secretary of State finds that such statement conforms to law, he shall, when all fees and franchise taxes have been paid as in this Act prescribed:

(1) Endorse on each of such duplicate originals the word "Filed", and the month, day and year of the filing thereof.

(2) File one of such duplicate originals in his office.

(3) Return the other duplicate original to the corporation or its representative.

§ 7. Defense of Ultra Vires

No act of a corporation and no conveyance or transfer of real or personal property to or by a corporation shall be invalid by reason of the fact that the corporation was without capacity or power to do such act or to make or receive such conveyance or transfer, but such lack of capacity or power may be asserted:

(a) In a proceeding by a shareholder against the cor-

poration to enjoin the doing of any act or the transfer of real or personal property by or to the corporation. If the unauthorized act or transfer sought to be enjoined is being, or is to be, performed or made pursuant to a contract to which the corporation is a party, the court may, if all of the parties to the contract are parties to the proceeding and if it deems the same to be equitable, set aside and enjoin the performance of such contract, and in so doing may allow to the corporation or to the other parties to the contract, as the case may be, compensation for the loss or damage sustained by either of them which may result from the action of the court in setting aside and enjoining the performance of such contract, but anticipated profits to be derived from the performance of the contract shall not be awarded by the court as a loss or damage sustained.

(b) In a proceeding by the corporation, whether acting directly or through a receiver, trustee, or other legal representative, or through shareholders in a representative suit, against the incumbent or former officers or directors of the corporation.

(c) In a proceeding by the Attorney General, as provided in this Act, to dissolve the corporation, or in a proceeding by the Attorney General to enjoin the corporation from the transaction of unauthorized business.

§ 8. Corporate Name

The corporate name:

(a) Shall contain the word "corporation," "company," "incorporated" or "limited," or shall contain an abbreviation of one of such words.

(b) Shall not contain any word or phrase which indicates or implies that it is organized for any purpose other than one or more of the purposes contained in its articles of incorporation.

(c) Shall not be the same as, or deceptively similar to, the name of any domestic corporation existing under the laws of this State or any foreign corporation authorized to transact business in this State, or a name the exclusive right to which is, at the time, reserved in the manner provided in this Act, or the name of a corporation which has in effect a registration of its corporate name as provided in this Act, except that this provision shall not apply if the applicant files with the Secretary of State either of the following: (1) the written consent of such other corporation or holder of a reserved or registered name to use the same or deceptively similar name and one or more words are added to make such name distinguishable from such other name, or (2) a certified copy of a final decree of a court of competent jurisdiction establishing the prior right of the applicant to the use of such name in this State.

A corporation with which another corporation, domestic or foreign, is merged, or which is formed by the reorganization or consolidation of one or more domestic or foreign corporations or upon a sale, lease or other disposition to or exchange with, a domestic corporation of all or substantially all the assets of another corporation, domestic or foreign, including its name, may have the same name as that used in this State by any of such corporations if such other corporation was organized under the laws of, or is authorized to transact business in, this State.

§ 9. Reserved Name

The exclusive right to the use of a corporate name may be reserved by:

(a) Any person intending to organize a corporation under this Act.

(b) Any domestic corporation intending to change its name.

(c) Any foreign corporation intending to make application for a certificate of authority to transact business in this State.

(d) Any foreign corporation authorized to transact business in this State and intending to change its name.

(e) Any person intending to organize a foreign corporation and intending to have such corporation make application for a certificate of authority to transact business in this State.

The reservation shall be made by filing with the Secretary of State an application to reserve a specified corporate name, executed by the applicant. If the Secretary of State finds that the name is available for corporate use, he shall reserve the same for the exclusive use of the applicant for a period of one hundred and twenty days.

The right to the exclusive use of a specified corporate name so reserved may be transferred to any other person or corporation by filing in the office of the Secretary of State a notice of such transfer, executed by the applicant for whom the name was reserved, and specifying the name and address of the transferee.

§ 10. Registered Name

Any corporation organized and existing under the laws of any state or territory of the United States may register its corporate name under this Act, provided its corporate name is not the same as, or deceptively similar to, the name of any domestic corporation existing under the laws of this State, or the name of any foreign corporation authorized to transact business in this State, or any corporate name reserved or registered under this Act.

Such registration shall be made by:

(a) Filing with the Secretary of State (1) an application for registration executed by the corporation by an officer thereof, setting forth the name of the corporation, the state or territory under the laws of which it is incorporated, the date of its incorporation, a statement that it is carrying on or doing business, and a brief statement of the business in which it is engaged, and (2) a certificate setting forth that such corporation is in good standing under the laws of the state or territory wherein it is organized, executed by the Secretary of State of such state or territory or by such other official as may have custody of the records pertaining to corporations, and

(b) Paying to the Secretary of State a registration fee in the amount of .... for each month, or fraction thereof, between the date of filing such application and December 31st of the calendar year in which such application is filed.

Such registration shall be effective until the close of the calendar year in which the application for registration is filed.

§ 11. Renewal of Registered Name

A corporation which has in effect a registration of its corporate name, may renew such registration from year to year by annually filing an application for renewal setting forth the facts required to be set forth in an original application for registration and a certificate of good standing as required for the original registration and by paying a fee of .... A renewal application may be filed between the first day of October and the thirty-first day of December in each year, and shall extend the registration for the following calendar year.

§ 12. Registered Office and Registered Agent

Each corporation shall have and continuously maintain in this State:

(a) A registered office which may be, but need not be, the same as its place of business.

(b) A registered agent, which agent may be either an

individual resident in this State whose business office is identical with such registered office, or a domestic corporation, or a foreign corporation authorized to transact business in this State, having a business office identical with such registered office.

§ 13. **Change of Registered Office or Registered Agent**

A corporation may change its registered office or change its registered agent, or both, upon filing in the office of the Secretary of State a statement setting forth:

(a) The name of the corporation.

(b) The address of its then registered office.

(c) If the address of its registered office is to be changed, the address to which the registered office is to be changed.

(d) The name of its then registered agent.

(e) If its registered agent is to be changed, the name of its successor registered agent.

(f) That the address of its registered office and the address of the business office of its registered agent, as changed, will be identical.

(g) That such change was authorized by resolution duly adopted by its board of directors.

Such statement shall be executed by the corporation by its president, or a vice president, and verified by him, and delivered to the Secretary of State. If the Secretary of State finds that such statement conforms to the provisions of this Act, he shall file such statement in his office, and upon such filing the change of address of the registered office, or the appointment of a new registered agent, or both, as the case may be, shall become effective.

Any registered agent of a corporation may resign as such agent upon filing a written notice thereof, executed in duplicate, with the Secretary of State, who shall forthwith mail a copy thereof to the corporation at its registered office. The appointment of such agent shall terminate upon the expiration of thirty days after receipt of such notice by the Secretary of State.

If a registered agent changes his or its business address to another place within the same ....,* he or it may change such address and the address of the registered office of any corporation of which he or it is registered agent by filing a statement as required above except that it need be signed only by the registered agent and need not be

*Supply designation of jurisdiction, such as county, etc., in accordance with local practice.

responsive to (e) or (g) and must recite that a copy of the statement has been mailed to the corporation.

§ 14. **Service of Process on Corporation**

The registered agent so appointed by a corporation shall be an agent of such corporation upon whom any process, notice or demand required or permitted by law to be served upon the corporation may be served.

Whenever a corporation shall fail to appoint or maintain a registered agent in this State, or whenever its registered agent cannot with reasonable diligence be found at the registered office, then the Secretary of State shall be an agent of such corporation upon whom any such process, notice, or demand may be served. Service on the Secretary of State of any such process, notice, or demand shall be made by delivering to and leaving with him, or with any clerk having charge of the corporation department of his office, duplicate copies of such process, notice or demand. In the event any such process, notice or demand is served on the Secretary of State, he shall immediately cause one of the copies thereof to be forwarded by registered mail, addressed to the corporation at its registered office. Any service so had on the Secretary of State shall be returnable in not less than thirty days.

The Secretary of State shall keep a record of all processes, notices and demands served upon him under this section, and shall record therein the time of such service and his action with reference thereto.

Nothing herein contained shall limit or affect the right to serve any process, notice or demand required or permitted by law to be served upon a corporation in any other manner now or hereafter permitted by law.

§ 15. **Authorized Shares**

Each corporation shall have power to create and issue the number of shares stated in its articles of incorporation. Such shares may be divided into one or more classes with such designations, preferences, limitations, and relative rights as shall be stated in the articles of incorporation. The articles of incorporation may limit or deny the voting rights of or provide special voting rights for the shares of any class to the extent not inconsistent with the provisions of this Act.

Without limiting the authority herein contained, a corporation, when so provided in its articles of incorporation, may issue shares of preferred or special classes:

(a) Subject to the right of the corporation to redeem any of such shares at the price fixed by the articles of incorporation for the redemption thereof.

(b) Entitling the holders thereof to cumulative, non-cumulative or partially cumulative dividends.

(c) Having preference over any other class or classes of shares as to the payment of dividends.

(d) Having preference in the assets of the corporation over any other class or classes of shares upon the voluntary or involuntary liquidation of the corporation.

(e) Convertible into shares of any other class or into shares of any series of the same or any other class, except a class having prior or superior rights and preferences as to dividends or distribution of assets upon liquidation.

§ 16. Issuance of Shares of Preferred or Special Classes in Series

If the articles of incorporation so provide, the shares of any preferred or special class may be divided into and issued in series. If the shares of any such class are to be issued in series, then each series shall be so designated as to distinguish the shares thereof from the shares of all other series and classes. Any or all of the series of any such class and the variations in the relative rights and preferences as between different series may be fixed and determined by the articles of incorporation, but all shares of the same class shall be identical except as to the following relative rights and preferences, as to which there may be variations between different series:

(A) The rate of dividend.

(B) Whether shares may be redeemed and, if so, the redemption price and the terms and conditions of redemption.

(C) The amount payable upon shares in the event of voluntary and involuntary liquidation.

(D) Sinking fund provisions, if any, for the redemption or purchase of shares.

(E) The terms and conditions, if any, on which shares may be converted.

(F) Voting rights, if any.

If the articles of incorporation shall expressly vest authority in the board of directors, then, to the extent that the articles of incorporation shall not have established series and fixed and determined the variations in the relative rights and preferences as between series, the board of directors shall have authority to divide any or all of such classes into series and, within the limitations set forth in this section and in the articles of incorporation, fix and determine the rela-

tive rights and preferences of the shares of any series so established.

In order for the board of directors to establish a series, where authority so to do is contained in the articles of incorporation, the board of directors shall adopt a resolution setting forth the designation of the series and fixing and determining the relative rights and preferences thereof, or so much thereof as shall not be fixed and determined by the articles of incorporation.

Prior to the issue of any shares of a series established by resolution adopted by the board of directors, the corporation shall file in the office of the Secretary of State a statement setting forth:

(a) The name of the corporation.

(b) A copy of the resolution establishing and designating the series, and fixing and determining the relative rights and preferences thereof.

(c) The date of adoption of such resolution.

(d) That such resolution was duly adopted by the board of directors.

Such statement shall be executed in duplicate by the corporation by its president or a vice president and by its secretary or an assistant secretary, and verified by one of the officers signing such statement, and shall be delivered to the Secretary of State. If the Secretary of State finds that such statement conforms to law, he shall, when all franchise taxes and fees have been paid as in this Act prescribed:

(1) Endorse on each of such duplicate originals the word "Filed," and the month, day, and year of the filing thereof.

(2) File one of such duplicate originals in his office.

(3) Return the other duplicate original to the corporation or its representative.

Upon the filing of such statement by the Secretary of State, the resolution establishing and designating the series and fixing and determining the relative rights and preferences thereof shall become effective and shall constitute an amendment of the articles of incorporation.

§ 17. Subscriptions for Shares

A subscription for shares of a corporation to be organized shall be irrevocable for a period of six months, unless otherwise provided by the terms of the subscription agreement or unless all of the subscribers consent to the revocation of such subscription.

Unless otherwise provided in the subscription

agreement, subscriptions for shares, whether made before or after the organization of a corporation, shall be paid in full at such time, or in such installments and at such times, as shall be determined by the board of directors. Any call made by the board of directors for payment on subscriptions shall be uniform as to all shares of the same class or as to all shares of the same series, as the case may be. In case of default in the payment of any installment or call when such payment is due, the corporation may proceed to collect the amount due in the same manner as any debt due the corporation. The by-laws may prescribe other penalties for failure to pay installments or calls that may become due, but no penalty working a forfeiture of a subscription, or of the amounts paid thereon, shall be declared as against any subscriber unless the amount due thereon shall remain unpaid for a period of twenty days after written demand has been made therefor. If mailed, such written demand shall be deemed to be made when deposited in the United States mail in a sealed envelope addressed to the subscriber at his last post-office address known to the corporation, with postage thereon prepaid. In the event of the sale of any shares by reason of any foreefiture, the excess of proceeds realized over the amount due and unpaid on such shares shall be paid to the delinquent subscriber or to his legal representative.

§ 18. Issuance of Shares

Subject to any restrictions in the articles of incorporation:

(a) Shares may be issued for such consideration as shall be authorized by the board of directors establishing a price (in money or other consideration) or a minimum price or general formula or method by which the price will be determined; and

(b) Upon authorization by the board of directors, the corporation may issue its own shares in exchange for or in conversion of its outstanding shares, or distribute its own shares, pro rata to its shareholders or the shareholders of one or more classes or series, to effectuate stock dividends or splits, and any such transaction shall not require consideration; provided, that no such issuance of shares of any class or series shall be made to the holders of shares of any other class or series unless it is either expressly provided for in the articles of incorporation, or is authorized by an affirmative vote or the written consent of the holders of at least a majority of the outstanding shares of the class or series in which the distribution is to be made.

§ 19. Payment for Shares

The consideration for the issuance of shares may be paid, in whole or in part, in money, in other property, tangible or intangible, or in labor or services actually performed for the corporation. When payment of the consideration for which shares are to be issued shall have been received by the corporation, such shares shall be non-assessable.

Neither promissory notes nor future services shall constitute payment or part payment for the issuance of shares of a corporation.

In the absence of fraud in the transaction, the judgment of the board of directors or the shareholders, as the case may be, as to the value of the consideration received for shares shall be conclusive.

§ 20. Stock Rights and Options

Subject to any provisions in respect thereof set forth in its articles of incorporation, a corporation may create and issue, whether or not in connection with the issuance and sale of any of its shares or other securities, rights or options entitling the holders thereof to purchase from the corporation shares of any class or classes. Such rights or options shall be evidenced in such manner as the board of directors shall approve and, subject to the provisions of the articles of incorporation, shall set forth the terms upon which, the time or times within which and the price or prices at which such shares may be purchased from the corporation upon the exercise of any such right or option. If such rights or options are to be issued to directors, officers or employees as such of the corporation or of any subsidiary thereof, and not to the shareholders generally, their issuance shall be approved by the affirmative vote of the holders of a majority of the shares entitled to vote thereon or shall be authorized by and consistent with a plan approved or ratified by such a vote of shareholders. In the absence of fraud in the transaction, the judgment of the board of directors as to the adequacy of the consideration received for such rights or options shall be conclusive.

§ 21. Determination of Amount of Stated Capital

[Repealed in 1979].

§ 22. Expenses of Organization, Reorganization and Financing

The reasonable charges and expenses of organization or reorganization of a corporation, and the reasonable expenses of and compensation for the sale or underwriting of its shares, may be paid or allowed by such corporation out of the consideration received by it in payment for its shares without thereby rendering such shares assessable.

§ 23. Shares Represented by Certificates and Uncertified Shares

The shares of a corporation shall be represented by certificates or shall be uncertificated shares. Certificates shall be signed by the chairman or vice-chairman of the board of directors or the president or a vice president and by the treasurer or an assistant treasurer or the secretary or an assistant secretary of the corporation, and may be sealed with the seal of the corporation or a facsimile thereof. Any of or all the signatures upon a certificate may be a facsimile. In case any officer, transfer agent or registrar who has signed or whose facsimile signature has been placed upon such certificate shall have ceased to be such officer, transfer agent or registrar before such certificate is issued, it may be issued by the corporation with the same effect as if he were such officer, transfer agent or registrar at the date of its issue.

Every certificate representing shares issued by a corporation which is authorized to issue shares of more than one class shall set forth upon the face or back of the certificate, or shall state that the corporation will furnish to any shareholder upon request and without charge, a full statement of the designations, preferences, limitations, and relative rights of the shares of each class authorized to be issued, and if the corporation is authorized to issue any preferred or special class in series, the variations in the relative rights and preferences between the shares of each such series so far as the same have been fixed and determined and the authority of the board of directors to fix and determine the relative rights and preferences of subsequent series.

Each certificate representing shares shall state upon the face thereof:

(a) That the corporation is organized under the laws of this State.

(b) The name of the person to whom issued.

(c) The number and class of shares, and the designation of the series, if any, which such certificate represents.

(d) The par value of each share represented by such certificate, or a statement that the shares are without par value.

No certificate shall be issued for any share until such share is fully paid.

Unless otherwise provided by the articles of incorporation or by-laws, the board of directors of a corporation may provide by resolution that some or all of any or all classes and series of its shares shall be uncertificated shares, provided that such resolution shall not apply to shares represented by a certificate until such certificate is surrendered to the corporation. Within a reasonable time after the issuance or transfer of uncertificated shares, the corporation shall send to the registered owner thereof a written notice containing the information required to be set forth or stated on certificates pursuant to the second and third paragraphs of this section. Except as otherwise expressly provided by law, the rights and obligations of the holders of uncertificated shares and the rights and obligations of the holders of certificates representing shares of the same class and series shall be identical.

§ 24. Fractional Shares

A corporation may (1) issue fractions of a share, either represented by a certificate or uncertificated, (2) arrange for the disposition of fractional interests by those entitled thereto, (3) pay in money the fair value of fractions of a share as of a time when those entitled to receive such fractions are determined, or (4) issue scrip in registered or bearer form which shall entitle the holder to receive a certificate for a full share or an uncertificated full share upon the surrender of such scrip aggregating a full share. A certificate for a fractional share or an uncertificated fractional share shall, but scrip shall not unless otherwise provided therein, entitle the holder to exercise voting rights, to receive dividends thereon, and to participate in any of the assets of the corporation in the event of liquidation. The board of directors may cause scrip to be issued subject to the condition that it shall become void if not exchanged for certificates representing full shares or uncertificated full shares before a specified date, or subject to the condition that the shares for which scrip is exchangeable may be sold by the corporation and the proceeds thereof distributed to the holders of scrip, or subject to any other conditions which the board of directors may deem advisable.

§ 25. Liability of Subscribers and Shareholders

A holder of or subscriber to shares of a corporation shall be under no obligation to the corporation or its creditors with respect to such shares other than the obligation to pay to the corporation the full consideration for which such shares were issued or to be issued.

Any person becoming an assignee or transferee of shares or of a subscription for shares in good faith and without knowledge or notice that the full consideration therefor has not been paid shall not be personally liable to the corporation or its creditors for any unpaid portion of such consideration.

An executor, administrator, conservator, guardian, trustee, assignee for the benefit of creditors, or receiver shall not be personally liable to the corporation as a holder of or subscriber to shares of a corporation but the estate and funds in his hands shall be so liable.

No pledgee or other holder of shares as collateral security shall be personally liable as a shareholder.

§ 26. Shareholders' Preemptive Rights

The shareholders of a corporation shall have no preemptive right to acquire unissued shares of the corporation, or securities of the corporation convertible into or carrying a right to subscribe to or acquire shares, except to the extent, if any, that such right is provided in the articles of incorporation.

§ 26A. Shareholders' Preemptive Rights [Alternative]

Except to the extent limited or denied by this section or by the articles of incorporation, shareholders shall have a preemptive right to acquire unissued shares or securities convertible into such shares or carrying a right to subscribe to or acquire shares.

Unless otherwise provided in the articles of incorporation,

(a) No preemptive right shall exist

(1) to acquire any shares issued to directors, officers or employees pursuant to approval by the affirmative vote of the holders of a majority of the shares entitled to vote thereon or when authorized by and consistent with a plan theretofore approved by such a vote of shareholders; or

(2) to acquire any shares sold otherwise than for money.

(b) Holders of shares of any class that is preferred or limited as to dividends or assets shall not be entitled to any preemptive right.

(c) Holders of shares of common stock shall not be entitled to any preemptive right to shares of any class that is preferred or limited as to dividends or assets or to any obligations, unless convertible into shares of common stock or carrying a right to subscribe to or acquire shares of common stock.

(d) Holders of common stock without voting power shall have no preemptive right to shares of common stock with voting power.

(e) The preemptive right shall be only an opportunity to acquire shares or other securities under such terms and conditions as the board of directors may fix for the purpose of providing a fair and reasonable opportunity for the exercise of such right.

§ 27. By-Laws

The initial by-laws of a corporation shall be adopted by its board of directors. The power to alter, amend or repeal the by-laws or adopt new by-laws, subject to repeal or change by action of the shareholders, shall be vested in the board of directors unless reserved to the shareholders by the articles of incorporation. The by-laws may contain any provisions for the regulation and management of the affairs of the corporation not inconsistent with law or the articles of incorporation.

§ 27A. By-Laws and Other Powers in Emergency [Optional]

The board of directors of any corporation may adopt emergency by-laws, subject to repeal or change by action of the shareholders, which shall, notwithstanding any different provision elsewhere in this Act or in the articles of incorporation or by-laws, be operative during any emergency in the conduct of the business of the corporation resulting from an attack on the United States or any nuclear or atomic disaster. The emergency by-laws may make any provision that may be practical and necessary for the circumstances of the emergency, including provisions that:

(a) A meeting of the board of directors may be called by any officer or director in such manner and under such conditions as shall be prescribed in the emergency by-laws;

(b) The director or directors in attendance at the meeting, or any greater number fixed by the emergency by-laws, shall constitute a quorum; and

(c) The officers or other persons designated on a list approved by the board of directors before the emergency, all in such order of priority and subject to such conditions, and for such period of time (not longer than reasonably necessary after the termination of the emergency) as may be provided in the emergency by-laws or in the resolution approving the list shall, to the extent required to provide a quorum at any meeting of the board of directors, be deemed directors for such meeting.

The board of directors, either before or during any

such emergency, may provide, and from time to time modify, lines of succession in the event that during such an emergency any or all officers or agents of the corporation shall for any reason be rendered incapable of discharging their duties.

The board of directors, either before or during any such emergency, may, effective in the emergency, change the head office or designate several alternative head offices or regional offices, or authorize the officers so to do.

To the extent not inconsistent with any emergency by-laws so adopted, the by-laws of the corporation shall remain in effect during any such emergency and upon its termination the emergency by-laws shall cease to be operative.

Unless otherwise provided in emergency by-laws, notice of any meeting of the board of directors during any such emergency may be given only to such of the directors as it may be feasible to reach at the time and by such means as may be feasible at the time, including publication or radio.

To the extent required to constitute a quorum at any meeting of the board of directors during any such emergency, the officers of the corporation who are present shall, unless otherwise provided in emergency by-laws, be deemed, in order of rank and within the same rank in order of seniority, directors for such meeting.

No officer, director or employee acting in accordance with any emergency by-laws shall be liable except for willful misconduct. No officer, director or employee shall be liable for any action taken by him in good faith in such an emergency in furtherance of the ordinary business affairs of the corporation even though not authorized by the by-laws then in effect.

§ 28. **Meetings of Shareholders**

Meetings of shareholders may be held at such place within or without this State as may be stated in or fixed in accordance with the by-laws. If no other place is stated or so fixed, meetings shall be held at the registered office of the corporation.

An annual meeting of the shareholders shall be held at such time as may be stated in or fixed in accordance with the by-laws. If the annual meeting is not held within any thirteen-month period the Court of . . . . may, on the application of any shareholder, summarily order a meeting to be held.

Special meetings of the shareholders may be called by the board of directors, the holders of not less than one-tenth of all the shares entitled to vote at the meet-

ing, or such other persons as may be authorized in the articles of incorporation or the by-laws.

§ 29. **Notice of Shareholders' Meetings**

Written notice stating the place, day and hour of the meeting and, in case of a special meeting, the purpose or purposes for which the meeting is called, shall be delivered not less than ten nor more than fifty days before the date of the meeting, either personally or by mail, by or at the direction of the president, the secretary, or the officer or persons calling the meeting, to each shareholder of record entitled to vote at such meeting. If mailed, such notice shall be deemed to be delivered when deposited in the United States mail addressed to the shareholder at his address as it appears on the stock transfer books of the corporation, with postage thereon prepaid.

§ 30. **Closing of Transfer Books and Fixing Record Date**

For the purpose of determining shareholders entitled to notice of or to vote at any meeting of shareholders or any adjournment thereof, or entitled to receive payment of any dividend, or in order to make a determination of shareholders for any other proper purpose, the board of directors of a corporation may provide that the stock transfer books shall be closed for a stated period but not to exceed, in any case, fifty days. If the stock transfer books shall be closed for the purpose of determining shareholders entitled to notice of or to vote at a meeting of shareholders, such books shall be closed for at least ten days immediately preceding such meeting. In lieu of closing the stock transfer books, the by-laws, or in the absence of an applicable by-law the board of directors, may fix in advance a date as the record date for any such determination of shareholders, such date in any case to be not more than fifty days and, in case of a meeting of shareholders, not less than ten days prior to the date on which the particular action, requiring such determination of shareholders, is to be taken. If the stock transfer books are not closed and no record date is fixed for the determination of shareholders entitled to notice of or to vote at a meeting of shareholders, or shareholders entitled to receive payment of a dividend, the date on which notice of the meeting is mailed or the date on which the resolution of the board of directors declaring such dividend is adopted, as the case may be, shall be the record date for such determination of shareholders. When a determination of shareholders entitled to vote at any meeting of shareholders has been made as provided in this section, such determination shall apply to any adjournment thereof.

§ 31. Voting Record

The officer or agent having charge of the stock transfer books for shares of a corporation shall make a complete record of the shareholders entitled to vote at such meeting or any adjournment thereof, arranged in alphabetical order, with the address of and the number of shares held by each. Such record shall be produced and kept open at the time and place of the meeting and shall be subject to the inspection of any shareholder during the whole time of the meeting for the purposes thereof.

Failure to comply with the requirements of this section shall not affect the validity of any action taken at such meeting.

An officer or agent having charge of the stock transfer books who shall fail to prepare the record of shareholders, or produce and keep it open for inspection at the meeting, as provided in this section, shall be liable to any shareholder suffering damage on account of such failure, to the extent of such damage.

§ 32. Quorum of Shareholders

Unless otherwise provided in the articles of incorporation, a majority of the shares entitled to vote, represented in person or by proxy, shall constitute a quorum at a meeting of shareholders, but in no event shall a quorum consist of less than one-third of the shares entitled to vote at the meeting. If a quorum is present, the affirmative vote of the majority of the shares represented at the meeting and entitled to vote on the subject matter shall be the act of the shareholders, unless the vote of a greater number or voting by classes is required by this Act or the articles of incorporation or by-laws.

§ 33. Voting of Shares

Each outstanding share, regardless of class, shall be entitled to one vote on each matter submitted to a vote at a meeting of shareholders, except as may be otherwise provided in the articles of incorporation. If the articles of incorporation provide for more or less than one vote for any share, on any matter, every reference in this Act to a majority or other proportion of shares shall refer to such a majority or other proportion of votes entitled to be cast.

Shares held by another corporation if a majority of the shares entitled to vote for the election of directors of such other corporation is held by the corporation, shall not be voted at any meeting or counted in determining the total number of outstanding shares at any given time.

A shareholder may vote either in person or by proxy executed in writing by the shareholder or by his duly authorized attorney-in-fact. No proxy shall be valid after eleven months from the date of its execution, unless otherwise provided in the proxy.

[Either of the following prefatory phrases may be inserted here: "The articles of incorporation may provide that" or "Unless the articles of incorporation otherwise provide"] ... at each election for directors every shareholder entitled to vote at such election shall have the right to vote, in person or by proxy, the number of shares owned by him for as many persons as there are directors to be elected and for whose election he has a right to vote, or to cumulate his votes by giving one candidate as many votes as the number of such directors multiplied by the number of his shares shall equal, or by distributing such votes on the same principle among any number of such candidates.

Shares standing in the name of another corporation, domestic or foreign, may be voted by such officer, agent or proxy as the by-laws of such other corporation may prescribe, or, in the absence of such provision, as the board of directors of such other corporation may determine.

Shares held by an administrator, executor, guardian or conservator may be voted by him, either in person or by proxy, without a transfer of such shares into his name. Shares standing in the name of a trustee may be voted by him, either in person or by proxy, but no trustee shall be entitled to vote shares held by him without a transfer of such shares into his name.

Shares standing in the name of a receiver may be voted by such receiver, and shares held by or under the control of a receiver may be voted by such receiver without the transfer thereof into his name if authority so to do be contained in an appropriate order of the court by which such receiver was appointed.

A shareholder whose shares are pledged shall be entitled to vote such shares until the shares have been transferred into the name of the pledgee, and thereafter the pledgee shall be entitled to vote the shares so transferred.

On and after the date on which written notice of redemption of redeemable shares has been mailed to the holders thereof and a sum sufficient to redeem such shares has been deposited with a bank or trust company with irrevocable instruction and authority to pay the redemption price to the holders thereof upon surrender of certificates therefor, such shares shall not be entitled to vote on any matter and shall not be deemed to be outstanding shares.

§ 34. Voting Trusts and Agreements Among Shareholders

Any number of shareholders of a corporation may create a voting trust for the purpose of conferring upon a trustee or trustees the right to vote or otherwise represent their shares, for a period of not to exceed ten years, by entering into a written voting trust agreement specifying the terms and conditions of the voting trust, by depositing a counterpart of the agreement with the corporation at its registered office, and by transferring their shares to such trustee or trustees for the purposes of the agreement. Such trustee or trustees shall keep a record of the holders of voting trust certificates evidencing a beneficial interest in the voting trust, giving the names and addresses of all such holders and the number and class of the shares in respect of which the voting trust certificates held by each are issued, and shall deposit a copy of such record with the corporation at its registered office. The counterpart of the voting trust agreement and the copy of such record so deposited with the corporation shall be subject to the same right of examination by a shareholder of the corporation, in person or by agent or attorney, as are the books and records of the corporation, and such counterpart and such copy of such record shall be subject to examination by any holder of record of voting trust certificates, either in person or by agent or attorney, at any reasonable time for any proper purpose.

Agreements among shareholders regarding the voting of their shares shall be valid and enforceable in accordance with their terms. Such agreements shall not be subject to the provisions of this section regarding voting trusts.

§ 35. Board of Directors

All corporate powers shall be exercised by or under authority of, and the business and affairs of a corporation shall be managed under the direction of, a board of directors except as may be otherwise provided in this Act or the articles of incorporation. If any such provision is made in the articles of incorporation, the powers and duties conferred or imposed upon the board of directors by this Act shall be exercised or performed to such extent and by such person or persons as shall be provided in the articles of incorporation. Directors need not be residents of this State or shareholders of the corporation unless the articles of incorporation or

by-laws so require. The articles of incorporation or by-laws may prescribe other qualifications for directors. The board of directors shall have authority to fix the compensation of directors unless otherwise provided in the articles of incorporation.

A director shall perform his duties as a director, including his duties as a member of any committee of the board upon which he may serve, in good faith, in a manner he reasonably believes to be in the best interests of the corporation, and with such care as an ordinarily prudent person in a like position would use under similar circumstances. In performing his duties, a director shall be entitled to rely on information, opinions, reports or statements, including financial statements and other financial data, in each case prepared or presented by:

(a) one or more officers or employees of the corporation whom the director reasonably believes to be reliable and competent in the matters presented,

(b) counsel, public accountants or other persons as to matters which the director reasonably believes to be within such person's professional or expert competence, or

(c) a committee of the board upon which he does not serve, duly designated in accordance with a provision of the articles of incorporation or the by-laws, as to matters within its designated authority, which committee the director reasonably believes to merit confidence,

but he shall not be considered to be acting in good faith if he has knowledge concerning the matter in question that would cause such reliance to be unwarranted. A person who so performs his duties shall have no liability by reason of being or having been a director of the corporation.

A director of a corporation who is present at a meeting of its board of directors at which action on any corporate matter is taken shall be presumed to have assented to the action taken unless his dissent shall be entered in the minutes of the meeting or unless he shall file his written dissent to such action with the secretary of the meeting before the adjournment thereof or shall forward such dissent by registered mail to the secretary of the corporation immediately after the adjournment of the meeting. Such right to dissent shall not apply to a director who voted in favor of such action.

§ 36. Number and Election of Directors

The board of directors of a corporation shall consist of one or more members. The number of directors shall be fixed by, or in the manner provided in, the articles of incorporation or the by-laws, except as to the number constituting the initial board of directors, which number shall be fixed by the articles of incorporation. The number of directors may be increased or decreased from time to time by amendment to, or in the manner provided in, the articles of incorporation or the by-laws, but no decrease shall have the effect of shortening the term of any incumbent director. In the absence of a by-law providing for the number of directors, the number shall be the same as that provided for in the articles of incorporation. The names and addresses of the members of the first board of directors shall be stated in the articles of incorporation. Such persons shall hold office until the first annual meeting of shareholders, and until their successors shall have been elected and qualified. At the first annual meeting of shareholders and at each annual meeting thereafter the shareholders shall elect directors to hold office until the next succeeding annual meeting, except in case of the classification of directors as permitted by this Act. Each director shall hold office for the term for which he is elected and until his successor shall have been elected and qualified.

§ 37. Classification of Directors

When the board of directors shall consist of nine or more members, in lieu of electing the whole number of directors annually, the articles of incorporation may provide that the directors be divided into either two or three classes, each class to be as nearly equal in number as possible, the term of office of directors of the first class to expire at the first annual meeting of shareholders after their election, that of the second class to expire at the second annual meeting after their election, and that of the third class, if any, to expire at the third annual meeting after their election. At each annual meeting after such classification the number of directors equal to the number of the class whose term expires at the time of such meeting shall be elected to hold office until the second succeeding annual meeting, if there be two classes, or until the third succeeding annual meeting, if there be three classes. No classification of directors shall be effective prior to the first annual meeting of shareholders.

§ 38. Vacancies

Any vacancy occurring in the board of directors may be filled by the affirmative vote of a majority of the remaining directors though less than a quorum of the board of directors. A director elected to fill a vacancy shall be elected for the unexpired term of his prede-

cessor in office. Any directorship to be filled by reason of an increase in the number of directors may be filled by the board of directors for a term of office continuing only until the next election of directors by the shareholders.

§ 39. Removal of Directors

At a meeting of shareholders called expressly for that purpose, directors may be removed in the manner provided in this section. Any director or the entire board of directors may be removed, with or without cause, by a vote of the holders of a majority of the shares then entitled to vote at an election of directors.

In the case of a corporation having cumulative voting, if less than the entire board is to be removed, no one of the directors may be removed if the votes cast against his removal would be sufficient to elect him if then cumulatively voted at an election of the entire board of directors, or, if there be classes of directors, at an election of the class of directors of which he is a part.

Whenever the holders of the shares of any class are entitled to elect one or more directors by the provisions of the articles of incorporation, the provisions of this section shall apply, in respect to the removal of a director or directors so elected, to the vote of the holders of the outstanding shares of that class and not to the vote of the outstanding shares as a whole.

§ 40. Quorum of Directors

A majority of the number of directors fixed by or in the manner provided in the by-laws or in the absence of a by-law fixing or providing for the number of directors, then of the number stated in the articles of incorporation, shall constitute a quorum for the transaction of business unless a greater number is required by the articles of incorporation or the by-laws. The act of the majority of the directors present at a meeting at which a quorum is present shall be the act of the board of directors, unless the act of a greater number is required by the articles of incorporation or the by-laws.

§ 41. Director Conflicts of Interest

No contract or other transaction between a corporation and one or more of its directors or any other corporation, firm, association or entity in which one or more of its directors are directors or officers or are financially interested, shall be either void or voidable because of such relationship or interest or because such director or directors are present at the meeting of the board of directors or a committee thereof which authorizes, approves or ratifies such contract or transaction or because his or their votes are counted for such purpose, if:

(a) the fact of such relationship or interest is disclosed or known to the board of directors or committee which authorizes, approves or ratifies the contract or transaction by a vote or consent sufficient for the purpose without counting the votes or consents of such interested directors; or

(b) the fact of such relationship or interest is disclosed or known to the shareholders entitled to vote and they authorize, approve or ratify such contract or transaction by vote or written consent; or

(c) the contract or transaction is fair and reasonable to the corporation.

Common or interested directors may be counted in determining the presence of a quorum at a meeting of the board of directors or a committee thereof which authorizes, approves or ratifies such contract or transaction.

§ 42. Executive and Other Committees

If the articles of incorporation or the by-laws so provide, the board of directors, by resolution adopted by a majority of the full board of directors, may designate from among its members an executive committee and one or more other committees each of which, to the extent provided in such resolution or in the articles of incorporation or the by-laws of the corporation, shall have and may exercise all the authority of the board of directors, except that no such committee shall have authority to (i) authorize distributions, (ii) approve or recommend to shareholders actions or proposals required by this Act to be approved by shareholders, (iii) designate candidates for the office of director, for purposes of proxy solicitation or otherwise, or fill vancancies on the board of directors or any committee thereof, (iv) amend the by-laws, (v) approve a plan of merger not requiring shareholder approval, (vi) authorize or approve the reacquisition of shares unless pursuant to a general formula or method specified by the board of directors, or (vii) authorize or approve the issuance or sale of, or any contract to issue or sell, shares or designate the terms of a series of a class of shares, provided that the board of directors, having acted regarding general authorization for the issuance or sale of shares, or any contract therefor, and, in the case of a series, the designation thereof, may, pursuant to a general formula or method specified by the board by resolution or by adoption of a stock option or other plan, authorize a committee to fix the terms of any contract for the sale of the shares and to fix the terms upon which such shares may be issued or sold, including, without limitation, the price, the dividend rate, provisions for redemption, sinking fund, conversion, voting or preferential rights, and provisions for other features of a class of shares, or a series of a class of shares, with full power in such committee to adopt any final resolution setting forth all the terms thereof and to authorize the statement of the terms of a series for filing with the Secretary of State under this Act.

Neither the designation of any such committee, the delegation thereto of authority, nor action by such committee pursuant to such authority shall alone constitute compliance by any member of the board of directors, not a member of the committee in question, with his responsibility to act in good faith, in a manner he reasonably believes to be in the best interests of the corporation, and with such care as an ordinarily prudent person in a like position would use under similar circumstances.

§ 43. Place and Notice of Directors' Meetings; Committee Meetings

Meetings of the board of directors, regular or special, may be held either within or without this State.

Regular meetings of the board of directors or any committee designated thereby may be held with or without notice as prescribed in the by-laws. Special meetings of the board of directors or any committee designated thereby shall be held upon such notice as is prescribed in the by-laws. Attendance of a director at a meeting shall constitute a waiver of notice of such meeting, except where a director attends a meeting for the express purpose of objecting to the transaction of any business because the meeting is not lawfully called or convened. Neither the business to be transacted at, nor the purpose of, any regular or special meeting of the board of directors or any committee designated thereby need be specified in the notice or waiver of notice of such meeting unless required by the by-laws.

Except as may be otherwise restricted by the articles of incorporation or by-laws, members of the board of directors or any committee designated thereby may participate in a meeting of such board or committee by means of a conference telephone or similar communications equipment by means of which all persons participating in the meeting can hear each other at the same time and participation by such means shall constitute presence in person at a meeting.

§ 44. Action by Directors Without a Meeting

Unless otherwise provided by the articles of incorporation or by-laws, any action required by this Act to be taken at a meeting of the directors of a corporation, or any action which may be taken at a meeting of the directors or of a committee, may be taken without a meeting if a consent in writing, setting forth the action so taken, shall be signed by all of the directors, or all of the members of the committee, as the case may be. Such consent shall have the same effect as a unanimous vote.

§ 45. Distributions to Shareholders

Subject to any restrictions in the articles of incorporation, the board of directors may authorize and the corporation may make distributions, except that no distribution may be made if, after giving effect thereto, either:

(a) the corporation would be unable to pay its debts as they become due in the usual course of its business; or

(b) the corporation's total assets would be less than the sum of its total liabilities and (unless the articles of incorporation otherwise permit) the maximum amount that then would be payable, in any liquidation, in respect of all outstanding shares having preferential rights in liquidation.

Determinations under subparagraph (b) may be based upon (i) financial statements prepared on the basis of accounting practices and principles that are reasonable in the circumstances, or (ii) a fair valuation or other method that is reasonable in the circumstances.

In the case of a purchase, redemption or other acquisition of a corporation's shares, the effect of a distribution shall be measured as of the date money or other property is transferred or debt is incurred by the corporation, or as of the date the shareholder ceases to be a shareholder of the corporation with respect to such shares, whichever is earlier. In all other cases, the effect of a distribution shall be measured as of the date of its authorization if payment occurs 120 days or less following the date of authorization, or as of the date of payment if payment occurs more than 120 days following the date of authorization.

Indebtedness of a corporation incurred or issued to a shareholder in a distribution in accordance with this Section shall be on a parity with the indebtedness of the corporation to its general unsecured creditors except to the extent subordinated by agreement.

§ 46. Distributions from Capital Surplus

[Repealed in 1979].

§ 47. Loans to Employees and Directors

A corporation shall not lend money to or use its credit to assist its directors without authorization in the particular case by its shareholders, but may lend money to and use its credit to assist any employee of the corporation or of a subsidiary, including any such employee who is a director of the corporation, if the board of directors decides that such loan or assistance may benefit the corporation.

§ 48. Liability of Directors in Certain Cases

In addition to any other liabilities, a director who votes for or assents to any distribution contrary to the provisions of this Act or contrary to any restrictions contained in the articles of incorporation, shall, unless he complies with the standard provided in this Act for the performance of the duties of directors, be liable to the corporation, jointly and severally with all other directors so voting or assenting, for the amount of such dividend which is paid or the value of such distribution in excess of the amount of such distribution which could have been made without a violation of the provisions of this Act or the restrictions in the articles of incorporation.

Any director against whom a claim shall be asserted under or pursuant to this section for the making of a distribution and who shall be held liable thereon, shall be entitled to contribution from the shareholders who accepted or received any such distribution, knowing such distribution to have been made in violation of this Act, in proportion to the amounts received by them.

Any director against whom a claim shall be asserted under or pursuant to this section shall be entitled to contribution from any other director who voted for or assented to the action upon which the claim is asserted and who did not comply with the standard provided in this Act for the performance of the duties of directors.

§ 49. Provisions Relating to Actions by Shareholders

No action shall be brought in this State by a shareholder in the right of a domestic or foreign corporation unless the plaintiff was a holder of record of shares or of voting trust certificates therefor at the time of the transaction of which he complains, or his shares or voting trust certificates thereafter devolved upon him by operation of law from a person who was a holder of record at such time.

In any action hereafter instituted in the right of any domestic or foreign corporation by the holder or holders of record of shares of such corporation or of voting trust certificates therefor, the court having jurisdiction, upon final judgment and a finding that the action was brought without reasonable cause, may require the plaintiff or plaintiffs to pay to the parties named as defendant the reasonable expenses, including fees of attorneys, incurred by them in the defense of such action.

In any action now pending or hereafter instituted or maintained in the right of any domestic or foreign corporation by the holder or holders of record of less than five per cent of the outstanding shares of any class of such corporation or of voting trust certificates therefor, unless the shares or voting trust certificates so held have a market value in excess of twenty-five thousand dollars, the corporation in whose right such action is brought shall be entitled at any time before final judgment to require the plaintiff or plaintiffs to give security for the reasonable expenses, including fees of attorneys, that may be incurred by it in connection with such action or may be incurred by other parties named as defendant for which it may become legally liable. Market value shall be determined as of the date that the plaintiff institutes the action or, in the case of an intervenor, as of the date that he becomes a party to the action. The amount of such security may from time to time be increased or decreased, in the discretion of the court, upon showing that the security provided has or may become inadequate or is excessive. The corporation shall have recourse to such security in such amount as the court having jurisdiction shall determine upon the termination of such action, whether or not the court finds the action was brought without reasonable cause.

§ 50. **Officers**

The officers of a corporation shall consist of a president, one or more vice presidents as may be prescribed by the by-laws, a secretary, and a treasurer, each of whom shall be elected by the board of directors at such time and in such manner as may be prescribed by the by-laws. Such other officers and assistant officers and agents as may be deemed necessary may be elected or appointed by the board of directors or chosen in such other manner as may be prescribed by the by-laws.

Any two or more offices may be held by the same person, except the offices of president and secretary.

All officers and agents of the corporation, as between themselves and the corporation, shall have such authority and perform such duties in the management of the corporation as may be provided in the by-laws, or as may be determined by resolution of the board of directors not inconsistent with the by-laws.

§ 51. **Removal of Officers**

Any officer or agent may be removed by the board of directors whenever in its judgment the best interests of the corporation will be served thereby, but such removal shall be without prejudice to the contract rights, if any, of the person so removed. Election or appointment of an officer or agent shall not of itself create contract rights.

§ 52. **Books and Records: Financial Reports to Shareholders; Examination of Records**

Each corporation shall keep correct and complete books and records of account and shall keep minutes of the proceedings of its shareholders and board of directors and shall keep at its registered office or principal place of business, or at the office of its transfer agent or registrar, a record of its shareholders, giving the names and addresses of all shareholders and the number and class of the shares held by each. Any books, records and minutes may be in written form or in any form capable of being converted into written form within a reasonable time.

Any person who shall have been a holder of record of shares or of voting trust certificates therefor at least six months immediately preceding his demand or shall be the holder of record of, or the holder of record of voting trust certificates for, at least five percent of all the outstanding shares of the corporation, upon written demand stating the purpose thereof, shall have the right to examine, in person, or by agent or attorney, at any reasonable time or times, for any proper purpose its relevant books and records of account, minutes, and record of shareholders and to make extracts therefrom.

Any officer or agent who, or a corporation which, shall refuse to allow any such shareholder or holder of voting trust certificates, or his agent or attorney, so to examine and make extracts from its books and records of account, minutes, and record of shareholders, for any proper purpose, shall be liable to such shareholder or holder of voting trust certificates in a penalty of ten per cent of the value of the shares owned by such shareholder, or in respect of which such voting trust certificates are issued, in addition to any other damages or remedy afforded him by law. It shall be a defense to any action for penalties under this section that the person suing therefor has within two years sold or offered for sale any list of shareholders or of holders of voting trust certificates for shares of such corporation or any other corporation or has aided or abetted any person in procuring any list of shareholders or of holders of voting trust certificates for any such purpose, or has improperly used any information secured through any prior examination of the books and records of account, or minutes, or record of shareholders or of holders of voting trust certificates for shares of such corporation or any other corporation, or was not acting in good faith or for a proper purpose in making his demand.

Nothing herein contained shall impair the power of any court of competent jurisdiction, upon proof by a shareholder or holder of voting trust certificates of proper purpose, irrespective of the period of time during which such shareholder or holder of voting trust certificates shall have been a shareholder of record or a holder of record of voting trust certificates, and irrespective of the number of shares held by him or represented by voting trust certificates held by him, to compel the production for examination by such shareholder or holder of voting trust certificates of the books and records of account, minutes and record of shareholders of a corporation.

Upon the written request of any shareholder or holder of voting trust certificates for shares of a corporation, the corporation shall mail to such shareholder or holder of voting trust certificates its most recent financial statements showing in reasonable detail its assets and liabilities and the results of its operations.

Each corporation shall furnish to its shareholders annual financial statements, including at least a balance sheet as of the end of each fiscal year and a statement of income for such fiscal year, which shall be prepared on the basis of generally accepted accounting principles, if the corporation prepares financial statements for such fiscal year on that basis for any purpose, and may be consolidated statements of the corporation and one or more of its subsidiaries. The financial statements shall be mailed by the corporation to each of its shareholders within 120 days after the close of each fiscal year and, after such mailing and upon written request, shall be mailed by the corporation to any shareholder (or holder of a voting trust certificate for its shares) to whom a copy of the most recent annual financial statements has not previously

been mailed. In the case of statements audited by a public accountant, each copy shall be accompanied by a report setting forth his opinion thereon; in other cases, each copy shall be accompanied by a statement of the president or the person in charge of the corporation's financial accounting records (1) stating his reasonable belief as to whether or not the financial statements were prepared in accordance with generally accepted accounting principles and, if not, describing the basis of presentation, and (2) describing any respects in which the financial statements were not prepared on a basis consistent with those prepared for the previous year.

§ 53. **Incorporators**

One or more persons, or a domestic or foreign corporation, may act as incorporator or incorporators of a corporation by signing and delivering in duplicate to the Secretary of State articles of incorporation for such corporation.

§ 54. **Articles of Incorporation**

The articles of incorporation shall set forth:

(a) The name of the corporation.

(b) The period of duration, which may be perpetual.

(c) The purpose or purposes for which the corporation is organized which may be stated to be, or to include, the transaction of any or all lawful business for which corporations may be incorporated under this Act.

(d) The aggregate number of shares which the corporation shall have authority to issue and, if such shares are to be divided into classes, the number of shares of each class.

(e) If the shares are to be divided into classes, the designation of each class and a statement of the preferences, limitations and relative rights in respect of the shares of each class.

(f) If the corporation is to issue the shares of any preferred or special class in series, then the designation of each series and a statement of the variations in the relative rights and preferences as between series insofar as the same are to be fixed in the articles of incorporation, and a statement of any authority to be vested in the board of directors to establish series and fix and determine the variations in the relative rights and preferences as between series.

(g) If any preemptive right is to be granted to shareholders, the provisions therefor.

(h) The address of its initial registered office, and the name of its initial registered agent at such address.

(i) The number of directors constituting the initial board of directors and the names and addresses of the persons who are to serve as directors until the first annual meeting of shareholders or until their successors be elected and qualify.

(j) The name and address of each incorporator.

In addition to provisions required therein, the articles of incorporation may also contain provisions not inconsistent with law regarding:

(1) the direction of the management of the business and the regulation of the affairs of the corporation;

(2) the definition, limitation and regulation of the powers of the corporation, the directors, and the shareholders, or any class of the shareholders, including restrictions on the transfer of shares;

(3) the par value of any authorized shares or class of shares;

(4) any provision which under this Act is required or permitted to be set forth in the by-laws.

It shall not be necessary to set forth in the articles of incorporation any of the corporate powers enumerated in this Act.

§ 55. **Filing of Articles of Incorporation**

Duplicate originals of the articles of incorporation shall be delivered to the Secretary of State. If the Secretary of State finds that the articles of incorporation conform to law, he shall, when all fees have been paid as in this Act prescribed:

(a) Endorse on each of such duplicate originals the word "Filed," and the month, day and year of the filing thereof.

(b) File one of such duplicate originals in his office.

(c) Issue a certificate of incorporation to which he shall affix the other duplicate original.

The certificate of incorporation, together with the duplicate original of the articles of incorporation affixed thereto by the Secretary of State, shall be returned to the incorporators or their representative.

§ 56. **Effect of Issuance of Certificate of Incorporation**

Upon the issuance of the certificate of incorporation, the corporate existence shall begin, and such certificate of incorporation shall be conclusive evidence that all conditions precedent required to be performed by the incorporators have been complied with and that the corporation has been incorporated under this Act, except as against this State in a proceeding to cancel or revoke the certificate of incorporation or for involuntary dissolution of the corporation.

§ 57. **Organization Meeting of Directors**

After the issuance of the certificate of incorporation an organization meeting of the board of directors named in the articles of incorporation shall be held, either within or without this State, at the call of a majority of the directors named in the articles of incorporation, for the purpose of adopting by-laws, electing officers and transacting such other business as may come before the meeting. The directors calling the meeting shall give at least three days' notice thereof by mail to each director so named, stating the time and place of the meeting.

§ 58. **Right to Amend Articles of Incorporation**

A corporation may amend its articles of incorporation, from time to time, in any and as many respects as may be desired, so long as its articles of incorporation as amended contain only such provisions as might be lawfully contained in original articles of incorporation at the time of making such amendment, and, if a change in shares or the rights of shareholders, or an exchange, reclassification or cancellation of shares or rights of shareholders is to be made, such provisions as may be necessary to effect such change, exchange, reclassification or cancellation.

In particular, and without limitation upon such general power of amendment, a corporation may amend its articles of incorporation, from time to time, so as:

(a) To change its corporate name.

(b) To change its period of duration.

(c) To change, enlarge or diminish its corporate purposes.

(d) To increase or decrease the aggregate number of shares, or shares of any class, which the corporation has authority to issue.

(e) To provide, change or eliminate any provision with respect to the par value of any shares or class of shares.

(f) To exchange, classify, reclassify or cancel all or any part of its shares, whether issued or unissued.

(g) To change the designation of all or any part of its shares, whether issued or unissued, and to change the preferences, limitations, and the relative rights in respect of all or any part of its shares, whether issued or unissued.

(h) To change the shares of any class, whether issued or unissued [sic] into a different number of shares of the same class or into the same or a different number of shares of other classes.

(i) To create new classes of shares having rights and preferences either prior and superior or subordinate and inferior to the shares of any class then authorized, whether issued or unissued.

(j) To cancel or otherwise affect the right of the holders of the shares of any class to receive dividends which have accrued but have not been declared.

(k) To divide any preferred or special class of shares, whether issued or unissued, into series and fix and determine the designations of such series and the variations in the relative rights and preferences as between the shares of such series.

(l) To authorize the board of directors to establish, out of authorized but unissued shares, series of any preferred or special class of shares and fix and determine the relative rights and preferences of the shares of any series so established.

(m) To authorize the board of directors to fix and determine the relative rights and preferences of the authorized but unissued shares of series theretofore established in respect of which either the relative rights and preferences have not been fixed and determined or the relative rights and preferences theretofore fixed and determined are to be changed.

(n) To revoke, diminish, or enlarge the authority of the board of directors to establish series out of authorized but unissued shares of any preferred or special class and fix and determine the relative rights and preferences of the shares of any series so established.

(o) To limit, deny or grant to shareholders of any class the preemptive right to acquire additional shares of the corporation, whether then or thereafter authorized.

§ 59. Procedure to Amend Articles of Incorporation

Amendments to the articles of incorporation shall be made in the following manner:

(a) The board of directors shall adopt a resolution setting forth the proposed amendment and, if shares have been issued, directing that it be submitted to a vote at a meeting of shareholders, which may be either the annual or a special meeting. If no shares have been issued, the amendment shall be adopted by resolution

of the board of directors and the provisions for adoption by shareholders shall not apply. If the corporation has only one class of shares outstanding, an amendment solely to change the number of authorized shares to effectuate a split of, or stock dividend in, the corporation's own shares, or solely to do so and to change the number of authorized shares in proportion thereto, may be adopted by the board of directors; and the provisions for adoption by shareholders shall not apply, unless otherwise provided by the articles of incorporation. The resolution may incorporate the proposed amendment in restated articles of incorporation which contain a statement that except for the designated amendment the restated articles of incorporation correctly set forth without change the corresponding provisions of the articles of incorporation as theretofore amended, and that the restated articles of incorporation together with the designated amendment supersede the original articles of incorporation and all amendments thereto.

(b) Written notice setting forth the proposed amendment or a summary of the changes to be effected thereby shall be given to each shareholder of record entitled to vote thereon within the time and in the manner provided in this Act for the giving of notice of meetings of shareholders. If the meeting be an annual meeting, the proposed amendment of such summary may be included in the notice of such annual meeting.

(c) At such meeting a vote of the shareholders entitled to vote thereon shall be taken on the proposed amendment. The proposed amendment shall be adopted upon receiving the affirmative vote of the holders of a majority of the shares entitled to vote thereon, unless any class of shares is entitled to vote thereon as a class, in which event the proposed amendment shall be adopted upon receiving the affirmative vote of the holders of a majority of the shares of each class of shares entitled to vote thereon as a class and of the total shares entitled to vote thereon.

Any number of amendments may be submitted to the shareholders, and voted upon by them, at one meeting.

§ 60. Class Voting on Amendments

The holders of the outstanding shares of a class shall be entitled to vote as a class upon a proposed amendment, whether or not entitled to vote thereon by the provisions of the articles of incorporation, if the amendment would:

(a) Increase or decrease the aggregate number of authorized shares of such class.

(b) Effect an exchange, reclassification or cancellation of all or part of the shares of such class.

(c) Effect an exchange, or create a right of exchange, of all or any part of the shares of another class into the shares of such class.

(d) Change the designations, preferences, limitations or relative rights of the shares of such class.

(e) Change the shares of such class into the same or a different number of shares of the same class or another class or classes.

(f) Create a new class of shares having rights and preferences prior and superior to the shares of such class, or increase the rights and preferences or the number of authorized shares, of any class having rights and preferences prior or superior to the shares of such class.

(g) In the case of a preferred or special class of shares, divide the shares of such class into series and fix and determine the designation of such series and the variations in the relative rights and preferences between the shares of such series, or authorize the board of directors to do so.

(h) Limit or deny any existing preemptive rights of the shares of such class.

(i) Cancel or otherwise affect dividends on the shares of such class which have accrued but have not been declared.

§ 61. Articles of Amendment

The articles of amendment shall be executed in duplicate by the corporation by its president or a vice president and by its secretary or an assistant secretary, and verified by one of the officers signing such articles, and shall set forth:

(a) The name of the corporation.

(b) The amendments so adopted.

(c) The date of the adoption of the amendment by the shareholders, or by the board of directors where no shares have been issued.

(d) The number of shares outstanding, and the number of shares entitled to vote thereon, and if the shares of any class are entitled to vote thereon as a class, the designation and number of outstanding shares entitled to vote thereon of each such class.

(e) The number of shares voted for and against such amendment, respectively, and, if the shares of any class are entitled to vote thereon as a class, the number of shares of each class voted for and against

such amendment, respectively, or if no shares have been issued, a statement to that effect.

(f) If such amendment provides for an exchange, reclassification or cancellation of issued shares, and if the manner in which the same shall be effected is not set forth in the amendment, then a statement of the manner in which the same shall be effected.

§ 62. Filing of Articles of Amendment

Duplicate originals of the articles of amendment shall be delivered to the Secretary of State. If the Secretary of State finds that the articles of amendment conform to law, he shall, when all fees and franchise taxes have been paid as in this Act prescribed:

(a) Endorse on each of such duplicate originals the word "Filed," and the month, day and year of the filing thereof.

(b) File one of such duplicate originals in his office.

(c) Issue a certificate of amendment to which he shall affix the other duplicate original.

The certificate of amendment, together with the duplicate original of the articles of amendment affixed thereto by the Secretary of State, shall be returned to the corporation or its representative.

§ 63. Effect of Certificate of Amendment

Upon the issuance of the certificate of amendment by the Secretary of State, the amendment shall become effective and the articles of incorporation shall be deemed to be amended accordingly.

No amendment shall affect any existing cause of action in favor of or against such corporation, or any pending suit to which such corporation shall be a party, or the existing rights of persons other than shareholders; and, in the event the corporate name shall be changed by amendment, no suit brought by or against such corporation under its former name shall abate for that reason.

§ 64. Restated Articles of Incorporation

A domestic corporation may at any time restate its articles of incorporation as theretofore amended, by a resolution adopted by the board of directors.

Upon the adoption of such resolution, restated articles of incorporation shall be executed in duplicate by the corporation by its president or a vice president and by its secretary or assistant secretary and verified by one of the officers signing such articles and shall set forth all of the operative provisions of the articles of incorporation as theretofore amended together with a statement that the restated articles of incorporation correctly set forth without change the corresponding provisions of the articles of incorporation as theretofore amended and that the restated articles of incorporation supersede the original articles of incorporation and all amendments thereto.

Duplicate originals of the restated articles of incorporation shall be delivered to the Secretary of State. If the Secretary of State finds that such restated articles of incorporation conform to law, he shall, when all fees and franchise taxes have been paid as in this Act prescribed:

(1) Endorse on each of such duplicate originals the word "Filed," and the month, day and year of the filing thereof.

(2) File one of such duplicate originals in his office.

(3) Issue a restated certificate of incorporation, to which he shall affix the other duplicate original.

The restated certificate of incorporation, together with the duplicate original of the restated articles of incorporation affixed thereto by the Secretary of State, shall be returned to the corporation or its representative.

Upon the issuance of the restated certificate of incorporation by the Secretary of State, the restated articles of incorporation shall become effective and shall supersede the original articles of incorporation and all amendments thereto.

§ 65. Amendment of Articles of Incorporation in Reorganization Proceedings

Whenever a plan of reorganization of a corporation has been confirmed by decree or order of a court of competent jurisdiction in proceedings for the reorganization of such corporation, pursuant to the provisions of any applicable statute of the United States relating to reorganizations of corporations, the articles of incorporation of the corporation may be amended, in the manner provided in this section, in as many respects as may be necessary to carry out the plan and put it into effect, so long as the articles of incorporation as amended contain only such provisions as might be lawfully contained in original articles of incorporation at the time of making such amendment.

In particular and without limitation upon such general power of amendment, the articles of incorporation may be amended for such purpose so as to:

(A) Change the corporate name, period of duration or corporate purposes of the corporation;

(B) Repeal, alter or amend the by-laws of the corporation;

(C) Change the aggregate number of shares or shares of any class, which the corporation has authority to issue;

(D) Change the preferences, limitations and relative rights in respect of all or any part of the shares of the corporation, and classify, reclassify or cancel all or any part thereof, whether issued or unissued;

(E) Authorize the issuance of bonds, debentures or other obligations of the corporation, whether or not convertible into shares of any class or bearing warrants or other evidences of optional rights to purchase or subscribe for shares of any class, and fix the terms and conditions thereof; and

(F) Constitute or reconstitute and classify or reclassify the board of directors of the corporation, and appoint directors and officers in place of or in addition to all or any of the directors or officers then in office.

Amendments to the articles of incorporation pursuant to this section shall be made in the following manner:

(a) Articles of amendment approved by decree or order of such court shall be executed and verified in duplicate by such person or persons as the court shall designate or appoint for the purpose, and shall set forth the name of the corporation, the amendments of the articles of incorporation approved by the court, the date of the decree or order approving the articles of amendment, the title of the proceedings in which the decree or order was entered, and a statement that such decree or order was entered by a court having jurisdiction of the proceedings for the reorganization of the corporation pursuant to the provisions of an applicable statute of the United States.

(b) Duplicate originals of the articles of amendment shall be delivered to the Secretary of State. If the Secretary of State finds that the articles of amendment conform to law, he shall, when all fees and franchise taxes have been paid as in this Act prescribed:

(1) Endorse on each of such duplicate originals the word "Filed," and the month, day and year of the filing thereof.

(2) File one of such duplicate originals in his office.

(3) Issue a certificate of amendment to which he shall affix the other duplicate original.

The certificate of amendment, together with the duplicate original of the articles of amendment affixed thereto by the Secretary of State, shall be returned to the corporation or its representative.

Upon the issuance of the certificate of amendment by

the Secretary of State, the amendment shall become effective and the articles of incorporation shall be deemed to be amended accordingly, without any action thereon by the directors or shareholders of the corporation and with the same effect as if the amendments had been adopted by unanimous action of the directors and shareholders of the corporation.

§ 66. Restriction on Redemption or Purchase of Redeemable Shares

[Repealed in 1979].

§ 67. Cancellation of Redeemable Shares by Redemption or Purchase

[Repealed in 1979].

§ 68. Cancellation of Other Reacquired Shares

[Repealed in 1979].

§ 69. Reduction of Stated Capital in Certain Cases

[Repealed in 1979].

§ 70. Special Provisions Relating to Surplus and Reserves

[Repealed in 1979].

§ 71. Procedure for Merger

Any two or more domestic corporations may merge into one of such corporations pursuant to a plan of merger approved in the manner provided in this Act.

The board of directors of each corporation shall, by resolution adopted by each such board, approve a plan of merger setting forth:

(a) The names of the corporations proposing to merge, and the name of the corporation into which they propose to merge, which is hereinafter designated as the surviving corporation.

(b) The terms and conditions of the proposed merger.

(c) The manner and basis of converting the shares of each corporation into shares, obligations or other securities of the surviving corporation or of any other corporation or, in whole or in part, into cash or other property.

(d) A statement of any changes in the articles of incorporation of the surviving corporation to be effected by such merger.

(e) Such other provisions with respect to the proposed merger as are deemed necessary or desirable.

§ 72. Procedure for Consolidation

Any two or more domestic corporations may consolidate into a new corporation pursuant to a plan of consolidation approved in the manner provided in this Act.

The board of directors of each corporation shall, by a resolution adopted by each such board, approve a plan of consolidation setting forth:

(a) The names of the corporations proposing to consolidate, and the name of the new corporation into which they propose to consolidate, which is hereinafter designated as the new corporation.

(b) The terms and conditions of the proposed consolidation.

(c) The manner and basis of converting the shares of each corporation into shares, obligations or other securities of the new corporation or of any other corporation or, in whole or in part, into cash or other property.

(d) With respect to the new corporation, all of the statements required to be set forth in articles of incorporation for corporations organized under this Act.

(e) Such other provisions with respect to the proposed consolidation as are deemed necessary or desirable.

§ 72A. Procedure for Share Exchange

All the issued or all the outstanding shares of one or more classes of any domestic corporation may be acquired through the exchange of all such shares of such class or classes by another domestic or foreign corporation pursuant to a plan of exchange approved in the manner provided in this Act.

The board of directors of each corporation shall, by resolution adopted by each such board, approve a plan of exchange setting forth:

(a) The name of the corporation the shares of which are proposed to be acquired by exchange and the name of the corporation to acquire the shares of such corporation in the exchange, which is hereinafter designated as the acquiring corporation.

(b) The terms and conditions of the proposed exchange.

(c) The manner and basis of exchanging the shares to be acquired for shares, obligations or other securities of the acquiring corporation or any other corporation, or, in whole or in part, for cash or other property.

(d) Such other provisions with respect to the proposed exchange as are deemed necessary or desirable.

The procedure authorized by this section shall not be deemed to limit the power of a corporation to acquire all or part of the shares of any class or classes of a corporation through a voluntary exchange or otherwise by agreement with the shareholders.

§ 73. **Approval by Shareholders**

(a) The board of directors of each corporation in the case of a merger or consolidation, and the board of directors of the corporation the shares of which are to be acquired in the case of an exchange, upon approving such plan of merger, consolidation or exchange, shall, by resolution, direct that the plan be submitted to a vote at a meeting of its shareholders, which may be either an annual or a special meeting. Written notice shall be given to each shareholder of record, whether or not entitled to vote at such meeting, not less than twenty days before such meeting, in the manner provided in this Act for the giving of notice of meetings of shareholders, and, whether the meeting be an annual or a special meeting, shall state that the purpose or one of the purposes is to consider the proposed plan of merger, consolidation or exchange. A copy or a summary of the plan of merger, consolidation or exchange, as the case may be, shall be included in or enclosed with such notice.

(b) At each such meeting, a vote of the shareholders shall be taken on the proposed plan. The plan shall be approved upon receiving the affirmative vote of the holders of a majority of the shares entitled to vote thereon of each such corporation, unless any class of shares of any such corporation is entitled to vote thereon as a class, in which event, as to such corporation, the plan shall be approved upon receiving the affirmative vote of the holders of a majority of the shares of each class of shares entitled to vote thereon as a class and of the total shares entitled to vote thereon. Any class of shares of any such corporation shall be entitled to vote as a class if any such plan contains any provision which, if contained in a proposed amendment to articles of incorporation, would entitle such class of shares to vote as a class and, in the case of an exchange, if the class is included in the exchange.

(c) After such approval by a vote of the shareholders of each such corporation, and at any time prior to the filing of the articles of merger, consolidation or exchange, the merger, consolidation or exchange may be abandoned pursuant to provisions therefor, if any, set forth in the plan.

(d) (1) Notwithstanding the provisions of subsections (a) and (b), submission of a plan of merger to a vote at a meeting of shareholders of a surviving corporation shall not be required if:

(i) the articles of incorporation of the surviving corporation do not differ except in name from those of the corporation before the merger,

(ii) each holder of shares of the surviving corporation which were outstanding immediately before the effective date of the merger is to hold the same number of shares with identical rights immediately after,

(iii) the number of voting shares outstanding immediately after the merger, plus the number of voting shares issuable on conversion of other securities issued by virtue of the terms of the merger and on exercise of rights and warrants so issued, will not exceed by more than 20 percent the number of voting shares outstanding immediately before the merger, and

(iv) the number of participating shares outstanding immediately after the merger, plus the number of participating shares issuable on conversion of other securities issued by virtue of the terms of the merger and on exercise of rights and warrants so issued, will not exceed by more than 20 percent the number of participating shares outstanding immediately before the merger.

(2) As used in this subsection:

(i) "voting shares" means shares which entitle their holders to vote unconditionally in elections of directors;

(ii) "participating shares" means shares which entitle their holders to participate without limitation in distribution of earnings or surplus.

§ 74. **Articles of Merger, Consolidation or Exchange**

(a) Upon receiving the approvals required by Sections 71, 72 and 73, articles of merger or articles of consolidation shall be executed in duplicate by each corporation by its president or a vice president and by its secretary or an assistant secretary, and verified by one of the officers of each corporation signing such articles, and shall set forth:

(1) The plan of merger or the plan of consolidation;

(2) As to each corporation, either (i) the number of shares outstanding, and, if the shares of any class are entitled to vote as a class, the designation and number of outstanding shares of each such class, or (ii) a statement that the vote of shareholders is not required by virtue of subsection 73(d);

(3) As to each corporation the approval of whose shareholders is required, the number of shares voted for and against such plan, respectively, and, if the shares of any class are entitled to vote as a class, the

number of shares of each such class voted for and against such plan, respectively.

(b) Duplicate originals of the articles of merger, consolidation or exchange shall be delivered to the Secretary of State. If the Secretary of State finds that such articles conform to law, he shall, when all fees and franchise taxes have been paid as in this Act prescribed:

(1) Endorse on each of such duplicate originals the word "Filed," and the month, day and year of the filing thereof.

(2) File one of such duplicate originals in his office.

(3) Issue a certificate of merger, consolidation or exchange to which he shall affix the other duplicate original.

(c) The certificate of merger, consolidation or exchange together with the duplicate original of the articles affixed thereto by the Secretary of State, shall be returned to the surviving, new or acquiring corporation, as the case may be, or its representative.

§ 75. **Merger of Subsidiary Corporation**

Any corporation owning at least ninety per cent of the outstanding shares of each class of another corporation may merge such other corporation into itself without approval by a vote of the shareholders of either corporation. Its board of directors shall, by resolution, approve a plan of merger setting forth:

(A) The name of the subsidiary corporation and the name of the corporation owning at least ninety per cent of its shares, which is hereinafter designated as the surviving corporation.

(B) The manner and basis of converting the shares of the subsidiary corporation into shares, obligations or other securities of the surviving corporation or of any other corporation or, in whole or in part, into cash or other property.

A copy of such plan of merger shall be mailed to each shareholder of record of the subsidiary corporation.

Articles of merger shall be executed in duplicate by the surviving corporation by its president or a vice president and by its secretary or an assistant secretary, and verified by one of its officers signing such articles, and shall set forth:

(a) The plan of merger;

(b) The number of outstanding shares of each class of the subsidiary corporation and the number of such shares of each class owned by the surviving corporation; and

(c) The date of the mailing to shareholders of the subsidiary corporation of a copy of the plan of merger.

On and after the thirtieth day after the mailing of a copy of the plan of merger to shareholders of the subsidiary corporation or upon the waiver thereof by the holders of all outstanding shares duplicate originals of the articles of merger shall be delivered to the Secretary of State. If the Secretary of State finds that such articles conform to law, he shall, when all fees and franchise taxes have been paid as in this Act prescribed:

(1) Endorse on each of such duplicate originals the word "Filed," and the month, day and year of the filing thereof,

(2) File one of such duplicate originals in his office, and

(3) Issue a certificate of merger to which he shall affix the other duplicate original.

The certificate of merger, together with the duplicate original of the articles of merger affixed thereto by the Secretary of State, shall be returned to the surviving corporation or its representative.

§ 76. **Effect of Merger, Consolidation or Exchange**

Upon the issuance of the certificate of merger or the certificate of consolidation by the Secretary of State, the merger or consolidation shall be effected.

When such merger or consolidation has been effective:

(a) The several corporations parties to the plan of merger or consolidation shall be a single corporation, which, in the case of a merger, shall be that corporation designated in the plan of merger as the surviving corporation, and, in the case of a consolidation, shall be the new corporation provided for in the plan of consolidation.

(b) The separate existence of all corporations parties to the plan of merger or consolidation, except the surviving or new corporation, shall cease.

(c) Such surviving or new corporation shall have all the rights, privileges, immunities and powers and shall be subject to all the duties and liabilities of a corporation organized under this Act.

(d) Such surviving or new corporation shall thereupon and thereafter possess all the rights, privileges, immunities, and franchises, of a public as well as of a private nature, of each of the merging or consolidating corporations; and all property, real, personal and mixed, and all debts due on whatever account, including subscriptions to shares, and all other choses in action, and all and every other interest of or belonging to or due to each of the corporations so merged or consolidated, shall be taken and deemed to be transferred to and vested in such single corporation without further act or deed; and the title to any real estate, or any interest therein, vested in any of such corporations shall not revert or be in any way impaired by reason of such merger or consolidation.

(e) Such surviving or new corporation shall thenceforth be responsible and liable for all the liabilities and obligations of each of the corporations so merged or consolidated; and any claim existing or action or proceeding pending by or against any of such corporations may be prosecuted as if such merger or consolidation had not taken place, or such surviving or new corporation may be substituted in its place. Neither the rights of creditors nor any liens upon the property of any such corporation shall be impaired by such merger or consolidation.

(f) In the case of a merger, the articles of incorporation of the surviving corporation shall be deemed to be amended to the extent, if any, that changes in its articles of incorporation are stated in the plan of merger; and, in the case of a consolidation, the statements set forth in the articles of consolidation and which are required or permitted to be set forth in the articles of incorporation of corporations organized under this Act shall be deemed to be the original articles of incorporation of the new corporation.

§ 77. Merger, Consolidation or Exchange of Shares Between Domestic and Foreign Corporations

One or more foreign corporations and one or more domestic corporations may be merged or consolidated in the following manner, if such merger or consolidation is permitted by the laws of the state under which each such foreign corporation is organized:

(a) Each domestic corporation shall comply with the provisions of this Act with respect to the merger or consolidation, as the case may be, of domestic corporations and each foreign corporation shall comply with the applicable provisions of the laws of the state under which it is organized.

(b) If the surviving or new corporation, as the case may be, is to be governed by the laws of any state other than this State, it shall comply with the provisions of this Act with respect to foreign corporations

if it is to transact business in this State, and in every case it shall file with the Secretary of State of this State:

(1) An agreement that it may be served with process in this State in any proceeding for the enforcement of any obligation of any domestic corporation which is a party to such merger or consolidation and in any proceeding for the enforcement of the rights of a dissenting shareholder of any such domestic corporation against the surviving or new corporation;

(2) An irrevocable appointment of the Secretary of State of this State as its agent to accept service of process in any such proceeding; and

(3) An agreement that it will promptly pay to the dissenting shareholders of any such domestic corporation the amount, if any, to which they shall be entitled under the provisions of this Act with respect to the rights of dissenting shareholders.

The effect of such merger or consolidation shall be the same as in the case of the merger or consolidation of domestic corporations, if the surviving or new corporation is to be governed by the laws of this State. If the surviving or new corporation is to be governed by the laws of any state other than this State, the effect of such merger or consolidation shall be the same as in the case of the merger or consolidation of domestic corporations except insofar as the laws of such other state provide otherwise.

At any time prior to the filing of the articles of merger or consolidation, the merger or consolidation may be abandoned pursuant to provisions therefor, if any, set forth in the plan of merger or consolidation.

§ 78. Sale of Assets in Regular Course of Business and Mortgage or Pledge of Assets

The sale, lease, exchange, or other disposition of all, or substantially all, the property and assets of a corporation in the usual and regular course of its business and the mortgage or pledge of any or all property and assets of a corporation whether or not in the usual and regular course of business may be made upon such terms and conditions and for such consideration, which may consist in whole or in part of cash or other property, including shares, obligations or other securities of any other corporation, domestic or foreign, as shall be authorized by its board of directors; and in any such case no authorization or consent of the shareholders shall be required.

§ 79. Sale of Assets Other Than in Regular Course of Business

A sale, lease, exchange, or other disposition of all, or substantially all, the property and assets, with or without the good will, of a corporation, if not in the usual and regular course of its business, may be made upon such terms and conditions and for such consideration, which may consist in whole or in part of cash or other property, including shares, obligations or other securities of any other corporation, domestic or foreign, as may be authorized in the following manner:

(a) The board of directors shall adopt a resolution recommending such sale, lease, exchange, or other disposition and directing the submission thereof to a vote at a meeting of shareholders, which may be either an annual or a special meeting.

(b) Written notice shall be given to each shareholder of record, whether or not entitled to vote at such meeting, not less than twenty days before such meeting, in the manner provided in this Act for the giving of notice of meetings of shareholders, and, whether the meeting be an annual or a special meeting, shall state that the purpose, or one of the purposes is to consider the proposed sale, lease, exchange, or other disposition.

(c) At such meeting the shareholders may authorize such sale, lease, exchange, or other disposition and may fix, or may authorize the board of directors to fix, any or all of the terms and conditions thereof and the consideration to be received by the corporation therefor. Such authorization shall require the affirmative vote of the holders of a majority of the shares of the corporation entitled to vote thereon, unless any class of shares is entitled to vote thereon as a class, in which event such authorization shall require the affirmative vote of the holders of a majority of the shares of each class of shares entitled to vote as a class thereon and of the total shares entitled to vote thereon.

(d) After such authorization by a vote of shareholders, the board of directors nevertheless, in its discretion, may abandon such sale, lease, exchange, or other disposition of assets, subject to the rights of third parties under any contracts relating thereto, without further action or approval by shareholders.

§ 80. Right of Shareholders to Dissent and Obtain Payment for Shares

(a) Any shareholder of a corporation shall have the right to dissent from, and to obtain payment for his shares in the event of, any of the following corporate actions:

(1) Any plan of merger or consolidation to which the corporation is a party, except as provided in subsection (c);

(2) Any sale or exchange of all or substantially all of the property and assets of the corporation not made in the usual or regular course of its business, including a sale in dissolution, but not including a sale pursuant to an order of a court having jurisdiction in the premises or a sale for cash on terms requiring that all or substantially all of the net proceeds of sale be distributed to the shareholders in accordance with their respective interests within one year after the date of sale;

(3) Any plan of exchange to which the corporation is a party as the corporation the shares of which are to be acquired;

(4) Any amendment of the articles of incorporation which materially and adversely affects the rights appurtenant to the shares of the dissenting shareholder in that it:

   (i) alters or abolishes a preferential right of such shares;

   (ii) creates, alters or abolishes a right in respect of the redemption of such shares, including a provision respecting a sinking fund for the redemption or repurchase of such shares;

   (iii) alters or abolishes a preemptive right of the holder of such shares to acquire shares or other securities;

   (iv) excludes or limits the right of the holder of such shares to vote on any matter, or to cumulate his votes, except as such right may be limited by dilution through the issuance of shares or other securities with similar voting rights; or

(5) Any other corporate action taken pursuant to a shareholder vote with respect to which the articles of incorporation, the bylaws, or a resolution of the board of directors directs that dissenting shareholders shall have a right to obtain payment for their shares.

(b) (1) A record holder of shares may assert dissenters' rights as to less than all of the shares registered in his name only if he dissents with respect to all the shares beneficially owned by any one person, and discloses the name and address of the person or persons on whose behalf he dissents. In that event, his rights shall be determined as if the shares as to which he has dissented and his other shares were registered in the names of different shareholders.

(2) A beneficial owner of shares who is not the record holder may assert dissenters' rights with respect to shares held on his behalf, and shall be treated as a dissenting shareholder under the terms of this section and section 31 if he submits to the corporation at the time of or before the assertion of these rights a written consent of the record holder.

(c) The right to obtain payment under this section shall not apply to the shareholders of the surviving corporation in a merger if a vote of the shareholders of such corporation is not necessary to authorize such merger.

(d) A shareholder of a corporation who has a right under this section to obtain payment for his shares shall have no right at law or in equity to attack the validity of the corporate action that gives rise to his right to obtain payment, nor to have the action set aside or rescinded, except when the corporate action is unlawful or fraudulent with regard to the complaining shareholder or to the corporation.

§ 81. Procedures for Protection of Dissenters' Rights

(a) As used in this section:

(1) "Dissenter" means a shareholder or beneficial owner who is entitled to and does assert dissenters' rights under section 80, and who has performed every act required up to the time involved for the assertion of such rights.

(2) "Corporation" means the issuer of the shares held by the dissenter before the corporate action, or the successor by merger or consolidation of that issuer.

(3) "Fair value" of shares means their value immediately before the effectuation of the corporate action to which the dissenter objects, excluding any appreciation or depreciation in anticipation of such corporate action unless such exclusion would be inequitable.

(4) "Interest" means interest from the effective date of the corporate action until the date of payment, at the average rate currently paid by the corporation on its principal bank loans, or, if none, at such rate as is fair and equitable under all the circumstances.

(b) If a proposed corporate action which would give rise to dissenters' rights under section 80(a) is submitted to a vote at a meeting of shareholders, the notice of meeting shall notify all shareholders that they have or may have a right to dissent and obtain payment for their shares by complying with the terms of this section, and shall be accompanied by a copy of sections 80 and 81 of this Act.

(c) If the proposed corporate action is submitted to a vote at a meeting of shareholders, any shareholder who wishes to dissent and obtain payment for his shares must file with the corporation, prior to the vote, a written notice of intention to demand that he be paid fair compensation for his shares if the proposed action is effectuated, and shall refrain from voting his shares in approval of such action. A shareholder who fails in either respect shall acquire no right to payment for his shares under this section or section 80.

(d) If the proposed corporate action is approved by the required vote at a meeting of shareholders, the corporation shall mail a further notice to all shareholders who gave due notice of intention to demand payment and who refrained from voting in favor of the proposed action. If the proposed corporate action is to be taken without a vote of shareholders, the corporation shall send to all shareholders who are entitled to dissent and demand payment for their shares a notice of the adoption of the plan of corporate action. The notice shall (1) state where and when a demand for payment must be sent and certificates of certificated shares must be deposited in order to obtain payment, (2) inform holders of uncertificated shares to what extent transfer of shares will be restricted from the time that demand for payment is received, (3) supply a form for demanding payment which includes a request for certification of the date on which the shareholder, or the person on whose behalf the shareholder dissents, acquired beneficial ownership of the shares, and (4) be accompanied by a copy of sections 80 and 81 of this Act. The time set for the demand and deposit shall be not less than 30 days from the mailing of the notice.

(e) A shareholder who fails to demand payment, or fails (in the case of certificated shares) to deposit certificates, as required by a notice pursuant to subsection (d) shall have no right under this section or section 80 to receive payment for his shares. If the shares are not represented by certificates, the corporation may restrict their transfer from the time of receipt of demand for payment until effectuation of the proposed corporate action, or the release of restrictions under the terms of subsection (f). The dissenter shall retain all other rights of a shareholder until these rights are modified by effectuation of the proposed corporate action.

(f) (1) Within 60 days after the date set for demanding payment and depositing certificates, if the corporation has not effectuated the proposed corporate action and remitted payment for shares pursuant to paragraph (3), it shall return any certificates that have been deposited, and release uncertificated shares from any transfer restrictions imposed by reason of the demand for payment.

(2) When uncertificated shares have been released from transfer restrictions, and deposited certificates have been returned, the corporation may at any later time send a new notice conforming to the requirements of subsection (d), with like effect.

(3) Immediately upon effectuation of the proposed corporate action, or upon receipt of demand for payment if the corporate action has already been effectuated, the corporation shall remit to dissenters who have made demand and (if their shares are certificated) have deposited their certificates the amount which the corporation estimates to be the fair value of the shares, with interest if any has accrued. The remittance shall be accompanied by:

   (i) the corporation's closing balance sheet and statement of income for a fiscal year ending not more than 16 months before the date of remittance, together with the latest available interim financial statements;

   (ii) a statement of the corporation's estimate of fair value of the shares; and

   (iii) a notice of the dissenter's right to demand supplemental payment, accompanied by a copy of sections 80 and 81 of this Act.

(g) (1) If the corporation fails to remit as required by subsection (f), or if the dissenter believes that the amount remitted is less than the fair value of his shares, or that the interest is not correctly determined, he may send the corporation his own estimate of the value of the shares or of the interest, and demand payment of the deficiency.

(2) If the dissenter does not file such an estimate within 30 days after the corporation's mailing of its remittance, he shall be entitled to no more than the amount remitted.

(h) (1) Within 60 days after receiving a demand for payment pursuant to subsection (g), if any such demands for payment remain unsettled, the corporation shall file in an appropriate court a petition requesting that the fair value of the shares and interest thereon be determined by the court.

(2) An appropriate court shall be a court of competent jurisdiction in the county of this state where the registered office of the corporation is located. If, in the case of a merger or consolidation or exchange of shares, the corporation is a foreign corporation without a registered office in this state, the petition shall be filed in the county where the registered office of the domestic corporation was last located.

(3) All dissenters, wherever residing, whose demands have not been settled shall be made parties to the proceeding as in an action against their shares. A copy of the petition shall be served on each such dissenter; if a dissenter is a nonresident, the copy may be served on him by registered or certified mail or by publication as provided by law.

(4) The jurisdiction of the court shall be plenary and exclusive. The court may appoint one or more persons as appraisers to receive evidence and recommend a decision on the question of fair value. The appraisers shall have such power and authority as shall be specified in the order of their appointment or in any amendment thereof. The dissenters shall be entitled to discovery in the same manner as parties in other civil suits.

(5) All dissenters who are made parties shall be entitled to judgment for the amount by which the fair value of their shares is found to exceed the amount previously remitted, with interest.

(6) If the corporation fails to file a petition as provided in paragraph (1) of this subsection, each dissenter who made a demand and who has not already settled his claim against the corporation shall be paid by the corporation the amount demanded by him, with interest, and may sue therefor in an appropriate court.

(i) (1) The costs and expenses of any proceeding under subsection (h), including the reasonable compensation and expenses of appraisers appointed by the court, shall be determined by the court and assessed against the corporation, except that any part of the costs and expenses may be apportioned and assessed as the court may deem equitable against all or some of the dissenters who are parties and whose action in demanding supplemental payment the court finds to be arbitrary, vexatious, or not in good faith.

(2) Fees and expenses of counsel and of experts for the respective parties may be assessed as the court

may deem equitable against the corporation and in favor of any or all dissenters if the corporation failed to comply substantially with the requirements of this section, and may be assessed against either the corporation or a dissenter, in favor of any other party, if the court finds that the party against whom the fees and expenses are assessed acted arbitrarily, vexatiously, or not in good faith in respect to the rights provided by this Section and Section 80.

(3) If the court finds that the services of counsel for any dissenter were of substantial benefit to other dissenters similarly situated, and should not be assessed against the corporation, it may award to these counsel reasonable fees to be paid out of the amounts awarded to the dissenters who were benefitted.

(j) (1) Notwithstanding the foregoing provisions of this section, the corporation may elect to withhold the remittance required by subsection (f) from any dissenter with respect to shares of which the dissenter (or the person on whose behalf the dissenter acts) was not the beneficial owner on the date of the first announcement to news media or to shareholders of the terms of the proposed corporate action. With respect to such shares, the corporation shall, upon effectuating the corporate action, state to each dissenter its estimate of the fair value of the shares, state the rate of interest to be used (explaining the basis thereof), and offer to pay the resulting amounts on receiving the dissenter's agreement to accept them in full satisfaction.

(2) If the dissenter believes that the amount offered is less than the fair value of the shares and interest determined according to this section, he may within 30 days after the date of mailing of the corporation's offer, mail the corporation his own estimate of fair value and interest, and demand their payment. If the dissenter fails to do so, he shall be entitled to no more than the corporation's offer.

(3) If the dissenter makes a demand as provided in paragraph (2), the provisions of subsections (h) and (i) shall apply to further proceedings on the dissenter's demand.

§ 82. Voluntary Dissolution by Incorporators

A corporation which has not commenced business and which has not issued any shares, may be voluntarily dissolved by its incorporators at any time in the following manner:

(a) Articles of dissolution shall be executed in duplicate by a majority of the incorporators, and verified by them, and shall set forth:

(1) The name of the corporation.

(2) The date of issuance of its certificate of incorporation.

(3) That none of its shares has been issued.

(4) That the corporation has not commenced business.

(5) That the amount, if any, actually paid in on subscriptions for its shares, less any part thereof disbursed for necessary expenses, has been returned to those entitled thereto.

(6) That no debts of the corporation remain unpaid.

(7) That a majority of the incorporators elect that the corporation be dissolved.

(b) Duplicate originals of the articles of dissolution shall be delivered to the Secretary of State. If the Secretary of State finds that the articles of dissolution conform to law, he shall, when all fees and franchise taxes have been paid as in this Act prescribed:

(1) Endorse on each of such duplicate originals the word "Filed," and the month, day and year of the filing thereof.

(2) File one of such duplicate originals in his office.

(3) Issue a certificate of dissolution to which he shall affix the other duplicate original.

The certificate of dissolution, together with the duplicate original of the articles of dissolution affixed thereto by the Secretary of State, shall be returned to the incorporators or their representative. Upon the issuance of such certificate of dissolution by the Secretary of State, the existence of the corporation shall cease.

§ 83. Voluntary Dissolution by Consent of Shareholders

A corporation may be voluntarily dissolved by the written consent of all of its shareholders.

Upon the execution of such written consent, a statement of intent to dissolve shall be executed in duplicate by the corporation by its president or a vice president and by its secretary or an assistant secretary, and verified by one of the officers signing such statement, which statement shall set forth:

(a) The name of the corporation.

(b) The names and respective addresses of its officers.

(c) The names and respective addresses of its directors.

(d) A copy of the written consent signed by all shareholders of the corporation.

(e) A statement that such written consent has been signed by all shareholders of the corporation or signed in their names by their attorneys thereunto duly authorized.

§ 84. Voluntary Dissolution by Act of Corporation

A corporation may be dissolved by the act of the corporation, when authorized in the following manner:

(a) The board of directors shall adopt a resolution recommending that the corporation be dissolved, and directing that the question of such dissolution be submitted to a vote at a meeting of shareholders, which may be either an annual or a special meeting.

(b) Written notice shall be given to each shareholder of record entitled to vote at such meeting within the time and in the manner provided in this Act for the giving of notice of meetings of shareholders, and, whether the meeting be an annual or special meeting, shall state that the purpose, or one of the purposes, of such meeting is to consider the advisability of dissolving the corporation.

(c) At such meeting a vote of shareholders entitled to vote thereat shall be taken on a resolution to dissolve the corporation. Such resolution shall be adopted upon receiving the affirmative vote of the holders of a majority of the shares of the corporation entitled to vote thereon, unless any class of shares is entitled to vote thereon as a class, in which event the resolution shall be adopted upon receiving the affirmative vote of the holders of a majority of the shares of each class of shares entitled to vote thereon as a class and of the total shares entitled to vote thereon.

(d) Upon the adoption of such resolution, a statement of intent to dissolve shall be executed in duplicate by the corporation by its president or a vice president and by its secretary or an assistant secretary, and verified by one of the officers signing such statement, which statement shall set forth:

(1) The name of the corporation.

(2) The names and respective addresses of its officers.

(3) The names and respective addresses of its directors.

(4) A copy of the resolution adopted by the shareholders authorizing the dissolution of the corporation.

(5) The number of shares outstanding, and, if the shares of any class are entitled to vote as a class, the designation and number of outstanding shares of each such class.

(6) The number of shares voted for and against the resolution, respectively, and, if the shares of any class are entitled to vote as a class, the number of shares of each such class voted for and against the resolution, respectively.

§ 85. Filing of Statement of Intent to Dissolve

Duplicate originals of the statement of intent to dissolve, whether by consent of shareholders or by act of the corporation, shall be delivered to the Secretary of State. If the Secretary of State finds that such statement conforms to law, he shall, when all fees and franchise taxes have been paid as in this Act prescribed:

(a) Endorse on each of such duplicate originals the word "Filed," and the month, day and year of the filing thereof.

(b) File one of such duplicate originals in his office.

(c) Return the other duplicate original to the corporation or its representative.

§ 86. Effect of Statement of Intent to Dissolve

Upon the filing by the Secretary of State of a statement of intent to dissolve, whether by consent of shareholders or by act of the corporation, the corporation shall cease to carry on its business, except insofar as may be necessary for the winding up thereof, but its corporate existence shall continue until a certificate of dissolution has been issued by the Secretary of State or until a decree dissolving the corporation has been entered by a court of competent jurisdiction as in this Act provided.

§ 87. Procedure after Filing of Statement of Intent to Dissolve

After the filing by the Secretary of State of a statement of intent to dissolve:

(a) The corporation shall immediately cause notice thereof to be mailed to each known creditor of the corporation.

(b) The corporation shall proceed to collect its assets, convey and dispose of such of its properties as are not to be distributed in kind to its shareholders, pay, satisfy and discharge its liabilities and obligations and do all other acts required to liquidate its business and affairs, and, after paying or adequately providing for the payment of all its obligations, distribute the remainder of its assets, either in cash or in kind, among its shareholders according to their respective rights and interests.

(c) The corporation, at any time during the liquidation of its business and affairs, may make application to a court of competent jurisdiction within the state and judicial subdivision in which the registered office or principal place of business of the corporation is situated, to have the liquidation continued under the supervision of the court as provided in this Act.

§ 88. Revocation of Voluntary Dissolution Proceedings by Consent of Shareholders

By the written consent of all of its shareholders, a corporation may, at any time prior to the issuance of a certificate of dissolution by the Secretary of State, revoke voluntary dissolution proceedings theretofore taken, in the following manner:

Upon the execution of such written consent, a statement of revocation of voluntary dissolution proceedings shall be executed in duplicate by the corporation by its president or a vice president and by its secretary or an assistant secretary, and verified by one of the officers signing such statement, which statement shall set forth:

(a) The name of the corporation.

(b) The names and respective addresses of its officers.

(c) The names and respective addresses of its directors.

(d) A copy of the written consent signed by all shareholders of the corporation revoking such voluntary dissolution proceedings.

(e) That such written consent has been signed by all shareholders of the corporation or signed in their names by their attorneys thereunto duly authorized.

§ 89. Revocation of Voluntary Dissolution Proceedings by Act of Corporation

By the act of the corporation, a corporation may, at any time prior to the issuance of a certificate of dissolution by the Secretary of State, revoke voluntary dissolution proceedings theretofore taken, in the following manner:

(a) The board of directors shall adopt a resolution recommending that the voluntary dissolution proceed-

ings be revoked, and directing that the question of such revocation be submitted to a vote at a special meeting of shareholders.

(b) Written notice, stating that the purpose or one of the purposes of such meeting is to consider the advisability of revoking the voluntary dissolution proceedings, shall be given to each shareholder of record entitled to vote at such meeting within the time and in the manner provided in this Act for the giving of notice of special meetings of shareholders.

(c) At such meeting a vote of the shareholders entitled to vote thereat shall be taken on a resolution to revoke the voluntary dissolution proceedings, which shall require for its adoption the affirmative vote of the holders of a majority of the shares entitled to vote thereon.

(d) Upon the adoption of such resolution, a statement of revocation of voluntary dissolution proceedings shall be executed in duplicate by the corporation by its president or a vice president and by its secretary or an assistant secretary, and verified by one of the officers signing such statement, which statement shall set forth:

(1) The name of the corporation.

(2) The names and respective addresses of its officers.

(3) The names and respective addresses of its directors.

(4) A copy of the resolution adopted by the shareholders revoking the voluntary dissolution proceedings.

(5) The number of shares outstanding.

(6) The number of shares voted for and against the resolution, respectively.

§ 90. Filing of Statement of Revocation of Voluntary Dissolution Proceedings

Duplicate originals of the statement of revocation of voluntary dissolution proceedings, whether by consent of shareholders or by act of the corporation, shall be delivered to the Secretary of State. If the Secretary of State finds that such statement conforms to law, he shall, when all fees and franchise taxes have been paid as in this Act prescribed:

(a) Endorse on each of such duplicate originals the word "Filed," and the month, day and year of the filing thereof.

(b) File one of such duplicate originals in his office.

(c) Return the other duplicate original to the corporation or its representative.

§ 91. Effect of Statement of Revocation of Voluntary Dissolution Proceedings

Upon the filing by the Secretary of State of a statement of revocation of voluntary dissolution proceedings, whether by consent of shareholders or by act of the corporation, the revocation of the voluntary dissolution proceedings shall become effective and the corporation may again carry on its business.

§ 92. Articles of Dissolution

If voluntary dissolution proceedings have not been revoked, then when all debts, liabilities and obligations of the corporation have been paid and discharged, or adequate provision has been made therefor, and all of the remaining property and assets of the corporation have been distributed to its shareholders, articles of dissolution shall be executed in duplicate by the corporation by its president or a vice president and by its secretary or an assistant secretary, and verified by one of the officers signing such statement, which statement shall set forth:

(a) The name of the corporation.

(b) That the Secretary of State has theretofore filed a statement of intent to dissolve the corporation, and the date on which such statement was filed.

(c) That all debts, obligations and liabilities of the corporation have been paid and discharged or that adequate provision has been made therefor.

(d) That all the remaining property and assets of the corporation have been distributed among its shareholders in accordance with their respective rights and interests.

(e) That there are no suits pending against the corporation in any court, or that adequate provision has been made for the satisfaction of any judgment, order or decree which may be entered against it in any pending suit.

§ 93. Filing of Articles of Dissolution

Duplicate originals of such articles of dissolution shall be delivered to the Secretary of State. If the Secretary of State finds that such articles of dissolution conform to law, he shall, when all fees and franchise taxes have been paid as in this Act prescribed:

(a) Endorse on each of such duplicate originals the

word "Filed," and the month, day and year of the filing thereof.

(b) File one of such duplicate originals in his office.

(c) Issue a certificate of dissolution to which he shall affix the other duplicate original.

The certificate of dissolution, together with the duplicate original of the articles of dissolution affixed thereto by the Secretary of State, shall be returned to the representative of the dissolved corporation. Upon the issuance of such certificate of dissolution the existence of the corporation shall cease, except for the purpose of suits, other proceedings and appropriate corporate action by shareholders, directors and officers as provided in this Act.

§ 94. Involuntary Dissolution

A corporation may be dissolved involuntarily by a decree of the . . . . court in an action filed by the Attorney General when it is established that:

(a) The corporation has failed to file its annual report within the time required by this Act, or has failed to pay its franchise tax on or before the first day of August of the year in which such franchise tax becomes due and payable; or

(b) The corporation procured its articles of incorporation through fraud; or

(c) The corporation has continued to exceed or abuse the authority conferred upon it by law; or

(d) The corporation has failed for thirty days to appoint and maintain a registered agent in this State; or

(e) The corporation has failed for thirty days after change of its registered office or registered agent to file in the office of the Secretary of State a statement of such change.

§ 95. Notification to Attorney General

The Secretary of State, on or before the last day of December of each year, shall certify to the Attorney General the names of all corporations which have failed to file their annual reports or to pay franchise taxes in accordance with the provisions of this Act, together with the facts pertinent thereto. He shall also certify, from time to time, the names of all corporations which have given other cause for dissolution as provided in this Act, together with the facts pertinent thereto. Whenever the Secretary of State shall certify the name of a corporation to the Attorney General as having given any cause for dissolution, the Secretary of State shall concurrently mail to the corporation at its registered office a notice that such certification has been made. Upon the receipt of such certification, the Attorney General shall file an action in the name of the State against such corporation for its dissolution. Every such certificate from the Secretary of State to the Attorney General pertaining to the failure of a corporation to file an annual report or pay a franchise tax shall be taken and received in all courts as prima facie evidence of the facts therein stated. If, before action is filed, the corporation shall file its annual report or pay its franchise tax, together with all penalties thereon, or shall appoint or maintain a registered agent as provided in this Act, or shall file with the Secretary of State the required statement of change of registered office or registered agent, such fact shall be forthwith certified by the Secretary of State to the Attorney General and he shall not file an action against such corporation for such cause. If, after action is filed, the corporation shall file its annual report or pay its franchise tax, together with all penalties thereon, or shall appoint or maintain a registered agent as provided in this Act, or shall file with the Secretary of State the required statement of change of registered office or registered agent, and shall pay the costs of such action, the action for such cause shall abate.

§ 96. Venue and Process

Every action for the involuntary dissolution of a corporation shall be commenced by the Attorney General either in the . . . . court of the county in which the registered office of the corporation is situated, or in the . . . . court of . . . . county. Summons shall issue and be served as in other civil actions. If process is returned not found, the Attorney General shall cause publication to be made as in other civil cases in some newspaper published in the county where the registered office of the corporation is situated, containing a notice of the pendency of such action, the title of the court, the title of the action, and the date on or after which default may be entered. The Attorney General may include in one notice the names of any number of corporations against which actions are then pending in the same court. The Attorney General shall cause a copy of such notice to be mailed to the corporation at its registered office within ten days after the first publication thereof. The certificate of the Attorney General of the mailing of such notice shall be prima facie evidence thereof. Such notice shall be published at least once each week for two successive weeks,

and the first publication thereof may begin at any time after the summons has been returned. Unless a corporation shall have been served with summons, no default shall be taken against it earlier than thirty days after the first publication of such notice.

§ 97. Jurisdiction of Court to Liquidate Assets and Business of Corporation

The . . . . courts shall have full power to liquidate the assets and business of a corporation:

(a) In an action by a shareholder when it is established:

(1) That the directors are deadlocked in the management of the corporate affairs and the shareholders are unable to break the deadlock, and that irreparable injury to the corporation is being suffered or is threatened by reason thereof; or

(2) That the acts of the directors or those in control of the corporation are illegal, oppressive or fraudulent; or

(3) That the shareholders are deadlocked in voting power, and have failed, for a period which includes at least two consecutive annual meeting dates, to elect successors to directors whose terms have expired or would have expired upon the election of their successors; or

(4) That the corporate assets are being misapplied or wasted.

(b) In an action by a creditor:

(1) When the claim of the creditor has been reduced to judgment and an execution thereon returned unsatisfied and it is established that the corporation is insolvent; or

(2) When the corporation has admitted in writing that the claim of the creditor is due and owing and it is established that the corporation is insolvent.

(c) Upon application by a corporation which has filed a statement of intent to dissolve, as provided in this Act, to have its liquidation continued under the supervision of the court.

(d) When an action has been filed by the Attorney General to dissolve a corporation and it is established that liquidation of its business and affairs should precede the entry of a decree of dissolution.

Proceedings under clause (a), (b) or (c) of this section shall be brought in the county in which the registered office or the principal office of the corporation is situated.

It shall not be necessary to make shareholders parties to any such action or proceeding unless relief is sought against them personally.

§ 98. **Procedure in Liquidation of Corporation by Court**

In proceedings to liquidate the assets and business of a corporation the court shall have power to issue injunctions, to appoint a receiver or receivers pendente lite, with such powers and duties as the court, from time to time, may direct, and to take such other proceedings as may be requisite to preserve the corporate assets wherever situated, and carry on the business of the corporation until a full hearing can be had.

After a hearing had upon such notice as the court may direct to be given to all parties to the proceedings and to any other parties in interest designated by the court, the court may appoint a liquidating receiver or receivers with authority to collect the assets of the corporation, including all amounts owing to the corporation by subscribers on account of any unpaid portion of the consideration for the issuance of shares. Such liquidating receiver or receivers shall have authority, subject to the order of the court, to sell, convey and dispose of all or any part of the assets of the corporation wherever situated, either at public or private sale. The assets of the corporation or the proceeds resulting from a sale, conveyance or other disposition thereof shall be applied to the expenses of such liquidation and to the payment of the liabilities and obligations of the corporation, and any remaining assets or proceeds shall be distributed among its shareholders according to their respective rights and interests. The order appointing such liquidating receiver or receivers shall state their powers and duties. Such powers and duties may be increased or diminished at any time during the proceedings.

The court shall have power to allow from time to time as expenses of the liquidation compensation to the receiver or receivers and to attorneys in the proceeding, and to direct the payment thereof out of the assets of the corporation or the proceeds of any sale or disposition of such assets.

A receiver of a corporation appointed under the provisions of this section shall have authority to sue and defend in all courts in his own name as receiver of such corporation. The court appointing such receiver shall have exclusive jurisdiction of the corporation and its property, wherever situated.

§ 99. **Qualifications of Receivers**

A receiver shall in all cases be a natural person or a corporation authorized to act as receiver, which corporation may be a domestic corporation or a foreign corporation authorized to transact business in this State, and shall in all cases give such bond as the court may direct with such sureties as the court may require.

§ 100. **Filing of Claims in Liquidation Proceedings**

In proceedings to liquidate the assets and business of a corporation the court may require all creditors of the corporation to file with the clerk of the court or with the receiver, in such form as the court may prescribe, proofs under oath of their respective claims. If the court requires the filing of claims it shall fix a date, which shall be not less than four months from the date of the order, as the last day for the filing of claims, and shall prescribe the notice that shall be given to creditors and claimants of the date so fixed. Prior to the date so fixed, the court may extend the time for the filing of claims. Creditors and claimants failing to file proofs of claim on or before the date so fixed may be barred, by order of court, from participating in the distribution of the assets of the corporation.

§ 101. **Discontinuance of Liquidation Proceedings**

The liquidation of the assets and business of a corporation may be discontinued at any time during the liquidation proceedings when it is established that cause for liquidation no longer exists. In such event the court shall dismiss the proceedings and direct the receiver to redeliver to the corporation all its remaining property and assets.

§ 102. **Decree of Involuntary Dissolution**

In proceedings to liquidate the assets and business of a corporation, when the costs and expenses of such proceedings and all debts, obligations and liabilities of the corporation shall have been paid and discharged and all of its remaining property and assets distributed to its shareholders, or in case its property and assets are not sufficient to satisfy and discharge such costs, expenses, debts and obligations, all the property and assets have been applied so far as they will go to their payment, the court shall enter a decree dissolving the corporation, whereupon the existence of the corporation shall cease.

§ 103. Filing of Decree of Dissolution

In case the court shall enter a decree dissolving a corporation, it shall be the duty of the clerk of such court to cause a certified copy of the decree to be filed with the Secretary of State. No fee shall be charged by the Secretary of State for the filing thereof.

§ 104. Deposit with State Treasurer of Amount Due Certain Shareholders

Upon the voluntary or involuntary dissolution of a corporation, the portion of the assets distributable to a creditor or shareholder who is unknown or cannot be found, or who is under disability and there is no person legally competent to receive such distributive portion, shall be reduced to cash and deposited with the State Treasurer and shall be paid over to such creditor or shareholder or to his legal representative upon proof satisfactory to the State Treasurer of his right thereto.

§ 105. Survival of Remedy after Dissolution

The dissolution of a corporation either (1) by the issuance of a certificate of dissolution by the Secretary of State, or (2) by a decree of court when the court has not liquidated the assets and business of the corporation as provided in this Act, or (3) by expiration of its period of duration, shall not take away or impair any remedy available to or against such corporation, its directors, officers, or shareholders, for any right or claim existing, or any liability incurred, prior to such dissolution if action or other proceeding thereon is commenced within two years after the date of such dissolution. Any such action or proceeding by or against the corporation may be prosecuted or defended by the corporation in its corporate name. The shareholders, directors and officers shall have power to take such corporate or other action as shall be appropriate to protect such remedy, right or claim. If such corporation was dissolved by the expiration of its period of duration, such corporation may amend its articles of incorporation at any time during such period of two years so as to extend its period of duration.

§ 106. Admission of Foreign Corporation

No foreign corporation shall have the right to transact business in this State until it shall have procured a certificate of authority so to do from the Secretary of State. No foreign corporation shall be entitled to procure a certificate of authority under this Act to transact in this State any business which a corporation organized under this Act is not permitted to transact.

A foreign corporation shall not be denied a certificate of authority by reason of the fact that the laws of the state or country under which such corporation is organized governing its organization and internal affairs differ from the laws of this State, and nothing in this Act contained shall be construed to authorize this State to regulate the organization or the internal affairs of such corporation.

Without excluding other activities which may not constitute transacting business in this State, a foreign corporation shall not be considered to be transacting business in this State, for the purposes of this Act, by reason of carrying on in this State any one or more of the following activities:

(a) Maintaining or defending any action or suit or any administrative or arbitration proceeding, or effecting the settlement thereof or the settlement of claims or disputes.

(b) Holding meetings of its directors or shareholders or carrying on other activities concerning its internal affairs.

(c) Maintaining bank accounts.

(d) Maintaining offices or agencies for the transfer, exchange and registration of its securities, or appointing and maintaining trustees or depositaries with relation to its securities.

(e) Effecting sales through independent contractors.

(f) Soliciting or procuring orders, whether by mail or through employees or agents or otherwise, where such orders require acceptance without this State before becoming binding contracts.

(g) Creating as borrower or lender, or acquiring, indebtedness or mortgages or other security interests in real or personal property.

(h) Securing or collecting debts or enforcing any rights in property securing the same.

(i) Transacting any business in interstate commerce.

(j) Conducting an isolated transaction completed within a period of thirty days and not in the course of a number of repeated transactions of like nature.

§ 107. Powers of Foreign Corporation

A foreign corporation which shall have received a certificate of authority under this Act shall, until a certificate of revocation or of withdrawal shall have been issued as provided in this Act, enjoy the same, but no greater, rights and privileges as a domestic corporation organized for the purposes set forth in the application pursuant to which such certificate of authority is issued; and, except as in this Act otherwise provided, shall be subject to the same duties, restrictions, penalties and liabilities now or hereafter imposed upon a domestic corporation of like character.

§ 108. Corporate Name of Foreign Corporation

No certificate of authority shall be issued to a foreign corporation unless the corporate name of such corporation:

(a) Shall contain the word "corporation," "company," "incorporated," or "limited," or shall contain an abbreviation of one of such words, or such corporation shall, for use in this State, add at the end of its name one of such words or an abbreviation thereof.

(b) Shall not contain any word or phrase which indicates or implies that it is organized for any purpose other than one or more of the purposes contained in its articles of incorporation or that it is authorized or empowered to conduct the business of banking or insurance.

(c) Shall not be the same as, or deceptively similar to, the name of any domestic corporation existing under the laws of this State or any foreign corporation authorized to transact business in this State, or a name the exclusive right to which is, at the time, reserved in the manner provided in this Act, or the name of a corporation which has in effect a registration of its name as provided in this Act except that this provision shall not apply if the foreign corporation applying for a certificate of authority files with the Secretary of State any one of the following:

(1) a resolution of its board of directors adopting a fictitious name for use in transacting business in this State which fictitious name is not deceptively similar to the name of any domestic corporation or of any foreign corporation authorized to transact business in this State or to any name reserved or registered as provided in this Act, or

(2) the written consent of such other corporation or holder of a reserved or registered name to use the same or deceptively similar name and one or more words are added to make such name distinguishable from such other name, or

(3) a certified copy of a final decree of a court of competent jurisdiction establishing the prior right of such foreign corporation to the use of such name in this State.

§ 109. Change of Name by Foreign Corporation

Whenever a foreign corporation which is authorized to transact business in this State shall change its name to one under which a certificate of authority would not be granted to it on application therefor, the certificate of authority of such corporation shall be suspended and it shall not thereafter transact any business in this State until it has changed its name to a name which is available to it under the laws of this State or has otherwise complied with the provisions of this Act.

§ 110. Application for Certificate of Authority

A foreign corporation, in order to procure a certificate of authority to transact business in this State, shall make application therefor to the Secretary of State, which application shall set forth:

(a) The name of the corporation and the state or county under the laws of which it is incorporated.

(b) If the name of the corporation does not contain the word "corporation," "company," "incorporated," or "limited," or does not contain an abbreviation of one of such words, then the name of the corporation with the word or abbreviation which it elects to add thereto for use in this State.

(c) The date of incorporation and the period of duration of the corporation.

(d) The address of the principal office of the corporation in the state or country under the laws of which it is incorporated.

(e) The address of the proposed registered office of the corporation in this State, and the name of its proposed registered agent in this State at such address.

(f) The purpose or purposes of the corporation which it proposes to pursue in the transaction of business in this State.

(g) The names and respective addresses of the directors and officers of the corporation.

(h) A statement of the aggregate number of shares which the corporation has authority to issue, itemized by classes and series, if any, within a class.

(i) A statement of the aggregate number of issued shares, itemized by class and by series, if any, within each class.

(j) An estimate, expressed in dollars, of the value of all property to be owned by the corporation for the following year, wherever located, and an estimate of the value of the property of the corporation to be located within this State during such year, and an estimate, expressed in dollars of the gross amount of business which will be transacted by the corporation during such year, and an estimate of the gross amount thereof which will be transacted by the corporation at or from places of business in this State during such year.

(k) Such additional information as may be necessary or appropriate in order to enable the Secretary of State to determine whether such corporation is entitled to a certificate of authority to transact business in this State and to determine and assess the fees and franchise taxes payable as in this Act prescribed.

Such application shall be made on forms prescribed and furnished by the Secretary of State and shall be executed in duplicate by the corporation by its president or a vice president and by its secretary or an assistant secretary, and verified by one of the officers signing such application.

§ 111. Filing of Application for Certificate of Authority

Duplicate originals of the application of the corporation for a certificate of authority shall be delivered to the Secretary of State, together with a copy of its articles of incorporation and all amendments thereto, duly authenticated by the proper officer of the state or country under the laws of which it is incorporated.

If the Secretary of State finds that such application conforms to law, he shall, when all fees and franchise taxes have been paid as in this Act prescribed:

(a) Endorse on each of such documents the word "Filed," and the month, day and year of the filing thereof.

(b) File in his office one of such duplicate originals of the application and the copy of the articles of incorporation and amendments thereto.

(c) Issue a certificate of authority to transact business in this State to which he shall affix the other duplicate original application.

The certificate of authority, together with the duplicate original of the application affixed thereto by the Secretary of State, shall be returned to the corporation or its representative.

§ 112. Effect of Certificate of Authority

Upon the issuance of a certificate of authority by the Secretary of State, the corporation shall be authorized to transact business in this State for those purposes set forth in its application, subject, however, to the right of this State to suspend or to revoke such authority as provided in this Act.

§ 113. Registered Office and Registered Agent of Foreign Corporation

Each foreign corporation authorized to transact business in this State shall have and continuously maintain in this State:

(a) A registered office which may be, but need not be, the same as its place of business in this State.

(b) A registered agent, which agent may be either an individual resident in this State whose business office is identical with such registered office, or a domestic corporation, or a foreign corporation authorized to transact business in this State, having a business office identical with such registered office.

§ 114. Change of Registered Office or Registered Agent of Foreign Corporation

A foreign corporation authorized to transact business in this State may change its registered office or change its registered agent, or both, upon filing in the office of the Secretary of State a statement setting forth:

(a) The name of the corporation.

(b) The address of its then registered office.

(c) If the address of its registered office be changed, the address to which the registered office is to be changed.

(d) The name of its then registered agent.

(e) If its registered agent be changed, the name of its successor registered agent.

(f) That the address of its registered office and the address of the business office of its registered agent, as changed, will be identical.

(g) That such change was authorized by resolution duly adopted by its board of directors.

Such statement shall be executed by the corporation by its president or a vice president, and verified by him, and delivered to the Secretary of State. If the Secretary of State finds that such statement conforms to the provisions of this Act, he shall file such statement in his office, and upon such filing the change of address of the registered office, or the appointment of a new registered agent, or both, as the case may be, shall become effective.

Any registered agent of a foreign corporation may resign as such agent upon filing a written notice thereof, executed in duplicate, with the Secretary of State, who shall forthwith mail a copy thereof to the corporation at its principal office in the state or country under the laws of which it is incorporated. The appointment of such agent shall terminate upon the expiration of thirty days after receipt of such notice by the Secretary of State.

If a registered agent changes his or its business address to another place within the same . . . .*, he or it may change such address and the address of the registered office of any corporation of which he or it is registered agent by filing a statement as required above except that it need be signed only by the registered agent and need not be responsive to (e) or (g) and must recite that a copy of the statement has been mailed to the corporation.

*Supply designation of jurisdiction, such as county, etc. in accordance with local practice.

§ 115. Service of Process on Foreign Corporation

The registered agent so appointed by a foreign corporation authorized to transact business in this State shall be an agent of such corporation upon whom any process, notice or demand required or permitted by law to be served upon the corporation may be served.

Whenever a foreign corporation authorized to transact business in this State shall fail to appoint or maintain a registered agent in this State, or whenever any such registered agent cannot with reasonable diligence be found at the registered office, or whenever the certificate of authority of a foreign corporation shall be suspended or revoked, then the Secretary of State shall be an agent of such corporation upon whom any such process, notice, or demand may be served. Service on the Secretary of State of any such process, notice or demand shall be made by delivering to and leaving with him, or with any clerk having charge of the corporation department of his office, duplicate copies of such process, notice or demand. In the event any such process, notice or demand is served on the Secretary of State, he shall immediately cause one of such copies thereof to be forwarded by registered mail, addressed to the corporation at its principal office in the state or country under the laws of which it is incorporated. Any service so had on the Secretary of State shall be returnable in not less than thirty days.

The Secretary of State shall keep a record of all processes, notices and demands served upon him under this section, and shall record therein the time of such service and his action with reference thereto.

Nothing herein contained shall limit or affect the right to serve any process, notice or demand, required or permitted by law to be served upon a foreign corporation in any other manner now or hereafter permitted by law.

§ 116. Amendment to Articles of Incorporation of Foreign Corporation

Whenever the articles of incorporation of a foreign corporation authorized to transact business in this State are amended, such foreign corporation shall, within thirty days after such amendment becomes effective, file in the office of the Secretary of State a copy of such amendment duly authenticated by the proper officer of the state or country under the laws of which it is incorporated; but the filing thereof shall not of itself enlarge or alter the purpose or purposes which such corporation is authorized to pursue in the transaction of business in this State, nor authorize such corporation to transact business in this State under any other name than the name set forth in its certificate of authority.

§ 117. Merger of Foreign Corporation Authorized to Transact Business in This State

Whenever a foreign corporation authorized to transact business in this State shall be a party to a statutory merger permitted by the laws of the state or country under the laws of which it is incorporated, and such corporation shall be the surviving corporation, it shall, within thirty days after such merger becomes effective, file with the Secretary of State a copy of the articles of merger duly authenticated by the proper officer of the state or country under the laws of which such statutory merger was effected; and it shall not be necessary for such corporation to procure either a new or amended certificate of authority to transact business in this State unless the name of such corporation be changed thereby or unless the corporation desires to pursue in this State other or additional purposes than those which it is then authorized to transact in this State.

§ 118. Amended Certificate of Authority

A foreign corporation authorized to transact business in this State shall procure an amended certificate of authority in the event it changes its corporate name, or desires to pursue in this State other or additional purposes than those set forth in its prior application for a certificate of authority, by making application therefor to the Secretary of State.

The requirements in respect to the form and contents of such application, the manner of its execution, the filing of duplicate originals thereof with the Secretary of State, the issuance of an amended certificate of authority and the effect thereof, shall be the same as in the case of an original application for a certificate of authority.

§ 119. Withdrawal of Foreign Corporation

A foreign corporation authorized to transact business in this State may withdraw from this State upon procuring from the Secretary of State a certificate of withdrawal. In order to procure such certificate of withdrawal, such foreign corporation shall deliver to the Secretary of State an application for withdrawal, which shall set forth:

(a) The name of the corporation and the state or country under the laws of which it is incorporated.

(b) That the corporation is not transacting business in this State.

(c) That the corporation surrenders its authority to transact business in this State.

(d) That the corporation revokes the authority of its registered agent in this State to accept service of process and consents that service of process in any action, suit or proceeding based upon any cause of action arising in this State during the time the corporation was authorized to transact business in this State may thereafter be made on such corporation by service thereof on the Secretary of State.

(e) A post-office address to which the Secretary of State may mail a copy of any process against the corporation that may be served on him.

(f) A statement of the aggregate number of shares which the corporation has authority to issue, itemized by class and series, if any, within each class, as of the date of such application.

(g) A statement of the aggregate number of issued shares, itemized by class and series, if any, within each class, as of the date of such application.

(h) Such additional information as may be necessary or appropriate in order to enable the Secretary of State to determine and assess any unpaid fees or franchise taxes payable by such foreign corporation as in this Act prescribed.

The application for withdrawal shall be made on forms prescribed and furnished by the Secretary of State and shall be executed by the corporation by its president or a vice president and by its secretary or an assistant secretary, and verified by one of the officers signing the application, or, if the corporation is in the hands of a receiver or trustee, shall be executed on behalf of the corporation by such receiver or trustee and verified by him.

§ 120. Filing of Application for Withdrawal

Duplicate originals of such application for withdrawal shall be delivered to the Secretary of State. If the Secretary of State finds that such application conforms to the provisions of this Act, he shall, when all fees and franchise taxes have been paid as in this Act prescribed:

(a) Endorse on each of such duplicate originals the word "Filed," and the month, day and year of the filing thereof.

(b) File one of such duplicate originals in his office.

(c) Issue a certificate of withdrawal to which he shall affix the other duplicate original.

The certificate of withdrawal, together with the duplicate original of the application for withdrawal affixed thereto by the Secretary of State, shall be returned to the corporation or its representative. Upon the issuance of such certificate of withdrawal, the authority of the corporation to transact business in this State shall cease.

§ 121. Revocation of Certificate of Authority

The certificate of authority of a foreign corporation to transact business in this State may be revoked by the Secretary of State upon the conditions prescribed in this section when:

(a) The corporation has failed to file its annual report within the time required by this Act, or has failed to pay any fees, franchise taxes or penalties prescribed by this Act when they have become due and payable; or

(b) The corporation has failed to appoint and maintain a registered agent in this State as required by this Act; or

(c) The corporation has failed, after change of its registered office or registered agent, to file in the office of the Secretary of State a statement of such change as required by this Act; or

(d) The corporation has failed to file in the office of the Secretary of State any amendment to its articles of incorporation or any articles of merger within the time prescribed by this Act; or

(e) A misrepresentation has been made of any material matter in any application, report, affidavit, or other document submitted by such corporation pursuant to this Act.

No certificate of authority of a foreign corporation shall be revoked by the Secretary of State unless (1) he shall have given the corporation not less than sixty days' notice thereof by mail addressed to its registered office in this State, and (2) the corporation shall fail prior to revocation to file such annual report, or pay such fees, franchise taxes or penalties, or file the required statement of change of registered agent or registered office, or file such articles of amendment or articles of merger, or correct such misrepresentation.

§ 122. Issuance of Certificate of Revocation

Upon revoking any such certificate of authority, the Secretary of State shall:

(a) Issue a certificate of revocation in duplicate.

(b) File one of such certificates in his office.

(c) Mail to such corporation at its registered office in this State a notice of such revocation accompanied by one of such certificates.

Upon the issuance of such certificate of revocation, the authority of the corporation to transact business in this State shall cease.

§ 123. Application to Corporations Heretofore Authorized to Transact Business in this State

Foreign corporations which are duly authorized to transact business in this State at the time this Act takes effect, for a purpose or purposes for which a corporation might secure such authority under this Act, shall, subject to the limitations set forth in their respective certificates of authority, be entitled to all the rights and privileges applicable to foreign corporations procuring certificates of authority to transact business in this State under this Act, and from the time this Act takes effect such corporations shall be subject to all the limitations, restrictions, liabilities, and duties prescribed herein for foreign corporations procuring certificates of authority to transact business in this State under this Act.

§ 124. Transacting Business Without Certificate of Authority

No foreign corporation transacting business in this State without a certificate of authority shall be permitted to maintain any action, suit or proceeding in any court of this State, until such corporation shall have obtained a certificate of authority. Nor shall any action, suit or proceeding be maintained in any court of this State by any successor or assignee of such corporation on any right, claim or demand arising out of the transaction of business by such corporation in this State, until a certificate of authority shall have been obtained by such corporation or by a corporation which has acquired all or substantially all of its assets.

The failure of a foreign corporation to obtain a certificate of authority to transact business in this State shall not impair the validity of any contract or act of such corporation, and shall not prevent such corporation from defending any action, suit or proceeding in any court of this State.

A foreign corporation which transacts business in this State without a certificate of authority shall be liable to this State, for the years or parts thereof during which it transacted business in this State without a certificate of authority, in an amount equal to all fees and franchise taxes which would have been imposed by this Act upon such corporation had it duly applied for and received a certificate of authority to transact business in this State as required by this Act and thereafter filed all reports required by this Act, plus all penalties imposed by this Act for failure to pay such fees and franchise taxes. The Attorney General shall bring proceedings to recover all amounts due this State under the provisions of this Section.

§ 125. Annual Report of Domestic and Foreign Corporations

Each domestic corporation, and each foreign corporation authorized to transact business in this State, shall file, within the time prescribed by this Act, an annual report setting forth:

(a) The name of the corporation and the state or country under the laws of which it is incorporated.

(b) The address of the registered office of the corporation in this State, and the name of its registered agent in this State at such address, and, in case of a foreign corporation, the address of its principal office in the state or country under the laws of which it is incorporated.

(c) A brief statement of the character of the business in which the corporation is actually engaged in this State.

(d) The names and respective addresses of the directors and officers of the corporation.

(e) A statement of the aggregate number of shares which the corporation has authority to issue, itemized by class and series, if any, within each class.

(f) A statement of the aggregate number of issued

shares, itemized by class and series, if any, within each class.

(g) A statement, expressed in dollars, of the value of all the property owned by the corporation, wherever located, and the value of the property of the corporation located within this State, and a statement, expressed in dollars, of the gross amount of business transacted by the corporation for the twelve months ended on the thirty-first day of December preceding the date herein provided for the filing of such report and the gross amount thereof transacted by the corporation at or from places of business in this State. If, on the thirty-first day of December preceding the time herein provided for the filing of such report, the corporation had not been in existence for a period of twelve months, or in the case of a foreign corporation had not been authorized to transact business in this State for a period of twelve months, the statement with respect to business transacted shall be furnished for the period between the date of incorporation or the date of its authorization to transact business in this State, as the case may be, and such thirty-first day of December. If all the property of the corporation is located in this State and all of its business is transacted at or from places of business in this State, then the information required by this subparagraph need not be set forth in such report.

(h) Such additional information as may be necessary or appropriate in order to enable the Secretary of State to determine and assess the proper amount of franchise taxes payable by such corporation.

Such annual report shall be made on forms prescribed and furnished by the Secretary of State, and the information therein contained shall be given as of the date of the execution of the report, except as to the information required by subparagraphs (g) and (h) which shall be given as of the close of business on the thirty-first day of December next preceding the date herein provided for the filing of such report. It shall be executed by the corporation by its president, a vice president, secretary, an assistant secretary, or treasurer, and verified by the officer executing the report, or, if the corporation is in the hands of a receiver or trustee, it shall be executed on behalf of the corporation and verified by such receiver or trustee.

§ 126. Filing of Annual Report of Domestic and Foreign Corporations

Such annual report of a domestic or foreign corporation shall be delivered to the Secretary of State between the first day of January and the first day of March of each year, except that the first annual report of a domestic or foreign corporation shall be filed between the first day of January and the first day of March of the year next succeeding the calendar year in which its certificate of incorporation or its certificate of authority, as the case may be, was issued by the Secretary of State. Proof to the satisfaction of the Secretary of State that prior to the first day of March such report was deposited in the United States mail in a sealed envelope, properly addressed, with postage prepaid, shall be deemed a compliance with this requirement. If the Secretary of State finds that such report conforms to the requirements of this Act, he shall file the same. If he finds that it does not so conform, he shall promptly return the same to the corporation for any necessary corrections, in which event the penalties hereinafter prescribed for failure to file such report within the time hereinabove provided shall not apply, if such report is corrected to conform to the requirements of this Act and returned to the Secretary of State within thirty days from the date on which it was mailed to the corporation by the Secretary of State.

§ 127. Fees, Franchise Taxes and Charges to be Collected by Secretary of State

The Secretary of State shall charge and collect in accordance with the provisions of this Act:

(a) Fees for filing documents and issuing certificates.

(b) Miscellaneous charges.

(c) License fees.

(d) Franchise taxes.

§ 128. Fees for Filing Documents and Issuing Certificates

The Secretary of State shall charge and collect for:

(a) Filing articles of incorporation and issuing a certificate of incorporation, ... dollars.

(b) Filing articles of amendment and issuing a certificate of amendment, ... dollars.

(c) Filing restated articles of incorporation, ... dollars.

(d) Filing articles of merger or consolidation and issuing a certificate of merger or consolidation, ... dollars.

(e) Filing an application to reserve a corporate name, ... dollars.

(f) Filing a notice of transfer of a reserved corporate name, ... dollars.

(g) Filing a statement of change of address of registered office or change of registered agent or both, ... dollars.

(h) Filing a statement of the establishment of a series of shares, ... dollars.

(i) Filing a statement of intent to dissolve, ... dollars.

(j) Filing a statement of revocation of voluntary dissolution proceedings, ... dollars.

(k) Filing articles of dissolution, ... dollars.

(l) Filing an application of a foreign corporation for a certificate of authority to transact business in this State and issuing a certificate of authority, ... dollars.

(m) Filing an application of a foreign corporation for an amended certificate of authority to transact business in this State and issuing an amended certificate of authority, ... dollars.

(n) Filing a copy of an amendment to the articles of incorporation of a foreign corporation holding a certificate of authority to transact business in this State, ... dollars.

(o) Filing a copy of articles of merger of a foreign corporation holding a certificate of authority to transact business in this State, ... dollars.

(p) Filing an application for withdrawal of a foreign corporation and issuing a certificate of withdrawal, ... dollars.

(q) Filing any other statement or report, except an annual report, of a domestic or foreign corporation, ... dollars.

§ 129. Miscellaneous Charges

The Secretary of State shall charge and collect:

(a) For furnishing a certified copy of any document, instrument, or paper relating to a corporation, ... cents per page and .... dollars for the certificate and affixing the seal thereto.

(b) At the time of any service of process on him as resident agent of a corporation, ... dollars, which amount may be recovered as taxable costs by the party to the suit or action causing such service to be made if such party prevails in the suit or action.

§ 130. License Fees Payable by Domestic Corporations

The Secretary of State shall charge and collect from each domestic corporation license fees, based upon the number of shares which it will have authority to issue or the increase in the number of shares which it will have authority to issue, at the time of:

(a) Filing articles of incorporation;

(b) Filing articles of amendment increasing the number of authorized shares; and

(c) Filing articles of merger or consolidation increasing the number of authorized shares which the surviving or new corporation, if a domestic corporation, will have the authority to issue above the aggregate number of shares which the constituent domestic corporations and constituent foreign corporations authorized to transact business in this State had authority to issue.

The license fees shall be at the rate of .... cents per share up to and including the first 10,000 authorized shares, ... cents per share for each authorized share in excess of 10,000 shares up to and including 100,000 shares, and .... cents per share for each authorized share in excess of 100,000 shares.

The license fees payable on an increase in the number of authorized shares shall be imposed only on the increased number of shares, and the number of previously authorized shares shall be taken into account in determining the rate applicable to the increased number of authorized shares.

§ 131. License Fees Payable by Foreign Corporations

The Secretary of State shall charge and collect from each foreign corporation license fees, based upon the proportion represented in this State of the number of shares which it has authority to issue or the increase in the number of shares which it has authority to issue, at the time of:

(a) Filing an application for a certificate of authority to transact business in this State;

(b) Filing articles of amendment which increased the number of authorized shares; and

(c) Filing articles of merger or consolidation which increased the number of authorized shares which the surviving or new corporation, if a foreign corporation, has authority to issue above the aggregate number of shares which the constituent domestic corporations and constituent foreign corporations authorized to transact business in this State had authority to issue.

The license fees shall be at the rate of .... cents per share up to and including the first 10,000 authorized shares represented in this State, ... cents per share for each authorized share in excess of 10,000 shares up to and including 100,000 shares represented in this State, and .... cents per share for each authorized share in excess of 100,000 shares represented in this State.

The license fees payable on an increase in the number of authorized shares shall be imposed only on the increased number of such shares represented in this State, and the number of previously authorized shares represented in this State shall be taken into account in determining the rate applicable to the increased number of authorized shares.

The number of authorized shares represented in this State shall be that proportion of its total authorized shares which the sum of the value of its property located in this State and the gross amount of business transacted by it at or from places of business in this State bears to the sum of the value of all of its property, wherever located, and the gross amount of its business, wherever transacted. Such proportion shall be determined from information contained in the application for a certificate of authority to transact business in this State until the filing of an annual report and thereafter from information contained in the latest annual report filed by the corporation.

§ 132. **Franchise Taxes Payable by Domestic Corporations**

The Secretary of State shall charge and collect from each domestic corporation an initial franchise tax at the time of filing its articles of incorporation at the rate of one-twelfth of one-half of the license fee payable by such corporation under the provisions of this Act at the time of filing its articles of incorporation, for each calendar month, or fraction thereof, between the date of the issuance of the certificate of incorporation by the Secretary of State and the first day of July of the next succeeding calendar year.

The Secretary of State shall charge and collect from each domestic corporation an annual franchise tax, payable in advance for the period from July 1 in each year to July 1 in the succeeding year, beginning July 1 in the calendar year in which such corporation is required to file its first annual report under this Act, (Alternative 1: at the rate of .... of .... per cent of the amount represented in this State of the stated capital of the corporation, as determined in accordance with accounting practices and principles that are reasonable in the circumstances, as disclosed by the latest report filed by the corporation with the Secretary of State) (Alternative 2: at the rate of .... cents per share up to and including the first 10,000 issued and outstanding shares, and .... cents per share for each

issued and outstanding share in excess of 10,000 shares up to and including 100,000 shares, and .... cents per share for each issued and outstanding share in excess of 100,000 shares).

[If Alternative 2 is enacted, the following paragraph should be deleted.]

The amount represented in this State of the stated capital of the corporation shall be that proportion of its stated capital which the sum of the value of its property located in this State and the gross amount of business transacted by it at or from places of business in this State bears to the sum of the value of all of its property, wherever located, and the gross amount of its business, wherever transacted.

§ 133. **Franchise Taxes Payable by Foreign Corporations**

The Secretary of State shall charge and collect from each foreign corporation authorized to transact business in this State an initial franchise tax at the time of filing its application for a certificate of authority at the rate of one-twelfth of one-half of the license fee payable by such corporation under the provisions of this Act at the time of filing such application, for each month, or fraction thereof, between the date of the issuance of the certificate of authority by the Secretary of State and the first day of July of the next succeeding calendar year.

The Secretary of State shall charge and collect from each foreign corporation authorized to transact business in this State an annual franchise tax, payable in advance for the period from July 1 in each year to July 1 in the succeeding year, beginning July 1 in the calendar year in which such corporation is required to file its first annual report under this Act, (Alternative 1: at the rate of .... per cent of the amount represented in this State of the stated capital of the corporation, as determined in accordance with accounting practices and principles that are reasonable in the circumstances, as disclosed by the latest annual report filed by the corporation with the Secretary of State) (Alternative 2: at a rate of .... cents per share up to and including the first 10,000 issued and outstanding shares represented in this State, and .... cents per share for each issued and outstanding share in excess of 10,000 shares up to and including 100,000 shares represented in this State, and .... cents per share for each issued and outstanding share in excess of 100,000 shares represented in this State).

[If Alternative 2 is enacted, the following paragraph should be deleted.]

The amount represented in this State of the stated capital of the corporation shall be that proportion of its stated capital which the sum of the value of its property located in this State and the gross amount of business transacted by it at or from places of business in this State bears to the sum of the value of all of its property, wherever located, and the gross amount of its business, wherever transacted.

§ 134. Assessment and Collection of Annual Franchise Taxes

It shall be the duty of the Secretary of State to collect all annual franchise taxes and penalties imposed by, or assessed in accordance with, this Act.

Between the first day of March and the first day of June of each year, the Secretary of State shall assess against each corporation, domestic and foreign, required to file an annual report in such year, the franchise tax payable by it for the period from July 1 of such year to July 1 of the succeeding year in accordance with the provisions of this Act, and, if it has failed to file its annual report within the time prescribed by this Act, the penalty imposed by this Act upon such corporation for its failure so to do; and shall mail a written notice to each corporation against which such tax is assessed, addressed to such corporation at its registered office in this State, notifying the corporation (1) of the amount of franchise tax assessed against it for the ensuing year and the amount of penalty, if any, assessed against it for failure to file its annual report; (2) that objections, if any, to such assessment will be heard by the officer making the assessment on or before the fifteenth day of June of such year, upon receipt of a request from the corporation; and (3) that such tax and penalty shall be payable to the Secretary of State on the first day of July next succeeding the date of the notice. Failure to receive such notice shall not relieve the corporation of its obligation to pay the tax and any penalty assessed, or invalidate the assessment thereof.

The Secretary of State shall have power to hear and determine objections to any assessment of franchise tax at any time after such assessment and, after hearing, to change or modify any such assessment. In the event of any adjustment of franchise tax with respect to which a penalty has been assessed for failure to file an annual report, the penalty shall be adjusted in accordance with the provisions of this Act imposing such penalty.

All annual franchise taxes and all penalties for failure to file annual reports shall be due and payable on the first day of July of each year. If the annual franchise tax assessed against any corporation subject to the provisions of this Act, together with all penalties assessed thereon, shall not be paid to the Secretary of State on or before the thirty-first day of July of the year in which such tax is due and payable, the Secretary of State shall certify such fact to the Attorney General on or before the fifteenth day of November of such year, whereupon the Attorney General may institute an action against such corporation in the name of this State, in any court of competent jurisdiction, for the recovery of the amount of such franchise tax and penalties, together with the cost of suit, and prosecute the same to final judgment.

For the purpose of enforcing collection, all annual franchise taxes assessed in accordance with this Act, and all penalties assessed thereon and all interest and costs that shall accrue in connection with the collection thereof, shall be a prior and first lien on the real and personal property of the corporation from and including the first day of July of the year when such franchise taxes become due and payable until such taxes, penalties, interest, and costs shall have been paid.

§ 135. Penalties Imposed Upon Corporations

Each corporation, domestic or foreign, that fails or refuses to file its annual report for any year within the time prescribed by this Act shall be subject to a penalty of ten per cent of the amount of the franchise tax assessed against it for the period beginning July 1 of the year in which such report should have been filed. Such penalty shall be assessed by the Secretary of State at the time of the assessment of the franchise tax. If the amount of the franchise tax as originally assessed against such corporation be thereafter adjusted in accordance with the provisions of this Act, the amount of the penalty shall be likewise adjusted to ten per cent of the amount of the adjusted franchise tax. The amount of the franchise tax and the amount of the penalty shall be separately stated in any notice to the corporation with respect thereto.

If the franchise tax assessed in accordance with the provisions of this Act shall not be paid on or before the thirty-first day of July, it shall be deemed to be delinquent, and there shall be added a penalty of one per cent for each month or part of month that the same is delinquent, commencing with the month of August.

Each corporation, domestic or foreign, that fails or refuses to answer truthfully and fully within the time prescribed by this Act interrogatories propounded by the Secretary of State in accordance with the provisions of this Act, shall be deemed to be guilty of a misdemeanor and upon conviction thereof may be fined in any amount not exceeding five hundred dollars.

§ 136. Penalties Imposed Upon Officers and Directors

Each officer and director of a corporation, domestic or foreign, who fails or refuses within the time prescribed by this Act to answer truthfully and fully interrogatories propounded to him by the Secretary of State in accordance with the provisions of this Act, or who signs any articles, statement, report, application or other document filed with the Secretary of State which is known to such officer or director to be false in any material respect, shall be deemed to be guilty of a misdemeanor, and upon conviction thereof may be fined in any amount not exceeding .... dollars.

§ 137. Interrogatories by Secretary of State

The Secretary of State may propound to any corporation, domestic or foreign, subject to the provisions of this Act, and to any officer or director thereof, such interrogatories as may be reasonably necessary and proper to enable him to ascertain whether such corporation has complied with all the provisions of this Act applicable to such corporation. Such interrogatories shall be answered within thirty days after the mailing thereof, or within such additional time as shall be fixed by the Secretary of State, and the answers thereto shall be full and complete and shall be made in writing and under oath. If such interrogatories be directed to an individual they shall be answered by him, and if directed to a corporation they shall be answered by the president, vice president, secretary or assistant secretary thereof. The Secretary of State need not file any document to which such interrogatories relate until such interrogatories be answered as herein provided, and not then if the answers thereto disclose that such document is not in conformity with the provisions of this Act. The Secretary of State shall certify to the Attorney General, for such action as the Attorney General may deem appropriate, all interrogatories and answers thereto which disclose a violation of any of the provisions of this Act.

§ 138. Information Disclosed by Interrogatories

Interrogatories propounded by the Secretary of State and the answers thereto shall not be open to public inspection nor shall the Secretary of State disclose any facts or information obtained therefrom except insofar as his official duty may require the same to be made public or in the event such interrogatories or the answers thereto are required for evidence in any criminal proceedings or in any other action by this State.

§ 139. Powers of Secretary of State

The Secretary of State shall have the power and authority reasonably necessary to enable him to administer this Act efficiently and to perform the duties therein imposed upon him.

§ 140. Appeal from Secretary of State

If the Secretary of State shall fail to approve any articles of incorporation, amendment, merger, consolidation or dissolution, or any other document required by this Act to be approved by the Secretary of State before the same shall be filed in his office, he shall, withi ten days after the delivery thereof to him, give wri' ɛn notice of his disapproval to the person or corporation, domestic or foreign, delivering the same, specifying the reasons therefor. From such disapproval such person or corporation may appeal to the .... court of the county in which the registered office of such corporation is, or is proposed to be, situated by filing with the clerk of such court a petition setting forth a copy of the articles or other document sought to be filed and a copy of the written disapproval thereof by the Secretary of State; whereupon the matter shall be tried de novo by the court, and the court shall either sustain the action of the Secretary of State or direct him to take such action as the court may deem proper.

If the Secretary of State shall revoke the certificate of authority to transact business in this State of any foreign corporation, pursuant to the provisions of this Act, such foreign corporation may likewise appeal to the .... court of the county where the registered office of such corporation in this State is situated, by filing with the clerk of such court a petition setting forth a copy of its certificate of authority to transact business in this State and a copy of the notice of revocation given by the Secretary of State; whereupon the matter shall be tried de novo by the court, and the court shall either sustain the action of the Secretary of State or direct him to take such action as the court may deem proper.

Appeals from all final orders and judgments entered by the .... court under this section in review of any ruling or decision of the Secretary of State may be taken as in other civil actions.

§ 141. Certificates and Certified Copies to be Received in Evidence

All certificates issued by the Secretary of State in accordance with the provisions of this Act, and all copies of documents filed in his office in accordance with the provisions of this Act when certified by him, shall be taken and received in all courts, public offices, and official bodies as prima facie evidence of the facts therein stated. A certificate by the Secretary of State under the great seal of this State, as to the existence or non-existence of the facts relating to corporations shall be taken and received in all courts, public offices, and official bodies as prima facie evidence of the existence or non-existence of the facts therein stated.

§ 142. Forms to be Furnished by Secretary of State

All reports required by this Act to be filed in the office of the Secretary of State shall be made on forms which shall be prescribed and furnished by the Secretary of State. Forms for all other documents to be filed in the office of the Secretary of State shall be furnished by the Secretary of State on request therefor, but the use thereof, unless otherwise specifically prescribed in this Act, shall not be mandatory.

§ 143. Greater Voting Requirements

Whenever, with respect to any action to be taken by the shareholders of a corporation, the articles of incorporation require the vote or concurrence of the holders of a greater proportion of the shares, or of any class or series thereof, than required by this Act with respect to such action, the provisions of the articles of incorporation shall control.

§ 144. Waiver of Notice

Whenever any notice is required to be given to any shareholder or director of a corporation under the provisions of this Act or under the provisions of the articles of incorporation or by-laws of the corporation, a waiver thereof in writing signed by the person or persons entitled to such notice, whether before or after the time stated therein, shall be equivalent to the giving of such notice.

§ 145. Action by Shareholders Without a Meeting

Any action required by this Act to be taken at a meeting of the shareholders of a corporation, or any action which may be taken at a meeting of the shareholders, may be taken without a meeting if a consent in writing, setting forth the action so taken, shall be signed by all of the shareholders entitled to vote with respect to the subject matter thereof.

Such consent shall have the same effect as a unanimous vote of shareholders, and may be stated as such

in any articles or document filed with the Secretary of State under this Act.

§ 146. Unauthorized Assumption of Corporate Powers

All persons who assume to act as a corporation without authority so to do shall be jointly and severally liable for all debts and liabilities incurred or arising as a result thereof.

§ 147. Application to Existing Corporations

The provisions of this Act shall apply to all existing corporations organized under any general act of this State providing for the organization of corporations for a purpose or purposes for which a corporation might be organized under this Act, where the power has been reserved to amend, repeal or modify the act under which such corporation was organized and where such act is repealed by this Act.

§ 148. Application to Foreign and Interstate Commerce

The provisions of this Act shall apply to commerce with foreign nations and among the several states only insofar as the same may be permitted under the provisions of the Constitution of the United States.

§ 149. Reservation of Power

The ....* shall at all times have power to prescribe such regulations, provisions and limitations as it may deem advisable, which regulations, provisions and limitations shall be binding upon any and all corporations subject to the provisions of this Act, and the ....* shall have power to amend, repeal or modify this Act at pleasure.

*Insert name of legislative body.

§ 150. Effect of Repeal of Prior Acts

The repeal of a prior act by this Act shall not affect any right accrued or established, or any liability or penalty incurred, under the provisions of such act, prior to the repeal thereof.

§ 151. Effect of Invalidity of Part of this Act

If a court of competent jurisdiction shall adjudge to be invalid or unconstitutional any clause, sentence, paragraph, section or part of this Act, such judgment or decree shall not affect, impair, invalidate or nullify the remainder of this Act, but the effect thereof shall be confined to the clause, sentence, paragraph, section or part of this Act so adjudged to be invalid or unconstitutional.

§ 152. Exclusivity of Certain Provisions [Optional]

In circumstances to which section 45 and related sections of this Act are applicable, such provisions supersede the applicability of any other statutes of this state with respect to the legality of distributions.

§ 153. Repeal of Prior Acts
(Insert appropriate provisions) ....

In view of the increasing importance of close corporations, both for the small family business and for the larger undertakings conducted by some small number of other corporations, this liberalizing trend has now been followed by the 1969 Amendments to the Model Act. The first sentence of section 35, providing that the business of the corporation shall be managed by a board of directors, was supplemented by a new clause "except as may be otherwise provided in the articles of incorporation." This permits the shareholders to take over and exercise the functions of the directors by appropriate provision to that effect in the articles, or to allocate functions between the directors and shareholders in such manner as may be desired. Taken with other provisions of the Model Act, which are here enumerated for convenience, this rounds out the adaptability of the Model Act for all the needs of a close corporation:

(1) By section 4(*l*) the by-laws may make any provision for the regulation of the affairs of the corporation that is not inconsistent with the articles or the laws of the incorporating state.

(2) By section 15 shares may be divided into several classes and the articles may limit or deny the voting rights of or provide special voting rights for the shares of any class to the extent not inconsistent with the Model Act. The narrow limits of this exception are revealed by section 33 which provides that each outstanding share, regardless of class, shall be entitled to one vote on each matter submitted to a vote at a meeting of the shareholders "except as may be otherwise provided in the articles of incorporation," thus expressly authorizing more than one vote per share or less than one vote per share, either generally or in respect to particular matters.

(3) By section 16 item (F) the shares of any preferred or special class may be issued in series and there may be variations between different series in numerous

respects, including specifically the matter of voting rights, if any.

(4) By section 32 the articles may reduce a quorum of shareholders to not less than one-third of the shares entitled to vote, or leave the quorum at the standard of a majority or, as confirmed by section 143, increase the number to any desired point.

(5) By section 34 agreements among shareholders regarding the voting of their shares are made valid and enforceable in accordance with their terms without limitation in time. These could relate to the election or compensation of directors or officers or the creation of various types of securities for new financing or the conduct of business of various kinds or dividend policy or mergers and consolidations or other transactions without limit.

(6) The flexibility permitted by the revision of section 35 in the distribution or reallocation of authority among directors and stockholders has already been mentioned.

(7) Under section 36 the number of directors may be fixed by the by-laws at one or such greater number as may best serve the interests of the shareholders and that number may be increased or decreased from time to time by amendment to, or in the manner provided in, the articles or the by-laws, subject to any limiting provision adopted pursuant to law, such as an agreed requirement for a unanimous vote by directors for any such change or a requirement that amendments to the by-laws be made by shareholder vote. Similarly, under section 53, the incorporation may be effected by a single incorporator or by more as may be desired.

(8) By section 37 directors may be classified. While this relates to directors classified in such manner that the term of office of a specified proportion terminates in each year, the Model Act does not forbid the election of separate directors by separate classes of stock.

(9) Section 40 permits the articles or the by-laws to require more than a majority of the directors to constitute a quorum for the transaction of business and also permits the articles or by-laws to require the act of a greater number than a majority of those present at a meeting where a quorum is present before any specified business may be transacted. Or a unanimous vote of all directors may be required. This may be utilized to confer a right of veto on any designated class in order to protect its special interests.

(10) By section 50 the authority and duties of the respective officers and agents of the corporation may be

tailored and prescribed in the by-laws, or consistently with the by-laws, in such manner as the needs of the shareholders may indicate.

(11) By section 54 the articles may include any desired provision for the regulation of the internal affairs of the corporation, including, in particular, "any provision restricting the transfer of shares." This expressly validates agreements for prior offering of shares to the corporation or other shareholders. All such restrictions must, of course, be clearly shown on the stock certificate as required by the Uniform Commercial Code. A similarly broad provision for the contents of the by-laws is contained in section 27.

(12) By sections 60, 73 and 79, respectively, a class vote may be required for an amendment to the articles, for any merger or consolidation or for a sale of assets other than in the regular course of business.

(13) Section 143 permits the articles to require, for any particular action by the shareholders, the vote or concurrence of the holders of a greater proportion of the shares, or of any class or series thereof, than the Model Act itself requires.

(14) Section 44 permits action by directors without a meeting and section 145 permits the same for shareholders, while section 144 contains a broad provision on waiver of notice. Thus the formality of meetings may, where desired, be eliminated in whole or in part, except for the annual meeting required by section 28.

Under these provisions protection may be afforded for a great diversity of interests. By way of illustration, the shares may be divided into different classes with different voting rights and each class may be permitted to elect a different director. Or some classes may be permitted to vote on certain transactions, but not all. Even more drastically, some classes may be denied all voting rights whatever. Thus a family could provide for equal participation in the profits of the venture, but restrict the power of management to selected members. The advantages of having a known group of business associates may be safeguarded by restrictions on the transfer of shares. Most commonly this takes the form of a requirement for *pro rata* offering

to the other shareholders before selling to an outsider. Or the other shareholders may be given an option, in the event of death or a proposed transfer, to buy the stock *pro rata*. The same option may be given to the corporation. The purchase price may be fixed by any agreed formula, such as adjusted book value or some multiple of recent earnings. Or stockholder agreements may be used to assure that, at least for a limited number of years, all shares will be voted for certain directors and officers, or in a certain way on other corporate matters. Cumulative voting may be provided for, by which each shareholder has a number of votes equal to the number of his shares multiplied by the number of directors to be elected, with the privilege of casting all of his votes for a single candidate, or dividing them as he may wish. This helps minorities obtain representation on the board of directors. Thus the holder of one-fourth of the shares voting, plus one share, is sure of electing one of three directors. The preemptive right is another important protection in the case of close corporations, since it assures each stockholder a right to maintain his proportionate interest. Still more definite protection is afforded by provisions in the articles that prohibit particular transactions except with the assent of a specified percentage of all outstanding shares or of each class of shares. Much the same protection can sometimes be obtained by requiring a specially large quorum for the election of directors, or a specially large vote, or even unanimous vote, by directors for the authorization of particular transactions. Quite the opposite situation exists if one of the participants is to be an inactive investor, for whom non-voting preferred stock, with its prior right to a return from earnings, may be sufficient. But even here he may require a veto power over major transactions, such as the issuance of debt, the issuance of additional preferred shares or mergers or consolidations. Or the preferred shareholders may be given as a class the right to elect one or more of the directors, particularly in the event that dividends should be in arrears.

These possibilities are listed merely as illustrations and not in any sense as exhausting the variations permissible under the Model Act.

DICTIONARY OF LEGAL TERMS

(Abridged and Adapted from Black's Law Dictionary)

A

ab initio Latin. From the beginning. E. g., void ab initio. An agreement is said to be "void ab initio" if it has at no time had any legal validity.

abrogate To annul; to repeal. A statute may abrogate a rule of the common law.

abstract of title A condensed history of the title to land, consisting of a synopsis or summary of the material or operative portion of all the conveyances, of whatever kind or nature, which in any manner affect said land, or any estate or interest therein, together with a statement of all liens, charges, or liabilities to which the same may be subject, and of which it is in any way material for purchasers to be apprised.

acceptance *In contracts and sales* The act of a person to whom a thing is offered or tendered by another, whereby he receives the thing with the intention of retaining it, such intention being evidenced by a sufficient act.

In negotiable instruments Acceptance of a bill of exchange. The act by which the person on whom a bill of exchange is drawn (called the "drawee") assents to the request of the drawer to pay it, or, in other words, engages, or makes himself liable to pay it when due. 2 Bl.Comm. 469. Under the negotiable Instruments Law, "the acceptance must be in writing and signed by the drawee."

accession An addition to one's property by increase of the original property or by production from such property. Instances are: The growth of a tree on A.'s land, although the tree overhangs the land of B.; the birth of a calf to the cow of A.; the innocent conversion of B.'s material by A. into a thing of different kind, so that its former identity no longer exists, as where A. innocently converts the wheat of B. into bread.

accident An unusual event, not expected by the person affected by it.

In equity "An occurrence in relation to a contract which was not anticipated by the parties when the same was entered into, and which gives an undue advantage to one of them over the other in a court of law. Jeremy, Eq. 358. This definition is objected to, because, as accidents may arise in relation to other things besides contracts, it is inaccurate in confining accidents to contracts; besides, it does not exclude cases of unanticipated occurrence resulting from the negligence or misconduct of the party seeking relief. In general, courts of equity will relieve a party who cannot obtain justice at law in consequence of an accident which will justify the interposition of a court of equity. The jurisdiction which equity exerts in case of accident is mainly of two sorts: Over bonds with penalties to prevent a forfeiture where the failure is the result of accident, as sickness, or where the bond has been lost, but, if the penalty be liquidated damages, there can be no relief; and, second, where a negotiable or other instrument has been lost, in which case no action lay at law, but where equity will allow the one entitled to recover upon giving proper indemnity. In some states it has been held that a court of law can render judgment for the amount, but requires the defendant to give a bond of indemnity. Relief against a penal bond can now be obtained in almost all common-law courts." Bouvier, Law Dict.

accommodation paper An accommodation bill or note is one to which the accommodating party, be he acceptor, drawer, or indorser, has put his name, without consideration, for the purpose of benefiting or accommodating some other party who desires to raise money on it and is to provide for the bill or note when due.

accord and satisfaction   An agreement between two persons, one of whom has a right of action against the other, that the latter should do or give, and the former accept, something in satisfaction of the right of action different from, and usually less than, what might be legally enforced. When the agreement is executed, and satisfaction has been made, it is called "accord and satisfaction." Accord and satisfaction is the substitution of another agreement between the parties in satisfaction of the former one, and execution of the latter agreement. Such is the definition of this sort of defense usually given. But a broader application of the doctrine has been made in later times, where one promise or agreement is set up in satisfaction of a prior one, unless it has been expressly accepted as such; as, where a new promissory note has been given in lieu of a former one, to have the effect of a satisfaction of the former, it must have been accepted on an express agreement to that effect.

account   A detailed statement of the mutual demands in the nature of debt and credit between parties, arising out of contracts or some fiduciary relation.

Account closed   An account to which no further additions can be made on either side, but which remains still open for adjustment and set-off, which distinguishes it from account stated.

Account current   An open or running or unsettled account between two parties.

Account rendered   An account made out by the creditor, and presented to the debtor for his examination and acceptance. When accepted, it becomes an account stated.

Account stated   The settlement of an account between the parties, with a balance struck in favor of one of them; an account rendered by the creditor, and by the debtor assented to as correct, either expressly or by implication of law from the failure to object.

acknowledgment   In conveyancing. The act by which a party who has executed an instrument of conveyance as grantor goes before a competent officer, or court, and declares or acknowledges the same as his genuine and voluntary act and deed.

The certificate of the officer on such instrument that it has been so acknowledged.

The term is also used of the act of a person who avows or admits the truth of certain facts which, if established, will entail a civil liability upon him. Thus, the debtor's acknowledgment of the creditor's demand or right of action will revive the enforceability of a debt barred by the statute of limitations.

action   A lawsuit. A right of action; i. e., a right to bring suit.

act of God   Any misadventure or casualty is said to be caused by the "act of God," when it happens by the direct, immediate, and exclusive operation of the forces of nature, uncontrolled and uninfluenced by the power of man, and without human intervention, and is of such a character that it could not have been prevented or escaped from by any amount of foresight or prudence, or by any reasonable degree of care or diligence, or by the aid of any appliances which the situation of the party might reasonably require him to use. Any accident produced by any physical cause which is irresistible, such as lightning, tempests, perils of the seas, inundations, earthquakes; and also the sudden death or illness of persons.

adjudication   The giving or pronouncing of a judgment in a case; also the judgment given. The term is principally used in bankruptcy proceedings; the adjudication being the order which declares the debtor to be a bankrupt.

administration   The management and settlement of the estate of an intestate decedent.

administrator   In the most usual sense, is a person to whom letters of administration—that is, an authority to administer the estate of a deceased person—have been granted by the proper court. He resembles an executor, but is appointed by the court, without any nomination by the deceased. An administrator of the estate is appointed, if the deceased has made no will, or has named no executor in his will.

admiralty   That system of law governing civil and criminal maritime cases.

adverse possession   The actual, open, and notorious possession and enjoyment of real property, or of any estate lying in grant, continued for a certain length of time, held adversely and in denial and opposition to the title of another claimant, or under circumstances which indicate an assertion or color of right or title on the part of the person maintaining it, as against another person who is out of possession.

affiant The person who makes and subscribes an affidavit. The word is used, in this sense, interchangeably with "deponent." But the latter term should be reserved as the designation of one who makes a deposition.

affidavit A written or printed declaration or statement of facts, made voluntarily, and confirmed by the oath or affirmation of the party making it, taken before an officer having authority to administer such oath.

a fortiori Latin. By a stronger reason.

agency A relation, created either by express or implied contracts or by law, whereby one party (called the principal) delegates the transaction of some lawful business or the power to do certain acts for him or in relation to his rights or property, with more or less discretionary power, to another person (called the agent, attorney in fact, or proxy) who undertakes to manage the affair and render him an account thereof.

agent One who represents and acts for another under the relation of agency.

alias Latin. At other times.

In practice An alias writ is one issued in a case wherein another writ the same in substance has been issued before. For instance, there may be an alias attachment, an alias summons, etc.

The word commonly precedes the assumed names under which a party to an action, usually a defendant in a criminal action, is known as the names are stated in the pleadings. For instance, "John Jones, alias John Smith," would indicate "John Jones, at other times known as John Smith."

alibi Latin. Elsewhere. In criminal cases, the defendant fequently pleads that he was elsewhere at the time of the perpetration of the alleged crime. In such a case, he is said to plead an alibi.

Apparently through the ignorance of some of those persons reporting court news to the daily papers, the word has been often very incorrectly and inexcusably used to signify a justification or an excuse.

alienation The transfer of property from one person to another.

allegation The assertion, declaration, or statement of a party to an action, made in a pleading, setting out what he expects to prove.

allege To state, recite, assert, or charge; to make an allegation.

animo contrahendi Latin. With the intention of contracting.

animus testandi Latin. An intention to make a last will and testament.

annul To cancel; make void; destroy. To annul a judgment or judicial proceeding is to deprive it of all force and operation, either ab initio or prospectively as to future transaction.

answer *In pleading* Any pleading setting up matters of facts by way of defense. In chancery pleading, the term denotes a defense in writing, made by a defendant to the allegations contained in a bill or information filed by the plaintiff against him. In pleading, under the Codes of Civil Procedure, the answer is the formal written statement made by a defendant setting forth the ground of his defense; corresponding to what, in actions under the common-law practice, is called the "plea."

antenuptial contract A contract made prior to marriage, usually between the prospective wife and the prospective husband, under which the wife gains certain advantages or suffers certain detriments. In some instances, the prospective wife, in consideration of the settling of a certain amount of real estate or of personalty upon her, gives up her right of dower in the property of the husband.

appeal *In civil practice* The complaint to a superior court of an injustice done or error committed by an inferior one, whose judgment or decision the court above is called upon to correct or reverse. The removal of a cause from a court of inferior to one of superior jurisdiction, for the purpose of obtaining a review and retrial.

appearance A technical coming into court as a party to an action, as plaintiff or as defendant. The party may actually appear in court, or he may, by his attorney, enter his appearance by filing written pleadings in the case, or by filing a formal written entry of appearance. The term first came into use at a time when the only appearance known was the actual physical appearance of a party in court.

appellant   A party who takes an appeal from one court to another.

appellee   The party in a cause against whom an appeal is taken; that is, the party who has an interest adverse to setting aside or reversing the judgment.

appraise   *In practice*   To fix or set a price or value upon; to fix and state the true value of a thing, and, usually, in writing.

appurtenances   Things that belong to another thing regarded as the principal thing. Things appurtenant pass as incident to the principal thing. Sometimes an easement consisting of a right of way over one piece of land will pass with another piece of land as being appurtenant to it.

arbitration   *In practice*   The investigation and determination of a matter or matters of difference between contending parties, by one or more unofficial persons, chosen by the parties, and called "arbitrators," or "referees."

arrest of judgment   *In practice*   The act of staying a judgment, or refusing to render judgment in an action at law, after verdict, for some matter intrinsic appearing on the face of the record, which would render the judgment, if given, erroneous or reversible.

assumpsit   Latin. He undertook; he promised. A promise or engagement by which one person assumes or undertakes to do some act or pay something to another. It may be either oral or in writing, but is not under seal. It is express, if the promisor puts his engagement in distinct and definite language; it is implied, where the law infers a promise (thouh no formal one has passed) from the conduct of the party or the circumstances of the case.

In practice   A form of action which lies for the recovery of damages for the non-performance of a parol or simple contract, or a contract that is neither of record nor under seal.

The ordinary division of this action is into (1) common or indebitatus assumpsit, brought for the most part on an implied promise; and (2) special assumpsit, founded on an express promise.

The action of assumpsit differs from trespass and trover, which are founded on a tort, not upon a contract; from covenant and debt, which are appropriate where the ground of recovery is a sealed instrument, or special obligation to pay a fixed sum; and from replevin, which seeks the recovery of specific property, if attainable, rather than of damages.

assurance   *In conveyancing*   A deed or instrument of conveyance. The legal evidences of the transfer of property are in England called the "common assurances" of the kingdom, whereby every man's estate is assured to him, and all controversies, doubts, and difficulties are either prevented or removed.

attachment   The act or process of taking, apprehending, or seizing a person's property, by virtue of a writ, and bringing the same into the custody of the law, used either for the purpose of bringing a person before the court, of acquiring jurisdiction over the property seized, to compel an appearance, to furnish security for debt or costs, or to arrest a fund in the hands of a third person who may become liable to pay it over. Also the writ or other process for the accomplishment of the purposes above enumerated, this being the more common use of the word.

attestation   The act of witnessing an instrument in writing, at the request of the party making the same, and subscribing it as a witness. Execution and attestation are clearly distinct formalities; the former being the act of the party, and the latter of the witnesses only.

Attestation clause   The clause commonly placed at the conclusion of an instrument, in which clause the witnesses certify that the instrument has been executed before them.

attesting witness   One who signs his name to an instrument as a witness thereto at the request of the parties, for the purposes of proof and identification.

attorney   In the most general sense, this term denotes an agent or substitute, or one who is appointed and authorized to act in the place or stead of another.

It is "an ancient English word, and signifieth one that is set in the turne, stead, or place of another; and of these some be private * * * and some be publike, as attorneys at law." Co. Litt. 51b.

One who is appointed by another to do something in his absence, and who has authority to act in the place and turn of him by whom he is delegated.

When used with reference to the proceedings of courts, the term always means "attorney at law."

auction A sale of property, conducted in public or after a notice to the general public, to the highest bidder.

auctioneer One who conducts an auction.

authorities Legislative enactments, judicial opinions, legal textbooks, and articles in law periodicals are recognized as authorities on the law. The weight given each of these classes of authorities is far from being equal to that given each of the others. Legislative enactments, if valid under the Constitution, represent the final word on what the present law is. Judicial opinions, until overruled, constitute another primary authority. Textbooks and legal articles, though important, are only secondary authorities, guiding into and interpreting the primary authorities, the statutes and decisions.

award v. To grant, concede, adjudge to. Thus, a jury awards damages; the court awards an injunction.

award n. The decision or determination rendered by arbitrators of commissioners, or other private or extrajudicial deciders, upon a controversy submitted to them; also the writing or document embodying such decision.

B

baggage Such articles of necessity or convenience as are carried by passengers for their general use. It includes clothing, books of the student, tools of the workman, etc.

bail v. To procure the release of a person from legal custody, by undertaking that he shall appear at the time and place designated and submit himself to the jurisdiction and judgment of the court.

bail n. *In practice* The sureties who procure the release of a person under arrest, by becoming responsible for his appearance at the time and place designated. Those persons who become sureties for the appearance of the defendant in court.

bailee In the law of contracts, one to whom goods are bailed; the party to whom personal property is delivered under a contract of bailment.

bailment A delivery of goods or personal property, by one person to another in trust for the execution of a special object upon or in relation to such goods, beneficial either to the bailor or bailee or both, and upon a contract, express or implied, to perform the trust and carry out such object, and thereupon either to redeliver the goods to the bailor or otherwise dispose of the same in conformity with the purpose of the trust.

bailor The party who bails or delivers goods to another, in the contract of bailment.

bankrupt A person who has committed an act of bankruptcy; one who has done some act or suffered some act to be done in consequence of which, under the laws of his country, he is liable to be proceeded against by his creditors for the seizure and distribution among them of his entire property.

barter A contract by which parties exchange goods or commodities for other goods. It differs from sale, in this: That in the latter transaction goods or property are always exchanged for money.

battery Any unlawful beating, or other wrongful physical violence or constraint, inflicted on a human being without consent.

beneficiary A person having the enjoyment of property of which a trustee, executor, etc., has the legal possession. The person to whom a policy of insurance is payable.

bequeath To give personal property by will to another.

bequest A gift by will of personal property; a legacy.

bid An offer by an intending purchaser to pay a designated price for property which is about to be sold at auction.

bill A formal declaration, complaint, or statement of particular things in writing. As a legal term, this word has many meanings and applications, the more important of which are enumerated below.

bill in equity   The first written pleading in a proceeding in equity. The complaint in a suit in equity.

bill of lading   *In common law*   The written evidence of a contract for the carriage and delivery of goods sent by sea for a certain freight. The term is often applied to a similar receipt and undertaking given by a carrier of goods by land. A bill of lading is an instrument in writing, signed by a carrier or his agent, describing the freight so as to identify it, stating the name of the consignor, the terms of the contract for carriage, and agreeing or directing that the freight be delivered to the order or assigns of a specified person at a specified place.

bill of particulars   *In practice*   A written statement or specification of the particulars of the demand for which an action at law is brought, or of a defendant's set-off against such demand (including dates, sums, and items in detail), furnished by one of the parties to the other, either voluntarily or in compliance with a judge's order for that purpose.

bill of sale   *In contracts*   A written agreement under seal, by which one person assigns or transfers his right to or interest in goods and personal chattels to another. An instrument by which, in particular, the property in ships and vessels is conveyed.

bona fide   Latin. In good faith.

C

capital   *Partnership*   "The capital of a partnership is the aggregate of the sums contributed by its members to establish or continue the partnership business." Gilmore on Partnership, p. 132.

Corporations   In reference to a corporation, it is the aggregate of the sum subscribed and paid in, or secured to be paid in, by the shareholders, with the addition of all gains or profits realized in the use and investment of those sums, or, if loss have been incurred, then it is the residue after deducting such losses.

capital stock   The common stock or fund of a corporation. The sum of money raised by the subscriptions of the stockholders, and divided into shares. It is said to be the sum upon which calls may be made upon the stockholders, and dividends are to be paid.

carrier   One who carries passengers or the goods of another. See *Common Carrier; Private Carrier.*

cause of action   Matter for which an action may be brought. The ground on which an action may be sustained. The right to bring a suit.

caveat emptor   Latin. Let the buyer take care. This maxim summarizes the rule that the purchaser of an article must examine, judge, and test it for himself, being bound to discover any obvious defects or imperfections.

certificate of deposit   *In the practice of bankers*
This is a writing acknowledging that the person named has deposited in the bank a specified sum of money, and that the same is held subject to be drawn out on his own check or order, or that of some other person named in the instrument as payee.

certificate of stock   A certificate of a corporation of joint-stock company that the person named is the owner of a designated number of shares of its stock; given when the subscription is fully paid and the "scrip certificate" taken up.

certiorari   A discretionary writ of review or inquiry. It is an appellate proceeding for reexamination and review of actions of an inferior court or tribunal or as auxiliary process to enable an appellate court to obtain further information in a pending cause. It is available for review of official, judicial or quasi-judicial actions.

cestui que trust   Anglo-French. He who has a right to a beneficial interest in and out of an estate the legal title to which is vested in another. The person who possesses the equitable right to property and receives the rents, issues, and profits thereof, the legal estate of which is vested in a trustee. It has been proposed to substitute for this uncouth term the English word "beneficiary," and the latter has come to be quite frequently used.

champerty   A bargain made by a stranger with one of the parties to a suit, by which such third person undertakes to carry on the litigation at his own cost and risk, in consideration of receiving, if he wins the suit, a part of the land or other subject sought to be recovered by the action.

chancellor In American law, this is the name given in some states to the judge (or the presiding judge) of a court of chancery. In England, besides being the designation of the chief judge of the Court of Chancery, the term is used as the title of several judicial officers attached to bishops or other high dignitaries and to the universities.

chancery Equity; equitable jurisdiction; a court of equity; the system of jurisprudence administered in courts of equity.

charter An instrument emanating from the sovereign power, in the nature of a grant, authorizing the formation of a corporation. Under modern statutes, a charter is usually granted by the state secretary of state, who acts under general statutory authority conferred by the state legislature.

charter party A contract by which an entire ship, or some principal part thereof, is let to a merchant for the conveyance of goods on a determined voyage to one or more places.

chattel An article of personal property; any species of property not amounting to a freehold or fee in land.

chattel mortgage An instrument of sale of personalty conveying the title of the property to the mortgagee with terms of defeasance; and, if the terms of redemption are not complied with, then, at common law, the title becomes absolute in the mortgagee.

check A draft or order upon a bank or banking house, purporting to be drawn upon a deposit of funds, for the payment at all events of a certain sum of money to a certain person therein named, or to him or his order, or to bearer, and payable instantly on demand.

chose in action A right to personal things of which the owner has not the possession, but merely a right of action for their possession. 2 Bl.Comm. 389, 397; 1 Chit.Pr. 99.

A right to receive or recover a debt, demand, or damages on a cause of action ex contractu, or for a tort connected with contract, but which cannot be made available without recourse to an action.

chose in possession A thing in possession, as distinguished from a thing in action.

civil In contradistinction to "criminal," it indicates the private rights and remedies of men, as members of the community, in contrast to those which are public and relate to the government; thus, we speak of civil process and criminal process, civil jurisdiction and criminal jurisdiction.

civil law The "Roman law" and the "civil law" are convertible phrases, meaning the same system of jurisprudence; it is now frequently denominated the "Roman civil law."

client A person who employs or retains an attorney, or counsellor, to appear for him in courts, advise, assist, and defend him in legal proceedings, and to act for him in any legal business.

close A portion of land, as a field, inclosed, as by a hedge, fence, or other visible inclosure.

code A collection or compendium of laws. A complete system of positive law, scientifically arranged, or promulgated by legislative authority.

cognovit Latin. He knew. The written authority of a debtor and his direction for entry of judgment against him. Defendant has confessed judgment and justice of the claim against him.

collateral By the side; at the side; attached upon the side. Not lineal, but upon a parallel or diverging line. Additional or auxilliary; supplementary; co-operating.

collateral security A security given in addition to the direct security, and subordinate to it, intended to guarantee its validity or convertibility or insure its performance; so that, if the direct security fails, the creditor may fall back upon the collateral security. Collateral security, in bank phraseology, means some security additional to the personal obligation of the borrower.

color An appearance or semblance, as distinguished from a reality. Hence, color of title.

comity of nations and states The most appropriate phrase to express the true foundation and extent of the obligation of the laws of one nation within the territories of another. It is derived altogether from the voluntary consent of the latter; and it is inadmissible when it is contrary to its known policy, or prejudicial to its interest. In the silence of any positive rule affirming or denying or restraining the operation of foreign laws, courts of sume the tacit adoption of them by their ⸳nment, unless repugnant to its policy, or preju⸳ ⸳al to its interests. It is not the comity of the courts, but the comity of the nation, which is administered and ascertained in the same way and guided by the same reasoning, by which all other principles of the municipal law are ascertained and guided.

commercial law A phrase used to designate the whole body of substantive jurisprudence applicable to the rights, intercourse, and relation of persons engaged in commerce, trade, or mercantile pursuits. It is not a very scientific or accurate term. As foreign commerce is carried on by means of shipping, the term has come to be used occasionally as synonymous with "maritime law;" but, in strictness, the phrase "commercial law" is wider, and includes many transactions or legal questions which have nothing to do with shipping or its incidents.

commercial paper The term "commercial paper" means bills of exchange, promissory notes, bank checks, and other negotiable instruments for the payment of money, which, by their form and on their face, purport to be such instruments as are, by the law-merchant, recognized as falling under the designation of "commercial paper."

commission A warrant or authority or letters patent, issuing from the government, or one of its departments, or a court, empowering a person or persons named to do certain acts, or to exercise jurisdiction, or to perform the duties and exercise the authority of an office (as in the case of an officer in the army or navy).

Also, in private affairs, it signifies the authority or instructions under which one person transacts business or negotiates for another.

In a derivative sense, a body of persons to whom a commission is directed. A board or committee officially appointed and empowered to perform certain acts or exercise certain jurisdiction of a public nature or relation; as a "commission of assize."

In commercial law The recompense or reward of an agent, factor, broker, or bailee, when the same is calculated as a percentage on the amount of his transactions or on the profit to the

principal. But in this sense the word often occurs in the plural.

commission merchant A factor.

committee A term applied, in some states, to the guardian of an insane person.

commodatum Latin. A loan of goods for use without pay, the goods to be returned in kind.

common carrier *Of goods* "One who holds himself out to transport for hire the goods of such as choose to employ him." Goddard on Bailments and Carriers, § 191.

Of passengers "Such as hold themselves out for hire to carry all persons indifferently who apply for passage." Id. § 317.

common counts Certain general counts or forms inserted in a declaration in an action to recover a money debt not founded on the circumstances of the individual case, but intended to guard against a possible variance, and to enable the plaintiff to take advantage of any ground of liability which the proof may disclose within the general scope of the action. In the action of assumpsit, these counts are as follows: For goods sold and delivered, or bargained and sold; for work done; for money lent; for money paid; for money received to the use of the plaintiff; for interest, or for money due on an account stated.

common law As distinguished from the Roman law, the modern civil law, the canon law, and other systems, the common law is that body of law and juristic theory which was originated, developed, and formulated and is administered in England, and has obtained among most of the states and peoples of Anglo-Saxon stock.

As distinguished from law created by the enactment of legislatures, the common law comprises the body of those principles and rules of action, relating to the government and security of persons and property, which derive their authority solely from usages and customs of immemorial antiquity, or from the judgments and decrees of the courts recognizing, affirming, and enforcing such usages and customs, and in this sense, particularly the ancient unwritten law of England.

As distinguished from equity law, it is a body of rules and principles, written or unwritten, which are of fixed and immutable authority, and which must be applied to controversies rigorously and in their entirety, and cannot be modified to suit the peculiarities of a specific case, or colored by any judicial discretion, and which rests confessedly upon custom or statute, as distinguished from any claim to ethical superiority.

complainant　The plaintiff in code pleading or in equity.

complaint　*In civil practice*　In those states having a Code of Civil Procedure, the complaint is the first or initiatory pleading on the part of the plaintiff in a civil action. It corresponds to the declaration in the common law practice.

In criminal law　A charge, preferred before a magistrate having jurisdiction, that a person named (or a certain person whose name is unknown) has committed a certain offense, with an offer to prove the fact, to the end that a prosecution may be instituted. It is a technical term, descriptive of proceedings before a magistrate.

composition　An agreement, made upon a sufficient consideration between an insolvent or embarrassed debtor and his creditors, whereby the latter, for the sake of immediate payment, agree to accept a dividend less than the whole amount of their claims, to be distributed pro rata, in discharge and satisfaction of the whole.

compos mentis　Latin. Sound of mind.

compounding a felony　The offense committed by a person who, having been directly injured by a felony, agrees with the criminal that he will not prosecute him, on condition of the latter's making reparation, or on receipt of a reward or bribe not to prosecute.

The offense of taking a reward for forbearing to prosecute a felony; as where a party robbed takes his goods again, or other amends, upon an agreement not to prosecute.

compromise　An arrangement arrived at, either in court or out of court, for settling a dispute upon what appears to the parties to be equitable terms, having regard to the uncertainty they are in regarding the facts or the law and the facts together.

conditional sale　A sale under the terms of which the passage of title is made to depend upon the performance of a condition. Usually the condition precedent to the passage of title is payment of the purchase price by the purchaser.

confession of judgment　The act of a debtor in permitting judgment to be entered against him by his creditor, for a stipulated sum, by a written statement to that effect or by warrant of attorney, without the institution of legal proceedings of any kind.

conflict of laws　An opposition, conflict, or antagonism between different laws of the same state or sovereignty upon the same subject-matter.

A similar inconsistency between the municipal laws of different states or countries, arising in the case of persons who have acquired rights or a status, or made contracts, or incurred obligations, within the territory of two or more states.

That branch of jurisprudence, arising from the diversity of the laws of different nations in their application to rights and remedies, which reconciles the inconsistency, or decides which law or system is to govern in the particular case, or settles the degree of force to be accorded to the law of a foreign country (the acts or rights in question having arisen under it), either where it varies from the domestic law, or where the domestic law is silent or not exclusively applicable to the case in point. In this sense it is more properly called "private international law."

connivance　The secret or indirect consent or permission of one person to the commission of an unlawful or criminal act.

consanguinity　Kinship; blood relationship; the connection or relation of persons descended from the same stock or common ancestor.

conservator　A guardian of an insane person's estate.

consideration　The inducement to a contract. The cause, motive, price, or impelling influence which induces a contracting party to enter into a contract.

Any benefit conferred, or agreed to be conferred, upon the promisor, by any other person, to which the promisor is not lawfully entitled, or any prejudice suffered, or agreed to be suffered, by such person, other than such as he is at the time of consent lawfully bound to suffer, as an inducement to the promisor, is a good consideration for a promise.

consignee *In mercantile law* One to whom a consignment is made. The person to whom goods are shipped for sale.

consignment The act or process of consigning goods; the transportation of goods consigned; an article or collection of goods sent to a factor to be sold; goods or property sent, by the aid of a common carrier, from one person in one place to another person in another place.

consignor One who sends or makes a consignment. A shipper of goods.

conspiracy *In criminal law* A combination or confederacy between two or more persons formed for the purpose of committing, by their joint efforts, some lawful or criminal act, or some act which is innocent in itself, but becomes unlawful when done by the concerted action of the conspirators, or for the purpose of using criminal or unlawful means to the commission of an act not in itself unlawful.

constructive That which is established by the mind of the law in its act of construing facts, conduct, circumstances, or instruments; that which has not the character assigned to it in its own essential nature, but acquires such character in consequence of the way in which it is regarded by a rule or policy of law; hence, inferred, implied, made out by legal interpretation.

    constructive assent An assent or consent imputed to a party from a construction or interpretation of his conduct; as distinguished from one which he actually expresses.

contra Latin. Opposite, contrary. Where a decision is said to be contra, it is on the opposite side of the question.

contract "In its broadest sense, an agreement whereby one or more of the parties acquire a right, in rem or in personam, in relation to some person, thing, act, or forbearance." Clark on Contracts (3d Ed.) p. 1.

contribution The sharing of a loss or payment among several. The act of any one or several of a number of codebtors, cosureties, etc., in reimbursing one of their number, who has paid the whole debt or suffered the whole liability, each to the extent of his proportionate share. In equity, a bill is brought by a surety that has paid the whole debt, for contribution by his cosureties. Such an action is also had at law.

conversion An unauthorized assumption and exercise of the right of ownership over goods or personal chattels belonging to another, to the alteration of their condition or the exclusion of the owner's rights.

    Constructive conversion An implied or virtual conversion, which takes place where a person does such acts in reference to the goods of another as amount in law to the appropriation of the property to himself.

convict Under the criminal law, to find guilty of an offense as charged in the indictment or information.

corporation An artificial person or legal entity, created by or under the authority of the laws of a state or nation, composed in same rare instances of a single person and his successors, being the incumbents of a particular office, but ordinarily consisting of an association of numerous individuals, who subsist as a body politic under a special denomination, which is regarded in law as having a personality and existence distinct from that of its several members, and which is, by the same authority, vested with the capacity of continuous succession, irrespective of changes in its membership, either in perpetuity or for a limited term of years, and of acting as a unit or single individual in matters relating to the common purpose of the association, within the scope of the powers and authorities conferred upon such bodies by law.

corporeal property Such as affects the senses, and may be seen and handled by the body, as opposed to incorporeal property which cannot be seen or handled, and exists only in contemplation. Thus, a house is corporeal, but the annual rent payable for its occupation is incorporeal. Corporeal property is, if movable, capable of manual transfer; if immovable, possession of it may be delivered up. But incorporeal property cannot be so transferred, but some other means must be adopted for its transfer, of which the most usual is an instrument in writing.

corpus Latin. Body.

corpus delicti Latin. The body of the wrong; the essential fact of the crime. The general rule is that no one can be convicted of a crime unless the actual doing of the crime has been proved. Laymen are accustomed to regard the requirements of this general rule as being much more rigid than they really are, and some convictions are on record in which the proof of the corpus delicti, while not entirely absent, was comparatively slight.

costs A pecuniary allowance, made to the successful party (and recoverable from the losing party), for his court costs in prosecuting or defending a suit or a distinct proceeding within a suit. Costs do not include attorney's fees, excepting where the parties have stipulated for them, or where a statute provides for their being included in costs.

counsel The one or more attorneys or counselors appearing for a party in a cause. Both theoretically and actually, attorneys are officers of the court, and, by virtue of their office, are expected to give advice to the court, through their briefs and arguments, as to the law involved in the case in hand. Thus they are, in a very real sense, counsel.

count n. *In pleading* The different parts of a declaration, each of which, if it stood alone, would constitute a ground for action, are the counts of the declaration. Used also to signify the several parts of an indictment, each charging a distinct offense.

counterclaim A claim presented by a defendant in opposition to or deduction from the claim of the plaintiff. A species of set-off or recoupment introduced by the codes of civil procedure in several of the states, of a broad and liberal character.

court *In practice* An organ of the government, belonging to the judicial department, whose function is the application of the laws to controversies brought before it and the public administration of justice.

court above—court below In appellate practice, the "court above" is the one to which a cause is removed for review, whether by appeal, writ of error, or certiorari; while the "court below" is the one from which the case is being removed.

covenant An agreement, convention, or promise of two or more parties, in deed in writing, signed, sealed, and delivered, by which either of the parties pledges himself to the other that something is either done or shall be done, or stipulates for the truth of certain facts. A promise contained in such an agreement.

covert Covered, protected, sheltered. A pound covert is one that is closed or covered over, as distinguished from pound overt, which is open overhead. A feme covert is so called, as being under the wing, protection or cover of her husband.

coverture The condition or state of a married woman.

crime A crime is an act committed or omitted, in violation of a public law, either forbidding or commanding it; a breach or violation of some public right or duty due to a whole community, considered as a community in its social aggregate capacity, as distinguished from a civil injury.

D

damage Loss, injury, or deterioration, caused by the negligence, design, or accident of one person to another, in respect of the latter's person or property.

damages 1. The plural of damage.

2. Compensation claimed or awarded in a judicial proceeding for damage or for the invasion of a legal right. Bauer on Damages, p. 1.

debt A sum of money due to certain and express agreement; as by bond for a determinate sum, a bill or note, a special bargain, or a rent reserved on a lease, where the amount is fixed and specific, and does not depend upon any subsequent valuation to settle it.

deceit A fraudulent and cheating misrepresentation, artifice, or device, used by one or more persons to deceive and trick another, who is ignorant of the true facts, to the prejudice and damage of the party imposed upon.

declaration The complaint in a civil proceeding at common law. It is the first pleading filed by the plaintiff upon beginning his action.

decree *In practice* The judgment of a court of equity or admiralty, answering to the judgment of a court of common law.

deed   A sealed instrument, containing a contract or covenant, delivered by the party to be bound thereby, and accepted by the party to whom the contract or covenant runs.

de facto   Latin. In fact; in deed; actually.

defendant   The party sued in an action. The person against whom the declaration or complaint is filed, and who is so named in such declaration or complaint.

de jure   Latin. Of right; legitimate; lawful; by right and just title.

del credere   An agreement by which a factor, when he sells goods on credit, for an additional commission (called a "del credere commission"), undertakes that the purchase price will be paid the seller. The del credere factor is usually held to have undertaken a primary and absolute liability, but some cases hold that he is a mere surety.

delictum   Latin. A tort.

delivery   The physical or constructive transfer of an instrument or of goods from the hands of one person to those of another.

demise   1. A conveyance of an estate to another for life, for years, or at will; a lease.

   2. Death or decease.

demurrer   *In pleading*   The formal mode of disputing the sufficiency in law of the pleading of the other side. In effect it is an allegation that, even if the facts as stated in the pleading to which objection is taken be true, yet their legal consequences are not such as to put the demurring party to the necessity of answering them or proceeding further with the cause.

   An objection made by one party to his opponent's pleading, alleging that he ought not to answer it, for some defect in law in the pleading. It admits the facts, and refers the law arising thereon to the court.

   It imports that the objecting party will not proceed, but will wait the judgment of the court whether he is bound so to do.

   In equity   An allegation of a defendant, which, admitting the matters of fact alleged by the bill to be true, shows that as they are therein set forth they are insufficient for the plaintiff to proceed upon or to oblige the defendant to answer, or that, for some reason apparent on the face of the bill, or on account of the omission of some matter which ought to be contained therein, or for want of some circumstances which ought to be attendant thereon, the defendant ought not to be compelled to answer to the whole bill, or to some certain part thereof.

de novo   Latin. Anew.

deponent   One who makes oath to a written statement.

deposit   *In banking law*   The act of placing or lodging money in the custody of a bank or banker, for safety or convenience, to be withdrawn at the will of the depositor or under rules and regulations agreed on; also the money so deposited.

deposition   The testimony of a witness taken upon interrogatories, not in court, but intended to be used in court.

depositum   Latin. A bailment having for its purpose that the bailee keep the goods for the bailor without reward.

descent   Hereditary succession.

descriptio personae   Latin. Description of the person.

detur digniori   Latin. Let it be given to him who is more worthy.

devastavit   Latin. He laid waste. The allegation, "He laid waste," in a suit brought against executor, administrator, guardian, or trustee, gave rise to the naming of the wrong "devastavit." In such a case, the defendant is alleged to have mismanaged and wasted assets of the estate intrusted to him and thereby caused a loss.

devise   A testamentary disposition of land or realty; a gift of real property by the last will and testament of the donor.

dictum   Latin. The word is generally used as an abbreviated form of obiter dictum, "a remark by the way;" that is, an observation or remark made by a judge in pronouncing an opinion upon a cause, concerning some rule, principle, or application of law, or the solution of a question suggested by the case at bar, but not necessarily involved in the case or essential to its determination; any statement of the law enunciated by the court merely by way of illustration, argument, analogy, or suggestion.

discount In a general sense, an allowance or deduction made from a gross sum on any account whatever. In a more limited and technical sense, the taking of interest in advance. By the language of the commercial world and the settled practice of banks, a discount by a bank means a drawback or deduction made upon its advances or loans of money, upon negotiable paper or other evidences of debt payable at a future day, which are transferred to the bank.

dishonor *In mercantile law and usage* To refuse or decline to accept a bill of exchange, or to refuse or neglect to pay a bill or note at maturity.

dividend A fund to be divided. The share allotted to each of several persons entitled to share in a division of profits or property. Thus, dividend may denote a fund set apart by a corporation out of its profits, to be apportioned among the shareholders, or the proportional amount falling to each. In bankruptcy proceedings, a dividend is a proportional payment to the creditors out of the insolvent estate.

domicile That place in which a man has voluntarily fixed the habitation of himself and family, not for a mere special or temporary purpose, but with the present intention of making a permanent home, until some unexpected event shall occur to induce him to adopt some other permanent home.

dormant partner See *Partners.*

dower The provision which the law makes for a widow out of lands or tenements of her husband, for her support and the nurture of her children. Co. Litt. 30a. Dower is an estate for life of the widow in a certain portion of the estate of her husband, to which she had not relinquished her right during the marriage.

drawee A person to whom a bill of exchange is addressed, and who is requested to pay the amount of money therein named.

drawer The person drawing a bill of exchange and addressing it to the drawee.

duebill A brief written acknowledgment of a debt. It is not made payable to order, like a promissory note.

duress Unlawful constraint exercised upon a person, whereby he is forced to do some act against his will.

E

earnest The payment of a part of the price of goods sold, or the delivery of part of such goods, for the purpose of binding the contract.

easement A right in the owner of one parcel of land, by reason of such ownership, to use the land of another for a special purpose not inconsistent with a general property in the owner. 2 Washb. Real Prop. 25.

A private easement is a privilege, service, or convenience which one neighbor has of another, by prescription, grant, or necessary implication, and without profit; as a way over his land, a gateway, watercourse, and the like. Kitch. 105.

ejectment An action of which the purpose is to determine whether the title to certain land is in the plaintiff or is in the defendant.

election The act of choosing or selecting one or more from a greater number of persons, things, courses, rights, or remedies.

emancipation The act by which an infant is set at liberty from the control of parent or guardian and made his own master.

embezzlement The fraudulent appropriation to his own use or benefit of property or money intrusted to him by another, by a clerk, agent, trustee, public officer, or other person acting in a fiduciary character.

emblements The vegetable chattels called "emblements" are the corn and other growth of the earth which are produced annually, not spontaneously, but by labor and industry, and thence are called "fructus industriales."

eminent domain Eminent domain is the right of the people or government to take private property for public use.

entirety The whole, in contradistinction to a moiety or part only. When land is conveyed to husband and wife, they do not take by moieties, but both are seised of the entirety. Parceners, on the other hand, have not an entirety of interest, but each is properly entitled to the whole of a distinct moiety.

The word is also used to designate that which the law considers as one whole, and not capable of being divided into parts. Thus, a judgment, it is held, is an entirety, and, if void as to one of the two defendants, cannot be valid as to the other. So, if a contract is an entirety, no part of the consideration is due until the whole has been performed.

eo nomine   Latin. By that name.

equitable   Just, fair, and right. Existing in equity; available or sustainable only in equity, or only upon the rules and principles of equity.

equitable assignment   An assignment which, though invalid at law, will be recognized and enforced in equity; e. g., an assignment of a chose in action, or of future acquisitions of the assignor.

equity   In one of its technical meanings, equity is a body of jurisprudence, or field of jurisdiction, differing in its origin, theory, and methods from the common law.

In a still more restricted sense, it is a system of jurisprudence, or branch of remedial justice, administered by certain tribunals, distinct from the common-law courts, and empowered to decree "equity" in the complex of well-settled and well-understood rules, principles, and precedents.

Equity also signifies an equitable right; i. e., a right enforceable in a court of equity. Hence a bill of complaint which did not show that the plaintiff had a right entitling him to relief was said to be demurrable for want of equity; and certain rights now recognized in all the courts are still known as "equities," from having been originally recognized only in the court of chancery.

equity of redemption   The right of the mortgagor of an estate to redeem the same after it has been forfeited, at law, by a breach of the condition of the mortgage, upon paying the amount of debt, interest and costs.

error   A mistaken judgment or incorrect belief as to the existence or effect of matters of fact, or a false or mistaken conception or application of the law.

Such a mistaken or false conception or application of the law to the facts of a cause as will furnish ground for a review of the proceedings upon a writ of error; a mistake of law, or false or irregular application of it, such as vitiates the proceedings and warrants the reversal of the judgment.

"Error" is also used as an elliptical expression for "writ of error"; as, in saying that error lies; that a judgment may be reversed on error.

Assignment of errors   In practice. The statement of the plaintiff's case on a writ of error, setting forth the errors complained of; corresponding with the declaration in an ordinary action. A specification of the erros upon which the appellant will rely, with such fullness as to give aid to the court in the examination of the transcript.

Harmless error   In appellat practice. An error committed in the progress of the trial below, but which was not prejudicial to the rights of the party assigning it, and for which, therefore, the court will not reverse the judgment; as, where the error was neutralized or corrected by subsequent proceedings in the case, or where, notwithstanding the error, the particular issue was found in that party's favor, or where, even if the error had not been committed, he could not have been legally entitled to prevail.

Reversible error   In appellate practice. Such an error as warrants the appellat court in reversing the judgment before it.

escrow   The state or condition of a deed which is conditionally held by a third person, or the possession and retention of a deed by a third person pending a condition; as when an instrument is said to be delivered "in escrow."

estate   The interest which any one has in lands, or in any other subject of property.

In another sense, the term denotes the property (real or personal) in which one has a right or interest; the subject-matter of ownership; the corpus of property.

In a wider sense, the term "estate" denotes a man's whole financial status or condition—the aggregate of his interests and concerns, so far as regards his situation with reference to wealth or its objects, including debts and obligations, as well as possessions and rights.

estoppel A bar or impediment raised by the law, which precludes a man from alleging or from denying a certain fact or state of facts, in consequence of his previous allegation or denial or conduct or admission, or in consequence of a final adjudication of the matter in a court of law.

eviction Dispossession by process of law; the act of depriving a person of the possession of lands which he has held, in pursuance of the judgment of a court.

evidence Any species of proof, or probative matter, legally presented at the trial of an issue, by the act of the parties and through the medium of witnesses, records, documents, concrete objects, etc., for the purpose of inducing belief in the minds of the court or jury as to their contention.

exception *In practice* A formal objection to the action of the court, during the trial of a cause, in refusing a request or overruling an objection; implying that the party excepting does not acquiesce in the decision of the court, but will seek to procure its reversal, and that he means to save the benefit of his request or objection in some future proceeding.

exchange *In conveyancing* A mutual grant of equal interests (in lands or tenements), the one in consideration of the other.

In commercial law A negotiation by which one person transfers to another funds which he has in a certain place, either at a price agreed upon or which is fixed by commercial usage.

In law of personal property Exchange of goods is a commutation, transmutation, or transfer of goods for other goods, as distinguished from "sale," which is a transfer of goods for money.

ex contractu Latin. From or out of a contract. In both the civil and common law, rights and causes of action are divided into two classes—those arising ex contractu (from a contract); and those arising ex delicto (from a delict or tort).

ex delicto Latin. From a delict, tort, fault, crime, or malfeasance. In both the civil and the common

law, obligations and causes of action are divided into two great classes—those arising ex contractu (out of a contract); and those ex delicto.

ex dolo malo non oritur actio Latin. Out of fraud no action arises; fraud never gives a right of action. No court will lend its aid to a man who founds his cause of action upon an immoral or illegal act.

executed Completed; carried into full effect; already done or performed; taking effect immediately; now in existence or in possession; conveying an immediate right or possession. The opposite of executory.

execution *In contracts* (1) The signing of a contract not under seal, or the signing, sealing, and delivering of a contract under seal. (2) The doing or accomplishing of the things stipulated in a contract to be done.

In criminal law The legal putting to death of a convict, in conformity with the terms of his sentence.

In civil practice The writ in which the court authorizes and orders the sheriff or similar officer to put into effect the court's final decree or judgment.

"Final execution is one which authorizes the money due on a judgment to be made out of the property of the defendant." Bouvier's Law Dictionary.

executor A person appointed by a testator to carry out the directions and requests in his will, and to dispose of the property according to his testamentary provisions after his decease.

executory That which is yet to be executed or performed; that which remains to be carried into operation or effect; incomplete; depending upon a future performance or event. The opposite of executed.

exemplary Punitive, punitory, for punishment

exemplary damages Damages on an increased scale, awarded to the plaintiff over and above what will barely compensate him for his property loss, where the wrong done to him was aggravated by circumstances of violence, oppression, malice, fraud, or wanton and wicked conduct on the part of the defendant, and are intended to punish the defendant for his evil behavior.

exemption   A privilege allowed by law to a judgment debtor, by which he may hold property to a certain amount, or certain classes of property, free from all liability to levy and sale on execution or attachment.

ex gratia   Latin. Out of grace; as a matter of favor or indulgence; gratuitous.

ex mero motu   Latin. Of his own mere motion; of his own accord.

exoneration   Latin, exonere; disburden; take the load off of. The lifting of a burden from a person or property.

In administration of estates   The taking of the burden of a mortgage debt, in certain instances, from mortgaged real estate, and the placing of the burden upon personalty.

In suretyship   The right of exoneration is an equitable right of a surety to have the burden of the debt lifted from his shoulders and placed upon those of the principal debtor. When a surety is sued by the creditor, he has sometimes filed a bill in equity, asking that the creditor be enjoined from prosecuting the action at law against the surety before suing the principal, and offering a bond to indemnify the creditor against loss.

ex parte   Latin. On one side only; by or for one party; done for, in behalf of, or on the application of, one party only.

express   Made known distinctly and explicitly, and not left to inference or implication. Declared in terms; set forth in words. Manifested by direct and appropriate language, as distinguished from that which is inferred from conduct. The word is usually contrasted with "implied."

ex turpi contractu non oritur actio   Latin. Out of an immoral or illegal contract an action does not arise. A contract founded upon an illegal or immoral consideration cannot be enforced by action. 2 Kent, Comm. 466.

F

factor   A commercial agent, employed by a principal to sell merchandise consigned to him for that purpose, for and in behalf of the principal, but usu-

ally in his own name, being intrusted with the possession and control of the goods, and being remunerated by a commission.

fee simple   *In English law*   A freehold estate of inheritance, absolute and unqualified. It stands at the head of estates as the highest in dignity and the most ample in extent; since every other kind of estate is derivable thereout, and mergeable therein.

fee tail   An estate of inheritance, descending only to a certain class or classes of heirs; e. g., an estate is conveyed or devised "to A. and the heirs of his body," or "to A. and the heirs male of his body," or "to A., and the heirs female of his body." Such estates have been common in England, but never very common in the United States. State statutes have dealt variously with estates tail, some statutes converting them into estates in fee simple. The entire plan of the estate tail is contrary to the spirit of American progress, contemplating, as the plan does, the continuance of the tenure in one class of persons, regardless of the changes in ownership often required by the progress of the community as a whole.

felony   *In American law*   The term has no very definite or precise meaning, except in some cases where it is defined by statute. For the most part, the state laws, in describing any particular offense, declare whether or not it shall be considered a felony. Apart from this, the word seems merely to imply a crime of a graver or more atrocious nature than those designated as "misdemeanors."

feme   L. Fr. A woman.

Feme covert   A married woman.

Feme sole   A single woman.

fiction   An assumption or supposition of law that something which is or may be false is true, or that a state of facts exists which has never really taken place.

fiduciary   As an adjective it means of the nature of a trust; having the characteristics of a trust; Analogous to a trust; relating to or founded upon a trust or confidence.

final process   A writ of execution. Such process is final, as contrasted with earlier process in the action. Process prior to judgment is known as mesne process.

final settlement The rendering of a final account by an executor or an administrator, at the closing of the business of the estate, approved by the probate court, and followed by the discharge of the executor or administrator.

fire insurance A contract under the terms of which the insurer agrees to indemnify the insured against loss caused by fire during a period specified in the contract.

fixtures (Authorities differ so much in their definitions of this term that it is deemed best to include several definitions, presenting varying conceptions.)

"A fixture is a thing which, though originally a chattel, is, by reason of its annexation to land, regarded as a part of the land, partaking of its character and belonging to its owner. Whether a chattel annexed to land is, in a particular case, to be so regarded as a part thereof, is determined usually by the mode of its attachment to the land, and the character of the chattel, as indicating the presumed intention of the annexor." Tiffany on Real Property, c. 9 (IV).

"Personal chattels affixed to real estate, which may be severed and removed by the party who has affixed them, or by his personal representative, against the will of the owner of the freehold. There is much dispute among the authorities as to what is a proper definition." Bouvier's Law Dict.

f. o. b. Free on board. "If a quotation is f. o. b., the seller undertakes for the price named to deliver the goods on board car or ship at a designated place, free of charges to the buyer." Whitaker's Foreign Exchange, p. 335.

forcible detainer The offense of violently keeping possession of lands and tenements, with menaces, force, and arms, and without the authority of law.

forcible entry An offense against the public peace, or private wrong, committed by violently taking possession of lands and tenements with menaces, force, and arms, against the will of those entitled to the possession, and without the authority of law.

foreclosure A proceeding by which the rights of the mortgagee of real property are enforced. This procedure varies greatly in different states. The property is commonly put up at public auction and sold to the highest bidder. The mortgagee gets out of the proceeds the amount of his debt, with costs. The remaining portion of the proceeds, if any, goes to the debtor, the mortgagor. If the property sells at a price less than the amount of the debt and costs, judgment is given against the mortgagor for the deficiency.

Foreclosure is now generally by court proceeding in the case of real estate mortgages, though formerly all mortgages were subject to "strict foreclosure"; i. e., foreclosure without judicial process.

forfeiture *In bonds* A bond is given as the absolute and sealed promise of the obligor to pay a certain sum of money, with a defeasance clause following the obligation. This clause states that, upon the happening of a certain event, such as the conveying of certain land or the faithful performance of the duties of a certain office during a specified term, the bond is to become null and void. If the condition subsequent stated in such defeasance clause does not occur, the obligor has forfeited his bond.

In insurance In a fire insurance policy, it is often stated that the policy shall be forfeited upon the occurrence of a certain event, such as nonpayment of the premium, storage of gasoline on the premises, vacancy of the premises, etc. A life insurance policy usually provides that it shall be forfeited for nonpayment of premiums. In the event of the happening of such a condition subsequent in an insurance policy, the insurer may declare a forfeiture or may waive the forfeiture and permit the insurance to continue.

forgery *In criminal law* The falsely making or materially altering, with intent to defraud, any writing which, if genuine, might apparently be of legal efficacy or the foundation of a legal liability.

forms of action Classes or kinds of action under the common law. "This term comprehends the various classes of personal action at common law, viz. trespass, case, trover, detinue, replevin, covenant, debt, assumpsit, scire facias, and revivor, as well as the nearly obsolete actions of account and annuity, and the modern action of mandamus. They are now abolished in England by Judicature Acts of 1873, and 1875, and in many of the states of the United States, where a uniform course of proceeding under codes of procedure has taken their place. But the principles regulating the distinctions between the common-law actions are still found applicable even where the technical forms are abolished." Bouvier's Law Dict.

franchise A special privilege conferred by government upon an individual or corporation, and which does not belong to the citizens of the country generally, of common right.

fraud Fraud consists of some deceitful practice or willful devise, resorted to with intent to deprive another of his right, or in some manner to do him an injury. As distinguished from negligence, it is always positive, intentional.

freehold An estate in land or other real property, of uncertain duration; that is, either of inheritance or which may possibly last for the life of the tenant at the least (as distinguished from a leasehold), and held by a free tenure.

fructus industriales Latin. Industrial fruits or fruits of industry. Those fruits of a thing, as of land, which are produced by the labor and industry of the occupant, as crops of grain; as distinguished from such as are produced solely by the powers of nature.

fructus naturales Latin. Those products which are produced by the powers of nature alone; as wool, metals, milk, the young of animals.

fungible things Movable goods, which may be estimated and replaced according to weight, measure, and number, things belonging to a class, which do not have to be dealt with in specie.

future estate An estate to begin in possession at or after the termination of the present estate; e. g., A. holds a life estate in a tract of land, and B. has a reversion therein, B.'s possession to begin on the termination of A.'s estate. B.'s reversion is one kind of future estate. The remainder is another common species of future estate.

G

garnish v. To issue process of garnishment against a person.

garnishee n. One garnished.

garnishment *In the process of attachment* A warning to a person in whose hands the effects of another are attached not to pay the money or deliver the property of the defendant in his hands to him, but to appear and answer the plaintiff's suit.

general and special issue The former is a plea which traverses and denies, briefly and in general and summary terms, the whole declaration, indictment, or complaint, without tendering new or special matter.

general verdict A verdict whereby the jury find either for the plaintiff or for the defendant in general terms; the ordinary form of verdict.

gratis dictum Latin. A voluntary assertion; a statement which a party is not legally bound to make, or in which he is not held to precise accuracy.

gravamen Latin. The burden or gist of a charge.

guaranty n. A promise to answer for the payment of some debt, or the performance of some duty, in case of the failure of another person, who, in the first instance, is liable to such payment or performance.

guardian A guardian is a person lawfully invested with the power, and charged with the duty, of taking care of the person and managing the property and rights of another person, who, for some peculiarity of status, or defect or age, understanding, or self-control, is considered incapable of administering his own affairs.

H

hearsay A term applied to that species of testimony given by a witness who relates, not what he knows personally, but what others have told him, or what he has heard said by others.

heir *At common law* A person who succeeds, by the rules of law, to an estate in lands, tenements, or hereditaments, upon the death of his ancestor, by descent and right of relationship.

hereditaments Things capable of being inherited, be it corporeal or incorporeal, real, personal, or mixed, and including not only lands and everything thereon, but also heirlooms, and certain furniture which, by custom, may descend to the heir together with the land.

I

implied This rod is used in law as contrasted with "express"; i. e., where the intention in regard to the subject-matter is not manifested by explicit and direct words, but is gathered by implication or necessary deduction from the circumstances, the general language, or the conduct of the parties.

inchoate Imperfect; unfinished; begun, but not completed; as a contract not executed by all the parties.

incorporeal Without body; not of material nature; the opposite of "corporeal."

indemnity An indemnity is a collateral contract or assurance, by which one person engages to secure another against an anticipated loss or to prevent him from being damnified by the legal consequences of an act or forbearance on the part of one of the parties or of some third person.

indenture A deed to which two or more persons are parties, and in which these enter into reciprocal and corresponding grants or obligations towards each other; whereas a deed poll is properly one in which only the party making it executes it, or binds himself by it as a deed, though the grantors or grantees therein may be several in number.

indicia Latin. Signs; indications.

indictment The formal written accusation of a crime, as presented by a grand jury. The indictment holds a place, in criminal pleading, analogous to the place held, in a civil case, by the declaration or complaint. The plaintiff, in a criminal case, is the state, and the proof introduced by the state must, in order to convict, sustain one or more of the counts named in the indictment, just as, in a civil case, the proof introduced by the plaintiff must sustain one or more counts in the declaration or complaint. In a criminal case, the state must sustain its case by proof beyond a reasonable doubt; in a civil case, the plaintiff need prove his case only by a preponderance of the evidence.

indorsee The person to whom a bill of exchange, promissory note, bill of lading, etc., is assigned by indorsement, giving him a right to sue thereon.

indorsement The act of a payee, drawee, accommodation indorser, or holder of a negotiable instrument in writing his name upon the back of same, with or without further words, whereby the property in same is transferred to another.

indorser He who makes an indorsement.

infant A person within age, not of age, or not of full age; a person under the age of twenty-one years; a minor.

information In the criminal law, an accusation made the basis of a prosecution for a crime, but not itself the result of a finding by a grand jury.

in haec foedera non venimus Latin. We did not enter into these bonds; we did not make this contract.

in invitum Latin. Against an unwilling party.

iniquum est ingenius hominibus non esse liberam rerum suarum alienationem Latin. Literally, it is unjust to freeborn men that the alienation of their own property should not be free. A better and freer translation would be: It is unjust that freeborn men should be unable freely to alienate their own property. This maxim states a reason underlying the rule against restraints upon alienation.

injunction A prohibitive writ issued by a court of equity, at the suit of a party complainant, directed to a party defendant in the action, or to a party made a defendant for that purpose, forbidding the latter to do some act, or to permit his servants or agents to do some act, which he is threatening or attempting to commit, or restraining him in the continuance thereof, such act being unjust and inequitable, injurious to the plaintiff, and not such as can be adequately redressed by an action at law.

injury Any wrong or damage done to another, either in his person, rights, reputation, or property.

in limine Latin. On or at the threshold; at the very beginning; preliminarily.

innkeeper The proprietor or keeper of a hotel or inn.

in pari delicto Latin. In equal fault; equally culpable or criminal.

In pari delicto, potior est conditio possidentis [defendantis] In a case of equal or mutual fault (between two parties), the condition of the party in possession [or defending] is the better one. This maxim is often applied to cases in which a plaintiff seeks to procure, under an illegal contract, money or other property in the possession of the defendant, or to get a judgment or decree of any kind, under such a contract.

in personam   Latin. Against the person. Actions or rights in personam are contrasted with actions or rights in rem, which are directed at specific property or at a specific right or status. A. sues B., in an action at law, for $100. This is one instance of an action in personam. All suits in equity were originally in personam, the bill and the decree being addressed directly to the person of the defendant and seeking to control his conduct.

in re   Latin. In the matter; e. g., "In re Jones" means "in the matter of Jones."

in rem   Latin. Against a thing; against the status; directed at specific property, or at a specific right or status. An action in admiralty against a certain vessel is in rem. A suit for the foreclosure of a mortgage is, in a sense, in rem. A divorce suit, while in a certain sense in personam, is actually directed against the status of marriage and is, in part, a suit in rem.

insolvency   The condition of a person who is insolvent; inability to pay one's debts; lack of means to pay one's debts. Such a relative condition of a man's assets and liabilities that the former, if all made immediately available, would not be sufficient to discharge the latter. Or the condition of a person who is unable to pay his debts as they fall due, or in the usual course of trade and business.

insolvent   Latin, insolvens; not paying.

In bankruptcy   In the federal Bankruptcy Act the following rule is stated: "A person shall be deemed insolvent within the provisions of this act whenever the aggregate of his property, exclusive of any property which he may have conveyed, transferred, concealed or removed, or permitted to be concealed or removed, with intent to defraud, hinder or delay his creditors, shall not, at a fair valuation, be sufficient in amount to pay his debts." Section 1, cl. 15.

In sales   The Uniform Sales Act gives the following rule: "A person is insolvent within the meaning of this act who either has ceased to pay his debts in the ordinary course of business or cannot

pay his debts as they fall due, whether he has committed an act of bankruptcy or not, and whether he is insolvent within the meaning of the federal bankruptcy law or not." Section 76.

in specie   Latin. In kind. Specific; specifically.

in statu quo   Latin. In the condition or state (in which it was).

insurable interest   Such a real and substantial interest in specific property as will sustain a contract to indemnify the person interested against its loss. If the assured had no real interest, the contract would be a mere wager policy.

insurance   A contract whereby, for a stipulated consideration, one party undertakes to compensate the other for loss on a specified subject by specified perils. The party agreeing to make the compensation is usually called the "insurer" or "underwriter"; the other, the "insured" or "assured"; the written contract, a "policy"; the events insured against, "risks" or "perils"; and the subject, right, or interest to be protected, the "insurable interest." Insurance is a contract whereby one undertakes to indemnify another against loss, damage, or liability arising from an unknown or contingent event.

insured   *In fire and other property insurance* The person whose property interest is insured.

In life insurance   The person whose life is insured.

insurer   The underwriter or insurance company with whom a contract of insurance is made.

interpleader   When two or more persons claim the same thing (or fund) of a third, and he, laying no claim to it himself, is ignorant which of them has a right to it, and fears he may be prejudiced by their proceeding against him to recover it, he may file a bill in equity against them, the object of which is to make them litigate their title between themselves, instead of litigating it with him, and such a bill is called a "bill of interpleader."

inter alia   Among other things. A term anciently used in pleading, especially in reciting statutes, where the whole statute was set forth at length. Inter alia enactatum fuit. Among other things it was enacted.

inter se, or **inter sese**   Latin. Between or among themselves.

interstate commerce commission A commission appointed by the President of the United States by authority of the Interstate Commerce Act of 1887. It is a corporate body, so that it may sue or be sued in the courts, and, by court action, its decisions, when valid, are enforced. Its work involves the rates and practices of interstate carriers.

intervener An intervener is a person who voluntarily interposes in an action or other proceeding with the leave of the court.

intestate Without making a will.

J

joint United; combined; undivided; done by or against two or more unitedly; shared by or between two or more.

A "joint" bond, note, or other obligation is one in which the obligors or makers (being two or more in number) bind themselves jointly, but not severally, and which must therefore be prosecuted in a joint action against them all. A "joint and several" bond or note is one in which the obligors or makers bind themselves both jointly and individually to the obligee or payee, and which may be enforced either by a joint action against them all or by separate actions against any one or more at the election of the creditor.

jointly Acting together or in concert or cooperation; holding in common or interdependently, not separately. Persons are "jointly bound" in a bond or note when both or all must be sued in one action for its enforcement.

Jointly and severally Persons who bind themselves "jointly and severally" in a bond or note may all be sued together for its enforcement, or the creditor may select any one or more as the object of his suit.

joint-stock company A partnership with a capital divided into transferable shares.

joint tenancy "Exists when a single estate in land is owned by two or more persons claiming under one instrument; its most important characteristic being that, unless the statute otherwise provides, the interest of each joint tenant, upon his death, inures to the benefit of the surviving joint tenant or tenants, to the exclusion of his own heirs, devisees, or personal representatives." Tiffany on Real Property, p. 368.

judgment The official and authentic decision of a court of justice upon the respective rights and claims of the parties to an action or suit therein litigated and submitted to its determination.

judgment debts Debts, whether on simple contract or by specialty, for the recovery of which judgment has been entered up, either upon a cognovit or upon a warrant of attorney or as the result of a successful action.

judgment in personam A judgment against a particular person, as distinguished from a judgment against a thing or a right or status. The former class of judgments are conclusive only upon parties and privies; the latter upon all the world.

judgment in rem A judgment in rem is an adjudication, pronounced upon the status of some particular subject-matter, by a tribunal having competent authority for that purpose. It differs from a judgment in personam, in this: That the latter judgment is in form, as well as substance, between the parties claiming the right; and that it is so inter partes appears by the record itself.

judgment note A promissory note, embodying an authorization to any attorney, or to a designated attorney, or to the holder, or the clerk of the court, to enter an appearance for the maker and confess a judgment against him for a sum therein named, upon default of payment of the note.

judgment n. o. v. Judgment non obstante verdicto in its broadest sense is a judgment rendered in favor of one party notwithstanding the finding of a verdict in favor of the other party. Originally, at common law, judgment non obstante verdicto was a judgment entered for plaintiff "notwithstanding the verdict" for defendant. The generally prevailing rule now is that either plaintiff or defendant may have a judgment non obstante verdicto.

judicial Belonging to the office of a judge; as judicial authority.

jurat The clause written at the foot of an affidavit, stating when, where, and before whom such affidavit was sworn.

jurisdiction The power and authority constitutionally conferred upon (or constitutionally recognized as existing in) a court or judge to pronounce the sentence of the law, or to award the remedies provided by law, upon a state of facts, proved or admitted, referred to the tribunal for decision, and authorized by law to be the subject of investigation or action by that tribunal, and in favor of or against persons (or a res) who present themselves, or who are brought, before the court in some manner sanctioned by law as proper and sufficient.

jury (From the Latin jurare, to swear.) A body of persons selected and summoned by law and sworn to try the facts of a case and to find according to the law and the evidence. In general, the province of the jury is to find the facts in a case, while the judge passes upon pure questions of law. As a matter of fact, however, the jury must often pass upon mixed questions of law and fact in determining the case, and in all such cases the instructions of the judge as to the law become very important.

K

kin Relationship; relationship by blood or marriage. The term is sometimes restricted to relationship by blood.

knowledge Information. "Knowledge" is a broader term than "notice," including, not only facts of which one is put on notice, but also facts of which one gets knowledge by means other than notice.

L

laches Negligence, consisting in the omission of something which a party might do, and might reasonably be expected to do, towards the vindication or enforcement of his rights. The word is generally the synonym of "remissness," "dilatoriness," "unreasonable or unexcused delay"; the opposite of "vigilance"; and means a want of activity and diligence in making a claim or moving for the enforcement of a right (particularly in equity) which will afford ground for presuming against it, or for refusing relief, where that is discretionary with the court.

landlord He of whom lands or tenements are holden. He who, being the owner of an estate in land, has leased the same for a term of years, on a rent reserved, to another person, called the "tenant."

lapse n. *In the law of wills* The failure of a testamentary gift in consequence of the death of the devisee or legatee during the life of the testator.

larceny *In criminal law* The wrongful and fraudulent taking and carrying away by one person of the mere personal goods of another from any place, with a felonious intent to convert them to his (the taker's) use, and make them his property, without the consent of the owner.

law merchant The system of rules, customs, and usages generally recognized and adopted by merchants and traders, and which either in its simplicity or as modified by common law or statutes, constitutes the law for the regulation of their transactions and the solution of their controversies.

lease A conveyance of lands or tenements to a person for life, for a term of years, or at will, in consideration of a return of rent or some other recompense. The person who so conveys such lands or tenements is termed the "lessor," and the person to whom they are conveyed, the "lessee"; and when the lessor so conveys lands or tenements to a lessee, he is said to lease, demise, or let them.

leasehold An estate in realty held under a lease; an estate for a fixed term of years.

legacy A bequest or gift of personal property by last will and testament.

legal tender That kind of coin, money, or circulating medium which the law compels a creditor to accept in payment of his debt, when tendered by the debtor in the right amount.

lessee He to whom a lease is made.

lessor He who grants a lease.

let v. In conveyancing. To demise or lease. "To let and set" is an old expression.

letters of administration The formal instrument of authority and appointment given an administrator by the proper court, empowering him to enter upon the discharge of his duties as administrator.

letters testamentary The formal instrument of authority and appointment given to an executor by the proper court, empowering him to enter upon the discharge of his office as executor.

levy v. To raise; execute; exact; collect; gather; take up; seize. Thus, to levy (raise or collect) a tax; to levy (raise or set up) a nuisance; to levy (acknowledge) a fine; to levy (inaugurate) war; to levy an execution—i. e., to levy or collect a sum of money on an execution.

lien A qualified right of property which a creditor has in or over specific property of his debtor, as security for the debt or charge or for performance of some act.

life estate An estate whose duration is limited to the life of the party holding it, or of some other person; a freehold estate, not of inheritance.

life tenant One who holds an estate in lands for the period of his own life or that of another certain person.

limitation *In conveyances* A defining or limiting, either by express words or by implication of law, of the time during which the estate granted is to be enjoyed; e. g., "to A. and his heirs forever," limits an estate in fee simple to A.; "to B. for life, remainder to C. and his heirs," limits a life estate to B., with a remainder in fee simple to C.

In statutes of limitation Under statutes of limitation, a certain limit of time is set, after the running of which, subsequent to the accruing of a cause of action, no action can be brought successfully, if the statute is pleaded.

limited partnership A partnership consisting of one or more general partners, jointly and severally responsible as ordinary partners, and by whom the business is conducted, and one or more special partners, contributing in cash payments a specific sum as capital to the common stock, and who are not liable for the debts of the partnership beyond the fund so contributed.

liquidated Ascertained; determined; fixed; settled; made clear or manifest. Cleared away; paid; discharged.

liquidated account An account whereof the amount is certain and fixed, either by the act and agreement of the parties or by operation of law; a sum which cannot be changed by the proof; it is so much or nothing; but the term does not necessarily refer to a writing.

liquidated and unliquidated damages The former term is applicable when the amount of the damages has been ascertained by the judgment in the action, or when a specific sum of money has been expressly stipulated by the parties to a bond or other contract as the amount of damages to be recovered by either party for a breach of the agreement by the other.

lis pendens Latin. A suit pending; that legal process, in a suit regarding land, which amounts to legal notice to all the world that there is a dispute as to the title. In equity the filing of the bill and serving a subpoena creates a lis pendens, except when statutes require some record.

locatio Latin. A hiring of goods for a reward.

locus poenitentiae Latin. A place for repentence; an opportunity for changing one's mind; a chance to withdraw from a contemplated bargain or contract before it results in a definite contractual liability. Also used of a chance afforded to a person, by the circumstances, of relinquishing the intention which he has formed to commit a crime, before the perpetration thereof.

lodging house A private house at which lodging is given for a consideration, as contrasted with a public house or inn or hotel.

l s An abbreviation for "locus sigilli," the place of the seal; i. e., the place where a seal is to be affixed, or a scroll which stands instead of a seal.

M

maintenance An unauthorized and officious interference in a suit in which the offender has no interest, to assist one of the parties to it, against the other, with money or advice to prosecute or defend the action.

malfeasance The wrongful or unjust doing of some act which the doer has no right to perform, or which he has stipulated by contract not to do. It differs from "misfeasance" and "nonfeasance" (which titles see).

malum in se Latin. A wrong in itself; an act or case involving illegality from the very nature of the transaction, upon principles of natural, moral, and public law. An act is said to be malum in se when it is inherently and essentially evil—that is, immoral in its nature and injurious in its consequences—without any regard to the fact of its being noticed or punished by the law of the state. Such are most or all of the offenses cognizable at common law (without the denouncement of a statute); as murder, larceny, etc.

malum prohibitum   Latin. A wrong prohibited; a thing which is wrong because prohibited; an act which is not inherently immoral, but becomes so because its commission is expressly forbidden by positive law; an act involving an illegality resulting from positive law. Contrasted with malum in se.

mandamus   Latin, we command. A legal writ compelling the defendant to do an official duty.

mandate   A bailment of property in regard to which the bailee engages to do some act without reward. Story, Bailm. § 137.

materialman   One who furnishes materials to be used in the construction or repair of ships or houses.

maturity   *In mercantile law*   The time when a bill of exchange or promissory note becomes due.

mechanic's lien   A species of lien created by statute in most of the states, which exists in favor of persons who have performed work or furnished material in and for the erection of a building. Their lien attaches to the land as well as the building, and is intended to secure for them a priority of payment.

merger   The fusion or absorption of one thing or right into another; generally spoken of a case where one of the subjects is of less dignity or importance than the other. Here the less important ceases to have an independent existence.

mesne   Intermediate.

Mesne process   Process issued between the beginning of a suit and final process.

Mesne profits   Profits from the use of land during wrongful occupancy, recovered, in ejectment or trespass, by the owner from the defendant in the action.

minor   An infant or person who is under the age of legal competence. A term derived from the civil law, which described a person under a certain age as less than so many years. Minor viginti quinque annis, one less than twenty-five years of age.

misdemeanor   *In criminal law*   A general name for criminal offenses of every sort, punishable by indictment or special proceedings, which do not in law amount to the grade of felony.

misfeasance   A misdeed or trespass. The doing what a party ought to do improperly. The improper performance of some act which a man may lawfully do.

Misfeasance, strictly, is not doing a lawful act in a proper manner, omitting to do it as it should be done, while malfeasance is the doing an act wholly wrongful, and nonfeasance is an omission to perform a duty, or a total neglect of duty. But "misfeasance" is often carelessly used in the sense of "malfeasance."

misrepresentation   An intentional false statement respecting a matter of fact, made by one of the parties to a contract, which is material to the contract and influential in producing it.

mortgage   An estate created by a conveyance absolute in form, but intended to secure the performance of some act, such as the payment of money, and the like, by the grantor or some other person, and to become void if the act is performed agreeably to the terms prescribed at the time of making such conveyance.

A conditional conveyance of land, designed as a security for the payment of money, the fulfillment of some contract, or the performance of some act, and to be void upon such payment, fulfillment, or performance.

A debt by specialty, secured by a pledge of lands, of which the legal ownership is vested in the creditor, but of which, in equity, the debtor and those claiming under him remain the actual owners, until debarred by judicial sentence or their own laches.

The foregoing definitions are applicable to the common-law conception of a mortgage. But in many states, in modern times, it is regarded as a mere lien, and not as creating a title or estate. It is a pledge or security of particular property for the payment of a debt, or the performance of some other obligation, whatever form the transaction may take, but is not regarded as a conveyance in effect, though it may be cast in the form of a conveyance.

mutuum Latin. In the law of bailments. A loan for consumption; a loan of chattels, upon an agreement that the borrower may consume them, returning to the lender an equivalent in kind and quantity.

N

negligence The omission to do something which a reasonable man, guided by those considerations which ordinarily regulate the conduct of human affairs, would do, or doing something which a prudent and reasonable man would not do. It must be determined in all cases by reference to the situation and knowledge of the parties and all the attendant circumstances.

Negligence, in its civil relation, is such an inadvertent imperfection, by a responsible human agent, in the discharge of a legal duty, as immediately produces, in an ordinary and natural sequence, a damage to another.

negligence vel non (A phrase of mixed English and Latin.) Negligence or not.

negotiable An instrument embodying an obligation for the payment of money is called "negotiable" when the legal title to the instrument itself and to the whole amount of money expressed upon its face, with the right to sue therefor in his own name, may be transferred from one person to another without a formal assignment, but by mere indorsement and delivery by the holder or by delivery only.

nemo plus juris ad alium transferre potest quam ipse haberet Latin. No one can transfer to another more of right than he himself has. This maxim, like most maxims, must not be taken as true without any limitations. It is well known that the bona fide purchaser of real or personal property, or the holder in due course of a negotiable instrument, does in many cases take a greater right than his transferor has had.

nil debet Latin. He owes nothing. A plea that the defendant owes nothing.

nisi pruis Latin. Literally, unless before. The expression has now so far departed from its original Latin signification as to mean substantially "at the trial." The words were originally words of some importance in the writ directing the sheriff to summon jurors. "A practice obtained very early, * * * in the trial of trifling causes, to continue the cause in the superior court from term to term, provided the justices in eyre did not sooner (nisi prius justiciari) come into the county where the cause of action arose, in which case they had jurisdiction when they so came." Bouvier's Law Dict.

nominal and substantial damages Nominal damages are a trifling sum awarded to a plaintiff in an action, where there is no substantial loss or injury to be compensated, but still the law recognizes a technical invasion of his rights or a breach of the defendant's duty, or in cases where, although there has been a real injury, the plaintiff's evidence entirely fails to show its amount.

nominal partner A person who appears to be a partner in a firm, or is so represented to persons dealing with the firm, or who allows his name to appear in the style of the firm or to be used in its business, in the character of a partner, but who has no actual interest in the firm or business.

non assumpsit Latin. The general issue in the action of assumpsit, being a plea by which the defendant avers that "he did not undertake" or promise as alleged.

non compos mentis Latin. Not sound of mind; insane.

non est factum Latin. It was not made.

nonfeasance The neglect of failure of a person to do some act which he ought to do.

non sequitur Latin. It does not follow. An inference which does not follow from the premise.

nonsuit Not following up the cause; failure on the part of a plaintiff to continue the prosecution of his suit. An abandonment or renunciation of his suit, by a plaintiff, either by omitting to take the next necessary steps, or voluntarily relinquishing the action, or pursuant to an order of the court. An order or judgment, granted upon the trial of a cause, that the plaintiff has abandoned, or shall abandon, the further prosecution of his suit.

notary public A public officer whose function is to attest and certify, by his hand and official seal, certain classes of documents, in order to give them credit and authenticity in foreign jurisdictions; to take acknowledgments of deeds and other conveyances, and certify the same; and to perform certain official acts, chiefly in commercial matters.

nudum pactum Latin. A naked pact; a bare agreement; a promise or undertaking made without any consideration for it.

nuisance That class of wrongs that arise from the unreasonable, unwarrantable, or unlawful use by a person of his own property, either real or personal, or from his own improper, indecent, or unlawful personal conduct, working an obstruction of or injury to the right of another or of the public, and producing such material annoyance, inconvenience, discomfort, or hurt that the law will presume a consequent damage.

O

oath An external pledge or asseveration, made in verification of statements made or to be made, coupled with an appeal to a sacred or venerated object, in evidence of the serious and reverent state of mind of the party, or with an invocation to a supreme being to witness the words of the party and to visit him with punishment if they be false.

obiter dictum Latin. A remark made, or opinion expressed, by a judge, in his decision upon a cause, "by the way"; that is, incidentally or collaterally, and not directly upon the question before him, or upon a point not necessarily involved in the determination of the cause, or introduced by way of illustration, or analogy or argument.

omnis ratihabitio retrotrahitur et mandato priori aequiparatur Latin. Every ratification relates back and is equivalent to a prior authority. Broom, Max. 757, 871.

ordinance The term is used to designate the enactments of the legislative body of a municipal corporation.

ore tenus Oral, word of mouth.

ostensible agency An implied or presumptive agency, which exists where one, either intentionally or from want of ordinary care, induces another to believe that a third person is his agent, though he never in fact employed him.

ostensible partner A partner whose name is made known and appears to the world as a partner, and who is in reality such.

outlawed When applied to a promissory note, means debarred by the statute of limitations.

oyer *In modern practice* A copy of a bond or specialty sued upon, given to the opposite party, in lieu of the old practice of reading it.

P

par *In commercial law* Equal; equality. An equality subsisting between the nominal or face value of a bill of exchange, share of stock, etc., and its actual selling value. When the values are thus equal, the instrument or share is said to be "at par"; if it can be sold for more than its nominal worth, it is "above par"; if for less, it is "below par."

pari passu Latin. By an equal progress; ratably; without preference.

particeps Latin. A participant; a sharer; anciently, a part owner, or parcener.

particeps criminis Latin. A participant in a crime; an accomplice. One who shares or co-operates in a criminal offense, tort, or fraud.

partition The dividing of lands held by joint tenants, coparceners, or tenants in common, into distinct portions, so that they may hold them in severalty. And, in a less technical sense, any division of real or personal property between co-owners or co-proprietors.

partnership A voluntary contract between two or more competent persons to place their money, effects, labor, and skill, or some or all of them, in lawful commerce or business, with the understanding that there shall be a proportional sharing of the profits and losses between them.

part performance The doing some portion, yet not the whole, of what either party to a contract has agreed to do.

patent n. A grant of some privilege, property, or authority, made by the government or sovereign of a country to one or more individuals.

In English law A grant by the sovereign to a subject or subjects, under the great seal, conferring some authority, title, franchise, or property; termed "letters patent" from being delivered open, and not closed up from inspection.

In American law The instrument by which a state or government grants public lands to an individual.

A grant made by the government to an inventor, conveying and securing to him the exclusive right to make and sell his invention for a term of years.

pawn n. A bailment of goods to a creditor, as security for some debt or engagement; a pledge. Story, Bailm. art. 7.

payee The person in whose favor a negotiable instrument is made or drawn; the person to whom a negotiable instrument is made payable.

payer, or **payor** One who pays, or who is to make a payment; particularly the person who makes or is to make payment of a negotiable instrument.

perform To perform an obligation or contract is to execute, fulfill, or accomplish it according to its terms. This may consist either in action on the part of the person bound by the contract or in omission to act, according to the nature of the subject-matter; but the term is usually applied to any action in discharge of a contract other than payment.

performance The fulfillment or accomplishment of a promise, contract, or other obligation according to its terms.

Part performance The doing some portion, yet not the whole, of what either party to a contract has agreed to do.

Specific performance Performance of a contract in the specific form in which it was made, or according to the precise terms agreed upon. This is frequently compelled by a bill in equity filed for the purpose. 2 Story, Eq. Pl. § 712 et seq. The doctrine of specific performance is that, where damages would be an inadequate compensation for the breach of an agreement, the contractor will be compelled to perform specifically what he has agreed to do. Sweet.

perjury *In criminal law* The willful assertion as to a matter of fact, opinion, belief, or knowledge, made by a witness in a judicial proceeding as part of his evidence, either upon oath or in any form allowed by law to be substituted for an oath, whether such evidence is given in open court, or in an affidavit, or otherwise, such assertion being known

to such witness to be false, and being intended by him to mislead the court, jury or person holding the proceeding.

perpetuity "A future limitation, whether executory or by way of remainder, and of real or personal property, which is not to vest till after the expiration of, or which will not necessarily vest within, the period prescribed by law for the creation of future estates, and which is not destructible by the person for the time being entitled to the property subject to the future limitation, except with the concurrence of the person interested in the contingent event." Lewis, Perp. c. 12.

per se Latin. By himself or itself; in itself; taken alone; inherently; in isolation; unconnected with other matters.

personalty Personal property; movable property; chattels.

personal property See *Personalty.*

pignus Latin. A pledge. A collateral pledge.

plaintiff A person who brings an action; the party who complains or sues in a personal action and is so named on the record.

plaintiff in error The party who sues out a writ of error to review a judgment or other proceeding at law.

plea *In common-law practice.* A pleading; any one in the series of pleadings. More particularly, the first pleading on the part of the defendant. In the strictest sense, the answer which the defendant in an action at law makes to the plaintiff's declaration, and in which he sets up matter of fact as defense, thus distinguished from a demurrer, which interposes objections on grounds of law.

In equity A special answer showing or relying upon one or more things as a cause why the suit should be either dismissed or delayed or barred.

plead To make, deliver, or file any pleading; to conduct the pleadings in a cause. To interpose any pleading in a suit which contains allegations of fact; in this sense the word is the antithesis of "demur." More particularly, to deliver in a formal manner the defendant's answer to the plaintiff's declaration, or to the indictment, as the case may be.

pleading The peculiar science or system of rules and principles, established in the common law, according to which the pleadings or responsive allegations of litigating parties are framed, with a view to preserve technical propriety and to produce a proper issue.

The process performed by the parties to a suit or action, in alternately presenting written statements of their contention, each responsive to that which precedes, and each serving to narrow the field of controversy, until there evolves a single point, affirmed on one side and denied on the other, called the "issue," upon which they then go to trial.

The act or step of interposing any one of the pleadings in a cause, but particularly one on the part of the defendant; and, in the strictest sense, one which sets up allegations of fact in defense to the action.

pledge n. A bailment of goods to a creditor, as security for some debt or engagement; a pawn. Story, Bailm. art. 7.

pledgee The party to whom goods are pledged, or delivered in pledge.

pledgor The party delivering goods in pledge; the party pledging.

police power The power vested in a state to establish laws and ordinances for the regulation and enforcement of public order and tranquillity. The power vested in the legislature to make, ordain, and establish all manner of wholesome and reasonable laws, statutes, and ordinances, either with penalties or without, not repugnant to the constitution, as they shall judge to be for the good and welfare of the commonwealth, and of the subjects of the same. The police power of the state is an authority conferred by the American constitutional system upon the individual states, through which they are enabled to establish a special department of police; adopt such regulations as tend to prevent the commission of fraud, violence, or other offenses against the state; aid in the arrest of criminals; and secure generally the comfort, health, and prosperity of the state, by preserving the public order, preventing a conflict of rights in the common intercourse of the citizens, and insuring to each an uninterrupted enjoyment of all the privileges conferred upon him by the laws of his country. It is true that the legislation which se-

cures to all protection in their rights, and the equal use and enjoyment of their property, embraces an almost infinite variety of subjects. Whatever affects the peace, good order, morals, and health of the community comes within its scope; and every one must use and enjoy his property subject to the restrictions which such legislation imposes. What is termed the "police power" of the state, which, from the language often used respecting it, one would suppose to be be an undefined and irresponsible element in government, can only interfere with the conduct of individuals in their intercourse with each other, and in the use of their property, so far as may be required to secure these objects.

policy of insurance A mercantile instrument in writing, by which one party, in consideration of a premium, engages to indemnify another against a contingent loss, by making him a payment in compensation, whenever the event shall happen by which the loss is to accrue.

post-date To date an instrument as of a time later than that at which it is really made.

power of appointment A power of authority conferred by one person by deed or will upon another (called the "donee") to appoint, that is, to select and nominate, the person or persons who are to receive and enjoy an estate or an income therefrom or from a fund, after the testator's death, or the donee's death, or after the termination of an existing right or interest.

power of attorney An instrument authorizing a person to act as the agent or attorney of the person granting it.

preference The payment of money or the transfer of property to one creditor in preference to other creditors. Where the debtor is solvent, he may legally make such a preference. Under the federal Bankruptcy Act, a debtor is said to have made a preference if, being insolvent, he has made a transfer of any of his property and the effect of the enforcement of such transfer will be to enable any one of his creditors to obtain a greater percentage of his debt than any other of such creditors of the same class.

premium The sum paid or agreed to be paid by an assured to the underwriter as the consideration for the insurance; being a certain rate per cent. on the amount insured.

prescription The acquisition of incorporeal hereditaments by user or enjoyment for a very long time; i. e. "from time immemorial," or for a certain time set by a statute of limitations. For instance, A. continues to cross the land of B. by a certain path each day for twenty years, the period within which an action must be brought or other means taken to cause a discontinuance of A.'s user, under the laws of the state in which B.'s land lies. A. then has the right "by prescription" to continue to cross the land of B. His easement is complete.

presentment The production of a bill of exchange to the drawee for his acceptance, or to the drawer or acceptor for payment; or of a promissory note to the party liable, for payment of the same.

presumption An inference affirmative or disaffirmative of the truth or falsehood of any proposition or fact drawn by a process of probable reasoning in the absence of actual certainty of its truth or falsehood, or until such certainty can be ascertained.

prima facie Latin. At first sight; on the first appearance; on the face of it; so far as can be judged from the first disclosure; presumably.

A litigating party is said to have a prima facie case when the evidence in his favor is sufficiently strong for his opponent to be called on to answer it.

principal In the law of agency. The employer or constitutor of an agent; the person who gives authority to an agent or attorney to do some act for him.

private carrier One who carries passengers or the goods of another without holding himself out to the general public as serving all persons that apply. The private carrier is contrasted with the common or public carrier.

probate The act or process of proving a will. The proof before an ordinary, surrogate, register, or other duly authorized person that a document produced before him for official recognition and registration, and alleged to be the last will and testament of a certain deceased person, is such in reality.

procedure The method and mechanism, so to speak, by which proceedings in a court are conducted.

process *In practice* This word is generally defined to be the means of compelling the defendant in an action to appear in court.

procuration Agency; proxy; the act of constituting another one's attorney in fact; action under a power of attorney or other constitution of agency. Indorsing a bill or note "by procuration" (or per proc.) is doing it as proxy for another or by his authority.

promissory note A promise or engagement, in writing, to pay a specified sum at a time therein limited, or on demand, or at sight, to a person therein named, or to his order, or bearer.

promoters In the law relating to corporations, those persons are called the "promoters" of a company who first associate themselves together for the purpose of organizing the company, issuing its prospectus, procuring subscriptions to the stock, securing a charter, etc.

prosecute To follow up; to carry on an action or other judicial proceeding; to proceed against a person criminally.

pro tanto Latin. For so much; as far as it goes.

protest A notarial act, being a formal statement in writing made by a notary under his seal of office, at the request of the holder of a bill or note, in which such bill or note is described, and it is declared that the same was on a certain day presented for payment (or acceptance, as the case may be), and that such payment or acceptance was refused, and stating the reasons, if any, given for such refusal, whereupon the notary protests against all parties to such instrument, and declares that they will be held responsible for all loss or damage arising from its dishonor.

proxy A person who is substituted or deputed by another to represent him and act for him, particularly in some meeting or public body. Also the instrument containing the appointment of such person.

Q

qua Latin. As; in the character or capacity of. E. g., "the trustee qua trustee."

quantum meruit   Latin. As much as he deserved.

In pleading   The common count in an action of assumpsit for work and labor, founded on an implied assumpsit or promise on the part of the defendant to pay the plaintiff as much as he reasonably deserved to have for his labor.

quasi   Latin. As if; as it were; analogous to. This term is used in legal phraseology to indicate that one subject resembles another, with which it is compared, in certain characteristics, but that there are also intrinsic differences between them.

quasi contract   In the civil law. A contractual relation arising out of transactions between the parties which give them mutual rights and obligations, but do not involve a specific and express convention or agreement between them.

quia emptores   Latin. The English statute (18 Edw. I) prohibiting subinfeudation.

quiet, v.   To pacify; to render secure or unassailable by the removal of disquieting causes or disputes. This is the meaning of the word in the phrase "action to quiet title," which is a proceeding to establish the plaintiff's title to land by bringing into court an adverse claimant and there compelling him either to establish his claim or be forever after estopped from asserting it.

quitclaim deed   A deed of conveyance operating by way of release; that is, intended to pass any title, interest, or claim which the grantor may have in the premises, but not professing that such title is valid, nor containing any warranty or covenants for title.

quo warranto   Latin. By what warrant? A name commonly applied, in the United States, to an "information in the nature of a quo warranto," an action compelling the defendant to show by what warrant he exercises certain powers or privileges. The proceeding is used to test the right of a person to public office, or the right of a private or public corporation to exercise certain franchises.

R

ratification   The confirmation of a previous act done either by the party himself or by another; confirmation of a voidable act.

real estate   See *Real Property*.

realty   See *Real Property*.

real property   A general term for lands, tenements, and hereditaments; property which, on the death of the owner intestate, passes to his heir. Real property is either corporeal or incorporeal.

receipt   A receipt is the written acknowledgment of the receipt of money, or a thing of value, without containing any affirmative obligation upon either party to it; a mere admission of a fact in writing.

Also the act or transaction of accepting or taking anything delivered.

receiver   A receiver is an indifferent person between the parties appointed by the court to collect and receive the rents, issues, and profits of land, or the produce of personal estate, or other things which it does not seem reasonable to the court that either party should do; or where a party is incompetent to do so, as in the case of an infant. The remedy of the appointment of a receiver is one of the very oldest in the court of chancery, and is founded on the inadequacy of the remedy to be obtained in the court of ordinary jurisdiction.

recognizance   An obligation of record, entered into before some court of record, or magistrate duly authorized, with condition to do some particular act; as to appear at the assizes, or criminal court, to keep the peace, to pay a debt, or the like. It resembles a bond, but differs from it in being an acknowledgment of a former debt upon record.

recoupment   Recoupment is a right of the defendant to have a deduction from the amount of the plaintiff's damages, for the reason that the plaintiff has not complied with the cross-obligations or independent covenants arising under the same contract.

"Recoupment" differs from "set-off" in this respect: that any claim or demand the defendant may have against the plaintiff may be used as a set-off, while it is not a subject for recoupment unless it grows out of the very same transaction which furnishes the plaintiff's cause of action.

recovery   The collection of a debt through an action at law.

Right of recovery   A plaintiff is said to have a right of recovery when he has a right of action under the facts of a given case.

redemption (From the Latin, redemptio; a buying back.) A buying back of property from the original purchaser by the original seller. A mortgage purports to convey title to the mortgagee, subject to a right of redemption in the mortgagor; i. e., the mortgagor has an "equity of redemption" in the property. The mortgagor has a right and a power to defeat the efficacy of his mortgage as a complete conveyance of the title, by paying the amount of the debt secured by the mortgage, thus meeting the condition subsequent stated in the "defeasance clause" of the mortgage.

reimbursement The equitable and legal right of reimbursement of a surety is the surety's right to be reimbursed by his principal in the amount of the principal's debt paid by the surety.

relator The person upon whose complaint, or at whose instance, an information or writ of quo warranto is filed, and who is quasi the plaintiff in the proceeding.

release The relinquishment, concession, or giving up of a right, claim, or privilege, by the person in whom it exists or to whom it accrues, to the person against whom it might have been demanded or enforced.

remainder An estate limited to take effect and be enjoyed after another estate is determined. As, if a man seised in fee-simple grants lands to A. for twenty years, and, after the determination of the said term, then to B. and his heirs forever, here A. is tenant for years, remainder to B. in fee.

remand Where a decision of a trial court is reversed in an appellate court, it is frequently sent back or "remanded" to the trial court for a new trial. In some cases, as where the plaintiff has been given judgment on a state of facts that could not, in any view, justify such judgment, the appellate court may reverse the judgment without remanding.

remedial Of or pertaining to the legal remedy, or to the form or procedural details of such remedy.

remedy The means by which the violation of a right is prevented, redressed, or compensated. Though a remedy may be by the act of the party injured, by operation of law, or by agreement between the injurer and the injured, we are chiefly concerned with one kind of remedy, the judicial remedy, which is by action or suit.

remittitur damna Latin. Usually shortened to *Remittitur.* An entry made on record, in cases where a jury has given greater damages than a plaintiff has declared for, remitting the excess.

rent The compensation, either in money, provisions, chattels, or labor, received by the owner of the soil from the occupant thereof.

replevin A personal action ex delicto brought to recover possession of goods unlawfully taken (generally, but not only, applicable to the taking of goods distrained for rent), the validity of which taking it is the mode of contesting, if the party from whom the goods were taken wishes to have them back in specie, whereas, if he prefer to have damages instead, the validity may be contested by action of trespass or unlawful distress.

replevin bond A bond executed to indemnify the officer who executed a writ of replevin and to indemnify the defendant or person from whose custody the property was taken for such damages as he may sustain.

rescission Rescission, or the act of rescinding, is where a contract is canceled, annulled, or abrogated by the parties, or one of them.

residence Living or dwelling in a certain place permanently or for a considerable length of time. The place where a man makes his home, or where he dwells permanently or for an extended period of time.

residuary Pertaining to the residue; constituting the residue; giving or bequeathing the residue; receiving or entitled to the residue.

residuary devisee The person named in a will, who is to take all the real property remaining over and above the other devises.

residuary estate The remaining part of a testator's estate and effects, after payment of debts and legacies; or that portion of his estate which has not been particularly devised or bequeathed.

residuary legatee The person to whom a testator bequeaths the residue of his personal estate, after the payment of such other legacies as are specifically mentioned in the will.

respondeat superior Latin. Let the master answer. This maxim means that a master is liable in certain cases for the wrongful acts of his servant, and a principal for those of his agent.

respondent The party who makes an answer to a bill or other proceeding in chancery.

The party who appeals against the judgment of an inferior court is termed the "appellant"; and he who contends against the appeal, the "respondent."

reverse An appellate court uses the term "reversed" to indicate that it annuls or avoids the judgment, or vacates the decree, of the trial court.

revocation The recall of some power, authority-,or thing granted, or a destroying or making void of some deed that had existence until the act of revocation made it void. It may be either general, of all acts and things done before; or special, to revoke a particular thing.

right of action The right to bring suit; a legal right to maintain an action, growing out of a given transaction or state of facts and based thereon.

right of entry A right of entry is the right of taking or resuming possession of land by entering on it in a peaceable manner.

right to redeem The term "right of redemption" or "right to redeem," is familiarly used to describe the estate of the debtor when under mortgage, to be sold at auction, in contradistinction to an absolute estate, to be set off by appraisement. It would be more consonant to the legal character of this interest to call it the "debtor's estate subject to mortgage."

S

satisfaction The act of satisfying a party by paying what is due to him (as on a mortgage, lien, or contract), or what is awarded to him, by the judgment of a court or otherwise. Thus, a judgment is satisfied by the payment of the amount due to the party who has recovered such judgment, or by his levying the amount.

scienter Latin. Knowingly.

scintilla Latin. A spark; a remaining particle; the least particle.

scire facias Latin. You may cause to know. In practice, a judicial writ, founded upon some record, and requiring the person against whom it is brought to show cause why the party bringing it should not have advantage of such record, or (in the case of a scire facias to repeal letters patent) why the record should not be annulled and vacated.

The most common application of this writ is as a process to revive a judgment, after the lapse of a certain time, or on a change of parties, or otherwise to have execution of the judgment, in which cases it is merely a continuation of the original action.

scroll or **scrawl** A mark intended to supply the place of a seal, made with a pen or other instrument of writing.

seal An impression upon wax, wafer, or some other tenacious substance capable of being impressed.

seisin Posession with an intent on the part of him who holds it to claim a freehold interest.

set-off A counterclaim or cross-demand; a claim or demand which the defendant in an action sets off against the claim of the plaintiff, as being his due, whereby he may extinguish the plaintiff's demand, either in whole or in part, according to the amount of the set-off.

set up To bring forward or allege, as something relied upon or deemed sufficient; to propose or interpose, by way of defense, explanation, or justification; as, to set up the statute of limitations—i. e., offer and rely upon it as a defense to a claim.

severance The cutting of the crops, such as corn, grass, etc., or the separating of anything from the realty. Brown.

Shelley's case, rule in "That rule is that, where a life estate is given to A. with a future interest to A.'s heirs (the use of the particular word 'heirs' being necessary), the whole gift is construed as one 'to A. and his heirs,' at once giving an estate to A. in fee." Albert M. Kales, in 5 Am.Law & Proced. 105.

silent partner Popular name for dormant partners or special partners.

simple contract A contract based upon consideration and not upon form.

special indorsement An indorsement in full, which specifically names the indorsee.

special partner A member of a limited partnership, who furnishes certain funds to the common stock, and whose liability extends no further than the fund furnished.

special property Property of a qualified, temporary, or limited nature; as distinguished from absolute, general, or unconditional property. Such is the property of a bailee in the article bailed, of a sheriff in goods temporarily in his hands under a levy, of the finder of lost goods while looking for the owner, of a person in wild animals which he has caught.

specialty A writing sealed and delivered, containing some agreement.

special verdict A special finding of the facts of a case by a jury, leaving to the court the application of the law to the facts thus found.

spoliation *In torts* Destruction of a thing by the act of a stranger, as the erasure or alteration of a writing by the act of a stranger, is called "spoliation." This has not the effect to destroy its character or legal effect.

ss An abbreviation used in that part of a record, pleading, or affidavit, called the "statement of the venue." Commonly translated or read "to wit," and supposed to be a contraction of "scilicet."

status The status of a person is his legal position or condition.

statute, n. An act of the legislature.

Statute of Frauds A celebrated English statute, passed in 1677, and which has been adopted, in a more or less modified form, in nearly all of the United States. Its chief characteristic is the provision that no action shall be brought on certain contracts unless there be a note or memorandum thereof in writing, signed by the party to be charged or by his authorized agent.

statute of limitation A statute prescribing limitations to the right of action on certain described causes of action; that is, declaring that no suit shall be maintained on such causes of action unless brought within a specified period after the right accrued.

statutory undertaking A penal bond, given, as required by statute, in connection with certain legal proceedings. "Common examples of statutory undertaking are: The bond given by a plaintiff in an injunction suit, as security to the defendant for damages caused by the issuance of an interlocutory injunction, such damages, within the amount of the penalty, to be collected by the defendant if the injunction is found to have been wrongfully issued; and the bond given for a very similar purpose in attachment or replevin." Bauer on Damages, p. 98, note.

stock *In corporation law* The capital or principal fund of a corporation or joint-stock company, formed by the contributions of subscribers or the sale of shares, and considered as the aggregate of a certain number of shares severally owned by the members or stockholders of the corporation; also the proportional part of the capital which is owned by an individual stockholder; also the incorporeal property which is represented by the holding of a certificate of stock, and in a wider and more remote sense, the right of a shareholder to participate in the general management of the company and to share proportionally in its net profits or earnings or in the distribution of assets on dissolution.

stoppage in transitu The act by which the unpaid vendor of goods stops their progress and resumes possession of them, while they are in course of transit from him to the purchaser, and not yet actually delivered to the latter.

strictissimi juris Latin. Of the strictest right or law.

subagent An under-agent; a substituted agent; an agent appointed by one who is himself an agent.

subinfeudation Under the feudal system, an inferior lord sometimes carved out of an estate which he held of a superior lord, a part which he granted to an inferior tenant, whose lord he in turn became. This under-feudalizing, so to speak, used in order to evade restraints on alienation, was known as subinfeudation, and was prohibited by the Statute of Quia Emptores (St. 18 Edw. I).

subpoena Latin. Sub, under, and poena, punishment or penalty. In the Latin writs early used in England, one was commanded to appear "sub poena," and these words have given the name to writs of those types in which they appeared.

Of a witness A process commanding a witness to appear in court at a certain time to testify in a given cause.

In chancery practice A process commanding a party or parties to a suit in equity to appear and answer matters alleged against them in the bill.

subrogation The substitution of one thing for another, or of one person into the place of another with respect to rights, claims, or securities.

Subrogation denotes the putting a third person who has paid a debt in the place of the creditor to whom he has paid it, so that he may exercise against the debtor all the rights which the creditor, if unpaid, might have done.

subscribe *In the law of contracts* To write under; to write the name under; to write the name at the bottom or end of a writing.

substantive law The part of the law which the courts are established to administer, as opposed to the rules according to which the substantive law itself is administered. That part of the law which creates, defines, and regulates rights, as opposed to adjective or remedial law, which prescribes the method of enforcing rights or obtaining redress for their invasion.

sui generis Latin. Of its own kind or class.

sui juris Latin. Of his own right; having legal capacity to manage his own affairs.

suit "Suit" is a generic term, of comprehensive signification, and applies to any proceeding in a court of justice in which the plaintiff pursues, in such court, the remedy which the law affords him for the redress of an injury or the recovery of a right.

summary, adj.   Immediate; peremptory; off-hand; without a jury; provisional; statutory.

summon *In practice* To serve a summons; to cite a defendant to appear in court to answer a suit which has been begun against him; to notify the defendant that an action has been instituted against him, and that he is required to answer to it at a time and place named.

summons *In practice* A writ, directed to the sheriff or other proper officer, requiring him to notify the person named that an action has been

commenced against him in the court whence the writ issues, and that he is required to appear, on a day named, and answer the complaint in such action.

surety A surety is one who at the request of another, and for the purpose of securing to him a benefit, becomes responsible for the performance by the latter of some act in favor of a third person, or hypothecates property as security therefor.

T

tenancy in common A tenancy under which each contenant has a distinct and several estate in the property. Under such a tenancy, the survivor from among the cotenants does not take the entire property as in the case of a joint tenancy.

tenant In the broadest sense, one who holds or possesses lands or tenements by any kind of right or title, whether in fee, for life, for years, at will, or otherwise. Cowell.

In a more restricted sense, one who holds lands of another; one who has the temporary use and occupation of real property owned by another person (called the "landlord"), the duration and terms of his tenancy being usually fixed by an instrument called a "lease."

tender An offer of money; the act by which one produces and offers to a person holding a claim or demand against him the amount of money which he considers and admits to be due, in satisfaction of such claim or demand, without any stipulation or condition.

Also, there may be a tender of performance of a duty other than the payment of money.

tenor In pleading the "tenor" of a document is sometimes said to be shown when an exact copy is set out in the pleading. Also, the word is often used to denote the true meaning or purport of an instrument.

tenure *In the law of public officers* The period during which an officer holds office.

In the law of real property The legal mode in which one owns an estate in lands.

term *Of court* The word "term" when used with reference to a court, signifies the space of time during which the court holds a session. A "session" signifies the time during the term when the court sits for the transaction of business, and the session commences when the court convenes for the term, and continues until final adjournment, either before or at the expiration of the term. The "term" of the court is the time prescribed by law during which it may be in "session." The "session" of the court is the time of its actual sitting.

testator One who makes or has made a testament or will; one who dies leaving a will.

title The means whereby the owner of lands or of personalty has the just possession of his property. See Co. Litt. 345; 2 Bl.Comm. 195.

tort Wrong; injury; the opposite of right. So called, according to Lord Coke, because it is "wrested," or crooked, being contrary to that which is right and straight. Co. Litt. 158b.

In modern practice, "tort" is constantly used as an English word to denote a wrong or wrongful act, for which an action will lie, as distinguished from a "contract." 3 Bl.Comm. 117.

A tort is a legal wrong committed upon the person or property independent of contract. It may be either (1) a direct invasion of some legal right of the individual; (2) the infraction of some public duty by which special damage accrues to the individual; (3) the violation of some private obligation by which like damage accrues to the individual. In the former case, no special damage is necessary to entitle the party to recover. In the two latter cases, such damage is necessary. Code Ga.1882, § 2951.

tort-feasor One who commits or is guilty of a tort.

tortious Wrongful; of the nature of a tort. Formerly certain modes of conveyance (e. g., feoffments, fines, etc.) had the effect of passing not merely the estate of the person making the conveyance, but the whole fee simple, to the injury of the person really entitled to the fee; and they were hence called "tortious conveyances." Litt. par. 611; Co. Litt. 271b, note 1; 330b, note 1. But this operation has been taken away. Sweet.

transitory action An action that is personal—i. e., brought against the person of the defendant— and possible to be brought in any county in which service of process upon the defendant is obtained.

trespass Any misfeasance or act of one man whereby another is injuriously treated or damnified. 3 Bl.Comm. 208.

An injury or misfeasance to the person, property, or rights of another person, done with force and violence, either actual or implied by law.

In the strictest sense, an entry on another's ground, without a lawful authority, and doing some damage, however inconsiderable, to his real property. 3 Bl.Comm. 209.

In practice A form of action, at the common law, which lies for redress in the shape of money damages for any unlawful injury done to the plaintiff, in respect either to his person, property, or rights, by the immediate force and violence of the defendant.

Trespass de bonis asportatis (Trespass for goods carried away.) In practice. The technical name of that species of trespass for injuries to personal property which lies where the injury consists in carrying away the goods or property.

Trespass on the case The form of action, at common law, adapted to the recovery of damages for some injury resulting to a party from the wrongful act of another, unaccompanied by direct or immediate force, or which is the indirect or secondary consequence of such act. Commonly called "case," or "action on the case."

Trespass quare clausum fregit (Trespass wherefore he broke the close, or trespass for breaking the close.) The common-law action for damages for an unlawful entry or trespass upon the plaintiff's land.

trover In common-law practice, the action of trover (or trover and conversion) is a species of action on the case, and originally lay for the recovery of damages against a person who had "found" another's goods and wrongfully converted them to his own use. Subsequently the allegation of the loss of the goods by the plaintiff and the finding of them by the defendant was merely fictitious, and the action became the remedy for any wrongful interference with or detention of the goods of another.

trust An equitable or beneficial right or title to land or other property, held for the beneficiary by another person, in whom resides the legal title or ownership, recognized and enforced by courts of chancery.

trust deed An instrument in use in many states, taking the place and serving the uses of a common-law mortgage, by which the legal title to real property is placed in one or more trustees, to secure the repayment of a sum of money or the performance of other conditions.

trustee The person appointed, or required by law, to execute a trust; one in whom an estate, interest, or power is vested, under an express or implied agreement to administer or exercise it for the benefit or to the use of another.

trustee process The name given in the New England states, to the process of garnishment or foreign attachment.

U

ultra vires Latin. Beyond the powers. A term used to express the action of a corporation which is beyond the powers conferred upon it by its charter, or the statutes under which it was instituted. 13 Am.Law Rev. 632.

undertaking A promise, engagement, or stipulation. Each of the promises made by the parties to a contract, considered independently and not as mutual, may, in this sense, be denominated an "undertaking."

underwriter The person who insures another in a fire or life policy; the insurer.

A person who joins with others in entering into a marine policy of insurance as insurer.

uniform statutes In general, statutes of substantially uniform substance, passed by various states, with the purpose of making the law of the subject uniform throughout the country. Such statutes have been drafted by the Commission on Uniform State Laws of the American Bar Association, and recommended for passage by the Legislatures of the various states. The most important of such statutes are the Negotiable Instruments Act, the Sales Act, and the Partnership Act, which have all been enacted in many of the states.

unilateral One-sided; ex parte; having relation to only one of two or more persons or things.

usury Unlawful interest; a premium or compensation paid or stipulated to be paid for the use of money borrowed or returned, beyond the rate of interest established by law. Webster.

V

valid Of binding force. A deed, will, or other instrument, which has received all the formalities required by law, is said to be valid.

validity This term is used to signify legal sufficiency, in contradistinction to mere regularity.

vendee A purchaser or buyer; one to whom anything is sold. Generally used of the transferee of real property, one who acquires chattels by sale being called a "buyer."

venditioni exponas Latin. You may expose to sale. This is the name of a writ of execution, requiring a sale to be made, directed to a sheriff when he has levied upon goods under a fieri facias, but returned that they remained unsold for want of buyers; and in some jurisdictions it is issued to cause a sale to be made of lands, seized under a former writ, after they have been condemned or passed upon by an inquisition. Frequently abbreviated to "vend. ex."

vendor The person who transfers property by sale, particularly real estate, "seller" being more commonly used for one who sells personalty.

venire Latin. To come; to appear in court. This word is sometimes used as the name of the writ for summoning a jury, more commonly called a "venire facias."

venire facias de novo Latin. A fresh or new venire, which the court grants when there has been some impropriety or irregularity in returning the jury, or where the verdict is so imperfect or ambiguous that no judgment can be given upon it, or where a judgment is reversed on error, and a new trial awarded.

verdict The formal and unanimous decision or finding of a jury, impaneled and sworn for the trial of a cause, upon the matters or questions duly submitted to them upon the trial.

vested Accrued; fixed; settled; absolute; having the character or giving the rights of absolute ownership; not contingent; not subject to be defeated by a condition precedent.

vindictive damages Exemplary damages are damages on an increased scale, awarded to the plaintiff over and above what will barely compensate him for his property loss, where the wrong done to him was aggravated by circumstances of violence, oppression, malice, fraud, or wanton and wicked conduct on the part of the defendant, and are intended to solace the plaintiff for mental anguish, laceration of his feelings, shame, degradation, or other aggravations of the original wrong, or else to punish the defendant for his evil behavior or to make an example of him, for which reason they are also called "punitive" or "punitory" damages or "vindictive" damages, and (vulgarly) "smart money."

void Null; ineffectual, nugatory; having no legal force or binding effect; unable, in law, to support the purpose for which it was intended.

voidable That may be avoided, or declared void; not absolutely void, or void in itself. Most of the acts of infants are "voidable" only, and not absolutely void.

voluntary Free; without compulsion or solicitation.

Without consideration; without valuable consideration; gratuitous.

volunteer *In conveyancing,* one who holds a title under a voluntary conveyance; i. e., one made without consideration, good or valuable, to support it.

A person who gives his services without any express or implied promise of remuneration in return is called a "volunteer," and is entitled to no remuneration for his services, nor to any compensation for injuries sustained by him in performing what he has undertaken. Sweet. Also one who officiously pays the debt of another.

W

wager A wager is a contract by which two or more parties agree that a certain sum of money or other thing shall be paid or delivered to one of them on the happening of an uncertain event or upon the ascertainment of a fact which is in dispute between them.

waiver The renunciation, repudiation, abandonment, or surrender of some claim, right, privilege, or of the opportunity to take advantage of some defect, iregularity, or wrong.

ward An infant or insane person placed by authority of law under the care of a guardian.

warrant, v. *In contracts.* To engage or promise that a certain fact or state of facts, in relation to the subject-matter, is, or shall be, as it is represented to be.

warrant, n. A writ or precept from a competent authority in pursuance of law, directing the doing of an act, and addressed to an officer or person competent to do the act, and affording him protection from damage, if he does it.

warranty *In real property law* A real covenant by the grantor of lands, for himself and his heirs, to warrant and defend the title and possession of the estate granted, to the grantee and his heirs, whereby either upon voucher, or judgment in the writ of warrantia chartae, and the eviction of the grantee by paramount title, the grantor was bound to recompense him with other lands of equal value.

In sales of personal property A warranty is a statement or representation made by the seller of goods, contemporaneously with and as a part of the contract of sale, though collateral to the express object of it, having reference to the character, quality, or title of the goods, and by which he promises or undertakes to insure that certain facts are or shall be as he then represents them.

A warranty is an engagement by which a seller assures to a buyer the existence of some fact affecting the transaction, whether past, present, or future.

In contracts An undertaking or stipulation, in writing, or verbally, that a certain fact in relation to the subject of a contract is or shall be as it is stated or promised to be.

A warranty differs from a representation in that a warranty must always be given contemporaneously with, and as part of, the contract; whereas, a representation precedes and induces to the contract. And, while that is their difference in nature, their difference in consequence or effect is this: that, upon breach of warranty (or false warranty), the contract remains binding, and damages only are recoverable for the breach; whereas, upon a false representation, the defrauded party may elect to avoid the contract, and recover the entire price paid. Brown.

will   A will is the legal expression of a man's wishes as to the disposition of his property after his death.

An instrument in writing, executed in form of law, by which a person makes a disposition of his property, to take effect after his death.

writ of entry   A real action to recover the possession of land where the tenant (or owner) has been disseised or otherwise wrongfully dispossessed.

writ of error   A writ issued from a court of appellate jurisdiction, directed to the judge or judges of a court of record, requiring them to remit to the appellate court the record of an action before them, in which a final judgment has been entered, in order that examination may be made of certain errors alleged to have been committed, and that the judgment may be reversed, corrected, or affirmed, as the case may require.

A writ of error is defined to be a commission by which the judges of one court are authorized to examine a record upon which a judgment was given in another court, and, on such examination, to affirm or reverse the same, according to law.

Y

year books   Books made up of reports of English cases from Edward II, 1292, to Henry VIII, early in the sixteenth century. They constitute an important source of information on the early English common law.

TABLE OF CASES

Principal cases are in italic type. Cases cited or discussed are in roman type.
References are to pages.

INDEX

†